Lecture Notes in Computer Science 7441

Commenced Publication in 1973
Founding and Former Series Editors:
Gerhard Goos, Juris Hartmanis, and Jan van Leeuwen

Luis Alvarez   Marta Mejail   Luis Gomez
Julio Jacobo (Eds.)

Progress in Pattern Recognition, Image Analysis, Computer Vision, and Applications

17th Iberoamerican Congress, CIARP 2012
Buenos Aires, Argentina, September 3-6, 2012
Proceedings

 Springer

Volume Editors

Luis Alvarez
Universidad de Las Palmas de Gran Canaria
Departamento de Informatica y Sistemas, CTIM (Imaging Technology Center)
Campus de Tafira, 35017, Las Palmas de Gran Canaria, Spain
E-mail: alvarez@dis.ulpgc.es

Marta Mejail
Julio Jacobo
Universidad de Buenos Aires
Facultad de Ciencias Exactas y Naturales, Departamento de Computación
1428 Ciudad Universitaria, Pabellón I, Buenos Aires, Argentina
E-mail: {marta, jacobo}@dc.uba.ar

Luis Gomez
Universidad de Las Palmas de Gran Canaria
Departamento de Ingeniería Electrónica y Automática
CTIM (Imaging Technology Center)
EITE, Campus Tafira, 35017, Las Palmas de Gran Canaria, Spain
E-mail: lgomez@ctim.es

ISSN 0302-9743   e-ISSN 1611-3349
ISBN 978-3-642-33274-6   e-ISBN 978-3-642-33275-3
DOI 10.1007/978-3-642-33275-3
Springer Heidelberg Dordrecht London New York

Library of Congress Control Number: 2012946104

CR Subject Classification (1998): I.5, I.4, I.2.10, I.2.7, F.2.2, J.3

LNCS Sublibrary: SL 6 – Image Processing, Computer Vision, Pattern Recognition, and Graphics

Typesetting: Camera-ready by author, data conversion by Scientific Publishing Services, Chennai, India

Printed on acid-free paper

Springer is part of Springer Science+Business Media (www.springer.com)

Preface

These proceedings include the papers of all the oral presentations and posters accepted at the 17th edition of the Iberoamerican Congress on Pattern Recognition, held at Buenos Aires, Argentina, during September 3–6, 2012.

This congress is an opportunity for the exchange and diffusion of knowledge, as well as for the promotion of collaboration among different research groups from Latin America, Spain, Portugal and the rest of the world.

Like previous editions, this event attracted contributions from many countries. The papers presented here came from Argentina, Austria, Belgium, Brazil, Chile, Colombia, Costa Rica, Cuba, Czech Republic, Guadeloupe, India, Iran, Italy, Malaysia, Mexico, The Netherlands, New Zealand, Peru, Portugal, Russian Federation, Slovenia, Spain, Thailand, Tunisia, USA and Uruguay.

The papers contained in this volume were selected by the Program Committee, consisting of Luis Alvarez Leon, Luis Gomez Deniz, Julio Jacobo, and Marta Mejail. Each submitted paper was carefully reviewed by about three reviewers in a double-blind peer-review process.

Six distinguished invited speakers gave two tutorials and four keynotes. One of the tutorials addressed the subject of human activity recognition with 2D and 3D cameras and was given by Zicheng Liu, from Microsoft Research; the other tutorial treated the subject of Markov random fields with emphasis on restricted Boltzmann machines, and was given by Christian Igel from the University of Copenhagen.

A keynote on pattern recognition in transportation was presented by José Antonio Rodriguez-Serrano, Research Scientist at the Xerox Research Centre Europe(XRCE) Group. Another keynote on optimal anti-Bayesian statistical pattern recognition was given by John Oommen from the School of Computer Science at Carleton University, Ottawa (Canada). "Robot, pass me the scissors"! was a keynote that addressed the problem of robots assistance in surgery, it was presented by Juan P. Wachs from Purdue University. A keynote on multi-class support vector machines was presented by Christian Igel from the University of Copenhagen.

A keynote on smooth signed distance surface reconstruction and applications was presented by Gabriel Taubin from Brown University.

To enhance the importance of this congress, extended versions of selected papers will be included in the Special Issue on *Computer Vision Applying Pattern Recognition Techniques (Pattern Recognition)*, in the *Special Issue on Robust Recognition Methods for Multimodal Interaction (Pattern Recognition Letters)*, in the *Special Issue on Real-Time Image and Video Processing for Pattern Recognition Systems and Applications (Journal of Real-Time Image Processing)* and in the *IPOL Publications of Algorithms.*

We wish to thank all those who submitted papers for consideration and all the Program Committee members for their excellent work. We also want to thank our colleagues and sponsors for their assistance and support, who contributed to the success of this CIARP 2012 conference.

September 2012

Luis Alvarez Leon
Marta Mejail
Luis Gomez Deniz
Julio Jacobo

Organization

Program Committee

Daniel Acevedo	Universidad de Buenos Aires, Argentina
Santiago Aja-Fernandez	Universidad de Valladolid
Miguel Aleman-Flores	University of Las Palmas de Gran Canaria, Spain
Andres Almansa	CNRS - Telecom ParisTech, France
Rene Alquezar	Universitat Politècnica de Catalunya, Spain
Luis Alvarez	Universidad de Las Palmas de Gran Canaria, Spain
Luis Alvarez	Universidad de Las Palmas de Gran Canaria, Spain
Helder Araujo	University of Coimbra, Portugal
Akira Asano	Kansai University, Japan
Virginia Ballarin	UNMdP, Argentina
Jose Miguel Benedi	DSIC, UPV
Jon Atli Benediktsson	University of Iceland
Rafael Berlanga-Llavori	Universitat Jaume I, Spain
Jose Bioucas-Dias	Instituto Superior Tecnico, Portugal
Isabelle Bloch	ENST - CNRS UMR 5141 LTCI, France
Jean-Francois Bonastre	Université d'Avignon et des Pays de Vaucluse, France
Dibio Borges	Universidade de Braslia, Brazil
Marcel Brun	UNMdP, Argentina
Maria Bucmi	Universidad de Buenos Aires, Argentina
A Campilho	University of Porto, Portugal
Sergio Cano	Universidad de Oriente
Jesus Ariel Carrasco-Ochoa	INAOE
Ana Casali	Universidad Nacional de Rosario, Argentina
Roberto Cesar	University of São Paulo, Brazil
Gerard Chollet	Centre National de la Recherche Scientifique, France
Bernard De Baets	Ghent University, Belgium
Pablo De Cristóforis	Universidad de Buenos Aires, Argentina
Mariana Del Fresno	UNCPBA
Alexandra Diehl	Universidad de Buenos Aires, Argentina
Marcos Dornellas	Universidad Santa Maria - RS

Jan Olof Eklundh	KTH - Royal Institute of Technology, Sweden
Jacques Facon	Pontificia Universidade Catolica do Parana, Brazil
Jialue Fan	North Western University
Alicia Fernandez	Universidad de la Republica, Uruguay
Gustavo Fernandez Dominguez	Austrian Institute of Technology, Austria
Francesc J. Ferri	Universitat de Valencia, Spain
J. Figueroa-Nazuno	Centro de Investigación en Computación, Instituto Politécnico Nacional
Alejandro Frery	Universidade Federal de Alagoas
Luis Garrido	Universitat de Barcelona, Spain
Lev Goldfarb	Faculty of CS, UNB
Herman Gomes	Universidade Federal de Campina Grande
Luis Gomez	University of Las Palmas de Gran Canaria, Spain
Luis Gomez	University of Las Palmas de Gran Canaria, Spain
Pilar Gomez-Gil	National Institute of Astrophysics, Optics and Electronics
Jordi Gonzàlez	Centre de Visió per Computador
Norberto Goussies	FCEyN, Universidad de Buenos Aires
Juan Pablo Graffigna	Universidad Nacional de San Juan
Manuel Grana	University of the Basque Country, Spain
Antoni Grau	Technical University of Catalonia, Spain
Francisco Gómez Fernández	Universidad de Buenos Aires, Argentina
Ana Haedo	Universidad de Buenos Aires, Argentina
Ana Haedo	Universidad de Buenos Aires, Argentina
Michal Haindl	Institute of Information Theory and Automation
Laurent Heutte	Université de Rouen, France
Vaclav Hlavac	Czech Technical University in Prague, Czech Republic
Julio Jacobo	Universidad de Buenos Aires, Argentina
Julio Jacobo	Universidad de Buenos Aires, Argentina
Xiaoyi Jiang	Universität Münster, Germany
Martin Kampel	Vienna University of Technology, Computer Vision Lab, Austria
Aggelos Katsaggelos	Northwestern University
Sang-Woon Kim	Myongji University
Vitaly Kober	CICESE
Walter Kosters	LIACS, Leiden University, The Netharlands
Tom Krajnik	Czech Technical University, Czech Republic
Karl Krissian	Universidad de las Palmas de Gran Canaria, Spain
Miren Lopez De Ipiña Peña	Universidad del Pais Vasco, Spain

José Ruiz Shulcloper	CENATAV
Javier Ruiz-Del-Solar	Universidad de Chile
Vladimir V. Ryazanov	Dorodnicyn Computing Centre of RAS, Russia
Agustín Salgado	University of Las Palmas de Gran Canaria, Spain
César San Martín	Universidad de La Frontera, Chile
João Sanches	Universidade Tecnica de Lisboa, Portugal
Jorge Sanchez	Universidad Tecnologica Nacional Regional Cordoba, Argentina
Jose Salvador Sanchez	Universitat Jaume I, Spain
Carlo Sansone	University of Naples "Federico II", Italy
Enrique Segura	Universidad de Buenos Aires, Argentina
Leticia Seijas	Universidad de Buenos Aires
Jean Serra	Université Paris-Est, France
Yoshiaki Shirai	Ritsumeikan University, Japan
Humberto Sossa Azuela	National Polytechnic Institute, Mexico
Beatriz Sousa-Santos	Universidade de Aveiro/IEETA, Portugal
Luis Enrique Sucar	INAOE
Javier Sánchez	University of Las Palmas de Gran Canaria, Spain
Alberto Taboada Crispi	Universidad Central de Las Villas
Mariano Tepper	Universidad de Buenos Aires, Argentina
Karl Tombre	INRIA
M. Inés Torres	Universidad del Pas Vasco, Spain
Sebastián Ubalde	Universidad de Buenos Aires, Argentina
Sebastián Ubalde	University of Buenos Aires, Argentina
Sebastian Vandalay	FEBA
Marcelo Venere	Universidad Nacional del Centro
Juan Vorobioff	Comision Nacional de Energia Atomica
Juan Pablo Wachs	Purdue University, USA
Shengrui Wang	University of Sherbrooke, Canada
Cornelio Yañez	CIC-IPN
Yehezkel Yeshurun	Tel Aviv University, Israel
Pablo Zegers	Universidad de los Andes, Colombia
Zhi-Hua Zhou	Nanjing University, China

Additional Reviewers

Aguena, Marcia
Argelles-Cruz, Amadeo Jos
Bechar, Avital
Bulacio, Pilar
Camacho-Nieto, Oscar
Cancela, Pablo
Cavalcanti, Claudio

Chen, Lifei
Chikhaoui, Belkacem
Cote, Marc-Alexandre
Deco, Claudia
Dias, Paulo
Escalante, Hugo Jair
Georgieva, Petia

Giorgieva, Petia
Hu, Ju-Hua
Huang, Sheng-Jun
Kiran, Bangalore Ravi
Lecumberry, Federico
Levada, Alexandre
Li, Nan
Lpez-Leyva, Luis Octavio
Lpez-Yez, Itzam
López-Monroy, Adrián Pastor
Martins, Ana Luisa Dinc
Molinar-Sols, Jess Ezequiel
Monasse, Pascal
Moura, Eduardo
Nitsche, Matias
Nitsche, Matias Alejandro

Pardo, Alvaro
Pereira, Eanes
Pire, Taihú
Planinc, Rainer
Ramirez, Ignacio
Rodriguez, Juan
Rosales-Perez, Alejandro
Salvadeo, Denis
Simmross, Federico
Sprechmann, Pablo
Torres-Garcia, Alejandro Antonio
Vallin Spina, Thiago
Vieira, Susana
Villatoro-Tello, Esaú
Wetzinger, Elisabeth
Zweng, Andreas

Table of Contents

Clustering

Fuzzy Methods

Human Actions and Gestures

Graphs

Image Processing and Analysis

Shape and Texture

Learning, Mining and Neural Networks

Medical Images

Robotics, Stereo Vision and Real Time

Remote Sensing

Signal Processing

Speech and Handwriting Analysis

Statistical Pattern Recognition

Theoretical Pattern Recognition

Video Analysis

Optimal "Anti-Bayesian" Parametric Pattern Classification Using Order Statistics Criteria

A. Thomas and B. John Oommen*

School of Computer Science, Carleton University, Ottawa, Canada : K1S 5B6

Abstract. The gold standard for a classifier is the condition of optimality attained by the Bayesian classifier. Within a Bayesian paradigm, if we are allowed to compare the testing sample with only *a single* point in the feature space from each class, the *optimal* Bayesian strategy would be to achieve this based on the (Mahalanobis) distance from the corresponding means. The reader should observe that, in this context, the mean, in one sense, is the most *central* point in the respective distribution. In this paper, we shall show that we can obtain optimal results by operating in a diametrically opposite way, i.e., a so-called "anti-Bayesian" manner. Indeed, we shall show the completely counter-intuitive result that by working with a *very few* (sometimes as small as two) points *distant* from the mean, one can obtain remarkable classification accuracies. Further, if these points are determined by the *Order Statistics* of the distributions, the accuracy of our method, referred to as Classification by Moments of Order Statistics (CMOS), attains the optimal Bayes' bound! This claim, which is totally counter-intuitive, has been proven for many uni-dimensional, and some multi-dimensional distributions within the exponential family, and the theoretical results have been verified by rigorous experimental testing. Apart from the fact that these results are quite fascinating and pioneering in their own right, they also give a theoretical foundation for the families of Border Identification (BI) algorithms reported in the literature.

Keywords: Classification using Order Statistics (OS), Moments of OS.

1 Introduction

Pattern classification is the process by which unknown feature vectors are categorized into groups or classes based on their features [1]. The age-old strategy for doing this is based on a Bayesian principle which aims to maximize the *a posteriori* probability. It is well known that when expressions for the latter are simplified, the classification criterion which attains the Bayesian optimal lower

---

* *Chancellor's Professor* ; *Fellow: IEEE* and *Fellow: IAPR*. This author is also an *Adjunct Professor* with the University of Agder in Grimstad, Norway. The work of this author was partially supported by NSERC, the Natural Sciences and Engineering Research Council of Canada. This paper was presented as a Keynote/Plenary talk at the conference.

L. Alvarez et al. (Eds.): CIARP 2012, LNCS 7441, pp. 1–13, 2012.

bound often reduces to testing the sample point using the corresponding distances/norms to the *means* or the "central points" of the distributions.

In this paper, we shall demonstrate that we can obtain optimal results by operating in a diametrically opposite way, i.e., a so-called "anti-Bayesian" manner. Indeed, we shall show the completely counter-intuitive result that by working with a *few* points *distant* from the mean, one can obtain remarkable classification accuracies. The number of points referred to can be as small as *two* in the uni-dimensional case. Further, if these points are determined by the *Order Statistics* of the distributions, the accuracy attains the optimal Bayes' bound! Thus, put in a nut-shell, we introduce here the theory of optimal pattern classification using Order Statistics of the features rather than the distributions of the features themselves. Thus, we propose a novel methodology referred to as Classification by Moments of Order Statistics (CMOS). It turns out, though, that this process is computationally not any more complex than working with the latter distributions.

1.1 Contributions of This Paper

The novel contributions of this paper are the following:

- We propose an "anti-Bayesian" paradigm for the classification of patterns within the parametric mode of computation, where the distance computations are not with regard to the "mean" but with regard to some samples "distant" from the mean. These points, which are sometimes as few as *two*, are the moments of OS of the distributions;
- We provide a theoretical framework for adequately responding to the question of why the border points are more informative for the task of classification;
- To justify these claims, we submit a formal analysis and the results of various experiments which have been performed for many distributions within the exponential family, and the results are clearly conclusive.

We conclude by mentioning that our results probably represent the state-of-the-art in BI!

2   Relevant Background Areas

2.1 Prototype Reduction Schemes and Border Identification Algorithms

If we fast-forward the clock by five decades since the initial formulation of Pattern Recognition (PR) as a research field, the informed reader will also be aware of the development of efficient classification methods in which the schemes achieve their task based on a *subset* of the training patterns. These are commonly referred to as "Prototype Reduction Schemes" (PRS)[2,3]. A PRS will be considered to be a generic method for reducing the number of training vectors, while simultaneously attempting to guarantee that the classifier built on the reduced design set performs as well, or nearly as well, as the classifier built on the original design set [4]. Thus, instead of considering all the training patterns for the classification, a subset of the whole set is selected based on certain criteria. The learning (or training) is then performed on this reduced training set, which is also called the "Reference" set. This Reference set not only contains the patterns which are closer to the true discriminant's boundary, but also the patterns from the other regions of the space that can adequately represent the entire training set. Zillions of PRS [5] techniques have developed over the years, and it is clearly impossible to survey all of these here. These include the Condensed Nearest Neighbor (CNN) rule [6], the Reduced Nearest Neighbor (RNN) rule [7], the Prototypes for Nearest Neighbor (PNN) classifiers [8], the Selective Nearest Neighbor (SNN) rule [9], the Edited Nearest Neighbor (ENN) rule [10], Vector Quantization (VQ) etc. Comprehensive survey of the state-of-the-art in PRSs can be found in [2,11,3]. The formal algorithms are also found in [12].

Border Identification (BI) algorithms, which form a distinct subset of PRSs, work with a Reference set which only contains "border" points. A PRS would attempt to determine the relevant samples in both the classes which are capable of achieving near-optimal classification. As opposed to this, a BI algorithm uses *only* those samples which lie close to the *boundaries* of the two classes. Important developments in this area were proposed by Duch [13], Foody [14] and Li [15]. Duch developed algorithms to obtain the reference set based on a border analysis of *every* training pattern, and those algorithms attempt to *add* patterns which are closer to the class boundary, to the reference set. According to Foody's approach, the training set is divided into two sets - the first comprising of the set of border patterns, and the second being the set of non-border patterns. A border training set should contain patterns from different classes, but which are close together in the feature space and which are thus in the proximity of the true classification boundary. According to Li, the border patterns obtained by the traditional approaches are considered to be the "Near" borders, and using the latter, the "Far" borders are identified from the remaining data points. It turns out that the final border points computed in this manner are more accurate than the initially identified "Near" borders. The "Near" and the "Far" borders collectively constitute the so-called "Full" border set for the training data. A detailed survey of these methods can be found in [12,16].

2.2 Order Statistics

Let $\mathbf{x}_1$, $\mathbf{x}_2$, ..., $\mathbf{x}_n$ be a univariate random sample of size n that follows a continuous distribution function Φ, where the probability density function (pdf) is $\varphi(\cdot)$. Let $\mathbf{x}_{1,n}$, $\mathbf{x}_{2,n}$, ..., $\mathbf{x}_{n,n}$ be the corresponding Order Statistics (OS). The rth OS, $\mathbf{x}_{r,n}$, of the set is the rth smallest value among the given random variables. The pdf of $\mathbf{y} = \mathbf{x}_{r,n}$ is given by:

$$f_{\mathbf{y}}(y) = \frac{n!}{(r-1)!(n-r)!} \left\{ \Phi(y) \right\}^{r-1} \left\{ 1 - \Phi(y) \right\}^{n-r} \varphi(y),$$

where $r = 1, 2, ..., n$. The reasoning for the above expression is straightforward. If the rth OS appears at a location given by $\mathbf{y} = \mathbf{x}_{r,n}$, it implies that the $r - 1$ smaller elements of the set are drawn independently from a Binomial distribution with a probability $\Phi(y)$, and the other $n - r$ samples are drawn using the probability $1 - \Phi(y)$. The factorial terms result from the fact that the $(r - 1)$ elements can be independently chosen from the set of n elements.

Although the distribution $f_{\mathbf{y}}(y)$ contains all the information resident in $\mathbf{y}$, the literature characterizes the OS in terms of quantities which are of paramount importance, namely its moments [17]. To better appreciate the results presented later in this paper, an understanding of the moments of the OS is necessary. This is briefly presented below.

Using the distribution $f_{\mathbf{y}}(y)$, one can see that the kth moment of $\mathbf{x}_{r,n}$ can be formulated as:

$$E[\mathbf{x}_{r,n}^k] = \frac{n!}{(r-1)!(n-r)!} \int_{-\infty}^{+\infty} y^k \Phi(y)^{k-1}(x)(1 - \Phi(y))^{n-r} \varphi(y) dy,$$

provided that both sides of the equality exist [18,19].

The fundamental theorem concerning the OS that we invoke is found in many papers [20,19,17]. The result is merely cited below inasmuch as the details of the proof are irrelevant and outside the scope of this study. The theorem can be summarized as follows.

Let $n \geq r \geq k + 1 \geq 2$ be integers. Then, since Φ is a nondecreasing and right-continuous function from $\mathbb{R} \to \mathbb{R}$, $\Phi(\mathbf{x}_{r,n})$ is uniform in $[0,1]$. If we now take the kth moment of $\Phi(\mathbf{x}_{r,n})$, it has the form [20]:

$$E[\Phi^k(\mathbf{x}_{r,n})] = \frac{B(r+k, n-r+1)}{B(r, n-r+1)} = \frac{n! \, (r+k-1)!}{(n+k)! \, (r-1)!}, \tag{1}$$

where $B(a,b)$ denotes the $Beta$ function, and $B(a,b) = \frac{(a-1)!(b-1)!}{(a+b-1)!}$ since its parameters are integers.

The above fundamental result can also be used for characterization purposes as follows [20]. Let $n \geq r \geq k + 1 \geq 2$ be integers, with Φ being nondecreasing and right-continuous. Let G be any nondecreasing and right-continuous function from $\mathbb{R} \to \mathbb{R}$ on the same support as Φ. The relation

$$E[G^k(\mathbf{x}_{r,n})] = \frac{n! \, (r+k-1)!}{(n+k)! \, (r-1)!} \tag{2}$$

holds if and only if $\forall x, \Phi(x) = G(x)$. In other words, $\Phi(\cdot)$ is the unique function that satisfies Eq. (2), implying that every distribution is characterized by the moments of its OS.

The implications of the above are the following:

1. If $n = 1$, implying that only a $single$ sample is drawn from $\mathbf{x}$, from Eq. (1),

$$E[\Phi^1(\mathbf{x}_{1,1})] = \frac{1}{2}, \implies E[\mathbf{x}_{1,1}] = \Phi^{-1}\left(\frac{1}{2}\right). \tag{3}$$

Informally speaking, the first moment of the 1-order OS would be the value where the cumulative distribution Φ equals $\frac{1}{2}$, which is the Median($\mathbf{x}$).

2. If $n = 2$, implying that only *two* samples are drawn from $\mathbf{x}$, we can deduce from Eq. (1) that:

$$E[\Phi^1(\mathbf{x}_{1,2})] = \frac{1}{3}, \implies E[\mathbf{x}_{1,2}] = \Phi^{-1}\left(\frac{1}{3}\right), \text{ and} \tag{4}$$

$$E[\Phi^1(\mathbf{x}_{2,2})] = \frac{2}{3}, \implies E[\mathbf{x}_{2,2}] = \Phi^{-1}\left(\frac{2}{3}\right). \tag{5}$$

Thus, from a computational perspective, the first moment of the first and second 2-order OS would be the values where the cumulative distribution Φ equal $\frac{1}{3}$ and $\frac{2}{3}$ respectively.

Although the analogous expressions can be derived for the higher order OS, for the rest of this paper we shall merely focus on the 2-order OS, and derive the consequences of using them in classification!

3 Optimal Bayesian Classification Using *Two* Order Statistics

3.1 The Generic Classifier

Having characterized the moments of the OS of arbitrary distributions, we shall now consider how they can be used to design a classifier.

Let us assume that we are dealing with the 2-class problem with classes ω_1 and ω_2, where their class-conditional densities are $f_1(x)$ and $f_2(x)$ respectively (i.e, their corresponding distributions are $F_1(x)$ and $F_2(x)$ respectively)[1]. Let ν_1 and ν_2 be the corresponding *medians* of the distributions. Then, classification based on ν_1 and ν_1 would be the strategy that classifies samples based on a *single* OS. We shall show the fairly straightforward result that for all symmetric distributions, the classification accuracy of this classifier attains the Bayes' accuracy.

This result is not too astonishing because the median is centrally located close to (if not exactly) on the mean. The result for higher order OS is actually far more intriguing because the higher order OS are not located centrally (close to the means), but rather distant from the means. Consequently, we shall show that for a large number of distributions, mostly from the exponential family, the classification based on *these* OS again attains the Bayes' bound.

We shall initiate this discussion by examining the Uniform distribution. The reason for this is that even though the distribution itself is rather trivial, the analysis will provide the reader with an insight into the mechanism by which the problem can be tackled, which can then be extended for other distributions.

---

[1] Throughout this section, we will assume that the *a priori* probabilities are equal. If they are unequal, the above densities must be weighted with the respective *a priori* probabilities.

3.2 The Uniform Distribution

The continuous Uniform distribution is characterized by a constant function $U(a, b)$, where a and b are the minimum and the maximum values that the random variable $\mathbf{x}$ can take. If the class conditional densities of ω_1 and ω_2 are uniformly distributed,

$$f_1(x) = \begin{cases} \frac{1}{b_1 - a_1} & \text{if } a_1 \leq x \leq b_1; \\ 0 & \text{if } x < a_1 \text{ or } x > b_1, \text{ and} \end{cases}$$

$$f_2(x) = \begin{cases} \frac{1}{b_2 - a_2} & \text{if } a_2 \leq x \leq b_2; \\ 0 & \text{if } x < a_2 \text{ or } x > b_2. \end{cases}$$

The reader should observe the following:

- If $a_2 > b_1$, the two distributions are non-overlapping, rendering the classification problem trivial.
- If $a_2 < b_1$, but $b_1 - a_1 \neq b_2 - a_2$, the optimal Bayesian classification is again dependent only on the heights of the distributions. In other words, if $b_2 - a_2 < b_1 - a_1$, the testing sample will be assigned to ω_2 whenever $x > a_2$. This criterion again is not related to the mean of the distributions at all, and is thus un-interesting to our current investigations.
- The meaningful scenario is when $b_1 - a_1$ is exactly equal to $b_2 - a_2$, and if $a_2 < b_1$. In this case, the heights of the two distributions are equal and the distributions are overlapping. This is really the interesting case, and corresponds to the scenario when the two distributions are identical. We shall analyze this in greater detail and demonstrate that the optimal Bayesian classification is also attained by using the OS.

Theoretical Analysis: Uniform Distribution - 2-OS. We shall now derive the formal properties of the classifier that utilizes the OS for the Uniform distribution.

Theorem 1. *For the 2-class problem in which the two class conditional distributions are Uniform and identical, CMOS, the classification using two OS, attains the optimal Bayes' bound.*

Proof. The proof of the result is done in two steps. We shall first show that when the two class conditional distributions are Uniform and identical, the optimal Bayesian classification is achieved by a comparison to the corresponding *means*. The equivalence of this to a comparison to the corresponding OS leads to the final result.

Without loss of generality let the class conditional distributions for ω_1 and ω_2 be $U(0, 1)$ and $U(h, 1 + h)$, with means $\mu_1 = \frac{1}{2}$ and $\mu_2 = h + \frac{1}{2}$, respectively. In this case, the optimal Bayes' classifier assigns x to ω_1 whenever $x < h$, x to ω_2 whenever $x > 1$, and x to ω_1 and to ω_2 with equal probability when $h < x < 1$. Since:

$$D\left(x,\ \mu_1\right) < D\left(x,\ \mu_2\right) \iff x - \frac{1}{2} < h + \frac{1}{2} - x$$
$$\iff 2x < 1 + h$$
$$\iff x < \frac{1+h}{2}, \tag{6}$$

we see that the optimal Bayesian classifier assigns the sample based on the proximity to the corresponding mean, proving the first assertion.

We now consider the moments of the OS of the distributions. If $\mathbf{x}_1$, $\mathbf{x}_2$, ..., $\mathbf{x}_n$ are n independent univariate random variables that follow the Uniform distribution $U(0,1)$, by virtue of Eq.(1), the expected values of the first moment of the k-order OS can be seen to be $E[\mathbf{x}_{k,n}] = \frac{k}{n+1}$. Thus, for $U(0,1)$, $E[\mathbf{x}_{1,2}] = \frac{1}{3}$ and $E[\mathbf{x}_{2,2}] = \frac{2}{3}$. Similarly, for the distribution $U(h, 1+h)$, the expected values are $E[\mathbf{x}_{1,2}] = h + \frac{1}{3}$ and $E[\mathbf{x}_{2,2}] = h + \frac{2}{3}$.

The OS-based classification is thus as follows: Whenever a testing sample comes from these distributions, the CMOS will compare the testing sample with $E[\mathbf{x}_{2,2}]$ of the first distribution, i.e., $\frac{2}{3}$, and with $E[\mathbf{x}_{1,2}]$ of the second distribution, i.e., $h + \frac{1}{3}$, and the sample will be labeled with respect to the class which minimizes the corresponding quantity. Observe that for the above rule to work, we must enforce the ordering of the OS of the two distributions, and this requires that $\frac{2}{3} < h + \frac{1}{3} \implies h > \frac{1}{3}$.

In order to prove that for $h > \frac{1}{3}$ the OS-based classification is identical to the mean-based classification, we have to prove that $D(x, \mu_1) < D(x, \mu_2) \implies D(x, O_1) < D(x, O_2)$, where O_1 is $E[\mathbf{x}_{2,2}]$ of the first distribution and O_2 is $E[\mathbf{x}_{1,2}]$ of the second distribution. By virtue of Eq.(6),

$$D(x, \mu_1) < D(x, \mu_2) \iff x < \frac{h+1}{2}. \tag{7}$$

Similarly,

$$D(x, O_1) < D(x, O_2) \iff D\left(x, \frac{2}{3}\right) < D\left(x, h + \frac{1}{3}\right)$$
$$\iff x - \frac{2}{3} < h + \frac{1}{3} - x$$
$$\iff x < \frac{h+1}{2}. \tag{8}$$

The result follows by observing that (7) and (8) are identical comparisons.

For the analogous result for the case when $h < \frac{1}{3}$, the CMOS will compare the testing sample with $E[\mathbf{x}_{1,2}]$ of the first distribution, i.e., $\frac{1}{3}$, and with $E[\mathbf{x}_{2,2}]$ of the second distribution, i.e., $h + \frac{2}{3}$. Again, the sample will be labeled with respect to the class which minimizes the corresponding quantity. The proofs of the equivalence of this to the Bayesian decision follows along the same lines as the case when $h > \frac{1}{3}$, and is omitted to avoid repetition.

Hence the theorem!   □

Experimental Results: Uniform Distribution - 2-OS. The CMOS method explained in Section 3.2 has been rigorously tested for various uniform distributions with 2-OS. In the interest of brevity, a few typical results are given below.

For each of the experiments, we generated 1,000 points for the classes ω_1 and ω_2 characterized by $U(0,1)$ and $U(h,1+h)$ respectively. We then invoked a classification procedure by utilizing the Bayesian and the CMOS strategies. In every case, CMOS was compared with the Bayesian classifier for different values of h, as tabulated in Table 1. The results in Table 1 were obtained by executing each algorithm 50 times using a 10-fold cross-validation scheme.

Table 1. Classification of Uniformly distributed classes by the CMOS 2-OS method for different values of h

h	0.95	0.90	0.85	0.80	0.75	0.70
Bayesian	97.58	95.1	92.42	90.23	87.82	85.4
CMOS	97.58	95.1	92.42	90.23	87.82	85.4

Observe that in every case, the accuracy of CMOS attained the Bayes' bound.

By way of example, we see that CMOS should obtain the Bayesian bound for the distributions $U(0,1)$ and $U(0.8,1.8)$ whenever $n < \frac{1+0.8}{1-0.8} = 9$. In this case, the expected values of the moments are $\frac{1}{10}$ and $\frac{9}{10}$ respectively. These results justify the claim of Theorem 1.

Theoretical Analysis: Uniform Distribution - k-OS. We have seen from Theorem 1 that the moments of the 2-OS are sufficient for the classification to attain a Bayes' bound. We shall now consider the scenario when we utilize other k-OS. The formal result pertaining to this is given in Theorem 2.

Theorem 2. *For the 2-class problem in which the two class conditional distributions are Uniform and identical as $U(0,1)$ and $U(h, 1+h)$, optimal Bayesian classification can be achieved by using symmetric pairs of the n-OS, i.e., the $n - k$ OS for ω_1 and the k OS for ω_2 if and only if $k > \frac{(n+1)(1-h)}{2}$.*

Proof. We know that for the uniform distribution $U(0,1)$, the expected values of the first moment of the k-order OS have the form $E[\mathbf{x}_{k,n}] = \frac{k}{n+1}$. Our claim is based on the classification in which we can choose any of the symmetric pairs of the n-OS, i.e., the $n - k$ OS for ω_1 and the k OS for ω_2, whose expected values are $\frac{n-k+1}{n+1}$ and $h + \frac{k}{n+1}$ respectively.

Consider the case when $h > 1 - \frac{2k}{n+1}$, the relevance of which will be argued presently. Whenever a testing sample comes, it will be compared with the corresponding k-OS symmetric pairs of the expected values of the n-OS, and the sample will be labeled with respect to the class that minimizes the distance.

Observe that for the above rule to work, we must again enforce the ordering of the OS of the two distributions, and this requires that:

$$\frac{n-k+1}{n+1} < h + \frac{k}{n+1} \implies k > \frac{(n+1)(1-h)}{2}. \tag{9}$$

Eq.(9) can be seen to be:

$$k > \frac{(n+1)(1-h)}{2} \implies h > 1 - \frac{2k}{n+1}, \tag{10}$$

which justifies the case under consideration. As we have already proved that the Bayesian bound can be achieved by a comparison to the corresponding means (in Eq.(6)), which in turn simplifies to $x \sim \omega_1 \iff x < \frac{h+1}{2}$, we need to show that to obtain optimal accuracy using these symmetric $n - k$ and k OS, $D(x, O_1) < D(x, O_2) \iff x < \frac{h+1}{2}$. Indeed, the OS-based classification also attains the Bayesian bound because:

$$D(x, O_1) < D(x, O_2) \iff D\left(x, \frac{n-k+1}{n+1}\right) < D\left(x, h + \frac{k}{n+1}\right)$$

$$\iff x - \frac{n-k+1}{n+1} < h + \frac{k}{n+1} - x$$

$$\iff x < \frac{h+1}{2}. \tag{11}$$

For the symmetric argument when $h < 1 - \frac{2k}{n+1}$, the CMOS will compare the testing sample with $E[\mathbf{x}_{k,n}]$ of the first distribution and $E[\mathbf{x}_{n-k,n}]$ of the second distribution and the classification is obtained based on the class that minimizes *this* distance. The details of the proof are analogous and omitted. Hence the theorem!   □

An alternate methodology to visualize the theorem and its consequences is given in [12,16], and is omitted here in the interest of space.

Experimental Results: Uniform Distribution - k-OS. The CMOS method has also been tested for the Uniform distribution for other k OS. In the interest of brevity, we merely cite one example where the distributions for ω_1 and ω_2 were characterized by $U(0, 1)$ and $U(0.8, 1.8)$ respectively. For each of the experiments, we generated 1,000 points for each class, and the testing samples were classified based on the selected *symmetric* pairs for values k and $n - k$ respectively. The results are displayed in Table 2.

To clarify the table, consider the row given by Trial No. 6 in which the 7-OS were invoked for the classification. Observe that the k-OS are now given by $\frac{n-k+1}{n+1}$ and $\frac{k}{n+1}$ respectively. In this case, the possible symmetric OS pairs could be $\langle 1, 6 \rangle$, $\langle 2, 5 \rangle$, and $\langle 3, 4 \rangle$ respectively. In every single case, the accuracy attained the Bayes' bound, as indicated by the results in the table.

The consequence of violating the condition imposed by Theorem 2 can be seen from the results given in the row denoted by Trial No. 9. In this case, the testing

Table 2. Results of the classification obtained by using the symmetric pairs of the OS for different values of n. The value of h was set to be 0.8. Note that in every case, the accuracy attained the Bayes' value whenever the conditions stated in Theorem 2 were satisfied.

Trail No.	Order(n)	Moments	OS_1	OS_2	CMOS	Pass/Fail
1	Two	$\{\frac{i}{3} \mid 1 \leq i \leq 2\}$	$\frac{2}{3}$	$h + \frac{1}{3}$	90.23	Passed
2	Three	$\{\frac{i}{4} \mid 1 \leq i \leq 3\}$	$\frac{3}{4}$	$h + \frac{1}{4}$	90.23	Passed
3	Four	$\{\frac{i}{5} \mid 1 \leq i \leq 4\}$	$\frac{4}{5}$	$h + \frac{1}{5}$	90.23	Passed
4	Five	$\{\frac{i}{6} \mid 1 \leq i \leq 5\}$	$\frac{4}{6}$	$h + \frac{2}{6}$	90.23	Passed
5	Six	$\{\frac{i}{7} \mid 1 \leq i \leq 6\}$	$\frac{4}{7}$	$h + \frac{2}{7}$	90.23	Passed
6	Seven	$\{\frac{i}{8} \mid 1 \leq i \leq 7\}$	$\frac{5}{8}$	$h + \frac{3}{8}$	90.23	Passed
7	Eight	$\{\frac{i}{9} \mid 1 \leq i \leq 8\}$	$\frac{6}{9}$	$h + \frac{3}{9}$	90.23	Passed
8	Nine	$\{\frac{i}{10} \mid 1 \leq i \leq 9\}$	$\frac{7}{10}$	$h + \frac{3}{10}$	90.23	Passed
9	Ten	$\{\frac{i}{11} \mid 1 \leq i \leq 10\}$	$\frac{10}{11}$	$h + \frac{1}{11}$	9.77	Failed
10	Ten	$\{\frac{i}{11} \mid 1 \leq i \leq 10\}$	$\frac{9}{11}$	$h + \frac{2}{11}$	90.23	Passed
11	Ten	$\{\frac{i}{11} \mid 1 \leq i \leq 10\}$	$\frac{7}{11}$	$h + \frac{4}{11}$	90.23	Passed
12	Ten	$\{\frac{i}{11} \mid 1 \leq i \leq 10\}$	$\frac{6}{11}$	$h + \frac{5}{11}$	90.23	Passed

attained the Bayes accuracy for the symmetric OS pairs $\langle 2, 9 \rangle$, $\langle 3, 8 \rangle$, $\langle 4, 7 \rangle$ and $\langle 5, 6 \rangle$ respectively. However, the classifier "failed" for the specific 10-OS, when the OS used were $\frac{10}{11}$ and $h + \frac{1}{11}$, as these values did not satisfy the condition $h > 1 - \frac{2k}{n+1}$. Observe that if $h < 1 - \frac{2k}{n+1}$, the symmetric pairs should be reversed, i.e., $\frac{k}{n+1}$ for the first distribution, and $h + \frac{n-k+1}{n+1}$ for the second distribution, to obtain the optimal Bayesian bound. The astonishing facet of this result is that one obtains the Bayes accuracy even though the classification requires only *two* points distant from the mean, justifying the rationale for BI schemes, and yet operating in an anti-Bayesian manner!

Remark: We believe that the CMOS, the classification by the moments of Order Statistics, is also true for multi-dimensional distributions. For a *prima facie* case, we consider two (overlapping) 2-dimensional uniform distributions U_1 and U_2 in which both the features are in $[0, 1]^2$ and $[h, 1 + h]^2$ respectively. Consequently, we can see that the overlapping region of the distributions forms a square. In this case, it is easy to verify that the Bayesian classifier is the diagonal that passes through the intersection points of the distributions. For the classification based on the moments of the 2-OS, because the features are independent for both dimensions, we can show that this is equivalent to utilizing the OS at position $\frac{2}{3}$ of the first distribution for both dimensions, and the OS at the position $h + \frac{1}{3}$ of the second distribution for both dimensions.

Table 3. Classification of Uniformly distributed 2-dimensional classes by the CMOS 2-OS method for different values of h. In the last two cases, the OS points of interest are reversed as explained in Section 3.2.

h	0.95	0.90	0.85	0.80	0.75	0.70	0.65	0.60
Bayesian	99.845	99.505	98.875	98.045	97.15	95.555	94.14	91.82
CMOS	99.845	99.505	98.875	98.045	97.15	95.555	94.14	91.82

The CMOS method for 2-dimensional uniform distributions U_1 (in $[0, 1]$ in both dimensions) and U_2 (in $[h, 1 + h]$ in both dimensions) has been rigorously tested, and the results are given in Table 3. A formal proof for the case when the second class is distributed in $[h_1, 1 + h_1] \times [h_2, 1 + h_2]$, and for multi-dimensional features is currently being devised. It will appear in a forthcoming paper.

3.3   The Laplace (or Doubly-Exponential) Distribution

The *Laplace distribution* is a continuous uni-dimensional pdf named after Pierre-Simon Laplace. It is sometimes called the *doubly exponential distribution*, because it can be perceived as being a combination of two exponential distributions, with an additional location parameter, spliced together back-to-back.

If the class conditional densities of ω_1 and ω_2 are doubly exponentially distributed,

$$f_1(x) = \frac{\lambda_1}{2} e^{-\lambda_1 |x - c_1|}, \quad -\infty < x < \infty, \text{and}$$

$$f_2(x) = \frac{\lambda_2}{2} e^{-\lambda_2 |x - c_2|}, \quad -\infty < x < \infty,$$

where c_1 and c_2 are the respective means of the distributions. By elementary integration and straightforward algebraic simplifications, the variances of the distributions can be seen to be $\frac{2}{\lambda_1^2}$ and $\frac{2}{\lambda_2^2}$ respectively.

If $\lambda_1 \neq \lambda_2$, the samples can be classified based on the heights of the distributions and their point of intersection. The formal results for the general case are a little more complex. However, to prove the analogous results of Theorem 1 for the Uniform distribution, we shall first consider the case when $\lambda_1 = \lambda_2$. In this scenario, the reader should observe the following:

- Because the distributions have the equal height, i.e. $\lambda_1 = \lambda_2$, the testing sample $\mathbf{x}$ will obviously be assigned to ω_1 if it is less than c_1 and be assigned to ω_2 if it is greater than c_2.
- Further, the crucial case is when $c_1 < \mathbf{x} < c_2$. In this regard, we shall analyze the CMOS classifier and prove that it attains the Bayes' bound even when one uses as few as *only* 2 OSs.

Theoretical Analysis: Doubly-Exponential Distribution. By virtue of Eq. (4) and (5), the expected values of the first moments of the two OS can be obtained by determining the points where the cumulative distribution function attains the values $\frac{1}{3}$ and $\frac{2}{3}$. Let u_1 be the point for the percentile $\frac{2}{3}$ of the first distribution, and u_2 be the point for the percentile $\frac{1}{3}$ of the second distribution. These points can be obtained as $u_1 = c_1 - \frac{1}{\lambda_1} \, log \left(\frac{2}{3}\right)$ and $u_2 = c_2 + \frac{1}{\lambda_2} \, log \left(\frac{2}{3}\right)$. With these points at hand, we can demonstrate that, for doubly exponential distributions, the classification based on the expected values of the moments of the 2-OS, CMOS, attains the Bayesian bound, and the proof can be seen in [21].

A similar argument can be raised for the classification based on the k-OS. For the 2-class problem in which the two class conditional distributions are Doubly Exponential and identical, the optimal Bayesian classification can be achieved by using symmetric pairs of the n-OS, i.e., the $n - k$ OS for ω_1 and the k OS for ω_2 if and only if $log \left(\frac{2k}{n+1}\right) > \frac{c_1 - c_2}{2}$, and this claim is also proved in [12,16].

Analogous results for the uni-dimensional Gaussian distribution are also available, but omitted here, in the interest of brevity. They can be found in [12,16].

4   Conclusions

In this paper, we have shown that the optimal Bayes' bound can be obtained by an "anti-Bayesian" approach named CMOS, Classification by Moments of Order Statistics. We have proved that the classification can be attained by working with a *very few* (sometimes as small as two) points *distant* from the mean. Further, if these points are determined by the *Order Statistics* of the distributions, the optimal Bayes' bound can be attained. The claim has been proved for many uni-dimensional distributions within the exponential family. The corresponding results for some multi-dimensional distributions have been alluded to, and the theoretical results have been verified by rigorous experimental testing. Apart from the fact that these results are quite fascinating and pioneering in their own right, they also give a theoretical foundation for the families of Border Identification (BI) algorithms reported in the literature.

References

1. Duda, R.O., Hart, P.: Pattern Classification and Scene Analysis. A Wiley Interscience Publication (2000)
2. Garcia, S., Derrac, J., Cano, J.R., Herrera, F.: Prototype Selection for Nearest Neighbor Classification: Taxonomy and Empirical Study. IEEE Transactions on Pattern Analysis and Machine Intelligence
3. Triguero, I., Derrac, J., Garcia, S., Herrera, F.: A Taxonomy and Experimental Study on Prototype Generation for Nearest Neighbor Classification. IEEE Transactions on Systems, Man and Cybernetics - Part C: Applications and Reviews
4. Kim, S., Oommen, B.J.: On Using Prototype Reduction Schemes and Classifier Fusion Strategies to Optimize Kernel-Based Nonlinear Subspace Methods. IEEE Transactions on Pattern Analysis and machine Intelligence 27, 455–460 (2005)

5. Kuncheva, L.I., Bezdek, J.C., Duin, R.P.W.: Decision Templates for Multiple Classifier Fusion: An Experimental Comparison. Pattern Recognition - The Journal of the Pattern Recognition Society 34, 299–314 (2001)
6. Hart, P.E.: The Condensed Nearest Neighbor Rule. IEEE Transactions on Information Theory 14, 515–516 (1968)
7. Gates, G.W.: The Reduced Nearest Neighbor Rule. IEEE Transactions on Information Theory 18, 431–433 (1972)
8. Chang, C.L.: Finding Prototypes for Nearest Neighbor Classifiers. IEEE Transactions on Computing 23, 1179–1184 (1974)
9. Ritter, G.L., Woodruff, H.B., Lowry, S.R., Isenhour, T.L.: An Algorithm for a Selective Nearest Neighbor Rule. IEEE Transactions on Information Theory 21, 665–669 (1975)
10. Devijver, P.A., Kittler, J.: On the Edited Nearest Neighbor Rule. In: Fifth International Conference on Pattern Recognition, pp. 72–80 (December 1980)
11. http://sci2s.ugr.es/pr/
12. Thomas, A.: Pattern Classification using Novel Order Statistics and Border Identification Methods. PhD thesis, School of Computer Science, Carleton University (to be submitted, 2013)
13. Duch, W.: Similarity based methods: a general framework for Classification, Approximation and Association. Control and Cybernetics 29(4), 937–968 (2000)
14. Foody, G.M.: Issues in Training Set Selection and Refinement for Classification by a Feedforward Neural Network. In: Proceedings of IEEE International Geoscience and Remote Sensing Symposium, pp. 409–411 (1998)
15. Li, G., Japkowicz, N., Stocki, T.J., Ungar, R.K.: Full Border Identification for Reduction of Training Sets. In: Proceedings of the Canadian Society for Computational Studies of Intelligence, 21st Conference on Advances in Artificial Intelligence, pp. 203–215 (2008)
16. Thomas, A., Oommen, B.J.: The Foundational Theory of Optimal "Anti-Bayesian" Parametric Pattern Classification Using Order Statistics Criteria (to be submitted, 2012)
17. Too, Y., Lin, G.D.: Characterizations of Uniform and Exponential Distributions. Academia Sinica 7(5), 357–359 (1989)
18. Ahsanullah, M., Nevzorov, V.B.: Order Statistics: Examples and Exercises. Nova Science Publishers, Inc. (2005)
19. Morris, K.W., Szynal, D.: A goodness-of-fit for the Uniform Distribution based on a Characterization. Journal of Mathematical Science 106, 2719–2724 (2001)
20. Lin, G.D.: Characterizations of Continuous Distributions via Expected values of two functions of Order Statistics. Sankhya: The Indian Journal of Statistics 52, 84–90 (1990)
21. Thomas, A., Oommen, B.J.: Optimal "Anti-Bayesian" Parametric Pattern Classification for the Exponential Family Using Order Statistics Criteria (to be submitted, 2012)

An Introduction
to Restricted Boltzmann Machines

Asja Fischer[1,2] and Christian Igel[2]

[1] Institut für Neuroinformatik, Ruhr-Universität Bochum, Germany
[2] Department of Computer Science, University of Copenhagen, Denmark

Abstract. Restricted Boltzmann machines (RBMs) are probabilistic graphical models that can be interpreted as stochastic neural networks. The increase in computational power and the development of faster learning algorithms have made them applicable to relevant machine learning problems. They attracted much attention recently after being proposed as building blocks of multi-layer learning systems called deep belief networks. This tutorial introduces RBMs as undirected graphical models. The basic concepts of graphical models are introduced first, however, basic knowledge in statistics is presumed. Different learning algorithms for RBMs are discussed. As most of them are based on Markov chain Monte Carlo (MCMC) methods, an introduction to Markov chains and the required MCMC techniques is provided.

1 Introduction

Boltzmann machines (BMs) have been introduced as bidirectionally connected networks of stochastic processing units, which can be interpreted as neural network models [1,16]. A BM can be used to learn important aspects of an unknown probability distribution based on samples from this distribution. In general, this learning process is difficult and time-consuming. However, the learning problem can be simplified by imposing restrictions on the network topology, which leads us to *restricted Boltzmann machines* (RBMs, [34]), the topic of this tutorial.

A (restricted) BM is a parameterized generative model representing a probability distribution. Given some observations, the training data, learning a BM means adjusting the BM parameters such that the probability distribution represented by the BM fits the training data as well as possible. Boltzmann machines consist of two types of units, so called visible and hidden neurons, which can be thought of as being arranged in two layers. The visible units constitute the first layer and correspond to the components of an observation (e.g., one visible unit for each pixel of a digital input image). The hidden units model dependencies between the components of observations (e.g., dependencies between pixels in images). They can be viewed as non-linear feature detectors [16].

Boltzmann machines can also be regarded as particular graphical models [22], more precisely undirected graphical models also known as Markov random fields. The embedding of BMs into the framework of probabilistic graphical models provides immediate access to a wealth of theoretical results and well-developed

L. Alvarez et al. (Eds.): CIARP 2012, LNCS 7441, pp. 14–36, 2012.

algorithms. Therefore, our tutorial introduces RBMs from this perspective. Computing the likelihood of an undirected model or its gradient for inference is in general computationally intensive, and this also holds for RBMs. Thus, sampling based methods are employed to approximate the likelihood and its gradient. Sampling from an undirected graphical model is in general not straightforward, but for RBMs Markov chain Monte Carlo (MCMC) methods are easily applicable in the form of Gibbs sampling, which will be introduced in this tutorial along with basic concepts of Markov chain theory.

After successful learning, an RBM provides a closed-form representation of the distribution underlying the observations. It can be used to compare the probabilities of (unseen) observations and to sample from the learnt distribution (e.g., to generate image textures [25,21]), in particular from marginal distributions of interest. For example, we can fix some visible units corresponding to a partial observation and sample the remaining visible units for completing the observation (e.g., to solve an image inpainting task [21]).

Boltzmann machines have been proposed in the 1980s [1,34]. Compared to the times when they were first introduced, RBMs can now be applied to more interesting problems due to the increase in computational power and the development of new learning strategies [15]. Restricted Boltzmann machines have received a lot of attention recently after being proposed as building blocks of multi-layer learning architectures called deep belief networks (DBNs, [19,17]). The idea is that the hidden neurons extract relevant features from the observations. These features can serve as input to another RBM. By stacking RBMs in this way, one can learn features from features in the hope of arriving at a high level representation.

It is an important property that single as well as stacked RBMs can be reinterpreted as deterministic feed-forward neural networks. Than they are used as functions from the domain of the observations to the expectations of the latent variables in the top layer. Such a function maps the observations to learnt features, which can, for example, serve as input to a supervised learning system. Further, the neural network corresponding to a trained RBM or DBN can be augmented by an output layer, where units in the new added output layer represent labels corresponding to observations. Then the model corresponds to a standard neural network for classification or regression that can be further trained by standard supervised learning algorithms [31]. It has been argued that this initialization (or unsupervised pretraining) of the feed-forward neural network weights based on a generative model helps to overcome problems observed when training multi-layer neural networks [19].

This introduction to RBMs is meant to supplement existing tutorials, such as the highly recommended review by Bengio [2], by providing more background information on Markov random fields and MCMC methods in Section 2 and Section 3, respectively. However, basic knowledge in statistics is presumed. We put an emphasis on topics that are – based on our experience – sometimes not familiar to people starting with RBMs. Restricted Boltzmann machines will be presented in Section 4. Section 5 will consider RBM training algorithms based on approximations of the log-likelihood gradient. This includes a discussion of contrastive divergence learning [15] as well as parallel tempering [10]. We will close by hinting at generalizations of RBMs in sections 6 and 7.

2   Graphical Models

Probabilistic graphical models describe probability distributions by mapping conditional dependence and independence properties between random variables on a graph structure (two sets of random variables X_1 and X_2 are conditionally independent given a set of random variables X_3 if $p(X_1, X_2|X_3) = p(X_1|X_3)p(X_2|X_3)$). Visualization by graphs can help to develop, understand and motivate probabilistic models. Furthermore, complex computations (e.g., marginalization) can be derived efficiently by using algorithms exploiting the graph structure.

There exist graphical models associated with different kind of graph structures, for example *factor graphs*, *Bayesian networks* associated with directed graphs, and *Markov random fields*, which are also called *Markov networks* or undirected graphical models. This tutorial focuses on the latter. A general introduction to graphical models for machine learning can, for example be found in [5]. The most comprehensive resource on graphical models is the textbook by Koller and Friedman [22].

2.1   Undirected Graphs and Markov Random Fields

First, we will summarize some fundamental concepts from graph theory. An *undirected graph* is a tuple $G = (V, E)$, where V is a finite set of nodes and E is a set of undirected edges. An edge consists out of a pair of nodes from V. If there exists an edge between two nodes v and w, i.e. $\{v, w\} \in E$, w belongs to the neighborhood of v and vice versa. The *neighborhood* $\mathcal{N}_v := \{w \in V : \{w, v\} \in E\}$ of v is defined by the set of nodes connected to v. A *clique* is a subset of V in which all nodes are pairwise connected. A clique is called *maximal* if no node can be added such that the resulting set is still a clique. In the following we will denote by $\mathcal{C}$ the set of all maximal cliques of an undirected graph. We call a sequence of nodes $v_1, v_2, \ldots, v_m \in V$, with $\{v_i, v_{i+1}\} \in E$ for $i = 1, \ldots, m-1$ a *path* from v_1 to v_m. A set $\mathcal{V} \subset V$ *separates* two nodes $v \notin \mathcal{V}$ and $w \notin \mathcal{V}$, if every path from v to w contains a node from $\mathcal{V}$.

We now associate a random variable X_v taking values in a state space Λ_v with each node v in an undirected graph $G = (V, E)$. To ease the notation, we assume $\Lambda_v = \Lambda$ for all $v \in V$. The random variables $X = (X_v)_{v \in V}$ are called *Markov random field* (MRF) if the joint probability distribution p fulfills the *(global) Markov property* w.r.t. the graph: For all disjunct subsets $\mathcal{A}, \mathcal{B}, \mathcal{S} \subset V$, where all nodes in $\mathcal{A}$ and $\mathcal{B}$ are separated by $\mathcal{S}$ the variables $(X_a)_{a \in \mathcal{A}}$ and $(X_b)_{b \in \mathcal{B}}$ are conditional independent given $(X_s)_{s \in \mathcal{S}}$, i.e. for all $x \in \Lambda^{|V|}$ it holds $p\left((x_a)_{a \in \mathcal{A}}|(x_t)_{t \in \mathcal{S} \cup \mathcal{B}}\right) = p\left((x_a)_{a \in \mathcal{A}}|(x_t)_{t \in \mathcal{S}}\right)$. A set of nodes $\text{MB}(v)$ is called the *Markov blanket* of node v, if for any set of nodes $\mathcal{B}$ with $v \notin \mathcal{B}$ we have

$p(v \mid \mathrm{MB}(v), \mathcal{B}) = p(v \mid \mathrm{MB}(v))$. This means that v is conditional independent from any other variables given $\mathrm{MB}(v)$. In an MRF, the Markov blanket $\mathrm{MB}(v)$ is given by the neighborhood $\mathcal{N}_v$ of v, a fact that is also referred to as *local* Markov property.

Since conditional independence of random variables and the factorization properties of the joint probability distribution are closely related, one can ask if there exists a general factorization form of the distributions of MRFs. An answer to this question is given by the *Hammersley-Clifford Theorem* (for rigorous formulations and proofs we refer to [23,22]). The theorem states that a strictly positive distribution p satisfies the Markov property w.r.t. an undirected graph G if and only if p factorizes over G. A distribution is said to factorize about an undirected graph G with maximal cliques $\mathcal{C}$ if there exists a set of non-negative functions $\{\psi_C\}_{C \subset \mathcal{C}}$, called *potential functions*, with

$$\forall \boldsymbol{x}, \hat{\boldsymbol{x}} \subset \Lambda^{|V|} : (x_c)_{c \in C} = (\hat{x}_c)_{c \in C} \Rightarrow \psi_C(\boldsymbol{x}) = \psi_C(\hat{\boldsymbol{x}}) \tag{1}$$

and

$$p(\boldsymbol{x}) = \frac{1}{Z} \prod_{C \in \mathcal{C}} \psi_C(\boldsymbol{x}). \tag{2}$$

The normalization constant $Z = \sum_{\boldsymbol{x}} \prod_{C \in \mathcal{C}} \psi_C(\boldsymbol{x}_C)$ is called *partition function*.

If p is strictly positive, the same holds for the potential functions. Thus we can write

$$p(\boldsymbol{x}) = \frac{1}{Z} \prod_{C \in \mathcal{C}} \psi_C(\boldsymbol{x}_C) = \frac{1}{Z} e^{\sum_{C \in \mathcal{C}} \ln \psi_C(\boldsymbol{x}_C)} = \frac{1}{Z} e^{-E(\boldsymbol{x})} \ , \tag{3}$$

where we call $E := \sum_{C \in \mathcal{C}} \ln \psi_C(\boldsymbol{x}_C)$ the *energy function*. Thus, the probability distribution of every MRF can be expressed in the form given by (3), which is also called *Gibbs distribution*.

2.2   Unsupervised Learning

Unsupervised learning means learning (important aspects of) an unknown distribution q based on sample data. This includes finding new representations of data that foster learning, generalization, and communication. If we assume that the structure of the graphical model is known and the energy function belongs to a known family of functions parameterized by $\boldsymbol{\theta}$, unsupervised learning of a data distribution with an MRF means adjusting the parameters $\boldsymbol{\theta}$. We write $p(\boldsymbol{x}|\boldsymbol{\theta})$ when we want to emphasize the dependency of a distribution on its parameters.

We consider training data $S = \{\boldsymbol{x}_1, \ldots, \boldsymbol{x}_\ell\}$. The data samples are assumed to be independent and identically distributed (i.i.d.). That is, they are drawn independently from some unknown distribution q. A standard way of estimating the parameters of a statistical model is maximum-likelihood estimation. Applied to MRFs, this corresponds to finding the MRF parameters that maximize the probability of S under the MRF distribution, i.e. training corresponds to finding the parameters $\boldsymbol{\theta}$ that maximize the likelihood given the training data. The likelihood $\mathcal{L} : \Theta \to \mathbb{R}$ of an MRF given the data set S maps parameters $\boldsymbol{\theta}$ from a parameter space Θ to $\mathcal{L}(\boldsymbol{\theta} \,|\, S) = \prod_{i=1}^{\ell} p(\boldsymbol{x}_i | \boldsymbol{\theta})$. Maximizing the likelihood is the same as maximizing the log-likelihood given by

$$\ln \mathcal{L}(\boldsymbol{\theta} \,|\, S) = \ln \prod_{i=1}^{\ell} p(\boldsymbol{x}_i | \boldsymbol{\theta}) = \sum_{i=1}^{\ell} \ln p(\boldsymbol{x}_i | \boldsymbol{\theta}) \ . \tag{4}$$

For the Gibbs distribution of an MRF it is in general not possible to find the maximum likelihood parameters analytically. Thus, numerical approximation methods have to be used, for example gradient ascent which is described below.

Maximizing the likelihood corresponds to minimizing the distance between the unknown distribution q underlying S and the distribution p of the MRF in terms of the *Kullback-Leibler-divergence* (KL-divergence), which for a finite state space Ω is given by:

$$\mathrm{KL}(q||p) = \sum_{\boldsymbol{x} \in \Omega} q(\boldsymbol{x}) \ln \frac{q(\boldsymbol{x})}{p(\boldsymbol{x})} = \sum_{\boldsymbol{x} \in \Omega} q(\boldsymbol{x}) \ln q(\boldsymbol{x}) - \sum_{\boldsymbol{x} \in \Omega} q(\boldsymbol{x}) \ln p(\boldsymbol{x}) \tag{5}$$

The KL-divergence is a (non-symmetric) measure of the difference between two distributions. It is always positive and zero if and only if the distributions are the same. As becomes clear by equation (5) the KL-divergence can be expressed as the difference between the entropy of q and a second term. Only the latter depends on the parameters subject to optimization. Approximating the expectation over q in this term by the training samples from q results in the log-likelihood. Therefore, maximizing the log-likelihood corresponds to minimizing the KL-divergence.

Optimization by Gradient Ascent. If it is not possible to find parameters maximizing the likelihood analytically, the usual way to find them is gradient ascent on the log-likelihood. This corresponds to iteratively updating the parameters $\boldsymbol{\theta}^{(t)}$ to $\boldsymbol{\theta}^{(t+1)}$ based on the gradient of the log-likelihood. Let us consider the following update rule:

$$\boldsymbol{\theta}^{(t+1)} = \boldsymbol{\theta}^{(t)} + \eta \underbrace{\frac{\partial}{\partial \boldsymbol{\theta}^{(t)}} \left(\sum_{i=1}^{N} \ln \mathcal{L}(\boldsymbol{\theta}^{(t)} | \boldsymbol{x}_i) \right) - \lambda \boldsymbol{\theta}^{(t)} + \nu \Delta \boldsymbol{\theta}^{(t-1)}}_{:= \Delta \boldsymbol{\theta}^{(t)}} \tag{6}$$

If the constants $\lambda \in \mathbb{R}_0^+$ and $\nu \in \mathbb{R}_0^+$ are set to zero, we have vanilla gradient ascent. The constant $\eta \in \mathbb{R}^+$ is the learning rate. As we will see later, it can be desirable to strive for models with weights having small absolute values. To achieve this, we can optimize an objective function consisting of the log-likelihood minus half of the norm of the parameters $\|\theta\|^2/2$ weighted by λ. This method called *weight decay* penalizes weights with large magnitude. It leads to the $-\lambda \boldsymbol{\theta}^{(t)}$ term in our update rule (6). In a Bayesian framework, weight decay can be interpreted as assuming a zero-mean Gaussian prior on the parameters. The update rule can be further extended by a *momentum* term $\Delta\boldsymbol{\theta}^{(t-1)}$, weighted by the parameter ν. Using a momentum term helps against oscillations in the iterative update procedure and can speed-up the learning process as known from feed-forward neural network training [31].

Introducing Latent Variables. Suppose we want to model an m-dimensional unknown probability distribution q (e.g., each component of a sample corresponds to one of m pixels of an image). Typically, not all variables $\boldsymbol{X} = (X_v)_{v \in V}$ in an MRF need to correspond to some observed component, and the number of nodes is larger than m. We split $\boldsymbol{X}$ into *visible* (or *observed*) variables $\boldsymbol{V} = (V_1, \ldots, V_m)$ corresponding to the components of the observations and *latent* (or *hidden*) variables $\boldsymbol{H} = (H_1, \ldots, H_n)$ given by the remaining $n = |V| - m$ variables. Using latent variables allows to describe complex distributions over the visible variables by means of simple (conditional) distributions. In this case the Gibbs distribution of an MRF describes the joint probability distribution of $(\boldsymbol{V}, \boldsymbol{H})$ and one is usually interested in the marginal distribution of $\boldsymbol{V}$ which is given by

$$p(\boldsymbol{v}) = \sum_{\boldsymbol{h}} p(\boldsymbol{v}, \boldsymbol{h}) = \frac{1}{Z} \sum_{\boldsymbol{h}} e^{-E(\boldsymbol{v},\boldsymbol{h})} \ , \tag{7}$$

where $Z = \sum_{\boldsymbol{v},\boldsymbol{h}} e^{-E(\boldsymbol{v},\boldsymbol{h})}$. While the visible variables correspond to the components of an observation, the latent variables introduce dependencies between the visible variables (e.g., between pixels of an input image).

Log-Likelihood Gradient of MRFs with Latent Variables. Restricted Boltzmann machines are MRFs with hidden variables and RBM learning algorithms are based on gradient ascent on the log-likelihood. For a model of the form (7) with parameters $\boldsymbol{\theta}$, the log-likelihood given a single training example $\boldsymbol{v}$ is

$$\ln \mathcal{L}(\boldsymbol{\theta} \mid \boldsymbol{v}) = \ln p(\boldsymbol{v} \mid \boldsymbol{\theta}) = \ln \frac{1}{Z} \sum_{\boldsymbol{h}} e^{-E(\boldsymbol{v},\boldsymbol{h})} = \ln \sum_{\boldsymbol{h}} e^{-E(\boldsymbol{v},\boldsymbol{h})} - \ln \sum_{\boldsymbol{v},\boldsymbol{h}} e^{-E(\boldsymbol{v},\boldsymbol{h})}$$

$$\tag{8}$$

and for the gradient we get:

$$\frac{\partial \ln \mathcal{L}(\boldsymbol{\theta} \mid \boldsymbol{v})}{\partial \boldsymbol{\theta}} = \frac{\partial}{\partial \boldsymbol{\theta}} \left(\ln \sum_{\boldsymbol{h}} e^{-E(\boldsymbol{v},\boldsymbol{h})} \right) - \frac{\partial}{\partial \boldsymbol{\theta}} \left(\ln \sum_{\boldsymbol{v},\boldsymbol{h}} e^{-E(\boldsymbol{v},\boldsymbol{h})} \right)$$

$$= -\frac{1}{\sum_{\boldsymbol{h}} e^{-E(\boldsymbol{v},\boldsymbol{h})}} \sum_{\boldsymbol{h}} e^{-E(\boldsymbol{v},\boldsymbol{h})} \frac{\partial E(\boldsymbol{v}, \boldsymbol{h})}{\partial \boldsymbol{\theta}} + \frac{1}{\sum_{\boldsymbol{v},\boldsymbol{h}} e^{-E(\boldsymbol{v},\boldsymbol{h})}} \sum_{\boldsymbol{v},\boldsymbol{h}} e^{-E(\boldsymbol{v},\boldsymbol{h})} \frac{\partial E(\boldsymbol{v}, \boldsymbol{h})}{\partial \boldsymbol{\theta}}$$

$$= -\sum_{\boldsymbol{h}} p(\boldsymbol{h} \mid \boldsymbol{v}) \frac{\partial E(\boldsymbol{v}, \boldsymbol{h})}{\partial \boldsymbol{\theta}} + \sum_{\boldsymbol{v},\boldsymbol{h}} p(\boldsymbol{v}, \boldsymbol{h}) \frac{\partial E(\boldsymbol{v}, \boldsymbol{h})}{\partial \boldsymbol{\theta}} \tag{9}$$

In the last step we used that the conditional probability can be written in the following way:

$$p(\boldsymbol{h} \mid \boldsymbol{v}) = \frac{p(\boldsymbol{v}, \boldsymbol{h})}{p(\boldsymbol{v})} = \frac{\frac{1}{Z} e^{-E(\boldsymbol{v}, \boldsymbol{h})}}{\frac{1}{Z} \sum_{\boldsymbol{h}} e^{-E(\boldsymbol{v}, \boldsymbol{h})}} = \frac{e^{-E(\boldsymbol{v}, \boldsymbol{h})}}{\sum_{\boldsymbol{h}} e^{-E(\boldsymbol{v}, \boldsymbol{h})}} \tag{10}$$

Note that the last expression of equality (9) is the difference of two expectations: the expected values of the energy function under the model distribution and under the conditional distribution of the hidden variables given the training example. Directly calculating this sums, which run over all values of the respective variables, leads to a computational complexity which is in general exponential in the number of variables of the MRF. To avoid this computational burden, the expectations can be approximated by samples drawn from the corresponding distributions based on MCMC techniques.

3 Markov Chains and Markov Chain Monte Carlo Techniques

Markov chains play an important role in RBM training because they provide a method to draw samples from 'complex' probability distributions like the Gibbs distribution of an MRF. This section will serve as an introduction to some fundamental concepts of Markov chain theory. A detailed introduction can be found, for example, in [6] and the aforementioned textbooks [5,22]. The section will describe Gibbs sampling as an MCMC technique often used for MRF training and in particular for training RBMs.

3.1 Definition of a Markov Chain and Convergence to Stationarity

A *Markov chain* is a time discrete stochastic process for which the *Markov property* holds, that is, a family of random variables $X = \{X^{(k)} | k \in \mathbb{N}_0\}$ which take values in a (in the following considerations finite) set Ω and for which $\forall k \geq 0$ and $\forall j, i, i_0, \ldots, i_{k-1} \in \Omega$ it holds

$$p_{ij}^{(k)} := P\left(X^{(k+1)} = j | X^{(k)} = i, X^{(k-1)} = i_{k-1}, \ldots, X^{(0)} = i_0\right) \tag{11}$$

$$= P\left(X^{(k+1)} = j | X^{(k)} = i\right) . \tag{12}$$

This means that the next state of the system depends only on the current state and not on the sequence of events that preceded it. If for all $k \geq 0$ the $p_{ij}^{(k)}$ have the same value p_{ij}, the chain is called *homogeneous* and the matrix $\mathbf{P} = (p_{ij})_{i,j \in \Omega}$ is called *transition matrix* of the homogeneous Markov chain.

If the starting distribution $\mu^{(0)}$ (i.e., the probability distribution of $X^{(0)}$) is given by the probability vector $\boldsymbol{\mu}^{(0)} = (\mu^{(0)}(i))_{i \in \Omega}$, with $\mu^{(0)}(i) = P(X^{(0)} = i)$, the distribution $\boldsymbol{\mu}^{(k)}$ of $X^{(k)}$ is given by $\boldsymbol{\mu}^{(k)\,\mathrm{T}} = \boldsymbol{\mu}^{(0)\,\mathrm{T}} \mathbf{P}^k$.

A distribution π for which it holds $\boldsymbol{\pi}^{\mathrm{T}} = \boldsymbol{\pi}^{\mathrm{T}} \mathbf{P}$ is called *stationary distribution*. If the Markov chain for any time k reaches the stationary distribution $\boldsymbol{\mu}^{(k)} = \boldsymbol{\pi}$ all subsequent states will be distributed accordingly, that is, $\boldsymbol{\mu}^{(k+n)} = \boldsymbol{\pi}$ for all $n \in \mathbb{N}$. A sufficient (but not necessary) condition for a distribution π to be stationary w.r.t. a Markov chain described by the transition probabilities $p_{ij}, i, j \in \Omega$ is that $\forall i, j \in \Omega$ it holds:

$$\pi(i)p_{ij} = \pi(j)p_{ji} \ . \tag{13}$$

This is called the *detailed balance condition.*

Especially relevant are Markov chains for which it is known that there exists an unique stationary distribution. For finite Ω this is the case if the Markov chain is *irreducible*. A Markov chain is irreducible if one can get from any state in Ω to any other in a finite number of transitions or more formally $\forall i, j \in \Omega$ $\exists k > 0$ with $P(X^{(k)} = j | X^{(0)} = i) > 0$.

A chain is called *aperiodic* if for all $i \in \Omega$ the greatest common divisor of $\{k | P(X^{(k)} = i | X^{(0)} = i) > 0 \wedge k \in \mathbb{N}_0\}$ is 1. One can show that an irreducible and aperiodic Markov chain on a finite state space is guarantied to converge to its stationary distribution (see, e.g., [6]). That is, for an arbitrary starting distribution μ it holds

$$\lim_{k \to \infty} d_V(\boldsymbol{\mu}^T \mathrm{P}^k, \boldsymbol{\pi}^T) = 0 \ , \tag{14}$$

where d_V is the *distance of variation*. For two distributions α and β on a finite state space Ω, the distance of variation is defined as

$$d_V(\boldsymbol{\alpha}, \boldsymbol{\beta}) = \frac{1}{2}|\boldsymbol{\alpha} - \boldsymbol{\beta}| = \frac{1}{2}\sum_{x \in \Omega} |\alpha(x) - \beta(x)| \ . \tag{15}$$

To ease the notation, we allow both row and column probability vectors as arguments of the functions in (15).

Markov chain Monte Carlo methods make use of this convergence theorem for producing samples from certain probability distribution by setting up a Markov chain that converges to the desired distributions. Suppose you want to sample from a distribution q with a finite state space. Then you construct an irreducible and aperiodic Markov chain with stationary distribution $\pi = q$. This is a non-trivial task. If t is large enough, a sample $X^{(t)}$ from the constructed chain is then approximately a sample from π and therefore from q. Gibbs Sampling [13] is such a MCMC method and will be described in the following section.

3.2   Gibbs Sampling

Gibbs Sampling belongs to the class of Metropolis-Hastings algorithms [14]. It is a simple MCMC algorithm for producing samples from the joint probability distribution of multiple random variables. The basic idea is to update each variable subsequently based on its conditional distribution given the state of the others. We will describe it in detail by explaining how Gibbs sampling can be used to simulate the Gibbs distribution of an MRF.

We consider an MRF $\boldsymbol{X} = (X_1, \ldots, X_N)$ w.r.t. a graph $G = (V, E)$, where $V = \{1, \ldots, N\}$ for the sake of clearness of notation. The random variables X_i, $i \in V$ take values in a finite set Λ and $\pi(\boldsymbol{x}) = \frac{1}{Z}e^{-\mathcal{E}(\boldsymbol{x})}$ is the joint probability distribution of $\boldsymbol{X}$. Furthermore, if we assume that the MRF changes its state during time, we can consider $X = \{\boldsymbol{X}^{(k)} | k \in \mathbb{N}_0\}$ as a Markov chain taking values in $\Omega = \Lambda^N$ where $\boldsymbol{X}^{(k)} = (X_1^{(k)}, \ldots, X_N^{(k)})$ describes the state of the MRF at time $k \geq 0$. At each transition step we now pick a random variable X_i, $i \in V$ with a probability $q(i)$ given by a strictly positive probability distribution q on V and sample a new value for X_i based on its conditional probability distribution given the state $(x_v)_{v \in V \setminus i}$ of all other variables $(X_v)_{v \in V \setminus i}$, i.e. based on $\pi\left(X_i | (x_v)_{v \in V \setminus i}\right) = \pi\left(X_i | (x_w)_{w \in \mathcal{N}_i}\right)$. Therefore, the transition probability $p_{\boldsymbol{xy}}$ for two states $\boldsymbol{x}, \boldsymbol{y}$ of the MRF $\boldsymbol{X}$ with $\boldsymbol{x} \neq \boldsymbol{y}$ is given by:

$$
p_{\boldsymbol{xy}} = \begin{cases} q(i)\pi\left(y_i | (x_v)_{v \in V \setminus i}\right), & \text{if } \exists i \in V \text{ so that } \forall v \in V \text{ with } v \neq i\colon x_v = y_v \\ 0, & \text{else .} \end{cases}
$$

(16)

And the probability, that the state of the MRF $\boldsymbol{x}$ stays the same, is given by:

$$
p_{\boldsymbol{xx}} = \sum_{i \in V} q(i)\pi\left(x_i | (x_v)_{v \in V \setminus i}\right) \ .
$$

(17)

It is easy to see that the joint distribution π of the MRF is the stationary distribution of the Markov chain defined by these transition probabilities by showing that the detailed balance condition (13) holds: For $\boldsymbol{x} = \boldsymbol{y}$ this follows directly. If $\boldsymbol{x}$ and $\boldsymbol{y}$ differ in the value of more than one random variable it follows from the fact that $p_{\boldsymbol{yx}} = p_{\boldsymbol{xy}} = 0$. Assume that $\boldsymbol{x}$ and $\boldsymbol{y}$ differ only in the state of exactly one variable X_i, i.e., $y_j = x_j$ for $j \neq i$ and $y_i \neq x_i$, then it holds:

$$
\pi(\boldsymbol{x})p_{\boldsymbol{xy}} = \pi(\boldsymbol{x})q(i)\pi\left(y_i | (x_v)_{v \in V \setminus i}\right) = \pi\left(x_i, (x_v)_{v \in V \setminus i}\right) q(i) \frac{\pi\left(y_i, (x_v)_{v \in V \setminus i}\right)}{\pi\left((x_v)_{v \in V \setminus i}\right)}
$$

$$
= \pi\left(y_i, (x_v)_{v \in V \setminus i}\right) q(i) \frac{\pi\left(x_i, (x_v)_{v \in V \setminus i}\right)}{\pi\left((x_v)_{v \in V \setminus i}\right)}
$$

$$
= \pi(\boldsymbol{y})q(i)\pi\left(x_i | (x_v)_{v \in V \setminus i}\right) = \pi(\boldsymbol{y})p_{\boldsymbol{yx}}. \quad (18)
$$

Since π is strictly positive so are the conditional probability distributions of the single variables. Thus, it follows that every single variable X_i can take every state $x_i \in \Lambda$ in a single transition step and thus every state of the whole MRF can reach any other in Λ^N in a finite number of steps and the Markov chain is irreducible. Furthermore it follows from the positivity of the conditional distributions that $p_{\boldsymbol{xx}} > 0$ for all $\boldsymbol{x} \in \Lambda^N$ and thus that the Markov chain is aperiodic. Aperiodicity and irreducibility guaranty that the chain converges to the stationary distribution π.

In practice the single random variables to be updated are usually not chosen at random based on a distribution q but subsequently in fixed predefined order. The corresponding algorithm is often referred to as *periodic Gibbs Sampler*. If $\boldsymbol{P}$ is the transition matrix of the Gibbs chain, the convergence rate of the periodic

Gibbs sampler to the stationary distribution of the MRF is bounded by the following inequality (see for example [6]):

$$|\boldsymbol{\mu}\mathbf{P}^k - \boldsymbol{\pi}| \le \frac{1}{2}|\boldsymbol{\mu} - \boldsymbol{\pi}|(1 - e^{-N\triangle})^k, \tag{19}$$

where $\triangle = \sup_{l \in V} \delta_l$ and $\delta_l = \sup\{|\mathcal{E}(\boldsymbol{x}) - \mathcal{E}(\boldsymbol{y})|; x_i = y_i \forall i \in V \text{ with } i \ne l\}$. Here μ is an arbitrary starting distribution and $\frac{1}{2}|\boldsymbol{\mu} - \boldsymbol{\pi}|$ is the distance in variation as defined in (15).

4   Restricted Boltzmann Machines

A RBM (also denoted as Harmonium [34]) is an MRF associated with a bipartite undirected graph as shown in Fig. 1. It consists of m visible units $\boldsymbol{V} = (V_1, ..., V_m)$ to represent observable data and n hidden units $\boldsymbol{H} = (H_1, ..., H_n)$ to capture dependencies between observed variables. In binary RBMs, our focus in this tutorial, the random variables $(\boldsymbol{V}, \boldsymbol{H})$ take values $(\boldsymbol{v}, \boldsymbol{h}) \in \{0,1\}^{m+n}$ and the joint probability distribution under the model is given by the Gibbs distribution $p(\boldsymbol{v}, \boldsymbol{h}) = \frac{1}{Z}e^{-E(\boldsymbol{v},\boldsymbol{h})}$ with the energy function

$$E(\boldsymbol{v}, \boldsymbol{h}) = -\sum_{i=1}^{n}\sum_{j=1}^{m} w_{ij}h_i v_j - \sum_{j=1}^{m} b_j v_j - \sum_{i=1}^{n} c_i h_i \ . \tag{20}$$

For all $i \in \{1, ..., n\}$ and $j \in \{1, ..., m\}$, w_{ij} is a real valued weight associated with the edge between units V_j and H_i and b_j and c_i are real valued bias terms associated with the jth visible and the ith hidden variable, respectively.

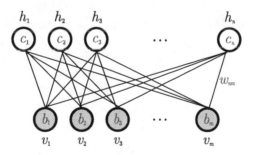

Fig. 1. The undirected graph of an RBM with n hidden and m visible variables

The graph of an RBM has only connections between the layer of hidden and visible variables but not between two variables of the same layer. In terms of probability this means that the hidden variables are independent given the state of the visible variables and vice versa:

$$p(\boldsymbol{h}\,|\,\boldsymbol{v}) = \prod_{i=1}^{n} p(h_i\,|\,\boldsymbol{v}) \ \text{ and } \ p(\boldsymbol{v}\,|\,\boldsymbol{h}) = \prod_{i=1}^{m} p(v_i\,|\,\boldsymbol{h}) \ . \tag{21}$$

The absence of connections between hidden variables makes the marginal distribution (7) of the visible variables easy to calculate:

$$p(\boldsymbol{v}) = \frac{1}{Z}\sum_{\boldsymbol{h}} p(\boldsymbol{v},\boldsymbol{h}) = \frac{1}{Z}\sum_{\boldsymbol{h}} e^{-E(\boldsymbol{v},\boldsymbol{h})}$$

$$= \frac{1}{Z}\sum_{h_1}\sum_{h_2}\cdots\sum_{h_n} e^{\sum_{j=1}^{m} b_j v_j} \prod_{i=1}^{n} e^{h_i\left(c_i + \sum_{j=1}^{m} w_{ij} v_j\right)}$$

$$= \frac{1}{Z} e^{\sum_{j=1}^{m} b_j v_j} \sum_{h_1} e^{h_1\left(c_1 + \sum_{j=1}^{m} w_{1j} v_j\right)} \sum_{h_2} e^{h_2\left(c_2 + \sum_{j=1}^{m} w_{2j} v_j\right)} \cdots \sum_{h_n} e^{h_n\left(c_n + \sum_{j=1}^{m} w_{nj} v_j\right)}$$

$$= \frac{1}{Z} e^{\sum_{j=1}^{m} b_j v_j} \prod_{i=1}^{n}\sum_{h_i} e^{h_i\left(c_i + \sum_{j=1}^{m} w_{ij} v_j\right)}$$

$$= \frac{1}{Z} \prod_{j=1}^{m} e^{b_j v_j} \prod_{i=1}^{n}\left(1 + e^{c_i + \sum_{j=1}^{m} w_{ij} v_j}\right) \tag{22}$$

This equation shows why a (marginalized) RBM can be regarded as a *product of experts* model [15,39], in which a number of "experts" for individual components of the observations are combined multiplicatively.

Any distribution on $\{0,1\}^m$ can be modeled arbitrarily well by an RBM with m visible and $k+1$ hidden units, where k denotes the cardinality of the support set of the target distribution, that is, the number of input elements from $\{0,1\}^m$ that have a non-zero probability of being observed [24]. It has been shown recently that even less units can be sufficient depending on the patterns in the support set [30].

The RBM can be interpreted as a stochastic neural network, where nodes and edges correspond to neurons and synaptic connections, respectively. The conditional probability of a single variable being one can be interpreted as the firing rate of a (stochastic) neuron with sigmoid activation function $\sigma(x) = 1/(1+e^{-x})$, because it holds:

$$p(H_i = 1\,|\,\boldsymbol{v}) = \sigma\left(\sum_{j=1}^{m} w_{ij} v_j + c_i\right) \tag{23}$$

and

$$p(V_j = 1\,|\,\boldsymbol{h}) = \sigma\left(\sum_{i=1}^{n} w_{ij} h_i + b_j\right) \ . \tag{24}$$

To see this, let $\boldsymbol{v}_{-l}$ denote the state of all visible units except the lth one and let us define

$$\alpha_l(\boldsymbol{h}) := -\sum_{i=1}^{n} w_{il} h_i - b_l \tag{25}$$

and

$$\beta(\boldsymbol{v}_{-l}, \boldsymbol{h}) := -\sum_{i=1}^{n} \sum_{j=1, j \neq l}^{m} w_{ij} h_i v_j - \sum_{j=1, j \neq l}^{m} b_i v_i - \sum_{i=1}^{n} c_i h_i . \tag{26}$$

Then $E(\boldsymbol{v}, \boldsymbol{h}) = \beta(\boldsymbol{v}_{-l}, \boldsymbol{h}) + v_l \alpha_l(\boldsymbol{h})$, where $v_l \alpha_l(\boldsymbol{h})$ collects all terms involving v_l and we can write [2]:

$$p(V_l = 1 \,|\boldsymbol{h}) = p(V_l = 1 \,|\boldsymbol{v}_{-l}, \boldsymbol{h}) = \frac{p(V_l = 1, \boldsymbol{v}_{-l}, \boldsymbol{h})}{p(\boldsymbol{v}_{-l}, \boldsymbol{h})}$$

$$= \frac{e^{-E(v_l=1, \boldsymbol{v}_{-l}, \boldsymbol{h})}}{e^{-E(v_l=1, \boldsymbol{v}_{-l}, \boldsymbol{h})} + e^{-E(v_l=0, \boldsymbol{v}_{-l}, \boldsymbol{h})}} = \frac{e^{-\beta(\boldsymbol{v}_{-l}, \boldsymbol{h}) - 1 \cdot \alpha_l(\boldsymbol{h})}}{e^{-\beta(\boldsymbol{v}_{-l}, \boldsymbol{h}) - 1 \cdot \alpha_l(\boldsymbol{h})} + e^{-\beta(\boldsymbol{v}_{-l}, \boldsymbol{h}) - 0 \cdot \alpha_l(\boldsymbol{h})}}$$

$$= \frac{e^{-\beta(\boldsymbol{v}_{-l}, \boldsymbol{h})} \cdot e^{-\alpha_l(\boldsymbol{h})}}{e^{-\beta(\boldsymbol{v}_{-l}, \boldsymbol{h})} \cdot e^{-\alpha_l(\boldsymbol{h})} + e^{-\beta(\boldsymbol{v}_{-l}, \boldsymbol{h})}} = \frac{e^{-\beta(\boldsymbol{v}_{-l}, \boldsymbol{h})} \cdot e^{-\alpha_l(\boldsymbol{h})}}{e^{-\beta(\boldsymbol{v}_{-l}, \boldsymbol{h})} \cdot \left(e^{-\alpha_l(\boldsymbol{v}_{-l}, \boldsymbol{h})} + 1\right)}$$

$$= \frac{e^{-\alpha_l(\boldsymbol{v}_{-l}, \boldsymbol{h})}}{e^{-\alpha_l(\boldsymbol{v}_{-l}, \boldsymbol{h})} + 1} = \frac{\frac{1}{e^{\alpha_l(\boldsymbol{h})}}}{\frac{1}{e^{\alpha_l(\boldsymbol{h})}} + 1} = \frac{1}{1 + e^{\alpha_l(\boldsymbol{v}_{-l}, \boldsymbol{h})}}$$

$$= \sigma(-\alpha_l(\boldsymbol{h})) = \sigma\left(\sum_{i=1}^{n} w_{il} h_i + b_j\right) \tag{27}$$

The independence between the variables in one layer makes Gibbs sampling especially easy: Instead of sampling new values for all variables subsequently, the states of all variables in one layer can be sampled jointly. Thus, Gibbs sampling can be performed in just two sub steps: sampling a new state $\boldsymbol{h}$ for the hidden neurons based on $p(\boldsymbol{h}|\boldsymbol{v})$ and sampling a state $\boldsymbol{v}$ for the visible layer based on $p(\boldsymbol{v}|\boldsymbol{h})$. This is also referred to as *block Gibbs sampling*.

As mentioned in the introduction, an RBM can be reinterpreted as a standard feed-forward neural network with one layer of non-linear processing units. From this perspective the RBM is viewed as a deterministic function $\{0,1\}^m \to \mathbb{R}^n$ that maps an input $\boldsymbol{v} \in \{0,1\}^m$ to $\boldsymbol{y} \in \mathbb{R}^n$ with $y_i = p(H_i = 1|\boldsymbol{v})$. That is, an observation is mapped to the expected value of the hidden neurons given the observation.

4.1   The Gradient of the Log-Likelihood

The log-likelihood gradient of an MRF can be written as the sum of two expectations, see (9). For RBMs the first term of (9) (i.e., the expectation of the energy gradient under the conditional distribution of the hidden variables given a training sample $\boldsymbol{v}$) can be computed efficiently because it factorizes nicely. For example, w.r.t. the parameter w_{ij} we get:

$$\sum_{h} p(h \mid v) \frac{\partial E(v,h)}{\partial w_{ij}} = \sum_{h} p(h \mid v) h_i v_j$$

$$= \sum_{h} \prod_{k=1}^{n} p(h_k \mid v) h_i v_j = \sum_{h_i} \sum_{h_{-i}} p(h_i \mid v) p(h_{-i} \mid v) h_i v_j$$

$$= \sum_{h_i} p(h_i \mid v) h_i v_j \underbrace{\sum_{h_{-i}} p(h_{-i} \mid v)}_{=1} = p(H_i = 1 \mid v) v_j = \sigma \left(\sum_{j=1}^{m} w_{ij} v_j + c_i \right) v_j \quad (28)$$

Since the second term in (9) can also be written as $\sum_{v} p(v) \sum_{h} p(h \mid v) \frac{\partial E(v,h)}{\partial \theta}$ or $\sum_{h} p(h) \sum_{v} p(v \mid h) \frac{\partial E(v,h)}{\partial \theta}$ we can also reduce its computational complexity by applying the same kind of factorization to the inner sum, either factorizing over the hidden variables as shown above or factorizing over the visible variables in an analogous way. However, the computation remains intractable for regular sized RBMs because its complexity is still exponential in the size of the smallest layer (the outer sum still runs over either 2^m or 2^n states).

Using the factorization trick (28) the derivative of the log-likelihood of a single training pattern v w.r.t. the weight w_{ij} becomes

$$\frac{\partial \ln \mathcal{L}(\theta \mid v)}{\partial w_{ij}} = -\sum_{h} p(h \mid v) \frac{\partial E(v,h)}{\partial w_{ij}} + \sum_{v,h} p(v,h) \frac{\partial E(v,h)}{\partial w_{ij}}$$

$$= \sum_{h} p(h \mid v) h_i v_j - \sum_{v} p(v) \sum_{h} p(h \mid v) h_i v_j$$

$$= p(H_i = 1 \mid v) v_j - \sum_{v} p(v) p(H_i = 1 \mid v) v_j \ . \quad (29)$$

For the mean of this derivative over a training set $S = \{v_1, \ldots, v_\ell\}$ often the following notations are used:

$$\frac{1}{\ell} \sum_{v \in S} \frac{\partial \ln \mathcal{L}(\theta \mid v)}{\partial w_{ij}} = \frac{1}{\ell} \sum_{v \in S} \left[-\mathbb{E}_{p(h \mid v)} \left[\frac{\partial E(v,h)}{\partial w_{ij}} \right] + \mathbb{E}_{p(h,v)} \left[\frac{\partial E(v,h)}{\partial w_{ij}} \right] \right]$$

$$= \frac{1}{\ell} \sum_{v \in S} \left[\mathbb{E}_{p(h \mid v)} \left[v_i h_j \right] - \mathbb{E}_{p(h,v)} \left[v_i h_j \right] \right]$$

$$= \langle v_i h_j \rangle_{p(h \mid v) q(v)} - \langle v_i h_j \rangle_{p(h,v)} \quad (30)$$

with q denoting the empirical distribution. This gives the often stated rule:

$$\sum_{v \in S} \frac{\partial \ln \mathcal{L}(\theta \mid v)}{\partial w_{ij}} \propto \langle v_i h_j \rangle_{\text{data}} - \langle v_i h_j \rangle_{\text{model}} \quad (31)$$

Analogously to (29) we get the derivatives w.r.t. the bias parameter b_j of the jth visible variable

$$\frac{\partial \ln \mathcal{L}(\theta \mid v)}{\partial b_j} = v_j - \sum_{v} p(v) v_j \quad (32)$$

and w.r.t. the bias parameter c_i of the ith hidden variable

$$\frac{\partial \ln \mathcal{L}(\boldsymbol{\theta} \mid \boldsymbol{v})}{\partial c_i} = p(H_i = 1 \mid \boldsymbol{v}) - \sum_{\boldsymbol{v}} p(\boldsymbol{v}) p(H_i = 1 \mid \boldsymbol{v}) \ . \tag{33}$$

To avoid the exponential complexity of summing over all values of the visible variables (or all values of the hidden if one decides to factorize over the visible variables beforehand) when calculating the second term of the log-likelihood gradient – or the second terms of (29), (32), and (33) – one can approximate this expectation by samples from the model distribution. These samples can be obtained by Gibbs sampling. This requires running the Markov chain "long enough" to ensure convergence to stationarity. Since the computational costs of such an MCMC approach are still too large to yield an efficient learning algorithm common RBM learning techniques – as described in the following section – introduce additional approximations.

5   Approximating the RBM Log-Likelihood Gradient

All common training algorithms for RBMs approximate the log-likelihood gradient given some data and perform gradient ascent on these approximations. Selected learning algorithms will be described in the following section, starting with contrastive divergence learning.

5.1   Contrastive Divergence

Obtaining unbiased estimates of log-likelihood gradient using MCMC methods typically requires many sampling steps. However, recently it was shown that estimates obtained after running the chain for just a few steps can be sufficient for model training [15]. This leads to *contrastive divergence* (CD) learning, which has become a standard way to train RBMs [15,4,18,3,17].

The idea of k-step contrastive divergence learning (CD-k) is quite simple: Instead of approximating the second term in the log-likelihood gradient by a sample from the RBM-distribution (which would require to run a Markov chain until the stationary distribution is reached), a Gibbs chain is run for only k steps (and usually $k = 1$). The Gibbs chain is initialized with a training example $\boldsymbol{v}^{(0)}$ of the training set and yields the sample $\boldsymbol{v}^{(k)}$ after k steps. Each step t consists of sampling $\boldsymbol{h}^{(t)}$ from $p(\boldsymbol{h}|\boldsymbol{v}^{(t)})$ and sampling $\boldsymbol{v}^{(t+1)}$ from $p(\boldsymbol{v}|\boldsymbol{h}^{(t)})$ subsequently. The gradient (equation (9)) w.r.t. $\boldsymbol{\theta}$ of the log-likelihood for one training pattern $\boldsymbol{v}^{(0)}$ is then approximated by

$$\mathrm{CD}_k(\boldsymbol{\theta}, \boldsymbol{v}^{(0)}) = -\sum_{\boldsymbol{h}} p(\boldsymbol{h}|\boldsymbol{v}^{(0)}) \frac{\partial E(\boldsymbol{v}^{(0)}, \boldsymbol{h})}{\partial \boldsymbol{\theta}} + \sum_{\boldsymbol{h}} p(\boldsymbol{h}|\boldsymbol{v}^{(k)}) \frac{\partial E(\boldsymbol{v}^{(k)}, \boldsymbol{h})}{\partial \boldsymbol{\theta}} \ . \tag{34}$$

The derivatives in direction of the single parameters are obtained by "estimating" the expectations over $p(\boldsymbol{v})$ in (29), (32) and (33) by the single sample $\boldsymbol{v}^{(k)}$. A batch version of CD-k can be seen in algorithm 1.

Algorithm 1. k-step contrastive divergence

Input: RBM $(V_1, \ldots, V_m, H_1, \ldots, H_n)$, training batch S
Output: gradient approximation Δw_{ij}, Δb_j and Δc_i for $i = 1, \ldots, n$,
        $j = 1, \ldots, m$
1   init $\Delta w_{ij} = \Delta b_j = \Delta c_i = 0$ for $i = 1, \ldots, n$, $j = 1, \ldots, m$
2   **forall the** $v \in S$ **do**
3   $\quad$ $v^{(0)} \leftarrow v$
4   $\quad$ **for** $t = 0, \ldots, k - 1$ **do**
5   $\quad\quad$ **for** $i = 1, \ldots, n$ **do** sample $h_i^{(t)} \sim p(h_i \mid v^{(t)})$
6   $\quad\quad$ **for** $j = 1, \ldots, m$ **do** sample $v_j^{(t+1)} \sim p(v_j \mid h^{(t)})$
7   $\quad$ **for** $i = 1, \ldots, n$, $j = 1, \ldots, m$ **do**
8   $\quad\quad$ $\Delta w_{ij} \leftarrow \Delta w_{ij} + p(H_i = 1 \mid v^{(0)}) \cdot v_j^{(0)} - p(H_i = 1 \mid v^{(k)}) \cdot v_j^{(k)}$
9   $\quad\quad$ $\Delta b_j \leftarrow \Delta b_j + v_j^{(0)} - v_j^{(k)}$
10 $\quad\quad$ $\Delta c_i \leftarrow \Delta c_i + p(H_i = 1 \mid v^{(0)}) - p(H_i = 1 \mid v^{(k)})$

Since $v^{(k)}$ is not a sample from the stationary model distribution the approximation (34) is biased. Obviously, the bias vanishes as $k \to \infty$. That CD is a biased approximation becomes also clear by realizing that it does not maximize the likelihood of the data under the model but the difference of two KL-divergences [15]:

$$\mathrm{KL}(q|p) - \mathrm{KL}(p_k|p) \ , \tag{35}$$

where q is the empirical distribution and p_k is the distribution of the visible variables after k steps of the Markov chain. If the chain already reached stationarity it holds $p_k = p$ and thus $\mathrm{KL}(p_k|p) = 0$ and the approximation error of CD vanishes.

The theoretical results from [3] give a good understanding of the CD approximation and the corresponding bias by showing that the log-likelihood gradient can – based on a Markov chain – be expressed as a sum of terms containing the k-th sample:

Theorem 1 (Bengio and Delalleau [3]). *For a converging Gibbs chain*

$$v^{(0)} \Rightarrow h^{(0)} \Rightarrow v^{(1)} \Rightarrow h^{(1)} \ldots$$

starting at data point $v^{(0)}$, *the log-likelihood gradient can be written as*

$$\frac{\partial}{\partial \boldsymbol{\theta}} \ln p(v^{(0)}) = - \sum_{h} p(h|v^{(0)}) \frac{\partial E(v^{(0)}, h)}{\partial \boldsymbol{\theta}}$$

$$+ E_{p(v^{(k)}|v^{(0)})} \left[\sum_{h} p(h|v^{(k)}) \frac{\partial E(v^{(k)}, h)}{\partial \boldsymbol{\theta}} \right] + E_{p(v^{(k)}|v^{(0)})} \left[\frac{\partial \ln p(v^{(k)})}{\partial \boldsymbol{\theta}} \right] \tag{36}$$

and the final term converges to zero as k goes to infinity.

The first two terms in equation (36) just correspond to the expectation of the CD approximation (under p_k) and the bias is given by the final term.

The approximation error does not only depend on the value of k but also on the rate of convergence or the mixing rate of the Gibbs chain. The rate describes how fast the Markov chain approaches the stationary distribution. The mixing rate of the Gibbs chain of an RBM is up to the magnitude of the model parameters [15,7,3,12]. This becomes clear by considering that the conditional probabilities $p(v_j|\boldsymbol{h})$ and $p(h_i|\boldsymbol{v})$ are given by thresholding $\sum_{i=1}^{n} w_{ij}h_i + b_j$ and $\sum_{j=1}^{m} w_{ij}v_j + c_i$, respectively. If the absolute values of the parameters are high, the conditional probabilities can get close to one or zero. If this happens, the states get more and more "predictable" and the Markov chain changes its state slowly. An empirical analysis of the dependency between the size of the bias and magnitude of the parameters can be found in [3].

An upper bound on the expectation of the CD approximation error under the empirical distribution is given by the following theorem [12]:

Theorem 2 (Fischer and Igel [12]). *Let p denote the marginal distribution of the visible units of an RBM and let q be the empirical distribution defined by a set of samples $\boldsymbol{v}_1, \ldots, \boldsymbol{v}_\ell$. Then an upper bound on the expectation of the error of the CD-k approximation of the log-likelihood derivative w.r.t some RBM parameter θ_a is given by*

$$\left| E_{q(\boldsymbol{v}^{(0)})} \left[E_{p(\boldsymbol{v}^{(k)}|\boldsymbol{v}^{(0)})} \left[\frac{\partial \ln p(\boldsymbol{v}^{(k)})}{\partial \theta_a} \right] \right] \right| \leq \frac{1}{2} \|q - p\| \left(1 - e^{-(m+n)\Delta} \right)^k \quad (37)$$

with

$$\Delta = \max \left\{ \max_{l \in \{1,\ldots,m\}} \vartheta_l, \; \max_{l \in \{1,\ldots,n\}} \xi_l \right\} \;,$$

where

$$\vartheta_l = \max \left\{ \left| \sum_{i=1}^{n} I_{\{w_{il}>0\}} w_{il} + b_l \right|, \left| \sum_{i=1}^{n} I_{\{w_{il}<0\}} w_{il} + b_l \right| \right\}$$

and

$$\xi_l = \max \left\{ \left| \sum_{j=1}^{m} I_{\{w_{lj}>0\}} w_{lj} + c_l \right|, \left| \sum_{j=1}^{m} I_{\{w_{lj}<0\}} w_{lj} + c_l \right| \right\} \;.$$

The bound (and probably also the bias) depends on the absolute values of the RBM parameters, on the size of the RBM (the number of variables in the graph), and on the distance in variation between the modeled distribution and the starting distribution of the Gibbs chain.

As a consequence of the approximation error CD-learning does not necessarily lead to a maximum likelihood estimate of the model parameters. Yuille [42] specifies conditions under which CD learning is guaranteed to converge to the maximum likelihood solution, which need not hold for RBM training in general. Examples of energy functions and Markov chains for which CD-1 learning does not converge are given in [27]. The empirical comparisons of the CD-approximation and the true gradient for RBMs small enough that the gradient is still tractable conducted in [7] and [3] shows that the bias can lead to a convergence to parameters that do not reach the maximum likelihood.

The bias, however, can also lead to a distortion of the learning process: After some learning iterations the likelihood can start to diverge (see figure 2) in the sense that the model systematically gets worse if k is not large [11]. This is especially bad because the log-likelihood is not tractable in reasonable sized RBMs, and so the misbehavior can not be displayed and used as a stopping criterion. Because the effect depends on the magnitude of the weights, weight decay can help to prevent it. However, the weight decay parameter λ, see equation (6), is difficult to tune. If it is too small, weight decay has no effect. If it is too large, the learning converges to models with low likelihood [11].

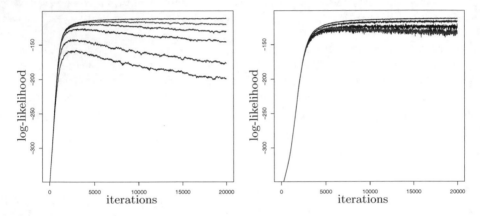

Fig. 2. Evolution of the log-likelihood during batch training of an RBM. In the left plot, CD-k with different values for k (from bottom to top $k = 1, 2, 5, 10, 20, 100$) was used. In the right plot, we employed parallel tempering (PT, see section 5.3) with different numbers M of temperatures (from bottom to top $M = 4, 5, 10, 50$). In PT the inverse temperatures were equally distributed in the interval $[0, 1]$, which may not be the optimal [9]. The training set was given by a 4×4 variant of the Bars-and-Stripes benchmark problem [28]. The learning rate was $\eta = 0.1$ for CD and $\eta = 0.05$ for PT and neither weight decay nor a momentum term were used ($\lambda = \nu = 0$). Shown are medians over 25 runs.

More recently proposed learning algorithms try to yield better approximations of the log-likelihood gradient by sampling from Markov chains with increased mixing rate.

5.2   Persistent Contrastive Divergence

The idea of *persistent contrastive divergence* (PCD, [36]) is described in [41] for log-likelihood maximization of general MRFs and is applied to RBMs in [36]. The PCD approximation is obtained from the CD approximation (34) by replacing the sample $v^{(k)}$ by a sample from a Gibbs chain that is independent from the sample $v^{(0)}$ of the training distribution. The algorithm corresponds to standard CD learning without reinitializing the visible units of the Markov chain with a training sample each time we want to draw a sample $v^{(k)}$ approximately from the RBM distribution. Instead one keeps "persistent" chains which are run for k Gibbs steps after each parameter update (i.e., the initial state of the current Gibbs chain is equal to $v^{(k)}$ from the previous update step). The fundamental idea underlying PCD is that one could assume that the chains stay close to the stationary distribution if the learning rate is sufficiently small and thus the model changes only slightly between parameter updates [41,36]. The number of persistent chains used for sampling (or the number of samples used to approximate the second term of gradient (9)) is a hyper parameter of the algorithm. In the canonical from, there exists one Markov chain per training example in a batch.

The PCD algorithm was further refined in a variant called *fast persistent contrastive divergence* (FPCD, [37]). Fast PCD tries to reach faster mixing of the Gibbs chain by introducing additional parameters w_{ij}^f, b_j^f, c_i^f (for $i = 1, \ldots, n$ and $j = 1, \ldots, m$) referred to as *fast* parameters. These new set of parameters is only used for sampling and not in the model itself. When calculating the conditional distributions for Gibbs sampling, the regular parameters are replaced by the sum of the regular and the fast parameters, i.e., Gibbs sampling is based on the probabilities $\tilde{p}(H_i = 1 \mid \boldsymbol{v}) = \sigma \left(\sum\limits_{j=1}^{m} (w_{ij} + w_{ij}^f)v_j + (c_i + c_i^f) \right)$ and $\tilde{p}(V_j = 1 \mid \boldsymbol{h}) = \sigma \left(\sum\limits_{i=1}^{n} (w_{ij} + w_{ij}^f)h_i + (b_j + b_j^f) \right)$ instead of the conditional probabilities given by (23) and (24). The learning update rule for the fast parameters equals the one for the regular parameters, but with an independent, large learning rate leading to faster changes as well as a large weight decay parameter. Weight decay can also be used for the regular parameters, but it was suggested that regularizing just the fast weights is sufficient [37].

Neither PCD nor FPCD seem to enlarge the mixing rate (or decrease the bias of the approximation) sufficiently to avoid the divergence problem as can be seen in the empirical analysis in [11].

5.3   Parallel Tempering

One of the most promising sampling technique used for RBM-training so far is *parallel tempering* (PT, [33,10,8]). It introduces supplementary Gibbs chains that sample form more and more smoothed replicas of the original distribution. This can be formalized in the following way: Given an ordered set of M temperatures $T_1, T_2, \ldots, T_M$ with $1 = T_1 < T_2 < \cdots < T_M$, we define a set of M Markov chains with stationary distributions

$$p_r(\boldsymbol{v}, \boldsymbol{h}) = \frac{1}{Z_r} e^{-\frac{1}{T_r} E(\boldsymbol{v}, \boldsymbol{h})} \tag{38}$$

for $r = 1, \ldots, M$, where $Z_r = \sum_{\boldsymbol{v}, \boldsymbol{h}} e^{-\frac{1}{T_r} E(\boldsymbol{v}, \boldsymbol{h})}$ is the corresponding partition function, and p_1 is exactly the model distribution.

Algorithm 2. k-step parallel tempering with M temperatures

Input: RBM $(V_1, \ldots, V_m, H_1, \ldots, H_n)$, training batch S, current state $\boldsymbol{v}_r$ of
Markov chain with stationary distribution p_r for $r = 1, \ldots, M$

Output: gradient approximation Δw_{ij}, Δb_j and Δc_i for $i = 1, \ldots, n$,
$j = 1, \ldots, m$

1 init $\Delta w_{ij} = \Delta b_j = \Delta c_i = 0$ for $i = 1, \ldots, n$, $j = 1, \ldots, m$

2 **forall the** $\boldsymbol{v} \in S$ **do**

3   **for** $r = 1, \ldots, M$ **do**

4          $\boldsymbol{v}_r^{(0)} \leftarrow \boldsymbol{v}_r$

5   **for** $i = 1, \ldots, n$ **do** sample $h_{r,i}^{(0)} \sim p(h_{r,i} \,|\, \boldsymbol{v}_r^{(0)})$

6   **for** $t = 0, \ldots, k-1$ **do**

7   **for** $j = 1, \ldots, m$ **do** sample $v_{r,j}^{(t+1)} \sim p(v_{r,j} \,|\, \boldsymbol{h}_r^{(t)})$

8   **for** $i = 1, \ldots, n$ **do** sample $h_{r,i}^{(t+1)} \sim p(h_{r,i} \,|\, \boldsymbol{v}_r^{(t+1)})$

9          $\boldsymbol{v}_r \leftarrow \boldsymbol{v}_r^{(k)}$

    /* swapping order below works well in practice [26]   */

10   **for** $r \in \{s \,|\, 2 \le s \le M \text{ and } s \bmod 2 = 0\}$ **do**

11   swap $(\boldsymbol{v}_r^{(k)}, \boldsymbol{h}_r^{(k)})$ and $(\boldsymbol{v}_{r-1}^{(k)}, \boldsymbol{h}_{r-1}^{(k)})$ with probability given by (40)

12   **for** $r \in \{s \,|\, 3 \le s \le M \text{ and } s \bmod 2 = 1\}$ **do**

13   swap $(\boldsymbol{v}_r^k, \boldsymbol{h}_r^k)$ and $(\boldsymbol{v}_{r-1}^k, \boldsymbol{h}_{r-1}^k)$ with probability given by (40)

14   **for** $i = 1, \ldots, n$, $j = 1, \ldots, m$ **do**

15          $\Delta w_{ij} \leftarrow \Delta w_{ij} + p(H_i = 1 \,|\, \boldsymbol{v}) \cdot v_j - p(H_i = 1 \,|\, \boldsymbol{v}_1^{(k)}) \cdot v_{1,j}^{(k)}$

16          $\Delta b_j \leftarrow \Delta b_j + v_j - v_{1,j}^{(k)}$

17          $\Delta c_i \leftarrow \Delta c_i + p(H_i = 1 \,|\, \boldsymbol{v}) - p(H_i = 1 \,|\, \boldsymbol{v}_1^{(k)})$

In each step of the algorithm, we run k (usually $k = 1$) Gibbs sampling steps in each tempered Markov chain yielding samples $(\boldsymbol{v}_1, \boldsymbol{h}_1), \ldots, (\boldsymbol{v}_M, \boldsymbol{h}_M)$. After this, two neighboring Gibbs chains with temperatures T_r and T_{r-1} may exchange particles $(\boldsymbol{v}_r, \boldsymbol{h}_r)$ and $(\boldsymbol{v}_{r-1}, \boldsymbol{h}_{r-1})$ with an exchange probability based on the Metropolis ratio,

$$\min\left\{1, \frac{p_r(\boldsymbol{v}_{r-1}, \boldsymbol{h}_{r-1}) p_{r-1}(\boldsymbol{v}_r, \boldsymbol{h}_r)}{p_r(\boldsymbol{v}_r, \boldsymbol{h}_r) p_{r-1}(\boldsymbol{v}_{r-1}, \boldsymbol{h}_{r-1})}\right\}, \tag{39}$$

which gives for RBMs

$$\min\left\{1, \exp\left(\left(\frac{1}{T_r} - \frac{1}{T_{r-1}}\right) * (E(\boldsymbol{v}_r, \boldsymbol{h}_r) - E(\boldsymbol{v}_{r-1}, \boldsymbol{h}_{r-1}))\right)\right\}. \tag{40}$$

After performing these swaps between chains, which enlarge the mixing rate, we take the (eventually exchanged) sample $\boldsymbol{v}_1$ of original chain (with temperature $T_1 = 1$) as a sample from the model distribution. This procedure is repeated L times yielding samples $\boldsymbol{v}_{1,1}, \ldots, \boldsymbol{v}_{1,L}$ used for the approximation of the expectation under the RBM distribution in the log-likelihood gradient (i.e., for the approximation of the second term in (9)). Usually L is set to the number of samples in the (mini) batch of training data as shown in algorithm 2.

Compared to CD, PT introduces computational overhead, but results in a faster mixing Markov chain and thus a less biased gradient approximation. The evolution of the log-likelihood during training using PT with different values of M can be seen in figure 2.

6   RBMs with Real-Valued Variables

So far, we considered only observations represented by binary vectors, but often one would like to model distributions over continuous data. There are several ways to define RBMs with real-valued visible units. As demonstrated by [18], one can model a continuous distribution with a binary RBM by a simple "trick". The input data is scaled to the interval $[0,1]$ and modeled by the probability of the visible variables to be one. That is, instead of sampling binary values, the expectation $p(V_j = 1|\boldsymbol{h})$ is regarded as the current state of the variable V_j. Except for the continuous values of the visible variables and the resulting changes in the sampling procedure the learning process remains the same. By keeping the energy function as given in (20) and just replacing the state space $\{0,1\}^m$ of $\boldsymbol{V}$ by $[0,1]^m$, the conditional distributions of the visible variables belong to the class of truncated exponential distributions. This can be shown in the same way as the sigmoid function for binary RBMs is derived in (27). Visible neurons with a Gaussian distributed conditional are for example gained by augmenting the energy with quadratical terms $\sum_j d_j v_j^2$ weighted by parameters $d_j, j = 1, \ldots, m$.

In contrast to the universal approximation capabilities of standard RBMs on $\{0,1\}^m$, the subset of real-valued distributions that can be modeled by an RBM with real-valued visible units is rather constrained [38].

More generally, it is possible to cover continuous valued variables by extending the definition of an RBM to any MRF whose energy function is such that $p(\boldsymbol{h}|\boldsymbol{v}) = \prod_i p(h_i|\boldsymbol{v})$ and $p(\boldsymbol{v}|\boldsymbol{h}) = \prod_j p(v_j|\boldsymbol{h})$. As follows directly from the Hammersley-Clifford theorem and as also discussed in [18], this holds for any energy function of the form

$$E(\boldsymbol{v}, \boldsymbol{h}) = \sum_{i,j} \phi_{i,j}(h_i, v_j) + \sum_j \omega_j(v_j) + \sum_i \nu_i(h_i)) \qquad (41)$$

with real-valued functions $\phi_{i,j}$, ω_j, and ν_i ,$i = 1, \ldots, n$ and $j = 1, \ldots, m$, fulfilling the constraint that the partition function Z is finite. Welling et al. [40] come to almost the same generalized form of the energy function in their framework for constructing *exponential family harmoniums* from arbitrary marginal distributions $p(v_j)$ and $p(h_i)$ from the exponential family.

7   Loosening the Restrictions

In this closing section, we will give a very brief outlook on selected extensions of RBMs that loosen the imposed restrictions on the bipartite network topology by introducing dependencies on further random variables or by allowing for arbitrary connections between nodes in the model.

Conditional RBMs. Several generalizations and extensions of RBMs exist. A notable example are *conditional RBMs* (e.g., example [35,29]). In these models, some of the parameters in the RBM energy are replaced by parametrized functions of some conditioning random variables, see [2] for an introduction.

Boltzmann Machines. Removing the "R" from the RBM brings us back to where everything started, to the general Boltzmann machine [1]. These are MRFs consisting of a set of hidden and visible variables where the energy is given by

$$E(\boldsymbol{v}, \boldsymbol{h}) =$$
$$-\sum_{i=1}^{n}\sum_{j=1}^{m} h_i w_{ij} v_j - \sum_{k=1}^{m}\sum_{l<k} v_k u_{kl} v_l - \sum_{k=1}^{n}\sum_{l<k} h_k y_{kl} h_l - \sum_{j=1}^{m} b_j v_j - \sum_{i=1}^{n} c_i h_i \; . \tag{42}$$

The graph corresponds to the one of an RBM with additional connections between the variables of one layer. These dependencies make sampling more complex (in Gibbs sampling each variable has to be updated independently) and thus training more difficult. However, specialized learning algorithms for particular "deep" graph structures have been developed [32].

8   Next Steps

The goal of this tutorial was to introduce RBMs from the probabilistic graphical model perspective. The text is meant to supplement existing tutorials, and it is biased in the sense that it focuses on material that we found helpful in our work. We hope that the reader is now equipped to move on to advanced models building on RBMs – in particular to deep learning architectures, where [2] may serve as an excellent starting point.

All experiments in this tutorial can be reproduced using the open source machine learning library Shark [20], which implements most of the models and algorithms that were discussed.

Acknowledgments. The authors acknowledge support from the German Federal Ministry of Education and Research within the National Network Computational Neuroscience under grant number 01GQ0951 (Bernstein Fokus "Learning behavioral models: From human experiment to technical assistance").

References

1. Ackley, D.H., Hinton, G.E., Sejnowski, T.J.: A learning algorithm for Boltzmann machines. Cognitive Science 9, 147–169 (1985)
2. Bengio, Y.: Learning deep architectures for AI. Foundations and Trends in Machine Learning 21(6), 1601–1621 (2009)
3. Bengio, Y., Delalleau, O.: Justifying and generalizing contrastive divergence. Neural Computation 21(6), 1601–1621 (2009)

4. Bengio, Y., Lamblin, P., Popovici, D., Larochelle, H., Montreal, U.: Greedy layer-wise training of deep networks. In: Schölkopf, B., Platt, J., Hoffman, T. (eds.) Advances in Neural Information Processing (NIPS 19), pp. 153–160. MIT Press (2007)
5. Bishop, C.M.: Pattern recognition and machine learning. Springer (2006)
6. Brémaud, P.: Markov chains: Gibbs fields, Monte Carlo simulation, and queues. Springer (1999)
7. Carreira-Perpiñán, M.Á., Hinton, G.E.: On contrastive divergence learning. In: 10th International Workshop on Artificial Intelligence and Statistics (AISTATS 2005), pp. 59–66 (2005)
8. Cho, K., Raiko, T., Ilin, A.: Parallel tempering is efficient for learning restricted Boltzmann machines. In: Proceedings of the International Joint Conference on Neural Networks (IJCNN 2010), pp. 3246–3253. IEEE Press (2010)
9. Desjardins, G., Courville, A., Bengio, Y.: Adaptive parallel tempering for stochastic maximum likelihood learning of RBMs. In: Lee, H., Ranzato, M., Bengio, Y., Hinton, G., LeCun, Y., Ng, A.Y. (eds.) NIPS 2010 Workshop on Deep Learning and Unsupervised Feature Learning (2010)
10. Desjardins, G., Courville, A., Bengio, Y., Vincent, P., Dellaleau, O.: Parallel tempering for training of restricted Boltzmann machines. In: JMLR Workshop and Conference Proceedings: AISTATS 2010, vol. 9, pp. 145–152 (2010)
11. Fischer, A., Igel, C.: Empirical Analysis of the Divergence of Gibbs Sampling Based Learning Algorithms for Restricted Boltzmann Machines. In: Diamantaras, K., Duch, W., Iliadis, L.S. (eds.) ICANN 2010, Part III. LNCS, vol. 6354, pp. 208–217. Springer, Heidelberg (2010)
12. Fischer, A., Igel, C.: Bounding the bias of contrastive divergence learning. Neural Computation 23, 664–673 (2011)
13. Geman, S., Geman, D.: Stochastic relaxation, Gibbs distributions and the Bayesian restoration of images. IEEE Transactions on Pattern Analysis and Machine Intelligence 6, 721–741 (1984)
14. Hastings, W.K.: Monte Carlo sampling methods using Markov chains and their applications. Biometrika 57(1), 97–109 (1970)
15. Hinton, G.E.: Training products of experts by minimizing contrastive divergence. Neural Computation 14, 1771–1800 (2002)
16. Hinton, G.E.: Boltzmann machine. Scholarpedia 2(5), 1668 (2007)
17. Hinton, G.E.: Learning multiple layers of representation. Trends in Cognitive Sciences 11(10), 428–434 (2007)
18. Hinton, G.E., Osindero, S., Teh, Y.W.: A fast learning algorithm for deep belief nets. Neural Computation 18(7), 1527–1554 (2006)
19. Hinton, G.E., Salakhutdinov, R.R.: Reducing the dimensionality of data with neural networks. Science 313(5786), 504–507 (2006)
20. Igel, C., Glasmachers, T., Heidrich-Meisner, V.: Shark. Journal of Machine Learning Research 9, 993–996 (2008)
21. Kivinen, J., Williams, C.: Multiple texture boltzmann machines. In: JMLR Workshop and Conference Proceedings: AISTATS 2012, vol. 22, pp. 638–646 (2012)
22. Koller, D., Friedman, N.: Probabilistic graphical models: Principles and techniques. MIT Press (2009)
23. Lauritzen, S.L.: Graphical models. Oxford University Press (1996)
24. Le Roux, N., Bengio, Y.: Representational power of restricted Boltzmann machines and deep belief networks. Neural Computation 20(6), 1631–1649 (2008)
25. Le Roux, N., Heess, N., Shotton, J., Winn, J.M.: Learning a generative model of images by factoring appearance and shape. Neural Computation 23(3), 593–650 (2011)

26. Lingenheil, M., Denschlag, R., Mathias, G., Tavan, P.: Efficiency of exchange schemes in replica exchange. Chemical Physics Letters 478, 80–84 (2009)
27. MacKay, D.J.C.: Failures of the one-step learning algorithm. Cavendish Laboratory, Madingley Road, Cambridge CB3 0HE, UK (2001), http://www.cs.toronto.edu/~mackay/gbm.pdf
28. MacKay, D.J.C.: Information Theory, Inference & Learning Algorithms. Cambridge University Press (2002)
29. Mnih, V., Larochelle, H., Hinton, G.: Conditional restricted Boltzmann machines for structured output prediction. In: Cozman, F.G., Pfeffer, A. (eds.) Proceedings of the Twenty-Seventh Conference on Uncertainty in Artificial Intelligence (UAI 2011), p. 514. AUAI Press (2011)
30. Montufar, G., Ay, N.: Refinements of universal approximation results for deep belief networks and restricted Boltzmann machines. Neural Comput. 23(5), 1306–1319
31. Rumelhart, D.E., Hinton, G.E., Williams, R.J.: Learning internal representations by error propagation. In: Rumelhart, D.E., McClelland, J.L. (eds.) Parallel Distributed Processing: Explorations in the Microstructure of Cognition, vol. 1: Foundations, pp. 318–362. MIT Press (1986)
32. Salakhutdinov, R., Hinton, G.E.: Deep Boltzmann machines. In: JMLR Workshop and Conference Proceedings: AISTATS 2009, vol. 5, pp. 448–455 (2009)
33. Salakhutdinov, R.: Learning in Markov random fields using tempered transitions. In: Bengio, Y., Schuurmans, D., Lafferty, J., Williams, C.K.I., Culotta, A. (eds.) Advances in Neural Information Processing Systems 22, pp. 1598–1606 (2009)
34. Smolensky, P.: Information processing in dynamical systems: Foundations of harmony theory. In: Rumelhart, D.E., McClelland, J.L. (eds.) Parallel Distributed Processing: Explorations in the Microstructure of Cognition, vol. 1: Foundations, pp. 194–281. MIT Press (1986)
35. Taylor, G.W., Hinton, G.E., Roweis, S.T.: Modeling human motion using binary latent variables. In: Schölkopf, B., Platt, J., Hoffman, T. (eds.) Advances in Neural Information Processing Systems (NIPS 19), pp. 1345–1352. MIT Press (2007)
36. Tieleman, T.: Training restricted Boltzmann machines using approximations to the likelihood gradient. In: Cohen, W.W., McCallum, A., Roweis, S.T. (eds.) International Conference on Machine learning (ICML), pp. 1064–1071. ACM (2008)
37. Tieleman, T., Hinton, G.E.: Using fast weights to improve persistent contrastive divergence. In: Pohoreckyj Danyluk, A., Bottou, L., Littman, M.L. (eds.) International Conference on Machine Learning (ICML), pp. 1033–1040. ACM (2009)
38. Wang, N., Melchior, J., Wiskott, L.: An analysis of Gaussian-binary restricted Boltzmann machines for natural images. In: Verleysen, M. (ed.) European Symposium on Artificial Neural Networks, Computational Intelligence and Machine Learning (ESANN), pp. 287–292. d-side publications, Evere (2012)
39. Welling, M.: Product of experts. Scholarpedia 2(10), 3879 (2007)
40. Welling, M., Rosen-Zvi, M., Hinton, G.: Exponential family harmoniums with an application to information retrieval. In: Saul, L.K., Weiss, Y., Bottou, L. (eds.) Advances in Neural Information Processing Systems (NIPS 17), pp. 1481–1488. MIT Press, Cambridge (2005)
41. Younes, L.: Maximum likelihood estimation of Gibbs fields. In: Possolo, A. (ed.) Proceedings of an AMS-IMS-SIAM Joint Conference on Spacial Statistics and Imaging. Lecture Notes Monograph Series, Institute of Mathematical Statistics, Hayward (1991)
42. Yuille, A.L.: The convergence of contrastive divergence. In: Saul, L., Weiss, Y., Bottou, L. (eds.) Advances in Neural Processing Systems (NIPS 17), pp. 1593–1600. MIT Press (2005)

Human Activity Recognition with 2D and 3D Cameras

Zicheng Liu

Microsoft Research
One Microsoft Way
Redmond WA 98052
zliu@microsoft.com

Abstract. This presentation will cover human activity recognition by using conventional 2D video cameras as well as the recently developed 3D depth cameras. I'll first give an overview on the interest- point based approach which has become a popular research direction in the past few years for 2D based activity recognition. In addition to the conventional classification problem, I'll discuss the problem of detection (spacetime localization) as well as the example-based search where the amount of labelled data is extremely small. The second part of the talk will focus on activity recognition with 3D depth cameras. I'll describe some of the recently developed visual representations and machine learning frameworks for 3D data analysis.

L. Alvarez et al. (Eds.): CIARP 2012, LNCS 7441, p. 37, 2012.
© Springer-Verlag Berlin Heidelberg 2012

Smooth Signed Distance Surface Reconstruction and Applications

Gabriel Taubin

Brown University, Providence RI 02912, USA
taubin@brown.edu
http://mesh.brown.edu/taubin

Abstract. We describe a new and simple variational formulation to reconstruct the surface geometry, topology, and color map of a 3D scene from a finite set of colored oriented points. Point clouds are nowadays obtained using a variety of techniques, including structured lighting systems, pasive multi-view stereo algorithms, and 3D laser scanning. In our formulation the implicit function is forced to be a smooth approximation of the signed distance function to the surface. The formulation allows for a number of different efficient discretizations, reduces to a finite dimensional least squares problem for all linearly parameterized families of functions, does not require the specification of boundary conditions, and it is particularly good at extrapolating missing and/or irregularly sampled data. The resulting algorithms are significantly simpler and easier to implement than alternative methods. In particular, our implementation based on a primal-graph octree-based hybrid finite element-finite difference discretization, and the Dual Marching Cubes isosurface extraction algorithm is very efficient, and produces high quality crack-free adaptive manifold polygon meshes. After the geometry and topology are reconstructed, the color information from the points is smoothly extrapolated to the surface by solving a second variational problem which also reduces to a finite dimensional least squares problem. The resulting method produces high quality polygon meshes with smooth color maps, which accurately approximate the source colored oriented points. An open source implementation of this method is available for download. We describe applications to digital archaeology, 3D forensics, and 3D broadcasting.

Keywords: surface reconstruction, multi-view stereo, geometry processing, digital archaeology, digital forensics.

1 Introduction

A new variational formulation was recently introduced [7,8] for the problem of reconstructing a watertight surface defined by an implicit equation $f(p) = 0$ from a finite set of oriented points $\{(p_1 n_1), \ldots, (p_N, n_N)\}$. Oriented point clouds are obtained from laser scanners, structured lighting systems, and multi-view

L. Alvarez et al. (Eds.): CIARP 2012, LNCS 7441, pp. 38–45, 2012.

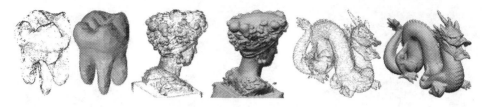

Fig. 1. We have developed a new method of reconstructing high resolution watertight surfaces from oriented points which is particularly good at extrapolating under-sampled areas, missing and irregularly sampled data [7]

stereo algorithms. This problem has received an immense amount of attention since the mid 80s. An extensive review of the literature and the state-of-the-art is provided in [7,8]. We have shown that this approach provides an interesting alternative to other popular methods, it is much simpler to implement, and performs particularly well on unevenly sampled data sets at comparable cost. The implicit surface $S = \{p : f(p) = 0\}$ is estimated by minimizing the energy function

$$E_1(f) = \frac{\alpha_0}{N} \sum_{i=0}^{N} f(p_i)^2 + \frac{\alpha_1}{N} \sum_{i=0}^{N} \|\nabla f(p_i) - n_i\|^2 + \frac{\alpha_2}{|V|} \int_V \|Hf(p)\|^2 dp \qquad (1)$$

where $\nabla f(p)$ is the gradient of the implicit function, V is a bounding volume, $|V|$ is the measure of this volume, $\|Hf(p)\|^2$ is the Frobenius norm of the Hessian of the implicit function (sum of squares of second order partial derivatives), and α_0, α_1 and α_2 are positive weights. In this formulation the first two terms of the energy function –the data terms– force the implicit function to approximate the signed distance function to the underlying surface, and the third term –the regularization term– forces the gradient of the function to be as close as possible to constant away from the data points. In our view this is a more natural regularization condition to impose, and it is responsible for the good behavior of the associated algorithms.

Various discretizations are possible with the problem reducing to the solution of a sparse linear system of equations. The resulting algorithms are simple and easy to implement, and produce results of quality comparable with state-of-the-art algorithms, if not better, particularly when the point cloud constitutes an uneven sampling of the subjacent surface. We have shown an efficient implementation based on a primal-graph octree-based hybrid finite element-finite difference discretization, and the Dual Marching Cubes isosurface extraction algorithm, which produces high quality crack-free adaptive manifold polygon meshes, as shown in Figure 5. A reference implementation of this algorithm, distributed as Open Source, can be downloaded from [8]. Leveraging this software, and targeting archaeology and forensics applications, we have build a processing pipeline for multi-view stereo surface reconstruction. This software, which is also distributed in Open Source, can be downloaded from [12]. The pipeline consists of three previously proposed methods that together reconstruct a complete 3D model from a collection of

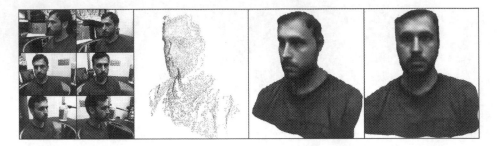

Fig. 2. Surface reconstructed from a colored oriented point cloud generated by the a multi-view stereo algorithm. This is an application to real-time view interpolation for face-to-face teleconferencing.

images taken from different camera viewpoints. The first step is to recover a set of camera parameters and 3D locations for keypoints in each image using Bundler [2], a method proposed to perform structure from motion (SfM) on unordered image collections. The second step is to generate a dense point cloud using PMVS [5], a patch-based multiview stereo method. The last step is to reconstruct the surface using our Smooth Signed Distance surface reconstruction method [7,8]. A precursor to this formulation, the VFIso algorithm introduced in [1], was used in our prior work on shape from depth discontinuities [3,4]. However, the VFIso implementation, based on finite differences on a regular voxel grid discretization, does not scale up gracefully.

2   Multi-view Stereo Surface Reconstruction

The problem of reconstructing colored 3D models from multiple images captured by inexpensive consumer level digital cameras has a wide range of applications in industry, entertainment, human-computer interaction, surveillance, navigation, archaeology, forensics, medicine, sports, architecture, and many other fields. Popular Multi-View Stereo algorithms such as [5,6] produce a dense colored oriented point cloud $\{(p_1, n_1, c_1), \ldots, (p_N, n_N, c_N)\}$ from a collection of images.

Originally targeting the needs of the REVEAL Digital Archaeology project [11,12], we have recently extended the SSD Surface Reconstruction method described above to produce colored surfaces. In our implementation the colored surface is represented as a polygon mesh with colors per vertex, which are then continuously interpolated within the faces by the rendering engine. The implicit surface color is represented as a color map function $c(p) = (r(p), g(p), b(p))$ defined on the bounding volume V. The color field is estimated independently of the geometry, by minimizing the following energy function

$$E_2(c) = \frac{\beta_0}{N} \sum_{i=0}^{N} \|c(p_i) - c_i\|^2 + \frac{\beta_2}{|V|} \int_V \|Dc(p)\|^2 dp \qquad (2)$$

where $Dc(p)$ is the Jacobian of the color map function, and β_0 and β_1 are positive constants.

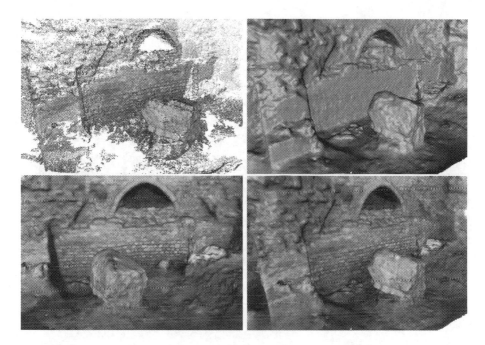

Fig. 3. Reconstruction of the side of a castle model: The input point cloud (top-left), Surface reconstructed by the proposed algorithm(top-right), Two views from the surface and color map reconstructed by the proposed algorithm (bottom)

In our octree-based implementation, after the geometry is reconstructed, a piecewise constant discretization with one RGB color value per octree cell is used to reduce the estimation of surface colors to a least square problem on the octree dual graph. This problem reduces to the solution of another (Laplacian) sparse linear system. Even a simple cascading multi-grid gradient descent algorithm (such as the Jacobi method) converges very fast to the solution. Figures 2, 3, 6, and 7 show applications to view interpolation for face-to-face teleconferencing, forensic 3D reconstruction of footprints where we have shown that this method is competitive with laser scanners [6], reconstruction of architecture from outdoors photography, and interesting problems in Archaeology.

Very often objects have relatively simple geometry but very detailed textures. In these cases it is convenient for a polygonal approximation scheme to represent the surface color data not as a color vector per vertex, face, or corner, but by using a coarsely tessellated polygon mesh and texture mapping. A tradeoff needs to be reached to determine where in between the two extremes the produced surface will be. Surfaces reconstructed from colored point clouds produced by multi-view stereo algorithms such as [5,6] usually result in polygon meshes of much lower resolution than can be derived from the input images, because the geometry is usually reconstructed from decimated images due to memory constraints. Using the process described above to estimate mesh color also results in degraded resolution, since the polygon mesh resolution is the limiting factor. One approach is to detect in the original images regions which may require high

REVEAL Archaeological Data Acquisition
Assisted Data Acquisition, Algorithmic Reconstruction, Integrated multi-format analysis

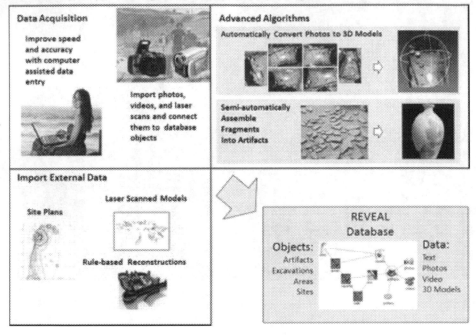

Fig. 4. The REVEAL Digital Archaeology System components

resolution and then modify the reconstruction process to refine the geometry of those regions alone, as will be discussed in a later section. Another possibility is to go back to the original high resolution images, and using the coarse reconstructed geometry and visibility information from the camera poses and surface geometry, create a texture atlas composed of non-overlapping charts cut from the original source images. If the main purpose of reconstructing the surface is visualization, then this approach is most efficient when the models to be created have low geometric complexity, but are highly textured. We are currently working on an extension of our surface reconstruction software which will create textured polygon mesh models.

3   Application to Digital Archaeology

REVEAL (Reconstruction and Exploratory Visualization: Engineering meets ArchaeoLogy) [11,12] is a four year NSF-funded project promoting paradigm shifts in archaeology. This is a project to create an environment for acquiring and presenting archaeological data in a way that streamlines the excavation process and supports and enhances the experts understanding of the data. REVEAL leverages three aspects of the technology: using vision algorithms to speed up or replace measurement and documentation tasks, using computer automation to speed up

REVEAL Archaeological Analysis

Data integrated and synchronized in tabular, plan drawing, 3D spatial, image, and video formats

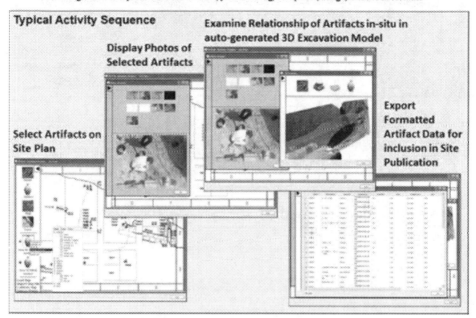

Typical Activity Sequence

Examine Relationship of Artifacts in-situ in auto-generated 3D Excavation Model

Display Photos of Selected Artifacts

Select Artifacts on Site Plan

Export Formatted Artifact Data for inclusion in Site Publication

Fig. 5. The REVEAL Analyze Software System

data entry tasks, using integrated 2D and 3D media to enhance data comprehension. Figure 6 illustrates a particular digital archaeology application of surface reconstruction from multi-view stereo data which requires surface reconstruction at high resolution, but only at selective places. In this case the ultimate goal is to be able to perform character recognition from the reconstructed geometry. Archeology experts are able to differentiate cuneiform writing styles from different authors. Sufficient information to perform these recognition tasks may not be present in low resolution 3D reconstructions. However, in practice reconstructing the geometry at the required resolution with the algorithms described above may result in polygon meshes too large to be processed. As a result we are currently developing adaptive methods, which based on processing the geometry of low resolution reconstructions as well as the source images, regions in the 3D bounding volume which require reconstruction at high resolution will be determined. Then we will modify our algorithms to refine the octree only where it is needed. We envision a user-driven adaptive recognition system where a coarse reconstruction is first produced by the system and shown to the user along with the source images. Using the camera pose information, we will establish correspondences between the images and the reconstructed geometry within the interactive system. Then the user will be able to select the region of interest by painting or drawing on the images and/or coarse geometry and the system will refine the selected areas at interactive rate. Also, because of the tree structure, reconstructed details which are no longer

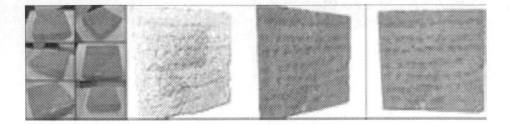

Fig. 6. Surface reconstructed from colored oriented point cloud generated by the PMVS multi-view stereo algorithm [5,6]. In this example we are exploring an application of the proposed techniques to Archaeology: the goal is to reconstruct the 3D geometry of a cuneiform tablet at sufficient resolution to be able perform 3D OCR.

of interest can be removed by cutting deep branches of the octree, and the surface re-estimated in real time.

4   Application to Forensics

Footwear impressions recovered from crime scenes are important to corroborate or refute hypotheses, or to narrow down the number of suspects. The long-standing standard used to obtain 3D models of 3D footwear impressions is casting. This method is slowly being replaced non-invasive techniques such as 3D laser scanning. In [10] we present an alternative method based on multi-view stereo data, which yields 3D models as accurate as those produced by 3D laser scanners, but at a much lower cost. We evaluated the results comparing our reconstructed 3D models with the ones acquired by 3D scanning, and we also examine the advantages and drawbacks of each method. Our solution relies on the pipeline developed for the REVEAL system mentioned above to reconstruct 3D surfaces using only digital photographs taken from the footwear print at the crime scene. In this work, we presented a pipeline to recover footwear impression from crime scenes based on a well known technique in Computer Vision, multi-view stereo, which has not been consider or analyzed for this kind of application

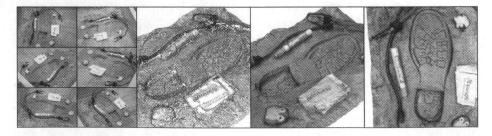

Fig. 7. Surface reconstructed from colored oriented point cloud generated by the PMVS algorithm [5,6]. This is an application to the forensic reconstruction of 3D shoeprints.

in the literature until now. Despite the simplicity for set up and acquisition, the reconstructed surfaces proved to be comparable with those produced by a 3D scanning system, a high-end technology used in practice, providing accurate 3D models of the shoe prints. A digital camera is the only equipment required to recover the evidence, which makes the process convenient and fast.

References

1. Sibley, P.G., Taubin, G.: Vectorfield Isosurface-Based Reconstruction from Oriented Points. In: ACM Siggraph 2005 Sketches, p. 29. ACM (2005)
2. Snavely, N., Seitz, S., Szeliski, R.: Photo Tourism: Exploring Photo Collections in 3D. ACM Transactions on Graphics 25, 835–846 (2006)
3. Crispell, D., Lanman, D., Sibley, P.G., Zhao, Y., Taubin, G.: Beyond silhouettes: Surface reconstruction using multi-flash photography. In: Third International Symposium on 3D Data Processing, Visualization, and Transmission (3DPVT 2006), pp. 405–412. IEEE (2006)
4. Lanman, D., Sibley, P., Crispell, D., Zhao, Y., Taubin, G.: Multi-Flash 3D Photography: Capturing Shape and Appearance. In: Siggraph 2006 Posters (August 2006)
5. Furukawa, Y., Ponce, J.: Accurate, Dense, and Robust Multi-View Stereopsis. IEEE Transactions on Pattern Analysis and Machine Intelligence 32(8), 1362–1376 (2010)
6. Furukawa, Y., Ponce, J.: Patch-Based Multi-View Stereo Software (PMVS - Version 2) (2010), http://grail.cs.washington.edu/software/pmvs/
7. Calakli, F., Taubin, G.: Smooth Signed Distance Surface Reconstruction. Computer Graphics Forum 30(7) (2011)
8. Calakli, F., Taubin, G.: Smooth Signed Distance Surface Reconstruction. Open source Software Released (2011), http://mesh.brown.edu/ssd
9. Andalo, F.A., Calakli, F., Taubin, G., Goldenstein, S.: Accurate 3D Footwear Impression Recovery From Photographs. In: Proceedings of the 4th International Conference on Imaging for Crime Detection and Prevention (ICDP 2011), Kington Upon Thames, London (November 2011)
10. Calakli, F., Taubin, G.: SSD-C: Smooth Signed Distance Colored Surface Reconstruction. In: Expanding The Frontiers of Visual Analytics and Visualization, Part 4, ch. 18, pp. 323–338. Springer (2012)
11. Cooper, D.B., et al.: Reconstruction and Exploratory Visualization: Engineering meets ArchaeoLogy (REVEAL), A System for Streamlined Powerful Sensing, Archiving, Extracting Information from, Visualizing and Communicating, Archaeological Site-excavation Data (2008–2008), http://vision.lems.brown.edu/project_desc/Reveal
12. Gay, E., et al.: REVEAL Analyze. Open Source Archaeological Database Browser and Analysis Software releases (2012), http://sourceforge.net/projects/revealanalyze/

Robot, Pass Me the Scissors! How Robots Can Assist Us in the Operating Room

Juan P. Wachs

Purdue University, West Lafayette, IN 47906, USA
jpwachs@purdue.edu

Abstract. The inclusion of robotics and automation to support and augment surgical performance offers the promise of shorter operating times, higher accuracy and fewer risks compared with traditional, human-only surgery. This paper discusses current research in the area of surgical robotics and human-robot collaboration. A multimodal robotic scrub nurse (Gestonurse) for the operating room (OR) is presented as a case study. Gestonurse assists the main surgeon by passing surgical instruments, thereby releasing the surgical technician to perform other tasks. Such a robotic system has the potential to reduce miscommunication and compensate for understaffing. The implications of the introduction of surgical robots, as assistants rather than autonomous agents, are discussed in terms of the societal and technological requirements. Quantitative and qualitative findings are presented as evidence to support the guidelines discussed.

Keywords: Gesture recognition, operating room, human computer interaction.

1 Introduction

Understaffing of nurses is a chronic problem in American hospitals that is expected to continue—a shortage of 260,000 registered nurses is (RNs) projected by 2025 [1]. Research conducted by the Robert Wood Johnson Foundation, NPR, and the Harvard School of Public Health found that the problem was not necessary nurses understaffing but nurses overworked. 34% of patients hospitalized during 2011 thought that nurses were not available when needed. While ideally the expectation is to have one nurse for every three patients in her ER, the reality makes the nurse to care for five patients to eight. This issue points to a shortage of nursing care in hospitals and other healthcare facilities. Moreover, there is a growing concern about the nursing staff being stretched even more thinly in the coming years. This shortage has been linked to an array of negative outcomes such as higher transmission rates of antibiotic resistant strains of illness, cardiac arrest and urinary tract infections [2]. Additionally, recent studies have shown that inpatient mortality risk is nearly 6% higher in units understaffed with nurses compared to fully staffed units [3]. As an example, another study [4] found that 11 to 14% patient mortality in Pennsylvania and New Jersey was directly related to unsuitable patient-to-nurse staffing ratios and burnout symptoms compared to other states in the US. A similar picture has been found in 12 countries in Europe [37].

L. Alvarez et al. (Eds.): CIARP 2012, LNCS 7441, pp. 46–57, 2012.

Because of this shortage, it is important to find new ways to use technological solutions for highly mechanistic tasks in health care settings. This frees nurses to focus on more complex tasks, allowing outcomes to be improved for all.

2   Why Do We Need Robots in the OR?

Currently, in the United States, errors in medical care delivery are the principal cause of inpatient mortality and morbidity (over 98,000 deaths annually). Research assessing verbal and non-verbal exchanges in the operating room (OR) shows that communication failures are frequent: commands are delayed, incomplete, not received at all, and frequently left unresolved. One study found that 31% of all communications in the OR represent failures, a third of which had a negative impact on the patient [5-8]. Another study found that 36% of communication errors were related to equipment use. New technologies could have a crucial impact on OR communication— Adaptable surgical robotic assistants that understand implicit and explicit communication can reduce the number of errors related to miscommunication. One of the uses of surgical robots is to augment the surgeon dexterity and physical abilities by offering a set of customizable set of skills while reducing errors intrinsic to humans [9]. Surgical assistants come in two flavors: surgeon extenders and auxiliary surgical support robots. The first type is controlled uniquely by the surgeon and can enhance the surgeon's dexterity during surgery (such as by eliminating hand's tremors). The second type works side-by-side with the surgeon and supports her task in a variety of functions, such as holding the endoscope. This type of robot can respond to joysticks, voice, touch-pads, and head trackers based interfaces. Natural verbal and nonverbal interfaces can allow surgeons to interact naturally with the robot (assistant) without requiring the surgeon learn in a new set of functions or wearing encumbering sensors. Within the social robotics community, the belief is that surgical robotic assistants, by reducing the miscommunications, will: 1) reduce morbidity and mortality risks; 2) treat of otherwise untreatable pathologies; and 3) reduce operating times. While such robotic systems in the operating room (OR) have been studied, nonverbal interaction as a means of robot interaction, has never been applied to the surgical theater.

3   Previous Work on Surgical Robots

Previous research on surgical extenders robots includes an assistive robot for object picking [10], haptic feedback controlled robots, such as SOFIE [11] or Agovic's [12] robot, and the commercially available da Vinci® surgical suite [13] which was developed to conduct minimally invasive and safer procedures for planned endoscopic and laparoscopic surgeries.

Robotic scrub nurses (RSN) is a type of auxiliary support robots that has some level of autonomy and cognitive capabilities. For example, Kochan et al., developed "Penelope" [14] which delivers and retrieves surgical instruments and is controlled by voice. Another voice-controlled robot developed by Carpintero et al., [15] relies on computer vision techniques to recognize, pick and return surgical instruments.

The EASOP [16] is a robotic endoscope holder controlled by means of speech. The RSN system developed by Yoshimitsu et al., [17] used voice control for handling laparoscopic surgeries. It also used depth-based action recognition for instrument use prediction. To assess the surgeon's action automatically, 3D point estimation and tracking is performed, requiring the surgeon to wear markers. These markers can compromise sterility.

Overall, the problem with voice-only systems and that they exhibit notable performance degradation [18] in loud environments such as the OR. Anesthesia machines, respirators, drills, side conversations, and other equipment affects the recognition accuracy—in such a setting, the surgeon may say "50,000 units" and the anesthetist may hear "15,000 units" [19]. Such errors could have catastrophic consequences for the patient.

Robots were developed by the military to reduce the fighters' exposure to unfriendly fire. These robots are capable to: (1) safely extract wounded from the battlefield; (2) diagnose and treat life threatening injuries within minutes; and (3) conduct surgery. The BEAR robot (The Battlefield Extraction-Assist Robot) [20] can extract wounded soldiers from the battleground. This robot is controlled remotely and understands speech commands. SRI's M7 surgical robot [21] is the first of its kind applied to a perform a tele-surgery (networked over 1,200 miles undersea) to simulate the conditions of outer space. In light of its success, it was integrated into an autonomous ultrasound-guided medical procedure under similar conditions. Trauma Pod [22] is a glimpse to the next generation of mobile robotic surgery platforms capable of conducting life-saving procedures in hostile environments. It is controlled through speech messages. A surgical deployed robot that responds to speech commands to deliver surgical tools retrieves them as soon as they are not longer needed [23] was developed by Treat et al. The instruments were recognized through computer vision, and a cognitive architecture was used for decision making. None of the robots discussed so far address the problem of multimodal interaction between surgeon and robot.

4   Gestonurse: A Robotic Assistant That Understands Verbal and Non-verbal Communication

A real-time RSN (Fig. 2) capable to passing surgical instruments to the surgeon when requested by speech and/or gesture has been developed by Jacob et al., [24]. This is the first time that non-verbal cues (hand gestures) were considered as a modality of interaction with surgical robots in the OR. Using gesture interaction has the advantage that it does not require surgeon total re-training and it is a totally sterile mean of control. Hand gestures are currently being used by surgeons to request the instruments as part of the OR technique [25-27] for surgery. Another advantage is that non-verbal communication is not affected by ambient noise in the OR.

Gestural commands are recognized from depth images acquired from a commodity camera (Kinect) and speech requests are gathered from a microphone. The FANUC robotic arm hands the required instrument to the surgeon (see Figure 2), as soon as the commands were recognized. Gestures were also used to switch between states in the RSN's state machine.

The system architecture of the robotic system is presented in Figure 3. The depth maps obtained from the Kinect sensor were processed by the gesture recognition module and in parallel the speech commands were captured by a microphone. These commands were interpreted using the speech recognition module. Once recognized, the command was sent through the network to the FANUC robotic arm using a Telnet interface. The robot, in turn, delivers the required surgical instrument to the surgeon and stays 'on hold' until the next command is received.

The system architecture, the computing and physical modules are briefly described in the following subsections.

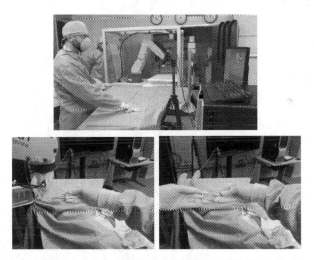

Fig. 1. (a). A prototype of the real-time RSN running at an OR (b) A sterile robot handing a surgical instrument (c) A nurse handing a surgical instrument

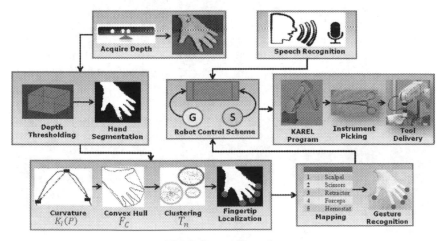

Fig. 2. System Overview

4.1   Pose Segmentation

Color and depth information were used for hand segmentation and compared to assess the strength of each method. Using color cues for segmentation required finding a background model of the scene and creating hand color model. Segmentation masks from the color models were added and morphologically processed so the largest blob in the image is selected. This region represents the mask of the hand once the noise was filtered out.

When using the depth cues, the segmentation involved extracting the user's hand from the scene using the depth map obtained from the Kinect sensor. Applying a threshold operation to the depth map and selecting the region closest to the camera resulted in the mask of the hand.

The contour and convex hull were found from the images including the hand masks. This information was passed to the fingertip localization module. Finally, the two methods of segmentation were compared and the one delivering the best results was selected (the depth-based method) as the main segmentation approach.

4.2   Fingertip Localization

To find the fingertip, the curvature value at each point on the contour of the hand mask was computed at multiple scales. For a point on the contour to be considered a fingertip candidate, it had to be the local minimum over several scales and its curvature lower than a given threshold. The set of candidate points included all those points that met the previous criteria after contour discretization, and those points affected by the presence of noisy segmentation. This set was reduced by discarding points too far from the convex hull and clustering the resulting points together. The true fingertip was represented by the centroid of each cluster.

4.3   Hand Gesture Recognition

The hand pose was recognized after the fingertips were detected and located within the hand. The number of fingertips in the image was one-to-one matched to the surgical instruments. Once the required instrument was detected from the image, this request was sent to the state machine.

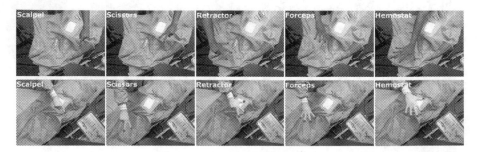

Fig. 3. Samples from the use-case with detected fingertips marked with red circles

4.4   Speech Recognition

The speech recognition module was responsible of recognizing each spoken command (from the surgeon) and sending the instrument request to the state machine for further processing. A fixed steered microphone was oriented towards the surgeon and it gathered acoustic information. The speech commands were recognized using the open source CMU Sphinx [28] toolkit.

4.5   State Machine

The state machine was responsible for processing requests coming from the gesture and speech recognition modules, and it was meant to deliver instruments, put the system 'on hold' (sleep mode), switch the system to "active" mode, or disable the speech recognition module. Disabling the speech modality was necessary in scenarios where the ambient noise was too loud which can result in false triggers. The gesture and speech recognition modules operate in parallel.

4.6   Instrument Pick and Delivery

A six degrees of freedom (DOF) FANUC robot was programmed using a combination of programming platforms, including: KAREL, a FANUC proprietary language used to control the robots and teach-pendant (TP) programs. The position of the surgical instruments was hard-coded and the corresponding coordinates were stored as part of the TP programs. The programs controlling the FANUC robot were each triggered when a request (gestural or verbal) was detected over the telnet interface. The robot proceeded to pick the instrument from its pre-programmed position using a latex-encapsulated magnetic gripper and passed it to the surgeon. When the instrument was delivered, the arm would return to its 'HOME' position and switch to the "wait" mode where it awaits a request for a new surgical instrument.

Fig. 4. (a) FANUC Robot (b) Latex-encased magnetic gripper

4.7   Human Robot Collaboration in a Mock Surgery

Experiments involving human-robot collaboration were performed using a patient's phantom simulator (Fig. 5). The performance of the system was assessed using common surgical task -- an abdominal incision and closure. The purpose of this surgical exercise was to penetrate the peritoneal cavity without puncturing an inflated balloon, manually examining the surroundings of the cavity, and final closing the abdominal wall without bursting the balloon. The task required the proper handing and use of surgical instruments such as scalpel and forceps Two types of subjects were involved in the experiment, the surgeon and an assistant, and two scenarios were studied: with robotic assistant to complete the task, and standard collaboration between surgeon and nurse without the robot. The economy of movements, learning times and recognition accuracy were assessed by comparing the performance of the mock surgical procedure under the two experimental conditions. It was found that that the robotic assistant improved the surgical procedure by reducing the number of movements (lower variance in the picking position) [29]. Robust recognition accuracy (97%) and short completion times after training (~250 seconds) were also reported by these studies [30, 31].

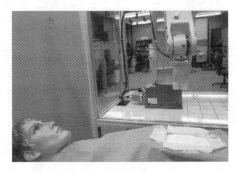

Fig. 5. A surgical simulator

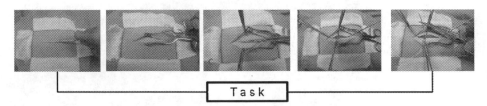

Fig. 6. Different stages of the mock abdominal incision. Stage (A). Incision; (B) Exposure of linea alba; (C) Enlarge the incision using scissors; (D) Incise the linea alba; (E) Close the incision.

5   Perception and Trust

While technically robots could complement/supplement personnel in hospitals, by working side by side with caregivers and patients, the robots need to be accepted socially by the hospital's staff. Robots need to be perceived as team-mates rather than threatening agents which purpose is taking away jobs. They need to build trust among the co-workers and patients, rapport must be built and responsibilities need to be shared.

5.1   Perception

Social acceptance is a fundamental key challenge for successful adoption of robots in hospitals. The main reason for this is that robots could replace and/or support highly educated workers in surgery with robot partners. Only a small number of studies have focus on the perception of robots as team co-workers in the OR. Wasen [32] looked at teamwork and human-robot interaction in surgery through ethnographic research tools to study social understanding and acceptance of surgical robots during a two-and-a-half-year study (2003-2005) involving four hospitals, one in the United States and three in Scandinavia. The case studies observed included coronary by-pass and prostate removal surgeries performed by surgeons with robotic assistance (AESOP, ZEUS and da-Vinci). The way that the AESOP system is designed implies that one surgical nurse is replaced by the robot which does the same job as the human assistant. Qualitative results of this study showed that surgeons were eager to accept surgical robots because "the robot's functionality provided them with additional support and increased their independence in the work place." [32]. From the surgical assistants stand point, the robotic assistant forced the assistants to participate in a very different way in the procedure due to the fact that the lead surgeon was in control of almost all the aspects related to the surgery. Anecdotic evidence shows that surgical nurses are more reluctant about the introduction of surgical robots to the OR due to the fact that they present a potential threat to their job stability.

5.2   Trust

Trust can affect the hospital's staff willingness to share existing surgical tasks, provide support to the robot [33], and provide information to enhance its performance. In healthcare contexts, a caregiver must trust that a robotic co-worker will protect the interests and welfare of the patients and to ensure the procedures' success with minimum risks. At the same time, the caregiver needs to trust that the robotic assistant will not "displace" the teammate from the task in hand. Trust allocation can have serious implications in the outcomes of the care, e.g. too much trust is placed on the robot can lead to physical risks to the patients - increasing mortality and morbidity risks (misuse) [34]. If too little trust is placed in the robot (disuse), the team may stop using the system altogether. An important observation is that trust decreases with more complex and cognitive demanding tasks, such as surgery, because the chances of error occurrences are higher and the costs (social and economic) of those errors are enormous; and therefore the team mate is more likely to rely on herself [35].

Even though trust assessment through objective measures is difficult to accomplish (mostly since the reported values are subjective), a number of factors have been suggested to estimate proxies for trust levels. Some of these factors include system usability, proximity of the robot, proxemics, situation awareness, and characteristics of the task and the environment [36]. A special emphasis should be given to ethnographic studies involving surgical nurses to clarify what are the issues that are concerning them the most. Findings can be used to create enhanced human-robot team models of trust, and help determine ways that mistrust may be mitigated, while assuring that there is a backup plan given that the system was over trusted.

6   Challenges and Recommendations

The entire human (perception, trust) and machine (accuracy) related characteristics may have implications for the future adoption of surgical robots as assistants in healthcare environment. Following specific recommendations and trying to address the existing challenges may reduce initial perception barriers and foster trust development by giving the user the option to participate in the implementation and integration of the robots in the OR. The surgical staff will be pivotal on the gathering of information about robot capabilities, system behaviors, and potential risks. In addition, a simple way to enhance the staff's perception about the robot is through fundamental training on how the tasks can be best shared among the participants, without fears but offering a fault-safe strategy to backup system errors. Based on previous findings, the following list of requirements was identified. This is not a comprehensive list, but it highlights the most common requirements that the surgical staff pointed out:

1) *Suitable dexterity:* Manipulation of surgical equipment requires a high level of dexterity (the hand has 27 DOF). For the most part, the surgical nurse needs to hand over the instrument to the surgeon, and pick them from the surgical site. A robotic arm with seven DOF and a gripper similar to tweezers may complete the task as good as a person. Nevertheless, more complex tasks such as opening a suture bag, or applying suction catheter may require more complex robots (e.g. dual arms) with more dexterous hands.

2) *Multimodality:* To successfully recognize the subtleties of communication that occur between humans, gestures, body language, gaze and speech need to be recognized. When more than one modality is used, the robot must be capable to resolve ambiguity (different requests expressed by different modalities).

3) *Fast response:* The action carried out by the robotic assistant must be promptly without delays due to actuators or due to processing requests. The immediate response should be as quick as an experienced assistant standing in the close proximity to the surgeon. Excessive speed is not advisable since it may come on the account of precision, or exhibit jerky movements.

4) *Prediction (mind readers):* Experienced nurses are also called mind readers because their ability to anticipate the surgeon's need. A robotic assistant must have robust inference and prediction mechanisms to perform the activity which is has been assigned to complete in support of the surgeon. Given that the prediction is not correct, ways to mitigate the mistakes and their consequences need to be included in the system.

5) *Predictable:* The surgical team will expect to see the robotic assistant to respond in the same fashion to similar requests under the same conditions every time. Unexpected behavior has the potential to distract the surgical team, create delays and even increase the risks of physical contact with the robot.

6) *Accuracy and Precision:* The surgeon's commands/requests must be interpreted accurately. A true hit rate over 99% with almost no false alarms is required to perform as good as a human assistant. This performance should be attainable in complex environment with variable light changes unfixed settings. Precise movements are also necessary to assure the grasp of cluttered small objects, like surgical equipment, sponges and gauzes.

7) *Safety:* Operator safety in industrial robotics has been addressed by defining a physical area (safety envelope) that is monitored for intrusions. This is not applicable for collaborative tasks in close human-robot interaction where physical contact is required. To avoid injuries due to collisions with sharp instruments, impact forces need to be reduced through effective design, or avoiding the collisions altogether through strategies for obstacle avoidance.

Based on this research, it is expected that some of these requirements and challenges will be addressed to allow the surgical team and robotic assistants to support intrinsically the development of effective, safe and more cost efficient human robot collaboration in the operating theater.

7   Conclusion

The shortage of nursing care in hospitals and other health care facilities has been linked to an array of negative outcomes such as higher transmission rates of antibiotic resistant strains of illness, cardiac arrest and urinary tract infections [5]. Inpatient mortality risk is nearly 6% higher in units understaffed with nurses compared to fully staffed units [7-8]. New technologies could have a crucial impact on OR communication— Adaptable surgical robotic assistants that understand implicit and explicit communication can reduce the number of errors related to miscommunication and make up for the lack of employed nurses.

The current research described a number of surgical robots designed to support the surgical team by being a co-worker rather than a tele-operated device. A robotic scrub nurse – Gestonurse - was presented as a case study of the existing challenges and limitations of robots in the OR. The system discussed, showed the feasibility for the implementation of a robot capable to understand non-verbal communication (hand gestures) and speech commands with a recognition accuracy of over 97%. Gestonurse has been validated in a mock surgery - an abdominal incision and closure. Results on economy of movements showed that the robotic assistant improved the surgical procedure by reducing the number of movements which is closely related to the concept of economy of movements in the operating room. Improving the effectiveness of the operating room can potentially enhance surgical outcomes without affecting the performance time.

In the last section of this work, it was described the requirements of surgical robotic assistants in terms of the technical and societal needs in today's operating room. While some of these requirements vary depending on the scope of the robot; there is a common theme– the need to be socially accepted and technically skilled as their team mates. Implications related to the introduction of surgical robots in the surgical setting, as assistants rather than autonomous agents, will have sociological and technological effects that are likely transform healthcare as we know it today. Scientific awareness of presented challenges to be addressed will guide the next generation of robots so they will play a central role in this transformation.

References

1. Buerhaus, P.I., Auerbach, D.I., Staiger, D.O.: The Recent Surge In Nurse Employment: Causes And Implications. Health Affairs 28(4), 657–668 (2009)
2. The Effect of Health Care Working Conditions on Patient Safety, Agency for Healthcare Research and Quality, Rockville, MD, Summary, Evidence Report/Technology Assessment: Number 74 AHRQ Publication No. 03-E024 (2003)
3. Needleman, D.J., Buerhaus, P., Pankratz, V.S., Leibson, C.L., et al.: Nurse staffing and inpatient hospital mortality. New England Journal of Medicine 364(11), 1037–1045 (2011)

4. McHugh, M.D., Brooks Carthon, M., Wu, E., Kelly, L., Sloane, D., Aiken, L.H.: Impact of nurse staffing mandates on safety-net hospitals: Lessons from California. The Milbank Quarterly 90, 160–186 (2012)
5. Firth-Cozens, J.: Why communication fails in the operating room. Qual. Saf. Health Care 13(5), 327 (2004)
6. Lingard, L., Espin, S., Whyte, S., et al.: Communication failures in the operating room: an observational classification of recurrent types and effects. Qual. Saf. Health Care 13, 330–334 (2004)
7. Healey, A.N., Undre, S., Vincent, C.A.: Defining the technical skills of teamwork in surgery. Qual. Saf. Health Care 15, 231–234 (2006)
8. Carthey, J., de Laval, M.R., Wright, D.J., et al.: Behavioural markers of surgical excellence. Safety Science 41, 409–425 (2003)
9. Taylor, R.H., Stoianovici, D.: Medical Robotics in Computer-Integrated Surgery. IEEE Transactions on Robotics and Automation 19(5) (2003)
10. Borenstein, J., Koren, Y.: A mobile platform for nursing robots. IEEE Transactions on Industrial Electronics (2), 158–165 (2007)
11. Bedem, V.L.: Realization of a demonstrator slave for robotic minimally invasive surgery. Ph.D. dissertation, Technische Universiteit Eindhoven (2010)
12. Agovic, A., Levine, S., Papanikolopoulos, N., Tewfik, A. (2010) Haptic interface design considerations for scrub nurse robots in microsurgery. 18th Mediterranean Conference on Control & Automation (MED), 2010 , pp.1573-1578.
13. Intuitive Surgical, da Vinci Surgical System, Online
14. Kochan, A.: Scalpel please, robot: Penelope's debut in the operating room. Industrial Robot: An International Journal 32(6), 449–451 (2005)
15. Carpintero, E., Perez, C., Morales, R., et al.: Development of a robotic scrub nurse for the operating theatre. In: 2010 3rd IEEE RAS and EMBS International Conference on Biomedical Robotics and Biomechatronics (BioRob), pp. 504–509 (2010)
16. Nathan, C., Chakradeo, V., Malhotra, K., D'Agostino, H., Patwardhan, R.: The Voice-Controlled Robotic Assist Scope Holder AESOP for the Endoscopic Approach to the Sella. Skull Base 12, 123–132 (2006)
17. Yoshimitsu, K., Miyawaki, F., Sadahiro, T., et al.: Development and evaluation of the second version of scrub nurse robot (SNR) for endoscopic and laparoscopic surgery. In: Intelligent Robots and Systems, IROS 2007, pp. 2288–2294 (2007)
18. McCulloch, P., Mishra, A., Handa, A., Dale, T., Hirst, G., Catchpole, K.: The effects of aviation-style non-technical skills training on technical performance and outcome in the operating theatre. British Medical Journal 18(2), 109 (2009)
19. Mitchell, L., Flin, R.: Non-technical skills of the operating theatre scrub nurse: literature review. Journal of Advanced Nursing 63(1), 15–24 (2009)
20. Purdy, E.: The Increasing Role of Robots in National Security. In: Greig, J.M. (ed.) Defense AT&L, vol. XXXVII (2008)
21. King, H., Low, T., Hufford, K., Broderick, T.: Acceleration compensation for vehicle based telesurgery on earth or in space. In: The International Conference on Intelligent Robots and Systems, IROS IEEE/RSJ 2008, pp. 1459–1464 (2008)
22. Garcia, P., Rosen, J., Kapoor, C., Noakes, M., Elbert, G., Treat, M., Ganous, T., Hanson, M., Manak, J., Hasser, C., Rohler, D., Satava, R.: Trauma pod: A semi-automated telerobotic surgical system. International Journal of Medical Robotics and Computer Assisted Surgery 5(2), 136–146 (2009)
23. Treat, M.R., Amory, S.E., Downey, P.E., Taliaferro, D.A.: Initial clinical experience with a partly autonomous robotic surgical instrument server. Surg. Endoscopy 20 (2006)

24. Jacob, M.G., Li, Y., Wachs, J.P.: A Gesture Driven Robotic Scrub Nurse. In: Proceedings of the 2011 IEEE International Conference on Systems, Man, and Cybernetics, Anchorage, Alaska, October 9-12 (2001)

25. Fulchiero, G.J., Vujevich, J.J., Goldberg, L.H.: Nonverbal hand signals: a tool for increasing patient comfort during dermatologic surgery. Dermatol Surg. 35(5), 856–857 (2009)

26. Phillips, N., Berry, E., Kohn, M.: Berry & Kohn's operating room technique. Mosby Inc. (2004)

27. Pezzella, A.: Hand Signals in Surgery. AORN Journal 63(4), 769 (1996)

28. CMU Sphinx: Open source toolkit for speech recognition. Carnegie Mellon University (2011)

29. Wachs, J.P., Jacob, M., Li, Y., Akingba, G.: Does a robotic scrub nurse improve economy of movements? In: SPIE Medical Imaging, Image-Guided Procedures, Robotic Interventions, and Modeling Conference, San Diego, California USA, February 4-9 (2012)

30. Jacob, M., Li, Y.T., Wachs, J.P.: Gestonurse: A Multimodal Robotic Scrub Nurse. In: Proc. of the 7th ACM/IEEE Intl Conf. on Human Robot Interaction (HRI 2012), Boston, Massachusetts, March 5-8 (2011)

31. Jacob, M., Li, Y.T., Akingba, G., Wachs, J.P.: 'Gestonurse' a robotic surgical nurse for handling surgical instruments in the operating room. Journal of Robotic Surgery, 1–11 (2011) ISSN: 1863-2483

32. Wasen, K.: Replacement of Highly Educated Surgical Assistants by Robot Technology in Working Life: Paradigm Shift in the Service Sector. I. J. Social Robotics 2(4), 431–438 (2010)

33. Freedy, A., DeVisser, E., Weltman, G., Coeyman, N.: Measurement of trust in human-robot collaboration. In: Proc. Int. Symp. Collaborative Technologies and Syst., Orlando, FL, pp. 106–114 (2007)

34. Parasuraman, R., Riley, V.: Humans and automation: Use, misuse, disuse, abuse. Human Factors 39(2), 230–253 (1997)

35. Adams, B.D., Bruyn, L.E., Houde, S., Angelopoulos, P.: Trust in automated systems literature review. Defense Research and Development Canada Toronto No. CR-2003-096 (2003)

36. Desai, M., Stubbs, K., Steinfeld, A., Yanco, H.: Creating trustworthy robots: Lessons and inspirations from automated systems. In: Proc. Artificial Intelligence and Simulation of Behaviour Conv.: New Frontiers in Human-Robot Interaction, Scotland (2009)

37. Aiken, L.H., Sermeus, W., Van den Heede, K., Sloane, D.M., et al.: Patient safety, satisfaction, and quality of hospital care: Cross-sectional surveys of nurses and patients in 12 countries in Europe and the United States. British Medical Journal (2012)

Pattern Recognition in Transportation

José Antonio Rodriguez-Serrano

Xerox Research Centre Europe
France
jose-antonio.rodriguez@xrce.xerox.com

Abstract. The research, development and design of Intelligent Transportation Systems worldwide relies on technologies that are able to enhance security and safety, increase efficiency, reduce congestion and promote environmental sustainability. In addition, transportation systems are becoming increasingly complex as they are required to deliver mobility to large, diverse and densely populated areas across multiple modes of transportation, e.g. cars, public transport, bicycles, electric cars, etc. Transportation systems able to cope with these challenges and scale will necessarily rely on smart sensors that monitor and act upon stimuli from the environment. Of all sensor options, visual sensors will continue to be a preferred choice since they provide data that humans can easily process and verify, e.g. it is estimated that every vehicle built after 2014 will come equipped with a rear-mounted camera.

As pattern recognition techniques mature, the demand for applications in the transportation domain will only grow. These applications range from automated vehicle detection and access control to safety systems for red-light, lane or speed management passing through traffic condition monitoring, incident detection, autonomous vehicles, etc. We will first take a look at the state-of-the-art of the different solutions with emphasis on those that present open research challenges. We will also take a look at the main trends in transportation in order to understand what research is likely to be of high relevance in future transportation systems.

L. Alvarez et al. (Eds.): CIARP 2012, LNCS 7441, p. 58, 2012.

The Intrinsic Dimensionality of Attractiveness: A Study in Face Profiles

Andrea Bottino and Aldo Laurentini

Politecnico di Torino, Dipartimento di Automatica e Informatica, Italy
{andrea.bottino,aldo.laurentini}@polito.it

Abstract. The study of human attractiveness with pattern analysis techniques is an emerging research field. One still largely unresolved problem is which are the facial features relevant to attractiveness, how they combine together, and the number of independent parameters required for describing and identifying harmonious faces. In this paper, we present a first study about this problem, applied to face profiles. First, according to several empirical results, we hypothesize the existence of two well separated manifolds of attractive and unattractive face profiles. Then, we analyze with manifold learning techniques their intrinsic dimensionality. Finally, we show that the profile data can be reduced, with various techniques, to the intrinsic dimensions, largely without loosing their ability to discriminate between attractive and unattractive faces.

Keywords: manifold learning, intrinsic dimensionality, dimensionality reduction, profiles, facial attractiveness.

1   Introduction

In recent years the scientific analysis of facial attractiveness has been a major research issue both in medical areas such as plastic surgery and orthodontics, and in human science fields such as psychology, psychobiology, anthropology, evolutionary biology, behavioral and cognitive sciences. Many thousands of relevant papers have been presented in these areas. Several results point to the objective nature of the human perception of attractiveness, suggesting that beauty is not, or not only, "in the eye of the beholder". Empirical rating studies have demonstrated high beauty rating congruence over ethnicity, social class, age, and sex ([1], [2], [3], [4]). Recent studies in psychophysiology and neuropsychology lead to the detection of the brain areas where the assessment of facial beauty is processed. Activity patterns related to explicit attractiveness judgement of face images, showed a non-linear response profile, with a greater response to highly attractive and unattractive faces. Finally, babies as young as three/six months, which are not affected by cultural standards about beauty, were found to be able to distinguish between faces previously rated as attractive or unattractive by adult raters ([5]). These results show that the human perception of attractiveness is essentially data-driven, and largely irrespective of the perceiver. They are the rationale of the use of pattern analysis/image processing techniques for objective attractiveness analysis. Computer analysis of attractiveness has several practical

L. Alvarez et al. (Eds.): CIARP 2012, LNCS 7441, pp. 59–66, 2012.

applications such as supporting studies in human science, planning plastic surgery and orthodontic treatments, suggesting the make-up and hairstyle more fitting to a particular face, selecting images for social networks or curricola. Using pattern analysis techniques for analyzing facial attractiveness is an emerging research area, and a number of paper on this subject have been recently published (see [5]). Although many interesting results have been obtained, they have not yet been combined in an overall framework. In particular, the main problems, that is: which are the objective elements of facial beauty, how they combine together and whether they can be expressed in some simple form, are far from being solved.

Using the face space paradigm ([6]), according to which faces represent a d-dimension manifold in the D-dimension space used to describe them, with d<<D, most of these unsolved problems can be expressed as the problem of learning the manifolds of faces rated for attractiveness. Manifold learning is an active area of research, aimed at discovering hidden relations between multidimensional data ([7]). Learning a manifold means first understanding its intrinsic dimensionality (ID), that is the number of independent parameters required for describing the manifold. The next step is reducing the high dimensionality of the original data into a space with dimensions near to ID, maintaining, as far as possible, the relations between data points relevant to the problem considered. Up to now, no such research has been performed in the face space with relation to attractiveness. Manifold learning techniques have been found useful for other face analysis, as human age estimation ([8]) and gender classification problems ([9]). Observe that an important requirement for manifold learning is a sufficiently dense sampling. Unfortunately, we have no clear idea of the meaning of "sufficiently dense" in the case of manifolds of faces rated for beauty. In [10] it has been observed that classification accuracy, that is coherence with human rating, increased with the number of samples without showing sign of saturation using around hundred 2D frontal expressionless samples. This and other facts point to a clear undersampling of the face space, in particular for very beautiful faces, even for monochromatic images.

In this paper, we present what to our knowledge is the first study that applies manifold learning techniques to the problem of facial attractiveness. In particular, we will deal with face profiles, in order to reduce possible undersampling problems (w.r.t. frontal images). Actually, profiles are very characterizing face features. In recent studies, they have been found to convey several information, sufficient, for instance, for identity recognition ([13], [14], [15]), for identifying gender and ethnicity ([12]), for planning plastic surgery ([11]), and for recognizing facial expressions ([16]). In addition, it has been demonstrated that beauty ratings of frontal and profile images are strongly correlated ([17]).

The aim of our work is the following. First of all, the research previously quoted that supports the objective nature of human attractiveness, also points to the existence in face space of two well separate manifolds, related to attractive and unattractive faces. This is also strongly supported by the fact that several approaches aimed at automatically rating face attractiveness report great accuracy for the higher and lower beauty levels, while average attractiveness judgments are much more uncertain both for automatic and human ratings ([22], [23], [24], [25]). Therefore, we first analyze the ID of the manifolds of attractive and unattractive face profiles. Then, we show that discriminating the two manifolds can be effectively performed with data reduced, with various techniques, to dimensions near to their ID. This has been done collecting a training set of face profile images rated for attractiveness by a human panel, and constructing, on the basis of the reduced image data, an automatic rater, to be compared for a test set with human ratings, assumed to be ground truth. Human raters are asked to score faces attractiveness with some integer numbers, from which the two classes of attractive and unattractive profiles can be separated. Therefore, attractiveness estimation is considered as a classification problem and its accuracy is evaluated as the percentage of test samples classified into the right class.

The rest of the paper is organized as follows. In section 2, we present the database used. In section 3, we briefly discuss the technique for estimating the ID related to the attractiveness classification. Section 4 is devoted to present and discuss the experimental results obtained.

2   Sampling the Manifolds of Pleasant and Unpleasant Faces

The first problem to face for this work, as well as for other 2D or 3D beauty research, is the lack of databases containing faces rated for attractiveness, and in particular beautiful faces. Therefore, we decided to build such a database, collecting an initial set of profile images, with different resolutions, selected from several sources (Bernard Achermann DB, Color FERET DB, CVL Face DB, Flickr and color photographs of volunteers participating to this research). Some examples can be seen in Fig. 1. The reference database contains 510 profile images with neutral expression, different age and ethnicity (45 Africans, 68 Asians and 397 Caucasians) and equally divided between the two genders. In order to identify samples belonging to the manifolds of attractive and unattractive faces for our investigation, we asked a panel of human raters to evaluate their attractiveness. The obtained scores have then been used, to separate these two sets from that of attractively average faces.

Fig. 1. profile images in the DB   **Fig. 2.** Nasion ans subnasal points

The samples in the DB were rated through a public website by a panel of students and colleagues of our University, who were asked to express a vote for each subject on a 10 levels scale, ranging from 1 (attractive) to 10 (unattractive). Prior to web evaluation images were properly cropped and scaled to focus raters on the profiles. The raters were almost equally divided between genders (53.3% males and 46.7% females). Since the scores of the human raters are not coincident, the attractiveness value for a profile is considered as the mean of the raters' votes. A total of 82,102 votes, with an average of 160 votes per image, were collected, showing a substantial rating congruence between male and female raters (Pearson correlation of 0.94), consistent with previously reported findings [5]. The final mean ratings were in the range [1.99, 7.91], with a 41% reduction of the initial available rating interval. As we expected, selecting faces from the available face databases strongly reduces the number of samples (very attractive and very unattractive) useful for our study. We underline the fact that this is a problem that seems to affect most of the data sets used in the literature for attractiveness related research.

In order to perform meaningful comparisons, the heterogeneous profiles in the DB have been normalized. This process was first aimed at aligning them and delimiting the same section for all profiles, including the most significant facial features (forehead, nose, mouth and chin) and then at reducing the effects of varying lighting conditions. Geometric normalization is based on the position of two landmarks in the profile contour (Fig. 2): nasion (the point in the skull where the nasal and frontal bone unite) and subnasal (the point, above the upper lip, where the nasal septum begins). These two landmarks are identified using the algorithm described in [18], which first extract the face silhouette by background subtraction and then processes its outline; landmarks are then aligned with two predefined points within a fixed area of interest, whose size is 200x100 pixels. Finally, normalized images are converted to grayscale and their histograms are equalized. Each profile is then represented as a one-dimensional vector of size 20.000, obtained concatenating grayscale image rows.

3   Intrinsic Dimensionality and Dimensionality Reduction

The intrinsic dimensionality ID of a data set with dimension D can be defined as the number of independent parameters that can be used to describe the data set without significant loss of information relative to the problem considered. In other terms, it means that the data points lie on a manifold of dimension ID, where $0 < ID \leq D$. Several methods have been reported in literature for ID estimation. In this work, we use a fractal-based estimator, called Correlation Dimension ([19]). The basic idea for this and other estimators is that the number of points enclosed into a hypersphere of radius r centred on a point of the manifold grows proportionally to r^{ID}. The Correlation Integral $C(r)$, defined as:

$$C(r) = \frac{2}{n(n-1)} \sum_{i=1}^{n} \sum_{j=i+1}^{n} c, \quad \text{where } c = \begin{cases} 1, \text{ if } \|x_i\text{-}x_j\| \leq r \\ 0, \text{ if } \|x_i\text{-}x_j\| > r \end{cases}$$

where x_i and x_j are points of the dataset, provides the relative amount of pairs of points lying into an hypersphere of radius r. $C(r)$ can be used to estimate ID of the dataset, by computing the limit: $\lim_{r \to 0} \log(C(r)) / \log(r)$

For a finite set of samples, this limit can be estimated considering the slope of the linear part of the curve $\log(C(r))/\log(r)$. As we already stated in the introduction, the reliability of the ID estimate has been tested by checking if attractiveness can be adequately discriminated in two classes by using ID dimension for each face sample. In other words, the human panel attractiveness scores are used to extract two subsets of attractive and unattractive profiles and discrimination is considered as a classification problem. Given the uncertainty about the adequateness of the density of sampling, we assume the ID computed with this technique as a rough estimation, and for classification we will experiment several other dimensions near ID. For conducting our tests, we have selected three different linear and non-linear dimensionality reduction methods: PCA, Isomap and Laplacian Eigenmaps ([7]).

4   Experimental Results

Our purpose is to estimate how many parameters are required for discriminating profiles belonging, according to attractiveness scores, to the manifolds of attractive and unattractive profiles. Hence, we first estimate the ID of the manifolds containing some of the best and worst classified profiles. The separation of the two classes of attractive and unattractive faces from that of attractively average faces, is given by the lower and upper percentile of all attractiveness scores. Then, to validate these estimates, we reduce dimensionality to various values near to the estimated ID using various techniques and attempt to discriminate classes with different attractiveness using these reduced dimensions. Validation has been done with different datasets to investigate the relevance to profile attractiveness classification of several factors: sex, number of samples and separation in attractiveness of the two manifolds.

Table 1. Attractiveness ratings of the samples in the reference database

	Female			Male			Mixed		
	1st	25th	50th	1st	25th	50th	1st	25th	50th
Attractive	7.91	5.72	5.11	7.46	5.07	4.48	7.91	6.07	5.52
Unattractive	1.99	3.06	3.35	2.23	2.92	3.14	1.99	2.71	3.00
Diff	5.92	2.66	1.76	5.23	2.15	1.34	5.92	3.36	2.52

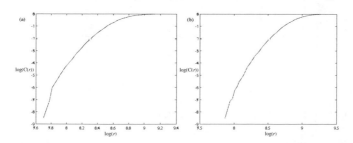

Fig. 3. The plot of Correlation Dimension for attractive (a) and unattractive (b) profile images

It is clear that more samples in each dataset provide a more dense coverage of the manifolds and a better training of the classifiers. It is also clear that the largest the distance, in terms of attractiveness between the classes of attractive and unattractive samples, the better the two classes are separated and, therefore, better classification results can be expected. Unfortunately, these requirements conflict, since increasing the dataset size reduces distances between classes, and vice-versa. This can be seen in Table 1, where the attractiveness ratings of the 1st, 25th and 50th best and worst samples of each class for the two distinct sexes and mixed sexes are listed. In order to keep a reasonable interval between the two classes, two datasets for each gender were created. The firsts comprise the 25 best and 25 worst rated profiles, the seconds the 50 best and 50 worst. Finally, we created two other sets of 50 and 100 samples combining the best and worst rated profiles, without regard of their sex.

An estimate of the ID of the manifolds of attractive and unattractive faces has been obtained applying the Correlation Dimension technique to two datasets, combining the 100 best and the 100 worst male and female profiles. The plots of the Correlation Dimension for these datasets are shown in Fig. 4. Since the plots are non linear, we selected three different intervals on that curve and evaluated the mean slope of the lines of best fit. We estimated 12 as ID for the attractive silhouettes (the results in the various intervals were d1=14, d2=12 and d3=9) and 11 for the unattractive ones (d1=13, d2=11 and d3=9). Since the ID evaluated with this technique can be considered only as a rough estimate, we performed classification experiments with several values near to the estimated IDs. After dimensionality reduction, three different classifiers were used: Support Vector Machines with radial basis kernel (SVM), whose parameters were optimized with a grid approach, Multi Layer Perceptron (MLP), with 10 training epochs and 5 hidden units, and k-Nearest Neighbours (kNN), with k=4. For assessing the classification results, in all experiments we applied a stratified 10-fold cross validation technique. In Table 2 we show a summary of the best classification results for different data sets (Female 50, Female 100, Male 50, Male 100, Mixed 50, Mixed 100) and reduced dimensionality spaces of size 3, 5, 10, 15, 20, 25 and 30, dropping the reference to dimensionality reduction and classification technique. The last column reports the highest classification accuracy obtained for each data set. We recall that ground truth values are given by human panel scores.

Table 2. Best classification accuracies

	3	5	10	15	20	25	30	max
Female 50	0,84	0,90	0,86	0,86	0,86	0,86	0,84	0,90
Female 100	0,82	0,83	0,86	0,87	0,85	0,84	0,87	0,87
Male 50	0,78	0,72	0,80	0,78	0,80	0,88	0,76	0,88
Male 100	0,67	0,71	0,77	0,77	0,77	0,84	0,81	0,84
Mixed 50	0,86	0,94	0,90	0,88	0,90	0,86	0,88	0,94
Mixed 100	0,76	0,80	0,87	0,85	0,86	0,88	0,88	0,88

The following main observations stems from the above table.

1. The main result is the effective profile attractiveness discrimination in low dimensionality spaces. Although the beauty rating separations between test datasets is rather low, the classification results in spaces with dimensionality near to the estimated ID in general can be considered in good agreement with the human ratings (94% accuracy for Mixed 50 and 90% for Female 50, both in a 5 dimension space). When the separation is lower, better results are achieved with a dimension somewhat higher (15 for Female 100, 25 for Male 50, Male 100 and Mixed 100), but still close to the estimated IDs.

2. Although not shown in the table, the classification results are not much affected from the data reduction techniques (linear, PCA, or non-linear, Isomap and Laplacian Eigenmaps,). This fact points to a good intrinsic separation of the manifolds of attractive and unattractive face profiles in the face space, which appears to

be an interesting result. As for different classifiers, SVM performed consistently better.

3. As expected, more effective classification is obtained for better separated datasets. As can be seen in the table: i) results achieved by 50 element datasets are better in all the cases than those obtained by 100 element datasets; ii) mixed datasets are better than female ones, which are in turn better than male datasets (according to their rating distances in Table 1).

4. Female datasets achieved better classification results than male datasets. One reason is that the average ratings of the attractive males was lower than that of attractive females. Another reason could be that attractive male faces have in general stronger features than attractive female features ([20], [21]), which hints at a worst sampling of the attractive male manifold. In general, according to various results presented in human sciences, as those stating that qualities as averageness and symmetry are much more related to female than male beauty ([5]), computer analysis of female beauty is likely to be easier than male beauty.

5   Conclusions and Future Work

In this paper, we presented what to our knowledge is the first study that applies manifold learning techniques to the analysis of facial attractiveness. Understanding the intrinsic dimensionality of the manifolds of attractive and unattractive faces is a first step toward understanding which facial elements are relevant to attractiveness, and how they must combine together. In order to reduce possible under-sampling problems, we analyzed the ID and dimensionality reduction techniques for face profiles. The analysis of data sets of attractive and unattractive faces has provided an intrinsic dimensionality ID not much far from 10. Several dimensionality reduction techniques have been experimented, and the discrimination of attractive and unattractive profiles in low dimensionality spaces has been compared with human ratings. The tests show that a number of independent parameters near to the estimated ID are sufficient for attractiveness ratings in good agreement with human judgement. Although we believe that these first results are interesting, much further work is needed to approach a full understanding of the elements of facial beauty and their relations. While the manifolds of attractive and unattractive faces have been shown to be well separated in low dimensionality spaces, the shape of these manifolds is still to determine, as well as the best data reduction techniques. A basic requirement of this research would be a dense sampling, in 2D, or better in 3D, of the manifolds of faces with high beauty ratings differences, and in particular of faces rated for high attractiveness. Since currently no such data set is available, we plan to construct it, starting from that of frontal 2D images.

References

[1] Bashour, M.: History and Current Concepts in the Analysis of Facial Attractiveness. Plastic and Reconstructive Surgery 118(3), 741–756 (2006)

[2] Cunningham, M.R., Roberts, A.R., Barbee, A.P., Druen, P.B.: Their ideas of beauty are, on the whole, the same as ours: Consistency and variability in the crosscultural perceptions of female attractiveness. Journ. Pers. and Social Psyc. 68, 261–279 (1995)

[3] Etcoff, N.: Beauty and the beholder. Nature 368, 186–187 (1994)

[4] Jones, D.: Physical Attractiveness and the Theory of Sexual Selection: Results from Five Populations. University of Michigan Press, Ann Harbour (1996)

[5] Bottino, A., Laurentini, A.: The Analysis of Facial Beauty: An Emerging Area of Research in Pattern Analysis. In: Campilho, A., Kamel, M. (eds.) ICIAR 2010. LNCS, vol. 6111, pp. 425–435. Springer, Heidelberg (2010)

[6] Sirovich, L., Kirby, M.: Low-dimensional procedure for the characterization of human faces. J. Opt. Soc. Am. 4, 519–524 (1987)

[7] van der Maaten, L.J.P.: An Introduction to Dimensionality Reduction Using Matlab. Int. Report MICC 07-07, Universiteit Maastricht, The Netherlands (2007)

[8] Guo, G., Fu, Y., Dyer, C.R., Huang, T.: Image-based human age estimation by manifold learning and locally adjusted robust regression. IEEE Trans. on Image Processing 17(7), 1178–1188 (2008)

[9] Buchala, S., Davey, N., Frank, R.J., Gale, T.M.: Dimensionality reduction of face images for gender classification. In: Proc. IEEE Conf. on Intell. Syst., pp. 88–93 (2004)

[10] Eisenthal, Y., Dror, G., Ruppin, E.: Facial Attractiveness: beauty and the machine. Neural Computation 18, 119–142 (2006)

[11] Ozkul, T., Ozkul, M.H.: Computer simulation tool for rhinoplasty planning. Comput. in Biol. and Med. 34, 697–718 (2004)

[12] Tariq, U., Hu, Y., Huang, T.S.: Gender and Ethnicity identification from silhouetted face profiles. In: IEEE Proc. ICIP, pp. 2441–2444 (November 2009)

[13] Kakadiaris, I.A., Abdelmunim, H., Yang, W., Theoharis, T.: Profile-based face recognition. In: IEEE Proc. FG 2008, pp. 1–8 (2008)

[14] Wu, C.J., Huang, J.S.: Human face profile recognitionby computer. Pattern Recognition 23, 255–259 (1990)

[15] Zhou, X., Bhanu, B.: Human recognition based onface profiles in video. In: Proc. IEEE CVPR, Washington, DC (June 2005)

[16] Pantic, M., Patras, I., Rothkrantz, L.: Facial action recognition in face profiles image sequences. In: Proc. IEEE ICME 2002, pp. 37–40 (2002)

[17] Davidenko, N.: Silhouetted face profiles: A new methodology for face perception research. Journal of Vision 7(4), 6, 1–17 (2007)

[18] Bottino, A., Cumani, S.: A fast and robust method for the identification of face landmarks in profile images. W. Trans. on Comp. 7(8), 1250–1259 (2008)

[19] Grassberger, P., Procaccia, I.: Measuring the Strangeness of Strange Attractors. Physica D: Nonlinear Phenomena 9(1-2), 189–208 (1983)

[20] Keating, C.F.: Gender and the physiognomy of dominance and attractiveness. Social Psychology Quarterly 48, 61–70 (1985)

[21] Zuk, M.: The role of parasites in sexual selection: current evidence and future directions. Advances in the Study of Behavior 21, 39–67 (1992)

[22] Aarabi, P., Hughes, D., Mohajer, K., Emami, M.: The automatic measurement of facial beauty. In: IEEE SMC 2004, pp. 2168–2174 (2004)

[23] Mao, H., Jin, L., Du, M.: Automatic classification of Chinese female facial beauty using Support Vector Machine. In: IEEE SMC 2009, pp. 4842–4846 (2009)

[24] Sutic, D., Breskovic, I., Huic, R., Jukic, I.: Automatic evaluation of facial attractiveness. In: MIPRO 2010, Opatija, May 24-28, pp. 1339–1342 (2010)

[25] Eisenthal, Y., Dror, G., Ruppin, E.: Facial Attractiveness: beauty and the machine. Neural Computation 18, 119–142 (2006)

A Hybrid of Principal Component Analysis and Partial Least Squares for Face Recognition across Pose

Ajay Jaiswal, Nitin Kumar, and R.K. Agrawal

School of Computer and Systems Sciences
Jawaharlal Nehru University, New Delhi, India
a_ajayjaiswal@yahoo.com {nitin2689,rkajnu}@gmail.com

Abstract. In this paper, we propose a simple and efficient hybrid approach based on the combination of principal component analysis and partial least squares. Principal component analysis is used to reduce the dimension of image in first step and partial least squares method is used to carry out pose invariant face recognition in second step. The performance of proposed method is compared with another popular method based on global linear regression on hybrid-eigenface (HGLR) in terms of classification accuracy and computation time. Experimental results on two well known publicly available face databases demonstrate the effectiveness of the proposed approach.

Keywords: Face recognition across pose, Partial least squares, Principal component analysis, Hybrid-eigenfaces, Linear regression.

1 Introduction

In controlled environment, the performance of face recognition system has already attained satisfactory levels. But still, there are many challenges associated with face recognition in presence of illumination variation, pose variation, occlusion etc. Face recognition across pose has been identified as one of the most challenging problem by research community [1]. Many methods have been proposed to tackle the problem of recognising faces across pose [2]. In recent years, few promising methods have been proposed such as global linear regression (GLR) [3], local linear regression (LLR) [3], GLR on hybrid eigenfaces (HGLR) [4] and face recognition based on partial least squares[5] etc. However, none of them is free from shortcomings.

HGLR involves generation of multiple virtual views to carry out face recognition. Hence, more storage and computation time is required. Similarly method based on partial least squares (PLS) performed on the images of larger size requires huge computation time. One way of reducing the computation time is to reduce the size of the image. But, it will lead to information loss in the image. Another approach is to reduce the dimensionality of the image with minimal loss of information. This can be achieved using principal component analysis (PCA) which reduces the redundant information of the image. Motivated by this, we propose to carry out face recognition in two steps. In first step, PCA is applied to reduce the dimensionality and in second step, face recognition is carried out with PLS. To check the efficacy, the performance of the proposed approach was evaluated in terms of classification accuracy and computation time. We also investigated the performance under different pose variations

L. Alvarez et al. (Eds.): CIARP 2012, LNCS 7441, pp. 67–73, 2012.

and different size of training data. The rest of the paper is organized as follows. Section 2 describes GLR and hybrid eigenfaces briefly. PLS is described in section 3. The proposed approach is discussed in section 4. Experimental results on two well known publicly available face databases are included in section 5. Finally, section 6 contains conclusions and future work.

2 Global Linear Regression (GLR) and Hybrid Eigenfaces

GLR [3] is based on the assumption that there exists a linear mapping between non-frontal face images and frontal images of the same person. Therefore, it is possible to transform a non-frontal face image to its corresponding frontal view or vice versa with some approximation. Chai et al. [3] formulated a method for virtual view generation in frontal pose from an input face image under p^{th} pose using GLR. This method involves two steps. In the first step, input face image in p^{th} pose (i^p_{in}) is decomposed into linear combination of N face images under the same pose using linear regression with face images as basis vectors and is given by

$$i^p_{in} = c^p_1 i^p_1 + c^p_2 i^p_2 + c^p_3 i^p_3 + \dots + c^p_N i^p_N \tag{1}$$

This can also be rewritten as

$$i^p_{in} = I^p c^p_{in} \quad \text{and} \quad c^p_{in} = (I^p)^\perp i^p_{in} \tag{2}$$

where $c^p_{in} = [c^p_1 \quad c^p_2 \quad \dots \quad c^p_N]^T$, $I^p = [i^p_1 \quad i^p_2 \quad \dots \quad i^p_N]$ and $(I^p)^\perp$ is the pseudo-inverse of I^p. In the second step, the corresponding virtual frontal view is obtained by linearly combining the face images under frontal pose using the same coefficient vector c^p_{in} i.e. $i^0_{in} = I^0 c^p_{in}$ and $I^0 = [i^0_1 \quad i^0_2 \quad \dots \quad i^0_N]$. GLR on coarsely aligned images does not provide realistic images and contain some artefacts especially around the corner of mouth and eyes [4]. To overcome this drawback, Sharma et al. [4] proposed GLR on H-eigenfaces. Brief description of HGLR is given here. Consider a face database consisting of face images of N subject with each subject having face images under different poses. A "mixed vector" is formed by stacking the face image vectors of same person under different pose [4]. For example, suppose a frontal-face vector of ith subject is denoted by x^0_i, then the mix vector ($\mathbf{m}_i$) is formed by appending the vector x^p_i below vector x^0_i one after another for all poses. The same was done for all the subjects and a matrix $\mathbf{M}$ was formed having vectors $\mathbf{m}_i$'s as columns, i=1, 2, …, N. The matrix $\mathbf{M}$ is given as

$$\mathbf{M} = \begin{bmatrix} x^0_1 & \dots & x^0_N \\ \dots & & \dots \\ x^p_1 & \ddots & x^p_1 \\ \dots & & \dots \\ x^q_1 & \dots & x^q_N \end{bmatrix} \quad and \quad \mathbf{g}_i = \begin{bmatrix} h^0_i \\ \dots \\ h^p_i \\ \dots \\ h^q_i \end{bmatrix} \tag{3}$$

In next step, PCA is applied on **M** to determine k dominant eigenvectors, $\mathbf{g_i}$ (i=1,..., k) to be used as basis vectors. Further, each of these eigenvectors, $\mathbf{g_i}$, is divided into $r+1$ sub-vectors, where r is the number of desired non-frontal viewpoints under which virtual views are required to be synthesized. The upper sub-vector belongs to the frontal face space and the subsequent lower parts belong to corresponding view-based face spaces in the same order in which they were stacked. These sub-vectors are termed as H-eigenfaces and used for generating virtual views.

3   Partial Least Squares (PLS)

PLS, based on the principle of statistical learning, is widely used in chemo metrics and bioinformatics etc. [6]. In recent years, it is also used in domains such as human detection [7], face recognition [8] etc. It models the relationship between two sets of variables by means of score vectors. All PLS methods work on the assumption that the observed data is generated by a process which is driven by a small number of latent variables [6]. Suppose N observed samples from two sets of variables are denoted as $\mathbf{X} = (x_1, x_2, \ldots, x_N)$ and $\mathbf{Y} = (y_1, y_2, \ldots, y_N)$ respectively, with $\mathbf{X} \in \Re^m$ and $\mathbf{Y} \in \Re^n$. Both **X** and **Y**, are normalized to zero mean. Using PLS, **X** and **Y** can be represented as [6]:

$$X = TP' + E$$
$$Y = UQ' + F \qquad (4)$$

where **T** and **U** are N×p matrices of the p extracted score vectors. The m×p matrix **P** and the n×p matrix **Q** are the loading matrices and the **E** and **F** are the matrices of residuals whose sizes are N×m and N×n respectively. The objective of PLS is to find weight vectors **b** and **c** such that

$$[\text{cov}\,(\mathbf{t}, \mathbf{u})]^2 = [\text{cov}\,(\mathbf{Xb}, \mathbf{Yc})]^2 = \max_{|b|=|c|=1} \text{cov}\,(\mathbf{Xw}, \mathbf{Yr})]^2 \qquad (5)$$

where **t** and **u** are the corresponding score vectors in **T** and **U**. Face recognition using PLS requires the coupled faces across different poses. If the training set is denoted as (**X**, **Y**) where **X** and **Y** correspond to two different poses, the samples in **X** and **Y** are coupled by identity [5] i.e. i^{th} row in **X** and **Y** correspond to image of ith identity in frontal and non-frontal pose respectively.

4   Proposed Approach

The proposed approach involves PCA in first step to reduce the dimensionality without sacrificing much information and PLS in second step for better recognition. Let **IX** and **IY** represent faces in frontal and non-frontal pose respectively. First, we normalize **IX** and **IY** to have zero mean and unit variance. Then we apply PCA separately on frontal (**IX**) and non-frontal (**IY**) images to obtain two subspaces corresponding to frontal images and non-frontal images. After this, PLS is used on the coupled training set to get optimized loading vectors **P** and **Q**. In the testing phase, the loading vectors are used to estimate score vectors for new samples. The score vectors are good pose invariant representation of faces. Face recognition across pose can be performed by directly matching the score vectors. Let us denote a gallery face (frontal) as **Ixt** and a probe face as **Iyt**. We reduce the dimension of **Ixt** and **Iyt** using PCA models obtained during training as given below.

$$xt = W_f Ixt$$
$$yt = W_p Iyt$$
(6)

where W_f and W_p are the transformation matrix obtained after applying PCA to **IX** and **IY** respectively. Based on Eq. (4) their corresponding score vectors **t** and **u** can be estimated using the loading vectors **P** and **Q**.

$$t = xt(P')^{-1}$$
$$u = yt(Q')^{-1}$$
(7)

The similarity s between **Ixt** and **Iyt** can be simply measured by the correlation between **t** and **u** which is given by $s = \dfrac{\langle t, u \rangle}{\|t\| \cdot \|u\|}$, where $\langle t, u \rangle$ denotes the inner product of **t** and **u**. In the recognition, test face is classified to the gallery face with highest similarity value (s).

5   Experimental Setup and Results

To check the efficacy of the proposed approach, we carried out experiments on two publicly available face databases PIE [9] and FERET [10]. For all the experiments, first the images were coarsely aligned according to two eyes position and two extreme mouth corners. Then images were cropped and resized to 50×50. The performance is evaluated in terms of classification accuracy and computation time. The classification accuracy is obtained in terms of 2- fold and 3-fold cross-validations. Each cross-validation is repeated 10 times to obtain average classification accuracy. In our experiments, images of seven poses from the PIE database are used, which covers the pose yawing over ±45 degree and the pitching variations in depth [9]. The poses used in our experiments a0re: P07, P09, P05, P29, P37, P11; and P27. Each pose class includes 68 subjects. The FERET database subset used in our experiments contains images of 196 subjects under nine poses (ba, bb, bc, bd, be, bf, bg, bh and bi). Example faces of both the databases are shown in figure 1.

Fig. 1. Example faces of PIE (left) and FERET (right) database

5.1   Experiments Using HGLR

To obtain H-eigenfaces, more explicitly, in 2-fold cross-validation, images in one pose are divided into two parts. One part is used to generate H-eigenfaces. The virtual views for other part are synthesized using GLR on H-eigenfaces. The virtual images are constructed for all the subjects with different number of H-eigenfaces. All experiments are carried out using single frontal image as a gallery image and two other poses as test images. Using gallery image, virtual frontal and non-frontal images in the poses present in test set are synthesized. Then, for each pose (including frontal), fifteen images under different illumination were generated using gray level transform resulting in a total of 15×3=45 virtual images. Then we used PCA+LDA to carry out face recognition. PCA is applied on the gallery images to obtain PCA subspace. All the virtual images are used as training samples for LDA. Before applying LDA, all the training images were first projected with PCA consisting of top few eigenfaces. The experiment is carried out with different number of eigenfaces. Euclidian distance is used to find the closest match of a probe image in all the experiments. Among the classification accuracies obtained with different combination of number of H-eigenfaces and number of eigenfaces, the best accuracy is reported. Similarly, we carry out 3-fold cross-validation experiments. Experiments on both the face databases are carried out in 3 modes. For PIE face database in mode 1, gallery set contains single frontal pose P27 and testing set comprises of images under poses P07, P09. Test set consists of poses P05 and P29 in mode 2. In mode 3, test set is replaced with images in poses P37 and P11. For FERET face database in mode 1, gallery set comprises of single frontal pose ba and testing set comprises of images under poses be and bf. In mode 2, probe set is replaced by poses bd and bg. In mode 3, test set consists of images in poses bc and bh. All the experiments were executed on Dell T3500 workstation running MATLAB 2010 on Windows 7 (64-bit) platform.

5.2 Experiments Using Proposed Approach

Images in frontal and one non-frontal pose are used at a time. Specifically, in 2-fold, images in one pose are divided into two parts. PCA is applied to first part of data to obtain transformation matrices with respect to frontal and non-frontal pose. Then PLS is applied to obtain loading vectors. Face recognition is performed on the second part of the data. Then training is done with second part and recognition is performed with first part. In this way face recognition is performed for all the subjects. In 3-fold cross-validation, two parts are used for training and face recognition is performed on third part. For PIE face database in mode 1, first we used frontal pose P27 and images under pose P07. Then images under pose P09 are used with frontal images. The average classification accuracy of two different poses (P07 and P09) is reported. Similarly, the average classification accuracy of poses in mode 2 and poses in mode 3 are determined. Similarly for FERET face database, the average classification accuracy of two different poses (be and bf) in mode 1, poses (bd and bg) in mode 2 and poses (bc and bh) in mode 3 are determined. Comparative classification accuracy of HGLR and the proposed approach for both the face databases are shown in Table 1. The comparative computation time is shown in Table 2. The following can be observed from Tables 1-2:

- The classification accuracy of the proposed method is significantly better in comparison to HGLR for both PIE and FERET database in all cases except in mode 1 of 2-fold cross-validation for FERET database.
- As pose variation increases (indicated by modes), the difference in classification accuracy of the two approaches increases significantly.
- Standalone PLS (without PCA) takes large computation time. With the use of PCA in first step of the proposed method, the computation time drops significantly while classification accuracy gets marginally affected. The computation time is significantly less in comparison to HGLR also. Similar observations are made for FERET face database.

Table 1. Comparative classification accuracy

Face database	Cross-validations	mode1		mode2		mode3	
		HGLR	HPCAPLS	HGLR	HPCAPLS	HGLR	HPCAPLS
PIE	2-fold	88.68	**99.63**	80.37	**99.49**	57.87	**96.25**
	3-fold	97.35	**99.93**	90.37	**99.57**	69.48	**98.98**
FERET	2-fold	**87.8**	87.45	76.48	**82.22**	56.22	**68.9**
	3-fold	90.66	**91.64**	82.7	**88.22**	65.56	**76.96**

Table 2. Variation in computation time for PIE face database(2-fold cross-validation)

Approach	Approx. Time taken (in sec.)
PLS on images after applying PCA	**0.88**
HGLR	98 .3
PLS on image of size 50×50	13140

The classification accuracy (Standalone PLS) for PIE database in mode 1 was found to be 99.70% in 2-fold cross validation which is comparable to that of proposed approach.

6   Conclusions

Experimental results demonstrate that the proposed approach performs significantly better than HGLR approach in terms both classification accuracy and computation time. In the proposed approach, there is no need to generate virtual views which reduces both computational time and memory requirement. In future, some other feature extraction methods can be explored for dimensionality reduction to further improve the performance.

References

1. Zhao, W., Chellappa, R., Phillips, P.J., Rosenfeld, A.: Face recognition: a literature survey. ACM Comput. Surv. 35(4), 399–459 (2003)
2. Zhang, X., Gao, Y.: Face recognition across pose: A review. Pattern Recognition 42, 2876–2896 (2009)

3. Chai, X., Shan, S., Chen, X., Gao, W.: Locally linear regression for pose-invariant face recognition. IEEE Trans. Image Process. 16(7), 1716–1725 (2007)
4. Sharma, A., Dubey, A., Tripathi, P., Kumar, V.: Pose invariant virtual classifiers from single training image using novel hybrid-eigenfaces. Neurocomputing 73, 1868–1880 (2010)
5. Li, A., Shan, S., Chen, X., Gao, W.: Cross-pose face recognition based on partial least squares. Pattern Recognition Letters 32(15), 1948–1955 (2011)
6. Rosipal, R., Kramer, N.: Overview and recent advances in partial least squares. Subspace Latent Struct. Feat. Select., 34–51 (2006)
7. Schwartz, W., Kembhavi, A., Harwood, D., Davis, L.: Human detection using partial least squares analysis. In: IEEE Internat. Conf. on Computer Vision, pp. 24–31. IEEE (2009)
8. Baek, J., Kim, M.: Face recognition using partial least squares components. Pattern Recognition 37(6), 1303–1306 (2004)
9. Sim, T., Baker, S., Bsat, M.: The CMU pose, illumination, and expression database. IEEE Trans. PAMI 25(12), 1615–1618 (2003)
10. Phillips, P.J., Wechsler, H., Huang, J., Rauss, P.: The FERET database and evaluation procedure for face recognition algorithms. Image Vision Comput. 16(5), 295–306 (1998)

Gender Classification in Large Databases

Enrique Ramón-Balmaseda, Javier Lorenzo-Navarro,
and Modesto Castrillón-Santana⋆

SIANI Universidad de Las Palmas de Gran Canaria Spain
enrique.de101@alu.ulpgc.es, {jlorenzo,mcastrillon}@siani.es

Abstract. In this paper, we address the challenge of gender classification using large databases of images with two goals. The first objective is to evaluate whether the error rate decreases compared to smaller databases. The second goal is to determine if the classifier that provides the best classification rate for one database, improves the classification results for other databases, that is, the cross-database performance.

Keywords: Gender Recognition, Local Binary Pattern, Large Facial Image Databases.

1 Introduction

Children with few years are able to quickly and easily determine the gender of the people who they interact with. For an automatic system, covering a larger population defines a more complex class border, making the process of classification more difficult. Due to the open challenges, gender classification is a current field of research in computer vision, with different application scenarios that include demographics, direct marketing, surveillance and forensics among others.

Automatic gender classification is therefore an active topic as evidenced by recent publications in major journals [2, 10, 11]. Nowadays, state-of-the-art approaches are based on the facial appearance, although some papers considering the analysis of context information are emerging. The interested reader should study the work by Mäkinen et al. [10], a valuable source presenting a comparison of classification results for this problem with automatically detected faces.

Until recently, FERET [12] has been the database mostly used to evaluate different gender classifiers due to the high quality of the images [2, 5, 6]. In this paper, we work with three large databases to evaluate gender classification: MORPH [9], The Images of Groups [7] database and the Labelled Faces in the Wild (LFW) [8] database. The first two databases contain more than 10,000 faces of people and the third one more than 5,000 images. These databases hhave recently attracted researchers due to the challenging variety of identities, ages, ethnicities, poses and the absence of controlled lighting conditions, they are therefore a source for testing algorithms of classification invariant to real world imagery. We will carry out an experimental analysis with normalized face

⋆ Work partially funded by the Spanish Ministry of Science and Innovation funds (TIN 2008-06068), and the Departamento de Informática y Sistemas at ULPGC.

L. Alvarez et al. (Eds.): CIARP 2012, LNCS 7441, pp. 74–81, 2012.

images at different resolutions, and including both the face area and the face area along with the local context. We use the Local Binary Pattern operator (LBP) [13] to extract images features, and Support Vector Machines (SVM) [14] for classification. The paper is organized as follows. In section 2 the LBP descriptor is introduced. In section 3 details about databases, methodology and experimental results and finally, our conclusions in section 4.

2 Local Binary Pattern

LBP [13] is a simple but efficient texture descriptor that labels the pixels of an image by thresholding the neighbourhood of each pixel with the central pixel value considering the result a binary code. Due to its capacity of discrimination and the simplicity of calculation, this texture descriptor has become a popular method that is used in several real world applications. The most important property of this operator is its robustness to monotonic gray-scale changes that may be caused, for example, by variations in lighting.

The original operator LBP, was introduced by Ojala et al. [1]. The operator labels each of the pixels of an image using the 3×3 neighbourhood, comparing each pixel with the central 3×3 window value. The result is considered as a binary number, and a histogram is calculated, and used as a texture descriptor of the image.

The original definition has been extended to a set of arbitrary circular neighbourhoods, and new definitions have been developed. However, the main idea is the same: a binary code that describes the pattern of the local texture is computed thresholding the neighbours by the center pixel gray value. The expression to compute the generalized LBP is the following:

$$LBP_{P,R} = \sum_{p=0}^{p-1} s(g_p - g_c)2^p \tag{1}$$

where, g_c is the gray level of p neighbours $g_p(p = 1, 2, \cdots, p - 1)$.The function $s(x)$ is defined as:

$$s(x) = \begin{cases} 1, x \geq 0 \\ 0, x < 0 \end{cases} \tag{2}$$

The LBP operator has multiple variants which reflect the attention received by the computer vision community. For the purposes of this work, we focus on one of them, the uniform patterns.

Uniform patterns can be used to reduce the length of the feature vector and to implement a simple descriptor invariant to rotations. This version was inspired by the fact that some binary patterns are more frequent than others. A LBP code is called uniform if the binary pattern contains a maximum of two transitions to bit-level, from 0 to 1 or vice versa, when the bit pattern is circularly travesed. For example, patterns of 00000000 (0 transitions), number 01110000 to (2 transitions) and 11001111 (2 transitions) are uniform, while the patterns of 11001001 (4 transitions) and 01010010 (6 transitions) are not. To get the LBP codification of an image using uniform patterns, each pixel is assigned the corresponding uniform pattern code, or a unique label for all non-uniform patterns. For example, when it is used (8, R) neighbourhood, there are a total of 256 patterns, 58 of which are uniform and the rest are not uniform, so that there are a total of 59 different labels.

2.1   Face Recognition with LBP

In texture classification, the LBP code occurrences in an image are described in a histogram. The classification is then performed using the simple calculation of histogram similarity. However, for facial recognition this approximation implies the loss of spatial information and, therefore, the location information must be coded somehow into the texture model. One way to achieve this goal is the use of LBP descriptors to construct several local descriptions of the face and combine them into a comprehensive description. Recently, this approach has gained adepts due to the limitations of the holistic representations. These methods based on local features are more robust to variations in the position or the lighting than the holistic methods.

The basic methodology for the extraction of features is proposed in [4]. The algorithm introduces a new approach to facial recognition because it considers not only the face shape but also the texture. In this algorithm the face is divided into small regions where the LBP operator is applied and later concatenated, following a Bag of Words scheme [15], into a single histogram that represents the image of the face. The textures of the facial regions are locally encoded by LBP, while the entire shape of the face is retrieved by the histogram of the face. The underlying idea of using LBP features, is that a face image can be seen as the composition of micro-patterns that are invariant to monotonic transformations of gray-scale. The combination of these micro-patterns generates a comprehensive description of the image of the face, as shown in Figure 1a. This histogram has a description of the face at three different levels:

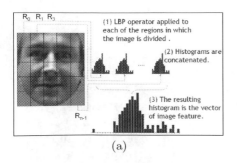

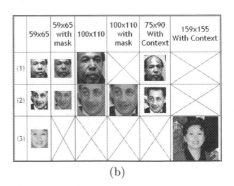

(a)   (b)

Fig. 1. (a) Face image feature vector computation. The final histogram is obtained by the concatenate of the respective cell histograms (b) Sample images of (1) MORPH (2) LFW and (3) The Image of Groups.

- The labels of the LBP histogram contain information about the patterns at pixel level.
- The labels are summarized in a small region to collect information at the local level.
- Region histograms are concatenated to create a comprehensive description of the face.

3   Datasets, Methodology and Experimental Results

Automatic gender classification would be of interest in scenarios where the number of people would be very high, e.g. direct marketing in a mall. In these scenarios, detected people would rarely be contained in the training set. In general, the works described in the literature make use of small dataset which is not representative of a real environment where the system must deal with thousands of people. Therefore, the challenge in this work is to cope with large databases of images in order to the percentage of correctly classified instances. The objective is therefore to use a large database of images to train, and a different database to evaluate the classification quality. In addition, we can determine if it is possible to keep the performance of state-of-the-art gender classifiers.

3.1   Datasets Description

The databases that have been used are MORPH, LFW (usig only one image per identity) and The Image of Groups. The next table summarizes the databases characteristics Figure 1 (b) shows examples of each database and image resolutions employed.

Table 1. Databases summary. (wm with mask), (wc with context).

Database	Female	Male	Sum	59x65	59x65wm	100x110	100x110wm	75x90wc	159x155wc
MORPH	8.488	46.646	55.134	x	x	x		x	
LFW	1.484	4.261	5.745	x	x	x	x	x	
Image of Groups	14.549	13.671	28.220	x					x

3.2   Methodology

The experimental procedure has been the following:

1. Each sample in the database is divided into a grid of nxn cells, where $n = 3, 5, 7, 9$. A LBP operator is applied to each grid cell: (LBP $\{8, 1\}$ or LBP$^{u2}\{8, 1\}$) and the resulting grid cell histograms are concatenated to obtain a new histogram. The resulting histogram is the corresponding feature vector, as seen in Figure (1).
2. The MORPH database was preprocessed, due to its size and the important unbalance between women and men (15% versus 85%), to randomly generate an additional balanced subset, i.e. with approximately equal number of females and males.

Table 2. Comparative MORPH all images or balanced set of females and males

Instances		Grid		
Learning	Test	3x3	5x5	7x7
14.244	3.560	94,39%	95,42%	96,27%
44.105	11.025	92,13%	94,27%	94,58%

3. A Support Vector Machine classifier with linear kernel is computed for each database.
4. The database that provides the best classification results is selected to analyze other versions of the LBP operator in order to determine which LBP configuration yields better results. If any LBP operator reports better classification results in the selected database, the process is repeated in the rest of the databases to confirm this fact.
5. Once we have the database and the LBP configuration providing the best classification results, the whole database is used to train the classifier and then the resulting classifier is tested with the other two databases. With this last test the aim is at comparing cross database classification results with those results achieved training and testing with the same database.

3.3 Experimental Results

First, the MORPH database was preprocessed as mentioned above to consider the original database or a balanced version of it. In this case we used the standard image size of 59x65 pixels, $LBP^{u2}\{8,1\}$ and SVM classifier, with the setup described in the preceding section.

The best results are obtained with the balanced subset with (8.488 females and 9,326 males), that reported an accuracy of 96,27% versus 94,58% with the original unbalanced database. In the rest of the work we make use only this balanced subset for this database. To build the balanced set, all female samples are used, while male samples are selected randomly. Identity intersection of the sets of training and test, in the worst cases, it is of one or two instances, and then we can see that the set of training examples and test are disjoint.

Then we apply the operator LBP^{u2} to generate a feature vector of lower dimension for each image, reducing the computational cost. With this experiment we select the database wih best accuracy.

The best results have been obtained with the MORPH database, achieving an accuracy of $97,64\%$ with a 9×9 grid applied on the images with context. The LFW database [6] reaches a $90,83\%$ with the LBP images computed using 120×105 pixels. In this paper, for this database, we reached $90,60\%$ for 75×90 pixel images. This difference is likely due to the lower image resolution, the reduced number of training samples, additionaly the absence of images of the same identity in both training and test sets, and the unbalanced number of female and male samples. In [6] the classification rates achieved for The Image of Group's database is a $86,34\%$. As shown in Table 3, we achieved $82,65\%$ using $LBP^{u2}\{8,1\}$, which significantly reduces the dimension of the feature vector, and uses normalized images of greater resolution. In [5] we can find the best

Table 3. Results apply $LBP^{u2}\{8,1\}$ to three databases

Database	Size	Instances		Grid			
		Learning	Test	3x3	5x5	7x7	9x9
MORPH	59x65	14.244	3.560	94,39%	95,42%	96,27%	96,18%
	59x65 with mask	14.244	3.560	94,34%	95,51%	96,49%	96,38%
	100x110	14.244	3.560	95,09%	96,49%	97,19%	97,06%
	75x90	14.244	3.560	95,23%	96,07%	97,06%	**97,64%**
LFW	59x65	4.596	1.149	87,12%	84,94%	88,34%	87,64%
	59x65 with mask	4.596	1.149	87,12%	85,64%	87,90%	87,90%
	100x110	4.596	1.149	87,82%	87,82%	87,47%	90,08%
	100x110	4.596	1.149	87,95%	86,95%	88,25%	89,82%
	75x90	4.596	1.149	86,86%	87,82%	89,56%	**90,60%**
The Image of Groups	59x65	22.529	5.632	80,43%	**82,65%**	82,34%	81,53%
	159x155	22.529	5.632	55,38%	54,27%	55,52%	n.a

Table 4. Results of applying different operator LBP to the MORPH database

LBP Operator	Instances		Grid			
	Learning	Test	3x3	5x5	7x7	9x9
$LBP\{8,1\}$	14.244	3.560	93,97%	95,93%	97,05%	**97,53%**
$LBP^{u2}\{8,1\}$	14.244	3.560	95,23%	96,07%	97,06%	**97,64%**
$LBP\{8,2\}$	14.244	3.560	94,28%	97,03%	97,22%	**97,25%**
$LBP^{u2}\{8,2\}$	14.244	3.560	95,32%	96,49%	96,52%	**96,69%**
$LBP\{4,1\}$	14.244	3.560	92,54%	95,63%	96,55%	**96,78%**
$LBP^{u2}\{4,1\}$	14.244	3.560	92,60%	95,81%	96,24%	**96,80%**
$LBP\{4,1\}$ concatenated with global histogram	14.244	3.560	92,74%	95,65%	96,63%	**96,75%**
$LBP^{u2}\{4,1\}$ concatenated with global histogram	14.244	3.560	92,65%	96,68%	96,16%	**96,77%**

Table 5. Cross-database results using MORPH database like training set and the other two databases like test set

Database test	Typo Size	LBP operator	Instances		Grid			
			Learning	Test	3x3	5x5	7x7	9x9
LFW	59x65	$LBP\{8,1\}$	14.244	1.149	59,23%	66,33%	69,68%	61,28%
		$LBP^{u2}\{8,1\}$	14.244	1.149	57,82%	**75,10%**	63,51%	50,47%
	59x65 with mask	$LBP\{8,1\}$	14.244	1.149	67,36%	72,16%	68,42%	61,28%
		$LBP^{u2}\{8,1\}$	14.244	1.149	67,53%	71,90%	69,00%	69,27%
The Image of Group	59x65	$LBP\{8,1\}$	14.244	5.632	65,54%	**76,74%**	68,15%	68,33%
		$LBP^{u2}\{8,1\}$	14.244	5.632	64,53%	53,37%	53,87%	52,80%
	159x155	$LBP\{8,1\}$	14.244	5.632	46,60%	51,23%	52,79%	51,99%
		$LBP^{u2}\{8,1\}$	14.244	5.632	53,61%	53,45%	53,25%	52,15%

results obtained with the database MORPH of 88% of accuracy in the gender classification. We have reached $97,64\%$, using a set of images with greater size for both training and test.

Other LBP operators have been applied to the MORPH database in order to test if better results can be obtained. In particular, we have used LPB$\{8,2\}$, LBP$^{u2}\{8,2\}$,the uniform, LBP$\{4,1\}$, LBP$^{u2}\{4,1\}$ and LBP$\{4,1\}$ plus its corresponding while image histogram. The best results, see Table 4, are obtained with a different operator the uniform $LPB\{8,1\}$, so the previous experiment was repeated to see if it improved with other databases.

The best results are achieved with the operator LBP$\{8,1\}$ and LBP$^{u2}\{8,1\}$, there is no additional tests in other databases.

Finally, we proceeded with the cross-database test, i.e. the training is performed with the set of images from a database, and evaluated with the data of other database to check the "quality" of the classifier. Note that the best results we got with images that contains part of the context is similar. However, the dimension of this type of images is not the same in the other databases, so we used the images without context for both training and test.

As we can see in Table 5 it does not exist any accuracy that improves the results presented in Table 3, the classifier performing the best for one databse is not able to do so with other databases.

4   Conclusions

We have achieved a very high recognition rate with the MORPH database, reaching $97,64\%$ accuracy. With the other databases under consideration, similar classification rates were not achieved, so the success of the method is not database independent. Indeed characteristics such as dimensions of the images, lighting, normalization procedure, total number of images, affect among others.

In addition, using the database with the best results as training set results, there has not been improvement of the accuracy rate of classification in the other databases, which confirms the assertion that there is a high dependency on the database.

Therefore, there are still open challenges in gender classification based on the facial pattern. The results achieved suggest that the problem is not completely solved and these results demonstrate that there are still areas where improvement must be done with new methods and procedures to get a database independent classifier. Thus a system trained under certain conditions may be used with images obtained and completely different from the training set and obtain similar classification rates.

References

[1] Ojala, T., Pietikäinen, M., Harwood, D.: A comparative study of texture measures with classification based on featured distributions. Pattern Recognition 29, 51–59 (1996)

[2] Bekios-Calfa, J., Buenaposada, J.M., Baumela, L.: Revisiting linear discriminant techniques in gender recognition. IEEE Transactions on Pattern Analysis and Machine Intelligence 33(4), 858–864 (2011)

[3] Ojala, T., Pietikäinen, M., Mänpä, T.: Multiresolution gray-scale and rotation invariant texture classification with local binary patterns. IEEE Trans. on Pattern Analysis and Machine Intelligence 24(7), 971–987 (2002)

[4] Ahonen, T., Hadid, A., Pietikäinen, M.: Face description with local binary patterns: Application to face recognition. IEEE Transactions on Pattern Analysis and Machine Intelligence 28(12) (December 2006)

[5] Chu, W.-S., Huang, C.-R., Chen, C.-S.: Identifying gender from unaligned facial images by set classification. In: International Conference on Pattern Recognition (ICPR), Istanbul, Turkey (2010)

[6] Dago-Casas, P., González-Jiménez, D., Long-Yu, L., Alba-Castro, J.L.: Single and cross database benchmarks for gender classification under unconstrained settings. In: Proc. First IEEE International Workshop on Benchmarking Facial Image Analysis Technologies (2011)

[7] Gallagher, A., Chen, T.: Understanding images of groups of people. In: Proc. CVPR (2009)

[8] Huang, G.B., Ramesh, M., Berg, T., Learned-Miller, E.: Labeled faces in the wild: A database for studying face recognition in unconstrained environments. Technical Report 07-49, University of Massachusetts (October 2007)

[9] Ricanek Jr., K., Tesafaye, T.: MORPH: A longitudinal image database of normal adult age-progression. In: IEEE 7th International Conference on Automatic Face and Gesture Recognition, Southampton, UK, pp. 341-345 (April 2006)

[10] Mäkinen, E., Raisamo, R.: Evaluation of gender classification methods with automatically detected and aligned faces. IEEE Transactions on Pattern Analysis and Machine Intelligence 30(3), 541-547 (2008)

[11] Moghaddam, B., Yang, M.-H.: Learning gender with support faces. IEEE Trans. on Pattern Analysis and Machine Intelligence 24(5), 707-711 (2002)

[12] Phillips, P.J., Wechsler, H., Huang, J., Rauss, P.J.: The FERET database and evaluation procedure for facerecognition algorithms. Image and Vision Computing 16(5), 295-306 (1998)

[13] Pietikäinen, M., Hadid, A., Zhao, G., Ahonen, T.: Computer Vision Using Local Binary Patterns. Springer (2011)

[14] Burges, C.J.C.: A tutorial on support vector machines for pattern recognition (1998)

[15] Csurka, G., Dance, C.R., Fan, L., Willamowski, J., Bray, C.: Visual categorization with bags of keypoints. In: Workshop on Statistical Learning in Computer Vision, ECCV, pp. 1-22 (2004)

Combining Face and Facial Feature Detectors for Face Detection Performance Improvement

Modesto Castrillón-Santana, Daniel Hernández-Sosa,
and Javier Lorenzo-Navarro*

SIANI
Universidad de Las Palmas de Gran Canaria, Spain
mcastrillon@iusiani.ulpgc.es

Abstract. In this paper, we experimentally study the combination of face and facial feature detectors to improve face detection performance. The face detection problem, as suggested by recent face detection challenges, is still not solved. Face detectors traditionally fail in large-scale problems and/or when the face is occluded or different head rotations are present. The combination of face and facial feature detectors is evaluated with a public database. The obtained results evidence an improvement in the positive detection rate while reducing the false detection rate. Additionally, we prove that the integration of facial feature detectors provides useful information for pose estimation and face alignment.

1   Introduction

Automatic facial analysis has become practical thanks to the robustness of recent reliable face detectors. Once the face is located, different applications, such as head pose, face aligment or gaze estimation, require its facial feature localization. Face alignment for instance, is indeed a necessary step before any further facial analysis. Though some authors do not observe any improvement using the face alignment in certain problems [11], its necessity is suggested by others [13], particularly if the classification is related to shape information [5,9].

However, face detectors are still unreliable in different hard scenarios where the pose and illumination are not controlled [8,12], or when a large-scale problem is tackled [4]. Therefore, face and facial element detection keeps being a common topic in the Computer Vision literature. Among the wide and recent literature on face detection, the Viola-Jones face detector [15] has received lots of attention within the community. The authors designed indeed a general object detection framework that requires a previous training stage. This stage is accomplished using a large set of roughly aligned samples of the object to detect (positive samples) and of images not containing the target (negative samples). To create a new classifier, positive and negative samples gathering, data annotation, data preparation and training phases must be accomplished.

---

* Work partially funded by the Spanish Ministry of Science and Innovation funds (TIN 2008-06068), and the Computer Science Department at ULPGC.

L. Alvarez et al. (Eds.): CIARP 2012, LNCS 7441, pp. 82–89, 2012.

Thanks to the OpenCV library [7], the training tools are available to a large community of researchers. As a result of their work, different classifiers specialized in face processing have been made publicly available [7] and compared [2]. The available implementation [10], and its successful results applied to face detection, have made the Viola-Jones framework based detectors to be frequently used as a baseline.

Face detectors are typically designed for the frontal face configuration. Therefore, their performance is sensitive to both in-plane and out-of plane rotations. In this paper, we study experimentally available face detectors, with the aim at proving that by combining both global face detection and local feature detection, the overall face detection performance can be substantially improved. In this sense, the reader must take into consideration the existence of works focused on the reduction of false positives [1].

Different datasets have been designed to analyze face detection performance. Most of them contain single faces in a reduced set of poses. As a remarkable exception, we would like to mention the CMU image database [14]. This dataset contains a collection of heterogeneous images, feature that from our point of view, allows for a better evaluation of the classifier performance. More recently, initiatives such as FIW [6] have introduced new challenging situations to test the performance of the face related detectors with much larger and heterogeneous imagery. Fortunately, the availability of annotation data referred to the face and facial feature location, such as those provided by FDDB [8], supports the comparison of face detectors. FDDB is used in our experiments because it includes a larger number of annotated faces in unrestricted situations.

Next section summarizes the Viola-Jones detection framework. Later, the experimental setup and results achieved are presented, finishing the paper with the conclusions.

2   Viola-Jones Based Face and Facial Feature Detection

Among the recent face detection approaches, we have selected the Viola-Jones object detection framework [15] for our experiments considering the public availability of face and facial feature detectors. However, we would like to make the reader evident that the combination approaches described below could be applied to any detection framework. Our emphasis is on the combination of cues not on the particular detector employed.

As mentioned above, the Viola-Jones framework requires a previous training stage, that makes use of a large set of positive roughly aligned samples of the object to detect, and images not containing the target. Both sets provide information about the target appearance space and its boundaries.

This training stage creates a boosted cascade of linear combinations of weak classifiers achieving a performance similar to a strong classifier, but reducing the processing cost (high for a strong classifier). The main idea behind the architecture is to waste less processing time in areas that are easy to classify. In fact, the reduction of processing cost allows the integration of object detectors based on this framework, in real-time applications.

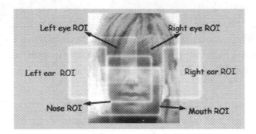

Fig. 1. Illustration of the ROIs areas defined in a face detection container to search the corresponding facial features. Left and right labels are related to the image.

To get a useful detector, these weak classifiers must be able to detect the target most of the time, and reject at least around half of the non target images. Once configured, a cascade of K weak classifiers under this architecture offers a target detection rate, D, and a false detection rate, F, that are given by the combination of each single stage weak classifier rates:

$$D = \prod_{i=1}^{K} d_i \quad F = \prod_{i=1}^{K} f_i$$

For example, assuming a cascade composed of 20 weak classifiers with a true detection rate, d_i, of at least 99% and a negative detection rate, f_i, not greater than 50%, its expected overall detection rate is 0.99^{20} with a false positive rate of $0.5^{20} \approx 0.9 * 10^{-6}$. A reduction in the number of stages increases both rates, i.e. is less restrictive, and reduces computational cost.

3   Experimental Results

3.1   Test Dataset

The facial annotation data provided with the FDDB dataset has been made available in terms of ellipses [8]. The authors suggest the use of a score based on the Jaccard index, to determine when a detection must be considered a true or positive detection. The match degree between a detection det_i and an annotation $anot_j$ is given by:

$$S\left(det_i, anot_j\right) = \frac{area\left(det_i\right) \bigcap area\left(anot_j\right)}{area\left(det_i\right) \bigcup area\left(anot_j\right)}$$

A large match means that both intersection and union overlap in a high degree. In our experiments we have considered that det_i is a positive detection when $S(det_i, anot_j) > 0.5$ [8]. The number of annotated faces contained in the face dataset, i.e. FDDB, is 5171.

3.2   Detection Results

Among the different face and head detectors included in the OpenCV release, we have chosen for our experiments FA2, labeled *haarcascade_frontalface_alt2* in the OpenCV distribution. This detector presents a good detection rate and speed, achieving a larger Area Under the Curve (AUC) in [2].

For facial feature detection, we have selected those exhibiting the best performance in [2,3] for eye, mouth, nose and ear detection. All of them are currently included in the OpenCV release. Our hypothesis is that we can get better performance introducing different heuristics in the face search. In this subsection we will compare different detection strategies:

- **F**: Face detection is performed using the FA2 classifier.
- **FC**: Face detection is performed using the FA2 classifier. Later, facial feature detection is applied within their respective expected Region of Interest (ROI), related to the detected face, see Figure 1. The fail in detecting at least four facial elements is used as a filter to remove likely false face detections. As a result, both positive and negative detection rates will be reduced. The different ROIs used, considering that sx and sy are respectively the width and height of the face container, are:
  - Left and right eyes: The left upper corner of their respective ROIs are $(0, 0)$ and $(sx \times 0.4, 0)$, their dimensions $(sx \times 0.6, sy * 0.6)$.
  - Nose: Left upper corner of the ROI are $(sx \times 0.2; sy \times 0.25)$ and its dimensions $(sx \times 0.6, sy \times 0.6)$.
  - Mouth: Left upper corner of the ROI are $(sx \times 0.1; sy \times 0.4)$ and its dimensions $(sx \times 0.8, sy \times 0.6)$.
  - Left and right ear: The left upper corner of their respective ROIs are $(-sx/3; sy \times 0.2)$ and $(sx/2; sy \times 0.2)$, and their dimensions $(sx/3 + sx/2, sy \times 0.6)$.
- **FC2**: This approach is similar to **FC**, but the face container is scaled up before searching the facial features. Ideally, the positive detection rate will be increased because the facial elements appear in more detail than in **FC**.
- **FFs**: No face detector is used, but facial feature detection is employed instead. The coocurrence of at least three coherently located detections gives support to a face presence. The basic rules applied to determine the coherence of two facial features detected are summarized as:
  - The mouth must be below any other facial feature, but not too far away.
  - The nose must be below both eyes, but above the mouth.
  - The centroid of the left eye must be to the left of any other facial feature and above nose and mouth.
  - The centroid of the right eye must be to the right of any other facial feature and above nose and mouth.
  - Ears must be on each side.
  - The separation distance must be coherent with the element size.
- **FFFs**: Combines **F** and **FFs** detection results, building a single set of detected faces. The objective is to be able to detect faces with hidden elements or slightly rotated, which are not easily removed using the **F** approach.

- **FCFFs**: Combines **FC** and **FFFs** to reduce the false positive rate.
- **FC2FFs**: Combines **FC2** and **FFFs** to both reduce the false positive rate, and increase the positive detection rate.
- **XXR**: All the previous approaches are also applied not only to the input image but to two slightly rotated images, ±15 degrees, to cope with more variations in the face pose.

The detection results obtained are presented in Table 1. We must point out that the FDDB annotation available is not completely exhaustive, i.e. no every face has been annotated. To avoid any artifact in the false detection rate, we have not considered as false detections those that are indeed non annotated faces. Their influence is particularly remarkable for facial features detection based approaches, as it is confirmed that if automatically considered false detections are revised by hand the false detection rate decreases drastically.

Table 1. True and false positive detection rates, respectivelly TPR and FPR, achieved for each approach

Approach	TPR	FPR
F	0.7117	0.0470
FC	0.6384	0.0015
FC2	0.6892	0.0041
FFs	0.5007	0.0019
FFFs	0.7248	0.0462
FCFFs	0.6511	0.0033
FC2FFs	0.7008	0.0054

Approach	TPR	FPR
FR	0.7401	0.1151
FCR	0.6693	0.0052
FC2R	0.7169	0.0126
FFsR	0.5691	0.0052
FFFsR	**0.7561**	0.1079
FCFFsR	0.6817	0.0044
FC2FFsR	**0.7289**	0.0112

The baseline given by the selected face detector reports a positive detection rate around 71%, and a negative detection rate around 5%. The criterion used to accept a detection is identical to the one used in [8], i.e. if the ratio of the intersection of a detected region with an annotated face region is greater than 0.5, a score of 1 is assigned to the detected region, and 0 otherwise.

Observe that when a face is validated only if at least two inner facial features are located (**FC** and **FC2**), both rates decrease, but the false positives decrease drastically. This suggests the importance of a simple heuristic on the face detection performance. Indeed, the **FC2** approach achieves a similar positive detection rate, while reducing more than ten times the false detection rate.

Table 1 includes also results achieved making use of an approach that detects faces based on face features detectors, **FFs**. We have accepted a valid face only if at least three inner features are detected. The results reported are clearly worse in terms of positive detection. Indeed only half of the faces are located, however the false detection rate is remarkable low. The rest of the table indicates the results achieved if both focuses are combined with the aim at improving the overall rate. The behavior is similar if faces are confirmed by means of its inner features or not. Some detection samples with and without the integration of facial features detection in the process are depicted in Figure 2.

Fig. 2. Face detection examples based on **F** (left) and **FC2FFs** (right). They illustrate the benefits of the integration of facial features detectors, serving to remove false detections (upper row) and undetected faces located by its facial features (bottom row).

If the search is applied not only in the input image but also in slightly rotated images the results achieved improve the detection rate. The best performances are achieved when face and facial features detection are combined. Compared to the **F** approach the improvement is evident, however we must remind the reader that there is an additional cost due to the fact that multiple detectors are employed, but it may be considered almost irrelevant thanks to the current multicore architectures.

To illustrate better the benefits, we have computed, for each approach excepting those involving only face features, the receiver operating characteristic (ROC) curve applying first the original face classifier, and two variants reducing its number of stages. Theoretically, this action must increase both correct, D, and false, F, detection rates. The results are presented in Figure 3a. Similar

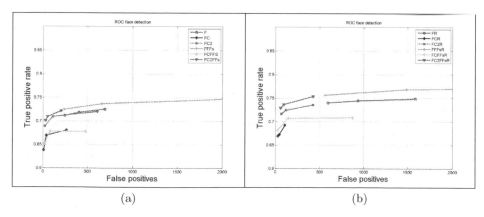

Fig. 3. Face detection results on the FDDB for the proposed approaches: (a) not including the search in rotated images, and (b) including the search in rotated images

88   M. Castrillón-Santana, D. Hernández-Sosa, and J. Lorenzo-Navarro

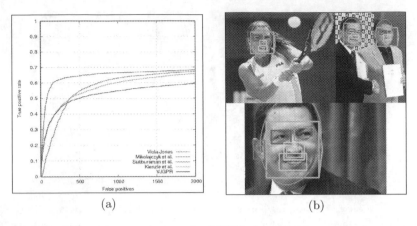

(a)   (b)

Fig. 4. (a) Face detection results on the FDDB for different approaches (extracted from [8]). (b) Examples of pose estimation based on the facial features detected.

graphs are shown in Figure 3b for the approaches that search the pattern in the original and rotated images. They present a slight improvement, but increasing three times the processing cost. The comparison with the results achieved in [8] for FDDB, see Figure 4a, evidences the better behavior exhibited by the approaches that combine face and facial features detectors. The improvement for 500 false positives is close to 10 percentage points.

An additional advantage of the integration of facial feature detectors in the process is that they provide useful information for other tasks. For example, the ear detection gives rough information of the head pose, as depicted in purple Figure 4b. Both ear detectors are designed for profile head poses. Thus, if just an ear is detected it could mean that the head is partially or totally rotated, we decide that according to the number of eyes detected for that particular face.

4   Conclusion

We have presented an experimental study on the FDDB of a set of face and facial features detectors based on the Viola-Jones framework. The study considers different face, head and facial feature detectors. We focus on the benefits that their combination based on common sense heuristics would bring in the face detection problem. In this way, we have reduced the number of false face detections by locating inner facial features within face containers, increased the number of detected faces by means of combining with facial feature based detection, and with searching in slightly rotated images. The results achieved suggest a better performance than other state of the art detectors. Facial feature detection provides not only the possibility of further face confirmation and help with slightly rotated faces, but also information about the face pose.

References

1. Atanasoaei, C., McCool, C., Marcel, S.: A principled approach to remove false alarms by modelling the context of a face detector. In: Proceedings of the British Machine Vision Conference (BMVC), pp. 1–11 (2010)
2. Castrillón, M., Déniz, O., Hernández, D., Lorenzo, J.: A comparison of face and facial feature detectors based on the viola-jones general object detection framework. Machine Vision and Applications 22(3), 481–494 (2011)
3. Castrillón, M., Hernández, D., Lorenzo, J.: An study on ear detection and its applications to face detection. In: Conferencia de la Asociación Española para la Inteligencia Artificial (2011)
4. Frome, A., Cheung, G., Abdulkader, A., Zennaro, M., Wu, B., Bissacco, A., Adam, H., Neven, H., Vincent, L.: Large-scale privacy protection in google street view. In: Proceedings of International Conference on Computer Vision (ICCV), pp. 2373–2380 (2009)
5. Heisele, B., Serre, T., Poggio, T.: A component-based framework for face detection and identification. International Journal of Computer Vision Research 74(2) (August 2007)
6. Huang, G.B., Ramesh, M., Berg, T., Learned-Miller, E.: Labeled faces in the wild: A database for studying face recognition in unconstrained environments. Technical Report 07-49, University of Massachusetts (October 2007)
7. Intel. Open Source Computer Vision Library, v2.3 (July 2011), http://opencv.willowgarage.com/wiki/ (last visited May 2012)
8. Jain, V., Learned-Miller, E.: FDDB: A benchmark for face detection in unconstrained settings. Technical report, University of Massachusetts (2010)
9. Lanitis, A., Taylor, C., Cootes, T.F.: Automatic interpretation and coding of face image using flexible models. IEEE Trans. on Pattern Analysis and Machine Intelligence 19(7) (July 1997)
10. Lienhart, R., Kuranov, A., Pisarevsky, V.: Empirical Analysis of Detection Cascades of Boosted Classifiers for Rapid Object Detection. In: Michaelis, B., Krell, G. (eds.) DAGM 2003. LNCS, vol. 2781, pp. 297–304. Springer, Heidelberg (2003)
11. Mäkinen, E., Raisamo, R.: Evaluation of gender classification methods with automatically detected and aligned faces. IEEE Transactions on Pattern Analysis and Machine Intelligence 30(3), 541–547 (2008)
12. Parris, J., Wilber, M., Helfin, B., Rara, H., El-barkouky, A., Farag, A., Movellanand, J., Castrillón-Santana, M., Lorenzo-Navarro, J., Teli, M.N., Marcel, S., Atanasoaei, C., Boult, T.: Face and eye detection on hard datasets. In: IEEE IAPR International Joint Conference on Biometrics, IJCB (2011)
13. Rabie, A., Lang, C., Hanheide, M., Castrillón, M., Sagerer, G.: Automatic initialization for facial analysis in interactive robotics. In: 6th International Conference on Computer Vision Systems, Vision for Cognitive Systems, pp. 517–526 (2008)
14. Schneiderman, H., Kanade, T.: A statistical method for 3D object detection applied to faces and cars. In: IEEE Conference on Computer Vision and Pattern Recognition, pp. 1746–1759 (2000)
15. Viola, P., Jones, M.J.: Robust real-time face detection. International Journal of Computer Vision 57(2), 151–173 (2004)

Randomized Face Recognition on Partially Occluded Images

Ariel Morelli Andres, Sebastian Padovani, Mariano Tepper,
Marta Mejail, and Julio Jacobo

Departamento de Computación, Facultad de Ciencias Exactas y Naturales,
Universidad de Buenos Aires, Argentina
{amorelli,spadovan,mtepper,marta,jacobo}@dc.uba.ar

Abstract. In this work we propose a new method for face recognition
that successfully handles occluded faces. We propose an innovative improvement that allows to detect and discard occluded zones of the face,
thus making recognition more robust in the presence of occlusion. We
provide experimental results that show that the proposed method performs well in practice.

1   Introduction

Face detection and recognition are being widely studied due to the large number
of applications they have. At present, we can find face recognition systems in
social networking sites, photo management software and access control systems,
to name a few.

Face recognition presents several difficulties. The image of the human face can
have large intra-subject variations (changes in the same individual) that make
it difficult to develop a recognition system. Variations may come, for example,
from head position variation when taking the picture, differences in lighting,
facial expression (laughter, anger, etc..), occlusion of parts of the face due to the
use of accessories such as lenses, sunglasses and scarves, facial hair (mustache,
beard, long hair, etc.), and changes in facial features due to aging. On the other
hand, inter-subject variations (differences between individuals) can be very small
between two people with similar traits, making correct identification difficult.

Presently there are various methods for face recognition. Among the most
popular are Eigenfaces [1] and Active Appearance Model [2,3,4]. However, when
the face is occluded, methods that extract global features (holistic features) (such
as Eigenfaces and Fisherfaces [5]) cannot be applied. While methods that use
local features are less affected by occlusion, useful information might be lost
when only local features are extracted [6].

In a seminal paper, Wright et al. [6] proposed a method for recognizing faces
that is robust to certain types and levels of occlusion. This method is based on
recent advances in the study of statistical signal processing, more specifically in
the area of compressed sensing [7,8,9]. The method fails when 33% of the image is
occluded in a single connected region. A straightforward solution is to partition

L. Alvarez et al. (Eds.): CIARP 2012, LNCS 7441, pp. 90–97, 2012.

the problem into smaller subproblems. To this end, the image is partitioned into smaller blocks and each block is then processed separately. Doing this entails several disadvantages, the main ones being that holistic features are lost and that the best way of partitioning the image can be hardly determined a priori.

Ideally, it would be best to detect which areas are occluded in the image and then discard them for recognition. There are other methods which seek to detect occlusion. For example, Lin et al. [10] presented a method that uses a Bayesian filter and Graph Cuts to do Face Inpainting to restore the occluded sections. Zhou et al. [11] proposed to detect and recognize occlusion using Markov Random Fields, but at a high computational cost. In this work we propose a method for detecting occlusion based on compressed sensing that obtains a better performance than the afore mentioned methods.

The rest of the paper is structured as follows. In Section 2 we present the face recognition method. Then we proceed to explain the proposed approach to handle occlusions in Section 3. We experimentally check the good performance of the proposed approach and provide concluding remarks in Section 4.

2   Face Recognition

In this section we model face recognition as an optimization problem in which we want to represent the query face as a sparse linear combination of the faces in a dictionary.

All the images to be used have the same size $width \times hight$. As usual, we assume that images are correctly cropped and aligned to the right size and position, respectively. These images represent a point in $\mathbb{R}^m$, where $m = width \times hight$, which is obtained by stacking their column vectors.

It has been shown that images of the same person under different lighting conditions and expressions fall (approximately) in a linear subspace of $\mathbb{R}^m$ of much lower dimension, called *faces subspace* [5,12,13].

A dictionary of n atoms is a matrix $A \in \mathbb{R}^{m \times n}$ where each of the n columns is an image in $\mathbb{R}^m$ of a person's face, whose identity is known. Let us assume that there are k $(1 < k \le n)$ different classes or individuals in A. We denote by W_j the images (columns fo A) corresponding to the j-th class.

Let $y \in \mathbb{R}^m$ be a query image. We represent image y by a linear combination of the atoms in A, so $y = Ax$, where $x \in \mathbb{R}^n$ is the vector of the coefficients used in the linear combination. Our goal is to find the most sparse solution, i.e. the one that uses the least number of atoms in the dictionary. This can be achieved by adding a constraint on the l^0 norm of x, unfortunately the resulting problem is non-convex. However, by using the l^1 norm, a sparse solution is obtained, while maintaining convexity [14]. We then define the problem as finding

$$\hat{x}_1 = \min ||x||_1 \quad \text{subject to} \quad y = Ax.$$

When the person to be evaluated is not represented in the dictionary, the solution x is usually dense and non-zero coefficients are distributed over the atoms of different people in the dictionary. However, if the individual to be evaluated is in the dictionary, most nonzero coefficients of x will correspond to that person's atoms.

In order to establish a rule to decide when the recognition is satisfactory, [6] defines a coefficient $SCI(x)$ (Sparsity Concentration Index) of a vector $x \in \mathbb{R}^n$ as

$$SCI(x) \triangleq \frac{k}{k-1} \cdot \left(\max_{1 \leq j \leq k} \left\| \delta_{W_j}(x) \right\|_1 / \left\| x \right\|_1 - 1 \right),$$

where $\delta_{W_j} : \mathbb{R}^n \to \mathbb{R}^n$ sets to zero those coefficients of x that do not correspond to atoms of class W_j.

If all the nonzero coefficients of x are concentrated in a single class, then $SCI(x) = 1$. Conversely, if all the nonzero coefficients of x are uniformly distributed among all classes, then $SCI(x) = 0$. Thus, by setting a threshold on the SCI we can determine whether or not a query person is in the dictionary of faces.

To determine the identity of a person already found in the dictionary, we define the residual $r_{W_j}(y) \triangleq \left\| y - A\, \delta_{W_j}(x) \right\|_2$. We consider the person's identity assigned to the class with the lowest residual, i.e. $\arg \min_j r_{W_j}(y)$.

When the face to be recognized is partially occluded, large errors appear that have to be modeled specifically. Consequently, one can think of occlusion as an error e that affects a portion of the image

$$y = Ax + e \tag{1}$$

where e has nonzero components only in the occluded portion of the image. The location of these errors is not known and their magnitudes are completely arbitrary. However, we assume that the portion affected by the occlusion is not overwhelmingly large with respect to the image size m.

To overcome this limitation, we develop a method that first detects the occluded zone and then performs recognition by using only the non-occluded parts.

3   Occlusion Detection

The problem of detecting occlusion is to determine which pixels in an image are showing a portion of a face and which pixels are not. We can think of occluded pixels as outliers in a face image. To detect the occlusion is then to detect those pixels with "outlier values" for a face image. We propose to use local image features to generate a new image that is similar to the one we want to recognize, but without occlusion. After obtaining this image, we find the difference between this image and the original query image and then apply a threshold τ. If the generated image is sufficiently similar to the query image, this procedure will yield the outlier pixels present in the occluded image.

To generate this image, let us consider that there is a non-occluded and possibly non-connected fragment F in the image domain. The procedure for generating this reconstructed image is described in Algorithm 1. We start by building

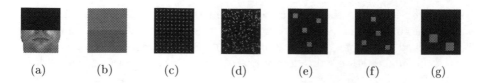

(a)   (b)   (c)   (d)   (e)   (f)   (g)

Fig. 1. An image and its occlusion map. Pixels in blue correspond to a non-occluded part, while pixels in red are occluded. We illustrate different ways of obtaining a fragment F.

the subimage y_F and the subdictionary A_F, where only the rows corresponding to pixels in F are kept. Then we try to recognize the identity of the person using the procedure described in the previous section. Of course, since we are only using partial information from the image, we obtain a less accurate result. We also obtain the vector of coefficients x that was used to represent y_F using A_F (step 3 in Algorithm 1). Using these coefficients, we obtain a reconstructed image $y' = Ax$, similar to the query image.

Algorithm 1. Algorithm to generate an image similar to y using pixels from fragment F only

---

Require: F, a set of pixels
1: Let y_F be the fragment F of the query image y.
2: Let A_F be the dictionary that results from selecting fragment F in each image of dictionary A.
3: Using image y_F and face dictionary A_F, we compute the sparse code x and error e so that $y_F = A_F x + e$.
4: return $y' = Ax$

The question now is: how to obtain an appropriate set of pixels F to be used algorithm 1? To this end, we consider the following four options: (1) to use predefined regions of the image, (2) to pick pixels from a fixed grid, (3) to sample pixels at random, and (4) to generate a sample of random blocks of contiguous pixels.

Let us first observe that occlusion usually occurs in blocks, i.e. it is usually concentrated in one or more connected portions of the image. Fig. 1(a) serves as a simple example, presenting a block occlusion of 50%. In this image, occlusion is concentrated in a single block, but in the following we make no assumptions in this respect.

The first method uses a predefined sets of pixels, taking into account the most common occlusions that can occur. That is, if many of the test images have dark glasses, it is desirable to try a set of pixels F that does not include pixels near the eye position. This is not difficult, since we assume that all images are aligned. As expected, this method is only to be used combined with others, because it is not possible to determine all types of occlusion that may arise.

Let us consider then the first randomized method for obtaining a set of pixels F, which involves considering pixels in a fixed uniform grid, as depicted in Fig. 1(c). The advantage of this method is that it captures well the global features of the image, however it clearly has two major disadvantages. First, since local traits usually span several pixels, the method fails at capturing these local image characteristics. The second and main disadvantage is that the proportion of occluded pixels in the set F is the same (or very similar) as in the original image. So, if the query image has a large number of pixels occluded (as in the example shown in the figure, where 50% of the pixels are occluded), the set F also will. Then, Algorithm 1 will yield a large error and the resulting reconstructed image will differ substantially from the query image in the non-occluded areas.

Our third method is a somewhat naive attempt to solve the problems of the first method and uses random selection of pixels. As shown in Figure 1(d), if the number of pixels selected is large enough, it is very likely that the selected pixels will be scattered throughout the image. This makes this method to have the same advantages and disadvantages as the first one.

The fourth method consists in selecting blocks of adjacent pixels at random. The more blocks we have and the smaller they are, then set F will have pixels scattered throughout the image. Contrarily, the larger these pixel blocks are, the fewer blocks we need for a given size of F. Moreover, if we use just a few large blocks, the pixels of set F will be more concentrated in some regions of the image, thus increasing the chance of not hitting the occluded region. Figures 1(e), 1(f) and 1(g) show examples of blocks of pixels selected at random. Considering that the occlusion is usually concentrated in some regions of the image, by choosing different positions of a few blocks of pixels, we obtain sets of pixels with different ratios of occluded pixels. For example, F contains 70% of occluded pixels in Figure 1(e), only 30% in Figure 1(f) and none in Figure 1(g).

However, the fact that the set of pixels F is concentrated in one region can have a negative effect on Algorithm 1 making it a less stable. Unfortunately there is no efficient way to determine the optimal number of blocks, this is why it is advisable to test with multiple block sizes and quantities. We cope with this effect by selecting multiple such sets $F_1, F_2, \ldots, F_t$ in a Monte Carlo-like approach, to finally select the one that achieves the best results.

Since we have multiple sets of pixels, we apply the Algorithm 1 several times, one for each set of pixels. We already stated that if in Algorithm 1 we use a set of pixels with a high proportion of occluded pixels, the resulting image is most likely to be very different from the query image. Given this, among all obtained images $y'_1, \ldots, y'_t$ we select y'_{max} such that $max = \arg\max_i \#P_i$, where $P_i = \{p \,,\, |y(p) - y'_i(p)| \leq \tau\}$, $\#S$ denotes the cardinal of set S, and τ is a given threshold. Algorithm 2 summarizes the proposed approach.

Algorithm 2. Occlusion detection algorithm

Require: occluded query image y, faces A, different sets of pixels $F_1, F_2, \ldots, F_t$ and threshold τ

1: **for** $i = 1 \ldots t$ **do**
2:    Obtain y_i' using algorithm 1 and set F_i
3:    Let $P_i = \{p ,\ |y(p) - y_i'(p)| \leq \tau\}$
4: **end for**
5: Let $max = \arg \max_i \#P_i$
6: Obtain y_{max}' using Algorithm 1 and fragment $F = P_{max}$
7: **return** $u = |y - y_{max}'| \leq \tau$

---

4   Results and Conclusions

In this section we present tests performed using the recognition algorithm described in Section 2, together with the proposed occlusion detection.

For testing purposes, we use the publicly available AR Database [15]. From this base we selected 60 people. From each individual, 8 non-occluded images were used for the faces dictionary and 4 occluded images were used for test: 2 occluded by sunglasses and 2 by a scarf.

The proposed occlusion detection approach (Algorithm 2) has several parameters. The main ones being the threshold τ, the number of pixels in each set F_i and how these sets are obtained. The sets F_i are selected by taking contiguous pixel blocks at random. We do this in order not to give any previous knowledge about occlusion to the detector.

We start by fixing the threshold $\tau = 20$ and vary the number of blocks. This was done for sets of 500 pixels (6.25%) and 1250 pixels (15.5%) from a total of 8064 pixels in the image. Figure 2(a) shows the obtained recognition rates .

As the number of blocks increases, the recognition rate with scarves begins to decay. This is due to the fact that, having more blocks, the probability that all blocks are in a non-occluded area is much lower. It can also be seen that the increase in the number of blocks does not affect so much images occluded with sunglasses. This phenomenon occurs because images with sunglasses have a lower proportion of occluded pixels than those with scarves and thus the probability of a pixel blocks containing non-occluded pixels is also smaller.

With regard to the number of pixels in each set F_i, we obtain the best and more stable results by using around 1250, that is 15% of the total number of pixels.

The second experiment involves fixing the number and the size of pixel blocks to 2 and 1250 pixels, respectively and then change the threshold τ. We obtained the best results using $\tau = 10$ (see Figure 2(b)).

Figure 3 presents an example of the detected occlusions. The performance is globally satisfactory. However, when analyzing carefully the occlusions maps, we see that there are small non-occluded regions which were detected as occluded and vice versa. Since the recognition algorithm in Section 2 is robust to small occluded areas, these small errors do not affect the recognition rate.

Fig. 2. Recognition rates obtained using occlusion detection. (a) We set $\tau = 20$, and for fragments F_i of 500 and 1250 pixels approximatively, we tested different number of blocks of contiguous pixels. We measured the recognition rate obtained in images with sunglasses and scarves. (b) We use fragments F_i with two blocks and 1250 pixels per block and test for different values of τ.

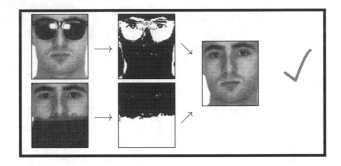

Fig. 3. Recognition in the presence of occlusion. On the left: two images from the same person, with different degrees of occlusion. On the center, the detected occlusions (in white). On the right, the non-occluded image of the recognized person.

Table 1. Recognition rates obtained with different face recognition methods in presence of occlusion

Algorithm	Sunglasses	Scarves	Total
Simple Model [6]	69.49%	12.71%	41.10%
Partitioned Model [6]	86.44%	95.76%	91.10%
Proposed method	**97.46%**	**99.15%**	**98.31%**

Finally, we compare our results with the state-of-the-art solutions proposed by Wright et al. [6]. They propose two different methods to perform face recognition in the presence of occlusion: the Simple and Partitioned Models. We obtain much higher recognition rates for the two different types of occlusion tested.

In conclusion, the method proposed in this paper presents an improvement in face recognition in the presence of occlusion compared to the performance obtained by the method proposed in [6]. Experiments have shown that successful recognition is strongly linked to the success of the occlusion detection. Likewise, one of the factors with a major impact in occlusion detection. Using blocks that are more adapted to the geometry of human faces can be a subject for further research.

References

1. Turk, M., Pentland, A.: Eigenfaces for recognition. Journal of Cognitive Neuroscience 3(1), 71–86 (1991)
2. Cootes, T.F., Edwards, G.J., Taylor, C.J.: Active appearance models. IEEE Transactions on Pattern Analysis and Machine Intelligence 23, 681–685 (2001)
3. Stegmann, M.B., Ersbøll, B.K., Larsen, R.: FAME - A Flexible Appearance Modelling Environment. IEEE Transactions on Medical Imaging 22(10), 1319–1331 (2003)
4. Kahraman, F., Kurt, B., Gokmen, M.: Robust face alignment for illumination and pose invariant face recognition. In: IEEE Computer Society Conference on Computer Vision and Pattern Recognition, pp. 1–7 (2007)
5. Belhumeur, P.N., Hespanha, J., Kriegman, D.J.: Eigenfaces vs. Fisherfaces: Recognition Using Class Specific Linear Projection. IEEE Transactions on Pattern Analysis and Machine Intelligence 19(7), 711–720 (1997)
6. Wright, J., Yang, A.Y., Ganesh, A., Sastry, S.S., Ma, Y.: Robust face recognition via sparse representation. IEEE Transactions on Pattern Analysis and Machine Intelligence 31(2), 210–227 (2009)
7. Candès, E.J., Romberg, J.K., Tao, T.: Stable signal recovery from incomplete and inaccurate measurements. Communications on Pure and Applied Mathematics 59(8), 1207–1223 (2006)
8. Candès, E.J., Tao, T.: Near-optimal signal recovery from random projections: Universal encoding strategies? IEEE Transactions on Information Theory 52(12), 5406–5425 (2006)
9. Candès, E.J., Wakin, M.B.: An introduction to compressive sampling. IEEE Signal Processing Magazine 25(2), 21–30 (2008)
10. Lin, D., Tang, X.: Quality-driven face occlusion detection and recovery. In: IEEE Computer Society Conference on Computer Vision and Pattern Recognition, pp. 1–7 (2007)
11. Zhou, Z., Wagner, A., Mobahi, H., Wright, J., Ma, Y.: Face recognition with contiguous occlusion using markov random fields. In: International Conference on Computer Vision, ICCV (2009)
12. Basri, R., Jacobs, D.W.: Lambertian reflectance and linear subspaces. IEEE Transactions on Pattern Analysis and Machine Intelligence 25(2), 218–233 (2003)
13. Lee, K.C., Ho, J., Kriegman, D.J.: Acquiring linear subspaces for face recognition under variable lighting. IEEE Transactions on Pattern Analysis and Machine Intelligence 27(5), 684–698 (2005)
14. Donoho, D.L.: For most large underdetermined systems of linear equations the minimal, L1-norm solution is also the sparsest solution. Communications on Pure and Applied Mathematics 59, 797–829 (2004)
15. Martinez, A.M., Benavente, R.: The AR face database. Technical Report 24, CVC (1998)

Face Recognition: Would Going Back to Functional Nature Be a Good Idea?

Noslen Hernández, Yoanna Martínez-Díaz, Dania Porro-Muñoz, and Heydi Méndez-Vázquez

Advanced Technologies Application Center, Havana, Cuba
{nhernandez,ymartinez,dpmunoz,hmendez}@cenatav.co.cu

Abstract. Traditional appearance-based methods for face recognition represent raw face images of size $u \times v$ as vectors in a $u \times v$-dimensional space. However in practice, this space can be too large to perform classification. For that reason, dimensionality reduction techniques are usually employed. Most of those traditional approaches do not take advantage of the spatial correlation of pixels in the image, considering them as independent. In this paper, we proposed a new representation of face images that takes into account the smoothness and continuity of the face image and at the same time deals with the dimensionality of the problem. This representation is based on Functional Data Analysis so, each face image is represented by a function and a recognition algorithm for functional spaces is formulated. The experiments on the AT&T and Yale B facial databases show the effectiveness of the proposed method.

Keywords: Face recognition, functional data analysis, biometrics.

1   Introduction

Face recognition has received significant attention due to its potential for a wide variety of applications [1]. Within the last several years, numerous face recognition algorithms have been developed [1,2]. Traditional face recognition methods are based on the fact that a class of patterns of interest, i.e. the face, resides in a subspace of the input image space [1]. The high dimensionality of face images is among the challenges that these algorithms have faced. In the context of face recognition, a $u \times v$ gray-scale image is usually identified with the vector $x \in R^{u \times v}$ given by stacking its columns. Performing face recognition in such a high dimensional space might result in several difficulties related to the curse of dimensionality. This matter has been addressed by transforming images to low-dimensional vectors in the face space. Different approaches have been introduced to achieve dimension reduction. They range from traditional approaches such as Principal Component Analysis (PCA) [4], Linear Discriminant Analysis (LDA) [5], Independent Component Analysis (ICA) [6] to more unconventional features such as downsampled images and random projections [7].

Many real-world data, as face images, have this high-dimensional nature. Some of these high-dimensional data usually have a functional nature. What does

L. Alvarez et al. (Eds.): CIARP 2012, LNCS 7441, pp. 98–105, 2012.

this mean? Although in practice, this data is observed and record discretely, the nature of the true process is not a finite vector of measurements, but an underlying continuous function that it is only measured at discrete points. The term functional refers to the intrinsic structure of the data rather than to their explicit form. When this is the case, Functional Data analysis (FDA) is a common way to overcome the effects of the curse of dimensionality [8,9].

Functional Data Analysis is a relatively new and growing research field that deals with the statistical description and modeling of such kind of (functional) data [8,9]. The basic rationale behind functional data analysis is that we should think of observed data functions as single entities described by a continuous real-valued function rather than merely a sequence of individuals observations. In this way, functional data are then supposed to have values in an infinite-dimensional space, often particularized as a Hilbert space.

In addition to handle the problem of dimensionality, why FDA can be considered a natural approach for representing and analyzing face images? A face image (and any image, in general) is a mathematical representation of a physical observation as a function over a spatial domain. Therefore we would like to treat a face image as defined over a continuous spatial domain, not as a mere collection of pixel values. All the aforementioned approaches used a classical discretization of the data as a sequence of numbers and loose some functional characteristics of the data like smoothness and continuity. On the contrary, FDA aggregates consecutive discrete measurements and views them as sampled values of a random variable, keeping track of order or smoothness.

The purpose of this paper is twofold. Firstly, to propose a new representation of face images using the functional data analysis framework. The central idea of this representation is just to describe a gray-scale face image as an observation of a functional random variable. And second, to formulate an algorithm for face identification using that functional representation.

The introduced face recognition algorithm can be categorized as a Nearest Subspace approach. It consists in a generalization to functional spaces of the ideas proposed by [10]. In this way, the proposed formulation lies on the key assumption that patterns from the same class lie on a linear subspace [5,11]. It is shown how our intuition for orthogonality and projections in R^m works fine in general Hilbert spaces which makes the formulation straightforward.

The remainder of the paper is organized as follows. Section 2 introduces the functional face recognition algorithm and describes how face images can be represented as functions. Section 3 analyzes the performance of the introduced approach on two standard public available face databases. Finally, some conclusions and future works are drawn in section 4.

2   Face Recognition in Functional Space

Let (X, Y) be a pair of random variables taking values in $\mathcal{X} \times \{1, 2, ..., N\}$, where $(\mathcal{X}, \langle \cdot, \cdot \rangle)$ is the space of square integrable functions from $[a, b] \times [c, d]$ to $\mathbb{R}$ (i.e., $L_2([a, b] \times [c, d])$) and $\{1, 2, ..., N\}$ represents the class labels for X, with

$N \in \mathbb{N}$ the number of distinguished classes. Suppose also that n independent and identically distributed (i.i.d) realizations of (X, Y) are given (training data), denoted by $(x_i, y_i), i = 1, ..., n$. The problem of interest is to build, from $(x_i, y_i)_i$, a predictor of the value of Y corresponding to a future observed value of X.

For convenience, the training data $(x_i, y_i)_i$ will be organized according to the class membership. Suppose then that, for each class $j \in \{1, ..., N\}$, n_j realizations of X are given, denoted by $(x_i^j), i = 1, ..., n_j$. This means that in the training data, each person j constitutes a class and we will have n_j images of this person.

For each class j, $(x_i^j)_i$ spans a (closed) finite-dimensional linear subspace M_j of the Hilbert space $\mathcal{X}$. Based on the concept that patterns from the same class lie on a linear subspace [5,11], any future observation x_0 belonging to class j must lie on M_j. Therefore, an estimate $\hat{y}_0$ of the class label y_0 corresponding to a new observation x_0, can be obtained by looking for, on each subspace M_j, the element $x_0^j \in M_j$ closest to x_0 (in the sense that it minimizes $d_j = \|x_0 - x_0^j\|$) and then, choosing the j for which d_j is minimized. Formally, this can be written as:

$$\hat{y}_0 = \min_{j \in \{1, ..., N\}} \|x_0 - x_0^j\|, \tag{1}$$

where $\| \cdot \|$ is the norm in $\mathcal{X}$ induced by the inner product.

We will see that such best approximations $x_0^j \in M_j$ exist, are unique and can be characterized in a way that they can be computed. It is known that if $(x_i^j)_i$ are elements of the Hilbert space $\mathcal{X}$, and $M_j = \text{span}\{x_i^j\}$ is a subspace of $\mathcal{X}$, for an arbitrary $x_0 \in \mathcal{X}$, there exist a unique $x_0^j \in M_j$ such that $\|x_0 - x_0^j\| = \inf_{x \in M_j} \|x_0 - x\|$. This unique minimizing vector is the orthogonal projection $x_0^j = P_{M_j}(x_0)$ of x_0 onto M_j.

The projection x_0^j can be written as $x_0^j = \sum_{k=1}^{n_j} \alpha_k^j x_k^j, \alpha_k^j \in \mathbb{R}$, and must satisfy $\langle x_0 - x_0^j, x_k^j \rangle = 0$, for $k = 1, ... n_j$, hence the $(\alpha_k^j)_k$ can be estimated by solving the following system of linear equations, called normal equations:

$$G^j(x_1^j, x_2^j, ..., x_{n_j}^j)\alpha^j = \beta^j, \tag{2}$$

where

$$G^j(x_1^j, x_2^j, ..., x_{n_j}^j) = \begin{pmatrix} \langle x_1^j, x_1^j \rangle & \langle x_2^j, x_1^j \rangle & \cdots & \langle x_{n_j}^j, x_1^j \rangle \\ \langle x_1^j, x_2^j \rangle & \langle x_2^j, x_2^j \rangle & \cdots & \langle x_{n_j}^j, x_2^j \rangle \\ & \cdots & & \\ \langle x_1^j, x_{n_j}^j \rangle & \langle x_2^j, x_{n_j}^j \rangle & \cdots & \langle x_{n_j}^j, x_{n_j}^j \rangle \end{pmatrix}$$

is called the Gram matrix of $\{x_1^j, x_2^j, ..., x_{n_j}^j\}$, and α^j and β^j are the column vectors $\alpha^j = (\alpha_1^j, \alpha_2^j, ..., \alpha_{n_j}^j)^T$ and $\beta^j = (\langle x_0, x_1^j \rangle, \langle x_0, x_2^j \rangle, ..., \langle x_0, x_{n_j}^j \rangle)^T$. Note that, although the normal equations do not possess a unique solution if the x_i^j's are linearly dependent, there is always at least one solution. Thus the degeneracy that could arise as a result of $det(G^j) = 0$ always results in a multiplicity of solutions rather than an inconsistent set of equations.

Once estimated α^j for each class j, the projections x_0^j can be obtained and consequently the class $\hat{y}_0$, by solving (1).

2.1   Functional Approximation of Face Images

The previous section presented the theoretical formulation of the introduced face recognition algorithm for an arbitrary Hilbert space. It is based on the fact that the face image is represented as a function $x \in L_2([a, b] \times [c, d])$. However, as stated in the introduction, what we observed in practice is a discretization $\tilde{x} \in \mathbb{R}^{u \times v}$ of the continuum data x. So, we need to construct an approximation of the functions x. This is usually done by a projection approach. Each image is approximated (smoothed) by a weighted sum (a linear combination) of basis functions, and the coefficients of the expansion are determined by fitting data by least squares. Each image is therefore, completely determined by the coefficients on this basis and each function is computable for any desired argument value (h, w).

Since we are interested in approximating functions of two variables, we need bivariate basis functions for the expansion. One way for obtaining such bivariate basis functions is through tensor product of univariate basis. In this way we can approximate the function $x(h, w)$ by

$$x(h, w) = \sum_i^p \sum_j^q c_{ij} g_{ij}(h, w) \tag{3}$$

where $g_{ij}(h, w) = e_i(h) f_j(w)$ is a basis on $L_2([a, b] \times [c, d])$, and $(e_i)_i$, $(f_j)_j$ are basis on $L_2[a, b]$ and $L_2[c, d]$, respectively.

We need not only that (3) approximates well the original function but also that the operations performed on the reconstructed functions approximate as exactly as possible the corresponding operations on the original functions. Let see how computing inner products and norms (integrals) between functions, which are mainly the involved operations in the algorithm, can be easily calculated.

Let E and F be the matrices defined by $E_{ij} = \langle e_i, e_j \rangle, i, j = 1, ..., p$ and $F_{kl} = \langle f_k, f_l \rangle, k, l = 1, ..., q$, and $E = R'_e R_e$, $F = R'_f R_f$ their corresponding Cholesky decompositions. It can be proved (we will not show this due to space limitations) that the inner product between two functions $x(h, w)$ (as expressed in (3)) and $z(h, w) = \sum_i^p \sum_j^q a_{ij} g_{ij}(h, w)$, with coefficients matrices $C = (c_{ij})$ and $A = (a_{ij})$ respectively, is equal to:

$$\langle x, z \rangle = \sum_i \sum_j \tilde{c}_{ij} \tilde{a}_{ij}, \tag{4}$$

where $\tilde{C} = (\tilde{c}_{ij}) = R'_e C R_f$ and $\tilde{A} = (\tilde{a}_{ij}) = R'_e A R_f$. With this, we have found an effective way to perform the operations between the functional approximations of face images involved in the algorithm.

3   Experimental Results

To validate the proposal, experiments were conducted on two standard public available face databases: AT&T (also known as ORL) [12] and Extended Yale B

[13]. The introduced Functional Near Subspace Classification (FNSC) algorithm is compared with existing methods that have been tested on these databases. The results reported in all of our experiments are given by the recognition rate, which measures the percent of face images well classified.

For the experiments on both databases, we shall use a tensor product of univariate B-spline basis of order 4 (which gives a suitable smooth approximation of the faces) over the rectangular domain of interest. An advantage of B-splines is their local character. B-splines capture the information locally, which is suitable for the problem at hand.

3.1   Results on the AT&T Database

The AT&T database consists of 400 face images from 40 subjects. It has 10 images per person with different variations in expressions and deviations from the frontal pose up to 20 degrees. Face images from some of the subjects have additional changes such as the use of glasses. We adopt here two evaluation protocols [10]. The first protocol (EP1) uses the first five images of each person for training, leaving the remaining five for testing. The second protocol (EP2) consists on the "leave-one-out" cross-validation strategy. In both experiments we have used the images of size 92×112 pixels as provided, without any further processing, i.e., no geometric or photometric normalization is applied.

As described in Section 2, we first have to represent face images through B-spline basis expansion. For this, we need to select the number of basis functions ($p \times q$ in Section 2.1) to be used. The choice of the number of basis is very important because it can be regarded as a smoothing parameter. Statistically, keeping a few coefficients in the expansion is equivalent to conducting heavy amount of smoothing for the original data. We have selected here the number of basis functions by expert knowledge (comparing row data images with its reconstructions) and by trial and error. A more reasoned approach like cross-validation could have been used in this step.

The number of basis functions used in this database is 49, i.e., $p = 7$ and $q = 7$. This imply that the image is characterized only by 49 coefficients in the basis expansion, which considerably reduce the dimension of the problem. We will not refer to this vector of coefficients as feature vector, because they are not going to be new features for us. There is some subtle but important difference that should be accounted for. Our data, is still a function and we operate on it like this: we have formulated an algorithm for that, we are performing norms and inner product in a functional sense. But in practice, as the calculations are reduced to operate on these coefficient matrices, we can argue that the dimension of the problem has been reduced to that number of coefficients.

Table 1 shows the results obtained on both evaluation protocols. For EP1, the introduced approach does not achieve the best results, but its recognition accuracy of 95.5% is comparable with the other methods based on subspace analysis. Only the 2D-PCA and the Eigenfeature Regularization and Extraction (ERE) algorithms outperform the proposal by a 0.5 % and 1.5 %, respectively. For the second protocol, FNSC reports the best results.

Table 1. Recognition rates on AT&T database

Method	EP1 Recognition Rate	EP2 Recognition Rate
PCA [14]	93.50 %	97.50 %
LDA [14]	94.50 %	98.50 %
ICA[14]	85.00 %	93.50 %
Kernel-PCA [14]	94.00 %	98.00 %
2D-PCA [14]	96.00 %	98.30 %
ERE [15]	97.00 %	99.25 %
LRC [10]	93.50 %	98.75 %
FNSC	**95.50 %**	**99.50 %**

3.2   Results on the Extended Yale B Database

The Extended Yale B database contains images of 38 subjects seen under 64 different illumination conditions, in which the angle between the light source direction and the camera axis was changed each time, in a way that the larger the angle, the more unfavorable the lighting conditions are. This database is usually divided into 5 subsets according to the angle of the incident illumination. Subset S1 is composed by 7 face images per subject with frontal or almost frontal incident lighting and is used as gallery. Subset S2 is composed by 456 images (12 per person) with incident lighting angle between $13^0 - 25^0$, S3 have also 456 images with angles between $26^0 - 50^0$, 532 images (14 per subject) with angles between $51^0 - 70^0$ are in S4 and S5 contains 722 images (19 per person) with angles greater than 70^0. Also in this case, the provided cropped version of the original images of size 168×192 are used without any pre-processing.

Figure 1 shows (for an image of this database) the original image and its functional representation. Also for this database, the number of basis functions was selected by expert knowledge to be $p = 31$ and $q = 35$, which gives a total of 1085 coefficients.

Also in this case, the dimensionality of the problem is considerably reduced. As was explained before, the number of coefficients chosen has the role of an smoothing parameter. This can be observed in this figure, where the functional

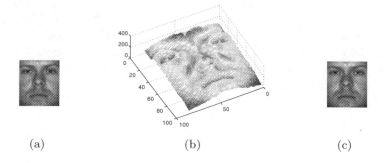

(a)   (b)   (c)

Fig. 1. a) Original image and b-c) its functional approximation

Table 2. Recognition rates on Extended Yale B database

Method	S2	S3	S4	S5
PCA [10]	98.46 %	80.04 %	15.79 %	24.38 %
ICA [10]	98.03 %	80.70 %	15.98 %	22.02 %
LRC [10]	100.0 %	100.0 %	83.27 %	33.61 %
FNSC	**100.0 %**	**100.0 %**	**87.97 %**	**38.50 %**

approximation shown in Figure 1(c) is smoother than the original image that appears in Figure 1(a).

The Extended Yale B database contains large illumination variations and it is usually used to test face recognition methods in front of this kind of problems. We are not addressing here the illumination problem and we have not applied any photometric normalization, although this could improve the results.

Table 2 shows the obtained results and comparisons with the Linear Regression Classification (LRC) algorithm and the other methods reported in [10]. The FNSC method reached the best results, achieving 100% of recognition rate in subset 2 and subset 3 and outperforming LRC in almost 5% on subsets 4 and 5.

4   Further Issues and Conclusions

This paper presents a new face recognition method based on Functional Data Analysis. First, a new representation of face images is proposed in which images are considered observations of functional random variables taking values in a Hilbert space. Second, a face recognition algorithm based on Near Subspace approach was generalized to functional spaces. Unlike the majority of the appearance-based methods for face recognition, our proposal attempts to take into account the smoothness and continuity of the face image.

Experiments were conducted on two popular face databases, AT&T and Yale B. Comparisons were done with previous approaches, and it was shown that the proposed face recognition method performs very well.

Although the obtained results are satisfactory, there are still many issues to investigate on the functional method proposed in this paper. One of these, is the selection of the basis. What is the more appropriate basis to represent face images? Is there a criteria to choose such a basis? Also, a two-dimensional basis can be obtained not only through tensor products of univariate basis. It is possible to use finite element analysis or thin-plate spline method to define bivariate basis over more complicated domains, such as non uniform grid. This new domain can be for example a Delaunay triangulation that takes better into account the structure of the face.

Another slightly more ambitious aspects would be to incorporate other kind of information in the construction of the functional approximation of the face image, not only the pixels intensity values. This would make the representation more robust to different problems affecting the image, like illumination variations.

Despite all that remains to be done or can be improved in this approach, we think that going back to the functional nature of face images could be very promising in the face recognition tasks, would you?

References

1. Jain, A.K., Li, S.Z.: Handbook of Face Recognition. Springer-Verlag New York, Inc., Secaucus (2005)
2. Zhao, W., Chellappa, R., Phillips, P.J., Rosenfeld, A.: Face recognition: A literature survey. ACM Comput. Surv. 35, 399–458 (2003)
3. Jafri, R., Arabnia, H.R.: A survey of face recognition techniques. Journal of Information Processing Systems 5(2) (2009)
4. Turk, M., Pentland, A.: Eigenfaces for recognition. J. Cognitive Neuroscience 3(1), 71–86 (1991)
5. Belhumeur, P.N., Hespanha, J.P., Kriegman, D.J.: Eigenfaces vs. Fisherfaces: recognition using class specific linear projection. IEEE Transactions on Pattern Analysis and Machine Intelligence 19(7), 711–720 (1997)
6. Yuen, P.: Face representation using independent component analysis. Pattern Recognition 35(6), 1247–1257 (2002)
7. Wright, J., Yang, A.Y., Ganesh, A., Sastry, S.S., Ma, Y.: Robust face recognition via sparse representation. IEEE Trans. Pattern Anal. Mach. Intell. 31(2), 210–227 (2009)
8. Ramsay, J., Silverman, B.: Functional data analysis. Springer series in statistics. Springer (2005)
9. Ferraty, F., Vieu, P.: Nonparametric Functional Data Analysis: Theory and Practice. Springer Series in Statistics. Springer-Verlag New York, Inc., Secaucus (2006)
10. Naseem, I., Togneri, R., Bennamoun, M.: Linear regression for face recognition. IEEE Trans. Pattern Anal. Mach. Intell. 32(11), 2106–2112 (2010)
11. Basri, R., Jacobs, D.W.: Lambertian reflectance and linear subspaces. IEEE Transactions on Pattern Analysis and Machine Intelligence 25, 218–233 (2003)
12. Samaria, F.S., Harter, A.C.: Parameterisation of a stochastic model for human face identification. In: Second IEEE Workshop Applications of Computer Vision (1994)
13. Lee, K.-C., Ho, J., Kriegman, D.J.: Acquiring linear subspaces for face recognition under variable lighting. IEEE Transactions on Pattern Analysis and Machine Intelligence 27(5), 684–698 (2005)
14. Yang, J., Zhang, D., Frangi, A.F., Yang, J.-y.: Two-dimensional pca: A new approach to appearance-based face representation and recognition. IEEE Transactions on Pattern Analysis and Machine Intelligence 26, 131–137 (2004)
15. Jiang, X., Mandal, B., Kot, A.: Eigenfeature regularization and extraction in face recognition. IEEE Trans. Pattern Anal. Mach. Intell. 30(3), 383–394 (2008)

Dissimilarity Representations Based on Multi-Block LBP for Face Detection

Yoanna Martínez-Díaz, Heydi Méndez-Vázquez, Yenisel Plasencia-Calaña, and Edel B. García-Reyes

Advanced Technologies Application Center. 7th Avenue ♯ 21812 % 218 and 222, Siboney, Playa, P.C. 12200, Havana, Cuba
{ymartinez,hmendez,yplasencia,egarcia}@cenatav.co.cu

Abstract. Face representation is one of the open problems in face detection. The recently proposed Multi-Block Local Binary Patterns (MB-LBP) representation has shown good results for this purpose. Although dissimilarity representation has proved to be effective in a variety of pattern recognition problems, to the best of our knowledge, it has never been used for face detection. In this paper, we propose new dissimilarity representations based on MB-LBP features for this task. Different experiments conducted on a public database, showed that the proposed representations are more discriminative than the original MB-LBP representation when classifying faces. Using the dissimilarity representations, a good classification accuracy is achieved even when less training data is available.

Keywords: face detection, dissimilarity representation, MB-LBP.

1 Introduction

Face detection is the first step in a face recognition system. The more precise this step, the more accurate any further processing [1]. Existing methods to detect faces in images can be grouped into four categories: knowledge-based methods, feature invariant approaches, template matching methods and appearance-based methods [2]. In general, appearance-based methods have shown the best performance, being the most studied and used [1]. However, how to represent and classify faces, are two key factors which are still unsolved problems [1].

Different kinds of features have been proposed for face detection. They are based on physical properties of faces, such as color intensity, texture, vertices, shape and facial features. Among them, the Haar-like features have been one of the most widespread and effectively used [3]. They encode the differences in average intensities of adjacent rectangular regions and can be efficiently computed through the integral image technique. However, the complete (or exhaustive) set of Haar-like features is very large, containing a lot of redundant information. Moreover, these features are not robust to extreme lighting conditions [1].

Object detectors based on the Local Binary Patterns (LBP) descriptor have become more popular, achieving highly competitive results [4]. This can be

L. Alvarez et al. (Eds.): CIARP 2012, LNCS 7441, pp. 106–113, 2012.

attributed to the tolerance of this operator against monotonic illumination variations and its computational simplicity [5]. Among different extensions of the original LBP operator, the Multi-Block LBP (MB-LBP) representation [6] has shown
to be more robust to noise and stable for face detection [4]. The MB-LBP compares average intensities of adjacent rectangular blocks in a neighborhood instead
of single pixels intensities. Compared to original LBP and Haar-like features, it
can capture more information about image structures and shows a better performance [6]. The MB-LBP also allows generating an exhaustive set of features with
different scales and locations [6]. This set is much smaller than the Haar-like one,
however it is still large and contains redundant information.

When exhaustive sets of features are used, boosting-based methods are usually
applied to select the most discriminative features and to build a strong classifier
[3,6]. The main drawbacks of these methods are that they need a large set of
training samples and the learning process is time consuming [1,7]. To overcome
some of these limitations, other learning strategies can be used for appearance-
based face detection [1,2,7].

A powerful alternative to those representations based on features are the
dissimilarity representations (DR) [8]. They are based on comparisons among
objects and can be obtained on top of feature representations. In this way, an
object is described by means of its dissimilarities with a set of prototypes [8]. If
a suitable dissimilarity measure is defined for the problem at hand, classifiers in
a dissimilarity space (DS) can provide very good results [8,9].

In this paper we propose new dissimilarity representations based on MB-LBP
features for the problem of face detection, which show to be more discriminative
than the original MB-LBP features space. The rest of this paper is organized
as follows. In Section 2 we review the MB-LBP representation and the methods
used for feature selection and classification. In Section 3, the dissimilarity representations based on MB-LBP features are presented. Experimental results and
discussion are drawn in Section 4. Finally, section 5 concludes this paper.

2   Multi-Block Local Binary Patterns Representation

Multi-Block Local Binary Patterns (MB-LBP) features were inspired by the
traditional Haar-like rectangular features [6]. In this case, the differences among
rectangular regions are encoded by the LBP operator [5]. MB-LBP compares the
average intensity of the central rectangle, r_c, with the average intensities of its
adjacent rectangular blocks $\{r_1, ..., r_8\}$ in a 3×3 neighborhood [6]. Afterwards,
it encodes the responses in a binary number, which can be further converted to
a decimal number:

$$\text{MB-LBP} = \sum_{i=1}^{8} S(r_i - r_c)2^i \qquad (1)$$

where,

$$S(\text{X}) = \begin{cases} 0 \text{ if X} \leq 0 \\ 1 \text{ if X} > 0 \end{cases} \qquad (2)$$

Since MB-LBP compares regions instead of pixels, they can capture larger scale structures than original LBP. Compared with Haar-like features, MB-LBP can encode more information, describing more complex image structures [6]. Similar to Haar-like features, the average intensities of rectangular blocks can be computed at constant time by using the integral image [6]. Given a sub-window size, the number of rectangles at various scales, locations and aspect ratios of MB-LBP features (exhaustive set) is about 5% of the total number of Haar-like features. Even when the exhaustive set of MB-LBP features is much smaller than the Haar-like features, it also contains a mass of redundant information [6]. Hence, a feature selection method should improve the classification accuracy and make the training process less expensive.

2.1   Feature Selection and Classification

Despite the successful advances on face detection [1,2], obtaining discriminative features and classifiers to achieve a good compromise between computational cost and classification accuracy, remains as a challenging issue. In previous works, AdaBoost algorithm [10] has been used both to select the most discriminative MB-LBP features and to construct a strong classifier [6]. In the boosting mechanisms used for face detection, each weak classifier is usually trained with a single feature and needs to evaluate thousands of features to minimize an error function. This process is very time consuming and usually requires a large set of training samples for a better performance [7]. Furthermore, if the data is noisy, the classifier can be trapped by local minima.

Other feature selection methods and learning approaches have been used to avoid the above limitations in the context of face detection, such as the Sequential Forward Selection algorithm [7] and the Support Vector Machines (SVM) [1]. As an alternative, the Minimal-Redundancy-Maximal-Relevance (MRMR) criterion, which has been effectively used for different face analysis problems [11], can be also used for the purpose of face detection.

Besides the mentioned strategies, there is another possibility which has not been exploited in the context of face detection. The so-called dissimilarity based classification has shown a good performance for high dimensional data such as images and for two class problems [8,9], therefore it could be useful for this task.

3   Dissimilarity Representations Based on MB-LBP

The DS was proposed in the context of dissimilarity-based classification. It was postulated as an Euclidean vector space, implying that classifiers proposed for feature spaces can be used there as well [8]. Under this framework, the objects are represented in terms of their dissimilarities to a set of so-called prototypes. Given a training set T, the prototypes $R = \{r_1, r_2, ..., r_k\}$ can be a subset from T, or T itself. The dissimilarity representation of an object x is then defined as:

$$D(x, R) = [d(x, r_1) \ d(x, r_2) \ ... \ d(x, r_k)],\tag{3}$$

where $d(x, r_i)$ is the dissimilarity value between x and each prototype $r_i, i = 1...k$. Finally, a dissimilarity matrix $D(T, R)$ of all objects against all prototypes is obtained.

More compact representations can be achieved using prototype selection methods [9]. They find the prototypes that better represent the data in the DS. In this way, a DS of lower dimensionality can be constructed, leading to lower computational and storage costs. Besides, the selection of a suitable dissimilarity measure is a key point in DR [8]. The aim of this work is to introduce the use of DR for face detection, so we have built two new DS based on MB-LBP features using Euclidean and L1 distances as dissimilarity measures.

4   Experimental Results and Discussion

In this section, two experiments are conducted in order to evaluate the DR based on MB-LBP features, for face representation and classification in the process of face detection. For this purpose we have used a dataset of 12788 gray-scales images of 24×24 pixels, divided into 4916 faces and 7872 non-faces [12]. Different configurations and learning schemes are evaluated, and three terms are used to measure the performance of the methods: False Positive rate (FP), False Negative rate (FN) and Error Rate (ER). FP measures the non-faces incorrectly classified as faces; FN indicates how many face images were incorrectly classified as non-faces; and ER is the ratio between the number of misclassified images (faces and non-faces) to the total number of analyzed images.

4.1   Classification in DS Based on the Exhaustive Set of MB-LBP

The first experiment was developed to compare our two DR based on the exhaustive set of MB-LBP features with the original MB-LBP features space. AdaBoost classifier [10] is then used on the different representations. Since AdaBoost selects a subset of features (prototypes in the DS) for classification, we decided to use all training data as prototypes. A subset composed by 6000 images (2000 faces + 4000 non-faces) of the dataset was used. It was randomly split into 2000 images for training and 4000 for testing. To reduce the variance of the estimation, this procedure was repeated 10 times and the comparison is then based on the averaged classification accuracy from all partitions. For each one of the 10 generated partitions, an AdaBoost classifier with 50 weak learners was trained and tested. From now on we will refer to this as Protocol 1.

Table 1 shows the performance of the AdaBoost classifier using the proposed representations and the original MB-LBP features space (FS), in terms of the average FN, FP and ER for the 10 partitions. In all cases, standard deviations are lower than 0.01. It can be seen from the table that the lowest errors are obtained for the two proposed DS, outperforming remarkably the original MB-LBP representation and achieving more than 99% of correct classification. The Euclidean distance on the MB-LBP features is slightly better than the L1 distance, but in general both measures performed very well. We can benefit from

Table 1. Performance of AdaBoost algorithm using MB-LBP features in DS and FS

	Average FN	Average FP	Average ER
MB-LBP in FS	0.0908	0.0379	0.0554
MB-LBP + Euclidean in DS	**0.0037**	**0.0028**	**0.0031**
MB-LBP + L1 in DS	0.0045	0.0034	0.0037

the use of DS constructed on top of MB-LBP features with this two common distances, since a more discriminative representation is obtained.

Moreover, the DR allow reducing the dimensionality of the training data. For the given sub-window size of 24×24, the dimension of the original MB-LBP exhaustive set is 8644. Despite the fact that we did not use prototype selection, in this case, the dimensionality of the DS obtained for training is only 2000. In order to analyze the behavior of the proposed representations when less training data is used, different training set sizes are evaluated. Figure 1 shows the obtained classification errors for the different representations. As it can be appreciated, the DS based on Euclidean and L1 distances always outperform the original representation of MB-LBP features, using AdaBoost classifier. We can see that, when the dissimilarities among objects are taken into account, a good classification accuracy can be obtained using even small training set sizes.

4.2   Classification in DS Based on a Subset of MB-LBP

In the second experiment our aim is to corroborate the robustness of the proposed representations using a different configuration. In this case, the MRMR criterion is used to select the most discriminative MB-LBP features and the two DS are obtained based on the reduced set of features. The basic idea of MRMR is to use information theory, finding the features that are maximally relevant on the target class but minimally redundant [11]. It allows one to select good features at very low cost, so the computation of the dissimilarity matrix become less expensive. Moreover, it removes the redundant information which might have influence on the DR. The two obtained DS are then compared with the reduced original MB-LBP features space, using AdaBoost and SVM classifiers. In this experiment the SVM classifier was used with a linear kernel, with the aim at making the computational cost less expensive.

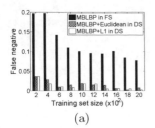 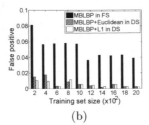 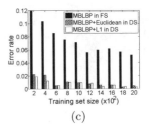

(a)   (b)   (c)

Fig. 1. Performance of MB-LBP features in DS and FS using AdaBoost algorithm with different training set sizes, in terms of (a) FN, (b) FP and (c) ER

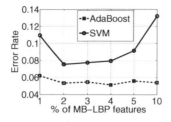

Fig. 2. Performance of Adaboost and SVM classifier with different dimensions of MB-LBP features selected by MRMR criterion

In order to choose an optimal number of features selected by the MRMR criterion, we have tested various percentages of the total number of features (8644), using the two classifiers in the original space. For this purpose, we have used a different subset of 3000 images, randomly divided into two equal parts for training and testing. The obtained error curves are plotted on Fig. 2. We decided to keep only 2% of the total number of features. It can be seen that, for this value a low error is achieved by the two classifiers.

We have constructed the DR based on the reduced set of MB-LBP features using both AdaBoost and SVM classifiers. The results obtained for AdaBoost are shown on Table 2. For this experiment we used the Protocol 1 defined on subsection 4.1. It can be seen from Table 2 that also using the reduced set of features, the DR remarkably outperform the original MB-LBP representation. Notice that although these results do not improve the ones presented on Table 1, the computation of the dissimilarity matrices is less expensive in this case.

We have decided to use a prototype selection method before applying the SVM classifier, with the aim to obtain a more compact DR, making the learning process less expensive. In order to choose a suitable method and an appropriate number of prototypes for the classification in the DS, we compared three methods with different numbers of prototypes. Based on results of previous works [9] we have tested: RandomC, KCentres and forward selection optimizing the leave-one-out nearest neighbor error in the training set (FS+NN error). For this experiment, a different subset of the dataset is used, composed by 500 face images and 1500 non-face images. The data was randomly divided into equal parts for training and testing, and the procedure was repeated 10 times. The classification accuracy of the SVM classifier in the obtained spaces, using both Euclidean and L1 distances, are compared in Fig. 3. In general, the KCentres method shows the

Table 2. Performance of AdaBoost algorithm using reduced set of MB-LBP features in DS and FS

	Average FN	Average FP	Average ER
MB-LBP in FS	0.1078	0.0523	0.0706
MB-LBP + Euclidean in DS	**0.0050**	**0.0025**	**0.0033**
MB-LBP + L1 in DS	0.0054	0.0035	0.0041

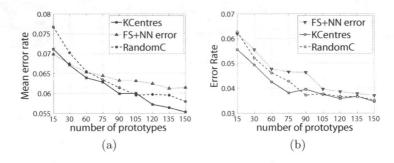

Fig. 3. Average error rates of the SVM classifier in DS using (a) Euclidean distance and (b) L1 distance with three prototypes selection methods

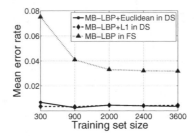

Fig. 4. Performance of SVM classifier with different training set sizes

lowest error rates. We decided to use this method selecting 60 prototypes, since this number of prototypes represents a good compromise between classification accuracy and computational cost.

The behavior of the SVM classifier on the DS obtained by using KCentres with 60 prototypes based on the reduced set of MB-LBP features, is compared with the classification in the reduced original MB-LBP feature space. The same images used on Protocol 1 are used in this experiment, but in this case different training set sizes are tested. For each one of the tested training sizes, the experiment was repeated 10 times, randomly splitting the data for training and testing. The average error rates are shown on Fig. 4. It can be seen that the classification accuracy of the SVM classifier on DS is significantly better for all tested training sizes. Moreover, it is shown that in the original MB-LBP feature space, the size of the training data has a direct influence on the classification accuracy, while the results on the DS exhibit a more stable behavior.

5   Conclusion and Future Work

In this paper we propose new dissimilarity representations based on MB-LBP features for face detection, using Euclidean and L1 distances. The proposed representations have shown to be more discriminative than the original MB-LBP features space. Moreover, they allow us to obtain a significantly better classification accuracy even when using a few amount of training data. Despite the fact that the redundant information in the exhaustive set of MB-LBP features does not have significative influence on the proposed representations, the use of the reduced set of features makes the computation of the dissimilarity matrices less expensive. This paper can be considered a good starting point for further developments on the use of dissimilarity representations for face detection. As future work we pretend to explore different DR based on other features using suitable dissimilarity measures.

References

1. Zhang, C., Zhang, Z.: A survey of recent advances in face detection. Technical Report MSR-TR-2010-66
2. Yang, M., Kriegman, D., Ahuja, N.: Detecting faces in images: A survey. IEEE Transactions on PAMI 24(1), 399–458 (2002)
3. Viola, P., Jones, M.: Rapid object detection using a boosted cascade of simple features. In: IEEE Computer Society Conference on CVPR, vol. 1, pp. 511–518 (2001)
4. Trefný, J., Matas, J.: Extended set of local binary patterns for rapid object detection. In: Proceedings of the Computer Vision Winter Workshop 2010 (2010)
5. Ojala, T., Pietikäinen, M., Harwood, D.: A comparative study of texture measures with classification based on featured distributions. Pattern Recognition 29(1), 51–59 (1996)
6. Zhang, L., Chu, R., Xiang, S., Liao, S., Li, S.: Face detection based on multi-block lbp representation. In: Proceedings of IAPR/IEEE ICB (2007)
7. Louis, W., Plataniotis, K.N.: Co-occurrence of local binary patterns features for frontal face detection in surveillance applications. In: EURASIP (2011)
8. Pekalska, E.: The Dissimilarity Representation For Pattern Recognition. Foundations and Applications. World Scientfic (2005)
9. Pekalska, E., Duin, R.P., Paclík, P.: Prototype selection for dissimilarity-based classifiers. Pattern Recognition 39(2), 189–208 (2006)
10. Freund, Y., Schapire, R.E.: A Decision-Theoretic Generalization of On-line Learning and an Application to Boosting. In: Vitányi, P.M.B. (ed.) EuroCOLT 1995. LNCS, vol. 904, pp. 23–37. Springer, Heidelberg (1995)
11. Akbaş, E., Yarman-Vural, F.T.: Design of a Feature Set for Face Recognition Problem. In: Levi, A., Savaş, E., Yenigün, H., Balcısoy, S., Saygın, Y. (eds.) ISCIS 2006. LNCS, vol. 4263, pp. 239–247. Springer, Heidelberg (2006)
12. Carbonetto, P.S.: Robust object detection using boosted learning. Technical report, Department of Computer Science,University of British Columbia, Vancouver, Canada (April 2002)

On the Vulnerability of Iris-Based Systems to a Software Attack Based on a Genetic Algorithm

Marta Gomez-Barrero, Javier Galbally, Pedro Tome, and Julian Fierrez

Biometric Recognition Group-ATVS, EPS, Universidad Autonoma de Madrid
C/ Francisco Tomas y Valiente 11, 28049 Madrid, Spain

Abstract. The vulnerabilities of a standard iris verification system to a novel indirect attack based on a binary genetic algorithm are studied. The experiments are carried out on the iris subcorpus of the publicly available BioSecure DB. The attack has shown a remarkable performance, thus proving the lack of robustness of the tested system to this type of threat. Furthermore, the consistency of the bits of the iris code is analysed, and a second working scenario discarding the fragile bits is then tested as a possible countermeasure against the proposed attack.

Keywords: Security, vulnerabilities, iris recognition, genetic algorithm, counter-measures.

1 Introduction

Due to their advantages over traditional security approaches, biometric security systems are nowadays being introduced into many applications where a correct identity assessment is a crucial issue, such as access control or sensitive data protection [1]. These systems perform automatic recognition of individuals based on anatomical (e.g., fingerprint, face, iris, etc.) or behavioural characteristics (e.g., signature, gait, keystroke dynamics). Among these traits, the iris has been traditionally regarded as one of the most reliable and accurate [1].

However, biometric systems are vulnerable to external attacks, that can be divided into two different groups, namely: *i) direct attacks*, carried out against the sensor using synthetic traits [2]; and *ii) indirect attacks*, carried out against one of the inner modules of the system [3], and thus requiring some knowledge about the inner working of the system. Several works have already studied the robustness of iris-based biometric systems against direct attacks, including attackers wearing contact lenses with artificial textures printed onto them [4] and fake iris images [5].

In the present paper, a novel indirect attack based on a genetic algorithm is presented. The point of attack are binary templates, as depicted in Fig. 1 (top), where a general hill-climbing attack is shown. Although other hill-climbing attacks have been proposed [6,3,7], none of them work on binary templates, but on real-valued feature vectors or directly on the sample images.

Although in commercial systems the number of consecutive unsuccessful access attempts is usually restricted, this countermeasure has been circumvented in different occasions or may even be used to compromise the system by performing an *account*

L. Alvarez et al. (Eds.): CIARP 2012, LNCS 7441, pp. 114–121, 2012.

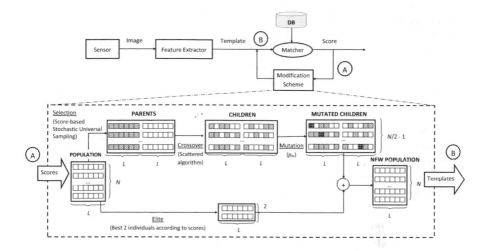

Fig. 1. Diagram of the general structure of a hill-climbing attack (top), with the specific modification scheme here implemented based on a genetic algorithm (bottom)

lockout attack (i.e., the intruder tries to access multiple accounts blocking all of them and collapsing the system). In the present work the consistency of the bits of the iris code is studied, and the use of the most consistent bits is analysed as a possible pure biometric countermeasure against the proposed attack.

The performance of the attack is evaluated on an iris recognition system adapted from the one developed by L. Masek [8] using the iris subcorpus of the BioSecure multimodal database [9]. The results show that most client accounts can be broken at the different operating points tested, even at a very high security one, requiring a similar number of matchings.

The paper is structured as follows: the attacking algorithm is introduced in Sect. 2. The system attacked is presented in Sect. 3, while the experimental protocol followed and the performance evaluation of the system are described in Sect. 4. The results obtained are shown in Sect. 5. Finally conclusions are drawn in Sect. 6.

2   Indirect Attack Based on a Genetic Algorithm

Most iris recognition systems use binary templates [10,11]. Therefore, given the good performance of genetic algorithms in binary optimization problems, they may be a very powerful tool to attack iris-based systems.

In the proposed attack to iris-based systems, the objective is to find an individual x (binary template), which is similar enough to the client being attacked, $\mathcal{C}$, according to a fitness function, $\mathcal{J}$, in this case being the similarity score (s) given by the matcher: $s = \mathcal{J}(\mathcal{C}, x)$

For this purpose, a genetic algorithm is used to optimize the similarity score (i.e., fitness function) starting from a randomly generated population, comprising a fixed number (N) of binary individuals (i.e., iris templates) of length L (in our particular case L will be the length of the iris code). As can be seen in Fig. 1 (bottom), four types of rules are used at each iteration to create the next optimized generation of individuals (templates) from the current population (being the input to the genetic algorithm the scores of the current population, and the output, the new templates):

- **Elite:** the two individuals (templates) with the maximum values for the fitness function (similarity scores) are kept for the next generation.
- **Selection rules:** certain individuals, the *parents*, are chosen by stochastic universal sampling. This way, the individuals with the highest fitness values (i.e., similarity scores) are more likely to be chosen as parents for the next generation: one subject can be selected 0 or many times.
- **Crossover rules:** parents are combined to form $N - 2$ *children* following a scattered crossover method, where a random binary vector is created and the genes are selected from the first parent where the bit is a 1, and from the second when it is a 0 (vice versa for the second child).
- **Mutation rules:** random changes are applied to the new children with a mutation probability p_m.

The genetic algorithm is used to iteratively produce new generations following the rules given above. Each of the generations will contain individuals more similar each time to the objective ($\mathcal{C}$) until one of them produces a score higher than the verification threshold (i.e., the account is broken) or until one of the other stopping criteria is fulfilled: the maximum number of generations allowed is reached or the fitness values vary less than a certain pre-established amount.

It should be noticed that the present work is not focused on the study of genetic algorithms, but on the evaluation of the vulnerabilities of iris recognition systems to attacks based on these optimization tools. Therefore, a thorough analysis of the different specific GA parameters fall out of the scope of the work. For a more detailed description of different architectures for genetic algorithms the reader is referred to [12,13].

3   Iris Verification System Attacked

In our experiments, we have used the iris recognition system developed by L. Masek[1] [8], which is widely used to obtain base results in many iris related publications. Although the performance of this system has been largely improved by different systems over the last years [14], the experimental results shown in Sect. 5 are still fully meaningful since, as will be explained in Sect. 4, they have been obtained at operating points corresponding to False Acceptance Rates (FAR) typical of any better recognition system (i.e., with lower False Rejection Rates, FRR, for those same FARs).

The system comprises four different steps, namely: i) segmentation, where the iris and pupil boundaries are modelled as two circles and detected using a circular Hough transform, as in [5]; ii) normalization, which maps the segmented iris region into a 2D array using a technique based on Daugman's rubber sheet model; iii) feature encoding,

---

[1] The source can be freely downloaded from
www.csse.uwa.edu.au/pk/studentprojects/libor/sourcecode.html

		BioSecure DS2 DB (210 Users)	
Session	Sample	170 Users	40 Users
1	1	Training	Test (Impostors)
	2		
2	1		
	2	Test (Clients)	

Fig. 2. Diagram showing the partitioning of the BioSecure DS2 DB according to the performance evaluation protocol defined in the present work

where the normalized iris pattern is convolved with 1D Log-Gabor wavelets, in order to produce a binary template of $20 \times 480 = 9,600$ bits and a corresponding noise mask that represents the eyelids areas; iv) matching, where the inverse of the Hamming distance, $1/HD$, is used for matching (a higher score implies a higher degree of similarity). This Hamming distance is modified so that it incorporates the noise mask, using only the significant bits:

$$HD = \frac{\sum_{j=1}^{L} X_j(XOR)Y_j(AND)\bar{X}n_j(AND)\bar{Y}n_j}{L - \sum_{k=1}^{L} Xn_k(OR)Yn_k}$$

where X_j and Y_j are the two bitwise templates to compare, Xn_j and Yn_j are the corresponding noise masks for X_j and Y_j, and L is the number of bits comprised by each template. $\bar{X}n_j$ denotes the logical not operation applied to Xn_j.

4   Experimental Protocol

The experiments are carried out on the iris subcorpus included in the DS2 of the BioSecure multimodal database [9]. BioSecure DB, publicly available through the BioSecure Foundation [2], was acquired thanks to the joint effort of 11 European institutions and has become one of the standard benchmarks for biometric performance and security evaluation.

The database comprises three datasets captured under different acquisition scenarios. The Desktop Dataset, DS2, comprises voice, fingerprints, face, iris, signature and hand of 210 users, captured in two time-spaced acquisition sessions. The iris subset used in this work includes four grey-scale images (two per session) per eye, all captured with the Iris Access EOU3000 sensor from LG.

The performance of the evaluated system is computed using the experimental protocol shown in Fig. 2. The database is divided into: *i)* a training set comprising the first three samples of 170 clients (enrolment templates); and *ii)* an evaluation set formed by the fourth image of the previous 170 clients (used to compute the genuine scores) and all the 4 images of the remaining 40 users (used to calculate the impostor scores).

The final score given by the system is the average of the scores obtained after matching the input binary vector to the three templates (i.e., iris codes) of the attacked client model C. For the experiments, we consider the left and right eyes of one person as different clients, thus having twice as many clients (340) and impostors (80). The system

---

[2] http://biosecure.it-sudparis.eu/AB

has an Equal Error Rate (EER) of 3.82%. The vulnerability of the system to the attack is evaluated at three operating points corresponding to: FAR = 0.1%, FAR = 0.05%, and FAR = 0.01%, which, according to [15], correspond to a low, medium and high security application. For completeness, the system is tested at a very high security operating point corresponding to FAR ≪ 0.01%.

4.1   Experimental Protocol for the Attacks

In order to generate the user accounts to be attacked with the genetic algorithm, we use the train set defined in the performance evaluation protocol (Fig. 2). The performance of the attack will be evaluated in terms of: $i)$ Success Rate (SR) or expected probability of breaking a given account, indicating how dangerous the attack is (the higher the SR, the bigger the threat); Efficiency (Eff) or inverse of the average number of matchings needed to break an account, thus giving an estimation of how easy it is for the attack to break into the system in terms of speed (the higher the Eff, the faster the attack). The SR is computed as the ratio between the number of broken accounts (A_B) and the total number of accounts attacked ($A_T = 170$): SR $= A_B/A_T$, and the Eff is defined as Eff $= 1/\left(\sum_{i=1}^{A_B} n_i/A_B\right)$, where n_i is the number of matchings computed to bypass each of the broken accounts.

5   Results

The experiments have two different goals, namely: $i)$ study the vulnerability of an automatic iris recognition system to the proposed attack, and $ii)$ find the most consistent bits in the iris code and analyse whether the use of those bits increases the robustness of the system to the attack.

5.1   Attack Performance

The performance of the attack is measured at four different operating points, namely: $i)$ FAR = 0.10%, $ii)$ FAR = 0.05%, $iii)$ FAR = 0.01%, and $iv)$ FAR ≪ 0.01%. As can be observed in Table 1, the attacking algorithm proposed in this work successfully breaks most of the attacked accounts: around 80% SR on average, and as many as 50% of broken accounts for an unrealistically high operating point (FA ≪ 0.01%). It is also worth noting the fact that the efficiency barely depends on the operating point attacked: the number of comparisons needed increases only about 25% between the operating points FAR = 0.1% and FAR = 0.01% (while a brute force attack using randomly chosen real irises to access the system would need about ten times as many matchings, ≃ 1/FAR).

5.2   Analysis of the Most Consistent Bits in the Iris Code

The results achieved by the hill-climbing attack based on a genetic algorithm against the iris recognition system considered in the experiments have shown its high vulnerability

Table 1. Eff and SR of the attack at the operating points tested

FAR	SR	Eff ($\times 10^{-4}$)
0.10%	91.18%	1.400
0.05%	80.89%	1.255
0.01%	62.36%	1.102
$\ll$0.01%	52.06%	1.051

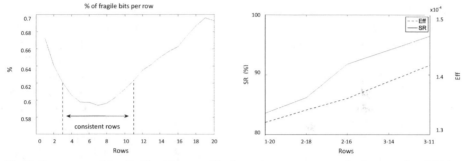

Fig. 3. Percentage of fragile bits (the ones flipping at least once across the images of an iris) in a row (left), and SR and Eff of the attack varying the number of rows used by the matcher (right)

against this type of attacking approach and the need to incorporate some attack protection method that increases its robustness against this threat. In this section we analyse the performance of using only the most consistent bits of the iris code for verification.

According to the analysis made by Hollingsworth *et al.* in [16], there are some bits more fragile than others in an iris code, that is, bits that flip between 0 and 1 in different images of the same iris with a high probability. Here we consider that a bit is consistent, (i.e., not fragile), when it does not flip in any of the four images available for each user. In order to determine the most consistent rows of bits in the iris code, we follow the method described in [16]: we compute the frequency (that must lie between 0% and 50%) that each unmasked bit flips, and take the average frequency across all bits in a row for each subject. All the codes of each user are previously aligned, keeping the rotation that gives the minimum Hamming distance to the first code of that user. In Fig. 3 (left), where the mean percentage of bits considered fragile in each row across all users is depicted, we can observe that rows 3 to 11 are the more consistent ones, having the lowest percentages of fragile bits.

Based on these results, we run some experiments testing the impact of reducing the number of rows of the iris codes: from using all rows (1 - 20) to only the best ones (3 - 11). The results, all obtained at an operating point of FAR = 0.05%, can be observed in Fig. 3 (right). The main reason for the increase in the performance of the attack (both in terms of SR and Eff) is that, by decreasing the number of rows, the number of bits drops drastically while the number of individuals in the population remains the same, thus increasing the diversity of the population and thereby enabling the genetic algorithm to find a maximum faster. Therefore, we may conclude that using only the most consistent bits in the iris code does not improve the robustness of the system against the proposed attacking algorithm.

6 Conclusions

In the present work, a novel indirect attack based on a genetic algorithm has been presented and used to evaluate a standard iris verification system to this type of threat. As many as 90% of the accounts are successfully broken in a similar number of generations for all the operating points considered, proving the vulnerabilities of such systems to this new attacking scheme.

The consistency of the bits of the iris code is then analysed as a possible countermeasure against the proposed attack, and a new scenario discarding the most fragile bits is considered. However, the algorithm reaches higher SRs needing even less comparisons.

Different analysis concerning the optimization of the specific genetic algorithm parameters may be considered in future works. However, these or other improvements fall outside the scope of this study, whose main objective is not to design a perfect method to break the security of biometric systems, but to encourage developers of algorithms and systems to seriously take into account this kind of attack and to implement specific protections and countermeasures.

The main objective of the work, is not to perform a thorough analysis of the different specific GA parameters, but to demonstrate the feasibility of such attacks and to encourage developers to take this security flaw seriously into account.

Acknowledgements. This work has been partially supported by projects Contexts (S2009/TIC-1485) from CAM, Bio-Challenge (TEC2009-11186) from Spanish MICINN, TABULA RASA (FP7-ICT-257289) and BEAT (FP7-SEC-284989) from EU, and *Cátedra UAM-Telefónica*.

References

1. Jain, A.K., Ross, A., Pankanti, S.: Biometrics: a tool for information security. IEEE TIFS 1(2), 125–143 (2006)
2. Matsumoto, T.: Gummy finger and paper iris: an update. In: Proc. WISR, pp. 187–192 (2004)
3. Martinez-Diaz, M., Fierrez, J., et al.: An evaluation of indirect attacks and countermeasures in fingerprint verification systems. Pattern Recognition Letters 32, 1643–1651 (2011)
4. Wei, Z., Qiu, X., et al.: Counterfeit iris detection based on texture analysis. In: Proc. ICPR, pp. 1–4 (2008)
5. Ruiz-Albacete, V., Tome-Gonzalez, P., Alonso-Fernandez, F., Galbally, J., Fierrez, J., Ortega-Garcia, J.: Direct Attacks Using Fake Images in Iris Verification. In: Schouten, B., Juul, N.C., Drygajlo, A., Tistarelli, M. (eds.) BIOID 2008. LNCS, vol. 5372, pp. 181–190. Springer, Heidelberg (2008)
6. Soutar, C., Gilroy, R., Stoianov, A.: Biometric system performance and security. In: Proc. IEEE AIAT (1999)
7. Galbally, J., McCool, C., Fierrez, J., Marcel, S.: On the vulnerability of face verification systems to hill-climbing attacks. Pattern Recognition 43, 1027–1038 (2010)
8. Masek, L., Kovesi, P.: Matlab source code for a biometric identification system based on iris patterns. Master's thesis, School of Computer Science and Software Engineering, University of Western Australia (2003)
9. Ortega-Garcia, J., Fierrez, J., others: The multi-scenario multi-environment BioSecure multimodal database (BMDB). IEEE TPAMI 32, 1097–1111 (2010)

10. Daugman, J.: How iris recognition works. IEEE TCSVT 14(1), 21–30 (2004)
11. Daugman, J.: 4. In: Iris Recognition, pp. 71–90. Springer (2008)
12. Goldberg, D.E.: Genetic Algorithms in Search, Optimization and Machine Learning. Addison-Wesley Longman Publishing Co., Inc. (1989)
13. Goldberg, D.: The design of innovation: lessons from and for competent genetic algorithms. Kluwer Academic Publishers (2002)
14. Grother, P., Tabassi, E., Quinn, G.W., Salamon, W.: Irex i: Performance of iris recognition algorithms on standard images. Technical report, National Institute of Standards and Technology (2009)
15. ANSI: Ansi.x9.84 ANSI X9.84-2001, Biometric Information Management and Security
16. Hollingsworth, K.P., Bowyer, K.W., Flynn, P.J.: The best bits in an iris code. IEEE TPAMI 31(6), 964–973 (2009)

On the Robustness of Kernel-Based Clustering

Fabio A. González[1], David Bermeo[1], Laura Ramos[1], and Olfa Nasraoui[2]

[1] BioIngenium Research Group, Universidad Nacional de Colombia, Bogotá
[2] Knowledge Discovery & Web Mining Lab, The University of Louisville
{fagonzalezo,jdbermeol,lmramoss}@unal.edu.co,
olfa.nasraoui@louisville.edu

Abstract. This paper evaluates the robustness of two types of unsupervised learning methods, which work in feature spaces induced by a kernel function, kernel k-means and kernel symmetric non-negative matrix factorization. The main hypothesis is that the use of non-linear kernels makes these clustering algorithms more robust to noise and outliers. The hypothesis is corroborated by applying kernel and non-kernel versions of the algorithms to data with different degrees of contamination with noisy data. The results show that the kernel versions of the clustering algorithms are indeed more robust, i.e. producing estimates with lower bias in the presence of noise.

1 Introduction

The presence of noise and outliers are a main source of data quality problems in statistics, data mining and machine learning. Many factors can cause noise and outliers, including errors in measurements, data entry and communication, as well as simple deviation of some data samples. These problems along with assumptions made about data are known to lead to incorrect and biased results. There has been a good amount of work devoted to dealing with noise and outliers. In some approaches, outliers are eliminated from the data as part of the data preprocessing stage. In other approaches, learning and inference algorithms are designed in such a way that they can resist noise and outliers; these algorithms are described as *robust*. *Robust statistics* is a field of statistics that deals with the development of techniques and theories for estimating the model parameters while dealing with deviations from idealized assumptions [7,10].

Data clustering is one of the most important data analysis tools with many applications and a great variety of algorithms. As with other learning algorithms, outliers in the data can result in bad parameter estimation, thus generating bad clusterings. The objective of this paper is to evaluate the robustness of an important type of clustering algorithms, namely those that are based on kernel methods. In particular, we evaluate how clustering algorithms behave when the input data is contaminated with increasing amounts of noisy data. The evaluated algorithms are the conventional versions and kernelized versions of k-means and Symmetric Non-negative Matrix Factorization . Our main hypothesis is that the use of a non-linear kernel may improve the robustness of the algorithm. The preliminary experimental results in this paper confirm this hypothesis, suggesting that kernel-based methods are a viable alternative for performing robust clustering.

L. Alvarez et al. (Eds.): CIARP 2012, LNCS 7441, pp. 122–129, 2012.

The rest of the paper is organized as follows: Section 2 discusses the problem of clustering and how it can be modeled as a matrix factorization problem; Section 3 introduces robust statistics and robust clustering; Section 4 presents the experimental evaluations; and finally, Sections 5 presents our conclusions and future work.

2 Clustering and Matrix Factorization

2.1 Clustering

Clustering is the most important problem in unsupervised learning. In general, the goal of a clustering algorithm is to find groups (called *clusters*) in a set of data samples., such that the clusters are homogeneous, i.e. contain similar data samples, while data samples from different clusters are different. Depending on the type of clustering algorithm, this goal could be accomplished in different ways. In this work we focus on a particular type of clustering algorithms which are based on the optimization of an objective function.

One of the most popular clustering algorithms is k-means., which represents the clusters by a set of centroids $M = \{m_1, \dots . m_k\}$ that minimize the following objective function:

$$SSE = \min_M \sum_{i=1}^{k} \sum_{x \in C_i} (x - m_i)^2 \tag{1}$$

where $\{C_1, \dots, C_k\}$ is a disjunct partition of the input data set X, such that $X = \bigcup_{l=1}^{k} C_l$. The minimization is accomplished by an optimization process that iteratively reassigns data points to clusters, thus refining the centroid estimations.

2.2 Non-negative Matrix Factorization

The general problem of matrix factorization is to decompose a matrix X into two factor matrices A and B :

$$X_{n \times l} = A_{n \times k} B_{k \times l} \tag{2}$$

This could be accomplished by different methods including: Singular Value Decomposition (SVD), Non-negative Matrix Factorization (NMF), and Probabilistic Latent Semantic Analysis, among others. The factorization problem can be formulated as an optimization problem:

$$\min {}_{A,B} d(X, AB) \tag{3}$$

where $d(,)$ is a distance or divergence function and the problem could have different types of restrictions. For instance, if $d(,)$ is the Euclidean Distance and there are no restrictions, the problem is solved by finding the SVD; if X, A and B are restricted to be positive, then the problem is solved by NMF.

This type of factorization may be used to perform clustering. The input data points are the columns of X (l n-dimensional data points). The columns of A correspond to the coordinates of the centroids. The columns of B indicate to which cluster each sample belongs, specifically if x_j belongs to C_i, then $B_{i,j} = 1$, otherwise $B_{i,j} = 0$. With this interpretation, the objective function in (1) is equivalent to the objective function in (3) using the Euclidean distance. An important advantage of this approach is that values in the matrix B are not required to be binary, in fact, they can take continuous values. These values can be interpreted as soft membership values of data samples to clusters, i.e., NMF can produce a soft clustering of the input data [3].

NMF has been shown to be equivalent to other unsupervised learning methods such as probabilistic latent semantic analysis and kernel k-means. Also, there are different versions of NMF which impose new restrictions or weaken some of its restrictions. For instance, Semi-NMF allows negative values in matrices X and A in (3), Convex-NMF imposes that A must be a combination of the data input, $A = XW$ [3]. In this work, we use a particular version of NMF, Symmetric-NMF (SNMF) which produces the following factorization:

$$(X_{lxn}^T X_{nxl}) = H_{lxk} H_{kxl}^T \tag{4}$$

An important characteristic of this version of NMF is that it is amenable to be used as a kernel method. This is discussed in the next subsection.

2.3 Kernel Methods

In contrast with traditional learning techniques, kernel methods do not need a vectorial representation of the data. Instead, they use a kernel function that allows kernel methods to be naturally applied to unstructured or complex structured data such as text, strings, trees and images [12].

Informally, a kernel function measures the similarity of two objects. Formally, a kernel function, $k : X \times X \to \mathbb{R}$, maps pairs (x, y) of objects in a set X, the problem space, to the space of real numbers. A kernel function implicitly generates a map, $\Phi : X \to F$, where F corresponds to a Hilbert space called the feature space. The dot product in F is calculated by k, specifically $k(x, y) = < \Phi(x), \Phi(y) >_F$. Given an appropriate kernel function, complex patterns in the problem space may correspond to simpler patterns in the feature space. For instance, non-linear boundaries in the problem space may be transformed to linear boundaries in the feature space.

Both k-means and SNMF have kernelized versions, which receive as input a kernel matrix instead of a set of data samples represented by feature vectors. The kernel version of k-means is called, unsurprisingly, kernel k-means (KKM). In the case of SNMF, the kernelized version works as follows [3].

SNMF starts with an initial estimation of the factor matrix H and iteratively updates it using the updating equation:

$$H_{i,k} = H_{i,k}(1 - \beta + \beta \frac{((X^T X)H)_{i,k}}{(HH^T H)_{i,k}})$$

The kernel version of the algorithm is obtained by using a kernel matrix K instead of the expression $(X^T X)$, where K is an $l \times l$ matrix with $K_{i,j} = k(x_i, x_j)$. There are different types of kernels, some of them general and some of them specifically defined for different types of data. The most popular general kernels are the linear kernel

$$k(x, y) = < x, y >, \tag{5}$$

the polynomial kernel

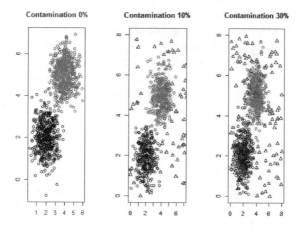

Fig. 1. Example of a data set with two clusters with different degrees of contamination

$$k(x,y) = p(<x,y>),$$

where $p(\ )$ is a polynomial with positive coefficients, and the Gaussian (or RBF) kernel

$$k(x,y) = e^{\frac{\|x-y\|^2}{2\sigma^2}}. \tag{6}$$

The cluster centroids estimated by the kernel versions of both algorithms are in the feature space, resulting from transforming the data via the mapping function Φ, and correspond to the points $C_j = \frac{1}{n}\sum_{x_i \in C_j} \Phi(x_i)$. However, we are interested in the pre-image in the original space of the centroids, i.e., points $\hat{C}_j$ such that $\Phi(\hat{C}_j) = C_j$. However, it is possible that an exact pre-image may not even exist, so we look for the $\hat{C}_j$ that minimizes the following objective function: $\min_{\hat{C}_j} \left\|\hat{C}_j - C_j\right\|^2$. According to Kwok et al. [9], the optimum C_j can be found by iterating the following fixed-point formula:

$$\hat{C}_j^{t+1} = \frac{\sum_{x_i \in C_j} \exp(\frac{-\|\hat{C}_j^t - x_i\|)}{s})x_i}{\sum_{x_i \in C_j} \exp(\frac{-\|\hat{C}_j^t - x_i\|}{s})} \tag{7}$$

3   Robust Clustering

Robust statistics is an area of statistics that deals with the problem of estimating the parameters of a parametric model while dealing with deviations from idealized assumptions [7,10]. These deviations could be caused by contamination of data by outliers, rounding and grouping errors, and departure from an assumed sample distribution. Outliers can cause classical estimators to heavily depart from the actual values of the parameters making them useless. Robust statistics provides theory and techniques to study and develop robust estimators.

In the particular case of clustering, outliers and noise are an important issue that could cause the incorrect detection of clusters, the detection of spurious clusters and a biased estimation of cluster parameters [5]. Figure 1 shows an example of a data set with two clusters and different degrees of contamination. It is important to notice that, in general, the source of contamination is not known, so it is difficult to make assumptions about the type of distribution or distribution parameters. A robust clustering algorithm is one that is able to deal with contaminated data in such a way that its estimations are not affected by the presence of contaminated data. There are different types clustering strategies, but in this work, we concentrate on partitional, prototype based methods such as k-means. In this case, clusters are characterized by centroids, which are in fact location estimators. A robust estimation of cluster centroids requires that the value of the estimation be affected as little as possible by the presence of contaminated data. Robust statistics provides different methods to measure the robustness of an estimator [8], such as the breakdown point, influence function and sensitivity curve. The goal is to measure how an estimator behaves with different proportions and values of contamination. In many cases, this analysis is performed assuming the worst conditions, such as using asymptotic analysis when the value of the contamination tends to infinity. But these extreme conditions are neither acceptable nor possible in most engineering applications [2]. In this work, and following [2], we assume a bounded contamination and perform a non-asymptotic analysis. The contamination model is given by

$$F = (1 - \varepsilon)G + \varepsilon E, \tag{8}$$

where G is the distribution of real, uncontaminated samples, E is the distribution of contaminated data and F is the overall sample distribution. The effect of contamination in the data is measured by the bias of the estimation:

$$\text{bias}(\hat{\Theta}, X) = \left\| \Theta - \hat{\Theta}(X) \right\|, \tag{9}$$

where Θ are the real parameters of G, X is a sample generated using the model in Eq. (8), $\hat{\Theta}$ is a estimator function and $\|\cdot\|$ is an appropriate norm. In this work, $\Theta = (C_1, \ldots, C_k)$ with $C_i \in \mathbb{R}^n$, the centroid of the i-th cluster, and $\|\cdot\|$ is the Euclidean norm.

Different robust estimators, for both location and scale, have been proposed. In the case of clustering, the development of robust methods has been studied since the nineties. Some of the representative works include: trimmed k-means [1], robust fuzzy clustering methods [11,2] and minimum covariance determinant estimator [6]. Interestingly, there has not been, to our knowledge, any work that explored the robustness of kernel-based clustering methods. While some works proposed kernel-based clustering methods that could be considered robust, their focus was not to study the robustness gained by the use of particular kernels but rather the implementation of certain robust strategies, e.g. minimum volume covering ellipsoid estimation[4], using kernel methods. The present work studies how the use of appropriate kernels provides a conventional clustering method, such a k-means, with robust properties.

4   Experimental Evaluation

The goal of the experimental evaluation is to study the influence of a popular non-linear kernel, the Gaussian kernel, in two kernel-based clustering algorithms. Both algorithms are applied to two data sets (one synthetic and one real) with different degrees of contamination. Two kernels are used: an identity kernel and a Gaussian kernel. The main hypothesis is that the Gaussian kernel makes the algorithms more resilient to contamination. The performance of the algorithms is evaluated by measuring the bias (Eq. (9)) and evaluating how it behaves when the amount of contamination is increased.

4.1 Datasets

Two datasets were used: a synthetic dataset and the real *iris flower* dataset. The synthetic dataset has 150 samples from a mixture of three multivariate Gaussians in $\mathbb{R}^4$, each Gaussian having a different mean and covariance matrix. The iris flower data set is a multivariate dataset that has been widely used in statistics and data mining. Each sample in the dataset corresponds to a flower characterized by four numerical features and a categorical attribute that indicates the species of the flower.

4.2 Experimental Setup

Both data sets are contaminated by adding a set of samples generated from a multivariate uniform distribution with a support that includes the range of the corresponding data set features. Different percentages of contamination are used: 0%, 5%, 10%, 15%, 20%, 25% and 30%. For instance, a data set with a ~30% of contamination is a dataset with 214 samples, 150 corresponding to the original samples and 64 corresponding to contamination. For each algorithm, two types of kernels are used: the identity kernel (Eq. (5)) and the Gaussian kernel (Eq. (6)). For the Gaussian kernel, different values of σ were tested following a logarithmic scale, $\sigma = 2^i$ for $i \in [-5, \dots, 5]$. Each algorithm configuration was run 10 times and the average bias is reported. The bias is calculated using Eq. (9), where $\hat{\Theta}(X)$ correspond to the cluster centroids estimated by each algorithm and, in the case of the configurations with the Gaussian kernel, are back-projected to the original space using Eq. (7).

4.3 Results and Discussion

Figures 2 and 3 show the evolution of the bias when the percentage of contamination increases, for both methods and for different kernels. Figures 2(a) and 3(a) show the results for KKM with three different kernels: linear kernel (equivalent to conventional k-means), Gaussian kernel with $\sigma = 2^{-2}$, and Gaussian kernel with $\sigma = 2^4$. In the case of the Gaussian kernel, a systematic evaluation of different values for the parameter σ was performed and the best performing value ($\sigma = 2^{-2}$) and an average performing value ($\sigma = 2^4$) are reported. Figures 2(b) and 3(b) show the corresponding results for SNMF, with the linear kernel corresponding to the conventional (non-kernelized) version.

For both algorithms, the worst performance is exhibited by the linear kernel, and the best performance is accomplished by the Gaussian kernel with $\sigma = 2^{-2}$. These results confirm the hypothesis that the use of a Gaussian kernel makes both algorithms more robust and resilient to noise and outliers. Also, it is clear that the robustness that is induced by the Gaussian kernel depends on the parameter σ. This parameter is related to the scale of the data and the results indicate that an appropriate identification of the scale has an important effect on the method's robustness.

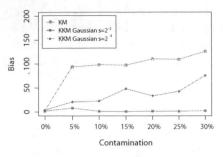 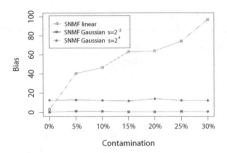

Fig. 2. Bias vs contamination in the Iris dataset using (left) K-Means (KM), Kernel K-Means (KKM) and (right) kernel Symmetric Non-negative Matrix Factorization (SNMF)

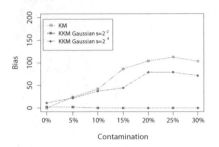 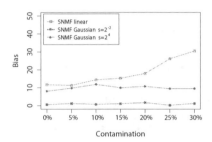

Fig. 3. Bias vs contamination in the synthetic dataset using (left) K-Means (KM), Kernel K-Means (KKM) and (right) kernel Symmetric Non-negative Matrix Factorization (SNMF)

The results also show that SNMF has a better performance, in terms of robustness, than KKM. A possible explanation is the fact that SNMF produces a soft clustering in contrast with the hard clustering produced by KKM. In fact, Davé et al. [2] found a connection between fuzzy membership functions and weight functions used in robust statistics.

5   Conclusions and Future Work

The main hypothesis of this work is that the robustness of kernel-based clustering methods is increased by the use of Gaussian kernels. The results of the exploratory experiments performed in this paper provide evidence to support this claim. Kernel methods are popular and well regarded machine learning methods thanks to their ability to learn complex non-linear models. This ability is due, in part, to the kernel trick, which allows finding non-linear patterns in the original problem space by learning linear patterns in a kernel-induced higher-dimensional space. The results of this study suggest an additional correspondence with useful applications: non-robust estimation in a Gaussian kernel-induced space corresponds to robust estimation in the original problem space.

The main question posed by our findings is why the use of the Gaussian kernel makes the corresponding algorithms more robust to noise and outliers. Our conjecture is that back-projection (Eq. 7) of a mean value from a Gaussian kernel-induced feature space can be considered as a robust W-estimator [10]. A deeper study of this conjecture is part of our future work.

Acknowledgements. This work was partially funded by the project "Sistema para la Recuperación de Imágenes Médicas utilizando Indexación Multimodal" number 110152128767. Part of this work was carried out while the first author was visiting the KD&WM Lab at the U of Louisville supported by the Fulbright Visiting Scholar Fellowship.

References

1. Cuesta-Albertos, J.A., Gordaliza, A., Matran, C.: Trimmed k-Means: An Attempt to Robustify Quantizers. The Annals of Statistics 25(2), 553–576 (1997)
2. Davé, R.N., Krishnapuram, R.: Robust clustering methods: a unified view. IEEE Transactions on Fuzzy Systems 5(2), 270–293 (1997)
3. Ding, C., Li, T., Jordan, M.I.: Convex and Semi-Nonnegative Matrix Factorizations. IEEE Transactions on Pattern Analysis and Machine Intelligence 32(1), 45–55 (2010)
4. Dolia, A., Harris, C., Shawetaylor, J., Titterington, D.: Kernel ellipsoidal trimming. Computational Statistics & Data Analysis 52(1), 309–324 (2007)
5. García-Escudero, L.A., Gordaliza, A., Matrán, C., Mayo-Iscar, A.: A review of robust clustering methods. Advances in Data Analysis and Classification 4(2-3), 89–109 (2010)
6. Hardin, J., Rocke, D.M.: Outlier detection in the multiple cluster setting using the minimum covariance determinant estimator. Computational Statistics & Data Analysis 44(4), 625–638 (2004)
7. Huber, P.J.: Robust Statistics. Wiley Series in Probability and Statistics. John Wiley & Sons, Inc., Hoboken (1981)
8. Hubert, M., Rousseeuw, P.J., Van Aelst, S.: High-Breakdown Robust Multivariate Methods. Statistical Science 23(1), 92–119 (2008)
9. Kwok, J.T.Y., Tsang, I.W.H.: The pre-image problem in kernel methods, vol. 15, pp. 1517–1525. IEEE (2004)
10. Maronna, R.A., Martin, R.D., Yohai, V.J.: Robust statistics. Wiley (2006)
11. Nasraoui, O., Krishnapuram, R.: A robust estimator based on density and scale optimization and its application to clustering. In: Proceedings of the Fifth IEEE International Conference on Fuzzy Systems, vol. 2, pp. 1031–1035. IEEE (1996)
12. Shawe-Taylor, J., Cristianini, N.: Kernel Methods for Pattern Analysis. Cambridge University Press, Cambridge (2004)

An Improved Multi-Class Spectral Clustering Based on Normalized Cuts

Diego Hernán Peluffo-Ordóñez, Carlos Daniel Acosta-Medina,
and César Germáan Castellanos-Domínguez

Signal Processing and Recognition Group, Universidad Nacional de Colombia,
Km. 9, Vía al aeropuerto, Campus la Nubia, Caldas, Manizales, Colombia
{dhpeluffoo,cdacostam,cgcastellanosd}@unal.edu.co

Abstract. In this work, we present an improved multi-class spectral clustering (MCSC) that represents an alternative to the standard k-way normalized clustering, avoiding the use of an iterative algorithm for tuning the orthogonal matrix rotation. The performance of proposed method is compared with the conventional MCSC and k-means in terms of different clustering quality indicators. Results are accomplished on commonly used toy data sets with hardly separable classes, as well as on an image segmentation database. In addition, as a clustering indicator, a novel unsupervised measure is introduced to quantify the performance of the proposed method. The proposed method spends lower processing time than conventional spectral clustering approaches.

1 Introduction

Spectral clustering has taken an important place within the context of pattern recognition, mainly, because this technique represents a very suitable alternative to solve problems when data are not labeled and classes are hardly separable. Derived from the normalized cuts-based clustering, described in detail in [1], many enhancing approaches have been proposed. For instance, kernel-based methods employing support vector machines (SVM) are discussed in [2–4], and methods with improved affinity or similarity matrices, proposed in [5]. Spectral clustering technique has been successfully applied in several applications such as image segmentation [6, 7] and has shown to be a powerful tool to determine information about initial data, namely, estimation of the group number [5, 8] and local scaling [9]. Commonly, the application of spectral clustering methods involves the determination of a new representation space, whose resultant dimension is lower than that from original data, and then a dimensionality reduction procedure should be accomplished. In that way, the relation among elements are conserved as well as possible. Thus, eigenvectors and eigenvalues based analysis takes place. This is because the information given by eigen-space (i.e, space generated by eigenvectors) is directly associated with the clustering quality. The computation of such eigen-space is usually a high time consuming computational procedure. Therefore, a computation of spectral clustering method with reasonable computational load, but keeping high clustering performance still remains an open issue.

In this work, an improved alternative to conventional k-way normalized cuts-based clustering is presented, which improves the computational cost avoiding the iterative

L. Alvarez et al. (Eds.): CIARP 2012, LNCS 7441, pp. 130–137, 2012.

search for tuning. Improved method also provides a better estimation of the initial parameter from the information given by the proposed solution. We solve the classical problem of spectral clustering without using any heuristical searching approach, instead, we accomplish a deterministic solution by means of solving an equation matrix of the form $ARB = C$, as discussed in [10]. This equation allows to determine the rotation matrix R, which generates an infinite number of solutions and is then chosen as that shows better convergence. Solving such equation matrix yields a solution that satisfies the condition given by the objective function but not the orthogonality condition. Therefore, we introduce a regularized form in order to obtain an orthonormal feasible solution. For assessing the performance of proposed method, we carry out experiments on toy data sets as well as the Berkeley Segmentation Dataset [11] to evaluate our method in terms of segmentation. As a clustering performance measure, we apply the total clustering performance taking advantage of the labels and segmented reference images and introduce an unsupervised measure that takes into consideration the quality clustering in terms of spectral information. Also, we include stages for estimating the number of groups and computing the affinity matrix as described in [5]. We compared our method with a conventional K-means and a K-way normalized-based clustering, as explained in [1].

2 Clustering Method

2.1 Multi-Class Spectral Clustering (MCSC)

A weighted graph can be represented as $\mathbb{G} = (\mathbb{V}, \mathbb{E}, W)$, where $\mathbb{V}$ is the set of either nodes or vertices, $\mathbb{E}$ is the edge set, and W represents the relationship among nodes, named, *affinity matrix*. Given that, each affinity matrix entry w_{ij} of $W \in \mathbb{R}^{N \times N}$ represents the weight of the edge between i-th and j-th element, it must be a non-negative value. Value N is the number of considered nodes. In addition, for a non-directed graph, it holds that $w_{ij} = w_{ji}$. Therefore, affinity matrix must be chosen as symmetric and positive semi-definite. After clustering procedure, a binary indicator matrix $M = [m_1| \dots |m_K]$ is accomplished, where each vector set m_k is a column vector formed by data point membership regarding cluster $k = 1, \dots, K$ and K is the number of groups. Each entry ik from the $N \times K$ dimensional matrix M is defined as $m_{ik} = \lfloor i \in \mathbb{V}_k \rfloor$, $i \in \mathbb{V}$, $k = 1, \dots, K$, where notation $\lfloor \cdot \rfloor$ stands for a binary indicator - it equals to 1 if its argument is true and, otherwise, 0. Also, because each node can only belong into one partition, the condition $M1_K = 1_N$ must be satisfied, where 1_d is a d-dimensional ones vector.

Then, the well-known k-way normalized cuts-based clustering, described in [1], can be written as:

$$\max \varepsilon(M) = \frac{1}{K} \frac{\operatorname{tr}(M^\top W M)}{\operatorname{tr}(M^\top D M)} \tag{1a}$$

$$\text{s. t.:} M \in \{0,1\}^{N \times K}, \quad M1_K = 1_N \tag{1b}$$

where $D = \operatorname{Diag}(W 1_N)$ is the degree matrix related to weights or affinity matrix. Notation $\operatorname{Diag}(\cdot)$ denotes a diagonal matrix formed by its argument vector. Expressions (1a) and (1b) are the formulation of normalized cuts optimization problem, named (*NCPM*).

In order to guarantee that M becomes binary it is needed that $||M||_F^2 = \mathrm{tr}(M^\top M) = \mathrm{tr}(E) = n$, where $E = \mathrm{Diag}(\sum_{i=1}^{n} m_{i1}, \cdots, \sum_{i=1}^{n} m_{iK})$. Therefore, the *NCPM* optimization problem can be expressed as:

$$\max \varepsilon(M) = \mathrm{tr}(M^\top W M) \quad \text{s. t.:} \quad \mathrm{tr}(M^\top D M) = \text{const.,} \quad M1_K = 1_N \quad (2)$$

2.2 Proposed *NCPM* Solution Based on an One Iteration Tuning

The *NCPM* optimization problem can be relaxed as follows. Let $P = D^{-1/2} W D^{-1/2}$ be a normalized affinity matrix. Then, a relaxed *NCPM* version can be expressed as:

$$\max \mathrm{tr}(L^\top P L), \quad \text{s. t.} \quad L^\top L = I_K \quad (3)$$

where $L = D^{-1/2} M$.

A feasible solution to this problem is $L^* = V_K R$, where V_K is any orthonormal basis of the K-dimensional principal subspace of P, and R is an arbitrary rotation matrix. At the end, a binarization process must be applied, e.g., by employing the sign function. Thus, there exists an infinite number of solutions. To overcome this issue with the aim to reach a deterministic solution without using an iterative algorithm, the following mathematical development is done.

According to the constraint given in (1b), we have:

$$M1_K = D^{1/2} L1_K = D^{1/2} V_K R1_K = 1_N \quad (4)$$

Therefore, a possible rotation matrix R can be chosen as $R = 1/k^2 V_K^\top D^{-1/2} 1_N 1_K^\top$. Yet, the previous solution do not satisfy the orthonormal condition given by (3), since it holds that $R^\top R = \frac{K}{N} D^{-1} \neq I_K$, and thus, $R^\top \neq R^{-1}$. So, as a way to avoid this drawback, a constrained optimization problem is introduced:

$$\min ||V_K R1_K - D^{-1/2} 1_N||_F^2, \quad \text{s. t.} \ R^\top R = I_K \quad (5)$$

where $|| \cdot ||_F$ stands for Frobenius norm.

For the sake of simplicity, let us define $A = V_K$, $B = 1_K$, $C = D^{-1/2}$. Also, we introduce a regularized orthonormal matrix $\widehat{R} = R + \alpha I_K$ to be determined that guarantees the orthogonality condition. Then, the optimization problem is rewritten as:

$$\min ||A\widehat{R}B - C||_F^2, \quad \text{s. t.} \ \widehat{R}^\top \widehat{R} = I_K \ \therefore \ ||\widehat{R}^\top \widehat{R} - I_K||_F^2 = 0 \quad (6)$$

By only considering the objective function to be minimized, the two following solutions are possible [10]: $\mathrm{vec}(R) = [B^\top \otimes A]^\dagger \mathrm{vec}(C)$ where $B^\dagger$ represents the pseudo-inverse matrix of B, and a real non-negative definite solution.

The latter solution, in its easiest form, is given by $R = A^- C B^- + Y - A^- AY BB^-$ requiring that the *Ben-Israel and Geville* condition be satisfied [12], where the $K \times K$ dimensional matrix Y is arbitrary and A^- denotes the inner inverse of A, such that $AA^- A = A$. Moreover, both solutions turn out to be no orthogonal and cannot be directly applied. Then, the *Gram-Schmidt* orthogonalization procedure is, perhaps, the most intuitive solution. But, despite the orthogonal condition be satisfied, however, the original problem remains unsolved, i.e, there is no a solution that satisfies the relaxed problem. Instead, we propose a solution based on Lagrange multipliers, as follows.

The Lagrangian corresponding to the problem (6) is written as follows:

$$\mathcal{L}(\boldsymbol{\lambda}, \boldsymbol{R}) = f(\alpha, \boldsymbol{R}) + \sum_{k=1}^{K} \lambda_k g_k(\alpha, \boldsymbol{R}) \tag{7}$$

where

$$f(\alpha, \boldsymbol{R}) = \text{tr}\left((A\widehat{\boldsymbol{R}}B - C)^{\top}(A\widehat{\boldsymbol{R}}B - C)\right)$$

$$\sum_{k=1}^{K} \lambda_k g_k(\alpha, \boldsymbol{R}) = \text{tr}\left((\boldsymbol{R}^{\top}\boldsymbol{R} - \boldsymbol{I}_K)^{\top}(\boldsymbol{R}^{\top}\boldsymbol{R} - \boldsymbol{I}_K)\boldsymbol{\Delta}\right)$$

Then, by solving $\frac{\partial f}{\partial \boldsymbol{R}} = 0$ and $\frac{\partial \sum_{k=1}^{K} \lambda_k g_k(\alpha, \boldsymbol{R})}{\partial \boldsymbol{R}} = \text{tr}(\frac{\partial f}{\partial \boldsymbol{R}})$, we obtain:

$$\boldsymbol{R} = 2\alpha A^{\top} C B^{\dagger} - \boldsymbol{I}_K \tag{8a}$$

$$\boldsymbol{\lambda} = \frac{1}{2} \text{diag}\left((\boldsymbol{R} + (\alpha - 1)\boldsymbol{I}_K)^{-1} \frac{\partial f}{\partial \boldsymbol{R}}\right) \tag{8b}$$

where $\boldsymbol{\Delta} = \text{Diag}(\boldsymbol{\lambda})$, $B^{\dagger}$ denotes the pseudo-inverse matrix of B and $\boldsymbol{\lambda}$ is the vector of Lagrange multipliers. At the end, a continuous estimation of matrix $\boldsymbol{M}$ can be written as $\widehat{\boldsymbol{M}} = D^{1/2}L - D^{1/2}V_K\widehat{\boldsymbol{R}}$, which is further binarized to determine the initial clustering problem solution $\boldsymbol{M}$. Parameter α is chosen at the minimal point of $\mathcal{L}$, i.e., where both f and g are minimum.

3   Experimental Setup

Experiments are carried out on two well-known database collections: Firstly, a toy data comprising the following several data sets (Swiss-roll, weird roll, fishbowl, and S-3D) shown in upper row of Fig. 1). Secondly, an image collection extracted from the free access Berkeley Segmentation Dataset [11]. In this work, we considered the first 100 train images from 2092 until 66039 (in ascendant order). In bottom row of Fig. 1, some samples from image database are shown. All considered images are size scaled at 20% and characterized per pixel by means of standard and normalized RGB color space, and XY position. Estimation of the number of groups, k, is based on calculation of the eigenvector set of the affinity matrix. In particular, the scaled exponential affinity matrix $\boldsymbol{W} = \{w_{ij}\}$ is employed that holds elements defined as follows [5]:

$$w_{ij} = \begin{cases} \exp(-\frac{\mathrm{d}^2(\boldsymbol{x}_i, \boldsymbol{x}_j)}{\sigma_i \sigma_j}), & i \neq j \\ 0, & i = j \end{cases} \tag{9}$$

where $\boldsymbol{X} \in \Re^{N \times p} = (\boldsymbol{x}_1^{\top}, \ldots, \boldsymbol{x}_n^{\top})^{\top}$ is the data matrix to be clustered, $\boldsymbol{x}_i \in \Re^p$ is its corresponding i-th data point, $\sigma_i = \mathrm{d}(\boldsymbol{x}_i, \boldsymbol{x}_n)$, $\boldsymbol{x}_n$ denotes the n-th nearest neighbor, and $d(\cdot, \cdot)$ stands for Euclidean distance. The value of n is experimentally set to be 7.

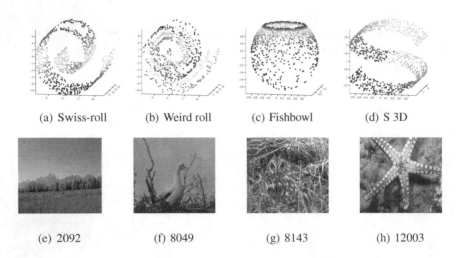

|(a) Swiss-roll | (b) Weird roll | (c) Fishbowl | (d) S 3D |

| (e) 2092 | (f) 8049 | (g) 8143 | (h) 12003 |

Fig. 1. Employed database collections for testing of discussed approach of multi-class spectral clustering. In upper row, exemplary of toy data comprising data sets (Swiss-roll, weird roll, fishbowl, and S-3D). In the bottom row, some numbered samples of image database.

Performance of discussed method is assessed by means of three considered clustering indicators: clustering performance, estimated number of groups, and the introduced cluster coherence as an unsupervised measure. The last measure is inferred from the optimization problem given in (1a), and its maximal value is 1, due to its normalization with respect to the affinity matrix degree. Then, after selecting a proper affinity matrix, cluster coherence measure indicates an adequate clustering whenever its value is close to 1. In addition, because of its descent monotonicity property, this measure automatically penalizes the group number. Table 1 shows the clustering performance measures with their description.

Table 1. Applied performance measures

Measure	Description
Clustering performance CP	Complement of standard error (e). $CP = 100 - e$
Cluster coherence ε_M	It is near to 1 when clustering is properly done. $\varepsilon_M = \dfrac{1}{k} \sum_{l=1}^{k} \dfrac{M_l^\mathsf{T} W M_l}{M_l^\mathsf{T} D M_l}$
Estimated number of groups ($\hat{k}$)	Eigenvectors-based estimation [5]

Lastly, testing within experimental framework is carried out by employing MATLAB Version 7.10.0.499 (R2010a) in a standard PC Intel(R) Core 2 Quad 2.8 GHz and 4 Gb RAM memory.

4   Results and Discussion

Table 2 shows the numerical results obtained for both toy data sets and image database. In general, we can note that the MCSC works significantly better than the conventional partitional clustering, showing the benefit of the spectral methods when clusters are not linearly separable. This fact can be appreciated in Fig. 2.

Table 2. Results for toy data sets

Method	Toy data sets			Image database		
	CP $(\mu - \sigma)$	ε_M $(\mu - \sigma)$	$\hat{k}$ $(\mu - \sigma)$	CP $(\mu - \sigma)$	ε_M $(\mu - \sigma)$	$\hat{k}$ $(\mu - \sigma)$
K-means	$63.25 - 9.07$	$0.58 - 0.13$		$59.25 - 10.55$	$0.54 - 0.09$	
MCSC	$89.50 - 4.21$	$0.86 - 0.05$	$5 - 0.47$	$68.62 - 6.51$	$0.76 - 0.02$	$8 - 0.75$
Improved MCSC	$89.50 - 3.67$	$0.90 - 0.02$		$70.37 - 8.09$	$0.78 - 0.04$	

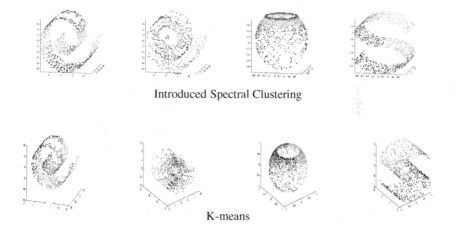

Introduced Spectral Clustering

K-means

Fig. 2. Clustering results after testing of considered databases

Then, for some applications it might be of benefit to increase the computational burden to improve significatively the performance. Nonetheless, to overcome this issue, we introduce a free iterative algorithm approach, in which instead of applying a complex or time-consuming procedures, we only need to determine parameter α for calculating the indicator binary matrix. Therefore, required time for estimating α becomes considerably lower than that one needed to binarize the clustering solution iteratively, as shown in Fig. 3. Computational time reduces since tuning of parameter α is, mostly, carried out by means of an heuristic search having inexpensive computational burden. In contrast, the conventional MCSC involves calculation of eigenvalues and eigenvector per iteration; both procedures being high time consuming.

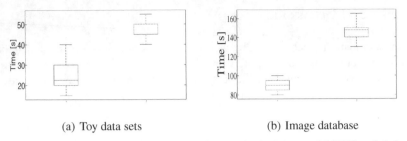

(a) Toy data sets   (b) Image database

Fig. 3. Box plots of time employed for clustering methods. Improved MCSC at left hand and classical MCSC at right hand.

For the Swiss-roll toy data set, Fig. 4 shows the penalization effect of measure ε_M when varying the group number. Testing is carried out computing the value ε_M for 10 iterations of the whole clustering procedure. As seen, the error bar corresponding to conventional is higher that the error achieved for the proposed MCSC method.

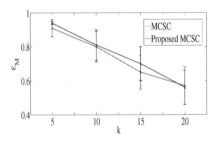

Fig. 4. Error bar comparing ε_M with the group number

5   Conclusions

This work introduces an improved multi-class spectral clustering method that is based on normalized cuts. Performance of discussed method is assessed by means of three considered clustering indicators: clustering performance, estimated number of groups, and the introduced cluster coherence. In terms of considered clustering indicators, the improved multi-class spectral clustering method exhibits a similar performance for tested databases including not linearly separable classes, because it employs the spectral information given by data and their transformations. Nonetheless, discussed method overperforms the conventional spectral methods, in terms of computational burden, since tuning of parameter α is, mostly, carried out by means of an heuristical search having inexpensive computational burden. In contrast, the conventional MCSC involves calculation of eigenvalues and eigenvector per iteration; both procedures being high time consuming.

Also, we introduced a non-supervised measure, associated with cluster coherence, that is inferred from a partition criterion, which showed to be a proper performance index. The cluster coherence measure, automatically, penalizes the number of groups and generates a value close to 1, whenever the grouping is rightly performed and the affinity matrix is properly chosen.

As a future work, another properties of spectral clustering algorithms should be explored to develop a method less sensitive to initialization, which enhances the trade-off between performance and computational cost. Such method should include proper initialization, estimation of number of groups, feature selection and grouping stages based on spectral analysis.

Acknowledgments. This research is carried out within the projects: "Beca para estudiantes sobresalientes de posgrado de la Universidad Nacional de Colombia" and "Programa de financiación para Doctorados Nacionales de Colciencias".

References

1. Yu, S.X., Jianbo, S.: Multiclass spectral clustering. In: ICCV 2003: Proceedings of the Ninth IEEE International Conference on Computer Vision, p. 313. IEEE Computer Society, Washington, DC (2003)
2. Alzate, C., Suykens, J.A.K.: Multiway spectral clustering with out-of-sample extensions through weighted kernel pca. IEEE Transactions on Pattern Analysis and Machine Intelligence 32(2), 335–347 (2010)
3. Suykens, J.A.K., Alzate, C., Pelckmans, K.: Primal and dual model representations in kernel-based learning. Statistics Surveys 4, 148–183 (2010)
4. Dhillon, I., Guan, Y., Kulis, B.: Kernel k-means: spectral clustering and normalized cuts. In: Proceedings of the tenth ACM SIGKDD International Conference on Knowledge Discovery and Data Mining, pp. 551–556. ACM (2004)
5. Zelnik-manor, L., Perona, P.: Self-tuning spectral clustering. In: Advances in Neural Information Processing Systems 17, pp. 1601–1608. MIT Press (2004)
6. O'Callaghan, R.J., Bull, D.R.: Combined morphological-spectral unsupervised image segmentation. IEEE Transactions on Image Processing 14(1), 49–62 (2005)
7. Tung, F., Wong, A., Clausi, D.A.: Enabling scalable spectral clustering for image segmentation. Pattern Recognition 43(12), 4069–4076 (2010)
8. Lee, S., Hayes, M.: Properties of the singular value decomposition for efficient data clustering. IEEE Signal Processing Letters 11(11), 862–866 (2004), doi:10.1109/LSP.2004.833513
9. Álvarez-Meza, A., Valencia-Aguirre, J., Daza-Santacoloma, G., Castellanos-Domínguez, G.: Global and local choice of the number of nearest neighbors in locally linear embedding. Pattern Recognition Letters 32(16), 2171–2177 (2011)
10. Cvetkovic-Ilic, D.S.: Re-nnd solutions of the matrix equation AXB= C. Journal of the Australian Mathematical Society 84(1), 63–72 (2008)
11. Martin, D., Fowlkes, C., Tal, D., Malik, J.: A database of human segmented natural images and its application to evaluating segmentation algorithms and measuring ecological statistics. In: Proc. 8th Int'l Conf. Computer Vision, vol. 2, pp. 416–423 (July 2001)
12. Ben-Israel, A., Greville, T.N.E.: Generalized inverses: theory and applications, vol. 15. Springer (2003)

A Simple Hybrid Method
for Semi-Supervised Learning

Hernán C. Ahumada[1,2,*] and Pablo M. Granitto[1]

[1] CIFASIS, French Argentine International Center for Information and Systems
Sciences, UPCAM, France / UNR-CONICET, Argentina
Bv. 27 de Febrero 210 Bis, 2000, Rosario, Argentina
[2] Facultad de Tecnología y Ciencias Aplicadas - Universidad Nacional de Catamarca
Maximio Victoria 55, 4700, Catamarca, Argentina
{ahumada,granitto}@cifasis-conicet.gov.ar

Abstract. We introduce and describe the Hybrid Semi-Supervised Method (HSSM) for learning. This is the first hybrid method aimed to solve problems with both labeled and unlabeled data. The new method uses an unsupervised stage in order to decompose the full problem into a set of simpler subproblems. HSSM applies simple stopping criteria during the unsupervised stage, which allows the method to concentrate on the difficult portions of the original problem. The new algorithm also makes use of a simple strategy to select at each subproblem a small subset of unlabeled samples that are relevant to modify the decision surface. To this end, HSSM trains a linear SVM on the available labeled samples, and selects the unlabeled samples that lie within the margin of the trained SVM. We evaluated the new method using a previously introduced setup, which includes datasets with very different properties. Overall, the error levels produced by the new HSSM are similar to other SSL methods, but HSSM is shown to be more efficient than all previous methods, using only a small fraction of the available unlabeled data.

Keywords: Semi-supervised learning, Hybrid methods, Classification.

1 Introduction

Semi-supervised learning (SSL) is a learning paradigm that recently has gained interest by researchers [3]. The main feature of SSL is its ability to use a few labeled examples together with many unlabeled examples. SSL has a high practical value in many real world applications where giving a label to an example is an expensive and consuming time task [14].

The goal of SSL methods is to improve the performance with respect to supervised methods when labeled data is scarce or expensive [14]. However, SSL methods usually need a large number of unlabeled examples to obtain similar or better results than supervised methods. Therefore, SSL methods are normally

---

* Author to whom all correspondence should be addressed. Authors acknowledge grant support from ANPCyT PICT 237.

L. Alvarez et al. (Eds.): CIARP 2012, LNCS 7441, pp. 138–145, 2012.

used on large datasets, which implies a high computational cost. Another problem, remarked by Singh et al. [12], is the fact that in many cases the addition of unlabeled examples is counterproductive to the learning process.

In this work we introduce a hybrid strategy for semi-supervised binary classification problems, which combines unsupervised, supervised and semi-supervised learning stages. This new strategy aims at dividing the dataset in many subproblems and then, in a smart way, choosing those unlabeled examples that are more relevant to the generation of the hypothesis. We evaluate the effectiveness and efficiency of the new method over some datasets proposed by Chapelle et al. [3] as a benchmark set for semi-supervised methods.

The rest of the paper is organized as follows. In the next section we shortly review previous works on semi-supervised problems. In Section 3 we introduce the HSSM method, which we evaluate in Section 4. Finally, in Section 5 we discuss the results and future lines of research.

2 Related Works

Semi-supervised methods can be divided in generative, graph based models and low density separation [14]. Generative methods try to model directly the probability density function that generated the data. They use the unlabeled examples to extract information that can help to find the best parameters for this task. Graph based methods build a graph whose nodes are the examples (with and without label) and whose arcs have weights proportional to the similarity among them. The idea of such methods is to spread labels from labeled nodes (examples) to nearby unknown label nodes [2]. Low density separation methods use unlabeled examples to find regions of low density, in which they place the decision surface [10,8]. Joachims [9] introduced one of the best known methods in this area, the semi-supervised support vector machine (S3VM), which seeks to maximize the margin of the solution considering both labeled and unlabeled examples. To this end, the method evaluates different assignments of labels to the unlabeled examples. Published methods differ in their strategy to assign the labels and to find the minimum of the cost function, including SVM-light [9], Branch and Bound [4] or the Low Density Separation (LDS) method [5].

Even if some semi-supervised methods can cope with big datasets, there are good reasons to select a reduced set of relevant unlabeled samples to use in SSL: accuracy and efficiency [11]. For example, Delalleau et al. [7] propose to start only with the supervised set, and to add unlabeled samples that are far away from each other, in order to cover the manifold in a uniform way. Then, in a second step, they propose to discard samples that are far away from the decision surface and to replace them with samples near the border. Li and Zhou [11] discuss the problem of the decrease in accuracy from a supervised method to a SSL method that can be observed in same datasets. Rather than selecting the unlabeled data used for training, their method selects the samples that will be predicted with the SSL classifier, switching to a simpler supervised method when appropriate.

HSSM

Input:
  D^l : The set of labeled samples.
  D^u : The set of unlabeled samples.
  $Cl()$: A clustering algorithm.
  $DF_{sup}()$: A classifier.
  $DF_{ssl}()$: A SSL method.
  $SC()$: A stopping criteria.
  $IS()$: An unlabeled samples selection function.

Function HSSM($D^l, D^u, Cl, DF_{sup}, DF_{ssl}, SC, IS$):
  1. Apply $Cl()$ to $D^l \cup D^u$ to create $(D^l \cup D^u)_1$ and $(D^l \cup D^u)_2$
  2. For $i = 1$ to 2:
      IF SC(D_i^l, D_i^u) THEN
          Train a classifier $DF_{sup}(D_i^l)$
          Apply $IS(D_i^u, DF_{sup})$ to produce S_i^u
          Train a SSL $DF_{ssl}(D_i^l, S_i^u)$
      ELSE
          Call $HSSM(D_i^l, D_i^u, Cl, DF_{sup}, DF_{ssl}, SC, IS)$:

Fig. 1. The pseudocode of HSSM

Ahumada et al. [1] proposed the use of a hybrid method to solve multiclass problems. The method has two steps, first it uses a clustering algorithm to construct a hierarchy of easier subproblems, and then it trains several SVMs to solve each individual subproblem. The authors claim that the clustering stage produce several easy-to-solve problems, including a high number of clusters containing only one class. To the best of our knowledge there are no applications of this kind of hybrid methods to SSL.

3   The Hybrid Semi-Supervised Method

The new Hybrid Semi-Supervised Method (HSSM) is a hybrid combination of unsupervised, supervised and semi-supervised methods. As with other hybrid methods [1], the objective is to decompose the original problem into a set of smaller and simpler subproblems, that can be solved more efficiently than the original problem. Also, when faced with a semi-supervised subproblem, the method uses a new simple strategy to select a subset of all the available unlabeled data.

Figure 1 shows the pseudocode of HSSM. The method is a recursion that builds an unsupervised decision tree. It starts by applying a given clustering method to all the input data (labeled and unlabeled samples together) in order to find two clusters. Then the method checks each cluster against the Stopping criteria. If the criteria is met, then the node is considered a leaf and the method fits a classifier to that cluster. In the opposite case the method is called in a recursive way on the corresponding cluster.

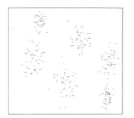  

Fig. 2. HSSM on an artificial problem. Left panel shows the partially labeled training set, center panel shows the clustering solution produced by the method and the right panel shows the classification output.

Any clustering algorithm can be used to create the hierarchy. For example, a partitioning method can be called at each recursion step to produce two clusters, or a hierarchical method can be used to build the complete hierarchy with a single call. In this work we use two well-known methods [13]: Average Linkage (AL) and Single Linkage (SL). In both cases the clustering method produces the complete hierarchy in an agglomerative way, thus in practice the HSSM method descends the tree checking where to prune according to the stopping criteria, and then replacing nodes with leaves (classifiers).

We used three simple conditions as stopping criteria. First, the division process is stopped if the "father node" has labeled samples from both classes but both "children nodes" have labeled samples from only one class. In this case it is highly probable that the decision surface goes through the "father node", so the last splitting is canceled and an SSL method is used on the "father node", as there is a potential advantage in adding unlabeled data to this learning problem. Second, when one (and only one) of the clusters has all its labeled samples from the same class, it is considered a leaf and there is no further splitting. In this case it is highly probable that the cluster is far away from the decision border, and all the samples in the cluster can be safely assigned to the present label. Third, if a cluster contains only unlabeled data, it is deleted from the tree structure, as it cannot help in determining the border and the most probable situation is that it contains a group of outliers. More elaborated stopping criteria can be used if needed, but our simple criteria gives a good balance between accuracy and efficiency, as we show in the next section.

Once a node has been selected as a leaf, we adjust a classifier to the corresponding cluster of labeled plus unlabeled data. If the node comes from the second stopping criteria, we use a trivial classifier that assigns all points to the only class present in the cluster. On the other hand, when the node comes from criteria i) we train a full SSL method on the data, but selecting only a subset of unlabeled data that can be helpful to the learning process. Again, any combination of SSL method plus selection method for the subset of unlabeled data can be used. In this work we use SVM-light [9] as the SSL method. Due to this choice, we use a linear SVM [6] to select the subset of unlabeled data. We fit the SVM to all the labeled data in the node, and then select all the unlabeled data that lie within the margin of the classifier to be used for the SSL process.

Table 1. Details of the six datasets used in this work. Row "n" shows the number of samples, "p" the number of variables

Dataset	g241c	g241d	digit1	USPS	BCI	text
n	1500	1500	1500	1500	400	1500
p	241	241	241	241	117	11960

In order to predict a new example, it is driven down the tree until it reaches a leaf. At each node, the example is assigned to a branch using the same criteria as the clustering method (for example, with single linkage the example is assigned to the clustering corresponding to its nearest neighbor) [1]. Once in a leaf, the corresponding classifier assigns a class to the example.

In Figure 2 we show a working example of HSSM. We produced an artificial binary dataset, where each class is formed by three normal distributions with the same variance. We sampled a total of 15 labeled samples for each class and 270 unlabeled samples. As can be seen in the figure, the clustering stage decompose the non-linear problem into 3 subproblem that can be easily solved by a linear SSL method.

4   Experimental Evaluation

To evaluate the new HSSM method we followed as close as possible the setup proposed in the book by Chapelle et al. [3], chapter 21, for SSL methods. We selected the six binary datasets described in Table 1. The evaluation setup includes two experiments for each dataset, one using 10 labeled points in total and the other using 100 labeled points. All the remaining samples are used as unlabeled data. For each experiment, the setup includes 12 replications with fixed labeled subsets [3]. The test set is always the full set of unlabeled samples.

Table 2. Classification errors for diverse methods on the six datasets considered in this work, with two different setups: 10 or 100 labeled points

	Dataset	SVM-L	Light-L	Light-NL	LDS	HSSM-AL	HSSM-SL
	g241c	46.91	20.99	21.40	24.71	44.63	45.22
	g241d	45.56	46.48	46.87	50.08	44.52	45.86
10	digit1	43.39	20.59	20.54	17.77	21.14	21.54
	USPS	19.98	30.70	30.59	25.20	20.64	18.75
	BCI	49.00	50.02	49.76	49.15	50.09	49.70
	text	49.41	28.60	28.80	31.21	32.81	41.25
	g241c	23.67	18.18	18.93	18.46	41.09	44.36
	g241d	25.76	23.76	30.70	22.42	33.83	43.67
100	digit1	49.19	18.05	16.95	6.15	8.20	7.30
	USPS	20.01	21.12	13.56	9.77	8.61	6.89
	BCI	38.33	42.67	42.72	33.25	45.94	47.69
	text	28.35	22.31	22.30	24.52	29.51	27.52

Table 3. Details on the tree structure created by HSSM using two different clustering methods (AL and SL) and two different number of labeled samples (10 and 100). For each possible type of leaf (One or two class leaves), the columns show the average number of leaves created by the method and, in brackets, the average percentage of samples used by those classifiers. The "Discarded" column shows the average percentage of samples that were discarded during the training process.

	Dataset	One class leaves	Two class leaves	Discarded
	g241c	7.1 (4.9%)	1.0 (2.3%)	92.7%
	g241d	5.1 (22.6%)	1.6 (2.2%)	75.2%
10 - AL	digit1	2.1 (37.6%)	1.5 (36.0%)	26.4%
	USPS	2.8 (32.0%)	1.2 (15.8%)	52.3%
	BCI	4.3 (50.6%)	2.0 (12.0%)	37.4%
	text	3.6 (13.5%)	1.5 (11.0%)	75.5%
	g241c	6.8 (0.6%)	1.0 (0.5%)	98.9%
	g241d	7.1 (0.6%)	1.0 (0.3%)	99.1%
10 - SL	digit1	5.8 (15.9%)	1.0 (16.7%)	67.5%
	USPS	2.3 (0.4%)	1.0 (1.0%)	98.5%
	BCI	6.1 (14.6%)	1.4 (4.1%)	81.3%
	text	6.2 (2.1%)	1.0 (1.3%)	96.6%
	g241c	59.8 (39.9%)	11.8 (7.3%)	52.8%
	g241d	68.0 (42.3%)	8.5 (5.1%)	52.6%
100 - AL	digit1	14.3 (87.0%)	3.9 (6.0%)	7.0%
	USPS	14.1 (72.1%)	3.5 (7.1%)	20.8%
	BCI	31.4 (45.7%)	21.0 (22.7%)	31.7%
	text	36.0 (63.4%)	11.7 (10.2%)	26.4%
	g241c	96.1 (8.6%)	1.2 (0.8%)	90.7%
	g241d	93.4 (8.7%)	2.3 (0.8%)	90.5%
100 - SL	digit1	49.7 (57.5%)	2.2 (6.4%)	36.1%
	USPS	39.4 (27.9%)	1.2 (2.9%)	69.2%
	BCI	60.5 (40.1%)	13.3 (11.7%)	48.2%
	text	76.0 (25.2%)	3.0 (1.3%)	73.5%

We evaluated two version of HSSM, one using Average Linkage as clustering method (HSSM-AL from here on) and the other using Single Linkage (HSSM-SL). In both cases we used a linear SVM as supervised method, and Joachims' SVM-light as SSL method. For the SVM, the C constant was fixed to 100, as it is difficult to do a model selection with 10 labeled points. For SVM-light, all constants where taken as suggested by Joachims [9].

As a comparison with the new method, we also included classification results using other methods, always evaluated with the same experimental setup. First, we included the results obtained with a linear SVM, without taking into account the unlabeled data. Then, we considered two version of Joachims' SVM-light, one with a linear kernel (Light-L in the tables) and another one with a Gaussian kernel (Light-NL). We also included the results obtained with Chapelle & Zien's Low Density Separation (LDS) method [5], another non-linear SSL method.

Table 2 show the corresponding results for the two different setups. As in Chapelle et al. [3], the results are shown as the average percentage of classification error over the 12 runs of each method. The six datasets are very different in structure and origin, as explained in [3]. The first two datasets, g241c and g241d, are artificial and were designed to fool SSL methods in some way. HSSM results are not very good on these problems. Only in g241d with 10 labeled samples the new method shows a good performance. Nevertheless, the artificial digit1 dataset has an structure that favors SSL methods. In this case the HSSM shows good results, equal or better than other SSL methods. The last 3 datasets are real world problems with different properties. The USPS dataset is highly imbalanced. In this problem again both HSSM versions show the best results. In the other two real world datasets the results are mixed. The BCI problem is highly difficult, and all methods show near random results (except for the LDS method with 100 points). The text dataset is sparse and high dimensional. HSSM is clearly better than the base supervised method but never better than the other SSL methods.

On Table 3 we show some details about the tree structures created by HSSM. Overall, it is remarkable the low number of SSL classifiers needed by the HSSM, and the small proportion of samples used by them. Comparing SL and AL structures, it is interesting to note that SL clustering always discard a higher proportion of samples, and always uses a lower number of SSL classifiers (two class leaves), which combined produce more efficient HSSM classifiers. This is a consequence of SL tendency to form small clusters, which are discarded or assigned a single class by HSSM most of the time. Another interesting finding is that the HSSM method always uses more unlabeled data on the digit1 than on other datasets, which is the artificial problem aimed to favor SSL methods, where it also shows the best results among all methods. As a last remark, the best result on the unbalanced USPS dataset is produced by HSSM-SL in both setups, using in most cases only one SSL classifier and less than 3% of the data, on average, to train it.

5   Conclusions

In this work we presented the HSSM for semi-supervised learning. This is the first hybrid method aimed to solve problems with labeled plus unlabeled data. The new method follows a typical strategy in hybrid methods, using an unsupervised stage in order to decompose the full problem into a set of simpler subproblems. Using simple stopping criteria during the unsupervised stage, we allow the method to concentrate on the difficult portions of the original problem.

We also introduced a simple method to select at each subproblem a small subset of unlabeled samples that are relevant to modify the decision surface. To this end we trained a linear SVM on the available labeled samples, and selected the unlabeled samples that lie within the margin of the trained SVM.

We evaluated the new method using a setup introduced by Chapelle et al. [3], which includes dataset with very different properties. Overall, the error levels produced by the new HSSM are similar to other SSL methods. The new method seems to be more aggressive than previous SSL methods, as it shows better results in problems appropriate for SSL, but also worst results in problems aimed at fooling SSL methods. We showed that HSSM is more efficient than other SSL methods, using in all cases only a small fraction of the available unlabeled data to produce equivalent results than other methods. As a last analysis, the use of the SL clustering methods always produced simpler and more efficient classifiers than the use of AL clustering, with a similar performance in classification accuracy.

Further work is needed in order to find better ways to regularize the method and improve its performance on problems less favorable to SSL methods.

References

1. Ahumada, H.C., Grinblat, G.L., Granitto, P.M.: Unsupervized Data Driven Partitioning of Multiclass Problems. In: Honkela, T. (ed.) ICANN 2011, Part I. LNCS, vol. 6791, pp. 117–125. Springer, Heidelberg (2011)
2. Blum, A., Chawla, S.: Learning from labeled and unlabeled data using graph min-cuts. In: ICML 18, pp. 19–26. Morgan Kaufmann, San Francisco (2001)
3. Chapelle, O., Schölkopf, B., Zien, A. (eds.): Semi-Supervised Learning. MIT Press, Cambridge (2006)
4. Chapelle, O., Sindhwani, V., Keerthi, S.: Branch and bound for semi-supervised support vector machines. In: NIPS 19. MIT Press, Cambridge (2007)
5. Chapelle, O., Zien, A.: Semi-supervised classification by low density separation. In: AISTATS 2005, pp. 57–64 (2005)
6. Cristianini, N., Shawe-Taylor, J.: An Introduction to Support Vector Machines. Cambridge University Press, Cambridge (2000)
7. Delalleau, O., Bengio, Y., Le Roux, N.: Large-scale algorithms. In: Chapelle, O., Schölkopf, B., Zien, A. (eds.) Semi-Supervised Learning, pp. 333–341. MIT Press, Cambridge (2006)
8. Grandvalet, Y., Bengio, Y.: Semi-supervised learning by entropy minimization. In: Actes de CAP 2005, pp. 281–296 (2005)
9. Joachims, T.: Transductive inference for text classification using support vector machines. In: ICML 16, pp. 200–209. Morgan Kaufmann Publishers, San Francisco (1999)
10. Lawrence, N.D., Jordan, M.I.: Semi-supervised learning via gaussian processes. In: NIPS 17, pp. 753–760. MIT Press, Cambridge (2004)
11. Li, Y.-F., Zhou, Z.-H.: Improving semi-supervised support vector machines through unlabeled instances selection. In: Burgard, W., Roth, D. (eds.) AAAI. AAAI Press (2011)
12. Singh, A., Nowak, R.D., Zhu, X.: Unlabeled data: Now it helps, now it doesn't. In: NIPS 21, pp. 1513–1520 (2008)
13. Sneath, P.H.A., Sokal, R.R.: Numerical Taxonomy. W.H. Freeman and Company, San Francisco (1973)
14. Zhu, X., Goldberg, A.B.: Introduction to Semi-Supervised Learning. Morgan & Claypool Publishers, California (2009)

Clustering of Incomplete Data and Evaluation of Clustering Quality

Vladimir V. Ryazanov

Institution of Russian Academy of Sciences Dorodnicyn Computing Centre of RAS
Vavilov st. 40, 119333 Moscow, Russia
http://www.ccas.ru

Abstract. Two approaches to solving the problem of clustering with gaps for a specified number of clusters are considered. The first approach is based on restoring the values of unknown attributes and solving the problem of clustering of calculated complete data. The second approach is based on solving a finite set of tasks of clustering of corresponding to incomplete data complete sample descriptions and the construction of collective decision. For both approaches, the clustering quality criteria have been proposed as functions of incomplete descriptions. Results of practical experiments are considered.

Keywords: clustering, missing data, gaps, clustering estimation.

1 Introduction

The problem of cluster analysis of incomplete data has high interest of researchers, since the real practical problems are usually with missing data.

Clustering is usually performed in two stages. Incomplete data is first converted to the full data, and then there is clustering of complete data. In recent years, various algorithms have been developed to the construction of complete data. Conventionally, they can be divided into two types: marginalization and imputation. In the first case, the objects with missing data (gaps) are removed simply from the sample. In the second case, the unknown values of features are replaced by best match estimates [1,2]. The simplest imputation methods are replacement gaps on statistical estimates of the average values of attributes (means, random, the nearest neighbor method, etc.). Their generalizations involve averaging of feature values in the neighborhood of the objects with gaps [3]. Many algorithms use regression models. Unknown feature value is calculated using the regression function was found from the known characteristics (linear regression, SVR [4]). Estimation minimization (EM) algorithm is based on probability model of dataset. It is the well-known and popular in this field. Based on the use of imputation \marginalization technique clustering has both advantages and disadvantages. It should be noted that the rate of missing values of features is usually assumed to be low. In constructing the regression model, it is assumed there are a sufficient number of objects without gapes. In these approaches some

L. Alvarez et al. (Eds.): CIARP 2012, LNCS 7441, pp. 146–153, 2012.
© Springer-Verlag Berlin Heidelberg 2012

information is lost. The advantage of these methods is their simplicity and the possibility of further use of standard software clustering of complete data. Frequently, the finding the estimates of unknown data is of independent interest.

Second approach to the clustering of incomplete data is to adapt the clustering methods to cases of incomplete data. This case does not require reconstruction of missing data. The paper [5] proposed the modification of fuzzy k-means clustering in case of missing data. There are some assumptions in this approach. The attribute with missing data linearly depends on the other features. Some parameters in distances calculation are the independent and identically distributed. The proposed method performs better results for some medical task in comparison with other imputation technique. Two methods for partitioning incomplete data set including missing values into linear fuzzy clusters by using local principal components have been proposed in [6]. One is the direct extension of fuzzy c- varieties method to an incomplete data set. It uses the least square criterion as the objective function. The other method is a hybrid technique of fuzzy clustering and principal component analysis with missing values. The direct clustering method has been proposed in [7]. For the constraining features the set of constraints based on known values is generated. Although there are already different approaches to solving the problem of clustering of incomplete data, the creation of new algorithms is till now an urgent task.

Another important aspect of missing data clustering is to assess the clustering quality as a function of the degree of incompleteness of data. Suppose that for some sample $X = \{\bar{x}_1, \bar{x}_2, ..., \bar{x}_m\}$ of incomplete data clustering $K = \{K_1, K_2, ..., K_l\}$ has been obtained. Let the sample $X' = \{\bar{x}'_1, \bar{x}'_2, ..., \bar{x}'_m\}$ of full descriptions corresponds to an initial sample X, and $K' = \{K'_1, K'_2, ..., K'_l\}$ is its clustering. What will be the "scatter" of the set of all admissible clusterings K' regarding clustering K? It is clear that the " scatter " must depend on many factors such as the clustering algorithm, data, rate of unknown characteristics, information content of missing data, etc.

In this paper we consider two problems associated with clustering of incomplete data: algorithms for clustering of incomplete data,and estimation of the quality of clustering as a function of data incompleteness.

In the first approach, some imputation is used. Degree of clustering certainty is calculated as an estimation of the stability of the obtained clustering result with respect to some sets of admissible complete sample. The second approach does not provide for reconstruction of features. At first, N complete samples which correspond to a given sample of partial descriptions are constructed. Next we solve independently N tasks of clustering and N clusterings are found. Finally, a collective solution of clustering task is computed. The degree of certainty of clustering is computed on the basis of estimation of the scatter difference of partial solutions with respect collective solution. The results of the comparison of degree of clustering certainty for different samples at different levels of data incompleteness are considered.

2   Clustering of Incomplete Data Based on the Features Imputation

Let a standard sample X of incomplete descriptions $\bar{x}_i = (x_{i1}, x_{i2}, ..., x_{in})$ of the objects in terms of features is given. We suppose the set $M_j \subseteq R, j = 1, 2, ..., n$ to be a finite set of values of j−th feature. It can be calculated by known feature values from training data. The unknown feature values (slips, gaps) will be denoted as Δ. We believe that $x_{ij} = \Delta, \forall j \in \Omega_i \subseteq \{1, 2, ..., n\}, i = 1, ..., m$. The set of unknown feature values is denoted as the set of pairs $J = \{\langle i, j \rangle, i = 1, 2, ..., m, j \in \Omega_i\}$. We use the local method of filling the gaps [8]. Obtained as a result sample of full descriptions will be denoted as $X^* = \{\bar{x}_1^*, \bar{x}_2^*, ..., \bar{x}_m^*\}$.

Let we solve a task of clustering of the sample X^* to l clusters using an algorithm A: $K = \{K_1, K_2, ..., K_l\}$, $K_i \subseteq X^*, i = 1, 2, ..., l$, $\bigcup_{i=1}^{l} K_i = X^*$, $K_i \bigcap K_j = \emptyset, i \neq j$. Denote $D_t = \{\bar{x}_t'\}$ the set of all possible $\bar{x}_t'$ corresponding to vector $\bar{x}_t$ (i.e. $x_{tj}' = \begin{cases} x_{tj}, & x_{tj} \neq \Delta, \\ \in M_j, & x_{tj} = \Delta. \end{cases}$).

Consider an arbitrary $\bar{x}_t^*$. Let $\bar{x}_t^* \in K_i$. Consider the partition $K' = \{K_1', K_2', ..., K_l'\}$ of sample $X' = X^* \setminus \{\bar{x}_t^*\} \bigcup \{\bar{x}_t'\}$, where $K_j' = K_j, j \neq i$, and $K_i' = K_i \setminus \{\bar{x}_t^*\} \bigcup \{\bar{x}_t'\}, \bar{x}_t' \in D_t$. Let $f_t(K)$ is the proportion of objects $\bar{x}_t'$ from D_t for which the partition K' is the result of clustering .

Definition 1. Degree of certainty $f(K)$ of the clustering K is the quantity $f(K) = \frac{1}{m} \sum_{t=1}^{m} f_t(K)$.

Consider the problem of calculating of $f(K)$ on the example of two well-known algorithms.

2.1   Clustering of Incomplete Data as the Minimization of Variance Criterion

It is known [9] that the condition for local optimality of clustering $K = \{K_1, K_2, ..., K_l\}$ with minimum value of the variance criterion is execution of the inequality

$$\frac{n_i}{(n_i - 1)} \left\| \bar{x}^* - \bar{m}_i^* \right\|^2 - \frac{n_j}{(n_j + 1)} \left\| \bar{x}^* - \bar{m}_j^* \right\|^2 \leq 0 \qquad (1)$$

for any pair K_i, K_j, and any $\bar{x}^* \in K_i$ (here $n_i = |K_i|$, $\bar{m}_i^* = \frac{1}{n_i} \sum_{\bar{x}^* \in K_i} \bar{x}^*$). We will use $\|\bar{x} - \bar{y}\| = \rho(\bar{x}, \bar{y}) = \sqrt{\sum_{j=1}^{n} (x_j - y_j)^2}$.

Let $\bar{x}_t' = (x_{t1}', x_{t2}', ..., x_{tn}') \in D_t$ is an arbitrary admissible vector corresponding to the vector $\bar{x}_t^* = (x_{t1}^*, x_{t2}^*, ..., x_{tn}^*) \in K_i$. We obtain the conditions under which the partition K' is the clustering. To do this, let's write the conditions (1) for all objects from X'. Denote $\delta \bar{x}_t = \bar{x}_t^* - \bar{x}_t'$, then

$$\bar{m}_i' = \bar{m}_i^* - \frac{\delta \bar{x}_t}{n_i} \qquad (2)$$

Partition K' is the clustering if the following conditions are satisfied:

$$\bar{x}_t' \in K_i', \frac{n_i}{(n_i - 1)} \left\| \bar{x}_t' - (\bar{m}_i^* - \frac{\delta \bar{x}_t}{n_i}) \right\|^2 - \frac{n_j}{(n_j + 1)} \left\| \bar{x}_t' - \bar{m}_j^* \right\|^2 \leq 0; \qquad (3)$$

$$\forall \bar{x}'_\alpha \in K_i, \alpha \neq t, \frac{n_i}{(n_i - 1)} \left\| \bar{x}^*_\alpha - (\bar{m}^*_i - \frac{\delta \bar{x}_t}{n_i}) \right\|^2 - \frac{n_j}{(n_j + 1)} \left\| \bar{x}^*_\alpha - \bar{m}^*_j \right\|^2 \leq 0; \quad (4)$$

$$\forall \bar{x}'_\alpha \in K_j, j \neq i, \frac{n_j}{(n_j - 1)} \left\| \bar{x}^*_\alpha - \bar{m}^*_j) \right\|^2 - \frac{n_i}{(n_i + 1)} \left\| \bar{x}^*_\alpha - \bar{m}^*_i + \frac{\delta \bar{x}_t}{n_i} \right\|^2 \leq 0. \quad (5)$$

Given (2),(3 - 5) can be rewritten as

$$\frac{n_i}{n_i - 1} \left\| \bar{x}^*_t - \bar{m}^*_i \right\|^2 - \frac{n_j}{(n_j + 1)} \left\| \bar{x}^*_t - \bar{m}^*_j \right\|^2 +$$

$$+ 2(\delta \bar{x}_t, \bar{m}^*_i - \frac{n_j}{(n_j + 1)} \bar{m}^*_j - \frac{1}{(n_j + 1)} \bar{x}^*_t) + \|\delta \bar{x}_t\|^2 \frac{(n_i - n_j - 1)}{n_i(n_j + 1)} \leq 0, \quad (6)$$

$$\frac{n_i}{n_i - 1} \left\| \bar{x}^*_\alpha - \bar{m}^*_i \right\|^2 - \frac{n_j}{(n_j + 1)} \left\| \bar{x}^*_\alpha - \bar{m}^*_j \right\|^2 +$$

$$+ 2(\delta \bar{x}_t, \frac{1}{(n_i - 1)} (\bar{x}^*_\alpha - \bar{m}^*_i)) + \|\delta \bar{x}_t\|^2 \frac{1}{n_i(n_i - 1)} \leq 0, \quad (7)$$

$$\frac{n_j}{n_j - 1} \left\| \bar{x}^*_\alpha - \bar{m}^*_j \right\|^2 - \frac{n_i}{(n_i + 1)} \left\| \bar{x}^*_\alpha - \bar{m}^*_i \right\|^2 -$$

$$- 2(\delta x_t, \frac{(x^*_\alpha - m^*_i)}{(n_i + 1)}) - \|\delta x_t\|^2 \frac{1}{n_i(n_i + 1)} \leq 0, \quad (8)$$

System (6 - 8) can be written as (9). Thus, the partition K' is the clustering, if for fixed $\bar{x}'_t$ system of m inequalities (9) is performed,

$$a_\lambda + \sum_{i \in \Omega_t} y_i c_{\lambda i} + b_\lambda \sum_{i \in \Omega_t} y_i^2 \leq 0, \lambda = 1, 2, ..., m, \quad (9)$$

where $a_\lambda, b_\lambda, c_{\lambda i}, i = 1, 2, ., k, \lambda - 1, 2, ..., m$ are constants for found K, and $y_i = \{x^*_{ti} - x'_{ti} : x'_{ti} \in M_i\}$. To calculate $f_t(K)$ we make enumeration for all admissible y_i (the systems (9) and calculate the number of executed systems (9). With a large enumeration, we estimate $f_t(K)$ on a random sample of allowed values of $f_t(K)$.

2.2 Clustering of Incomplete Data Using k-means Algorithm

Let K be the clustering X^* using k-means algorithm [9]. This means, $\forall \bar{x}^*_t \in K_i$ there is

$$\left\| \bar{x}^*_t - \bar{m}^*_i \right\| \leq \left\| \bar{x}^*_t - \bar{m}^*_j \right\|, \forall j \neq i, \quad (10)$$

Partition K' is the clustering if

$$\left\| \bar{x}^*_t - \delta \bar{x}_t - \bar{m}^*_i + \frac{\delta \bar{x}_t}{n_i} \right\|^2 \leq \left\| \bar{x}^*_t - \delta \bar{x}_t - \bar{m}^*_j \right\|^2, \bar{x}'_t \in K'_i, j \neq i, \quad (11)$$

$$\left\| \bar{x}^*_\alpha - \bar{m}^*_i + \frac{\delta \bar{x}_t}{n_i} \right\|^2 \leq \left\| \bar{x}^*_\alpha - \bar{m}^*_j \right\|^2, j \neq i, \forall \bar{x}'_\alpha \in K_i, \alpha \neq t, \quad (12)$$

$$\left\| \bar{x}^*_\alpha - \bar{m}^*_j \right\|^2 \leq \left\| \bar{x}^*_\alpha - \bar{m}^*_i + \frac{\delta \bar{x}_t}{n_i} \right\|^2, \forall \bar{x}'_\alpha \in K_j, j \neq i. \quad (13)$$

After elementary transformations we obtain a system similar to (9). The calculation of $f_t(K)$ is also carried out similarly.

3   Clustering of Sample with Missing Data without Imputation

By using X we make N samples of full descriptions $X'^{(i)} = \{\bar{x}_1'^{(i)}, \bar{x}_2'^{(i)}, ..., \bar{x}_m'^{(i)}\}, i = 1, 2, ..., N$, where $x_{tj}'^{(i)} = \begin{cases} x_{tj}, & x_{tj} \neq \Delta, \\ \in M_j, & x_{tj} = \Delta \end{cases}$ (probability of assigning a value from M_j to $x_{tj}'^{(i)}$ is equal to its frequency of occurrence in the training sample X). For each of the resulting complete samples, we solve the problem of clustering on l clusters and find N solutions $K^{(i)} = \{K_1^{(i)}, K_2^{(i)}, ..., K_l^{(i)}\}, i = 1, 2, ..., N$. Further, the collective clustering $K = \{K_1, K_2, ..., K_l\}$ is build and considered as a solution of the clustering task with missing data.

Denote $< t_1, t_2, ..., t_l >$ a permutation of $< 1, 2, ..., l >$.

Definition 2. Degree of certainty $\Phi(K)$ of clustering $K = \{K_1, K_2, ..., K_l\}$ is the quantity

$$\Phi(K) = \sum_{i=1}^{N} \max_{<t_1, t_2, ..., t_l>} \sum_{j=1}^{l} \left| K_j \bigcap K_{t_j}^{(i)} \right| / mN.$$

Definition 3. Degree of certainty $F(K)$ of clustering $K = \{K_1, K_2, ..., K_l\}$ is the quantity $F(K) = \min_{i=1,...,N} \max_{<t_1, t_2, ..., t_l>} \sum_{j=1}^{l} \left| K_j \bigcap K_{t_j}^{(i)} \right| / m$.

Quantity $\max_{<t_1, t_2, ..., t_l>} \sum_{j=1}^{l} \left| K_j \bigcap K_{t_j}^{(i)} \right|$ characterizes the proximity of clustering results K and $K^{(i)}, i = 1, 2, ..., N$. Criterion $\Phi(K)$ characterizes the normalized average the proximity of collective clustering with respect to clustering of admissible samples. Criterion $F(K)$ meets the worst case.

The task of collective clustering construction and the committee algorithm for its solution were proposed in [10,11]. Earlier, a collective clustering for some sample was based on using some algorithm that combines the set of clusterings obtained for the same sample by different clustering methods. In our case, the collective solution will be built as application of some clustering algorithm to the set of clusterings obtained by fixed method for different full samples $X'^{(i)}$. The results of the clustering of samples $X'^{(i)}$ by some clustering method can be written in the form of three-dimensional information matrix

$$\left\| \alpha_{ij}^{\nu} \right\|_{m \times l \times N}, \alpha_{ij}^{\nu} \in \{0, 1\}, \sum_{j=1}^{l} \alpha_{ij}^{\nu} = 1, i = 1, ..., m, j = 1, ..., l, \nu = 1, ..., N.$$

Its submatrix $\left\| \alpha_{ij}^{\nu} \right\|_{l \times N}, i = 1, 2, ..., m$, can be regarded as a new description of $\bar{x}_i$. As a collective solution of main cluster analysis task was considered the clustering of given m matrix descriptions by k - means method.

4   The Results of Experiments on Simulated and Practical Data

Proposed clustering algorithms of incomplete data were tested on simulated and practical problems. As a model problem we used a sample mixture of normal distributions with independent features ($n = 10, l = 4, m_i = 50, i = 1, 2, 3, 4$). Expectation and variance of the classes are chosen such that the result of their clustering coincided with their a priori classification. Considered training samples were transformed into descriptions of the samples with gaps at various levels of data incompleteness. Unknown values of features in each training object on the uniform law of distribution is set, and $w\%$ feature values were unknown. Separately, we solved the problem of clustering of incomplete samples by means of collective clustering. Visualization of a model example for the four classes (the "projection" of the multidimensional data on the plane of generalized features [9]) is shown in Fig. 1. Fig. 3,4 demonstrate the proposed criteria $f(K), \Phi(K)$, $F(K)$ and parameters $\varphi(K) = \max\limits_{<t_1, t_2, \ldots, t_l>} \sum_{j=1}^{l} |K_j \cap K^*| / m$, $\varphi_{avr}(K) = \max\limits_{<t_1, t_2, \ldots, t_l>} \sum_{j=1}^{l} |K_j'' \cap K^*| / m$ as functions of incompleteness rate w. Here $K^* = \{K_1^*, K_2^*, \ldots, K_l^*\}$ is a priori classification of the initial sample, K is a collective clustering of sample with gaps, and $K'' = \{K_1'', K_2'', \ldots, K_l''\}$ is a sample clustering after replacing the gaps on the average feature values. In Figures 1-2 and 3-4 , respectively, visualizations and graphics of a model and the practical task of "breast cancer" [12] are shown. Task "breast cancer" is a sample of 344 descriptions of patients with benign or malignant tumor ($n = 9, l = 2, m_1 = 218, m_2 = 126$). The task has a cluster structure that agrees well with a priori classification. The experimental results are the preliminary, but the form of obtained dependences corresponds to a priori expectations. Criterion $F(K)$ corresponds to the worst-case of possible clusterings $K^{(i)}, i = 1, 2, \ldots, N$, and its value decreases rapidly with w increasing.

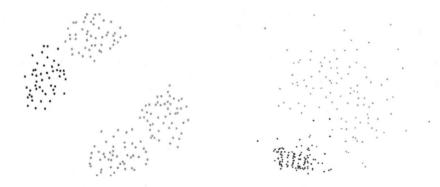

Fig. 1. Mixture of normal distributions   **Fig. 2.** The problem of breast cancer

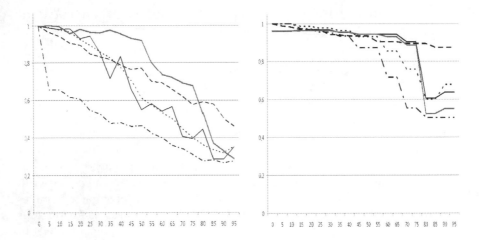

Fig. 3. Dependencies of criteria and parameters for incomplete data in the model
task

Fig. 4. Dependencies of criteria and parameters for incomplete data in the task
of breast cancer

Table 1. Notations of graphics of criteria and indicators

————————	index $\varphi(K)$	·· ·· ·· ·· ·· ·· ·· ··	criterion $\Phi(K)$
····················	index$\varphi_{avr}(K)$	▬ ▬ ▬ ▬ ▬	criterion $f(K)$
▬ ·· ▬ ·· ▬	criterion$F(K)$		

Nevertheless, it can be very useful in practice. The beginning of its fall corresponds to the maximal level of missing data, in which the incompleteness of the
data does not affect to clustering. In the task "breast cancer" clusters are well separated. They are calculated even with a gaps rate 45% when $F(K)$ begins to decrease sharply. High values of $\varphi_{avr}(K)$ are the outcome of the simplicity of the
structures of data. Criteria $\varphi(K)$ and $\Phi(K)$ are well correlated, due, apparently,
to the use of collective clustering. The graphics show also the correlation of the
criteria $f(K)$ and $\Phi(K)$. Value of the criterion $\Phi(K)$ seems more objective than of
$f(K)$, as the $f(K)$ calculation is based on variations of only the individual objects.

5   Conclusion

In report [13], it was proposed a leave-one-out approach to evaluation of clustering quality that had been based on an estimation of the clustering stability.
Clustering quality evaluation belongs to the interval [0,1] and is not associated
with any a priori classifications or probability nature of data. It is interesting
to study the relationships between the criteria [13] and the criteria of degree of

clustering certainty introduced in this paper. The proposed criteria are simple and interpretable. Of course, the results of experiments are preliminary. Nevertheless, we hope that the methods of clustering of incomplete data and criteria for evaluating the degree of clustering certainty proposed here will be useful in solving practical tasks.

Acknowledgments. I would like to thank students of M.V.Lomonosov Moscow State University A.S. Schichko and K.V.Tishin for experiments performed. This work was supported by RAS Presidium program number 15 and "Basic Sciences for Medicine, Program number 2 of Department of Mathematical Sciences of RAS, RFBR 12-01-00912, 11-01-00585.

References

1. Little, R.J.A., Rubin, D.B.: Statistical Analysis with Missing Data. Wiley, New York (1987)
2. Zloba, E.: Statistical methods of reproducing of missing data. J. Computer Modelling & New Technologies 6(1), 51–61 (2002)
3. Zhang, S.: Parimputation: From imputation and null-imputation to partially imputation. IEEE Intelligent Informatics Bulletin 9(1), 32–38 (2008)
4. Honghai, F., Guoshun, C., Cheng, Y., Bingru, Y., Yumei, C.: A SVM Regression Based Approach to Filling in Missing Values. In: Khosla, R., Howlett, R.J., Jain, L.C. (eds.) KES 2005. LNCS (LNAI), vol. 3683, pp. 581–587. Springer, Heidelberg (2005)
5. Sarkar, M., Leong, T.-Y.: Fuzzy k-means Clustering with Missing Values. In. AMIA Symp., pp. 588–592 (2001)
6. Honda, K., Ichihashi, H.: Linear Fuzzy Clustering Techniques With Missing Values and Their Application to Local Principal Component Analysis. IEEE Transactions on Fuzzy Systems 12(2), 183–193 (2004)
7. Wagstaff, K.: Clustering with missing values: No imputation required. In: Meeting of the International Federation of Classification Societies "Classification, Clustering, and Data Mining", pp. 649–658. Springer (2004)
8. Ryazanov, V.: Some Imputation Algorithms for Restoration of Missing Data. In: San Martin, C., Kim, S.-W. (eds.) CIARP 2011. LNCS, vol. 7042, pp. 372–379. Springer, Heidelberg (2011)
9. Duda, R.O., Hart, P.E., Stork, D.G.: Pattern Classification, 2nd edn. Wiley Interscience (2001)
10. Ryazanov, V.V.: The committee synthesis of pattern recognition and classification algorithms, Zh. Vychisl. Mat. i Mat. Fiziki 21(6), 1533–1543 (1981) (in Russian) (Printed in Great Britain, 1982. Pergamon Press. Ltd.)
11. Biryukov, A.S., Ryazanov, V.V., Shmakov, A.S.: Solving Clusterization Problems Using Groups of Algorithms. Zh. Vychisl. Mat. i Mat. Fiziki 48(1), 176–192 (2008) (Printed in Great Britain, 2008. Pergamon Press. Ltd.)
12. Mangasarian, O.L., Wolberg, W.H.: Cancer diagnosis via linear programming. SIAM News 23(5), 1–18 (1990)
13. Arseev, A.S., Kotochigov, K.L., Ryazanov, V.V.: Universal criteria for clustering and stability problems. In: 13th All-Russian Conference "Mathematical Methods for Pattern Recognition", pp. 63–64. S.-Peterburg (2007) (in Russian)

A New Classifier Combination Scheme Using Clustering Ensemble

Miguel A. Duval-Poo, Joan Sosa-García, Alejandro Guerra-Gandón,
Sandro Vega-Pons, and José Ruiz-Shulcloper

Advanced Technologies Application Center (CENATAV), Havana, Cuba
{mduval,jsosa,aguerra,svega,jshulcloper}@cenatav.co.cu

Abstract. Combination of multiple classifiers has been shown to increase classification accuracy in many application domains. Besides, the use of cluster analysis techniques in supervised classification tasks has shown that they can enhance the quality of the classification results. This is based on the fact that clusters can provide supplementary constraints that may improve the generalization capability of the classifiers. In this paper we introduce a new classifier combination scheme which is based on the Decision Templates Combiner. The proposed scheme uses the same concept of representing the classifiers decision as a vector in an intermediate feature space and builds more representatives decision templates by using clustering ensembles. An experimental evaluation was carried out on several synthetic and real datasets. The results show that the proposed scheme increases the classification accuracy over the Decision Templates Combiner, and other classical classifier combinations methods.

Keywords: Classifier Combination, Decision Templates, Clustering Ensemble.

1 Introduction

There are several areas in pattern recognition where the use of reliable and accurate classifiers is necessary. Traditionally, these problems have been solved with the use of a single classifier. However, one single classifier cannot always reach the desired classification accuracy for a specific problem. One way to improve the results of a single classifier is by combining multiple base classifiers [1].

On the other hand, the idea of combining different clustering results (clustering ensemble) emerged as an alternative approach to improve the quality of clustering algorithms [2]. This is possible because the combination process can compensate possible errors in individual clustering results.

Recently, new methods for combining supervised classifiers that use cluster analysis as a tool for improving the classification results have been presented [3, 4, 5]. Some even combine both ensembles of classifiers and clusterers [6]. The main motivations for doing such combinations is that the use of unsupervised models can provide a variety of supplementary constraints for classifying new data [6].

L. Alvarez et al. (Eds.): CIARP 2012, LNCS 7441, pp. 154–161, 2012.

Classifiers output can be categorized into three levels: abstract level (class label), rank level (rank order of class labels), and measurement level (soft labels) [7]. Depending on the form of the information delivered by base classifiers, different schemes has been proposed for combining multiple classifiers decisions. The simplest and more frequently considered rule to combine class labels is the Majority Vote. In this scheme, base classifiers output is used as class votes and the most voted class is returned. There are other class labels combiners like Bayesian Combination and Behavior Knowledge Space [1]. On the other hand, soft labels can be combined by using simple rules like the sum, product and average of the support values given by the base classifiers to each class [8]. Others schemes like Fuzzy Integral [8] and Dempster−Shafer [9] can be also used for combining soft labels. Another way to combine soft classifiers results is to see them as features in an intermediate feature space. At this point any classifier, also called meta-classifier, can be applied to make the final class decision. Following this approach, one of the most widely used method is the *Decision Templates Combiner* (DTC) [10]. DTC is a robust scheme that builds class templates in the intermediate feature space by using the true class labels of the objects in a training set. Then, a new object is classified by comparing the base classifiers output for this object, to each class template.

In this paper, we introduce a new classifier combination scheme that uses clustering ensemble tools for finding more representative templates for a class. To do that, we combine partitions obtained by two different procedures. First, a set of partitions is generated by grouping objects taking into account their proximity values in the intermediate feature space. In the second case, another partition is obtained by using the information of the true class labels in the training set. Finally, all partitions are combined to obtain a consensus one, where each cluster centroid can be viewed as a new decision template.

The remainder of this paper is organized as follows: In Section 2 the DTC is described. The proposed combination scheme is introduced in Section 3. Section 4 presents an experimental study performed on several datasets, in which the proposed scheme is compared to DTC and other classifier combination methods. Finally, conclusions and future works are presented in Section 5.

2   Decision Templates Combiner

Let us view the problem of classifying an object $\mathbf{x}$ into c classes using L individual classifiers, where $\mathbf{x}$ is a tuple of some n-dimensional space $\mathbb{F}^n$. Let $\Omega = \{\omega_1, \omega_2, \ldots, \omega_c\}$ be the set of class labels and $\mathbb{D} = \{D_1, D_2, \ldots, D_L\}$ be the ensemble of supervised classifiers. Each classifier D_i is a function $D_i : \mathbb{F}^n \to \mathbb{R}^c$ that returns a c-dimensional vector $[d_{i,1}(\mathbf{x}), d_{i,2}(\mathbf{x}), \ldots, d_{i,c}(\mathbf{x})]$ where $d_{i,j}(\mathbf{x})$ denote the support that classifier D_i gives to the hypothesis that $\mathbf{x}$ belongs to the class ω_j. In addition, let us assume that a labeled data set $\mathbf{Z} = \{\mathbf{z}_1, \mathbf{z}_2, \ldots, \mathbf{z}_N\}$, $\mathbf{z}_i \in \mathbb{F}^n$ is available, which is used to train the classifier combination scheme: both the individual classifiers and the combiner.

Kuncheva [1] proposed to organize the L classifiers output for a particular input $\mathbf{x}$ as a matrix called *decision profile* $(DP(\mathbf{x}))$.

$$DP(\mathbf{x}) = \begin{bmatrix} d_{1,1}(\mathbf{x}) \ldots d_{1,j}(\mathbf{x}) \ldots d_{1,c}(\mathbf{x}) \\ d_{i,1}(\mathbf{x}) \ldots d_{i,j}(\mathbf{x}) \ldots d_{i,c}(\mathbf{x}) \\ d_{L,1}(\mathbf{x}) \ldots d_{L,j}(\mathbf{x}) \ldots d_{L,c}(\mathbf{x}) \end{bmatrix} \tag{1}$$

One way of using the $DP(\mathbf{x})$ matrix for combining classifiers is to treat the values $d_{i,j}(\mathbf{x})$ as features in a new space called *intermediate feature space*. Then, another supervised classifier returns the class label taking as input the data in this space. One of the most widely used method that follows this approach is the Decision Templates Combiner (DTC).

The idea behind the DTC is to remember the most typical decision profile for each class ω_j, which is called *decision template* (DT_j). The decision template DT_j for class ω_j is the average of the decision profiles of the elements of the training set $\mathbf{Z}$, labeled in class ω_j:

$$DT_j = \frac{1}{N_j} \sum_{\substack{\mathbf{z}_k \in \mathbf{Z} \\ l(\mathbf{z}_k) = \omega_j}} DP(\mathbf{z}_k) \tag{2}$$

where N_j is the number of elements in $\mathbf{Z}$ that belong to the class ω_j and $l(\mathbf{z})$ represents the class label of $\mathbf{z}$. After constructing the DTs matrices in the training phase, when a new object $\mathbf{x}$ is submitted for classification, the DTC scheme matches $DP(\mathbf{x})$ to DT_j, $j = 1, \ldots, c$ and produces soft class labels by:

$$\mu_j(\mathbf{x}) = S(DP(\mathbf{x}), DT_j), \quad j = 1, \ldots, c \tag{3}$$

where S is a similarity measure. The higher the similarity between the $DP(\mathbf{x})$ and the DT_j, the higher the support for the class ω_j.

3   Classifier Combination Using Clustering Ensemble

As we previously said, this method is based on the idea of representing objects with the support values given by the base classifiers for each class. In other words, each object $\mathbf{x}$ can be represented in the $(L \cdot c)$ - dimensional intermediate feature space as a vector $dv(\mathbf{x})$ obtained by concatenating its $DP(\mathbf{x})$ rows. This way the training set $\mathbf{Z}$ is mapped into a new set $\mathbf{Y}$ in the intermediate feature space in the following way $\mathbf{Y} = \{\mathbf{y}_i \in \mathbb{R}^{L \cdot c} \mid \mathbf{y}_i = dv(\mathbf{z}_i), i = 1, \ldots, N\}$.

In this space, the original DTs in (2) can be viewed as the centroids of the clusters in the *ground-truth* partition. The *ground-truth* partition of $\mathbf{Y}$ is defined as $P^{gt} = \{G_1^{gt}, G_2^{gt}, \ldots, G_c^{gt}\}$, where each cluster $G_j^{gt} = \{\mathbf{y}_k \in \mathbf{Y} \mid l(\mathbf{y}_k) = \omega_j\}$. DTC represents in a single DT the most typical decision behavior for each class. However, in some cases, there could be more than one typical behavior for a group of objects belonging to the same class. In other words, there could be cluster centroids in P^{gt} with a low representative power. In these cases, representing a class by a single DT can lead to a not representative template for this class.

Therefore, to build more representative DTs we propose to use cluster analysis tools. In particular, we use clustering ensemble to combine partitions in which objects are grouped by they decision behavior with the *ground-truth* partition. As result, a new *consensus partition* is build where each cluster centroid can be view as a more representative DT. Each one of these DTs, instead of being associated to a single class label, gives a support value to each class.

Formally, a set $\mathbb{P}^{db} = \{P_1, P_2, \ldots, P_M\}$ of partitions of $\mathbf{Y}$ is generated by using different clustering algorithms or the same algorithm with different parameter initialization. In each $P_i = \{G_1^i, G_2^i, \ldots, G_{q_i}^i\}$, G_j^i is the jth cluster of the ith partition, for all $i = 1, \ldots, M$. Next, a partition ensemble $\mathbb{P}$ is build by joining the partition set $\mathbb{P}^{db}$ with the *ground-truth* partition, i.e. $\mathbb{P} = \mathbb{P}^{db} \cup \{P^{gt}\}$. Then, the *consensus partition* $P^* = \{G_1^*, G_2^*, \ldots, G_{q_*}^*\}$ is built as

$$P^* = \arg \max_{P \in \mathbb{P}_{\mathbf{Y}}} \sum_{i=1}^{M+1} b_i \Gamma(P, P_i) \tag{4}$$

where $\mathbb{P}_{\mathbf{Y}}$ is the set of all possible partitions with the set of objects $\mathbf{Y}$, and Γ is a similarity measure between partitions. Each b_i is a weight associated to the partition P_i. In particular, P_{M+1} represents the *ground-truth* partition P^{gt} and b_{M+1} is its associated weight. The influence of $\mathbb{P}^{db}$ and P^{gt} in the combination process can be handled by using the b_i weights.

Finally, for each cluster G_k^* in the *consensus partition*, a centroid e_k is calculated and used as a DT. Besides, a class support vector $[\mu_1^k, \mu_2^k, \ldots, \mu_c^k]$ is computed. Each μ_j^k denotes the support given by the cluster centroid e_k to the fact that an object belongs to class ω_j. This support is defined as:

$$\mu_j^k = \frac{|\{\mathbf{y} \in G_k^* \mid l(\mathbf{y}) = \omega_j\}|}{|G_k^*|} \tag{5}$$

where the numerator represents the number of elements of the cluster G_k^* that belong to class ω_j and the denominator is the total number of elements in the cluster G_k^*.

Once the model is trained, we obtain a collection of q_* centroids and support vectors. When a new object $\mathbf{x}$ is wanted to be classified, the similarity between its representative vector $dv(\mathbf{x})$ in the intermediate feature space and all the e_k centroids is computed. Finally, the proposed scheme returns the support values of the most similar centroid to $\mathbf{x}$:

$$\mu_j(\mathbf{x}) = \mu_j^r, \quad r = \arg \max_k S(DP(\mathbf{x}), e_k) \tag{6}$$

Notice that the final *consensus partition* does not have to necessary possess c clusters. Therefore, a class can be represented by more than one DT. In addition, the DTC can be viewed as a particular case of the proposed scheme when the partition ensemble only contains the *ground-truth* partition, $\mathbb{P} = \{P^{gt}\}$. In this case, the *consensus partition* will be in fact the same *ground-truth* partition and its clusters centroid will be the original DTs. Although the class supports will not be the same that the originally calculated by the DTC (3), notice that both will return the same class label, wherever the class with maximum support value is selected as crisp label.

4   Experimental Evaluation

Experiments with six numerical datasets were conducted to evaluate the proposed scheme. Three datasets were selected from the UCI Machine Learning Repository [11] (Iris, Wine, SPECT) while the other three are 2D synthetic datasets (Half-Rings, Cassini, Smiley), see Fig. 1. A description of the datasets is presented in Table 1.

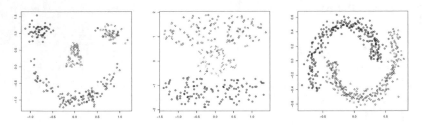

Fig. 1. 2D synthetic datasets. Smiley (Left), Cassini (Center), Half-Rings (Right).

Table 1. Description of the datasets

Dataset	No. Instances	No. Classes	No. Attributes	Instances per classes
Smiley	200	4	2	33-33-50-84
Cassini	300	3	2	120-60-120
Half-Rings	200	2	2	100-100
Iris	150	3	4	50-50-50
Wine	178	3	13	59-71-48
SPECT	267	2	22	55-212

Ten *fast decision tree learners* (REPTree), implemented in Weka [12], were used as the classifier ensemble. Each classifier in the ensemble was configured with their default parameters and with a different random seed. The criterion used for measuring the results was the classification accuracy.

In all experiments, each dataset was divided in 3 groups of equal size in which objects were randomly assigned. The first group was used to train the classifier ensemble. In this case, each base classifier was trained with 70% of the objects in the group, randomly selected with replacement. The second group was used for training the combination schemes and the third for testing. This process was repeated 100 times and the final accuracy was calculated as an average over the 100 iterations.

For the proposed method, an alpha parameter, $\alpha \in [0, 1]$, was used for assigning the partition weights. The weight used for the *ground-truth* partition was $b_{gt} = 10(1 - \alpha)$. Besides, $M = \lfloor 10\alpha \rfloor$ partitions were generated by using k-means with euclidian distance and a random number of clusters k between c and $3c$. Each one of these partitions was assigned with a weight $b_i = 1$, $i = 1, \ldots, M$. The α parameter is used to simultaneously control the weight of the *ground-truth* partition and the number of partitions in $\mathbb{P}^{db}$. Notice that the *ground-truth* partition is more taken into account in the combination process as the α value decreases. On the contrary, higher α values increase the influence of $\mathbb{P}^{db}$ partitions in the combination process.

In order to find the *consensus partition*, the following procedure [13] is used. First, a co-association matrix is build, where each position (i, j) of this matrix has a value that represents how many times the objects x_i and x_j are in the same cluster for all partitions in $\mathbb{P}$. This co-association matrix is used as a similarity measure between objects. Then, the *consensus partition* is obtained by applying a hierarchial clustering algorithm. In this case, we use the Group Average algorithm and the *highest lifetime* criterion to select the most representative level in the hierarchy.

The similarity measure S used in our experiments is defined based on the euclidian distance in the following way:

$$S(x, y) = 1 - \frac{1}{L \cdot c} \|x - y\|_2 \qquad (7)$$

Two experiments were carried out. In the first, the accuracy was evaluated with different values of the α parameter, see Fig. 2. The effect of the $\mathbb{P}^{db}$ partitions on the accuracy can be analyzed by the application of different α values.

In the second experiment (Table 2), the proposed scheme (CCCE) was tested on each dataset and then compared with the classifier ensemble average (CEA), the best (BBC) and worst (WBC) base classifier of the ensemble. Also was compared with other combination methods like: Majority Vote (MV), the average combination function (AVG), the Dempster–Shafer Combination (D-F) and the

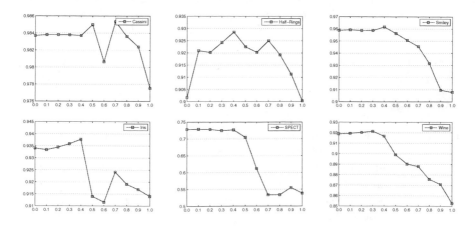

Fig. 2. Accuracy of DTCE on the datasets with different values of the α parameter

Table 2. Accuracy (%) for the different methods over the six datasets

Method	Synthetic			Real		
	Smiley	Cassini	Half-Rings	Iris	Wine	SPECT
WBC	89.863	97.022	84.157	86.324	77.377	57.191
CEA	91.716	97.249	85.826	88.127	78.933	59.864
BBC	92.427	97.752	86.908	90.648	80.016	61.419
MV	95.303	98.197	87.917	92.901	90.259	58.135
AVG	95.627	98.212	88.852	92.923	90.474	57.135
D-F	95.901	98.280	88.803	93.242	90.835	72.413
DTC	95.876	98.370	90.162	93.404	91.892	72.485
CCCE	**96.160**	**98.533**	**92.852**	**93.770**	**92.142**	**72.865**

Decision Template Combiner (DTC). For the DTC, the similarity measure in (7) was used. Besides, for the proposed CCCE, the α parameter employed in each dataset was the one for which the highest accuracy was reached in the first experiment.

4.1 Results

Notice that in the first experiment, when $\alpha = 0$, CCCE is equivalent to the DTC. However, as the α parameter is increased, the partitions in $\mathbb{P}^{db}$ will have more influence in the determination of the consensus partition. As Fig. 2 shows, the use of those partitions can improve the accuracy. However, when the partitions in $\mathbb{P}^{db}$ are more taken into account in the determination of the consensus partition, the accuracy drastically decreases. That is why it is very important to establish a correct balance between the number of partitions in $\mathbb{P}^{db}$ and the *ground-truth*, by adjusting the partitions weights.

In the second experiment, the results in Table 2 show that the proposed CCCE outperforms the accuracy of the base classifiers in the ensemble and the other combination methods, particularly the DTC. This shows that using the information of the $\mathbb{P}^{db}$ partitions, instead of only using the *ground-truth* partition like in the DTC, more representative *DT*s can be build. This way, the accuracy can be increased.

5   Conclusions

In this paper, we have proposed a new scheme to combine multiple classifiers by using clustering ensemble. It uses the main idea of the DTC of building class templates in an intermediate feature space. The use of unsupervised learning tools, specially clustering ensemble, helps to build more representative class templates in the intermediate feature space. An experimental comparison was carried out with other classifier combination methods, including the DTC, on several datasets. The results show that the proposed scheme improves the accuracy of the classifier ensemble and the other combination methods. This supports the idea that ensembles of supervised and not supervised classifiers can complement to each other and produce high quality classification results. As future work, we will perform a more exhaustive experimental evaluation using more complex datasets. Additionally, we will evaluate different clustering algorithms, consensus functions, the weights b_i associated with each partition as well as new distance measures.

References

[1] Kuncheva, L.I.: Combining Pattern Classifiers. Methods and Algorithms. John Wiley & Sons, New York (2004)

[2] Vega-Pons, S., Ruiz-Shulcloper, J.: A survey of clustering ensemble algorithms. International Journal of Pattern Recognition and Artificial Intelligence 25(3), 337–372 (2011)

[3] Jurek, A., Bi, Y., Wu, S., Nugent, C.: Classification by Cluster Analysis: A New Meta-Learning Based Approach. In: Sansone, C., Kittler, J., Roli, F. (eds.) MCS 2011. LNCS, vol. 6713, pp. 259–268. Springer, Heidelberg (2011)

[4] Gao, J., Liangy, F., Fanz, W., Sun, Y., Han, J.: Graph-based consensus maximization among multiple supervised and unsupervised models. In: 23rd Annual Conference on Neural Information Processing Systems, pp. 1–9 (2009)

[5] Ma, X., Luo, P., Zhuang, F., He, Q., Shi, Z., Shen, Z.: Combining supervised and unsupervised models via unconstrained probabilistic embedding. In: Proceedings of the Twenty-Second International Joint Conference on Artificial Intelligence (2011)

[6] Acharya, A., Hruschka, E.R., Ghosh, J., Acharyya, S.: C^3E: A Framework for Combining Ensembles of Classifiers and Clusterers. In: Sansone, C., Kittler, J., Roli, F. (eds.) MCS 2011. LNCS, vol. 6713, pp. 269–278. Springer, Heidelberg (2011)

[7] Xu, L., Krzyzak, A., Suen, C.: Methods of combining multiple classifiers and their applications to handwriting recognition. IEEE Transactions on Systems, Man and Cybernetics 22(3), 418–435 (1992)

[8] Kuncheva, L.: Combining classifiers: Soft computing solutions, pp. 427–452. World Scientific (2001)

[9] Rogova, G.: Combining the results of several neural network classifiers. Neural Networks 7(5), 777–781 (1994)

[10] Kuncheva, L., Bezdek, J., Duin, R.: Decision templates for multiple classifier fusion: an experimental comparison. Pattern Recognition 34(2), 299–314 (2001)

[11] Frank, A., Asuncion, A.: UCI machine learning repository (2010),
http://archive.ics.uci.edu/ml

[12] Hall, M., Frank, E., Holmes, G., Pfahringer, B., Reutemann, P., Witten, I.H.: The weka data mining software: An update. SIGKDD Explorations 11(1) (2009)

[13] Fred, A., Jain, A.: Combining multiple clustering using evidence accumulation. IEEE Transactions on Pattern Analysis and Machine Intelligence 27(6), 835–850 (2005)

Nested Dichotomies Based on Clustering

Miriam Mónica Duarte-Villaseñor, Jesús Ariel Carrasco-Ochoa, José Francisco Martínez-Trinidad, and Marisol Flores-Garrido

Instituto Nacional de Astrofísica, Óptica y Electrónica
Luis Enrique Erro #1, 72840, Santa María Tonantzintla, Puebla, Mexico
{mduarte,ariel,fmartine,mflores}@inaoep.mx

Abstract. Multiclass problems, i.e., classification problems involving more than two classes, are a common scenario in supervised classification. An important approach to solve this type of problems consists in using binary classifiers repeated times; within this category we find nested dichotomies. However, most of the methods for building nested dichotomies use a random strategy, which does not guarantee finding a good one. In this work, we propose new non-random methods for building nested dichotomies, using the idea of reducing misclassification errors by separating in the higher levels those classes that are easier to separate; and, in the lower levels those classes that are more difficult to separate. In order to evaluate the performance of the proposed methods, we compare them against methods that randomly build nested dichotomies, using some datasets (with mixed data) taken from the UCI repository.

Keywords: Nested Dichotomies, Binarization, Multiclass Problems, Supervised Classification.

1 Introduction

Supervised classification is one of the main issues in pattern recognition, which is applied in different fields such as medicine, astronomy, and economy, among others. In the most well-known scenario there are only two different classes to which each object can be assigned (binary classification), however, it is common to find problems in which more than two classes are involved (multiclass classification). Although multiclass classifiers have been developed to deal with multiclass problems, these problems become harder when the number of classes grows and, therefore, it is more likely to make classification mistakes.

An alternative approach to solve a multiclass problem consists in decomposing the problem into several binary classification problems; in this way the original problem is simplified and it is expected to achieve better classification accuracy. This later alternative is called binarization and among its most important approaches we find *One-vs-One* (OVO) [1], *One-vs-All* (OVA) [2] and nested dichotomies [3].

In a nested dichotomy, a multiclass problem is divided into several binary classificacion problems by using a binary tree whose root contains the set of all the problem classes. Then, the classes are split into two subsets of classes,

L. Alvarez et al. (Eds.): CIARP 2012, LNCS 7441, pp. 162–169, 2012.
© Springer-Verlag Berlin Heidelberg 2012

called superclasses, and a model is created to differentiate between them. This process is repeated, splitting superclasses until they contain a single class from the original set, i.e., each leaf of the tree contains only one class. In order to classify a new object, the constructed tree is traversed using a binary model to choose the branch that must be followed at each level; when a leaf is reached, its associated class is assigned to the object.

For each multiclass problem, it is possible to construct different nested dichotomies; finding a good one could help to reduce classification mistakes. There are several ways to build a nested dichotomy proposed in the literature [3–5], but most of them separate classes in a random way, which does not guarantee finding a good nested dichotomy. In this work, we propose three deterministic methods to build a nested dichotomy that separates first, at the upper levels of the tree, the more easily separable classes and leaves to lower levels the separation among classes that are hard to distinguish from each other. In a nested dichotomy, errors that appear in certain level cannot be corrected in lower levels and, therefore, they become classification errors in the final result. For this reason, it makes sense to try to reduce classification errors in upper levels and we believe that this can be achieved by following the proposed strategy, obtaining, as a consequence, a better classification accuracy.

The rest of this paper is organized as follows: in Section 2, we present some previous work on nested dichotomies. Section 3 contains a description of the proposed methods: Nested Dichotomy based on Clustering (NDC), Nested Dichotomy based on Clustering using Radius (NDCR) and Nested Dichotomy based on Clustering using Average Radius (NDCA). In Section 4, we show a series of experiments in which the proposed methods are compared against other state-of-the-art methods that use a random strategy. Finally, in Section 5, we present some conclusions and future research lines.

2   Previous Work

Choosing a nested dichotomy, given a multiclass problem, is not a trivial issue. Each multiclass problem can be decomposed in many different nested dichotomies. In [4] it is shown the recurrence relation that gives the number of nested dichotomies for a problem with n classes $(t(n) = (2n - 3)t(n - 1))$; for a problem with 12 classes, for instance, there are 13749310575 possible nested dichotomies. The classification results obtained by different nested dichotomies can vary, since each nested dichotomy contains different binary problems to be solved. Most of the works on nested dichotomies randomly choose the order in which the classes are separated. We can mention at least three of them.

In 2004, Frank and Kramer [3] propose the use of a binary tree that recursively splits the class set into dichotomies. At each internal node of the tree, including the root, the class set is partitioned into two subsets. The authors state that there is no reason to prefer a dichotomy over another one, and, therefore, they randomly choose the classes that go into every set partition. They also propose the use of an ensamble of nested dichotomies (END) in order to get better classification results.

Later, in 2005, Dong *et al.* [4] use an ensamble of nested dichotomies in which they consider only balanced dichotomies, i.e., when building a nested dichotomy, they randomly split the classes at each internal node but taking care of keeping an equilibrium between the number of classes at each child node; they call this method ECBND. They also propose a variant of the method (EDBND) in which the data (instead of the number of classes) is kept balanced at each internal node.

In 2010, Rodriguez *et al.* [5] consider that ensamble methods frequently generate better results than individual classifiers and propose the use of nested dichotomies of decision trees as base classifiers in an ensemble; they call this approach *Forest of Nested Dichotomies* (FND). In order to form the ensambles they consider three strategies: bagging [6], AdaBoost [7] and MultiBoost [8].

Finally, it is important to mention the work of Aoki and Kudo [9], who, in 2010, propose a top down method for building class decision trees, which are similar to nested dichotomies. However, class decision trees allow using multiclass classifiers to separate two groups of classes. The method proposed by Aoki and Kudo decides which classes must be separated, in each node, by testing different classifiers, and selecting those groups of classes producing lower error rates. Additionally, this method applies feature selection before evaluating the error rate of a classifier. Since the selection of the best classifier and the best subset of features for separating the best separable groups of classes, the method proposed by Aoki and Kudo is very expensive in time, and not always produces good results.

As stated before, when constructing a nested dichotomy, following certain criteria can help to obtain better classification quality. For this reason, in this paper we propose three methods that allow to build a nested dichotomy in a non-random and inexpensive way.

3 Proposed Methods

When a binary classifier in a nested dichotomy makes a mistake, the error is spread to lower levels of the tree, where it cannot be corrected. For this reason, it is important to reduce the number of errors in the upper levels of the tree. Following this idea, we propose to build nested dichotomies in which classes that are more easily separable are considered first, at the upper levels of the tree, and those classes that are harder to differentiate are postponed until lower levels.

3.1 Nested Dichotomy Based on Clustering (NDC)

The basic idea of the Nested Dichotomy based on Clustering (NDC) method is that classes with greater distance between each other are easier to separate and, therefore, they should be separated at the upper levels of a nested dichotomy. To determine the distance among classes, we compute the centroid of each class and measure the distance among them. Once these distances are computed, we find the two classes with centroids furthest away from each other, say m_1 and

m_2, and the rest of the classes are clustered into two groups using m_1 and m_2 as group centers.

We next describe the proposed method NDC, distinguishing between two main phases: the construction of the nested dichotomy and the classification process itself.

1. **Construction of the nested dichotomy.** Given a dataset of class-labeled objects, where each object is described by a set of attributes:
   (a) Choose the mean of each class as centroid of the class, taking into account all dataset instances. If there are non-numeric attributes, we choose, for each class, the object with the greatest similarity, on average, to all other instances of its class.
   (b) Create the tree root with all the classes and the centroids chosen in the previous step.
   (c) Create a dichotomy. This step is performed recursively, over each node containing two or more classes, until there is only one a class at each tree leaf.
      i. Choose the two classes whose centroids have the greatest distance between each other. Use the identified centroids as group centers.
      ii. Each class at the current node is grouped with the closest center, considering the distance between its class centroid and the defined group centers. If the distance toward the two centers is equal, the class is put into the first group.
      iii. A child node is created for each of the groups and the process is repeated.
   (d) Once the tree is built, a binary classifier is trained at each internal node of the tree in order to separate the groups of classes of its child nodes. For this purpose, all the instances from the training set corresponding to the classes grouped at each child node are used.
2. **Classification process.** Given an instance:
   (a) The tree is traversed, starting from the root and following the branches indicated by each binary classifier, until a leaf node is reached.
   (b) The class associated with the final tree leaf is assigned to the instance.

3.2   Nested Dichotomy Based on Clustering Using Radius (NDCR)

A drawback of the NDC method is that there can be classes that, despite having centroids that are far from each other, are difficult to separate due to considerable overlapping. The opposite case is also possible, i.e., classes with close centroids that, however, do not have overlap among them and, as a consequence, these classes are easy to separate. For this reason, we propose a variant of the NDC method that involves each class radius to compute the distance among classes. The class radius is computed as the distance between the class centroid and the element, within the class, furthest away from the centroid. Thus, in order to measure the distance between two classes, C_1 and C_2, given the centroid of each

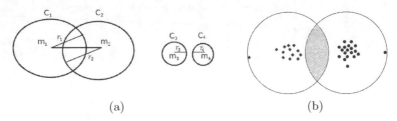

Fig. 1. (a) Representation of the distance between classes using their radius. (b) Example that shows the drawback of obtaining the class radius by computing the distance to the furthest away instance.

class, m_1 and m_2 respectively, the distance between them, $d(m_1, m_2)$, and the radius of each class, r_1 and r_2, we propose the function

$$D(C_1, C_2) = \frac{d(m_1, m_2)}{r_1 + r_2} \tag{1}$$

as a measure of the distance between classes. Note that $D = 1$ indicates that the classes are next to each other but they do not overlap, $D > 1$ that the classes are separated, and $D < 1$ that there is overlapping between the classes. The Fig. 1a shows, in general, the distance between two classes using their radius. In this figure, the centroids of classes C_1 and C_2, m_1 and m_2 respectively, are far from each other, but since both radius, r_1 and r_2, are big, there is overlapping between classes C_1 and C_2. Therefore, according to our distance, these classes are close to each other. On the other hand, the centroids of C_3 and C_4, m_3 and m_4 respectively, are close to each other, but since both radius, r_3 and r_4 are small, there is not overlapping between classes C_3 and C_4. Therefore, according to our distance, these classes are far from each other.

We call this method Nested Dichotomy based on Clustering using Radius (NDCR). The steps of the method are similar to the ones described for NDC, except that the Phase 1 requires an aditional step in which the radius of each class is computed, and that distance D, given in (1), is used in the step 1c instead of the distance between centroids.

3.3   Nested Dichotomy Based on Clustering Using Average Radius (NDCA)

A shortcoming of the method described in the previous section is its sensitivity to outliers. If an element of a class is far away from the rest of the class elements, the radius of the class will be big and, when it is used to compute the distance D, will mislead to think that there is overlapping between classes when, in fact, this might not be true; see Fig. 1b for an example. In order to deal with this scenario, we propose to compute each class radius as the average of the distance between the class centroid and all the elements of the class. Thus, this method is similar to NDCR, but the function used to measure the distance between classes is given by

$$D'(C_1, C_2) = \frac{d(m_1, m_2)}{r'_1 + r'_2} \qquad (2)$$

where r'_i represents the average of the distance between the centroid m_i and the elements within the class C_i.

4   Experimental Results

We conducted experiments on 20 datasets taken from the UCI Machine Learning repository [11] that have been commonly used to evaluate methods for constructing nested dichotomies; the Table 1 shows details of these datasets.

In all the experiments, we used 10-fold cross validation, using the same folds for all the methods. The binary classifiers that we use are C4.5, Random Forest, 1-NN, 3-NN and Naive Bayes taken from Weka 3.7.1. In our methods, as well as for 1NN and 3NN, we used, as distance function, the Heterogeneous Euclidean-Overlap Metric (HEOM) [10], which allows comparing object descriptions that include numerical and non-numerical attributes (mixed data). We compared our methods against: ND [3], ND-CB (Class Balanced) and ND-DB (Data Balanced) [4], as well as ensembles based on these methods, all of them also taken from Weka 3.7.1. The proposed methods are implemented in Java. All the experiments were conducted on a PC with a Pentium Dual-Core processor at 2.9 Ghz and 3Gb of RAM, running Linux-Ubuntu 11.04.

The Table 2 shows the results obtained in our experiments. The columns show the average accuracy, over the 20 datasets, of the different methods to build nested dichotomies using different base classifiers, as well as the results obtained with nested-dichotomies ensembles built using bagging [6], AdaBoost [7] and MultiBoost [8] approaches. The best result for each classifier is highlighted in bold.

In the Table 2, for each method, it is also shown the average accuracy over all the used base classifiers. In all the cases, the methods NDC and NDCR got the highest average accuracy (this is even more clear in the general average shown at the bottom of the table), suggesting that a better classification quality is achieved through the nested dichotomies built in a non-random way.

Table 1. Datasets used in the experiments

Dataset	Instances	Attributes Num.	Nom.	Classes	Dataset	Instances	Attributes Num.	Nom.	Classes
Anneal	898	6	32	6	Optdigits	5620	64	0	10
Audiology	226	0	69	24	Page-blocks	5473	10	0	5
Balance-scale	625	4	0	3	Pendigits	10992	16	0	10
Car	1728	0	6	4	Primary-tumor	339	0	17	22
Dermatology	366	1	33	6	Segment	2310	19	0	7
Mfeat-factors	2000	216	0	10	Soybean	683	0	35	19
Mfeat-Karhunen	2000	64	0	10	Vehicle	846	18	0	4
Mfeat-morphological	2000	6	0	10	Vowel-context	990	10	2	11
Mfeat-pixel	2000	0	240	10	Waveform	5000	40	0	3
Nursey	12960	0	8	5	Zoo	101	1	15	7

Table 2. Results of the performed experiments using individual nested dichotomies as well as ensembles of them. The columns show the average of the accuracy obtained by each method, using different base classifiers; the first three columns correspond to the proposed methods.

	Base Classifier	Method					
		NDC	NDCR	NDCA	ND	ND-DB	ND-CB
	C4.5	**88.81**	88.58	88.48	87.22	87.63	88.02
	RandomForest	93.07	92.89	92.73	93.51	**93.63**	93.52
	1-NN	93.65	**93.74**	93.50	93.64	93.63	93.65
	3-NN	88.97	88.76	88.78	88.92	88.87	**88.99**
	Naive Bayes	77.32	**78.35**	78.01	73.10	72.59	72.60
	Average	88.37	**88.46**	88.30	87.28	87.27	87.36
Bagging	C4.5	91.60	91.72	91.70	92.33	92.22	**92.68**
Ensemble:	RandomForest	94.32	94.17	93.94	94.47	94.38	**94.50**
	1-NN	93.33	93.36	93.32	93.40	**93.43**	93.41
	3-NN	**90.24**	89.29	89.32	90.01	90.01	89.99
	Naive Bayes	**82.61**	80.56	79.49	80.32	80.49	80.65
	Average	**90.42**	89.82	89.55	90.11	90.11	90.25
AdaBoost	C4.5	93.83	93.69	93.47	93.79	93.64	**93.97**
Ensemble:	RandomForest	94.36	94.23	94.36	94.55	94.37	**94.58**
	1-NN	**93.31**	93.28	93.28	93.19	93.28	93.19
	3-NN	92.51	92.49	92.46	92.55	92.48	**92.65**
	Naive Bayes	83.55	**83.62**	82.70	80.22	81.15	81.31
	Average	**91.51**	91.46	91.25	90.86	90.98	91.14
MultiBoost	C4.5	93.37	93.29	93.21	93.40	**93.59**	93.47
Ensemble:	RandomForest	94.30	94.12	94.17	94.34	**94.36**	94.32
	1-NN	93.35	**93.47**	93.33	93.30	93.31	93.27
	3-NN	91.11	**91.32**	91.34	91.22	91.20	91.02
	Naive Bayes	82.39	**83.44**	82.39	80.45	80.70	80.16
	Average	90.90	**91.13**	90.89	90.54	90.63	90.45
	Gral. Average	**90.30**	90.22	90.00	89.70	89.75	89.80

5   Conclusions

We proposed three methods, NDC, NDCR and NDCA, to build nested dichotomies in a non-random way. The main idea in these methods is to separate in the upper levels of the tree the classes that are easier to separate and separate in the lower levels the classes that are harder to separate. The first method determines which classes are easier to separate by clustering the classes using the distance among the centroids of the classes. The second method takes into account, besides the distances among centroids, the radius of each class, trying to determine if there is overlapping among the classes. Finally, the third method replaces the radius of each class by the average of the distance between the class centroid and all other elements within the class.

Experiments were performed on individual nested dichotomies and ensembles of nested dichotomies. The three proposed methods showed, in average, better classification accuracy than ND, ND-CB (Class-Balanced) and ND-DB (Data-Balanced), which build nested dichotomies in a random way. It must be also highlighted that, whereas the proposed methods are deterministic, the methods that build nested dichotomies in a random way could show variations in their classification accuracy in different runs (sometimes for the worst). Although in the proposed methods there is an additional cost (respect to random methods) for choosing the separable classes at each level of the nested dichotomy, the proposed separability criteria are inexpensive to evaluate, compared to other approaches previously proposed in the literature.

In the future, it would be important to explore different ways to assess the overlapping among classes, for instance, measuring how many objects are located in regions where most of the objects belong to other classes. In addition, methods of attribute and/or instance selection could be used in the binary classifiers, in order to improve the classification accuracy.

References

1. Hastie, T., Tibshirani, R.: Classification by pairwise coupling. Ann. Statist. 26(2), 451–471 (1998)
2. Rifkin, R., Klautau, A.: In defense of one-vs-all classification. J. Mach. Learn. Res. 5, 101–141 (2004)
3. Frank, E., Kramer, S.: Ensembles of Balanced Nested Dichotomies for Multi-class Problems. In: 21st International Conference on Machine Learning, ICML 2004, pp. 305–312. ACM, New York (2004)
4. Dong, L., Frank, E., Kramer, S.: Ensembles of Balanced Nested Dichotomies for Multi-class Problems. In: Jorge, A.M., Torgo, L., Brazdil, P.B., Camacho, R., Gama, J. (eds.) PKDD 2005. LNCS (LNAI), vol. 3721, pp. 84–95. Springer, Heidelberg (2005)
5. Rodrguez, J.J., Garca-Osorio, C., Maudes, J.: Forests of Nested Dichotomies. Pat. Rec. Lett. 31(2), 125–132 (2010)
6. Breiman, L.: Bagging predictors. Mach. Learn. 24(2), 123–140 (1996)
7. Freund, Y., Schapire, R.E.: Game theory, on-line prediction and boosting. In: 9th Annual Conference on Computational Learning Theory, COLT 1996, pp. 325–332 (1996)
8. Webb, G.I.: MultiBoosting: A Technique for Combining Boosting and Wagging. Mach. Learn. 40(2), 159–196 (2000)
9. Kazuaki, A., Mineichi, K.: A top-down construction of class decision trees with selected features and classifiers. In: International Conference on High Performance Computing and Simulation, HPCS, pp. 390–398 (2010)
10. Wilson, D.R., Martinez, T.R.: Improved heterogeneous distance functions. J. Art. Intell. Res. 6, 1–34 (1997)
11. Frank, A., Asuncion, A.: UCI Machine Learning Repository. University of California, School of Information and Computer Science, Irvine, CA (2010), http://archive.ics.uci.edu/ml

Combining Re-Ranking and Rank Aggregation Methods

Daniel Carlos Guimarães Pedronette and Ricardo da S. Torres

Recod Lab - Institute of Computing
University of Campinas
Campinas, Brazil

Abstract. Content-Based Image Retrieval (CBIR) aims at retrieving the most similar images in a collection by taking into account image visual properties. In this scenario, accurately ranking collection images is of great relevance. Aiming at improving the effectiveness of CBIR systems, *re-ranking* and *rank aggregation* algorithms have been proposed. However, different re-ranking and rank aggregation approaches produce different image rankings. These rankings are complementary and, therefore, can be further combined aiming at obtaining more effective results. This paper presents novel approaches for combining re-ranking and rank aggregation methods aiming at improving the effectiveness of CBIR systems. Several experiments were conducted involving shape, color, and texture descriptors. Experimental results demonstrate that our approaches can improve the effectiveness of CBIR systems.

1 Introduction

Given a query image, a Content-Based Image Retrieval (CBIR) system aims at retrieving the most similar images in a collection by taking into account image visual properties (such as, shape, color, and texture). CBIR systems use visual similarity for judging semantic similarity, which may be problematic due to the *semantic gap* related to the mismatch between low-level features and higher-level concepts. In order to reduce the semantic gap, several approaches have been proposed, as *re-ranking* and *rank aggregation* algorithms.

In general, CBIR systems consider only pairwise image analysis, that is, compute similarity measures considering only pairs of images, ignoring the rich information encoded in the relations among several images. In the past few years, there has been considerable research on exploiting *contextual information* for improving the distance measures and *re-ranking images* in CBIR systems [9,15,16,18,25,26]. Another approach for improving CBIR systems is based on using *rank aggregation* techniques [2,5]. Basically, rank aggregation techniques aim at combining different and complementary rankings in order to obtain a more accurate one.

Although a lot of efforts have been employed to develop new re-ranking and rank aggregation methods, few initiatives aim at combining existing approaches. Different re-ranking and rank aggregation methods produce different and complementary rankings, and therefore, can also be combined to obtain more effective results. Considering this scenario, we propose three novel approaches for

L. Alvarez et al. (Eds.): CIARP 2012, LNCS 7441, pp. 170–178, 2012.
© Springer-Verlag Berlin Heidelberg 2012

combining re-ranking and rank aggregation methods aiming at improving the effectiveness of CBIR systems. This paper presents new approaches to combine *(i)* re-ranking algorithms; *(ii)* rank aggregation algorithms, and both *(iii)* re-ranking and rank aggregation algorithms. A large evaluation protocol was conducted involving shape, color, and texture descriptors, different datasets and comparisons with baseline methods. Experimental results demonstrate that our combination approaches can further improve the effectiveness of CBIR systems.

2 Combining Re-Ranking and Rank Aggregation

2.1 Problem Definition

Let $\mathcal{C}=\{img_1, img_2, \ldots, img_N\}$ be an *image collection*. Let $\mathcal{D}$ be an *image descriptor*, which defines a distance measure $\rho(img_i, img_j)$ between two given images. The distance $\rho(img_i, img_j)$ among all images $img_i, img_j \in \mathcal{C}$ can be computed to obtain an $N \times N$ distance matrix A, such that $A_{ij} = \rho(img_i, img_j)$. Given an image query img_q, we can compute a ranked list $R_q=\{img_1, img_2, \ldots, img_N\}$ in response to the query, based on distance matrix A. We also can take every image $img_i \in \mathcal{C}$ as an image query img_q, in order to obtain a set $\mathcal{R} = \{R_1, R_2, \ldots, R_N\}$ of ranked lists for each image of the collection $\mathcal{C}$.

We can formally define a *re-ranking* method as a function f_r that takes as input the distance matrix A and the set of ranked lists $\mathcal{R}$ for computing a new and more effective distance matrix $\hat{A}$, such that $\hat{A} = f_r(A, \mathcal{R})$.

Let $\mathcal{D} = \{D_1, D_2, \ldots, D_m\}$ be a set of m image descriptors. The set of descriptors $\mathcal{D}$ can be used for computing a set of distances matrices $\mathcal{A} = \{A_1, A_2, \ldots, A_m\}$ (and associated set of ranked lists $\mathcal{R}_{\mathcal{A}}$). The objective of *rank aggregation* methods is to use the sets $\mathcal{A}$ and $\mathcal{R}_{\mathcal{A}}$ as input for computing a new (and more effective) distance matrix $\hat{A}_c$, such that $\hat{A}_c = f_a(\mathcal{A}, \mathcal{R}_{\mathcal{A}})$.

2.2 Cascading Re-Ranking

Both input and output of a re-ranking method defined by a function f_r is a distance matrix (the set of ranked lists $\mathcal{R}$ can be computed based on the distance matrix). In this way, an output matrix obtained from a given function f_{r_1}, implemented by a re-ranking algorithm can be used as input of other re-ranking algorithm f_{r_2}, aiming at further improving its effectiveness. We call this combination approach as *"cascading re-ranking"*, as it can be applied to a chain of re-ranking algorithms. The main motivation of this approach is based on two facts: *(i)* different re-ranking algorithms exploit contextual information in different ways and can be complementary (one algorithm can improve the quality of ranked lists that others did not); *(ii)* the second re-ranking algorithm can take advantage of improvements obtained by the first one. Figure 1 illustrates this combination approach, considering two re-ranking algorithms.

2.3 Re-Ranking with Rank Aggregation Combination

A single image descriptor can be submitted to different re-ranking algorithms, defined by a set of functions $\{f_{r_1}, f_{r_2}, \ldots, f_{r_m}\}$. In this scenario, a different distance matrix is produced for each re-ranking algorithm. However, the results can be complementary (one re-ranking can exploit contextual information that others did not). In this way, a rank aggregation method can combine the results of different re-ranking algorithms in order to obtain a single, and more effective distance matrix. Figure 2 illustrates this process, considering the use of two re-ranking methods followed by a rank aggregation step.

2.4 Agglomerative Rank Aggregation

The two previous combination approaches consider that only one image descriptor is available. This sections presents the *"agglomerative rank aggregation"* approach that uses several image descriptors as input. Given a set of image descriptors, different rank aggregation methods can be employed for combining them. However, each rank aggregation method produces a different output. In this way, another rank aggregation method can be used for combining the results of the first rank aggregation methods. This combination approach uses a hierarchical agglomerative method, in which the rank aggregation approaches are divided into layers. Figure 3 illustrates our approach for a two-layer rank aggregation scenario.

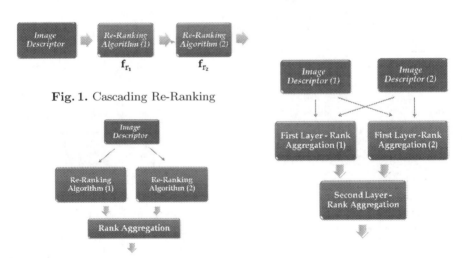

Fig. 1. Cascading Re-Ranking

Fig. 2. Re-Ranking with Rank Aggregation   **Fig. 3.** Aglomerative Rank Aggregation

3 Used Re-Ranking and Rank Aggregation Methods

This section briefly describes the re-ranking and rank aggregation methods considered for combination in our experimental evaluation.

3.1 Re-Ranking Methods

• **Contextual Re-Ranking:** The Contextual Re-Ranking (CRR) [15] algorithm re-ranks images by taking into account *contextual information* encoded in ranked lists and distance among images. The algorithm uses a *gray scale image* representation of distance matrices computed by CBIR descriptors, referenced as *context image*. The context image is constructed for the k-nearest neighbors of a query image and analyzed using image processing techniques.

• **RL-Sim Re-Ranking Algorithm:** The RL-Sim Re-Ranking [18] algorithm is based on the conjecture that *contextual information encoded in the similarity between ranked lists can provide resources for improving effectiveness of CBIR descriptors.* An iterative approach is used for improving the effectiveness of ranked lists.

3.2   Rank Aggregation Methods

• **Contextual Rank Aggregation:** The *Contextual Rank Aggregation (CRA)* [17] algorithm combines the results of different descriptors. The main idea consists in applying the Contextual Re-Ranking [15] algorithm, but using the affinity matrix W for accumulating updates of different descriptors at the first iteration. In this way, different matrices $A_d \in \mathcal{A}$ of different descriptors are combined.

• **RL-Sim Rank Aggregation:** Let $\mathcal{C}$ be an image collection and let $\mathcal{D} = \{D_1, \ldots, D_m\}$ be a set of descriptors. We use the set of descriptors $\mathcal{D}$ for computing a set of distances matrices $\mathcal{A} = \{A_1, \ldots, A_m\}$. The approach used by the RL-Sim Algorithm [18] combines the set $\mathcal{A}$ in a unique matrix A_c. For the matrices combination a multiplicative approach is used. Each position (i, j) of the matrix is computed as follows: $A_c[i,j] = (1 + A_1[i,j]) \times (1 + A_2[i,j]) \times \ldots (1 + A_m[i,j])$.

• **Set Rank Aggregation:**   we propose a simple rank aggregation method to be used in the *second layer* of the agglomerative approach combination. We call this method as *Set Rank Aggregation (SetRA)* . We consider the strategy of modelling the ranked lists as *sets* of different sizes, also used by the RL-Sim [18] algorithm. We use the function ψ to compute the similarity between ranked lists. The objective of function ψ, based on the intersection metric [6], is to compute a more effective distance between two images considering the contextual information encoded in the first K positions of their ranked lists. The function ψ computes the intersection between the subsets of two ranked lists considering different values of k, such that $k \leq K$, as follows ψ: $\psi(R_x, R_y, K) = \frac{\sum_{k=1}^{K} |KNN(R_x,k) \cap KNN(R_y,k)|}{K}$. The main idea is to compute the similarity between ranked lists considering each descriptor being combined, and add this similarity scores in order to obtain a new combined score. Let m be the number of matrices being combined and R_{i_x} be the ranked list produced by matrix A_i for image img_x and R_{i_y} for image img_y, the new combined similarity score ψ_c is computed as follows: $\psi_c(img_x, img_y, K) = \sum_{i=1}^{m} \psi(R_{i_x}, R_{i_y}, K)$.

4   Experimental Evaluation

This section presents conducted experiments for assessing the effectiveness of the three proposed combination approaches. We analysed our approaches under several aspects and compared our results with baselines from the literature. Three datasets and twelve descriptors (six shape descriptors, three color descriptors and three texture descriptors) are considered. We briefly describe the datasets in the following:

• **MPEG-7:** the MPEG-7 dataset [11] is a well-known shape dataset, commonly used for re-ranking and post-processing methods evaluation and comparison. The dataset is composed by 1400 shapes divided into 70 classes.

• **Brodatz:** the Brodatz [4] dataset is a popular dataset for texture descriptors evaluation. The Brodatz dataset are composed of 111 different textures. Each texture is divided into 16 blocks, such that 1776 images are considered.

• **Soccer:** the Soccer dataset [24] is composed by images from 7 soccer teams, containing 40 images per class.

As effectiveness measures, we use the Mean Average Precision (MAP). In addition to MAP, we consider the bullseye score ($Recall@40$) for the MPEG-7 dataset, which counts all matching objects within the 40 most similar candidates. Since each class consists of 20 objects, the retrieved score is normalized with the highest possible number of hits.

4.1   Cascading Re-Ranking

The evaluation of the *Cascade Re-Ranking* approach considers the MPEG-7 dataset and four different re-ranking methods: the Distance Optimization Algorithm (DOA) [16], the Mutual kNN Graph [9], the Contextual Re-Ranking [15], and RL-Sim [18] algorithms. We also considered the Contextual Re-Ranking [15] and RL-Sim [18] combined with all algorithms. Table 1 presents the results for $Recall@40$ measure. We can observe that the gains are positives for all combinations, ranging from +0.11% to +1.99%. Those results demonstrate that, even with contextual information already exploited by the first re-ranking employed, the second re-ranking can further improve the effectiveness when combined by our cascading approach.

Table 1. Cascading Re-Ranking Methods on the MPEG-7 dataset *(Recall@40)*

Descriptor	Score	Re-Ranking Algorithm 1	Score	Re-Ranking Algorithm 2	Cascade Score	Gain
CFD [16]	84.43%	Distance Optimization [16]	92.56%	Contextual Re-Ranking [15]	**93.39%**	+10.61%
CFD [16]	84.43%	Distance Optimization [16]	92.56%	RL-Sim Re-Ranking [18]	**94.40%**	+11.81%
IDSC [12]	85.40%	Mutual kNN Graph [9]	93.40%	Contextual Re-Ranking [15]	**93.68%**	+9.70%
IDSC [12]	85.40%	Mutual kNN Graph [9]	93.40%	RL-Sim Re-Ranking [18]	**94.09%**	+10.18%
CFD [16]	84.43%	RL-Sim Re-Ranking [18]	94.13%	Contextual Re-Ranking [15]	**94.23%**	+11.61%
CFD [16]	84.43%	Contextual Re-Ranking [15]	95.71%	RL-Sim Re-Ranking [18]	**95.94%**	+13.63%

4.2   Combining Re-Ranking Methods with Rank Aggregation

This section presents the evaluation of our approach for combining re-ranking with rank aggregation algorithms, considering three datasets and twelve descriptors, including shape, color, and texture descriptors. We consider the Contextual Re-Ranking (CRR) [15] and the RL-Sim [18] re-ranking algorithms, and the Set Rank Aggregation. Table 2 presents the MAP scores for RL-Sim [18] and Contextual Re-Ranking [15] algorithms in isolation (as baselines), and considering our combination approach. As we can observe, for almost all descriptors our combination approach presents a higher MAP score than both baselines, with significant gains. Exceptions are the LBP [14] and LAS [22] descriptors, in which the RL-Sim [18] presents low gains. However, we should note that, even for those cases, our combination approach presents a MAP score higher than the worst re-ranking method. Our approach also presents a higher average score when compared with both re-ranking algorithms.

Table 2. Re-Ranking with Rank Aggregation Combination on CBIR Tasks *(MAP)*

Image Descriptor	Type	Dataset	Score	Re-Ranking 1: *RL-Sim [18]*	Re-Ranking 2: *CRR [15]*	Rank Aggregation: *SetRA*	Gain
SS [19]	Shape	MPEG-7	37.67%	43.06%	44.79%	**47.33%**	+25.64%
BAS [1]	Shape	MPEG-7	71.52%	74.57%	76.60%	**78.31%**	+9.49%
IDSC [12]	Shape	MPEG-7	81.70%	86.75%	87.39%	**88.66%**	+8.52%
CFD [16]	Shape	MPEG-7	80.71%	88.97%	92.76%	**92.94%**	+15.15%
ASC [13]	Shape	MPEG-7	85.28%	88.81%	89.82%	**90.62%**	+6.26%
AIR [7]	Shape	MPEG-7	89.39%	93.54%	94.49%	**97.15%**	+8.68%
GCH [21]	Color	Soccer	32.24%	33.66%	33.02%	**33.78%**	+4.78%
ACC [8]	Color	Soccer	37.23%	43.54%	39.86%	**46.60%**	+25.17%
BIC [20]	Color	Soccer	39.26%	43.45%	43.04%	**47.27%**	+20.40%
LBP [14]	Texture	Brodatz	48.40%	47.77%	49.06%	**47.93%**	-0.97%
CCOM [10]	Texture	Brodatz	57.57%	62.01%	63.67%	**64.20%**	+11.52%
LAS [22]	Texture	Brodatz	75.15%	77.81%	78.48%	**77.89%**	+3.65%
Average			61.34%	65.32%	66.08%	**67.72%**	+11.52%

Table 3. Re-Ranking and Rank Aggregation Combination for Shape Descriptors

Shape Descriptor	Score	Re-Ranking 1: *RL-Sim [18]*	Re-Ranking 2: *CRR [15]*	Rank Aggregation: *SetRA*	Gain
SS [19]	43.99%	53.15%	51.38%	**54.69%**	+24.32%
BAS [1]	75.20%	82.94%	82.43%	**83.51%**	+11.06%
IDSC [12]	85.40%	92.18%	91.84%	**92.16%**	+7.92%
CFD [16]	84.43%	94.13%	95.71%	**95.98%**	+13.67%
ASC [13]	88.39%	94.69%	93.07%	**93.80%**	+6.12%
AIR [7]	93.67%	99.90%	99.80%	**99.99%**	+6.75%
Average	78.51%	86.17%	85.71%	**86.69%**	+10.42%

We also considered the bullseye score (*Recall@40*) for shape descriptors on the MPEG-7 dataset. Table 3 presents the effectiveness results considering the *Recall@40* measure. Similar results to the use of the MAP measure are observed. Our combination approach also presents better average scores (86.69%) than both re-ranking algorithms.

4.3   Agglomerative Rank Aggregation

For the experimental evaluation of our proposed Agglomerative Rank Aggregation approach, we select two descriptors for each visual property (shape, color, and texture). Table 4 presents the MAP scores of our combination approach. We can observe that significant gains are obtained when compared with the results of the use of descriptors in isolation and of the first-layer rank aggregation method.

Table 4. Agglomerative Rank Aggregation Combination for CBIR Tasks *(MAP)*

Descriptor	Type	Dataset	First Layer - Rank Aggregation	Second Layer - Rank Aggregation	Score (MAP)
CFD [16]	Shape	MPEG-7	-	-	80.71%
ASC [13]	Shape	MPEG-7	-	-	85.28%
CFD [16] + ASC [13]	Shape	MPEG-7	RL-Sim [18]	-	98.75%
CFD [16] + ASC [13]	Shape	MPEG-7	CRA [17]	-	98.77%
CFD [16] + ASC [13]	**Shape**	**MPEG-7**	**RL-Sim + CRA**	**Set Rank Aggregation**	**99.41%**
ACC [8]	Color	Soccer	-	-	37.23%
BIC [20]	Color	Soccer	-	-	39.26%
BIC [20] + ACC [8]	Color	Soccer	RL-Sim [18]	-	44.49%
BIC [20] + ACC [8]	Color	Soccer	CRA [17]	-	42.14%
BIC [20] + ACC [8]	**Color**	**Soccer**	**RL-Sim + CRA**	**Set Rank Aggregation**	**49.00%**
CCOM [10]	Texture	Brodatz	-	-	57.57%
LAS [22]	Texture	Brodatz	-	-	75.15%
LAS [22] + CCOM [10]	Texture	Brodatz	RL-Sim [18]	-	80.26%
LAS [22] + CCOM [10]	Texture	Brodatz	CRA [17]	-	81.63%
LAS [22] + CCOM [10]	**Texture**	**Brodatz**	**RL-Sim +CRA**	**Set Rank Aggregation**	**83.70%**

4.4   Comparison with Other Approaches

We also evaluated our combination approaches in comparison with other state-of-the-art re-ranking an rank aggregation methods, applied to various shape descriptors. Table 5 presents the results of our approach in comparison with other methods. We consider the re-ranking with rank aggregation combination, using the RL-Sim [18] and Contextual Re-Ranking [15] for re-ranking and the Set Rank Aggregation method. We can observe that our combination approach achieves very high effectiveness performance, being comparable to the best scores reported in literature. Our methods are also compared with other rank aggregation approaches on the MPEG-7 dataset. Three baselines are considered: the traditional Borda Count method; the recently proposed Reciprocal Rank Fusion [5] method; and the Co-Transduction [2] method, recently proposed for CBIR applications. Our agglomerative approach were considered for comparison. We can observe that our method outperforms the considered baselines.

Table 5. Re-Ranking methods comparison on MPEG-7 dataset

Algorithm	Descriptor	Score	Gain
Shape Descriptors			
CFD [16]	-	84.43%	-
IDSC [12]	-	85.40%	-
ASC [13]	-	88.39%	-
AIR [7]	-	93.67%	-
Re-Ranking Methods			
DOA [16]	CFD [16]	92.56%	+9.63%
LCDP [25]	IDSC [12]	93.32%	+9.27%
Mutual kNN [9]	IDSC [12]	93.40%	+9.37%
RL-Sim [18]	CFD [16]	94.13%	+7.13%
CRR [15]	CFD [16]	95.71%	+13.36%
LCDP [25]	ASC [13]	95.96%	+8.56%
SetRA (CRR+RL-Sim)	**CFD [16]**	**95.98%**	**+13.68%**
CRR [15]	AIR [7]	99.80%	+6.54%
RL-Sim [18]	AIR [7]	99.90%	+6.66%
TPG [25]	AIR [7]	99.99%	+6.75%
SetRA (CRR+RL-Sim)	**AIR [7]**	**99.99%**	**+6.75%**

Table 6. Rank aggregation comparison on the MPEG-7 dataset

Shape Descriptor	Rank Aggregation	Score [%]
Shape Descriptors		
DDGM [23]	-	80.03%
CFD [16]	-	84.43%
IDSC [12]	-	85.40%
SC [3]	-	86.80%
ASC [13]	-	88.39%
Rank Aggregation Methods		
CFD [16]+IDSC [12]	Borda Count	91.92%
CFD [16]+ASC [13]	Borda Count	93.51%
CFD [16]+IDSC [12]	Reciprocal [5]	94.98%
CFD [16]+ASC [13]	Reciprocal [5]	96.25%
IDSC [12]+DDGM [23]	Co-Transduction [2]	97.31%
SC [3]+DDGM [23]	Co-Transduction [2]	97.45%
SC [3]+IDSC [12]	Co-Transduction [2]	97.72%
CFD [16]+ASC [13]	CRA [17]	99.38%
CFD [16]+ASC [13]	RL-Sim [18]	99.44%
CFD [16]+ASC [13]	SetRA (RL-Sim + CRA)	99.50%

5   Conclusions

We have presented novel combination approaches for re-ranking and rank aggregation methods. The main idea of the our work consists in exploiting complementary rankings obtained by different methods in order to obtain more effective results. We conducted a large set of experiments and experimental results demonstrate that our approaches can further improve the effectiveness of image retrieval tasks based on shape, color and texture descriptors. In future work, we intend to investigate the use of other re-ranking and rank aggregation methods in a iterative combination approach.

Acknowledgments. Authors thank AMD, CAPES, FAPESP, FAEPEX, and CNPq for financial support. Authors also thank DGA/UNICAMP for its support in this work.

References

1. Arica, N., Vural, F.T.Y.: Bas: a perceptual shape descriptor based on the beam angle statistics. Pattern Recognition Letters 24(9-10), 1627–1639 (2003)
2. Bai, X., Wang, B., Wang, X., Liu, W., Tu, Z.: Co-transduction for shape retrieval. In: Daniilidis, K. (ed.) ECCV 2010, Part III. LNCS, vol. 6313, pp. 328–341. Springer, Heidelberg (2010)
3. Belongie, S., Malik, J., Puzicha, J.: Shape matching and object recognition using shape contexts. PAMI 24(4), 509–522 (2002)
4. Brodatz, P.: Textures: A Photographic Album for Artists and Designers. Dover (1966)
5. Cormack, G.V., Clarke, C.L.A., Buettcher, S.: Reciprocal rank fusion outperforms condorcet and individual rank learning methods. In: SIGIR 2009, pp. 758–759 (2009)
6. Fagin, R., Kumar, R., Sivakumar, D.: Comparing top k lists. In: SODA 2003, pp. 28–36 (2003)
7. Gopalan, R., Turaga, P., Chellappa, R.: Articulation-invariant representation of non-planar shapes - supplementary material. In: Daniilidis, K. (ed.) ECCV 2010, Part III. LNCS, vol. 6313, pp. 286–299. Springer, Heidelberg (2010)
8. Huang, J., Kumar, S.R., Mitra, M., Zhu, W.J., Zabih, R.: Image indexing using color correlograms. In: CVPR 1997, p. 762 (1997)
9. Kontschieder, P., Donoser, M., Bischof, H.: Beyond Pairwise Shape Similarity Analysis. In: Zha, H., Taniguchi, R.-i., Maybank, S. (eds.) ACCV 2009, Part III. LNCS, vol. 5996, pp. 655–666. Springer, Heidelberg (2010)
10. Kovalev, V., Volmer, S.: Color co-occurence descriptors for querying-by-example. In: MMM 1998, p. 32 (1998)
11. Latecki, L.J., Lakmper, R., Eckhardt, U.: Shape descriptors for non-rigid shapes with a single closed contour. In: CVPR, pp. 424–429 (2000)
12. Ling, H., Jacobs, D.W.: Shape classification using the inner-distance. PAMI 29(2), 286–299 (2007)
13. Ling, H., Yang, X., Latecki, L.J.: Balancing Deformability and Discriminability for Shape Matching. In: Daniilidis, K. (ed.) ECCV 2010, Part III. LNCS, vol. 6313, pp. 411–424. Springer, Heidelberg (2010)

14. Ojala, T., Pietikäinen, M., Mäenpää, T.: Multiresolution gray-scale and rotation invariant texture classification with local binary patterns. PAMI 24(7), 971–987 (2002)
15. Pedronette, D.C.G., da S. Torres, R.: Exploiting Contextual Information for Image Re-ranking. In: Bloch, I., Cesar Jr., R.M. (eds.) CIARP 2010. LNCS, vol. 6419, pp. 541–548. Springer, Heidelberg (2010)
16. Pedronette, D.C.G., da, S., Torres, R.: Shape retrieval using contour features and distance optmization. In: VISAPP, vol. 1, pp. 197–202 (2010)
17. Pedronette, D.C.G., da, S., Torres, R.: Exploiting contextual information for rank aggregation. In: ICIP, pp. 97–100 (2011)
18. Guimarães Pedronette, D.C., da S. Torres, R.: Image Re-ranking and Rank Aggregation Based on Similarity of Ranked Lists. In: Real, P., Diaz-Pernil, D., Molina-Abril, H., Berciano, A., Kropatsch, W. (eds.) CAIP 2011, Part I. LNCS, vol. 6854, pp. 369–376. Springer, Heidelberg (2011)
19. da, S., Torres, R., Falcão, A.X.: Contour Salience Descriptors for Effective Image Retrieval and Analysis. Image and Vision Computing 25(1), 3–13 (2007)
20. Stehling, R.O., Nascimento, M.A., Falcão, A.X.: A compact and efficient image retrieval approach based on border/interior pixel classification. In: CIKM 2002, pp. 102–109 (2002)
21. Swain, M.J., Ballard, D.H.: Color indexing. IJCV 7(1), 11–32 (1991)
22. Tao, B., Dickinson, B.W.: Texture recognition and image retrieval using gradient indexing. JVCIR 11(3), 327–342 (2000)
23. Tu, Z., Yuille, A.L.: Shape Matching and Recognition – Using Generative Models and Informative Features. In: Pajdla, T., Matas, J(G.) (eds.) ECCV 2004, Part III. LNCS, vol. 3023, pp. 195–209. Springer, Heidelberg (2004)
24. van de Weijer, J., Schmid, C.: Coloring Local Feature Extraction. In: Leonardis, A., Bischof, H., Pinz, A. (eds.) ECCV 2006, Part II. LNCS, vol. 3952, pp. 334–348. Springer, Heidelberg (2006)
25. Yang, X., Koknar-Tezel, S., Latecki, L.J.: Locally constrained diffusion process on locally densified distance spaces with applications to shape retrieval. In: CVPR, pp. 357–364 (2009)
26. Yang, X., Latecki, L.J.: Affinity learning on a tensor product graph with applications to shape and image retrieval. In: CVPR, pp. 2369–2376 (2011)

Extracting Understandable 3D Object Groups with Multiple Similarity Metrics

Antonio Adán and Miguel Adán

Departamento Ingeniería E. E. A. C. Universidad de Castilla La Mancha. Spain
{Antonio.Adan,Miguel.Adan}@uclm.es

Abstract. Some of the main difficulties involved in the clustering problem are the interpretation of the clusters and the choice of the number of clusters. The imposition of a complete clustering, in which all the objects must be classified might lead to incoherent and not convincing groups. In this paper we present an approach which alleviates this problem by proposing incomplete but reliable clustering strategies. The method is based on two pillars: using a set of different metrics which are evaluated through a *clustering confidence measure* and achieving a hard/soft clustering consensus. This method is particularly addressed to 3D shape grouping in which the objects are represented through geometric features defined over mesh models. Our approach has been tested using eight metrics defined on geometrical descriptors in a collection of free-shape objects. The results show that in all cases the algorithm yields coherent and meaningful groups for several numbers of clusters. The clustering strategy here proposed might be useful for future developments in the unsupervised grouping field.

Keywords: 3D shape representation, 3D Shape similarity, 3D Object Clustering.

1 Incomplete Grouping

Different clustering techniques, either hierarchical or partitional based strategies, aim to categorize similar objects together using any type of similarity metrics. Agglomerative clustering methods [1], place all objects into singleton clusters and iteratively merge them one at a time. Others, like spectral clustering [2] and graph partitioning [3] methods, partition the data into relatively dense subgraphs, minimizing the edges between the subgraphs. In addition, semi-supervised (or constrained) clustering methods have recently attracted considerable attention [4, 5].

In all those cases, the use of a unique metric and the imposition of a complete clustering (in which all the objects of the dataset must be classified in a particular cluster) might lead to incoherent solutions. The group coherence is broken when outliers (objects clearly different to the rest in the group) are included. In this paper we propose an approach which eliminates these two constraints. The paper's originality can be synthesized in two aspects: a clustering consensus between several similarity metrics, which will guarantee coherent groups, and an incomplete clustering proposal, which signifies that some objects might not belong to any cluster.

L. Alvarez et al. (Eds.): CIARP 2012, LNCS 7441, pp. 179–186, 2012.

Traditional clustering methods have been developed to analyze complete data sets. However there exist some examples which deal with clustering in incomplete data-sets. Cheng et al. [6] produce fine clusters on incomplete high-dimensional data space. Hathaway et al. [7] introduce four strategies for doing fuzzy c-means (FCM) clustering of incomplete data sets. Incomplete data consists of vectors that are missing one or more of the feature values. All approaches are tested using real and artificially generated incomplete data sets. In [8] the so-called kernel fuzzy c-means algorithm adopts a new kernel-induced metric in the data space to replace the original Euclidean norm metric in FCM. It is used to cluster incomplete data. Himmelspach et al. [9] present an extension for existing fuzzy c-means clustering algorithms for incomplete data, which uses the information about the dispersion of clusters.

Although algorithms dealing with clustering in incomplete datasets are relatively frequents in literature ([6-9]), to the best of our knowledge there are no works focused on incomplete clustering, in which we understand the term "incomplete" as that explained above, that is "some objects might not belong to any cluster".

Another clear difference between our approach and the aforementioned works is that we compare the clustering results for several similarity measures and, finally, we make decisions by integrating the clustering results. Most of the works just evaluate different approaches and select the most convenient but they do not integrate metrics. Some examples can be found in [10] and [11]. Jayanti et al [10] evaluate the clustering results on a classified benchmark database of 3D models after using two different approaches. The authors solely compare the clustering effectiveness of these two approaches, and do not integrate the methods. In [11] three existing 3D similarity search methods were chosen but no integration of methods is therefore performed.

Our approach is explained in the following sections. Sections 2 and 3 tackle the evaluation and clustering procedure. We present the term *confidence measure* as the parameter which globally evaluates the clustering result from each particular similarity metric and explain how incomplete clusters are extracted after a simple voting strategy. Section 4 is devoted to showing the experimental work and results. Our conclusions are provided in Section 5.

2   Clustering Evaluation for Different Metrics

Since our method is used in the object clustering research context, from here on we will talk about object clustering or, in general, 3D shape clustering.

Let us assume an object database with n objects O_i , i=1,...n and a set of metrics $d_p, p = 1, ... r$ which have previously been defined. We define r, nxn Similarity Matrices S_p as follows:

$$S_{p,ij} = d_p(O_i, O_j), \qquad i, j = 1,...n, p = 1, ...r \qquad (1)$$

Note that each Similarity Matrix stores the entire similarity information in a database, depending on the metric used. These Similarity Matrices S_p are used to carry out the clustering process. We specifically apply the Ward's hierarchical clustering method [12] based on the Similarity Matrices of equation (1). As is known, in hierarchical strategies, the data (in our case S) are not partitioned into a set of groups in a single step. Instead, a series of partitions takes place, which may run from a single cluster containing all objects to n clusters, each containing a single object. Hierarchical clustering is subdivided into agglomerative methods, which proceed by a series of fusions of the n objects into groups, and divisive methods, which separate n objects into successively finer groupings. The result may be represented by a dendogram which illustrates the fusions or divisions that take place in each successive stage of analysis. In each step, the clusters are defined by minimizing an objective function which usually measures the separation between clusters.

Ward's linkage uses the incremental sum of squares; that is, the increase in the total within-cluster sum of squares as a result of joining two clusters. The within-cluster sum of squares is defined as the sum of the squares of the distances between all objects in the cluster and the centroid of the cluster. For example, for clusters C_i and C_j, the Ward's equivalent distance is given by:

$$D^2(C_i, C_j) = \langle C_i \rangle \langle C_j \rangle \frac{\left\| \bar{x}_{C_i} - \bar{x}_{C_j} \right\|^2}{\langle C_i \rangle + \langle C_j \rangle} \tag{2}$$

where $\| \ \|$ signifies Euclidean distance, $\bar{x}_{C_i}$ and $\bar{x}_{C_j}$ are the centroids, and $\langle C_i \rangle$ and $\langle C_j \rangle$ are the respective number of objects in cluster C_i and C_j.

Let us now assume that the set of objects has been grouped into w clusters C_j, $j=1,...w$, $w<n$ following our hierarchical clustering approach. In order to evaluate the goodness of the grouping result we propose the object confidence value K which measures how well a particular object is assigned to a certain cluster. Equation (3) shows the object confidence value when object O_i is assigned to cluster C_k after using a metric d_p.

$$K_p(O_i | O_i \in C_k) = \frac{\min\{\hat{d}_p(O_i, C_j), \forall j \neq k\} - \hat{d}_p(O_i, C_k)}{\max\{\min\{\hat{d}_p(O_i, C_j), \forall j \neq k, \hat{d}_p(O_i, C_k)\}\}} \qquad p = 1, ...r \tag{3}$$

$$\hat{d}_p(O_i, C_j) = \frac{\sum_{\forall O_h \in C_j} d_p(O_i, O_h)}{\langle C_j \rangle} \tag{4}$$

Equation (4) calculates the mean inter-cluster distance of object O_i, and symbol $\langle . \rangle$ signifies the cardinal of a set.

Given a clustering proposal, the mean of the object confidence values for all the objects in the database is taken as the overall evaluation parameter. Thus, the *clustering confidence measure* for metric p, $\bar{K}_p$, is eventually defined as follows:

$$\bar{K}_p = \frac{\sum_{i=1}^{n} K_p(O_i)}{n} \qquad p = 1, ...r \tag{5}$$

3   Hard/Soft Incomplete Clustering

The definitive groups are built by using the *clustering confidence measures* for each metric and setting the number of clusters. Let us assume that p metrics are used and that up to w clusters can be taken in an object database. A *clustering confidence matrix* $M(pxw)$ containing parameters $\bar{K}_p$ for p rows, each corresponding to a particular metric, and w columns, each for a particular number of clusters, is then obtained. The objective is to extract the most suitable numbers of clusters and the best metrics for each case.

The system extracts a vector containing the number of clusters which reports the highest $\overline{K}_p$ value per row in M and obtains the median of the vector as the most reliable choice. The best metrics are also chosen for each column of M, penalysing the cases which yield unitary clusters. Let $\hat{w}$, $\hat{w} < w$, and $\hat{p}$, $\hat{p} < p$, be the number of selected clusters and metrics.

The next stage consists of achieving a common cluster labeling for all the metrics considered. A common labeling is imposed on all the clusters from each metric by considering the maximum concordance between them. The main idea is that the same label is assigned to the clusters belonging to different metrics in which the intersection is maximum. This is synthesized in equation (6). A short explanation follows.

Let $\hat{p} \leq p$ and $\hat{w} \leq w$ be the number of metrics and clusters established in the earlier stage, C_k^j be the k-th cluster after applying the j-th metric, $\langle A \cap B \rangle$ be the number of common objects in generic clusters A and B, $\langle C_m^1 \cap \{C_k^j\}_{k=1...\hat{w}} \rangle$ be the $\hat{w}$-vector which contains the number of common objects in the m-th cluster of the first metric with each one of the clusters obtained with the j-th metric. Assume also that the labeling of the first metric is denoted as $\Lambda(C_k^1) = k$, $k = 1, ... \hat{w}$.

In equation (6), $\Lambda(m)$ is a $\hat{p}$-vector containing the indices of the m-th group for each particular metric. Figure 1 a) presents an explicatory example of the labeling stage.

$$\Lambda(m) = \left\{ \arg max_k \langle C_m^1 \cap \{C_k^j\}_{k=1...\hat{w}} \rangle \right\}_{j=2...\hat{p}}, \quad m = 1, ... \hat{w} \tag{6}$$

In case of a certain metric h provides equal number of common objects for two or more clusters, the indexation of j in (6) is updated so that $j = 1 ... h - 1, h + 1, .. \hat{p}, h$. That is, the turn corresponding to the metric h is postponed at the end of the list.

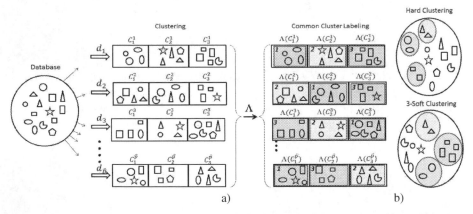

a)   b)

Fig. 1. Explanatory picture of the common cluster labeling process. a) The figure represents fourteen objects which are grouped in three cluster according $\hat{p}$ metrics. Labels 1, 2, and 3 are depicted in different colors. b) Incomplete clustering using *hard* and *3-soft coincidence* criteria taking $\hat{p} = 4$.

The third step concerns the integration and definition of the definitive incomplete clusters, taking a simple voting-consensus strategy. We defined two performance parameters to quantitatively evaluate the clustering concordance of an object from different metrics. We thus distinguish between *hard coincidence* and *soft coincidence*.

Hard coincidence occurs when all metrics classify the object in the same labeled cluster, whereas *j-soft coincidence* occurs if at least j, $(1<j<\hat{p})$, metrics do so. It is consequently possible to obtain the respective *hard coincidence groups* and *j-soft coincidence groups*. Figure 1 b) illustrates the clustering results after taking four metrics. Note that the clustering is incomplete for *hard* and *3-soft coincidence*.

4   Experimental Results

Our approach has been tested to cluster 3D shapes. To characterize a 3D shape we chose the representation model based on *RC-images* and took eight different metrics. Definition and metrics based on *RC*-images can be found in [13]. Basically a *RC-image* is an image in which the pixel (r, c) contains the relative voting frequency of features r and c in the nodes of the mesh model; r being the distance of the node to the mesh center and c being the absolute value of the curvature around the node. The *RC-image* is normalized, so that $r \in [0,1]$ and $c \in [0,\pi/2]$.

We built a model database with 45 real free-form shapes and studied the performance of the method through the parameter $\overline{K}_p$ for a different number of classes and similarity metrics. We then selected the three best metrics and analyzed the concordance between the respective clusters obtained. As will be shown, our method was able to provide coherent-incomplete clustering results after establishing a voting-consensus between metrics.

The first analysis stage consisted of calculating the *clustering confidence matrix* M. Table 1 shows M for $w - 6$ and $p = 8$. Each row corresponds to a particular metric d_p and each column for a particular number of clusters w. The last row and column corresponds to the average values of $\overline{K}_p$ per metric and per number of clusters respectively. Taking the highest $\overline{K}_p$ value per row, the optimum numbers of cluster are {3,5,2,2,6,6,3,2}, and we therefore chose the three most voted cases, that is $w_1 = 2, w_2 = 3, w_3 = 6$. With regard to the best metrics, we performed a selection for each w, bearing in mind several aspects such as: the average $\overline{K}_p$ values and the number of unitary clusters. The criterion is that if any unitary cluster appears for all the number of clusters selected, the metric is refused. The selected triplets were

Table 1. Clustering *confidence measure* calculated for metrics d_1 to d_8 and two to six clusters

#clusters Metric	#2	#3	#4	#5	#6	Average
d_1	0,3164	0,3328	0,2631	0,2461	0,2637	0,2844
d_2	0,3124	0,3162	0,3333	0,3638	0,3006	0,3252
d_3	0,3563	0,3342	0,3049	0,3269	0,3398	0,3324
d_4	0,6053	0,4339	0,1859	0,2033	0,2151	0,3287
d_5	0,2226	0,2202	0,237	0,2397	0,2656	0,2370
d_6	0,1365	0,1687	0,2084	0,2365	0,2631	0,2026
d_7	0,2963	0,322	0,306	0,2926	0,3163	0,3067
d_8	0,4749	0,351	0,3009	0,3019	0,3157	0,3489
Average	0,3022	0,2922	0,2791	0,2868	0,295	0,2910

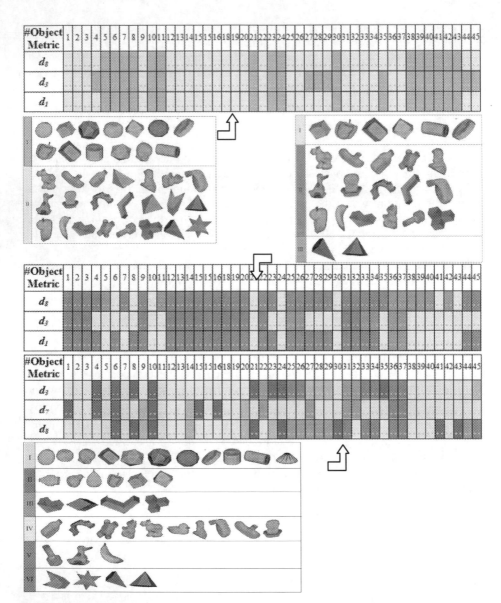

Fig. 2. Incomplete clustering results. *Hard coincidence* groups for two and three clusters and *2-Soft coincidence* groups for six clusters.

(d_1, d_3, d_8), (d_1, d_3, d_8) and (d_3, d_7, d_8). Note that the metric d_4 was not selected in cases $w_1 = 2$ and $w_2 = 3$ for not verifying the unitary cluster criterion. Thus, in the experimentation presented in this paper, *hard coincidence* cases occur when all three metrics classify the object in the same cluster. As regards *soft coincidence*, it is reduced to the case $j=2$.

Figure 2 shows the mesh models of the objects belonging to each group. The visual representation provides a qualitative evaluation of the curvature in the color scale which goes from yellow (low values) to red (high values). This color representation is used in order to better argue the discussion concerning the global geometry properties of each of the groups. The groups are also identified by colors in the tables introduced. Note that our method is able to provide coherent-incomplete clustering results after establishing a voting-consensus between metrics. Several comments follow.

In the case $w=2$ (first colored table)), note that the models in Group I have large flat zones and small high-curvature areas, signifying that parameter c in a large part of the model is low and is only high in a few nodes. Also note that there is a slight variation of the parameter r in the majority of the objects. Group II contains objects with high-curvature nodes which have disparate r values and, in general, the curvature distribution is more uniform than in Group I. Similar comments can be made for case $w=3$ (second table)) with regards Groups I and II. The objects in Group I have large flat and small high-curvature areas, whereas Group II contains objects which have disparate r values and, in general a more uniform curvature distribution than in Group I. Group III is composed solely of two pyramids. For six clusters ($w=6$) see the last table. In all groups it is possible to find a common property of the objects which makes these results compelling. For example, Group I is composed of more or less round objects, Group II contains round objects with some kind of tip or stalk, Group III contains parallelepide shapes, Group IV consists of typical smooth free form shapes which are extended to Group V but including pointed zones on the objects. Finally, all the objects in Group VI are polyhedral with extremely sharp areas.

5   Conclusions

In this paper we present a new approach to generate incomplete but reliable clusters. The method has been applied to cluster 3D objects through their mesh model representations. The clustering process is carried out under a consensus algorithm in which a set of metrics are considered for each particular database. In the classification process, the goodness of each metric is globally evaluated through the *clustering confidence measure*. The consensus algorithm finally establishes the so-called *hard* and *soft coincidence* parameters inside each of the groups, and decides which objects are definitively classified from different metrics.

This clustering approach has successfully been tested on a set of mesh models belonging to a wide variety of objects. The results proved in all those cases in which *hard* or *soft coincidences* between metrics were considered, very coherent clusters were obtained.

The idea of recovering coherent 3D shape groups using a consensus between different similarity metrics is interesting and may provide promising results in the future. Unfortunately, it is difficult to evaluate the quality of our results in comparison to other methods, principally owing to the lack of similar approaches and to the fact that it depends largely on the details of our test database. Our future lines of work are focused on labeling reliable groups of objects using extended databases with the aim of discovering the applicability of our method in a real environment. The goal in this case is to extract, from a large set of objects, specific subgroups of objects with a clear particularity. This will certainly be our objective in the future.

Acknowledgments. This research has been supported by the Spanish DPI2009-14024-C02-01 project.

References

1. Tan, P., Steinbach, M., Kumar, V.: Introduction to Data Mining. Addison Wesley (2005)
2. Shi, J., Malik, J.: Normalized cuts and image segmentation. IEEE Trans. Pattern Analysis and Machine Intelligence 22(8), 888–905 (2000)
3. Ertoz, L., Steinbach, M., Kumar, V.: Finding clusters of different sizes, shapes, and densities in noisy, high dimensional data. In: Proceedings of SDM 2003, SIAM Int'l Conf on Data Mining, San Francisco, CA (2003)
4. Basu, S., Bilenko, M., Mooney, R.: A probabilistic framework for semi-supervised clustering. In: Proceedings of the 10th ACM SIGKDD International Conference on Knowledge Discovery and Data Mining, Seatle, WA (2004)
5. Davidson, I., Ravi, S.: Clustering with constraints: feasibility issues and the k-means algorithm. In: Proceedings of SDM 2006: SIAM International Conference on Data Mining, Newport Beach, CA (2005)
6. Cheng, Z., Zhou, D., Wang, C., Guo, J., Wang, W., Ding, B., Shi, B.-L.: CLINCH: Clustering Incomplete High-Dimensional Data for Data Mining Application. In: Zhang, Y., Tanaka, K., Yu, J.X., Wang, S., Li, M. (eds.) APWeb 2005. LNCS, vol. 3399, pp. 88–99. Springer, Heidelberg (2005)
7. Hathaway, R.J., Bezdek, J.C.: Fuzzy c-means clustering of incomplete data. IEEE Trans. System Man and Cybernetic Part B 31(5), 735–744 (2001)
8. Zhang, D.-Q., Chen, S.-C.: Clustering incomplete data using kernel-based fuzzy c-means Algorithm. Neural Processing Letters 18(3), 155–162 (2003)
9. Himmelspach, L., Conrad, S.: Fuzzy clustering of incomplete data based on cluster dispersion. In: 13th International Conference on Information Processing and Management of Uncertainty
10. Jayanti, S., Kalyanaraman, Y., Ramani, K.: Shape-based clustering for 3D CAD objects: A comparative study of effectiveness. In: Computer-Aided Design, vol. 41(12), pp. 999–1007 (2009)
11. Chakraborty, T.: Shape-based Clustering of Enterprise CAD Databases. Computer-Aided Design & Applications 2(1-4), 145–154 (2005)
12. Ward, J.H.: Hierarchical Grouping to Optimize an Objective Function. Journal of the American Statistical Association 58(301), 236–244 (1963)
13. Adán, A., Adán, M.: Incomplete-Clustering Consensus Strategy Using RC-images. Pattern Recognition. 3DVC&R, UCLM Technical Report (2012)

Semantic Representation of Geospatial Objects Using Multiples Knowledge Domains

Rainer Larin Fonseca and Eduardo Garea Llano

Advanced Technologies Application Centre, 7ma A # 21406, Playa, Havana - 12200, Cuba
{rlarin,egarea}@cenatav.co.cu

Abstract. Geographical data is obtained through abstractions made from objects in the real world. Generally, each of these abstractions is obtained by taking into account only one point of view about the object being analyzed. When different abstractions are made on the same object different data sources regarding to it are produced. These data sources are generally heterogeneous. Thus the semantic processing of these objects become challenge since different data sources must be combined to obtain good results in tasks such as information retrieval and analysis for decision-making. This paper presents an approach based on ontologies to enrich the semantic representation of geospatial objects taking into account different abstractions made on them. The experimental results show the usefulness of this approach and how it is possible to make a multidimensional semantic representation automatically using classification algorithms and search techniques on trees.

Keywords: Ontology, Classification, Semantic Representation, Geospatial Data.

1 Introduction

Usually the objects in the geospatial field can be analyzed from different semantic points of view. Thus the semantic processing of these objects becomes a challenging task, since heterogeneous data sources regarding to these objects must be combined to obtain results in tasks such as data retrieval and analysis for decision-making.

There are several approaches regarding to the representation of different semantic point of view about a same object [1-7]. A conceptual spaces theory is presented in [1] by Peter Gärdenfors. The Gärdenfors' idea proposes that the different domains can be defined as a set of quality dimensions with a geometrical or topological structure. Then, an object in the conceptual space can be seen as a vector $v = (d_1, d_2, ..., d_n)$ where each $d_i \ \forall \ i = 1 ... n$ is a quality of this object referred to the related domain. In this approach the object is formed with qualities from different domains.

This paper presents a new ontology-based approach for making a semantic representation of geospatial objects taking into account several knowledge domains. Thus, is enabled the representation of different semantic of point of views about geospatial objects. It also enables the semantic representation of objects stored in heterogeneous data sources. This paper continues with Section 2 which deals about main elements of the proposed approach. The Section 3 presents a method for reducing the search space in the classification process of these objects. Section 4 presents experimental results that validate the proposed approach and finally Section 5 presents the main conclusions.

L. Alvarez et al. (Eds.): CIARP 2012, LNCS 7441, pp. 187–195, 2012.

2   The Fifth Dimension of Geographical Objects

Geospatial objects are usually described based on four conventional dimensions. These dimensions are referred to the location and behavior over time of these objects. In the last years there has been a new trend based on describe semantically geospatial objects. This new type of description can be named as the fifth dimension of these objects which is referred to the semantic nature of geospatial objects and the way which they should be understood by both humans and machines.

Geospatial objects have different meanings for different specialist. This fact implies that they assign different terms to the same object; e.g. "*The Zapata Swamp*" can be defined as "*Nature Reserve*". But this designation does not take into account all the semantic nature of this object, since it also can be defined as "*Historic Place*". When we are assigning a meaning to an object we are making a semantic representation of this object. This representation takes place in the "Semantic Space". The fact that the semantics of a particular object covers several disjoint domains can be defined as "*Multidimensional Semantics*" (MS). With the word *"Semantics"* we refer to the meaning of the object taking into account all the knowledge domains that define it. Then, we can say that the semantics is the set of all possible definitions related to the object nature. Taking into account whole the semantics of an object is hard enough; it usually takes into account only a subset of these definitions. In this way a *"Semantic Abstraction"* (SA) of the object is made. Formally we can define the Multidimensional Semantics (MS) of an object as follows:

Let $D_o = (d_1, d_2, ..., d_n)$ be the set of all domains of knowledge that define the semantic nature of an object "o", which satisfies that $d_i \cap d_j = \emptyset$ with $i \neq j$ and $n \geq 1$. Thus we can define the Multidimensional Semantic Abstraction (MSA) of an object as a subset of D_o. The representation of semantic abstraction of geographical objects brings great benefits since it enables different systems to process these objects more efficiently avoiding problems such as incompatibilities between heterogeneous formats.

Geospatial objects can be represented in the "*Semantic Space*" (SS) based on their semantic abstraction which is defined as "*Context*". The Context defines the knowledge area over which these objects are processed from semantic point of view.

Each object represented in the Semantic Space has only one context and a context can contain more than one object. Geospatial objects belonging to different contexts can be linked together through relationships between them, see Fig. 1.

Explicitly, an object in the Semantic Space can be seen as a vector $e = (s_1, s_2, ..., s_n)$ where each $s_i \forall i = 1..n$ is the similarity value regarding to the domain d_i.

To formally define the Semantic Space, it is necessary to state some definitions:

- Let $A = (a_1, a_2, ..., a_k)$ be the finite set of attributes.
- Let $B = (b_1, b_2, ..., b_h)$ be the finite set of axioms.
- Let $\hat{a}$ be an attribute that contains the geo-reference value of the geographical objects.
- Let $C = (c_1, c_2, ..., c_p)$ be the finite set of concepts where for each $c_i \subseteq A \forall c_i \in C$.

- Let $X = (x_1, x_2, ..., x_n)$ be the finite set of concepts referring to geographical objects where $x_j \subseteq A \cup \{\hat{a}\} \; \forall \; x_j \in X$.
- Let $U = X \cup C$ be the finite set of all possible concepts.
- Let $R = (r_1, r_2, ..., r_t)$ be the finite set of Relationships where $r_s \subseteq U \times U \; \forall \; r_s \in R$.
- Let $r' \subseteq X \times C$ be relationships of instantiation.
- Let $\mathbb{O} = (O_1, O_2, ..., O_q)$ be the finite set of Ontologies where $O_l = (\mathcal{U}_l, \mathcal{R}_l, \mathcal{B}_l)$ such that $\mathcal{U}_l \subseteq U, \mathcal{R}_l \subseteq R, \mathcal{B}_l \subseteq B$.

For each $x_i \in X$ the context t_j is defined as follows:

- Let $t_j = (N, E)$ be the jth context, where N is the finite set of concepts that have relationships of instantiation with the geographical objects x_i and E is the finite set of Ontologies linked with these objects, defined as below:
  - $N = (c \in C : x_i \; r' \; c).$ (1)
  - $E = (O_t = (\mathcal{U}_t, \mathcal{R}_t, \mathcal{B}_t) \in \mathbb{O} : \exists \; c \in N \wedge c \in \mathcal{U}_t).$ (2)

Then we can define the Semantic Space as follows:

- Let $T = (t_1, t_2, ..., t_n)$ be the Semantic Space defined by a finite set of contexts where t_j is the context referring to $x_j \in X$. Note that x_i, x_j with $i \neq j$ can have the same context.

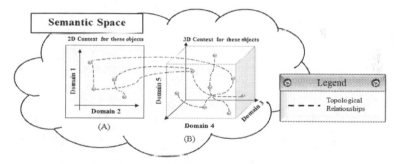

Fig. 1. Two different contexts represented in the Semantic Space. In (A) a 2D context defined by two domains is shown, in (B) a 3D context defined by three domains is shown.

In this approach, the semantic abstraction of geospatial objects is made by Data-Representation Nodes and together form the Data-Representation Ontology (DRO)[8]. Based on the Semantic Space definition we can define the DRO as a graph $G = (V, Z)$ where one hand we have that $V = (v_1, v_2, ..., v_n)$ is the finite set of DRN such as for each geographical object x_i the corresponding DRN v_i exists. On the other hand we have that Z is the finite set of edges where $z_{ij} \in Z$ exists among the DRN v_i and v_j if and only if the geographical objects x_i and x_j are linked by a relationship $r \in R$. Similarly, the Higher-Level Ontologies (HLO) [8] in this space are defined by the expression 2 (E). The main advantage of this approach is the representation of more information about the geographical objects, which implies obtaining better results in tasks such as information retrieval and analysis for decision making.

3   Search Space Reduction in DRN Classification

As is described in [8] each geospatial object in the DRO is represented by a DRN. To set an interrelationship among the DRO and the domain ontologies (HLO) is necessary to classify the DRN regarding to existing concepts in HLO based on semantic similarity criteria. To automatically achieve this, a method based on the paradigm of the tree search with heuristic using nearest neighbor rule with rejection (1-NN_R) is presented. This new method is a variant of the method proposed in [8] which take advantage of the underlying taxonomy in the HLO to reduce the search space in the classification process. Thus, the HLO taxonomy can be defined as a finite set of concepts such that there is at least one (c^*), which can be named as *"Root"* because it is the most abstract concept from which other concepts are defined. The remaining concepts in the taxonomy are descendants of the Root; they can be named as *"child-concepts"* for those who have a relationship of type *"subclass_of"* with others including the Root. These concepts can be divided into p disjoint sets named as *"sub-taxonomies"*. Those concepts that do not have descendants can be named as *"leaf concepts"*.

From this abstraction, the DRN classification ($x_i \leftrightarrow drn_i$) can be faced using search trees methods. Thus a concept $c_i \in C$ defined by drn_i can be obtained without having to process whole concepts in C, see pseudo code (A) in Fig. 2.

```
Inputs: C, X, R
Output: R
 1:  for ô = 0 to q do
 2:      M* = getSuccOf(Cô)
 3:      for n̂ = 0 to n do
 4:          U = D(Xn̂, Cô)
 5:          repeat
 6:              S(m*, isCorrect, dis) = get1NN_R(Xn̂, M*, U, R)
 7:              U = S → dis
 8:              if S → isCorrect then
 9:                  Set W = {(Xn̂, S → m*)}
10:                  Add W to R
11:              else
12:                  M* = getSuccOf(S → m*)
13:              end if
14:          until S → isCorrect ≠ true
15:      end for
16:  end for
```

```
Inputs: DRNi, M*, U, R
Output: S
 1:  Set minDis = D(DRNi, m*₁)
 2:  Set S = {m*₁, false, minDis}
 3:  for j = 1 to p do
 4:      if minDis > D(DRNi, m*ⱼ) then
 5:          Set minDis = D(DRNi, m*ⱼ)
 6:          if minDis < R then
 7:              Set S = {m*ⱼ, true, minDis}
 8:          else
 9:              Set S = {m*ⱼ, false, minDis}
10:          end if
11:      end if
12:  end for
13:  if S → minDis > U then
14:      Set S → m* = getAntOf(S → m*)
15:  end if
16:  return S
```

(A)   (B)

Fig. 2. (A) Pseudo code of the algorithm 1-NN_R-BFS. (B) Pseudo code of the algorithm 1-NN_R. Algorithms used for classification of NRD.

Where:
Let M^* be the finite set of concepts $m_j^* \in C$ that are input parameters in the proposed method. M^* is defined as below:

$$M^* = \{m_1^*, m_2^*, \dots, m_p^*\} / M^* \subseteq C \tag{3}$$

Likewise S is the result of the 1NN_R algorithm described in the pseudo code (B) of Fig. 2. Is defined as below:

$$S = (m^*, \text{isCorrect}, \text{dis}) \tag{4}$$

Where:

- m^* : It is the concept that better defines to drn_i.
- isCorrect: Variable that denote if the nrd_i was classified or not.
- dis: It is the computed dissimilarity between nrd_i and m_j^*.

In the pseudo code (B) the 1NN_R modified algorithm is shown. This algorithm is used by the proposed algorithm (1NN_R-BFS), which is presented in pseudo code (A), see Fig. 2.

For the pseudo code B we have that:

- $D(\text{drn}_i, m_j^*)$: Function that computes the dissimilarity among drn_i and m_j^*.
- $\mathcal{R}$: Denotes the rejected threshold for the DRN classification.
- getAntOf(m^*): Function that returns the concept $m^{*\prime}$ which is an antecessor of m^* in the taxonomy.
- U: Denotes the computed dissimilarity to the concept $m^{*\prime}$ whose descendant are contained in M^*. U is used as stopping criterion of the algorithm.

The 1-NN_R algorithm let to know if the drn_i was classified or not at each iteration. S contains the concept m_j^* which better defines to drn_i, the value of if the classification was correct and the computed similarity value. This paper proposes the Jaccard distance [9] to determine the similarity between both DRN (x_i) and Concepts (c_i) based on their features. For a better understanding of this pseudo code (A) of Fig. 2 it is necessary to define that:

- m^*: Denotes the Root /Sub-root concept in the HLO taxonomy for all HLO processed.
- $\mathbb{C}$: Denotes the finite set of Root /Sub-root taken into account by the $1 - \text{NN\_R} - \text{BFS}$ algorithm, see the expression (5):

$$\mathbb{C} = \{c_1^*, c_2^*, \dots, c_q^*\} \tag{5}$$

- X: Denotes the finite set of DRN to be classified, see the expression (6):

$$X = \{\text{nrd}_1, \text{nrd}_2, \dots, \text{nrd}_n\} \tag{6}$$

- getSuccOf(c^*) : Is the function that returns in M^* those concepts $m_j^* \; \forall j = 1 \dots p$ which are successors of m^* in the HLO taxonomy.
- get1NN_R($\text{nrd}, M^*, U, \mathcal{R}$) : Is the function that executes the $1 - \text{NN\_R}$ algorithm.
- $\mathbb{R}$: Denotes the finite set W_i of pairs of m_j^* and nrd_i that have a taxonomic relationship between them, see the expressions (7) and (8):

$$\mathbb{R} = \{W_1, W_2, \dots, W_k\} \quad (7) \qquad W = \{(\text{nrd}_i, m_j^*)\} \tag{8}$$

The underlying idea behind this method is to take the shortest path to the concept m^* that better defines to the nrd_i that is being processed. This method follows the heuristic that the similarity increases when the drn_i being close to the concept m_j^* with which it can be classified and decreases when the drn_i being away from it.

4   Experimental Results

4.1   Automatic Representation of Geographical Data in the Multidimensional Semantic Space

To validate the proposed method, the use of geographical objects that can be seen from different semantic domains was taken. Each of these domains is represented by a different ontology. Three domains for representing the set of objects have been selected. These domains are: N*ature Reserve (NR), Tourist Attraction (TA) and Historic Place (HP)*. The selected objects are: *Playa Girón (PG), Castillo de los Tres Reyes del Morro (CM), Parque Baconao (PB), Sierra del Rosario (SR), Ciénaga de Zapata (CZ), Sierra Maestra (SM), Cayo Coco (CC), Catedral de La Habana (CLH), Sierra del Escambray (SE), Centro Histórico de Camagüey (CHC)*. Each of these objects contains features that are taken for the classification process. The Table 1 shows the binary vectors that represent the existence or absence of these features for both objects and domains.

Table 1. The obtained vectors of common features for both concepts in HLO and DRN and the ground true of the objects classification taking into account expert criteria is presented

Domains	Binary Vectors for the Domains																		
NR	1	1	1	1	1	1	1	1	0	0	0	0	0	0	0	0	0	0
TA	1	1	0	0	0	0	0	0	1	1	1	1	1	1	0	0	0	0
HP	1	1	0	0	0	0	0	0	0	0	0	0	1	1	1	1		

Objects	Binary Vectors for the Objects																		Ground True
PG	1	1	1	0	1	1	1	0	1	0	1	1	0	1	1	1	1	0	NR, TA, HP
CM	1	1	0	0	0	0	0	0	1	0	1	1	1	1	1	1	1	1	- , TA, HP
PB	1	1	1	1	0	1	1	1	1	1	0	1	1	1	1	1	1	0	NR, TA, HP
SR	1	1	1	1	0	1	0	1	0	0	0	0	0	0	0	0	0	0	NR, -, -
CZ	1	1	1	1	0	1	0	1	0	0	1	0	1	1	0	0	0	0	NR, TA,-
SM	1	1	1	1	0	1	1	1	0	0	0	0	0	1	1	0	0	0	NR, -, HP
CC	1	0	0	0	0	0	0	0	1	1	0	1	1	0	0	0	0	0	-, TA, -
CLH	1	1	0	0	0	0	0	0	1	1	0	1	1	0	1	1	1	1	-, TA, HP
SE	1	1	1	1	1	1	1	1	0	0	0	0	0	0	1	1	1	1	NR, -, HP
CHC	1	1	0	0	0	0	0	0	0	0	0	0	0	1	0	1	1		-, -, HP

The classification was made in MATLAB[10] using the Jaccard Distance implementation of PRTools toolbox [11, 12]. The Fig. 3-A shows the belonging values obtained for each geospatial object regarding to the domains. Axes are indicating the semantic domains. The objects are represented based on the value of belonging to each of these domains. In this figure can be shown as geospatial objects semantically different are distant between them while similar objects are close. The Fig. 3-B shows these geospatial objects represented in the multidimensional Semantic Space using the viewer Protégé 4.0.

The main contribution of the proposed approach is that it provides more information about the objects represented in the Multidimensional Semantic Space. This fact enables the data-analysis from different points of view improving conventional tasks such as information retrieval and analysis for decision-making. The experiment also shows the feasibility of carrying out this type of representation automatically taking into account different domains of knowledge from which geospatial objects can be defined.

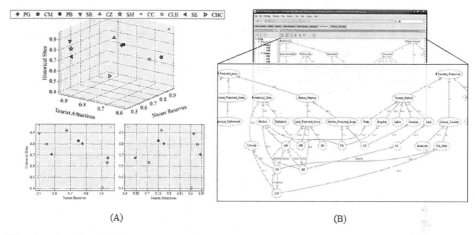

(A)   (B)

Fig. 3. (A) Graphic Representation of the belonging values of the geographical objects regarding to the domains. (B) Graphical Representation of the Generated Ontology (ORD + ONS) using the Protégé viewer.

4.2   Comparative Results between 1-NN_R and 1-NN_ R-BFS Algorithms

The main objective of this experiment is compare the performance of the 1-NN_R-BFS algorithm regarding to 1-NN_R algorithm based on the number of transactions in the classification process. Thus, the search space is reduced taking advantage of the taxonomic structure of the ONS. The used datasets have the structure shown in expression 11 and the results are shown in Table 3.

$$DS = (G_{ds}, O_{ds}) \tag{11}$$

Where:

- G_{ds}: It is the geospatial dataset that contains geospatial objects (X) to be used.
- O_{ds}: It is the ontological dataset that contains the HLO (E) to be used.

For this experiment has been used three datasets (DS) described to below:

- DS_1: For this dataset we have that:
    - G_{ds_1}: It is the set of geospatial data layers that contains information about two types of objects: soil and geology.
    - O_{ds_1}: For this dataset we have used a *Land Cover Ontology*. This HLO is a domain ontology which contains the semantic abstraction of the geospatial dataset explicitly defined by the Geology and Soil concepts.
    The goal of this dataset is to show the performance of both algorithms taking into account a high amount of geospatial objects. The geospatial objects are semantically defined by one domain ontology (*Land Cover Ontology*).
- DS_2: For this dataset we have that:
    - G_{ds_2}: This geographical dataset is the same of the dataset DS_1, but taking one data layer for each type of objects (geology and soil).

- O_{ds_2}: For this dataset we have used three HLO, they are: The Land Cover Ontology (previously used in the dataset DS_1), the Rocks Classification Ontology and the Soil Classification Ontology.

  The goal of this dataset is to show the performance of both algorithms taking into account a multidimensional context into the Semantic Space. The context is defined by three different Ontologies. Some of these objects belong to one or several domain.

- DS_3: For this dataset we have that:
  - G_{ds_3}: It is the same geographical dataset used in the dataset DS_1.
  - O_{ds_3}: It is the same ontological dataset used in the dataset DS_2.

  The goal of this dataset is to show the performance of both algorithms taking into account many geospatial objects over a multidimensional context.

Table 2. Transactions effected by each algorithm on each dataset

Datasets	Algorithms $\widehat{A}$	$\ddot{A}$	Saved Transaction
$DS_{1_{(D^+,O^-)}}$	194940	58482	70 %
$DS_{2_{(D^-,O^+)}}$	114855	30870	73,11 %
$DS_{3_{(D^+,O^+)}}$	604314	337896	44,08 %

$\widehat{A}$: 1-NN_R Algorithms.
$\ddot{A}$: 1-NN_R-BFS Algorithms.
D^+: A lot of data in the geographical dataset.
D^-: Few data in the geographical dataset.
O^+: Multidimensional ontological dataset.
O^-: One-dimensional ontological dataset.

The performance results of each algorithm for each of the datasets are shown in Table 2. Each of these datasets is focused on different variants of processing that might be encountered in real applications, these are: A large amount of objects in a one-dimensional context (D^+, O^-), a few objects in a multidimensional context (D^+, O^-) and a large amount of objects in a multidimensional context (D^+, O^-). As result we can see that in all cases the number of transactions performed by the 1-NN_R algorithm is bigger than those made by the 1-NN_R-BFS algorithm. This is because on one hand the 1-NN_R algorithm processes all the objects in each data set, making unnecessary transactions. On the other hand we have that the 1-NN_R-BFS algorithm optimizes the processing through reducing the search space taking advantage of the taxonomic structure of the ONS.

5   Conclusions

The proposed approach seeks to lay the groundwork for representing geographical objects from semantic point of view automatically. The main advantage of this approach lies in the proposal for a mechanism that can contain different semantic abstractions made from geographical objects. This makes it possible to represent these objects closer to their semantic nature. This results in the representation of more information about these objects. Thus, tasks like information retrieval and analysis for decision making can be improved. In addition the use of the algorithm 1-NN_R-BFS decreases the number of transactions made over the sets of data. This fact brings the additional advantage that these methods can be used in real applications.

References

1. Gärdenfors, P.: Conceptual spaces as a framework for knowledge representation. Mind and Matter 2, 9–27 (2004)
2. Raubal, M.: Formalizing Conceptual Spaces. Formal Ontology in Information Systems. In: Proceedings of the Third International Conference (FOIS 2004), p. 114 (2004)
3. Carmagnola, F., et al.: A Semantic Framework for Adaptive web-based Systems. In: Proceedings of the 9th Conference on Advances in Artificial Intelligence, pp. 370–380 (2005)
4. Balley, S., Parent, C., Spaccapietra, S.: Modelling geographic data with multiple representations. International Journal of Geographical Information Science 18, 329–354 (2004)
5. Adnani, M.E., Yétongnon, K., Benslimane, D.: A multiple layered functional data model to support multiple representations and interoperability of GIS: application to urban management systems. In: Proceedings of the 9th ACM International Symposium on Advances in Geographic Information Systems, pp. 70–75 (2001)
6. Strang, T., Linnhoff-Popien, C., Frank, K.: CoOL: A Context Ontology Language to Enable Contextual Interoperability. In: Stefani, J.-B., Demeure, I., Zhang, J. (eds.) DAIS 2003. LNCS, vol. 2893, pp. 236–247. Springer, Heidelberg (2003)
7. Ahlqvist, O.: A Parameterized Representation of Uncertain Conceptual Spaces. Transactions in GIS 8(4), 493–514 (2004)
8. Larin-Fonseca, R., Garea-Llano, E.: Automatic Representation of Geographical Data from Semantic Point of View throughout a New Ontology and Classification Techniques. Transaction in GIS 15(1) (2011)
9. Jaccard, P.: Étude comparative de la distribution florale dans une portion des Alpes et des Jura. Bulletin de la Société Vaudoise des Sciences Naturelles 37, 547–579 (1901)
10. MATLAB, version 7.10.0 (R2010a). The MathWorks Inc., Natick (2010)
11. Duin, R.P.W., et al.: PRTools4 A Matlab Toolbox for Pattern Recognition Version 4.1.5. Delft Pattern Recognition Research, Faculty EWI - ICT, Delft University of Technology, The Netherlands (2009), http://prtools.org
12. Duin, R.P.W., et al.: DisTools A Matlab Toolbox for Pattern Recognition Delft Pattern Recognition Research, Faculty EWI - ICT, Delft University of Technology, The Netherlands (2009), http://prtools.org

Feature Extraction and Classification for Insect Footprint Recognition

Bok-Suk Shin[1], James Russell[2,3], and Reinhard Klette[1]

[1] Department of Computer Science, The University of Auckland
b.shin@auckland.ac.nz
[2] School of Biological Sciences, The University of Auckland
[3] Department of Statistics, The University of Auckland
Private Bag 92019, Auckland, New Zealand

Abstract. We propose a method to extract and classify insect footprints for the purpose of recognition. Our four-level procedural feature extraction model is defined as follows: First, images produce new data via the trace transform. Second, for reducing the dimensionality of the produced data, we apply some mathematical conversions. Third, dimensionality-reduced data are converted into frequency components. Finally, characteristic signals with significant components of representative values are created by excluding insignificant factors such as those related to noise. For classification, based on uncertain features, we propose a decision method defined by fuzzy weights and a fuzzy weighted mean. The proposed fuzzy weight decision method estimates weights according to degrees of contribution. Weights are assigned by ranking the degree of a feature's contribution. We present experimental results of classification by using the proposed method on scanned insect footprints. Experiments show that the proposed method is suitable for noisy footprints with irregular directions, or symmetrical patterns in the extracted segments.

1 Introduction

A method for monitoring small animals is defined by the use of tracking tunnels [1]. Tracks are collected on white *tracking cards* having a pre-inked middle part. Animals, attracted by lures, walk through the tracking tunnel and leave their footprints on the tracking card. In environmental surveillance, footprint analysis helps for solving monitoring tasks, for example by verifying the presence of some rodents or insects, or for more detailed ecological or biological studies as supported by those footprints [2,3]. The identification requires that individual footprints are extracted, and then clustered into meaningful track patterns. In general it is even difficult for experts to analyse, extract, or classify footprints.

A track of footprints typically has a symmetrical structure (left and right feet centring on the body, see Fig. 1), but are translated or rotated into irregular directions. Thus we can expect to extract similar prints for the left side and right side, but affected by affine transformations. Binarization of collected images needs to be adaptive to deal with varying intensities, but the binarization process will also contribute to uncertainties. The applied classification method can only use the described incomplete information for footprint identification.

L. Alvarez et al. (Eds.): CIARP 2012, LNCS 7441, pp. 196–203, 2012.
© Springer-Verlag Berlin Heidelberg 2012

Fig. 1. Footprints in areas of tracking cards; left to right: black cockroach (*Platyzosteria* sp.; class A in our experiments), native bush cockroach (*Celatoblatta* sp.; class B), and ground weta (*Hemiandrus* sp.; class C)

In order to overcome these difficulties, we propose a new feature extraction and classification method. For extracting features, we use a 4-level procedural model that is suitable for footprints having characteristics invariant to affine transformations. For pattern recognition and classification, we propose a fuzzy weight decision, where weights are based on degrees of contributions, considering the possibilities of image degradations.

2   A 4-Level Procedural Feature Extraction Model

We propose a 4-level procedural feature extraction model. This model is suitable for extracting features for noisy footprints of insects, small mammals and so forth, having irregular directions, a symmetrical pattern structure, and a few singularities in extracted segments [4]. The *4-level procedural feature extraction method* (4-level FEM) is summarized as follows. First, images produce new 2D data (the *trace matrix*) through the trace transform [5]. Second, the trace matrix is processed for reducing the dimensionality of the data by several mathematical conversions. Third, dimensionality-reduced data are converted into frequency components. Finally, *characteristic signals* (CS-feature) with significant components of representative values are created by excluding insignificant factors.

At *Level 1*, a footprint segment produces new data (basic features) through the trace transform. The trace transform can create feature values of an input image that are invariant to rotation, translation, and even reflection of the input image. Thus it is appropriate to extract feature values from various shapes of animal footprint segments, even if deformed by rotation, translation or reflection. The *trace transform*, as used in this paper, is as follows:

Let F denote an image. We position a 2D coordinate system in the image (e.g., origin at the centre) and represent features of image F with respect to straight lines $l(\theta, p)$ (called *trace lines*), where θ is the angle with the horizontal axis, and p the distance to the origin. See Fig. 2, left. We have $l = \{(x, y) : x \cos \theta + y \sin \theta = p\}$. Assuming that we have a *trace function* T, we finally have the trace transform defined by $T_F(\theta, p)$. The position of the origin is not

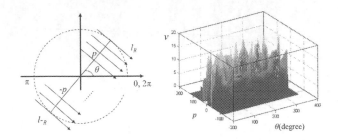

Fig. 2. Left: parameters θ (angle) and p (distance) define a straight line l_R. Right: a 3D visualization of a trace matrix, with V (value) as the third axis.

important for the qualitative analysis of the resulting trace matrix $\mathbf{T}_F$. See Fig. 2, right, with $v = T_F(\theta, p)$. We do not use subscript F if not needed.

Following [5], if the original image rotates then its trace matrix shifts along the horizontal axis; if the original image translates by some vector then its trace matrix also undergoes defined changes: columns remain unchanged and stay in their places but may shift up or down. A shift vector specifies numbers a and b such that a column with coordinate θ_i shifts vertically to $a\cos(\theta_i - b)$. Because of the characteristics, feature values extracted from an input image by the trace transform are always invariant to translation and rotation. Altogether, Level 1 is defined by the following:

1-1. The trace transform is determined by the trace function T.

1-2. The trace-line l is decided using the distance p from the origin to l, and the angle θ, the trace-line l is represented by the formula $l = \{(x, y) : x\cos\theta + y\sin\theta = p\}$.

1-3. A trace matrix $\mathbf{T}_F$ is generated by the trace transform; matrix $\mathbf{T}_F$ can be visualized in 3D space using axes θ, p, and v; the range of θ is $[0, 2\pi]$, and the range of p is $[p_{\min}, p_{\max}]$.

1-4. Two different trace functions $T(\theta, p) = T_F(\theta, p)$ are defined as follows:

$$T_1(\theta, p) = \int_{k \in l} \eta(k)\,\mathrm{d}k \quad \text{and} \quad T_2(\theta, p) = \int_{k \in l} t^2\eta(k)\,\mathrm{d}k \qquad (1)$$

where k is a pixel location in image F, function η outputs a value at pixel k along trace line l, $t = \eta(k) - c$, and c is the mean of all $\eta(k)$ along trace line l in image F.

At *Level 2*, the produced data are processed for reducing the dimensionality of the data by several mathematical conversions. Level 2 is defined by the following:

2-1. A diametric signal ρ is generated by a *diametric function* P; the range of the diametric signal ρ is for all θ in $[0, 2\pi]$.

2-2. Four different diametric functions $P(\theta)$, for $t = \eta(h) - median\{\eta(h)\}$:

$$P_1(\theta) = \int_p \eta(h)\,\mathrm{d}h \quad \text{and} \quad P_2(\theta) = \int_p t^2\eta(h)\,\mathrm{d}k \qquad (2)$$

$$P_3(\theta) = \max_p\{\eta(h)\} \quad \text{and} \quad P_4(\theta) = \mathrm{var}_p\{\eta(h)\} \qquad (3)$$

where $h = (\theta, p)$, and function η outputs a value at point h. Figure 3, left, shows ρ signal generated by Level 2.

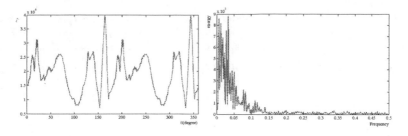

Fig. 3. Left: ρ signal through function P. Right: frequency signal ϕ

At *Level 3*, dimensionality-reduced data are converted into frequency components. We extract frequency components from the data set to get the range of signal waves regardless of the data translation by the Fourier transform. A frequency transform divides a signal into high or low frequency parts in order to adjust them, to analyse a cycle of a specific signal wave, or to obtain the range of a signal wave. Level 3 is defined by the following:

3-1. The signal ϕ is acquired by the *circus function* Φ using parameter θ; the range of signal ϕ is $[0, 2\pi]$.

3-2. The circus function Φ is defined by $\phi = FFT(\rho)$.

Figure 3, right, shows signal ϕ generated by Level 3.

Finally, at *Level 4*, characteristic signals with significant components of representative values are created by excluding insignificant factors such as noise. A *characteristic function* ζ is a filtering method that chooses n high energy elements on the frequency axis. This ensures comparison of strong harmonic signals, excluding meaningless features in the frequency components. A strong characteristic signal is a way to represent a spectrum's shape. The characteristic function ζ defines values $\Lambda = \zeta(\phi)$ CS-features are extracted by the 4-level FEM, which is the feature used in the final pattern classification step.

3   A Fuzzy Network for Classification

In the case of scanned tracks of footprints, insect footprints are 'tiny' scattered spots and form delicate patterns. The intensity of a footprint mostly depends on ink quantity on a pad. Those images of footprints have frequently not only a few incomplete spots that are not filled with black ink, but also sliding (smearing) footprints, missing toe footprints, or overlapped footprints because of movements. In addition, footprint segments show lots of noise not yet removed in the process of segmentation. Fuzzy theory is used for appropriate evaluation of, or decisions on, uncertain data [6]. Membership functions of fuzzy sets can take on any shape, such as triangular, trapezoidal, exponential, Gaussian, or cosine. In this paper, we generate membership values by using a triangular membership function [7]. We use a fuzzy network consisting of 6 layers.

Layer 1. Let f be a set of input features for one of the classes $i = 1$ to k. Each input set f defines a fuzzy function, represented by a data array of size $1 \times e$, where e is the number of features.

Layer 2. Membership values are determined by a triangular membership function in the unit interval $[0, 1]$, with mean $m(f)$ at maximum membership value 1, and interval borders $v(f)_{min}$ and $v(f)_{max}$ at minimum membership value 0. The triangular membership function is represented as follows:

$$u_{ji}(f_i) = \begin{cases} \frac{1}{(m_i - v_{i_{\min}})}(f_i - m_i) + 1 \\[2mm] -\frac{1}{(v_{i_{\max}} - m_i)}(f_i - m_i) + 1 \end{cases} \tag{4}$$

Layer 3. Weights are computed by fuzzy weighted mean.

Layer 4. The membership value is multiplied with the weight and used as input to Layer 5: $U_i(f) = u_i(f) \cdot w_j$.

Layer 5. The output of Layer 5 equals $\hat{h}_i = \sum_{j=1}^{e}(U_j(f))$.

Layer 6. This layer finds the highest membership among all outputs of Layer 5. The class i having the highest membership value $\hat{h}_i$ is the final classification result, for $i = 1, 2, \ldots, k$.

4   Fuzzy Weights Decisions

We propose a decision method for fuzzy weights by estimating the weight according to degrees of contribution. The weights are assigned by ranking the degrees of the contribution. The degrees of contribution are decided by parameters comparing the classes. If one of the feature values defines a distinct difference for deciding classification, a high weight is assigned to this feature. Calculated weights determine membership values by fuzzy membership functions. Objects are classified into that class which has a superior value.

We assign to each feature its weight according to parameters such as its variance, gap, or overlap with other classes. Decided weights are assigned by the fuzzy weighted mean method. The fuzzy weighted mean equation is as follows:

$$u_{ji}(f_i) = \sum_{j=1}^{e}(u_{ji}(f) \cdot N_{w_j}) = \sum_{j=1}^{e}(U_{ji}(f)) \tag{5}$$

Membership function values are real numbers. A triangular graph is used to define how each point in the input space is labelled by a membership value between 0 and 1. Such a triangular membership graph is defined by classes which are separated by straight line segments. A *gap* between two straight lines defines a *gradient*; the gap is defined by variance. Therefore, membership graphs have gradient and variance data assigned. Such graphs may be non-disjoint for different classes. We use mean and variance in non-empty intersections of membership graphs for deciding about weights. Consider classes A and B with *centroids* A_c and B_c. For the distance between class A and class B we take the distance between A_c and B_c.

We decide about weights based on a degree of contribution. In the proposed method we use parameters such as mean and variance, the ratio of variance in a class, and the distance between two classes. See Fig. 4.

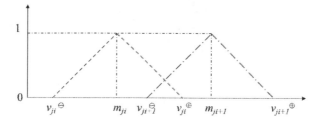

Fig. 4. Variables for adjusting weights

Let C be a class. Let V be the variance of C and m its mean. $V(m)$ is the variance of means of other classes, g^n is the distance of separation among other classes, and g is overlapping among other classes. The weight w_{ji} is defined as follows:

$$w_i = -\frac{\sum g_i^n + 1}{\sum g_{ji}} \times (V(m_{ji}) + 1) \tag{6}$$

$$g_{ji}^n = -\frac{d_{ij}}{V(m_{ji})} \quad \text{if} \quad d_{ij} > 0 \quad \text{and} \quad g_{ji} = -\frac{d_{ij}}{V(m_{ji})} \quad \text{if} \quad d_{ij} < 0 \tag{7}$$

where, if $\sum g_{ji} = 0$ then use $\sum g_{ji} = 1$, and $d_{ji} = v_{ji+1}^{\ominus} - v_{ji}^{\oplus}$ for $i = a$ is the number of classes, $j = a$ the number of features, and $V(m_{ji}) = \left\| v_{ji}^{\oplus} - v_{ji}^{\ominus} \right\|$. Let $w_j^{\Omega} = (w_j - (w_j)^{Min})/((w_j)^{Max} - (w_j)^{Min})$. Let N_{w_i} be the normalized weight w_j^{Ω} such that $\sum_{j=1}^{e} N_{w_j} = 1$.

5   Footprint Classification and Experiments

In order to classify footprints, we need to extract different singular features from segments and to compose patterns by combining feature sets. It is possible to classify footprints based on uniquely identified patterns. We can compare using the variance of features if they are distinct (i.e. their 'character' is reflected in their distribution). Therefore, we generate CS-features by using the 4-level FEM. For footprint classification, we consider gradually 2-step classifications to increase the reliability of evaluation. The 4-level FEM is able to generate n kinds of features. In

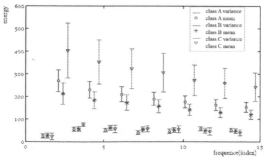

Fig. 5. Distribution of extracted CS-features

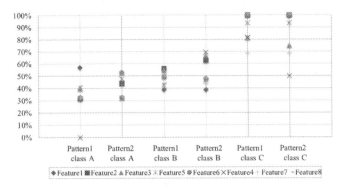

Fig. 6. Recognition results by the first classification step

other words, we can obtain n membership values as well as n results of classification decided by n membership values. We reclassify using n results of classification.

In a primary classification, classification happens by the proposed fuzzy weighted-mean model; n results of classification are made, which show different results or the same result of classification, h is the result of classification, and h^* is the highest value of the class. In a secondary classification, in the case of different results, we need to decide a final result to determine which class. We use a majority voting approach. There are n values h^* after primary classification. We choose the classification based on voting: let h^* be the set Υ defined as $\{h_1^*, h_2^*, \cdots, h_n^*\}$; the final result is $\hat{\Upsilon} = vote\,[\Upsilon]$.

In our experiments, we extracted CS-features from improved segments by using the 4-level FEM, and we generated patterns by combining each of the eight kinds of features. We used footprints of three insect species: black cockroach (*class A*), native bush cockroach (*class B*), and ground weta (*class C*). Figure 1 shows three kinds of footprints on a tracking card. The number of samples used was *class A*=102, *class B*=61, and *class C*=16. Figure 5 shows the distribution of CS-features

Table 1. Recognition results by the second classification step

Insect Class	Card No.	Voting result			Recognition
		Class A	Class B	Class C	
Class A	#1	9	5	1	True
	#2	4	7	4	False
	#3	8	5	4	True
	#4	8	7	-	True
	#5	8	5	4	True
	#6	5	2	5	-
	#7	5	6	-	False
Class B	#1	3	5	2	True
	#2	5	1	1	False
	#3	3	4	3	True
	#4	2	9	-	True
	#5	1	6	-	True
	#6	-	7	1	True
	#7	1	7	-	True
Class C	#1	-	-	4	True
	#2	-	-	4	True
	#3	-	-	3	True
	#4	-	-	5	True

extracted from segments of footprints, which are extracted by 4-level FEM. Each class has mean and variance as defined above. In our experiments, we performed gradually a 2-step classification. The first step is recognition depending on fuzzy membership values of segments (see Fig. 6). This shows recognition results by the first classification. For recognition evaluation, we used eight kinds of features, defining two types of patterns. See the case of *class C* in Fig. 6; Feature 4 has a recognition rate of 69%, Feature 6 has a recognition rate of 100% when using the first pattern (see Tab. 1). This table shows recognition results by the second classification step (i.e. voting with the results after the first classification). For example, regarding the *class A* insect and Card #3, 8 segments of footprints indicate that they are *class A*, 5 segments of footprints say that they are *class B*, and 4 segments of footprints say that they are *class C*. Therefore, the majority is *class A*. On seven cards we had *class A* or *class B*, and on four cards *class C*.

6   Conclusions

This paper proposed a feature extraction method and a classification method for the purpose of diverse small species recognition by using their footprint images. We proposed a 4-level FEM. This model is suitable for extracting features of species with irregular directions, symmetrical structure patterns, and noisy prints with a few singularities in the extracted segments. For classification, based on uncertain features, we proposed a decision method defined by fuzzy weights and a fuzzy weighted mean. We presented experimental results of classification by using the proposed method on scanned insect footprints of three species.

Acknowledgement. The data used in this paper were provided by the insect track recognition project at The University of Auckland. The project was initiated in 2003, in collaboration with Connovation Ltd., Auckland.

References

1. Blackwell, G.L., Potter, M.A., McLennan, J.A.: Rodent density indices from tracking tunnels, snap-traps and fenn traps: do they tell the same story? New Zealand J. Ecology 26, 43–51 (2002)
2. Russell, J.C., Hasler, N., Klette, R., Rosenhahn, B.: Automatic track recognition of footprints for identifying cryptic species. Ecology 90, 2007–2013 (2009)
3. Whisson, D.A., Engeman, R.M., Collins, K.: Developing relative abundance techniques (RATs) for monitoring rodent population. Wildlife Research 32, 239–244 (2005)
4. Shin, B.-S., Cha, E.-Y., Kim, K.-B., Cho, K.: -W., Klette, R., and Woo, Y. W., Effective feature extraction by trace transform for insect footprint recognition. J. Computational Theoretical Nanoscience 7, 868–875 (2010)
5. Petrou, M., Kadyrov, A.: Affine invariant features from the trace transform. IEEE Trans. Pattern Analysis Machine Intelligence 26, 30–44 (2004)
6. Jin, Y.: Fuzzy modelling of high-dimensional systems complexity reduction and interpretability improvement. IEEE Trans. Fuzzy Systems 8, 212–221 (2000)
7. Olunloyo, V.O.S., Ajofoyinbo, A.M.: On the systematic computation of membership functions of union and intersection of triangular fuzzy. European J. Scientific Research 41, 135–149 (2010)

Vector Transition Classes Generation
from Fuzzy Overlapping Classes

Enguerran Grandchamp[1], Sébastien Régis[1], and Alain Rousteau[2]

[1] LAMIA Laboratory, French West Indies University, Guadeloupe, France
[2] DUNECAR Laboratory, French West Indies University, Guadeloupe, France
{egrandch,sregis,aroustea}@univ-ag.fr

Abstract. We present in this paper a way to create transition classes and to represent them with vector structures. These classes are obtained using a supervised classification algorithm based on fuzzy decision trees. This method is useful to classify data which have a space evolution following a gradient such as forest, where transitions are spread over hundreds of meter, or other natural phenomenon. The vector representation is well adapted for integration in Geographical Information Systems because it is a more flexible structure than the raster representation. The method detailed takes into account local environmental conditions and leads to non regular gradient and fuzzy structures. It allows adding classes, called transition classes, when transition areas are too spread instead of fixing an arbitrary border between classes.

Keywords: GIS, decision tree, fuzzy, classification.

1 Introduction

Geographical Information Systems (*GIS*), and their applications, followed a spectacular increase during the last years. Data modeled with these systems are based on geographical positions which could represent simple points or very complex structures such as cities or natural phenomenon (hurricane, rain), networks (water, electric).

Each *GIS* tool allows manipulating raster data (such as satellite images or results of spatial analysis) or vector data (series of points, lines or polygons).

Since 1997, in the conclusions of the special edition *Spatial Data Types for Database Systems* 18, the authors underline the importance of data structures in *GIS* and their lack of adaptation to fuzzy data. Even if some ways have been investigated, the implementation and modeling difficulties as much as computation complexity lead, more than 10 years later, to a very shy advance in this field.

In 1986, Peter Burrough has done the first work concerning fuzzy 2D modeling [3]. Most of the studies on representation and manipulation of 2D fuzzy data use a raster representation ([13], [15], [20], [21]). This representation is based on a regular square partition of the space. The main drawbacks of such models have often been underlined in the literature ([1], [7], [8], [12], [18]). They are linked to *(i)* a lack of flexibility *(ii)* a high computation time *(iii)* a large size of the data *(iv)* the degradation of the precision linked to the approximation of the rasterization.

L. Alvarez et al. (Eds.): CIARP 2012, LNCS 7441, pp. 204–211, 2012.
© Springer-Verlag Berlin Heidelberg 2012

A vector representation uses simple geometric models (points, lines, polygons) to represent the scenes. It is the most adapted structure for *GIS* and could receive contextual information (semantic) [13]. The main drawback for fuzzy representation is that they are based on strict structures. Only rare studies introduce a vector dimension to fuzzy geo-processing ([2], [17]). They propose modeling fuzzy set with series of regular buffers around the classes.

In this paper, we propose a fuzzy vector model based on non regular structures allowing a more reliable representation of the data. Secondly we propose a strict representation of a set of fuzzy classes by introducing transition classes instead of fixing an arbitrary border to split the space. Indeed, we present a method to create transition classes from a supervised classification based on fuzzy decision trees. This method is particularly useful for the strict classification of data having fuzzy borders. This is the case of the studied forest, where transitions are spread over hundreds of meters and depend on local environmental conditions.

Section 2 presents the modeling with fuzzy classes using decision trees and also gives raw and simplified representations of the classes. Section 3 presents the algorithm to generate the transition classes. Section 4 gives illustrations of the two previous sections and define the reference data. Section 5 gives some perspectives to this work and section 6 is the conclusion.

2   Fuzzy Vector Classes Modeling

Let $V = \{V_i, i \in \{1, ..., M\}\}$ be the vector objects obtained by the union of N information layers ($L = \{L_1, ..., L_N\}$). V is considered as a partition of the space [10], [11]. Each V_i represents a uniform area regarding the information coming from the layers and is then associated to an attribute vector $F_i = \{F_{i1}, F_{i2}, ..., F_{iN}\}$. Figure 1, illustrates the building of V from two layers.

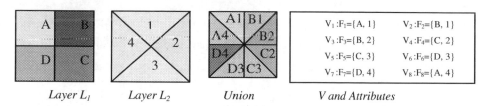

$V_1 : F_1 = \{A, 1\}$	$V_2 : F_2 = \{B, 1\}$
$V_3 : F_3 = \{B, 2\}$	$V_4 : F_4 = \{C, 2\}$
$V_5 : F_5 = \{C, 3\}$	$V_6 : F_6 = \{D, 3\}$
$V_7 : F_7 = \{D, 4\}$	$V_8 : F_8 = \{A, 4\}$

Layer L_1   *Layer L_2*   *Union*   *V and Attributes*

Fig. 1. Layers union

We consider now the fuzzy classification of the V_i using F_i. The classes are obtained using fuzzy supervised classification methods. We use decision trees such as Functional Trees (FT, [7]) and C4.5 trees [14].

We consider a set of n classes (C_k, $k \in \{1 ... n\}$) and a set $A \subset V$ of labelized V_i for learning and cross validation steps.

After the learning step, the decision trees used give for each V_i a vector $\mu_i = \{\mu_{i1}, ..., \mu_{in}\}$ which indicates the trust degree of the affectation of the V_i to each class (μ_{ik} =trust degree in the assertion V_i belongs to class k).The trust degrees are computed with a logistic regression [9] giving the membership probability of a sample to each class. The regression function used is defined as a linear combination of the attributes used during the learning step.

The heart of the class C_k is defined by   : $H_k = \{V_i \mid i \in \{1 \ \dots \ M\}, \mu_{ik} = 1\}$
The interior of the class C_k is defined by : $E_k = \{V_i \mid i \in \{1 \ \dots \ M\}, \mu_{ik} > 0\}$
The exterior of the class C_k is defined by : $\overline{E_k} = \{V_i \mid i \in \{1 \ \dots \ M\}, \mu_{ik} = 0\}$

So each class C_k is a fuzzy vector map based on the values of the trust degrees of the V_i restricted to the class: $m_k = \{\mu_{1k}, \dots, \mu_{Mk}\}$. The display of this kind of map is classic and the grey level depends on the trust degree (0 for black and 1 for white).

This is a vector representation because each V_i is a vector object. Even if this kind of structure is a reliable internal representation it represents a lot of data (due to the continuous aspect of the membership function) and it could be simplified for more visibility. To solve this problem we propose different simplified views by building groups of spatially close V_i having close trust degrees.

The parameters defining a view v are the number of groups g_v and the limits of the intervals of the trust degrees $I^v = \{I_0^v, I_2^v, \dots, I_{g_v}^v\}$ with $I_0^v = 0$, $I_{g_v}^v = 1$ and $I_p^v < I_{p+1}^v$.

The pth group ($p \in \{1 \ \dots \ g_v\}$) of the class C_k ($k \in \{1 \ \dots \ n\}$) regarding the view v is defined by

$$G_{kp}^v = \{V_i \mid I_{p-1}^v < \mu_{ik} \le I_p^v\}$$

Adjacent V_i belonging to the same group are joined to form a unique vector object.
With such notations

$$\forall v, \ E_k = U_{p=1}^{g_v} G_{kp}^v, \quad V = U_{p=1}^{g_v} G_{kp}^v \ U \overline{E_k} \qquad \text{and} \qquad H_k \subseteq G_{kg_v}^v$$

The choice of the limits allows underlying different aspects of the class. Different ways to fix the limits have been identified:

1. Regular partition of [0,1]. In this case $I_p^v = \dfrac{p}{g_v}$

2. Intervals centered on most represented values of the trust degrees. I_p^v is fixed in order to have $|G_{kp}^v| \simeq \dfrac{M}{g_v}$ (|.| returns the cardinal and M is the number of V_i, $M = \sum_{p=1}^{g_v} |G_{kp}^v|$). In this case we choose the intervals in order to minimize $\sum_{p=1}^{g_v} (|G_{kp}^v| - \dfrac{M}{g_v})^2$.

3. Intervals centered on the highest values of the trust degrees. In this case we have to respect the following rule $I_{p+1}^v - I_p^v < I_p^v - I_{p-1}^v$. Every function f which is strictly increasing and concave from [0,1] to [0,1] (with $f(0) = 0$ et $f(1) = 1$) could be used from a regular partition : $I_p^v = f(\dfrac{p}{g_v})$.

3   Transition Class Generation

We are now interested on the research of extended transition areas in order to deduce transition classes. This identification allows displaying all classes in a unique map instead of one map per class as in previous modeling. These areas are identified using a thresholding of the trust degrees in the following way:

1. Let S be a threshold ($S \epsilon [0,1]$)
2. For each V_i we sort the classes by decreasing order of the trust degrees :
$$\{\mu_{ij_1} \geq \mu_{ij_2} \geq \cdots \mu_{ij_n}\} \rightarrow \{C^i_{j_1}, C^i_{j_2}, .., C^i_{j_n}\}, i \in \{1 \ ... \ M\}, \ j_p \epsilon \{1 \ ... \ n\}$$
3. We   affect   to   each V_i the   shortest   class   list   such   as
$$E_i(S) = \{C^i_{j_1}, C^i_{j_2}, .., C^i_{j_p} | \Sigma^p_{k=1} \mu_{ij_k} > S\}$$

For each V_i: $E_i(0) = \{C^i_{j_1}\}$. So we obtain a unique class for each V_i which is equivalent to the generation of a strict classification from a set of n fuzzy classes by choosing the class having the highest trust degree. More generally, if $E_i(S)$ is a singleton, there is no ambiguity concerning the class. In the other case, we are confronted to a transition class. Depending on the value of the threshold the number of transition areas varies but the space evolution of these areas is not regular.

By varying S from 0 to 1 we obtain a hierarchy of the transitions. If a transition appears for a low value of S the uncertainty concerning the class affectation is high. If a transition is spatially extended it indicates a slow gradient. The choice of S allows fixing the transition to take into account.

Theoretically every transition between classes is possible and the hierarchy could leads to 2^n transitions. But in our case, the spatial coherence of the classes leads to a limited number of transitions.

4   Applications

Now we are going to apply our approach to a concrete classification of fuzzy sets. We study various types of forests following a progressive evolution (with a gradient covering hundreds of meters).

Indeed, the classification of the forest is based on their floristic composition (species, maturity, etc.) which is a continuous parameter.

As if the granularity of the classes could be discussed the transition aspect of the forests is attested by the experts. We are especially interested in this study to the forest covering the Basse-Terre Island of the Guadeloupe archipelagos.

4.1   The Reference Map

We compare our results to a reference map obtained by biologists [16] in 1996. 14 classes $\{C_1, ..., C_{14}\}$ were identified from the statistical analysis of the floristic composition of 47 observation areas. The map has been manually drawn by the experts taking into account the geographical repartition of the classes and local environmental conditions.

4.2   Data Used for Supervised Classification

V is obtained using four information layers about topography (slope, altitude, exposition and hillside) (L= $\{L_1, L_2, L_3, L_4\}$) which generate *417 273* V_i (*M = 417 273*).

These layers give attributes to the V_i which will be used during the learning step ($F_i = \{slope(V_i), altitude(V_i), exposition(V_i), hillside(V_i)\}$).

We use the class defined by the experts. The learning set (A) is obtained by selecting the V_i containing the 47 observations.

4.3   Strict Classification ($S=0$)

In order to compare our approach with the existing classification we apply the algorithm with $S=0$. This naturally leads to a classification without transition classes.

Figure 2 shows two extracts of the National Park of Guadeloupe obtained with FT and C4.5 decision trees. A first visual analysis shows coherence between the two results and also between these results and the reference map.

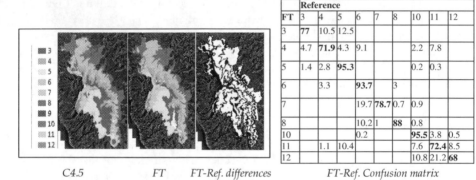

	Reference								
FT	3	4	5	6	7	8	10	11	12
3	77	10.5	12.5						
4	4.7	71.9	4.3	9.1			2.2	7.8	
5	1.4	2.8	95.3				0.2	0.3	
6		3.3		93.7		3			
7				19.7	78.7	0.7	0.9		
8				10.2	1	88	0.8		
10					0.2		95.5	3.8	0.5
11		1.1	10.4				7.6	72.4	8.5
12							10.8	21.2	68

C4.5   FT   FT-Ref. differences   FT-Ref. Confusion matrix

Fig. 2. Automatic classification extracts and differences

Indeed the map in the middle of Figure 2 presents the differences (black) between the reference map and FT classification. We observe that the two classifications are globally identical (few differences). Conflicts areas are localized at the border of the classes. Some borders are exactly localized at the same place and others have more extended differences.

The confusion matrix gives a dominant diagonal with a good classification rate from 68% to 95.5% (average 82.3%). Regarding that the reference classification has been made manually we can validate the algorithm and the obtained classifications.

4.4   Fuzzy Classification and Representation

We give now an illustration of the fuzzy maps and their simplified views $m_k = \{\mu_{1k}, ..., \mu_{Mk}\}$. Figure 3 shows the m_9 raw and simplified maps. The simplified map in the middle is based on 5 intervals ($g_v = 5$) centered on the more represented values of the trust degree ($|G_{kp}^v| \simeq \frac{M}{5}$) $I=\{0, 0.03, 0.07, 0.13, 0.22, 1\}$, and in the right part with 10 intervals ($g_v = 10$) centered on the highest values $I = \{0, 0.14, 0.5, 0.65, 0.73, 0.80, 0.86, 0.91, 0.95, 0.98, 1\}$. This last map is the most interesting for our application. We observe the non regular aspect of the different areas compared to regular buffers presents in the literature.

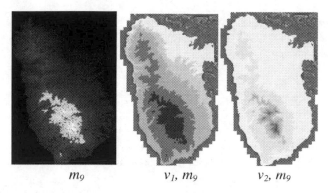

$$m_9 \qquad\qquad v_1,\ m_9 \qquad\qquad v_2,\ m_9$$

Fig. 3. Fuzzy vectorial map (raw : left, simplified : middle and right)

4.5 Transition Classes

We now illustrate the localization of the transition classes (in black in figure 4) for two threshold values ($S=0.8$ and 0.9). Transition areas are localized at the border of a class. Some transition are very short such as between class 3 (red) and 5 (yellow).

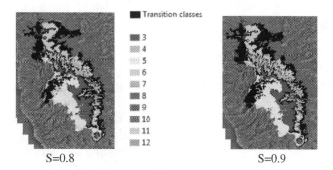

Fig. 4. Transition classes

Table 1. Transition hierachy

S	Transitions	Surface
0		0
0.1	**6-7, 6-8, 7-8**	1.2 %
0.3	6-7, 6-8, 7-8, **10-12, 11-12**	2.1 %
0.5	6-7, 6-8, **6-11**, 7-8, **8-11, 10-11**, 10-12, 11-12	4.4 %
0.7	**3-4, 4-6**, 6-7, 6-8, 6-11, 7-8, 8-11, 10-11, 10-12, 11-12	21.4 %
0.9	3-4, 4-6, **4-11**, 6-7, 6-8, 6-11, 7-8, 8-11, 10-11, 10-12, 11-12	25.1 %
1	3-4, 4-6, 4-11, 6-7, 6-8, 6-11, 7-8, 8-11, 10-11, 11-12, **6-7-8, 6-8-11, 10-11-12,**	27.2 %

Table 1 presents the hierarchy of the transitions obtained by varying S from 0 to 1. For each value of S the transition set is indicated. We obtain between 3 and 13 transition classes. The first transition that appears is between classes 6, 7 and 8. The transition between *6* and *8* grow rapidly with *S* (also between classes *10* and *11* which appears for *S=0.5*). These two transition classes are interesting because they show extended uncertain areas.

5   Perspectives

The first perspective of the work is the integration of the *OKM* (*Overlap K-Means*) algorithm to have an unsupervised approach ([4], [5], [6]). By using a distance in the attributes space, the algorithm allows the affectation of a sample to the union of two or more classes instead of a unique class.

This algorithm could also be applied to the transition areas, after localizing them as described in our approach. The *OKM* algorithm will allow refining the transition classes.

A second perspective aims to automatically determine the transition classes to take into account by using the importance of the transition (low value of *S*) and it's extend.

Then, the localization of the transition areas could guide the choice of the limits of the intervals of the views in order to have well adapted simplified models.

6   Conclusion

In a first time, we present in this paper an adaptive fuzzy vector model for spatial data. This model is useful for data having fuzzy borders and well adapted for integration into GIS. The advantage of this structure is its vector representation and its non uniform evolution, in space, instead of regular series of buffers. This takes into account the irregular evolution of the trust degree translating the local environmental conditions.

In a second time, we propose an algorithm allowing, from fuzzy models, the generation of transition classes. The main objective is to identify transition classes when uncertain areas are too spread. The resulting classifications are visually and numerically coherent with the reference classification which allows validating the approach.

References

1. Altman, D.: Fuzzy set theoretic approaches for handling imprecision in spatial analysis. Internat. J. Geographical Inform. Systems 8(3), 271–289 (1994)
2. Benz, U.C., et al.: Multi-resolution, object-oriented fuzzy analysis of remote sensing data for GIS-ready information. ISPRS Journal of Photogrammetry & Remote Sensing 5839–258 (2004)
3. Burrough, P.A., Frank, A.U.: Geographic Objects with Indeterminate Boundaries, ch. 12, pp. 171–187. Taylor & Francis, London (1987)
4. Cleuziou, G.: OKM: une extension des k-moyennes pour la recherche de classes recouvrantes. In: 7èmes journées d'Extraction et de Gestion des Connaissances (EGC 2007), pp. 691–702 (2007)

5. Cleuziou, G.: An extended version of the k-means method for overlapping clustering. In: 19th International Conference on Pattern Recognition (ICPR 2008), pp. 1–4 (2008)
6. Cleuziou, G.: Two Variants of the OKM for Overlapping Clustering. In: Guillet, F., Ritschard, G., Zighed, D.A., Briand, H. (eds.) Advances in Knowledge Discovery and Management. SCI, vol. 292, pp. 149–166. Springer, Heidelberg (2010)
7. Cross, V.V.: Fuzzy extensions for relationships in a generalized object model. International Journal on Intelligent Systems 16, 843–861 (2001)
8. Fisher, P.: Sorites paradox and vague geographies. Fuzzy Sets and Systems 113, 7–18 (2000)
9. Gama, J.: Functional Trees. In: Landwehr, N., Hall, M., Frank, E. (eds.) Logistic Model Trees (2005)
10. Grandchamp, E.: GIS information layer selection directed by remote sensing for ecological unit delineation. In: IGARSS (2009)
11. Grandchamp, E.: Raster-vector cooperation algorithm for GIS. In: GeoProcessing (2010)
12. Kainz: Introduction to Fuzzy Logic and Applications in GIS – Example (2011)
13. Mukhopadhyay, B.: Integrating exploration dataset in GIS using fuzzy inference modeling, GISdevelopment
14. Quinlan, R.: C4.5: Programs for Machine Learning. Morgan Kaufmann Publishers, San Mateo (1993)
15. Raines, G.L., et al.: New fuzzy logic tools in ArcGIS 10. ESRI Communication (2010)
16. Rousteau, A.: Carte écologique de la Guadeloupe. 3 feuilles au 1/75.000ème et notice (36 p.). Conseil Général de la Guadeloupe, Office National des Forêts et Parc National de la Guadeloupe (1996)
17. Sawatzky, D., Raines, G.L., Bonham-Carter, G.: Spatial Data Modeller. Technical Report (2008)
18. Schneider, M.: Spatial Data Types for Database Systems, Finite Resolution Geometry for Geographic Information Systems. LNCS, vol. 1288, 275 p. Springer, Heidelberg (1997)
19. Schneider, M.: Uncertainty Management for Spatial Data in Databases: Fuzzy Spatial Data Types. In: Güting, R.H., Papadias, D., Lochovsky, F.H. (eds.) SSD 1999. LNCS, vol. 1651, pp. 330–351. Springer, Heidelberg (1999)
20. Sunila, R., Horttanainen, P.: Fuzzy Model of Soil Polygons for Managing the Imprecision Interfacing GeoStatistics and GIS (2009)
21. Zhu, A.X., et al.: Soil Mapping Using GIS Expert Knowledge, and Fuzzy Logic. Simonson, Soil Sci. Soc. Am. J. 65, 1463–1472 (2001)

Infant Cry Classification Using Genetic Selection of a Fuzzy Model

Alejandro Rosales-Pérez[1], Carlos A. Reyes-García[1], Jesus A. Gonzalez[1], and Emilio Arch-Tirado[2]

[1] National Institute of Astrophysics, Optics and Electronics (INAOE)
Computer Science Department
Tonantzintla, Puebla, Mexico
{arosales,kargaxxi,jagonzalez}@ccc.inaoep.mx
[2] National Institute of Rehabilitation (INR). Laboratory of Bioacoustics
Mexico City, Mexico
earch@inr.gob.mx

Abstract. In the last years, infant cry recognition has been of particular interest because it contains useful information to determine if the infant is hungry, has pain, or a particular disease. Several studies have been performed in order to differentiate between these kinds of cries. In this work, we propose to use Genetic Selection of a Fuzzy Model (GSFM) for classification of infant cry. GSFM selects a combination of feature selection methods, type of fuzzy processing, learning algorithm, and its associated parameters that best fit to the data. The experiments demonstrate the feasibility of this technique in the classification task. Our experimental results reach up to 99.42% accuracy.

Keywords: Infant Cry Classification, Model Selection, Genetic Algorithms.

1 Introduction

Infant cry is the only initial communication way babies have in their earlier stages of life. By crying, the baby can express either the cause of the crying (pain, hunger, etc.) or the presence of physical abnormalities (pathology or disease). Generally, most parents learn to distinguish causes of crying and interpret the baby's need, but it is not easy to distinguish normal from pathological cry, and even less to distinguish one pathology from another. It has been shown that the acoustic characteristics of the sound of crying are influenced by physical or psychological aspects of the infant as well as external stimuli [11]. In this sense, the crying wave contains useful information to distinguish different states of the infant.

Several studies have been performed around infant cry recognition. In signal processing Mel Frequency Cepstral Coefficients (MFCC) and Linear Prediction Coefficient (LPC) techniques have been applied to extract features to represent the audio signals. Several pattern recognition techniques have been used for the classification task. Among these techniques, artificial neural networks have been

L. Alvarez et al. (Eds.): CIARP 2012, LNCS 7441, pp. 212–219, 2012.
© Springer-Verlag Berlin Heidelberg 2012

one of the most widely used [6,9,14,16]. It has also been explored the use of support
vector machines [3,19], hidden Markov models [12,13], as well as several hybrid approaches that combine fuzzy logic with neural networks [15,20,21,22], fuzzy logic
with support vector machines [2] or evolutionary strategies with neural networks
[8]. These works have reported promising results in infant cry recognition. However, many efforts had to be devoted in the manual design of the classifiers with
the intend to determine the set of adequate parameters for each technique to get
the right classification of infant cry. In order to avoid many drawbacks, alternative
approaches that combine genetic algorithms with fuzzy logic and neural networks
have been proposed [1,17], but most of the works only determine the parameters
for a specific learning algorithm. In this work we propose to explore the use of Genetic Selection of a Fuzzy Model (GSFM) for infant cry classification. GSFM was
recently proposed and it was applied to acute leukemia classification [18]. A genetic algorithm is used in GSFM for selecting the right combination of a feature
selection method, the type of fuzzy processing, a learning algorithm, and their associated parameters that better fit to a data set.

The rest of the paper is organized as follows: in section 2 we describe the
data set used in our work. In section 3 our classification approach is described.
Next, in section 4 the experiments and results are shown. Finally, in section 5
the conclusions and future work are presented.

2   Data Set Description

The infant cry samples were collected directly by specialized physicians. The
samples were labeled in the moment of their recording. Labels contain information about the cause of the cry or the pathology presented.

Recordings were divided in segments of one second, each segment is then
taken as an individual sample of cry. Samples were divided in frames of 50
milliseconds. The MFCC technique was applied to the samples and 16 coefficients
were extracted from each frame, getting vectors with 304 coefficients. The Pratt
[5] tool was used to extract the coefficients.

The infant cry corpus has 340 samples of cries of asphyxia, 192 for pain, 350
for hunger, 879 cries of babies who are deaf and 157 of normal cries. Pain and
hunger cries come from normal babies, so they are also part of the normal cries
collection. This corpus was used to build different binary data sets: asphyxia
vs normal and hunger, deaf vs normal and hunger and hunger vs pain. Table
1 shows the different data sets and the number of samples of each case. These
data sets were used in our experiments.

3   Classification Approach

A genetic algorithm, proposed by Holland [10] in the 70s, is a heuristic search
technique which is inspired in the Darwin's evolutionary theory to solve problems using computational models. The genetic algorithm is based on the idea
of the survival of the individual's fitness and, reproduction strategies, where

Table 1. Description of infant cry data sets

Data set	No. Samples	Samples by class
Asphyxia vs Normal and Hungry	847	Asphyxia: 340 Normal and Hungry: 507
Deaf vs Normal and Hungry	1386	Deaf: 879 Normal and Hungry: 507
Hungry vs Pain	542	Hungry:350 Pain:192

stronger individuals have a higher chance to create offsprings, and consequently are considered in the evolution process. Generally, a genetic algorithm has five basic components: an encoding scheme, in a form of chromosomes or individuals, that represents the potential solutions to the problem, a form to create potential initial solutions, a fitness function to measure how close a chromosome is to the desired solution, selection operations and reproduction operators [7].

In this work we use GSFM for infant cry classification. For each data set, described in section 2, we applied GSFM to select a model. The obtained model was trained with a training data set, and this model was used to predict the testing set. Next, the GSFM technique is described.

3.1   Genetic Selection of a Fuzzy Model

The process of the construction of a fuzzy model is shown in Fig. 1. A labeled data set is the input. Given that each sample is described by a set of N features, and that N is usually large, the first step is to reduce the dimensionality of the data set. This task is done by applying a feature selection method. Then, the subset of selected features is converted into fuzzy values, which is the fuzzification step. Next, the parameters of fuzzy membership are fitted to reduce the overlapping degree. Finally, with the fuzzy features a fuzzy classifier is built. Given a pool of feature selection methods, fuzzy processing and learning algorithms, GSFM selects the combination of them that minimizes the error.

GSFM has the advantage to consider different methods, Table 2 describes each of methods considered by GSFM. Nevertheless, searching across the model space is computationally intractable. In GSFM, each model (combination of different methods) is represented by a chromosome, also known as individual. For each generation in the genetic algorithm, a set of chromosomes is evaluated and these chromosomes are used to generate new models for the next generation. A fitness function is required to asses the models, in this case we considered the balance error rate (BER). However, the error of each model is not known *a priori*, for that reason we used 2 fold cross validation over the training set to estimate it (a detailed description of GSFM can be found in [18]). BER is computed as follows:

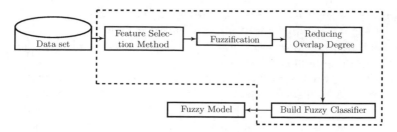

Fig. 1. Process for building a model

$$BER = \frac{1}{j} \sum_{i=1}^{j} e_i \qquad (1)$$

where j is the number of classes in the data set and e_i is the error in the ith class.

Table 2. Methods considered in GSFM. The combination of feature selection method, type of fuzzy processing, and fuzzy classifier is done with a genetic algorithm.

Method	Number of Parameters	Description
Feature Selection		
ReliefF	3	Ranking of features based on the ReliefF algorithm.
χ^2	1	Ranking of features based on the χ^2 statistical test.
InfoGain	1	Features are ranked according to their information gain.
Correlation	2	A subset of features is selected according to the correlation among themselves.
Fuzzy Processing		
NLP	1	Defines the number of linguistic properties. It can take the values: 3 (Low, Medium, and High), 5 (Very Low, Low, Medium, High, and Very High), and 7 (Very Low, Low, More or Less Low, Medium, More or Less High, High, and Very High).
TMF	1	The type of fuzzy membership function. It can take the values of Trapezoid, Triangle, Gaussian, and Bell.
Fuzzy Classifier		
FDT	1	A fuzzy decision tree.
FDF	2	A fuzzy decision forest.
FKNN	2	A fuzzy version of the k nearest neighbor algorithm.
FRNN	5	A fuzzy relational neural network classifier.

4   Experiments and Results

For our experiments we used the Baby chillanto® infant cry data base property of INAOE-CONACyT, Mexico. This data set has samples of cries from deaf babies and with asphyxia, hunger, pain, and normal, as described in section 2.

We performed several experiments considering binary classification. First, we considered the binary problems identifying between asphyxia and normal[1] cries, deaf and normal, and finally hungry and pain cries. For each experiment, we used GSFM to determine the best model.

The evaluation was done using 10 fold cross validation. This technique divides the data set into 10 disjoint subsets, and in each fold a subset is left apart for testing and the remaining subsets for training. This process is repeated until all subsets have been used for testing and training. As evaluation metrics we used accuracy (ACC), true positive rate (TPR), true negative rate (TNR) and area under the ROC[2] curve (AUC) [4].

Table 3 shows the best obtained results in our experiments and the reported by Rosales-Pérez et al. [17]. Even though other works have tackled the infant cry classification problem, a direct comparison among those is not performed, because they do not apply 10 fold cross validation. Nonetheless, accuracy percentages of 99% and of 95% are reported in [9] and [19], respectively, for asphyxia vs normal cries. Table 3 also shows that our approach clearly outperforms the reported in [17]. However, we performed the Wilcoxon signed rank test [23] to determine whether the difference is statistically significant or not. This test was done across the obtained results in each fold. Table 4 shows this test and whether the difference for each data set is significant or not.

Table 3. Percentual classification results for each experiment. Results are the average of using 10 fold cross validation. Reported results by Rosales-Pérez et al. [17] are also shown. The best result is shown in bold font for each case.

ID	Data Set	Accuracy		TPR		TNR		AUC	
		GSFM	[17]	GSFM	[17]	GSFM	[17]	GSFM	[17]
1	Asphyxia vs Normal	**90.68**	88.67	85.29	**90.00**	**94.29**	87.78	**95.79**	92.85
2	Deaf vs Normal	**99.42**	97.55	**100.00**	98.75	**98.42**	95.47	**100.00**	99.75
3	Hungry vs Pain	**97.96**	96.03	**99.43**	95.59	95.26	**96.67**	**98.89**	98.35

Table 4. Statistical test on the infant cry data set. T^+ is the sum of possitive differences, T^- is the sum of negative difference and T is the minimum between T^+ and T^-. The significance level, α, is set to 0.05, for that level T should be less than 8

ID	T^+	T^-	T	significant?
1	46	6	6	YES
2	41	7	7	YES
3	40	9	9	NO

Finally, Table 5 describes the obtained models for each case. For each model, the feature selection method (FSM), type of membership function (TMF), number of linguistic properties (NLP), the learning algorithm (LA), and its associated parameters are shown.

---

[1] We considered the hungry cries as normal cries.

[2] Receiver Operating Characteristic.

Table 5. Selected models for infant cry data sets using GSFM

ID	FSM	TMF	NLP	LA	Parameters
1	Correlation	Trapezoid	3	FKNN	nn = 7
					sm = correlation
2	InfoGain	Bell	7	FDT	cv = 0.87
3	InfoGain	Gauss	3	FKNN	nn = 5
					sm = chord

5 Conclusion and Future Work

In this work we described the application of GSFM for the task of infant cry classification. Our approach allows to select an adequate model to differentiate between each type of cry. Among the main advantages of the adopted approach we highlight that the user does not have to perform several experiments in order to determine a good combination of methods. Our experimental results show that our approach outperforms results reported in the literature from methods that only consider one learning algorithm.

As a future work we would like to explore the use of other techniques to extract features from the audio signals, as well as to test strategies such as ensembles of different models. We will also try infant cry classification as a multiclass problem.

Acknowledgements. The firts author (register number 234672) wants to thank to CONACyT for the financial support given to his postgraduate studies.

References

1. Barajas, S., Reyes, C.: Your fuzzy relational neural network parameters optimization with a genetic algorithm. In: The 14th IEEE International Conference on Fuzzy Systems, FUZZ 2005, pp. 684–689. IEEE (2005)
2. Barajas-Montiel, S., Reyes-García, C.: Fuzzy Support Vector Machines for Automatic Infant Cry Recognition. In: Huang, D.-S., Li, K., Irwin, G. (eds.) Intelligent Computing in Signal Processing and Pattern Recognition. LNCIS, vol. 345, pp. 876–881. Springer, Heidelberg (2006)
3. Barajas-Montiel, S.E., Reyes-García, C.A., Arch-Tirado, E., Mandujano, M.: Improving Baby Caring with Automatic Infant Cry Recognition. In: Miesenberger, K., Klaus, J., Zagler, W.L., Karshmer, A.I. (eds.) ICCHP 2006. LNCS, vol. 4061, pp. 691–698. Springer, Heidelberg (2006)
4. Beck, J., Shultz, E., et al.: The use of relative operating characteristic (roc) curves in test performance evaluation. Archives of Pathology & Laboratory Medicine 110(1), 13 (1986)
5. Boersma, P., Weenink, D.: Praat v. 4.0. 8. A system for doing phonetics by computer. Institute of Phonetic Sciences of the University of Amsterdam (2002)

6. Cano Ortiz, S.D., Escobedo Beceiro, D.I., Ekkel, T.: A Radial Basis Function Network Oriented for Infant Cry Classification. In: Sanfeliu, A., Martínez Trinidad, J.F., Carrasco Ochoa, J.A. (eds.) CIARP 2004. LNCS, vol. 3287, pp. 374–380. Springer, Heidelberg (2004)
7. Engelbrecht, A.: Computational intelligence: an introduction. Wiley (2007)
8. Galaviz, O.F.R., García, C.A.R.: Infant Cry Classification to Identify Hypo Acoustics and Asphyxia Comparing an Evolutionary-Neural System with a Neural Network System. In: Gelbukh, A., de Albornoz, Á., Terashima-Marín, H. (eds.) MICAI 2005. LNCS (LNAI), vol. 3789, pp. 949–958. Springer, Heidelberg (2005)
9. Hariharan, M., Yaacob, S., Awang, S.A.: Pathological infant cry analysis using wavelet packet transform and probabilistic neural network. Expert Systems with Applications 38(12), 15377–15382 (2011),
http://www.sciencedirect.com/science/article/pii/S0957417411009201
10. Holland, J.: Adaptation in natural and artificial systems. University of Michigan Press, Ann Arbor MI (1975)
11. Lederman, D.: Automatic classification of infants cry. Ben Gorion University. M.Sc. Thesis P, pp. 1–11 (2002)
12. Lederman, D., Cohen, A., Zmora, E., Wermke, K., Hauschildt, S., Stellzig-Eisenhauer, A.: On the use of hidden markov models in infants' cry classification. In: The 22nd Convention of Electrical and Electronics Engineers in Israel, pp. 350–352. IEEE (2002)
13. Lederman, D., Zmora, E., Hauschildt, S., Stellzig-Eisenhauer, A., Wermke, K.: Classification of cries of infants with cleft-palate using parallel hidden markov models. Medical and Biological Engineering and Computing 46, 965–975 (2008)
14. Orozco-García, J., Reyes-García, C.A.: A Study on the Recognition of Patterns of Infant Cry for the Identification of Deafness in Just Born Babies with Neural Networks. In: Sanfeliu, A., Ruiz-Shulcloper, J. (eds.) CIARP 2003. LNCS, vol. 2905, pp. 342–349. Springer, Heidelberg (2003)
15. Reyes-Galaviz, O.F., Tirado, E.A., Reyes-Garcia, C.A.: Classification of Infant Crying to Identify Pathologies in Recently Born Babies with ANFIS. In: Miesenberger, K., Klaus, J., Zagler, W.L., Burger, D. (eds.) ICCHP 2004. LNCS, vol. 3118, pp. 408–415. Springer, Heidelberg (2004)
16. Reyes-Galaviz, O.F., Verduzco, A., Arch-Tirado, E., Reyes-García, C.A.: Analysis of an Infant Cry Recognizer for the Early Identification of Pathologies. In: Chollet, G., Esposito, A., Faúndez-Zanuy, M., Marinaro, M. (eds.) Nonlinear Speech Modeling. LNCS (LNAI), vol. 3445, pp. 404–409. Springer, Heidelberg (2005)
17. Rosales-Pérez, A., Reyes-García, C.A., Gómez-Gil, P.: Genetic Fuzzy Relational Neural Network for Infant Cry Classification. In: Martínez-Trinidad, J.F., Carrasco-Ochoa, J.A., Ben-Youssef Brants, C., Hancock, E.R. (eds.) MCPR 2011. LNCS, vol. 6718, pp. 288–296. Springer, Heidelberg (2011)
18. Rosales-Pérez, A., Reyes-García, C.A., Gómez-Gil, P., Gonzalez, J.A., Altamirano, L.: Genetic Selection of Fuzzy Model for Acute Leukemia Classification. In: Batyrshin, I., Sidorov, G. (eds.) MICAI 2011, Part I. LNCS, vol. 7094, pp. 537–548. Springer, Heidelberg (2011)
19. Sahak, R., Mansor, W., Lee, Y.K., Yassin, A.I.M., Zabidi, A.: Performance of combined support vector machine and principal component analysis in recognizing infant cry with asphyxia. In: 2010 Annual International Conference of the IEEE Engineering in Medicine and Biology Society (EMBC), pp. 6292–6295. IEEE (2010)

20. Suaste-Rivas, I., Díaz-Méndez, A., Reyes-García, C.A., Reyes-Galaviz, O.F.: Hybrid Neural Network Design and Implementation on FPGA for Infant Cry Recognition. In: Sojka, P., Kopeček, I., Pala, K. (eds.) TSD 2006. LNCS (LNAI), vol. 4188, pp. 703–709. Springer, Heidelberg (2006)
21. Suaste-Rivas, I., Reyes-Galaviz, O.F., Diaz-Mendez, A., Reyes-Garcia, C.A.: A Fuzzy Relational Neural Network for Pattern Classification. In: Sanfeliu, A., Martínez Trinidad, J.F., Carrasco Ochoa, J.A. (eds.) CIARP 2004. LNCS, vol. 3287, pp. 358–365. Springer, Heidelberg (2004)
22. Suaste-Rivas, I., Reyes-Galviz, O.F., Diaz-Mendez, A., Reyes-Garcia, C.A.: Implementation of a Linguistic Fuzzy Relational Neural Network for Detecting Pathologies by Infant Cry Recognition. In: Lemaître, C., Reyes, C.A., González, J.A. (eds.) IBERAMIA 2004. LNCS (LNAI), vol. 3315, pp. 953–962. Springer, Heidelberg (2004)
23. Wilcoxon, F.: Individual comparisons by ranking methods. Biometrics Bulletin 1(6), 80–83 (1945)

Intention, Context and Gesture Recognition for Sterile MRI Navigation in the Operating Room

Mithun Jacob, Christopher Cange, Rebecca Packer, and Juan P. Wachs

Purdue University, West Lafayette, IN 47906, USA
{mithunjacob,ccange,rpacker,jpwachs}@purdue.edu

Abstract. Human-Computer Interaction (HCI) devices such as the keyboard and the mouse are among the most contaminated regions in an operating room (OR). This paper proposes a sterile, intuitive HCI to navigate MRI images using freehand gestures. The system incorporates contextual cues and intent of the user to strengthen the gesture recognition process. Experimental results showed that while performing an image navigation task, mean intent recognition accuracy was 98.7% and that the false positive rate of gesture recognition dropped from 20.76% to 2.33% with context integration at similar recognition rates.

Keywords: Gesture recognition, operating room, human computer interaction.

1 Introduction

Recent advances in computer-assisted surgery are taking user centered interfaces to the operating room (OR) in more and more hospitals and outpatient clinics. Since HCI devices are possible sources of contamination due to the difficulty in sterilization, clinical protocols have been devised to delegate control of the terminal to a sterile human assistant [1], [2]. Nevertheless, this mode of communication has been shown to be cumbersome [3], prone to errors [1] and overall, inefficient. This paper proposes a sterile method for the surgeon to naturally, and efficiently manipulate MRI images through touchless, freehand gestures. Image manipulation through gestural devices has been shown to be natural and intuitive [4] and does not compromise the sterility of the surgeon. The system extends a system previously developed by the authors [5] with the use of dynamic two-handed gestures and contextual knowledge.

2 System Overview

2.1 MRI Image Browser

Users interact with an image browser developed to navigate and manipulate MRI images. The browser (developed with OpenGL and OpenCV libraries) displays several sequences on the left side of the screen for selection and a single slice from the selected sequence on the right side of the screen (see Fig. 1(a)). The user then selects an image representing an anatomical structure of interest. This image is then manipulated through several actions such as increasing/decreasing image brightness, and rotating the image in the clockwise or counter-clockwise directions.

L. Alvarez et al. (Eds.): CIARP 2012, LNCS 7441, pp. 220–227, 2012.
© Springer-Verlag Berlin Heidelberg 2012

The images are accessed entirely through gestural commands (one gesture for each command). The lexicon consists of ten gestures (see Fig. 2(a)) which were selected from interviews with nine veterinary surgeons. The gestures encompass image navigation and manipulation tasks such as browsing (*up*, *down*, *left*, and *right*), zooming (*zoom-in*, and *zoom-out*), rotation (*clockwise*, and *counter-clockwise*) and brightness change (*brightness-up*, and *brightness-down*). The system can also be used independently of a fixed display such as a television or monitor; Fig. 1(b) shows the system being used with a pico-projector hanging around the user.

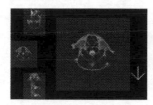 

Fig. 1. (a) MRI Image Browser (b) Browser with the pico-projector

2.2   Gesture Recognition

A Microsoft Kinect using the OpenNI SDK was used to capture the user's skeleton thus providing the positions of various landmark positions on the human body from depth data (see Fig. 2(b)). The positions of the left and right shoulders, and the head were quantized and delivered to a decision tree, as visual cues to gauge the user's intention. If the user intends to use the system, the position of the left and right hands are tracked and the trajectories are classified with a set of 10 Hidden Markov Models (HMMs). Additionally, non-visual contextual cues such as the sequence of commands issued by the user was modeled as a Markov chain and the time between commands were also used as contextual cues to aid in gesture recognition. The recognized command is then sent to the MRI image browser.

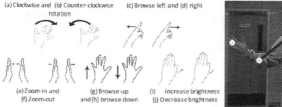 

Fig. 2. (a) Gesture Lexicon (b) Skeleton model and tracked marker-less points

3   Gesture Recognition with Contextual Cues

Gaze has been established as a critical cue in establishing attention which stems from the intention of a user to interact with a person or a device [6]. Other fundamental cues are head orientation, body posture and the position of the hands w.r.t the body [7]. The following sections describe how visual and non-visual contextual cues are used to recognize the performed gestures.

3.1   Intention Recognition

The intention recognition module decides whether a performed gesture is intentional or not based on anthropometric and kinematic features of the human body. The torso orientation (T_θ), head orientation confidence (H_θ), hand orientation w.r.t. the torso (L_θ, R_θ) are combined to form the visual context feature vector,

$$V = [T_\theta \quad H_\theta \quad L_\theta \quad R_\theta]^T \tag{1}$$

The information encapsulated in this feature vector allows us to successfully determine whether the user "intends" to perform a gesture or not. The cues are explained in detail below:

- **Torso orientation:** The orientation of the torso helps determine whether the user is facing the system and is thus intending to use it. The 3D position of the left and right shoulder $(\vec{L}_s, \vec{R}_s)$ is used to compute the azimuth orientation of the torso w.r.t. the X-axis, i.e. $T_\theta = \cos^{-1}\left(\frac{(\vec{L}_s - \vec{R}_s)}{|\vec{L}_s - \vec{R}_s|} \cdot [1 \quad 0 \quad 0]^T\right)$.

- **Head orientation:** The location of the head is obtained from the skeleton and is used to reduce the search space of the Viola-Jones frontal face detector [8]. A continuous estimate H_θ of the confidence that the head of the user is forward-facing is computed by sliding a 10×1 mean filter over the output of the frontal face detector per frame. This cue provides information regarding the gaze of the user.

- **Hands position:** Arm orientation with respect to the torso is an indication of whether the user wants to gesticulate towards the camera, or instead, is engaged in a surgical task. The 3D position of each hand is used to compute its orientation with the waistline providing the inclination of each hand (i.e. L_θ, R_θ) with respect to the zenith angle.

Integration of Visual Contextual Cues

A dataset of 2100 sample sequences of "intentional" behavior, and 2650 samples of "unintentional" behavior were captured from users and manually annotated (I and U, respectively). Then, each sequence was quantized into a feature vector (see Equation 1). The data set was used to train a decision tree which was pruned to produce a minimum-cost tree of 63 nodes.

3.2   Gesture Spotting

Once intent has been determined, the gesture was segmented from the trajectory of the user's hands. Gesture spotting [7] is the process of automatically determining the start and the end of a gesture. Low-level features such as gesture acceleration [9] serve as a proxy to segment each gesture (gestures are preceded and succeeded by sudden acceleration and deceleration respectively). The segmented observations were used as inputs to the discrete HMMs.

Let the velocity of hand h at time t be $V_h(t)$, and t_1 and t_N the start and end times of a sliding window, respectively ($t \in \{t_1, \ldots t_k, \ldots, t_N\}$). If the variance $\sigma^2(V_h(t_k))$ exceeds the threshold α (an empirically determined), t_k is set as the start point of the gesture. The end-point is similarly determined. If the length of the segmented gesture exceeds a threshold, a gesture has been spotted.

3.3   Pre-selection of Gesture Classes

The contextual information used so far is a good proxy for gestural intent; nevertheless it does provide much information about the likelihood of a given gestural occurrence. A combined measure of gesture likelihood is obtained using two non-visual contextual cues. These cues are learned independently of the gesture interface, since they are intrinsic to the task alone. All the non-visual cues were gathered after observing a large number of MRI browsing tasks completed by the users of the system.

- **Delay between commands:** The time between commands t_D provides predictive information. For example, navigational commands exhibit shorter delays between commands whereas image manipulation commands image have a longer delay. A normal distribution was fitted to the observed delays between commands, so each gesture class k (mapped to a command) has a normal distribution $\mathcal{N}(\mu_k, \sigma_k)$ assigned to it.
- **Command history:** The command history provides information regarding which commands are more probable to occur given the previous command. Since all commands are not equiprobable, the command history helps in reducing the possible set of gestures by using the knowledge of the previously evoked command C_{t-1}. The sequence of commands is modeled as a first-order Markov chain and a transition matrix A is learned from user-interactions.

Integration of Non-visual Contextual Cues
Given a command delay, and a current command, the probability of the next gesture k from the gesture lexicon Γ was computed by finding the joint probability between the gesture class given the delay time t_D, and the probability of transition to the current command. Formally,

$$P_k = P(k|t_D)P(k|C_{t-1}) \ \forall k \in \Gamma \tag{2}$$

All hand trajectories corresponding to gestures where $P_k > \epsilon$, were classified using chains of HMM detailed in the next subsection.

3.4   Post-selection of Gesture Classes

The motion of the centroids of the hands from the skeleton model is fed to the gesture recognition algorithm. This algorithm attempts to classify the spotted trajectory (see section 3.2) as belonging to one of the ten gestures in the surgical gesture lexicon Γ. The input to the gesture recognition algorithm is the feature vector u which encodes the velocity of each hand along each axis in $\mathbb{R}^3$. Given that the centroids of the first and second hand in the nth frame are given by $(x_{f;n}, y_{f,n}, z_{f;n})$ and $(x_{s;n}, y_{s,n}, z_{s;n})$ respectively, then the feature vector for a frame n is computed as u,

$$[x_{f;n} - x_{f;n-1}, \ y_{f;n} - y_{f;n-1}, \ z_{f;n} - z_{f;n-1}, \ x_{s;n} - x_{s;n-1}, \ y_{s;n} - y_{s;n-1}, \ z_{s;n} - z_{s;n-1}] \tag{3}$$

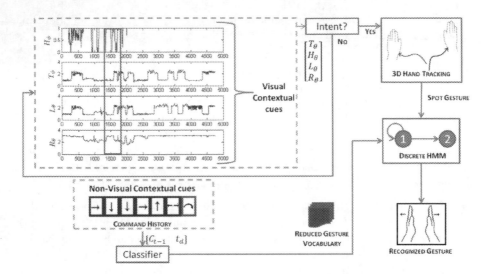

Fig. 3. Pruning the gesture lexicon with visual and non-visual contextual cues

A subset $\Lambda \subseteq \Gamma$ (determined in the pre-selection process) of discrete HMMs (one corresponding to each gesture), was used to recognize the trajectories. Each HMM is a left-right model [10] with 5 states. Each element in the vector u (velocities of the hands along each axis in $\mathbb{R}^3$) was quantized to three possible symbols; $\{+, 0, -\}$. If $|u_i| \leq \tau$, then u was considered static (0 symbol). Else, the sign corresponding to the velocity along the corresponding axis was assigned.

Each vector u was quantized to 3^6 representations which form the set of observation symbols for each HMM. Ten HMMs (an HMM $\lambda_k = (A_k, B_k, \pi_k)$ per gesture k) was trained with labeled data with the Baum-Welch [10] algorithm. A gesture k was said to be recognized if λ_k resulted in the highest probability of the set of quantized observations $O = [O_1, ..., O_T]^T$. The probabilities were computed using the Viterbi algorithm [10] on the segmented trajectories, i.e.

$$k = \text{argmax}_k \, P(O|\lambda_k) \, \forall k = 1, ..., |\Lambda| \tag{4}$$

4   Experiments

The following section discusses the experiments conducted to validate the hypothesis that contextual information (intention) can be used to detect accurately the gestures evoked by the user.

4.1   Experiment 1: Intention Detection

The first experiment tested the prediction of intention based on contextual cues, as described in section 3.1. A dataset of 4750 observations was collected to train and test the decision tree, of which 44% represented "intentional" behavior, and the rest "unintentional" behavior. An ROC curve (see Fig. 4) was generated through 2-fold cross-validation for ten discrete values of κ, the maximum depth of the decision tree (κ varied from 6-15). The ROC curve indicates that the peak operating point of the classifier has recognition accuracy of 97.9% with 1.36% false positive rate. A true positive is obtained when the user is correctly found to be facing the screen.

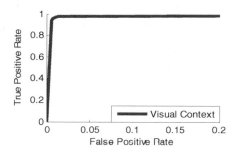

Fig. 4. ROC curve for intention recognition

4.2 Experiment 2: Gesture Recognition

The gesture recognition performance of the HMM was evaluated in this experiment. A dataset of 1000 gestures were performed by 10 users (10 gestures per user per class). Also, several configurations of the left-right HMM model with various discretization thresholds τ were tested over the dataset through 10-fold cross-validation. The value of $\tau = 28mm$ was found to be optimal (see Fig. 5). The performance per class at this optimal operating point is described by the confusion matrix, presented in Fig. 6. Mean recognition accuracy of 97.23% was obtained. Fig.6 also shows that the *left* and *right* gestures have relatively lower mean accuracy since they are respectively sub-gestures of the *clockwise* and *counter-clockwise* gestures and are thus susceptible to be confused.

4.3 Experiment 3: In-task Recognition Performance

Twenty two students were asked to perform a specific browsing and manipulation task using the MRI image browser in a laboratory environment. The task consisted of searching for a landmark image and performing image manipulation tasks on the landmark image. All the data was recorded over 220 trials (10 per student) and each performed gesture was manually annotated. Data from 2 users were discarded as outliers due to the failure of the Kinect to reliably determine the skeleton of the user. A total of 4445 gestures were collected from users performing this task. At the end of each trial, each user was asked to assemble a surgical box. This activity served as a controlled way to force the user shift the focus of attention from the image browser. Without contextual information, such activity could potentially trigger accidental gestures. Fig. 7 displays the isolated gesture recognition accuracy of the 4445 annotated gestures captured when the user was interacting with the system. During the "non-intentional" phase of each trial, the gesture spotter was executed and the segmented gestures (false positives) were recognized. Intent was correctly determined 98.7% of the time and mean gesture recognition accuracy (ACC) of 92.58% and 93.6% was obtained for the system with and without context respectively.

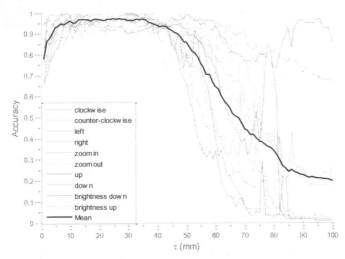

Fig. 5. Mean gesture recognition accuracy vs. discretization threshold. On the vertical axis is the accuracy of each gesture (in different colored line), and on the horizontal is the discretization threshold used to convert trajectories to sequences of discrete symbols.

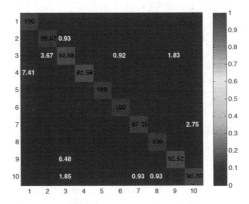

Fig. 6. Confusion matrix for $\tau = 28mm$. The rows represent the true class of the gestures labels and the columns represent the class assigned by the algorithm. High values on the diagonal elements indicate high gesture recognition accuracy.

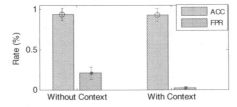

Fig. 7. Comparison of gesture recognition with and without context

The main advantage of incorporating context is visible in the reduction of the false positive rate (FPR) of 20.76% without context to 2.33% with context.

5   Discussion and Conclusion

The hypothesis that contextual information integrated with hand trajectory gesture information can significantly improve the overall system recognition performance was validated. It has been shown that the false positive rate is significantly reduced using context without affecting recognition performance. The intent recognition and gesture recognition systems have been shown to perform well (98.5% and 93.6% respectively) on data collected from user interactions. In the dataset of gestures, the average isolated gesture recognition rate was found to be 97.23%.

Future work includes building a more sophisticated gesture spotter which uses the gestural knowledge as well as local features of the trajectory to segment gestures. Additionally, tracking skeletal joints independently is required to handle the possible situation of failure in skeletal tracking by the OpenNI SDK.

Acknowledgments. This project was supported by grant number R03HS019837 from the Agency for Healthcare Research and Quality (AHRQ). The content is solely the responsibility of the authors and does not necessarily represent the official views of the AHRQ. We would also like to thank all the students who helped.

References

1. Albu, A.: Vision-based user interfaces for health applications: a survey. Advances in Visual Computing, 771–782 (2006)
2. Schultz, M., Gill, J., Zubairi, S., Huber, R., Gordin, F.: Bacterial contamination of computer keyboards in a teaching hospital. Infection Control and Hospital Epidemiology 24(4), 302–303 (2003)
3. Maintz, J., Viergever, M.A.: A survey of medical image registration. Medical Image Analysis 2(1), 1–36 (1998)
4. Ebert, L.C., Hatch, G., Ampanozi, G., Thali, M.J., Ross, S.: You Can't Touch This: Touch-free Navigation Through Radiological Images. Surg. Innov. (November 2011)
5. Wachs, J.P., Stern, H.I., Edan, Y., Gillam, M., Handler, J., Feied, C., et al.: A Gesture-Based Tool for Sterile Browsing of Radiology Images. J. Am. Med. Inf. Assoc. 15(3), 321–323 (2008)
6. Emery, N.: The eyes have it: the neuroethology, function and evolution of social gaze. Neuroscience & Biobehavioral Reviews 24(6), 581–604 (2000)
7. Langton, S.R.H.: The mutual influence of gaze and head orientation in the analysis of social attention direction. The Quarterly Journal of Experimental Psychology: Section A 53(3), 825–845 (2000)
8. Viola, P., Jones, M.J.: Robust real-time face detection. International Journal of Computer Vision 57(2), 137–154 (2004)
9. Kang, H., Woo Lee, C., Jung, K.: Recognition-based gesture spotting in video games. Pattern Recognition Letters 25(15), 1701–1714 (2004)
10. Rabiner, L.R.: A tutorial on hidden Markov models and selected applications in speech recognition. Proceedings of the IEEE 77(2), 257–286 (1989)

Facilitated Gesture Recognition Based Interfaces for People with Upper Extremity Physical Impairments

Hairong Jiang[1], Juan P. Wachs[1], and Bradley S. Duerstock[1,2]

[1] School of Industrial Engineering, Purdue University, West Lafayette, IN, USA
[2] Weldon School of Biomedical Engineering, Purdue University, West Lafayette, IN, USA
{jiang115,jpwachs,bsd}@purdue.edu

Abstract. A gesture recognition based interface was developed to facilitate people with upper extremity physical impairments as an alternative way to perform laboratory experiments that require 'physical' manipulation of components. A color, depth and spatial information based particle filter framework was constructed with unique descriptive features for face and hands representation. The same feature encoding policy was subsequently used to detect, track and recognize users' hands. Motion models were created employing dynamic time warping (DTW) method for better observation encoding. Finally, the hand trajectories were classified into different classes (commands) by applying the CONDENSATION method and, in turn, an interface was designed for robot control, with a recognition accuracy of 97.5%. To assess the gesture recognition and control policies, a validation experiment consisting in controlling a mobile service robot and a robotic arm in a laboratory environment was conducted.

Keywords: Gesture recognition, particle filter, dynamic time warping (DTW), CONDENSATION.

1   Introduction

Effective, natural and intuitive human computer interfaces (HCI) are critical aspects in the development of assistive technologies [1]. Voice, facial expressions, gaze and hand gestures have been widely used as communication channels for unimodal or multimodal interfaces for people with upper mobility impairments. Those interfaces were used for intelligent wheelchairs control, wellness monitoring and home medical alert systems [2,3], to mention a few. Upper limb gesturing is of particular use, since people already use gestures for communicating desired actions (e.g. pointing destination, indicating direction and motion), thus having to learn a series of atypical body movements is avoided. For those individuals who are able to move their hands and upper arms to some degree, gesture-based HCI is an extremely promising alternative or complement to existing interface techniques.

Hand gesture recognition algorithms involve the hand segmentation, tracking, and trajectories recognition. A common method for hand segmentation involves modeling the user skin color [4]. Depending purely on color information is unreliable, brightness, unstructured backgrounds, and clutter affects object segmentation. If the focus is on the gestures' trajectories, instead of the hand shape, classic tracking approaches

L. Alvarez et al. (Eds.): CIARP 2012, LNCS 7441, pp. 228–235, 2012.
© Springer-Verlag Berlin Heidelberg 2012

can be adopted. For example, *Camshift* is a well-established and basic algorithm for object tracking and was previously used for hand tracking [5]. Other more complex and robust approaches include the CONDENSATION algorithm developed by Isard and Black [6]. Particle filter is a common stochastic based technique for object tracking that can be easily parallelized. Perez applied the color-based appearance model to a particle filter framework to enhance tracking under complex backgrounds and occlusions [7]. In terms of gestures classification, the predominant approach is still Hidden Markov Models (HMM) (see Bilal for an extensive review of HMM applied to hand posture and gesture recognition [8]). Common problems with HMM involve finding a good set of parameters (e. g. initial probabilities) and trajectory spotting for gesture temporal segmentation. Black and Jepson [9] proposed a CONDENSATION-based trajectory gesture recognition algorithm to this end. Nevertheless the gestures segmentation was not addressed in that work.

In this paper, particle filters and the CONDENSATION algorithm were combined for hand tracking and gesture classification in a simplistic yet robust fashion, which made it appropriate for human robot interaction (HRI) in assistive technologies.

2   System Architecture

The architecture of this system is illustrated in Fig. 1. The hand gesture based recognition system includes foreground segmentation, color-based detection, tracking, and trajectories recognition. A detailed description of the system is given in Section 3.

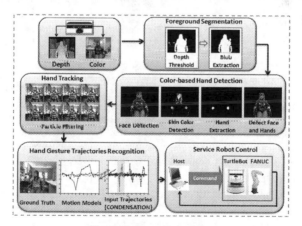

Fig. 1. System Overview

3   Gesture Recognition

3.1   Foreground Segmentation

To detect the user's movements, the user's body was treated as the foreground object. Two steps were employed to segment the foreground (refer to algorithm 1). The first step was to exclude pixels based on their distance to the camera (depth thresholding).

The second step required ruling out small areas and keeping the largest blob in the remaining image as the foreground (blob cleaning). In the first step, the depth information was assessed through a Kinect sensor (fig. 2(a)). Two absolute depth thresholds (a low threshold T_{DL} and a high threshold T_{DH}) were manually set by the user according to their relative distance to the sensor. T_{DL} is set to no less than a constant which is the minimum distance that can be observed by the depth sensor (due to its physical limitations). T_{DH} is set to be the maximum distance that can be reached by the user[1]. Only those pixels with a depth value between the two thresholds were kept in a mask image (fig. 2(b)). The mask image was used to compute the area of the biggest region (blob), denoted as (B_{SH}). All the remaining blobs with a smaller area than B_{SH} were deleted (fig. 2(c)). If the largest blob is not the face or hands, it will be discarded in a later stage since tracking is performed based on color and spatial information.

Algorithm 1: Foreground Segmentation

Input: T_{DL}; T_{DH}; depth Image $D(i, j)$;

$$D_1(i, j) = \begin{cases} 1: & T_{DL} \leq D(i,j) \leq T_{DH} \\ 0: & \text{otherwise} \end{cases}$$

$T_{SH} = \max(\text{Area}(B_i))$ //B_i is the ith blob in the mask image D_1

$$D_2(i, j) = \begin{cases} 1: & D_1(i,j) \in B_i \ \& \ \text{Area}(B_i) == T_{BH} \\ 0: & \text{otherwise} \end{cases}$$

(a)Depth Image   (b) Depth Threshold Mask   (c) Foreground Mask

Fig. 2. Foreground Segmentation

3.2   Hand Detection

Before detecting the hands, a face detection method [10] was used to obtain the initial face region (as shown in fig. 3(a)). The result was used to remove the face region from the target image. Skin and non-skin color histogram models were constructed by using the Compaq database [11]. The probability of a pixel to be part of the hand was calculated as the division of the two histograms (which is a proxy of the distinctiveness- the higher the ratio, the more likely the two pixels belong to different color distributions). The mask image was obtained by applying the histogram ratio and back-projecting the probabilities of each pixel back in the image (as show in fig. 3(b)). To obtain the hand regions without the face, the region detected by the face detector was removed from the target image. After this, the two largest blobs were selected as hand regions (fig. 3(c), (d)). This hand detection procedure is only used to provide automatic initialization to particle filter tracking. Afterwards the hands positions were assessed through continuous tracking done by the particle filter.

---

[1] These values were chosen since they resulted in the best performance; however other thresholds will impact the results differently.

(a)Face Detection   (b) Skin Color Detection   (c) Hand Extraction   (d) Localization

Fig. 3. Face and Hand Detection

3.3   Hand Tracking

A color and spatial information based Sequential Importance Resampling (SIR) particle filter framework was proposed to track both face and hands through frames in video sequences [7, 12]. The Particle filter algorithm consists of three main phases: predicting, measuring and resampling. In the prediction phase, a second order auto-regressive (AR) was selected as the dynamic motion model as in equation (1):

$$x_{t+1} = A_1(x_t - x_0) + A_2(x_{t-1} - x_0) + x_0 + Bv_t, v_t \sim \mathcal{N}(0, \Sigma) \tag{1}$$

where A_1, A_2, B and Σ were the parameter matrices that best matched the real motion of the tracked object; x was the state of particles. In the measuring stage, both color and spatial information were incorporated in the particle filter framework to calculate the likelihood function. The method in [8] was used to calculate the color likelihood function:

$$\omega^i \propto \exp(-\lambda D_i^2) \tag{2}$$

where λ is the Bhattacharyya similarity coefficient ((is empirically set to 20) following the practice in [8] which delivered satisfactory results). The spatial likelihood function included three parts: the Euclidian distance between the centroid of face and hand blob (defined as D_{fhx}, x=1 or 2), the two hands blobs (defined as D_{hh}) and each particle and the centroid of blob in the previous video frame (defined as D_{pc}). The spatial part of likelihood is then:

$$\omega^i \propto \exp(k_1 D_{fhx} + k_2 D_{hh} + k_3(1/D_{pc})) \tag{3}$$

Combining equation (2) and (3), the likelihood function is:

$$\omega^i = \beta * \exp(-\lambda D_i^2 + k_1 D_{fhx} + k_2 D_{hh} + k_3(1/D_{pc})) \tag{4}$$

where β is a normalization factor; k_1, k_2, k_3 are parameters that were set to change the weight of each feature for optimal tracking.

3.4   Hand Trajectory Classification

The positions of the hands in each frame of the video sequence were acquired from the tracking stage. The motion model for each gesture trajectory was created based on the data collected from eight subjects. Although gestures performed by each subject may have similar trajectories, the precise duration of each sub-trajectory within the trajectory were different. To normalize the trajectories, temporal alignment was conducted. The dynamic time warping (DTW) method was employed to accommodate differences in timing between different trajectories to the construct motion models [13]. The following procedure was proposed to obtain the motion models (Algorithm 2).

Algorithm 2: Procedure to Construct Motion Models

Input: Number of gestures G; number of subjects S; number of sampling trajectories from each subject T; horizontal and vertical velocity for left and right hand V_p^m, m=1,...,S*T.

> for k = 1: G
>> for j=1:S
>>> for i=1:T-1
>>>> Align V_p^i with V_p^{i+1} to obtain V_{ap}^i
>>>
>>> **end for**
>>> Align V_p^T with V_p^1 to obtain V_{ap}^T
>>> $V_p^j = \sum_{i=1}^T V_{ap}^i / T$
>>
>> **end for**
>> for j=1:S-1
>>> Align V_p^j with V_p^{j+1} to obtain V_{ap}^j
>>
>> **end for**
>> Align V_p^S with V_p^1 to obtain V_{ap}^S
>> $V_p^k = \sum_{i=1}^S V_{ap}^i / S$
>
> **end for**

The CONDENSATION algorithm [9] was used to recognize the hand gesture trajectories. The original algorithm was extended to work for two hands. A state at time t is described as a parameter vector:

$$s_t = (\mu, \Phi^x, \alpha^x, \rho^x) \tag{5}$$

Where, μ was the index of the motion models, ϕ was the current phase in the model, α was an amplitude scaling factor, ρ was a time dimension scaling factor, x denoted the hand used x∈ {left hand, right hand}.

4   Experimental Results

4.1   Recognition Accuracy

An eight-gesture lexicon (as shown in fig. 4) was selected according to results from an interview with individuals with physical disabilities. The size of the gesture lexicon is eight because more gestures were difficult for the users to remember, while less was not enough due to the number of functions required. It was tested by eight users and resulted in an average cross validation accuracy of 97.5%. Ten sessions were used for cross validation of each gesture (k-fold with k=10). In each session, 72 gestures were used for training and 8 gestures were used for testing. A confusion matrix was computed using a temporal window size of w=20 (fig. 5). The ROC curve to demonstrate the system performance was obtained by changing the size of the window from 10 to 24 to different values (fig. 6).

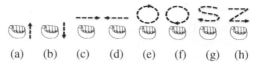

(a)   (b)   (c)   (d)   (e)   (f)   (g)   (h)

Fig. 4. Gesture Lexicon

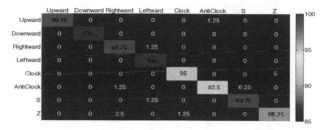

Fig. 5. Confusion Matrix with the window size- w =20

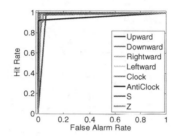

Fig. 6. ROC Curve showing recognition performance for each gesture

4.2   Laboratory Experiment

A laboratory case study was completed five times by one able bodied individual with each mode of operation. While the task completion time depends on the user performing the experiment, general trends can be observed in this pilot experiment regarding task completion time that can be generalized to larger pools of users. In this experiment, a mobile robot was controlled by the gesture algorithm to transport a beaker to a position near a robotic arm. The robotic arm would then be activated by the operator to add a reagent to the beaker and the mobile robot would be summoned back to the beginning point. To control the mobile robot and the robotic arm, the gestures in the lexicon from (a)-(h) were mapped to the following commands: 'change mode', 'robotic arm action', 'go forward', 'go backward', 'turn left', 'turn right', 'stop' and 'enable robotic arm'. Two modes were used to control the mobile robot: *discrete* and *continuous* mode. In *discrete* mode, the robot moved an increment of distance, every time that a command was issued. While the *continuous* mode, the robot responded to the given command, until the 'stop' command was issued. To switch between these two modes one distinctive gesture ('upward') was used. In the experiment, the discrete, continuous and combined (continuous plus discrete) control modes were tested. The resulting average task completion times were of 205, 109.8 and 143.2 seconds, respectively (fig. 7). Each recognition process required only 47ms for face and both hand recognition. The map for the lab and the trajectories of the robot for discrete (red star line), continuous (blue solid line), and combined (black dash line) control modes were recorded to test for correlation between average completion time for a task with fixed distance and the used control mode (fig. 8).

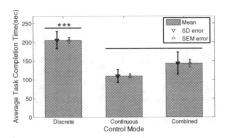

Fig. 7. Average Task Completion Time, Unpaired t-test, p<0.001

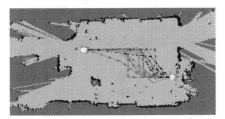

Fig. 8. Robot trajectories for different control modes

5   Conclusions and Future Work

A hand gesture recognition based interfaces was developed for people with limited upper limb mobility. The depth information was used to segment the human body from a non-static background. An automatic initialization procedure for the particle filter method was engineered by combining blob extraction, face detection, image dilation, erosion and color histograms techniques. Both color and spatial information were considered when applying the particle filter framework. A training procedure was proposed to obtain motion models for each gesture in the lexicon. The CONDENSATION algorithm was used to classify the bimanual gestures. The gesture recognition algorithm designed was found to reach a recognition accuracy of 97.5%. A laboratory task experiment was conducted to validate real time performance of the gesture interface to assist in conducting a typical biomedical lab procedure with the help of two robots. From the results, the continuous mode required the least average task completion time, while the discrete control mode required the most. Therefore, the authors recommend continuous control mode is used most of the time and the discrete is used only when the robot is very near to the target. Future work includes: (1) Determining automatically the depth thresholds for the Kinect sensor and their effect in the segmentation results. (2) Study additional robust techniques for hand tracking to tackle the problem of resilience to occlusions (when one hand occludes the other). (3) Recruit more users in the future versions of system for gesture lexicon testing to enhance the system's robustness.

Acknowledgement. This work was partially funded by the National Institutes of Health NIH Director's Pathfinder Award to Promote Diversity in the Scientific Workforce, grant number DP4-GM096842-01.

References

1. Jacko, J.A.: Human-Computer Interaction Design and Development Approaches. In: 14th HCI International Conference, pp. 169–180 (2011)
2. Moon, I., Lee, M., Ryu, J., Mun, M.: Intelligent Robotic Wheelchair with EMG-, Gesture-, and Voice-based Interfaces. In: International Conference on Intelligent Robots and Systems, pp. 3453–3458. IEEE Press (2003)
3. Reale, M., Liu, P.: Yin. L.J.: Using eye gaze, head pose and facial expression for personalized non-player character interaction. In: IEEE Computer Society Conference on Computer Vision and Pattern Recognition Workshops, pp. 13–18. IEEE Press (2011)
4. Soriano, M., Martinkauppi, B., Huovinen, S., Laaksonen, M.: Skin detection in video under changing illumination conditions. In: 15th International Conference on Pattern Recognition, vol. 1, pp. 839–842 (2000)
5. Bradski, G.R.: Computer vision face tracking as a component of a perceptual user interface. In: Workshop on Applications of Computer Vision, Princeton, NJ, pp. 214–219 (1998)
6. Isard, M., Black, A.: CONDENSATION: Conditional density propagation for visual tracking. International Journal of Computer Vision 29, 5–28 (1998)
7. Pérez, P., Hue, C., Vermaak, J., Gangnet, M.: Color-Based Probabilistic Tracking. In: Heyden, A., Sparr, G., Nielsen, M., Johansen, P. (eds.) ECCV 2002, Part I. LNCS, vol. 2350, pp. 661–675. Springer, Heidelberg (2002)
8. Bilal, S., Akmeliawati, R., Shafie, A.A., Salami, M.J.E.: Hidden Markov Model for human to computer interaction: a study on human hand gesture recognition. In: Artificial Intelligence (2011)
9. Black, M.J., Jepson, A.D.: A Probabilistic Framework for Matching Temporal Trajectories: CONDENSATION-Based Recognition of Gestures and Expressions. In: Burkhardt, H.-J., Neumann, B. (eds.) ECCV 1998, Part I. LNCS, vol. 1406, pp. 909–924. Springer, Heidelberg (1998)
10. Viola, P., Jones, M.: Rapid object detection using a boosted cascade of simple features. In: International Conference on Computer Vision and Pattern Recognition, pp. 511–518 (2001)
11. Jones, M.J., Rehg, J.M.: Statistical color models with application to skin detection. In: IEEE Computer Society Conference on Computer Vision and Pattern Recognition, vol. 46, pp. 81–96 (2002)
12. Hess, R., Fern, A.: Discriminatively Trained Particle Filters for Complex Multi-Object Tracking. In: IEEE Computer Society Conference on Computer Vision and Pattern Recognition, pp. 240–247 (2009)
13. Aach, J., Church, G.M.: Alignment gene expression time series with time warping algorithms. J. Bioinformatics 17(6), 495–508 (2001)

A Performance Evaluation of HMM and DTW for Gesture Recognition

Josep Maria Carmona and Joan Climent

Barcelona Tech (UPC), Spain

Abstract. It is unclear whether Hidden Markov Models (HMMs) or Dynamic Time Warping (DTW) techniques are more appropriate for gesture recognition. In this paper, we compare both methods using different criteria, with the objective of determining the one with better performance. For this purpose we have created a set of recorded gestures. The dataset used includes many samples of ten different gestures, with their corresponding ground truth obtained with a kinect. The dataset is made public for benchmarking purposes.

The results show that DTW gives higher performance than HMMs, and strongly support the use of DTW.

Keywords: Hidden Markov Models, Dynamic Time Warping, Gesture Recognition, Kinect.

1   Introduction

Visual recognition of hand gestures provides an attractive alternative to cumbersome interface devices for human-computer interaction. This has motivated a very active research concerned with computer vision-based analysis and interpretation of hand gestures. Computer vision and pattern recognition techniques, involving feature extraction, object detection, clustering, and classification, have been successfully used for many gesture recognition systems [4][7]. Preliminary works on vision-based gesture interpretation were focused on the recognition of static hand gestures or postures. However, hand gestures are dynamic actions and the motion of the hands conveys much more information than their posture does. While static gesture (pose) recognition can typically be accomplished by template matching and pattern recognition techniques, the dynamic gesture recognition problem involves the use of techniques such as Dynamic Time Warping (DTW) [6] or Hidden Markov Models (HMM) [8] [3].

There are some similarities between gesture and speech recognition [6] so that HMM or DTW, generally used for speech recognition, are also used for gesture recognition. In speech recognition applications, a hard task has been to recognize spoken words independent of their duration and variation in pronunciation. HMMs have shown to solve these tasks successfully. A HMM is associated with each different unit of language, while in gesture recognition each gesture can also be associated with a different HMM.

Although DTW and HMM have been applied in a large amount of works concerning gesture recognition, no previous work has done an exhaustive comparative study between both techniques. The objective of this paper is to compare the results of dynamic gesture recognition obtained using these two methods, according to recognition rates, sensitivity to the amount of training samples, optimal parameters, and computing times.

L. Alvarez et al. (Eds.): CIARP 2012, LNCS 7441, pp. 236–243, 2012.

The basics of HMM, DTW, and a description of the features commonly extracted from images are given in next section. Section 3 outlines the details of the experiments. The results are shown in section 4, and section 5 concludes the paper.

2   Preliminaries

2.1   Feature Extraction

The selection of the right features to be extracted from image sequences plays an important role in gesture recognition. Usually, the selected features are location, orientation, or velocity.

To determine the location, the coordinates are extracted directly from sequence frames, and they can be referenced to different coordinate origins. In some works, the hand location points are referenced to the distance from head. Others, like [1] use as origin the centroid of the hand trajectory, or the starting point of the hand gesture path. Holt et al. [2] use the position (x,y,z) relative to the head, of the left and right hand to recognize gesture from the standard vocabulary of Sign language of the Netherlands.

A second feature widely used is the orientation, which represents the direction of the hand at every point of the gesture path. It is computed as the displacement vector of every point and is represented by the orientation relative to the centroid of the gesture path, the orientation between two consecutives points or the orientation between the starting point and the current gesture point.

The third feature is the velocity, which plays an important role in recognition phase, particularly in some critical situations. It is computed as the distance between two successive points divided by the time measured in number of frames.

Ming-Hsuan et al. [9] use the position, velocity, and angle, to introduce the feature vector (x,y,v,θ) into a classifier whose outputs are the classes corresponding to each gesture.

2.2   Hidden Markov Models

A HMM λ (Fig. 1) consists of N states and a transition matrix $A=\{a_{ij}\}$, where a_{ij} is the probability of the transition from S_i state to S_j. Each state has assigned an output probability distribution function b_{im}, which gives the probability of the state S_i generating observation Om under the condition that the system is in S_i.

A HMM is a triple $\lambda=(A, B, \Pi)$ as follows:

- A set of N states S= $\{s_1,s_2,...s_N\}$.
- An initial probability for each state Π_i; $i=1,2,...,N$ such that $\Pi_i =P(Si)$ in the initial step.
- A $N x N$ transition matrix $A=\{a_{ij}\}$ where a_{ij} is the probability of the transition from S_i state to S_j; $1 \le i, j \le N$.
- A set of T possible emission $O = \{o_1,o_2,...,o_T\}$.
- A set of M discrete symbols $V = \{v_1, v_2,..., v_M\}$.
- An $N x M$ observation matrix $B=b_{im}$ where b_{im} gives the probability of emitting symbol v_m from state S_i .

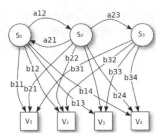

Fig. 1. HMM

In the training process, the parameters *(A, B, Π)* are modified to find the model that best describes the spatio-temporal dynamics of the desired gesture. Training is usually achieved by optimizing the maximum likelihood measure *log(P(observation|model))* over a set of training examples for the particular gesture. Such optimization involves the use of computationally expensive expectation-maximization procedures, like the Baum-Welch algorithm [5].

In the recognition stage, a gesture trajectory is tested over the set of trained HMMs in order to decide to which one it belongs. A probability of the gesture being produced by each HMM is evaluated using the Viterbi algorithm [5].

There are three main different topologies in HMMs; Fully connected (Ergodic model), where any state can be reached from any other state, Left-Right model (LR), such that any state can be iterate over itself or to next states, and Left-Right Banded (LBR) model that any state can only iterate over itself or to next state.

2.3   Dynamic Time Warping

The dynamic time warping algorithm computes an optimal matching path between two signals. The DTW algorithm calculates also the distance between the two signals computing the cumulative distance between each possible pair of points of both signals in terms of their associated feature values. The algorithm computes the local distance between the elements of two sequences $(a_1, a_2, ..., a_n)$ and $(b_1, b_2, ..., b_m)$ with lengths n and m respectively. The result is a distance matrix having n rows and m columns of terms:

$$d_{ij} = |a_i - b_j|, \quad i = 1, n \quad j = 1, m \tag{1}$$

From local distances, the minimal distance matrix between two sequences is calculated using a dynamic programming algorithm following the next optimization objective:

$$t_{ij} = d_{ij} + \min\left(t_{i-1,j-1}, t_{i-1,j}, t_{i,j-1}\right) \tag{2}$$

Being t_{ij} the minimum distance between $(a_1, a_2, ..., a_i)$ and $(b_1, b_2, ..., b_j)$.

A (n,m)-warping path is a sequence $(a_{11}, ..., a_{nm})$ satisfying the following three conditions.

- Boundary condition: The path starts in left-down corner t_{11} and ends in right-up corner t_{nm}.

- Monotonicity condition: the path will not turn back on itself, that means that both i and j indexes either stay the same or increase, but never decrease.
- Step size condition: The path advances gradually. The indices i and j increase, at most, a single unit on each step.

3   The Experiment

We have compared DTW and HMMs recognition responses for a set of different gestures. For this purpose, we have created a dataset composed by 75 samples of ten different gestures corresponding to the numbers from 0 to 9. Therefore, our dataset is composed by 750 different samples. The gestures were made by three different persons, and different distances to the camera in order to ensure that the samples had different length and morphology.

The sequences have been obtained using a Microsoft's Kinect device. From the skeleton obtained using OpenNI libraries we get the coordinates of the position of the hands (Fig 2). Once we have these coordinates in each frame, the construction of the feature vector generated by hand movement, becomes an easy task. Kinect response is very robust to indoor illumination changes; therefore the coordinates obtained are not much dependent on the illumination conditions.

Fig. 2. Gesture path for number 3 captured from Kinect

Elmezain et al. analyze in [1] the performance of the three described main features: location, orientation, and velocity of the hand centroid. They prove that orientation is the most discriminant feature among the three, velocity has a lower discrimination power than orientation, and location feature has the lowest discriminative rate. Therefore, in our work, we have used as feature the orientations of the hand path between two consecutives frames.

We assign a codeword to each orientation. Our feature vector consists of a sequence of codewords corresponding to the directions, quantified in 18 bins. Thus, we have 75 feature vectors for each gesture, where each vector is composed by a sequence of codes from 1 to 18. The length of each of these sequences will vary according to gesture path length. Due to the angular nature of these features (our codebook is cyclic), we have adapted feature comparisons to circular arithmetic in order to avoid the zero-crossing problem.

We use exactly the same features for both experiments using DTW and HMM techniques, in order to avoid the influence of the chosen features.

In [1], they also study the optimal topology and number of states of HMMs. They compare Ergodic, LR and LRB topologies with a different number of states ranging from 3 to 10, and conclude that LRB topology is always better than LR and Ergodic topologies. Therefore, we use a LRB topology in our experiments.

DTW is a technique that does not recognize gestures directly, just gives distances between feature vectors. Thus, once we have got these distances, we use a K-NN classifier to determine which class is the most likely for a captured gesture. K-NN is a simple and effective classification procedure: decision surfaces are non-linear, it has a high capacity without training, and the quality of predictions assimptotically improves with the amount of data.

First, we have determined the optimum parameters for the HMM and the DTW algorithms. This is the first experiment. For HMMs we have studied the recognition rate using different number of states, ranging from 1 to 10. For DTW the objective is to determine the optimum number of neighbours, k, for the K-NN classifier.

Next, the second experiment determines the influence of the amount of training samples on the recognition rate.

In a third experiment we have studied the maximum, minimum and average recognition rates obtained using HMM and DTW. For each gesture class in the dataset, we have partitioned its sample group into two subgroups, performing the training using the first (training) subgroup, and cross-validating the analysis on the other (test) subgroup. In order to avoid the dependence on the samples chosen as training subgroup, we have used a bootstrap technique in all the evaluation experiments, repeatedly picking random subgroups of samples chosen from the dataset. The average performance using bootstraping is reported in the results section.

Finally, we have measured the training and recognition computing times for both methods.

4   Results

First of all we have to determine the optimal parameters for tuning both algorithms. For this purpose, we have first studied the classification results using HMMs, with LRB topology, for a different amount of states. We have tried from 1 state up to 10 states to evaluate which HMM achieved the highest recognition rate.

For each different gesture class, we have used 50 random subgroups consisting of 25 test samples and 50 training samples. Therefore, we have tested 1250 samples for each class. Fig 3(a) shows the average recognition rate, and fig. 3(b) shows the individual recognition rates obtained for each different gesture class. The best average recognition rate is 96% obtained with 5-state HMMs.

DTW method has been studied observing the recognition rate according the *K-NN* classifier. Only a single parameter k is needed, and it can be easily tuned by cross-validation. Again, we have used 50 random subgroups with 25 test samples and 50 training samples for each gesture class. Fig 4 shows the results. We can see that the best results are obtained with $k=3$, reaching 98.9% average recognition rate.

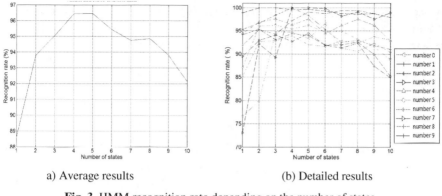

a) Average results   (b) Detailed results

Fig. 3. HMM recognition rate depending on the number of states

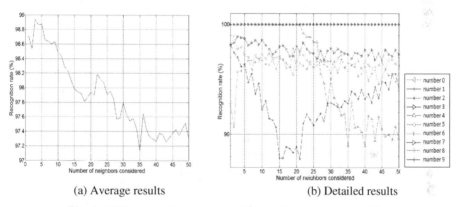

(a) Average results   (b) Detailed results

Fig. 4. DTW recognition rate depending on the number of neighbours

The next experiment is to determine the needed amount of training samples. We have tested the recognition rate of both algorithms using 25 test samples, and an increasing number of training samples from 1 to 50. Fig 5 shows the average recognition rates. We can see that recognition rates on DTW easily reach 90% with just 3 training samples, while HMMs need around 50 samples to achieve the same rates.

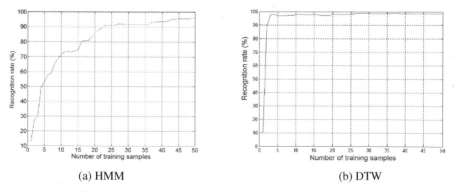

(a) HMM   (b) DTW

Fig. 5. Recognition rate according number of training samples

Once we have the optimal parameters obtained from previous experiments, we can test HMM and DTW responses to determine their recognition rates. For each gesture class, we have randomly selected 100 groups of samples from original dataset. Each group consists of 25 test samples and 50 training samples, that is, we have tested 2500 samples of each gesture for both recognition techniques. We have used 5-state HMMs, and 3-Nearest neighbour classifier to classify gestures from DTW distances, since these were the optimal values obtained in the previous experiments. We have measured the recognition rate for each group of samples and computed the maximum, minimum and average recognition rate. Table 1 shows the recognition rates.

Table 1. Recognition rates

	Min	Max	Avg.
HMM	92,8%	99,2%	96,46%
DTW	97,2%	100%	98,84%

Finally, we have measured the computing times required for training and recognition. The average time needed to train a HMM with 50 samples for each gesture class is 17,3ms. DTW has no training stage. The average time taken for a HMM to classify a gesture feature vector is 3,6 ms. Using DTW, we need 0,2 ms. to compare two gesture feature vectors. We need 3 model samples with DTW in order to achieve an equal error rate with a HMM trained with 50 samples, therefore, comparing a test sample with 3 model samples for each gesture class, we obtain an average recognition time around 6 ms. All calculations have been performed with an Intel® Core™ 3.10GHz CPU.

5   Conclusions

We have constructed a set of experiments to test which one of the related recognition methods gives better results. We are not aware of such evaluation in previous literature. The most popular method used to identify gestures is by far HMM, but surprisingly, DTW gets better scores in all our experiments. Tuning both algorithms with the obtained optimal parameters, we obtain a 98.8% average recognition rate for DTW, whereas for HMM is only 96.46%.

We have also studied the sensitivity of the recognition rate to the number of training samples, and the conclusion is that HMMs need many more training samples than DTW to obtain similar recognition rates. This is an important fact to decide which method should be chosen according to the amount of samples available in user's dataset.

Moreover, we have constructed a dataset specifically designed to test both methods. It consists of different sequences of gesture images obtained with a kinect, together with their corresponding ground truth of hand positions. The dataset is freely downloadable from http://urus.upc.edu/datasets/gestures/.

Recognition time is lower on HMM than DTW, 3,6ms in front of 6 ms., but we must bear in mind that recognition times using DTW are directly proportional to the number of comparisons, and we have just proved that a small training database is enough to obtain excellent rates using DTW. Even so, recognition time on DTW is more than acceptable for most applications.

The results obtained strongly encourage the use of DTW instead of HMMs.

Acknowledgments. This research was partially supported by Consolider Ingenio 2010, project (CSD2007-00018) and CICYT project DPI2010-17112.

References

1. Appenrodt, J., Elmezain, M., Al-Hamadi, A., Michaelis, B.: A hidden markov model-based isolated and meaningful hand gesture recognition. International Journal of Electrical, Computer, and Systems Engineering 3, 156–163 (2009)
2. ten Holt, G.A., Reinders, M.J.T., Hendriks, E.A.: Multi-Dimensional Dynamic Time Warping for Gesture Recognition. In: Thirteenth Annual Conference of the Advanced School for Computing and Imaging (2007)
3. Lee, H., Kim, J.: An HMM-based threshold model approach for gesture recognition. IEEE Trans. Pattern Analysis and Machine Intelligence 21(10), 961–973 (1999)
4. Pavlovic, V.I., Sharma, R., Huang, T.S.: Visual interpretation of hand gestures for human computer interaction. IEEE Trans. Pattern Anal. Mach. Intell. 19(7), 677–695 (1997)
5. Rabiner, L.R.: A Tutorial on Hidden Markov Models and Selected Applications in Speech Recognition. Proc. IEEE 77, 257–286 (1989)
6. Sakoe, H., Chiba, S.: Dynamic programming algorithm optimization for spoken word recognition. IEEE Trans. Acoustics, Speech, and Signal Processing 26(1), 43–49 (1978)
7. Wexelblat, A.: An approach to natural gesture in virtual environments. ACM Transactions on Computer-Human Interaction 2(3), 179–200 (1995)
8. Wilson, A.D., Bobick, A.F.: Parametric hidden Markov models for gesture recognition. IEEE Trans. Pattern Analysis and Machine Intelligence 21(9), 884–900 (1999)
9. Yang, M.-H., Ahuja, N.: Recognizing Hand Gestures Using Motion Trajectories. In: IEEE Conference on Computer Vision and Pattern Recognition, vol. 1, pp. 466–472 (1999)

Human Gait Identification Using Persistent Homology

Javier Lamar-León, Edel B. García-Reyes, and Rocío Gonzalez-Diaz

Patterns Recognition Dept., Advanced Technologies Application Center, Cuba
Applied Math Dept., School of Computer Engineering, Univ. of Seville, Spain
{jlamar,egarcia}@cenatav.co.cu, rogodi@us.es

Abstract. This paper shows an image/video application using topological invariants for human gait recognition. Using a background subtraction approach, a stack of silhouettes is extracted from a subsequence and glued through their gravity centers, forming a 3D digital image I. From this 3D representation, the border simplicial complex $\partial K(I)$ is obtained. We order the triangles of $\partial K(I)$ obtaining a sequence of subcomplexes of $\partial K(I)$. The corresponding filtration F captures relations among the parts of the human body when walking. Finally, a topological gait signature is extracted from the persistence barcode according to F. In this work we obtain 98.5% correct classification rates on CASIA-B database[1].

1 Introduction

Gait recognition is a challenging problem that gives the possibility to identify persons at a distance, without any interaction with the subjects, which is very important in real surveillance scenario [9]. Methods based on feature extraction using silhouettes or contour of silhouettes have been frequently used [3,10,6,1]. However, many silhouettes obtained during the process are incomplete due to illumination changes, occlusions, and others. These factors severely affect the recognition accuracy. Even though, a recent study [3] is aimed at suppressing the effect of silhouette incompleteness to improve performance on previous approach, we do not pre-process the silhouettes in this paper.

The stability of geometric descriptors is affected by deformation in the silhouette shape. Even for the same individual, little changes on the walking direction, illumination variation and the way the clothes fit to the human body may cause variability of the geometric features. In this paper, the changes of silhouettes induced by gait are considered as a moving nonrigid object. In pattern recognition tasks, it is important to achieve an object description which is discriminative and invariant to different geometric transformations. Topological descriptions based on the persistence of the homology classes seem to be more invariant to these kind of transformations than classical approaches for gait recognition which are affected by changes and noise in the silhouette shape, as we have experimentally shown at the end of this paper. Even without improving the silhouettes, our

---

[1] http://www.cbsr.ia.ac.cn/english/GaitDatabases.asp

L. Alvarez et al. (Eds.): CIARP 2012, LNCS 7441, pp. 244–251, 2012.

results are better to the existing methods, like [3]. To the best of the authors knowledge this approach has never been applied to gait recognition.

Topology has been previously used to match nonrigid shapes [8]. Homology is a topological invariant frequently used in practice [2]. It could be a robust representation since the shapes of connected components and holes may change under geometric transformations, but the number of components and holes could remain the same. Nevertheless, it is not enough to reach the invariance for the representation, a set of discriminative features is also needed.

In this paper, a 2D border simplicial complex $\partial K(I)$ is obtained from a stack of silhouettes extracted from a subsequence and glued through their gravity centers. We then use incremental algorithm [5] to compute persistent homology on a particle filtration of $\partial K(I)$. We propose a novel topological representation for gait recognition from a simplification of the persistence barcode obtained from the given filtration. We test this representation on the CASIA-B database.

The rest of the paper is organized as follows. In Section 2 we explain how to obtain the simplicial complex $\partial K(I)$. We present a brief reviewing of the incremental algorithm for persistent homology in Section 3. Section 4 is devoted to describe the new method in detail. Experimental results are then reported in Section 5. We conclude this paper and discuss some future work in Section 6.

2   The Simplicial Complex $\partial K(I)$

First, the moving object (person) is segmented for each frame applying background modeling and subtraction. The sequence of silhouettes is analyzed to extract one subsequence of representation, which include at least a gait cycle [9]. One subsequence of representation is selected for each sequence.

The 3D binary digital picture $I = (\mathbb{Z}^3, 26, 6, B)$ (where $B \subset \mathbb{Z}^3$ is the *foreground*, $B^c = \mathbb{Z}^3 \backslash B$ the *background*, and $(26, 6)$ is the adjacency relation for the foreground and background, respectively of a subsequence of representation is built stacking silhouettes aligned by their gravity centers (gc) (see Fig. 1.a).

The border simplicial complex $\partial K(I)$ associated with I is constructed as follows. First, we compute the 3D cubical complex $Q(I)$ (whose geometric building blocks are vertices, edges, squares and cubes). Second, we visit all the point of B, from down to up and from left to right. Let $v = (i, j, k) \in B$. If the following 7 neighbors of v $\{(i+1, j, k), (i, j+1, k), (i, j, k+1), (i+1, j+1, k), (i+1, j, k+1), (i, j+1, k+1), (i+1, j+1, k+1)\}$ are also in B then, the point v and its 7 neighbors form a unit cube which is added to $Q(I)$ together with all its faces (vertices, edges and squares). This way, we do not consider the small artifacts of I. Then, the cells of the 2D cubical complex $\partial Q(I)$ are all the squares of $Q(I)$ which are shared by a voxel of B and a voxel of B^c, together with all their faces (vertices and edges). The simplicial representation $\partial K(I)$ of I is obtained from $\partial Q(I)$ by subdividing each square of $\partial Q(I)$ in 2 triangles together with all their faces (see Fig. 3.a). Finally, coordinates of the vertices of $\partial K(I)$ are normalized to coordinates (x, y, t), where $0 \leq x, y \leq 1$ and t is the number of silhouette of the subsequence of representation.

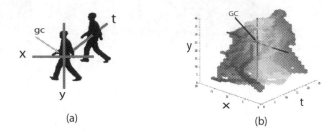

Fig. 1. (a) Silhouettes aligned by their gravity centers (*gc*). (b) The 3D binary digital picture I obtained from the silhouettes. GC is the gravity center of I.

3   Incremental Algorithm for Persistent Homology

In this section, we briefly explain incremental algorithm for computing persistent homology [5]. Let K be a simplicial complex which is a collection of simplices (vertices, edges, triangles, tetrahedra). Incremental algorithm needs an ordering $\sigma_1, \sigma_2, \ldots, \sigma_m$ of the simplices of K. The ordering is given by a *filter function* that assigns a positive integer value to each simplex in K. The value of a simplex can not be smaller than those of its faces. Simplices of K are listed in ascending order. Then, for each i, $K_i = \{\sigma_1, \sigma_2, \ldots, \sigma_i\}$ is a subcomplex of K. The sequence of simplices σ_i (the number i denotes the order of the simplex in the sequence) is called *filter* and the sequence of subcomplexes $\emptyset = K_0 \subseteq K_1 \subseteq \cdots \subseteq K_m = K$ *filtration*. When σ_i is added to K_{i-1}, the Betti numbers of K_i can be computed from σ_i and the Betti numbers of K_{i-1}. If σ_i completes a d-cycle in K_i (d is the dimension of σ_i), then $\beta_d(K_i) = \beta_d(K_{i-1}) + 1$. Otherwise, $\beta_{d-1}(K_i) = \beta_{d-1}(K_{i-1}) - 1$. Looking at a filtration as a growing simplicial complex, homology classes are born and die. The difference between their birth and death time is called *persistence*, which quantifies the significance of a topological attribute. The life interval of a homology class is a horizontal line (interval) in a plane, where birth and death time correspond to start and end points of the intervals. This representation is called *persistence barcode*, which is robust under noise, since features have long lives, while noise is short-lived. A Matlab implementation of the incremental algorithm of easy handling[2] or C++ implementation[3] are available on the Internet.

4   The New Method

Fig. 2 shows the process chain to obtain the gait signature for gait classification. From the border simplicial complex $\partial K(I)$ associated with a gait silhouette, we obtain a concrete filter (ordering of the simplices) depending on the direction of view (see Subsection 4.1). In Subsection 4.2, the persistence barcode associated

---

[2] http://comptop.stanford.edu/programs/plex-2.0.1-windows.zip
[3] http://hg.mrzv.org/Dionysus/

Fig. 2. Extracting the gait topological signature

with the previous filter is then computed. Only the intervals of the barcode that provide useful topological information is considered and a similarity measure for comparing two gait sequences is given.

4.1 A Filter for $\partial K(I)$

The topology of the border simplicial complex $\partial K(I)$ associated with a subsequence of representation is, in general, very poor. In this subsection we present a filtration on $\partial K(I)$ to get a signature using persistence barcode. This filtration captures relations among the parts of the human body when walking.

Recall that $\partial K(I)$ is a 2D simplicial complex, that is, only vertices, edges and triangles belong to it. Now, the triangles of $\partial K(I)$ are represented by their smallest vertices (considering the lexicographical order). If an horizontal (resp. vertical) direction is considered, then the triangles of $\partial K(I)$ are ordered by the first (resp. second) coordinate of the smallest vertex of each triangle. In general, given a direction of view d, a normal plane to d across the origin is computed (see Fig. 3.b). Then the triangles of $\partial K(I)$ are ordered by the distance of the smallest vertex of each triangle to the plane.

Fixing a direction of view, we construct two filters A and B. The triangles of $\partial K(I)$ (together with all their faces) are added to A (resp. B) in increasing (resp. decreasing) order. Only the first half of the simplices in the filters will be considered for the topological gait signature. Let us denote these last ordered sets by $K_{[a,GC]}$ and $K_{[b,GC]}$, respectively.

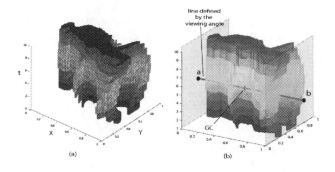

Fig. 3. (a) Border simplicial complex $\partial K(I)$. (b) A direction of view and its normal plane.

4.2 Topological Gait Signature

The gait signature is obtained based on the topological invariants extracted from persistence barcode after removing the intervals that do not provide useful information.

First, persistence barcodes are computed for $K_{[a,GC]}$ and $K_{[b,GC]}$. Second, we reduce the barcodes removing the intervals $[i,j]$ such that the number of triangles in $[i, j-1]$ is less than 2 (i.e., homology classes with low persistence are ignored).

Now, n cuts are performed homogeneously in the sets $K_{[a,GC]}$ and $K_{[b,GC]}$, being n a given positive integer, as follows: Suppose $K_{[a,GC]} = \{\sigma_0, \ldots, \sigma_m\}$. Construct the subsets $P_i^a = \{\sigma_{\lfloor \frac{(i-1)m}{n} \rfloor + 1}, \ldots, \sigma_{\lfloor \frac{im}{n} \rfloor - 1}\}$, $1 \leq i \leq n$. Fixed i, the reduced persistence barcode shows: (a) Homology classes that were born or persist when the simplex $\sigma_{\lfloor \frac{(i-1)m}{n} \rfloor}$ is added, and, persist or die when the simplex $\sigma_{\lfloor \frac{im}{n} \rfloor}$ is added. (b) Homology classes that were born in P_i^a. An analogous process is done for $K_{[b,GC]}$. A vector of dim. $2n$ is then formed counting the number of homology classes classified as explained above.

For example, consider the border simplicial complex $\partial K(I)$ given in Fig. 4 which consists in 136474 simplices. We perform $n = 5$ cuts on the set $K_{[a,GC]}$ (resp. $K_{[b,GC]}$). See the green lines in the persistence barcode representations in Fig. 4. For instance, consider the set $K_{[b,GC]}$ and fix $i = 2$. According to Fig. 4, the number of homology classes that persist or were born in σ_{13648}, and, persist or die in σ_{27296} are $H_0 = 5$ in dim. 0 and $H_1 = 1$ in dim. 1. The number of the homology classes that were born in P_2^b are $H_0 = 2$ in dim. 0 and $H_1 = 5$ in dim. 1.

The *topological signature for a gait subsequence considering a fixed direction of view* consists in four $2n$-dimensional vectors: (V_1, V_2, V_3, V_4) constructed as explained above.

In our example, we have four 10-dimensional vectors: V_1 (resp. V_2) is the first (resp. second) column of the table on the left in Fig. 4. V_3 (resp. V_4) is the first (resp. second) column of the table on the right in Fig. 4. The similarity value for the topological signatures (V_1, V_2, V_3, V_4) and (W_1, W_2, W_3, W_4) for two gait subsequences considering a fixed direction of view is done by computing, first, the angle between the two vectors V_i and W_i, for $i = 1, 2, 3, 4$ using Eq. 1:

$$S_i = \cos^{-1} \left(\frac{V_i \cdot W_i}{||V_i|| \quad ||W_i||} \right) \tag{1}$$

Then, four angles (S_1, S_2, S_3, S_4) are obtained, since for each subsequence of representation, four vectors were computed. The total similarity value for two gait subsequences considering a fixed direction of view, O_1 and O_2, is the weighted sum of the four similarity measures (angles) computed before:

$$S(O_1, O_2) = w_1 S_1 + w_2 S_2 + w_3 S_3 + w_4 S_4 \tag{2}$$

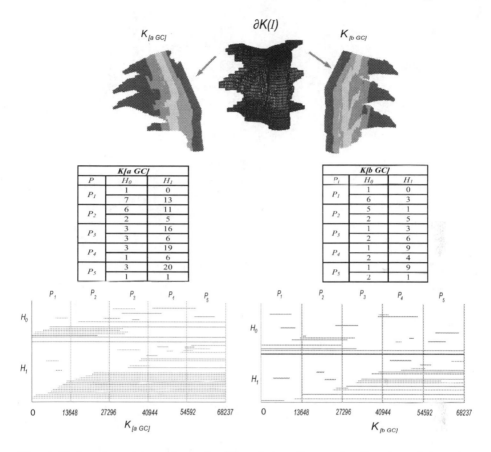

Fig. 4. Reduced persistence barcodes filtered according to the direction of view given in Fig. 3.b. Five cuts are done on the sets $K_{[a,GC]}$ and $K_{[b,GC]}$.

5   Experimental Results

In this section, we test the proposed method on 11 directions of view of the CASIA-B database, which contains 124 subjects. There are 6 normal walking sequences for each person. CASIA-B database provides image sequences with background subtraction for each person.

In this experiment the subsequence of representation is all the walking sequence, which approximately consists in two gait cycles. We have used 4 direction of view: The first one is horizontal (axe X), the second one is vertical (axe Y), the third one forms 45 degrees with the axes X and Y and is orthogonal to the axe T (see Section 2). The fourth direction of view is orthogonal to the axe T and to the third direction of view. See Fig. 5. Besides, in our experiment, the number of cuts in each direction of view is $n = 23$ (see Subsection 4.2). Finally, the value of w_i, $i = 1, 2, 3, 4$, according to Eq. 2 is 1.

(a)   (b)   (c)   (d)

Fig. 5. Directions of view used in our experiments

The experiment was carried out using 4 sequences for training, and 2 as testing set. The results are compared with the ones in [6,3,10]. Table. 1 shows the cross validation average (15 combinations) of correct classification rates at rank 1 from the candidate list. It is also considered the correct classification rate when at least one subject of the two used as test is correctly classified (ALS). The correct classification rate (CCR) provides accuracy over the whole test set. However, the at-least-one subject criterion (ALS) shows an idea of the accuracy by classes.

Table 1. Correct classification rates (CCR in %)

Method	0	18	36	54	72	90	108	126	144	162	180	**Avg**
Goffredo. M, et al [6]	–	–	72.1	79.5	85.0	86.5	82.3	81.1	–	–	–	81.1
Wavelet(FD) [3]	100	100	100	93.4	81.1	90.3	90.3	83.3	91.9	92.7	97.6	93.0
Gait energy image [10]	99.2	99.6	97.6	97.2	97.2	97.6	95.6	96.8	96.4	98.4	99.6	97.7
Our method												
rank 1	99.3	99.1	98.8	98.3	97.6	98.0	98.3	98.3	98.2	98.2	99.0	98.5
ALS 1	100	100	100	100	99.0	100	100	100	99.4	98.9	99.1	99.7

To evaluate the discriminative power of the features, we use the first 50 persons from 90 degree view of the CASIA-B data base. The evaluation was carried out

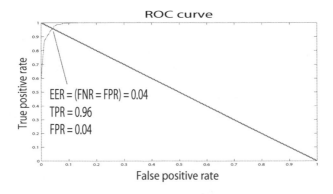

Fig. 6. Receiver operating characteristic (ROC) curve

using 4 sequences for training, and 2 as testing set. Fig. 6 shows the receiver operating characteristic (ROC) curve, which provides detailed information on the trade-off between the two types of errors, False Positive Rate (FPR) and False Negative Rate (FNR). The intersection of the ROC curve with the diagonal (see Fig. 6, blue line) is the means of the equal error rate (EER), i.e, where $FPR = FNR$. In our experiment EER= 0.04, FPR= 0.04 and therefore, True Positive Rate (TPR) is 0.96.

6   Conclusion and Future Work

In this paper we propose a new representation based on topological invariants for human gait recognition. A new approach called reduced persistence barcode is used to improve the discriminative capacity of the representation. This approach adds the possibility to use more discriminative topological invariants such as cup product [7]. Furthermore, we plan to use the bottleneck distance as similarities measures between barcodes, which guarantees stability in Persistent Homology. For this, we need a filtration associated to a continuous tame real-valued function [4]. We want to extend these experiments using other database. On the other hand, we want to evaluate the diversity in order to combine classifiers based on geometric and topological features.

References

1. Bouchrika, I., Goffredo, M., Carter, J.N., Nixon, M.S.: Covariate Analysis for View-Point Independent Gait Recognition. In: Tistarelli, M., Nixon, M.S. (eds.) ICB 2009. LNCS, vol. 5558, pp. 990–999. Springer, Heidelberg (2009)
2. Carlsson, G., Zomorodian, A., Collins, A., Guibas, L.: Persistence barcodes for shapes. In: Proc. of SGP 2004, pp. 124–135 (2004)
3. Chen, C.H., Liang, J.M., Zhao, H., Hu, H.H., Tian, J.: Frame difference energy image for gait recognition with incomplete silhouettes. PRL 30(11) (2009)
4. Cohen-Steiner, D., Edelsbrunner, H., Harer, J.: Stability of persistence diagrams. Discrete & Computational Geometry 37(1) (2007)
5. Edelsbrunner, H., Letscher, D., Zomorodian, A.: Topological persistence and simplification. Discrete & Comput. Geometry 28(4), 511–533 (2002)
6. Goffredo, M., Bouchrika, I., Carter, J.N., Nixon, M.S.: Self-calibrating view-invariant gait biometrics. IEEE Transactions on Systems, Man, and Cybernetics, Part B 40(4), 997–1008 (2010)
7. Gonzalez-Diaz, R., Umble, R., Lamar-León, J.: Cup Products on Polyhedral Approximations of 3D Digital Images. In: Aggarwal, J.K., Barneva, R.P., Brimkov, V.E., Koroutchev, K.N., Korutcheva, E.R. (eds.) IWCIA 2011. LNCS, vol. 6636, pp. 107–119. Springer, Heidelberg (2011)
8. Hilaga, M., Shinagawa, Y., Kohmura, T., Kunii, T.L.: Topology matching for fully automatic similarity estimation of 3d shapes. In: Proc. of the 28th Conf. on Computer Graphics and Interactive Techniques, SIGGRAPH 2001, pp. 203–212 (2001)
9. Nixon, M.S., Carter, J.N.: Automatic recognition by gait. Proc. of IEEE 94(11), 2013–2024 (2006)
10. Yu, S.Q., Tan, D.L., Tan, T.N.: A framework for evaluating the effect of view angle, clothing and carrying condition on gait recognition. In: ICPR, pp. IV:441–IV:444 (2006)

STOP: Space-Time Occupancy Patterns for 3D Action Recognition from Depth Map Sequences

Antonio W. Vieira[1,2], Erickson R. Nascimento[1], Gabriel L. Oliveira[1],
Zicheng Liu[3], and Mario F.M. Campos[1,*]

[1] DCC - Universidade Federal de Minas Gerais, Belo Horizonte, Brazil
{awilson,erickson,gabriel,mario}@dcc.ufmg.br
[2] CCET - Unimontes, Montes Claros, Brazil
[3] Microsoft Research, Redmond, USA
zliu@microsoft.com

Abstract. This paper presents Space-Time Occupancy Patterns (STOP), a new visual representation for 3D action recognition from sequences of depth maps. In this new representation, space and time axes are divided into multiple segments to define a 4D grid for each depth map sequence. The advantage of STOP is that it preserves spatial and temporal contextual information between space-time cells while being flexible enough to accommodate intra-action variations. Our visual representation is validated with experiments on a public 3D human action dataset. For the challenging cross-subject test, we significantly improved the recognition accuracy from the previously reported 74.7% to 84.8%. Furthermore, we present an automatic segmentation and time alignment method for online recognition of depth sequences.

Keywords: Pattern recognition, Machine Learning, Human action.

1 Introduction

Human action recognition has been an active research topic for many years. It has a wide range of applications including senior home monitoring, video surveillance, video indexing and search, and human robot interaction, to name a few. So far, most of the work has been focused on using 2D video sequences as input due to the ubiquity of conventional video cameras.

State-of-the-art algorithms for action recognition use silhouettes, Space-Time Interest Point (STIP) and skeletons. Skeletons can be obtained from motion capture systems using body joint markers or directly tracked from depth maps. However, tracking of body joints from depth maps is not a completely-solved problem. For example, the joint positions returned by XBOX Kinect skeleton tracker are quite noisy [9].

A recently published work that uses depth maps for action recognition is described by Li et al. [9]. For the depth map in any given frame, their method uses the silhouettes projected onto the coordinate planes and samples a small set

---

* This work is supported by grants from CNPq, CAPES and FAPEMIG.

L. Alvarez et al. (Eds.): CIARP 2012, LNCS 7441, pp. 252–259, 2012.

of 3D points, which are the interest points. The dissimilarity between two depth maps is computed by the Hausdorff distance between the two sets of interest points. One limitation of this approach is that the spatial context information between interest points is lost. Furthermore, due to noise and occlusions in the depth maps, the silhouettes viewed from the side and from the top may not be very reliable. This makes it very difficult to robustly sample the interest points given the geometry and motion variations between different persons. This is probably why they reported low recognition accuracy for cross-subject tests.

Our approach represents the depth sequence in a 4D space-time grid and uses a saturation scheme to enhance the roles of the sparse cells which typically consist of points on the silhouettes or moving parts of the body. These cells contain important information for action recognition. We will show that the feature vectors obtained by using this scheme perform much better than the original histogram vectors without saturation. In addition, we use an action graph based system to learn a statistical model for each action class and use a state machine to segment long depth sequences using a neutral pose classifier.

Related Work. Action recognition methods can be classified in global or local methods. The methods in the first category use global features such as silhouettes [10,8] and space-time volume information [15,4]. The methods in the second category use local features for which a set of interest points are extracted from a video and a feature descriptor is computed for each interest point. These locally extracted features are used to characterize actions for recognition [3,13]. Compared to action recognition from 2D data, the amount of work from 3D data has been quite limited due to the difficulty of 3D data acquisition.

One way to obtain 3D data is by using marker-based motion capture systems such as those made by MoCap. These systems capture the 3D positions of the markers which are attached to the joints of a performer. One dataset like this can be downloaded from [1]. Han et al. [6] developed a technique to learn a low-dimensional subspace from the high dimensional space of joint positions, and perform action recognition in the learned low-dimensional space.

The second way to obtain 3D data is to use multiple 2D video streams to reconstruct 3D information. Gu et al. [5] developed a system that generates volumetric data from multiple views as in [14]. Furthermore, they recovered the joint positions which are used as features for action and gait recognition.

The third way to obtain 3D data is to use depth sensors. One type of depth sensor is based on the time-of-flight principle [7]. Breuer et al. [2] proposed to use a 3D articulated hand model as a template to match the 3D point cloud captured by a time-of-flight camera. The other type of depth sensor uses structured light patterns. A number of systems used visible structured light patterns as in [11].

Using visible lights has the drawback that it is invasive. Recently, Microsoft released a depth camera, called Kinect, which uses invisible structured lights. Li et al. [9] developed a technique for action recognition from depth maps captured by a depth camera similar to Kinect. They captured a dataset with various people performing different actions. This dataset is used in our experiments.

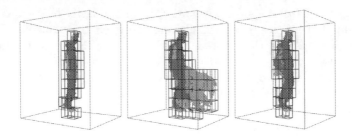

Fig. 1. Space-time cells of a depth sequence of the action *Forward Kick*. For each time segment, we place all the frames together in the same space. The red points are those in the cells with more than p points.

2   Space-Time Occupancy Patterns

To construct our visual representation, we consider a given depth sequence of someone performing an action as a set $A = \{(x_i, y_i, z_i, t_i), i = 1 \ldots N\}$ into a space-time box B where the fourth dimension is the frame index t_i which specifies time. This space-time box is then partitioned into a 4-dimensional grid with m 4D cells. We use c_i to denote the ith cell. The set of cells is called a *partition*, denoted as $C = \{c_1, ..., c_m\}$. For each cell c_i, we denote by A_i its intersection with the set of 4-dimensional points A, that is, $A_i = A \cap c_i$. The occupancy value of c_i is defined as

$$P\left(c_i\right) = \begin{cases} 1, \text{ if } & |A_i| \geq p \\ \frac{|A_i|}{p}, & \text{otherwise} \end{cases}, \tag{1}$$

where p is a predefined saturation parameter, empirically selected to maximize recognition accuracy. Our experiments discuss the saturation parameter effect by presenting the recognition accuracies for different values of p. To construct our feature vector for a given depth sequence A and partition C, we denote $f\left(A, C\right) = \left(P\left(c_1\right), P\left(c_1\right), \ldots, P\left(c_m\right)\right)^T$.

$f(A, C)$ is an m-dimensional vector, which is called the Space-Time Occupancy Pattern (STOP) of A with respect to the partition C. In our offline classification, B is partitioned in 10 segments along x, y and z, and 3 segments along time axis, so the dimension of $f(A, C)$ is 3000.

Figure 1 illustrates the space-time cells from a depth sequence of the action Forward Kick. The sequence is divided into three time segments, and each segment is comprised of about 20 frames. Only the non-empty cells are drawn. The red points are those in the cells which contain more than p points.

In general, a STOP feature vector is quite sparse, that is, the majority of its elements are zero. This motivated us to perform a dimensionality reduction using a modified version of Principal Component Analysis (PCA), called Orthogonal Class Learning (OCL), as presented in [12], to obtain, for each STOP feature f_i, a low dimensional feature e_i that we call PCA-STOP. In our experiments, the dimension of a PCA-STOP feature is 300.

2.1 Offline Recognition

For offline recognition, we consider training and testing sets with segmented actions where start and end frame of each action in a depth sequence is well segmented and we use a simple classifier based on the cosine distance.

Let H denote the number of action classes and E_h denote the set with L PCA-STOP feature vectors in the training data of action class h, $h = 1, ..., H$. Given any PCA-STOP feature vector e to be classified, the distance from e to action class h is given by

$$D_h(e) = 1 - \frac{1}{L} \sum_{\hat{e} \in E_h} \frac{<e, \hat{e}>}{\|e\|\|\hat{e}\|}. \tag{2}$$

2.2 Online Recognition

To perform online recognition, we compute a short-time STOP feature vector, from every 5 frames, and obtain the short-time PCA-STOP features. These features are used to train a neutral pose classifier using a Support Vector Machine (SVM) in order to address temporal segmentation. For the back-end classifier, we use an approach called action graph [8] which was proposed by Li et al. for video action recognition.

Compared to the offline classifier, the action graph classifier has the advantage that it can perform classification (decoding) without having to wait until an action is finished. Similar to Hidden Markov Models (HMM), action graph is flexible in handling performing speed variations and takes into account the temporal dependency. Compared to HMM, action graph has the advantage that it requires less training data and allows different actions to share the states.

Figure 2 is an overview of the online system. It maintains two states: Idle state and Action state. Please note that these two states are different from the states in the action graph. For every 5 frames, the system computes the short-time PCA-STOP descriptor, and applies the SVM neutral pose classifier. If the current state is Idle while seeing a neutral pose, it stays in the Idle state. If it sees a non-neutral pose, it transitions to Action state. While it is in Action state, the action graph performs decoding whenever a new short-time PCA-STOP is

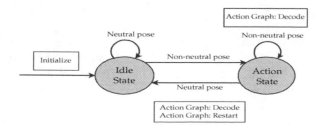

Fig. 2. Overview of the online action recognition system.

added. When the system detects a neutral pose, it transitions back to the neutral state. In the meantime, it restarts the action graph to prepare for the next action.

2.3   Action Graph

Formally, an action graph is a system composed of a set $A = \{a_1, a_2, \ldots, a_H\}$ with H trained action classes, a set with t key poses $V = \{v_1, v_2, \ldots, v_t\}$, a set $\Sigma = \{p(e|v_1), p(e|v_2), \ldots, p(e|v_t)\}$ with observation model of a feature vector e with respect to key poses $v_i \in V$ and a set $\Gamma = \{P_1, P_2, \ldots, P_H\}$ with H matrices, $t \times t$, to model the transition probability between key poses for a given action class.

Given a test depth map sequence, we obtain a sequence of short-time PCA-STOP features $T = \{e_1, e_2, \ldots, e_r\}$, and compute the probability of occurrence of T with respect to each trained action class $h \in A$. The resulting class $\bar{h}$ is given by $\bar{h} = arg \max_h \{p(T|h)\}$.

The decoding process to compute $\bar{h}$ uses a dynamic programing scheme to save computational time. More details can be found in [8].

To learn the key poses, we cluster all training feature vectors from all action types using a K-means. This is different from [9] because we have a single feature vector per frame while [9] uses a set of unorganized points as their visual description. The resulting key poses V are the nodes (also called states) of the action graph. For each cluster $v_j \in V$, we fit a Gaussian distribution and estimate the observation likelihood model $p(e|v_j) \in \Sigma$.

The transition matrix $P_h \in \Gamma$ is computed as $p(j|i) = \frac{N_{(i \to j)}}{N_i}$, where $N_{(i \to j)}$ is the number of transitions from key pose i to j in the training data that belongs to action h, and N_i is the number of times state i is observed in the training data that belongs to action h.

3   Experiments

In this section we present our experimental results. Firstly, our offline classification method is compared with another offline method using a public dataset. Then, experiments with our online classification method shows that we are able to classify unsegmented depth sequences while addressing time alignment.

3.1   Offline Experiments

We used the public MSR Action3D Dataset [9] to validate our offline classification technique. It was recorded by using a depth camera similar to the Kinect device that uses infra-red light, capturing depth maps of 640×480 at about 15 frames per second. There are 20 action types, and 10 subjects. Each subject performs each action 2-3 times. In [9] the 20 action types are divided into three subsets AS1, AS2 and AS3, each having 8 action types. In order to present a comparison, we present our recognition results on the three subsets. As in [9], all depth maps are firstly down-sampled by factor of 2.

For each subset of action types, three tests were performed. In Test I, $\frac{1}{3}$ of the instances were used in the training phase while the rest was used in actual testing. In Test II, $\frac{2}{3}$ of the instances were used for training while the rest was used for testing. Test III is a cross-subject test where instances performed by half of the subjects were used for training and the rest was used as testing. In other words, the subjects in the test data are not seen in the training data. The recognition results obtained by our method and by Li et al. [9] on the three action subjects are shown in Table 1.

Table 1. Comparison of offline recognition accuracies (%)

Set	Test I			Test II			Test III		
	Li et al.	Skt	Our	Li et al.	Skt	Our	Li et al.	Skt	Our
AS1	89.50	68.00	98.23	93.30	72.97	99.12	72.90	40.28	84.70
AS2	89.00	73.86	94.82	92.90	70.67	96.95	71.90	50.00	81.30
AS3	96.30	78.67	97.35	96.30	83.78	98.67	79.20	73.91	88.40
Avg	91.36	73.51	96.80	94.20	75.81	98.25	74.70	54.73	84.80

In order to show that our PCA-STOP features are more discriminative for action recognition than skeletons obtained from depth maps, we used the recorded skeletons of the same dataset for classification. There are different ways to encode the skeleton joint positions as a feature descriptor for classification. We found that the best recognition accuracy is obtained by using Fast Fourier Transform (FFT) coefficients on the curves of the joint positions over time. In Table 1, column Skt shows the classification results using the skeleton feature. We can readily see that our method outperforms the other two methods in all the test cases. In the more challenging cross-subject test (Test III), we have improved the average recognition accuracy from 74.70% to 84.80%.

To demonstrate the effect of the saturation parameter, Figure 3 shows the cross-subject recognition rates of our PCA-STOP for different saturation parameter values. Notice that the recognition accuracy is quite stable for small values of saturation and that performance decreases as the saturation parameter gets too large.

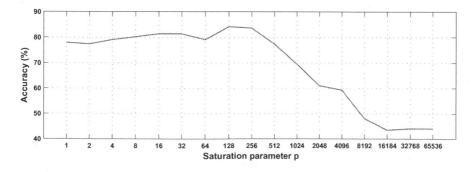

Fig. 3. Recognition accuracies for different values of saturation parameter p

3.2 Online Experiments

For our online experiments, we used long unsegmented depth sequence where several actions are performed over time. Our neutral pose and action graph is used for classification with temporal segmentation and alignment. We used unsegmented sequences with the same set of actions as used in our offline experiments. For this experiment, we used 511 depth sequences from 9 subjects as training set and 56 depth sequences from a different subject as test set. The training set is used to learn the action graph. The sequences in the test set are concatenated together to form a long sequence for testing. We do this 10 times, each with a different partition where the subject in the test set are not seen in the training set. The overall accuracy for this ten-fold cross classification was 98.41% in a test using all 20 action types, which emphasizes that, by addressing time alignment, online classification improves cross-subject recognition.

In order to illustrate segmentation and classification we show, in Figure 4, an example of classification using a long unsegmented sequence. The figure presents a matrix, where columns stands for frame number and rows stands for action classes. The actual action segmentation of each sequence along time is shown by horizontal black bars and, in gray bars, the predicted action segmentation and classification based on our online approach. Notice that a neutral pose is classified before and after the performance of each action. This is coherent with the dataset where each subject rested in a neutral pose between the performance of two different actions.

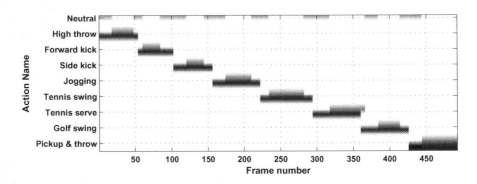

Fig. 4. Example of online action segmentation and recognition in a long depth sequence. Black horizontal bars show actual action segmentation along time and gray bars show the predicted action segmentation and classification.

4 Conclusions

We presented Space-Time Occupancy Patters (STOP), a novel feature descriptor for classifying human action from depth sequences. It leverages the spatial and temporal contextual information while allowing for intra-action variations. It is particularly suited for recognizing short and non-repetitive actions. The accuracy of our STOP features for action classification has shown to be superior in a comparison with previous work using public dataset. Furthermore, we developed an online action recognition system based on short-time STOP features, which handles automatic segmentation and temporal alignment.

References

1. Carnegie mellon university motion capture database, http://mocap.cs.cmu.edu
2. Breuer, P., Eckes, C., Müller, S.: Hand Gesture Recognition with a Novel IR Time-of-Flight Range Camera–A Pilot Study. In: Gagalowicz, A., Philips, W. (eds.) MIRAGE 2007. LNCS, vol. 4418, pp. 247–260. Springer, Heidelberg (2007)
3. Dollar, P., Rabaud, V., Cottrell, G., Belongie, S.: Behavior recognition via sparse spatio-temporal features. In: IEEE Int. Workshop on Visual Surveillance and Performance Evaluation of Tracking and Surveillance, San Diego, CA (2005)
4. Gorelick, L., Blank, M., Shechtman, E., Irani, M., Basri, R.: Actions as space-time shapes. IEEE Trans. PAMI 29(12) (2007)
5. Gu, J., Ding, X., Wang, S., Wu, Y.: Action and gait recognition from recovered 3D human joints. IEEE Trans. on Systems, Man, and Cybernetics-Part B: Cybernetics 40(4) (2010)
6. Han, L., Wu, X., Liang, W., Hou, G., Jia, Y.: Discriminative human action recognition in the learned hierarchical manifold space. Image Vision Comput. 28, 836–849 (2010)
7. Iddan, G.J., Yahav, G.: 3D imaging in the studio. In: Proc. SPIE 4298 (2001)
8. Li, W., Zhang, Z., Liu, Z.: Expandable data-driven graphical modeling of human actions based on salient postures. IEEE Transactions on Circuits and Systems for Video Technology 18(11) (2008)
9. Li, W., Zhang, Z., Liu, Z.: Action recognition based on a bag of 3D points. In: CVPR Workshop for Human Communicative Behavior Analysis, San Francisco, CA (June 2010)
10. Lv, F., Nevatia, R.: Single view human action recognition using key pose matching and Viterbi path searching. In: Proc. CVPR (2007)
11. Malassiotis, S., Tsalakanidou, F., Mavridis, N., Giagourta, V., Grammalidis, N., Strintzis, M.G.: A face and gesture recognition system based on an active stereo sensor. In: Proc. ICPR, Thessaloniki, Greece, vol. 3 (October 2001)
12. Oliveira, G.L., Nascimento, E.R., Vieira, A.W., Campos, M.F.M.: Sparse spatial coding: A novel approach for efficient and accurate object recognition. In: Proc. ICRA, St. Paul, MN (May 2012)
13. Sun, J., Wu, X., Yan, S., Cheong, L., Chua, T., Li, J.: Hierarchical spatio-temporal context modeling for action recognition. In: Proc. CVPR, Miami, FL (June 2009)
14. Weinland, D., Ronfard, R., Boyer, E.: Free viewpoint action recognition using motion history volumes 104(2) (2006)
15. Yilmaz, A., Shah, M.: Actions sketch: a novel action representation. In: Proc. CVPR, vol. 1 (2005)

Human Activity Recognition by Class Label LLE

Juliana Valencia-Aguirre[1], Andrés M. Álvarez-Meza[1], Genaro Daza-Santacoloma[1], Carlos Acosta-Medina[1,2], and Germán Castellanos-Domínguez[1]

[1] Signal Processing and Recognition Group, Universidad Nacional de Colombia, Manizales, Colombia
[2] Scientific Computing and Mathematical Modeling Group, Universidad Nacional de Colombia, Manizales, Colombia
{jvalenciaag,amalvarezme,gdazas,cdacostam,cgcastellanosd}@unal.edu.co

Abstract. Human motion analysis has emerged as an important area of research for different fields and applications. However, analyzing image and video sequences to perform tasks such as action recognition, becomes a challenge due to the high dimensionality of this type of data, not mentioning the restrictions in the recording conditions (lighting, angle, distances, etc). In that sense, we propose a framework for human action recognition, which involves a preprocessing stage that decreases the influence of the record conditions in the analysis. Further, our proposal is based on a new supervised feature extraction technique that includes class label information in the mapping process, to enhance both the underlying data structure unfolding and the margin of separability among classes. Proposed methodology is tested on a benchmark dataset. Attained results show how our approach obtains a suitable performance using straightforward classifiers.

Keywords: Motion recognition, video processing, dimensionality reduction.

1 Introduction

Human action recognition is a growing area of study, which arises a lot of associated applications of interest, e.g. detection of suspicious behavior for security systems, development of interactive game environments, performance evaluation of sport players, motion assessment for patients in rehabilitation programs, among others. As known, the main purpose of human action recognition is to assign a specific label to a motion [1]. Previous approaches found in the state-of-the-art report adequate performance in the recognition of different human actions, traditionally, running and walking. However, some of these works analyze data recorded under constrained conditions such as: distance from the camera to the subject must be fixed, lightning and angle can not have several changes, the background must present homogeneity along the video, among others.

Generally, there are two tightly related steps in building a motion recognition system: extracting motion features and training a classifier using these features.

L. Alvarez et al. (Eds.): CIARP 2012, LNCS 7441, pp. 260–267, 2012.

The most relevant works about motion recognition focuses on motion feature selection, including extracting features from 2-D tracking data [2], 3-D tracking information [3], or extracting motion information directly from images [1,4,5]. Some works use Support Vector Machines (SVM) to perform human motion recognition [1,3]. Moreover, in [6], the motion representation strategy is based on local spatial and temporal features, and the learning procedure is achieved by employing the k-means clustering algorithm. In [3], a 3-D characterization of the spatial and temporal correspondences for each frame are used to describe the motion behavior, next, a SVM classifies the activities. The major disadvantage of these works is to find suitable values for the SVM parameters.

In this work, we propose a framework for human action recognition, which involves a preprocessing stage that detects frames with no motion in the video and decreases the influence of the record conditions and noise in the analysis. Also, an Infinite Impulse Responde (IIR) filter is used in order to extract motion information from the video frames. Further, our proposal is based on a new supervised nonlinear dimensionality reduction technique that includes class label information in the mapping process, to enhance both the underlying data structure and the classification performance. In this regard, our scheme searches a low-dimensional space, in which a straightforward classifier can be used, for obtaining a suitable human action recognition performance. This work is organized as follows. Section 2 introduces the proposed methodology for human action recognition. In Section 3, the experimental results are described and discussed. Finally, in Section 4, we conclude about the attained results.

2 Motion Analysis

In order to analyze videos taken under real conditions, we proposed a methodology (see Figure 1) that is less sensitive to restrictions such as lighting control, specific distance between the subject and the camera, cloth control, angle, etc. The main purpose is to consider as few constrains as possible in the input data.

Fig. 1. Proposed methodology

2.1 Motion Detection

It is possible to find videos that do not present activity or motion 100% of the time. Thence, perform motion detection becomes an essential step. Let $\mathbf{X}_{n_v \times p}$ the input data, n_v is the number of analyzed videos and p is the input dimension. Then $\mathbf{X} = \begin{bmatrix} \mathbf{V}_1 \ \mathbf{V}_2 \cdots \ \mathbf{V}_{n_v} \end{bmatrix}^\top$, where $\mathbf{V}_r \in \mathbb{R}^{n_{fr} \times p}$, n_{fr} is the number of frames of r-th video, $r \in \{1, 2, \ldots, n_v\}$, $p = h * w$, being h the number of rows pixels and w the number of column pixels for each frame in gray scale.

The first step in this stage is to apply a median filter to each frame in $\mathbf{X}$. Given a video $\widehat{\mathbf{V}}_r = \begin{bmatrix} \mathbf{v}_1 \ \mathbf{v}_2 \cdots \ \mathbf{v}_{n_{fr}} \end{bmatrix}^\top$, where $\mathbf{v}_i \in \mathbb{R}^{1 \times p}$ are the vectorized version of the filter frames, we propose to detect motion in each $\widehat{\mathbf{V}}_r$ by $\mathbf{d}_i = |\mathbf{v}_i - \mathbf{v}_{i-1}|$, being $\mathbf{d}_i$ the derivative of $\mathbf{v}_i$, and $i = 1, 2, \ldots, n_{fr}$. This operation allows to detect significant changes between video frames, in order to eliminate parts of the video with minimum variability. As a result we obtain the derivative matrix $\mathbf{De} = \begin{bmatrix} \mathbf{d}_1 \ \mathbf{d}_2 \cdots \ \mathbf{d}_{n_{fr}-1} \end{bmatrix}^\top$.

Now, a series of morphological operations are applied to $\mathbf{De}$, to facilitate the detection of constant frames, and to avoid consider noise as motion in the video: Calculate the extended-maxima transform, perform a morphological closing on the images, and finally fill holes in the binary images. Afterward this procedure, the constant frames are identifying by performing a sum of the derivative value pixel by pixel. When the number of pixels with intensity 0 in a frame are more than an specific value (e.g. 90%) then is consider with no motion. Once we know if there is motion and where is located, then we proceed to extract the frames with no movement. As a result we obtained the matrix $\mathbf{Z}_r = \begin{bmatrix} \mathbf{T}_1 \ \mathbf{T}_2 \cdots \ \mathbf{T}_{n_s} \end{bmatrix}^\top$, where $\mathbf{T}_j \in \mathbb{R}^{n_{fT} \times p}$, being n_{fT} the amount of frames that have motion in constant sequence, $n_{fT} \in [n_{fT_{\min}}, n_{fT_{\max}}]$, $j \in \{1, 2, \ldots, n_s\}$, and n_s is the number of sub-sequences with motion detected in $\mathbf{V}_r$.

2.2   Recursive Filtering - IIR Filter

The IIR filter response acts like a measure that allows to identify recent motion. It works by adding a fraction of a previous frame to the current frame, then, the added fraction represents the degree of filtering. As the degree of filtering is increased, moving objects are also blurred in time. This can make moving objects appear to have a *ghost* or *comet-tail*, which we used as motion information. At each frame, motion information is represented by a feature image [4].

Considering a subsequence $\mathbf{T}_j = \begin{bmatrix} \mathbf{t}_1 \ \mathbf{t}_2 \cdots \ \mathbf{t}_{n_{fT}} \end{bmatrix}^\top$ found in a video $\mathbf{V}_r$, a weighted average at time a, is computed as $\boldsymbol{\rho}_a = \tau \mathbf{t}_{a-1} + (1 - \tau) \boldsymbol{\rho}_{a-1}$, where $\boldsymbol{\rho}_a \in \mathbb{R}^{1 \times p}$, $\mathbf{t}_a \in \mathbb{R}^{1 \times p}$ is the image at time a, $a = 1, 2, \ldots, n_{fT}$, and τ is a scalar between 0 and 1. The feature image $\mathbf{f}_a$ is calculated by $\mathbf{f}_a = |\boldsymbol{\rho}_a - \mathbf{t}_a|$.

Then, for $\mathbf{T}_j$, the filter output is $\mathbf{F}_j = \begin{bmatrix} \mathbf{f}_1 \ \mathbf{f}_2 \cdots \ \mathbf{f}_{n_{fT}} \end{bmatrix}^\top$, with $\mathbf{F}_j \in \mathbb{R}^{n_{fT} \times p}$. If $\tau = 1$ then $\mathbf{t}_a$ will be equal to the previous frame, if $\tau = 0$ then $\mathbf{t}_a$ will remain constant, and thence $\mathbf{F}_j$ will be equal to the foreground. The idea is that the feature image captures the temporal changes in the video sequence, and therefore, moving objects result in blurring.

Finally, to remove possible noise present after the IIR filter, a median filter is applied to $\mathbf{F}_j$, and a morphological filter is employed to facilitate the next stage. This morphological operation sets a pixel to 1 if five or more pixels in its 3-by-3 neighborhood are 1s; otherwise, it sets the pixel to 0 (considering a binary image). The outcome of the morphological filter is noted as $\mathbf{Fm}_j = \begin{bmatrix} \mathbf{fm}_1 \ \mathbf{fm}_2 \cdots \ \mathbf{fm}_{n_{fT}} \end{bmatrix}^\top$. It is important to emphasize that the main advantage of the recursive filtering, is that is suitable for real-time applications.

2.3 Region of Interest Detection and Resize

To identify what kind of activity is generating the motion, a region of interest is found (i.e. for hand waving, the region of interest should be located around the hands and arms, which are the ones that produce changes between frames). Considering $\mathbf{Fm}_j$, the idea is to find the height and width of the subjects by calculating their position in each image, thence, we look for changes in pixel intensity to determine the first pixel in both rows and columns, in which begin the silhouette of the subject.

Regarding to the resize stage, the goal is to set a standard resolution for the video frames. Thus, the images were resized to an specific number of rows and columns, $h_r \times w_r$. This process is performed using a bicubic interpolation and antialiasing. Then, output pixel value is a weighted average of pixels in the nearest 4-by-4 neighborhood, and an antialiasing is performed when shrinking the images. The resize operation is executed considering the region of interest found based on $\mathbf{Fm}_j$. Thence, the obtained output is $\tilde{\mathbf{F}}_j \in \mathbb{R}^{n_{fT} \times p_r}$, being $p_r = h_r w_r$, h_r is the resized height and w_r is the resized width.

2.4 Class Label Locally Linear Embedding – CLLE

In [7] an extension of the LLE method is presented, which we called Class Label Locally Linear Embedding - CLLE. This technique employs class labels as extra information to guide the dimensionality reduction procedure, to preserve the local geometry of the data while providing a discriminative strategy during the mapping. Given the input data matrix $\mathbf{A} \in \mathbb{R}^{N \times p_r}$, containing the N total number of preprocessed frames with constant motion from a set of videos $\mathbf{X}$ (see section 2.1), the weight matrix $\mathbf{W} \in \mathbb{R}^{N \times N}$ is computed by minimizing $\varepsilon(\mathbf{W}) = \sum_{i=1}^{N} \| \mathbf{a}_i - \sum_{j=1}^{N} w_{ij} \mathbf{a}_j \|^2$, subject to $w_{ij} = 0$ if $\mathbf{a}_j$ is not k-neighbor of $\mathbf{a}_i$, and $\sum_{j=1}^{N} w_{ij} = 1$. Then, C-LLE computes a low-dimensional space $\mathbf{Y} \in \mathbb{R}^{N \times m}$ ($m \leq p_r$), by minimizing

$$\min_{\mathbf{Y}} \Psi(\mathbf{Y}, \beta) = \min_{\mathbf{Y}} \left\{ \sum_{i=1}^{N} \left\| \mathbf{y}_i - \sum_{j=1}^{N} w_{ij} \mathbf{y}_j \right\|^2 - \beta \sum_{i=1}^{N} \left\| \mathbf{y}_i - \sum_{j=1}^{N} \gamma_{ij} \mathbf{y}_j \right\|^2 \right\}, \quad (1)$$

with $\beta \in \Re^{+}$, and subject to $\sum_{i=1}^{N} \mathbf{y}_i = \mathbf{0}$ and $\sum_{i=1}^{N} \mathbf{y}_i \mathbf{y}_i^{\top} / N = \mathbf{I}_{m \times m}$. Furthermore, $\gamma_{ij} = 0$ if $i = j$, $\gamma_{ij} = \frac{1}{N-1}$, if $i = j$ if $\mathcal{P}(\mathbf{y}_i) \neq \mathcal{P}(\mathbf{y}_j)$, and $\gamma_{ij} = -\frac{1}{N-1}$ if $\mathcal{P}(\mathbf{y}_i) = \mathcal{P}(\mathbf{y}_j)$, being $\mathcal{P}(\cdot)$ a function that determines the class label of the objects, and β is a tradeoff between the preservation of the data local geometry and the representation induced by the class labels. For solving the minimization problem, it is possible to rewrite (1) as

$$\min_{\mathbf{Y}} \Psi(\mathbf{Y}, \beta) = \min_{\mathbf{Y}} \left\{ \mathrm{tr} \left(\mathbf{Y}^{\top} \left(\mathbf{M} - \beta \tilde{\mathbf{M}} \right) \mathbf{Y} \right) \right\} \quad \text{s.t.} \quad \begin{cases} \mathbf{1}_{1 \times N} \mathbf{Y} = \mathbf{0}_{1 \times N} \\ \frac{1}{N} \mathbf{Y}^{\top} \mathbf{Y} = \mathbf{I}_{m \times m} \end{cases},$$
$$(2)$$

where $\mathbf{M} = \left(\mathbf{I}_{N \times N} - \mathbf{W}^{\top}\right)\left(\mathbf{I}_{N \times N} - \mathbf{W}\right)$, and $\tilde{\mathbf{M}} = \left(\mathbf{I}_{N \times N} - \Gamma^{\top}\right)\left(\mathbf{I}_{N \times N} - \Gamma\right)$, being $\Gamma \in \Re^{N \times N}$ a matrix whose elements γ_{ij} are computed as mentioned above. It is possible to calculate the m eigenvectors of $\mathbf{M} - \beta\tilde{\mathbf{M}}$ associated to its m smallest eigenvalues, discarding the eigenvector related to some eigenvalue equal to zero. Obtained eigenvectors constitute the embedding space $\mathbf{Y}$. Note that the β parameter in (1) is a tradeoff between the reconstruction error and the margin between objects belonging to different classes. If $\beta = 0$, we have the original mapping of LLE, and as β increases the separation between classes is larger. For a given β it is possible to find the output $\mathbf{Y}_{\beta}$ that minimizes the cost function (1). Next, the reconstruction error e_R and the margin μ can be computed as $e_R(\beta) = \text{tr}\left(\mathbf{Y}_{\beta}^{\top}\mathbf{M}\mathbf{Y}_{\beta}\right)$, and $\mu(\beta) = \text{tr}\left(\mathbf{Y}_{\beta}^{\top}\tilde{\mathbf{M}}\mathbf{Y}_{\beta}\right)$. Looking forward the minimization of $e_R(\beta)$ and the maximization of $\mu(\beta)$, the parametric plot $e_R(\beta)$ vs $\mu(\beta)$ can be used to study the behavior of these quantities [7].

3   Experimental Results

In order to validate the proposed methodology, we provide comparison with commonly known techniques for different processing conditions. Firstly, the pre-processing stage is carried out, but without performing dimensionality reduction. Then, based on the scheme described in Figure 1, besides proposed CLLE, we use three dimensionality reduction techniques: the traditional linear Principal Components Analysis (PCA) and as nonlinear algorithms, the Locally Linear Embedding (LLE) and Laplacian Eigenmaps (LEM) are employed [8,9]. Testing of considered methods is carried out on a real world database, namely, the Action dataset, which is a benchmark in the state-of-the-art [6]. The database is conformed by six kinds of human actions (walking, jogging, running, boxing, handwaving and handclapping) performed by 25 subjects. All sequences were taken with a static camera with 25 fps. The sequences having four-seconds-length in average were down-sampled to 120×160 pixels. For testing, the videos with scale variation (zoom) and/or noticeable shadows were discarded. Besides, we randomly choose 30 videos ($n_v = 30$); 5 videos for each one of the six considered activities. Figure 2 shows some Action dataset samples.

The generalization abilities for the provided experimental conditions are tested by using a 10-folds-cross-validation scheme. In regard to the early stages of the proposed methodology, the parameters are set as follows: the median filter applied in the motion detection stage is performed using a 3-by-3 neighborhood. A morphological filter $disc$ type is used. Then for the motion detection, a minimum window of 10 and maximum 20 frames is established to extract those parts of the video with no activity. The frames are removed if the 90% (or more) of the image pixels are zero content, otherwise, a frame is considered as motion. The parameter τ in the IIR filter is set to 0.5. The final frame size is set to 25×30. As a result, 141 videos (sub-video sequences found in the motion detection stage) are employed for training and testing. We obtained an space $\tilde{\mathbf{F}}$ with $n_{fT} = 141$, $p = 750$ and $C = 6$, considering the resizing procedure. The specific amount of videos for each activity is: Walking - 25, Jogging - 21, Running - 20, Boxing - 25, Hanwaving - 25, Handclapping - 25.

The number of nearest neighbors for LLE, LEM and CLLE is chosen using a proposed approach in [10], which computes an specific number of neighbors for each input object. The dimension of the embedding space is fixed looking for a 95% of expected local variability, leading in an output dimension of $m = 4$. Three classifiers are tested: linear discriminant classifier (LDC), quadratic discriminant classifier (QDC), and k-nearest neighbors classifier (KNNC). The number of neighbors for this classifier is optimized with respect to the leave-one-out error of the training set. Finally, the procedure to analyze new samples after training the system is shown in Figure 3.

Fig. 2. Action dataset samples

Fig. 3. Scheme used for new samples

Table 1. Classification Accuracy and Confidence Interval

	Classification Accuracy ± Standard Deviation				
	Without DR	PCA	LLE	LEM	CLLE
LDC	48.7473 ± 11.3255	50.3883 ± 7.7237	52.5238 ± 13.7744	33.7573 ± 16.0388	85.8832 ± 5.3789
	CI = [40.64, 56.84]	CI = [44.86, 55.91]	CI = [42.67, 62.37]	CI = [22.28, 45.22]	CI = [82.03, 89.730]
QDC	18.4725 ± 3.7750	63.5788 ± 10.4543	60.1575 ± 14.3836	50.9240 ± 10.5782	90.1360 ± 5.4782
	CI = [15.77, 21.17]	CI = [56.10, 71.05]	CI = [49.86, 70.44]	CI = [43.35, 58.49]	CI = [86.21, 94.05]
KNN	90.8022 ± 9.5041	87.4615 ± 8.2779	75.7106 ± 7.4377	73.4840 ± 9.9066	91.8246 ± 8.0512
	CI = [84.00, 97.60]	CI = [81.53, 93.38]	CI = [70.45, 80.96]	CI = [66.39, 80.57]	CI = [86.06, 97.58]

Regarding to the PCA results (see Table 1, Figure 4(b)), this simplest re- duction dimension approach exhibits a poor performance for simple classifiers (LDC, QDC), showing that linear transformations are not suitable to unfold the underlying data structure. Indeed, PCA decreases the classification accuracy for the KNN classifier in comparison to the case when dimensionality reduction is not carried out. According to Figure 4(b), the greatest difficulties become when identifying Jogging, Running, Handwaving and Handclapping.

In case of the nonlinear methods (LLE and LEM), the achieve classification accuracy decreases. In particular, these techniques have drawbacks to identify properly between Walking, Jogging and Running, and between Handwaving and

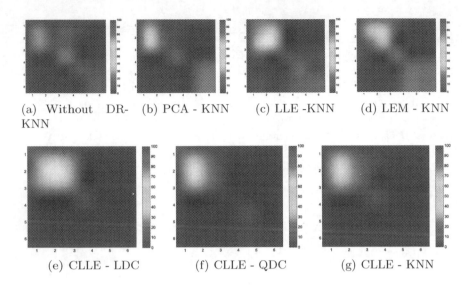

(a) Without DR-KNN   (b) PCA - KNN   (c) LLE -KNN   (d) LEM - KNN

(e) CLLE - LDC   (f) CLLE - QDC   (g) CLLE - KNN

Fig. 4. Confusion matrices best classification results. Order of the actions: Walk, Jog, Run, Box, H. Waving, H. Clapping

Handclapping (see Figure 4(c) and 4(d)). LLE and LEM have some limitations when data is coming from different manifolds. In contrast, discussed CLLE approach preserves the local geometry of the data, and provides a discriminative strategy during the embedding procedure. Thus, CLLE improves the classification results in comparison to conventional LLE or other techniques like LEM, as can be corroborated in Table 1 and Figures 4(e), 4(f) and 4(g). According to the attained results, CLLE allows to use a classifier with very simple decision boundary, and therefore, leading to high classification performance. Improved performance may be explained, since the technique can unfold the non-linear input data structures. Hence, obtained mappings produce simpler low dimensional manifolds, which preserves the high-dimensional data topology while the class label information is considered, ensuring the class separability. In this sense, one may infer that CLLE technique does not require complex classifiers.

It must be quoted that due to the characteristics of the KNN classifier, it exhibits a good performance even without the dimensionality reduction procedure, and for each technique tested, this classifier always obtained the best results. So, the main contribution of the proposed methodology is that CLLE improves the performance of the classification stage even for simpler classifiers such as LDC, also decreasing the standard deviation of the average accuracy.

4   Conclusion

In this paper, a new human action recognition methodology is proposed. This methodology involves a preprocessing stage that is robust to noise and perturbations, and that allows to extract frames with no motion in the input data.

Moreover, the motion information is extracted directly from the frames by an IIR filter. On the other hand, we used a supervised form of LLE, called CLLE, proposed in [7], for the dimensionality reduction process. However, we tested with other unsupervised feature extraction techniques (PCA, LEM and LLE), and we also consider no dimensionality reduction. According to the results, CLLE allows to use a classifier with very simple decision boundary and obtain high classification performance. The proposed methodology is robust against noise conditions and/or unexpected changes of the given environment, and it improves the performance of the classification stage even for simpler classifiers such as LDC.

Acknowledgments. Research carried out under grants provided by a PhD. scholarship and the project 20201006570 funded by Universidad Nacional de Colombia, and project 20201006594 funded by Universidad Nacional de Colombia and Universidad de Caldas.

References

1. Cao, D., Masoud, O.T., Boley, D., Papanikolopoulos, N.: Human motion recognition using support vector machines. Comput. Vis. Image Underst. 113, 1064–1075 (2009)
2. Efros, A., Berg, A., Mori, G., Malik, J.: Recognizing action at a distance. In: Proceedings of Ninth IEEE International Conference on Computer Vision, vol. 2, pp. 726–733 (2003)
3. Mori, T., Shimosaka, M., Sato, T.: Svm-based human action recognition and its remarkable motion features discovery algorithm. In: ISER 2004. Springer Tracts in Advanced Robotics, vol. 21, pp 15–25. Springer (2004)
4. Masoud, O., Papanikolopoulos, N.: A method for human action recognition. Image and Vision Computing 21, 729–743 (2003)
5. Meng, H., Pears, N., Freeman, M., Bailey, C.: Motion history histograms for human action recognition. Embedded Computer Vision 139, 139–162 (2009)
6. Schuldt, C., Laptev, I., Caputo, B.: Recognizing human actions: A local svm approach. In: ICPR, pp. 32–36 (2004)
7. Daza-Santacoloma, G., Castellanos-Dominguez, G., Principe, J.C.: Locally linear embedding based on correntropy measure for visualization and classification. Neurocomputing 80(0), 19–30 (2012)
8. Saul, L.K., Roweis, S.T.: Think globally, fit locally: Unsupervised learning of low dimensional manifolds. Machine Learning Research 4, 119–155 (2003)
9. Belkin, M., Niyogi, P.: Laplacian eigenmaps for dimensionality reduction and data representation. Neural Computation 15(6), 1373–1396 (2003)
10. Álvarez Meza, A., Valencia-Aguirre, J., Daza-Santacoloma, G., Castellanos-Domínguez, G.: Global and local choice of the number of nearest neighbors in locally linear embedding. Patter Recognition Letters 32(16), 2171–2177 (2011)

Fast Non-parametric Action Recognition

Sebastián Ubalde and Norberto Adrián Goussies

Departamento de Computación, Facultad de Ciencias Exactas y Naturales,
Universidad de Buenos Aires, Buenos Aires, Argentina
{seubalde,ngoussie}@dc.uba.ar

Abstract. In this work we propose a method for action recognition which needs no intensive learning stage, and achieves state-of-the-art classification performance. Our work is based on a method presented in the context of image classification. Unlike that method, our approach is well-suited for working with large real-world problems, thanks to an efficient organization of the training data. We show results on the KTH and IXMAS datasets. On the challenging IXMAS dataset, the average running time is reduced by 50% when using our method.

Keywords: action recognition, nearest neighbor, image-to-class distance.

1 Introduction

The problem of automatically identifying an action performed in a video is receiving a great deal of attention in the computer vision community. The fields of application for action recognition are varied, and include video summarization, video indexing, video surveillance, human-computer interaction, etc. The problem is challenging because, on one hand, the appearance of an action can vary considerable in different videos and, on the other hand, different actions can look very similar to each other.

Several approaches to the problem have been proposed. An entire body of work [1–4] is based on a global representation of the video. Once the actor is localized in the video, movement information is encoded as a whole.

More related to our work are those approaches based on local descriptors. The basic idea is to characterize a video using descriptors of spatio-temporal patches extracted from certain interest points. A wide range of methods [5–9] have been used both for interest point detection and for descriptor computation. Many works use descriptor quantization in order to work with low-dimensional data. In [5, 6, 10–12], descriptors are clustered and cluster centers are selected as codewords. Videos are therefore represented as histograms of codewords. This approach is commonly known as *bag-of-features*. A classifier is trained using the set of histograms from the training videos. Nearest neighbor and support vector machines are among the most used.

Recently, Boiman et al. [13] proposed a method for image classification referred to as *Naive-Bayes Nearest-Neighbor* (*NBNN*), with several attractive features. First, it is a *non-parametric* classifier, which means that it needs no intensive learning phase. This is extremely useful when working with large training databases that are subject to frequent updates. Second, it achieves a performance comparable to that of the top *learning-based* methods. Learning based methods require an intensive parameter learning phase, and

L. Alvarez et al. (Eds.): CIARP 2012, LNCS 7441, pp. 268–275, 2012.

can usually achieve a better classification performance than non-parametric methods. According to [13], the success of the NBNN method is due to the avoidance of local descriptors quantization and to the use of *Image-to-Class* (I2C) distance instead of *Image-to-Image* (I2I) distance. As an extra advantage, the idea behind the method is fairly simple.

Despite its good qualities, the NBNN method is not well-suited for most real-world problems [14]. The number of training features required at those scenarios to achieve a state-of-the-art performance is usually very large. This makes I2C computation expensive and results in prohibitive classification times. In Sect. 3 we propose an alternative method to NBNN (named *NBNNTree*), by which we aim at lowering the amount of time consumed for classification.

Few studies ([14, 15]) have used NBNN for action recognition. In this work, we thoroughly tested NBNN and NBNNTree on two very popular action recognition datasets: the KTH dataset and IXMAS multiview dataset. To the best of our knowledge, this is the first time the NBNN approach is tested on the challenging IXMAS dataset.

2   The NBNN Method

While in the work of Boiman et al. NBNN is used for image classification, this paper deals with action recognition. Because of that, we use a slightly different terminology here, to reflect the fact that we are working with *videos* and *actions* instead of *images* and *classes*.

Let V be a query video, and let $d_1, d_2, \ldots, d_n$ be its local descriptors. The NBNN method chooses the action $\hat{A}$ performed in V according to the following equation:

$$\hat{A} = \operatorname*{argmin}_{A} \sum_{i=1}^{n} \|d_i - NN_A(d_i)\|^2. \tag{1}$$

where $NN_A(d_i)$ is the nearest neighbor of d_i within the descriptors of action A. Descriptors of action A are gathered from every training video labeled with A. As Boiman et al. show [13], the summation in (1) approximates a *Video-to-Action* (V2A) KL-distance. In other words, NBNN computes an approximated distance from V to every possible action, and chooses the action with the minimum distance.

As shown in [14], NBNN requires a large number of local descriptors in the training set to achieve state of the art performance. This makes the computation of $NN_A(d_i)$ in (1) very expensive for real-world sets (which are usually built extracting more than 10000 descriptors per training instance). This is the main computational bottleneck, even when approximate searches (using KD-trees as in [13]) are performed.

Based on the previous observation, it seems reasonable to expect that a reduction in the number of NN searches would lead to a more time efficient method. A first step in this direction is to notice the sequential nature of the NBNN method. Only after computing the V2A distance for every action, the method chooses the closest action. This may seem like a fair strategy, but it doesn't take advantage of a very common phenomena in action recognition problems. In most of them, actions can be easily arranged in sets of look-alike actions, each set containing actions similar to each other but not similar to actions in other sets.

For example, in the KTH dataset [16] two sets are distinguishable at first glance: the one consisting of actions *boxing*, *hand waving* and *hand clapping* and the one consisting of actions *running*, *jogging* and *walking*. It would take a very bad classifier to classify a *running* video as belonging to any action in the first set, or a *boxing* video as belonging to any action in the second set. Taking this into account, it seems inefficient to compute the V2A distance for every action. It would be much more efficient to quickly discard the wrong set, concentrating the efforts in choosing an action within the right set. This is precisely the idea behind our proposed method.

3   The NBNNTree Method

Our method is based on a particular organization of the descriptors in the training dataset. Instead of grouping descriptors according to their action (as in NBNN), we group them according to their *action-set*. An action-set is just a set of actions (e.g. the set $\{boxing, hand\ waving, hand\ clapping\}$).

The method requires a training step in which all actions are organized in an *action-set tree*. An action-set tree is a binary tree in which every subtree is labeled at its root with an action-set. For the purposes of our method, we are interested only in those action-set trees which are *valid*. A valid action-set tree t can be described as follows. If t is a leaf, then it should be labeled with an action-set consisting of a single action. If t is not a leaf, then the following conditions should be met:

1. Let s be the action-set label of t. Let s_l and s_r be the action-set labels of t's left and right subtree respectively. Then, $\{s_l, s_r\}$ should be a partition of s, with $|s_l| = \lfloor \frac{|s|}{2} \rfloor$ and $|s_r| = \lceil \frac{|s|}{2} \rceil$.
2. The left subtree of s should be a valid action-set tree.
3. The right subtree of s should be a valid action-set tree.

Figure 1 shows two examples of action-set trees. Every action-set in the picture is tagged with a letter for future reference. Figure 1 (b) shows an invalid tree. The tree is invalid for several reasons. First, $\{B, C\}$ is not a partition of A. Also, $|C| \neq \lceil |A|/2 \rceil$. Second, $\{D, E\}$ is not a partition of C. And third, B is at a leaf, but $|B| > 1$.

Based on the action-set tree, a *descriptor tree* is built. A descriptor tree is just an action-set tree in which every subtree stores at its root descriptors of the actions in its associated action-set. Descriptors are selected randomly from the training descriptor dataset. The exact number of descriptors q to select is chosen based on the confusion matrix obtained from our NBNN tests. Let s, s_l and s_r be defined as before. Let z be the number of descriptors per action in the training dataset, and m the confusion matrix for NBNN. The degree of confusion between actions in s_l and actions in s_r is given by $d(s_l, s_r, m) = \sum_{(a,b) \in (s_l \times s_r)} m(a, b) + m(b, a)$. To compute q, we first normalize $d(s_l, s_r, m)$, dividing it by $2|s_l||s_r|\alpha$, where α is just a reasonable confusion value between actions (we used 1% for all our experiments). Whenever q results larger than z, we simply discard it and use z instead.

Given a query video, both its local descriptors and the descriptor tree are used by the NBNNTree method for classification. The algorithm for the NBNNTree classifier is detailed in Algorithm 1. We use $left(t)$ and $right(t)$ to designate the left and right

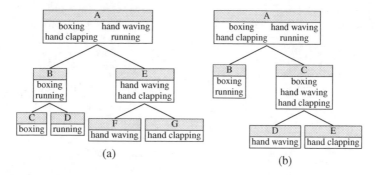

Fig. 1. Examples of valid and invalid action-set trees. Figure 1b shows an invalid tree. Figure 1a shows a valid tree.

subtrees of t respectively, $action\text{-}set(t)$ to designate the label at the root of t and $descriptors(t)$ to designate the set of descriptors stored at the root of t.

$NBNNTree(d_1, \ldots, d_n, t)$

Returns an action for a given set of descriptors $d_1, \ldots, d_n$ and a descriptor tree t

Steps:

1. If t is a leaf, return the only action in $action\text{-}set(t)$.
2. Let $L = descriptors(left(t))$ and $R = descriptors(right(t))$.
3. $\forall d_i$ compute the nearest neighbor of d_i in L: $NN_L(d_i)$.
4. Compute $D_L = \sum_{i=1}^{n} \|d_i - NN_L(d_i)\|^2$.
5. $\forall d_i$ compute the nearest neighbor of d_i in R: $NN_R(d_i)$.
6. Compute $D_R = \sum_{i=1}^{n} \|d_i - NN_R(d_i)\|^2$.
7. If $D_L < D_R$, $t_{next} = left(t)$, else $t_{next} = right(t)$.
8. Recursively call $NBNNTree(d_1, \ldots, d_n, t_{next})$.

Algorithm 1. NBNNTree algorithm

The algorithm starts from the root of the tree and descends one level at a time. At each level, the distance D_L between the video and the action-set in the left subtree is compared to the distance D_R between the video and the action-set in the right subtree. The algorithm descends to the subtree with smaller distance and the process is repeated. When a leaf is reached, its action-set (consisting of a single action) is returned.

Our method avoids the sequential strategy of the NBNN method. This was motivated by the observation that actions can be arranged into increasingly smaller sets of look-alike actions, yielding an action-set tree. But the question remains of how to build that tree. At this work we use a recursive method based on the confusion matrix from our NBNN tests. The method is shown in Algorithm 2.

$$c(s_l, s_r, m) = \sum_{a,b \in s_l \wedge a \neq b} m(a,b) + m(b,a) \ + \sum_{a,b \in s_r \wedge a \neq b} m(a,b) + m(b,a) \quad (2)$$

$BuildTree(s, m)$

Builds an action-set tree t from a given set of actions s and a given confusion matrix m

Steps:

1. $action\text{-}set(t) = s$.
2. If $|s| = 1$ return.
3. Split s into two subsets s_l and s_r, such that $c(s_l, s_r, m)$ (see (2)) is maximized, with $|s_l| = \lfloor \frac{|s|}{2} \rfloor$ and $|s_r| = \lceil \frac{|s|}{2} \rceil$.
4. $left(t) = BuildTree(s_l, m), right(t) = BuildTree(s_r, m)$.

Algorithm 2. Building the action-set tree

At each step, the algorithm evaluates every possible partition of the set of actions s into a pair of sets s_l and s_r. The chosen partition is the one that maximizes $c(s_l, s_r, m)$. As shown in (2), $c(s_l, s_r, m)$ is the sum of confusion values between actions in s_l plus the sum of confusion values between actions in s_r. Thus, s_l and s_r are chosen in such a way that actions belonging to the same set are often confused with each other by the NBNN classifier.

3.1 Time Complexity of the NBNNTree Method

As shown in the previous section, NBNNTree performs several steps at each level of the tree (numbered from 1 to 8 in Algorithm 1). Of these steps, 1, 2, 7 and 8 are clearly $\mathcal{O}(1)$. Step 3 computes $NN_L(d_i)$ for each of the n descriptors of the query video. Following [13], we used an approximate nearest neighbor algorithm [17] for the computation of $NN_L(d_i)$. The expected time for this nearest neighbor search is logarithmic in $|L|$. Thus, step 3 is $\mathcal{O}(n \log(|L|))$. Step 4 is clearly $\mathcal{O}(n)$, because it involves only $\mathcal{O}(1)$ computations over n values. Step 3 to 4 together are therefore $\mathcal{O}(n \log(|L|))$. Likewise, steps 5 to 6 are $\mathcal{O}(n \log(|R|))$. In our experiments, every node in the descriptor tree stores at most z descriptors, where z is the number of training descriptors for a single action. Replacing $|L|$ and $|R|$ for z in the previous expressions yields a time complexity of $\mathcal{O}(n \log(z))$ for the steps $1 - 8$ performed at each level of the tree. Since t is built from a valid action-set tree, its height is logarithmic in the total number of actions k. Thus, the time complexity of the NBNNTree classifier is $\mathcal{O}(\log(k)n \log(z))$. This is a substantial speed-up over the NBNN method, which has a time complexity of $\mathcal{O}(kn \log(z))$.

4 Experiments

We tested NBNN and NBNNTree on two well-known action recognition datasets: the KTH dataset [16] and the IXMAS dataset [18]. For all the experiments, descriptor datasets were built following [6]. Parameters for NBNN were set as suggested in [13].

The KTH dataset contains 6 actions, performed several times by 25 actors in 4 different scenarios of appearance, illumination and scale. Both camera location and orientation of actors remain constant for most videos. In total, the dataset consists of 2391 videos. Figure 2 shows some example frames.

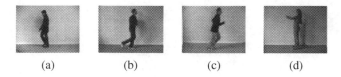

Fig. 2. Example frames from KTH dataset: *walking* (a), *jogging* (b), *running* (c), *boxing* (d)

We used leave-one-out cross-validation (LOOCV) on the actors. That is, videos were divided into 25 sets, each including exactly the videos of one actor. In each of 25 experiments, the classifier was trained using the videos from 24 sets and tested on the videos from the remaining set. We report average precision (both global and by action) over the 25 experiments. Figure 3 shows confusion matrices for NBNN and NBNNTree. Our method obtains similar results to those of NBNN for all the actions. Table 1 (a) compares our results on KTH with those of existing approaches.

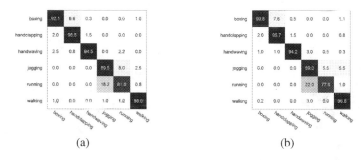

Fig. 3. Confusion matrices for the KTH dataset using NBNN (a) and IXMAS (b)

The average running time for classification is reduced by 10% when using NBNNTree, compared to NBNN. This improvement came almost entirely from the strategy used to select the number of stored descriptors at each node, detailed in Sect. 3. For some of the nodes, only 8% of the total number of descriptors for that node action-set were enough to achieve the results reported in Fig. 3 (b), which is impressive. Because of the small number of actions of the KTH dataset, the main improvement in time complexity provided by NBNNTree is not fully exploited.

The IXMAS dataset contains 13 actions, performed 3 times by 12 actors. Each action execution was recorded by fixed cameras at 5 different positions. We use the videos of the 4 cameras usually considered in literature. Actors arbitrarily chose position and orientation. Figure 4 shows some example frames.

We used 6-fold cross-validation on the actors, and report average precision (both global and by action) over the 6 experiments. Classifiers were trained using the videos taken by the four cameras, and tested on the videos of one designated camera. Table 1 (b) compares the results achieved by several approaches. Both NBNN and NBNNTree perform better than the rest of the methods. Confusion matrices are shown in Fig. 5. Average running time for classification is reduced by 50% when using NBNNTree,

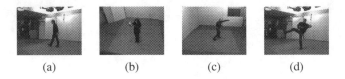

| (a) | (b) | (c) | (d) |

Fig. 4. Example frames for the dataset IXMAS: *walk* (a), *wave* (b), *punch* (c), *kick* (d)

Table 1. Average precision (in %) of different methods. Table (a) shows results for the KTH dataset. Table (b) shows results for the IXMAS dataset.

(a)

Method	Precision
Dollar et al. [6]	80.66
Liu et al. [11]	94.16
Laptev et al. [5]	91.8
Nowozin et al. [19]	84.72
NBNN	91.73
NBNNTree	90.58

(b)

Method	Cam 0	Cam 1	Cam 2	Cam 3
Weinland et al. [2]	65.4	70	54.3	66
Yan et al. [3]	72	53	68	63
Liu et al. [11]	76.67	73.29	71.97	72.99
NBNN	79.4	76.15	74.04	74.13
NBNNTree	78.8	75.83	71.07	71.75

| (a) | (b) |

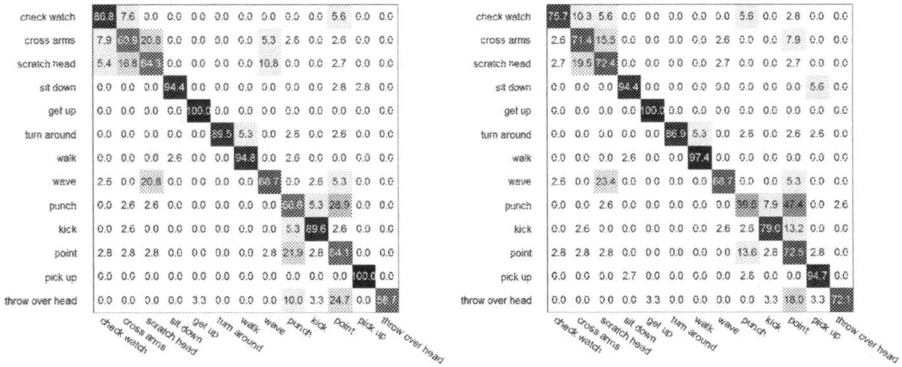

Fig. 5. Confusion matrices for the IXMAS dataset, using NBNN (a) and NBNNTree (b)

compared to NBNN. Due to the larger number of actions, the benefits of using the descriptor tree are more clearly visible with IXMAS than with KTH.

5 Conclusions

We proposed a method that significantly reduces the time complexity of NBNN while achieving a similar classification accuracy. Our approach benefits from the good qualities of non-parametric methods, and is better suited for real world problems. On the challenging IXMAS dataset, the average running time is reduced by 50% when using our method, compared to NBNN. In the future, we hope to explore new criterias to organize descriptors, in an effort to further improve classification time.

References

1. Davis, J., Bobick, A.: The representation and recognition of action using temporal templates. In: CVPR 1997, pp. 928–934 (1997)
2. Weinland, D., Boyer, E., Ronfard, R.: Action recognition from arbitrary views using 3d exemplars. In: ICCV 2007, pp. 1–7 (2007)
3. Yan, P., Khan, S., Shah, M.: Learning 4d action feature models for arbitrary view action recognition. In: CVPR 2008, pp. 1–7 (2008)
4. Zelnik-manor, L., Irani, M.: Event-based analysis of video. In: Proc. CVPR, pp. 123–130 (2001)
5. Laptev, I., Marszalek, M., Schmid, C., Rozenfeld, B.: Learning realistic human actions from movies. In: CVPR 2008, pp. 1–8 (2008)
6. Dollar, P., Rabaud, V., Cottrell, G., Belongie, S.: Behavior recognition via sparse spatio-temporal features. In: PETS 2005, pp. 65–72 (2005)
7. Le, Q., Zou, W., Yeung, S., Ng, A.: Learning hierarchical invariant spatio-temporal features for action recognition with independent subspace analysis. In: CVPR 2011, pp. 3361–3368 (2011)
8. Goussies, N.A., Liu, Z., Yuan, J.: Efficient search of top-k video subvolumes for multi-instance action detection. In: ICME 2010, pp. 328–333 (2010)
9. Yu, G., Goussies, N., Yuan, J., Liu, Z.: Fast action detection via discriminative random forest voting and top-k subvolume search. MultMed. 13(3), 507–517 (2011)
10. Sivic, J., Zisserman, A.: Video google: A text retrieval approach to object matching in videos. In: ICCV 2003, pp. 1470–1477 (2003)
11. Liu, J., Shah, M.: Learning human actions via information maximization. In: CVPR 2008, pp. 1–8 (2008)
12. Bregonzio, M., Gong, S., Xiang, T.: Recognising action as clouds of space-time interest points. In: CVPR 2009, pp. 1948–1955 (2009)
13. Boiman, O., Shechtman, E., Irani, M.: In defense of nearest-neighbor based image classification. In: CVPR 2008, pp. 1–8 (2008)
14. Wang, Z., Hu, Y., Chia, L.: Learning instance-to-class distance for human action recognition. In: ICIP 2009, pp. 3545–3548 (2009)
15. Yuan, J., Liu, Z., Wu, Y.: Discriminative video pattern search for efficient action detection. PAMI 33, 1728–1743 (2011)
16. Laptev, I.: On space-time interest points. IJCV 64, 107–123 (2005)
17. Muja, M., Lowe, D.G.: Fast approximate nearest neighbors with automatic algorithm configuration. In: International Conference on Computer Vision Theory and Application, VISSAPP 2009, pp. 331–340. INSTICC Press (2009)
18. Zelnik Manor, L., Irani, M., Weinland, D., Ronfard, R., Boyer, E.: Free viewpoint action recognition using motion history volumes. CVIU 103, 249–257 (2006)
19. Nowozin, S., Bakir, G., Tsuda, K.: Discriminative subsequence mining for action classification. In: ICCV 2007, pp. 1–8 (2007)

An Human-Computer Interface Using Facial Gestures for the Game of *Truco*

Gonzalo Castillo, Santiago Avendaño, and Norberto Adrián Goussies

Departamento de Computación,
Facultad de Ciencias Exactas y Naturales,
Universidad de Buenos Aires
Ciudad Universitaria, C1428EGA, Buenos Aires, Argentina
{gcastilo,savendano,ngoussie}@dc.uba.ar

Abstract. In this work we present a method to detect and recognize the signs of the card game of *Truco* which are a subset of facial gestures. The method uses temporal templates to represent motion and later extract features. The proposed method works in real time, allowing to use it as an human-computer interface , for example, in the context of the card game of *Truco* . To the best of our knowledge this is the first work that uses detection of facial gestures in the context of a game.

Keywords: facial gesture, temporal templates, truco.

1 Introduction

The *Truco* is a card game originary from Spain and played in South-America. One of its main objectives is to deceive the opponent in order to get a higher score. It is played using a spanish deck by two, four or six players divided into two teams. In order to develop a common strategy it is important that teammates inform each other the cards that they have in the hand. The players of each team use a set of facial gestures to secretly inform the others players of the same team the cards they have. The most generally accepted gestures are shown in Figure 1.

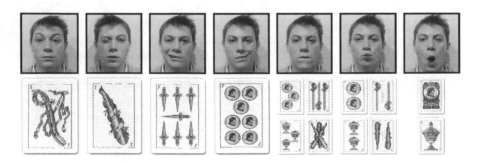

Fig. 1. Truco gestures and their corresponding cards. From left to right: ace of swords, ace of clubs, seven of swords, seven of gold, any three, any two, any other ace.

L. Alvarez et al. (Eds.): CIARP 2012, LNCS 7441, pp. 276–283, 2012.

In this paper we address the problem of detection and recognition of *Truco* signs which could be integrated into a computer *Truco* player in order to replace one of the human players by a computer player. The proposed interface will give the other players a more realistic and comfortable experience.

In other words, we present a novel human-computer interface that understands commands using facial gestures. This is a different type of interface to previous human-computer interfaces which usually understands commands using upper-body gestures [1, 2]. Additionally, the goal of this paper is different to the one of [3–6] where authors propose a system to understand human emotions using facial gestures. Note that when we design a facial gesture interface we should allow the user to do gesticulations that are not part of the interface, a challenge that is not present for other facial analysis systems. Also, the interface should work for different people and have a fast response time.

Our proposal presented in this paper uses temporal templates [2] to represent motion and later extract facial features. In addition, we developed a real-time on-line *Truco* sign recognition system. Figure 2 gives an overview of our system. First, we locate frontal faces [7] in each frame and at the same time we update the temporal template. Next, if the a *Truco* sign is spotted we extract features and recognize the type of *Truco* gesture.

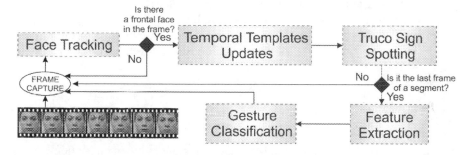

Fig. 2. Overview of the proposed system

The remainder of this paper is organized as follows: Section 2 provides an overview of related work. In Section 3 we describe the representation of the facial motion. In Section 4 we present different features for the facial motion. In Section 5 we explain the *Truco* gesture spotting method. We show experimental results in Section 6. Finally we conclude our work in Section 7.

2   Related Work

In this Section we mention the most relevant contributions for our work. Initially in [8] Kalman filters were used to predict and track the position of certain facial features in real time. Using these positions it is possible to detect gestures such as: yes, no, maybe, look up or down.

In [9–12] methods to detect facial gestures are proposed. In [9] vector spaces of facial gestures are built using the method of eigenfaces. Using these vector spaces, the facial gestures are represented by a limited number of descriptors. A different representation based on optical flow was proposed in [10] to detect and recognize the six universal facial expressions (happiness, sadness, surprise, fear, anger and disgust). A cylindrical 3D model was built in [11] to perform face tracking. Additionally, the residual error was modeled as a linear combination of templates of facial movement to deduce the expression a person was doing. Another 3D model was proposed in [12] to detect the position and tilt of the face. Furthermore, the problem of detecting facial gestures in the presence of head movement was studied.

New methods for the problem of recognition of Action Units [13] were proposed in [3, 4, 6]. Temporal templates originary proposed to recognize human actions [2] were adapted in [3] for recognition of Action Units using nearest neighbor. In [4] the authors proposed a system that detects Action Units and analyses the temporal behavior, using spatio-temporal features computed by tracking 20 facial points. Both gestures and their temporal segments were recognized by Supports Vectors Machines. Later, [6] suggested two approaches based on dynamic textures to recognize Action Units and their temporary models. The first is an extension of the method of temporal templates based on Motion History Image. The second method relies on nonrigid registration using free-form deformations.

Our approach extends the work of [3, 6] on temporal templates and Motion History Images for facial gesture recognition. We use Directional Motion History Images [14] in order to overcome the problem of self-occluding gestures. Although the *Truco* gestures can be partly mapped to Action Units and there are methods based on temporal templates for recognizing Action Units, our method is not only able of recognize facial gestures but also performs real-time detection.

3   Motion Representation

The gestures of the face are described by temporal templates based on Motion History Image (MHI) and Motion Energy Image (MEI) presented by Bobick and Davis in [2]. The MHI is a scalar-valued image where intensity is a function of recency of motion. The MEI represents where motion has occurred in an image sequence. A temporal template is a vector-valued image where each component of each pixel is some function of the motion at that pixel location, for example the MEI and the MHI.

Let $\mathbf{I} = (I_1, \ldots, I_t)$ be an image sequence of t frames, ψ_k is a binary image indicating associated the motion in the I_k frame :

$$\psi_k(x,y) = \begin{cases} true & \text{if } \Delta_k^\beta(x,y) \geq \mu \\ false & \text{if } \Delta_k^\beta(x,y) < \mu \end{cases} \tag{1}$$

$$\Delta_k^\beta(x,y) = \begin{cases} |I_k(x,y) - I_1(x,y)| & \text{if } k \leq \beta \\ |I_k(x,y) - I_{k-\beta}(x,y)| & \text{if } k > \beta \end{cases} \tag{2}$$

where $\mu \in \mathbb{N}$ is the threshold of motion and $\beta \in \mathbb{N}$ is the temporal gap between subtracted frames.

In our work, we assume that the Truco gestures have a maximum duration of α frames. Therefore, we do not need to take into account all the frames but only α previous frames when computing the temporal template for a given frame $i \leq t$. We encode the motion information for the range of time in the MHI M as follows:

$$M_i^\alpha(x,y) = \begin{cases} \min(i,\alpha) & \text{if } \psi_i(x,y) \\ M_{i-1}^\alpha(x,y) & \text{if } \neg\psi_i(x,y) \text{ and } i < \alpha \\ \max(0, M_{i-1}^\alpha(x,y) - 1) & \text{if } \neg\psi_i(x,y) \text{ and } i \geq \alpha \end{cases} \qquad (3)$$

The range of the MHI are the natural numbers in $[0, \alpha]$. The pixels with highest value are those that had motion most recently in the last α frames. The comparison of two MHIs with different α is meaningless because their range depends on α. In order to solve this problem we define the Normalized MHI, $NMHI$, whose range is $[0, 1]$:

$$NMHI_i^\alpha(x,y) = \begin{cases} 0 & \text{if } t = 0 \\ M_i^\alpha(x,y)/t & \text{if } 1 < t < \alpha \\ M_i^\alpha(x,y)/\alpha & \text{if } t \geq \alpha \end{cases} \qquad (4)$$

The Motion Energy Image E^α can be computed using the MHI M^α:

$$E_i^\alpha(x,y) = M_i^\alpha(x,y) > 0 \qquad (5)$$

3.1 Directional Motion History Image (DMHI)

Most of the Truco signs can be separated in three different stages. In the first stage the facial muscles are contracted. Then, the sign is maintained for a few frames. Finally, the facial muscles are relaxed. Since, the stages are performed in the same spatial area, if we use the MHI as defined above each stage overrides the information of the previous one. In other words, the Truco signs are self-occluding. In order to solve this problem in [14, 15] the authors proposed to extend the information coded in the MHI. In their approach, gradient-based optical flow is calculated between two consecutive frames and split it into four channels. Based on such a strategy, a four-directional motion templates for left, right, up and down directions can be obtained. The Directional Motion History Image (DMHI) is defined as:

$$DM_t^{\alpha,\gamma}(x,y) = \begin{cases} M_t^\alpha(x,y) & \text{if } \angle_t^\alpha(x,y) \in \gamma \\ DM_{t-1}^{\alpha,\gamma}(x,y) & \text{if } \angle_t^\alpha(x,y) \notin \gamma \text{ and } i < \alpha \\ \max(0, DM_{t-1}^{\alpha,\gamma}(x,y) - 1) & \text{if } \angle_t^\alpha(x,y) \notin \gamma \text{ and } i \geq \alpha \end{cases} \qquad (6)$$

where γ is one of the possible directions : left, right, up and down. The function $\angle$ is defined as:

$$\angle_t^\alpha(x,y) = \arctan\left(\frac{G_y * M_t^\alpha}{G_x * M_t^\alpha}\right) \qquad (7)$$

where $G_y * MHI_t$ and $G_x * MHI_t$ are the images resulting from convolving the MHI with the vertical and horizontal Sobel filters respectively. The function $\angle_t$ provides a good approximation of the motion angle at each pixel. Although there are more exact implementations for obtaining the motion angle (for example [6]) we have chosen this one because is the fastest one, allowing the system to work in real-time.

4   Feature Extraction and Classification

In this section we describe the feature extraction method which will be used as input for the classifiers. Two main types of features has been proposed for MHIs. The first type are based on image moments [16] and are common features for body motion [2]. The second type are features common in face motion [6] and aggregate the motion in different areas of the face. In this work we use the second type of feature.

The first step is to divide the face using an uniform grid of r rows and c columns [3]. The features computed using a regular grid have tolerance to small rotations, displacements and scale changes. The level of tolerance is given by the number of cells in the grid. In this work we use cells without overlapping of the same size.

Then, the motion of a DMHI, NMHI or MEI I is aggregated for each region R. We use the function C_R defined as:

$$C_R(I) = \frac{1}{|R|} \sum_{(x,y) \in R} I(x,y) \tag{8}$$

Note that the function C_R assigns higher values to recent facial motion than to motion that occurs further in the past when computed over a NMHI or DMHI while this is not true for MEI. The final feature vector consists of the concatenation for all regions R of the values $C_R(NM^\alpha)$, $C_R(E^\alpha)$ and $C_R(DM_t^{\alpha,\gamma})$ and for all directions γ. As a result the feature vector has information about where and how the motion is present and the direction of that motion.

We use the LIBSVM [17] implementation of Support Vector Machines (SVM). We use the one-versus-one approach for mutliclass classification with the radial basis function. Given a feature vector x our classifier f outputs a vector y containing one probability per *Truco* sign which are estimated using the implementation of [18].

5   *Truco* Sign Spotting

During the development of a round in the *Truco* the teammates talk and make facial gestures that are not always *Truco* signs. Therefore it is important to distinguish between the *Truco* signs and other types of gestures. This is an important requirement so the players can enjoy the game without any restrictions. In other words in this step the objective is to distinguish relevant gestures from other type of movements. The output of this step is the temporal location of the gestures, i.e. the first and last frame of a *Truco* gesture.

This is an extremely difficult task because there is a huge number of facial gestures that has similar motion patterns and occur in the same facial area. Furthermore, we are interested in building a system that works online, i.e. we do not have the entire image sequence in advance, each frame arrives as it is captured by the camera. Therefore, the method proposed here has to find the beginning and ending of the gesture using only the information prior the current frame.

A similar problem was studied in the design of human-computer interfaces for video games using computer vision techniques [1, 19]. The main difference with this work is that the methods proposed by those authors are mostly for recognition of upper-body gestures but in this paper we are concerned with facial gestures. It is interesting to note that this problem has not received much attention in the area of facial gestures, probably because previous work in the area was not focused in human-computer interfaces using facial gestures.

Bearing in mind that we are interested in spotting *Truco* gestures and that they are only sent to the other teammate when both players are looking at each other, the first step in our gesture spotting method is to consider only the frames that have a frontal face.

In the following step we look for facial movements that are a potential *Truco* gesture. Again, we are going to use specific knowledge on *Truco* gestures. First we note that *Truco* gestures are expressed moving parts of the face that have approximately the same size. Therefore when a *Truco* gesture is signaled areas of approximately the same size must appear in the MEI. Following this idea we define the amount of motion at frame k as:

$$AM_k = C_R(E_k^\alpha) \tag{9}$$

where C_R is the function defined in Eq. (8) and R is the union of the regions of the face.

We define two thresholds τ, δ as the minimum and maximum of AM_k, respectively, that a frame must have in order to be considered as part of a gesture. The definition of a maximum amount of motion helps to differentiate motion generated by a gesture as opposed to motion produced by movement of the head. Also, *Truco* gestures have a minimum duration, therefore we define another threshold v as the minimum number of continuous frames of motion a gesture must have. Experimentally we determined that $\tau = 0.02$, $\delta = 0.14$, $v = 10$ gives excellent results. To sum up, we only consider intervals such that the amount of motion for each frame is between τ and δ and have at least v frames.

6 Experiments

Two types of experiments were performed: off-line isolated *Truco* sign recognition and real-time on-line gesture recognition. The goal of the first set is to examine the effectiveness of the features as well as the classification performance and generalization. In the second set the complete Truco sign system is tested.

6.1 Isolated Truco Sign Recognition

Two subjects were asked to perform all the Truco signs in front of a video camera. The total number of Truco signs samples collected were 229. Each sample gesture lasts about 1s and runs at 25 frames per second, the spatial resolution is 640×480 pixels and the face is at least 100×100 pixels.

To test robustness and generalization ability we train using the samples of one subject and test using the samples of the other subject. This way, we can also find out if the system works with different people without having to be trained for each person. When we train using Subject A and test on Subject B we obtain an accuracy of 89%, in the other case we obtain an accuracy of 92%. As expected, the *Truco* signs that have motion in the area of the mouth, are the ones that were harder to differentiate.

6.2 Real-Time Truco Signs Spotting and Recognition

Here we analyze the experiments for the real-time on-line system to detect and recognize the Truco gestures. Our system was run on a desktop computer having four core AMD Phenom II X4 64bits and 4 Gb of RAM. We trained the system using the complete dataset of 229 samples. The accuracy of the on-line system ranged from 90% to 100%. The system runs at 22 frames per second, most of the time was spent in updating the MHI and DMHI.

7 Conclusions

We described a real-time on-line system for detecting and recognizing *Truco* signs. As far as we know this is the first paper in developing an human-computer interface that understands commands using facial gestures in the context of a game. Finally, our approach works with different people without having to be trained for each person.

In the future we hope to develop a complete *Truco* computer player, capable of sending and receiving signs and build a strategy for the round. Also, the player should have a verbal interface in order to understand the different commands of the teammate and the other players.

References

1. Kang, H., Lee, C.W., Jung, K.: Recognition-based gesture spotting in video games. Pattern Recogn. Lett. 25, 1701–1714 (2004)
2. Davis, J.W., Bobick, A.F.: The Representation and Recognition of Human Movement Using Temporal Templates. In: CVPR 1997: Proceedings of the 1997 Conference on Computer Vision and Pattern Recognition (CVPR 1997). IEEE Computer Society Press (1997)
3. Valstar, M.F., Patras, I., Pantic, M.: Facial action unit recognition using temporal templates. In: Proceedings of IEEE Int'l Workshop on Robot-Human Interaction (RO-MAN 2004), Kurashiki, Japan, pp. 253–258 (September 2004)
4. Valstar, M.F., Pantic, M.: Fully automatic facial action unit detection and temporal analysis. In: Proceedings of IEEE Int'l Conf. Computer Vision and Pattern Recognition (CVPR 2006), New York, USA, vol. 3, p. 149 (June 2006)
5. Valstar, M., Pantic, M., Patras, I.: Motion history for facial action detection from face video. In: Proceedings of IEEE Int'l Conf. Systems, Man and Cybernetics (SMC 2004), The Hague, Netherlands, pp. 635–640 (October 2004)
6. Koelstra, S., Pantic, M., Patras, I.: A dynamic texture based approach to recognition of facial actions and their temporal models. IEEE Transactions on Pattern Analysis and Machine Intelligence 32, 1940–1954 (2010)
7. Viola, P., Jones, M.: Robust real-time face detection. International Journal of Computer Vision 57, 137–154 (2004)
8. Zelinsky, A., Zelinsky, E., Heinzmann, J.: Real-time visual recognition of facial gestures for human-computer interaction. In: Proceedings of the Int. Conf. on Automatic Face and Gesture Recognition, pp. 351–356. IEEE Computer Society Press (1996)
9. Algorri, M.E., Escobar, A.: Facial gesture recognition for interactive applications. In: Proceedings of the Fifth Mexican International Conference in Computer Science, pp. 188–195. IEEE Computer Society, Washington, DC (2004)

10. Naghsh-Nilchi, A.R., et al.: An efficient algorithm for motion detection based facial expression recognition using optical flow (2006)
11. La Cascia, M., Valenti, L., Sclaroff, S.: Fully automatic, real-time detection of facial gestures from generic video. In: IEEE 6th Workshop on Multimedia Signal Processing 2004, pp. 175–178 (2004)
12. Liao, W.-K., Cohen, I.: Classifying facial gestures in presence of head motion. In: Proceedings of the 2005 IEEE Computer Society Conference on Computer Vision and Pattern Recognition (CVPR 2005) Workshops, vol. 03, p. 77. IEEE Computer Society, Washington, DC (2005)
13. Ekman, P., Friesen, W.: Facial Action Coding System: A Technique for the Measurement of Facial Movement. Consulting Psychologists Press, Palo Alto (1978)
14. Ahad, M.A.R., Ogata, T., Tan, J.K., Kim, H., Ishikawa, S.: Motion recognition approach to solve overwriting in complex actions. In: FG, pp. 1–6. IEEE (2008)
15. Ahad, M., Tan, J., Kim, H., Ishikawa, S.: Solutions to motion self-occlusion problem in human activity analysis. In: 11th International Conference on Computer and Information Technology, ICCIT 2008, pp. 201–206 (December 2008)
16. Hu, M.-K.: Visual pattern recognition by moment invariants. IRE Transactions on Information Theory 8, 179–187 (1962)
17. Chang, C.-C., Lin, C.-J.: Libsvm: A library for support vector machines. ACM Trans. Intell. Syst. Technol. 2, 27:1–27:27 (2011)
18. Lin, H.-T., Lin, C.-J., Weng, R.C.: A note on platt's probabilistic outputs for support vector machines. Mach. Learn. 68, 267–276 (2007)
19. Freeman, W.T., Anderson, D.B., Beardsley, P.A., Dodge, C.N., Roth, M., Weissman, C.D., Yerazunis, W.S., Kage, H., Kyuma, K., Miyake, Y., Tanaka, K.-i.: Computer vision for interactive computer graphics. IEEE Comput. Graph. Appl. 18, 42–53 (1998)

Using Word Graphs as Intermediate Representation of Uttered Sentences

Jon A. Gómez and Emilio Sanchis

Departament de Sistemes Informàtics i Computació,
Universitat Politècnica de València, Spain
{jon,esanchis}@dsic.upv.es
http://elirf.dsic.upv.es/

Abstract. We present an algorithm for building graphs of words as an intermediate representation of uttered sentences. No language model is used. The input data for the algorithm are the pronunciation lexicon organized as a tree and the sequence of acoustic frames. The transition between consecutive units are considered as additional units.

Nodes represent discrete instants of time, arcs are labelled with words, and a confidence measure is assigned to each detected word, which is computed by using the phonetic probabilities of the subsequence of acoustic frames used for completing the word.

We evaluated the obtained word graphs by searching the path that best matches with the correct sentence and then measuring the word accuracy, i.e. the oracle word accuracy.

Keywords: word graphs, word lattices, lexical tree, confidence measures.

1 Introduction

Word graphs are directed acyclic graphs (DAGs) where each arc is labelled with a word and each node is labelled with a discrete time mark. Each arc represents a word detected between two instants of time and contains a confidence measure.

There are a lot of works using weighted word graphs as intermediate representation of uttered sentences in automatic speech recognition (ASR) systems or in spoken language understanding (SLU) systems [1–7]. Some authors use the concept of word lattice and other ones use the concept of word confusion network (WCN). There maybe differences at the implementation level, but the purpose is the same, that is to obtain a compact and efficient representation of the n-best recognized sentences. Then, word-graphs/word-lattices/WCN can be used as the input to modules operating at higher levels of knowledge, for example the understanding module in a spoken dialog (SD) system.

In [1], a bigram language model is used to obtain a word graph from each uttered sentence. The used algorithm is an extension of their one-pass beam search strategy using lexical trees. A variation of the approach presented in [1] is presented in [2]. The difference between both approaches resides in the strategy used for exploring the search space. Several confidence measures to be used in weighted word graphs are presented and discussed in [3, 4].

L. Alvarez et al. (Eds.): CIARP 2012, LNCS 7441, pp. 284–291, 2012.
© Springer-Verlag Berlin Heidelberg 2012

A SLU system where the output of the ASR module is a lattice of word hypotheses is described in [5]. Finite state transducers (FST) are used in a translation process for generating hypotheses of conceptual constituents from the lattice of word hypotheses. In [6], word lattices are used to be converted into word confusion networks (WCN), the authors presented the *"pivot"* algorithm for reducing a word lattice and obtaining as a result a WCN. The main idea of this algorithm is to normalize the topology of input graphs.

In [7], it is presented a two-stage strategy for building word graphs: the first stage is "forward–decoding" and the second one is "backward–decoding". The first stage is an interesting extension of the Viterbi algorithm that stores several predecessor words for each word, then the second one explores backward the n-best final states until the initial state is reached. Word graphs are generated as a result of the backward-decoding phase.

Our approach does not use a language model for building word graphs, it explores the sequence of acoustic frames in order to complete phonetic sequences corresponding to words. The pronunciation lexicon with all the possible phonetic sequences of each word is organized as a tree. This way of representing the pronunciation lexicon has been used by many researchers [1]. The confidence measure of each detected word is computed using only the phonetic probabilities estimated by the acoustic models. In other words, our approach for the construction of word graphs only uses the following sources of knowledge: acoustical, phonetic and lexical. The syntactic knowledge provided by language models can be used in a decoder that takes word graphs as starting point for recognizing. In [9], the understanding module combines two sources of knowledge, syntactic and semantic, for detecting semantic units related with the concepts defined as goals in a dialogue system.

The rest of the paper is organized as follows. Section 2 describes the details of the lexical tree used in our approach. Section 3 presents and explains the algorithm for building word graphs. Section 4 describes the experiments and presents the results. Finally conclusions are discussed in Section 5.

2   Lexical Tree or *Trie*

Figure 1 shows an example of the lexical tree or *Trie* used in our system for representing the phonetic transcriptions of all the words in the vocabulary. Terminal nodes are grey coloured and labelled with the words which are completed when reaching these nodes. In fact, each terminal node points to a list with all the words that share the same phonetic transcription.

Table 1 presents an example of file containing the words in the vocabulary with their possible phonetic transcriptions. The process of building the *Trie* takes into account the set of phonetic units (phonemes + silence) and the transitions between two consecutive phonetic units. Transitions are considered as additional units and are represented with a plus sign between the labels of two consecutive units. Not all possible transitions are used, only those which appear frequently enough in the set of training sentences are considered.

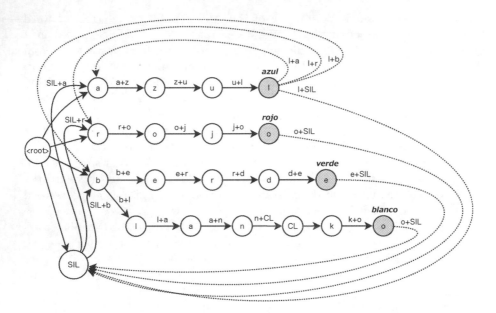

Fig. 1. Example of lexical tree o Trie for representing the phonetic transcriptions of all the words in the vocabulary. Arcs are labelled with units representing transitions between consecutive phonemes. Dotted arcs are special arcs for connecting terminal nodes with the ones representing word-initial phonemes. For clarity, not all the arcs of this kind are represented, only the arcs leaving from the terminal node corresponding to the word *"azul"* and the ones reaching the silence.

Nodes represent phonetic units. Arcs are labelled with the transition between two phonetic units when the transition is used, otherwise arcs are λ labelled. An example is shown in Figure 1, where the arc connecting nodes CL and k of word *"blanco"* is not labelled because the transition CL+k is not allowed. CL represents the closure before plosive consonants. Root node doesn't represent any unit. SIL node represents all possible silences in the recording of an utterance: initial silence, final silence and pauses between words.

As Figure 1 shows, there are special arcs leaving from terminal nodes pointing to initial nodes. These arcs are drawn with dotted lines and their role is taking into account the transition between the ending phoneme of a word and the initial phoneme of the next one. The use of this kind of arcs simplifies the algorithm for building word graphs.

3   Algorithm for Building Word Graphs

Our proposed algorithm for building word graphs will be easy to understand keeping in mind the described *Trie*, and putting special attention to arcs that connect terminal nodes with nodes representing the word-initial phonemes. This

Table 1. Example of the list representing all the possible phonetic transcriptions of the words in the vocabulary. Each line contains a pair orthographic transcription – phonetic transcription. The different possible phonetic sequences of a word are in different lines.

Orthographic transcription	Phonetic transcription
azul	a z u l
rojo	r o x o
verde	b e r d e
blanco	b l a n CL k o

algorithm explores the sequence of acoustic frames that represents each pronounced sentence, and maintains a list of word hypotheses that is updated for each incoming acoustic frame.

A hypothesis is defined as a 5-tuple, $hyp = \{n, a, t_0, t, score\}$, where n is a node in the *Trie*, a is an arc in the *Trie*, a hypothesis can only be located in either a node or an arc, no both. t is the current time, t_0 is the time instant this word hypothesis begins, and *score* is the sum of the logarithms of the phonetic probabilities corresponding to the acoustic frames from t_0 up to t.

Figure 2 shows the block diagram of our ASR system. Only modules related with the word graph builder are represented. Each module runs in an independent execution thread. FIFO queues are used in order to manage the data flow between each pair of connected modules. Due to this, no process becomes locked when sending its output data and the whole system takes advantage of microprocessors with multiple cores.

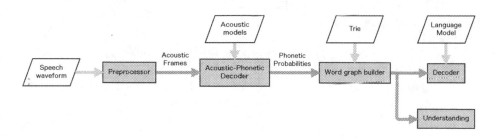

Fig. 2. Block diagram of our ASR system. Each module runs in an independent execution thread and modules are connected by means of FIFO queues. Word graphs are sent to several modules (understanding, decoder, ...) depending on the selected configuration.

The acoustic-phonetic decoder converts the sequence of acoustic frames into a sequence of vectors with phonetic probabilities [8]. The word graph builder processes sequentially the stream of vectors with phonetic probabilities. It is connected by means of a FIFO queue with the output of the acoustic-phonetic decoder. The process of building word graphs begins with a unique hypothesis located at the root node of the *Trie*. The first incoming vector with phonetic probabilities is used to expand this initial word hypothesis in order to reach nodes corresponding to word-initial phonemes. The normal operation of the algorithm consists of expanding hypotheses in the list of hypotheses (LH) for each vector with phonetic probabilities extracted from the FIFO queue. Not all the hypotheses in LH are expanded, a beam search strategy is applied. A word is inserted into the graph every time that one hypothesis reaches a word-initial phoneme (or silence) from a terminal node.

Algorithm 1. Expanding of the list of hypotheses

Input: $logProb$: vector with phonetic probabilities estimated at frame t
Input: t : index frame representing time
Global variables:
    $bestScore$: real
    $BEAM$: real
    LH : list of hypotheses expanded up to frame $t-1$
Local variables:
    LH' : temporal list of hypotheses
    nbs : real   ▷ New best score

  $LH' \leftarrow \{\}$
  $nbs \leftarrow -\infty$
  for all $h \in LH$ **do**
    if $score(h)$ is worse than $(bestScore + BEAM)$ **then**
        do nothing
    else if $node(h)$ is not $null$ **then**
        if $node(h)$ is a terminal node **and** h is in the last state of the acoustic
model **then**
            insert into the graph all words completed at $node(h)$
        end if
        $u \leftarrow label(node(h))$ ▷ Hypothesis which continues in the same node
        $h' \leftarrow (node(h), null, t_0(h), t, score(h) + logProb[u])$
        $LH' \leftarrow LH' + \{h'\}$; $nbs \leftarrow \max(nbs, score(h'))$
        for all $a \in arcsFrom(node(h))$ **do**
            if $label(a)$ is not $null$ **then**
                $u \leftarrow label(a)$ ▷ New hypothesis in a labelled arc
                $h' \leftarrow (null, a, t_0(h), t, score(h) + logProb[u])$
            else
                $n' \leftarrow node(a)$
                $u \leftarrow label(n')$ ▷ New hypothesis in a node
                if n' is a word-initial node **then**
                    $h' \leftarrow (n', null, t, t, score(h) + logProb[u])$
                else
                    $h' \leftarrow (n', null, t_0(h), t, score(h) + logProb[u])$
                end if
            end if

$LH' \leftarrow LH' + \{h'\}$; $nbs \leftarrow \max(nbs, score(h'))$
    end for
  else $\triangleright$ Then $arc(h)$ is not $null$
    $a \leftarrow arc(h)$
    $u \leftarrow label(a)$ $\triangleright$ Hypothesis which continues in the same arc
    $h' \leftarrow (null, a, t_0(h), t, score(h) + logProb[u])$
    $LH' \leftarrow LH' + \{h'\}$; $nbs \leftarrow \max(nbs, score(h'))$

    $n' \leftarrow node(arc(h))$
    $u \leftarrow label(n')$
                  $\triangleright$ New hypothesis in the node pointed by the current arc
    if n' is a word-initial node **then**
        $h' \leftarrow (n', null, t, t, score(h) + logProb[u])$
    else
        $h' \leftarrow (n', null, t_0(h), t, score(h) + logProb[u])$
    end if
    $LH' \leftarrow LH' + \{h'\}$; $nbs \leftarrow \max(nbs, score(h'))$
  end if
end for
$LH \leftarrow LH'$;
$bestScore \leftarrow nbs$

Algorithm 1 shows the pseudo-code corresponding to the body of the loop that processes the stream of vectors with phonetic probabilities. Each iteration of this loop processes one vector for expanding all hypotheses in LH. The operation for inserting new hypotheses in LH' checks if the hypothesis is going to be pruned in the next iteration. A new hypothesis will be rejected if its score is worse than $(nbs + BEAM)$. As pointed out in [6, 7], word graphs are an efficient way of storing a high number of sentence hypotheses, but they can grow hugely if it is not applied a pruning strategy in the building process. Additionally, we use a histogram based pruning strategy for limiting the number of words between each pair of nodes. This value was adjusted empirically to five words in a trade-off between performance and word accuracy.

4 Experimentation

We used two Spanish speech corpora for measuring the quality of the obtained word graphs: *Albayzin* [10] and DIHANA [11].

Albayzin corpus is divided into two subcorpus, one phonetic and one geographical. We used the phonetic subcorpus: 6,800 uttered sentences obtained by making groups from a set of 700 distinct sentences pronounced by 40 different speakers. We used the suggested training/test subdivision.

DIHANA corpus is also divided into two subcorpus. One subcorpus has 3,594 uttered sentences. We used all these uttered sentences for training. The other subcorpus has 6,277 uttered sentences corresponding to 900 human-machine dialogues regarding information about train timetables, fares, destinations and services. 4,928 uttered sentences were used for training and 1,349 for testing. Working with this corpus is a difficult task due to the spontaneity of the speech.

4.1 Evaluation Results

For evaluation purposes, it was extracted from each word graph the sequence of words corresponding to the path which best matches the reference sentence. The criterion used for evaluating the quality of word graphs consists of measuring the oracle word accuracy O-WA $= 100 \times \frac{Correct}{Correct+Insertions+Substitutions+Deletions}$.

Another parameter of interest in relation with word graphs is the branching factor, i.e. the average number of arcs leaving from nodes.

Table 2. Oracle word accuracy and branching factor estimated for both Spanish corpora *Albayzin* and DIHANA, and word accuracy for DIHANA obtained in [7]

Corpus	Oracle WA	Branching factor	Oracle WA in [7]
Albayzin	98.8%	367	
DIHANA	88.8%	189	86.9%

Table 2 shows the results obtained by evaluating the graphs generated by using our ASR system. Our algorithm has a high rate for detecting words, as the obtained results confirm. We have to point out that DIHANA corpus is composed by spontaneous speech dialogues acquired by telephone. It is considered a very difficult task. As a reference, the O-WA obtained in [7] when working with DIHANA corpus and using a language model for building graphs is also shown in Table 2.

The values of the branching factor may seem too high, specially in the case of *Albayzin* corpus, but it is important to point out that the obtained word graphs have a lot of arcs labelled with the same word. This happens because we allow several alternatives for each detected word, each alternative begins and ends at different nodes. This feature allows to simplify the algorithms to be used for working with these graphs.

5 Conclusions

We have presented an algorithm for building word graphs as an intermediate representation of uttered sentences. The main difference with respect to previous works is that our algorithm does not use a language model, therefore, the strategy for detecting words is quite different. The rules used for deciding whether a word has to be inserted into the graph are also different. Furthermore, words are inserted into the graph just when their phonetic sequence is completed, in a way different from other approaches, that generate the graphs in a backward process once the end of the sentence is reached. Usually, these other algorithms build

the graph from the lattice obtained in the Viterbi decoding process or from the
n-best recognized sentences.

The obtained oracle word accuracy shows that our algorithm has a high capacity for detecting words, but there are some aspects we have to improve in order to obtain less dense graphs.

Acknowledgments. This work was supported by the Spanish MICINN under contract TIN2011-28169-C05-01 and the Vic. d'Investigació of the UPV under contract 20110897.

References

1. Ortmanns, S., Ney, H., Aubert, X.: A word graph algorithm for large vocabulary continuous speech recognition. Computer Speech and Language 11, 43–72 (1997)
2. Ney, H., Ortmanns, S., Lindam, I.: Extensions to the word graph method for large vocabulary continuous speech recognition. In: Proceedings of IEEE ICASSP 1997, Munich, Germany, vol. 3, pp. 1791–1794 (1997)
3. Wessel, F., Schlüter, R., Macherey, K., Ney, H.: Confidence Measures for Large Vocabulary Continuous Speech Recognition. IEEE Transactions on Speech and Audio Processing 9(3), 288–298 (2001)
4. Ferreiros, J., San-Segundo, R., Fernández, F., D'Haro, L.-F., Sama, V., Barra, R., Mellén, P.: New word-level and sentence-level confidence scoring using graph theory calculus and its evaluation on speech understanding. In: Proceedings of INTERSPEECH 2005, Lisbon, Portugal, pp. 3377–3380 (2005)
5. Raymond, C., Béchet, F., De Mori, R., Damnati, G.: On the use of finite state transducers for semantic interpretation. Speech Communication 48, 288–304 (2006)
6. Hakkani-Tür, D., Béchet, F., Riccardi, G., Tur, G.: Beyond ASR 1-best: Using word confusion networks in spoken language understanding. Computer Speech and Language 20, 495–514 (2006)
7. Justo, R., Pérez, A., Torres, M.I.: Impact of the Approaches Involved on Word-Graph Derivation from the ASR System. In: Vitrià, J., Sanches, J.M., Hernández, M. (eds.) IbPRIA 2011. LNCS, vol. 6669, pp. 668–675. Springer, Heidelberg (2011)
8. Gómez, J.A., Calvo, M.: Improvements on Automatic Speech Segmentation at the Phonetic Level. In: San Martin, C., Kim, S.-W. (eds.) CIARP 2011. LNCS, vol. 7042, pp. 557–564. Springer, Heidelberg (2011)
9. Calvo, M., Gómez, J.A., Sanchis, E., Hurtado, L.F.: An algorithm for automatic speech understanding over word graphs. Procesamiento del Lenguaje Natural (48) (accepted, pending of publication, 2012)
10. Moreno, A., Poch, D., Bonafonte, A., Lleida, E., Llisterri, J., Mariño, J.B., Nadeu, C.: Albayzin Speech Database: Design of the Phonetic Corpus. In: Proceedings of Eurospeech, Berlin, Germany, vol. 1, pp. 653–656 (September 1993)
11. Benedí, J.M., Lleida, E., Varona, A., Castro, M., Galiano, I., Justo, R., López, I., Miguel, A.: Design and acquisition of a telephone spontaneous speech dialogue corpus in Spanish: DIHANA. In: Proc. of LREC 2006, Genova, Italy (2006)

Image Classification Using Frequent Approximate Subgraphs

Niusvel Acosta-Mendoza, Annette Morales-González, Andrés Gago-Alonso,
Edel B. García-Reyes, and José E. Medina-Pagola

Advanced Technologies Application Center (CENATAV), Havana, Cuba
{nacosta,amorales,agago,jmedina,egarcia}@cenatav.co.cu

Abstract. Frequent approximate subgraph (FAS) mining is used in applications where it is important to take into account some tolerance under slight distortions in the data. Following this consideration, some FAS miners have been developed and applied in several domains of science. However, there are few works related to the application of these types of graph miners in classification tasks. In this paper, we propose a new framework for image classification, which uses FAS patterns as features. We also propose to compute automatically the substitution matrices needed in the process, instead of using expert knowledge. Our approach is tested in two real image collections showing that it obtains good results, comparable to other non-miner solutions reported, and that FAS mining is better than the exact approach for this task.

Keywords: Approximate graph mining, frequent approximate subgraphs, graph-based image representation, image classification.

1 Introduction

Data in multiple domains can be naturally modeled as graphs [11] since graphs are general and powerful data structures that can be used to represent diverse types of objects. Several authors have developed graph-based techniques and methods for satisfying the need of converting large volumes of data into useful information [6]. The frequent approximate subgraph (FAS) discovery is an example of such techniques [1,4,5]. These techniques have become important topics in mining tasks where the mined patterns are detected taking into account distortions in the data.

The aforementioned techniques have been successfully used in several domains of the science. An important area of intelligent data analysis is the development of classifiers using FAS as features. However, from the reported FAS miners, only *APGM* [5] and *VEAM* [1] use FASs as features in classification tasks. APGM is used in both synthetic data set and real data set of protein structure pattern identification and structure classification, while VEAM is used in several synthetic data sets for image classification.

In this work we propose a framework using FAS mining methods for image classification. APGM and VEAM are used to detect the FASs in a graph collection, where the approximation consists in considering some variations of the

L. Alvarez et al. (Eds.): CIARP 2012, LNCS 7441, pp. 292–299, 2012.

data through the substitution probability, preserving the topology of graphs. In this paper, we propose a graph-based image representation and a classification framework using FASs as features on a real image collection. We also propose to compute automatically the substitution matrices employed by FAS miners, in contrast to other approaches [1,5] where such task is usually left in hands of human experts. Several graph miners are used to evaluate our proposed framework.

Very few approaches have been reported relating image classification with graph mining techniques. Among them, we find [7,15], where they use frequent subgraph mining to build a vocabulary, following the bag-of words approach [10]. The differences with our proposal lies in the graph-based image representation and in the use of an exact subgraph mining algorithm. We advocate the idea that using FAS is a better choice to model slight image variations.

The basic outline of this paper is as follows. Section 2 provides some basic concepts and the approximate pattern definitions used. The graph-based image representation is presented in Section 3. The framework for image classification is explained in Section 4 and the experimental results in a real image collection are discussed in Section 5. Finally, conclusions of the research and some ideas about future directions are exposed in Section 6.

2 Background

In this section, we start by providing the background knowledge and notation used in the following sections. Next, the definition of approximate patterns, which is the subject of this paper, is showed. Finally, the frequent approximate subgraph mining problem is formalized.

2.1 Basic Concepts

This work is focused on simple undirected labeled graphs; henceforth, when we refer to graph we assume this type of graph. Before presenting their formal definition, we will define the domain of labels.

Let L_V and L_E be label sets, where L_V is a set of vertex labels and L_E is a set of edge labels. The domain of all possible labels is denoted by $L = L_V \cup L_E$.

A *labeled graph* in L is a 4-tuple, $G = (V, E, I, J)$, where V is a set whose elements are called *vertices*, $E \subseteq \{\{u, v\} \mid u, v \in V, u \neq v\}$ is a set whose elements are called *edges* (the edge $\{u, v\}$ connecting the vertex u with the vertex v), $I : V \to L_V$ is a *labeling function* for assigning labels to vertices and $J : E \to L_E$ is a *labeling function* for assigning labels to edges.

Let $G_1 = (V_1, E_1, I_1, J_1)$ and $G_2 = (V_2, E_2, I_2, J_2)$ be two graphs, we say that G_1 is a *subgraph* of G_2 if $V_1 \subseteq V_2$, $E_1 \subseteq E_2$, $\forall u \in V_1, I_1(u) = I_2(u)$, and $\forall e \in E_1, J_1(e) = J_2(e)$. In this case, we use the notation $G_1 \subseteq G_2$.

Given G_1 and G_2, we say that f is an *isomorphism* between these graphs if $f : V_1 \to V_2$ is a bijective function, where $\forall u \in V_1, f(u) \in V_2 \wedge I_1(u) = I_2(f(u))$ and $\forall \{u, v\} \in E_1, \{f(u), f(v)\} \in E_2 \wedge J_1(\{u, v\}) = J_2(\{f(u), f(v)\})$. When there is an isomorphism between G_1 and G_2, we say that G_1 and G_2 are *isomorphic*.

Let Ω be the set of all possible labeled graphs in L, the *similarity* between two elements $G_1, G_2 \in \Omega$ is defined as a function $sim : \Omega \times \Omega \to [0, 1]$. We say that the elements are very different if $sim(G_1, G_2) = 0$, the higher the value of $sim(G_1, G_2)$ the more similar the elements are and if $sim(G_1, G_2) = 1$ then there is an isomorphism between these elements.

Let $D = \{G_1, \ldots, G_{|D|}\}$ be a graph collection and let G be a labeled graph in L, the *support* value of G in D is obtained through the following equation:

$$supp(G, D) = \sum_{G_i \in D} sim(G, G_i)/|D| \tag{1}$$

If $supp(G, D) \geq \delta$, then the graph G is approximately frequent in the collection D, saying that G is a *FAS* in D. Notice that when we refer to a graph collection we assume that it is the representation built from a real graph collection. The value of the support threshold δ is in $[0, 1]$ assuming that the similarity is normalized to 1. *FAS mining* consists in finding all the FASs in a collection of graphs D, using a similarity function sim and a support threshold δ.

2.2   Approximate FAS Methods Considered

In APGM [5] and VEAM [1] algorithms, the idea that not always a vertex label or an edge label can be replaced by any other is upheld. Therefore, these algorithms specify which vertices, edges or labels can replace others using substitution matrices to perform the frequent subgraph mining. APGM only deals with the variations among vertex labels, while VEAM performs the mining process using the vertex and edge label sets. These methods use the substitution matrix that can have a probabilistic interpretation and they offer frameworks for each frequent subgraph mining task.

A *substitution matrix* $M = (m_{i,j})$ is an $|L| \times |L|$ matrix indexed by a label set L. An entry $m_{i,j}$ ($0 \leq m_{i,j} \leq 1, \sum_j m_{i,j} = 1$) in M is the probability that the label i is replaced by the label j. When M is diagonally dominant (i.e. $M_{i,i} > M_{i,j}, \forall j \neq i$) then M is known as *stable matrix*.

Let $G_1 = (V_1, E_1, I_1, J_1)$ and $G_2 = (V_2, E_2, I_2, J_2)$ be two labeled graphs in L, MV be a substitution matrix indexed by L_V, ME be a substitution matrix indexed by L_E, and τ be the isomorphism threshold. We say that G_1 is *approximate isomorphic* to G_2, denoted by $G_1 =_A G_2$, if there exists a bijection $f : V_1 \to V_2$ such that:

- $\forall \{u, v\} \in E_1, \{f(u), f(v)\} \in E_2,$
- $S_f(G_1, G_2) = \prod_{u \in V_1} \frac{MV_{I_1(u), I_2(f(u))}}{MV_{I_1(u), I_1(u)}} * \prod_{e = \{u, v\} \in E_1} \frac{ME_{J_1(e), J_2(\{f(u), f(v)\})}}{ME_{J_1(e), J_1(e)}} \geq \tau.$

The bijection f is an approximate isomorphism between G_1 and G_2, and $S_f(G_1, G_2)$ is the product of normalized probabilities called *approximate isomorphism score* of f. When G_1 is approximate isomorphic to a subgraph of G_2, we say that G_1 is *approximate sub-isomorphic* to G_2. Notice that this is a generalization of the APGM approach [5].

The *approximate matching score* between two graphs, denoted by $S_{max}(G_1, G_2)$, is the largest approximate isomorphism score.

$$S_{max}(G_1, G_2) = max_f\{S_f(G_1, G_2)\} \qquad (2)$$

Given a graph collection D and an isomorphism threshold τ, the *approximate support* of a graph G, denoted by $supp(G, D)$, is the average score of the graph in the collection, where G is approximate isomorphic to a subgraph of graphs in the collection:

$$supp(G, D) = \sum_{G_i \in D} S_{max}(G, G_i)/|D| \qquad (3)$$

If $supp(G, D) \geq \delta$, then the graph G is approximately frequent in the collection D, saying that G is a *frequent approximate subgraph* in D, with δ as support threshold. Notice that the values of the products of normalized probabilities $S_f(G_1, G_2)$ is in the interval $(0, 1]$. The value of the support threshold δ is in $[0, 1]$ assuming that $S_{max}(G, G_i)$ is normalized. The *frequent subgraph mining* task used in this paper consists in finding all the connected frequent subgraphs in a collection of graphs D, using (3), δ as support threshold, and τ as isomorphism threshold.

3 Graph-Based Image Representation

In order to use graph mining techniques for image classification, it is necessary to obtain a graph-based image representation. For this purpose, we used the approach presented in [11,12]. We construct an irregular pyramid for each image [2], which provides a hierarchy of partitions at different levels of resolution. Each level is a region adjacency graph (RAG) where each region of the partition is a vertex in this graph, and an edge exists between two vertices, if the underlying regions are adjacent. The pyramid is built from bottom to top, being the base level (level 0) the whole image (i.e. each vertex of the base level represents one pixel in the image, and the edges are the 4-connections of each pixel). Each level l is constructed from its previous level $l - 1$, by means of contraction kernels, which are sets of vertices in level $l - 1$ that are selected to be contracted into a surviving vertex. In the new level l, each surviving vertex will represent all the vertices from level $l - 1$ in its contraction kernel, and will keep a connection to them. Further information regarding the construction of the pyramid can be obtained in [2,8].

Once we have the pyramid for an image, its vertices and edges are labeled using the image regions and graph information at each level. The vertices, which represent regions, will contain a color histogram which will be computed using 16 bins per channels in the RGB color model, yielding a 48 bin histogram. Also, local binary patterns (LBP) [14] will represent the texture information of the region, distributed into a 256 bin histogram. The edges will store the spatial descriptor (binary vector) proposed in [11], representing several topological and orientation relationships between pairs of regions. This graph labeling corresponds to the one used in [11,12].

Each image is represented by a single graph, therefore, in order to select which level of he pyramid should be selected, we used the B measure proposed in [12]. This measure evaluates each level of the pyramid against a border map of the image, in terms of how much each partition preserves the borders present in the map. The best level evaluated by B is selected to represent the image.

3.1   Automatically Building Substitution Matrices

In order to compute the substitution matrix for the vertices, it is necessary to reduced the set of vertices labels. According to the pyramid representation explained before, there will be as much labels as possible pairs of different color and texture histograms. To reduce the set of vertices labels, we use a clustering algorithm to group similar features. The centroid of each cluster will be the new label of all the vertices with features belonging to this cluster. Then, the substitution matrix will be a $n \times n$ matrix, where n is the number of labels (clusters). Each element of this matrix will store the similarity between two labels, given by the similarity between the centroids of the clusters they belong to. In this case, we decided to use the Euclidean distance between the concatenation of the color and LBP histogram for each node. This means that an element of this matrix can be interpreted as the confidence to substitute a node with label x with a node with label y in a matching scheme.

The substitution matrix for edges is easier to construct, since using the spatial descriptor representation we can have only 27 possible configurations of spatial relations. The value that will be stored in the elements of the matrix is obtained by the Sokal-Michener measure proposed in [11] for computing the similarity between spatial descriptors.

4   Classification Framework

Given a set of pre-labeled real images, we obtain the graph collection that represents these images by producing the graph-based image representations presented in Section 3. After that, the FAS miners are used to obtain all the FASs of the mentioned graph collection. The FASs extracted from the graph collection are considered an analogy to the vocabulary obtained in the bag-of-features approach, converting our proposal in a sort of bag-of-subgraphs approach. Having this vocabulary composed of subgraphs, the feature vectors of the original images are built using those FASs as features. The dimension of the new feature will be the number of FASs found in the collection. In our framework, as well as proposed by [1], the feature vectors are built taking into account the approximation values in each image of the collection. That means that for every subgraph in the vocabulary, if it is present in an image, then its corresponding value in the new feature is the highest similarity value of its occurrence in the image.

When all the new features are built, a classifier generator (SVM using 10 cross-validation) is used having such vectors as data to produce an image classifier. The complete flowchart of our classification framework is shown in Fig. 1.

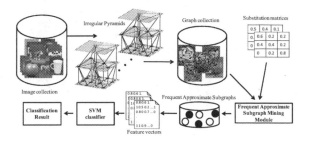

Fig. 1. Framework of graph-based image classification

5 Experimental Results

We chose two well known databases to test our approach: the COIL-100 [13] and the ETH-80 [9] image sets. Both databases contain images of simple objects taken from different viewpoints. We represented all images by a single graph, which corresponds to the "best" segmented level of each pyramid (See Section 3). The COIL-100 image set is a database of color images of 100 objects having 72 poses per object. In Figure 2 some examples are shown. We took 25 objects randomly selected from this dataset to test our classification framework. The ETH-80 Image Set database contains 80 objects from 8 categories. Each object is represented by 41 different views yielding a total of 3280 images (See Figure 2). This database is more challenging than the COIL-100 database in the sense of the viewpoint diversity. For the experiment in this database we took the same 6 categories employed by [11]: *apples, cars, cows, cups, horses* and *tomatoes*.

Fig. 2. Example images from the COIL-100 Image Set database (first 6 images), and from the ETH-80 Image Set database (last 6 images)

The results of the experiment are presented in Table 1. In this table we can see the comparison of our framework using three different graph miners, i.e, gdFil [3], APGM and VEAM. The first one represents the exact methods and the last two are FAS miners. Columns show different support thresholds (δ) used in the experiments. For the case of APGM and VEAM, the isomorphism threshold was set to $\tau = 0.4$. The first thing to notice is that the approximate graph miners achieve a higher accuracy in most cases than the exact ones, showing the relevance of allowing slight differences in real data. Regarding the approximate methods, for the case of the COIL-100 database, we can see that the VEAM obtained better accuracies than APGM, which indicates that the use of the edge distortion in the FAS mining can provide additional cues for classification. In the ETH-80 dataset, the edge distortions did not provided any relevant information though.

Table 1. Accuracies achieved by gdFil, APGM and VEAM algorithms

a) COIL database using 25 random classes.

Algorithm	70%	60%	50%	40%	30%	20%	10%
				Support (δ)			
gdFil	-	-	-	-	23.06%	60.39%	**85.89%**
APGM	**21.94%**	**57.11%**	90.28%	91.39%	90.94%	87.83%	84.33%
VEAM	**21.94%**	**57.11%**	**91.35%**	**92.18%**	**91.52%**	**89.24%**	84.69%

b) ETH-80 database using 6 classes.

Algorithm	70%	60%	50%	40%	30%	20%	10%
				Support (δ)			
gdFil	-	-	-	-	28.70%	47.80%	76.63%
APGM	**26.75%**	**31.67%**	**51.91%**	**82.03%**	**82.03%**	**82.03%**	**81.38%**
VEAM	**26.75%**	**31.67%**	**51.91%**	**82.03%**	**82.03%**	81.83%	76.54%

We compared our proposal with other classification methods that do not use FAS mining techniques. In the COIL-100 dataset, the method proposed by [12] obtained 91.6% while our method scored 92.18%. For the case of ETH-80 dataset, our method obtained 82.03%, which is comparable to other state-of-the-art methods according to the comparison performed by [12], where the results range from 76% to 88%.

These results show that the proposed framework, which involves using FAS mining and automatically computing the substitution matrices (and not using expert knowledge in this process), is able to provide good outcomes for real image classification.

6   Conclusions

In this paper we proposed a framework for image classification using FASs as features, which are obtained using FAS miners reported in the literature. They are able to detect FAS patterns in graph collections allowing slight semantic differences among graphs. Within our framework, we also propose to use substitution matrices computed automatically based on image features, which proves that not using expert knowledge for this task can also produce good results. The graph-based image representation was extracted from irregular graph pyramids, relabeling the vertices using clustering techniques. Since our approach is an application of FAS mining for real graph-based collections, the classification accuracy results obtained by traditional miners are smaller than the obtained by FAS miners in most cases. Also, the experimental results show that our proposal is comparable with other state-of-the-art methods for image classification.

As future work, we are going to develop new ways for taking advantage of FAS selection strategies for improving graph classification (such as, using discriminative FASs, representative FASs, etc.). These strategies in combination with FAS miners could be useful for reducing dimensionality and improving the efficiency of graph classifiers.

References

1. Acosta-Mendoza, N., Gago-Alonso, A., Medina-Pagola, J.E.: Frequent Approximate Subgraphs as Features for Graph-Based Image Classification. Knowledge-Based Systems 27, 381–392 (2012)
2. Brun, L., Kropatsch, W.: Introduction to combinatorial pyramids. In: Digital and Image Geometry: Advanced Lectures, pp. 108–128 (2001)
3. Gago-Alonso, A., Carrasco-Ochoa, J.A., Medina-Pagola, J.E., Martínez-Trinidad, J.F.: Full Duplicate Candidate Pruning for Frequent Connected Subgraph Mining. Integrated Computer-Aided Engineering 17, 211–225 (2010)
4. Holder, L.B., Cook, D.J., Bunke, H.: Fuzzy Substructure Discovery. In: Proceedings of the Ninth International Workshop on Machine Learning, San Francisco, CA, USA, pp. 218–223 (1992)
5. Jia, Y., Zhang, J., Huan, J.: An efficient graph-mining method for complicated and noisy data with real-world applications. Knowledge Information Systems 28(2), 423–447 (2011)
6. Jiang, C., Coenen, F., Zito, M.: A Survey of Frequent Subgraph Mining Algorithm. To appear in Knowledge Engineering Review (2012)
7. Jiang, C., Coenen, F.: Graph-based image classification by weighting scheme. In: Proceedings of the Artificial Intelligence, pp. 63–76. Springer, Heidelberg (2008)
8. Kropatsch, W., Haxhimusa, Y., Pizlo, Z., Langs, G.: Vision pyramids that do not grow too high. Pattern Recognition Letters 26(3), 319–337 (2005)
9. Leibe, B., Schiele, B.: Analyzing Appearance and Contour Based Methods for Object Categorization. In: IEEE Conference on Computer Vision and Pattern Recognition (CVPR 2003), pp. 409–415 (2003)
10. Li, F.F., Perona, P.: A Bayesian Hierarchical Model for Learning Natural Scene Categories. In: Proceedings of the 2005 IEEE Computer Society Conference on Computer Vision and Pattern Recognition (CVPR 2005), pp. 524–531 (2005)
11. Morales-González, A., García-Reyes, E.: Assessing the Role of Spatial Relations for the Object Recognition Task. In: Bloch, I., Cesar Jr., R.M. (eds.) CIARP 2010. LNCS, vol. 6419, pp. 549–556. Springer, Heidelberg (2010)
12. Morales-González, A., García-Reyes, E.B.: Simple object recognition based on spatial relations and visual features represented using irregular pyramids. In: Multimedia Tools and Applications, pp. 1–23. Springer, Netherlands (2011), http://dx.doi.org/10.1007/s11042-011-0938-3
13. Nene, S., Nayar, S., Murase, H.: Columbia Object Image Library (COIL-100). Technical Report, Department of Computer Science, Columbia University CUCS-006-96 (1996)
14. Ojala, T., Pietikainen, M.: A comparative study of texture measures with classification based on featured distribution. Pattern Recognition 29(1), 51–59 (1996)
15. Ozdemir, B., Aksoy, S.: Image Classification Using Subgraph Histogram Representation. In: Proceedings of the 2010 20th International Conference on Pattern Recognition, pp. 1112–1115 (2010)

Using Rough Sets and Maximum Similarity Graphs for Nearest Prototype Classification

Yenny Villuendas-Rey[1,3], Yailé Caballero-Mota[2], and María Matilde García-Lorenzo[3]

[1] Computer Science Department, University of Ciego de Ávila, Carr. a Morón km 9 ½, Cuba
yennyv@informatica.unica.cu
[2] Computer Science Department, University of Camagüey, Circunv. Norte km 3 ½, Cuba
yaile.caballero@reduc.edu.cu
[3] Computer Science Department, University of Las Villas, Carr. a Camajuaní, km 5 ½, Cuba
mmgarcia@uclv.edu.cu

Abstract. The nearest neighbor rule (NN) is one of the most powerful yet simple non parametric classification techniques. However, it is time consuming and it is very sensitive to noisy as well as outlier objects. To solve these deficiencies several prototype selection methods have been proposed by the scientific community. In this paper, we propose a new editing and condensing method. Our method combines the Rough Set theory and the Compact Sets structuralizations to obtain a reduced prototype set. Numerical experiments over repository databases show the high quality performance of our method according to classifier accuracy.

Keywords: nearest neighbor, prototype selection, editing methods.

1   Introduction

The nearest neighbor (NN) classifier is one of the most popular supervised classification methods in Pattern Recognition. However, it suffers from two important drawbacks: (i) High storage and computational requirements: it storages the entire training set, requiring large space. Moreover, to determine the class of a new object, it needs to compare it with every prototype in the training set, and (ii) Sensitivity: the NN classification rule is quite sensitive to noisy and outlier objects.

To overcome these drawbacks researchers have proposed prototype selection methods. These methods aim to obtain a reduced set of representative objects (prototypes) to be used for classification. In the literature, these techniques are known as prototype selection and prototype generation methods. The former obtain a reduced set composed by objects in the original training set, and the later may create artificial prototypes, not present in the original data [1]. Another challenge with the NN classifiers is handling mixed as well as incomplete data. This kind of data affects most prototype generation methods, by lacking of the properties of vector spaces. Some prototype selection methods based on geometric properties of the data space are also inapplicable, because the objects are defined in a Cartesian space instead of a Metric space. Among prototype selection methods, there is a distinction between error based editing and condensing methods. Error based editing methods are focused on remove noisy as well as outlier objects, and aim at smoothing the class boundaries, improving

L. Alvarez et al. (Eds.): CIARP 2012, LNCS 7441, pp. 300–307, 2012.
© Springer-Verlag Berlin Heidelberg 2012

accuracy. On the contrary, condensing methods aim at reducing redundant objects, and to obtain training set as small as possible. Although they have a different goal, combining both techniques may result into a small training set, with high classifier accuracy. In this paper, we combine the Rough Set Theory and the Compact Set structuralization to achieve this objective, and also to handling mixed and incomplete data sets.

The paper is organized as follows: section two reviews some of the previous work done in prototype selection, section three introduces the proposed method, section four shows the results of the numerical experiments and section five offers some conclusions.

2   Previous Works on Prototype Selection

Since the introduction of Nearest Neighbor classifier, reducing the training set have been an active research area in the Pattern Recognition and Artificial Intelligence field. In this section we only address methods capable of handling mixed as well as incomplete data. The methods to reduce the training set can be divided in editing methods and condensing methods. Condensing methods aim at reducing redundant objects, and to obtain a training set as small as possible. Several condensing methods have been proposed, and among them we can mention the Minimal Consistent Set (MCS) [2], the Generalized Condensed Nearest Neighbor (GCNN) [3], the Prototype Relevance Selection (PRS) [4], the Gray Based Reduction (GBR1, GBR2) [5] and the CSESupport [6]. Recently, several algorithms have been proposed, such as Multiple Instance Learning [7] and Class Boundaries Preserving (CBP) [8].

Opposite to condensing methods, editing methods try to smooth class boundaries, by removing noisy or outlier objects. Usually, editing methods do not reduce a significant amount of objects, but in some cases may improve classifier accuracy. The first method to accomplish this task was the Edited Nearest Neighbor (ENN) by Wilson [9]. It removes every object misclassified by a k-NN classifier, with k value as used defined parameter. Among editing methods are NENN [10], editing based on Rough Sets (EditRS1, EditRS2) [11] and editing based on Maximum Similarity Graphs (MSEditA, MSEditB) [12].

Although editing and condensing methods achieve complementary objectives, the smoothing power of editing methods, and the high reduction rates of condensing algorithms have not been sufficiently exploited by combining both approaches into a single algorithm. The analysis of previous prototype selection methods reveals that improving NN in both accuracy and computational requirements by reducing the training set is still an open problem. Previous methods cannot accurately deal with both objectives, which is the basic motivation of the method introduced in this paper.

3   Editing Based on Rough Sets and Compact Sets

3.1   Rough Sets and Maximum Similarity Graphs

Rough Set Theory (RST) has been an excellent mathematical tool for data analysis and it has offered an interesting theoretic base for the solution of many problems within knowledge discovery. Rough Sets Theory was proposed by Pawlak in 1982 [13]. In RST, a training set can be represented as a Decision System. First, an Information System is a pair S= (U, A), where U is a non-empty finite set of objects called the Universe and A is a non-empty finite set of attributes, and a Decision System is any information system of the form $DS = A \cup \{c\}$, where $c \notin A$ is the decision attribute. Classical definitions of lower and upper approximations were originally introduced with reference to an indiscernible relation which assumed to be an equivalence relation. Let B⊆A and X⊆U. B defines an equivalence relation and X is a concept. X can be approximated using only the information contained in B by constructing the B-lower and B-upper approximations of X, denoted by B^*X and B_*X respectively. The objects in B_*X are sure members of X, while the objects in B^*X are possible members of X. Rough set model has several advantages to data analysis, especially to edit training sets. It is based on the original data only and does not need any external information; no assumptions about data are necessary, and it is suitable for analyzing both quantitative and qualitative features [11].

Maximum Similarity Graph (MSG) are a useful tool for structuralizing data in the Pattern Recognition field [14]. A Maximum Similarity Graph is a directed graph, such as it connects each object with its most similar neighbor. Formally, let be $G = (X, \theta)$ a MSG for a set of objects X, with arcs θ. Two objects $x_i, x_j \in X$ form an arc $(x_i, x_j) \in \theta$ if $\max_{x \in X}\{sim(x_i, x)\} = sim(x_i, x_j)$, where $sim(x_i, x_j)$ is a similarity function, usually $sim(x_i, x_j) = 1 - \Delta(x_i, x_j)$ and $\Delta(x_i, x_j)$ is a dissimilarity function. In case of ties, the maximum similarity graph establishes a connection between the object and each of its nearest neighbors (figure 1).

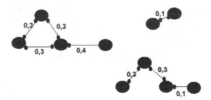

Fig. 1. Maximum similarity graph, using 1- Δ(.,.) as similarity function

Among the advantages of Maximum Similarity Graphs we can mention that they do not need parameters for their construction, except of the similarity function to compare two objects. In addition, the objects form arcs only to their most similar objects in the training matrix, which is valuable information particularly in high Bayes risk zones. The arcs between objects also contribute to predict the certainty of the correct classification of an object [12].

In a Maximum Similarity Graph, each connected component is called a Compact Set. In figure 2 we show the Compact Sets of figure 1. Formally, a subset $N \neq \emptyset$ of X is a compact group if and only if [14]:

$$a) \forall x_j \in X \left[x_i \in N \wedge \left(\begin{array}{c} \max\limits_{\substack{x_i \in X \\ x_i \neq O_j}}\{sim(x_i, x_j)\} = sim(x_i, x_j) \\ \vee \max\limits_{\substack{x_i \in X \\ x_i \neq x_j}}\{sim(x_j, x_i)\} = sim(x_j, x_i) \end{array} \right) \right] \Rightarrow x_j \in N$$

$$b) \forall x_i, x_j \in N, \exists x_{i_1}, \cdots, x_{i_q} \in N \begin{bmatrix} x_i = x_{i_1} \wedge x_j = x_{i_q} \wedge \forall p \{1, \cdots, q-1\} \\ \begin{bmatrix} \max_{\substack{x_t \in X \\ x_t \neq 0_{i_p}}} \left\{ \text{sim}\left(x_{i_p}, x_t\right) \right\} = \text{sim}\left(x_{i_p}, x_{i_{p+1}}\right) \\ \vee \max_{\substack{x_t \in X \\ x_t \neq x_{i_p}}} \left\{ \text{sim}\left(x_{i_{p+1}}, x_t\right) \right\} = \text{sim}\left(x_{i_{p+1}}, x_{i_p}\right) \end{bmatrix} \end{bmatrix}$$

c) Every isolated object is a compact set, degenerated.

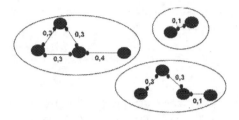

Fig. 2. Compact sets of the objects. Each ellipse corresponds to a compact set.

Compact Sets are formed by highly similar objects, and have been used successfully to edit nearest neighbor classifiers [12].

3.2   Hybridizing Rough Sets and Compact Sets

In order to consider the advantages of both Rough Sets and Compact Sets, we use the definition of Neighborhood Rough Sets introduced by Hu et al. [15]. Given an arbitrary object $x_i \in X$ and a set of attributes $B \subseteq A$, the neighborhood $\partial_B(x_i)$ of x_i in feature space B is defined as the set of objects which dissimilarity values with respect x_i, taking into consideration only the attributes in B, is lower than a threshold ∂.   Formally, $\partial_B(x_i) = \left\{ x_j \mid x_j \in X, \Delta^B(x_i, x_j) \leq \partial \right\}$,   where Δ is   a dissimilarity function. As mention by Hu et al., a neighborhood granule degrades to an equivalent class if the threshold $\partial = 0$. In this case, the objects in the same neighborhood granule are equivalent to each other. Consequently, the neighborhood rough sets are a generalization of Pawlak´s rough sets. In our case, we want to obtain neighborhood granules without fixing the threshold ∂, so we redefine the neighborhood $\partial_B(x_i)$ of x_i in feature space B, as a Minimum Neighborhood Rough Set, taking as the ∂ value the minimum dissimilarity between x_i and every other object in the data.

$$\partial_B(x_i) = \left\{ x_j \mid x_j \in X, \Delta^B(x_i, x_j) = \min_{x_j \in X}(\Delta^B(x_i, x_j)) \right\} \tag{1}$$

Given a Decision System $DS = A \cup \{C\}$, the lower approximation of the decision is defined as the union of the lower approximation of each decision class. The lower approximation of the decision is also called the positive region of the decision. The minimum neighborhood $\partial_B(x_i)$ of x_i in feature space B can be rewritten as:

$$\partial_B(x_i) = \{x_j | (x_i, x_j) \in \theta\} \tag{2}$$

where   are the arcs in a Maximum Similarity Graph, using as similarity function $1 - \Delta^B$. In a Minimum Neighborhood Rough Set, the positive region of a decision class, $POS_B(c)$ is composed by all objects connected in a Maximum Similarity Graph with objects of the same class. The positive region will be formed by objects which are sure members of one of the decision classes, and can be correctly classified by a NN classifier, while boundary region is the set of samples which may be misclassified by a NN classifier. Opposite, the objects in the boundary region are connected to objects from more than one decision class.

$$POS_B(c) = \left\{x_i \middle| x_i \in X, \forall_{(x_i, x_j) \in \theta}, C(x_i) = C(x_j) = c\right\} \tag{3}$$

where $C(x_i)$ denotes the decision class of object x_i.

Our method (Figure 3) first computes the positive region of each decision class. Then, it computes compact sets of the positive region of each decision class, grouping the objects in subclasses according to its similarity (dissimilarity). Then, we condense each compact set to a single object, the representative prototype p. We select as prototype the object that maximizes the similarity with respect to other objects in the compact set CS, that is, the object for which the similarity value is the maximum:

$$p = \underset{o \in CS}{\operatorname{argmax}} \left\{ \sum_{i \in CS} sim(o, i) \right\} \tag{4}$$

Our approach gracefully handles mixed and incomplete data, because it is based on Maximum Similarity Graph computation and Neighborhood Rough Sets, which do not assume any metric or geometric property of data.

Prototype Editing based on Rough sets and Compact sets (PERC)
Inputs: Training set T, Attribute set B, Dissimilarity Δ. Outputs: Prototype set P

1. $P = \emptyset$
 2.   Obtain a Maximum Similarity Graph, $G = (T, \theta)$ of the objects in T
 3.   For each decision class c:
      3.1. Compute $POS_B(c) = \{x_i | x_i \in T, \forall \theta(x_i, x_j), C(x_i) = C(x_j) = c\}$
      3.2. Compute compact sets CS_c of $POS_B(c)$
          For each $cs \in CS_c$
          3.2.1. Select a representative prototype p using equation 4, $P = P \cup \{p\}$
 4.   Return P

Fig. 3. The PERC algorithm for prototype selection

Summarizing, our algorithm to edit and condense the training matrix obtains the positive region of each decision class, then computes compacts set of each positive region and returns as the edited set the set of selected representative prototypes, one of each compact set. Our approach takes advantages of the discriminative power of Rough Sets, as well as the structuralization abilities of Compact Sets. The PERC algorithm smoothes the class boundaries by taking into consideration only the positive region of the decision, and obtains a highly condensed set, by taking representatives of the compact set structuralization of the positive region of each class. Our proposal also handles mixed and incomplete data sets.

4   Experimental Analysis

In order to compare the performance of the propose algorithm, we carried out some numerical experiments in a wide range of databases with both numerical and categorical attributes from the Machine Learning repository of the University of California at Irvine [16]. The description of used databases is given in table 1. We perform 10-fold cross validation and average the results in both classifier accuracy and object reduction rates. We use in our experiments as dissimilarity functions the HEOM and HVDM proposed by Wilson and Martínez [17].

We compare our method against 12 classical and state of the art editing and condensing prototype selection methods. We use the Wilcoxon test to establish the statistical significance of the differences in performance of the studied methods. We set as null hypothesis no difference in performance between each pair of methods, and set a significant value of 0.05, for a 95% of confidence. In table 2, we summarize the results of the Wilcoxon test, using both HEOM and HVDM dissimilarities, according to classifier error and object retention rates.

Table 1. Description of the databases used in numerical experiments

Databases	Attributes (Categorical -Numerical)	Obj.	Missing values	Databases	Attributes (Categorical -Numerical)	Obj.	Missing values
autos	10-16	205	x	heart-h	7-6	294	x
balance	0-4	625		hepatitis	13-6	155	x
breast-c	9-0	286	x	iris	0-4	150	
breast-w	0-9	299		labor	6-8	57	
colic	15-7	368	x	lymph	15-3	148	
credit-a	9-6	690	x	sonar	0-60	208	
dermat.	1-33	366	x	vote	16-0	435	x
glass	0-10	214		wine	13-0	178	
heart-c	7-6	303	x	zoo	16-1	101	

Each cell of the table 2 is formed by a pair (x,y), which x represents the significance value of the Wilcoxon test comparing our method with respect to other algorithm using the HEOM dissimilarity and y, using the HVDM dissimilarity. In bold are represented the values when our method outperforms the other method. The PRS method deletes all objects with the HVDM dissimilarity, being excluded of the statistical comparison (a - sign).

Table 2. Results of the Wicoxon test comparing our method aginst others

Condensing methods	Error	Object reduction	Editing methods	Error	Object reduction
MCS	0.809,0.12	**0.007,0.003**	ENN	0.126,0.289	**0,0**
GCNN	0.171,0.122	**0,0**	NENN	0.687,0.077	**0,0**
GBR1	0.084,0.455	**0.001,0.003**	EditRS1	0.147,0.230	**0,0**
GBR2	**0.049,0.001**	**0.024,0.005**	EditRS2	0.147,0.230	**0,0**
PRS	**0.033,0.001**	**0,-**	MSEditA	0.036*,0.305	**0,0**
CSESupport	0.629,0.099	**0.009,0.004**	MSEditB	0.059,0.050	**0,0**

* our method had worse performance

The results obtained of the experimental comparison show that our proposal obtains similar results with both dissimilarity functions. It obtains the best results according to object reduction, being significantly better than every other method. According to classifier error, the PERC method achieves very good results. It outperforms the GBR1 and GBR2 methods using both dissimilarities, and the PRS method with the HEOM dissimilarity, and ties with all other methods. Our prototype selection schema losses with respect to the MSEditA using the HEOM dissimilarity, but ties this method with the HVDM function. It is important to point out that our method maintains the classifier accuracy using only a very reduced prototype set. The above results show that combining Rough Sets and Compact Sets leads to an edited set with high accuracy and also with much less objects than the original training set.

5   Conclusions

Prototype selection for improving the classifiers accuracy is a very important task in supervised classification problems with the NN classifier. In this paper a novel method is introduced, resulting from hybridizing Rough Sets with Maximum Similarity Graphs. Our method smooth decision boundaries, by using positive decision regions, and condenses the training data by selecting representative objects from compact sets structuralizations. The method is also able deal with databases containing objects described by features no exclusively numeric or categorical. Experimental results carried out over several repository data show the high performance of the proposed method.

References

1. Triguero, I., Derrac, J., García, S., Herrera, F.: A taxonomy and Experimental Study on prototype generation for Nearest Neighbor classification. IEEE Transactions on Systems, Man, and Cybernetics (2012), doi:10.1109/TSMCC.2010.2103939
2. Dasarathy, B.D.: Minimal consistent set (MCS) identification for optimal nearest neighbor decision systems design. IEEE Transactions on Systems, Man and Cybernetics 24, 511–517 (1994)

3. Chou, C.H., Kuo, B.A., Cheng, F.: The Generalized Condensed Nearest Neighbor rule as a data reduction technique. In: 18th International Conference on Pattern Recognition, pp. 556–559 (2006)

4. Olvera-López, J.A., Carrasco-Ochoa, J.A., Martínez-Trinidad, J.F.: Prototype Selection Via Prototype Relevance. In: Ruiz-Shulcloper, J., Kropatsch, W.G. (eds.) CIARP 2008. LNCS, vol. 5197, pp. 153–160. Springer, Heidelberg (2008)

5. Huang, C.-C.: A novel gray-based reduced NN classification method. Pattern Recognition 39, 1979–1986 (2006)

6. García-Borroto, M., Villuendas-Rey, Y., Carrasco-Ochoa, J.A., Martínez-Trinidad, J.F.: Finding Small Consistent Subset for the Nearest Neighbor Classifier Based on Support Graphs. In: Bayro-Corrochano, E., Eklundh, J.-O. (eds.) CIARP 2009. LNCS, vol. 5856, pp. 465–472. Springer, Heidelberg (2009)

7. Zafra, A., Gibaja, E.L., Ventura, S.: Multiple instance learning with multiple objective genetic programming for web mining. Applied Soft Computing 11, 93–102 (2011)

8. Nikolaidis, K., Goulemas, J.Y., Wu, Q.H.: A class boundary preserving algorithm for data condensation. Pattern Recognition 44, 704–715 (2011)

9. Wilson, D.L.: Asymptotic properties of nearest neighbor rules using edited data. IEEE Transactions on Systems, Man and Cybernetics SMC-2, 408–421 (1972)

10. Hattori, K., Takanashi, M.: A new edited k-nearest neighbor rule in the pattern classification problem. Pattern Recognition 33, 521–528 (2000)

11. Caballero, Y., Bello, R., Salgado, Y., García, M.M.: A method to edit training set based on rough sets. International Journal of Computational Intelligence Research 3, 219–229 (2007)

12. García-Borroto, M., Villuendas-Rey, Y., Carrasco-Ochoa, J.A., Martínez-Trinidad, J.F.: Using Maximum Similarity Graphs to Edit Nearest Neighbor Classifiers. In: Bayro-Corrochano, E., Eklundh, J.-O. (eds.) CIARP 2009. LNCS, vol. 5856, pp. 489–496. Springer, Heidelberg (2009)

13. Pawlak, Z.: Rough Sets. International Journal of Information & Computer Sciences 11, 341–356 (1982)

14. Ruiz-Shulcloper, J., Abidi, M.A.: Logical combinatorial pattern recognition: A Review. In: Pandalai, S.G. (ed.) Recent Research Developments in Pattern Recognition. Transword Research Networks, USA, pp. 133–176 (2002)

15. Hu, Q., Yu, D., Liu, J., Wu, C.: Neighborhood rough sets based heterogeneous feature selection. Information Sciences 178, 3577–3594 (2008)

16. Merz, C.J., Murphy, P.M.: UCI Repository of Machine Learning Databases. University of California at Irvine, Department of Information and Computer Science, Irvine (1998)

17. Wilson, R.D., Martinez, T.R.: Improved Heterogeneous Distance Functions. Journal of Artificial Intelligence Research 6, 1–34 (1997)

Hierarchical Elastic Graph Matching
for Hand Gesture Recognition

Yu-Ting Li and Juan P. Wachs[*]

Department of Industrial Engineering, Purdue University, West Lafayette IN, U.S.A
{yutingli,jpwachs}@purdue.edu

Abstract. This paper proposes a hierarchical scheme for elastic graph matching hand posture recognition. The hierarchy is expressed in terms of weights assigned to visual features scattered over an elastic graph. The weights in graph's nodes are adapted according to their relative ability to enhance the recognition, and determined using adaptive boosting. A dictionary representing the variability of each gesture class is proposed, in the form of a collection of graphs (a bunch graph). Positions of nodes in the bunch graph are created using three techniques: manually, semi-automatic, and automatically. The recognition results show that the hierarchical weighting on features has significant discriminative power compared to the classic method (uniform weighting). Experimental results also show that the semi-automatically annotation method provides efficient and accurate performance in terms of two performance measures; cost function and accuracy.

Keywords: Elastic bunch graph, Graph matching, Feature hierarchy, Hand gesture recognition.

1   Introduction

With the growing development of smaller, cheaper and versatile sensors, human-computer interaction (HCI) relies more on natural communication, as among humans, and less in standard interfaces such as the mice or keyboard [1,2]. This is reflected by the users' subjective satisfaction, the extent of the expressiveness and the overall experience perceived by the users of such systems [3]. Gestures are found extensively as the main channel used to interact with computers in sign language interpretation [2], assistive technologies [4], and game control applications [5]. Recently gestures were adopted in new areas where sterility is essential to the task completion (e.g. browsing medical images in the operating room) [6]. Nevertheless, to make gesture recognition technologies to gain popularity in the HCI common market, high recognition accuracy with low false alarms must be achieved through new pattern recognition techniques.

Elastic graph matching (EGM) is a technique used for object recognition [7], where an object is represented by a labeled graph. The graph is matched against the target image by computing filter responses at each node in the graph, and minimizing

---

[*] Corresponding author.

L. Alvarez et al. (Eds.): CIARP 2012, LNCS 7441, pp. 308–315, 2012.

a cost function based on some metric applied to the nodes in a template image and a target image. This method was used previously for face and gesture recognition on clutter and complex backgrounds. Elastic Bunch Graph Matching (EBGM) is proposed to recognize the facial images where features were extracted at fiducial points (e.g. the pupils, the nose, and the corners of the mouth) [7]. Triesch et al. employed EBGM to develop a classification approach of hand gestures against complex background [8]. Our improvement with respect to the classic method developed by Triesch et al, consists of assigning an hierarchy to each node in the graph. Those nodes which features are found with higher likelihood on the target image receive a higher hierarchy compared to those nodes which their features are not consistent with the graph model. In other words, nodes with low hierarchy have a reduced effect on the accuracy of the recognition, and thus the matching process can be skipped for them, saving valuable computation time and increasing the accuracy of recognition. Enhancement on the recognition rate is achieved by weighting the linear combination of features in order to assign greater discriminative power to those nodes with higher hierarchies. To summarize, the contribution of this paper are to introduce (1) a hierarchical scheme for elastic graph matching to enhance the hand gesture recognition performance. (2) a study on efficient annotation techniques to create the bunch graph.

The rest of the paper is organized as follows: in Section 2 the EBGM and Adaptive Boosting algorithm are described. Section 3 derives the proposed annotation methods and the hierarchical hand gesture recognition algorithm. Experimental results in Section 4 demonstrate the feasibility and efficiency of the proposed techniques. Finally the discussion and conclusions are presented in Section 5.

2   Fundamentals of Proposed Algorithms

2.1   Elastic Bunch Graph

Bunch graphs are used to represent and recognize hand posture [8,9]. Each bunch graph is a collection of individual graphs representing a posture. Each node is associated with a vector of complex responses (called jet). The jets are obtained by convolving a set of images (the dictionary set) with a bank of Gabor filters and extracting the responses on specific locations on the images (labeled nodes). The vector of complex responses at a given pixel $\vec{x}$ follows the form:

$$\psi_k(x) = \frac{\vec{k}^2}{\sigma^2} \exp\left(-\frac{\vec{k}^2 \vec{x}^2}{2\sigma^2}\right) \left[\exp\left(i\vec{k}\vec{x}\right) - \exp\left(-\frac{\sigma^2}{2}\right)\right] \tag{1}$$

where $\psi_k(x)$ is the Gabor-based kernels where the wave vector $\vec{k}$ describes the variation of spatial frequencies and orientations, which are represented by the index $v \in [0, \dots, L-1]$ and $\mu \in [0, \dots, D-1]$. The different values of $\vec{k}$ are found using:

$$k_{v\mu} = k_v \begin{pmatrix} cos\phi_\mu \\ sin\phi_\mu \end{pmatrix} \text{ with } k_v = \frac{k_{max}}{f^v}, \phi_\mu = \frac{\mu\pi}{D} \tag{2}$$

where L is the number of frequency levels and D is the number of orientations. These values were chosen according to what was suggested in previous work [8] and since this choice yielded the best performance: f is chosen to be $1/\sqrt{2}$, and $k_{max} = 1.7$. The width of the Gaussian envelope function is σ/k with $\sigma = 2.5$. The jet is a complex vector consisting of $L \times D$ filter responses and it is defined as $J_j = a_j \exp(i\phi_j)$. Once the node positions are annotated on the dictionary images, the bunch graph is created by extracting the responses of the filters on those positions (the nodes). The similarity between the bunch graph and target image is used to measure to likelihood of classification of a given image as a gesture. The similarity function in Eq. (3) uses the magnitude and phase of the jet to find a matching score between the bunch graph and the images.

$$S_{pha}(J,J') = \frac{1}{2}(1 + \frac{\sum_j a_j a_j' \cos(\phi_j - \phi_j')}{\sqrt{\sum_j a_j^2 \sum_j a_j'^2}})$$ (3)

where a_j' and ϕ_j' is obtained from $J_j' = a_j' \exp(i\phi_j')$, the jet from the target image. The phase based similarity in (3) varies rapidly between continuous pixels, resulting in multiple local maxima; thus it is advantageous to have a good initial estimate about the position of the hand within the target image. During the matching process, the best fitting jet is selected according to the maximum similarity score among the bunch. When all the nodes in each bunch are visited and compared, the total score of the matching is given by a linear combination of the scores between the nodes in the bunch graph and the target image. Additionally, total score of the matching considers the distortion of the nodes by introducing the penalty cost to prevent excessive distortion of the graph. Correspondence between the nodes is established automatically according to their relative position on graph. The classification is determined by the maximum score over all the detectors.

2.2   Adaptive Boosting

Boosting [10,11,12], is a general machine learning technique used to design and train classifiers by combining a series of weak classifiers to create a strong classifier. This technique was adopted in our posture recognition algorithm to reflect the hierarchy of nodes in the bunch graphs. In boosting technique, a family of weak classifiers forms an additive model:

$$F(v) = \sum_{m=1}^{M} f(v)$$ (4)

where $f(v)$ denotes a weak detector, v is a feature vector , and M is the number of iterations (or number of weak detectors) to form a strong classifier, $F(v)$. When training the samples, a set of weights is applied to the training samples and they are updated in each iteration. The updates increase the weight of the samples which are misclassified at the current iteration, and decrease the weights of those which were classified correctly. The weights $\omega_i = e^{-z_i F(v_i)}$ for each training sample i with class label z_i, are defined so the cost of misclassification is minimized by adding a new optimal weak classifier:

$$\operatorname{argmin}_{f_m} \sum_{i=1}^{N} \omega_i \big(z_i - f_m(v_i)\big)^2 \tag{5}$$

Upon choosing the weak classifier and added to $F(v_i)$, the estimates are updated: $F(v_i) = F(v_i) + f_m(v_i)$. Accordingly, the weights over the samples are updated by:

$$\omega_i = \omega_i e^{-z_i f_m(v_i)} \tag{6}$$

In this paper, the gentleboost cost function [10] is used to minimize the error (Eq. 5).

3   Hand Gesture Recognition Methodology

3.1   Node Annotation Techniques

To create the bunch graph described earlier, posture images have to be annotated (their inner nodes and those over the contour (outer) selected). We compare three methods to accomplish this: the manual, semi-automatic and automatic. A single bunch graph consists of six graphs for each posture. To compare the effectiveness of the proposed annotation methods, two metrics are computed and evaluated: (1) Costs entailed to align the nodes. Nodes need to be aligned with respect to their peers within the bunch graph. Relative displacements of the nodes with respect to each other in the different graphs result in an alignment 'cost'.(2) Recognition accuracy given a bunch graph annotated using different approaches.

The difference among these three techniques is the manner on which the nodes are selected within the hand region. For the semi-automatic and automatic methods, first select a graph among six to be the reference (randomly selected). The silhouette of all the six graphs is annotated manually. Once the outer nodes were identified, the interesting points within the hand region are those highly textured regions within the hand, found using a Harris corner detector. For the five remaining graphs, each graph is aligned with respect to the reference graph. The nodes inside the hand region are selected from a larger set of candidates in the following way: apply a linear assignment problem (the formulation is provided in Eq. (7)) to find the points in the current graph that better correspond (with least displacement) to those points in the reference graph.

$$\min_{z_i} \big(\sum_{i=1}^{N_1 \times N_2} z_i d_i\big) \tag{7}$$

$$s.t. \sum_{j=1}^{N_2} z_j = N_1, z_j = 0 \; or \; 1 \tag{8}$$

where $d_k = \|(x_i^1, y_i^1) - (x_i^2, y_i^2)\|$ is the Euclidian distance ($i = 1 \ldots N_1, j = 1 \ldots N_2$), (x_i^1, y_i^1) is the node of the reference graph, and (x_i^2, y_i^2) is the node of the graph to be matched. The semi-automatic approach allows users to correct manually those points that were detected automatically by subjective observation, while the automatic method does not allow re-placing the nodes. Thus, the automatic approach saves time however can result in greater assignment cost, and thus worse recognition rates.

3.2   Hierarchical Weighting on Features

The standard approach for graph matching equally weights the similarity function; meaning every node has the same importance in the same bunch graph. However, it is well-known that some features of the posture are more dominant than others, in terms of their discriminative power. Thus, this importance is expressed in terms of assigning a weight (hierarchy) to each node to reflect this attribute within the total similarity metric $\hat{S}_{pha}$. The similarity metric is weighted by the vector c that represents the discriminatory degree of nodes:

$$\hat{S}_{pha} = \sum_{k=1}^{K} c_k S_{pha}(B^{(k)}, J(x^{(k)})) \tag{9}$$

where B is the bunch graph with node index k, and $J(x)$ is the jet from target graph taken at node vector x. For different postures, the classifiers are trained separately using the adaptive boosting. Positive and negative feature vectors are extracted from each image to form the training set. Figure 1 shows the similarity response of an example image when the metric is computed with and without hierarchy (the bunch graph is scanned over the image with an increment of 4 pixels). In the left image (with hierarchy) the response is more 'focused' than in the right image (without hierarchy). The similarity scores of the entire image are more discriminative when hierarchy is applied over the classifier. This focused response results in fewer local maxima.

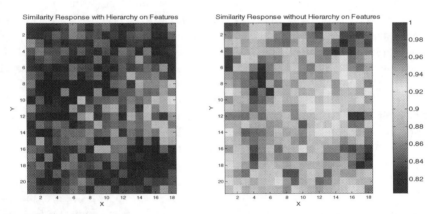

Fig. 1. Similarity response of bunch graph matched to an example image

4   Experimental Results

The proposed algorithms were validated with the Triesch hand posture dataset [13]. The dataset consists of 730 128x128 grey-scale images with10 different hand gestures against complex, light, and dark backgrounds; performed by 24 people. Each bunch graph is created by selecting two instances of a given posture performed by three subjects against light and dark backgrounds. The geometry of nodes (their position) on the bunch graph is averaged from six graphs. 60 images were used to create the bunch graph. The remaining 650 images were used for the training and testing. The bunch graphs matched on 10 hand postures are presented in Figure 2.

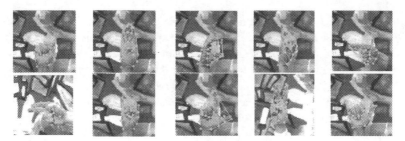

Fig. 2. Ten classes of sample hand gesture images

4.1 Hand Gesture Classification

Two metrics are used to evaluate the hand gesture classification performance. First, if the classified score was greater than a threshold (empirically found), then it was regarded as a true positive, otherwise it was a miss. If the negative classes were detected, then those were considered as false alarms. According to these values, a Receiver Operating Characterisic (ROC) curve was plotted to present the relationship between the true positives and false alarms. Figure 3 shows the ROC curves which were generated using 5-fold cross-validation for the 10 hand gestures. The average recognition accuracy was 91.84%.

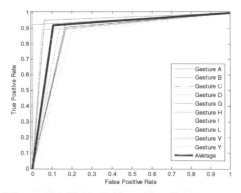

Fig. 3. ROC curve for Hierarchy-based hand gesture recognition

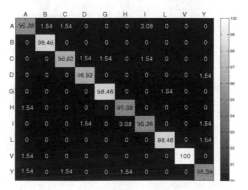

Fig. 4. Confusion Matrix for 10 Gestures

The second metric was the maximum score over 10 classifiers – this metric always delivered a single detection (correct or incorrect), and no false alarms. If the incorrect gesture was detected, that was considered as confusion. To this end, the confusion matrix (see Figure 4) was obtained by comparing the scores and taking the maximum from all the classifiers applied to the image. The average accuracy of correct classification over the confusion matrix reached 97.08%. Both these values show better performance to those reported in the literature [8].

4.2   Performance on Different Annotation Techniques

In this section the performance of each annotation technique used to create the bunch graphs is discussed. Highly textured points inside the hand were detected and considered candidate nodes in the semi-automatic and automatic techniques. The semi-automatic method allowed nodes to be adjusted manually. The results displayed in Figure 5 illustrates that the recognition rate for those classifiers trained using a bunch graph created using a semi-automatic technique tested with light and dark background images (92.12%) was better than the other two methods (90.91%, and 89.26% for manually and automatically, respectively).The normalized alignment cost was the highest for the automatic technique due to the inconsistency of the nodes' position among the graphs. However, the costs between manual and semi-automatic approaches were comparable. Therefore, the proposed semi-automatic technique shows to be an efficient annotation method for building up the bunch graph.

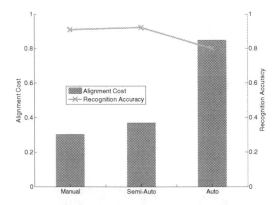

Fig. 5. Alignment cost and recognition accuracy for different annotation techniques

5   Discussions and Conclusions

This research proposed an enhanced graph based method for hand posture recognition incorporating the concept of nodes hierarchy. The proposed algorithm was tested in a standard dataset of postures using three backgrounds: light, dark and complex. The algorithm suggested classified the postures with a gesture recognition accuracy of 97.08% on average. This indicates that incorporating hierarchy in the bunch graphs improves the overall performance, since it stressed the discriminatory power of key nodes in every posture. Further work will show a major advantage of hierarchy based graphs: they can save computation time; for those nodes with a weight below a threshold, the matching function does not need to be computed.

Another important contribution of this work is a method for fast and reliable annotation of bunch graphs. A semi-automatic annotation technique was proposed which allows the flexible selection of nodes which are consistent between images of the same posture. This method showed to deliver the highest recognition accuracy compared to the manual (traditional) method to construct bunch graphs. Future work will include the validation of this method with a larger and more complex datasets of gestures, and experimenting with different bank of filters other than the Gabor.

References

1. Poppe, R., Rienks, R., van Dijk, B.: Evaluating the Future of HCI: Challenges for the Evaluation of Emerging Applications. In: Huang, T.S., Nijholt, A., Pantic, M., Pentland, A. (eds.) ICMI/IJCAI Workshops 2007. LNCS (LNAI), vol. 4451, pp. 234–250. Springer, Heidelberg (2007)
2. Roomi, S.M.M., Priya, R.J., Jayalakshmi, H.: Hand Gesture Recognition for Human-Computer Interaction. Journal of Computer Science 6(9), 1002–1007 (2010)
3. Rautaray, S.S., Agrawal, A.: Interaction with virtual game through hand gesture recognition. In: International Conference on Multimedia, Signal Processing and Communication Technologies (IMPACTs), December 17-19, pp. 244–247 (2011)
4. Chang, Y.-J., Chen, S.-F., Chuang, A.-F.: A gesture recognition system to transition autonomously through vocational tasks for individuals with cognitive impairments. Research Developmental Disabilities 32(6), 2064–2068 (2011)
5. Leyvand, T., Meekhof, C., Wei, Y.-C., Sun, J., Guo, B.: Kinect Identity: Technology and Experience. Computer 44(4), 94–96 (2011)
6. Wachs, J.P., Stern, H.I., Edan, Y., Gillam, M., Handler, J., Feied, C., Smith, M.: A gesture-based tool for sterile browsing of radiology images. Journal of the American Medical Informatics Association 15(3), 321–323 (2008)
7. Wiskott, L., Fellous, J.-M., Kruger, N., von der Malsburg, C.: Face recognition by elastic bunch graph matching. In: Int'l Conference on Image Processing, vol. 1, pp. 129–132 (1997)
8. Triesch, J., von der Malsburg, C.: Robust classification of hand postures against complex backgrounds. In: Proceedings of the Second International Conference on Automatic Face and Gesture Recognition, October 14-16, pp. 170–175 (1996)
9. Kumar, P.P., Vadakkepat, P., Poh, L.A.: Graph matching based hand posture recognition using neuro-biologically inspired features. In: 11th International Conference on Control Automation Robotics & Vision (ICARCV), December 7-10, pp. 1151–1156 (2010)
10. Friedman, J., Hastie, T., Tibshirani, R.: Additive logistic regression: a statistical view of boosting. Annals of Statistics 28(2), 337–374 (2000)
11. Torralba, A., Murphy, K.P., Freeman, W.T.: Sharing features: efficient boosting procedures for multiclass object detection. In: Proceedings of the 2004 IEEE Computer Society Conference on Computer Vision and Pattern Recognition, June 27-July 2, vol. 2, pp. II-762–II-769 (2004)
12. Torralba, A., Murphy, K.P., Freeman, W.T.: Sharing Visual Features for Multiclass and Multiview Object Detection. IEEE Transactions on Pattern Analysis and Machine Intelligence 29(5), 854–869 (2007)
13. Sebastien marcel hand posture and gesture datasets: Jochen triesch static hand posture database, http://www.idiap.ch/resource/gestures/

On Speeding up Frequent Approximate Subgraph Mining

Niusvel Acosta-Mendoza, Andrés Gago-Alonso, and José E. Medina-Pagola

Advanced Technologies Application Center (CENATAV), Havana, Cuba.
{nacosta,agago,jmedina}@cenatav.co.cu

Abstract. Frequent approximate subgraph (FAS) mining has become an interesting task with wide applications in several domains of science. Most of the previous studies have been focused on reducing the search space or the number of canonical form (CF) tests. CF-tests are commonly used for duplicate detection; however, these tests affect the efficiency of mining process because they have high computational complexity. In this paper, two prunes are proposed, which allow decreasing the label space, the number of candidates and the number of CF-tests. The proposed prunes are already used and validated in two reported FAS miners by speeding up their mining processes in artificial graph collections.

Keywords: Approximate graph mining, approximate graph matching, frequent approximate subgraphs, labeled graphs.

1 Introduction

In recent years, the necessity to use approximate matching in graph mining tasks has increased [7]. In fact, there are concrete problems where exact matching could not be applicable with positive outcome [5]. Sometimes, interesting subgraphs show slight differences throughout datasets. This means that we should tolerate certain level of geometric distortion, slight semantic variations, vertices or edges mismatch in frequent pattern search. For this reason, it is required to evaluate the similarity between graphs allowing some structural differences, i.e. considering approximate matching.

Taking into account these facts, several algorithms have been developed for FAS mining which use different approximate graph matching techniques in different domains of science [1, 4–6, 8–11]. However, only *APGM* [6] and *VEAM* [1] detect the FASs in a graph collection, where the approximation consists in considering some variations of the data through the substitution probability, keeping the topology of the graphs. These algorithms specify which vertices, edges or labels can replace others. Thus, the idea that not always a vertex label or an edge label can be replaced by any other is defended. APGM only deals with the variations between the vertex labels while VEAM perform the mining process using the vertex and edge label sets.

On the other hand, candidates are represented by a unique code called CF for frequency counting. In order to obtain the occurrences of the candidates are

L. Alvarez et al. (Eds.): CIARP 2012, LNCS 7441, pp. 316–323, 2012.

performed CF-tests to each of them. However, the computational complexity of a CF-test is very high [3]. In this paper, we introduce several prunes for improving FAS mining in an approximate framework related to APGM and VEAM approaches. Using these prunes it is possible to reduce the label space and the search space, as well as number of candidates. This fact also allows us to reduce the number of CF-tests.

The basic outline of this paper is as follows. Section 2 provides some basic concepts. The prunes for speeding up approximate methods are provided in section 3. The experimental results are discussed in section 4. Finally, conclusions of the research and some ideas about future directions are exposed in Section 5.

2 Basic Concepts

This work is focused on simple undirected labeled graphs. Henceforth, when we refer to graph we assume this type of graph. Before presenting their formal definition, we define the domain of labels.

Let L_V and L_E be label sets, where L_V is a set of vertex labels and L_E is a set of edge labels. The domain of all possible labels is denoted by $L = L_V \cup L_E$.

A *labeled graph* in L is a 4-tuple, $G = (V, E, I, J)$, where V is a set whose elements are called *vertices*, $E \subseteq \{\{u, v\} \mid u, v \in V, u \neq v\}$ is a set whose elements are called *edges* (the edge $\{u, v\}$ connecting the vertex u with the vertex v), $I : V \to L_V$ is a *labeling function* for assigning labels to vertices and $J : E \to L_E$ is a *labeling function* for assigning labels to edges.

Let $G_1 = (V_1, E_1, I_1, J_1)$ and $G_2 = (V_2, E_2, I_2, J_2)$ be two graphs, we say that G_1 is a *subgraph* of G_2 if $V_1 \subseteq V_2$, $E_1 \subseteq E_2$, $\forall u \in V_1, I_1(u) = I_2(u)$, and $\forall e \in E_1, J_1(e) = J_2(e)$. In this case, we use the notation $G_1 \subseteq G_2$ and we say that G_2 is a *supergraph* of G_1.

Given two graphs $G_1 = (V_1, E_1, I_1, J_1)$ and $G_2 = (V_2, E_2, I_2, J_2)$, where $G_1 \subseteq G_2$, we say that $e = \{u, v\} \in E_2$ is an *extension* of G_1 if: $V_2 = V_1 \cup \{v\}$ and $E_1 = E_2 \setminus \{e\}$. This fact can be denoted by $G_2 = G_1 \diamond e$. We say that e is a *backward extension* if $v \in V_1$, otherwise we say that it is a *forward extension* (it extends the vertex set of G_1).

Given G_1 and G_2, we say that f is an *isomorphism* between these graphs if $f : V_1 \to V_2$ is a bijective function, where $\forall u \in V_1, f(u) \in V_2 \wedge I_1(u) = I_2(f(u))$ and $\forall \{u, v\} \in E_1, \{f(u), f(v)\} \in E_2 \wedge J_1(\{u, v\}) = J_2(\{f(u), f(v)\})$. When there is an isomorphism between G_1 and G_2, we say that G_1 and G_2 are *isomorphic*.

Let Ω be the set of all possible labeled graphs in L, the *similarity* between two elements $G_1, G_2 \in \Omega$ is defined as a function $sim : \Omega \times \Omega \to [0, 1]$. We say that the elements are very different if $sim(G_1, G_2) = 0$, the higher the value of $sim(G_1, G_2)$ the more similar the elements are and if $sim(G_1, G_2) = 1$ then there is an isomorphism between these elements.

Let $G_1 = (V_1, E_1, I_1, J_1)$, $G_2 = (V_2, E_2, I_2, J_2)$ and $T = (V_T, E_T, I_T, J_T)$ be three labeled graphs in L, where $T \subseteq G_2$. Using an isomorphism threshold τ, we say that T is an *embedding* of G_1 in G_2 if $sim(G_1, T) \geq \tau$. The *embedding set* of G_1 in G_2 is denoted by $O(G_1, G_2)$.

Let T be an embedding of G_1 in $G_2 = (V_2, E_2, I_2, J_2)$, using an isomorphism threshold τ. The *extension set* of T is denoted by $ExtSet(T) = \{e \in E_2 \mid e$ is an extension of $T\}$.

Let $D = \{G_1, \ldots, G_{|D|}\}$ be a graph collection and let G be a labeled graph in L, the *support* value of G in D is obtained through the following equation:

$$supp(G, D) = \sum_{G_i \in D} sim(G, G_i)/|D| \tag{1}$$

If $supp(G, D) \geq \delta$, then the graph G is approximately frequent in the collection D, saying that G is a *FAS* in D. Notice that when we refer to a graph collection we assume that it is the representation built from a real graph collection. The value of the support threshold δ is in $[0, 1]$ assuming that the similarity is normalized to 1. *FAS mining* consists in finding all the FASs in a collection of graphs D, using a similarity function *sim* and a support threshold δ.

3   Prunes for Mining

In this section, we introduce two prunes for FAS mining. These prunes can be used in any FAS miner which uses substitution matrices and they are based on the downward closure property [2]. VEAM and APGM are used as basis for showing the improves.

The candidate generation process consists of extending a subgraph pattern by an edge. This is done searching the possible approximate label set of the new edge e and for every possible label of e seeking the possible label set of the new vertex if e is a forward extension. Finally, candidates are generated using those labels that satisfy definitions *"Vertex Approximate Sub-isomorphism[1]"* and *"Approximate Sub-isomorphism[2]"* presented by Acosta-Mendoza et al. [1]. In the above mentioned label sets, there are labels that could replace another ones with a similarity less than the threshold τ. Using these labels it is not possible to obtain candidates; however, the algorithms lose time checking these extensions. To formalize the previous assertions the following definition is presented.

Definition 1 (Useful label set). *Let $l_v \in L_V$, $l_e \in L_E$ be a vertex label and an edge label respectively, we say that the label sets, for a vertex label l_v and an edge label l_e, are useful label sets if they are obtained by the functions $U_V^\tau : L_V \to P_{L_V}$ and $U_E^\tau : L_E \to P_{L_E}$ such that:*

- $U_V^\tau(l_v) = \{l \in L_V \mid \frac{MV_{l,l_v}}{MV_{l,l}} \geq \tau\}$,
- $U_E^\tau(l_e) = \{l \in L_E \mid \frac{ME_{l,l_e}}{ME_{l,l}} \geq \tau\}$;

where, P_{L_V} and P_{L_E} are the power sets of L_V and L_E respectively[3].

---

[1] Definition used as similarity function in APGM
[2] Definition used as similarity function in VEAM
[3] For a set X, the power set of X is $P_X = \{Y \mid Y \subseteq X\}$.

Notice that, for each $l_v \in L_V$, $U_V^\tau(l_v) \neq \emptyset$, since at least $l_v \in U_V^\tau(l_v)$. In the same way, for each $l_e \in L_E$, $U_E^\tau(l_e) \neq \emptyset$, since at least $l_e \in U_E^\tau(l_e)$.

Theorem 2. *Let G be a labeled graph, let MV and ME be a substitution matrix indexed by vertex labels and a substitution matrix indexed by edge labels respectively; let v, v' be two vertices with labels l_v and $l_{v'}$ respectively, and let $e = \{u, v\}, e' = \{u, v'\}$ be two edges with labels l_e and $l_{e'}$ respectively. Then the following statements are true:*

1. *If $l_{v'} \notin U_V^\tau(l_v)$, then $G \diamond e' \neq_A G \diamond e$ (in the same way $G \diamond e' \neq_a G \diamond e$).*
2. *If $l_{e'} \notin U_E^\tau(l_e)$, then $G \diamond e' \neq_A G \diamond e$.*

Proof. In these statements, the definitions of approximate sub-isomorphism of APGM and VEAM are used. These definitions use a product of substitution probabilities with the requirement that its result should be greater than or equal to τ. These substitution probability values are in the interval $[0, 1]$. Therefore, if a factor of this product is lesser than τ then its value is less than τ too and does not generate an approximate subgraph candidate. □

On the other hand, in APGM and VEAM, the approximation is based on the semantic of labels. For this reason, we proposed a heuristic to reduce the search space, according to some rules that can be applied by these FAS miners. These rules are: (1) The vertices (and its corresponding edges), which are not used as an embedding of a single-vertex FAS, are removed from each graph in D; (2) The edges, which are not used as an embedding of a single-edge FAS, are removed from each graph in D.

Theorem 3. *Let $L_U^V \subseteq L_V$ be the label set used by the single-vertex FASs in a collection D and u be a vertex with label $l_u \in L_V$. The following statements are true:*

1. *The vertex u is not used as an embedding by any single-vertex FAS if and only if $L_U^V \cap U_V^\tau(l_u) = \emptyset$.*
2. *If $L_U^V \cap U_V^\tau(l_u) = \emptyset$ then a non-frequent subgraph is obtained when $e = \{v, u\}$ extends an existing FAS G in D, where u is the new vertex of this forward extension.*

Proof. First, we will prove statement 1. Suppose that the vertex u is used as an embedding by a single-vertex FAS $Y = (\{w\}, \emptyset, I_Y, J_Y)$. If this occurs, then the label $l_w \in L_U^V$ of the vertex w replaces the label l_u with a value greater than or equal to τ, i.e. $l_w \in U_V^\tau(l_u)$, and $L_U^V \cap U_V^\tau(l_u) \neq \emptyset$. Therefore, if $L_U^V \cap U_V^\tau(l_u) = \emptyset$, then the vertex u is not used as an embedding by any single-vertex FAS. On the other hand, assuming that $L_U^V \cap U_V^\tau(l_u) \neq \emptyset$, then u is not used as an embedding by any single-vertex FAS because their labels replace l_u with values less than τ. Therefore, if u is used as an embedding by a single-vertex FAS, then $L_U^V \cap U_V^\tau(l_u) = \emptyset$.

Next, we will prove the second statement. Suppose that we have a forward extension $e = \{v, u\}$, with u as the new vertex, of an existing FAS G in D.

If $L_U^V \cap U_V^\tau(l_u) = \emptyset$ then the vertex u is not used as an embedding by any single-vertex FAS, according to the first part of the Theorem and, as a directly consequence, the single-vertex subgraph $T = (\{u\}, \emptyset, I_T, J_T)$ is non-frequent. As $T \subseteq_A G \diamond e$, applying the downward closure, we have $supp(G \diamond e, D) \le supp(T, D)$, then $G \diamond e$ is a non-frequent pattern because T is a non-frequent. Therefore, to prune the vertices with label l_u of D does not change the frequent pattern output. □

Theorem 4. *Let $L_U^E \subseteq L_E$ be the label set used by the single-edge FASs in a collection D and an edge e with label $l_e \in L_E$, the following statements are true:*

1. *The edge e is not used as an embedding by any single-edge FAS if and only if $L_U^E \cap U_E^\tau(l_e) = \emptyset$.*
2. *If $L_U^E \cap U_E^\tau(l_e) = \emptyset$ then a non-frequent subgraph is obtained if e extends a FAS G in D.*

Proof. First, we will prove statement 1. Suppose that the edge e is used as an embedding by a single-edge FAS $Y = (V_Y, \{e'\}, I_Y, J_Y)$. If this occurs, then the label $l_{e'} \in L_U^E$ of the edge e' replaces the label l_e with a value greater than or equal to τ, i.e. $l_{e'} \in U_V^\tau(l_e)$, and $L_U^E \cap U_E^\tau(l_e) \ne \emptyset$. Therefore, if $L_U^E \cap U_E^\tau(l_e) = \emptyset$, then the edge e is not used as an embedding by any single-edge FAS. On the other hand, assuming that $L_U^E \cap U_E^\tau(l_e) \ne \emptyset$, then e is not used as an embedding by any single-edge FAS because their labels replace l_e with values less than τ. Therefore, if e is used as an embedding by a single-edge FAS, then $L_U^E \cap U_E^\tau(l_e) = \emptyset$.

Next, we will prove the second statement. Suppose that we have an extension e of an existing FAS G in D. If $L_U^E \cap U_E^\tau(l_e) = \emptyset$ then the edge e is not used as an embedding by any single-edge FAS, according to the first part of the Theorem and, as a directly consequence, the single-edge subgraph T with l_e as edge label is non-frequent. As $T \subseteq_A G \diamond e$, applying the downward closure, we have $supp(G \diamond e, D) \le supp(T, D)$, then $G \diamond e$ is a non-frequent pattern because T is a non-frequent. Therefore, to prune the edges with label l_e of D does not change the frequent pattern output. □

VEAM and APGM are shown through three pseudo-codes where the common main algorithm consists in finding the single-vertex FAS and single-edge FAS sets, then the first set is stored in set F and only the second one is stored in set C (see Algorithm 1 in Figure 1). A prune using Theorem 3 as basis is performed in line 2. After obtaining the single-edge FAS set, a prune using Theorem 4 as basis is performed in line 5. As we can see, in order to apply the last prune, a breadth-first search (BFS) is required to obtain the approximate frequent edges in the initial process. Later, for each pattern in C the algorithm *Search* is invoked. When all single-edge FASs in C have been extended, then the set F of all FASs in D is returned.

The other common pseudo-code of VEAM and APGM performs the extension of subgraph patterns on one edge using DFS (see Algorithm 2 in Figre 1). Thus, all candidate subgraphs are created using the label set obtained through the "*appLSetVEAM*" algorithm, in the VEAM case, or "*appLSetAPGM*" algorithm, in the APGM case, in line 2. In Algorithm 3 (see lines 1 and 4) and in Algorithm 4 (see line 3), a prune using theorem 2 as basis is included, where only the labels in $U_E^\tau(J(e))$ and $U_V^\tau(I(v))$ are used.

Algorithm 1: *Main*

Input: D : A graph collection, MV : Substitution matrix indexed by L_V, ME : Substitution matrix indexed by L_E, τ : Isomorphism threshold, δ : Support threshold.

Output: F : Frequent approximate subgraph set.

1 $F \leftarrow$ *the frequent approximate single-vertex set in D;*
2 Remove from D the vertices with label l_v such that $L_U^V \cap U_V^\tau(l_v) = \emptyset$;
3 $C \leftarrow$ *the frequent approximate single-edge set in D;*
4 $F \leftarrow F \cup C$;
5 Remove from D the edges with label l_e such that $L_U^E \cap U_E^\tau(l_e) = \emptyset$;
6 foreach $T \in C$ do
7 | Search$(T, D, MV, ME, \tau, \delta, F)$;

Algorithm 2: *Search*

Input: $T = (V_t, E_t, I_t, J_t)$: A frequent approximate subgraph, D : Graph collection, MV : Substitution matrix indexed by L_V, ME : Substitution matrix indexed by L_E, τ : Isomorphism threshold, δ : Support threshold, F : Frequent approximate subgraph set.

Output: F : Frequent approximate subgraph set.

1 foreach $o_j \in O(T, G_i)$, *where* $G_i \in D$ do
2 | foreach $e = ExtSet(o_j)$ do
3 | | $CL \leftarrow$ appLSet$(T, MV, ME, G_i, o_j, e, \tau)$;
4 | | foreach $(elabel, vlabel) \in CL$ do
5 | | | The candidate X is built using the tuple $(elabel, vlabel)$;
6 | | | The code CAM of X is computed and stored in $codeCAM(X)$;
7 | | | $C \leftarrow C \cup \{(X, codeCAM(X), score)\}$;
8 foreach $T_1 \in C$ do
9 | if $sup_G(T_1, D) \geq \delta$ *and* $codeCAM(T_1) \notin F$ then
10 | | Insert T_1 in F;
11 | | Search$(T_1, D, MV, ME, \tau, \delta, F)$;

Algorithm 4: *appLSetAPGM*

Input: T : A candidate graph, MV : Substitution matrix indexed by L_V, $G = (V, E, I, J)$: A graph of the collection, G' : Embedding of T in G, $e = \{u, v\}$: An extension of G', τ : Isomorphism threshold.

Output: CL : A set of candidate 2-tuples $(elabel, vlabel)$.

1 $l_{uv} = J(e)$;
2 if e *is a forward extension of G'* then
3 | foreach $i \in U_V^\tau(I(v))$ do
4 | | $score \leftarrow S_{max}(T, G') * \frac{MV_{i,I(v)}}{MV_{i,i}}$;
5 | | if $score \geq \tau$ then $CL \leftarrow CL \cup \{(l_{uv}, i)\}$;
6 else $CL \leftarrow CL \cup \{(l_{uv}, \emptyset)\}$;

Algorithm 3: *appLSetVEAM*

Input: T : A candidate graph, MV : Substitution matrix indexed by L_V, ME : Substitution matrix indexed by L_E, $G = (V, E, I, J)$: A graph of the collection, G' : An extension of G', τ : Isomorphism threshold.

Output: CL : A set of candidate 2-tuples $(elabel, vlabel)$.

1 foreach $j \in U_E^\tau(J(e))$ do
2 | $scoreE \leftarrow S_{max}(T, G') * \frac{ME_{j,J(e)}}{ME_{j,j}}$;
3 | if e *is a forward extension of G'* then
4 | | foreach $i \in U_V^\tau(I(v))$ do
5 | | | if i *is less than or equal to the largest of the vertex labels of T* then
6 | | | | $score \leftarrow scoreE * \frac{MV_{i,I(v)}}{MV_{i,i}}$;
7 | | | | if $score \geq \tau$ then $CL \leftarrow CL \cup \{(j, i)\}$;
8 | else if $scoreE \geq \tau$ then $CL \leftarrow CL \cup \{(j, \emptyset)\}$;

Fig. 1. Pseudo-code of VEAM and APGM using the proposed prunes

4   Experimental Results

All our experiments were carried out using a personal computer (x64 platform) Intel (R) Core (TM) 2 Quad CPU Q9450 @ 2.66 GHz with 4 Gb main memory. We used ANSI C language and we compiled the algorithms using gcc compiler of GNU/Linux.

In this paper, the mining process is performed in the several image collections used by Acosta-Mendoza *et al.* [1]. The impact of our prunes in FAS mining on image collections is evaluated with the aim of showing the usefulness of these prunes. The performance of VEAM and APGM[4] with and without our prunes in several collections are compared as follows. Note that in Table 1 are shown only the results of the algorithms in two collections (D700 and D600) due to space restrictions.

First, VEAM and APGM with and without the prunes proposed are compared regarding the number of exhaustive CF-tests that they perform in their mining strategies (see subtable a) in Table 1). Note that the original algorithms are denoted by VEAM and APGM, and the algorithms with our prunes are denoted by *VEAMwP* and *APGMwP*. These CF-tests become much more complex to great extent with the increase of the candidate size. In this comparison, the number

---

[4] The APGM version used in our experiments was implemented by us to detect all frequent vertex approximate subgraphs and not just the clique subgraphs as proposed [6].

of such expensive CF-tests, in most of the cases, were reduced in 30% when our prunes are used. The fact that these prunes reduce the number of candidates to be processed impacts in a positive manner in the algorithm's performance.

Second, the performance, in terms of runtime, of APGM and VEAM with and without the prunes proposed are compared. In this comparison the runtimes were reduced, in most of the cases, in 15%, when our prunes are used. Notice that we use the same support threshold and isomorphism threshold values presented by Acosta-Mendoza et al. [1] with the purpose of showing the improvement achieving the same accuracies obtained by them.

Table 1. Comparison between VEAM and VEAMwP, and between APGM and APGMwP in image collections using $\tau = 0.4$

a) Number of CF-tests computed

Algorithm	Support (δ)								
	20%	25%	30%	35%	40%	45%	50%	55%	60%
	D700								
APGM	153524	48437	11927	3555	1407	992	992	904	829
APGMwP	**67197**	**21709**	**4478**	**1131**	**303**	**187**	**187**	**180**	**174**
	D600								
APGM	58300	24453	8278	2515	1081	963	963	883	808
APGMwP	**28950**	**12133**	**3245**	**848**	**257**	**186**	**186**	**179**	**173**
	D700								
VEAM	350589	114907	33423	11105	5212	2600	2302	2118	1687
VEAMwP	**259034**	**67405**	**17264**	**5505**	**2522**	**477**	**453**	**428**	**371**
	D600								
VEAM	157751	79555	26160	8241	4374	2526	2236	2056	1641
VEAMwP	**113005**	**47699**	**13662**	**4167**	**2049**	**475**	**452**	**427**	**370**

b) Runtimes (s)

Algorithm									
	D700								
APGM	58.61	9.95	2.13	0.76	0.42	0.36	0.35	0.33	0.30
APGMwP	**31.24**	**6.61**	**1.60**	**0.59**	**0.29**	**0.17**	**0.17**	**0.16**	**0.15**
	D600								
APGM	11.00	3.69	1.27	0.46	0.29	0.28	0.28	0.26	0.23
APGMwP	**7.24**	**2.71**	**0.96**	**0.36**	**0.19**	**0.13**	**0.13**	**0.12**	**0.12**
	D700								
VEAM	133.78	25.50	6.51	2.43	1.41	0.94	0.88	0.81	0.67
VEAMwP	**114.93**	**20.34**	**5.53**	**2.15**	**1.24**	**0.42**	**0.40**	**0.39**	**0.34**
	D600								
VEAM	29.91	12.69	4.19	1.57	0.98	0.72	0.68	0.63	0.52
VEAMwP	**25.47**	**10.37**	**3.53**	**1.34**	**0.83**	**0.33**	**0.30**	**0.29**	**0.26**

In summary, we can conclude that our prunes positively impact the performance of APGM and VEAM. The prune based on Theorem 2 is very effective when the number of dissimilarities between labels or the number of candidates are increased. The prune using Theorems 3 and 4 is considered effective when the collection has many non-frequent vertices and edges, and its graphs are dense. In general, the new prunes help us to reduce runtimes of VEAM and APGM. These results ensure the usefulness of the prunes proposed in this paper.

5   Conclusions and Future Work

In this paper, we introduced a prune which is useful to reduce the number of CF-tests during the FAS mining. This prune allows decreasing the search space of collection's graphs. Another prune, which uses only the label set that comply with the isomorphism threshold, was proposed. These prunes are implemented and tested in already reported FAS miners, APGM and VEAM. As can be seen in the experimental results, the number of CF-tests is notably reduced, and the improvement in time is appreciable.

As future work, we are going to develop new ways for taking advantage of the candidate reduction in order to achieve better performance in FAS mining. This allows us to accelerate the support calculation by the reduction of the number of test sub-isomorphism, and in turn, the number of embedded to keep.

References

1. Acosta-Mendoza, N., Gago-Alonso, A., Medina-Pagola, J.E.: Frequent Approximate Subgraphs as Features for Graph-Based Image Classification. Knowledge-Based Systems 27, 381–392 (2012)
2. Agrawal, R., Srikant, R.: Fast Algorithms for Mining Association Rules. In: In Proceedings of the 1994 International Conference on Very Large Data Bases (VLDB 1994), Santiago, Chile, pp. 487–499 (1994)
3. Borgelt, C.: Canonical Forms for Frequent Graph Mining. In: Proceedings of the 30th Annual Conference of the Gesellschaft für Klassifikation e.V., pp. 8–10. Universitat Berlin (2006)
4. Chen, C., Yan, X., Zhu, F., Han, J.: gApprox: Mining Frequent Approximate Patterns from a Massive Network. In: IEEE International Conference on Data Mining, ICDM 2007, pp. 445–450 (2007)
5. Holder, L.B., Cook, D.J., Bunke, H.: Fuzzy substructure discovery. In: Proceedings of the 9th International Workshop on Machine Learning, San Francisco, CA, USA, pp. 218–223 (1992)
6. Jia, Y., Zhang, J., Huan, J.: An Efficient Graph-Mining Method for Complicated and Noisy Data with Real-World Applications. Knowledge Information Systems 28(2), 423–447 (2011)
7. Jiang, C., Coenen, F., Zito, M.: A Survey of Frequent Subgraph Mining Algorithms. To appear: Knowledge Engineering Review (2012)
8. Song, Y., Chen, S.: Item Sets Based Graph Mining Algorithm and Application in Genetic Regulatory Networks. In: Proceedings of the IEEE International Conference on Granular Computing, Atlanta, GA, USA, pp. 337–340 (2006)
9. Xiao, Y., Wu, W., Wang, W., He, Z.: Efficient Algorithms for Node Disjoint Subgraph Homeomorphism Determination. In: Haritsa, J.R., Kotagiri, R., Pudi, V. (eds.) DASFAA 2008. LNCS, vol. 4947, pp. 452–460. Springer, Heidelberg (2008)
10. Zhang, S., Yang, J.: RAM: Randomized Approximate Graph Mining. In: Ludäscher, B., Mamoulis, N. (eds.) SSDBM 2008. LNCS, vol. 5069, pp. 187–203. Springer, Heidelberg (2008)
11. Zou, Z., Li, J., Gao, H., Zhang, S.: Mining Frequent Subgraph Patterns from Uncertain Graph Data. IEEE Transactions on Knowledge and Data Engineering 22(9), 1203–1218 (2010)

Segmentation of Building Facade Domes

Gayane Shalunts[1,*], Yll Haxhimusa[2], and Robert Sablatnig[1]

[1] Vienna University of Technology, Computer Vision Lab
{shal,sab}@caa.tuwien.ac.at
[2] Vienna University of Technology, Pattern Recognition and Image Processing Lab
yll@prip.tuwien.ac.at

Abstract. Domes are architectural structural elements typical for ecclesiastical and secular grand buildings, like churches, mosques, palaces, capitols and city halls. The current paper targets the problem of segmentation of domes within the framework of architectural style classification of building facades. We perform segmentation of building facade domes by combining bilateral symmetry detection, graph-based segmentation approaches and image analysis and processing technics into a single method. Our algorithm achieves good segmentation results on buildings belonging to variety of architectural styles, such as Renaissanse, Neo-Renaissance, Baroque, Neo-Baroque, Neoclassical and Islamic.

Keywords: Building facade domes, bilateral symmetry, segmentation.

1 Introduction

Architectural styles are phases of development that classify architecture in the sense of historic periods, regions and cultural influences. Automatic classification of building facade images by architectural styles will allow indexing of building image databases into subdatabases belonging to certain historic periods. Such a semantic categorization limits the search of building image databases to certain category portions for the purposes of building recognition [17,16], Content Based Image Retrieval (CBIR) [6], 3D reconstruction, 3D city-modeling [2] and virtual tourism [14]. Architectural style classification system may also be applicable in real tourism, provided with smart phones. Our main focus is on historic styles, which combine style-typical architectural elements and obey to certain design rules for building construction. Unlike historic architecture, modern architecture is not confined by any rules and is difficult to categorize.

Facade images either do not have labels related to styles or such labels are inaccurate. To know the style of an observed building, one should search for the building name. Since most buildings lack names, visual information of facades remains the only clue to their styles. While an automatic system for classification of facade images by architectural styles still does not exist, the first steps towards creating such a computer vision system are done in [12,13,9]. The authors in [12]

---

* Supported by the Doctoral College on Computational Perception.

L. Alvarez et al. (Eds.): CIARP 2012, LNCS 7441, pp. 324–331, 2012.

classify facade windows of Romanesque, Gothic and Baroque styles. The approach proposed in [13] classifies architectural element tracery into Gothic class and elements pediment and balustrade - into Baroque class. In [9] classification of Flemish Renaissance, Haussmannian and Neoclassical styles is performed on complete facade images.

Our method of architectural style classification of facades consists of 3 major steps: (i) facade segmentation by architectural structural elements, (ii) classification of the segmented elements by architectural styles and (iii) style voting of the classified elements. The algorithm is capable to classify partly occluded facades by a single style-typical element and facades, which are a mixture of styles. Buildings of historic, religeous and cultural importance are of special interest to us. And as it is the privilege of such buildings to feature domes, we focus on segmentation and classification of domes. The previous work, related to facade segmentation by an architectural element, is limited to detection of windows [1,11,10,5]. The current paper addresses the problem of segmentation of facade domes and is the first to do so. We present a multi-step algorithm, integrating bilateral symmetry detection, graph-based segmentation approaches and image analysis and processing technics. Our approach manipulates the visual features of domes, such as specificity of bilateral symmetricity, raising out of the main building and roundness, to reach robust segmentation of domes. The experiments prove that the method is capable to handle buildings in complex scenes and achieves accurate segmentation on 96% of the test images.

The paper is organized as follows: Sect. 2 gives architecture review of the types of domes, which are segmented by our methodology. Sect. 3 explains the proposed methodology for the segmentation of domes. The experiments and results are presented in Sect. 4. And finally Sect. 5 concludes the paper.

2   Building Facade Domes

Dome is a convex roof. Hemispherical domes have a circular base with a semicircular section and are characteristic for grand buildings of Renaissance, Neo-Renaissance, Baroque, Neo-Baroque and Neoclassical architecture. Here Neo-styles refer to revived styles, e.g. Neo-Baroque refers to Baroque Revival. The essence of the phenomenon called architectural revivalism is the imitation of past architectural styles. In Fig. 1a, Fig. 1b, Fig. 1c are shown respectively St. Charles's Baroque Church in Vienna, California Neoclassical Capitol in Sacramento and San-Francisco Neoclassical City Hall featuring this type of dome. Onion domes have a circular or polygonal base and an onion-shaped section. This type of dome is a typical feature of Islamic mosques, palaces, etc. Taj Mahal in India (Fig. 1d) is the most famous landmark featuring an onion dome. Architectural definitions are taken from the Illustrated Architecture Dictionary[1].

---

[1] Illustrated Architecture Dictionary:
   http://www.buffaloah.com/a/DCTNRY/vocab.html

a) St. Charles's Church   b) California Capitol   c) SF City Hall   d) Taj Mahal

Fig. 1. Examples of buildings with domes and segmentation of domes

3   Segmentation of Domes

Building facade dome segmentation is a highly complex task, being a high-level semantic segmentation by an architectural element. Color-based segmentation approaches are not applicable, since color is not a distinctive feature and a single dome contains multiple color segments. Though domes have certain geometric forms, defined as hemispherical, onion, etc, shape analysis is also not suitable for segmentation, as these shapes may not be modeled owing unlimited variety.

Using symmetry as a feature is logical, since facades, like any artefacts, are highly symmetrical. Facades have symmetry specificities. Firstly, dominant symmetry axes are vertical. Secondly, whereas bilateral symmetry is common for historic facades, translational and rotational symmetries also take place. For dome segmentation purpose bilateral symmetry is of interest to us, since domes are 3D objects preserving bilateral symmetry related to the vertical axis passing through their center in 2D projections. Thus at the first step the image bilateral symmetry axes are detected using the method proposed by Loy et al [8]. In [8] matches of symmetric points are found using modern feature-based methods, such as [7], from which bilateral symmetry axes or centers of rotational symmetry are determined. The method is independent of the feature detector and descriptor used, requiring only robust, rotation-invariant matching and an orientation measure for each feature [8]. This method is sucessfully used also for detecting repeated structures on facades [15]. Fig. 2a shows an example image with a tilted dome. Image bilateral symmetry axes and supporting symmetric points are displayed in Fig. 2b. In case multiple symmetry axes are found, we choose the axis with the strongest symmetry magnitude (supported by the biggest number of symmetry points). As the dominant symmetry axis passes through the dome center and is vertical, we rectify the image by rotation, making the strongest symmetry axis vertical (Fig. 2c). Images, whose strongest symmetry axis is vertical, skip this step. Bilateral symmetry detection [8] is performed once more on the rotated image to find the position (column) of the strongest symmetry axis. At the second

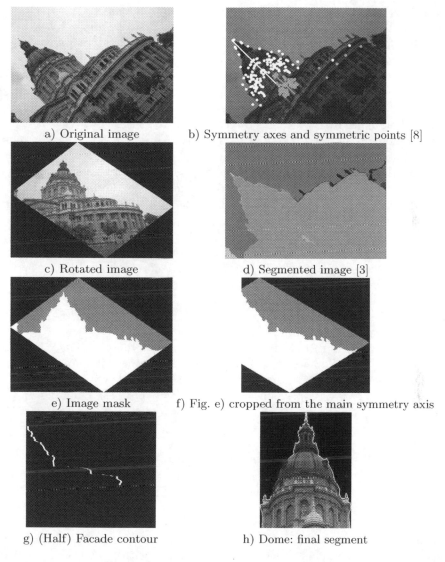

a) Original image

b) Symmetry axes and symmetric points [8]

c) Rotated image

d) Segmented image [3]

e) Image mask

f) Fig. e) cropped from the main symmetry axis

g) (Half) Facade contour

h) Dome: final segment

Fig. 2. Dome segmentation algorithm steps

step segmentation of the original image background and foreground is performed. As domes are situated high above the buildings, the sky and clouds form their background. We segment the original image using the methodology introduced by Felzenszwalb et al. [3] (Fig. 2d). The pairwise comparison of neighboring vertices, i.e. partitions is used to check for similarities [3,4]. In [3] a definition of a pairwise group comparison function $Comp(\cdot, \cdot)$ is given, judging if there is evidence for a boundary between two image segments or not. $Comp(\cdot, \cdot)$ contains a scale parameter k, where bigger k prefers larger segmented regions. The function measures the difference along the boundary of two components relative

328 G. Shalunts, Y. Haxhimusa, and R. Sablatnig

to a measure of differences of components' internal differences. This definition tries to encapsulate the intuitive notion of contrast. Images are preprocessed by Gaussian blurring with σ before the segmentation, as well as postprocessed by merging small regions with the biggest neighboring one [3]. After the segmented image is also rotated to make the strongest symmetry axis vertical.

As our image is already justified so that the sky is on the top of it, we find the segment (color) of the sky by looking for the first non-black pixel starting from the first upper row, which is located on the strongest symmetry axis. Then the image foreground mask is obtained by setting all sky pixels to background color and non-sky pixels - to foreground color (Fig. 2e).

Having the image foreground mask found, our task is to analyze its shape in order to crop the dome. As domes are symmetric, for optimization we analyze only the image part cropped to the right from the strongest symmetry axis (Fig. 2f). The strongest symmetry axis is expected to pass through the center of the dome, i.e. through the highest point of the dome. For images, whose symmetry axis position is shifted left or right from the dome center due to perspective distortions, the symmetry axis position is corrected by looking on the image mask for the foreground maxima in the symmetry axis local neighborhood. This milestone of our methodology means, if the initial detected vertical symmetry axis lies on the dome, it justifies itself to the correct position, making the approach robust to high perspective distortions.

Now our purpose is to find the bottom row of the segmented dome. Here we use a visual feature of domes: domes raise out of the main building. This means that the facade contour, formed by the foreground pixel followed by a backgroud pixel in each row (Fig. 2g), has a leap on the row where the dome meets the main building. The observed leap is found by scanning down row by row the facade contour in Fig. 2g until the condition in Eq. 1 is satisfied:

$$\text{Leap} / (\text{Row}(k) - \text{Row}(1)) > 0.15 \ \&\& \ \text{Leap} > \text{minLeapThreshold} \qquad (1)$$

where Leap is the column difference of contour pixels on kth and $(k-1)$th sequential rows: $\text{Leap} = \text{Col}(k) - \text{Col}(k-1)$.

$\text{Row}(k) - \text{Row}(1)$ is a normalization factor and is the difference of the kth and first rows of the contour. minLeapThreshold excludes too small leaps between two subsequent rows and is set to 18 pixels for images with resolution lower than 1 million pixels and to 26 pixels otherwise. After the image mask is cropped from the found row to discard the image part below, which does not contain the segment of interest. In order to obtain the final dome segment, we pick up the blob through which the main symmetry axis passes and discard all the other blobs formed by clouds, trees and any other objects present in the image. Multiplication of the blob mask with the same segment of the original image delivers the segmented dome (Fig. 2h).

Still we take a further step by incorporating feature roundness for domes, to address the following types of complex images: i) the strongest symmetry axis does not pass through the dome center, due to too high perspective distortions or other symmetric objects in the image, ii) the strongest symmetry axis is located on the dome, but is horizontal, iii) the facade is reflected in water, thus the strongest symmetry axis is horizontal. Feature roundness is calculated by Eq. 2.

$$\text{Roundness} = 4 * \text{Area} / (\pi * \text{MajorAxisLength}^2) \qquad (2)$$

$$\text{Roundness} > 0.37 \;\&\&\; \text{DomeBoundingBox} > 1500 \qquad (3)$$

If the dome blob roundness and bounding box resolution pass the thresholds in Eq. 3, the dome segmentation is considered successful. The thresholds in Eq. 1 and Eq. 3 were found by experimenting on multiple images. Setting a threshold for dome bounding box resolution excludes too small blobs. In case the condition in Eq. 3 is not met, the whole segmentation algorithm is rerun by taking the 2nd strongest symmetry axis in the initial step. After the condition in Eq. 3 is checked again and if not satisfied, the algorithm is rerun by the 3rd strongest symmetry axis and so on. We limit our dome segment search by the 5th strongest symmetry axis (if such exists), since experimentally was found (Sect. 4) that further search is useless.

4   Experiments of Dome Segmentation and Results

To test for robustness and evaluate our segmentation approach we created an image database of buildings featuring domes, as to the best knowledge of the authors such a database did not exist so far. The database is collected from our own and Flickr[2] image databases and exhibits Renaissanse, Neo-Renaissance, Baroque, Neo-Baroque, Neoclassical and Islamic buildings. Our database includes 550 images of 77 buildings, among those the most famous world landmarks, like St. Peter's Basilica in Vatican, Florence Cathedral, St. Paul's Cathedral in London, Pantheon in Paris, United States Capitol in Washington, capitol buildings of 24 US states and Taj Mahal in India. The resolution of the images ranges from 108×82 to 3681×5522 pixels, proving the algorithm to be resolution-independent. We handle both day and night images, since our method is color-independent. The only limitations of our methodology are: 1) segmentation of occluded domes is not supported, 2) the rare cases when the dome background is formed by cityscape, not the sky, as a result of shooting from a level higher than the ground (building roofs, helicopter, etc) are also not handled. The allowed tilt of the dome is (-90 to 90) degrees related to vertical axis. We do not consider this a limitation, since our search showed that building images taken upside down or tilted more than 90 degrees related to vertical axis are very rare.

The default value for both parameters of graph-based segmentation algorithm [3] σ and k is 2000. The chosen big value is explained by the fact that we need a coarse segmentation of sky and non-sky segments. For images taken by night illumination, foggy weather condition or having low resolution the values of σ and k should be tuned down to obtain the non-sky segment with the precise dome edge. Whereas for images with strong cloud edges in the dome vicinity the values of σ and k should be tuned up to blur the cloud edges. Clouds not

---

[2] http://www.flickr.com

Table 1. Segmentation rate vs. symmetry axis magnitude

	1st	2nd	3rd	4th	5th	Segmented domes	Total
Segmentation rate	504	11	7	5	1	528 (96% of Total)	550
% of segmented domes	95.45%	2.08%	1.33%	0.95%	0.19%	100%	

touching the dome do not affect the segmentation output, as they are discarded segments. For our database both σ and k are in the range from 50 to 16000.

We demonstrate our segmentation results on building examples in complex scenes - St. Charles's Church (Fig. 1a), California Capitol (Fig. 1b), San-Francisco City Hall (Fig. 1c) and Taj Mahal (Fig. 1d) and the respective segmented domes located below each image in Fig. 1. The accurately segmented dome was obtained on 528 out of the 550 tested images, which yields an average 96% rate for our approach (Table 1). On 504 out of 528 images, i.e. on 95.45% of the correctly segmented images, the segmentation was accomplished by looking for the dome in the vicinity of the 1st strongest symmetry axis (Table 1). And it is only on 4.55% of the correctly segmented images that the dome is segmented by trying symmetry axis weaker in magnitude than the 1st strongest symmetry axis, i.e. on 11 images the dome segment was found in the neigbourhood of the 2nd strongest symmetry axis, on 7 images - 3rd, on 5 images - 4th and on 1 image - 5th (Table 1). We also analyzed the reasons of unsuccessful segmentation for all 22 images. On 18 images the symmetry axis passing through the dome was not detected or was weakly detected, due to too high perspective distortions, other dominant symmetries present in the image vast panorama or building reflection in water. Images, where the dome top touches the image top fail, since the segmentation algorithm [3] fails to deliver 1 sky segment, but ends up with 2 sky segments on each side of the dome. This leads to attachment of one of sky segments to the foreground mask, further resulting in either delivering the dome segment with having one sky segment on the background or failing to obtain the dome due to not overcoming the roundness threshold. Our database happened to contain 2 such images. 1 image failed because of clouds touching the dome, the strong edges of which segmentation method [3] failed to ignore. As a result they appeared as a part of the foreground mask, leading to analysis of a false facade contour. And on 1 image finding the leap row between the dome and the main building was unsuccessful owing high perspective distortions.

5   Conclusion

We presented a pioneer method for segmentation of building facade domes, as a milestone in a computer vision system for architectural style classification of building facades. Taking into account the visual features of domes, our methodology integrated bilateral symmetry detection, graph-based segmentation approaches and image analysis and processing technics. We proved experimentally that accurate dome segmentation is performed on images of facades of a variety of architectural styles, in complex scenes and under high perspective distortions. Future work in the scope of architectural style classification of facades includes segmentation and classification of other architectural elements.

References

1. Ali, H., Seifert, C., Jindal, N., Paletta, L., Paar, G.: Window detection in facades. In: Proc. of 14th ICIAP, pp. 837–842. Springer (2007)
2. Cornelis, N., Leibe, B., Cornelis, K., Gool, L.V.: 3d urban scene modeling integrating recognition and reconstruction. IJCV 78, 121–141 (2008)
3. Felzenszwalb, P.F., Huttenlocher, D.P.: Efficient graph-based image segmentation. IJCV 59(2), 167–181 (2004)
4. Guigues, L., Herve, L.M., Cocquerez, J.P.: The hierarchy of the cocoons of a graph and its application to image segmentation. PRL 24(8), 1059–1066 (2003)
5. Haugeard, J.E., Philipp-Foliguet, S., Precioso, F.: Windows and facade retrieval using similarity on graphs of contours. In: ICIP, pp. 269–272 (2009)
6. Li, Y., Crandall, D., Huttenlocher, D.: Landmark classification in large-scale image collections. In: Proc. of IEEE 12th ICCV, pp. 1957–1964 (2009)
7. Lowe, D.G.: Distinctive image features from scale-invariant keypoints. IJCV 60(2), 91–110 (2004)
8. Loy, G., Eklundh, J.-O.: Detecting Symmetry and Symmetric Constellations of Features. In: Leonardis, A., Bischof, H., Pinz, A. (eds.) ECCV 2006. LNCS, vol. 3952, pp. 508–521. Springer, Heidelberg (2006)
9. Mathias, M., Martinovic, A., Weissenberg, J., Hacgler, S., Gool, L.V.: Automatic architectural style recognition. In: Proc. of the 4th International Workshop on 3D Virtual Reconstruction and Visualization of Complex Architectures. International Society for Photogrammetry and Remote Sensing, Trento, Italy (2011)
10. Recky, M., Leberl, F.: Window detection in complex facades. In: Proc. of 2nd EUVIP, pp. 220–225 (2010)
11. Recky, M., Leberl, F.: Windows detection using k-means in cie-lab color space. In: Proc. of 20th ICPR, pp. 356–360 (2010)
12. Shalunts, G., Haxhimusa, Y., Sablatnig, R.: Architectural Style Classification of Building Facade Windows. In: Bebis, G., Boyle, R., Parvin, B., Koracin, D., Wang, S., Kyungnam, K., Benes, B., Moreland, K., Borst, C., DiVerdi, S., Yi-Jen, C., Ming, J. (eds.) ISVC 2011, Part II. LNCS, vol. 6939, pp. 280–289. Springer, Heidelberg (2011)
13. Shalunts, G., Haxhimusa, Y., Sablatnig, R.: Classification of gothic and baroque architectural elements. In: Proc. of the 19th IWSSIP, Vienna, Austria, pp. 330–333 (2012)
14. Snavely, N., Seitz, S.M., Szeliski, R.: Photo tourism: exploring photo collections in 3d. ACM Transaction on Graphics 25, 835–846 (2006)
15. Wenzel, S., Drauschke, M., Förstner, W.: Detection of repeated structures in facade images. Pattern Recognition and Image Analysis 18(3), 406–411 (2008)
16. Zhang, W., Kosecka, J.: Hierarchical building recognition. Image and Vision Computing 25(5), 704–716 (2004)
17. Zheng, Y.T., Zhao, M., Song, Y., Adam, H., Buddemeier, U., Bissacco, A., Brucher, F., Chua, T.S., Neven, H.: Tour the world: building a web-scale landmark recognition engine. In: Proc. of ICCV and PR, pp. 1085–1092 (2009)

Human Relative Position Detection Based on Mutual Occlusion

Víctor Borjas, Michal Drozdzal, Petia Radeva, and Jordi Vitrià

Universitat de Barcelona,
Facultat de Matemàtiques & Centre de Visiò per Computador,
Campus UAB

Abstract. In this paper, we propose, within the field of automatic social context analysis, a novel method to identify the mutual position between two persons in images. Based on the idea that mutual information of head position, body visibility and bodies' contour shapes may lead to a good estimation of mutual position between people, a predictor is constructed to classify the relative position between both subjects. We advocate the use of superpixels as the basic unit of the human analysis framework. We construct a Support Vector Machine classifier on the feature vector for each image. The results show that this combination of features, provides a significantly low error rate with low variance in our database of 366 images.

1   Introduction

When two persons are facing an audience or facing a camera for a shot, it is common that one of the subjects occludes part of the other's body. This occlusion may be originated by both physical or social atributes. For example, physically shorter people (usually, females or children) tend to stand in front of the other subject producing the occlusion, or socially more important people tend to stand in a closer plane to the camera or audience. Fig. 1 sketches the situation addressed. In these images we can observe couples in a frontal view from camera. In these cases, the relative position can denote political, hierarchical or leadership status between them. These social relations can be of great importance when analyzing social and cultural behavior like social hierarchy, political importance or leadership. Multiple characteristics of the scene are involved like head and body position, clothing color, pose analysis, and many others.

Up to our knowledge, the amount of papers related to analyze faces as a group instead of individuals, and the physical mutual relation of people within a scene is surprisingly low, usually in the context of identifying people in collection of photos like in [5], [7] and [8]. In [6], the authors analyze people in images using contextual features extracted from relative head position and size that encapsulate the structure of the scene to perform tasks like demographic recognition, calculating scene and camera parameters, and event recognition. They show that factors like age or gender influence the position of subjects in an image.

L. Alvarez et al. (Eds.): CIARP 2012, LNCS 7441, pp. 332–339, 2012.

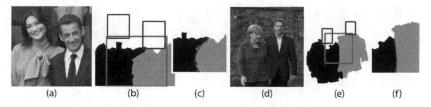

Fig. 1. (a) and (d) Original images; (b) and (e) Head Detection boundaries in blue, intersection zone in red and Body Segmentation labels: white for Background, black for Left and grey for Right; (c) and (f) Curve Fitting in the intersection zone

Our goal is to develop an automatic method to detect relative position of people in frontal images in terms of mutual human body occlusions. First, using a Head Detection Algorithm [9], faces are detected (see Fig. 1 (b) and (e)). Next, the image is then converted into superpixels to act as the basic element of all operations. Skin superpixels are identified and eliminated from the image to avoid confusion and misclassification. The parameters of three RGB Gaussian Mixture Models (GMM) corresponding to the background and both persons are computed. A previously stated body hypothesis is projected on the image to delimit body prior boundaries. An energy minimization cut is performed in an undirected graph, where each node is a superpixel (Fig. 1 (b) and (e)). Edges are extracted from the "uncertainty" zone between both bodies and curves are fitted to analyze the image structure (Fig. 1 (c) and (f)). Finally, a Support Vector Machine (SVM) is trained to classify the mutual position.

2   Our Approach

Given the problem of detecting mutual position of persons, we propose to extract a feature vector that represents scene in terms of head position, body visibility and bodies' contour shapes.

2.1   Superpixels

In order to simplify the image into a new representation that is more meaningful and easier to analyze, we use the geometric flows method [2] to extract the superpixels from the images. Superpixels represent regions of pixels that have nearly the same color and brightness. This algorithm produces segments that on one hand respect local image boundaries, while on the other hand limit under-segmentation through a compactness constraint. Pixels are guaranteed to maintain an uniform size along the image, giving an advantage for GMM calculation and skin detection. Fig. 2 (a) and (b) show an example of this extraction.

2.2   Skin Detection

Images with high percentage of skin may lead to misclassification since they reduce the effectiveness of the GMM as a basic superpixel classifier. To this

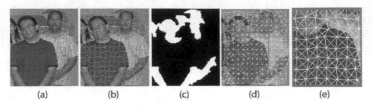

Fig. 2. (a) Original image. (b) Superpixels. (c) Skin detection. (d) Connected Super-pixel Graph. (e) Closer Visualization of Graph

purpose, we disable skin pixels in the images for contributing to the classification process. According to [10], one of the fastest and more reliable ways of identifying skin pixels in an image is presented in [3]. Three basic threshold operations (see Eq. (1)) over three terms built from RGB colors proved to have above 90% of precision. An example of the resulting skin class mask is shown in Figure 2 (c).

$$\frac{3br^2}{(r+g+b)^3} > 0.1276 \ \& \ \frac{r+g+b}{3r} \ \frac{r-g}{(r+g+b)} \le 0.9498 \ \& \ \frac{rb+g^2}{gb} \le 2.7775 \quad (1)$$

2.3 Body Visibility

Aiming to extract an attribute that defines body visibility, we need to perform body segmentation. Using GMM to represent section or classes in an image have been widely used and proved to be effective. In [11], the authors perform background/foreground segmentation based on iterative graph cuts via energy minimization. He aims for a quick foreground segmentation simplifying user interaction. In respect to that, a foreground and background GMM is defined from user input and a k value (GMM correspondence) to every pixel is assigned. Secondly, GMM means and covariances are updated, with the corresponding weights. To perform final segmentation, the author performs graph cut via energy minimization as in [13] giving each pixel in the image a label l. This process is repeated iteratively until the minimum energy is reached.

In our algorithm, a weighted GMM model in RGB color space is used as initial pixel classification. Models are built for *Background, Left Person* and *Right Person*. We follow a practice that is already used for soft segmentation [14]. Each GMM is taken to be a full-covariance Gaussian mixture with K components (we use $K = 2$ for foreground/bodies and $K = 3$ for background).

GMM 'A Priori' Classification. In previous recognition work using cloth-ing [4], either a rectangular region below the face is assumed to be clothing, or the clothing region is modeled using operator-labeled clothing from many im-ages. Similar to [1], we use a non-rectangular mask (Fig. 3(a)), computed from a set of body labeled images, projecting it into the image scaling it according to each face size. From this projection, we create two masks identifying both body hypothesis useful for further operations as shown in Fig. 3 (c) and (d).

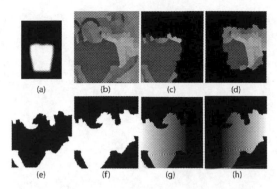

Fig. 3. (a) Body Mask. (b) Turbopixel segmentation. (c) and (d) Left and Right body mask projections. (e) Background mask. (f) Foreground mask. (g) and (h) Left and Right weighted masks for GMM training.

The hypothetical foreground and background regions in the image are obtained joining both body hypothesis as shown in Fig. 3 (c) and (d). Skin superpixels are added to the background as explained in Section 2.2. Both foreground GMM (Left and Right) are then computed assigning weights to the pixels, assuming that the most-left pixels within the foreground belong to the left-hand person. The pixel weights decrease as the position in the horizontal axis increases for the Left GMM and viceversa. Fig. 3 *Bottom Row* shows an example of how weights behave within the foreground.

Finally, GMM for each label are trained using the corresponding weights and pixels stated previously. The weighted means μ_l and weighted covariance matrices Σ_l for each model are stored for further likelihood calculation. Assuming weights are normalized $\sum_{i=1}^{N} \omega_i = 1$, where N is the number of pixels, means and covariance matrices for each label l are computed as follows:

$$\mu^l = \sum_{i=1}^{N} \omega_i^l x_i , \quad \{\Sigma_l\}_{jk} = \frac{\sum_{i=1}^{N} \omega_i^l}{(\sum_{i=1}^{N} \omega_i^l)^2 - \sum_{i=1}^{N} (\omega_i^l)^2} \sum_{i=1}^{N} \omega_i^l (x_{i,j}^l - \mu_j^l)(x_{i,k}^l - \mu_k^l) \quad (2)$$

where x is the RGB value of each pixel and l denotes the label (Background, Left or Right).

Body Segmentation and Graph Cut via Energy Minimization. An energy function E is defined so that its minimum should correspond to a good segmentation guided by the observed foreground and background GMM, and reflecting solidity of objects. This is captured by a "Gibbs" energy of the form: $E(L, \theta, Z) = U(L, \theta, Z) + V(L, Z)$, where $L = \{l_i\}_{i=1,...,N} = \{1, 2, 3\}$ is the set of possible labels, θ is the set of GMM and Z is the set of pixels. The data term U evaluates the probability of assigning label l_i to pixels in Z given the GMM θ: $U(L, \theta, Z) = \sum_{z_i \in Z} -log(P(z_i|l_i))$. The smoothness term can be written

as: $V(L, Z) = \sum\limits_{(m,n)\in H} [l_m \neq l_n] \exp\left(-\beta(z_m - z_n)^2\right)$ where H is the set of connected nodes, $[\cdot]$ acts as a factor that allows summation only pairs of nodes with
different assigned label l and β is a smoothness term also known as Ising prior.
This energy term encourages coherence in regions of similar RGB values. Good
results are obtained by defining nodes to be connected if their distance in image
coordinates is below a given threshold t:

$$t = \frac{\sum\limits_{i=1}^{N} d(z_i)}{N} \tag{3}$$

where $d(\cdot)$ is a function that returns the longest possible diameter of a given
superpixel. This limits the neighbor to those nodes within a diameter distance
in any direction as sketched on Fig. 2 (d) and (e).

A reliable value of β is $\beta = \left(2\langle(z_m - z_n)^2\rangle\right)^{-1}$ where $\langle z_m - z_n\rangle^2$ represents
the Euclidean distance in the RGB color space between pixels z_m and z_n [13].
Minimization of $E(L, \theta, Z)$ is done using the standard minimum cut algorithm
defined in [13].

2.4   Curve Fitting

Once the bodies are segmented in the image, we perform a curve fitting process
on important edges along the intersection of them. Assuming an overlapping
between body hypothesis, we use their intersection as the "uncertainty zone"
(see Fig. 1 (b) and (e)). We extract this zone from the labeled image and detect
edges using Sobel filters. Considering that edges belonging to background should
not be taken into account for curve fitting, we filter them by performing basic
morphologic operations in the edge image (See Fig. 1 (c) and (f)). This procedure
leaves only edges that correspond to boundaries between both bodies.

Afterwards, a polynomial curve is fitted on the edge points. In this case, we
used second order polynomial since we are aiming for a simple quadratic function
curve that corresponds to shoulder-like shapes. Once the curve is fitted, mean
normal vectors are computed. Since the direction and magnitude of these vectors
represent the shape or type of curve, this vector is directly used as a feature, n^*.

2.5   SVM Training

We use a SVM classifier with a third grade polynomial Kernel function to classify each new image as *Left* or *Right* human occlussion. Each image is then
represented as a 3D feature vector:

$$F = [y^*, r^*, n^*] \ , \ y^* = \frac{y_i - y_j}{\frac{a_i + a_j}{2}} \ , \ r^* = \frac{\sum\limits_{\{z_i | l_i = right\}} 1 - \sum\limits_{\{z_j | l_j = left\}} 1}{N} \tag{4}$$

where y^* is the normalized difference in vertical position of both detected heads
in the image. Normalization is done over the average scale $\bar{s}$ of heads obtained as

the head area $a_i = w_i \cdot h_i$, where w_i represents the head width and h_i represents the head height in the image. The term r^* represents the difference in percentage of labels in the "uncertainty zone" graph cut segmentation. Normals n^* come directly from the edge detection and curvature step in Section 2.4. Figure 4 sketches the three components of the feature vector.

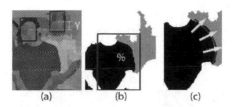

(a)   (b)   (c)

Fig. 4. (a) Relative height difference (y^*), (b) Body visibility likelihhod (r^*), and (c) Contour shape estimated from the curve fitting (n^*)

3   Experiments

3.1   Database

We constructed a dataset that consists of 366 images with ground truth annotations in the form of *Left* and *Right* overlapping. Each image includes only two persons in frontal view to the camera and one is partially occluding the other. Since there is no proper public domain database, we created one by randomly downloading from internet and cropping the images in situations when more than two persons appeared close to each other and an overlapping is possible to occur. The database is available for downloading in the first author's website.

3.2   Evaluation

We performed a ten-fold cross-validation measuring the mean score and variance of all possible combinations of features. Fig. 5(a) shows how the classifier performs, noticing that the highest mean score and the lowest variance, are obtained by combinations of the explained features, y^*, r^* and n^*. Additionally, very low variance values are important to notice.

Fig. 5(b) sketches the precision of our system in function of number of superpixels in which the image is represented. It shows that the best results are obtained with 200 superpixels per image, corresponding to 10-15 superpixels per face. This is an important fact because it tells how general a representation of an image can be avoiding image details and still be able to perform GMM, graph cut segmentation and curve fitting.

Failures can occur mainly in three cases shown in the *Right Column* of Fig. 6: (a) when skin detection is not precise, either it gives false positives like labeling clothing as skin, or false negatives like not labeling a face as skin; (b) both persons clothing has the same distribution of color, like both dressed in black which can lead to a weak segmentation in "uncertainty zone"; (c) uncommon human poses, lead to a wrongly determined "uncertainty zone", therefore producing a wrong segmentation and an inaccurate curve fitting.

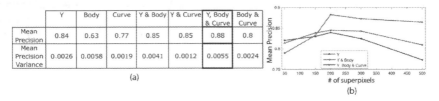

	Y	Body	Curve	Y & Body	Y & Curve	Y, Body & Curve	Body & Curve
Mean Precision	0.84	0.63	0.77	0.85	0.85	0.88	0.8
Mean Precision Variance	0.0026	0.0058	0.0019	0.0041	0.0012	0.0055	0.0024

(a)

(b)

Fig. 5. (a) Mean Precision and Mean Precision Covariance. (b) Mean Precision as function of number of superpixels.

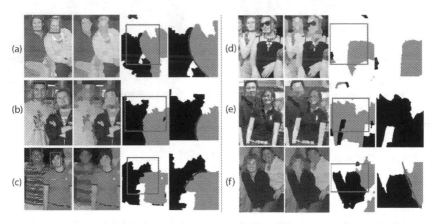

Fig. 6. From Left to Right: Original image with Head Detection; Superpixel representation; Graph Cut result in greyscale labels and "Uncertainty Zone" in red; and Curve Fitting in blue. *(a)*, *(b)* & *(c)* sketch correct classification. *(d)* Too much skin in the image leads to lack of information for further processes. *(e)* Color similarity between both persons' clothes produces graph cut errors. *(f)* Uncommon human pose leads to curve fitting errors.

4   Conclusions and Future Work

In this paper, up to our knowledge, for the first time an automatic detection of mutual occlusion of persons is addressed. We presented a novel method to identify the mutual position between two persons in the same plane of an image. Our system relies on an efficient feature vector construction from both simple and complex characteristics of the scene. It resulted in a reliable classification system in uncontrolled datasets obtaining an accuracy of 88%.

The framework described here allows for exploration in a wide set of directions to enrich the model like: new GMM class for skin recognition and interpretation on possible arm and head poses, learning the likelihoods of edge orientation according to face or upper body appearance.

Acknowledgments. This work was partially supported by MICINN grants TIN2009- 14404-C02, CONSOLIDER-INGENIO 2010 (CSD2007-00018) and the AGAUR grant to SGR696.

References

1. Sivic, J., Zitnick, C., Szeliski, R.: Finding people in repeated shots of the same scene. In: Proc. BMVC (2006)
2. Levinshtein, A., Stere, A., Kutulakos, K.N., Fleet, D.J., Dickinson, S.J., Siddiqi, K.: TurboPixels: Fast Superpixels Using Geometric Flows. TPAMI (2009)
3. Gomez, G., Morales, E.F.: Automatic feature construction and a simple rule induction algorithm for skin detection. In: Proc. ICML Workshop on Machine Learning in Computer Vision
4. Gallagher, A., Chen, T.: Clothing cosegmentation for recognizing people. In: Proc. CVPR (2008)
5. Gallagher, A., Chen, T.: Using group prior to identify people in consumer images. In: Proc. CVPR SLAM Workshop (2007)
6. Gallagher, A., Chen, T.: Understanding Images of Groups of People. In: Proc. CVPR (2009)
7. Naaman, M., Yeh, R., Garcia Molina, H., Paepcke, A.: Leveraging context to resolve identity in photo albums. In: Proc. JCDL (2005)
8. Stone, Z., Zickler, T., Darrell, T.: Autotagging facebook: Social network context improves photo annotation. In: Proc. CVPR, Internet Vision Workshop (2008)
9. Drozdzal, M., Hernández, A., Segu, S., Baro, X., Escalera, S., Lapedriza, A., Masip, D., Radeva, P., Vitria, J.: Combining Detectors for Human Layout Analysis. In: Proc. ECCV, The Pascal Visual Object Classes Challenge Workshop (2010)
10. Vezhnevets, V., Sazonov, V., Andreeva, A.: A Survey on Pixel-Based Skin Color Detection Techniques. In: Proc. GRAPHICON (2003)
11. Rother, C., Kolmogorov, V., Blake, A.: GrabCut, interactive foreground extraction using iterated graph cuts. ACM Trans. SIGGRAPH (2004)
12. Fulkerson, B., Vedaldi, A., Soatto, S.: Class segmentation and object localization with superpixel neighborhoods. In: Proc. ICCV (2009)
13. Boykov, Y., Jolly, M.: Interactive graph cuts for optimal boundary and region segmentation of objects in N-D images. In: Proc. ICCV (2001)
14. Ruzon, M., Tomasi, C.: Alpha estimation in natural images. In: Proc. CVPR (2000)

Online Matrix Factorization
for Multimodal Image Retrieval

Juan C. Caicedo and Fabio A. González

Universidad Nacional de Colombia

Abstract. In this paper, we propose a method to build an index for image search using multimodal information, that is, using visual features and text data simultaneously. The method combines both data sources and generates one multimodal representation using latent factor analysis and matrix factorization. One remarkable characteristic of this multimodal representation is that it connects textual and visual content allowing to solve queries with only visual content by implicitly completing the missing textual content. Another important characteristic of the method is that the multimodal representation is learned online using an efficient stochastic gradient descent formulation. Experiments were conducted in a dataset of 5,000 images to evaluate the convergence speed and search performance. Experimental results show that the proposed algorithm requires only one pass through the data set to achieve high quality retrieval performance.

1   Introduction

Consider the problem of finding useful images by querying a system with an example image, i.e., the user provides an image to retrieve other semantically related images from a large collection [1]. This kind of search —also known as the query-by-example paradigm for image retrieval [2]— can be of potential benefit in different situations such as people taking pictures with mobile phones [3], or physicians comparing a new medical image with respect to the hospital's archive [4]. Regardless of the specific task, the main problem of finding useful images with an example query is the semantic gap [2]: images with similar visual features computed by a machine can have different semantic meanings for users observing them.

Then, the main research agenda in image retrieval systems has been devoted to design methods able to automatically understand image contents, and so, image search systems will have the ability to deliver more accurate results. The most popular approach is based on auto-annotation, which consists on analyzing the visual content of an image and generating tags associated to what can be seen on it [5]. However, one of the main drawbacks of this approach is scalability: most of these methods only work with a few tens of labels or tags. For large scale image search systems, the ability to handle large numbers of tags would be a desirable property. Also, methods for large scale image search are required to handle large amounts of images, which can be very expensive in computational terms.

In this paper, we explore the ability of matrix factorization algorithms to build large scale multimodal image indices. First, the image collection is organized in a table of images vs. features, which encodes the visual contents of images. This table is actually a

L. Alvarez et al. (Eds.): CIARP 2012, LNCS 7441, pp. 340–347, 2012.

matrix of visual data, that can be analyzed and processed to extract meaningful patterns. Second, a similar matrix is build for text data associated to training images, i.e., a matrix of images vs. tags, which can handle any number of keywords simultaneously.

The goal of the method proposed in this paper is to find relationships between these two matrices, using multimodal analysis. We propose the use of matrix factorization algorithms to decompose a training data set, and find correspondences between visual patterns and text terms. These correspondences are expressed as latent factors that can be computed from the input matrices described before. Under this formulation, a system for image search can directly handle multiple tags or labels for a single image, and can handle new images that do not have annotations at all. Furthermore, the proposed decomposition algorithms are formulated using stochastic gradient descent, which allows to manipulate very large image collections.

The main contribution of this paper is the formulation of the matrix factorization algorithms as online processes and its application to multimodal image representation. The contents of this paper are organized as follows: Section 2 reviews related work. Section 3 discusses the visual representation and similarity measures for image search. Section 4 presents the proposed matrix factorization algorithms. Section 5 shows an experimental evaluation and Section 6 presents some concluding remarks.

2 Related Work

Multimodal representations for images are usually related to the combination of two sources of information: visual features and text data [6]. The goal of combining these data sources is to complement the possible representations of image contents using semantic information extracted from text data. Previous works include probabilistic models [7] and matrix factorization algorithms [8]. These approaches require solving large optimization problems or computing expensive updating rules, which make them infeasible for large image collections. Our approach differs from the others, since the algorithm formulation can be gracefully scaled up to large image databases.

The strategy that we follow to scale up the matrix factorization algorithms is based on stochastic approximations. Mairal et al. [9] proposed an online setting for matrix factorization, specially designed for sparse coding. We follow similar ideas, with a simpler formulation that follows the stochastic gradient descent structure. Also, our main research focus is to generate multimodal image representations instead of sparse coding.

3 Image Representation

In this work, we consider the problem of image retrieval using as queries example pictures. So, users are expected to upload an image file to the retrieval system, and the system is expected to analyze its visual content to identify potentially relevant images. Those images selected by the system are presented to the user as results of his/her search. This image retrieval system requires a representation of the visual contents for each image. In this work, we follow the Bag-of-Features (BoF) approach to model image descriptors for search. Basically, this representation accounts for the occurrence of visual patterns that can be seen in an image, with respect to a predefined dictionary or codebook. The final representation of images is a histogram that represents the visual structure of images.

Given the BoF descriptors for a database of images, we can build a matrix of visual patterns vs. images in the collection. Also, given the BoF descriptors for a query image, the system can compute the similarity of it with respect to images in the database using the histogram intersection.

4   Multimodal Indexing Using Matrix Factorization

A multimodal representation for images is proposed, with the goal of improving the response of a system that uses only visual data to search similar images. The approach used in this paper to build the multimodal representation is based on latent factors. A common latent space for visual and text data is learned, i.e., any of both data modalities can be projected from its original representation space to the common latent space. In this way, the resulting multimodal space to represent images incorporates semantic information together with visual contents, and so, can provide a better mechanism to match similar images.

The computational methods used in this work for learning such a multimodal space are based on matrix factorization. The proposed algorithm simultaneously decompose the matrices of visual and text data to find a low rank approximation of them, by solving an optimization problem. To this end, assume the availability of two matrices of data, one for visual features $V \in \mathbb{R}^{n \times l}$ and the second for text data $T \in \mathbb{R}^{m \times l}$. Both matrices have the same number of columns, corresponding to the number of images in the database: l. Let n be the number of visual features, i.e., the number of rows in the visual matrix, and let m be the number of text terms, i.e., the number of rows in the text matrix. The problem of multimodal decomposition is to find the matrices P, Q and H such that

$$V \approx PH$$
$$T \approx QH$$

where $H \in \mathbb{R}^{r \times l}$ is an encoding matrix for the multimodal latent representation of images, $P \in \mathbb{R}^{n \times r}$ and $Q \in \mathbb{R}^{m \times r}$ are the multimodal transformations for visual and text data respectively. The main idea behind this model is to find a common representation H for the visual and text data, which is known as the latent representation, together with the corresponding transformations from the latent space to the source data. The dimensionality of the latent space, r, is a fixed parameter, which indicates how many latent factors should be extracted from the data.

This simultaneous factorization of V and T can be found by solving an optimization problem that minimizes the following objective function:

$$\min_{P,Q,H} \quad \frac{1}{2} \left(\|V - PH\|_F^2 + \|T - QH\|_F^2 \right) \\ + \frac{\lambda}{2} \left(\|P\|_F^2 + \|Q\|_F^2 + \|H\|_F^2 \right) \tag{1}$$

where $\|\cdot\|_F$ is the Frobenius norm, and λ is a regularization parameter for the unknowns in the problem.

Gradient Descent Solution. The problem above has a non-convex objective function. However, the function is differentiable for all unknowns and the solution can be computed using gradient descent as follows:

$$P_{\tau+1} = P_\tau + \gamma \left(V H_\tau^T - P_\tau H_\tau H_\tau^T - \lambda P_\tau \right) \tag{2}$$

$$Q_{\tau+1} = Q_\tau + \gamma \left(T H_\tau^T - Q_\tau H_\tau H_\tau^T - \lambda Q_\tau \right) \tag{3}$$

$$H_{\tau+1} = H_\tau + \gamma \left(P_\tau^T V - P_\tau^T P_\tau H_\tau + Q_\tau^T T - Q_\tau^T Q_\tau^T H_\tau - \lambda H_\tau \right) \tag{4}$$

In the updating rules shown above, the subindex τ represents the solution at the iteration τ, and γ is the step size in the gradient descent algorithm. The solution above presents a batch formulation of the solution, i.e., at each step or iteration, the algorithm requires the full matrices V and T to decide the new direction of the solution. This can be quite expensive or even infeasible for large image collections, that can not be fit in memory. Alternative formulations of this problem run in parallel mode. However, our proposal is to formulate this problem using a stochastic gradient descent approximation.

Online Matrix Factorization. The idea of online learning using stochastic approximations is to compute the new solution for each unknown in the problem using only one data sample at a time [10]. Then, we can scan large data sets without memory restrictions, and this can be potentially scaled up to large image datasets. The stochastic gradient descent formulation for the multimodal matrix factorization problem is as follows:

$$h_\tau = \left(\lambda I + P_\tau^T P_\tau + Q_\tau^T Q_\tau \right)^{-1} \left(P_\tau^T v_\tau + Q_\tau^T t_\tau \right) \tag{5}$$

$$P_{\tau+1} = (1 - \gamma\lambda) P_\tau + \gamma v_\tau h_\tau^T - \gamma P_\tau h_\tau h_\tau^T \tag{6}$$

$$Q_{\tau+1} = (1 - \gamma\lambda) Q_\tau + \gamma t_\tau h_\tau^T - \gamma Q_\tau h_\tau h_\tau^T \tag{7}$$

where v_τ and t_τ are vectors of visual features and text features, respectively, for one image, and h_τ is the multimodal representation for that pair of vectors. This approach learns the matrices P and Q using one image with its corresponding text data at a time, and then, the image is discarded. For the image used in the iteration τ, the multimodal representation is approximated using the solution for h_τ, but this is also discarded with the image vectors v_τ and t_τ. Then, a final pass over the data would be required to recover the multimodal latent representation H for the full database, using the same expression for all images, and without updating P and Q.

Minibatch Extension. A minibatch extension of the algorithm presented in equations 6, 7 and 5 can be easily obtained by assuming that v_τ, t_τ and h_τ are not single vectors, but small matrices containing several vectors. The minibatch extension allows to process several images at the same time to make an update in the unknown parameters of the objective. Actually, the batch algorithm is an special case of the minibatch extension, in which the number of images in the minibatch is equal to the number of images in the training set.

Indexing New Images. The algorithm and the solution presented are useful to learn the transformation matrices P and Q from a training image set that has visual and text data, and also to index a database by computing H using equation 5. For new images not included in the factorization analysis, we assume that all these matrices are already learned and are available. To index a new image, all what is required is the transformation matrices P and Q with a visual vector v for the new image. Since we expect queries with no text data, the following expression can be evaluated to project the new image to the multimodal latent space: $h_q = \left(\lambda I + P^T P + Q^T Q\right)^{-1} \left(P^T v\right)$. Other query strategies such as text queries and multimodal queries can also be supported in this framework, following similar extensions to those proposed in [8].

Searching in the Multimodal Space. After all images in the collection have been indexed, a new matrix with the latent representation that fuses visual features and text data is obtained: H. This matrix has as many columns as images in the database, so each image has a column vector $h \in \mathbb{R}^r$, with dimensionality r as the number of multimodal latent factors. Query images can be projected in the same space as well. So, to search in the multimodal latent space, we will use the dot product between these vectors, which accounts for the degree of similarity between two latent representations. Our assumption is that images with similar semantic interpretations will have similar multimodal factors in this representation.

5   Experimental Evaluation

Data. The image collection used in this work is the Corel 5k image dataset, which is composed of 5,000 photographs organized in 50 categories, and has been used in different image retrieval evaluations by many researchers [7,11]. It consists of text annotations for each image, using a text dictionary with 374 terms. Also, the dataset has been organized in 3 parts to allow other researchers to reproduce experimental results: training (4,000 images), validation (500 images) and test (500 images). This data set is used to simulate retrieval performance using the 50 initial categories as ground truth. We follow the same experimental setup in this study. The visual matrix representation is built using a bag-of-features extracted with the same features as [8]: DCT coefficients in all color channels for local features and a dictionary of visual words with 2,000 clusters. The text matrix is built using a boolean vector representation: 1 for terms attached to images and 0 otherwise.

Algorithm Convergence. The first evaluation conducted in this work is the analysis of convergence of the algorithm using the batch and online approaches. The input matrices for training are $V \in \mathbb{R}^{2000 \times 4000}$ and $T \in \mathbb{R}^{374 \times 4000}$. We set the parameter $r = 50$, which defines the size of the multimodal latent space (or the number of latent factors). Then, the expected output matrices after the learning algorithm is run are $P \in \mathbb{R}^{2000 \times 50}$, $Q \in \mathbb{R}^{374 \times 50}$ and $H \in \mathbb{R}^{50 \times 4000}$.

Both strategies, the batch and online algorithms, require the definition of the parameter λ for regularization, as well as the parameter γ, the gradient descent step size. We set both parameters with the same values for both algorithms, using $\lambda = 0.1$ and defining γ as a decreasing function of time [10]: $\gamma(\tau) = \dfrac{\gamma_0}{1 + \gamma_0 \lambda \tau}$, where $\gamma_0 = 0.1$ is the initial parameter, and τ is the iteration number. Both algorithms were run during the same number of epochs, where an epoch is defined as a complete scan over the dataset.

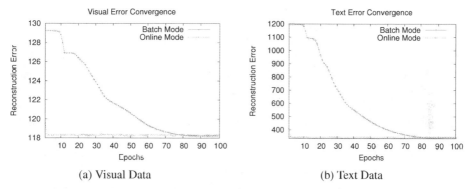

(a) Visual Data   (b) Text Data

Fig. 1. Evolution of the reconstruction error per epochs

Figure 1 present the findings of error convergence for 100 epochs, for both data modalities. These results show the evolution of the reconstruction error for the visual and text matrices for each epoch of the algorithm. The scale of the error units are specific for this data set. The results show that the online algorithm achieve the lowest reconstruction error from the very first epoch, converging much more faster than the batch algorithm. This means that the online algorithm provides a large reduction in the computational cost with respect to the batch counterpart, mainly because the online algorithm requires very few epochs to reach a stable solution. This tendency suggest that no more than 5 epochs are required to achieve a good factorization of the multimodal data.

To investigate how many iterations are actually needed to achieve a good performance, not in terms of reconstruction error, but in terms of retrieval accuracy, we run the algorithm for 20 epochs and evaluated the resulting model at each epoch by conducting information retrieval experiments. The experiments consist of using example images to search in the multimodal index, as is described in the next Subsection. The performance is measured using Mean Average Precision (MAP). In terms of MAP, the higher the value the better, since it suggests a more accurate response with respect to the results expected by users. The results show that the factorization achieves very good retrieval performance (a MAP of 0.2159), in contrast to the baseline based on image matching using visual contents only, which has a significantly lower performance (a MAP of 0.1239). More importantly, the improvement showed by the online multimodal indexing method is obtained with a single pass over the training data. Running the algorithm for more epochs does not seem to improve or hurt the quality of the factorization in a significant way. This is a very important result that supports the idea of scaling the algorithm to very large data sets with minimum processing effort: no more than a single scan on the available training data.

Retrieval Evaluation. To evaluate the retrieval performance, the validation data set is used as queries for the system. This allows to simulate a total number of 500 queries from 50 different categories. The queries in this system are received as image examples alone with no attached text or labels. However, the database has been indexed using multimodal data. Since queries do not have any text, it is reasonable to search using the BoF descriptor only to observe the benefit of using multimodal indexing strategies. Besides the proposed algorithm, we implemented and tested two different multimodal indexing algorithms recently proposed in the literature, which are based on Nonnegative Matrix Factorization (NMF): Multimodal NMF [12] and Asymmetric NMF [8].

Table 1 compares the retrieval performance of different indexing methods using MAP. The results show that using multimodal data for image search improves upon the baseline that uses only visual information, i.e., a multimodal indexing strategy for image retrieval can be used to deliver more meaningful results for users. The proposed online algorithm provides the second best retrieval performance in these experiments, with a very competitive result.

In addition, one of the most important aspects of the proposed algorithm is its ability to process the data set very quickly. For this experiment all the algorithms were implemented in Matlab and run in multithreading mode on a 12 core computer. The Table presents execution times and number of epochs required to achieve the reported retrieval performance for each method. The proposed online algorithm runs from 13 to 25 times faster than the other algorithms, even though an online approach does not fully exploit multithreading as the other algorithms do. This demonstrates the potential of our approach to process really large image databases.

Table 1. Retrieval performance for image search using Mean Average Precision (MAP). The learning time and the number of epochs to achieve that performance are also reported.

Method	MAP	Learning Time	Epochs
Visual Matching	0.1239	N.A.	N.A
Online Multimodal MF	0.2159	**2.3 secs**	1
Batch Multimodal MF	0.2115	58.6 secs	100
Asymmetric NMF [8]	0.2203	36.7 secs	100
Multimodal NMF [12]	0.2096	29.3 secs	100

6   Conclusions and Future Work

This paper has presented a matrix factorization algorithm for multimodal data analysis. The most remarkable characteristic of the proposed algorithm is its online formulation, which leads to very fast convergence over the batch algorithm. Experimental results show significant difference between the convergence speed of the algorithms, showing that only one pass through the data is enough to obtain state-of-the-art performance. As part of our future work, we plan to process bigger datasets with potentially hundreds of thousands of images to test the ability of the proposed algorithm to deal with large collections in terms of processing time as well as learning power.

References

1. Rasiwasia, N., Moreno, P.J., Vasconcelos, N.: Bridging the gap: Query by semantic example. IEEE Transactions on Multimedia 9(5), 923–938 (2007)
2. Datta, R., Joshi, D., Li, J., Wang, J.Z.: Image retrieval: Ideas, influences, and trends of the new age. ACM Comput. Surv. 40(2), 1–60 (2008)
3. Fan, X., Xie, X., Li, Z., Li, M., Ma, W.: Photo-to-search: using multimodal queries to search the web from mobile devices. In: Proceedings of the 7th ACM SIGMM International Workshop on Multimedia Information Retrieval, pp. 143–150. ACM, Hilton (2005)
4. Muller, H., Michoux, N., Bandon, D., Geissbuhler, A.: A review of content-based image retrieval systems in medical applications: Clinical benefits and future directions. International Journal of Medical Informatics 73, 1–23 (2004)
5. Makadia, A., Pavlovic, V., Kumar, S.: A New Baseline for Image Annotation. In: Forsyth, D., Torr, P., Zisserman, A. (eds.) ECCV 2008, Part III. LNCS, vol. 5304, pp. 316–329. Springer, Heidelberg (2008)
6. Atrey, P., Hossain, M., El Saddik, A., Kankanhalli, M.: Multimodal fusion for multimedia analysis: a survey. Multimedia Systems (2010)
7. Duygulu, P., Barnard, K., de Freitas, J.F.G., Forsyth, D.: Object Recognition as Machine Translation: Learning a Lexicon for a Fixed Image Vocabulary (chapter 7). In: Heyden, A., Sparr, G., Nielsen, M., Johansen, P. (eds.) ECCV 2002, Part IV. LNCS, vol. 2353, pp. 97–112. Springer, Heidelberg (2002)
8. Caicedo, J.C., BenAbdallah, J., González, F.A., Nasraoui, O.: Multimodal representation, indexing, automated annotation and retrieval of image collections via non-negative matrix factorization. Neurocomput. 76, 50–60 (2012)
9. Mairal, J., Bach, F., Ponce, J., Sapiro, G.: Online learning for matrix factorization and sparse coding. J. Mach. Learn. Res. 11, 19–60 (2010)
10. Bottou, L.: Large-scale machine learning with stochastic gradient descent. In: Proceedings of the 19th International Conference on Computational Statistics (2010)
11. Hare, J.S., Samangooei, S., Lewis, P.H., Nixon, M.S.: Semantic spaces revisited: investigating the performance of auto-annotation and semantic retrieval using semantic spaces. In: CIVR 2008: Proceedings of the 2008 International Conference on Content-based Image and Video Retrieval, pp. 359–368. ACM, New York (2008)
12. Akata, Z., Thurau, C., Bauckhage, C.: Non-negative matrix factorization in multimodality data for segmentation and label prediction. In: 16th Computer Vision Winter Workshop (2011)

Improved HSI Color Space for Color Image Segmentation

Rodolfo Alvarado-Cervantes and Edgardo M. Felipe-Riveron[*]

Center for Computing Research, National Polytechnic Institute, Juan de Dios Batiz w/n, Col.
Nueva Industrial Vallejo, P.O. 07738, Mexico
`ateramex@gmail.com, edgardo@cic.ipn.mx`

Abstract. We present an interactive, semiautomatic image segmentation method that processes the color information of each pixel as a unit, thus avoiding color information scattering. The color information of every pixel is integrated in the segmented image by an adaptive color similarity function designed for direct color comparisons. The border between the achromatic and chromatic zones in the HSI color model has been transformed in order to improve the quality of the pixels segmentation when their colors are very obscure and very clear. The color integrating technique is direct, simple and computationally inexpensive, and it has also good performance in low chromaticity and low contrast images. It is shown that segmentation accuracy is above 95% as average and that the method is fast. These results are significant when compared to other solutions found in the current literature.

Keywords: Color image segmentation, Adaptive color similarity function, Improved HSI color model, Achromatic zone definition.

1   Introduction

At present, several segmentation techniques are available for color images, a good amount of them are monochromatic methods applied on the individual planes in different color spaces where the results are combined later in different ways [3]. A common problem to this approach is that when the color components of a particular pixel are processed separately the color information is so scattered in its components that most of the color information is lost [1] [3] [4].

In this work, an interactive, semiautomatic image segmentation method is presented that uses the color information for each pixel as a whole, thus avoiding color information scattering.

One weakness in the characterization of the achromatic region as presented in [5], [7] and [10] is its poor performance in the border regions of achromatic and chromatic zones, both in low and high brightness, due to the fact that the commonly used HSI color model does not take into account the human visual response at low and high brightness. Human vision has a nonlinear perceptual response to luminance [11]. This

---

[*] Corresponding author.

L. Alvarez et al. (Eds.): CIARP 2012, LNCS 7441, pp. 348–354, 2012.
© Springer-Verlag Berlin Heidelberg 2012

problem was overcome by modifying the saturation value of every pixel by a factor that reflects the human exponential response to brightness. We show this improvement in Section 3 comparing the achromatic zone obtained by both methods.

The results tabulated in Section 3 show that the segmentation method presented in this paper offers a useful and efficient alternative for the segmentation of objects with different colors in relatively complex color images with good performance in the presence of the unavoidable additive noise. It has also good performance in gray level and low contrast images [5].

2   Description of the Method

The segmentation method proposed in this paper relies on the calculation of a color similarity function for every pixel in a RGB 24-bit true color image to form what we call a Color Similarity Image (CSI), which is a gray level image. The color similarity function allows the clustering of the many thousands of colors representing the same perceived color in a single gray output image. The CSI is then automatically thresholded and the output can be used as a segmentation layer, or it can be modified with morphological operators to introduce geometric enhancements if they are needed. The generation of a CSI only requires calculating Eq. 1 (below) for every pixel in the RGB input image. Thus the complexity is linear with respect to the number of pixels of the source image and for that reason inexpensive computationally.

Firstly, we compute the color centroid and color standard deviation of a small sample consisting of few pixels (less than 3-4 pixels per color). The computed centroid represents the desired color to be segmented using the technique we designed for that purpose.

Then, our color similarity function uses the color standard deviation calculated from the pixel sample to adapt the level of color scattering in the comparisons. The result of a particular similarity function calculation for every pixel and the color centroid (meaning the similarity measure between the pixel and the representative color value) generates the CSI.

The CSI can be thresholded with any automatic thresholding method. To obtain the results presented in this work we used Otsu's method [8] [9].

To obtain the CSI we calculate for every pixel (i, j) in the image the following color similarity function   (Eq. 1).

$$S_{i,j} = e^{(\frac{-\Delta_h^2}{2\sigma_h^2})} * e^{(\frac{-\Delta_s^2}{2\sigma_s^2})} * e^{(\frac{-\Delta_i^2}{2\sigma_i^2})} \tag{1}$$

where Δ_h is the hue distance between *hue(i,j)* and the *average_hue*; Δ_s is the saturation distance between *saturation(i,j)* and the *average_saturation*; Δ_i is the intensity distance between *intensity()* and the *average_intensity*; σ_h is the hue standard deviation of the sample; σ_s is the saturation standard deviation of the sample; σ_i is the intensity standard deviation of the sample. In Equation (1) the color information is integrated giving high importance to perceptual small changes in hue, as well as giving wide or narrow tolerance to the intensity and saturation values depending on the initial sample, which is representative to the desired color to be segmented.

The common disadvantages attributed to the HSI color space such as the irremovable singularities of hue in very low saturations or the periodical nature of hue [7], which is lost in its standard representation as an, are overcome in our technique using vector representation in $\Re^2$, in the separation of chromatic and achromatic regions, and in the definition of the Δ_h, Δ_s and Δ_i distances.

2.1   Pixel Sample Selection

The pixel sample is a representation of the desired color(s) to be segmented from a color image. From this pixel sample we calculate two values to feed our segmentation algorithm: the color centroid and a measure of the dispersion from this centroid, in our case the standard deviation, they can be consulted for reference in [5] and [10].

2.2   The Achromatic Zone G

The achromatic zone G is the region in the HSI color space where no hue is perceived by the human. This means that color is perceived only as a gray level because the color saturation is very low or the intensity is either too low or too high.

In order to model better the human visual response in the abrupt corners regions near the union zones of the two cones with the cylinder of the singularity zone G, as presented in [5], [7] and [10], we found convenient to modify the characterization of the HSI color model for colors belonging to regions with very low or very high brightness. This step will permit us to differentiate the colors in these extreme regions, because the human response to brightness does not have this possibility. In order to adjust the zone G to a better model nearer to the human response to brightness we introduced an exponential function with three parameters to define the improved singularity of zone G: saturation threshold (st), inflection point (ip), and Slope (Fig 1). Then, the saturation image will be affected now by a factor calculated from the inflection point (ip), and Slope for every pixel (P) as shown in Eq.(2):

$$New\_Saturation\_(P) = \left(1 - Slope * \left(e\right)^{abs(ip - \text{int} ensity(P))}\right) * Saturation\_(P) \quad (2)$$

where Slope is a parameter representing the degree of affectation of the exponential factor to the saturation attribute for every pixel; abs( ) represents the absolute value function and intensity( ) is defined as an average of the RGB channels in Eq. (6) in [5]. After calculating the New_Saturation values for the source image, it is thresholded with the saturation threshold (st) to obtain the effects of the improved achromatic zone G.

We found good performance with the parameters empirically determined in the following ranges: st ϵ [0.07, 0.1], ip ϵ [0.5, 0.6], and Slope ϵ [1, 1.5].

The statistical values needed in Eq. (1) are calculated from the pixel sample using the common statistics formulae adapted to our model. The details about all this can be consulted in [5] and [10].

3   Experiments and Results

In this section we describe the experiments and present the results achieved from our segmentation method applied to two classical color images in RGB 24-bit true color format. These experiments consisted of segmenting color regions according to the following two steps:

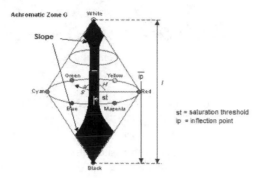

Fig. 1. The new achromatic zone G

Selection of the pixel sample. This is the only step to be left up to the user, and [5] can be consulted .as a guide. This step is automatic; its output is a gray image showing the similarity of each pixel of the RGB true color image to the color centroid formed with the chosen pixel sample taken from of the region of interest to be segmented, being white for 100% of similarity and black for 0%.

The user can now threshold the CSI using, for example, the non-supervised Otsu thresholding method [8], [9] as in this case.

We can also separate the achromatic area to obtain a better segmentation. This achromatic zone can be subdivided later using only intensity as a discriminative characteristic. In figures 2, 3 and Table 1 we show the improved results of our new definition of G in Eq. (2) with respect to the former results presented in [5], [7] and [10].

In all the composite images we used the XOR logical function to avoid the possibility that one pixel could belong simultaneously to two different color-segmented zones or regions.

Next, we demonstrate the effectiveness of the proposed color segmentation method in some relatively complex color images.

Figure 2 (left) shows the results of the application of our method to the RGB color image (sized 200 x 200 pixels and with 33 753 different colors) of the popular baboon image. In this image we can see four main hues of colors despite the many thousands of actual RGB values to represent them: The red part of the baboon's nose, the blue part of the nose, the orange eyes and the yellow-orange part of the fur.

In our experiments we do not use any preprocessing at all. We obtained 95.5% of pixels segmented properly (See Table 1). In figure 2 we show the results with the old (center) and new achromatic region G (right) for appreciation. The improvement in quality is significant.

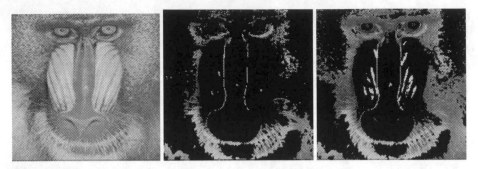

Fig. 2. Composite image of 5 segmented colors (left) and results obtained with the old (center) and the new achromatic zone G (right)

In order to evaluate the efficiency of the color segmentation method and due to the difficulty of obtaining a ground-truth for each complex image to which we applied the method or to compare the results from different methods, the evaluation was based on the number of pixels not segmented with respect to the total number of pixels in the corresponding image. This ratio combines the pixels not belonging to any color cluster and those selected by two or more clusters (obtained by means of the XOR operation) with respect to the total number of pixels in the image It gives us a measure of the segmentation efficiency.. In general the number of selected pixels for the samples depends on the complexity of the image (texture of objects), on the diversity of colors and on their spatial distribution in the image. As it can be observed from Table 1, the average accuracy of the color segmentation in both complex images, without an exhaustive selection of colors and a few numbers of pixels (4-5 as average) per color sample, is 95.91%.

In Figure 3 (left) a composite image of 5 segmented colors (with the non-segmented pixels in pseudocolor) of a color fabric is shown; it contains an achromatic region with high saturation but low brightness that is very difficult to separate with the former G zone (Figure 3 center) but easily separated with the new one shown in Fig. 3 (right). Figure 3 shows the original and a composite with the non-segmented pixels in pseudocolor. We obtained 95.3% of pixels segmented.

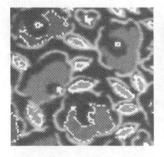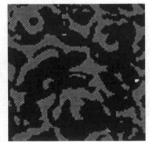

Fig. 3. Composite image of 5 segmented colors (left) and results obtained with the old (center) and the new achromatic zone G (right)

When we compare the new achromatic region G with the former one, the difference is astonishing whereas the new achromatic area seems correctly segmented the former one segmented only a couple of pixels.

Table 1 show the results obtained in the segmentation of two images. The last column of Table 1 shows the percent of segmented pixels obtained in these images.. In all cases, the possibility that one pixel could belong to two different colors segmented zones or regions have been avoided by means of the application of the XOR logical function (of two or more partial segmentations). A result with many black pixels indicates that has been coincidence in segmented pixels from two or more partial segmentations considered in the XOR operation.

As it can be observed from Table 1, the average accuracy of the color segmentation in both complex images, without an exhaustive selection of colors and a few numbers of pixels (4-5 as average) per color sample, is 95.4%.

Table 1. Results of the global segmentation per image

No.	Image	Number of pixels in image	Number of colors (levels)	Number of colors (levels) selected	Total number of pixels used as samples	Number of non-segmented pixels	% of segmented pixels
1	Baboon	40000	33753	5	31	1803	95.5
2	Fabric	9900	9349	5	23	465	95.3

4   Conclusions

The results in the previous section, demonstrate that the color segmentation method presented in this paper offers a useful and efficient alternative for the segmentation of objects with different colors in relatively complex color images with good performance in the presence of the unavoidable additive noise, and in images with low contrast, and with very low chromaticity.

The steps required to obtain a good segmentation of regions with different colors by using the proposed methodology are usually straightforward, simple and repetitive. If color is a discriminative characteristic in the layer of interest, only the selection of a given threshold to the color similarity image CSI is needed to obtain a good segmentation result. From many experiments we have observed that a good percentage of colors were segmented in a straightforward way only by thresholding the Color Similarity Image. The method discriminates whichever type of different color objects independently on their shapes and tonalities in a very straightforward way.

The new characterization of the achromatic region improves its performance, compared to that presented in [5], [7] and [10], due to the affectation of saturation by an exponential factor in an effort to better model the human visual response in case of very low or very high brightness. The improvement in quality of its results is significant and can be visually appreciated in examples of Section 3.

One of the inconveniences of the proposed color segmentation method is the degree of human intervention, summarized in the necessity of selecting a pixel sample. This sample has to be carefully chosen in order to obtain the best results. An associated problem of the use of a pixel sample is to obtain the number of data points necessary to capture the color distribution. These related problems will be treated in future developments of the algorithm enforced to obtain a complete automatic version.

Acknowledgements. The authors of this paper wish to thank the Computing Research Center (CIC), Mexico; Research and Postgraduate Secretary (SIP), Mexico, and National Polytechnic Institute (IPN), Mexico, and CONACyT, Mexico, for their support to this work.

References

1. Alvarado-Cervantes, R.: Segmentación de patrones lineales topológicamente diferentes, mediante agrupamientos en el espacio de color HIS. M. Sc. Thesis, and Center for Computing Research, National Polytechnic Institute, Mexico (2006)
2. Felipe-Riveron, E.M., García-Ramos, M.E., Levachkine, S.P.: Problemas potenciales en la digitalización automática de los mapas cartográficos en colores. In: Proceedings of International Congress on Computation CIC IPN, Mexico City, Mexico (2000)
3. Cheng, H., Jiang, X., Sun, Y., Wang, J.: Color image segmentation: Advances and prospects. Pattern Recognition 34(12), 2259–2281 (2001)
4. Hanbury, A., Serra, J.A.: 3D-polar coordinate colour representation suitable for image analysis. Technical Report PRIP-TR-77, Austria (2002)
5. Alvarado-Cervantes, R., Felipe-Riveron, E.M.: An Adaptive Color Similarity Function for Color Image Segmentation. In: San Martin, C., Kim, S.-W. (eds.) CIARP 2011. LNCS, vol. 7042, pp. 113–124. Springer, Heidelberg (2011)
6. Gonzalez, R.C., Woods, R.E.: Digital Image Processing, 3rd edn. Prentice-Hall, USA (2008)
7. Plataniotis, K.N., Venetsanopoulos, A.N.: Color Image Processing and Applications, 1st edn. Springer, Germany (2000)
8. Otsu, N.: A Threshold Selection Method from Gray-Level Histograms. IEEE Transactions on Systems, Man and Cybernetics 9(1), 62–66 (1979)
9. Sezgin, M., Sankur, B.: Survey over image thresholding techniques and quantitative performance evaluation. Journal of Electronic Imaging 13(1), 146–165 (2003), doi:10.1117/1.1631315
10. Alvarado-Cervantes, R., Felipe-Riveron, E.M., Sanchez-Fernandez, L.P.: Color Image Segmentation by Means of a Similarity Function. In: Bloch, I., Cesar Jr., R.M. (eds.) CIARP 2010. LNCS, vol. 6419, pp. 319–328. Springer, Heidelberg (2010)
11. Poynton, C.: (2002), http://www.poynton.com/PDFs/GammaFAQ.pdf
12. Dubey, A., Bhattacharya, I., Godbole, S.: A Cluster-Level Semi-supervision Model for Interactive Clustering. In: Balcázar, J.L., Bonchi, F., Gionis, A., Sebag, M. (eds.) ECML PKDD 2010, Part I. LNCS, vol. 6321, pp. 409–424. Springer, Heidelberg (2010)

Wavelet-FFT Filter Applied to Non Uniformity Correction in Infrared Imaging System

Cesar San Martin[1,2], Carlos Deocares [1,2], S. Godoy[2], P. Meza[2], and Daniela Bonilla[1,2]

[1] Information Processing Laboratory, Electrical Engineering Department,
Universidad de La Frontera, Casilla 54-D, Temuco Chile
cesarsanmartin@ufro.cl
[2] Center for Optics and Photonics, Chile

Abstract. In this paper, we use the recently presented wavelet-FFT filter [1] to reduce the nonuniformity noise that affect almost all infrared imaging systems. The wavelet-FFT filter was originally developed to compensate the one-dimensional noise known as stripping noise. We perform an extension of this methodology in order to compensate the two-dimensional noise that degrades infrared imagery. The principal hypothesis of this work is that the two-dimensional focal-plane array can be considered as the composition of vertical and horizontal one-dimensional array sensors. Under this assumption we use a specific design of the wavelet filter to synthesize a replica of the two-dimensional noise and then recover the real incident radiation. The method is evaluated using real mid- and long-wave infrared data from two cameras. The results show the promising performance of the wavelet-FFT filter when is applied in infrared imaging system such as self heating effect.

1 Introduction

The noise that corrupts the one- and two-dimensional imaging systems is an artifact common to all the focal-plane array—based imaging systems. This noise becomes more important in systems that acquire infrared (IR) radiation due to the low level of radiant energy collected by the sensors. In addition, the IR detectors in a focal-plane array (FPA) normally have physical differences even though they are fabricated under the same specifications. These differences give rise to a no uniform photo response in the sensors array that creates a fixed-pattern noise (FPN). The principal characteristic of this noise is that the pattern does not change significantly in time [2]. The sensors array can be found in both one- or two-dimensional form. If we have a horizontal (vertical) one-dimensional array of sensors, the images are created performing a vertical (horizontal) scanning. Considering this fact, the FPN present in the raw data is called stripping noise because it can be seen as vertical (horizontal) lines across the image, [3]. The one-dimensional arrays are typically used in remote sensing technology, satellite applications, spectroradiometry, multi- and hyper-spectral images, etc. For two-dimensional arrays, the FPN is normally referred in the literature as the non-uniformity (NU) of noise. As was aforementioned, the that NU noise is presented in

L. Alvarez et al. (Eds.): CIARP 2012, LNCS 7441, pp. 355–363, 2012.
© Springer-Verlag Berlin Heidelberg 2012

IR imaging technology mainly due to the low energy presented at 3-5 um (mid-wave) and 8-14 um (long-wave) wavelengths IR ranges. The reduction of the stripping noise is an active area in the digital image processing field [3–5] due to their applications in several scientific studies. On the other hand, nonuniformity correction (NUC) is an active research field that is normally classified in two subareas of development: reference- and scene-based methods. The reference-based methods require a flat field of radiation emitted from black-bodies at different temperatures. Using this uniform-and-known input as reference, we can obtain a direct relationship between the reference and the readout data. The relationship allows us to estimate the two-dimensional noise in a very accurate way, which is desirable for thermographics applications. Depending of the number of measurement considered the method is called one-, two- or multi-point calibrations. Nonetheless these methods are accurate, simple and reliable; the references are not always available due to the high cost of black body radiators [6]. In the scene-based method, the NUC can be performed using mathematical or statistical operations in time, no requiring halt the normal operation of the camera. Several examples can be seen in [2, 7, 8]. Some methods work in the pixel basis, and others assume some spatial relations between pixel neighborhoods.

Munch et al. in [1] report a fast and stable filter based on wavelet and Fourier transform, that they called wavelet-FFT filter. Briefly, this method has two key steps: wavelet decomposition and damping process. The first one permits to separate the information into horizontal, vertical and diagonal details in several scales. For vertical stripping noise, the vertical detail band contains the principal stripe artifacts. Therefore the Fourier transform is applied only in this band in order to reduce the stripping noise by means of a Gaussian high-pass filter. The de-stripe image is then reconstructed using the inverse wavelet transform. In order to tune the performance of the filter, we can adjust two parameters: decomposition level of wavelet transform, and the damping factor of the high pass filter. The decomposition level allows us to select the frequency band where the filter is applied and the damping factor modifies the filter bandwidth. The lower the damping factor, the higher the bandwidth.

In this paper, we use the wavelet-FFT filter to perform NUC for IR imaging system. The principal assumption of this work is that the two-dimensional FPA can be considered as the composition of vertical and horizontal one-dimensional arrays. Under this assumption we select the best decomposition alternative, generating two stripping-noises—like images from the decomposed virtual arrays. We applied the wavelet-FFT to this virtual 1D array to denoise the readout data. With the noise-free imagery, we estimate the real two-dimensional noise in order to denoise the following frames in the image sequence. The performance of the metric is evaluated using real data in mid- and long-IR wavelength range and compares with state-of-art NUC methods.

2   Wavelet-FFT Filter as NUC Method

The typical mathematical model used to describe the input-output relationship for each sensor in a FPA is given by:

$$Y(n,m) = A(n,m)I(n,m) + B(n,m), \tag{1}$$

where $A(n,m)$ and $B(n,m)$ are the gain and offset of the (n,m)-*th* pixel in the array. $I(n,m)$ is the input irradiance and $Y(n,m)$ is the readout signal for the same pixel. Gain and offset summarize the principal factors that generate the no uniform photo response in IR FPA sensors [6]. The result of these no uniform parameters gives rise to the NU noise present in IR images. This mathematical model represents both the 1D and the 2D sensors array, with the difference that for 1D arrays, one of the spatial coordinates must be set equal to unity: $n = 1$ for horizontal arrays or $m = 1$ for vertical arrays. To generate the 2D image from a 1D array the scene must be scanned in time by moving the target or the camera. This implies that a horizontal array will generate a vertical stripping noise, and the gain and offset from eq. (1) will be given by:

$$A(n,m) = A_m \delta(m), \tag{2}$$

$$B(n,m) = B_m \delta(m), \tag{3}$$

presenting variations only in the coordinate m. The principal characteristic of the stripping noise is that, in the Fourier domain, it concentrates the vertical (horizontal) stripes in horizontal (vertical) frequency components. In fact, taking the Fourier transform to eq. (2) and (3) we obtain:

$$F\Lambda(u,v) = \sum_{m=0}^{M-1} A_n e^{-jmv} \delta(u), \tag{4}$$

$$FB(u,v) = \sum_{m=0}^{M-1} B_m e^{-jmv} \delta(u). \tag{5}$$

Using this results in the frequency-domain of the stripping noise, a wavelet-FFT filter was proposed in [1] in order to improve the quality of the raw image $Y(n,m)$. Let us refer to eq. (1). In the frequency domain, the offset is located only for $u = 0$, which is the easiest case and was evaluated in the corresponding reference, [1]. When we face a problem that includes gain –as in our case-- more elaborated analysis must be done. Recall that in the frequency-domain the image corrupted by the nonuniform gain is given by the convolution between the Fourier transform of the gain and the Fourier transform of the image. This implies that the gain noise is not concentrated in any frequency, but is dispersed around $u = 0$. Indeed, the noise produced by the gain has a bandwidth that is commonly called stripping frequency band (SFB) that can also include the offset effects. Based on this analysis, it is possible to postulate that a simple way to cancel the stripping noise is by the reduction of the SFB. In order to perform this we can use a filter with the form [1]:

$$g(u) = 1 - e^{-\frac{u^2}{D^2}}, \tag{6}$$

where D is the damping factor that is selected accordingly with the SFB.

The well-known wavelet transform allow us to separate an image in four images (first decomposition level): diagonal, vertical and horizontal details and the approximation image. If the multi-resolution algorithm is applied, consecutively the approximation images are decomposed in another four images. Then, the filter g is applied only in vertical details, which gives an improvement of the filter performance. As a consequence, the wavelet-FFT filter requires the adjustment of two parameters: the damping factor and the decomposition level of the wavelet transform. The best pair of values that improve the filter performance are obtained by trial-and-error. The effectiveness of the filter is given by the resolution in the frequency domain: the more the information in the vertical direction, the more effective is the use of the filter given by eq. (6).

2.1   Realignment of 2D FPA into 1D FPA

As was aforementioned, the principal assumption of this work is that the two-dimensional FPA can be decomposed in two one-dimensional virtual arrays. The procedure to realignment the 2D FPA is addressed in this section. Let us consider a N×M FPA sensor. Since the frames are captures at discrete-time basis we can capture a block of K frames, forming a tree-dimensional matrix of data, as it is shown in the Fig. 1.

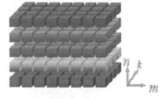

Fig. 1. Constructions of N×M×K variable in which the rows are the n-positions, the columns are denoted by m and k is sample time o frame number. Each row has different color (from up to down): blue, cyan, green, orange and red; representing each image with stripe noise.

During the last years, the nonuniformity has been well documented and its principal characteristic is that presents fixed-patterns during blocks of time [2, 7, 8]. Under this scenario, we can observe that the patters present among rows (columns) are fixed during a block of K frames, so stripping-noise—like images can be obtained from a row-to-row (column-to-column) analysis across time. Let us be focused on the row-to-row analysis. For each row in the Fig. 1, we consider only m and k dimensions, in order to generate N images of M×K virtual pixels. Therefore, each image given by a different color in Fig. 1, can be considered as images captured by one-dimensional virtual FPAs with M detectors. The wavelet-FFT filter previously described is applied to each one of these virtually generated images, and the one-dimensional--compensated block is restored again in the real N×M×K block of data. Further, for each column the process is repeated but considering that the striping-noise--like images are obtained in n and k directions generating M images captured by a one-dimensional virtual FPA with N detectors.

3   Results

In this section, the proposed method is evaluated and compared with two state-of-art NUC methodologies using real infrared data from two different cameras that are corrupted by two-dimensional noise. This comparison is made based on both classical metrics that we present below and naked-eye evaluation of the final results. For this paper, in all cases Daubechies basis has been fixed as wavelet function with 12 coefficients in order to obtain a first approach of the methodology.

3.1   Metrics

Two quality metrics are used in this paper with comparison purposes. The first one corresponds to the root-mean-square error (RMSE) given by:

$$RMSE^2 = \frac{1}{NM} \sum_i \sum_j \left(I(i,j) - X(i,j) \right)^2 , \tag{7}$$

where I is the real image (reference image) and X is the corrected image with the NUC method under study. The RMSE require the knowledge of the real incident infrared radiation, which in our case can be approximated with a black-body–corrected image [2].

Nonetheless, in some cases this reference is not disposable, becoming necessary a reference-free quality index. A good example of this is the roughness index given by:

$$\rho = \frac{\left\| h \otimes X \right\|_2 + \left\| h^T \otimes X \right\|_2}{\left\| X \right\|_2} , \tag{8}$$

where h is a 1D high pass filter, T transpose and $\otimes$ denote convolution. The comparison of the roughness index must be used in conjunction with naked-eye evaluation because it only shows if the correction is producing a smooth image or not, leaving out any radiometric modifications.

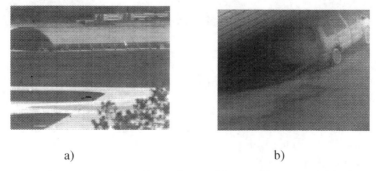

a)   b)

Fig. 2. Example of IR data used in this work: a) mid-wave IR image, and b) long-wave IR image

3.2   Infrared Data

In this paper two real infrared data has been used to evaluate the proposed method. The first sequence has been collected using a 128×128 InSb FPA cooled camera (Amber Model AE-4128) operating in the 3 – 5 um range. An example of the readout data of this camera is depicted in Fig. 2(a). For this dataset, data of black-body radiators is available, so the quantity $I(i,j)$ can be obtained using a two-point calibration method. The second sequence of infrared data has been recorded using a 320 × 240 HgCdTe FPA cooled camera (CEDIP Jade) operating in the 8 – 12 um range. An example of the readout data of this camera is depicted in Fig. 2(b). Since we do not have black-body data or this dataset, only roughness index is used as comparison.

3.3   Results

In the Fig. 3 we resume the steps used in this section, accordingly with the afore explained procedure. The first step of the proposed method is build the N×M×K variable (Fig. 1) using a sequence of consecutive frames as shown in Fig. 3a. The aim is to obtain image with stripping noise (Fig. 3b). The wavelet-FFT filter is applied over each one of these images, obtaining a corrected version (Fig. 3c). Further, transposing the 2D FPA, new image with vertical stripping noise is obtained, and the process is repeated.

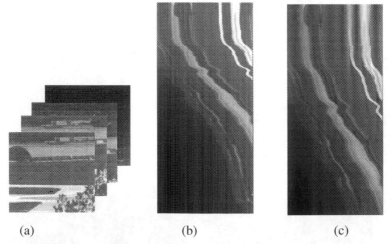

(a)   (b)   (c)

Fig. 3. Realignment of the 2D FPA to 1D FPA. (a) shows the construction of the variable presented in Fig.1; b) shows the image with stripe noise; and c) is the corrected image using wavelet-FFT filter.

Some results of this methodology can be observed in Fig. 4. The corrupted image (readout data) is presented in Fig. 4a. Fig. 4b is the corrected version of the same image using the proposed method. Fig. 4c and 4d are the corresponding corrected frame using the statistical algorithm proposed in [8] and the Kalman filter proposed in [2]. This method use a block of frame in order to obtain the gain and offset, and then, the NUC is performed. Note that the proposed method is based in the use of a block of frames in order to build the image with stripping noise. In the Fig. 4 is easy to see that the proposed method presents a comparative behavior with other techniques. In order to compare the performance of those methods as function of the length of the block of frames, six values are selected. For all of these cases the RMSE is computed using the corrected data from black-body radiators. Table 1 resumes the principal results. Clearly, the proposed method exhibits the best values for the RMSE. This is due to the fact that the wavelet-FFT filter maintains the radiometric range of the original imagery.

Note that the RMSE is actually an average RMSE over all pixels in a frame. Of course, the lower the value of RMSE, the better the NUC achieved.

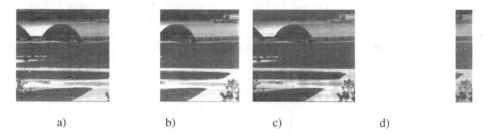

a)   b)   c)   d)

Fig. 4. Results using the mid-wave IR data: a) corrupted data, b) corrected using the proposed method; c) statistical algorithm and d) Kalman filtering. Comparative correction is obtained using the wavelet-FFT in same sequence.

The second experiment considers data from long-wave infrared camera (Fig. 2b). Table 2 resumes the results using the roughness parameter. Clearly the performance of the proposed method is consistent with the performance of statistical algorithm and Kalman filter. But, using the naked-eye analysis in a particular frame (Fig. 5) the proposed method generates lower ghosting artifacts than the other methods under study. Based on a subjective analysis over the image contrast, from Fig. 5b is possible to conclude that the method preserve the radiometric range. Fig. 5c and 5d do not show the same behavior. Additionally, the ghosting generated by the car presented in Fig. 2b is showed in both images, whereas it is reduced in Fig. 5b.

Table 1. RMSE using three NUC methods: statistical algorithm, Kalman filter and the proposed method. The RMSE is calculated for 1000 frames.

Frames	Statistical algorithm	Kalman filter	Proposed method
50	5.4963	3.1459	0.6494
100	5.3372	2.8570	0.6097
150	5.3320	2.6561	0.6427
200	5.3372	2.7410	0.6392
250	5.4779	2.7600	0.6627
300	5.3322	2.8668	0.6378

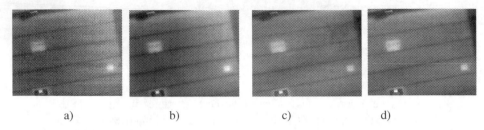

a)   b)   c)   d)

Fig. 5. Results using the long-wave IR data: a) corrupted data, b) corrected using the proposed method; c) statistical algorithm and d) Kalman filtering. Note that in the proposed method no ghosting effect is presented.

Table 2. Roughness index using three NUC methods: statistical algorithm, Kalman filter and the proposed method. The roughness index is calculated for 1000 frames.

Frames	Statistical algorithm	Kalman filter	Proposed method
25	0.6622	0.6866	0.9892
50	0.7038	0.7022	0.7296
100	0.7038	0.7185	0.7184
150	0.7125	0.7213	0.7087

4   Conclusions and Future Work

In this paper, a wavelet-FFT filter is adapted to reduce FPN in infrared imaging system. The principal hypothesis is that the 2D FPA can be decomposed in two 1D FPA, and then, a de-stripping algorithm is applied. The performance of the method has been evaluated using two real IR sequences: mid and long wave IR data. In both cases, the performance of the method is compared with two techniques presenting a similar behavior. The proposed method exhibit two advantages: i) the radiometric range is preserved and ii) the method generate reduced ghosting artifact. Then, the wavelet-FFT filter is a promising tool to apply in NUC problems. The future work include more numerical experiments and analysis using real IR data specially when ghosting is presented in thermal images considering the influence of the kind of wavelet used.

Acknowledgements. This work was partially supported by Proyecto DI-UFRO DI12-0064 and Center for Optics and Photonics CEFOP FB0824/2008. The authors wish to thank Ernest E. Armstrong (OptiMetrics Inc., USA) and Pierre Potet (CEDIP Infrared Systems) for collecting the data, and the United States Air Force Research Laboratory, Ohio, USA.

References

1. Munch, B., Trtik, P., Marone, F., Stampanoni, M.: Stripe and ring artifact removal with combined wavelet-Fourier filtering. Opt. Express 17, 8567–8591 (2009)
2. Torres, S., Hayat, M.: Kalman Filtering for Adaptive Non uniformity Correction in Infrared Focal Plane Arrays. The JOSA-A Opt. Soc. of America 20, 470–480 (2003)

3. Liu, J.G., Morgan, G.L.K.: FFT Selective and Adaptive Filtering for Removal of Systematic Noise in ETM+Imageodesy Images. IEEE Trans. Geosci. Remote Sens. 44, 3716–3724 (2006)
4. Zhang, Z., Shi, Z., Guo, W., Huang, S.: Adaptively Image De-striping through Frequency Filtering. In: ICO20: Opt. Inf. Proc., Proc. SPIE 6027, p. 60273V (2006)
5. Wang, Z., Fu, Y.: Frequency-domain Regularized Deconvolution for Images with Stripe Noise. In: ICIG Proc. 4th Intl Conf. Image and Graphics, pp. 110–115 (2007)
6. Godoy, S., Torres, S., Pezoa, J., Hayat, M., Wang, Q.: Nonuniformity correction algorithm based on a noise-cancellation system for infrared focal-plane arrays. In: Proc. SPIE, vol. 6542 (2007) 65423S
7. Torres, S., Pezoa, J., Hayat, M.: Scene-based Nonuniformity Correction for Focal Plane Arrays Using the Method of the Inverse Covariance Form. OSA App. Opt. Inf. Proc. 42, 5872–5881 (2003)
8. Hayat, M., Torres, S., Amstrong, E., Cain, S., Yasuda, B.: Statistical algorithm for non uniformity correction in focal plane arrays. Applied Optics 38, 773–780 (1999)

Concealing Damaged Coded Images
Using Improved FSE with Critical Support Area

Alejandro A. Ramírez-Acosta[1], Mireya S. García-Vázquez[2], and Sunil Kumar[3]

[1] MIRAL. R&D, 1047 Palm Garden,
Imperial Beach, 91932 USA
[2] Instituto Politécnico Nacional, Unidad CITEDI,
Tijuana, B.C. México 22510
[3] SDSU, San Diego,CA, USA
mgarciav@citedi.mx, ramacos10@hotmail.com, skumar@mail.sdsu.edu

Abstract. The transmission over error-prone networks of block-based coded images may results in the lost of the several images blocks, degrading drastically the visual quality of images. Consequently, if retransmission is not feasible, then applications of error concealment techniques are required to reduce this degradation caused mainly by the missing information. This paper proposes an adaptive and effective method to select the required support area, using suited base functions and optimal expansion coefficients, in order to conceal the damaged blocks in critical error situations. This method outperforms the concealment done by the conventional frequency selective extrapolation approach. It also performs well in current situations where significant loss of information is present and the data of the past reference images are also not available. The proposed method and the reviewed algorithms were implemented, tested and compared. Experimental results show that the proposed approach outperforms existing methods by up to 7.2 dB.

Keywords: Image, spatial error concealment, video, adaptive frequency selective extrapolation, critical support area, H.264/AVC.

1 Introduction

The original coded image signal can be affected when it is transmitted over error-prone networks. This may lead to loss of information. Therefore, application of error concealment techniques are required if no retransmission is possible. Error concealment (EC) techniques for compressed image or video attempt to exploit correctly received information to recover corrupted regions that are lost [1-3]. In the past, several spatial error concealment algorithms restoring missing blocks from surrounding correctly received blocks in the same image have been proposed in the literature [4-12]. Most of these conventional approaches consider the eight neighboring macroblocks availability for suitable operation and performance. However, one problem derived from this is that these methods cannot work well, especially over high burst error condition since a great of neighboring information

L. Alvarez et al. (Eds.): CIARP 2012, LNCS 7441, pp. 364–373, 2012.
© Springer-Verlag Berlin Heidelberg 2012

have been corrupted or lost (called 'critical situations'). This has therefore prompted the needed to design new error concealment methods or improve the existing ones, which allow a suitable quality image reconstruction over bursty error environments, such as current wireless communication systems. Thus, in this paper we propose an adaptive and effective method to select the required support area, using suited base functions and optimal expansion coefficients, in order to conceal the damaged blocks in critical error situations. This method outperforms the concealment done by the conventional frequency selective extrapolation approach. It also performs well in situations where significant loss of information is present and the data of the past reference images are not also available. The idea is then that this method can alleviate the disadvantages of the conventional methods effectively and provide better performance considering the critical situation of having at least one neighbor macroblock correctly received or already concealed of the considered lost or corrupted macroblock.

The remainder of this paper is organized as follows. Section 2 reviews existing spatial error concealment schemes used in MPEG-4 H.264/AVC decoders; in section 3 discusses the proposed new method. Implementation, results and discussion are presented in section 4. Finally, in section 5, we draw discussion and give suggestions for future work.

2   Spatial Error Concealment Methods

2.1   Weighted Average Approach in MPEG-4 H.264/AVC decoder

This well-known and highly influential ancient spatial error concealment technique was proposed in [12] as a non-normative algorithm in the MPEG-4 H.264/AVC standard [1,3,13,14]. It uses weighted averaging interpolation (WAI) of four pixel values located at vertically and horizontally neighboring boundaries of a damaged macroblock (MB) consisting usually of 16x16 pixels. A pixel value in a damaged or lost MB is replaced with the reconstructed pixel value using WAI as following:

$$P = \frac{P_R d_L + P_L d_R + P_T d_B + P_B d_T}{d_L + d_R + d_B + d_T} \tag{1}$$

where P indicates a pixel value in a damaged MB, P_T, P_B, and P_L, P_R, are vertically (top, bottom) and horizontally (left, right) neighboring boundary pixels values, and d_T, d_B, d_L, d_R indicate the distance between the interpolated pixel. The original WAI's method assumes that the top, bottom, left and right MBs are usually available to apply error concealment process. However, it may be not true for some applications. For instance, in the MPEG-4 H.264/AVC decoder standard, the WAI's method, applied for intra-frames [13,15], works if at least two neighboring MBs in the horizontal or vertical direction are correct or already concealed. However, one major drawback is that this method does not consider the edge characteristics of images. Thus, this method is relatively effective in the region that has no edge, whereas it causes noticeable visual degradation in the region including the edges (cf. section 4, figs. 2a-4a).

2.2   Frequency Extrapolation Using DFT

The idea in this approach is to estimate the missing image blocks using the signal extrapolation principle [16,17], which is based on the extending of a signal beyond a limited number of known samples. Various methods have been proposed which solve the extrapolation task for two dimensional signals by applying spectral estimation [6,16-19] and spectral deconvolution [20,21]. For the images EC application, Kaup et al [22-24] proposed a frequency selective extrapolation (FSE) approach based on successive approximation technique [25,26]. So, the image content (see fig. 1a) of the known blocks (support area $\mathcal{R}$) is successively approximated through a parametric model $g(m,n)$ and the missing block (missing area $\mathcal{L}$) is obtained by extrapolation according to an error criterion based on the energy weighted function, described as follows:

$$E_{\mathcal{R}} = \sum_{(m,n)\in Q} w(m,n)[f(m,n) - g(m,n)]^2, \quad \forall\{Bk \in \mathcal{R}\} \tag{2}$$

where

$$Bk = \sum_{m}^{M}\sum_{n}^{N} f(m,n), \quad \{m,n \in \mathcal{R}\}, k = \{0,1,\dots,7\} \tag{3}$$

$w(m,n)$ is the weighting function, $f(m,n)$ are the values of the samples in the area Q, $g(m,n)$ is the parametric model and Bk is the MB in the support area $\mathcal{R}$. The parametric model in each iteration is:

$$g^{(v)}(m,n) = \sum_{(p,q)\in\mathcal{P}_v} c_{p,q}^{(v)}\varphi_{p,q}(m,n), \quad \{m,n \in Q\} \tag{4}$$

$\mathcal{P}_v$ denoting the set of basis functions $\varphi_{p,q}(m,n)$ weighted by the expansion coefficients $c_{p,q}^{(v)}$ used in the iteration v, m,n indicates the row and column index. The number of available basis functions equals the number of samples in the entire area Q.

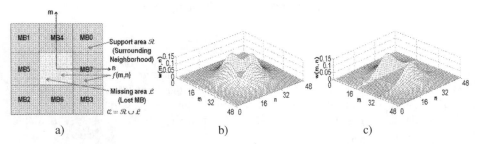

Fig. 1. a) Representation of missing and support area. Weighting function: b) Isolated lost block, c) Consecutive lost block.

The FSE algorithm of Kaup et al [22-24], presupposes, as does WAI's method, that all eight neighboring MBs (support area $\mathcal{R}$) are usually available to apply error concealment process over the damage MB (missing area $\mathcal{L}$). Considering this assumption, the FSE method can have good performance if there is only a dominant edge orientation in the considered support area $\mathcal{R}$. However, it causes noticeable visual degradation in the region when multiple edges are present or when the resulting dominant edge orientation is slightly different of each MB of the considered support area $\mathcal{R}$ (cf. section 4, figs. 2b-4b).

3   Proposed Method

The FSE's method which is applied for intra-frames [22-24], takes all eight surrounding MBs (support area $\mathcal{R}$), as above was mentioned, to restore the lost one (missing area $\mathcal{L}$). If any of the neighboring MBs is not correctly received, the FSE's method doesn't perform well (cf. section 4, figs. 2b-4b). To alleviate the disadvantages of the FSE's method effectively and provide better performance considering critical situations as having at least one correctly received or concealed neighbor MB, we focus on the challenge of providing the necessary conditions to correctly estimate the signal in the available support area $\mathcal{R}$ through a suited base functions and an optimal expansion coefficients to suitably reconstruct the damaged MB with minimal information.

3.1   Computing Basis Functions and Expansion Coefficients

For emphasizing closer regions to missing area $\mathcal{L}$, Kaup et al [22-24] use a weighting function $w(m,n)$ (see eq.2) based on an isotropic model $\rho(m,n)$.

$$w(m,n) = \begin{cases} \rho(m,n) = \hat{\rho}^{\sqrt{\left(m-\frac{M}{2}\right)^2 + \left(n-\frac{N}{2}\right)^2}}, & 0 < \hat{\rho} < 1, \{m,n \in \mathcal{R}, \forall Bk \in \mathcal{R}\} \\ 0, & \{m,n \in \mathcal{L}\} \end{cases} \quad (5)$$

Figure 1b depicts the resulting weighting function for a single lost MB. This lost MB is located in the center of this weighting function having zero intensities and all surrounding MB's area has a certain weight defined by ρ.

Kaup et al [22-24], also treat the consecutive macroblock loss. The resulting weighting function $w(m,n)$ on the available support area $\mathcal{R}$, for the case of consecutive macroblock loss, is shown in figure 1c. In this figure, the macroblock MB7 is not available and macroblock MB5 has been concealed (extrapolated). Then, in order to include the MB5 in the concealment procedure, Kaup et al [22-24] limit their influence by assigning a weight of 0.1 trying to prevent the spread of approximation errors. It is known that the influence of the weighting function decreases radial symmetrically with distance from the center of the lost area at $(M/2, N/2)$, then, we compute the contribution of each sub-area (surrounding MBs) in the support area $\mathcal{R}$ in terms of energy: $MB0 = MB1 = MB2 = MB3 = 0.14096 \times 10^{-4}$ J/Hz, and for horizontal and vertical macroblocks: $MB4 = MB5 = MB6 = MB7 = 1.6858 \times 10^{-4}$ J/Hz. Based on this results, we propose to use the information of the concealed neighbors MB's throughout the support area $\mathcal{R}$, under the same conditions as the correctly received MB's. So, we apply the weighting function in the area of the concealed MB without limiting its influence. Our FSE algorithm optimization allows the concealment of the lost MB for any error pattern structure present in the Intra frame. The implemented optimization algorithm is described as follows:

1. Establishment of the weighting function

In the proposed method, the resulting weighting function is variable because it depends on the available support area $\mathcal{R}$ for each lost MB that needs to be concealed. This condition can be represented as follows:

$$w_{Bk}(m,n) = \begin{cases} \rho(m,n) = \hat{\rho}^{\sqrt{\left(m-\frac{M}{2}\right)^2+\left(n-\frac{N}{2}\right)^2}}, & 0 < \hat{\rho} < 1, \{m,n \in \mathcal{R}\} \\ & \{\forall Bk \in \mathcal{R} \wedge Bk \neq 0\} \\ 0, & \{m,n \in \mathcal{L}\} \end{cases} \tag{6}$$

Bk is the MB correctly received or concealed in the variable support area $\mathcal{R}$.

2. Initialization of the parametric model

The parametric model is initialized as Kaup et al [22-24], $g^{(0)}(m,n) = 0$.

3. Initialization of the approximation weighted residual error

The initialization $\{v = 0\}$ of the approximation weighted residual error is done by the following:

$$r_{w_{Bk}}^{(v)}(m,n) = w_{Bk}(m,n) \times r^{(v)}(m,n), \quad \{m,n \in \mathcal{R}\}, \forall\{Bk \in \mathcal{R} \wedge Bk \neq 0\} \tag{7}$$

where

$$r^{(v)}(m,n) = \left[f(m,n) - g^{(v)}(m,n)\right] \tag{8}$$

4. Iterative Procedure of Frequency Successive Approximation

4.1. Best Fitting Basis Function Determination

Based on the equation 2 as well as the conditions presented in equations 6 and 7, and using the 2D Discrete Fourier Transform (DFT) base functions, the maximal decrease of the weighted error criterion to select the best fitting basis function in the frequency domain (by DFT of $r^{(v)}(m,n): R^{(v)}(m,n)$ and $w_{Bk}(m,n): W_{Bk}(m,n)$) can be expressed as follows:

$$\Delta E_{\mathcal{R}_{Bk}}^{(v)} = \frac{R_{w_{Bk}}^{(v)}[p,q]^2}{W_{Bk}[0,0]}, \quad \forall\{Bk \in \mathcal{R} \wedge Bk \neq 0\} \tag{9}$$

4.2. Expansion Coefficients Determination

After doing some mathematical simplifications from equation 2, the expansion coefficient update Δc for each iteration v can expressed in the frequency domain as:

$$\Delta c = MN\frac{R_{w_{Bk}}^{(v)}[u,v]}{W_{Bk}[0,0]}, \quad \forall\{Bk \in \mathcal{R} \wedge Bk \neq 0\} \tag{10}$$

The expansion coefficient $c_{u,v}^{(v+1)}$ is then update by

$$c_{u,v}^{(v+1)} = c_{u,v}^{(v)} + \Delta c \tag{11}$$

4.3. Updating the Parametric Model

The parametric model $g^{(v)}(m,n): G^{(v)}(m,n)$ is updated for each iteration v based on the proposed conditions mentioned before, allowing obtain suitable base functions and optimal expansion coefficients to correctly estimate the available support area $\mathcal{R}$.

4.4. New Approximation Error Determination

To obtain the weighted residual error signal in the next iteration $v + 1$, the following equation is computed:

$$R_{W_{Bk}}^{(v+1)}[p,q] = R_{W_{Bk}}^{(v)}[p,q] - \frac{1}{MN}\Delta c W_{Bk}[p-u, q-v], \quad \forall\{Bk \in \mathcal{R} \wedge Bk \neq 0\} \tag{12}$$

4.5. The Final Parametric Model

After all iterations are done, the final parametric model is obtained by an inverse DFT. This parametric model is then, the closest approximation to the signal data in the available support area $\mathcal{R}$:

$$g[m,n] = IDFT_{M,N}\{G[p,q]\} \tag{13}$$

Finally, the proper concealed lost MB is obtained from the parametric model which is optimized for the available support area $\mathcal{R}$.

4   Implementation and Results

In order to evaluate the performance of the proposed approach and to compare it with three other spatial concealment methods, experiments were conducted using corrupted representative Intra Images with significant losses (20% to 42%) and with different errors distributions. Table 1, summarizes the details of our experiments. It is important to highlight that the select images are a major challenge for the EC algorithms. They show multiples edges and rich textures than need to be suitably concealed.

As it is shown in the Table 1, we compared the performances of the following spatial error concealment methods: WAI method [12,15], FSE method with all MBs correctly received [22-24], FSE method for consecutive macroblock loss (FSE weighted 0.1) [22-24] and our proposed method. In order to evaluate the quality of reconstruction of an image Intra we use the peak to signal-to-noise ratio of its YUV color space luminance component (Y-PSNR). According to the results shown in the Table 1, in general, the proposed method outperforms existing methods by up to 7.2 dB on average.

Table 1. Performance of the spatial error concealment methods

Image Intra	Error distribution	% losses	WAI	FSE (all MBs)	FSE weighted 0.1	Our method
Lena	Bursty	42.48	22.82 dB	10.93 dB	26.37 dB	26.59 dB
	Checkerboard	41.02	23.13 dB	23.42 dB	---	28.34 dB
	Uniform	21.97	25.83 dB	30.71 dB	---	30.71 dB
Baboon	Bursty	42.48	21.15 dB	10.43 dB	22.21 dB	22.35 dB
	Checkerboard	41.02	21.35 dB	21.24 dB	---	23.13 dB
	Uniform	21.97	24.02 dB	26.04 dB	---	26.04 dB
Foreman	Bursty	38.38	22.65 dB	9.52 dB	26.84 dB	27.25 dB
	Checkerboard	35.88	23.06 dB	23.52 dB	---	30.09 dB
	Uniform	20.20	26.00 dB	32.67 dB	---	32.67 dB

Figures 2-5 present some concealed images Intra applying the spatial error concealment methods discussed in this paper. The error distributions are the bursty and checkerboard for these figures. As shown in these figures, the best spatial error concealment method (proposed method) yields the best performance according to Y-PSNR criteria and the visual quality. This can be explained by the fact that our method takes into account only the correctly received neighboring MBs or concealed neighboring MBs to compute the frequency selective extrapolation. Moreover, it selects the proper neighboring MBs according to the formulation done in section 3.1. On the other hand, the WAI's method works well in regions with smooth texture area. However, as we can see in the figures, it causes important visual degradations in the region including edges. The conventional FSE's method [22-24] presents good results when all neighboring MBs have been correctly received (uniform error distribution). On the contrary, it shows catastrophic results taking into account all eight neighboring MBs without considering their availability to compute the frequency selective extrapolation and the reconstruction of the lost MB.

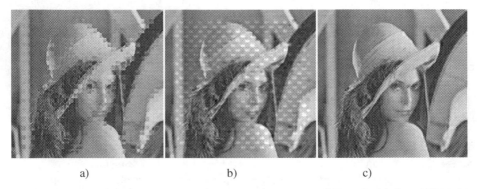

a)   b)   c)

Fig. 2. Error distribution: checkerboard. Concealed image Intra of "Lena" with the: a) WAI, Y-PSNR=23.13dB; b) FSE all 8 MB's, Y-PSNR=23.42dB; c) Our method, Y-PSNR=28.34dB.

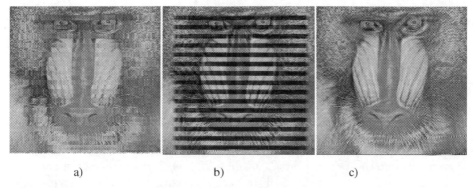

Fig. 3. Error distribution: bursty. Concealed image Intra of "Baboon" with the: a) WAI, Y-PSNR=21.15dB; b) FSE all 8 MB's, Y-PSNR=10.43dB; c) Our method, Y-PSNR=22.35dB.

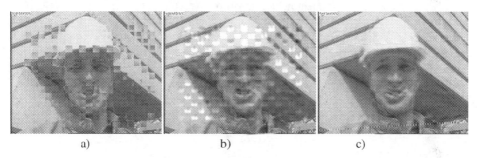

Fig. 4. Error distribution: checkerboard. Concealed image Intra of "Foreman" with the: a) WAI, Y-PSNR=23.06dB; b) FSE all 8 MB's, Y-PSNR=23.52dB; c) Our method, Y-PSNR=30.09dB.

For consecutive macroblock loss, our method has on average of Y-PSNR=0.27 dB which is superior to FSE weighted 0.1 [22-24] (see Table 1). The figure 5 shows that the FSE weighted 0.1 method generates blocking effects, this is due to the weight assigned of 0.1 to MB5 in the support area. It is also shown that our method has better performance in avoiding error propagation.

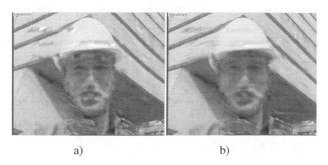

Fig. 5. Error distribution: bursty. Concealed image Intra of "Foreman" with the: a) FSE weighted 0.1, Y-PSNR=26.84dB; b) Our method, Y-PSNR=27.25dB.

5   Discussions and Further Work

As opposed to several studies of spatial error concealment that have been more concerned about devising new complex techniques to improve the visual quality with loss of information up to 25%, we investigate how to resolve the problem of significant loss of information (42% of errors with different distributions) due to node congestion or excessive delay in mobile communications. Thus, in this paper we proposed an adaptive and effective method to select the required support area, using suited base functions and optimal expansion coefficients, in order to conceal the damaged blocks in critical error situations. This method outperformed the concealment done by the conventional frequency selective extrapolation approach. It also performed well in current environments, where the images Intra are corrupted with different errors distributions covering up to 42% of the image area. Compared with three spatial error concealment algorithm, WAI [12,15], frequency selective extrapolation with all 8 MB's [22-24] and frequency selective extrapolation with weighted 0.1 [22-24], the adaptive proposed technique has the best results against several errors distribution, according to the metric Y-PSNR. The proposed method provide better performance considering the critical situation of having at least one neighbor macroblock correctly received or already concealed of the considered lost or corrupted macroblock. The proposed method can be combined with temporal replacement algorithms to provide improved error concealment for block-based video sequence coding.

Acknowledgment. This research was supported by grant SIP2012 from IPN.

References

1. Richardson, I.E.G.: H.264 and MPEG-4 Video Compression, Video Coding for Next – generation Multimedia. John Wiley & Sons, Ltd. (2004)
2. Wang, Y., Zhu, Q.-F.: Error Control and Concealment for Video Communication: A Review. Proceedings of the IEEE 86(5), 985–995 (1998)
3. Kumar, S., Xu, L., Mandal, M.K., Panchanathan, S.: Error Resiliency Schemes in H.264/AVC standard. Visual Communications & Image Representation 17(2) (2006)
4. Alkachouh, Z., Bellanger, M.G.: Fast DCT-Based Spatial Domain Interpolation of Blocks in Images. IEEE Trans. Image Processing 9(4), 729–732 (2000)
5. Wang, Y., Zhu, Q.F., Shaw, L.: Maximally Smooth Image Recovery in Transform Coding. IEEE Trans. Communication 41, 1544–1551 (1993)
6. Sun, H., Kwok, W.: Concealment of Damaged Block Transform Coded Images Using Projections onto Convex Sets. IEEE Trans. Image Processing 4(4), 470–477 (1995)
7. Yang, H., Yan, B.: A Novel Spatial Error Concealment Method for Wireless Video Transmission. In: Int. Conf. Wireless Comm., Netw. and Mobile Comp., China, pp. 1–4 (September 2009)
8. Chen, Y., Yu, K., Li, J., Li, S.: An error concealment algorithm for entire frame loss in video transmission. Microsof. Reasearch, 1–4 (December 2004)

9. Wang, J., Zhu, X.: Content Adaptive Intra Error Concealment Method. In: 12th IEEE International Conference on Communication Technology, China, pp. 1224–1227 (January 2010)
10. Ndjiki-Nya, P., Koppel, M., Doshkov, D., Wiegand, T.: Automatic Structure-Aware Inpainting for Complex Image Content. In: Int. Sym. on Visual Computing (November 2008)
11. Seiler, J., Kaup, A.: A Fast Algorithm for Selective Signal Extrapolation with Arbitrary Basis Functions. Journal on Advances in Signal Processing (2011)
12. Varsa, V., Hannuksela, M.M., Wang, Y.K.: Non-normative error concealment algorithms, ITU-T VCEG-N62 (September 2001)
13. Joint Video Team (JVT) of ISO/IEC MPEG & ITU-T VCEG: Draft ITU-T Recommendation and Final Draft International Standard of Joint Video Specification (ITU-T Rec. H.264 – ISO/IEC 14496-10 AVC), Doc. JVT-G050r1 (May 2003)
14. Wiegand, T., Sullivan, G.J., Bjøntegaard, G., Luthra, A.: Overview of the H.264/AVC Video Coding Standard. IEEE Trans. Circ. and Syst. for Vid. Tech. 13(7) (July 2003)
15. H.264/AVC Codec Software: JM14.2 Video Coding Standard
16. Papoulis, A.: A new algorithm in spectral analysis and band –limited extrapolation. IEEE Trans. Circuits Syst. 22, 735–742 (1975)
17. Papoulis, A., Chamzas, C.: Detection of hidden periodicities by adaptive extrapolation. IEEE Trans. Acoustics Speech Signal Process. 27, 492–500 (1979)
18. Aach, T.: Missing data interpolation by transform-based successive approximation. In: Proc. of the Workshop on Spectral Methods and Multirate Signal Processing, SMMSP 2001 (2001)
19. Lakshman, H., Ndjiki-Nya, P., Koppel, M., Doshkov, D., Wiegand, T.: An automatic structure-aware image extrapolation applied to error concealment. In: ICIP (2009)
20. Clark, A.A., Thomas, B.T., Campbell, N.W., Greenway, P.: Texture deconvolution for the Fourier-based analysis of non-rectangular regions. In: British Machine Vision Conference, pp. 193–202 (September 1999)
21. Aach, T., Metzler, V.: Defect interpolation in digital radiography - how object oriented transform coding helps. In: SPIE Medical Imaging 2001, vol. 4322 (February 2001)
22. Kaup, A., Meisinger, K., Aach, T.: Frequency selective signal extrapolation with applications to error concealment in image communication. Int. J. of Elect. Comm. 59, 147–156 (2005)
23. Meisinger, K., Kaup, A.: Minimizing a weighted error criterion for spatial error concealment of missing image data. In: Proc. IEEE Int. Conf. on Image Proc., ICIP 2004, pp. 813–816 (2004)
24. Meisinger, K., Kaup, A.: Spatial error concealment of corrupted image data using frequency selective extrapolation. In: ICASSP 2004, pp. 209–212 (May 2004)
25. Kaup, A., Aach, T.: Efficient prediction of uncovered background in inter frame coding using spatial extrapolation. In: ICASSP 1994, pp. 501–504 (April 1994)
26. Kaup, A., Aach, T.: Coding of segmented images using shape independent basis functions. IEEE Trans. Image Process. 7, 937–947 (1998)

Sketchable Histograms of Oriented Gradients for Object Detection

Ekaterina Zaytseva[1], Santi Seguí[1,2], and Jordi Vitrià[1,2]

[1] Computer Vision Center, Universitat Autònoma de Barcelona
{ezaytseva,ssegui}@cvc.uab.es, jordi.vitria@ub.edu
[2] Dept. de Matemàtica Aplicada i Anàlisi, Universitat de Barcelona

Abstract. In this paper we investigate a new representation approach for visual object recognition. The new representation, called sketchable-HoG, extends the classical histogram of oriented gradients (HoG) feature by adding two different aspects: the *stability* of the majority orientation and the *continuity* of gradient orientations. In this way, the sketchable-HoG locally characterizes the complexity of an object model and introduces global structure information while still keeping simplicity, compactness and robustness. We evaluated the proposed image descriptor on publicly Catltech 101 dataset. The obtained results outperforms classical HoG descriptor as well as other reported descriptors in the literature.

Keywords: Object Recognition, Feature stability, Centrality measures, Histogram of Oriented Gradients.

1 Introduction

In his seminal book, David Marr [8] conjectured that the path to object recognition could benefit from the use of a first level representation of images in terms of simple features. This representation, called primal sketch, was supposed to be a parsimonious but sufficient to reconstruct the original image without much perceivable distortions.

State of the art object recognition systems are not making use of this concept and, instead, are based on representing visual information with local edge statistics or patch based features. This paper focuses on applying the concept of sketchable representation to one of the most used representations: the histogram of oriented gradients (HoG) [4]. This image descriptor has been widely used and it is represented in several forms in the most of state of the art methods for object recognition. In this context, our goal is to go one step beyond the use of local edge statistics by considering additional information to improve upon this cutting-edge descriptor. In spite of this addition, the resulting descriptor keeps the simplicity and robustness of the original one.

The original structure of a HoG is implemented by dividing the image into a set of small connected regions and for each region, or cell, compiling a histogram of gradient directions for the pixels within the cell. This structure is shown in figure 1(b). HoG descriptor can be then built by concatenating the values of the

L. Alvarez et al. (Eds.): CIARP 2012, LNCS 7441, pp. 374–381, 2012.

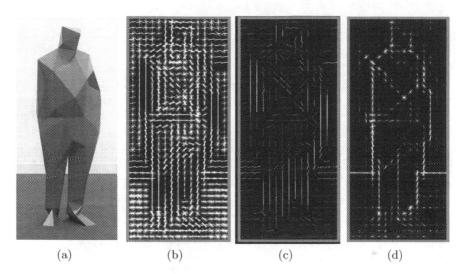

(a)   (b)   (c)   (d)

Fig. 1. (a) Original image; (b) HoG features of (a); (c) Stable orientations of (b); (d) Cells of (b) with high continuity values

bins of all histograms, getting a high-dimensional vector $I = (x_1, \ldots, x_n)$ that represents the image. The final step when using this representation for object recognition is to feed the descriptors into a discriminative learning method such as Support Vector Machine.

In this paper we propose the addition of two characteristics for each histogram cell that represent a more abstract feature of the image: (i) a measure of the *stability* of the most probable orientation in a cell and (b) a measure of the *continuity* of the cell orientation with respect to the whole model. The first characteristic identifies for each object model those cells of the HoG representation that clearly represent an oriented edge of the object. The second one reinforces those cells that represent a continuous oriented gradient field with respect to the neighboring cells.

In figure 1 we show (a) an image of an object and its corresponding (b) HoG model as defined in [4]. In 1(c) we show a new version of (b) where each orientation has been weighted by a value proportional to its stability. It can be easily seen that the stability feature reduces noise but highlights the most well defined edges of the model. Finally, in 1(d) we show a version of (b) where each orientation has been weighted according to its continuity value. As can be easily seen, the resulting models are simpler but sufficient representations of the object and for this reason we call it *sketchable* histograms of oriented gradients.

In summary, this paper shows a way for deriving sketchable histograms from images and that this new feature constitutes a more abstract layer of visual information that allows to build better models even from a few images.

2   Image Description

In order to represent visual object models we propose the addition to the classical HoG representation of two new image features that can be readily derived from it. In the first case, the derived feature is called *stability* and it assigns a value that represents the homogeneity of the gradient vector field that corresponds to a HoG cell. In the second case, the feature is called *continuity* and it represents the level of continuity of the object edges that are represented by that cell.

Our main hypothesis is that these features constitute a parsimonious and sufficient representation of the Histogram of Oriented Gradients. Image representation, obtained by concatenation of stability, continuity and original HOG values, is called sketchable-HoG descriptor. The use of this representation should increase the performance of classifiers because more abstract information is readily accessible to it. In the following sections we defined both features and check the expected increment of performance in a standard dataset.

2.1   Stability

In a HoG representation, each pixel contributes a weighted vote for an edge orientation based on the orientation of the gradient element centered on it. Votes, which are a function of the gradient magnitude at the pixel, are accumulated into orientation bins h_i over local spatial regions that we call cells.

Let $H = (h_1, \ldots, h_9)$ be the vector representing the values of the bins of a standard HoG cell. To define its *stability* we can use the Hoeffding inequality [9], which relates the empirical mean of a bounded random variable to its true mean.

Let $x_1, x_2, \ldots, x_k$ be iid random variables with values in $[0, 1]$. Then, for any $\delta > 0$, the following inequality holds with probability at least $1 - \delta$,

$$E[x] \leq \frac{1}{k}\sum_{i=1}^{k} x_i + \sqrt{\frac{\ln(1/\delta)}{2k}} \qquad (1)$$

In our case, and considering that each pixel contributes with its gradient magnitude to its corresponding orientation bin, we can state, with probability at least $1 - \delta$, that we can associate to h_i a confidence interval $[h_i^{LB}, h_i^{UB}]$, derived from (1), within we expect the true value of h_i to be.

We will say that a cell H is *stable* if its most voted orientation i is *admissible*, in the sense that its estimated value incurs at most β times as much error as any other orientation:

$$H \text{ is stable} \iff \exists i, (1 - h_i^{LB}) < \beta \cdot min_{i' \neq i}(1 - h_{i'}^{UB}) \qquad (2)$$

In our experiments the value of β parameter was fixed at 1. It means that we consider orientation i admissible if the lower bound of the most voted orientation is greater than the upper bound of the second most voted orientation (see figures 2 and 3).

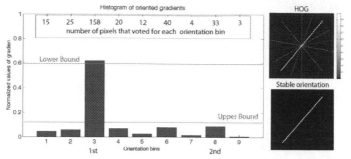

Fig. 2. In the case of a well defined distribution of gradient orientations, the lower bound of the most voted orientation is higher than the upper bound of the second most-voted orientation

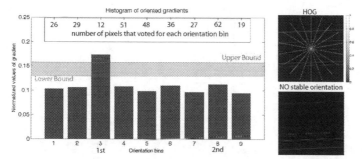

Fig. 3. In the case of an ill defined distribution of gradient orientations, the lower bound of the most voted orientation is lower than the upper bound of the second most-voted orientation. Please note that for the estimation of the lower bound of the fist most probable orientation bin and the upper bound of the second most probable orientation bin both the gradient histograms and the number of voted pixels for each histogram bins are important.

The concept behind the stability indicates that easier visual classes are characterized by higher stability values whilst harder classes have fewer admissible orientations. To check this hypothesis, we have considered the twenty object classes of the PASCAL VOC Challenge 2009. For each class we have computed its HoG model and its mean stability. The complexity of the class has been represented by the average precision (AP) value obtained by state of the art detection methods in the PASCAL VOC Challenge 2009. Finally, we have computed the Spearman's rank correlation coefficient ρ between mean stability of the model and the average precision (AP) value of the class, resulting in a $\rho = 0.81$. As it is shown in figure 4, this value corresponds to a significant correlation between the mean stability and the complexity of the class, corroborating the idea that, when considering state of the art methods [5], easier classes to detect are those presenting higher mean stability values.

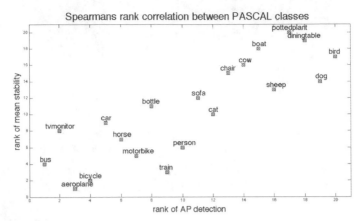

Fig. 4. The Spearman's rank correlation coefficient between the mean stability of a HoG model and the average precision (AP) value of its class in the PASCAL VOC Challenge 2009 is 0.81, which clearly shows a relationship between visual class complexity and stability of its HoG features

2.2   Continuity

In order to represent continuity, we will consider the centrality measure of the nodes of a graph G defined from a HoG descriptor $\{H^j\}_{j=1,...,m}$, where m is the total number of cells of the descriptor. Each node v_j of the graph G corresponds to a cell H^j and the edges $e_{i,k}$ connect neighboring HoG cells H^i and H^k (we have considered a 8-connectivity structure).

The cost of an edge $e_{i,k}$ is assigned by taking into account the values of the histogram bins that correspond to angles which are similar to the angle between both HoG cells. That is, if the node v_i corresponds to an image location that is oriented by angle α with respect to the node v_k, the cost of $e_{i,k}$ is computed by adding the value of the bins from H^i and H^k that correspond to the following angles: $\alpha - 22.5°$ to $\alpha + 22.5°$. In this way, edges which correspond to neighboring cells that represent aligned gradient fields will get higher values (see figure 5).

We have selected the *betweenness* measure proposed in [7] to represent the centrality of each node $v_j \in V$ of the graph . The betweeness measure of a node v_j is equal to the number of shortest paths from all vertices to all others that pass through v_j. This value is then normalized by dividing through the number of pairs of vertices not including v_j. Formally, this continuity measure can be defined as:

$$C(v_j) = \sum_{s \neq v_j \neq t \in G} \frac{\sigma_{st}(v_j)}{\sigma_{st}} \tag{3}$$

where σ_{st} is the total number of paths from node s to node t and $\sigma_{st}(v_j)$ is the total number of shortest paths from node s to node t that pass through v_j. The resulting descriptor is a vector C of size m.

In order to estimate the betweeness we use the Brandes' algorithm [3]. This algorithm is, up to date, the fastest exact algorithm with a complexity $\mathcal{O}(VE + V^2 log(V))$. The method solves n SSSP (Single Source Shortest Path) problems by using Dijkstra's algorithm, where n is the number of vertices, and then adds counter values from the leaves to the root.

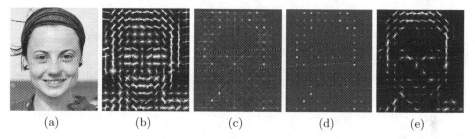

| (a) | (b) | (c) | (d) | (e) |

Fig. 5. (a) Original image; (b) HoG features of (a); (c) Graph constructed using (b) indicating with jet colormap (blue/lower value to red/higher value) the obtained continuity values; (d) Continuity value of cells from (b); (e) Cells of (b) with continuity values

3   Results

In order to evaluate the discriminative power of the proposed feature descriptor, the performance of this descriptor was evaluated by training a One-against-All Support Vector Machine (SVM) [10] classifier for the Caltech-101 dataset [6]. This dataset consists of images from 101 different classes, and contains 30 to 800 images per class. The performance was obtained by averaging results from 10 different trials. In each trial of the evaluation, 15 random training images and 50 random testing images were selected per class. In those classes with less samples than needed fewer images were used for test set. We use this protocol to be able to compare with results reported in [1] and [2].

The achieved results are presented in Table 1. In this table we compare the results obtained using the proposed sketchable HoG descriptor with results of classical HoG descriptor and Berg in [1] and Bileschi in [2]. In order to do a comparison with reported results we used a Linear SVM. As it can be seen, the proposed sketchable HoG descriptor obtains the best performance ($52.71\% \pm 0.80\%$) outperforming all other image descriptors. Table 1 also shows results, obtained by sketchable and classical HoG descriptors using a SVM with rbf-kernel. Sigma parameter of rbf kernel was fixed as the $1/d$ where d is the dimensionality of the image descriptor. In this case, the sketchable HoG descriptor gets an accuracy of $58.80\% \pm 0.57\%$ outperforming classical HoG by more than 4%.

Figure 3 shows the confusion matrix for sketchable HoG and classical HoG descriptors using SVM with rbf-kernel. The confusion matrix denotes the absolute difference in the accuracy between classes. For simplicity, the figure only presents the 5 classes for which the performance increases the most, and the 5 classes for which the performance decreases the most. Moreover, for each of these classes

Table 1. Caltech 101 classification results

Method	% Accuracy
Lineal SVM	
Berg et.al.[1]	45
Bileschi et.al.[2]	48.26% ± 0.91%
HOG	47.71% ± 0.80%
sketchable-HoG	52.71% ± 0.61%
RBF SVM	
HOG	54.35% ± 0.80%
sketchable-HoG	58.80% ± 0.57%

we show its most confusing class. As it can be seen in this confusion matrix, for some classes the performance increases on 20%, when we use a sketchable HoG descriptor instead of classical HOG, while, in those classes where the accuracy decreases the most, the decrease is only 2%.

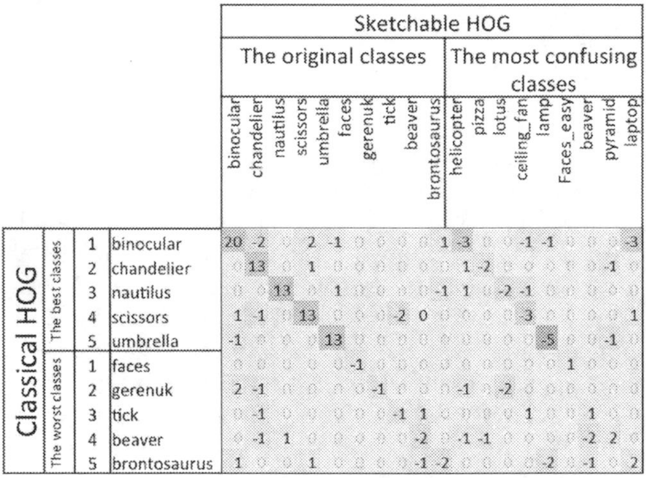

Fig. 6. Confusion matrix for Caltech-101 dataset using sketchable-HoG and classical HoG with RBF-SVM. We show the 5 classes for which the performance increases the most, and the 5 classes for which the performance decreases the most. Each of these classes are paired with its most confusing class.

4   Discussion and Future Work

The most similar approach to our method was proposed by Bileschi and Wolf in [2]. This method defines 4 different image features based on continuity, symmetry, closure and repetition. The main difference between this method and the proposed sketchable-HoG is that this image representation, extends the classical (HoG) descriptor by adding two different aspects: the stability of the majority orientation and the continuity of gradient orientations. As can be seen in Table 1, the proposed sketchable-HoG outperforms in a significant way the results obtained by classical HoG descriptor and the method proposed by Bileschi and Wolf.

These results point towards a clear objective for object recognition systems: to go one step beyond classical local gradient descriptors and develop mid level image descriptors that represent more abstract object characteristics such as stability and continuity. Our option has been not to define a brand new descriptor, but to leverage a powerful one, the HoG. As it is observed in [2], the idea that more meaningful image representations can produce significantly better recognition results is attractive, but it is not trivial to demonstrate. We think that in this work contributes to this research objective in a clear way.

Acknowledgements. This work was partially supported by MEC grants TIN2009- 14404-C02-01 and CONSOLIDER-INGENIO 2010 (CSD2007-00018).

References

1. Berg, A., Berg, T., Malik, J.: Shape matching and object recognition using low distortion correspondences. In: IEEE Computer Society Conference on Computer Vision and Pattern Recognition, CVPR 2005, vol. 1, pp. 26–33 (2005)
2. Bileschi, S.M., Wolf, L.: Image representations beyond histograms of gradients: The role of gestalt descriptors. In: CVPR. IEEE Computer Society (2007)
3. Brandes, U.: A faster algorithm for betweenness centrality. Journal of Mathematical Sociology 25, 163–177 (2001)
4. Dalal, N., Triggs, B.: Histograms of oriented gradients for human detection. In: CVPR, pp. 886–893 (2005)
5. Everingham, M., Van Gool, L., Williams, C.K.I., Winn, J., Zisserman, A.: The PASCAL Visual Object Classes Challenge (VOC2009) Results (2009),
   http://www.pascal-network.org/challenges/VOC/
   voc2009/workshop/index.html
6. Fei-Fei, L., Fergus, R., Perona, P.: Learning generative visual models from few training examples: an incremental Bayesian approach tested on 101 object categories. In: Workshop on Generative-Model Based Vision (2004)
7. Freeman, L.C.: A Set of Measures of Centrality Based on Betweenness. Sociometry 40(1), 35–41 (1977)
8. Marr, D.: Vision: A Computational Investigation into the Human Representation and Processing of Visual Information. Henry Holt and Co., Inc., New York (1982)
9. Serfling, R.J.: Probability Inequalities for the Sum in Sampling without Replacement. The Annals of Statistics 2(1), 39–48 (1974)
10. Vapnik, V.N.: The nature of statistical learning theory. Springer-Verlag New York, Inc., New York (1995)

Supervised Biometric System
Using Multimodal Compression Scheme

Wafa Chaabane[1], Régis Fournier[1], Amine Naït-ali[1,*], Julio Jacobo[2], Marta Mejail[2],
Marcelo Mottalli[2], Heitor Ramos[3], Alejandro C. Frery[3], and Leonardo Viana[3]

[1] Université Paris-Est Créteil (UPEC), LiSSi. Biometrics Research Group, France
`{wafa.chaabane,rfournier,naitali}@u-pec.fr`
[2] Universidad de Buenos Aires, Argentina
`{julio.jacobo,marta.mejail,mottalli}gmail.com`
[3] Universidade Federal de Alagoas, Brazil
`acfrery@gmail.com, lpviana@lccv.ufal.br`

Abstract. This work is a part of a project supported by STIC Am-Sud where
the main objective is to design an intelligent vision system to protect children
from some critical information accessible from the Internet, from some videos
or from some video games that are related to violence, wars, pornography, etc.
Considered definitively not appropriate for their age, such multimedia contains
can significantly offend young people. More specifically, in this paper, we are
interested in discussing a general concept of a supervised biometric system that
is controlled by specific tags embedded in video frames through a multimodal
compression. Using a spiral insertion scheme, specific frequencies (TAGs) are
compressed jointly with video frames in the region of insertion and then extracted for supervision purpose. The multimodal compression is considered here
because it allows high-level robustness regarding the bitrates and down-
sampling.

Keywords: Face recognition, biometrics, Intelligent system, Lossy compression, Multimodal Compression.

1   Introduction

Nowadays, televisions and computers are more and more used in daily routine for
both personal and professional purposes. Since, such devices are used permanently by
various categories of people, including young and very young people. It happens
hence that some multimedia contains, not appropriate, can significantly offend them
(e.g. wars, violence, pornography, etc). Without control, dramatic consequences can
occur.

The question that may arise is: how one can protect young people and children
from such contains?

---

* Corresponding author.

L. Alvarez et al. (Eds.): CIARP 2012, LNCS 7441, pp. 382–389, 2012.

It is well known that some proposed systems require the use of passwords to protect the access to resources or require the installation of some specific software to filter illegal websites or those considered not appropriate for children. Generally, the process of filtering requires using IP addresses or some keywords, but the problem is that these solutions are known to be very limited and can be easily bypassed.

This work is a part of a project called BIOCHIP, organized between France, Argentina and Brazil and supported by STIC Am-SUD [1]. The purpose is to develop a system that allows identifying persons, estimating their ages and controlling any vision system (e.g. TV/computer) by filtering automatically, the multimedia information, based on the contains and the user age (see Fig.1). In other words, the system should define who is using the computer, watching the TV or playing the video game. Somehow, the purpose of this intelligent system is to allow efficient and safe interaction between the device and the user.

Fig. 1. Supervised intelligent TV system based on face recognition (*images used separately from the Internet*)

In this work, after describing briefly the concept, a special interest is given to the multimedia part that requires tagging the information (i.e. video) according to the category of its contains. For this purpose, no watermarking is used, but instead the video/images are compressed jointly with TAG, considered here as a signal having a specific frequency. This task is performed thanks to a multimodal compression scheme [4], [5] allowing a high robustness regarding the bitrates and which can be less sensitive to down-sampling.

This paper is organized as follows: in section 2, a general concept of face recognition module is presented. The multimodal compression scheme using a spiral mixing function is presented in section 3. Afterwards, some preliminary results are provided in section 4, and finally a conclusion is given in the last section 5.

2   PCA-Based Identification

Face detection and recognition are widely studied nowadays due to a requirement in identifying automatically persons [2]. They are used commonly for security and access control purposes.

Face recognition systems do not require any physical contact since the image capture can be performed at a distance using a simple camera. In our system, principal component analysis (PCA) technique developed by Turk and Pentland [3] has been considered, after detecting faces.

This statistical technique requires the following processing steps:

1. The mean of the detected face images is removed,
2. Covariance matrix is calculated,
3. Eigenvectors (called also *eigenfaces*) are calculated from the covariance matrix,
4. Each face image is projected on the *eigenfaces* corresponding to the most significant eigenvalues. Consequently, each face image k is characterized by a set of parameters $\{\alpha_{1k}, \alpha_{2k} ... \alpha_{Mk}\}$.

The proposed system operates according a supervised mode. It required an enrolment phase and a control phase, described as follows:

1. **Enrolment Phase:** in this phase, the administrator should enrol the users that are supposed to watch the TV. A face recognition system extracts the parameters $\{\alpha_{1k}, \alpha_{2k} ... \alpha_{Mk}\}$ from each acquired image using PCA method, as described above. Afterwards, the administrator attributes priorities for each user according to his age and the recommendation that should be given by the provider. For instance, if we consider the French legislation, one can attribute priorities according to the following categories:

-Category I: free program,
-Category II: not recommended for under 10 years old,
-Category III: not recommended for under 12 years old,
-Category IV: not recommended for under 16 years old,
-Category V: not recommended for under 18 years old.

Table 1. Matching face features and allowed priorities

Person	Code	Priority
1	$\{\alpha_{11}, \alpha_{21} ... \alpha_{M1}\}$	$\in \{I, II, ... V\}$
2	$\{\alpha_{12}, \alpha_{22} ... \alpha_{M2}\}$	$\in \{I, II, ... V\}$
...	...	
N	$\{\alpha_{1N}, \alpha_{2N} ... \alpha_{MN}\}$	$\in \{I, II, ... V\}$

Based on the same principle, other categories can be considered for video games that can differ from one country to another. Consequently, a priority i is associated to a category i (see Table 1).

2. **Control Phase:** during this phase, the system extracts tags from the analysed video frames and user face images in front the computer/TV are detected then identified in real time. Afterwards, a matching is performed between the identified category and the priority that corresponds to the youngest user (see Table 1, Fig. 2).

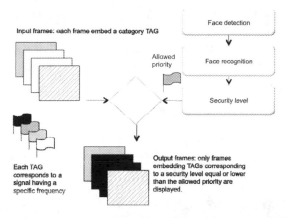

Fig. 2. Scheme showing the concept of biometric system supervision. Tags are embedded in input video frames before compression. Once decoded, only frames corresponding to a security level, equal or lower than the allowed priority are displayed.

3   Multimodal Compression Tagging

The idea of the multimodal compression consists in inserting "or embedding" signal samples into an image, before encoding the entire data mixture using only a single encoder [3]. As shown in a generic scheme of Fig. 3, the function allowing this mixture will be called "Mixing function". For the decoding, an inverse function, "Separation function" is applied to the decoded mixture. As evoked previously, in order to avoid any possible confusion, this technique shouldn't be considered as watermarking because the constraints and the purpose are not the same. Generally, when dealing with watermarking, one has to hide some data inside an image. This is not the case here.

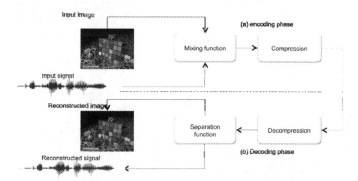

Fig. 3. Generic scheme of the multimodal compression showing a joint encoding image/signal

In our application, we have proposed a set of Tags where each Tag is a specific signal that corresponds to a given category. These Tags are embedded in the video frames according to a spiral mixing function, described bellow. These Tags correspond to five different frequencies f_1, f_2, f_3, f_4, f_5. When dealing with low compression ratios, it is indeed not necessary to insert these frequencies in each frame.

Actually, when a frequency f_i is detected, the priority i is applied until the detection of another frequency. Whereas, when videos are compressed using high compression ratios, embedding Tags in each frame to create a redundancy is useful because, once extracted Tag signals can be averaged in order to reduce the noise due to the compression process (Fig. 6).

3.1   Spiral Insertion Based Mixing Function

Let's I denotes a $M \times N$ frame and s_i a K samples Tag signal f_i. The insertion phase consists of replacing each sample/2 of a selected pathway that belongs to the frame, by Tag signal samples. In this work, we are considering a spiral pathway as shown in Fig. 4.

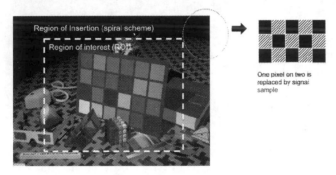

One pixel on two is replaced by signal sample

Fig. 4. Spatial insertion of samples in the Region of insertion. Tag signal samples are interleaved as shown (one pixel on two corresponds to Tag sample). No insertion is performed in ROI in order to avoid any potential distortion of the image quality.

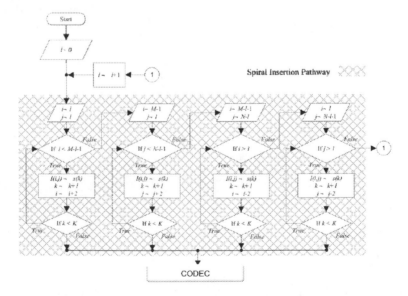

Fig. 5. Encoding flowchart corresponding multimodal compression scheme, using spiral insertion

The insertion pathway should belong to the external insertion region (around the borders) because generally, Region of Interests (ROI) are basically located at the centre of the image. In such a case, the maximum of samples that can be inserted in an image without defining a ROI is $K \leq (M \times N)/2$. This is referred as, the capacity of insertion. If a ROI is pre-defined in the frame (i.e. no insertion is allowed in that region), the capacity will be bounded by $((M - N) - S)/2$ where S denotes the size of the ROI.

The insertion algorithm is provided in the flowchart of the Fig. 5. Afterwards, the entire mixture is encoded.

3.2 Spiral Separation

At the decoding phase, the frame is first decoded. Afterwards, a separation function is achieved in order to separate the Tag signal from the frame. In this phase, signal samples are extracted from the spiral pathway to form the Tag signal (Figure 5). In order to reconstruct the original frame, pixels initially replaced by Tag signal samples should be estimated by a simple interpolation method.

In order to obtain high compression ratios, videos are generally compressed according to lossy compression standards (we used here the H.264 codec). Consequently, the quality of compressed images and the extracted Tags can be affected if the compression ratio is high. Since we present in this work only preliminary results, the PSNR (Peak Signal to Noise Ratio) function is used to evaluate the quality of the compressed images.

This PSNR should be evaluated in two regions, namely the global region denoted by $PSNR_{global}$ and the region where no Tag should be inserted ($PSNR_{local}$).

To evaluate the quality of the extracted Tag signal, one can use a time domain criterion such as the PRD (percent root-mean-square difference). In the frequency domain, the estimated frequency $\widehat{f}_i$ can be compared to the original one by a simple calculation of Euclidian distance (Fig. 6). In such a case, a threshold should be defined.

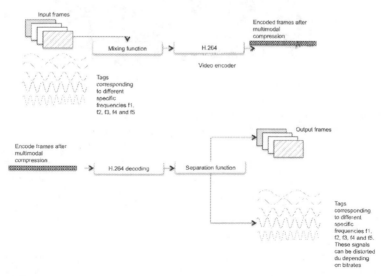

Fig. 6. Example of mixing/separation process using the multimodal compression scheme. Tags signals correspond to specific frequencies.

4   Some Preliminary Results

To validate the proposed multimodal compression scheme, we have considered a speech signal (as a validation tool) before using Tag signals, since the speech signal contains a large number of frequencies. This signal is embedded into two different videos "Foreman" (Fig.7) and "Claire" using the spiral scheme mixing function. Afterwards, the mixture is compressed using H.264 codec. After the decoding process, the reconstructed frames as well as the reconstructed speech signal are evaluated in terms of quality. For example, Fig.8.(left), show that the quality of the decoded videos using H. 264 without multimodal compression is close to the quality obtained when considering multimodal compression. This means that for the same bitrate, the multimodal compression allows compressing an additional signal without affecting the quality of the video nor the quality of the embedded signal as shown in Fig 8.(right) Here, bitrate is set so that the visual quality of videos remains visually acceptable and without significant distortion.

Based on this result, Tag signals of the following frequencies are used 2000 Hz, 2500 Hz, 3000 Hz, 3500 Hz and 4000 Hz that can be regarded as tones. The frequency sampling is set at 22050 Hz. These signals are periodically embeded in each frame so that their extraction by averaging becomes possible even if the bitrate is low. As it has been reported previously, when dealing with high bitrates, it is not important to embed a Tag in each frame. Actually, a Tag signal should be embedded in a frame each time the video category changes. The same priority should be used until detecting a new Tag signal in the video.

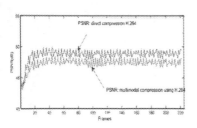

Fig. 7. Foreman video sequence used for the evaluation process

Consequently, using the multimodal compression based on a single encoder, an efficient encoding of both frames and the Tag signals are obtained.

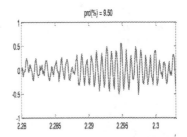

Fig. 8. Left: Mean video quality with and without embedding Tags. Right: Input embedded signal and the output superimposed (PRD=9.50%), highlighting the minimal distorsion.

5   Conclusion

We have considered in this paper a supervised vision system that is controlled through Tags embedded in video sequences and encoded using a multimodal compression scheme. The main advantage of this scheme is its robustness regarding the compression ratio. No significant distortion is observed on decoded videos, and good Tags quality is obtained whatever the used frequency, (validation achieved on speech signals). For a future work, it would be interesting to optimize both the mixing function and the shape of Tags in order to reduce the computing complexity.

References

1. BIOCHIP (2012),
   http://international-education-biometrics.net/biochip/
2. Zhao, W., Chellapa, R., Phillips, P.: Face recognition: a literature survey. ACM Computing Surveys 35(4), 399–458 (2003)
3. Turk, M., Pentland, A.: Eigenfaces For Recognition. Journal of Cognitive Neuroscience 3, 71–86 (1991)
4. Naït-ali, A., Zeybek, E., Drouot, X.: Introduction to Multimodal Compression of Biomedical data. book: Advanced Biosignal Processing, pp. 353–375. Springer (2009)
5. Fournier, R., Nait-ali, A., Zeybek, E.H.: A novel supervised model for multimodal compression. Journal of Signal and Information Processing (in press, 2012)

A New Morphological Measure
of Histogram Bimodality

Miguel Angel Cataño and Joan Climent

[1] Pontificia Universidad Católica del Perú
[2] Barcelona Tech (UPC), Spain

Abstract. The presence of multiple modes in a histogram gives important information about data distribution for a great amount of different applications. The dip test has been the most common statistical measure used for this purpose.

Histograms of oriented gradients (HOGs) with a high bimodality have shown to be very useful to detect highly robust keypoints. However, the dip test presents serious disadvantages when dealing with such histograms. In this paper we describe the drawbacks of the dip test for determining HOGs bimodality, and present a new bimodality test, based on mathematical morphology, that overcomes them.

Keywords: Keypoint detection, Bimodality test, Histograms of Oriented Gradients, Mathematical Morphology, Dynamics.

1 Introduction

Histograms of oriented gradients (HOGs) have become increasingly popular in the computer vision community in recent years. Among other applications, they are used for object detection [3], as keypoint descriptors (i.e., SIFT [8]), or for keypoint detection [2]. The basic idea is that local shapes can be characterized rather well by the distribution of local gradient directions. The use of directions gives robustness to lighting changes. HOGs are implemented by dividing the image into small windows, called cells, each cell accumulating a 1-D histogram of gradient directions of all pixels within the cell. The main advantage of HOG representation is the high invariance to translations and rotations.

Recent works have shown that HOGs can be used for the detection of singular points, giving very robust keypoints. They use the bimodality of the HOGs as a measure of the significance of a keypoint. The dip test of bimodality [5] is used for this purpose. Figure 1 shows the HOGs corresponding to the cells selected in the image of figure 2a. The bimodality of each histogram is computed for each pixel using the dip test. Figure 2b shows the bimodality image extracted from figure 2a. As it can be seen, peaks of the bimodality image correspond to keypoints of the original image.

However, the dip measure has some drawbacks, mainly due to the fact that HOGs are cyclic, and the extension of the dip test to cyclic histograms is not

L. Alvarez et al. (Eds.): CIARP 2012, LNCS 7441, pp. 390–397, 2012.

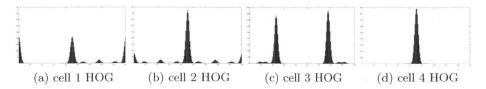

| (a) cell 1 HOG | (b) cell 2 HOG | (c) cell 3 HOG | (d) cell 4 HOG |

Fig. 1. HOGs of selected areas of figure 2a

trivial. Furthermore, it presents a remarkable lack of linearity, specially in the particular case where the histogram has samples only in two neighboring bins.

In this paper we present a new bimodality measure, based on the dynamics, that will be used to improve the detection of keypoints. The dynamics is a mathematical morphology concept introduced by Grimaud [4]. It has usually been used as a concise and powerful measure of contrast for the identification of regions of interest in the image, but in our work we use dynamics to quantify the modes of the histograms. The dynamics of the histogram peaks are used to define a new bimodality measure, that makes possible to establish a hierarchy of interest points.

After presenting the basics of the dip test and the dynamics in section 2, we give the implementation details of our proposal in section 3. In the results section, the limitations of the dip measure are shown, and we compare its response to histogram transformations with the response of our method.

2   Preliminaries

2.1   The Dip Measure

The most popular measure of bimodality is the dip Test [5]. It was first used for globular cluster studies. The dip test is based on the cumulative distribution of the input sample. The dip statistic is the maximum distance between the cumulative input distribution and the best-fitting unimodal distribution. The dip test searches specifically for a flat step in the cumulative distribution function, which corresponds to a 'dip' in the histogram representation. Formally, the dip

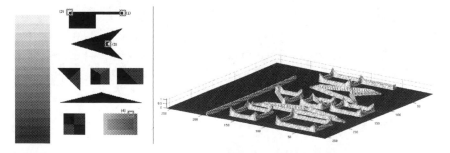

Fig. 2. (a) A synthetic image (b) A 3D representation of the bimodality image

of a distribution function F is defined by $D(F) = \rho(F, \zeta)$, being ζ the class of unimodal distribution functions, and

$$\rho(F, \zeta) = inf_{G \in \zeta} \{sup_x |F(x) - G(x)|\}. \tag{1}$$

To test the null hypothesis that F has a unimodal density Hartigan and Hartigan [5] proposed the statistic $D(Fn)$, where Fn is the empirical distribution function of a random sample of size n. The distribution of $D(Fn)$ is compared with the distribution of $D(F)$, where F is the uniform distribution on $[0; 1]$. Although the dip test was originally reported as an unimodality measure, it is commonly used for computing the bimodality of distributions. Hartigan and Hartigan showed that the dip is asymptotically larger for the uniform distribution than for any other unimodal distribution. Therefore, histograms with high unimodality result in low scores of the dip test. High scores of the dip test correspond to highly bimodal histograms.

The algorithm for computing the dip test is published in [6]. Open source code used to compute the dip can be found in www.cran.r-project.org/web/packages/diptest/

2.2   The Dynamics

The dynamics [4], is a morphological measure associated to each regional extrema of an image. This measure is a powerful tool to quantify the saliency of a maximum or minimum. The dynamics of a regional minimum is defined as the minimum height we have to climb starting from this minimum to reach another one with strictly higher dynamics, the climb being the difference in altitude between the highest point of the path and the regional minimum under study. Formally: Let M be a regional minimum of a function f. The dynamics of M is defined as:

$$\min \left\{ \max_{s \in [0,1]} \{f(\gamma(s)) - f(\gamma(0))\} \mid \gamma : [0,1] \to \Re^2, f(\gamma(1)) < f(\gamma(0)), \gamma(0) \in M \right\} \tag{2}$$

where γ is a path linking two points.

Note that the dynamics are not defined for the global minimum of the image, as there is no pixel with strictly lower altitude. However, in morphological image processing is assumed that the image f has a global minimum on its boundary. This makes possible the valuation of the global minimum inside the domain of definition of f.

Grimaud [4], presents dynamics of regional minima instead of maxima. However, we need the dynamics of the maxima of the histogram to compute the bimodality. Dynamics of a regional maximum M is the minimum height that we should fall, to reach another regional maximum higher than M.

3   Computing the HOG Bimodality

The algorithm for extracting the dynamics is based on the watershed algorithm proposed by Vincent and Soille [15]. It consists in flooding from the minima, level by level, until water from a catchment basin meets water from another one. The meeting point between two basins is a saddle point, and this is the point where we can compute the dynamics of one of the two basins: the basin with the lowest value floods the other one, and the dynamics of the basin with the lowest minimum is equal to the grey-value of the saddle point minus the grey-value of the minima.

Organizing the image as a set of regions enables a faster implementation of dynamics. In this sense, the Component Tree [7, 9] is a structure formed by the decomposition of a grey-level image by thresholds, and very useful for dynamics determination [1] . It is especially interesting because it requires only the adjacency definition for its construction, and there exist several quasi-linear time algorithms for constructing it [10].

Max-tree refers to the algorithm introduced by Salembier [12] for an efficient implementation of the component tree. Silva and Lotufo describe in [14] an efficient computation of the dynamics, based on the incremental determination of attributes from the max-tree construction, in linear time.

We have used the implementation presented in [14] (Available from http://parati.dca.fee.unicamp.br/adesso/), and modified the original algorithm to make it able to work with cyclic histograms. As mentioned earlier, the dynamics of the absolute maximum of an image is computed considering that the image boundary has a virtual higher value. Since we are dealing with cyclic histograms, we cannot make this assumption because a circular structure has no boundaries. Thus, the global maximum of the histogram will be always considered the maximum with highest dynamics, and quantified with its height.

The other variation introduced to the original algorithm also concerns the circularity of HOGs. We have modified the original algorithm in order to avoid the zero crossing discontinuity. We have considered the circularity of the histogram in the flooding process, and taken into account that a saddle point can split two domes whose maxima are at both sides of the histogram origin. The zero crossing could also split a single dome in two, giving as a result two regional maxima, one at each side of the histogram origin. Due to the nature of the flooding process, this modification of the algorithm does not translate into any additional computational cost.

Once we have the values of the two highest dynamics, dyn_1 and dyn_2, the bimodality of the histogram is computed using equation 3

$$BM = \frac{dyn_1 \cdot dyn_2}{\sqrt{dyn_1^2 + dyn_2^2}} \qquad (3)$$

The product of the dynamics is divided by the Euclidean norm for normalization purposes.

4   Results

We have computed the bimodality of a set of histograms, using both the dip test and our method based on dynamics. The objective is to establish a comparison

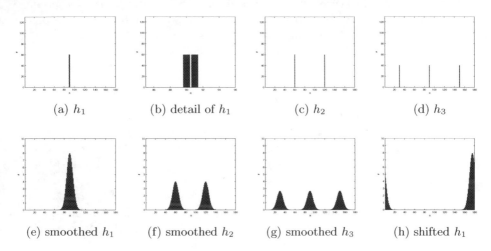

(a) h_1 (b) detail of h_1 (c) h_2 (d) h_3

(e) smoothed h_1 (f) smoothed h_2 (g) smoothed h_3 (h) shifted h_1

Fig. 3. Test histograms

between the responses of both algorithms. First we use synthetic histograms specially designed to detect anomalies in the bimodality measures. Next, we use the HOGs extracted from real images with the objective of evaluating the bimodality tests for non-ideal histograms.

h_1 is an unimodal histogram consisting of two non-empty neighbour bins. It is very usual when constructing HOGs, that the orientation of a single straight line count into two neighbour bins due to discretization. h_1 is a synthetic model of this situation. h_2 and h_3 are pure bimodal and trimodal histograms respectively. All histograms have the same amount of samples (120) and bins (180).

The first experiment is the response to histogram smoothing. In real images, the gradient direction, computed by means of convolution masks, is not always accurate. The measure of orientation is affected by blurring and lack of contrast of the image. This inaccuracy causes that HOG neighboring bins share samples from pixels with similar orientations, giving the typical modal shaped histogram. For this purpose we have smoothed the synthetic histograms h_1, h_2 and h_3, shown in figure 3, with a Gaussian filter with an increasing standard deviation.

Figure 4 shows the responses of bimodality tests for the 3 sets of filtered histograms. It should be noticed that the dip test gives a higher bimodality score to h_3 than to h_2 for high smoothing levels, while using our test, the bimodality of h_2 is always higher than h_3 for any given value of σ. But the main drawback of the dip test is that it gives the highest bimodality score (0,25) to h_1. For descriptors such as HOGs, h_1 should always be considered as a pure unimodal histogram. Using our measure, h_1 gets the minimum bimodality score for all smoothing levels.

The second experiment is shift invariance. For a robust keypoint detection, rotational invariance is mandatory. Rotations of the image translate into cyclic shifts of the HOG. We have shifted the histograms shown in figures 3e-3g by all possible values from 1 to 180. The bimodality tests for the three sets of 180

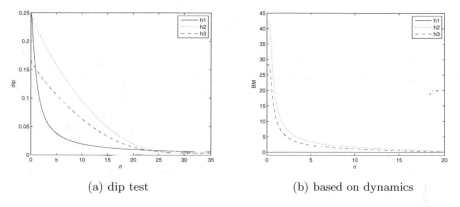

(a) dip test   (b) based on dynamics

Fig. 4. Bimodality measures of smoothed histograms

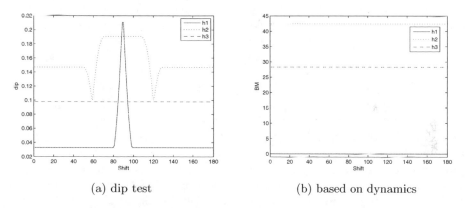

(a) dip test   (b) based on dynamics

Fig. 5. Bimodality measures of shifted histograms

histograms have been computed, and the results are shown in figure 5. Due to the fact that the algorithm presented works with cyclic vectors, our bimodality measure remains constant for all possible shifts of every histogram. On the other hand, figure 5a shows the effects of the zero crossing in the dip test. An unimodal histogram such as h_1, gets a high bimodality score when the mode is splitted in two parts at both sides of the histogram origin (like the one shown in figure 3h). A variation of the dip test for dealing with cyclic histograms is not an easy task, and we are not aware of any published implementation. However, a partial solution for using the dip algorithm with cyclic vectors, is to shift the histogram up to the global minimum before computing the dip test, but this solution doesn't work when the HOG has several global minima.

Finally, the third experiment is a comparison of the repeatability of the keypoints detected with both bimodality measures.

(a) Blocks image   (b) Keypoints   (c) 45°transform   (d) Keypoints

Fig. 6. Test image, a projective transform, and keypoints detected

Using the integral histogram [11], a HOG is computed for every pixel of the image within a cell of 21x21 pixels. We construct the bimodality images (like the one shown in figure 2b) assigning the bimodality value of each histogram to the center pixel of each cell. Peaks of the bimodality image are candidates for being keypoints. We select the keypoints locating the relative maxima of the bimodality image. The bimodality scores make possible to establish a hierarchy of keypoints based on their saliency.

In order to test the robustness of the keypoints detected, we change the image point of view with a projective transform (see figure 6). Then, the whole process is repeated for both bimodality tests, computing new bimodality images and extracting the keypoints of the transformed images. Repeatability [13] is the standard measure for testing the robustness of a keypoint detector to image transforms. The repeatability rate, $r(I,\psi(I))$, is defined as the number of points present in both the original and the transformed image, with respect to the total number of detected points. Keypoints that are not present within a certain neighborhood in both images, decrease the repeatability measure. We have computed the repeatability $r(\psi_\alpha(Keyp(I)),Keyp(\psi_\alpha(I)))$ for all projective transforms ψ_α from $\alpha=0°$ to $\alpha=70°$. $Keyp(I)$ is an image containing the keypoints of image I. It is computed for both bimodality measures selecting the most salient maxima of the bimodality images. As it could be expected from previous experiments, we have obtained a higher repeatability using the bimodality measure based on dynamics than using the dip test. Concretely, using the dip test we obtain a mean repeatability $\bar{r}=66.2\%$, while using our measure the mean repeatability is $\bar{r}=78,8\%$.

5   Conclusions

The dip test of bimodality presents some drawbacks that create big problems when computing the bimodality of HOGs: it does not deal with cyclic histograms, unimodal histograms consisting of two neighboring bins are considered bimodal, and it does not preserve the order of the scores when the smoothing level is increased.

We have presented a new algorithm for computing the bimodality of an histogram based on the dynamics of its domes. This algorithm overcomes the drawbacks of the dip test. The keypoints detected in real images by means of HOG bimodality, have shown to have a higher repeatability using our measure.

Acknowledgments. This research was partially supported by Consolider Ingenio 2010, project (CSD2007-00018) and CICYT project DPI2010-17112.

References

1. Bertrand, G.: On the dynamics. Image Vision Comput. 25(4), 447–454 (2007)
2. Cataño, M.A., Climent, J.: Keypoint detection based on the unimodality test of hOGs. In: Bebis, G. (ed.) ISVC 2012, Part I. LNCS, vol. 7431, pp. 189–198. Springer, Heidelberg (2012)
3. Dalal, N., Triggs, B.: Histograms of Oriented Gradients for Human Detection. In: IEEE Conference on CVPR , vol. 1, pp. 886–893 (2005)
4. Grimaud, M.: New measure of contrast: the dynamics. Image Algebra and Morphological Image Processing III 1769(1), 292–305 (1992)
5. Hartigan, J.A., Hartigan, P.M.: The Dip Test of Unimodality. Ann. Stat. 13(1), 70–84 (1985)
6. Hartigan, P.M.: Algorithm as 217: Computation of the dip statistic to test for unimodality. J. Roy. Stat. Soc. C-App. 34(3), 320–325 (1985)
7. Jones, R.: Connected filtering and segmentation using component trees. Comput. Vis. Image Und. 75(3), 215–228 (1999)
8. Lowe, D.G.: Distinctive Image Features from Scale-Invariant Keypoints. International Journal of Computer Vision 60(2), 91–110 (2004)
9. Mattes, J., Richard, M., Demongeot, J.: Tree Representation for Image Matching and Object Recognition. In: Bertrand, G., Couprie, M., Perroton, L. (eds.) DGCI 1999. LNCS, vol. 1568, pp. 298–312. Springer, Heidelberg (1999)
10. Najman, L., Couprie, M.: Building the component tree in quasi-linear time. IEEE T. Image Process. 15(11), 3531–3539 (2006)
11. Porikli, F.: Integral histogram: A fast way to extract histograms in cartesian spaces. In: IEEE Computer Vision and Pattern Recognition (CVPR), pp. 829–836 (2005)
12. Salembier, P., Oliveras, A., Garrido, L.: Antiextensive connected operators for image and sequence processing. IEEE T. Image Process. 7(4), 555–570 (1998)
13. Schmid, C., Mohr, R., Bauckhage, C.: Comparing and Evaluating Interest Points. In: ICCV, pp. 230–235 (1998)
14. Silva, A.G., de Alencar Lotufo, R.: Efficient computation of new extinction values from extended component tree. Pattern Recogn. Lett. 32(1), 79–90 (2011)
15. Vincent, L., Soille, P.: Watersheds in digital spaces: An efficient algorithm based on immersion simulations. IEEE T. Pattern Anal. 13(6), 583–598 (1991)

Street Detection with Asymmetric Haar Features

Geovany A. Ramirez and Olac Fuentes

Computer Science Department, University of Texas at El Paso
garamirez@miners.utep.edu, ofuentes@utep.edu

Abstract. We present a system for object detection applied to street detection in satellite images. Our system is based on asymmetric Haar features. Asymmetric Haar features provide a rich feature space, which allows to build classifiers that are accurate and much simpler than those obtained with other features. The extremely large parameter space of potential features is explored using a genetic algorithm. Our system uses specialized detectors in different street orientations that are built using AdaBoost and the C4.5 rule induction algorithm. Experimental results show that Asymmetric Haar features are better than basic Haar features for street detection.

Keywords: Object Detection, Asymmetric Haar Features, Machine Learning, Street Detection.

1   Introduction

Object detection has received a great deal of attention in the last few years. Most recent approaches to this problem pose it as a binary classification problem, where one needs to classify every window in an image as belonging to the class of interest (i.e. streets), or not. Recent research contributions have focused mostly on two main aspects of the problem: feature engineering and classifier design. Feature engineering consists of designing and selecting classes of features that can improve the performance of the classifiers that are based on them. Work on classifier design consists of adapting existing classification algorithms to the detection and recognition problems, or of designing special-purpose algorithms that are targeted to these problems.

In a series of papers, Viola and co-workers advocated an approach to object recognition based on Haar features, which are equivalent to the difference of the sum of the intensity levels of two contiguous equal-sized rectangular image regions (see Figure 1a). They presented an algorithm for computing these features in constant time, which makes them suitable for real-time performance [13]. Using Haar features, a cascade of classifiers based on the Adaboost algorithm was constructed, yielding accurate detection, albeit at the expense of long training times. Successful applications of this methodology were presented in face detection [13], image retrieval [11], and pedestrian detection [14]. There are some extensions to the original set of Haar features proposed by Viola and

L. Alvarez et al. (Eds.): CIARP 2012, LNCS 7441, pp. 398–405, 2012.

Jones such as the work of Lienhart and Maydt, which introduced rotated Haar features as shown in Figure 1b [6]. Another extension was presented by Ramirez and Fuentes, which proposed asymmetric Haar features, which can have regions with either different width or height, but not both [10]. This results in a more expressive feature space, which, as they showed, allows to build classifiers that are much simpler than those obtained with the standard features.

Road extraction is a problem where the goal is to segment roads in satellite/aerial images. It is typically performed in three steps: image pre-processing, road detection, and road following [3]. Road detection consists of determining what regions of the images are likely to be roads. The goal of road following is to build a road network by connecting all the road segments found using road detection. Street extraction is a subproblem of road extraction, where the goal is to extract the roads in satellite/aerial images in urban areas. In this paper we focus on the subproblem of automatic street detection in satellite images. We use the extensions to the the original set of Haar features proposed by Ramirez and Fuentes [10]. We present experimental results that show that our method can attain better results than the original set of Haar features proposed by Viola and Jones [13] for street detection.

2   Related Work

Street detection, has received some attention in recent years. Vosselman and Knecht detect roads matching the average gray value of a road model with pixels of some manually selected segments of the image [15]. With the matches they obtain some parameters that describe the shape and position of the road. The parameters are used in combination with the Kalman filter to predict the position of the complete road.

Doucette *et al.* presents an algorithm for automatic building of road maps in multi-spectral images [2]. The algorithm is inspired by Kohonen's self-organizing map neural network algorithm. First a human-supervised segmentation of roads is performed, then the segmented image is given as input to a K-medians algorithm. The points that represent the road are initialized in a uniform grid. After that they use a minimum spanning tree algorithm to derive the road topology.

Tupin *et al.* presents a road detection method for synthetic aperture radar images [12]. They used a line detector that is based on thresholding. After that, they contruct a graph using the interconnected segments. To identify a road, they minimize an energy function associated with the graph.

Yan and Zhao presents a method based on segmentation [16]. The segmentation is performed using region growing based on three rules: gray comparability, width consistency, and continuity. After segmenting, they measure some features such as parallelism and connectivity and also fuse information from different image channels to obtain more precise road detection. Péteri and Ranchin presents a road extractor based on a multi-resolution analysis [8]. They used the Canny edge detector and a wavelet transform to construct a multi-resolution image representation. Then they use double active contours called double snakes. They fit a street minimizing an energy function that represents continuity, curvature and parallelism. A drawback is that the search has to be initialized near the road to ensure convergence.

Christophe and Inglada presents a road detector based on color and geometric properties of roads [1]. The detector needs user interaction to define the color of the road to be detected. The detector's output is a set of vectors that can be integrated to GIS software. Guo *et al.* presents a method for road extraction on a large set of aerial images [4]. The method is based on detection of road footprints. A footprint describes the geometric characteristics of a possible road segment. To build a road network the authors used a growing algorithm to connect all the road segments.

3   Haar Features

Haar features are based on Haar wavelets, which are functions that consist of a brief positive impulse followed of a brief negative impulse. In image processing, a Haar feature is the difference of the sums intensities of all pixels in two or more contiguous regions. Papageorgiou *et al.* were the first to use Haar features for face detection [7]. They used three types of Haar features of size 2×2 and 4×4 pixels, for a total of 1,734 different features in a 19×19 face image. Viola and Jones proposed a basic set of four types of Haar features that are shown in Figure 1a [13]. The value of Haar feature is given by the sum of intensities of the pixels in the light region minus the sum of intensities in the dark region. Using all possible sizes, they generate around 180,000 features for a 24×24 pixel image. Lienhart and Maydt presented an extension to the basic set with rotated Haar features as shown in Figure 1b [6]. Using a straightforward implementation, the time required to perform the sum of pixels increases linearly with the number of pixels. Viola and Jones proposed to use the integral image as preprocessing to compute the sum of regions of any size in constant time [13]. Each element of the integral image contains the sum of pixels in the original image that are above and to the left of that pixel; using this idea allows to compute a two-region Haar feature using only six memory access and a three-region Haar feature with only eight.

(a)   (b)

Fig. 1. (a) Haar features introduced by Viola and Jones [13]. (b) Some Haar features variations proposed by Lienhart and Maydt [6].

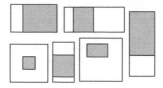

Fig. 2. Asymmetric Haar features used

4   Proposed Algorithm

In contrast with basic Haar features, the features we presented in [10] can have regions with different width or height, but not both (see Fig. 2). By allowing asymmetry, the number of possible configurations for Haar features grows exponentially and is an overcomplete set. For the 6 Haar features shown in Figure 2, there are around 200 million possible configurations for a 24×24 image. Using all the possible configurations is unfeasible, therefore, to deal with this limitation we use a Genetic Algorithm to select a subset of features.

We use specialized detectors to detect streets with different orientations. We build a specialized detector for every 30 degrees in orientation to cover the 360 degree in-plane rotation of each possible street orientation. Each specialized detector consists of a cascade of strong classifiers created with the AdaBoost algorithm used by Viola and Jones [13]. We use a weak classifier based on the C4.5 rule induction algorithm [9] that is associated with only one Haar feature. We only need to train detectors for 0 and 30 degrees; the remaining ten detectors can be created by combinations of 90-degree rotations and inversions of original Haar features as shown in Figure 3. Since a street is symmetric horizontal and vertically, we require only 6 specialized detectors to cover the 360 degree in-plane rotation.

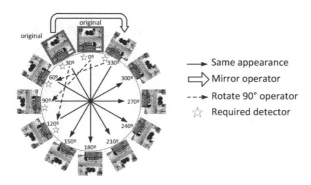

Fig. 3. Specialized detector for streets

4.1   Selecting Haar Features with a Genetic Algorithm

Training a specialized detector using all the possible configurations of the asymmetric region Haar features would be impractical. For instance, using an initial training set of 4,000 examples and all the possible Haar configurations, we would need about 4 months on a 2.5GHz Intel Xeon computer for only one specialized detector. Therefore, to reduce the number of possible Haar features, we use a Genetic Algorithm (GA) to select the width and the height of the regions associated with a feature. In the GA, one individual is a weak classifier (WC) that contains only one Haar feature and is trained with the C4.5 algorithm. The fitness of each individual corresponds to the classification accuracy on an initial training set. We compute a WC for each place on the image and for each type of feature, for a total of 2,431 Haar features. We use a decimal representation that avoids the creation of invalid individuals by crossover. For mutation, we generate an uniformly distributed random value inside the allowed range. We use two point crossover with a deterministic crossover model presented in [5]. This model consists of combining the best and the worst individuals in the population, then the second best with the second worst, and so on. With this crossover model, it is possible to perform a larger exploration on the search space. The best result was obtained with a 10% mutation rate. Using the GA to select a subset of Haar features, we can reduce training time to 6 hours on our 2.5GHz Intel Xeon computer; this corresponds to a 99.8% reduction in time.

4.2   Training a Specialized Detector

A specialized detector is a cascade of strong classifiers (SC). We can create a cascade of SC using the same algorithm presented in [10]. After obtaining a subset of WC with GA, new examples are added to the training set and then the AdaBoost algorithm is used to create a new SC. AdaBoost ends when the minimum detection rate and the maximum false positive rate per layer in the cascade are attained. If the target false positive rate is achieved, the algorithm ends. Otherwise all negative examples correctly classified are eliminated and the training set is balanced adding negative examples using a bootstrapping technique. With the training set updated, all the WCs are retrained and then used in AdaBoost.

5   Experimental Results

We use satellite images taken from Google Earth. We use 20 high resolution images from urban places and manually crop square regions that contain streets. A total of 800 regions were cut and normalized in rotation to 0 degrees and a size of 24×24 pixels. For each region we add 4 variations in angle inside the range of ±15 degrees for a total of 4,000 positive images. To generate negative samples, we replaced the streets in the 20 original images with other parts of the image that do not contain streets. Then we randomly selected 4,000 regions

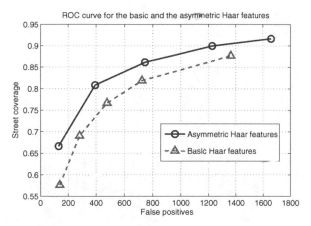

Fig. 4. Comparison between the basic and the asymmetric Haar features

as negative samples for the training set. The training set contains a total of 8,000 examples and can be transformed for any rotation angle in order to create other specialized detectors. In addition, we use 160 scenery images with the streets replaced with image regions without streets to add negative examples using bootstrapping. We trained 2 specialized detectors, one in 0 degrees and other in 30 degrees, the other 4 detectors were created rotating 90 degrees of inverting the Haar features of the original detectors as shown in Fig. 3. For comparison, we also trained specialized detectors using the implementation of the original set of Haar features proposed by Viola and Jones [13] provided by OpenCV. To detect streets in any rotation angle, we combined the output of the 6 specialized detectors. For testing we created a set of 40 satellite images at a resolution of 1280×900 pixels. For each image we manually segmented the street regions to create the ground truth data. The performance of the full detectors was measured as the percentage of the streets that were corrected detected by the detectors and we called it *street coverage*. We found that on average, our detector based on asymmetric Haar features has 35% fewer false positives than the detector based on basic Haar features when they have similar levels of street coverage as we can see in the ROC curve showed in Fig. 4.

Table 1. Comparison of Haar features sets

Haar features set	Number of layers	Total number of Haar features	Training time
Basic	16	0 degrees: 970, 30 degrees: 891	88 hours
Asymmetric	5	0 degrees: 452, 30 degrees: 436	6 hours

Table 1 shows a comparison of the Haar features sets used in our experiments. As we can see, we only need about 7% of the time for training a detector using our proposed approach in comparison with the exhaustive approach used by OpenCV. Also, our detector based on asymmetric Haar features only needs around half of the features to archive a better performance for street detection.

A lower number of features results is a faster detection. Figure 5 shows some results of our street detector.

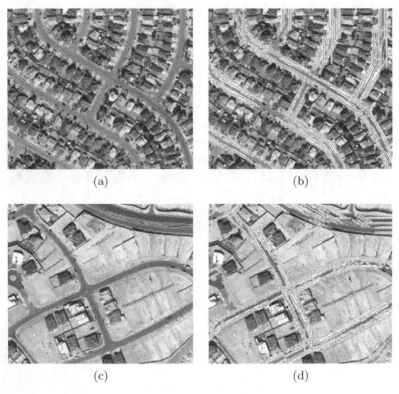

(a)   (b)

(c)   (d)

Fig. 5. Some results for street detection. (a) and (c) Input images. (b) and (d) After use our street detector.

6   Conclusions and Future Work

In this paper we have presented a street detection system based on asymmetric Haar features. According to our experiments, these new features can represent object appearance more accurately than basic Haar features. We used a genetic algorithm to reduce the training time; this allowed us to exploit the expressive advantage of asymmetric features while requiring only 0.02% of the time that would be required using the full feature set. Our detector has on average 11% better performance than the detector based on basic Haar features. Future work will include testing our system in other object detection problems such as car detection in aerial images. In addition, we will perform experiments using other classification algorithms such as FloatBoost and Real AdaBoost.

References

1. Christophe, E., Inglada, J.: Robust road extraction for high resolution satellite images. In: IEEE International Conference on Image Processing, ICIP 2007, October 16-19, vol. 5, pp. V-437–V-440 (2007)
2. Doucette, P., Agouris, P., Stefanidis, A., Musavi, M.: Self-organised clustering for road extraction in classified imagery. ISPRS Journal of photogrammetry and Remote Sensing 55(5-6) (2001)
3. Gruen, A., Li, H.: Road extraction from aerial and satellite images by dynamic programming. ISPRS Journal of Photogrammetry and Remote Sensing 50(4), 11–20 (1995)
4. Guo, X., Dean, D., Denman, S., Fookes, C., Sridharan, S.: Evaluating automatic road detection across a large aerial imagery collection. In: 2011 International Conference on Digital Image Computing Techniques and Applications (DICTA), pp. 140–145 (December 2011)
5. Kuri-Morales, A.F.: Efficient compression from non-ergodic sources with genetic algorithms. In: Fourth Mexican International Conference on Computer Science, pp. 324–329 (2003)
6. Lienhart, R., Maydt, J.: An extended set of Haar-like features for rapid object detection. In: International Conference on Image Processing, vol. 1, pp. I-900–I-903 (2002)
7. Papageorgiou, C.P., Oren, M., Poggio, T.: A general framework for object detection. In: ICCV 1998: Proceedings of the Sixth International Conference on Computer Vision, p. 555. IEEE Computer Society, Washington, DC (1998)
8. Péteri, R., Ranchin, T.: Multiresolution snakes for urban road extraction from ikonos and quickbird images. In: 23rd EARSeL Symposium Remote Sensing in Transition (2003)
9. Quinlan, J.R.: C4.5: programs for machine learning. Morgan Kaufmann Publishers Inc., San Francisco (1993)
10. Ramirez, G.A., Fuentes, O.: Multi-pose face detection with asymmetric haar features. In: IEEE Workshop on Applications of Computer Vision, WACV 2008, pp. 1–6 (January 2008)
11. Tieu, K., Viola, P.: Boosting image retrieval. International Journal of Computer Vision 56(1-2), 17–36 (2004)
12. Tupin, F., Houshmand, B., Datcu, M.: Road detection in dense urban areas using sar imagery and the usefulness of multiple views. IEEE Trans. Geosci. and Remote Sensing 40(11) (2002)
13. Viola, P., Jones, M.: Rapid object detection using a boosted cascade of simple features. In: Proceedings of 2001 IEEE International Conference on Computer Vision and Pattern Recognition, pp. 511–518 (2001)
14. Viola, P., Jones, M., Snow, D.: Detecting pedestrians using patterns of motion and appearance. International Journal of Computer Vision 63(2), 153–161 (2005)
15. Vosselman, G., Knecht, J.: Road tracing by profile matching and kalman filtering. In: Automatic Extraction of Man-Made Objects from Aerial and Space Images (1995)
16. Yan, D., Zhao, Z.: Road detection from quickbird fused image using ihs transform and morphology. In: IEEE International Geoscience and Remote Sensing Symposium (2003)

Automatic Camera Pose Recognition in Planar View Scenarios

Luis Alvarez, Luis Gomez, Pedro Henriquez, and Luis Mazorra

CTIM (Centro de Tecnologías de la Imagen),
Universidad de Las Palmas de Gran Canaria, Spain
{lalvarez,lgomez,phenriquez,lmazorra}@ctim.es
http://www.ctim.es

Abstract. The main goal of this paper is to recognize automatically camera pose from a single image of a planar view scenario. We apply this technique to sport event scenarios using as information the white lines/circles dividing the different parts of the sport court. Using these court primitives we define a loss function that we minimize to obtain the best perspective transformation (homography) matching the actual sport court with its projection in the image. From such homography we recover the camera pose (position and orientation in the 3D space). We present numerical experiments in simulated and real sport scenarios.

Keywords: camera calibration, sport scenarios, lens distortion.

1   Introduction

Camera calibration is an important issue in computer vision. In particular, the broadcasting of sport events increasingly introduces the processing of video sequences for a wide variety of purposes, such as mosaicing, change of the view point or insertion of virtual objects. Some of these tasks require a highly precise calibration of the cameras. In this paper we address the problem of automatic camera pose recognition in the context of planar view scenarios as sport events where the court the sport is played in a planar surface with known dimensions and with a number of lines or circles (usually in white) dividing the different parts of the court. This is a quite common situation in sport scenarios, for instance, tennis, basketball or soccer courts satisfied this assumption. The court primitives we use to recover the camera pose are the white lines/circles dividing the different parts of the sport court.

As we will show below, when we take a photo of the planar sport court, the position of the court primitives in the image is given by a perspective transformation (an homography) of their actual position. In figure 1 we illustrate this perspective transformation. We will show in this paper that if a minimum number of court primitives are visible in the scene then we can recover the homography which transforms the image scene court to the actual reference court. Then from this homography (and assuming that some internal camera parameters are known) we can recover the camera pose, that is the position and orientation of

L. Alvarez et al. (Eds.): CIARP 2012, LNCS 7441, pp. 406–413, 2012.

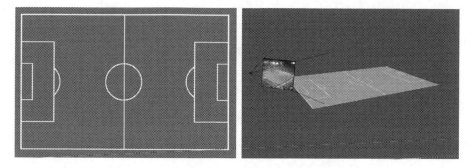

Fig. 1. On the left, illustration of actual Soccer Court. On the right Camera Pose.

the camera. So the method we propose in this paper to automatically recognize and recover camera pose can be divided in the following steps:

1. Court primitives extraction (white lines/circles) in the image.
2. To define and minimize a loss function, using the extracted court primitives, which allow us to evaluate the quality of the matching between actual and image court for an specific perspective transformation (homography)
3. To recover the camera pose from the estimated homography.

The organization of the paper is as follows : in section 2, we present some related work. Section 3 is devoted to briefly explain the camera model we use. In section 4 we study the problem of court primitives extraction. In section 5 we introduce the loss function we use to perform camera pose recognition and we design methods to estimate, automatically, the homography which minimizes the loss function. In section 6 we study how to recover camera pose from the homography. In section 7 we present some numerical experiments on simulated and real scenarios. Finally, in section 8 we present some conclusions.

2   Related Works

Most line extraction methods applied to sport events commonly use a segmentation with dominant colour detection using HSV space [1] or Gaussian mixture models [2]. But to be able to extract lines when dealing with interlaced images, HD definition images, or scenarios with significant contrast variations between the background and the lines, we use the method described in [3]. In the following step, we need to estimate the lens distortion model to obtain an accurate evaluation of the quality of the matching between actual and image court. To deal with lens distortion we use the approach detailed in [5,6]. Finally, to calculate the extrinsic parameters of the camera (rotation and focus) some methods based on soccer lines/circles have been proposed as [4],and using court models as in [7,8]. Also, there are another methods which use the vanishing points of the lines as [9].

3   Camera Model

The camera model we use in this work is called pinhole model, where we include a radial lens distortion model. Using this camera model, a 3D point (X, Y, Z) is projected in the image in a 2D point (x, y) in projective coordinates given by:

$$
\begin{pmatrix} d_x(x, y) \\ d_y(x, y) \\ 1 \end{pmatrix} = sAR \begin{pmatrix} 1\ 0\ 0 & -c_x \\ 0\ 1\ 0 & -c_y \\ 0\ 0\ 1 & -c_z \end{pmatrix} \begin{pmatrix} X \\ Y \\ Z \\ 1 \end{pmatrix} \tag{1}
$$

Where R is the rotation matrix and $C = (c_x, c_y, c_z)$ is the focus. They are called extrinsic parameters. A is the intrinsic parameters 3×3 matrix and $(d_x(x, y), d_y(x, y))$ is the lens distortion correction model.

4   Court Primitives Extraction

We obtain image court primitive points using standard algorithms to extract centre line points on the white image court primitives (see for instance [3]). So our starting point is the set P given by :

$$
P = \{p_i = (x_i, y_i) \ \in \ \text{Image court primitives}\} \tag{2}
$$

We apply the Hough transform to extract lines from the set P. In figures 7 of the numerical experiments section we illustrate the collection of extracted lines in different images. We observe that some of the lines corresponds to tangents to circles projection in the image. Although, initially, these tangents can be considered as faults in Hough transformation line estimation, in fact, the information of such tangents can be use to extract the associated ellipse equation. To build the ellipse equation from the tangents we use the nice and classic work [11] (published in 1885). In this work, different methods of building ellipse equation are shown using different kind of information. In particular, using this work approach, we can easily deduce that using 2 tangents of the ellipse with their correspondence contact points and a third line passing by the ellipse centre we can extract ellipse equation. So using this technique we can extract ellipse from the image using just line information. Of course this is much faster and robust than to look for ellipses in the image using standard techniques based on using just primitive point information.

5   Loss Function: Definition and Minimisation

Let us note by C the collection of actual court primitives. Given an homography H (a 3×3 matrix) and a 2D point p we denote by $H(p)$ the perspective transformation induced by H on point p. We define the loss function $L(H)$ as :

$$
L(H) = \sum_{p_i \in P} distance(H(p_i), C)^2 \tag{3}
$$

Find the minima of the above loss function is a quite difficult problem. The method we propose is based on building homography candidates using the collection of primitive lines we have extracted in the image. We observe (see the numerical experiments) that the number of lines we manage is quite small, so the number of potential configuration we have to manage is also small. We separate our analysis in 2 cases according to the scene configuration:

Case 1: There are at least four visible primitives lines in the image. In this case we build homography candidates by putting in correspondence 4 visible lines in the scene with 4 lines in the actual court. We observe that for each pair of lines put in correspondence between the image court and the actual court, we obtain the relation:

$$\begin{pmatrix} h_1 & h_2 & h_3 \\ h_4 & h_5 & h_6 \\ h_7 & h_8 & h_9 \end{pmatrix}^T \begin{pmatrix} a_i' \\ b_i' \\ c_i' \end{pmatrix} = S \begin{pmatrix} a_i \\ b_i \\ c_i \end{pmatrix} \tag{4}$$

From the above relation we deduce 2 linear equations in the coefficients of H

$$(a_i' h_1 + b_i' h_4 + c_i' h_7) \, b_i = (a_i' h_2 + b_i' h_5 + c_i' h_8) \, a_i \tag{5}$$

$$(a_i' h_1 + b_i' h_4 + c_i' h_7) \, c_i = (a_i' h_3 + b_i' h_6 + c_i' h_9) \, a_i \tag{6}$$

Collecting the above linear equations for the 4 line correspondence we obtain the equation system $Bh = 0$ where B is a $8x9$ matrix, The system solution is obtained by minimising $\|Bh\|^2$, and we can deduce that the homography H is given by the minimum eigenvector of $B^T T B$ matrix.

Case 2: The centre circle and the half-way line are visible in the image. Additionally, it will be supposed that it is also visible one touchline or the court centre spot. This case is more complex to analyze and its solution is based on work done by Luis Alvarez and Vicent Caselles in [10], where they show a method to recover the homography from this scenario (we refer to [10] for more details).

We observe that we do not have "a priori" information about the scenario configuration we deal with. So we check both configurations (case 1 and case 2) and for each configuration we build different homographies by considering potential combination of lines in the image and primitives in the actual court. Finally, we keep the homography with the loss function lowest value.

6   Camera Pose Recognition

We fix a 3D coordinate system where the actual court is included in the plane $z = 0$. To recover the camera pose we need to manage the intrinsic parameter matrix A and the homography H given by :

$$A = \begin{pmatrix} f & 0 & x_c \\ 0 & f \cdot r & y_c \\ 0 & 0 & 1 \end{pmatrix} \qquad H = sAR \begin{pmatrix} 1 & 0 & -c_x \\ 0 & 1 & -c_y \\ 0 & 0 & -c_z \end{pmatrix} \tag{7}$$

We assume that intrinsic camera parameters are known, except the focal distance f which varies according to zoom parameter setting. To recover the focal distance from H we observe than from the above equation we obtain:

$$H^T A^{-T} A^{-1} H = s^2 \begin{pmatrix} 1 & 0 & -c_z \\ 0 & 1 & -c_y \\ -c_z & -c_y & (c_y)^2 + 2(c_z)^2 \end{pmatrix} \tag{8}$$

Replacing A with its value we obtain :

$$H^T \begin{pmatrix} 1 & 0 & -x_c \\ 0 & \frac{1}{r^2} & -\frac{1}{r^2} y_c \\ -x_c & -\frac{1}{r^2} y_c & \frac{1}{r^2} y_c^2 + x_c^2 + f^2 \end{pmatrix} H = s \begin{pmatrix} 1 & 0 & -c_z \\ 0 & 1 & -c_y \\ -c_z & -c_y & (c_y)^2 + 2(c_z)^2 \end{pmatrix} \tag{9}$$

With $b = (b_1, b_2, b_3, b_4) = (\frac{1}{r^2}, x_c, -\frac{1}{r^2} y_c, -\frac{1}{r^2} y_c^2 + x_c^2 + f^2)$. From the previous equation we obtain two equations in the b coefficients:

$$h_{21}(b_1 h_{21} + b_3 h_{31}) + h_{11}(b_2 h_{31} + h_{11}) + h_{31}(b_2 h_{11} + b_3 h_{21} + b_4 h_{31}) -$$
$$h_{22}(b_1 h_{22} + b_3 h_{32}) + h_{12}(b_2 h_{32} + h_{12}) + h_{32}(b_2 h_{12} + b_3 h_{22} + b_4 h_{32}) = 0$$
$$h_{22}(b_1 h_{21} + b_3 h_{31}) + h_{12}(b_2 h_{31} + h_{11}) + h_{32}(b_2 h_{11} + b_3 h_{21} + b_4 h_{31}) = 0 \tag{10}$$

As b_1, b_2 and b_3 are known, the only unknown is b_4, therefore, from only one camera it is possible to calculate b_4 and subsequently the focal distance f.

Next, to calculate the extrinsic parameters (rotation and focus) from the homography and the intrinsic parameters, we use the following relationships: The homography H, that projects the reference field on the image field, is shown in expression 7. From that equation we can obtain the following expression:

$$R = s A^{-1} H \begin{pmatrix} 1 & 0 & -c_x \\ 0 & 1 & -c_y \\ 0 & 0 & -c_z \end{pmatrix} = s A^{-1} H \begin{pmatrix} 1 & 0 & -\frac{c_x}{c_z} \\ 0 & 1 & -\frac{c_y}{c_z} \\ 0 & 0 & -\frac{1}{c_z} \end{pmatrix} \tag{11}$$

Equating the first two columns of the matrixes in expression 11 we obtain the rotation matrix. Equating the third column we obtain the focus.

We will assume that the internal parameters of the camera such as the pixel aspect ratio and the projection of the camera focus in the camera projection plane are known.

7   Numerical Experiments and Results

We have tested our method on different images using both, scale models (1440 x 809 frames) and real scenes from soccer matches (1920 x 1080). Moreover, we have tested the method in the 2 different cases, when at least 4 lines are visible and when the centre circle, the half-way line and a touchline are visible. In the table 1 we can see the results obtained when we applied the method to an image of each case. The second column contains the number of points which

Fig. 2. Scale model and real images: Images on top are the detected lines. Bottom images are illustrations of the estimated pose of the camera in each top image.

have been labelled as a primitive point with the morphological thick line center detection [3]. In the third column we can see the number of lines extracted after applying the Hough transform. Finally, we show the loss function average, measured in metres, and we can see that the results are very accurate. Indeed, in the worst case we obtain only a 2 centimetres error, being usual an error of some milimetres.

On the other hand, we have used the estimated camera pose to build a 3D representation of each camera. In the figure 2 some examples are shown. In that images we can observe image pairs, where one of them (top ones) is the real image with the detected lines painted in different colours, and the other one (bottom ones) is a 3D illustration with the estimated camera pose represented by a image miniature and 4 lines determining the view. We can see with those images that the camera position and orientation have been properly calculated.

Table 1. Quantitative results for images in Fig. 2. we show the number of court primitives points and lines used and the loss function point average measured in metres

Images from Fig. 2	Points	Lines	Loss function average
Area (scaled court model image)	4146	9	5.5921e-004
Centre (scaled court model image)	2705	9	8.0006e-004
Corner (real court image)	5986	12	9.8619e-003
Area (real court image)	4977	11	8.9835e-003
Centre (real court image)	3174	10	3.7095e-002
General view (real court image)	3880	10	2.9171e-002

8   Conclusions

In this paper we study the problem of camera pose estimation in scenarios where there are usually a small number of visible primitives which can be considered to perform the estimation. We have shown that if a minimum number of court primitives are visible in the scene then we can recover the homography which transforms the image scene court to the actual reference court. We have proposed a method based on building homography candidates using the collection of primitive lines we have extracted in the image to find the homography which minimizes the loss function. Then from this homography we can recover the camera pose, that is the position and orientation of the camera. We present some experiments using HD images of soccer matches in both, scale models and real scenarios. The numerical results we present are precise and we show some examples with 3D illustration of the estimated camera poses.

Acknowledgement. This research has partially been supported by the MICINN project reference MTM2010-17615 (Ministerio de Ciencia e Innovación. Spain). We acknowledge MEDIAPRODUCCION S.L. for providing us with the real HD video we use in the numerical experiments.

References

1. Ekin, A., Tekalp, A.M., Mehrotra, R.: Automatic Soccer Video Analysis and Summarization. IEEE Transactions on Image Processing 12(7) (July 2003)
2. Liu, Y., Huang, Q., Ye, Q., Gao, W.: A new method to calculate the camera focusing area and player position on play field in soccer video. In: Visual Communications and Image Processing (2005)
3. Alemán-Flores, M., Alvarez, L., Henríquez, P., Mazorra, L.: Morphological Thick Line Center Detection. In: Campilho, A., Kamel, M. (eds.) ICIAR 2010. LNCS, vol. 6111, pp. 71–80. Springer, Heidelberg (2010)
4. Li, Q., Luo, Y.: Automatic Camera Calibration for Images of Soccer Match. Proceedings of World Academy of Science, Engineering and Technology 1, 170–173 (2005)
5. Alvarez, L., Gomez, L., Sendra, J.R.: An algebraic approach to lens distortion by line rectification. Journal of Mathematical Imaging and Vision 35, 36–50 (2009)
6. Alvarez, L., Gomez, L., Sendra, J.R.: Accurate Depth Dependent Lens Distortion Models: An Application to Planar View Scenarios. Journal of Mathematical Imaging and Vision 39, 75–85 (2011)
7. Farin, D., Krabbe, S., de With, P.H.N., Effelsberg, W.: Robust camera calibration for sport videos using court models. Storage and Retrieval Methods and Applications for Multimedia 5307, 80–91 (2004)
8. Jiang, B., Songyang, L., Liang, B.: Automatic line mark recognition and its application in camera calibration in soccer video. In: IEEE International Conference on Multimedia and Expo (ICME), pp. 1–6 (2011)
9. Babaee-Kashany, V., Reza Pourreza, H.: Camera Pose Estimation in Soccer Scenes Based on Vanishing Points. In: 9th IEEE International Symposium on Haptic Audio-Visual Environments and Games, pp. 157–162 (2010)
10. Alvarez, L., Caselles, V.: Calibration method for a TV and video camera. European Patent 09380137.1 (issued, February 2011)
11. Eagles, T.H.: Constructive geometry of plane curves. Macmillan and Co. (1885)

Texture Image Retrieval
Based on Log-Gabor Features

Rodrigo Nava[1], Boris Escalante-Ramírez[2], and Gabriel Cristóbal[3]

[1] Posgrado en Ciencia e Ingeniería de la Computación,
Universidad Nacional Autónoma de México, Mexico City, Mexico
urielrnv@uxmcc2.iimas.unam.mx
[2] Departamento de Procesamiento de Señales, Facultad de Ingeniería,
Universidad Nacional Autónoma de México, Mexico City, Mexico
boris@servidor.unam.mx
[3] Instituto de Óptica, Spanish National Research Council (CSIC), Serrano 121,
Madrid 28006, Spain
gabriel@optica.csic.es

Abstract. Since Daugman found out that the properties of Gabor filters match the early psychophysical features of simple receptive fields of the Human Visual System (HVS), they have been widely used to extract texture information from images for retrieval of image data. However, Gabor filters have not zero mean, which produces a non-uniform coverage of the Fourier domain. This distortion causes fairly poor pattern retrieval accuracy. To address this issue, we propose a simple yet efficient image retrieval approach based on a novel log-Gabor filter scheme. We make emphasis on the filter design to preserve the relationship with receptive fields and take advantage of their strong orientation selectivity. We provide an experimental evaluation of both Gabor and log-Gabor features using two metrics, the Kullback-Leibler (D_{KL}) and the Jensen-Shannon divergence (D_{JS}). The experiments with the USC-SIPI database confirm that our proposal shows better retrieval performance than the classic Gabor features.

Keywords: Gabor filters, Image retrieval, Jensen-Shannon divergence, Log-Gabor filters, Texture analysis.

1 Introduction

Due to the massive amount of digital image collections, visual information retrieval has become an active research area. The content-based image retrieval approach (CBIR) is based on extracting the content of visual information such as color [1] or textures [2] and its goal is to retrieve images from a data bank using features that best describe objects in a query image [3]. Image characterization by feature extraction is used to catch similarities among images. Hence, it is a crucial stage in CBIR. Theoretically, having more features implies a greater ability to discriminate images. However, this is not always true, because not all features are important for understanding or representing a visual scene [4].

L. Alvarez et al. (Eds.): CIARP 2012, LNCS 7441, pp. 414–421, 2012.
© Springer-Verlag Berlin Heidelberg 2012

Texture is one of the most important features in image retrieval [5], [6]. It provides a robust mathematical description of the spatial distribution of gray levels within a bounded neighborhood and refers to visual patterns that have properties of homogeneity [7]. However, texture characterization is not an easy problem because some spatial patterns can be quite simple as stripes while others can exhibit complex behavior like those in natural images. From a mathematical point of view, it is usual to analyze the spatial distributions as intensity variations from deterministic –where textures contain periodic patterns– to randomness – where textures look like unstructured noise. Since texture is a fundamental image property that describes a perceptually homogeneous region, the HVS requires that textures can be extracted and processed in an optimal way.

Spectral methods for characterizing textures have proven to be powerful tools [8]. These methods collect a distribution of filter responses and extract features from the first and second order statistics [9]. Especially, the use of Gabor filters in texture analysis was motivated due to the studies of Daugman on visual modeling of simple cells. He found out that the experimental findings on orientation selectivity of visual cortical neurons were previously observed by Hubel and Wiesel in human beings and cats [10], [11], [12]. Gabor filters represent time-varying signals in terms of functions that are localized in both time and frequency domains. These functions described by the product of a Gaussian function and a sinusoid constitute a unique family of linear filters that behave optimally in the sense that their simultaneous resolution in both domains is maximal [13].

Manjunath and Ma in [14] proposed a method for texture analysis. The input images are filtered using a set of Gabor filters and the mean and standard deviation are taken to build a feature vector. Their method is generally accepted as a benchmark method for texture retrieval. However, Gabor filters have not zero mean, which produces a non-uniform coverage of the Fourier domain. This distortion may cause fairly poor pattern retrieval accuracy [15].

In this paper, we propose a simple yet efficient image retrieval approach based on a novel log-Gabor filter scheme. In Section 2, the classic Gabor filter and the log-Gabor model proposal are presented. In Section 3, the D_{KL} and D_{JS} are described. In Section 4, we compare retrieval accuracy of both Gabor and log-Gabor filter banks over the USC-SIPI database [16]. Finally, our work is summarized in Section 5.

2   Bio-Inspired Models for Texture Feature Extraction

Daugman [11] proposed a 2D extension of the Gabor filters –receptive fields are deployed in two dimensions– and showed that they occupy an irreducible volume in the four-dimensional (4D) hyperspace where the four orthogonal axes correspond to spatial (x, y) and frequency (u, v) variables. The joint 2D resolution achieves the lower bound of the 2D uncertainty principle as follows: $(\Delta x)(\Delta y)(\Delta u)(\Delta v) \geq \frac{1}{16\pi^2}$.

The canonical 2D Gabor filter in spatial domain is defined as:

$$g(x, y) = e^{-\frac{1}{2}\left(\frac{(x-x_0)^2 + \gamma^2(y-y_0)^2}{\alpha^2}\right) + i(2\pi[u_0(x-x_0) + v_0(y-y_0)] + \phi)} \tag{1}$$

where (x_0, y_0) are the center of the filter, (u_0, v_0) and ϕ represent the radial frequency and the phase of the sinusoidal signal respectively. (α, γ) are the space constants of the Gaussian envelope along x and y axes respectively and they control the filter bandwidth.

Here, we assume the use of real Gabor filters (just the even part) centered at the origin. Therefore, we obtain the next expression that provides a suitable symmetric filter for detecting salient edges [17] as follows:

$$g\left(x, y\right) = e^{-\frac{1}{2}\left(\frac{x^2 + \gamma^2 y^2}{\alpha^2}\right)} \cos\left(2\pi u_0 x\right) \tag{2}$$

Using the rotation matrix, $R_\theta = [\cos\theta, -\sin\theta; \sin\theta, \cos\theta]$ and applying in Eq. 2 yields the 2D polar Gabor representation as follows:

$$g\left(x, y\right) = e^{-\frac{1}{2}\left(\frac{\tilde{x}^2 + \gamma^2 \tilde{y}^2}{\alpha^2}\right)} \cos\left(2\pi u_0 \tilde{x}\right) \tag{3}$$

with

$$\begin{aligned} \tilde{x} &= x\cos\theta - y\sin\theta \\ \tilde{y} &= x\sin\theta + y\cos\theta \end{aligned} \tag{4}$$

The frequency and orientation selectivity properties of Gabor filters can be more explicit in Fourier domain. The Fourier transform of $g\left(x, y\right)$ is given by:

$$\begin{aligned} \hat{G}\left(u, v\right) &= e^{-2\pi^2\alpha^2\left[(\tilde{u} - u_0\cos\theta)^2 + \frac{1}{\gamma^2}(\tilde{v} + u_0\sin\theta)^2\right]} \\ &+ e^{-2\pi^2\alpha^2\left[(\tilde{u} + u_0\cos\theta)^2 + \frac{1}{\gamma^2}(\tilde{v} - u_0\sin\theta)^2\right]} \end{aligned} \tag{5}$$

where $(\tilde{u}, \tilde{v}) = (u\cos\theta + v\sin\theta, -u\sin\theta + v\cos\theta)$.

$\hat{G}\left(u, v\right)$ represents a rotated Gaussian function by an angle θ with u_0 frequency units shifted along the axes.

Psychophysical experiments showed that frequency bandwidths of simple cells are about one octave apart [11], [18], [19]. The half-amplitude bandwidth of the frequency response, B_u, satisfies this condition and is linked to central frequency u_0 as follows:

$$\alpha = \frac{\sqrt{\log\left(2\right)}\left(2^{B_u} + 1\right)}{\sqrt{2}\pi u\left(2^{B_u} - 1\right)} \tag{6}$$

In order to determine the optimum angular bandwidth B_θ we considered an isotropic Gabor filter. Hence, we forced $\gamma = 1$.

$$\frac{\alpha}{\gamma} = \frac{\sqrt{\log\left(2\right)}}{\sqrt{2}\pi u \tan\left(\frac{B_\theta}{2}\right)} \tag{7}$$

in this way, $B_\theta \approx 36°$ is obtained, but for computational efficiency $B_\theta = \frac{\pi}{6}$ was chosen.

Although Gabor filters possess a number of interesting mathematical properties (they have a smooth and indefinitely differentiable shape and they do not have side lobes neither in space nor frequency domain) they present a main drawback, the filter averaging is not null and therefore the DC component influences intermediate bands. They overlap more at lower frequencies than in higher ones yielding a non-uniform coverage of the Fourier domain, (see Fig. 1(a)).

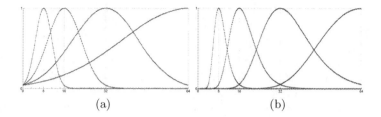

Fig. 1. Profiles of the frequency response of (a) Gabor and (b) log-Gabor filters. Note that the DC component is minimized by introducing the ln function.

2.1 Log-Gabor Filters

Log-Gabor filters, firstly proposed by D. Field [20], are defined in the frequency domain as Gaussian functions shifted from the origin due to the singularity of the log function. They always have a null DC component and can be optimized to produce filters with minimal spatial extent in an octave scale multiresolution scheme, (see Fig. 1(b)). Log-Gabor filters can be splited into two components: radial and angular filters, $\hat{G}(\rho, \theta) = \hat{G}_\rho \hat{G}_\theta$, as follows:

$$\hat{G}(\rho, \theta) = e^{-\frac{1}{2}\left[\frac{\log\left(\frac{\rho}{u_0}\right)}{\log\left(\frac{\alpha_\rho}{u_0}\right)}\right]^2} e^{-\frac{1}{2}\left[\frac{(\theta - \theta_0)}{\alpha_\theta}\right]^2} \tag{8}$$

where (ρ, θ) represent the polar coordinates, u_0 is the central frequency, θ_0 is the orientation angle. α_ρ and α_θ determine the scale and the angular bandwidth respectively. We set $\alpha_\rho = 0.75$ that results in minimal overlap among scales one octave apart and $\alpha_{theta} = \frac{pi}{6}$ as it was mentioned before. In order to better cover the Fourier plane even scales are rotated by a constant factor consisting of the half a distance between filter centers, (see Fig. 2(c)), [21].

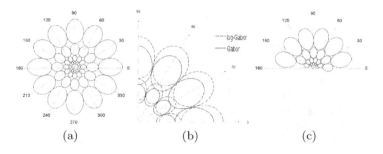

Fig. 2. Half-amplitude bandwidth of the frequency response of (a) an ensemble of Gabor filters. (b) Contour comparison between Gabor and log-Gabor filters before rotating the log-Gabor even bands. (c) Log-Gabor filters (1 octave bandwidth).

3   Texture Retrieval Based on Entropy Information

As in [14], any image coefficient, $C_{(s,\theta)}$, defined as $C_{(s,\theta)} = I\left(x,y\right) \star g\left(x,y\right)_{(s,\theta)}$ where $I\left(x,y\right)$ is the given image, $g\left(x,y\right)_{(s,\theta)}$ is the filter at the scale s and orientation θ, and $\star$ indicates the convolution, represents texture characteristics in a particular scale and orientation. Thus, energy signatures such as the mean $\mu_{(s,\theta)}$ and the variance $\sigma^2_{(s,\theta)}$ can be used as texture features for constructing a feature vector as follows:

$$\bar{t} = \left[\mu_{(0,0)}, \sigma^2_{(0,0)}, \ldots, \mu_{(s-1,\theta-1)}, \sigma^2_{(s-1,\theta-1)}\right] \tag{9}$$

Although the Kullback-Leibler divergence –a generalization of Shannon's entropy– is not a true metric rather it is a relative entropy, it can be used as a suitable descriptor for measuring distances between histograms or feature vectors. Then, the distance between two texture images A and B with $\overline{t_A}$ and $\overline{t_B}$ as the corresponding feature vectors is defined as:

$$D_{KL}\left(A,B\right) = \sum_{i=0}^{b-1} \overline{t_B}\left(i\right) \log\left(\frac{\overline{t_B}\left(i\right)}{\overline{t_A}\left(i\right)}\right) \tag{10}$$

where b is the length of the feature vectors $\overline{t_A}$ and $\overline{t_B}$.

In addition, the Jensen-Shannon divergence [22] denoted by ψ can be used for evaluating distance between two textures as follows:

$$\psi = \sqrt{2D_{JS}\left(A,B\right)} \tag{11}$$

where

$$D_{JS}\left(A,B\right) = \frac{1}{2}D_{KL}\left(A, \frac{A+B}{2}\right) + \frac{1}{2}D_{KL}\left(B, \frac{A+B}{2}\right) \tag{12}$$

4   Experimental Results

We used the USC-SIPI texture database [16], to measure retrieval accuracy (RA) of both Gabor and log-Gabor filters. USC-SIPI consists of twenty gray-scale textures of 512×512 pixels. Each image was divided into sixteen 128×128 non-overlapping patches, thus creating a database of 320 texture images. The resulted patches were processed with a filter bank (4 scales and 6 orientations) in order to form 320 feature vectors of 48 bins-length each. Each feature vector is a query pattern and was used to calculate distances among the 320 textures. The distances were sorted in increasing order and the closest sixteen patches were retrieved. We must note that in [14] the mean and the standard deviation were used to form a query image. Here we use the mean and the variance because they improve the retrieval performance.

The average retrieval rate (ARR) is the standard metric for evaluating CBIR systems and is listed in Table 1 for the different texture images used in this study. ARR is calculated by the following procedure: First, each texture (D*) is

Table 1. ARR for the 20 texture images, D* indicates the Brodatz texture. ARR is computed using Gabor and log-Gabor filter banks and both D_{KL} and D_{JS} metrics.

	Gabor filters				log-Gabor filters			
	D_{KL}		D_{JS}		D_{KL}		D_{JS}	
texture	# patches	(%)	# patches	(%)	# patches	(%)	# patches	(%)
D1	256	100	256	100	256	100	256	100
D3	186	72.65	181	70.70	177	69.14	175	68.35
D4	256	100	256	100	256	100	256	100
D5	220	85.93	224	87.5	227	88.67	229	89.45
D6	256	100	256	100	256	100	256	100
D9	231	90.23	233	91.01	254	99.21	254	99.21
D10	191	74.60	194	75.78	217	84.76	221	86.32
D11	256	100	256	100	256	100	256	100
D15	183	71.48	179	69.92	194	75.78	187	73.04
D20	256	100	256	100	256	100	256	100
D24	240	93.75	238	92.96	243	92.92	242	94.53
D26	256	100	256	100	256	100	256	100
D56	256	100	256	100	253	98.82	256	100
D66	178	69.53	178	69.53	200	78.12	202	78.90
D93	231	90.23	234	91.40	242	94.53	244	95.31
D104	256	100	256	100	256	100	256	100
D105	136	53.12	136	53.12	205	80.07	203	79.29
D106	**134**	**52.34**	**136**	**53.12**	**173**	**67.57**	**177**	**69.14**
D109	163	63.67	163	53.67	227	88.67	227	88.67
D112	200	78.12	198	77.34	190	74.21	191	74.60

Table 2. FRR for Gabor and log-Gabor filters. Given a single query (patch), all the sixteen patches that belong to the same texture are retrieved.

	Gabor filters		log-Gabor filters	
distance	# patches	(%)	# patches	(%)
D_{KL}	146	45.62	**165**	**51.56**
D_{JS}	147	45.93	**167**	**52.18**

divided into 16 patches, from which each patch is used as a query. In the best case, one single query returns the 16 patches belonging to the same texture, and evaluating all the 16 queries return up to 256 patches from the same texture.

Note that for the Gabor scheme, the lower rate achieved was with the D106 texture, the ARR was 52.34% and 53.12% using D_{KL} and D_{JS} respectively. On the contrary, the log-Gabor scheme achieved 67.57% and 69.14% of accuracy respectively, which represents 39 and 41 more patches classified correctly with D_{KL} and D_{JS} metrics respectively.

In the ideal case, given a single query, all the sixteen patches that belong to the same texture should be retrieved. An important metric that assesses this specific case is called full retrieval rate (FRR) which measures the number of query patterns fully retrieved correctly. Our proposal achieves 52.18% of query patterns fully retrieved, it means a 6.56% higher rate compare to the Gabor scheme with 45.62%, (see Table 2).

An overall retrieval rate (ORR) is presented in Table 3. The Gabor scheme achieves 84.78% and 84.80% of patches retrieved correctly with D_{KL} and D_{JS} respectively. On the other hand, the proposal here presented achieves 89.72%

Table 3. ORR for Gabor and log-Gabor schemes

distance	Gabor filters (%)	log-Gabor filters (%)
D_{KL}	84.78	**89.72**
D_{JS}	84.80	**89.84**

and 89.84% of patches retrieved correctly with D_{KL} and D_{JS} respectively. This represents an increase in the classification rate up to 4.94% using D_{KL} and 5.04% using D_{JS}.

5   Conclusions

Here we presented the classic Gabor scheme for texture analysis and summarized its properties and drawbacks. Further, a novel scheme for CBIR was presented. This proposal based on log-Gabor filters has a strong correlation with the HVS. It may say that the proposal is a bio-inspired model where the parameters agreed with simple cells in the visual cortex. In addition, we evaluate the texture distances using two metrics, the well-known D_{KL} and the Jensen-Shannon divergence, which boosts the retrieval process. The log-Gabor filtering approach outperforms the retrieval performance for the analyzed textures in comparison with the Gabor filters.

Acknowledgments. This work has been sponsored by the grant UNAM PA-PIIT IN113611 and TEC2010-20307 from the Spanish Ministry of Science and Innovation. R. Nava gives a special thank to Consejo Nacional de Ciencia y Tecnología for the doctoral scholarship 167161.

References

1. Xing-yuan, W., Zhi-feng, C., Jiao-jiao, Y.: An effective method for color image retrieval based on texture. Computer Standards & Interfaces 34(1), 31–35 (2012)
2. Huang, P.W., Dai, S.K.: Image retrieval by texture similarity. Pattern Recognition 36(3), 665–679 (2003)
3. Jie, Y., Qiang, Z., Liang, Z., Wuhan, C.Y.: Research on texture images retrieval based on the Gabor wavelet transform. In: International Conference on Information Engineering, ICIE 2009, vol. 1, pp. 79–82 (2009)
4. ElAlami, M.E.: A novel image retrieval model based on the most relevant features. Knowledge-Based Systems 24(1), 23–32 (2011)
5. Zhang, G., Ma, Z.M.: Texture feature extraction and description using Gabor wavelet in content-based medical image retrieval. In: International Conference on Wavelet Analysis and Pattern Recognition, ICWAPR 2007, vol. 1, pp. 169–173 (2007)
6. Turner, M.R.: Texture discrimination by Gabor functions. Biological Cybernetics 55, 71–82 (1986)

7. Nava, R., Cristóbal, G., Escalante-Ramírez, B.: A comprehensive study of texture analysis based on local binary patterns. In: Optics, Photonics, and Digital Technologies for Multimedia Applications II 8436-1, 84360E. SPIE (2012)
8. Randen, T., Husøy, J.H.: Filtering for texture classification: A comparative study. IEEE Trans. Pattern Anal. Mach. Intell. 21, 291–310 (1999)
9. Nava, R., Escalante-Ramírez, B., Cristóbal, G.: A comparison study of Gabor and log-Gabor wavelets for texture segmentation. In: 7th International Symposium on Image and Signal Processing and Analysis (ISPA), pp. 189–194 (2011)
10. Kong, A.W.-K.: An Analysis of Gabor Detection. In: Kamel, M., Campilho, A. (eds.) ICIAR 2009. LNCS, vol. 5627, pp. 64–72. Springer, Heidelberg (2009)
11. Daugman, J.G.: Uncertainty relation for resolution in space, spatial frequency, and orientation optimized by two-dimensional visual cortical filters. J. Opt. Soc. Am. A 2, 1160–1169 (1985)
12. Hubel, D.H., Wiesel, T.N.: Brain and Visual Perception: The Story of a 25-year Collaboration. Oxford University Press, Oxford (2005)
13. Gabor, D.: Theory of communication. J. Inst. Elec. Eng. (London) 93(III), 429–457 (1946)
14. Manjunath, B.S., Ma, W.Y.: Texture features for browsing and retrieval of image data. IEEE Transactions on Pattern Analysis and Machine Intelligence 18(8), 837–842 (1996)
15. Sastry, C.S., Ravindranath, M., Pujari, A.K., Deekshatulu, B.: A modified Gabor function for content based image retrieval. Pattern Recognition Letters 28(2), 293–300 (2007)
16. Brodatz, P.: USC-SIPI (2012), http://sipi.usc.edu/database/database.php?volume=rotate (Online accessed March 1, 2012)
17. Redondo, R., Šroubek, F., Fischer, S., Cristóbal, G.: Multifocus image fusion using the log-Gabor transform and a multisize windows technique. Information Fusion 10(2), 163–171 (2009)
18. Bovik, A.C., Clark, M., Geisler, W.S.: Multichannel texture analysis using localized spatial filters. IEEE Transactions on Pattern Analysis and Machine Intelligence 12, 55–73 (1990)
19. Clausi, D.A., Jernigan, M.E.: Designing Gabor filters for optimal texture separability. Pattern Recognition 33(11), 1835–1849 (2000)
20. Field, D.J.: Relations between the statistics of natural images and the response properties of cortical cells. J. Opt. Soc. Am. A 4(12), 2379–2394 (1987)
21. Gross, M., Koch, R.: Visualization of multidimensional shape and texture features in laser range data using complex-valued Gabor wavelets. IEEE Transactions on Visualization and Computer Graphics 1(1), 44–59 (1995)
22. Lin, J.: Divergence measures based on the Shannon entropy. IEEE Transactions on Information Theory 37(1), 145–151 (1991)

Image Retrieval Using Low Level Features of Object Regions with Application to Partially Occluded Images

E.R.Vimina[1,*] and K. Poulose Jacob[2]

[1] Department of Computer Science, Rajagiri College of Social Sciences,
Kochi, Kerala, India
vimina_er@yahoo.com
[2] Department of Computer Science, Cochin University of Science and Technology,
Kochi, Kerala, India
kpj@cusat.ac.in

Abstract. This paper proposes an image retrieval system using the local colour and texture features of object regions and global colour features of the image. The object regions are roughly identified by segmenting the image into fixed partitions and finding the edge density in each partition using edge thresholding and morphological dilation. The colour and texture features of the identified regions are computed from the histograms of the quantized HSV colour space and Gray Level Co- occurrence Matrix (GLCM) respectively. A combined colour and texture feature vector is computed for each region and Euclidean distance measure is used for computing the distance between the features of the query and target image. Preliminary experimental results show that the proposed method provides better retrieving result than retrieval using some of the existing methods. Also promising results are obtained for 50% and 75% occluded query images.

Keywords: Content Based Image Retrieval, GLCM, Colour histogram.

1 Introduction

The volume of image database is growing at an exponential rate with the steady growth of computer power, declining cost of storage and increasing access to Internet. To effectively manage the image information, it is imperative to advance automated image learning techniques. In the traditional method of text-based image retrieval the image search is mostly based on textual description of the image found on the web pages containing the image and the file names of the image [1]. The problem here is that the accuracy of the search result highly depends on the textual description associated with the image. Also un-annotated image collection cannot be searched. An alternate method is to retrieve image information based on the content of the image. The goal is to retrieve images that are semantically related to the user's query from a database. In Content based image retrieval systems the visual contents of the image

---

* Corresponding author.

L. Alvarez et al. (Eds.): CIARP 2012, LNCS 7441, pp. 422–429, 2012.

such as colour, texture, shape or any other information that can be automatically extracted from the image itself are extracted and is used as a criterion to retrieve content related images from the database. The retrieved images are then ranked according to the relevance between the query image and images in the database in proportion to a similarity measure calculated from the features [2][3].

Many early CBIR systems perform retrieval based on the global features of the query image [4][5][9]. Such systems are likely to fail as the global features cannot sufficiently capture the important properties of individual objects. Recently, much research has focused on region-based techniques [2][3][6]that allow the user to specify a particular region of an image and request that the system retrieve images that contain similar regions. Our research focuses on automatic identification of object regions and computing the feature vectors for comparison purpose. The object regions are roughly identified by performing morphological operations on the image and segmenting the image into fixed partitions.

2   Object Region Identification

The images are resized to 128×192 and divided into 3×3 equal sub-blocks. To identify the object regions, first the grayscale image is computed for the resized image and edge map is detected using Sobel edge filter with a threshold value of τ ($\tau <1$ so that the edges are boosted). The gaps in the edge map are bridged by dilating it with 'line' structuring element, that consists of three 'on' pixels in a row, in the 0, 45, 90 and 135 directions. The holes in the resultant image are then filled to get the approximate location of the objects. The objects are identified correctly if the background is uniform.

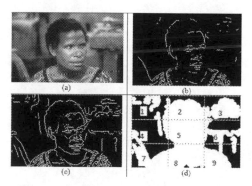

Fig. 1. (a)Original image (b)Edge map after sobel edge filtering (c) Edge map after edge thresholding (d)Region identification

A sub-block is identified as region of interest (ROI) if $\tau'\%$ of the sub-block is part of the object region. Ie., if the number of white pixels in that sub-block is greater than τ', it is identified as a region of interest. Here we have taken $\tau'=30\%$. For example in Fig.1, regions 2,3,5,7,8 and 9 are the ROIs. Only these sub-blocks take part in further computations for calculating the similarity along with the global colour features of the image. For each sub-block that is identified as ROI, the colour and texture features are computed. Colour features are extracted from the histograms of quantized HSV colour space and texture features are computed from the gray-level co-occurrence matrix. Euclidean distance measure is used for calculating the distance between the query and the candidate images in the database.

3   Feature Extraction

After identifying the image sub-blocks/ prominent regions of object, colour and texture features for each region are computed. We have used HSV colour space for extracting the colour features. The HSV space is uniformly quantized to 18 bins for hue, 3 bins for saturation and 3 bins for value. The histogram of each of these channels are extracted resulting in a 24 dimensional colour feature vector that is normalized in the range of [0,1]. For each image both global and local colour features are extracted.

Texture features are computed using the gray-level co-occurrence matrix (GLCM) [7]. It is a matrix showing how often a pixel with the intensity (gray-level) value i occurs in a specific spatial relationship to a pixel with the value j. It is defined by $P(i,j|d,\Theta)$, which expresses the probability of the couple of pixels at Θ direction and d interval. We have taken d=1 and Θ = 0, 45, 90 and 135. Energy, contrast, correlation and homogeneity are calculated in all the four directions and entropy of the whole block only is computed resulting in 17 texture feature vectors for each sub-block.

4   Similarity Measure

Euclidean distance is used for computing the similarity between the given pair of images. It is given by,

$$d_{(I1,I2)}=\sqrt{(F_{I1}-F_{I2})^2} \tag{1}$$

where FI1 and FI2 are the feature vectors of image I1 and I2.

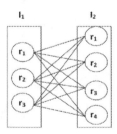

Fig. 2. Each ROI of image I_1 is compared with that of I_2

For each ROI in the query image, the colour and texture features are computed and is compared with each ROIs of the target images (Fig.2). Assume that image I_1 has m ROIs represented by R_1= {r_1, r_2,......,r_m} and I_2 has n ROIs represented by R_2={ r'_1, r'_2,......r'_n}. Let the distance between ri and r'j be d(ri,rj) denoted as di,j. Every region ri of R_1 is compared with every region rj of R_2. This results in 'n' comparisons for a single region in R_1 and n distance measures. These distances are stored in ascending order in an array and the minimum distance only is taken for the final computation of the distance D; the distance between I_1 and I_2. Thus out of the m × n distances m lowest distances are added to get the distance D. This means that if image I_1 is compared with itself, D will be equal to zero.

The algorithm for computing the minimum distance between two images is described below:

```
Input: R1, R2; the ROIs of the query and the target image
Output: minimum distance between I₁ and I₂
begin
  for each region in the query image I₁, i=1 to m do
    for each region in the target image I₂, j=1 to n do
      compute distance d[j]=d_{i,j};
    end
    Sort distance array 'd' in ascending order;
    D=D+d[1];
  end
end
```

'd' is the array containing the distances between the r_i of R_1 with the n regions of R_2. The final distance between I1 and I2 is given by

$$D' = D + d_{global\_colour\_feature} \qquad (2)$$

Where, $d_{global\_colour\_feature}$ is the Euclidean distance between the global colour feature vectors of I_1 and I_2.

5   Experimental Results

The Wang's image database [9] of 1000 images consisting of 10 categories is used for evaluating the performance of the proposed method. Each category contains 100 images. A retrieved image is considered to be correct if and only if it is in the same category as the query. For each query, a preselected number of images are retrieved which are illustrated and listed in the ascending order of the distance between the query and the retrieved images.

The results of the proposed method is compared with that of [10] and [11] in terms of average precision. Precision (P) of N retrieved results is given by

$$P(k) = n_k/N \qquad (3)$$

Where N is the number of retrieved images, n_k is the number of relevant images in the retrieved images.

Table1. shows the average precision of the retrieved images for different methods.

Table 1. Average Precision (N=20) of retrieved images using different methods

Category	Jhanwar et al[11]	Hung and Dai's [10]	Proposed method
Africa	0.4525	0.4240	0.6747
Beaches	0.3975	0.4455	0.3655
Buildings	0.3735	0.4105	0.4645
Bus	0.7410	0.8515	0.8445
Dinosaur	0.9145	0.5865	0.9830
Elephant	0.3040	0.4255	0.6030
flowers	0.8515	0.8975	0.8565
Horse	0.5680	0.5890	0.8750
Mountain	0.2925	0.2680	0.3005
Food	0.3695	0.4265	0.6005
Average	**0.5264**	**0.5324**	**0.6568**

5.1   Retrieval of Partially Occluded Images

Further to evaluate the efficiency of the proposed method, we have partially occluded the query images and presented to the retrieval system. For this purpose 10 randomly chosen images from each category are occluded 50% and 75% and presented as query images to the proposed system and the global features based retrieval system for comparison purpose. Experimental results show that the proposed method outperforms retrieval using global features based method. Table 2. shows retrieved results for 50% occluded query images for different values of N and Table 3. shows the same for 75% occluded query images.

Table 2. Average precision (N=20) of retrieved images for 50% occluded query images

Category	Global HSV Histogram+GLCM Texture	Proposed Method
Africa	0.8608	0.8204
Beaches	0.4090	0.3045
Buildings	0.4200	0.6175
Bus	0.6675	0.8350
Dinosaur	0.9675	0.9525
Elephant	0.3525	0.3975
flowers	0.9900	0.8750
Horse	0.6295	0.8550
Mountain	0.2795	0.3022
Food	0.4000	0.5850
Average	**0.5977**	**0.6545**

Table 3. Average precision (N=20) of retrieved images for 75% occluded query images

Category	Global HSV Histogram+GLCM Texture	Proposed Method
Africa	0.5337	0.7625
Beaches	0.2750	0.2475
Buildings	0.4162	0.4950
Bus	0.5537	0.7887
Dinosaur	0.9225	0.8800
Elephant	0.2000	0.2862
flowers	0.8962	0.7900
Horse	0.4987	0.6212
Mountain	0.1587	0.2175
Food	0.3400	0.4525
Average	**0.4795**	**0.5541**

(a)

(b)

Fig. 3. Retrieved images using query images occluded by 50%. (a) Using global colour histogram and texture features.(b) Using proposed method.

Fig. 4. Retrieved images using query images occluded by 75%. (a) Using global colour histogram and texture features.(b) Using proposed method.

Fig.3. depicts the top 14 retrieved images for sample query images occluded 50% using proposed method and global HSV histogram+ GLCM texture based retrieval. In each set, on top left corner is the query image and the retrieved images are listed according to their distance with the query image. (a) shows the retrieved results using global colour and texture features and (b) shows that using the proposed method. Fig.4 depicts the same for the 75% occluded query images. The marked image is the original image part of which is given as query.

6   Conclusion and Future Work

A content based image retrieval system using the colour and texture features of automatically extracted object regions is proposed. The colour features are extracted from the histograms of the quantized HSV color space and texture features are computed from GLCM. Experimental results show that the proposed method provides better retrieving result than some of the existing methods. Unlike other sub-block based retrieval systems that require all the sub-blocks to participate in similarity comparison, the proposed method requires only the identified sub-blocks be compared with that of the candidate image sub-blocks reducing complexity and time required for retrieval. Preliminary results of the 50% and 75% occluded query images using the proposed method also outperforms that using global colour and texture features. Future work aims at the generation of fuzzy rules that may improve the retrieval precision.

References

1. Li, J., Wang, J.Z.: Real-time computerized annotation of pictures. In: Proceedings of the 14th Annual ACM International Conference on Multimedia, pp. 911–920 (2006)
2. Chen, Y., Wang, J.Z., Krovetz, R.: CLUE: Cluster-based retrieval of images by unsupervised learning. IEEE Transactions on Image Processing 14(8), 1187–1201 (2005)
3. Wang, J.Z., Li, J., Wiederhold, G.: SIMPLIcity.: Semantics-sensitive Integrated Matching for Picture LIbraries. IEEE Transactions on Pattern Analysis and Machine Intelligence 23(9), 947–963 (2001)
4. Flickner, M., Sawhney, H., Niblack, W., Ashley, J., Huang, Q., Dom, B., et al.: Query by Image and Video Content: The QBIC System. IEEE Computer 28, 23–32 (1995)
5. Pentland, A., Picard, R., Sclaroff, S.: Photobook.: Content-based Manipulation of Image Databases. In: Proc. SPIE Storage and Retrieval for Image and Video Databases II, San-Jose, CA, pp. 34–47 (1994)
6. Carson, C., Thomas, M., Belongie, S., Hellerstein, J.M., Malik, J., Blobworld: A System for Region-Based Image Indexing and Retrieval. In: Proc. Visual Information Systems, pp. 509–516 (1999)
7. Haralick, R.M., Shanmugan, K., Dinstein, I.: Textural Features for Image Classification. IEEE Transactions on Systems, Man, and Cybernetics SMC-3, 610–621 (1973)
8. Murala, S., Gonde, A.B., Maheshwari, R.P.: Color and Texture Features for Image Indexing and Retrieval. In: 2009 IEEE International Advance Computing Conference (IACC 2009), pp. 1411–1416 (2009)
9. http://wang.ist.psu.edu/docs/related/
10. Huang, P.W., Dai, S.K.: Image retrieval by texture similarity. Pattern Recognition 36(3), 665–679 (2003)
11. Jhanwar, N., Chaudhuri, S., Seetharaman, G., Zavidoviqu, B.: Content based image retrieval using motif co-occurrence matrix. Image Vis. Computing 22(14), 1211–1220 (2004)

Continuous Multi-way Shape Measure for Dissimilarity Representation

Diana Porro-Muñoz[1,2], Robert P.W. Duin[2],
Mauricio Orozco-Alzate[3], and Isneri Talavera Bustamante[1]

[1] Advanced Technologies Application Center (CENATAV), Cuba
{dporro,italavera}@cenatav.co.cu
[2] Pattern Recognition Lab, TU Delft, The Netherlands
r.duin@ieee.org
[3] Universidad Nacional de Colombia - Sede Manizales, Colombia
morozcoa@bt.unal.edu.co

Abstract. For many applications, a straightforward representation of objects is by multi-dimensional arrays e.g. signals. However, there are only a few classification tools which make a proper use of this complex structure to obtain a better discrimination between classes. Moreover, they do not take into account context information that can also be very beneficial in the classification process. Such is the case of multi-dimensional continuous data, where there is a connectivity between the points in all directions, a particular (differentiating) shape in the surface of each class of objects. The dissimilarity representation has been recently proposed as a tool for the classification of multi-way data, such that the multi-dimensional structure of objects can be considered in their dissimilarities. In this paper, we introduce a dissimilarity measure for continuous multi-way data and a new kernel for gradient computation. It allows taking the connectivity between the measurement points into account, using the information on how the shape of the surface varies in all directions. Experiments show the suitability of this measure for classifying continuous multi-way data.

Keywords: Classification, Continuous multi-way data, Dissimilarity representation, Object representation.

1 Introduction

Representation of objects by matrices or higher-order arrays has become very popular in many application areas. These multi-dimensional structures of objects can be created for some specific purpose or they can be obtained directly from acquisition equipments e.g. excitation-emission autofluorescence measurements and time-frequency representation of signals.

Tools that make a proper use of these multi-way structures are needed. Traditional multivariate methods are not suitable for it. Data would have to be re-arranged in a vector, thus the information of the multi-way structure is lost

L. Alvarez et al. (Eds.): CIARP 2012, LNCS 7441, pp. 430–437, 2012.

and huge-dimensional problems are created. Several methods have been proposed for multi-way data analysis, mainly in the psychometrics and chemometrics fields. However, most of them aim for regression or exploratory analysis [1]. The development of tools for multi-way classification is rather poor in comparison with the large amount of methods for other purposes. There are basically three main multi-way classification approaches, namely: NPLS-DA, traditional classifiers on the scores of multi-way decomposition methods like PARAFAC [2], and NSIMCA [3]. These methods succeed in making use of the multi-way structure. However, this might not be enough for a proper analysis of the data. Continuous data, for example, are just numerically analyzed as a set of sampled, individual features. Features are in this paper the measurement directions of a multi-way data set. Important discriminative information, like connectivity between features and their shape is not considered in the analysis.

Recently, the Dissimilarity Representation (DR) approach was introduced for multi-way data classification [4]. The DR approach consists in representing objects by their proximities with respect to other objects [5]. As classes of objects are determined by how (dis)similar they are, the authors advocate that for classification, a representation based on dissimilarities between objects may be more informative than the traditional feature based representation.

One of the goals and advantages of this approach is the possibility of introducing discriminative context information in the representation of objects by the dissimilarity measure. In the case of 2D or any-dimensional continuous data, e.g. spectroscopic data, it could be important for their analysis to consider their continuous nature. Several 2D measures have been proposed for image comparison; however most of them are just based on pairwise comparison of objects, ignoring the continuous nature of images [6]. Recently, the 2Dshape [4] measure was introduced for this purpose. In order to reflect the continuous shape of the data, comparison of objects is based on the differences between the first Gaussian derivatives in each direction. However, it is based on the combination of 1D dissimilarities; hence it does not analyze the combined 2D shape changes [1].

In this paper, we propose a new dissimilarity measure, the Continuous Multiway Shape (CMS) measure, that exploits the information on the whole structure of multi-dimensional continuous data. It is based on differences between gradients of objects, so shape changes of the surfaces are considered. The computation of the gradient components is usually based on convolution kernel operators. We introduce a gradient kernel operator where each partial derivative is computed as the derivative of a polynomial fitted to the analyzed points. The proposed measure will be compared to 2Dshape [4], and to two 2D measures [6], which are not designed for continuous data. It is shown that considering the continuous nature of data can be beneficial to improve its classification.

The paper is organized as follows. Fundamentals of the dissimilarity representation approach are presented in the first part of Section 2. In the second part, the new measure and its generalization are detailed. Experiments and results are discussed in Section 3. Conclusions are presented in Section 4.

---

[1] The naming of the procedure given in paper [4], 2Dshape, can be confusing.

2   Dissimilarity Representation for Multi-way Data

In the DR [5] approach, new features are defined for the objects, such that they are represented by their proximities to a set of representative objects of each class. The fact (property) that dissimilarities should be smaller for similar objects and larger for different ones, suggests that they could be used as more discriminative features, if a suitable measure is used.

Thus, in this approach, given a set of training objects $\mathbf{X} = \{x_1, x_2, ..., x_l\}$, a representation set (a set of prototypes for each class) $\mathbf{R} = \{r_1, r_2, ..., r_p\}$, and a dissimilarity measure; the distance between each object $x_i \in \mathbf{X}$ to each object $r_h \in \mathbf{R}$ will be defined as $d(x_i, r_h)$. The representation set $\mathbf{R}$ can be a subset of $\mathbf{X}$, $\mathbf{R} \subseteq \mathbf{X}$ or $\mathbf{X}$ itself, being then $\mathbf{D}(\mathbf{X}, \mathbf{X})$ a square dissimilarity matrix, or $\mathbf{R}$ and $\mathbf{X}$ can be completely different sets. There are a number of approaches to select prototypes of the representation set [5].

Let us assume we have a multi-way or n-dimensional array $\underline{Y} \in \mathbb{R}^{I_1 \times I_2 \times ... \times I_n}$ (training set), where object $\underline{Y_i} \in \mathbb{R}^{I_1 \times I_2 \times ... \times I_{n-1}}$. To build the dissimilarity space, the mapping $\phi(\cdot, \mathbf{R}) : \mathbb{R}^{I_1 \times I_2 \times ... \times I_{n-1}} \to \mathbb{R}^h$ is defined, such that for every object $\phi(\underline{Y_i}, \mathbf{R}) = [d(\underline{Y_i}, r_1), d(\underline{Y_i}, r_2), ..., d(\underline{Y_i}, r_h)]$. We need then a $(n\text{-}1)$-dimensional dissimilarity measure for its computation. Classifiers are built in this space, as in any feature space. Consequently, the relationship between all objects in the training and representation sets is used for classification. If a suitable measure is chosen, the compactness property (objects from the same class should be similar and objects from different classes should be different) of the classes should be more pronounced. Therefore, it should be easier for the classifiers to discriminate between them, since linear classifiers in the dissimilarity space may correspond to non-linear classifiers in the feature space. In general, any arbitrary classifier operating on features can be used [5].

3   Continuous Multi-way Shape Measure

A measure that somehow respects the multi-way structure of the data (considers the relationship of different directions) is needed. It should also make use of the continuity and shape information of the multi-dimensional continuous data.

Given a $n - 1$ dimensional object, each point in the multi-dimensional surface could be analyzed with a $n - 1$ dimensional window, such that shape changes in all directions can be taken into account. Thus, the comparison between two objects should be based on the differences of their multi-way shape, considering the connectivity that exists between the neighboring points in the different directions. In the case of 1D continuous data e.g. spectral data, derivatives are the commonly used tool to evaluate shape changes. For multi-dimensional functions, the gradient is the natural extension of the derivative concept.

Although data may have a continuous nature, they are captured by the sampling procedures of sensors as a collection of discrete values. As derivatives are undefined for discrete functions, they need to be estimated somehow to be used on these data. A widely used method for approximating the derivative of a discrete function is the application of linear filters by convolution.

Given the multi-dimensional discrete functions $\underline{Y}$ and $\underline{H}$, a convolution operation is defined as $\underline{Y}' = \underline{Y} * \underline{H}$, where $*$ is the convolution operator [7]. Thus, given two objects $\underline{Y_a}$ and $\underline{Y_b}$, they can be compared by computing the difference between the gradients of the surfaces that represent these objects. As derivatives and therefore the gradient are very noise sensitive, data should be smoothed before performing these operations. A common way to smooth data is by convolving it with a Gaussian filter. Following the previous ideas, the Continuous Multi-way Shape (CMS) measure is defined as:

Definition 1. *Let $\underline{Y}$ be a n-way data set and let $\underline{Y_a}$, $\underline{Y_b}$ be two objects from this data set. The dissimilarity between $\underline{Y_a}$ and $\underline{Y_b}$ can be computed as:*

$$d_G(\underline{Y_a}, \underline{Y_b}) = \left\| \sum_{i=1}^{f} \underline{Y_a} * \underline{G_\sigma} * H_i - \underline{Y_b} * \underline{G_\sigma} * H_i \right\|_F \tag{1}$$

where $\| \cdot \|_F$ is the Frobenius norm for tensors [8], $\underline{G_\sigma}$ a Gaussian convolution kernel to smooth the data first, $\underline{H_i}$ is a partial derivative kernel and f is the amount of partial derivatives in the different directions in order to obtain the gradient.

3.1 Gradient Kernels

The Prewitt and Sobel operators [7] are 2D convolution kernels based on linear filters that compute the average gradient components of three adjacent lines and columns to overcome the noise sensitivity. They differ in that central weights for the smoothing are higher. Horizontal and vertical Prewitt and Sobel kernels are then defined as follows:

$$H_x^P = \begin{array}{|c|c|c|} \hline -1 & 0 & 1 \\ \hline -1 & 0 & 1 \\ \hline -1 & 0 & 1 \\ \hline \end{array} \quad H_y^P = \begin{array}{|c|c|c|} \hline -1 & -1 & -1 \\ \hline 0 & 0 & 0 \\ \hline 1 & 1 & 1 \\ \hline \end{array} \quad H_x^S = \begin{array}{|c|c|c|} \hline -1 & 0 & 1 \\ \hline -2 & 0 & 2 \\ \hline -1 & 0 & 1 \\ \hline \end{array} \quad H_y^S = \begin{array}{|c|c|c|} \hline -1 & -2 & -1 \\ \hline 0 & 0 & 0 \\ \hline 1 & 2 & 1 \\ \hline \end{array} \tag{2}$$

The previous gradient operators are based on approximating a partial derivative at a point p by computing the slope of the line that fits the previous and next point of p in the direction of the derivative. Extensions of these filters to diagonal directions and to higher dimensions can be found [9], and the same idea of a line fitting is kept.

3.2 Gradient Polynomial-Based Kernel for the CMS Measure

We propose to approximate each partial derivative in point p as the derivative of the polynomial of degree t, which is obtained by interpolating p and its t nearest points in the direction of the derivative.

For a 2D kernel of size $[3 \times 3]$ this approach is equivalent to applying the Prewitt operator. So, the particular case of a 2D kernel of size $[5 \times 5]$ will be explained here. For 2D objects, we want to analyze the derivatives in four directions (horizontal, vertical and the two diagonals). Without loss of generality, let us see the case for the horizontal direction. Assume there are five points $p_0 = (-2, y_0)$, $p_1 = (-1, y_1)$, $p_2 = (0, y_2)$, $p_3 = (1, y_3)$ and $p_4 = (2, y_4)$, so a fourth degree polynomial should be approximated to compute the derivative in each direction. We chose these values for x just for simplicity, but it really does not matter, the shape of the polynomial is the same: $P(x) = ax^4 + bx^3 + cx^2 + dx + e$. Its derivative is the cubic polynomial $P'(x) = 4ax^3 + 3bx_2 + 2cx + d$ and, evaluated in point p_2, it is reduced to $P'(0) = d$. If we solve the system of equations from evaluating all points in $P(x)$, we obtain $P'(0) = d = \frac{y_0 - 8y_1 + 8y_3 - y_4}{12}$, which can be wrapped in a filter kernel.

As for Prewitt and Sobel operators where adjacent lines are averaged, an approximated average polynomial of the adjacent set of points can be obtained. Then, the following convolution kernels for horizontal, vertical, main diagonal and secondary diagonal are defined respectively:

$$
H_x^L = \begin{bmatrix} 1 & -8 & 0 & 8 & 1 \\ 1 & -8 & 0 & 8 & 1 \\ 1 & -8 & 0 & 8 & 1 \\ 1 & -8 & 0 & 8 & 1 \\ 1 & -8 & 0 & 8 & 1 \end{bmatrix} \quad
H_y^L = \begin{bmatrix} 1 & 1 & 1 & 1 & 1 \\ -8 & -8 & -8 & -8 & -8 \\ 0 & 0 & 0 & 0 & 0 \\ 8 & 8 & 8 & 8 & 8 \\ -1 & -1 & -1 & -1 & -1 \end{bmatrix} \quad
H_{md}^L = \begin{bmatrix} 0 & 0 & 0 & 1 & 1 \\ 0 & 0 & -8 & -8 & 1 \\ 0 & 8 & 0 & -8 & 0 \\ -1 & 8 & 8 & 0 & 0 \\ -1 & -1 & 0 & 0 & 0 \end{bmatrix} \quad
H_{sd}^L = \begin{bmatrix} 1 & 1 & 0 & 0 & 0 \\ 1 & -8 & -8 & 0 & 0 \\ 0 & -8 & 0 & 8 & 0 \\ 0 & 0 & 8 & 8 & -1 \\ 0 & 0 & 0 & -1 & -1 \end{bmatrix} \tag{3}
$$

The same idea can be generalized to larger windows, but higher order polynomials are used. These filters can also be extended to n-way arrays. Polynomials will be determined in the same manner according to the size of the window, but now there will be more directions to be analyzed. For example, in the case of a 4-way array where objects are 3D, if we use a $[3 \times 3 \times 3]$ window, 13 directions can be analyzed as in the following figure:

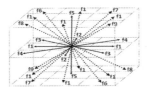

Fig. 1. The 13 directions to be analyzed in a 3D object

The proposed CMS measure can be seen as a generalization of the idea of the 2Dshape [4] measure for 2D objects. Both measures are based on smoothing surfaces with a Gaussian kernel and their partial derivatives are compared in order to take the shape of the functions into account. However, in the case of the 2Dshape measure, a 1D Gaussian derivative is computed independently for every feature in the horizontal and vertical directions of a 2D object, treating the feature as a 1D signal, without taking into account the relationship between the features in the two directions. Differences in each direction are then combined.

In contrast, the CMS measure already considers 2D information in the smoothing process by applying a 2D Gaussian kernel. Moreover, with 2D gradient kernel operators, more global information (relationship between features) is considered. As partial derivatives are computed on the average line obtained from a number of rows/columns (depending on the kernel size), information from the neighboring signals is used. The most remarkable feature of the CMS measure is that it is not restricted to measure the shape in two directions only. Although CMS is based on the idea of the gradient of an image, which is mathematically defined by a vector of 2 components i.e. horizontal and vertical, this measure allows analyzing other directions e.g. diagonals. This way, more accurate approximations of the information on the shape of objects and dependencies in the different directions are computed for the comparison. With the introduced polynomial-based kernels, the partial derivatives can be approximated as the derivative of higher-degree polynomials instead of a simple line. Consequently, it is to be expected that the multi-way shape information can be better modeled with the proposed CMS measure, leading to a better discrimination of these types of objects. At last, the CMS measure has been defined for continuous multi-way objects in general, while 2Dshape can only be applied to 2D objects.

4   Experimental Setup and Discussion

In this section, we present experiments with a Regularized Linear Discriminant classifier based on dissimilarities. Experiments are conducted on five 2D continuous data sets of different sources. Our aim is to compare the performance of classifiers on the two shape-based measures, 2Dshape and the proposed CMS measure for multi-way continuous data. These performances will also be compared with the non-shape based measures Frobenius and Yang, which are versions of the AMD [6] distance with weights $p = 2$ and $p = 1$ respectively.

For the different data sets, experiments were carried out differently. For small data sets (Parma ham and St John's), classification errors were obtained in a 10 times k-fold cross-validation (CV). The Enzyme data has a training and test set, so the classifier is evaluated on the test set. In the case of Colon and Volcano data, 10 different training and test sets were randomly chosen and the error values were averaged. For the three bigger data sets, i.e. Enzyme, Colon and Volcano, a part of the data was used to optimize the measures parameters in a CV procedure. The rest was then used as explained before. For the other two, as they are too small, the parameters were optimized with the whole data sets.

The first data set is private and it comes from 1200 patches of 1024×1024 pixels of 36 colon tissue slides from Atrium hospital in Heerlen, The Netherlands. Patches were filtered with Laplace filters in 90 different scales using $\sigma = 2.\hat{\ }[0.1 : 0.1 : 9]$. The log-squares of the results are summarized in 60 bin normalized histograms with bin centres $[-50 : 1 : 9]$. Thus, a 90×60 array is obtained for every patch, leading to a three-way array of $1200 \times 90 \times 60$. The patches are labeled in two classes: Normal and Tumor. A representation set of 550 prototypes was randomly chosen from the training set. The second data set corresponds to seismic signals from Nevado del Ruiz volcano in the Colombian Andes. The data set is composed of 12032-point signals of two classes of volcanic events: Long-Period earthquakes, and Volcano-Tectonic earthquakes. A 2D time-frequency representation was computed for each signal with a 256-points (window size) Short-Time Fourier Transform (STFT), with 50% overlap. The concatenation of the obtained spectrograms results in a $470 \times 93 \times 129$ three-way array. The dissimilarity matrix has a size of 470×100.

The third and fourth data sets are from public domains and they are both obtained by Fluorescence spectroscopy. The first of them consists of a training set of size $323 \times 15 \times 15$ and a test set of $53 \times 15 \times 15$. The two variable directions correspond to excitation and emission wavelengths respectively. The classification problem consists in determining the quality (Low or High) of a process according to the enzyme activity [10]. A representation set of 100 prototypes was randomly chosen from the training set, thus the dissimilarity matrices have a size of 323×100 and 53×100 for training and test sets respectively. The other data set has a size of $67 \times 11 \times 13$ and the purpose is to determine the age range of a Parma ham sample: raw (0 months), salted (3 months), matured (11 and 12 months) and aged (15 and 18 months) [3]. The last data set consists of 108 samples of carrot juice, which have been crystallized, with the aim of describing their quality (Good/Bad) [11]. Images of size 528×528 of each biocrystallized sample were taken. Gabor filters with a bank of 128 filters from 16 orientations was applied, resulting in a four-way data set of $108 \times 528 \times 528 \times 128$. Thus, 128 dissimilarity matrices were computed with 2D measures on the 528×528 matrices of each filter and latter averaged. All objects were used as representation set in the DR.

Table 1. Classification error with different measures: CMS measure with Prewitt, Prewitt in 4 directions (including diagonals), Sobel, Sobel in 4 directions and Polynomial filter, 2Dshape measure, Frobenius and Yang

| Data | CMS | | | | | | No shape | |
	Prew.	Prew.(4d)	Sob.	Sob.(4d)	Polyn.	2Dshape	Frob	Yang
Colon cancer	11.0	11.5	11.2	12.0	**9.5**	12.7	13.3	13.3
Volcano	28.0	25.6	28.2	23.4	23.4	**20.9**	40.0	28.7
Enzyme	9.4	**5.7**	9.4	9.4	9.4	13.2	9.4	9.4
Parma ham	3.7	**2.4**	3.7	2.5	3.7	2.9	4.5	4.3
Carrot juice	**7.2**	**6.0**	**7.2**	6.3	**7.1**	8.3	9.8	10.7

Results are shown in Table 1. It can be seen that as expected, measures which take the continuous information of data into account give the best results. The CMS measure, with most filters, outperforms the results obtained with the 2Dshape measure in general, corroborating our previous analysis. The selection of the kernel to be applied should depend on the problem at hand and how rough shape changes are. Larger kernels should be able to capture better the changes in the surface when these are not so sudden. However, if there are shape changes in small regions, they might be averaged in a large window. Thus, small windows should work better in these cases. It is shown that results are improved by using the diagonal directions in the Prewitt and Sobel operators. This supports the previously discussed argument that if more directions are analyzed, there can be more information which contributes to a better discrimination of the classes.

5   Conclusions

We introduced a multi-dimensional dissimilarity measure for multi-way continuous data based on the computation of the gradient. This was proposed with the aim of applying the DR approach as a classification tool for this type of data. The new measure allows taking into account the complex multi-dimensional structure, such that the connectivity and shape information of the surfaces (objects) can be considered in the dissimilarity representation of the objects. The way the measure has been defined, allows to use different gradient convolution kernels, according to the problem at hand. This measure was compared to the 2Dshape measure and other non-shape based measures for the classification of 2D objects. Results have corroborated the presented argument that considering the continuous multi-way nature of these types of data in their analysis can lead to better results. Moreover, it is shown that by taking into account the information in more directions, results can be improved.

References

[1] Smilde, A.K., Bro, R., Geladi, P.: Multi-way Analysis. In: Applications in the Chemical Sciences. Wiley Publisher, England (2004)
[2] Acar, E., Aykut-Bingol, C., Bingol, H., Bro, R., Yener, B.: Multiway analysis of epilepsy tensors. Bioinformatics 23, i10–i18 (2007)
[3] Durante, C., Bro, R., Cocchi, M.: A classification tool for N-way array based on SIMCA methodology. Chem. and Intell. Lab. Syst. 106, 73–85 (2011)
[4] Porro-Muñoz, D., Duin, R.P.W., Talavera, I., Orozco-Alzate, M.: Classification of three-way data by the dissimilarity representation. Signal Processing 91(11), 2520–2529 (2011)
[5] Pekalska, E., Duin, R.P.W.: The Dissimilarity Representation For Pattern Recognition. Foundations and Applications. World Scientific, Singapore (2005)
[6] Zuo, W., Zhang, D., Wang, K.: An assembled matrix distance metric for 2DPCA-based image recognition. Pattern Recognition Letters 27, 210–216 (2006)
[7] Gonzalez, R.C., Woods, R.E.: Digital Image Processing, 3rd edn. Prentice-Hall, Inc., Upper Saddle River (2006)
[8] Lathauwer, L., De Moor, B.: From matrix to tensor: Multilinear algebra and signal processing. In: Proc. 4th Int'l Conf. on Mathematics in Signal Processing, vol. 1, pp. 1–11 (1996)
[9] Jetto, L., Orlando, G., Sanfilippo, A.: The edge point detection problem in image sequences: Definition and comparative evaluation of some 3D edge detecting schemes. In: Proc. of the 7th Mediterranean Conference on Control and Automation (MED 1999), pp. 2161–2171 (1999)
[10] Mortensen, P.P., Bro, R.: Real time monitoring and chemical profiling of a cultivation process. Chem. and Intell. Lab. Syst. 84(1-2), 106–113 (2005)
[11] Busscher, N., Kahl, J., Andersen, J., Huber, M., Mergardt, G., Doesburg, P., Paulsen, M., Ploeger, A.: Standardization of the biocrystallization method for carrot samples. Biological Agriculture and Horticulture 27, 1–23 (2010)

Improving Spider Recognition
Based on Biometric Web Analysis

Carlos M. Travieso Gonzalez[1], Jaime Roberto Ticay-Rivas[1], Marcos del Pozo-Baños[1],
William G. Eberhard[2], and Jesús B. Alonso-Hernández[1]

[1] Signals and Communications Department
Institute for Technological Development and Innovation in Communications
University of Las Palmas de Gran Canaria
Campus University of Tafira, 35017, Las Palmas de Gran Canaria, Las Palmas, Spain
[2] Smithsonian Tropical Research Institute and Escuela de Biologia
Universidad de Costa Rica, Ciudad Universitaria, Costa Rica
{ctravieso,jalonso}@dsc.ulpgc.es, {jrticay,mpozo}@idetic.eu,
william.eberhard@ucr.ac.cr

Abstract. This work presents an improvement of the automatic and supervised
spider identification approach based on biometric spider web analysis. We have
used as feature extractor, a Joint Approximate Diagonalization of Eigenmatrixes Independent Component Analysis applying to a binary image with a
reduced size (20×20 pixels) from the colour original image. Finally, we have
applied a least square support vector machine as classifier, reaching over
98.15% in our hold-50%-out validation. This system is making easier Biologists' tasks in this field, because they can have a second opinion or have a tool
for this work.

Keywords: Spider webs, spider classification, independent component analysis,
support vector machine.

1 Introduction

The pollution and socioeconomic growth is generating serious problems in our actual
world and one of big handicap is the loss diversity in natural environments. Therefore,
biodiversity conservation has become a priority for researchers [1]. Knowledge about
species is critical to understand and protect the biodiversity of life on Earth. Sadly,
spiders have been one of most unattended groups in conservation biology [2]. These
arachnids are plentiful and ecologically crucial in almost every terrestrial and semi-
terrestrial habitat [3-5]. Moreover, they present a series of extraordinary qualities,
such as the ability to react to environmental changes and anthropogenic impacts [5-6].

Several works have studied the spider behaviour. Some of them analyse the use of
the way spiders build their webs as a source of information for species identification
[7-8]. Artificial intelligent systems have been proven to be of use for the study of the
spider nature. In [9], Authors proposed a system for spider behaviour modelling,
which provides simulations of how specific spider specie builds its web. In [10], it is

L. Alvarez et al. (Eds.): CIARP 2012, LNCS 7441, pp. 438–446, 2012.
© Springer-Verlag Berlin Heidelberg 2012

recorded how spiders build their webs in a controlled scenario for further spatial-temporal analysis.

Due to spider webs carry an incredibly lot of information, this work proposed the used of them as a source of information for spider specie identification. From our point of view, this work has improved the first version [11], increasing the success on 4%. Independent Component Analysis has been used as biometric features for this purpose. This feature extraction, added to image processing tools for preparing images, and Least Square Support Vector Machines for classification, has reached an improvement vs. our previous work [11].

The remainder of this paper is organized as follow. First, our pre-processing system is presented in order to detect the spider webs from the background. Section 3 explains how feature extraction images were applied. Least Square Support Vector Machine is introduced in section 4. Next, experimental settings are shown by the dataset, the experimental methodology, results and the discussion. Finally in section 6, conclusions derived from the results are presented.

2   Pre-processing System

Spider web images were taken in both controlled and uncontrolled environments. Thus, the pre-processing step was vital in order to isolate the spider webs and remove possible effects of background in the system's results.

Fig. 1. Examples of full spider web images after preprocessing corresponding to *Allocyclosa*, *Anapisona Simoni*, and *Micrathena Duodecimspinosa, Zosis Geniculata,* respectively

Fig. 2. Examples of centre spider web images after preprocessing corresponding to *Allocyclosa*, *Anapisona Simoni*, and *Micrathena Duodecimspinosa, Zosis Geniculata,* respectively

To enhance the contour of cobweb's threats an increase of colour contrast was first applied. Then, images were multiplied by two to further intensify the spider webs in relation to the background. Once images have been enhanced, they were binarized by

Otsu's Method [12] and cleaned up by morphological transformations [13]. Finally, the spider webs were cropped following two criterions. As results, two full set of spider web images were obtained. One of both contains the full web and another one shows only the central area. Examples of these sets can be seen in Fig. 1 and 2 respectively. Finally, all images were normalized to dimensions 20 x 20 pixels.

3   Feature Extraction: Joint Approximate Diagonalization of Eigen-Matrixes Independent Component Analysis

Independent Component Analysis (ICA) is a particularization of Principal Component Analysis (PCA) to extract components that are, at the same time, non-gaussian and statistically independent [14]. When used on images, ICA obtains independent base images which are not necessarily orthogonal. Application of these base images extracts between pixels information related to high order statistics.

In this study, an approach based on Joint Approximate Diagonalization of Eigenmatrixes Independent Component Analysis (JADE-ICA) has been used to implement this tool. JADE-ICA is based on joint diagonalization of cumulant matrixes. For simplicity, the case of symmetric distributions is considered, where the odd-order cumulants vanish. Let $X_1, \ldots, X_4$ be random variables, and defined $X_i^* = X_i + E(X_i)$. The second order cumulants can be written as:

$$C(X_1, X_2) = E(X_1^*, X_2^*) \tag{1}$$

And the fourth-order cumulants as:

$$C(X_1, X_2, X_3, X_4) = E(X_1^*, X_2^*, X_3^*, X_4^*) - E(X_1^*, X_2^*)E(X_3^*, X_4^*) -$$
$$E(X_1^*, X_3^*)E(X_2^*, X_4^*) - E(X_1^*, X_4^*)E(X_2^*, X_3^*) \tag{2}$$

In addition, the definitions of variance and kurtosis of a random variable X are:

$$\sigma^2 = C(X, X) = E(X^{*2})$$
$$kurt(X) = C(X, X, X, X) = E(X^{*4}) - 3E^2(X^{*4}) \tag{3}$$

Now, under a linear transformation $Y=AX$, the cumulants of fourth-order transformation became:

$$C(Y_i, Y_j, Y_k, Y_l) = \sum_{p,q,r,s} a_{ip} a_{jq} a_{kr} a_{ls} C(X_p, X_q, X_r, X_s) \tag{4}$$

with a_{ij} the i-th row and j-th column entry of matrix A. Since the ICA model ($X=AS$) is linear, using the assumption of independence by $C(S_p, S_q, S_r, S_s) = kurt(S_q)\delta_{pqrs}$ where:

$$\delta_{pqrs} = \begin{cases} 1 & if \quad p = q = r = s \\ 0 & otherwise \end{cases} \tag{5}$$

and S has independent entries:

$$C(Y_i, Y_j, Y_k, Y_l) = \sum_{m=1}^{n} kurt(S_m) a_{im} a_{jm} a_{km} a_{lm} \tag{6}$$

the cumulants of the ICA model are obtained.

Given any $n \times n$ matrix M and a random $n \times 1$ vector X, we consider a cumulant matrix $Q_x(M)$ defined by:

$$Q_X(M) = \sum_{m=1}^{n} C(X_i, X_j, X_k, X_i) M_{ki} \tag{7}$$

If X is centered, the definition of (4) shows that:

$$Q_X(M) = E\{(X^T M X^T) X X^T\} - R^X tr(MR^X) - \\ R^X M R^X - R^X M^T R^X \tag{8}$$

where $tr(B)$ denotes the trace of matrix B and $[R_X]_{ij} = C(X_i, X_j)$.

The structure of a cumulant $Q_x(M)$ in ICA model is easily deduced from (9) as:

$$Q_X(M) = A\Delta(M)A^T \tag{9}$$

with:

$$\Delta(M) = diag(kurt(S_1)a_1^T M a_1, ..., kurt(S_n)a_n^T M a_n \tag{10}$$

where a_i is the i-th column of A.

Now, let W be a whitening matrix and $Z=WX$. Let us assume that the independent sources matrix S has unit variance, so that S is white. Thus $Z=WX=WAS$ is also white, and the matrix $U=WA$ is orthonormal. Similarly, the previous techniques can be applied into (13) for any $n \times n$ matrix M.

First, the whitening matrix W and the cumulant matrix Z are estimated. Then, the estimation of an orthonormal matrix denoted by U, is calculated. Therefore, an estimated matrix A denoted by A is obtained from $W^{-1}U$, and the sources matrix S is calculated by $A^{-1}X$.

To measure non-diagonality of a matrix B, $off(B)$ is defined as the sum of the squares of the non-diagonal elements:

$$off(B) = \sum_{i \neq j} (b_{ij})^2 \tag{11}$$

where b_{ii} are elements of the matrix B. In particular $off(U^T Q_Z(M_i)U) = U\Delta_i U^T) = off(\Delta_i) = 0$ since $Q_Z(M_i) = U\Delta_i U^T$ and U is orthogonal. For any matrix set M and orthonormal matrix V, the joint diagonality criterion is defined as:

$$D_M(V) = \sum_{M_i \in M} off(V^T Q_Z(M_i)V) \tag{12}$$

which measures diagonality far from the matrix V and bring the cumulants matrixes from the set M.

4   Classification System

At this section, the system has got the useful information from the input images by JADE-ICA. Now, the classification component uses this information to take a decision on behalf the spider specie from the spider web biometric as input. To do so, this work uses the well known Support Vector Machine (SVM) [15].

The SVM is a structural risk minimization learning method of separating functions for pattern classification, which was derived from the statistical learning theory elaborated by [16]. In other words, SVM is a tool able to differ between classes characterized by parameters, after a training process.

What makes this tool powerful is the way it handles non-linearly separable problems. In these cases, the SVM transforms the problem into a linearly separable one by projecting samples into a higher dimensional space. This is done using an operator called kernel, which in this study is set to be a Radial Basis Function (RBF). Then, efficient and fast linear techniques can be applied in the transformed space. This technique is usually known as the kernel trick, and was first introduced by [17].

For simplicity, we configure the SVM to work as a verification system. In this particular case, the positive class (1) corresponds to spider specie to verify and the negative class (-1) to the rest of spider species. As a result, the classifier answers the "is the actual spider specie to verify?" question. The output of the SVM is a numeric value between -1 and 1 named score. A threshold has to be set to define a border between actual spider specie (1) and other different spider species (-1) responses.

However, if all samples are used for training, there are no new samples for setting the threshold, and using the training samples for this purpose will lead to bad adjustments. Therefore, a 30 iterations hold-50%-out validation procedure is used over the training samples to obtain scores. These scores are then used to set error rate. The system's margin, defined as the distance of the closest point to the threshold line, is also measured. All these measures are referred to as validation measures.

When the threshold is finally set, the SVM is available to work in test mode. Because no big differences exist in the number of training samples used for this final training and the validation, we can expect the system to have a very similar threshold than that computed before.

In particular, the Least Squares Support Vector Machines (LS-SVM) implementation is used [18]. Given a training set of N data points $\{y_i, x_i\}_{K=1}^{N}$, where x_i is the k-th input sample and y_i its corresponding produced output, we can assume that:

$$\begin{cases} w^T \phi(x_i) + b \geq 1 & if \quad y_i = +1 \\ w^T \phi(x_i) + b \leq 1 & if \quad y_i = -1 \end{cases} \tag{13}$$

where ϕ is the kernel function that maps samples into the higher dimensional space. The LS-SVM solves the classification problem:

$$\min L_2(w,b,e) = \frac{\mu}{2} w^T w + \frac{\zeta}{2} \sum_{i=1}^{N} e_{c,i}^2 \tag{14}$$

where μ and ξ are hyper-parameters related to the amount of regularization versus the sum square error. Moreover, the solution of this problem is subject to the constraints:

$$y_i \left[w^T \phi(x_i) + b \right] = 1 - e_{c,i}, \quad i = 1, ..., N \qquad (15)$$

5   Experimental Settings

5.1   Database

The database contains spider web images of four different species named *Allocyclosa*, *Anapisona Simoni, Micrathena Duodecimspinosa and Zosis Geniculata*. Each class has 28, 41, 39 and 42 images, respectively, in total, 150 images (see Fig. 3).

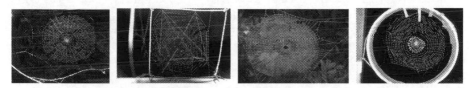

Fig. 3. Examples of spider web images from the data base corresponding to *Allocyclosa, Anapisona Simoni, Micrathena Duodecimspinosa and Zosis Geniculata,* respectively

5.2   Experimental Methodology

Our proposal used the first M components obtained from the JADE-ICA of the spider webs images as inputs for a RBF-kernel LS-SVM with specific regularization and kernel parameters. These two parameters (the number of components and the kernel parameters) were automatically optimized by iteration using validation results. To obtain more reliable results the available samples were divided into training and test sets, so that the system is trained and tested with totally independent samples, according to supervised classification. We have done two experiments, in order to find our best approach.

Our first experiment will be to determine where the most discriminate information is, comparing the whole the spider web or only the central part. We have used 20 components from the pre-processing image to 20 x 20 pixels. This experiment will be done under hold-50%-out validation techniques.

Our second experiment will be to adjust these two parameters (the number of components and the kernel parameters) for the most discriminate information, obtained from previous experiment; under the well known K-Folds cross-validation techniques, which have been used to obtain the final results. In particular, experiments with K equal 3, 5, 7, and 10 were run. Too, multiple hold-out validation has been used in this experiment. In Table 2, accuracy rates can be observed.

All the experiments have been repeated 30 times, showing our accuracy rates in averages and standard deviation.

5.3   Results and Discussions

From our first experiment (see Table 1), we can see the most of the information are located on the central part of the spider web, with over 5% of accuracy rate. This goal agrees with the Biological point of view, because the Biologists use this central part in order to try to do a manual identification. Besides, this goal will design the following experiment, because the tests with whole spider web will be removed.

Table 1. Accuracy Rates in processing images of 20 x 20 pixels for 20 independent components using LS-SVM under 50% hold out cross-validation techniques

Type of image	Whole spider web	Central part of spider web
Accuracy Rate	91.85% ± 4.92	97.16% ± 2.47

The second experiment has been done for the central part of spider web. The Fig. 4 shows the evolution of the number of independent components for 50% hold-out validation techniques. This evolution is done from 1 to 50 independent components, with a step of 5. It can be seen in Fig. 4 that the best accuracy rate versus the number of independent components is 10. Therefore, the rest of experiment will be done with that condition, and the kernel parameter of LS-SVM will be automatically searched (see Section 4) when the mayor accuracy rate is found (see Table 2).

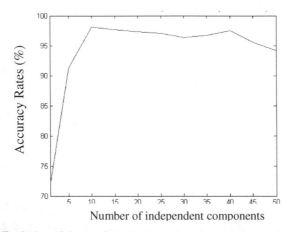

Fig. 4. Evolution of the number of independent components vs. Accurate Rates

Table 2. Accuracy Rates for different validation methodologies

K-Fold	Accuracy Rate	Hold-out	Accuracy Rate
10	96.16% ± 0.89	50	98.15% ± 3.96
7	95.17% ± 1.03	40	98.06% ± 4.09
5	94.60% ± 1.52	30	96.59% ± 5.22
3	94.18% ± 2.06	20	94.40% ± 6.74

From Table 2, we can observe our approach is working over 98%, in order to identify the spider specie using the central part of the spider web as biometric information. Therefore, the error between species is low, when that central part of the spider web is used.

About the computational time, our approach uses 435 milliseconds in order to do the pre-processing and the extraction of 10 independent components using JADE-ICA. Besides, it uses 0.25 milliseconds in order to test one sample. Therefore, our algorithm runs need 435.25 milliseconds in order to evaluate on test sample. This was implemented using AMD Phenom^{TM} II X6 1090T 3.2GHz Processor with 6GB RAM memory, programmed on MATLAB.

6   Conclusions

An automatic identification approach is implemented in this work for the spider classification from its spider web, reaching an accuracy rate of 98.15%. Our computational time is minor to 500 milliseconds, given good efficiency between accuracy rate and this time.

The future lines will be to increase the dataset and to search a new parameterization system in order to improve our present system. These advances give very important biological information, because it validates the Biologists' work, showing the objective way, as it is possible to have an automatic system for identifying spider species, as it is done by biologists.

Acknowledgement. This work has been supported by Spanish Government, in particular by *"Agencia Española de Cooperación Internacional para el Desarrollo"* under funds from D/027406/09, D/033858/10 and A1/039089/11 for 2012.

References

1. Sytnik, K.M.: Preservation of biological diversity: Top-priority tasks of society and state. Ukrainian Journal of Physical Optics 11(suppl. 1), 2–10 (2010)
2. Carvalho, J.C., Cardoso, P., Crespo, L.C., Henriques, S., Carvalho, R., Gomes, P.: Biogeographic patterns of spiders in coastal dunes along a gradient of mediterraneity. Biodiversity and Conservation, 1–22 (2011)
3. Johnston, J.M.: The contribution of microarthropods to aboveground food webs: A review and model of belowground transfer in a coniferous forest. American Midland Naturalist 143, 226–238 (2000)
4. Peterson, A.T., Osborne, D.R., Taylor, D.H.: Tree trunk arthropod faunas as food resources for birds. Ohio Journal of Science 89(1), 23–25 (1989)
5. Cardoso, P., Arnedo, M.A., Triantis, K.A., Borges, P.A.V.: Drivers of diversity in Macaronesian spiders and the role of species extinctions. J. Biogeogr. 37, 1034–1046 (2010)
6. Finch, O.D., Blick, T., Schuldt, A.: Macroecological patterns of spider species richness across Europe. Biodivers. Conserv. 17, 2849–2868 (2008)
7. Eberhard, W.G.: Behavioral Characters for the Higher Classification of Orb-Weaving Spiders. Evolution, Society for the Study of Evolution 36(5), 1067–1095 (1982)

8. Eberhard, W.G.: Early Stages of Orb Construction by Philoponella Vicina, Leucauge Mariana, and Nephila Clavipes (Araneae, Uloboridae and Tetragnathidae), and Their Phylogenetic Implications. Journal of Arachnology, American Arachnological Society 18(2), 205–234 (1990)
9. Eberhard, W.G.: Computer Simulation of Orb-Web Construction. J. American Zoologist, 229–238 (1969)
10. Suresh, P.B., Zschokke, S.: A computerised method to observe spider web building behaviour in a semi-natural light environment. In: 19th European Colloquium of Arachnology, Denmark (2000)
11. Ticay-Rivas, J.R., del Pozo-Baños, M., Eberhard, W.G., Alonso, J.B., Travieso, C.M.: Spider Recognition by Biometric Web Analysis. In: Ferrández, J.M., Álvarez Sánchez, J.R., de la Paz, F., Toledo, F.J. (eds.) IWINAC 2011, Part II. LNCS, vol. 6687, pp. 409–417. Springer, Heidelberg (2011)
12. Otsu, N.: A thresholding selection method from gray-level histogram. IEEE Transactions on Systems, Man, and Cybernetics 9(1), 62–66 (1979)
13. Gonzalez, R.C., Woods, R.E., Eddins, S.L.: Digital Image Processing. Pearson Prentice Hall (2003)
14. Hyvärinen, A.: Independent Component Analysis: Algorithms and Applications. Neural Networks 13(4-5), 411–430 (2000)
15. Schölkopf, B., Smola, A.J.: Learning with Kernels. Support Vector Machines, Regularization, Optimization, and Beyond. The MIT Press (2002)
16. Vapnik, V.: The Nature of Statistical learning Theory. Springer, New York (1995)
17. Yan, F., Qiang, Y., Ruixiang, S., Dequan, L., Rong, Z., Ling, C.X., Wen, G.: Exploiting the kernel trick to correlate fragment ions for peptide identification via tandem mass spectrometry. Bioinformatics 20(12), 1948–1954 (2004)
18. Suykens, J.A.K., Van Gestel, T., De Brabanter, J., De Moor, B., Vandewalle, J.: Least Squares Support Vector Machines. World Scientific, Singapore (2002)

Legume Identification by Leaf Vein Images Classification

Mónica G. Larese[1,2,*], Roque M. Craviotto[2], Miriam R. Arango[2],
Carina Gallo[2], and Pablo M. Granitto[1]

[1] CIFASIS, French Argentine International Center for Information and Systems
Sciences, UAM (France) / UNR-CONICET (Argentina)
Bv. 27 de Febrero 210 Bis, 2000, Rosario, Argentina
{larese,granitto}@cifasis-conicet.gov.ar
[2] Estación Experimental Oliveros, Instituto Nacional de Tecnología Agropecuaria
Ruta Nacional 11 km 353, 2206 Oliveros, Santa Fe, Argentina
{rcraviotto,marango,cgallo}@correo.inta.gov.ar

Abstract. In this paper we propose an automatic algorithm able to classify legume leaf images considering only the leaf venation patterns (leaf shape, color and texture are excluded). This method processes leaf images captured with a standard scanner and segments the veins using the Unconstrained Hit-or-Miss Transform (UHMT) and adaptive thresholding. We measure several morphological features on the veins and classify them using Random forests. We applied the process to recognize several legumes (soybean, white bean and red bean). We analyze the importance of the features and select a small set which is relevant for the recognition task. Our automatic procedure outperforms the expert manual classification.

Keywords: Leaf images automatic classification, Legume automatic recognition, Image analysis, Random forests, Unconstrained Hit-or-Miss Transform.

1 Introduction

In the recent literature, many works have been proposed aimed at automatically analyzing leaf images in order to classify them or to perform plant image retrieval. The most common approach consists in considering the leaf shape [1,2,3,4,5,6]. Other works, additionally, take into account the color information [7,8]. Moreover, the leaf texture can also be included [9,10].

However, in many practical situations there are not evident differences in the shape, size, color or texture features of the leaves for the plants under study. This is the case, for example, when identifying individuals from the same specie but which belong to different varieties or cultivars, so their leaves share the same visual properties. In recent studies [11,12,13], the authors highlighted the

* Author to whom all correspondence should be addressed. MGL and PMG acknowledge grant support from ANPCyT PICT 237.

L. Alvarez et al. (Eds.): CIARP 2012, LNCS 7441, pp. 447–454, 2012.

importance of considering the vein architecture to perform leaf-based plant identification. As recent works in the literature demonstrate [14,15], there exists a
correlation between the leaf venation characteristics and the leaf properties such
as, for example, damage and drought tolerance. If the plants under study have
different physiological characteristics, there is a chance that these properties can
be reflected in their veins even if the leaves look similar. Then, the motivation of
this work consists in developing an automatic procedure to perform leaf recognition exclusively analyzing the morphological traits from the leaf venation system,
i.e., no leaf shape, size, color or texture information is considered.

We perform the leaf segmentation using the Unconstrained Hit-or-Miss Transform (UHMT)[18] and adaptive image thresholding in order to extract the veins
from the gray scale images. The UHMT is a mathematical morphology operator useful to perform template matching in gray scale images, extracting all the
pixels with a certain foreground and background neighboring configuration.

Then we measure simple morphological features and employ the Random
forests algorithm [17] for the recognition task. This is a recent ensemble algorithm which uses a set of de-correlated trees as individual classifiers. It performs
comparably well against the most powerful state of the art classifiers. It is also
able to estimate the importance of the input variables, which we use to discuss
the relevance of the venation features for our particular problem.

We apply the whole method to recognize three classes of legumes, namely
soybean (*Glycine max (L) Merr*), red and white beans (*Phaseolus vulgaris*).
Red and white beans are two varieties from the same specie, with very similar
leaves. The only exception is the color of the veins, which are dark for the red
bean. However, we do not consider color information in this work, but only vein
morphological measures computed on the gray scale images.

We quantitatively assess the performance of the whole procedure by means
of computing the classification accuracies for each class. We also report the
accuracy obtained by expert manual classification for comparison, showing the
improved results achieved by the automatic classifier.

The rest of the paper is organized as follows. In Section 2.1 we describe the leaf
images dataset. Sections 2.2 and 2.3 explain the segmentation procedure that
we employed to extract the leaf venation system. We summarize the measures
that we computed on the segmented veins in Section 2.4. We briefly describe the
Random forests classification algorithm in Section 2.5. We present and discuss
the results in Section 3, where we assess the performance of the procedure and
analyze the relevant features. Finally, we draw some conclusions in Section 4.

2   Materials and Methods

2.1   Leaf Images Dataset

Our dataset consists of a total number of 866 RGB leaf images provided by
Instituto Nacional de Tecnología Agropecuaria (INTA, Oliveros, Argentina). The
dataset is divided in the following way: 422 images correspond to soybean leaves,
272 images to red bean leaves and 172 to white bean leaves. They are the images

of the first foliage leaves (pre-formed in the seed) of 433 specimens (211 soybean plants, 136 red bean plants and 86 white bean plants). First foliage leaves were selected for the analysis, after 12 days of seedling grow, since their characteristics are less influenced by the environment. We did not use any chemical or biological procedure to physically enhance the leaf veins. Instead, a fast, inexpensive and simple imaging procedure was used: the leaves were scanned using a Hewlett Packard Scanjet-G 3110 scanner, at a resolution of 200 pixels per inch and stored as 24-bit RGB TIFF images.

2.2   Unconstrained Hit-or-Miss Transform (UHMT)

The UHMT is an extension of the Hit-or-Miss Transform (HMT) for gray scale images [18]. It extracts all the pixels matching a certain foreground and background neighboring configuration. A composite structuring element $\mathbf{B}$ is employed, which is a disjoint set formed by one structuring element that specifies the foreground configuration, B_{fg}, and one structuring element for the background setting, B_{bg}. The origin of the composite structuring element matches the foreground.

The UHMT is defined as

$$UHMT_{\mathbf{B}}(Y)(y) = \max\left\{\varepsilon_{B_{fg}}(Y)(y) - \delta_{B_{bg}}(Y)(y), 0\right\}, \tag{1}$$

where Y is a gray scale image with set of pixels y and $\mathbf{B}$ is a composite structuring element. It can be computed as the difference between an erosion with B_{fg}, $\varepsilon_{B_{fg}}(Y)(y)$, and a dilation with B_{bg}, $\delta_{B_{bg}}(Y)(y)$, if $\delta_{B_{bg}}(Y)(y) < \varepsilon_{B_{fg}}(Y)(y)$. Otherwise it equals 0.

2.3   Vein Segmentation

Since we are only interested in the vein morphology, we removed all the color information by converting the RGB images to gray scale. We thresholded the gray scale image Y and filled its holes using morphological reconstruction [18]. After deleting all the connected components except the largest one, we obtained a binary mask for the leaf.

On the other hand, we computed the UHMT on 5 different sized versions of Y, namely at 100%, 90%, 80%, 70% and 60%. Each version is intended to highlight a different level of vein detail. Next, we resized back to the original size each resulting UHMT and summed them to obtain the combined UHMT, which highlights both small and large visible veins simultaneously. We used the 4 composite structuring elements (foreground and background configurations) shown in Fig. 1 to detect leaf veins in 4 directions (vertical, horizontal, +45°and -45°). After that, we enhanced the contrast of the combined UHMT and binarized the result by means of a standard adaptive thresholding algorithm. We removed all the connected components with less than 20 pixels.

Finally, we computed the product between the result of the segmentation and the previously computed leaf binary mask.

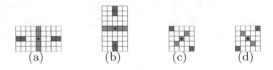

Fig. 1. The four pairs of flat composite structuring elements used for the UHMT to detect veins in four directions: (a) Vertical, (b) horizontal, (c) +45°and (d) -45°. Foreground and background pixel configurations are shown in red and green, respectively. The center of the composite structuring element is marked with a black dot.

2.4   Vein Measurements

In order to avoid the influence of the leaf shape we cropped a centered 100×100-pixel patch from the combined UHMT for each leaf, and measured all the features on these patches. We adapted LeafGUI [16] measures to extract a set of features of interest for veins and areoles. For our particular problem aimed at leaf classification, the individual vein/areole measures computed by LeafGUI are not suitable. For this reason, we computed the median, minimum and maximum feature values for veins and areoles where it was appropriate. The interested reader can found in the paper by Price et al. [16] a detailed explanation of each feature as well as the computation procedure. An exception is the edge orientation (not available in LeafGUI), which we computed as the angle (in the range [-90°, 90°]) between the x-axis and the major axis of the ellipse with the same second order moments as the vein.

We measured the following features: Total number of veins (VNE); Total number of nodes (VNN), i.e., number of connecting nodes between veins; Total network length (VTNL; in mm); Median/min/max edge length (VMeL/VmL/VML; in mm); Median/min/max edge width (VMeW/VmW/VMW; in mm); Median/min/max edge 2D area (VMeA/VmA/VMA; in mm^2); Median/min/max edge surface area (VMeSA/VmSA/VMSA; in mm^2); Median/min/max edge volume (VMeV/VmV/VMV; in mm^3); Median/min/max edge orientation (VMeO/VmO/VMO; in degrees); Total number of areoles (AN) in the image patch; Median/min/max areole perimeter (AMeP/AmP/AMP; in mm); Median/min/max areole area (AMeA/AmA/AMA; in mm^2); Median/min/max areole convex area (AMeCA/AmCA/AMCA; in mm^2); Median/min/max areole solidity (AMeS/AmS/AMS; dimensionless in [0,1]); Median/min/max areole major axis (AMeMaA/AmMaA/AMMaA; in mm); Median/min/max areole minor axis (AMeMiA/AmMiA/AMMiA; in mm); Median/min/max areole eccentricity (AMeE/AmE/AME; dimensionless between 0 -a circle- and 1 -a line-); Median/min/max areole equivalent diameter (AMeEq/AmEq/AMEq; in mm); Median/min/max areole mean distance (AMeMD/AmMD/AMMD; in mm); Median/min/max areole variance distance (AMeVD/AmVD/AMVD; in mm). Altogether, these measures make a feature vector of 52 components.

2.5   Random Forests

Random forests [17] is a recent ensemble algorithm where the individual classifiers are a set of de-correlated trees. They perform comparably well to other state of the art classifiers and are also very fast. Random forests also allows to estimate the importance of input variables (in their original dimensional space).

The algorithm constructs a set of unpruned trees from B random samples with replacement (bootstrap versions) of the original training dataset. For each random forest tree f_b, a random sample of m variables from the full set of p variables ($m \leq p$) is selected to split the data at each node and grow the decision tree. The final classification result $F(\mathbf{d}_i)$ is the class corresponding to the majority vote of the ensemble of trees,

$$F(\mathbf{d}_i) = \text{majority vote } \{f_b(\mathbf{d}_i)\}_{b=1}^{B} \tag{2}$$

Random forests has a built-in procedure to estimate the relevance of the input variables. After training the model, the features are shuffled one at a time. An out-of-bag estimation of the prediction error is made on this permuted dataset. Intuitively, a feature that is not relevant to the model will not alter significantly the classification performance when shuffled. On the other hand, if the model made strong use of a given feature, modifying its values will produce an important decrease in performance. The relative loss in performance between the original dataset and the shuffled dataset is therefore related to the relative relevance of the feature affected by the process.

In this work we used 500 trees and a standard value of $m = \sqrt{p}$ for the number of variables randomly sampled as candidates at each split.

3   Results and Discussion

We show in Fig. 2 an example of the segmentation results for a soybean leaf, a white bean leaf and a red bean leaf, as well as the 100×100-pixel central patches used for feature extraction. Figures 2(b), (e) and (h) are the combined UHMT images segmented according to Section 2.3. As it can be noticed from this figure, mainly primary order veins are extracted. Higher order veins (e.g. terminal veins) are not possible to segment since they are not visible (the images were scanned with no clearing or amplification procedures, as explained in Section 2.1).

We computed the 52 features described in Section 2.4 for each leaf patch. However, we had to discard 13 features since they presented a constant value for all the leaves (except for a few outliers), namely: VmL, VmO, VMO, AmA, AmCA, AmE, AmEq, AmMaA, AmMia, AmP, AmMD, AMS and AmVD. Thus, we used for classification 39 out of the 52 originally computed features.

We report in Table 1 the results for the classification of the 3 different legume species performing leave-one-out cross validation (LOOCV). The accuracies we obtained using 39 features are depicted in the first row of Table 1, showing that the identification rates are very good: in average, only 18 leaves out of 422 are misclassified for soybean and 39 out of 272 are misclassified for red bean. The

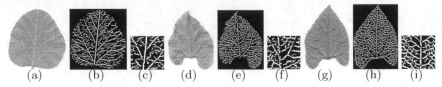

Fig. 2. (a) Soybean leaf. (b) Vein segmentation for (a). (c) 100×100-pixel central patch from (b). (d) White bean leaf. (e) Vein segmentation for (d). (f) 100 × 100-pixel central patch from (e). (g) Red bean leaf. (h) Vein segmentation for (g). (i) 100 × 100-pixel central patch from (h).

classification of white bean leaves seems to be the most difficult, although the results are quite satisfactory (in average 49 out of 172 images are misclassified).

Our automatic procedure with 39 features achieves an improvement of 16.22% over manual classification based on the same central patches (average of 5 experts; shown in the third row of Table 1) for red bean recognition, and 5.08% for the white bean.

However, the computation of the correlation matrix between the features (not included because of lack of space) shows that some of these features are strongly correlated one to each other (Pearson coefficient $|r| \geq 0.9$), e.g., the vein median volume (VMeV) with the vein median length (VMeL), the vein median area (VMeA) and the vein median surface area (VMeSA). This means that some of the features are redundant, and could lead to some overfitting of the data.

In order to find a small set of non-redundant relevant features able to describe the vein differences between soybean, white bean and red bean, we report in Fig. 3 the 30 most relevant traits according to Random forests. From this figure, it can be noticed that there is a differentiated small group of 7 features which achieve a mean decrease accuracy of more than 0.7 [1]. These features are, in order of priority, the vein median width (VMeW), the areole minimum solidity (AmS), the vein median orientation (VMeO), the vein median volume (VMeV), the number of areoles (AN), the vein maximum volume (VMV) and the total network length (VTNL).

In order to analyze the degree of independence between these 7 features we also computed the correlation matrix for them and concluded that there were not strong correlations ($|r| < 0.9$). Performing classification with only this small subset achieves the accuracies shown in the second row of Table 1.

This small set of 7 uncorrelated features achieves a performance similar to the one obtained by using the 39 original features (the accuracy improves slightly for the white bean while it diminishes a little for the red bean, still providing an improvement of 12.55% over manual classification), having the advantage that they are a reduced number of non-redundant properties and much easier to handle. In both cases the experts achieve a better recognition for soybean, although the automatic procedure has a high degree of accuracy (over 95%).

---

[1] The procedure followed for feature selection is the one suggested by Breiman at http://www.stat.berkeley.edu/~breiman/RandomForests/cc_home.htm#varimp.

Table 1. Accuracy for legume detection using different numbers of relevant features

Number of features	Soybean	White bean	Red bean
39	95.74%	71.51%	85.66%
7	95.50%	72.67%	81.99%
Manual classification	98.29%	66.43%	69.44%

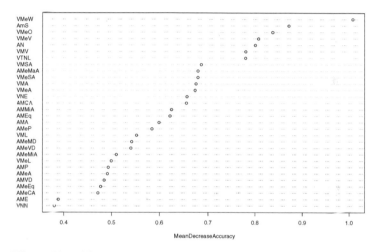

Fig. 3. Variable importance showing the 30 most relevant features

4   Conclusions

In this work we propose an automatic legume recognition procedure based only on the analysis of leaf vein morphology. The leaves are captured using a standard scanner and do not require any clearing or staining treatment. In order to perform segmentation, we used the UHMT and adaptive thresholding. We measured several morphological features on the segmented venation network from a small central patch of the images, and classified them with Random forests.

We found a small subset of 7 uncorrelated features ($|r| < 0.9$) which improve expert manual classification for two of the three classes (white bean and red bean). Although the recognition for soybean is better done by humans, the automatic algorithm achieves over 95% of accuracy. Overall, the automatic method improves the results obtained by human experts, with clear advantages in repetibility, confiability and economy. The 7 relevant features are, in order of priority: the vein median width, the areole minimum solidity, the vein median orientation, the vein median volume, the number of areoles, the vein maximum volume and the total network length.

Since this procedure shows to be successful to identify different legume species, we are currently working on extending this method to separate different cultivars from a single specie.

References

1. Im, C., Nishida, H., et al.: Recognizing plant species by leaf shapes-a case study of the Acer family. In: ICPR, vol. 2, pp. 1171–1173 (1998)
2. Agarwal, G., Ling, H., et al.: First steps toward an electronic field guide for plants. Taxon, J. of the International Association for Plant Taxonomy 55, 597–610 (2006)
3. Camargo Neto, J., Meyer, G.E., et al.: Plant species identification using Elliptic Fourier leaf shape analysis. Comput. Electron. Agric. 50, 121–134 (2006)
4. Du, J.X., Wang, X.F., et al.: Leaf shape based plant species recognition. Applied Mathematics and Computation 185(2), 883–893 (2007), special Issue on Intelligent Computing Theory and Methodology
5. Solé-Casals, J., Travieso, C.M., et al.: Improving a leaves automatic recognition process using PCA. In: IWPACBB, pp. 243–251 (2008)
6. Chaki, J., Parekh, R.: Designing an automated system for plant leaf recognition. Int. Journal of Advances in Engineering & Technology 2(1), 149–158 (2012)
7. Horgan, G.W., Talbot, M., et al.: Towards automatic recognition of plant varieties. In: British Computer Society Electronic Workshops in Computing: The Challenge of Image Retrieval (1998)
8. Perez, A., Lopez, F., et al.: Colour and shape analysis techniques for weed detection in cereal fields. Comput. Electron. Agric. 25, 197–212 (2000)
9. Golzarian, M.R., Frick, R.A.: Classification of images of wheat, ryegrass and brome grass species at early growth stages using principal component analysis. Plant. Methods 7(28) (2011)
10. Bama, B.S., Valli, S.M., et al.: Content based leaf image retrieval (CBLIR) using shape, color and texture features. Indian Journal of Computer Science and Engineering 2(2), 202–211 (2011)
11. Clarke, J., Barman, S., Remagnino, P., Bailey, K., Kirkup, D., Mayo, S., Wilkin, P.: Venation Pattern Analysis of Leaf Images. In: Bebis, G., Boyle, R., Parvin, B., Koracin, D., Remagnino, P., Nefian, A., Meenakshisundaram, G., Pascucci, V., Zara, J., Molineros, J., Theisel, H., Malzbender, T. (eds.) ISVC 2006. LNCS, vol. 4292, pp. 427–436. Springer, Heidelberg (2006)
12. Park, J., Hwang, E., et al.: Utilizing venation features for efficient leaf image retrieval. J. Syst. Softw. 81(1), 71–82 (2008)
13. Valliammal, N., Geethalakshmi, S.: Hybrid image segmentation algorithm for leaf recognition and characterization. In: PACC 2011, pp. 1–6 (July 2011)
14. Sack, L., Dietrich, E.M., et al.: Leaf palmate venation and vascular redundancy confer tolerance of hydraulic disruption. PNAS USA 105, 1567–1572 (2008)
15. Scoffoni, C., Rawls, M., et al.: Decline of leaf hydraulic conductance with dehydration: relationship to leaf size and venation architecture. Plant Physiology 156, 832–843 (2011)
16. Price, C.A., Symonova, O., et al.: Leaf extraction and analysis framework graphical user interface: Segmenting and analyzing the structure of leaf veins and areoles. Plant Physiology 155, 236–245 (2011)
17. Breiman, L.: Random forests. Machine Learning 45, 5–32 (2001)
18. Soille, P.: Morphological Image Analysis: Principles and Applications. Springer (1999)

CAR-NF$^+$: An Improved Version of CAR-NF Classifier

Raudel Hernández-León[1], José Hernández-Palancar[1],
Jesús Ariel Carrasco-Ochoa[2], and José Francisco Martínez-Trinidad[2]

[1] Centro de Aplicaciones de Tecnologías de Avanzada (CENATAV), 7a ♯ 21812
e/ 218 and 222, Rpto. Siboney, Playa, C.P. 12200, La Habana, Cuba
{rhernandez,jpalancar}@cenatav.co.cu
[2] Computer Science Department
Instituto Nacional de Astrofísica, Óptica y Electrónica (INAOE)
Luis Enrique Erro No. 1, Sta. María Tonantzintla, Puebla, CP:72840, México
{ariel,fmartine}@ccc.inaoep.mx

Abstract. In this paper, we propose two improvements to CAR-NF classifier, which is a classifier based on Class Association Rules (CARs). The first one, is a theoretical proof that allows selecting the minimum Netconf threshold, independently of the dataset, that avoids ambiguity at the classification stage. The second one, is a new coverage criterion, which aims to reduce the number of non-covered unseen-transactions during the classification stage. Experiments over several datasets show that the improved classifier, called CAR-NF$^+$, beats the best reported classifiers based on CARs, including the original CAR-NF classifier.

Keywords: Data mining, Supervised classification, Class association rules.

1 Introduction

Associative Classification is a well-known data mining technique that aims to build a classifier based on CARs to determine the class of unseen transactions [1]. A classifier based on CARs usually consists in computing an ordered CAR list l, and applying a mechanism for classifying unseen transactions using l [1,2,6,10,14,15]. Nowadays, Associative Classification is been used in real world applications, such as detection of breast cancer [11], prediction of protein-protein interaction types [12] and prediction of consumer behavior [13], among others.

In Associative Classification, similar to Association Rule Mining (ARM), a set of items $I = \{i_1, \ldots, i_n\}$, a set of classes C, and a set of labeled transactions D, are given. Each transaction in D is represented by a set of items $X \subseteq I$ and a class $c \in C$. The Support of an itemset $X \subseteq I$ is the fraction of transactions in D containing X (see Eq. 1). A CAR is a expression $X \Rightarrow c$, where $X \subseteq I$ and $c \in C$. The interest of a CAR $X \Rightarrow c$ is usually evaluated using the Support and Confidence measures (see Eq. 2 and Eq. 3), where Support is the fraction of transactions in D containing $X \cup \{c\}$ and Confidence is the probability of finding

L. Alvarez et al. (Eds.): CIARP 2012, LNCS 7441, pp. 455–462, 2012.

c in transactions containing X.

$$Sup(X) = \frac{|D_X|}{|D|} \tag{1}$$

where D_X is the set of transactions in D containing X and $|\cdot|$ represents the cardinality.

$$Sup(X \Rightarrow c) = Sup(X \cup \{c\}) \tag{2}$$

$$Conf(X \Rightarrow c) = \frac{Sup(X \Rightarrow c)}{Sup(X)} \tag{3}$$

Several authors have mentioned some drawbacks of these measures [3,8,15]. In order to overcome these drawbacks, in [15], the authors introduced the use of the Netconf measure (see Eq. 4) instead of Support and Confidence for computing the CARs, and additionally, they proved that a Netconf threshold value of 0.5 avoids ambiguity at classification stage. However, they did not prove that, independently of the dataset, 0.5 is the minimum Netconf threshold value that avoids ambiguity at the classification stage. Two CARs are ambiguous if they have the same antecedent implying different classes.

$$Netconf(X \Rightarrow Y) = \frac{Sup(X \Rightarrow Y) - Sup(X)Sup(Y)}{Sup(X)(1 - Sup(X))} \tag{4}$$

At the classification stage, in order to classify an unseen transaction t, the best rules covering t are selected. In previous works [1,2,15], a CAR $X \Rightarrow c$ satisfies or covers a transaction t iff the transaction t contains all the items of X. Furthermore, in these works when no rule covers a transaction, the default class (majority class in all cases) is assigned, which could influence positively or negatively the results, hiding the real classification accuracy.

In this paper, we introduce and prove a new proposition, which guarantees to use the minimum Netconf threshold that avoids ambiguity at the classification stage, independently of the dataset. Additionally, we propose a relaxed coverage criterion, which allows to reduce the number of non-covered unseen-transactions. The relaxed coverage criterion together with the use of the introduced proposition allows CAR-NF$^+$ to have better accuracy than HARMONY, DDPMine and CAR-NF, the best classifiers based on CARs reported in the literature.

2   Our Proposal

In this section we introduce the improvements made to CAR-NF classifier. As was mentioned above, in [15], the authors introduced and proved the following proposition:

Proposition 1. *Let $C = \{c_1, c_2, \ldots, c_m\}$ be the set of predefined classes, for each itemset X we can obtain at most one rule $X \Rightarrow c_k$ $(c_k \in C)$ with Netconf value greater than 0.5.*

Based on this proposition, if we set the Netconf threshold to 0.5, we can avoid ambiguity at the classification stage. However, in [15] it was not proved that, for all datasets, 0.5 is the minimum Netconf threshold value that avoids ambiguity at classification stage. In this paper, we propose and prove a more robust proposition that guarantees, no matter the dataset, the minimum Netconf threshold value that must be used for avoiding ambiguity at the classification stage:

Proposition 2. *Let X be an itemset and $C = \{c_1, c_2, \ldots, c_m\}$ be the set of predefined classes, independently of the dataset, we have that:*

a) *If $|C| > 2$ then 0.5 is the minimum Netconf threshold value that avoids ambiguity in CARs having X as antecedent.*
b) *If $|C| = 2$ then 0 is the minimum Netconf threshold value that avoids ambiguity in CARs having X as antecedent.*

Proof.

a) If $|C| > 2$, we just have to find a dataset containing an itemset X where any Netconf value smaller than 0.5 does not avoid ambiguity in CARs having X as antecedent. Suppose a dataset D having m classes $\{c_1, c_2, ..., c_m\}$ such that $|D_{\{c_1\}}| = |D_{\{c_2\}}|, |D_{\{c_3\}}| = ... = |D_{\{c_m\}}| = 1$, and containing the itemset X in all transactions of classes c_1 and c_2, and only in these transactions (see Table 1).

Table 1. Dataset D used for the proof of Proposition 2

Id_transaction	Itemset	Class
t_1	$\cdots X \cdots$	c_1
$\ldots$	$\ldots$	$\ldots$
t_n	$\cdots X \cdots$	c_1
t_{n+1}	$\cdots X \cdots$	c_2
$\ldots$	$\ldots$	$\ldots$
t_{2n}	$\cdots X \cdots$	c_2
t_{2n+1}	$\cdots Y \cdots$	c_3
$\ldots$	$\ldots$	$\ldots$
t_{2n+m-2}	$\cdots Y \cdots$	c_m

In the dataset D, for all Netconf threshold $\alpha < 0.5$ we have two CARs $X \Rightarrow c_1$ and $X \Rightarrow c_2$ having Netconf values greater than α (see Eq. 5).

$$Netconf(X \Rightarrow c_1) = Netconf(X \Rightarrow c_2) = \frac{\frac{n}{2n+m-2} - \frac{2n}{2n+m-2}\frac{n}{2n+m-2}}{\frac{2n}{2n+m-2}(1 - \frac{2n}{2n+m-2})}$$
$$= \frac{\frac{n}{2n+m-2}(1 - \frac{2n}{2n+m-2})}{\frac{2n}{2n+m-2}(1 - \frac{2n}{2n+m-2})} = 0.5 > \alpha \tag{5}$$

Therefore, we can conclude that when we have more than two classes, 0.5 is the minimum Netconf threshold value that avoids CAR ambiguity at classification stage, independently of the dataset.

b) If $|C| = 2$, we first will show that 0 avoids ambiguity by proving that:

$$Netconf(X \Rightarrow c_1) + Netconf(X \Rightarrow c_2) = 0 \qquad (6)$$

Since we have only two classes (c_1 and c_2), and each transaction has one and only one class, the following statements are satisfied:

$$\sum_{i=1}^{2} Sup(X \Rightarrow c_i) = Sup(X) \qquad (7)$$

$$\sum_{i=1}^{2} Sup(\{c_i\}) = 1 \qquad (8)$$

From equations 4, 7 and 8:

$$\sum_{i=1}^{2} Netconf(X \Rightarrow c_i) = \frac{\sum_{i=1}^{2} Sup(X \Rightarrow c_i) - \sum_{i=1}^{2} Sup(X)Sup(\{c_i\})}{Sup(X)(1 - Sup(X))}$$

$$= \frac{\sum_{i=1}^{2} Sup(X \Rightarrow c_i) - Sup(X) \sum_{i=1}^{2} Sup(\{c_i\})}{Sup(X)(1 - Sup(X))} \qquad (9)$$

$$= \frac{Sup(X) - Sup(X) * 1}{Sup(X)(1 - Sup(X))} = 0$$

Therefore, $Netconf(X \Rightarrow c_1) = Netconf(X \Rightarrow c_2) = 0$ or both Netconf values have different signs. In both cases, we can obtain at most one CAR with Netconf value greater than 0, avoiding the ambiguity.

On the other hand, for all Netconf threshold $\alpha < 0$ we can find sets of transactions (see Table 2) where $Netconf(X \Rightarrow c_1) = Netconf(X \Rightarrow c_2) = 0$ and hence, greater than α (see Eq. 10).

$$Netconf(X \Rightarrow c_1) = Netconf(X \Rightarrow c_2) = \frac{\frac{n}{2n+2} - \frac{2n}{2n+2}\frac{n+1}{2n+2}}{\frac{2n}{2n+2}(1 - \frac{2n}{2n+2})} = 0 \qquad (10)$$

Table 2. Set of transactions with only two classes, where CARs $X \Rightarrow c_1$ and $X \Rightarrow c_2$ have a Netconf value equal to 0

Id_transaction	Itemset	Class
t_1	$\cdots X \cdots$	c_1
$\cdots$	$\cdots$	$\cdots$
t_n	$\cdots X \cdots$	c_1
t_{n+1}	$\cdots Y \cdots$	c_1
t_{n+2}	$\cdots X \cdots$	c_2
$\cdots$	$\cdots$	$\cdots$
t_{2n+1}	$\cdots X \cdots$	c_2
t_{2n+2}	$\cdots Y \cdots$	c_2

Therefore, we can conclude that when we have only two classes, 0 is the minimum Netconf value that avoids CAR ambiguity at classification stage, independently of the dataset.

□

Taking into account the previous proposition, we propose to compute the CARs using a Netconf threshold value equal to 0 when we have only two classes, and a Netconf threshold value equal to 0.5 when we have more than two classes.

As it was mentioned in section 1, in previous works, a CAR r covers a transaction t if the antecedent of the rule r is a subset of t (exact coverage). Using this criterium, for the set of interesting CARs shown in Table 3, if you want to classify the transactions $\{i_2, i_3\}$ or $\{i_2, i_3, i_4\}$ then the majority class will be assigned (or the classifier refuses to classify) because, using exact coverage, these transactions will not be covered by any CAR of Table 3 although $\{i_2, i_3\}$ and $\{i_2, i_3, i_4\}$ appear in the antecedents of some rules.

Table 3. Example of a set of interesting CARs

CAR	Netconf
$\{i_1\} \Rightarrow c$	0.53
$\{i_1, i_2\} \Rightarrow c$	0.53
$\{i_1, i_2, i_3\} \Rightarrow c$	0.55
$\{i_1, i_2, i_3, i_4\} \Rightarrow c$	0.57
$\{i_5\} \Rightarrow c$	0.52
$\{i_5, i_6\} \Rightarrow c$	0.54
$\{i_5, i_6, i_7\} \Rightarrow c$	0.54

In order to reduce the number of non-covered unseen-transactions for those cases where the exact coverage does not work, we propose to relax the coverage criterion as follows; given a CAR $X \Rightarrow c$, with $|X| = n \geq 2$, it will cover a transaction t if there is an itemset $X' \subset t$ such that $X' \subset X$ and $|X'| = n - 1$.

Using the relaxed coverage criterion, the transactions $\{i_2, i_3\}$ and $\{i_2, i_3, i_4\}$ of our example would be covered by the CARs $\{i_1, i_2, i_3\} \Rightarrow c$ and $\{i_1, i_2, i_3, i_4\} \Rightarrow c$ respectively. This coverage criterion allows reducing the number of non-covered unseen-transactions, which could positively influence the results. The CAR-NF$^+$ classifier is the result of applying the Proposition 2 jointly with the relaxed coverage criterion in the classification phase. Similar to the CAR-NF classifier, CAR-NF$^+$ classifies an unseen transaction t applying the "Best K rules" satisfaction mechanism [15]. We first use the CARs that exactly cover t; if no CAR exactly covers t then CAR-NF$^+$ applies the relaxed coverage criterion. The class with highest average Netconf is assigned to t. If there is a tie, one of the tied classes is randomly assigned. If no rule covers t (exactly or not), CAR-NF$^+$ refuses to classify t, and such abstentions are counted as errors.

3   Experimental Results

In this section, we present the results of our experimental comparison between CAR-NF$^+$ and the main classifiers based on CARs reported in the literature: HARMONY [6], DDPMine [10] and CAR-NF[15]. The codes of DDPMine and CAR-NF were provided by their authors and for HARMONY, we used the accuracy values reported in [6]. All our experiments were done using ten-fold cross-validation reporting the average over the ten folds. The same folds were used for

Table 4. Classification accuracy

Dataset	HARMONY	DDPMine	CAR-NF	CAR-NF+
adult	81.90	82.82	83.42	**84.50**
anneal	91.51	90.86	93.43	**95.38**
breast	**92.42**	86.53	85.26	85.43
connect4	**68.05**	67.80	62.18	62.18
dermatology	62.22	63.42	78.78	**79.66**
ecoli	63.60	64.25	82.36	**84.01**
flare	75.02	77.10	86.31	**86.45**
glass	49.80	53.61	67.89	**68.92**
heart	56.46	57.19	56.79	**57.34**
hepatitis	83.16	82.29	85.87	**87.02**
horseColic	82.53	81.07	83.25	**83.56**
ionosphere	92.03	**93.25**	84.34	86.02
iris	93.32	94.03	**96.67**	**96.67**
led7	74.56	73.98	74.53	**75.88**
letRecog	**76.81**	76.12	71.14	73.42
mushroom	99.94	**100.00**	99.52	99.52
pageBlocks	91.60	93.24	92.44	**94.93**
penDigits	96.23	**97.87**	78.04	78.32
pima	72.34	75.22	77.65	**78.53**
waveform	80.46	**83.83**	74.68	75.22
Average	79.20	79.72	80.73	**81.65**

all classifiers. All the tests were performed on a PC with an Intel Core 2 Duo at 1.86 GHz CPU with 1 GB DDR2 RAM, running Windows XP SP2.

Similar to other works [1,2,6,10,15], we used several datasets, specifically 20 datasets also reported in [6,10,15]. The chosen datasets were originally taken from the UCI Machine Learning Repository [9], and their numerical attributes were discretized by Frans Coenen using the LUCS-KDD [4] discretized/normalized ARM and CARM Data Library.

In Table 4, the results show that CAR-NF+ yields an average accuracy higher than all other evaluated classifiers, having a difference of 0.92% with respect to the classifier in the second place (CAR-NF). The used datasets have between 2 and 26 classes [15]. In order to show the accuracy of CAR-NF+ on the different datasets, we grouped them according to the number of classes, in three groups: (1) datasets with 2 or 3 classes; (2) datasets with 4,5, 6 or 7 classes and (3) datasets with more than 7 classes. In Table 5, we report the average accuracy of CAR-NF+ and CAR-NF (the second best) classifiers over these three groups of datasets. From Table 5, we can see that CAR-NF+ obtained the best results, independently of the number of classes in the datasets.

Table 5. Average accuracy of CAR-NF and CAR-NF+ over datasets grouped by number of classes

# classes	CAR-NF	CAR-NF+
2 or 3	85.63	**86.27**
4, 5, 6 or 7	75.25	**76.40**
more than 7	78.48	**79.62**

In Table 6, we show the percent of abstentions and the accuracy of CAR-NF⁺ using exact coverage and relaxed coverage. When we used relaxed coverage, CAR-NF⁺ had, in average, 1.26% less abstentions than using exact coverage and its average accuracy was improved in 0.82%. Additionally, in Table 6, we highlight the datasets with only two classes in order to show how using 0 as Netconf threshold improves the accuracy results (see the accuracy of the original CAR-NF classifier, in Table 4, for the highlighted datasets).

Table 6. Percentage of abstentions (%Abst.) and accuracy (Acc.) of CAR-NF⁺ using exact coverage (EC) and relaxed coverage (RC)

| | CAR-NF⁺ (EC) | | CAR-NF⁺ (RC) | |
Dataset	%Abst.	Acc.	%Abst.	Acc.
adult	1.55	**83.76**	0.44	84.50
anneal	3.46	93.43	0.99	95.38
breast	6.84	**85.32**	5.56	85.43
connect4	0.86	62.18	0.85	62.18
dermatology	5.16	78.78	3.34	79.66
ecoli	1.98	82.36	0.33	84.01
flare	1.20	86.31	1.04	86.45
glass	4.15	67.89	2.60	68.92
heart	5.13	56.79	3.67	57.34
hepatitis	2.87	**86.45**	0.72	87.02
horseColic	2.72	**83.25**	1.81	83.56
ionosphere	5.70	**85.12**	3.80	86.02
iris	1.48	96.67	0.74	96.67
led7	2.19	74.53	0.49	75.88
letRecog	3.01	71.14	0.56	73.42
mushroom	0.27	**99.52**	0.23	99.52
pageBlocks	3.19	92.44	2.50	94.93
penDigits	6.19	78.04	5.70	78.32
pima	4.63	**77.91**	3.04	78.53
waveform	1.96	74.68	0.96	75.22
Average	3.23	80.83	1.97	81.65

Table 7. Pairwise comparison between all evaluated classifiers. Each cell (i, j) contains the number of datasets where the classifier i significantly Win/Lose to the classifier of column j, over the 20 selected datasets.

	HARMONY	DDPMine	CAR-NF	CAR-NF⁺
HARMONY		2/7	4/11	4/13
DDPMine	7/2		5/9	5/12
CAR-NF	11/4	9/5		0/7
CAR-NF⁺	13/4	12/5	7/0	

Finally, in order to determine if the results shown in Table 4 are statistically significant, we performed a pairwise comparison between all tested classifiers. Each cell (i, j) in Table 7 contains the number of datasets where the classifier of row i significantly Win/Lose to the classifier of column j. We detected ties using a one-tailed T-Test [7] with significance level of 0.05. The results in the pairwise comparison reveal that CAR-NF⁺ beats in accuracy all other evaluated classifier, including CAR-NF, over most of the tested datasets.

4   Conclusions

In this paper, an improved version of the CAR-NF classifier, called CAR-NF$^+$, was presented. CAR-NF$^+$ combines the use of an appropriated Netconf threshold value that avoids ambiguity at classification stage with a novel relaxed coverage criterion, which reduces the number of non-covered unseen-transactions. Experiment results show that CAR-NF$^+$ beats the best classifiers based on CARs reported in the literature, including the original CAR-NF classifier.

References

1. Liu, B., Hsu, W., Ma, Y.: Integrating classification and association rule mining. In: Proceedings of the KDD, New York, NY, USA, pp. 80–86 (1998)
2. Li, W., Han, J., Pei, J.: CMAR: accurate and efficient classification based on multiple class-association rules. In: Proceedings of the ICDM, pp. 369–376 (2001)
3. Berzal, F., Blanco, I., Sánchez, D., Vila, M.A.: Measuring the accuracy and interest of association rules: A new framework. Intelligent Data Analysis 6(3), 221–235 (2002)
4. Coenen, F.: The LUCS-KDD discretised/normalised ARM and CARM Data Library (2003), http://www.csc.liv.ac.uk/~frans/KDD/Software/LUCS-KDD-DN
5. Ahn, K.I., Kim, J.Y.: Efficient Mining of Frequent Itemsets and a Measure of Interest for Association Rule Mining. Information and Knowledge Management 3(3), 245–257 (2004)
6. Wang, J., Karypis, G.: HARMONY: Efficiently mining the best rules for classification. In: Proceedings of SDM, pp. 205–216 (2005)
7. Demšar, J.: Statistical Comparisons of Classifiers over Multiple Data Sets. J. Mach. Learn. Res. 7, 1–30 (2006)
8. Steinbach, M., Kumar, V.: Generalizing the notion of confidence. Knowl. Inf. Syst. 12(3), 279–299 (2007)
9. Asuncion, A., Newman, D.J.: UCI Machine Learning Repository (2007), http://www.ics.uci.edu/~mlearn/MLRepository.html
10. Cheng, H., Yan, X., Han, J., Philip, S.: Yu: Direct Discriminative Pattern Mining for Effective Classification. In: Proceedings of the ICDE, pp. 169–178 (2008)
11. Karabatak, M., Ince, M.C.: An expert system for detection of breast cancer based on association rules and neural network. Expert Syst. Appl. 36, 3465–3469 (2009)
12. Park, S.H., Reyes, J.A., Gilbert, D.R., Kim, J.W., Kim, S.: Prediction of protein-protein interaction types using association rule based classification. BMC Bioinformatics 10(1) (2009)
13. Bae, J.K., Kim, J.: Integration of heterogeneous models to predict consumer behavior. Expert Syst. Appl. 37, 1821–1826 (2010)
14. Hernández, R., Carrasco, J.A., Martínez, J.: Fco. and Hernández, J.: Classifying using Specific Rules with High Confidence. In: Proceedings of the MICAI, pp. 75–80 (2010)
15. Hernández, R., Carrasco, J.A., Martínez, J.F., Hernández, J.: CAR-NF: A Classifier based on Specific Rules with High Netconf. Intelligent Data Analysis 16(1) (2012)

Recognition of Patterns of Health Problems and Falls in the Elderly Using Data Mining

Bogdan Pogorelc[1,2,3] and Matjaž Gams[1,2,3]

[1]Jožef Stefan Institute, Department of Intelligent Systems, Ljubljana, Slovenia
[2] Špica International d. o. o.
[3] Jozef Stefan International Postgraduate School, Slovenia
{bogdan.pogorelc,matjaz.gams}@ijs.si

Abstract. We present a generalized data mining approach to the detection of health problems and falls in the elderly for the purpose of prolonging their autonomous living. The input for the data mining algorithm is the output of the motion-capture system. The approach is general since it uses a k-nearest-neighbor algorithm and dynamic time warping with the time series of all the measurable joint angles for the attributes instead of a more specific approach with medically defined attributes. Even though the presented approach is more general and can be used to differentiate other types of activities or health problems, it achieves very high classification accuracies, similar to the more specific approaches described in the literature.

Keywords: health problems, activities, falls, elderly, machine learning, data mining.

1   Introduction

The number of elderly people in the developed countries is increasing [19], and they tend to lead isolated lives away from their offspring. In many cases they fear being unable to obtain help if they are injured or ill. In recent decades this fear has resulted in research attempts to find assistive technologies to make the living of elderly people easier and more independent. The aim of this study is to provide ambient assistive-living services to improve the quality of life of older adults living at home.

We propose a generalized approach to an intelligent care system to recognize a few of the most common and important health problems in the elderly, which can be detected by observing and analyzing the characteristics of their movement.

It is a two-step approach as shown in Figure 1. In the first step it classifies the person's activities into five activities, including two types of falls. These are: fall (F), unconscious fall (UF), walking (W), standing/sitting (SS), lying down/lying (L). In the second step it classifies classified walking instances from the first step into five different health states: one healthy (N) and four unhealthy. The types of abnormal health states are: hemiplegia (H), Parkinson's disease (P), pain in the leg (L), pain in the back (B).

L. Alvarez et al. (Eds.): CIARP 2012, LNCS 7441, pp. 463–471, 2012.

The movement of the user is captured with a motion-capture system, which consists of tags attached to the body, whose coordinates are acquired by sensors located in the apartment. The output time series of the coordinates are modeled with the proposed data-mining approach in order to recognize the specific activity or health problem. The architecture of the system is presented in Figure 1.

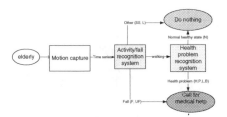

Fig. 1. Architecture of the system

In related studies the motion is normally captured with inertial sensors [18, 1], computer vision and also with a specific sensor for measuring the angle of joint deflection [15] or with electromyography [20]. In our study an infra-red (IR) sensor system with tags attached to the body [5] was used.

We do not only address the recognition of activities of daily living, such as walking, sitting, lying, etc. and the detection of falling, which has been addressed many times [3, 10], but also the recognition of health problems based on motion data.

Using a similar motion-capture system to that in our approach, the automatic distinction between health problems such as hemiplegia and diplegia is presented [9]. However, a much more common approach to the recognition of health problems is the capturing of movement that is later manually examined by medical experts [15, 4, 12]. Such an approach has a major drawback in comparison to ours, because it needs to be constantly monitored by medical professionals.

The paper [11] presented a review of assistive technologies for care of the elderly. The first technology consists of a set of alarm systems installed at people's homes. The system includes a device in the form of a mobile phone, a pendant or a chainlet that has an alarm button. They are used to alert and communicate with a control center. However, such devices are efficient only if the person recognizes the emergency and has the physical and mental capacity to press the alarm button. The second technology presented in [11] is video-monitoring. The problems of the presented solution are ethical issues, since elderly users do not want to be monitored by video [3]. Moreover, such an approach requires the constant attention of the emergency center. Miskelly [11] also presented a technology based on health monitors. The health monitor continuously monitors the pulse, skin temperature and movement. At the beginning of the system's use, the pattern for the user is learned. Afterwards, any deviations are detected and alarms are sent to the emergency center. Such a system detects collapses, faints, blackouts, etc.

Another presented technology is the group of fall detectors. They measure the accelerations of the person using tags worn around the waist or the upper chest. If the accelerations exceed a threshold during a time period, an alarm is raised and sent to the community alarm service. Bourke et al. [2] presented the acceleration data produced during the activities of daily living and when a person falls. The data was acquired by monitoring young subjects performing simulated falls. In addition, elderly people performed the activities of daily living. Then, by defining the appropriate threshold it is possible to distinguish between the accelerations during falls and the accelerations produced during the normal activities of daily living. In this way accelerometers with a threshold can be used to monitor elderly people and recognize falls. However, threshold-based algorithms produce mistakes, for instance, quickly standing up from or sitting down on a chair could result in crossing the threshold, which is erroneously recognized as a fall.

Perolle et al. [13] described an elderly-care system that consists of a mobile module worn by the user all the time that is able to locate the user, detect falls and monitor the user's activity. In addition, this device is connected to a call center, where the data is collected, analyzed, and emergency situations are managed. The mobile module is worn on a belt. It produces an alarm, provides the possibility to cancel it, shows the battery status, etc. In addition, it monitors the user activity and gives it three classifications: low, medium and high. Once a day, the data is sent to the call center for analysis.

The studies [14, 21] differentiate between the same five health states as presented in this study, but are more specific due to the use of 13 medically defined attributes. The currently presented study instead uses very general attributes of the angles between body parts, allowing the system to use the same attributes and the same classification methods for differentiating between five activities and between five health states.

The aim of this study is to realize an automatic classifier that is able to support the autonomous living of the elderly by detecting falls and health problems that are recognizable through movement. Earlier works (e.g., [7]) describe machine-learning techniques employed to analyze activities based on the static positions and recognized postures of the users. Although these kinds of approaches can leverage a wealth of machine-learning techniques, they fail to take into account the dynamics of the movement. The present work has instead the aim to recognize movements by observing the time series of the movements of the users. Better activity-recognition performance can be achieved by using pattern-matching techniques, which take into account all of the sensors' readings, in parallel, considering their time course.

2   Materials and Methods

2.1   Targeted Activities and Health Problems for Detection

The proposed system uses a two-step approach for the recognition of important situations. All the situations that we are recognizing were suggested by the collaborating medical expert on the basis of occurrence in the elderly aged over 65, the medical significance and the feasibility of their recognition from movements. Thus, in the first step we are recognizing five activities: accidental fall, unconscious fall, walking, standing/sitting, lying down/lying. We are focusing on differentiating between "accidental fall" and "unconscious fall":

- **Accidental fall:** as the name suggests it happens due to an accident. The types of accidental falls are, e.g., stumbling and slipping. If the person does not hurt him/herself after it, he/she does not need medical attention.
- **Unconscious fall:** this happens due to an illness or a short loss of consciousness. In most cases the person who falls in this way needs medical attention.

The other three activities of interest are common activities at home, also known as the activities of daily living (ADL).

In the second step we focused on four health problems and normal walking as a reference in accordance with the suggestions received from the collaborating medical expert. The following four health problems were chosen as the most appropriate [4]:

- **Parkinson's disease:** a degenerative disease of the brain (central nervous system) that often impairs motor skills, speech, and other functions. The symptoms are frequently tremor, rigidity and postural instability. The rate of the tremor is approximately 4–6 Hz. The tremor is present when the involved part(s), usually the arms or neck, are at rest. It is absent or diminished with sleep, sedation, and when performing skilled acts.
- **Hemiplegia:** is the paralysis of the arm, leg and torso on the same side of the body. It is usually the result of a stroke, although diseases affecting the spinal cord and the brain are also capable of producing this state. The paralysis hampers movement, especially walking, and can thus cause falls.
- **Pain in the leg:** resembles hemiplegia in that the step with one leg is different from the step with the other. In the elderly this usually means pain in the hip or in the knee.
- **Pain in the back:** this is similar to hemiplegia and pain in the leg in terms of the inequality of steps; however, the inequality is not as pronounced as in walking with pain in the leg.

The classification into five activities and into five health problems was made using the k-nearest-neighbor machine-learning algorithm and dynamic time warping for the similarity measure.

2.2 Attributes for Data Mining

The recordings consisted of the position coordinates for the 12 tags that were worn on the shoulders, the elbows, the wrists, the hips, the knees and the ankles, sampled at 10 Hz. The tag coordinates were acquired with a Smart IR motion-capture system with a 0.5-mm standard deviation of noise.

From the motion-capture system we obtain the position of each tag in x-y-z coordinates. Achieving the appropriate representation of the user's behavior activity was a challenging part of our research. The behavior needs to be represented by simple and general attributes, so that the classifier using these attributes will also be general and work well on behaviors that are different from those in our recordings. It is not difficult to design attributes specific to our recordings; such attributes would work well on them. However, since our recordings captured only a small part of the whole range of human behavior, overly specific attributes would likely fail on general behavior.

Considering the above mentioned, we designed attributes such as the angles between adjacent body parts: left and right shoulder angles with respect to the upper torso, left and right hip angles with respect to the lower torso, the angle (orientation) of the upper and of the lower torso, left and right elbow angles, left and right knee angles. The angles between body parts that rotate in more than one direction are expressed with quaternions.

2.3   Dynamic Time Warping

We will present dynamic time warping (DTW) as a robust technique to measure the "distance" between two time series [8]. Dynamic Time Warping aligns two time series in such a way that some distance measure is minimized (usually the Euclidean distance is used). Optimal alignment (minimum distance warp path) is obtained by allowing the assignment of multiple successive values of one time series to a single value of the other time series and therefore the DTW can also be calculated on time series of different lengths.

The time series have similar shapes, but are not aligned in time. While the Euclidean distance measure does not align the time series, the DTW does address the problem of time difference. By using DTW an optimal alignment is found among several different warp paths. This can be easily represented if two time series $A = (a_1, a_2, ..., a_n)$ and $B = (b_1, b_2, ..., b_m)$, $a_i, b_j \in R$ are arranged to form a n-by-m grid. Each grid point corresponds to an alignment between the elements $a_i \in A$ and $b_j \in B$. A warp path $W = w_1, w_2, ..., w_k, ... w_K$ is a sequence of grid points where each w_k corresponds to a point $(i, j)_k$ – the warp path W maps elements of sequences A and B.

From all possible warp paths the DTW finds the optimal one [22]:

$$DTW(A, B) = \min_W \left[\sum_{k=1}^{K} d(w_k) \right]$$

The $d(wk)$ is the distance between the elements of the time series.

The purpose of DTW is to find the minimum distance warp path between two time series. Dynamic programming can be used for this task. Instead of solving the entire problem all at once, solutions to sub-problems (sub-series) are found and used to repeatedly find the solution to a slightly larger problem. Let $DTW(A, B)$ be the distance of the optimal warp path between time series $A = (a_1, a_2, ..., a_n)$ and $B = (b_1, b_2, ..., b_m)$ and let $D(i, j) = DTW(A', B')$ be the distance of the optimal warp path between the prefixes of the time series A and B:

$$D(0,0) = 0$$
$$A' = (a_1, a_2, ..., a_i), B' = (b_1, b_2, ..., b_j)$$
$$0 \le i \le n, 0 \le j \le m$$

DTW(A, B) can be calculated using the following recursive equations:

$$D(0,0) = 0$$
$$D(i, j) = \min(D(i-1, j), D(i, j-1), D(i-1, j-1))$$
$$+d(a_i, b_j),$$

The distance between two values of the two time series (e.g. the Euclidean distance) is $d(a_i, b_j)$. The most common way of calculating *DTW(A, B)* is to construct a $n*m$ cost matrix M, where each cell corresponds to the distance of the minimum distance warp path between the prefixes of the time series *A* and *B*:

$$M(i, j) = D(i, j)$$
$$1 \leq i \leq n, 1 \leq j \leq m$$

Procedure starts by calculating all the fields with small indexes and then progressively continues to calculate the fields with higher indexes:

```
for i = 1...n
  for j = 1...m
    M(i,j) = min(M(i-1,j), M(i,j-1), M(i,j)) +
dst(a , b )
```

The value in the cell of a matrix *M* with the highest indexes *M(n,m)* is the distance corresponding to the minimum distance warp path. A minimum distance warp path can be obtained by following cells with the smallest values from *M(n,m)* to *M(1, 1)*.

Many attempts to speed up DTWs have been proposed [17]; these can be categorized as constraints. Constraints limit the minimum distance warp path search space by reducing the allowed warp along the time axis. The two most commonly used constraints are the Sakoe-Chiba Band [16] and Itakura Parallelogram [6].

2.4   Modification of the Algorithm for Multidimensional Classification

The DTW algorithm commonly described in the literature is suitable for aligning one-dimensional time series. This work employed a modification of the DTW, which makes it suitable for multidimensional classification.

First, each time point of the captured time series consisting of the positions of the 12 tags coming out of the motion-capture system is transformed into angle attribute space, as defined before. The classification is then performed in the transformed space.

To align an input recording with a template recording (on which the classifier was trained), we first have to compute the matrix of local distances, *d(i,j)*, in which each element *(i, j)* represents the local distance between the *i*-th time point of the template and the input at the time *j*. Let C_{js} be a generic attribute-vector element relative to a template recording, and Q_{is} be the attribute-vector element relative to a new input recording to recognize, where $1 \leq s \leq N$ is the considered attribute.

For the definition of distance the Euclidean distance was used, defined as follows:

$$d_{Euc} = \sqrt{\sum_{s=1}^{N}\left(C_{js} - Q_{is}\right)^2}$$

The value of the minimum global distance for the complete alignment of the DTW procedure, i.e., the final algorithm output, is found in the last column and row, $D(Tr, Tr)$. The optimal alignment can also be efficiently found by back tracing through the matrix: the alignment path starts from $D(Tr, Tr)$, then it proceeds, at each step, by selecting the cell that contains the minimum cumulative distance between those cells allowed by the alignment path constraints until $D(1, 1)$ is reached.

3   Experiments and Results

The DTW algorithm attempts to stretch and compress an input time series in order to minimize a suitably chosen distance measure from a given template. We used a nearest-neighbor classifier based on this distance measure to design the algorithm as a fall detector and a disease classifier. The classification process considers one input time series, comparing it with the whole set of templates, computing the minimum global distance for each alignment and assuming that the input recording is in the same class of the template with which the alignment gives the smallest minimum global distance (analogous to instance-based learning).

The proposed algorithms were tested with the methodology and the data set described in the study. The 10-fold cross-validation for the 5-nearest-neighbor classifier resulted in a classification accuracy of 97.5 % and 97.6 % for the activities and health problems, respectively.

Table 1 shows the confusion matrices, i.e., how many examples of a certain true class (in rows) are classified in one of five possible classes (in columns). The results show that in the proposed approach false positives/negatives are very rare, i.e., they would not cause many unnecessary ambulance costs. Since the method accurately classified most real health problems, it represents high confidence and safety for its potential use in the care of the elderly.

Table 1. Confusion matrices of k-nearest-neighbor classifier, where in a) F=fall, UF= unconscious fall, W=walking, SS=standing/sitting, L=lying down/lying, and in b) H=hemiplegia, L=pain in the leg, N=normal (healthy) walking, P=Parkinson's disease and B=Pain in the back. Numbers denote the quantity of the classified examples.

		classified as				
		F	UF	W	SS	L
true	F	30	0	0	0	0
class	UF	0	30	0	0	0
	W	1	0	124	1	1
	SS	0	0	0	24	1
	L	0	3	1	0	26

		classified as				
		H	L	N	P	B
true	H	42	2	1	0	0
class	L	0	25	0	0	0
	N	1	0	24	0	0
	P	0	0	0	25	0
	B	0	0	0	0	21

4   Conclusion

This study presented a generalized approach to the discovery of the patterns of health problems and falls in the elderly. It is general in the sense that it does not use specific medically defined attributes but the general approach of a combined k-nearest-neighbor algorithm with multidimensional dynamic time warping. It is a two-step approach. In the first step it classifies the person's activities into five activities, including different types of falls. In the second step it classifies walking patterns into five different health states: one healthy and four unhealthy. Even though the new approach is more general and can also be used to classify other types of activities or health problems, it still achieves high classification accuracies, similar to the more specific kind of approach.

Acknowledgements. This work was partially financed by the European Union, the European Social Fund.

References

1. Bourke, A.K., et al.: An optimum accelerometer configuration and simple algorithm for accurately detecting falls. In: Proc. BioMed., pp. 156–160 (2006)
2. Bourke, A.K., O'Brien, J.V., Lyons, G.M.: Evaluation of a threshold-based tri-axial accelerometer fall detection algorithm. Gait & Posture 26, 194–199 (2007)
3. Confidence Consortium. Ubiquitous Care System to Support Independent Living, http://www.confidence-eu.org
4. Craik, R., Oatis, C.: Gait Analysis: Theory and Application. Mosby-Year Book (1995)
5. eMotion. Smart motion capture system, http://www.emotion3d.com/smart/smart.html
6. Itakura, F.: Minimum prediction residual principle applied to speech recognition. IEEE Transactions on Acoustics, Speech and Signal Processing 23(1), 67–72 (1975)
7. Kaluža, B., Mirchevska, V., Dovgan, E., Luštrek, M., Gams, M.: An Agent-Based Approach to Care in Independent Living. In: de Ruyter, B., Wichert, R., Keyson, D.V., Markopoulos, P., Streitz, N., Divitini, M., Georgantas, N., Mana Gomez, A. (eds.) AmI 2010. LNCS, vol. 6439, pp. 177–186. Springer, Heidelberg (2010)
8. Keogh, E., Ratanamahatana, C.A.: Exact indexing of dynamic time warping. Knowl. Inf. Syst. 7(3), 358–386 (2005)
9. Lakany, H.: Extracting a diagnostic gait signature. Patt. Recognition 41, 1627–1637 (2008)
10. Luštrek, M., Kaluža, B.: Fall detection and activity recognition with machine learning. Informatica 33, 2 (2009)
11. Miskelly, F.G.: Assistive technology in elderly care. Age and Ageing 30, 455–458 (2001)
12. Moore, S.T., et al.: Long-term monitoring of gait in Parkinson's disease. Gait Posture (2006)
13. Perolle, G., Fraisse, P., Mavros, M., Etxeberria, L.: Automatic fall detection and acivity monitoring for elderly. COOP-005935 – HEBE Cooperative Research Project- CRAFT. Luxembourg (2006)
14. Pogorelc, B., Bosnić, Z., Gams, M.: Automatic recognition of gait-related health problems in the elderly using machine learning. Multimed Tools Appl. (2011), doi:10.1007/s11042-011-0786-1

15. Ribarič, S., Rozman, J.: Sensors for measurement of tremor type joint movements. MIDEM 37(2), 98–104 (2007)
16. Sakoe, H., Chiba, S.: Dynamic programming algorithm optimization for spoken word recognition. IEEE Transactions on Acoustics, Speech and Signal Processing 26(1), 43–49 (1978)
17. Salvador, S., Chan, P.: Toward accurate dynamic time warping in linear time and space. Intell. Data Anal. 11(5), 561–580 (2007)
18. Strle, D., Kempe, V.: MEMS-based inertial systems. MIDEM 37(4), 199–209 (2007)
19. Toyne, S.: Ageing: Europe's growing problem. BBC News, http://news.bbc.co.uk/2/hi/business/2248531.stm
20. Trontelj, J., et al.: Safety Margin at mammalian neuromuscular junction – an example of the significance of fine time measurements in neurobiology. MIDEM 38(3), 155–160 (2008)
21. Dovgan, E., Luštrek, M., Pogorelc, B., Gradišek, A., Burger, H., Gams, M.: Intelligent elderly-care prototype for fall and disease detection from sensor data. Zdrav. Vestn. 80, 824–831 (2011)
22. Strle, B., Mozina, M., Bratko, I.: Qualitative approximation to Dynamic TimeWarping similarity between time series data. In: Proceedings of the Workshop on Qualitative Reasoning (2009)

SVMTOCP: A Binary Tree Base SVM Approach through Optimal Multi-class Binarization

Diego Arab Cohen[1] and Elmer Andrés Fernández[1,2]

[1] Biomedical Data Mining Group, Facultad de Ingeniería,
Universidad Católica de Córdoba, Argentina
[2] CONICET
{diego.arab,elmerfer}@gmail.com

Abstract. The tree architecture has been employed to solve multi-class problems based on SVM. It is an alternative to the well known OVO/OVA strategies. Most of the tree base SVM classifiers try to split the multi-class space, mostly, by some clustering like algorithms into several binary partitions. One of the main drawbacks of this is that the natural class structure is not taken into account. Also the same SVM parameterization is used for all classifiers. Here a preliminary and promising result of a multi-class space partition method that account for data base class structure and allow node's parameter specific solutions is presented. In each node the space is split into two class problem possibilities and the best SVM solution found. Preliminary results show that accuracy is improved, lesser information is required, each node reaches specific cost values and hard separable classes can easily be identified.

Keywords: multi-class classification, SVM, Binary Tree.

1   Introduction

Over the last few years one of the most used techniques to solve binary classification problems (K=2) has been Support Vector Machines (SVM). It has several advantages compared to other competitors. From a data mining point of view it provides much more information about the problem at hand such as class margin, class separability (if it is a hard or soft problem) and which data from the data base was used to build the solution. Its extension to multi-class problems (K >2) relies on transforming the multi-class problem space into several binary space problems, where each of these can now be solved by a single SVM. Different algorithms have been developed for this purpose such as One-against-All (OvA), One-against-One (OvO)[1], Direct Acyclic Graph SVM (DAGSVM)[2] and Binary Tree SVM (BTSVM)[3] . In OVA each class is faced to the rest of the classes resulting in building as much SVM classifiers as available classes. Classification of a new sample is defined according to the maximum output over all SVM classifiers. In OvO and DAGSVM all the classes are contrasted to each other requiring K(K-1)/2 SVM classifiers and a new sample is labeled according to a voting schema. Binary Trees based SVM multi-class follows a quite different approach. Instead of a contrast in a pairwise or OvA fashion, it builds K-1 SVM classifiers and for each of them recursively splits the multi-class space into two "new classes"

L. Alvarez et al. (Eds.): CIARP 2012, LNCS 7441, pp. 472–478, 2012.

for each of the K-1 SVMs. A new sample is labeled according to the label of the reached leaf of the tree. Different methods were proposed to split the multi-class space. They are mainly based on some kind of clustering and re-assignment technique. One of them is named Multistage SVM (MSVM), introduced by Liu et al [4]. They proposed to split a multi-class space into a two class space through unsupervised Support Vector Clustering (SVC) [5] and then re-label the samples according to the SVC solution. However this approach requires adjusting SVC parameters to find only two clusters each time. In addition it does not guarantee that the input class structure will be preserved (samples for the same class could be re-labeled to a different class) and the resulted tree may not be balanced, requiring, in addition, a balancing step. A second one called Binary Tree SVM (BTS) [3], randomly choses a pair of classes and then builds SVM classifiers for these two and "re-classifies" the remaining samples according to this SVM. Then, re-classified samples feed the child nodes of the previous one, repeating the process until a leaf is reached. Although this approach does not require SVC, it does not solve the drawbacks of the MSVM. The third approach is also a re-assignation procedure, but instead of randomly choosing two classes from the original space to build the SVM classifier, it applies a kind of k-means algorithm with $k=2$, using as a starting point the "gravity centres" of the two most disjointed classes and then reassigning remaining samples to these two classes. However, In order to build "gravity centres" in a feature space it is required to know the mapping function and this is not always the case as in the Gaussian kernel SVMs and it does not take into account class structure as in previously mentioned strategies.

Here we propose a new approach to split a K>2 multi-class problem into two class problem for each node in the tree by looking for the input class combinations that produce the best SVM performance in a specific tree node. This implies to solve for node "i"

$$L_i = \eta \cdot \frac{K_i!}{r!(K_i - r)!} \tag{1}$$

binary problems, where $\eta=1$ for K odd and 0.5 for K even and r=[K/2]. Once the best solution if found for node "i" r classes are passed to the child nodes and the process repeated until reaching a leaf. Despite the training phase is time and computationally expensive, the proposed approach always produces a balanced tree and the original class structure is preserved. The last property is very important from a Data Mining point of view because the reached solution allows identifying which of the class combinations provides soft or hard margin solutions (tree nodes could have different kernel parameters) and automatically identifies what are the most difficult input classes to split. These are very important properties for data analysts who need to extract hidden knowledge from a multivariate data base.

2   Support Vector Machines

Here we briefly present the SVM theory. Support vector machines are learning machines with a very nice theoretical background, the Statistical Learning Theory, which provides insights through which can then be used to improve the performance in practical real applications [6]. In the classification context, SVM provides a way to find

Maximal Margin Hyperplane giving a specific configuration of the machine. In a general setting, the learning algorithm finds the optimum weight vector that solves the following problem: Given the set of samples $\{(\mathbf{x}_i, y_i)\}_{i=1}^{N}$ where $\mathbf{x_i} \in R^p$ is the input pattern for the ith example and $y_i \in \{-1,1\}$ the desired class response, the Hyperplane that separate the data should satisfy

$$y_i\left(\mathbf{w}^T\mathbf{x}_i + b\right) \geq 1 + \xi \tag{2}$$

where the weight vector $\mathbf{w} \in R^p$ and the slack variable ξ allows the incorporation of some errors in the solution. The weight vector $\mathbf{w}$ can be obtained by the minimization of (primal form)

$$\Phi(\mathbf{w},\xi) = 0.5 \cdot \|\mathbf{w}\|^2 + C\sum_{i=1}^{N}\xi_i \tag{3}$$

constrained to Eq.1. By the introduction of Lagrange multipliers the problem can be formulated in the dual form as

$$\Phi(\alpha) = \sum_{i=1}^{N}\alpha_i + 0.5\sum_{i=1}^{N}\sum_{j=1}^{N}\alpha_i\alpha_j y_i y_j \mathbf{x}_i^T\mathbf{x}_j \tag{4}$$

Subject to the constrains

$$\sum_{i=1}^{N}\alpha_i y_i = 0 \tag{5}$$

$$0 \leq \alpha_i \leq C \text{ for } i=1,2,..,N.$$

Where C, the cost parameter, is a user specified positive value. In practice if all $\alpha_i <$ C, the data set can be linearly separated without error (all ξ_i =0) and the problem is said to be a "hard-margin" problem" if not, a "soft-margin" one. The bridge between primal and dual form is given by

$$\mathbf{w} = \sum_{i=1}^{N}\alpha_i y_i\mathbf{x}_i = \sum_{i\in SV}\alpha_i y_i\mathbf{x}_i \tag{6}$$

where SV is the set of input vectors for which $\alpha_i \neq 0$ (the support vectors). The squared norm of the weight vector can be calculated as

$$\|\mathbf{w}\|^2 = \sum_{i=1}^{N}\alpha_i - \frac{\|\alpha\|^2}{C} \tag{7}$$

and the maximum distance between the closest patterns in the hyper-geometrical space R^p is given by

$$2\gamma = \frac{2}{\|\mathbf{w}\|^2} \tag{8}$$

[7] In the case of a "hard margin" solution the second term of Eq. 7 vanishes.

3   SVM Tree Structure

The proposed method uses multiple SVMs arranged in a binary tree structure [3,7] (See Fig.1)). Each node in the tree will constitute the solution of a binary problem which represents a particular partition of the multiclass space. In order to find the best solution of a particular binary problem the best partition of the K classes should be found. At node "i" the class space is split in $L_i = c \cdot \dfrac{K_i!}{r!(K_i - r)!}$ disjoint partitions.

Each partition is solved by an optimized SVM and the one with the best performance (i.e less error and less number of support vectors) is chosen to represent this "i-th" node in the tree. For instance, if we have four classes ($K=4$) $mc=\{A,B,C,D\}$ they are divided in $L_i = 0.5 \cdot \dfrac{4!}{2!\,2!} = 3$ binary problems, i.e $\{A,B\}$vs$\{C,D\}$, $\{A,C\}$vs$\{B,D\}$

and $\{A,D\}$vs$\{B,C\}$. Then $L_i = 3$ SVMs trained in the root node, and from these binary problems (partitions) the one achieving the lowest error rate and the fewest amount of support vectors will represent the root node. Then a $K/2=2$ class problem is passed to each of its child nodes. If $K=5$, ten (10) SVMs are required in the root node, then 3 classes will be passed to the left child node and 2 classes to the right child (or vice-versa).

For each of the I_{-i} SVM, the best SVM cost C (eq.3) is found. In order to avoid expensive cross validation procedures, we chose the SVMpath algorithm [8]. This algorithm permits setting the best cost for Linear and Gaussian kernels without cross validation. The proposed algorithm was implemented in R (www.r-project.org) using svmpath and e1071 libraries. The last one is based on the well known LibSVM C++ library [9].

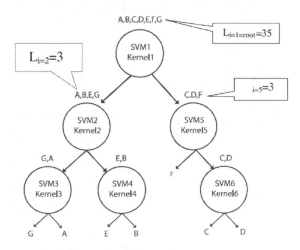

Fig. 1. A seven class problem example

4   Training and Validation

In this work, even though all the SVM parameters could be optimized, the unique tuned SVM parameter was the cost C of eq.3. In this context the used kernel function was radial /Gaussian with $\delta=1$ in all cases. For SVM OVO, the "svm" and "tune.svm" functions were used to set the optimum C cost value (they are available in the e1071 R library). The C value was spanned into the [C_{min} , C_{max}] range. If the best achieved SVM implies a cost equal to C_{min} or C_{max}, the process was repeated expanding the C range until the best SVM satisfied $C_{min} < C < C_{max}$.

For the SVMTree algorithm proposed here, the svmpath function from the "svmpath" R library was used. This algorithm fits the entire path of SVM solutions for every value of the cost parameter, with essentially the same computational cost as fitting one SVM model [8].

In all cases a 5-fold cross validation over 80% of the data base was applied to evaluate the reached solution over different partitions of the data base, and the remaining 20% of the data was used to test the final model.

4.1   Data Sets

Three well known UCI repository data sets were used - Iris, Glass and Yeast, see table 1 for a description of each one.

5   Results

In Table 1, performance of the best 5-fold cross validation models are shown. It is possible to observe that SVMTOCP achieves lowers or almost equal prediction errors but much less support vectors (between 6% and 15% less than in the OVO case). This means a robust solution through the SVMTOCP algorithm. In addition, it is clear that the solution for each of the binary problems does not necessarily imply the same cost. The last columns of Table 1 could range for low to high cost values. The TOCP strategy also achieves higher Hard Margin Solutions (HMS) than OVO strategy.

Table 1. Data Base summary (N: #samples, Cls: #classes and Vars: #variables) and SVM strategy performance (%Err: percentage error, %SV: percentage of SV over the total number of training samples, %HMS: Percentage of Hard Margin Solutions)

Data Base	N	Classes	Vars	SVM multiclass strategy							
				OVO				TOCP			
				%Err	%SV	C	%HMS	%Err	%SV	C [min-max]	%HMS
Iris	150	3	3	6.66	44.2	3	50	0	40	[0.9 -30.83]	50
Glass	216	6	10	41.8	82.5	5	60	39.6	77.7	[0,55 – 39.79]	60
Yeast	1479	10	9	41.9	93.6	5	11	43.6	79.6	[0.24 -90.1]	56

In Fig. 2 the SVMTOCP achieved for Yeast data set is shown. The tree is balanced and no further step is required. The class structure is preserved, meaning that no sample re-allocation is necessary providing a way to identify those classes more difficult to separate from each other (a nice property from an information discovery point of view). For instance in the Yeast data set, classes NUC and CYT are, despite having several data points, very difficult to separate, remaining together until the corresponding leaf has been reached. This conclusion can be achieved since their solution requires a high C value and produces large classification errors.

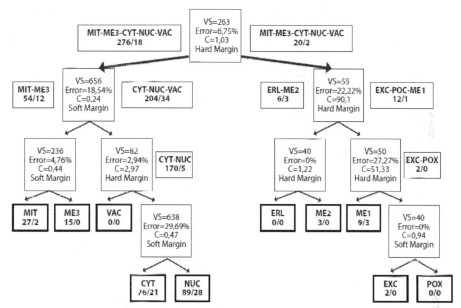

Fig. 2. SVMTOCP for Yeast data set. Square box contains class decision and an amount of correct/bad classification over 20% of testing data. It is also possible to see which nodes achieve a hard margin solution.

6 Conclusion and Future Work

The proposed method is computationally expensive; however it can be easily parallelized (work in progress) by speeding up the best SVM selection for each node. The proposed splitting method always produces a balanced tree and at the end of the training process $K-1$ SVM classifiers are obtained and at most $[\log_2 K]$ SVMs are required to consult to classify a new sample. The achieved solution requires a lesser number of support vectors favorably impacting in the margin width and in solution robustness. It has been shown that the SVM for each node does not necessarily require the same cost parameters as in the previously published SVM tree based methods as well as in OVO, OVA and DAGSVM strategies.

From a Data Mining point of view, this method has several advantages. For instance, any kind of kernel could be used in each node and then, each one treated as an independent problem over the rest. By exploring nodes, it is possible to query if a particular class partition reaches a hard ($0 < \alpha_i < C$) or soft ($0 < \alpha_i \leq C$, i.e at least some $\alpha_i = C$) margin solution. In addition, the classes that remain together deep in the tree are those most difficult to classify or separate. For instance for the Yeast Data Set a higher number of hard margin solutions were achieved (i.e: linear separable cases) compared to OVO. This information is very important when analyzing large data bases in high dimensional problems, providing useful information for the problem at hand.

Further work is required to fully evaluate error performance, since a particular solution (particular C value) could also imply choosing a particular kernel parameter (the gamma parameter in case of Gaussian/Radial kernel). Also optimizing the other kernel parameters could improve the reached solution as in the other strategies such as OVO and OVA. This will also be evaluated.

References

1. Rifkin, R., Klautau, A.: Defence of OneVs.-All Classification. Journal of Machine Learning 5, 101–141 (2004)
2. Platt, C.N., Shawe-Taylor, J.: Large margin DAGSVMs for multiclass classification. In: Advances in Neural Information Processing System, vol. 12, pp. 547–553 (2000)
3. Fei, B., Liu, J.: Binary Tree of SVM: A New fast Multiclass Training and Classification algorithm. IEEE Trans. on Neural Networks 17, 3 (2006)
4. Madzarov, G., Gjorgjevikj, D., Chorbev, I.: A multi-class SVM Classifier Utilizing Binary Decision Tree. Informatica 33, 233–241 (2009)
5. Liu, X.P., Xing, H., Wang, X.: A multistage support vector machine. In: Proc. 2nd Conf. on Mach. Learning and Cybernetics, Xi'an (2003)
6. Ben-Hur, A., Horn, D.: Support vector Clustering. The Journal of Machine Learning Research Archive 2(3/1) (2002)
7. Cristianini, N., Shawe-Taylor, J.: An introduction to Support Vector Machines and other kernel-based learning methods. Cambridge Univ. Press (2000)
8. Gjorgji, M., Dejan, G., Ivan, C.: A Multiclass SVM Classifier Utilizing Binary Decision Tree. Informatica 33, 233–241 (2009)
9. Hastie, T.: http://www-stat.stanford.edu/~hastie/Papers/svmpath.pdf
10. Chang, C.C., Lin, C.J.: LIBSVM: a library for support vector machines. ACM Transactions on Intelligent Systems and Technology 2, 27:1–27:27 (2011)

On the Comparison of Structured Data

Jyrko Correa-Morris[1] and Noslen Hernández[2]

[1] Institute for Pure and Applied Mathematics (IMPA), RJ - Brazil
[2] Advanced Technologies Application Center (CENATAV) - Cuba
jyrkoc@gmail.com, nhernandez@cenatav.co.cu

Abstract. This paper introduces a theoretical framework to characterize measures on structured data. We firstly describe the lattice of structured data. Then, four basic and intuitive properties which any measure
on structure data must fulfill are formally introduced. Metrics and kernel
functions are studied as particular cases of (dis)similarity measures. In
the case of metrics we prove that the well-known edit distances meet all
the desirable properties. We also give sufficient conditions for a kernel
function to satisfy those properties. Some examples are given for particular kinds of structured data.

Keywords: structured data, kernel functions, metrics.

1 Introduction

Structured data can be found everywhere. These sophisticated data provide the
technical machinery for modeling problems in which, besides observations and
measurements, we are interested in representing relations. For this reason, they
are very useful in many fields of pattern recognition, artificial intelligence and
computer vision. Some examples are the applications they found in biometrics [1–
4], image processing and image segmentation [5], clustering [6], object detection,
information retrieval, document analysis [7], among others.

In most of the aforecited applications, to compare objects represented by some
kind of structured data is a primary task. Many measures have been proposed for
comparing these data [8–13]. To decide what measure can be more appropriate
for a particular problem is a challenge. A measure is good in as much as it solves
the problem at hand. However, there are intuitive properties that any good
measure should fulfills independently of the problem being solved. That's why
this work does not focus on introducing a new criterion to comparing structured
data, but on providing some theoretical elements that allow characterizing what
a competent measure is, as well as a better understanding of the various classes
of existing measures for structured data.

In order to characterize a good measure for comparing structured data we
must first know in detail the space in which such data lie and then to formulate
which properties would be desirable for such a measure. With this as a guiding philosophy, this paper introduces four simple intuitive properties which any
measure on structured data must meet. These properties are based on the lattice

L. Alvarez et al. (Eds.): CIARP 2012, LNCS 7441, pp. 479–486, 2012.

structure of all spaces of structured data (e.g., the space of strings, the space of graphs, etc.). Recall that a lattice is a pair $(L, \preceq)$ formed by a set L and an order relation $\preceq$ (i.e., a reflexive, antisymmetric, and transitive binary relation) such that any pair of elements in L has a supremum (or joint) and an infimum (or meet), both in L. For any space of structured data we count with a natural order relation which is closely connected to the intrinsic notion of (dis)similarity, say "is a substructure of". Several existing measures for comparing structured data are studied on the basis of the introduced properties.

The rest of the paper is organized as follows. Section 2 briefly describes the lattice of structured data. In section 3, the desirable properties for measures on structured data are introduced. Section 4 studies metrics and kernels as special kind of measures. Finally, some conclusions are drawn in Section 5.

2   The Lattice of Structured Data

Structured data represents relations between objects in a determined environment. For example, given an alphabet A we have the set $\mathcal{S}_A$ of all possible strings whose characters lie in A; given a finite set X we have the set $\mathcal{G}_X$ of all possible graphs with vertices in X, and the set $\mathcal{P}_X$ of all possible partitions of X. When we refer to a set of structured data without taking into account the explicit form of its element, we write S_X. We frequently use this notation to state results which are valid both for strings, graphs, partitions, and so on.

S_X is naturally endowed with an order structure: we say that $s \in S_X$ is less or equal than $s' \in S_X$ if s is a substructure of s', in notation $s \preceq s'$. This order relation takes a specific form in each of the aforementioned sets: in $\mathcal{S}_A$, $s \preceq s'$ if s is a substring of s', while in $\mathcal{G}_X$ (resp. $\mathcal{P}_X$), $s \preceq s'$ if s is a subgraph of s' (resp. s refines s'). Notice that given any two structures s and s', not necessarily one of them is a substructure of the other. If this is the case, we say that s and s' are not *comparable*.

The relation $\preceq$ on S_X has another important property: given two any structures s and s' it is always possible to find a structure $s \wedge s'$ which is both a substructure of s and s'; and if any other structure s'' has this property then, s'' is a substructure of $s \wedge s'$. This structure $s \wedge s'$ is called the *meet* of s and s'. Note that $s \wedge s'$ keeps what is common to both structures.

3   Structural Properties

Let Γ be a dissimilarity measure on S_X, we will require that Γ satisfy the following properties:

Property 1. (Symmetry) Γ is symmetric.

This property is a standard requirement for any measure responsible for the comparison of the dissimilarity between two objects belonging to a data set. It is based on the simple fact that the likeness among objects does not depend on the order in which they are selected.

Property 2. (Collinear monotonicity) If $s \preceq s' \preceq s''$ then, $\Gamma(s, s') \leq \Gamma(s, s'')$.

What is the intuition behind this property? If we have a structure s and we gradually transform s into $\hat{s}$ by adding more structure on it, then the dissimilarity between s and $\hat{s}$ increases as the structure $\hat{s}$ grows. Thinking of s' and s'' as being two instances of $\hat{s}$, s' with less structure than s'', the property arises.

Property 3. (Dual collinear monotonicity) If $s \preceq s' \preceq s''$ then, $\Gamma(s'', s) \leq \Gamma(s'', s')$.

This property is analogous to the previous. The difference is that in this case we transform the structure s'' by removing structure. Then, the dissimilarity with respect to s'' increases as the structure declines.

Property 4. (Meet predominance) For all $s, s' \in S_X$, $\Gamma(s, s \wedge s') \leq \Gamma(s, s')$.

This property is based on the principle that the dissimilarity between two objects is determined by the things they have in common. The characteristics that concern only one of them just make the difference. Since $s \wedge s'$ only includes what is common to s and s', the property is natural.

The important point to note here is that these properties furnish some guidelines for the proper performance of a measure to compare structured data. They formalize the fact that the "is a substructure of" relation induces an organization of the elements in S_X which is compatible with the most elementary notion of dissimilarity. Hereafter, we will refer to these properties as $P1, P2, P3$ and $P4$, respectively.

Another property that could also be included in the above group is collinear additivity: if $s \preceq s' \preceq s''$ then $\Gamma(s, s'') = \Gamma(s, s') + \Gamma(s', s'')$. We instead enunciate $P2$ and $P3$ which capture the essence of collinear additivity, without requiring additivity because this condition can be in general very restrictive. Nevertheless, whenever appropriate, reference to it will be made.

Note also that the property perhaps more intuitive and basic of any dissimilarity measure was not included among the introduced properties. This is because it is a consequence of $P1 - P4$, as it is shown in the following Lemma.

Lemma 1. *Let Γ be a dissimilarity measure on S_X that satisfies $P1-P4$. Then, for all $s, s' \in S_X$, $\Gamma(s, s) \leq \Gamma(s, s')$. That is, no object is more similar to a given object s than the same s.*

Proof. Indeed, if $s \preceq s'$ then the result follows clearly from $P2$. If $s' \preceq s$ then the result is immediate from $P3$. Now, if s and s' are not comparable, then by applying $P4$ we have that $\Gamma(s, s \wedge s') \leq \Gamma(s, s')$. Since $s \wedge s' \preceq s$, this case is reduced to that previously analyzed. We thus get $\Gamma(s, s) \leq \Gamma(s, s \wedge s') \leq \Gamma(s, s')$, which completes the proof.

Although those properties were only introduced for dissimilarity measures, all of them have an analogous to similarity measures. It is easily seen that if we reverse the order of the inequality in $P2 - P4$, then such analogous properties are obtained.

4   Metrics and Kernels for Structured Data

In this section some of the existing measures for structured data are studied in terms of the introduced properties. Given that metrics and kernels are honorable representatives of the classes of dissimilarity and similarity measures, respectively; we studied them separately.

4.1   Metrics

Among the most flexible measures for comparing structured data are the edit distances. They have as a tenet to compare structured data by counting the structural distortions (also referred as edit transformations) needed to obtain one structure from another. By structural distortion we mean a change in the structure of the datum (e.g., to insert a character in a string, to insert a vertex in a graph, etc.). Each edit distance has its proper set τ of edit transformations allowed to be performed. The next theorem shows that an edit distance with all its edit transformation being invertible, meets all of the properties afore-introduced.

Theorem 1. *Let τ be a set of invertible edit transformations. Let Γ be the edit distance so that for all $s, s' \in \mathrm{S}_X$, $\Gamma(s, s')$ is the minimum number of τ-distortions needed to transform s into s'. Then, Γ satisfies all of the properties $P1 - P4$. In addition, Γ is a metric.*

Proof. The symmetry of Γ follows immediately from the fact that all edit transformations in τ are invertible. Thus, if for transforming s into s', we need to apply $\tau_i \in \tau$ n_i times; then by applying the inverse transformation τ_i^{-1} also n_i times, we transform s' into s. This gives $P1$.

Consider now $s \preceq s' \preceq s''$. If the edit transformation $\tau_i \in \tau$ is required to transform s into s', then it is also needed in the process of transforming s into s''. This is because edit transformations are those changes to be performed with the purpose of transforming one structure into another, so since the structure of s is contained in s' and the structure s' is contained in the structure of s'', to pass from s to s' is part of the process of passing from s to s''. This proves $P2$. The same argument shows that $P3$ holds.

In order to prove $P4$ it suffices to note that when we transform s into s' we firstly need to remove from s everything that is not in s''. Thereafter it only remains in s what is common to s and s'. This is just $s \wedge s'$. We thus get P4.

Finally, since Γ is a non-negative and symmetric function, what is left is to show that (1) $\Gamma(s, s') = 0$ if and only if $s = s'$, and (2) Γ satisfies the triangular inequality. (1) is immediate from the fact that we do not need to perform any edit transformations if and only if $s = s'$. (2) is a consequence of the fact that when we transform s into s'' and after s'' into s', then we obtain s' from s. This process requires $\Gamma(s, s'') + \Gamma(s'', s')$ edit transformations to be done. Because $\Gamma(s, s')$ is the minimum number of edit transformations needed to obtain s' from s, we can conclude that $\Gamma(s, s') \leq \Gamma(s, s'') + \Gamma(s'', s')$. This completes the proof.

Note that in this case we can say more: any edit measure satisfying the hypotheses of Theorem 1 meets the collinear additivity property.

Let see now applications of Theorem 1 to some particular examples.

Example 1. (An edit distance for strings)
Let Γ_s be the edit distance in $\mathcal{S}_A$ whose set of edit transformations is $\tau_s = \{\tau_1, \tau_2\}$, where τ_1 is to insert a character, and τ_2 is to remove a character. Since τ_1 and τ_2 are inverses of each other, Theorem 1 has the following corollary.

Corollary 1. Γ_s *satisfies* $P_1 - P_4$.

Example 2. (An edit distance for graphs)
In the case of graphs, we consider the traditional edit distance Γ_g which has edit transformations: τ_1: insert a vertex, τ_2: remove a vertex, τ_3: insert an edge, and τ_4: remove an edge. Because $\tau_1 = \tau_2^{-1}$ and $\tau_3 = \tau_4^{-1}$, we have the following corollary of Theorem 1.

Corollary 2. Γ_g *fulfills properties* $P_1 - P_4$.

Example 3. (An edit distance for partitions)
Mirkin measure Γ_p is the most known example of edit distance for partitions. Its edit transformations are: τ_1: insert a pair, and τ_2: remove a pair. Again we have $\tau_1 = \tau_2^{-1}$ and therefore, the following corollary.

Corollary 3. Γ_p *fulfills properties* $P_1 - P_4$.

To some extent, these results were expected, because it is known that edit distances are fairly good measures and, as was pointed out before, the required properties are very basics for structured data. For the particular case of partitions, an analogous study was done for Variation of Information metric, Dogen metric and the Classification Error metric [14].

4.2   Kernels

Let us study in this section under what conditions kernel functions for structured data satisfy properties $P1 - P4$.

Theorem 2. *Let k be a kernel function on S_X and φ its feature map (i.e., $k(s, s') = \langle \varphi(s), \varphi(s') \rangle = \sum_i \varphi(s)^i \varphi(s')^i$). If the following conditions hold:*

C1 *For all $s \in S_X$, $\varphi(s)$ has all of its components non-negative;*
C2 *Let $s \prec s'$. If $\varphi(s)^i > 0$ then $\varphi(s)^i \geq \varphi(s')^i > 0$;*
C3 *If $s \prec s' \prec s''$ then,*

$$\sum_i \varphi(s'')^i \varphi(s)^i - \sum_{i, \varphi(s)^i \neq 0} \varphi(s'')^i \varphi(s')^i < \sum_{j, \varphi(s)^j = 0} \varphi(s'')^j \varphi(s')^j;$$

C4 *If $\varphi(s)^i$ and $\varphi(s')^i$ are simultaneously no-null, then also is $\varphi(s \wedge s')^i$;*
then, k satisfies properties $P1 - P4$.

Proof. The proof is a simple verification of the properties $P1 - P4$. Symmetry (i.e., $P1$) follows immediately from the fact that k is kernel.

Now, if $s \preceq s' \preceq s''$ we have that

$$k(s, s') = \sum_i \varphi(s)^i \varphi(s')^i \geq \sum_i \varphi(s)^i \varphi(s'')^i = k(s, s''),$$

because if $\varphi(s'')^i \neq 0$, then $\varphi(s')^i \neq 0$, and condition $C2$ assures that $\varphi(s')^i > \varphi(s'')^i$. This shows that k satisfies $P2$.

Using condition $C3$ we obtain

$$k(s'', s') = \sum_{i, \varphi(s)^i \neq 0} \varphi(s'')^i \varphi(s')^i + \sum_{j, \varphi(s)^j = 0} \varphi(s'')^j \varphi(s')^j > \sum_i \varphi(s'')^i \varphi(s)^i,$$

and as the last term equals $k(s'', s)$, we thus get $P3$.

It remains to prove that k satisfies $P4$. Since $k(s, s \wedge s') = \sum_i \varphi(s)^i \varphi(s \wedge s')^i$ and $k(s, s') = \sum_i \varphi(s)^i \varphi(s')^i$, we can use condition $C4$ for getting that $k(s, s \wedge s')$ has more no-null terms than $k(s, s')$. Moreover, by virtue of condition $C2$, we also have that $\varphi(s \wedge s')^i > \varphi(s')^i$. Therefore, we can conclude $k(s, s \wedge s') > k(s, s')$.

As the reader may have noticed, the previous theorem has an analogous one which is a consequence of simple variations on conditions $C2$ and $C3$.

Theorem 3. *If in addition of conditions $C1$ and $C4$, the following statements hold:*

C'2 *Let $s \prec s'$. If $\varphi(s')^i > 0$ then $\varphi(s')^i \geq \varphi(s)^i > 0$.*
C'3 *If $s \prec s' \prec s''$ then,*

$$\sum_i \varphi(s)^i \varphi(s'')^i - \sum_{i, \varphi(s'')^i \neq 0} \varphi(s)^i \varphi(s')^i < \sum_{j, \varphi(s'')^j = 0} \varphi(s)^j \varphi(s')^j.$$

Then k satisfies properties $P1 - P4$.

Example 4. (Kernel for partitions)
Perhaps the simplest example of a kernel that satisfies Theorem 2 is given by the set significance based kernels for partitions (see [12]). The significance $\mu(A/P)$ of subset $A \subseteq X$ with respect to a partition P of X is defined as $\frac{|A|}{|C|}$, provided that there exists a cluster C of P containing A, and 0 otherwise. Putting all subsets of X in a determined order $A_1, A_2, \ldots, A_{2^n}$, n the number of objects in X, we can assign the vector V_P whose i^{th} component is $\mu(A_i/P)$ to the partition P. Thus, $k(P, P') = \langle V_P, V_{P'} \rangle$.

The fulfillment of conditions $C1 - C4$ of Theorem 2 is a consequence of the following fact: if $P \preceq P'$, then the clusters of $\mathcal{P}$ are smaller than the clusters of $\mathcal{P}'$ and therefore, the component associated to the subset A_i in V_P (if non-null) is greater than its analog in $V_{P'}$. However, as there are subsets $A_i's$ contained in a cluster of P', but not in a cluster of P, $V_{P'}$ has more non-null components than V_P. We thus get the following corollary.

Corollary 4. *The set significance based kernel satisfies P1-P4.*

Example 5. (Kernel for graphs. A counterexample)
An example of a kernel that has an arbitrary behavior with respect to properties $P1 - P4$ is the selection prototypes based kernels [10]. These kernels use the edit distance (see Section 2) to compare each graph g with a set $T = \{t_1, t_2, \ldots, t_m\}$ of prototypes, and thus, to associate g with the vector V_g whose i^{th} component is $\Gamma_g(g, t_i)$. The similarity between two graphs g and g' is then computed as the inner product between V_g and $V_{g'}$. We shall evince that these kernels, although defined from the edit distance which is a measure as good and flexible as expected, do not meet any of the properties $P2 - P4$, whatever the prototypes.

Let $g \prec g'$. If for obtaining g from a prototype t_i we need to add a vertex or an edge to t_i, then this vertex or edge is also needed to be added when obtaining g' from t_i. We can not make the same claim in the case where a vertex or an edge needs to be removed from t_i because it is possible that such vertex or edge is not in g, but does in g'. This is the reason why $d_g(t_i, g)$ and $d_g(t_i, g')$ do not always have the same order, and as a consequence the kernel fails to satisfy properties $P2 - P4$.

For instance, consider $t_1 = \{V_1 = \{v_1, v_2, v_3\}, E_1 = \{(v_1, v_2), (v_2, v_3)\}\}$ and $t_2 = \{V_2 = \{v_1, v_2, v_3, v_4\}, E_2 = V_2 \times V_2 - Diag(V_2)\}$ as prototypes, and set:

$$g = \{V = \{v_1, v_2\}, E = \{(v_1, v_2)\}\},$$
$$g' = \{V' = \{v_1, v_2, v_3\}, E' = \{(v_1, v_2), (v_1, v_3)\}\} \cong t_1,$$
$$g'' = \{V'' = \{v_1, v_2, v_3, v_4, v_5\}, E'' = E_2 \bigcup \{(v_1, v_5), (v_4, v_5)\}\}.$$

It is easily seen that $V_g = (2, 7)$, $V_{g'} = (0, 5)$, and $V_{g''} = (8, 3)$, and hence, $P2$ and $P3$ fails.

What this example is trying to illustrate is that given any set of prototypes we can always find graphs making the properties fail. This is not difficult to achieve and the reader can easily construct their own examples. It is worthy to mention that these kernels can easily be introduced in the partitions and strings scopes, and even in these scenarios they continue having the same deficiencies.

Although we do not have a rigorous proof, we feel that the marginalized kernels for comparing labeled graphs [9] satisfy the desired properties $P1 - P4$.

5   Conclusions

Structured data are becoming increasingly important in many applications. Although various measures for comparing structured data have been introduced, there is a lack for theoretical studies analyzing what a good measure is and how we could choose-between different measures. The present paper is an attempt to provide a theoretical framework for characterizing measures on structured data. For this, four basic and intuitive properties that must fulfill such kind of measures were formally introduced. On the basis of these properties, different existing measures were studied. It was shown how competent measures, as for example the edit distances, fulfilled all the properties. It can be concluded that the introduced theoretical framework is useful not only in the development of new measures but also in the analysis and understanding of the existing ones. For the case of kernel functions, this work establishes sufficient conditions that a kernel function must meets in order to fulfill the introduced properties. A comparative study including the analysis of more measures can be done as future work.

References

1. Chen, H., Jain, A.K.: Dental biometrics: Alignment and matching of dental radiographs. IEEE Trans. Pattern Anal. Mach. Intell. 27(8), 1319–1326 (2005)
2. Dinu, L.P., Sgarro, A.: A low-complexity distance for dna strings. Fundam. Inform. 73(3), 361–372 (2006)
3. Zhu, E., Hancock, E.R., Ren, P., Yin, J., Zhang, J.: Associating Minutiae between Distorted Fingerprints Using Minimal Spanning Tree. In: Campilho, A., Kamel, M. (eds.) ICIAR 2010, 235–245. LNCS, vol. 6112, Springer, Heidelberg (2010)
4. Dinu, L.P., Ionescu, R.: A genetic approximation of closest string via rank distance. In: SYNASC, pp. 207–214 (2011)
5. González-Díaz, R., Ion, A., Ham, M.I., Kropatsch, W.G.: Invariant representative cocycles of cohomology generators using irregular graph pyramids. Computer Vision and Image Understanding 115(7), 1011–1022 (2011)
6. Correa-Morris, J., Espinosa-Isidrón, D.L., Álvarez-Nadiozhin, D.R.: An incremental nested partition method for data clustering. Pattern Recognition 43(7), 2439–2455 (2010)
7. Bunke, H., Riesen, K.: Recent advances in graph-based pattern recognition with applications in document analysis. Pattern Recognition 44(5), 1057–1067 (2011)
8. Bunke, H., Shearer, K.: A graph distance metric based on the maximal common subgraph. Pattern Recognition Letters 19(3-4), 255–259 (1998)
9. Kashima, H., Tsuda, K., Inokuchi, A.: Marginalized kernels between labeled graphs. In: Proceedings of the Twentieth International Conference on Machine Learning, pp. 321–328. AAAI Press (2003)
10. Bunke, H., Riesen, K.: A Family of Novel Graph Kernels for Structural Pattern Recognition. In: Rueda, L., Mery, D., Kittler, J. (eds.) CIARP 2007. LNCS, vol. 4756, pp. 20–31. Springer, Heidelberg (2007)
11. Riesen, K., Bunke, H.: Approximate graph edit distance computation by means of bipartite graph matching. Image Vision Comput. 27(7), 950–959 (2009)
12. Vega-Pons, S., Correa-Morris, J., Ruiz-Shulcloper, J.: Weighted partition consensus via kernels. Pattern Recognition 43(8), 2712–2724 (2010)
13. Thor, A.: Toward an adaptive string similarity measure for matching product offers. In: GI Jahrestagung (1), 702–710 (2010)
14. Meila, M.: Comparing clusterings: an axiomatic view. In: ICML, pp. 577–584 (2005)

A Modification of the Lernmatrix
for Real Valued Data Processing

José Juan Carbajal-Hernández[1,2], Luis P. Sánchez-Fernández [2],
Luis A. Sánchez-Pérez[2], Jesús Ariel Carrasco-Ochoa[1],
and José Francisco Martínez-Trinidad[1]

[1] Computer Science Department, National Institute of Astrophysics, Optics and Electronics,
Luis Enrique Erro #1, Santa Maria Tonantzintla, Puebla, México
[2] Center of Computer Research – National Polytechnic Institute. Av. Juan de Dios Bátiz s/n,
Nueva. Industrial Vallejo, Gustavo A. Madero, México D.F., México
juancarvajal@sagitario.cic.ipn.mx

Abstract. An associative memory is a binary relationship between inputs and
outputs, which is stored in an M matrix. In this paper, we propose a
modification of the Steinbuch Lernmatrix model in order to process real-valued
patterns, avoiding binarization processes and reducing computational burden.
The proposed model is used in experiments with noisy environments, where the
performance and efficiency of the memory is proven. A comparison between
the proposed and the original model shows a good response and efficiency in
the classification process of the new Lernmatrix.

Keywords: Associative memories, artificial intelligence, neurocomputing,
pattern processing, classifier.

1   Introduction

An associative memory can be seen as a particular kind of neural network specially
designed to recall output patterns in terms of input patterns that might appear altered
by some kind of noise. Associative memories have demonstrated usefulness in the
pattern processing field and considerable importance in the developed activities of
numerous researchers, mainly in theory, recognition and pattern classification
applications [2]. Karl Steinbuch developed the first associative memory in 1961,
which works as a binary patterns classifier: the Lernmatrix [19, 20]. Researchers have
tackled the problem of generating models of associative memories, achieving
important results [5], [9], [13], [22] – [25]. In 1982, the John Hopfield work was a
very important contribution of research in this field [8], due to Hopfield model works
as an associative memory and as a neural network, unifying both research fields [1].
The Lernmatrix is a crucial precedent in the development of current associative
memories models and is one of the first successful attempts to encode information in
an arrangement, known as crossbar grids [16 – 18].

A particular limitation with data information is that associative memories in
general, are based on processing binary patterns; real values ($\Re$) must be binarized,

L. Alvarez et al. (Eds.): CIARP 2012, LNCS 7441, pp. 487–494, 2012.

which implies huge information loss and high computational burden. In order to resolve this gap, different works implement algorithms for building associative memories with real valued data, using new or classical models as [13] and Vázquez and Sossa [21]. In this sense, the aim of this work is to introduce a new algorithm for storing and recovering real valued patterns in the Lernmatrix.

2   Associative Memories

An associative memory (**M**) is a system of inputs and outputs that relates as follows: $x \rightarrow [M] \rightarrow y$. The input pattern is represented by a column vector denoted as x and the output pattern by a column vector y. The goal of an associative memory is to restore full patterns from input patterns that can be altered [12], [14], [15]. Each input pattern forms an association with the corresponding output pattern as (x, y).

An associative memory **M** is represented by a matrix, whose ij^{th} component is m_{ij}. The **M** matrix is generated by a finite set of associations known as a fundamental set [12]. The set cardinality is denoted as p. For a positive integer μ, the corresponding association will be denoted as follows:

$$\left\{ \left(x^{\mu}, y^{\mu} \right) \middle| \mu = 1,2,...,p \right\} . \tag{1}$$

The patterns that build the fundamental set associations are called fundamental patterns. If it holds that $x^{\mu} = y^{\mu} \ \forall \ \mu = 1,2,...p$, then the memory is autoassociative; otherwise it is heteroassociative. Each column vector that represents an input pattern has n components that fall within the set A, where $A=\{0,1\}$ and each column vector that represents an output pattern has m components that fall within the set A as follows:

$$x^{\mu} \in A^{n} \ and \ y^{\mu} \in A^{m} \ \forall \ \mu = 1,2,...,p . \tag{2}$$

An associative memory works in two clearly established phases:

1.   Learning phase (creation of the associative memory **M**)
2.   Recalling phase (operation of the associative memory **M**)

3   The Steinbuch's Lernmatrix

The Lernmatrix is a heteroassociative memory that works as a classifier of binary patterns if output patterns are properly chosen. It is a system of input-output that accepts as input binary patterns $x^{\mu} \in A^{n}$, and produces output binary patterns such like $y \in A^{m}$ [17], [19], [20]. It should be noted that there are m different classes, each one coded with a single rule: class $k \in \{1, 2,..., m\}$ will be represented by a column vector whose components will be assigned by $y_{k}^{\mu} = 1, y_{j}^{\mu} = 0$ for $j = 1,2,...,k-1,k+1,...,m$.

Learning Phase

The learning phase consists in finding the way to generate a matrix **M** that will store the information of the p associations of the fundamental set $\{(x^{1}, y^{1}),.., (x^{p}, y^{p})\}$ [3],

[4]. The process for determining each of the m_{ij} components can be described following two steps: 1) each of the m_{ij} components of **M** is initialized with zero; 2) each of the m_{ij} components must be updated according the following rule:

$$m_{ij} = m_{ij} + \Delta m_{ij}.$$ (3)

where Δm_{ij} can be computed using the following expression:

$$\Delta m_{ij} = \begin{cases} \varepsilon & if \ x_j^\mu = 1 = y_i^\mu \\ -\varepsilon & if \ x_j^\mu = 0 \ and \ y_i^\mu = 1 \\ 0 & otherwise \end{cases}$$ (4)

where ε is a positive constant previously chosen.

Recalling Phase

The recalling phase consists in determining the corresponding class of an input pattern $x^\omega \in A^n$. Finding the class means to obtain $y^\omega \in A^m$ that corresponds to $x^\omega \in A^n$; according to the methodology for constructing the y^μ patterns, the class should be obtained without ambiguity [10], [15].

The ith component of y^ω can be determined using the following expression, where $\vee$ is the maximum operator.

$$y_i^\omega = \begin{cases} 1 & if \ \sum_{j=1}^n m_{ij} x_j^\omega = \bigvee_{h=1}^m \left[\sum_{j=1}^n m_{hj} x_j^\omega \right] \\ 0 & otherwise \end{cases}.$$ (5)

4   Our Proposed Modification in the Lernmatrix Model

Our proposed algorithm is an addendum to the Lernmatrix learning and recalling phase, since the new algorithm is applied for real valued patterns that will be stored in the associative memory, avoiding the binarization process and reducing computational burden.

4.1   New Learning Phase

The new learning phase consists on storing the original input vector in the associative memory M in order to compute the complete information of real-valued patterns. The process for determining each of the m_{ij} components can be described following the next steps: a) inicialization process can be determined using steps 1 and 2 of section 3; b) Δm_{ij} can be determined using the following expression:

$$\Delta m_{ij} = \begin{cases} x_i & if \ x_i^\mu = 1 = y_i^\mu \\ 0 & otherwise \end{cases}.$$ (6)

where ε is a positive constant previously chosen.

4.2   New Recalling Phase

The following concepts define the steps to follows in order to recover real valued patterns; those concepts are well documented and represent a novelty for the actual associative memory.

Definition 1. Let $A=\{0,1\}$ and $x^{\omega} \in A^n$ be a pattern, then the adjusted vector a_i is defined as follows:

$$a_i = \begin{cases} x_i^{\omega} & if \ x_i^{\omega} \neq 0 \\ \\ \varepsilon & if \ x_i^{\omega} = 0 \end{cases} \tag{7}$$

Definition 2. Let a_i be the adjusted vector, then the inverse vector z_i^{ω} is defined as follows:

$$z_i = \frac{1}{a_i} \ . \tag{8}$$

Definition 3. Let z_i be the inverse vector and m_{ij} be the ij^{th} component of an associative memory M, then the multiplicative matrix q_{ij} can be defined as follows:

$$q_{ij} = m_{ij} \cdot z_j \ . \tag{9}$$

Definition 4. Let q_{ij} be the multiplicative matrix, then the asymptotic matrix s_{ij} can be defined as follows:

$$s_{ij} = \tanh\left(q_{ij} - 1\right) \ . \tag{10}$$

Definition 5. Let s_{ij} be the asymptotic matrix, then the class vector s_i^{ω} is defined as follows:

$$C_i^{\omega} = \sum_{j=1}^{n} \left| s_{ij} \right| \ . \tag{11}$$

Using the previous definitions, it is possible to enunciate the new Lernmatrix recalling rule. The ith component of y^{ω} is computed according to the following rule:

$$y_i^{\omega} = \begin{cases} 1 & if \ C_i^{\omega} = \bigwedge_{h=1}^{m} \left[C_h^{\omega} \right] \\ 0 & otherwise \end{cases} \ . \tag{12}$$

where $\wedge$ is the minimum operator.

5   Numerical Examples

For a better understanding of the proposed algorithm, this section exemplifies the operation of the new Lernmatrix. Due to space limitations, one pattern is recovered in order to show the real-valued Lernmatrix operation; however, the reader can easily recover the rest of the proposed input patterns. Suppose a fundamental set with $p = 3$, $n = 5$ and $m = 3$ and the fundamental associations expressed as ordered pairs: $\{(x^1, y^1), (x^2, y^2), (x^3, y^3)\}$ as follows:

$$
x^1 = \begin{pmatrix} 5.3 \\ 7.2 \\ 1 \\ -4 \\ 1.2 \end{pmatrix} \quad y^1 = \begin{pmatrix} 1 \\ 0 \\ 0 \end{pmatrix} \quad x^2 = \begin{pmatrix} 3.1 \\ -3.2 \\ 0 \\ -5 \\ 2 \end{pmatrix} \quad y^2 = \begin{pmatrix} 0 \\ 1 \\ 0 \end{pmatrix} \quad x^3 = \begin{pmatrix} 4.2 \\ -6.4 \\ -1.3 \\ 2.1 \\ 0 \end{pmatrix} \quad y^3 = \begin{pmatrix} 0 \\ 0 \\ 1 \end{pmatrix}
$$

Learning phase

To create the matrix $\mathbf{M}$ using the p associations of the fundamental set, it is necessary to follow steps 1 and 2 of section 4.1:

Step 1   Step 2

$$
M = \begin{pmatrix} 0 & 0 & 0 & 0 & 0 \\ 0 & 0 & 0 & 0 & 0 \\ 0 & 0 & 0 & 0 & 0 \end{pmatrix} \qquad M = \begin{pmatrix} 5.3 & 7.2 & 1 & -4 & 1.2 \\ 3.1 & -3.2 & \varepsilon & -5 & 2 \\ 4.2 & -6.4 & -1.3 & 2.1 & \varepsilon \end{pmatrix}
$$

In this case, we have chosen $\varepsilon = 0.001$, due to it provides a good performance of our algorithm. Once the learning phase is computed and the associative memory $\mathbf{M}$ is determined, the next step is to compute the recalling phase.

Recalling phase

The recalling phase for the proposed method using the input pattern x^1 is computed using the matrix $\mathbf{M}$. According to Definition 1 and 2, the inverse vectors z_i is calculated using Eq. (7) and (8) as follows:

$$
z^1 = \begin{pmatrix} 0.188 \\ 0.138 \\ 1 \\ -0.25 \\ 0.833 \end{pmatrix}
$$

According to Definition 3, the multiplicative matrices q_{ij} can be computed using expression (9) as follows:

$$
q^1_{ij} = \begin{pmatrix} 5.3 & 7.2 & 1 & -4 & 1.2 \\ 3.1 & -3.2 & \varepsilon & -5 & 2 \\ 4.2 & -6.4 & -1.3 & 2.1 & \varepsilon \end{pmatrix} \begin{pmatrix} 0.188 \\ 0.138 \\ 1 \\ -0.25 \\ 0.833 \end{pmatrix} = \begin{pmatrix} 1 & 1 & 1 & 1 & 1 \\ 5.84 & -0.44 & \varepsilon & 1.25 & 1.66 \\ 0.79 & -0.88 & -1.3 & -0.52 & 0.8\varepsilon \end{pmatrix}
$$

According to Definition 4, the asymptotic matrices s_{ij} can be calculated using (10):

$$
s^1_{ij} = tanh(q^1_{ij} - 1) = \begin{pmatrix} 0 & 0 & 0 & 0 & 0 \\ -0.392 & -0.894 & -0.761 & 0.244 & 0.582 \\ -0.204 & -0.955 & -0.980 & -0.909 & -0.761 \end{pmatrix}
$$

Using Definition 5, the subclass vector C_i^ω is obtained using the expression (11) as follows:

$$
C^1_{ij} = \sum_{j=1}^{n} |s^1_{ij}| = \begin{pmatrix} 0 + 0 + 0 + 0 + 0 \\ 0.392+0.894+0.761+0.244+0.582 \\ 0.204+0.955+0.980+0.909+0.761 \end{pmatrix} = \begin{pmatrix} 0 \\ 2.876 \\ 3.810 \end{pmatrix} \rightarrow \begin{pmatrix} 1 \\ 0 \\ 0 \end{pmatrix} \rightarrow y^1
$$

Finally, the output class y^ω is obtained according to expression (12).

6   Experimental Results

Noise can be defined as the presence of an undesirable signal, since it degrades the accuracy and precision of analysis [11]. In binary codes, noise can appear in different forms. When one or several zeros are changed to one, it is known as additive noise. When one or several ones are changed to zero, it is known as subtractive noise. The combination between additive and subtractive noise is known as combined noise [6], [7]. In this case, true color images (24 bits image depth) of flowers (Fig. 1) with a 65 × 65 pixel resolution were used as fundamental set in order to estimate the performance of the proposed algorithm with real data information. A true color pixel has a valued range from 0 to 0xFFFFFF. Therefore, additive noise changes the value of selected pixels to the maximum value allowed for RGB pixels (0×FFFFFF). Subtractive noise changes the value of selected pixels to the minimum value allowed for RGB pixels (0×000000). Mixed noise changes values of selected pixels to the minimum value or maximum value allowed for RGB pixels randomly. Gaussian noise changes the value of selected pixels between the minimum and maximum value allowed for RGB using a Gaussian distribution function.

A comparison between models (original and proposed) was performed using a database of 20 patterns. Those patterns were binarized for making experiments with the original associative memory. Different levels of mixed and Gaussian noises were introduced in the fundamental pattern set in order to estimate the behavior of the proposed model with a density from 5% to 40% respectively.

Fig. 1. 20 flower images compound the fundamental set of patterns

a)   b)

Fig. 2. Different levels of a) mixed and b) Gaussian noises alter the input patterns (0, 5, 10, 15, 20, 25, 30, 35 and 40% of density)

Table 1. Comparison between the Steinbuch Lernmatrix and the Real-valued Lernmatrix

	Steinbuch Lernmatrix		Real Lernmatrix	
Noise	Combined	Gaussian	*Combined*	*Gaussian*
Density	Recalled patterns	Recalled patterns	*Recalled patterns*	*Recalled patterns*
0%	20	20	*20*	*20*
5%	18	18	*20*	*20*
10%	16	17	*20*	*20*
15%	15	16	*20*	*20*
20%	14	16	*20*	*20*
25%	14	15	*20*	*20*
30%	12	13	*20*	*20*
35%	12	12	*19*	*20*
40%	11	11	*18*	*19*

7   Conclusions

In this paper a modification for building a real valued data classifier was proposed using the Steinbuch's Lernmatrix. This model is one-shot trained and also is capable for storing and recalling real-valued patterns. Algorithms based on the original Lernmatrix work their computational processes only with binary patterns; this behavior increases the computational burden and presents information loss when real-valued patterns must be binarized. The proposed modification to the Lernmatrix worked perfectly with real patterns and increased the effectiveness in the pattern recalling phase against the original associative memory (Table 1).

Experimental results using true-color patterns and with different kinds of noise levels showed good performance on the recalling process of the proposed model and in this case, a better recovering of the input patterns. This improvement to the original Lernmatrix provides an alternative solution for the pattern processing field.

References

1. Abu, M., Jacques, J.: Information capacity of the Hopfield model. IEEE Transactions on Information Theory, IT-31(4), 461–464 (1985)
2. Acevedo, M.: Memorias asociativas bidireccionales alfa – beta. Ph.D. Thesis, Centre of Computer Research, Institute Polytechnic National, Mexico (2006)
3. Amari, S.: Learning patterns and pattern sequences by self-organizing nets of threshold elements. IEEE Transaction on Computers C-21(11), 1197–1206 (1972)
4. Anderson, J., Bower, G.: Memoria Asociativa, México, Limusa (1977)
5. Austin, J.: ADAM: a distributed associative memory for scene analysis. In: Proceedings of First International Conference on Neural Networks, pp. 285–295 (1987)
6. Flores, R., Yáñez, C.: Memorias asociativas alfa beta basadas en código Johnson Möbius modificado. Ms.C. Thesis. Center of Computer Research, Institute Polytechnic National, Mexico (2006)
7. Hassoun, M.: Associative Neural Memories. Oxford University Press, New York (1993)

8. Hopfield, J.J.: Neural networks and physical systems with emergent collective computational abilities. Proceedings of the National Academy of Sciences 79, 2554–2558 (1982)
9. Kohonen, T.: Correlation matrix memories. IEEE Transactions on Computers C-2I(4), 353–359 (1972)
10. Kosko, B.: Bidirectional associative memories. IEEE Transactions on Systems, Man and Cybernetics 18(1), 49–60 (1998)
11. Lidner, D.: Introducción a las señales y los sistemas. McGraw Hill (1997)
12. Palm, G., Schwenker, F., Sommer, F.T., Strey, A.: Neural associative memories. In: Krikelis, A., Weems, C.C. (eds.) Associative Processing and Processors, pp. 307–326. IEEE Computer Society, Los Alamitos (1997)
13. Ritter, G., Sussner, P., Días de León, J.: Morphological associative memories. IEEE Transactions on Neural Networks 9, 281–293 (1998)
14. Román, G., López, I., Yáñez, M.: A new classifier based on Associative Memories. In: Proc. 15th International Conference on Computing CIC, pp. 55–59. IEEE Computer Society, Los Alamitos (2006)
15. Sánchez, F., Días de León, J., Yáñez, C.: Lernmatrix de Steinbuch: condiciones necesarias y suficientes para recuperación perfecta de patrones. Research on Computing Science 10, 91–102 (2002)
16. Sánchez, A., Díaz de León, S., Yáñez, C.: New results on the Lernmatrix properties. Research in Computing Science 10, 91–102 (2004a)
17. Sánchez, A., Díaz de León, S., Yáñez, C.: Lernmatrix de Steinbuch: Avances Teóricos. Computación y Sistemas 7(3), 175–189 (2004b)
18. Simpson, P.K.: Artificial Neural Systems. Pergamon Press, New York (1990)
19. Steinbuch, K.: Die Lernmatrix. Kybernetik 1(1), 36–45 (1961)
20. Steinbuch, K., Frank, H.: Nichtdigitale Lernmatrizen als perzeptoren. Kybernetik 1(3), 117–124 (1961)
21. Vázquez, H., Sossa, H.: A bidirectional hetero-associative memory for true – color patterns. Neural Processing Letters 28, 131–153 (2008)
22. Willshaw, D., Buneman, O., Longuet-Higgins, H.: Non-holographic associative memory. Nature 222, 960–962 (1969)
23. Yáñez, C.: Memorias Asociativas basadas en relaciones de orden y operadores binarios. Ph.D. Thesis. Center of Computer Research, Institute Polytechnic National, Mexico (2002)
24. Yáñez, C., Díaz de León, J.: 2003a. Memorias Autoasociativas Morfológicas max: condiciones suficientes para convergencia, aprendizaje y recuperación de patrones. IT-I75, Serie Azul, CIC-IPN, Mexico (2003) ISBN 970-36-0035-2
25. Yáñez, C., Díaz de León, J.: Memorias Autoasociativas Morfológicas min: condiciones suficientes para convergencia, aprendizaje y recuperación de patrones. IT-I77, Serie Azul, CIC-IPN, Mexico (2003b) ISBN 970-36-0036-0

Automatic Design of Binary W-Operators Using Artificial Feed-Forward Neural Networks Based on the Weighted Mean Square Error Cost Function

Marco Benalcázar[1,2,3], Marcel Brun[1], Virginia Ballarin[1], Isabel Passoni[4],
Gustavo Meschino[4], and Lucía Dai Pra[4]

[1] Grupo de Procesamiento de Imágenes, Universidad Nacional de Mar del Plata, Argentina
[2] Consejo Nacional de Investigaciones Científicas y Técnicas, Argentina
[3] Secretaría Nacional de Educación Superior Ciencia, Tecnología e Innovación, Ecuador
marco_benalcazar@hotmail.com
http://www3.fi.mdp.edu.ar/imagenes
[4] Laboratorio de Bioingeniería, Universidad Nacional de Mar del Plata, Argentina

Abstract. One of the main issues concerning automatic design of W-operators is the one of generalization. Considering the designing of W-operators as a particular case of designing a pattern recognition system, in this work we propose a new approach for the automatic design of binary W-operators. This approach consists on a functional representation of the conditional probabilities for the whole set of patterns viewed by a given window, instead the values of the characteristic function. The estimation of its parameters is achieved by means of a nonlinear regression performed by an artificial feed-forward neural network based on a weighted mean square error cost function. Experimental results show that, for the applications presented in this work, the proposed approach leads to better results than one of the best existing methods of generalization within the family of W-operators, like is the case of pyramidal multiresolution.

Keywords: W-operators, pattern recognition, artificial neural network, nonlinear regression, weighted mean square error, pyramidal multiresolution.

1 Introduction

The W-operators are a class of nonlinear operators, within the domain of Computational Mathematical Morphology [1,2]. The designing process of these operators is based on the estimation of joint probabilities [3], or conditional probabilities [4], for the patterns viewed by a given window. The estimation is made from training examples, formed by pairs of observed and ideal images. Observed images represent the problem to be solved and ideal images correspond to the desired output. Using these probabilities, W-operators are designed and characterized by characteristic functions that minimize some given cost function or error measure.

One of the main issues that appear in the automatic design of W-operators is the one of generalization. It occurs when certain patterns are not found during training.

L. Alvarez et al. (Eds.): CIARP 2012, LNCS 7441, pp. 495–502, 2012.
© Springer-Verlag Berlin Heidelberg 2012

Some approaches have been proposed to circumvent this problem such as: automatic programming of binary morphological machines, pyramidal multiresolution [1], decision trees, genetic algorithms, adaptive algorithms, incremental splitting intervals (ISI), and multilevel training [3].

In this paper we propose a new approach for generalization in the design of W-operators: instead of generalizing the characteristic function, computed from the estimation of the conditional probabilities, we apply artificial neural networks to approximate the conditional probabilities, and then deduce the characteristic function from this approximation. We chose artificial neural networks because of their ability of generalization and because they may generate complex nonlinear boundaries [6]. Finally, the network learning is based on the weighted mean square error (WMSE) cost function [7].

Following this introduction, Section 2 recalls the formulation of the statistical design of binary W-operators. Section 3 describes the proposed approach. In Section 4, we present two application examples, and finally, in Section 5, we summarize this work and outline future possible developments.

2   W-Operators

Let consider a *binary image* as a function $H: E \rightarrow \{0,1\}$, where E is a rectangular subset of $\mathbf{Z}^2$. The set of all possible images from E to $\{0,1\}$ will be denoted by $\{0,1\}^E$. A *point* $t = (x, y)$ of this image, or *pixel*, is a coordinate in E, where x and y are integer numbers. Finally, a *window* $W = \{w_1, w_2, ..., w_n\}$ is another small subset of $\mathbf{Z}^2$, usually including the origin of coordinates of E: $(0,0) \in W$, with $w_k \in \mathbf{Z}^2$, denoting the size of the window W by $n = |W|$.

Given a binary image H, an arbitrary point t of this image, and a window W. A *window configuration*, or *observation* $\mathbf{u}_{H(t)} = (u_1, ..., u_n)$, is a vector composed of n binary values: $u_k \in \{0,1\}$, where each value is defined by $u_k = H(t + w_k)$; i.e., by the image value at the point $w_k + t$ of the window W_t, where W_t denotes the translation of W at the point t: $W_t = \{w + t : w \in W\}$. Thus, $\mathbf{u}_{H(t)}$ can be expressed as follows:

$$\mathbf{u}_{H(t)} = \left(H(w_1 + t), H(w_2 + t), ..., H(w_n + t)\right) \tag{1}$$

Since $\mathbf{u}_{H(t)} \in \{0,1\}^n$, the number of possible observations for a given window W is 2^n. On the other hand, a *W-operator*, $\mathbf{\Psi}$, is a function of the form $\mathbf{\Psi} : \{0,1\}^E \rightarrow \{0,1\}^E$ that, applied to the binary image H, produces other binary image $G = \mathbf{\Psi}(H)$. Moreover, W-operators are characterized by binary functions, called *characteristic functions*, whose form is $\psi : \{0,1\}^n \rightarrow \{0,1\}$, such that, for each point $t \in E$:

$$G(t) = \mathbf{\Psi}(H)(t) = \psi(H(w_1 + t), H(w_2 + t), ..., H(w_n + t)) = \psi(\mathbf{u}_{H(t)}) \tag{2}$$

Finally, W-operators fulfill two important properties: *translation invariance*, which means that $\Psi(H_t)=\Psi(H)_t$; and *local definition* within W, which implies that $\Psi(H)(t)=\Psi(H\cap W_t)(t)$. The last property indicates that knowing only the values of H in the neighborhood of W_t, we can determine the value of $\Psi(H)(t)$ [1,2].

2.1   Statistical Design of Binary W-Operators

To perform the statistical design of W-operators, we model the images to be processed (i.e., observed images) and their desired images (i.e., ideal images) as realizations of two stationary and stochastic processes $\mathbf{O}$ and $\mathbf{I}$, respectively [1,2]. In this context, the goal of the statistical design is to find a W-operator ψ such that, given realizations (I,O) from the processes $(\mathbf{I},\mathbf{O})$, $\psi(O)$ must be as close as possible to I. Using the mean square error (MSE) as the closeness measure between I and $\psi(O)$, we can establish, at the origin of coordinates $(0,0)=0$, the following relationship as the cost function for the statistical design of binary W-operators:

$$MSE = \sum_{\{\mathbf{u}:\,\mathbf{u}\in O\cap W_{(0)}\}} \Pr\big(I(0)\neq \psi(\mathbf{u})\big|\mathbf{u}\big)\Pr(\mathbf{u}) \qquad (3)$$

In the above equation, $\Pr\big(I(0)\neq \psi(\mathbf{u})\big|\mathbf{u}\big)$ is the conditional probability, given the observation $\mathbf{u}\in O\cap W_{(0)}$, that $I(0)$ is different from the result of applying the characteristic function ψ to the observation $\mathbf{u}$; while $\Pr(\mathbf{u})$ represents the marginal probability, or frequency, that $\mathbf{u}$ occurs in the image $O\cap W_{(0)}$. Therefore, the optimal binary W-operator $\Psi_{\mathbf{opt}}$, represented by its characteristic function ψ_{opt}, minimizes equation (3). Formally, ψ_{opt} is defined by the following expression:

$$\psi_{opt}(\mathbf{u})=\begin{cases}1 & \text{if} & \Pr\big(I(0)=1\big|\mathbf{u}\big)\geq \Pr\big(I(0)=0\big|\mathbf{u}\big) \\ 0 & \text{if} & \Pr\big(I(0)=1\big|\mathbf{u}\big)< \Pr\big(I(0)=0\big|\mathbf{u}\big)\end{cases} \qquad (4)$$

Due to the fact that in practice the conditional probabilities $\Pr\big(I(0)=1\big|\mathbf{u}\big)$ and $\Pr\big(I(0)=0\big|\mathbf{u}\big)$ are not known, we may estimate their values using pairs of training images, and then determine the value of the characteristic function $\psi(\mathbf{u})$ by applying equation (4) [2]. On the other hand, in order to use equation (4), the values of $\hat{\Pr}\big(I(0)=1\big|\mathbf{u}\big)$ and $\hat{\Pr}\big(I(0)=0\big|\mathbf{u}\big)$, for a given observation $\mathbf{u}$, need to be known. Since good estimation of probabilities in practice is not always possible because the amount of training data is limited, and also considering that the number of possible window configurations grows exponentially with the size of the window W, we propose to use artificial neural networks to approximate the conditional probabilities for the whole set of window configurations $\{\mathbf{u}_i:\; i=1,...,2^n;\; n=|W|\}$, depending on the available training data, instead of generalizing the class labels of the window configurations.

3   Generalizing Conditional Probabilities Using Artificial Feed-Forward Neural Networks

In this section, we describe the proposed generalization for the automatic design of binary W-operators. This approach consists of finding two functions that, for any window configuration $\mathbf{u}$, approximate the estimated values of the conditional probabilities $\Pr(I(0)=1|\mathbf{u})$ and $\Pr(I(0)=0|\mathbf{u})$. In order to achieve such generalization, we use neural networks, a supervised learning tool from Machine Learning, that are widely used to solve classification and regression problems [6-8]. In our case, the neural networks are used to estimate the parameters of a nonlinear regression.

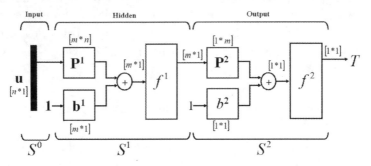

Fig. 1. Three layer artificial feed-forward neural network architecture

Based on the fact that an artificial feed-forward neural network of three layers is capable of approximating any Borel measurable function [9], for the network architecture shown in Fig. 1 (using the representation from [8]), where the layer S^1 is composed of m neurons, with sigmoid transfer functions f^1, and the single one neuron of the layer S^2 has a linear transfer function $f^2(z)=z$, the response T, for an input vector $\mathbf{u}=(u_1,...,u_n)$, is given by the following equation:

$$T(\mathbf{u})= f^2\left(\mathbf{P}^2 f^1\left(\mathbf{P}^1\mathbf{u}+\mathbf{b}^1\right)+b^2\right)=\mathbf{P}^2 f^1\left(\mathbf{P}^1\mathbf{u}+\mathbf{b}^1\right)+b^2 , \qquad (5)$$

where, $\mathbf{P}^1$ and $\mathbf{P}^2$ represent the weight matrices of S^1 and S^2, respectively, whereas $\mathbf{b}^1$ represents the bias matrix of S^1, and b^2 is the bias of S^2.

Moreover, starting from the second axiom of probability, for any observation $\mathbf{u}$, the sum of conditional probabilities must satisfy: $\Pr(I(0)=1|\mathbf{u})+\Pr(I(0)=0|\mathbf{u})=1$. Adding 2δ to both sides of this expression, where $\delta\in\Re^+$ is an infinitesimal number (e.g. the distance between 1 and the closest double-precision number: 2^{-52}), and conveniently grouping terms, we obtain: $(\Pr(I(0)=1|\mathbf{u})+\delta)+(\Pr(I(0)=0|\mathbf{u})+\delta)=1+2\delta$. Then, computing the natural logarithm of the ratio between the two terms on the left side of this equation, we have: $\phi(\mathbf{u})= Ln\left(\dfrac{\Pr(I(0)=1|\mathbf{u})+\delta}{\Pr(I(0)=0|\mathbf{u})+\delta}\right)= Ln\left(\dfrac{\Pr(I(0)=1|\mathbf{u})+\delta}{1-\Pr(I(0)=1|\mathbf{u})+\delta}\right)$. In this equation, if $\delta = 0$, the resulting expression resembles that one used for defining a logistic regression. Also, It is worth noticing that δ allows us to represent, with finite values, the cases when $\Pr(I(0)=1|\mathbf{u})=0$ and $\Pr(I(0)=0|\mathbf{u})=1$, or $\Pr(I(0)=1|\mathbf{u})=1$ and $\Pr(I(0)=0|\mathbf{u})=0$. Furthermore, approximating the right side of equation (5) with the right side of the last expression, we obtain the following relationship that defines a nonlinear regression:

$$Ln\left(\frac{\Pr(I(0)=1|\mathbf{u})+\delta}{\Pr(I(0)=0|\mathbf{u})+\delta}\right) = Ln\left(\frac{\Pr(I(0)=1|\mathbf{u})+\delta}{1-\Pr(I(0)=1|\mathbf{u})+\delta}\right) = \mathbf{P}^2 f^1(\mathbf{P}^1\mathbf{u}+\mathbf{b}^1)+b^2 \tag{6}$$

From the above equation, it follows that the function that generalizes the conditional probability $\Pr(I(0)=1|\mathbf{u})$, for the window configuration $\mathbf{u}$, has the following form:

$$\Pr(I(0)=1|\mathbf{u}) = \frac{\exp(\mathbf{P}^2 f^1(\mathbf{P}^1\mathbf{u}+\mathbf{b}^1)+b^2)(1+\delta)-\delta}{1+\exp(\mathbf{P}^2 f^1(\mathbf{P}^1\mathbf{u}+\mathbf{b}^1)+b^2)}, \tag{7}$$

while $\Pr(I(0)=0|\mathbf{u})$ is generalized by the following expression:

$$\Pr(I(0)=0|\mathbf{u}) = \frac{(1-\exp(\mathbf{P}^2 f^1(\mathbf{P}^1\mathbf{u}+\mathbf{b}^1)+b^2))\delta+1}{1+\exp(\mathbf{P}^2 f^1(\mathbf{P}^1\mathbf{u}+\mathbf{b}^1)+b^2)} \tag{8}$$

Therefore, given the conditional probabilities $\Pr(I(0)=1|\mathbf{u}_j)$ and $\Pr(I(0)=0|\mathbf{u}_j)$, estimated in a first stage of the proposed designing process by means of the relative frequencies $\frac{freq(I=1|\mathbf{u}_j)}{freq(I=0|\mathbf{u}_j)+freq(I=1|\mathbf{u}_j)}$ and $\frac{freq(I=0|\mathbf{u}_j)}{freq(I=0|\mathbf{u}_j)+freq(I=1|\mathbf{u}_j)}$, respectively, with $j=1,...,l$, where l is the total number of different configurations collected by shifting the window in the training images, the goal of a second stage is to estimate the weights $\mathbf{P}^1$ and $\mathbf{P}^2$, and the bias $\mathbf{b}^1$ and b^2 for an artificial feed-forward neural network, using equation (6). Moreover, the network training will be based on the WMSE cost function, allowing us to use the marginal probability, or frequency, $\Pr(\mathbf{u}_j)$ of each observation $\mathbf{u}_j$ collected in the first stage.

3.1   Training an Artificial Feed-Forward Neural Network Based on the Weighted Mean Square Error Cost Function

The use of the WMSE function MSE_W, defined by equation (9), as the cost function for training an artificial neural network has two important advantages compared with the MSE: 1) the noise-contaminated observations have less influence on the cost function and 2) if there are no noisy observations, the network can avoid over-fitting [7].

$$MSE_W = \frac{1}{l}\sum_{j=1}^{l}\left((T(\mathbf{u}_j)-\phi(\mathbf{u}_j))^2 \frac{\Pr(\mathbf{u}_j)}{max(\{\Pr(\mathbf{u}_1),...,\Pr(\mathbf{u}_l)\})}\right) \tag{9}$$

In equation (9), $T(\mathbf{u}_j)$ is the network output, $\phi(\mathbf{u}_j)$ is the expected output and $\Pr(\mathbf{u}_j)$ is the marginal probability with that the observation $\mathbf{u}_j$ appears in the training images.

As in the case of $\Pr(I(0)=1|\mathbf{u})$ and $\Pr(I(0)=0|\mathbf{u})$ that are not known, $\Pr(\mathbf{u})$ is also unknown, therefore, in equation (9) we must work with its estimate $\hat{\Pr}(\mathbf{u})$. Finally, to complete the definition of the network architecture to perform the nonlinear regression, we determined heuristically based on trial and error, that the best results were obtained when the number of neurons of S^1 is $m = 4\sqrt{n}$, where $n = |W|$, and the transfer functions for the neurons of this layer are $f^1 = \text{tansig}(z) = \dfrac{2}{1+\exp(-2z)} - 1$. The method to be employed for the network training is the Levenberg-Marquardt method, using equation (9) as the cost function to be minimized.

4   Experimental Results

In this section, we present two applications of the proposed approach. The goal of the first experiment is to filter the noise in images of retinal angiographies. The angiographies were segmented using an algorithm based on Fuzzy Mathematical Morphology (FMM) [10]. The dataset of this experiment is formed by 4 pairs of observed and ideal images of 565x584 pixels. Observed images are the segmented ones, and their associated ideal images are taken from the DRIVE database [11].

The goal of the second experiment is to detect edges in objects contained in noisy images. For this case, the dataset is composed of 4 noiseless images of the following sizes: 350x156, 300x270, 637x563 and 401x393 pixels. Observed images are obtained adding synthetic salt-pepper noise, with a density of 0.1, to images from the dataset. Each ideal image (i.e., image with the edges) is obtained by applying the morphological gradient $H - \varepsilon_B(H)$ to each noiseless image H, where $\varepsilon_B(H)$ denotes the erosion of the image H by the structuring element B. For the current experiment, we use a square structuring element of size 3x3 pixels (connectivity 8 border).

Table 1 summarizes the results from noise filtering in images of retinal angiographies, both before and after the application of W-operators. According to these values, the proposed approach produces a substantial reduction of noise in the segmentation of angiographies, compared with pyramidal multiresolution, which can be corroborated by the error rate (ER) and the false positive rate (FPR) values. In the case of the false negative rate (FNR), multiresolution has a slight advantage over W-operators designed using neural networks.

Table 1. Results of noise filtering in images of retinal angiographies

	ER [%]	FPR [%]	FNR [%]
Original values (FMM algorithm)	4.53	1.89	32.78
Nonlinear regression with neural network	3.94	1.50	28.86
Pyramidal multiresolution	4.15	1.85	27.66

Fig. 2 shows an example of the generalization with neural networks (Fig. 2-c) and pyramidal multiresolution (Fig. 2-d) to the sample image of Fig. 2-b. The image shown in Fig. 2-b is the result of applying FMM segmentation to image of Fig. 2-a.

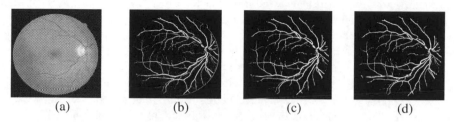

(a)   (b)   (c)   (d)

Fig. 2. (a) Original image, (b) segmented image with FMM; noise filtering by a W-operator based on: (c) neural network and (d) pyramidal multiresolution

Table 2 summarizes the results obtained applying W-operators for edge detection in noisy images. According to the ER, FPR and FNR values, the proposed approach seems more robust to noise compared with pyramidal multiresolution and morphological gradient. Moreover, it is worth noticing that the automatic methods to design W-operators lead to better results than the heuristic method.

Table 2. Results of edge detection in noisy images

	ER [%]	FPR [%]	FNR [%]
Nonlinear regression with neural network	1.55	0.46	17.49
Pyramidal multiresolution	2.17	0.60	24.33
Morphological gradient	22.36	18.37	94.83

Fig. 3 shows an example of the result of applying the generalization with neural networks (Fig. 3-b), pyramidal multiresolution (Fig. 3-c) and morphological gradient (Fig. 3-d) to the sample image of Fig. 3-a.

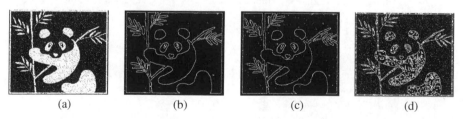

(a)   (b)   (c)   (d)

Fig. 3. (a) Salt-pepper noisy image; edge detection using W-operators based on: (b) neural network, (c) pyramidal multiresolution, and (d) morphological gradient

5   Concluding Remarks

In this paper we have proposed a new approach for the automatic design of binary W-operators. The idea behind this work is to consider the design of W-operators as a particular case of designing a pattern recognition system. Thus, the method consist in the estimation of the parameters of two functions that generalize the conditional probabilities for the whole set of window configurations. The estimation is achieved by nonlinear regression performed by an artificial feed-forward neural network of three layers, whose training is based on the minimization of the WMSE cost function.

This approach allows us to represent W-operators by the parameters of the trained neural network, avoiding the storage of the large amount of data needed to represent characteristic functions, as in techniques like ISI or pyramidal multiresolution.

The experimental results show that, for the examples presented in this work, the proposed approach allows us to achieve better results than one of the best existing methods for the generalization of characteristic functions of W-operators, like is the case of the pyramidal multiresolution.

Further work should include the extension of the proposed method for the automatic design of W-operators to process gray-scale and color images.

References

1. Hirata Jr., R., Brun, M., Barrera, J., Dougherty, E.R.: Aperture filters: theory, application, and multiresolution analysis. In: Advances in Nonlinear Signal and Image Processing, New York (2006)
2. Barrera, J., Banon, G., Dougherty, E.R.: Automatic design of morphological operators. Space Structure and Randomness. In: Bickel, P., Diggle, P., Fienberg, S., Gather, U., Olkin, I. (eds.) LNS, vol. 183, pp. 257–278. Springer (2005)
3. Santos, C., Hirata, N.S., Hirata, R.: An Information Theory framework for two-stage binary image operator design. Pattern Recognition 31(4), 297–306 (2010)
4. Benalcázar, M., Padín, J., Bouchet, A., Brun, M., Ballarin, V.: Diseño Auto-mático de Operadores Morfológicos Aplicado a la Segmentación de Angiograf-ías Retinales. In: JAIIO 2011, Argentina, pp. 137–147 (2011)
5. Hirata Jr., R., Dougherty, E.R., Barrera, J.: Aperture Filters. Signal Processing 80(4), 697–721 (2000)
6. Egmont-Petersen, M., Ridder, D., Handels, H.: Image processing with neural network - a review. Pattern Recognition 35 (2002)
7. Sai, Y., Jinxia, R., Zhongxia, L.: Learning of Neural Networks Based on Weighted Mean Squares Error Function. In: IEEE - Computational Intelligence and Design, pp. 241–244 (2009)
8. Hagan, M., Demuth, H., Beale, M.: Neural Network Design, Boston (1996)
9. Hornik, K., Stinchcombe, M., White, H.: Multilayer feed forward networks are universal approximators. Neural Networks 2(5), 359–366 (1989)
10. Bouchet, A., Brun, M., Ballarin, V.: Morfología Matemática Difusa aplicada a la segmentación de angiografías retinales. Revista Argentina de Bioingeniería 16(1), 7–10 (2001)
11. Staal, J., Abramoff, M., Niemeijer, M., Viergever, M., Van Ginneken, B.: Ridge based vessel segmentation in color images of the retina. IEEE Transactions on Medical Imaging 23(4), 501–509 (2004)

On Using Asymmetry Information
for Classification in Extended Dissimilarity
Spaces

Yenisel Plasencia-Calaña[1,2], Edel B. García-Reyes[1],
Robert P.W. Duin[2], and Mauricio Orozco-Alzate[3]

[1] Advanced Technologies Application Center,
7ma A ♯ 21406, Playa, Havana - 12200, Cuba
`{yplasencia,egarcia}@cenatav.co.cu`
[2] Faculty of Electrical Engineering, Mathematics and Computer Sciences,
Delft University of Technology, The Netherlands
`r.duin@ieee.org`
[3] Departamento de Informática y Computación, Universidad Nacional de Colombia -
Sede Manizales. Kilómetro 7 vía al Aeropuerto, Campus La Nubia – Bloque Q,
Piso 2, Manizales, Colombia
`morozcoa@unal.edu.co`

Abstract. When asymmetric dissimilarity measures arise, asymmetry correction methods such as averaging are used in order to make the matrix symmetric. This is usually needed for the application of pattern recognition procedures, but in this way the asymmetry information is lost. In this paper we present a new approach to make use of the asymmetry information in dissimilarity spaces. We show that taking into account the asymmetry information improves classification accuracy when a small number of prototypes is used to create an extended asymmetric dissimilarity space. If the degree of asymmetry is higher, improvements in classification accuracy are also higher. The symmetrization by averaging also works well in general, but decreases performance for highly asymmetric data.

Keywords: asymmetric dissimilarity, dissimilarity spaces, prototype selection, extended dissimilarity spaces.

1 Introduction

Dissimilarity representations [1] arose as an alternative to feature-based representations when the definition and extraction of good features is difficult or intractable while a robust dissimilarity measure can be defined more easily for the problem at hand. Research in this field has focused on several topics: prototype selection [2,3] or generation [4], classification in dissimilarity spaces [5,6], among others. One open issue corresponds to the information usage in dissimilarity matrices: they can be asymmetric but most of the traditional classification and clustering methods are thought for symmetric dissimilarity matrices. In case

L. Alvarez et al. (Eds.): CIARP 2012, LNCS 7441, pp. 503–510, 2012.

of asymmetry, the typical approach is to symmetrize the matrix with any known symmetrization method, and then apply the methods on the symmetric variant. This might carry a loss of useful information.

Asymmetric dissimilarity or similarity measures can arise in several situations; see [7] for a general analysis of the causes of non-Euclidean data. Measures resulting from a matching process may appear to be asymmetric due to a suboptimal procedure. Also, measures designed using expert knowledge for the problem might not be symmetric. One example is fingerprint matching [3], where measures are often asymmetric. When various dissimilarity matrices are combined, the final matrix can also be asymmetric. One of the most widely used methods for symmetrization is the average method. In [1], before embedding asymmetric dissimilarity matrices into Pseudo-Euclidean spaces, the average method is used to make the matrix symmetric. In [2], the dissimilarity matrix is symmetrized using the average method in order to allow the use of some prototype selection algorithms in the dissimilarity space (DS). Other authors, in the context of kernel-based classification, proposed the use of a positive semidefinite matrix $K^t K$, where K denotes a nonsymmetric kernel [8].

Different variants of the Multidimensional Scaling algorithm have incorporated asymmetry in an intuitive way, by defining a skew symmetric term [9]. In [10], the authors proposed modifications to Self Organizing Map and Sammon Mapping in order to deal with asymmetric proximities showing that the proposed algorithms outperformed their symmetric variants. In [11], the authors compared several symmetrization methods of asymmetric kernel matrices for their use in the context of Support Vector Machines. They also proposed a simple supervised symmetrization method that outperformed the other methods compared.

One question that arises is whether the asymmetry information can be useful for classification in dissimilarity spaces, instead of ignoring it or using a symmetrization method. Another question is how we can use the asymmetry information in the context of classification in dissimilarity spaces. In this paper we propose a new approach for using asymmetry information in what we called the extended asymmetric dissimilarity space (EADS). As the dimension of the EADS space is twice the dimension of the original DS, the use of prototype selection is needed in order to reduce the dimensions before the EADS is constructed. Results are provided comparing classification errors in both the DS and EADS for four standard asymmetric dissimilarity data sets.

2   Dissimilarity Space and Extended Dissimilarity Space

Dissimilarity representations arose from the idea that the classes are constituted by similar objects, so the nearness information is more fundamental than features to discriminate between the classes [1]. In this context, the DS was proposed in [1] as follows. Let $R = \{r_1, r_2, ..., r_k\}$ be the representation set: a collection of prototypes that may be a subset of the training set T. Let d be a dissimilarity measure for the problem at hand. The DS is created by a mapping of the objects to the space defined by the dissimilarities to the prototypes, where each dimension corresponds to the dissimilarities to a given prototype. The representation d_x of an object x is:

$$d_x = [d(x, r_1) \ d(x, r_2) \ ... \ d(x, r_k)].\tag{1}$$

The DS was postulated as a Euclidean vector space, making suitable the use of traditional classifiers for feature spaces like Bayesian ones. The cardinality of the representation set defines the dimension of the DS. For the reduction of the representation set, prototype selection methods are used. They allow one to determine the desired tradeoff between classification accuracy and representation cardinality.

In this section we present the EADS. The motivation for this proposal is that when projecting asymmetric data in the DS, asymmetry information is lost because we only use dissimilarities from the objects to the prototypes, and not from prototypes to objects. If the matrix is previously symmetrized, we are also neglecting the asymmetry present in the data. In order to take advantage of the asymmetry information in both directions, we explore the use of an extended representation of the initial asymmetric dissimilarity matrix in an EADS. We propose to create the EADS using the prototypes selected from the original dissimilarity matrix as it is given. Then, having those prototypes $R = \{r_1, r_2, ..., r_k\}$, the representation of an object in the EADS is defined by:

$$d_x = [d(x, r_1) \ d(x, r_2) \ ... \ d(x, r_k) \ d(r_1, x) \ d(r_2, x) \ ... \ d(r_k, x)].\tag{2}$$

In order to represent the training set and the objects submitted for classification in the EADS, we need to measure the dissimilarities from the objects to the prototypes and from the prototypes to the objects. As a result, the dimension of the EADS space is twice the dimension of the DS. Classifiers can be trained in the EADS in the same way they are trained in the DS.

3   Experiments

In this section the discriminative power of the EADS is compared to the discriminative power of the non-symmetrized version and the one symmetrized by averaging. Classification errors are presented using different numbers of prototypes in DS and EADS. Prototypes are the same for both spaces, but in the DS only dissimilarities in one direction are used. In the EADS, dissimilarities from the two directions are used. This leads to a space of dimension twice the size of the DS dimension.

3.1   Data Sets and Experimental Setup

For the experiments we used four data sets: Chickenpieces-20-60, Chickenpieces-35-45, CoilYork, and Zongker. Some important characteristics of the data sets can be found in Table 1. The Asymmetry column shows an asymmetry coefficient ac for each data set, this was computed using the following equation:

$$ac = \frac{1}{n(n-1)} \frac{\sum |d_{ij} - d_{ji}|}{\min(d_{ij}, d_{ji})}, i = 1...n-1, j = i+1...n, \qquad (3)$$

where n is the number of objects in the data set. We assume that dissimilarities between different objects will not be zero. In case it is known beforehand that in the data it may exist any dissimilarity with value zero between two different objects, a term with a very small value such as 0.0001 must be added in the denominator to avoid the indefinite result of the division by zero.

Table 1. Characteristics of the data sets, the $|X|$ column is the number of training objects, and $|T|$ is the number of test objects

Data sets	# Classes	# Obj. per class	Asymmetry	$\|X\|$	$\|T\|$
ChickenPieces-20-60	5	117,76,96,61,96	0.05	222	224
ChickenPieces-35-45	5	117,76,96,61,96	0.08	222	224
CoilYork	4	4x72	0.009	144	144
Zongker	10	10x200	0.18	400	1600

As classifier it was used the Linear Bayes Normal (BayesL) in both the DS and EADS, it is a simple and fast classifier that is optimal for normally distributed classes with equal covariances. Experiments were repeated twenty times using equal-sized random partitions for training and testing for ChickenPieces and CoilYork data sets, and twenty and eighty percent for training and testing respectively in the Zongker data set. Results were averaged over the twenty experiments. As prototype selectors, two different methods are used: the systematic forward selection optimizing the leave-one-out nearest neighbour error on the training set as in [2] (FS+NN error), and the random selection. The methods selected 5, 10, 15, 20 and 25 prototypes. The BayesL and prototype selectors were trained using the training data, and the classification results were computed in the test set for the DS and EADS generated using the prototypes selected with the different methods. Regularization parameter of BayesL is 0.01.

3.2   Results and Discussion

Figure 1 shows the curves of error rates for increasing number of prototypes in the original asymmetric representation in the DS and the representation in the EADS. Figure 2 shows the curves of error rates for an increasing number of prototypes comparing the symmetrized representation in the DS using the average and the representation in the EADS. Solid lines represent the approaches in EADS; dashed lines represent the approaches in DS. The same symbol is assigned for the results in DS and EADS using the same prototype selector. Standard deviations are between 0.007 and 0.08.

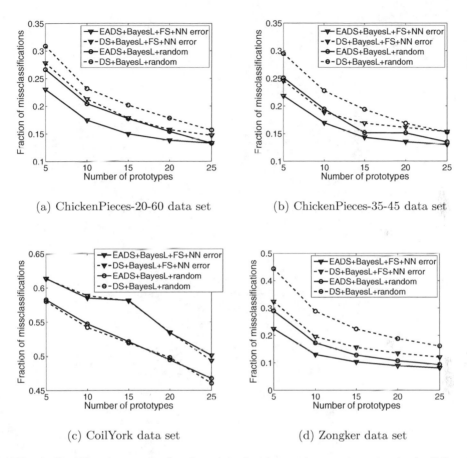

(a) ChickenPieces-20-60 data set

(b) ChickenPieces-35-45 data set

(c) CoilYork data set

(d) Zongker data set

Fig. 1. Classification results for the original asymmetric representation in the DS and the EADS in the data sets, the dimension of the associated DS is equal to the number of prototypes, and the dimension of the associated EADS is twice the number of prototypes

From the results in Fig. 1 we can see that in three of the four data sets —the ChickenPieces-20-60, ChickenPieces-35-45, and Zongker— classification in EADS outperforms classification in DS using both the systematic and the random prototype selectors. These are the data sets with the higher degree of asymmetry as measured by the asymmetry coefficient. In the CoilYork data set, which has the smallest asymmetry degree, the results in the EADS were a little worse than those in the DS. Except for the CoilYork data set, when the number of prototypes increases, the difference between the error rates in EADS and DS decreases. This implies that the asymmetry information is more useful if small sets of prototypes are used, and having more dimensions compensates for not using asymmetry information.

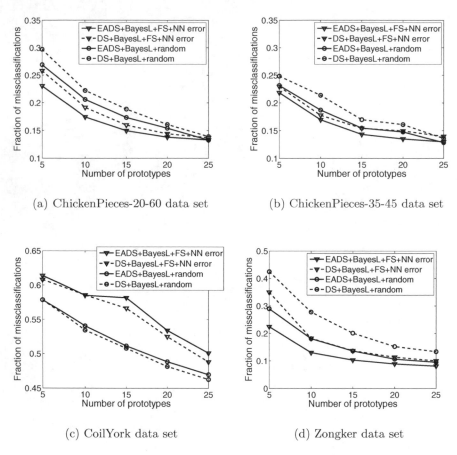

(a) ChickenPieces-20-60 data set

(b) ChickenPieces-35-45 data set

(c) CoilYork data set

(d) Zongker data set

Fig. 2. Classification results for the representation in the DS symmetrized by averaging and the EADS in the data sets, the dimension of the associated DS is equal to the number of prototypes, and the dimension of the associated EADS is twice the number of prototypes

From Fig. 2 we can see that once the dissimilarities are symmetrized by averaging, incorporating the asymmetry information does not improve classification in the same extent as by using the non-symmetrized version. This shows that the symmetrization by averaging is a good alternative for dealing with asymmetric data. In the CoilYork data set, the EADS performed worse than the DS using the symmetrized dissimilarities. In this case, where the asymmetry coefficient has a very small value, the use of asymmetry information leads to a slight decrease in classification performance. The symmetrization by averaging becomes less useful when the asymmetry degree of the data increases as it can be deduced from the similar classification errors in the original DS (see Fig. 1, (d)) and the DS symmetrized by averaging (see Fig. 2, (d)) in the Zongker data.

From the results, we made a characterization of the relationship between the amount of asymmetry present in each data set measured by the asymmetry coefficient and the improvements obtained in classification in the EADS compared to the non-symmetrized DS. First, we sorted the asymmetry coefficients of each data set in increasing order, and plotted the classification improvements in EADS compared to DS measured by the differences between the curves for the same prototype selection method in both spaces. The sum of these differences was plotted for each data set with its related asymmetry coefficient, see Fig. 3.

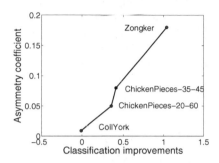

Fig. 3. Classification improvements in EADS compared to DS as a function of the asymmetry coefficient

In the function we can see a positive linear correlation between the two variables, as the value of the asymmetry coefficient increases, the value of the improvements in classification also increases. The value of the correlation coefficient was 0.99. This means that it is important to take the asymmetry information into account in order to improve classification rates when the asymmetry degree is perceivable, and while the data is more asymmetric the classification improvement increases. In the CoilYork dataset we obtained a negative value of improvement equal to -0.01, since the EADS performed slightly worse than the DS.

4 Conclusions

We proposed the EADS that proved to be suitable for exploiting the asymmetry information from the dissimilarities. This is especially useful for small prototype sets. For a data set with a very small degree of asymmetry, it might not be necessary and can even be slightly detrimental to use asymmetry information. Another conclusion is that the symmetrization by averaging is a good alternative for dealing with asymmetric data, although it becomes less useful when the asymmetry degree of the data increases. In our results, the improvements achieved in classification in EADS are positively correlated to the degree of asymmetry in each data set. The use of EADS can be beneficial when one has a very small set of informative prototypes with a highly asymmetric data set. The symmetrization operation may depend on the cause of asymmetry, e.g. averaging can be good for asymmetry caused by noise, the minimum can be useful for asymmetry caused by a shortest path optimization to compute the dissimilarities. Further work will be devoted to study these operations and the EADS for asymmetry caused by expert knowledge incorporated in the dissimilarity measure, noise or suboptimal procedures.

References

1. Pekalska, E., Duin, R.P.W.: The Dissimilarity Representation for Pattern Recognition: Foundations and Applications (Machine Perception and Artificial Intelligence). World Scientific Publishing Co., Inc., River Edge (2005)
2. Pekalska, E., Duin, R.P.W., Paclík, P.: Prototype selection for dissimilarity-based classifiers. Pattern Recogn. 39(2), 189–208 (2006)
3. Bunke, H., Riesen, K.: Graph Classification Based on Dissimilarity Space Embedding. In: da Vitoria Lobo, N., Kasparis, T., Roli, F., Kwok, J.T., Georgiopoulos, M., Anagnostopoulos, G.C., Loog, M. (eds.) S+SSPR 2008. LNCS, vol. 5342, pp. 996–1007. Springer, Heidelberg (2008)
4. Orozco-Alzate, M., Duin, R.P.W., Castellanos-Domínguez, G.: A generalization of dissimilarity representations using feature lines and feature planes. Pattern Recogn. Lett. 30(3), 242–254 (2009)
5. Pekalska, E., Duin, R.P.W.: Beyond traditional kernels: Classification in two dissimilarity-based representation spaces. IEEE Trans. Syst. Man Cybern. C, Appl. Rev. 38(6), 729–744 (2008)
6. Pekalska, E., Paclik, P., Duin, R.P.W.: A generalized kernel approach to dissimilarity-based classification. J. Mach. Learn. Res. 2, 175–211 (2002)
7. Duin, R.P.W., Pękalska, E.: Non-Euclidean Dissimilarities: Causes and Informativeness. In: Hancock, E.R., Wilson, R.C., Windeatt, T., Ulusoy, I., Escolano, F. (eds.) SSPR & SPR 2010. LNCS, vol. 6218, pp. 324–333. Springer, Heidelberg (2010)
8. Schölkopf, B., Mika, S., Burges, C.J.C., Knirsch, P., Müller, K.R., Rätsch, G., Smola, A.J.: Input space versus feature space in kernel-based methods. IEEE Trans. Neural Netw. 10(5), 1000–1017 (1999)
9. Okada, A., Imaizumi, T.: Nonmetric multidimensional scaling of asymmetric proximities. Behaviormetrika 14(21), 81–96 (1987)
10. Martín-Merino, M., Muñoz, A.: Self Organizing Map and Sammon Mapping for Asymmetric Proximities. In: Dorffner, G., Bischof, H., Hornik, K. (eds.) ICANN 2001. LNCS, vol. 2130, pp. 429–435. Springer, Heidelberg (2001)
11. Muñoz, A., de Diego, I.M., Moguerza, J.M.: Support vector machine classifiers for asymmetric proximities. In: Kaynak, O., Alpaydın, E., Oja, E., Xu, L. (eds.) ICANN 2003 and ICONIP 2003. LNCS, vol. 2714, pp. 217–224. Springer, Heidelberg (2003)

Improving Convergence of Restricted Boltzmann Machines via a Learning Adaptive Step Size

Noel Lopes[1,2] and Bernardete Ribeiro[1,3]

[1] CISUC - Center for Informatics and Systems of University of Coimbra, Portugal
`noel@ipg.pt, bribeiro@dei.uc.pt`
[2] UDI/IPG - Research Unit, Polytechnic Institute of Guarda, Portugal
[3] Department of Informatics Engineering, University of Coimbra, Portugal

Abstract. Restricted Boltzmann Machines (RBMs) have recently received much attention due to their potential to integrate more complex and deeper architectures. Despite their success, in many applications, training an RBM remains a tricky task. In this paper we present a learning adaptive step size method which accelerates its convergence. The results for the MNIST database demonstrate that the proposed method can drastically reduce the time necessary to achieve a good RBM reconstruction error. Moreover, the technique excels the fixed learning rate configurations, regardless of the momentum term used.

Keywords: Restricted Boltzmann Machines, Deep Belief Networks, Deep learning, Adaptive step size.

1 Introduction

Restricted Boltzmann Machines (RBMs) are becoming increasingly popular due to their unsupervised learning characteristics and inherent ability to cope with missing data [12], but mostly due to their potential to integrate more complex and deeper architectures. Deep architectures have recently gain momentum, raising the interest of machine learning researchers [6] due to theoretical and empirical results suggesting that they can be exponentially more efficient than shallow ones [11]. Much of this interest derived from the development of Deep Belief Networks (DBNs), recently proposed by Hinton et al. [4].

DBNs have been successfully applied to several domains including classification, regression, dimensionality reduction, object segmentation, information retrieval, robotics, natural language processing, and collaborative filtering among others [2]. DBNs are composed of several RBMs stacked on top of each other. The idea is to progressively extract higher-level dependencies from the original input data, thereby improving the ability of the network as a whole to capture the underlying regularities of the data [10].

Each RBMs learns a generative model from the data distribution, using the Contrastive Divergence (CD) algorithm, which is an approximation of the true gradient of the data likelihood, since calculating the later is not feasible [12].

L. Alvarez et al. (Eds.): CIARP 2012, LNCS 7441, pp. 511–518, 2012.

Training a DBNs is often a computationally expensive process that involves training independently several RBMs and may require a considerable amount of time. Moreover the proper choice of the learning rate and momentum parameters is a fundamental aspect of the training procedure that may affect considerably the networks convergence. In particular the learning rate is correlated with the learning speed [12]. In this paper we propose the use of an adaptive step size technique, which solves the difficulty of choosing an adequate learning rate and accelerates the training convergence.

The remainder of this paper is organized as follows. Section 2 details both the RBMs and DBNs. Section 3 describes the proposed adaptive step size technique. Section 4 presents and discusses the results. Finally, section 5 summarizes the paper contributions and addresses directions for future work.

2   Restricted Boltzmann Machines

An RBM is an energy-based generative model that consists of a layer of binary visible units, $\mathbf{v}$, and a layer of binary hidden units, $\mathbf{h}$, connected by symmetrically weighted connections [5], as depicted in Figure 1.

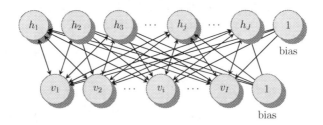

Fig. 1. Schematic representation of a Restricted Boltzmann Machine (RBM)

Given an observed state, the energy of the joint configuration of the visible and hidden units $(\mathbf{v}, \mathbf{h})$ is given by (1):

$$E(\mathbf{v}, \mathbf{h}) = -\sum_{i=1}^{I} a_i v_i - \sum_{j=1}^{J} b_j h_j - \sum_{j=1}^{J}\sum_{i=1}^{I} w_{ji} v_i h_j \; , \tag{1}$$

where a_i represents the bias of the visible unit i, b_j the bias of the hidden unit j and w_{ji} the weight associated to the connection between unit i and unit j.

The RBM assigns a probability for each configuration $(\mathbf{v}, \mathbf{h})$, using the energy function given by (2):

$$p(\mathbf{v}, \mathbf{h}) = \frac{e^{-E(\mathbf{v}, \mathbf{h})}}{Z} \; , \tag{2}$$

where Z is the partition function, obtained by summing the energy of all possible $(\mathbf{v}, \mathbf{h})$ configurations:

$$Z = \sum_{v,h} e^{-E(\mathbf{v}, \mathbf{h})} \; . \tag{3}$$

Given a random input configuration $\mathbf{v}$, the state of the hidden unit j is set to 1 with probability:

$$p(h_j = 1|\mathbf{v}) = \sigma(b_j + \sum_{i=1}^{I} v_i w_{ji}) \,, \tag{4}$$

where $\sigma(x)$ is the sigmoid function $\frac{1}{(1+e^{-x})}$. Similarly, given a random hidden vector the state of the visible unit i can be set to 1 with probability:

$$p(v_i = 1|\mathbf{h}) = \sigma(a_i + \sum_{j=1}^{J} h_j w_{ji}) \,. \tag{5}$$

The probability assigned to a visible vector, $\mathbf{v}$, is given by (6):

$$p(\mathbf{v}) = \sum_{\mathbf{h}} p(\mathbf{v}, \mathbf{h}) = \sum_{\mathbf{h}} p(\mathbf{v}|\mathbf{h})p(\mathbf{h}) \tag{6}$$

Hence, the probability assigned to a specific training vector $\mathbf{v}$ can be raised by adjusting the weights and the biases of the network in order to lower the energy of that particular vector while raising the energy of all the others. To this end, we can performing a stochastic gradient ascent on the log-likelihood surface of the training data, by computing the derivative of the log probability with respect to the weights of the network, which is given by (7):

$$\frac{\partial \log p(\mathbf{v})}{\partial w_{ij}} = \langle v_i h_j \rangle_0 - \langle v_i h_j \rangle_\infty \tag{7}$$

where $\langle \cdot \rangle_0$ denotes the expectations for the data distribution (p_0) and $\langle \cdot \rangle_\infty$ denotes the expectations for the model distribution (p_∞) [7]. Unfortunately, computing $\langle v_i h_j \rangle_\infty$ is intractable as it requires performing alternating Gibbs sampling for a very long time [5]. To solve this problem, Hinton et al. proposed a much faster learning procedure – the Contrastive Divergence (CD-k) algorithm [3,5], whereby $\langle . \rangle_\infty$ is replaced by $\langle \cdot \rangle_k$ for small values of k [7].

Using the specified procedure the following rules can be applied in order to correct the weights and bias of the network:

$$\Delta w_{ij} = \gamma(\langle v_i h_j \rangle_0 - \langle v_i h_j \rangle_k) \tag{8}$$
$$\Delta b_j = \gamma(\langle h_j \rangle_0 - \langle h_j \rangle_k) \tag{9}$$
$$\Delta a_j = \gamma(\langle v_i \rangle_0 - \langle v_i \rangle_k) \tag{10}$$

where γ represents the learning rate.

An RBM by itself is limited in what it can represent and its true potential emerges when several RBMs are stacked together to form a DBN [8].

2.1   Deep Belief Networks

RBMs, were recently proposed by Hinton et al. along with an unsupervised greedy learning algorithm for constructing the network one layer at a time [4].

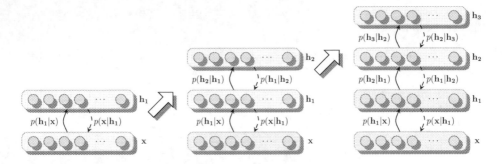

Fig. 2. Training process of a Deep Belief Network (DBN) with one input layer, $\mathbf{x}$, and three hidden layers $\mathbf{h_1}$, $\mathbf{h_2}$, $\mathbf{h_3}$. From left to right, layers with lighter color represent those already trained, while layers with darker color belong to the RBM being trained.

The idea is to train independently each layer using an RBM network that models the output of the previous layer. This approach represents an efficient way of learning an otherwise complicated model, by combining multiple and simpler (RBM) models, learned sequentially [4]. Figure 2 represents this process.

The first layers of the network are expected to extract low-level features from the input data while the upper layers are expected to gradually refine previously learn concepts, therefore producing more abstract concepts [7]. The training process is done in an unsupervised manner allowing the system to learn complex functions by mapping the input to the output directly from data, without depending on human-crafted features [2]. However, the output of the top layer can easily be fed to a conventional supervised classifier [5,10].

Although CD-1 does not provide a very good estimate of the maximum-likelihood, this is not an issue when the features learned serve as inputs for an higher-level RBM [5]. In fact, for RBMs that integrate a DBN, it is not necessarily a good idea to use another form of CD-k that may provide closer approximations to the maximum-likelihood, but does not ensure that the hidden features retain most of the information contained in the input data vectors [5]. This is consistent with the results obtained by Swersky et al. for the MNIST dataset, where the best DBN results were obtained for CD-1 [14].

3   Proposed Approach

Numerous techniques have been proposed for accelerating the convergence of the Back-Propagation (BP) algorithm. An analysis of these can be found in Zainuddin et al. [15]. Among those, the adaptive step size, proposed by Silva and Almeida [13,1], consists of using an individual learning rate (step size) parameter, γ_{ji}, for each weight connection, w_{ji}, instead of a global learning rate for all the network. Adapting this idea for the case of an RBM, at each CD-k iteration, the step sizes are adjusted according to the sign changes:

$$\gamma_{ji} = \begin{cases} u\gamma_{ji}^{old} & \text{if } (\langle v_i h_j \rangle_0 - \langle v_i h_j \rangle_k)(\langle v_i h_j \rangle_0^{old} - \langle v_i h_j \rangle_k^{old}) > 0 \\ d\gamma_{ji}^{old} & \text{if } (\langle v_i h_j \rangle_0 - \langle v_i h_j \rangle_k)(\langle v_i h_j \rangle_0^{old} - \langle v_i h_j \rangle_k^{old}) < 0 \end{cases} \quad (11)$$

where $u > 1$ (up) represents the increment factor for the step size and $d < 1$ (down) the decrement factor. If two consecutive updates have the same direction the step size of that particular weight is increased. For updates with opposite directions the step size is decreased, thus avoiding oscillations in the learning process due to excessive learning rates. The underlying ideas of this procedure is to find near-optimal step sizes that would allow to bypass ravines on the error surface. Moreover, the technique is especially effective for ravines that are parallel (or almost parallel) to some axis [1].

Additionally, each connection has its own momentum, $\alpha_{ji} = \gamma_{ji}\alpha$, proportional to the global momentum configuration, α, and to the step sizes. Moreover, according to our tests, it is advantageous to clamp α_{ji}, such that $0.1 \leq \alpha_{ji} \leq 0.9$.

4   Results and Discussion

4.1   Experimental Setup

In order to evaluate the performance of the proposed technique, we conducted several tests using the MNIST database of handwritten digits, available at http://yann.lecun.com/exdb/mnist/. This database contains 60,000 training samples. However, for the tests conducted in this work we only use the first 1,000 samples. Each sample consists of a 28×28 pixel image of a hand-written digit. Hence, each sample has 784 inputs.

The tests were conducted using our Graphics Processing Units (GPU) implementation of RBMs [9] on a Core 2 Quad CPU Q9300 (2.5 GHz) with an NVIDIA GTX 280.

The adaptive step size technique was compared with three different fixed learning rate settings ($\gamma = 0.1$, $\gamma = 0.4$ and $\gamma = 0.7$), while using three distinct momentum terms ($\alpha = 0.1$, $\alpha = 0.4$ and $\alpha = 0.7$). For adaptive step size technique the initial learning rate of each connection was set to 0.1 and the increment, u and decrement, d, factors were set respectively to 1.2 and 0.8. Altogether, twelve configuration settings were used (three for the adaptive step technique and nine for the fixed learning rates). For statistical significance, we conducted 30 tests per configuration, using an RBM with 784 inputs and 100 outputs. Each test starts with a different set of weights, but for fairness all the configurations use the same weight settings according to the test being performed.

4.2   Benchmark Results

Figure 3 show the evolution of the Root Mean Square Error (RMSE) of the reconstruction, according to to the learning rate, γ, and momentum, α, settings.

Independently of the learning rate used, the best results were obtained for a momentum $\alpha = 0.1$, while the worst solutions were obtained for $\alpha = 0.7$.

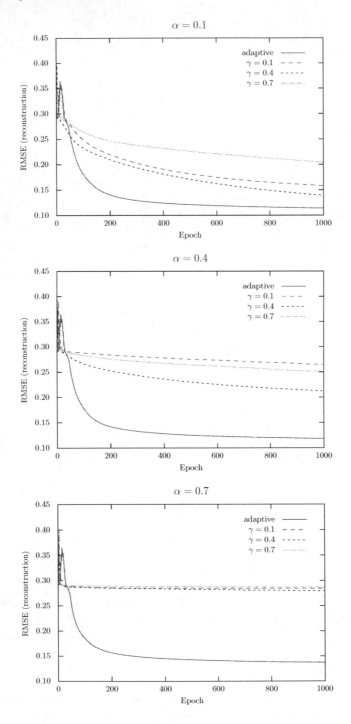

Fig. 3. Average reconstruction RMSE according to the learning parameters

Adaptive Step Sizes   Fixed (optimized) learning rate $\gamma = 0.4$

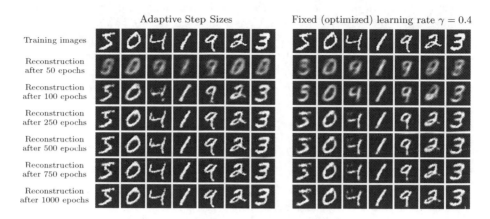

Fig. 4. Impact of the step size technique on the convergence of an RBM ($\alpha = 0.1$)

As expected the adaptive step size technique excels all the fixed learning rate configurations, regardless of the momentum term used. The discrepancy is quite significant (2.51%, 9.39% and 14.20% relatively to the best fixed learning rate solution, respectively for $\alpha = 0.1$, $\alpha = 0.4$ and $\alpha = 0.7$) and demonstrates the usefulness of the proposed technique and its robustness to an inadequate choice of the momentum. Moreover, in order to achieve better results than those obtained after 1000 epochs, using a fixed learning rate, we would only require 207, 68 and 48 epochs, respectively for $\alpha = 0.1$, $\alpha = 0.4$ and $\alpha = 0.7$.

Figure 4 shows the quality of the reconstruction of the original images in the database, for both the best network trained with a fixed learning rate ($\gamma = 0.4$, $\alpha = 0.1$) and the best network trained with the step size technique.

Training a network for 1,000 epochs (in the hardware configuration described earlier) using the adaptive step size takes on average 76.63 ± 0.09 seconds, while training the same network with a fixed learning rate takes 76.12 ± 0.05 seconds. Thus the overhead of using this method is not significant, while the convergence of the network is considerably enhanced.

Additionally, by using the adaptive step size technique, we are no longer required to search for a suitable γ parameter. Moreover, the step size method can easily recover from a bad choice of the initial learning rate [1] and the parameters u and d are easily tuned (the values chosen for this problem will most likely yield good results for other problems).

5   Conclusions and Future Work

The CD-k algorithm performs an efficient gradient ascent approximation. Nevertheless training an RBM is a difficult task. Experimental results suggest that finding a suitable learning rate is fundamental to successfully accomplish this task. In this paper we presented an adaptive step size method that solves this problem by using a different learning rate and momentum for each connection. At each iteration the technique seeks to find the near-optimal step sizes in order to improve convergence. The proposed method yielded excellent results in the MNIST handwritten, reducing drastically the reconstruction error. Moreover, the running overhead in the GPU is imperceptible.

Future work will focus on applying the proposed technique to real-world problems.

References

1. Almeida, L.B.: C1.2 Multilayer perceptrons. In: Handbook of Neural Computation, pp. C1.2:1–C1.2:30. IOP Publishing Ltd. and Oxford University Press (1997)
2. Bengio, Y.: Learning deep architectures for AI. Foundations and Trends in Machine Learning 2(1), 1–127 (2009)
3. Hinton, G.E.: Training products of experts by minimizing contrastive divergence. Neural Comput. 14, 1771–1800 (2002)
4. Hinton, G.E., Osindero, S., Teh, Y.W.: A fast learning algorithm for deep belief nets. Neural Comput. 18, 1527–1554 (2006)
5. Hinton, G.: A practical guide to training restricted boltzmann machines. Tech. rep., Dep. of Computer Science, University of Toronto (2010)
6. Larochelle, H., Erhan, D., Courville, A., Bergstra, J., Bengio, Y.: An empirical evaluation of deep architectures on problems with many factors of variation. In: Proc. of the 24th Intl. Conference on Machine Learning, pp. 473–480. ACM (2007)
7. Le Roux, N., Bengio, Y.: Representational power of restricted boltzmann machines and deep belief networks. Neural Comput. 20, 1631–1649 (2008)
8. Lee, H., Grosse, R., Ranganath, R., Ng, A.Y.: Convolutional deep belief networks for scalable unsupervised learning of hierarchical representations. In: Proc. of the 26th Annual Intl. Conference on Machine Learning, pp. 609–616. ACM (2009)
9. Lopes, N., Ribeiro, B.: Restricted boltzmann machines and deep belief networks on multi-core processors. In: IEEE World Congress on Computational Intelligence (2012)
10. Ranzato, M., Boureau, Y., LeCun, Y.: Sparse feature learning for deep belief networks. In: Advances in Neural Information Processing Systems, vol. 20 (2007)
11. Roux, N.L., Bengio, Y.: Deep belief networks are compact universal approximators. Neural Computation 22(8), 2192–2207 (2010)
12. Schulz, H., Müller, A., Behnke, S.: Investigating convergence of restricted boltzmann machine learning. In: NIPS 2010 Workshop on Deep Learning and Unsupervised Feature Learning, Whistler, Canada (2010)
13. Silva, F.M., Almeida, L.B.: Acceleration Techniques for the Backpropagation Algorithm. In: Almeida, L.B., Wellekens, C. (eds.) EURASIP 1990. LNCS, vol. 412, pp. 110–119. Springer, Heidelberg (1990)
14. Swersky, K., Chen, B., Marlin, B., de Freitas, N.: A tutorial on stochastic approximation algorithms for training restricted boltzmann machines and deep belief nets. In: Information Theory and Applications Workshop (2010)
15. Zainuddin, Z., Mahat, N., Hassan, Y.A.: Improving the convergence of the backpropagation algorithm using local adaptive techniques. Intl. Journal of Computational Intelligence, 172–175 (2005)

Robust Asymmetric Adaboost[*]

Pablo Ormeño[1], Felipe Ramírez[1],
Carlos Valle[1], Héctor Allende-Cid[1], and Héctor Allende[1,2]

[1] Departamento de Informática, Universidad Técnica Federico Santa María
Avenida España 1680, Valparaíso, Chile
[2] Factultad de Ingeniería y Ciencia, Universidad Adolfo Ibáñez
Avenida Padre Hurtado 750, Viña del Mar, Chile

Abstract. In real world pattern recognition problems, such as computer-assisted medical diagnosis, events of a given phenomena are usually found in minority, making it necessary to build algorithms that emphasize the effect of one of the classes at training time. In this paper we propose a variation of the well-known Adaboost algorithm that is able to improve its performance by using an asymmetric and robust cost function. We assess the performance of the proposed method on two medical datasets and synthetic datasets with different levels of imbalance and compare our results against three state-of-the-art ensemble learning approaches, achieving better and comparable results.

Keywords: ensemble learning, adaboost, asymmetric cost functions, robust methods.

1 Introduction

Over the past years machine learning methods for automatic pattern recognition have obtained successful results in a variety of real-world applications. Learning from data has proved to be very useful for aiding decision making on matters such as planning, forecasting, visualization, process control, etc. In some domains, however, traditional pattern recognition algorithms fail to provide adequate solutions given the difficulties inherent to some phenomena. One of such difficulties is the asymmetry in the distribution of certain observable events, as occurs in computer-assisted diagnosis of rare diseases.

This problem has been recently studied and a considerable number of algorithms have been proposed to provide more suitable solutions given its particular features [7,6]. Two major trends of pattern recognition methods have made substantial contributions in the field: cost-sensitive learning and ensemble methods.

One of the most popular ensemble-based techniques is Adaboost [3], a sequential iterative approach that fits an additive model through a forward stage-wise

[*] This work was supported by the following Research Grants: Fondecyt 1110854 and FB0821 Centro Científico Tecnológico de Valparaíso. Partial support was also received from CONICYT (Chile) Ph.D. Grant 21080414.

L. Alvarez et al. (Eds.): CIARP 2012, LNCS 7441, pp. 519–526, 2012.
© Springer-Verlag Berlin Heidelberg 2012

approach [5], by training a single predictor to minimize the residual of the previous ensemble in each round. In other words, this algorithm combines a set of weak classifiers weighting them according to their individual performances in the training phase. Thus, the weight of wrongly classified samples increases and the weight of correctly classified samples decreases.

Since its introduction, several variations of Adaboost have been proposed to solve different not previously-considered issues [4,10]. One of the major problems of the original version of Adaboost is that it is unable to handle the presence of outlying observations in the data, which causes an excessive increase of their sampling weights as they are most likely misclassified in each iteration. The authors of [1] proposed an improvement to Adaboost to address this flaw. The algorithm is termed Robust Alternating Adaboost (Radaboost) because it operates by literally alternating between Adaboost and its inverse variation [8]. The authors report that the proposed method outperforms the original version when the data has outlier samples [11].

However, none of these techniques are appropriate in pattern recognition problems where class distributions are imbalanced or the misclassification costs are not equivalent. Often, these problems appear simultaneously, as in the aforementioned example, where observations of ill patients are heavily outnumbered by the observations of healthy ones, and it is more important to detect the disease rather than the absence of it. In other words, the cost of false negatives (also called *type-II errors*) is much greater than that of false positives (also called *type-I errors*). Hence, a different treatment for each kind of error is needed, which often means to penalize more one than the other.

In this work we propose an algorithm that incorporates robustness and asymmetry allowing to solve the problem of imbalance by differentiating the kinds of errors committed. The remainder of the paper is organized as follows: in Section 2 we give a brief literature review on the methods that inspired this work, in Section 3 we describe in detail our proposal, in Section 4 we perform an experimental comparative study with the proposed method and the previously described related literature approaches, and finally in Section 5 we conclude and discuss possible further work.

2   Boosting Algorithms

In this section we show details of the algorithms that inspired our work and whose understanding is required to proceed to introduce our improvement. We begin by introducing the traditional form of the Adaboost algorithm with its inverse variation, then we explain briefly the Radaboost algorithm, and finally we cite a cost-sensitive boosting algorithm.

The Adaboost algorithm [3] takes as input a training set $\mathcal{Z} = \{(x_1, y_1)...(x_n, y_n)\}$ where each x_i is a variable that belongs to $\mathcal{X} \subset \mathbb{R}^d$ and each y_i is some label in $\mathcal{Y}$. In this particular paper we assume that $\mathcal{Y} = \{-1, 1\}$. Adaboost calls a weak or base learning algorithm repeatedly in a sequence of stages $t = 1...T$.

The main idea of AdaBoost is to maintain a sampling distribution over the training set, which is used to train the learner at each round t. Let $\mathcal{D}_t(i)$ be the sampling weight assigned to example i on round t. At the beginning of the algorithm the distribution is uniform, *i.e.* $\mathcal{D}_1(i) = \frac{1}{n} \forall i$, and at each round, the weights of the misclassified examples are increased, so that the following base learner is forced to focus on the *hard* examples of the training set. The job of each learner is to find an appropriate hypothesis $h_t : \mathcal{X} \to \{-1, 1\}$ for the distribution $\mathcal{D}_t$. The goodness of the obtained hypothesis can be quantified as the weighted error $\epsilon_t = Pr_{i \sim \mathcal{D}_t}[h_t(x_i) \neq y_i] = \sum_{i: h_t(x_i) \neq y_i} \mathcal{D}_t(i)$. Note that the error is measured with respect to the distribution $\mathcal{D}_t$ on which the weak learner was trained.

Once the weak hypothesis h_t is obtained, its relevance is computed $\alpha_t = \frac{1}{2} \ln \left(\frac{1-\epsilon_t}{\epsilon_t} \right)$ and the sampling distribution is updated according to the rule $\mathcal{D}_{t+1}(i) = \frac{1}{Z_t} \mathcal{D}_t(i) e^{-\alpha_t y_i h_t(x_i)}$, where Z_t is a normalization factor. This rule has the aforementioned effect on the sampling weights of correctly classified and misclassified objects. After a sequence of T rounds have been performed, the final hypothesis H is computed as

$$H_T(x) = sign \left(\sum_{t=1}^{T} \alpha_t h_t(x) \right) \tag{1}$$

The Inverse Adaboost algorithm is a variation of the original form that operates with an inverse distribution updating rule $\mathcal{D}_{t+1}(i) = \frac{1}{Z_t} \mathcal{D}_t(i) e^{\alpha_t y_i h_t(x_i)}$. This rule basically underweights misclassified observations and vice versa, contrary to the original approach. Thus, the base learners are forced to focus more on the *easy* examples of the training set.

The Radaboost algorithm [1] was proposed to address the problem of data with outliers. It operates by alternating between the classic and the inverse versions of Adaboost to create a more stable algorithm, which limits the influence of the empiric distribution by detecting and decreasing the weight of problematic examples to achieve better classification overall.

The authors introduce an alternative way to compute α_t to prevent excessive increases in sampling weights of difficult examples. As the sampling distribution is updated in every stage, after a few iterations the weight of misclassified samples will be considerably higher than that of the rest. To avoid this, two variables are introduced: the inverse variable $\beta(i)$ and the epoch variable $age(i)$ for each example $i = 1, ..., n$ in the training set. If $\beta(i)$ is equal to 1, it means that the original Adaboost is being used to update the weights. Otherwise, if $\beta(i)$ is equal to -1, the inverse approach is being used. The $age(i)$ variable counts the number of times that the samples was sequentially misclassified. If this value is higher than a given threshold τ, then $\beta(i)$ takes the value -1 and alternates.

As mentioned earlier, one of the limitations of Adaboost is that it focuses on minimizing the overall classification error not taking into account the difference between the costs of the two possible types of error, given a certain problem. To solve this issue, Asymmetric Adaboost [12] was proposed, which works by introducing a non-uniform initial sampling distribution according to the asymmetry in the misclassification costs of the problem.

3   Robust Asymmetric Adaboost

As described in the latter section, Radaboost only focuses on solving the problem of outlying examples and does not provide special treatment for cases with asymmetric misclassification costs. In this section we propose a considerable number of modifications for the Radaboost algorithm in order to provide it with cost-sensitiveness in the context of medical applications. Our proposal consists in a cost-sensitive updating function that allows the algorithm to find solutions more suitable for a given problem considering its particular cost asymmetry.

We first define a non-uniform initial sampling distribution using a k_i parameter, which measures how many times the majority class outnumbers the minority class for samples i that belong to the minority class. Thus, the values of the positive examples are increased, allowing the algorithm to focus in minimizing the false negative rate.

$$D_1(i) = \frac{k_i}{\sum_i^m k_i}, \forall i = 1, ..., m. \tag{2}$$

Note that the parameter k_i characterizes the level of imbalance in the class distribution of the training.

Then, based on the original Radaboost algorithm, we modify the limit for α_t taking the rth root, with $r \in N$, to values of ϵ_t lower than a given γ:

$$\alpha_t = \begin{cases} \frac{1}{2}\sqrt[r]{ln(\frac{1-\epsilon_t}{\epsilon_t})} + \alpha_\gamma & \epsilon_t < \gamma \\ \frac{1}{2}ln(\frac{1-\epsilon_t}{\epsilon_t}) & \epsilon_t \geq \gamma \end{cases} \tag{3}$$

where $\alpha_\gamma = \frac{1}{2}ln(\frac{1-\gamma}{\gamma}) - \frac{1}{2}\sqrt[r]{ln(\frac{1-\gamma}{\gamma})}$ is a constant needed to maintain the continuity of equation (3). This prevents the sampling weights of problematic examples to grow excessively in one iteration.

We also define a cost-sensitive pseudo-loss function ϵ, which takes into account that the cost of false negatives is greater than that of false positives in the context of medical applications. An important thing to note is that the new value of ϵ that is introduced in the equation (5), maintains its continuity.

Finally, we propose a new updating rule for the sampling distribution that takes into account the level of imbalance in the class distribution of the training set. In each iteration the distribution is computed for every example i as follows

$$D_{t+1}(i) = \frac{exp(-\alpha_t y_i \sum_t h_t(x_i))exp(y_i log\sqrt{k(i)})}{Z_t}, \tag{4}$$

where Z_t is a normalization factor. This rule overweights positive examples by means of the k_i parameter previously used to the define the initial distribution. As a result, more minority class objects will be sampled for training and, in turn, learners of further iterations will be fed with balanced training data.

All aforementioned modifications to the Radaboost method can be seen in Algorithm 1. In this particular study, we used as base classifier the Support Vector Machine (SVM) [9].

Algorithm 1. Robust Asymmetric Adaboost

1: Given the training set $Z = \{(x_1, y_1), ..., (x_n, y_n)\}$ where $x_i \in X$, $y_i \in Y = \{-1, +1\}$; define σ_{ini}, σ_{min}, and σ_{dec}

2: Initialize the parameters: choose the k value, the threshold of epochs τ, the threshold of the error γ, σ with σ_{ini}, the robust parameter r, the sample distribution $D_1(i) = \frac{k_i}{\sum_{i=1}^{n} k_i}, \forall i = 1, ..., n$, the inverse variable $\beta(i) = 1$ and the variable $age(i) = 0$ for each data in the sample (x_i, y_i), $i = 1, .., n$.

3: **for** t= 1,...,T **do**

4:    **while** $(\sigma > \sigma_{min})$ **do**

5:       Take the weak hypothesis $h_t : X \rightarrow \{-1, +1\}$

6:       Compute the error of the base classifier

$$\epsilon_t = \sum_i D_t(i) \frac{(1 - h_t(x_t)y_t)}{2} \tag{5}$$

7:       **if** $\epsilon_t > 0.5$ **then**

8:          Decrease the value of σ, in σ_{dec} and go to step 5.

9:       **end if**

10:      Calculate α_t with the equation (3)

11:      Update the weights distribution as in equation (4)

12:      **if** The sample (x_i, y_i) is correctly classified by $H_T(x)$ ($H_T(x_i)y_t > 0$) **then**

13:         $age(i) = 0$ and $\beta(i) = 1$

14:      **else**

15:         Increase $age(i)$ in one.

16:         **if** $age(i) > \tau$ **then**

17:            $\beta(i) = -1$ and $age(i) = 0$

18:         **end if**

19:      **end if**

20:    **end while**

21: **end for**

22: Calculate the final strong hypothesis as in equation (1)

---

4 Experimental Results

In this section we present the results obtained with our proposal (*Robust Asymmetric* for short) and the other three related literature approaches: the classic Adaboost algorithm, the Radaboost algorithm (*Robust* for short) and the Asymmetric Adaboost algorithm (*Asymmetric* for short). We used the *Breast Cancer* and *Liver Desease* datasets from the UCI Machine Learning Repository [2], along with a synthetic dataset to assess the performance of the methods with different imbalance rates.

Each experiment was run 20 times to report the mean values and the variability of the performance measures. An 80% of the data was used for training and the remaining 20% for testing. The *Breast Cancer* dataset, has a total of 568 examples, where 212 correspond to the positive class (malignant tumor) and 356 to the negative class (benign tumor). The *Liver Desease* dataset has 345 examples, 145 of which are positive (presence of the disease) and 200 are negative.

The γ and r parameters were chosen empirically. The values of γ were set to 0.05, 0.1 and 0.2. The robustness parameter r was set to 2, 3 and 5. The k value, as stated earlier, is the rate of the number of examples from the majority class over the number of examples of the minority. For the *Breast Cancer* data set the value was $k = 1.69$ and for the *Liver Desease* data set was $k = 1.37$. The values σ and C, for the SVM with gaussian kernel were tuned using the methodology proposed in [9]. The performance measures used to compare the 4 models are the classification error and sensitivity over the testing set, where the latter is a performance measure related to the false negative type of error.

Figures 1 and 2 show the two performance measures as a function of the number of boosting iterations with the *Breast Cancer* and *Liver Disease* datasets, respectively.

In the *Breast Cancer* case we can clearly see that our approach outperforms all other methods in both measures, and has the lower variability as well. Meanwhile, in the *Liver Disease* case, we can see that our method has comparable classification error mean and variability, and it has the higher sensitivity mean, but was outperformed by the *Asymmetric* approach in variability.

Note that the sensitivity has a direct relation with the type-II error: the higher its value, the lower the probability of committing false negatives will be, which is often required in medical applications such as automated diagnosis. Hence, given the above results, our method is the most appropriate for these kinds of problem.

We also synthetically generated instances of the *Breast Cancer* dataset to evaluate the performance of the methods against the imbalance ratio of the data. The proportions tested were 10-90%, 30-70% and 50-50%. Table 1 shows the results of the experiments with the three synthetic instances at 20 boosting

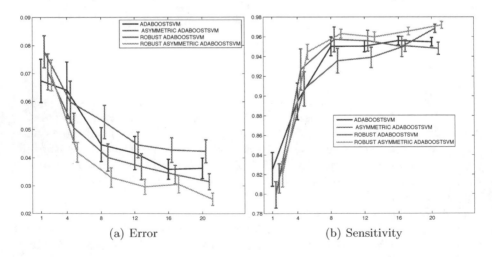

(a) Error   (b) Sensitivity

Fig. 1. Performance measures of *Breast Cancer* data set as a function of the number of boosting iterations

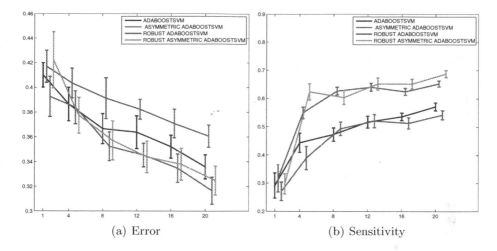

(a) Error   (b) Sensitivity

Fig. 2. Performance measures of *Liver Desease* data set as a function of the number of boosting iterations

iterations. We can see that our proposal outperforms the other three methods in classification error for all the cases, however, in sensitivity our results are comparable with those of the *Asymmetric* approach.

Table 1. Results with synthetically imbalanced data

Proportion	Algorithm	Error	Sensitivity
10 - 90	Adaboost	0.0326 ± 0.0100	0.8801 ± 0.0689
	Asymmetric	0.0217 ± 0.0141	0.9452 ± 0.0774
	Robust	$0.0253 \pm \mathbf{0.0073}$	0.9037 ± 0.0581
	Robust Asymmetric	$\mathbf{0.0127} \pm 0.0103$	$\mathbf{0.9489} \pm \mathbf{0.0481}$
30 - 70	Adaboost	0.0357 ± 0.0168	0.9246 ± 0.0497
	Asymmetric	0.0374 ± 0.0160	$\mathbf{0.9304} \pm 0.0729$
	Robust	0.0357 ± 0.0137	$0.9239 \pm \mathbf{0.0388}$
	Robust Asymmetric	$\mathbf{0.0272} \pm \mathbf{0.0113}$	$\mathbf{0.9304} \pm 0.0397$
50 - 50	Adaboost	0.0391 ± 0.0178	$\mathbf{0.9754} \pm \mathbf{0.0209}$
	Asymmetric	$0.0408 \pm \mathbf{0.0094}$	0.9647 ± 0.0295
	Robust	$0.0408 \pm \mathbf{0.0094}$	0.9550 ± 0.0328
	Robust Asymmetric	$\mathbf{0.0238} \pm 0.0097$	0.9647 ± 0.0295

5   Conclusion and Future Work

In this paper we have proposed a cost-sensitive variation of the Radaboost algorithm that aims not only to improve the performance of the positive class, but to preserve the robustness of its original form against outlying observations. We conducted an experimental study and compared our technique with three related state-of-the-art approaches over real and synthetic datasets. The results show that our method is at least comparable with literature approaches in sensitivity, and outperforms them in overall accuracy. It also proved to be robust against the class imbalance rate achieving a steady low error in comparison to the growing error of the other approaches as the imbalance increases.

We conclude that our method successfully solves the data asymmetry issue, providing a solid alternative to address problems of this nature. Future work may consider a study of the convergence of the algorithm to improve its computational performance by using simpler base learners without hindering its classification accuracy.

References

1. Allende-Cid, H., Salas, R., Allende, H., Ñanculef, R.: Robust Alternating AdaBoost. In: Rueda, L., Mery, D., Kittler, J. (eds.) CIARP 2007. LNCS, vol. 4756, pp. 427–436. Springer, Heidelberg (2007)
2. Frank, A., Asuncion, A.: UCI machine learning repository (2010), http://archive.ics.uci.edu/ml
3. Freund, Y., Schapire, R.E.: A decision-theoretic generalization of on-line learning and an application to boosting (1997)
4. Friedman, J., Hastie, T., Tibshirani, R.: Additive logistic regression: a statistical view of boosting. Annals of Statistics 28, 2000 (1998)
5. Hastie, T., Tibshirani, R., Friedman, J.: The elements of statistical learning. Springer (2003)
6. Japkowicz, N., Myers, C., Gluck, M.: A novelty detection approach to classification. In: Proceedings of the Fourteenth Joint Conference on Artificial Intelligence, pp. 518–523 (1995)
7. Japkowicz, N., Stephen, S.: The class imbalance problem: A systematic study. Intell. Data Anal. 6, 429–449 (2002)
8. Kuncheva, L.I., Whitaker, C.J.: Using Diversity with Three Variants of Boosting: Aggressive, Conservative, and Inverse. In: Roli, F., Kittler, J. (eds.) MCS 2002. LNCS, vol. 2364, pp. 81–90. Springer, Heidelberg (2002)
9. Li, X., Wang, L., Sung, E.: Adaboost with SVM-based component classifiers. Eng. Appl. Artif. Intell. 21(5), 785–795 (2008)
10. Nock, R., Nielsen, F.: A generalization of discrete adaboost. Artificial Intelligence 171(1), 25–41 (2007)
11. Takenouchi, T., Eguchi, S.: Robustifying adaboost by adding the naive error rate. Neural Computation 16(4), 767–787 (2004)
12. Wang, Z., Fang, C., Ding, X.: Asymmetric real adaboost. In: ICPR 2008, pp. 1–4 (2008)

Enhancing the Performance of AdaBoost Algorithms by Introducing a Frequency Counting Factor for Weight Distribution Updating

Diego Alonso Fernández Merjildo and Lee Luan Ling

Department of Communications, DECOM
School of Electrical and Computer Engineering, FEEC
State University of Campinas, UNICAMP
Campinas, 13083-852, Brazil
{diegofer,lee}@decom.fee.unicamp.br

Abstract. This work presents a modified Boosting algorithm capable of avoiding training sample overfitting during training procedures. The proposed algorithm updates weight distributions according to amount of misclassified samples at each iteration training step. Experimental tests reveal that our approach has several advantages over many classical AdaBoost algorithms in terms of error generalization capacity, overfitting avoidance and superior classification performance.

Keywords: AdaBoost Algorithm, Weights Update, Frequency Factor, Misclassified Samples, Machine Learning.

1 Introduction

AdaBoost algorithm was probably the very first boosting algorithm widely used in real-time systems, due to its simplicity and adaptability. Freund and Schapire [1] introduced the adaptive Boosting algorithm (AdaBoost) based on a simple boosting algorithms developed by Valiant [2] and Schapire [3]. The Real AdaBoost algorithm is considered as the first variant of AdaBoost seeking to optimize the cost function of classifiers [4]. The Gentle AdaBoost uses Newton stepping to produce more stable and reliable ensembles [5]. The Modest AdaBoost provides lower generalization error but higher classification error rate during training stages when compared to the Gentle AdaBoost [6]. The FloatBoost removes less significant weak classifiers in order to reduce classification error rate [7]. The EmphasisBoost uses the so-called emphasis function of, in this case each sample is weighted according to a criterion defined by a parameter such that the training process focuses on critical samples [8].

Dietterich [9], Ratsch et al. [10] and Servedio [11] showed that AdaBoost algorithm has great tendencies to cause sample overfitting in the presence of high noise data. In order to avoid sample overfitting phenomena, Li et al. [12] proposed a modified method to update weights, focusing on the samples being

L. Alvarez et al. (Eds.): CIARP 2012, LNCS 7441, pp. 527–534, 2012.
© Springer-Verlag Berlin Heidelberg 2012

misclassified by assigning large weights to samples erroneously classified. The proposed weight updating procedure may cause considerable distortion in weight distribution, cumulatively augmented by repeated iterations. In this sense, in this work we propose a new method to update sample weight distribution in order to avoid sample overfitting problems.

2   The Proposed AdaBoost Algorithm

2.1   The Conventional AdaBoost Algorithm

Adaboost algorithm combines several weak classifiers in such a way that the ensemble can improve their performance. The training ensemble consists of a set of samples $x_i \in X, i = 1 \dots N$, with labels $y_i \in \{-1, 1\}$. At each round $t = 1, \dots, T$, a new weak classifier is added implementing a function $h_t(x_i) : X \rightarrow [-1, 1]$. Through a gradient descent procedure, a classic AdaBoost algorithm attempts to minimize an exponential error function. $W_{t,i}$ denotes the weight that the tth classifier function assign to x_i. Initially, a common weight value is adopted, $W_{1,i} = 1/N$. Then, the weight distribution is updated according to $W_{t+1,i} = W_{t,i}exp(-\alpha_t h_t(x_i)y_i)/Z_t$, where Z_t is a normalization factor assuring that $\sum_{i=1}^{N} W_{t,i} = 1$, and α_t is the importance assigned to the tth weak classifier.

At each iteration, AdaBoost linearly combines weak classifiers as $F(x) = \sum_{j=1}^{T} \alpha_j h_j(x)$ in order to achieve a classification accuracy better than each weak classifier individually. As a result, the generalization error of the resulting linearly combined classifier becomes smaller and smaller as training iteration proceeds, possibly achieving zero classification error after several iterations.

2.2   The Improved AdaBoost Algorithm

In order to solve the overfitting problem detected during training processes, this work suggests a modified method to update the weight distribution, by introducing a new variable, denoted by δ_i, which is associated to each training sample. The proposed updating process is similar to that of the classical AdaBoost algorithm; thus, at each iteration step we add a weak classifier to the set of classifiers that are linearly combined to build a single strong classifier $F(x)$. In this way, the set of new variables, $\delta_i \in \Delta = \{0, \dots, k\}$ is involved in the training and is responsible for preventing the increase of weights of misclassified samples.

Notice that in a classical Boosting procedure when a sample is misclassified, the associated weight has its value increased; on the other hand, when a sample is correctly classified, the associated weight is diminished. This weight updating strategy may cause sample overfitting due to excessive weight value accumulated in repeated iterations. In order to avoid this problem, in this work, we change the weight updating procedure by considering the frequency of occurrence of misclassified samples. In other words, the weights are only changed when the number of a sample being misclassified is above a predetermined threshold value, denoted by k frequency samples. Thus, the rise of the weight is not always

---

Algorithm 1. Proposed modified AdaBoost algorithm

– Given dataset $S = \{(x_i, y_i), ..., (x_n, y_n)\}$, where $y_i \in \{-1, +1\}$, with $\delta_i \in \Delta = \{0, ..., k\}$
– Initializing $\delta_i = 0$
– For $t = 1, ..., T$
  1. Normalizing the sample distribution: $W_{t,i}$
  2. Calling weak classification algorithm, and choosing the best weak classifier $h_t : S\{-1, +1\}$ with the lowest error ϵ_t
  3. Choosing $\alpha_t = \frac{1}{2} \ln \frac{1+\epsilon_t}{1-\epsilon_t}$
  4. Updating the sample weight distribution.

$$W_{t+1,i} = \begin{cases} W_t(i)exp(-\alpha_t) & h_t(x_i) = y_i \\ W_t(i)exp(\alpha_t) & h_t(x_i) \neq y_i \wedge \delta_i \geq k \\ W_t(i) & \text{otherwise} \end{cases} \qquad (1)$$

  5. Updating the misclassified count (Frequency).

$$\delta_i = \begin{cases} \delta_i + 1 & h_t(x_i) \neq y_i \wedge \delta_i < k \\ 0 & \delta_i > k \\ \delta_i & \text{otherwise} \end{cases} . \qquad (2)$$

– The final strong classifier is introduced as:

$$F(x) = sign(\sum_{t+1}^{T} \alpha_t h_t(x)) \qquad (3)$$

---

performed continuously from iteration to iteration. The weight of a misclassified sample will be increased only if it was misclassified k times or more (see (1)).

According to Algorithm 1, during the training phase, a dummy variable δ_i, belonging to the set $\{0, 1, 2, ..., k\}$, is used to indicating the number of times sample has already been misclassified. δ_i remains unchanged when the sample is classified correctly. δ_i is reset to zero when it is saturated, i.e. when $\delta_i = k$. The updating procedure of the variable δ_i is shown by (2) in Algorithm 1.

3 Experimental Investigation

The main objective of the experiments (computational trials) developed in this work consists in comparing the performance of the proposed method with those offered by other boosting approaches. Accordingly, most Boosting algorithms, reported in the literature, rely on a cost function optimization. We adopted the real data sets described in [13] and two artificially generated data sets in our experimental evaluation. Each dataset is splitted into a training set and a testing set under the 80:20 proportion. The maximum value for variable δ_i is limited to $k = 20$. We explicitly compare the performance of the proposed method with that given by the Real AdaBoost Algorithm as illustrated by six classification error curves for six different data in Fig. 1 and 2. In addition, in Table 1 we compare the performance, in terms of average classification error rates, observed in both training and testing phases using thirteen different datasets [13].

According to [14] the Ringnorm dataset has a sphere surface separation. Such a geometric format prevents the Adaboost algorithms to guarantee good classification results. To contrast, our boosting method offered better performance for the testing subset with lower error rate almost in every iteration (see Figure 1a). The proposed method was designed to resist sample overfitting; in fact, our method outperforms the classical AdaBoost algorithm when data samples are noisy or separation surfaces are complex. As illustration, according to [14], the Twonorm dataset presents a planar separation surface what implies an easier classification task than the above case of the Ringnorm dataset (see Figures 1a and 1b). It is important to highlight that the comparison results are valid for all classical Adaboost algorithms (Real AdaBoost, GentleBoost, Modest AdaBoost, FloatBoost, EmphasisBoost, etc.), because the improved method described in this work can be introduced into these variants.

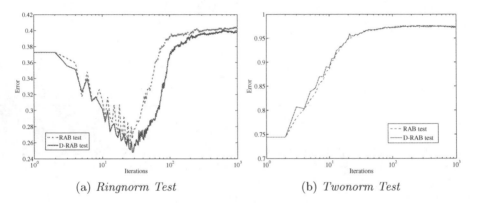

(a) *Ringnorm Test*   (b) *Twonorm Test*

Fig. 1. Test error curves of classical approach (RAB - Real AdaBoost) and the approach of this work (D-RAB). The x-axis is on a logarithmic scale for easier comparison.

We also observed that there are significant differences between the proposed method and the Real AdaBoost in terms of error and convergence of the training process. As illustrated by Table 1, the proposed approach consistently performs better for the following datasets: *Australian, Bcancer, Diabetes, Fourclass, Liver, Splice, Svmguide1, W1a, Spam*. In terms of convergence speed, the proposed approach is higher than the classical approaches and also provides lower training errors. This is due to the fact the proposed updating scheme (using δ_i counter) has eliminated unnecessary and redundant weight updating steps. As a result, it is possible to use a reduced number of weak classifiers to build strong classifiers. Certainly this is a desirable property for real time applications such as real-time object detection. Figures 2a and 2b show that the method developed in this work may converge faster than the classical approaches (in this case, when compared to the Real Ad-aBoost algorithm), in terms of the number of iterations (up to 1000 iterations).

Table 1. Results of Real Adaboost (RAB) and Real Adaboost using the δ_i variable (D-RAB) for training error and test error

Data set	Algorithm	Average Training error	Average Test error
australian	RAB	0.073797 ± 0.022533	0.73868 ± 0.016918
	D-RAB	**0.056123 ± 0.023557**	**0.73222 ± 0.032643**
bcancer	RAB	0.0020888 ± 0.0067642	**0.7033 ± 0.013678**
	D-RAB	**0.0017302 ± 0.0054692**	0.70771 ± 0.015291
diabetes	RAB	0.12941 ± 0.026878	0.41084 ± 0.0042467
	D-RAB	**0.11787 ± 0.029094**	**0.39325 ± 0.0041971**
fourclass	RAB	0.43295 ± 0.011658	-3.9745 ± 19.4456
	D-RAB	**0.37657 ± 0.039754**	**-4.4004 ± 30.8115**
heart	RAB	**0.0186255 ± 0.03319**	0.41922 ± 0.012025
	D-RAB	0.018817 ± 0.029935	**0.41492 ± 0.0099736**
ionosphere	RAB	**0.0018697 ± 0.011596**	**0.37 ± 0.016583**
	D-RAB	0.0020264 ± 0.011412	0.37452 ± 0.021583
liver	RAB	0.080236 ± 0.045446	**0.50874 ± 0.00487**
	D-RAB	**0.077945 ± 0.045223**	0.51065 ± 0.00466
sonar	RAB	**0.00187 ± 0.0156**	**0.51398 ± 0.00681**
	D-RAB	0.00205 ± 0.0159	0.51489 ± 0.00686
splice	RAB	0.017477 ± 0.02460	0.31484 ± 0.01243
	D-RAB	**0.017088 +0.02410**	**0.30438 ± 0.01441**
svmguise1	RAB	0.01529 ± 0.00687	0.63523 ± 0.001161
	D-RAB	**0.01294 ± 0.00571**	**0.63519 ±0.000723**
svmguide3	RAB	**0.05238 ± 0.03806**	0.38258 ± 0.04875
	D-RAB	0.05560 ± 0.03602	**0.36418 ± 0.04123**
w1a	RAB	0.017522 ± 0.005182	**0.010509 ± 0.000903**
	D-RAB	**0.016046 ±0.005242**	0.011638 ± 0.001349
spam	RAB	0.038357 ± 0.0011447	-0.41031 ± 2.0464
	D-RAB	**0.034284 ⊥ 0.0010706**	**-0.50353 ± 2.2454**

On the other hand, it was computed the test error in terms of the general-ization ability. The behavior of the classical approaches may generate sample overfitting on several cases; that is, the performance on the training examples still increases while the performance on unseen data becomes worse, as presented by Dietterich [9], Ratsch et al. [10] and Servedio [11]. However, the experiments developed in this work (computational trials) showed that this approach may be more resistant to overfitting problems. Table 1 also shows the performance of the algorithms in the testing phase. Real AdaBoost algorithm is slightly bet-ter in five cases (*bcancer, ionosphere, liver, sonar, w1a*), while our method has better performance, in terms of better lower average test error, in eight distinct cases (*australian, diabetes, fourclass, heart, splice, svmguide1, smguide3, spam*). Now, in terms of generalization ability our approach is considerably better than those classical AdaBoost ones. This fact is illustrated by Fig. 2c when using the

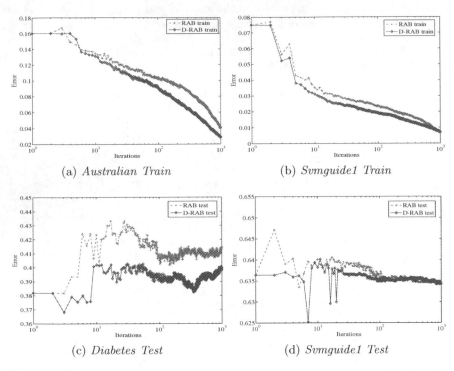

Fig. 2. Train error curves and Test error curves of classical approach (RAB - Real AdaBoost) and the approach of this work (D-RAB). The x-axis is on a logarithmic scale for easier comparison.

diabetes database. Similar results were obtained for the *svmguide* dataset (see Figure 2d), where a lower average test error is obtained.

4   Discussion and Conclusions

4.1   Algorithm Structure and Capabilities

In this section, we provide some insights into the quality of the proposed method. For this, we use the margin theory proposed by Schapire et al. [15] who provided one the most popular explanations to the success of AdaBoost, i.e, it tends to improve the *margin* even after the error. The *margin* of an example with respect to a classifier is a measure of the confidence of the classification result. Thus, consider binary classification problems, where the examples are drawn independently according to an underlying distribution W over $X \times \{-1, +1\}$, and X is an instance space. Let to include H variable as a classifier space. A weak classifier $h \in H$ is a mapping from X to $-1, +1$. A linear convex combination is of the form $F(x) = \sum \alpha_i h_i(x)$, where $\sum \alpha_i = 1, \alpha_i \geq 0$. An error occurs on an example (x, y) if and only if:

$$yF(x) \leq 0. \tag{4}$$

The value of $yF(x)$ reflects the confidence of the prediction. Therefore, $yF(x)$ is called the *margin* for (x, y) with respect to F, where $yF(x)$ is the difference between the weights assigned to those weak classifiers that correctly classify (x, y) and the weights assigned to those that misclassify the example. We use $P_X(F(x, y))$ to denote the probability with respect to choosing an example (x, y) uniformly at random from the training set X, where, $P_X(yf(x) \leq 0)$ is the generalization error which we want to bound. Considering the margins over the whole set of training examples, we can regard $P_X(yF(x) \leq \beta)$ as a distribution over $\beta(-1 \leq \beta \leq 1)$, which is the fraction of training examples whose margin is at most β. This distribution is referred to as the margin distribution. On the other hand, during weights update process performed at each iteration of the training process, the misclassified samples in previous iterations are focused, i.e, those misclassified samples have a *low margin*. In each subsequent iteration, the classic AdaBoost algorithm try to increase the margins of those training samples; thus the distribution at each step can also rewritten as:

$$W_t(i) = \frac{exp(-yf(x_i))}{Z} \tag{5}$$

where, it is possible to assign high weights to samples misclassified in previous iterations. However, this operation may result in provoking misclassification of samples with *higher margin* at a given iteration; and, therefore, reducing their *margins*. Under such a circumstance, it is natural to ask whether it is a good practice to reduce the *margin* in the beginning of the training process. Apparently it is not a wise measure because it could also reduce the *margins* of samples that are not "truly" misclassified, since this could decrease generalization ability of the AdaBoost algorithm; and, therefore, causing higher errors in testing stages. Such a phenomenon is known as overfitting. In order to solve this overfitting problem, we introduce and use δ_i variable to monitoring the misclassification rate of those samples with *low margins*, avoiding excessive reduction of *margins* and simultaneously maintaining its generalization ability.

4.2   Conclusions

In this paper, we present and introduce a novel weight updating procedure to improve the performance of the AdaBoost algorithm. Experimental results validated the proposed method which has the following qualities:

- The proposed method enables faster convergence than the Classical AdaBoost, providing lower misclassification error rates. The fast convergence is the consequence of using a smaller number of weak classifiers to build the strong classifier. Such structure simplification has some desirable implication including real time applications such as object detection, where on line response is critical.
- The approach described in this work makes boosting algorithms less noise sensitive.

References

[1] Freund, Y., Schapire, R.E.: A Decision-Theoretic Generalization of On-line Learning and an Application to Boosting. In: Vitányi, P.M.B. (ed.) EuroCOLT 1995. LNCS, vol. 904, pp. 23–37. Springer, Heidelberg (1995)

[2] Valiant, L.G.: A theory of the learnable. Commun. ACM 27, 1134–1142 (1984)

[3] Schapire, R.E.: The strength of weak learnability. Mach. Learn. 5, 197–227 (1990)

[4] Schapire, R.E., Singer, Y.: Improved boosting algorithms using confidence-rated predictions. Mach. Learn. 37, 297–336 (1999)

[5] Friedman, J., Hastie, T., Tibshirani, R.: Additive Logistic Regression: a Statistical View of Boosting. The Annals of Statistics 38(2) (2000)

[6] Vezhnevets, A., Vezhnevets, V.: 'modest adaboost' - teaching adaboost to generalize better. In: GRAPHICON

[7] Li, S., Zhang, Z.: Floatboost learning and statistical face detection. IEEE Transactions on Pattern Analysis and Machine Intelligence 26(9), 1112–1123 (2004)

[8] Gómez-Verdejo, V., Ortega-Moral, M., Arenas-García, J., Figueiras-Vidal, A.R.: Boosting by weighting critical and erroneous samples. Neurocomput. 69, 679–685 (2006)

[9] Dietterich, T.G.: Ensemble Methods in Machine Learning. In: Kittler, J., Roli, F. (eds.) MCS 2000. LNCS, vol. 1857, pp. 1–15. Springer, Heidelberg (2000)

[10] Rätsch, G., Onoda, T., Müller, K.R.: Soft margins for adaboost. Mach. Learn. 42, 287–320 (2001)

[11] Servedio, R.A.: Smooth boosting and learning with malicious noise. J. Mach. Learn. Res. 4, 633–648 (2003)

[12] Li, G., Xu, Y., Wang, J.: An improved adaboost face detection algorithm based on optimizing skin color model. In: 2010 Sixth International Conference on Natural Computation (ICNC), vol. 4, pp. 2013–2015 (August 2010)

[13] Chang, C.C., Lin, C.J.: LIBSVM: A library for support vector machines. ACM Transactions on Intelligent Systems and Technology 2, 27:1–27:27 (2011), Software http://www.csie.ntu.edu.tw/~cjlin/libsvm

[14] Breiman, L.: Arcing classifiers. Annals of Statistics 26(3), 801–824 (1998)

[15] Schapire, R.E., Freund, Y., Bartlett, P., Lee, W.S.: Boosting the margin: a new explanation for the effectiveness of voting methods. Annals of Statistics 26(5), 1651–1686 (1998)

Significative Learning Using Alpha-Beta Associative Memories

Catalán-Salgado Edgar Armando[1], Yáñez-Márquez Cornelio[2],
and Figueroa-Nazuno Jesus[3]

[1] ESCOM-IPN, Av. Juan de Dios Batiz s/n, GAM, Mexico DF
ecatalanb05@sagitario.cic.ipn.mx
www.edgarcatalan.com
[2] CIC, Av. Juan de Dios Batiz s/n, GAM, Mexico DF
cyanez@cic.ipn.mx
www.alfabeta.org
[3] CIC, Av. Juan de Dios Batiz s/n, GAM, Mexico DF

Abstract. The main goal in pattern recognition is to be able to recognize interest patterns, although these patterns might be altered in some way. Associative memories is a branch in AI that obtains one generalization per class from the initial data set. The main problem is that when generalization is performed much information is lost. This is mainly due to the presence of outliers and pattern distribution in space. It is believed that one generalization is not sufficient to keep the information necessary to achieve a good performance in the recall phase. This paper shows a way to prevent information loss and make more significative learning allowing better recalling results.

1 Introduction

One of the main tasks in AI is pattern recognition. In pattern recognition the goal is to train a model to be able to recognize certain patterns of interest although these might be affected in some way. In supervised learning this training is performed by a set of patterns called the fundamental set. With this set the model obtains its generalization in the learning phase. In the recall phase the model is asked for the pattern class.

The first models of learning matrices appeared more than four decades ago[1,2]. Associative memories have attracted researchers due to its properties, including their efficiency, tolerance to noise and ease of implementation that facilitates the development of applications[1,3,4].

Alpha-Beta associative memories have had a noteworthy development. Since their creation[5,6] an algorithm that speeds up learning[7] has been developed and they (or a variant) are used in different applications[8,9].

In Alpha-Beta associative memories however, due to the nature of the memories, the presence of outliers affects their recall capacity; reducing it greatly. A similar problem arises when learning a great quantity of patterns in some class. This problem is called memory saturation. This paper proposes a method to

L. Alvarez et al. (Eds.): CIARP 2012, LNCS 7441, pp. 535–542, 2012.

avoid these problems and increase memory efficiency. This is achieved through the use of sub-generalizations.

Section 2 first describes the original Alpha-Beta associative memories and introduce the Alpha and Beta operators. Section 3 describes our proposal beginning with all the necessary definitions in order to build an Alpha-Beta associative committee. Learning and recall algorithms are shown in this section. Section 4 shows the experimentation and finally Section 5 presents conclusions and future work.

2   Alpha-Beta Associative Memories

In Alpha-Beta associative memories an input pattern of n attributes is denoted by a column vector $\mathbf{x} = [x_1, x_2, ..., x_n]$ and an output pattern of m attributes is denoted by a column vector $\mathbf{y} = [y_1, y_2, ..., y_m]$, where $m, n \in \mathbf{N}$.

$(\mathbf{x}^\mu, \mathbf{y}^\mu)$ is written to denote that input vector x^μ is associated to output vector y^μ, with $\mu \in \{1, 2, .., p\}$ and p is the number of associations. The set of associations used in the learning phase is know *a priori*, it is finite and called the fundamental set. The patterns belonging to the fundamental set are called fundamental patterns. The input and output patterns are represented as follows:

$$\mathbf{x}^\mu = \begin{bmatrix} x_1^\mu \\ x_2^\mu \\ ... \\ x_n^\mu \end{bmatrix} \in A^n \qquad \mathbf{y}^\mu = \begin{bmatrix} y_1^\mu \\ y_2^\mu \\ ... \\ y_m^\mu \end{bmatrix} \in A^m$$

where A={0,1}. An associative memory $\mathbf{M}$ is a system that relates an input pattern $\mathbf{x}^\mu$ with its respective output pattern $\mathbf{y}^\mu$ for each $\mu \in \{1, 2, .., p\}$. These memories have two phases.

The first phase is called learning phase; in it the memory establishes the association between the input pattern $\mathbf{x}^\mu$ and output pattern $\mathbf{y}^\mu$. Since $\mathbf{M}$ is a matrix generated by these associations, the transposition of $\mathbf{x}^\mu$, denoted as $(\mathbf{x}^\mu)^t$ is used.

$$(\mathbf{x}^\mu)^t \rightarrow \boxed{\mathbf{M}} \leftarrow \mathbf{y}^\mu$$

An associative memory $\mathbf{M}$ is represented by a matrix with ij-th component m_{ij}. If $\mathbf{x}^\mu = \mathbf{y}^\mu$ for all $\mu \in \{1, 2, .., p\}$ then $\mathbf{M}$ is auto-associative, otherwise it is hetero-associative. In the later it is possible to establish that $\mu \in \{1, 2, .., p\}$ for which $\mathbf{x}^\mu \neq \mathbf{y}^\mu$.

The second phase is called recall phase. In it an input pattern $\tilde{\mathbf{x}}$ is presented to the memory. This pattern may be an unknown or altered pattern, as the resulting memory gives an output pattern $\mathbf{y}$:

$$(\tilde{\mathbf{x}})^t \rightarrow \boxed{\mathbf{M}} \rightarrow \mathbf{y}$$

If the input pattern $\tilde{\mathbf{x}} = \mathbf{x}^\mu$ for some $\mu \in \{1, 2, .., p\}$ and the memory recalls the output pattern $\mathbf{y} = \mathbf{y}^\mu$, then it is said that recall is correct.

The Alpha-Beta associative memories are based in order relations and binary operators[5]. For the learning stage the operator uses α, and for the recall phase the operator uses β. These operators are defined as follows:

x	y	$\alpha(x,y)$
0	0	1
0	1	0
1	0	2
1	1	1

x	y	$\beta(x,y)$
0	0	0
0	1	0
1	0	1
1	1	1
2	0	2
2	1	2

Learning Phase. There are two kinds of Alpha-Beta associative memories, the Alpha-Beta associative memory MAX, denoted by $\mathbf{M}$ and the Alpha-Beta associative memory MIN, denoted by $\mathbf{W}$. $\wedge$ is used to denote minimum operator, and $\vee$ for the max operator. The ij-th entries of the associative memories $\mathbf{M}$ and $\mathbf{W}$ are defined by:

$$m_{ij} = \bigvee_{\mu=1}^{p} \alpha\left(y_i^\mu, x_j^\mu\right) \qquad w_{ij} = \bigwedge_{\mu=1}^{p} \alpha\left(y_i^\mu, x_j^\mu\right)$$

respectively.

Recalling Phase. To obtain the output vector $\mathbf{y}$, the associative memory $\mathbf{M}$ or $\mathbf{W}$ will be operated with the input pattern $\tilde{\mathbf{x}}$. The i-th entry y_i of the output pattern $\mathbf{y}$ is obtained as follows:

$$y_i = \bigwedge_{j=1}^{n} \beta\left(m_{ij}, \tilde{x}_j\right) \qquad y_i = \bigvee_{j=1}^{n} \beta\left(w_{ij}, \tilde{x}_j\right)$$

for $\mathbf{M}$ and $\mathbf{W}$ respectively.

In either case $\mathbf{y}$ is called the recalled pattern. It is important to note that the associative memory $\mathbf{M}$ is robust to additive noise but sensitive to subtractive noise, and the associative memory $\mathbf{W}$ is robust to subtractive noise but sensitive to additive [5].

3   Alpha Beta Associative Memory Committee

In associative memories the learning phase carries the responsibility to obtain a generalization that achieves a good performance in recall phase. Enhancing this performance necesitates making multiple sub-generalizations per class. In order to generate these multiple sub-generalizations an Alpha-Beta Associative Memory Committee (ABAMC)is created. The ABAMC contains m associative memories, each one specialized in one class. These sub-generalizations are made creating dynamically representative patterns using a similarity measure in the learning phase.

3.1 Definitions

Definition 1 (one-hot vector). *A one hot vector is a vector* $\mathbf{y} = [y_1, y_2, ..., y_m]$ *with the characteristic that just one of its components is equal to one.*

Definition 2 (Representative Pattern). *Let* $\mathbf{x}^1, \mathbf{x}^2, \ldots, \mathbf{x}^l$ *be fundamental input patterns which are members of the same class* c, *where* $l \in (1, 2, ..., p)$. *A representative pattern* $\mathbf{r} = [r_1, r_2, ..., r_n]$ *is an* n *dimensional column vector with* $\mathbf{r} = \mathbf{x}^1 \cap \mathbf{x}^2 \cap \ldots \cap \mathbf{x}^l$, *where* $\cap$ *denotes intersection.*

Definition 3 (Representative pattern identifier). *Let* r *be a representative pattern, let* $q \in [1, ..., p]$ *be an integer value that indicates the number of representative patterns in a class. A representative pattern identifier is a one-hot column vector* $\mathbf{v} = [v_1, v_2, .., v_q]$ *associated to* $\mathbf{r}$ *used to identify it.*

Definition 4 (Operator ζ). *Let* $\mathbf{x} = [x_1, x_2, ..., x_n]$ *be an* n *dimensional one-hot vector. The operator* ζ *returns the unique position* i,*such that* $x_i = 1$, *i.e.*

$$\zeta(\mathbf{x}) = i \text{ where } x_i = 1$$

Definition 5 (Operator ζ^{-1}). *Let* $a \in [1, 2, .., n]$ *be an integer value. The operator* ζ^{-1} *is the inverse of* ζ, *i.e.*

$$\zeta^{-1}(a) = [x_1, x_2, ..., x_i, ..., x_n] \text{ where } x_i = \begin{cases} 0 \ i \neq a \\ 1 \ i = a \end{cases}$$

Definition 6 (Alpha-Beta Max associative memory committee). *Let* $c \in [1, 2, ...m]$ *be an integer value that indicates a class in the fundamental set, let* $\mathbf{r}^{c1}, \mathbf{r}^{c2}, ..., \mathbf{r}^{cq}$ *be the* q *representative patterns for the class* c, *let* $\mathbf{v}^{c1}, \mathbf{v}^{c2}, ..., \mathbf{v}^{cq}$ *be the pairwise distinguishing one-hot patterns, where* r^{ck} *is associated to* $\mathbf{v}^{ck}$ *for* $k \in [1, 2, ..., q]$. *An associative memory committee is the set of associative memories* $\{\mathbf{M}^c | c \text{ is a class}\}$, *where* $\mathbf{M}^c$ *is the Max associative memory of the class* c *that results in the learning of all associations* $(\mathbf{r}^{ck}, \mathbf{v}^{ck})$. *The ij-th component* m_{ij}^c *of* $\mathbf{M}^c$ *is defined as follows*

$$m_{ij}^c = \alpha \left(v_i^{ck}, r_j^{ck} \right)$$

Definition 7 (Additive difference). *Let n be an integer value, $\mathbf{x}$ and $\mathbf{y}$ two patterns of dimension n. The additive difference is defined as the number of $y_i = 1$ and $x_i = 0$, and can be obtained using the following equation*

$$\delta(\mathbf{x}, \mathbf{y}) = h\left((\mathbf{x} \cap \mathbf{y}), \mathbf{y}\right)$$

where $\cap$ denotes intersection and $h\left((\mathbf{x} \cap \mathbf{y}), \mathbf{y}\right)$ is the hamming distance from intersection to pattern $\mathbf{y}$

Definition 8 (Representative pattern loss limit). *Let r be a representative pattern, a representative pattern loss limit $a \in \{0, 1, 2, \ldots, n\}$ is a integer value that indicates the maximum number of $r_i = 1$ that can change to $r_i = 0$*

Definition 9 (Input pattern loss limit). *Let x be an input pattern, a input pattern loss limit $b \in \{0, 1, 2, \ldots, n\}$ is a integer value that indicates the maximum number of $x_i = 1$ that can change to $x_i = 0$*

Definition 10 (operator ψ). *Let $x \in \{0, 1, 2\}$ and $y \in \{0, 1\}$. The operator ψ is defined as follows*

x	y	$\psi(x, y)$
0	*0*	*1*
0	*1*	*1*
1	*0*	*0*
1	*1*	*1*
2	*0*	*0*
2	*1*	*0*

Definition 11 (Operator η). *Let $\mathbf{x}$ be a n dimensional patter. Operator η realizes a count of positions x_i with $x_i = 1$, is defined as follows:*

$$\eta = \sum_{i=1}^{n} x_i$$

Definition 12 (Conditional similarity). *Let n be an integer value, $\mathbf{x}$ and $\mathbf{y}$ two patters of dimension n. The conditional similarity between $\mathbf{x}$ and $\mathbf{y}$ is defined as follows*

$$\varrho(\mathbf{x}, \mathbf{y}) = \begin{cases} \left(\frac{\eta(\mathbf{x}) - h(\mathbf{x} \wedge \mathbf{y}, \mathbf{x})}{\eta(\mathbf{x})} + \frac{\eta(\mathbf{y}) - h(\mathbf{x} \wedge \mathbf{y}, \mathbf{y})}{\eta(\mathbf{y})} \right) * \frac{1}{2} & \text{if } \eta(\mathbf{x}) \neq 0, \eta(\mathbf{y}) \neq 0 \\ 0 & \text{Otherwise} \end{cases}$$

3.2 Learning Phase Algorithm

The learning phase is shown with the following flow diagram.

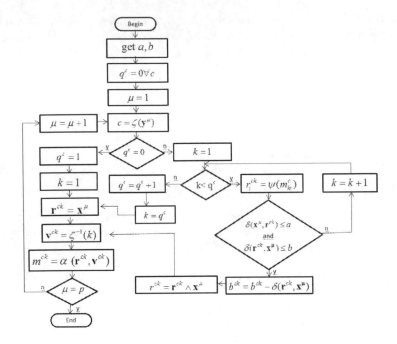

3.3   Recalling Phase Algorithm

The recalling phase is shown using the following flow diagram

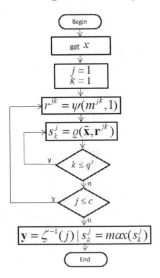

4   Experimentation

This section shows the result of experimentation made with the proposed algorithm.

The algorithm was tested with three popular databases[10]: iris plant, wine and lung cancer, with every database we ran our algorithm several times with different loss values a and b; these values and validation using 10 fold cross validation are shown. A comparison based on efficiency with other models in literature was made. Experiments with these models were realized using Weka[11,12]. It is important to note the preprocessing realized to data before the experiments. This preprocessing consists of the following points:

1. Normalize numerical data to [0,100]
2. Convert this normalized data to Jonhson-Moebius code[13]
3. Convert the class label into a One-Hot vector.

Experiments were made in a Intel core i5 computer with 4gb RAM, and are focused to show the efficiency with different learning schema, so two bayesian classifiers (BayesNet[14],NaiveBayes[15]), one function based classifier (Simple Logistic[16]), two meta-classifiers (AdaBoostM1[17], MultiClassClassifier[18]) and one decision tree classifier(RandomForest[19]) were used. The following table shows comparative efficiency between these models and ABAMC.

	Iris Plant	Wine	Lung cancer
BayesNet	94.63	98.31	50
NaiveBayes	94.63	94.94	62.5
Simple Logistic	95.97	95.5	62.2
AdaBoostM1	95.3	88.2	46.87
MulticlassClassifier	96.64	94.38	46.87
RandomForest	94.63	97.75	56.25
ABAMC	97.33(a=10, b=35)	95.56(a=30,b=30)	87.5 (a=47,b=48)

The experimentation shows that the best efficiency with Iris plant and lung cancer databases was achieved by the proposed algorithm but was second in the wine database. This was anticipated in accordance with *no free lunch theorem*. The most promising result is with lung cancer database where ABAMC achieved 87.5 (25 percent more efficiency than other models).

5   Conclusion and Future Work

This model was conceived based on the hypothesis that the sub-generalizations obtained through representative patterns preserving useful information that is lost with only one generalization, and this preservation allows better recalling results. The experimentation confirms this hypothesis and provides motivation to test more challenging databases.

Future work would be in the following way:

1. It is highly desirable to find optimal ways to obtain the best loss value for an input pattern and for representative patterns.
2. Processes or modifications that enhance efficiency.
3. Complexity analysis for learning and recalling phase.

References

1. Steinbuch, K., Piske, U.A.W.: Learning matrices and their applications. IEEE Transactions on Electronic Computers 12(6), 846–862 (1963)
2. Steinbuch, K.: Die lernmatrix. Kybernetik 1(3), 148–152 (1961)
3. Anderson, J.A.: A memory storage model utilizing spatial correlation. Kybernetik 5(3), 113–119 (1968)
4. Anderson, J.A.: A simple neural network generating an interactive memory. Mathematical Biosciences 14, 197–220 (1972)
5. Yáñez Márquez, C.: Associative memories based in binary operators and order relations. PhD thesis, Center for Computer Research (2002)
6. Yáñez Márquez, C., Diaz de Leon, J.L.: Associative memories based on order relations and binary operators. Computation and Systems 6(4), 300–311 (2003) (in Spanish)
7. Catalán-Salgado, E.A., Yáñez Márquez, C., José, A.C.A.: Simplification of the learning phase in the alpha-beta associative memories. In: CERMA 2008, pp. 428–433 (2008)
8. Yáñez, C., Felipe-Riveron, E., López-Yáñez, I., Flores-Carapia, R.: A Novel Approach to Automatic Color Matching. In: Martínez-Trinidad, J.F., Carrasco Ochoa, J.A., Kittler, J. (eds.) CIARP 2006. LNCS, vol. 4225, pp. 529–538. Springer, Heidelberg (2006)
9. López-Yáñez, I., Yáñez Márquez, C., de la Sáenz-Morales, G.: Application of the gamma classifier to environmental data prediction. In: CERMA 2008, pp. 80–84. IEEE (2008)
10. Asuncion, A., Newman, D.: Uci machine learning repository (2007), http://archive.ics.uci.edu/ml/
11. Hall, M., Frank, E., Holmes, G., Pfahringer, B., Reutemann, P., Witten, I.H.: The weka data mining software: An update. SIGKDD Explorations 11(1), 10–18 (2009)
12. Hall, M., Frank, E., Holmes, G., Pfahringer, B., Reutemann, P., Witten, I.H.: Weka 3: Data mining software in java, http://www.cs.waikato.ac.nz/ml/weka/
13. Yáñez-Márquez, C., Sánchez-Fernández, L.P., López-Yáñez, I.: Alpha-Beta Associative Memories for Gray Level Patterns. In: Wang, J., Yi, Z., Żurada, J.M., Lu, B.-L., Yin, H. (eds.) ISNN 2006. LNCS, vol. 3971, pp. 818–823. Springer, Heidelberg (2006)
14. Christofides, N.: G.t.: An algorithmic approach. In: Press, A., (ed.): Computer Science and Applied Mathematics, Orlando, FL, USA (1975)
15. John, G.H., Langley, P.: Estimating continuous distributions in bayesian classifiers. In: Eleventh Conference on Uncertainty in Artificial Intelligence, pp. 338–345. Morgan Kaufmann, San Mateo (1995)
16. Sumner, M., Frank, E., Hall, M.: Speeding Up Logistic Model Tree Induction. In: Jorge, A.M., Torgo, L., Brazdil, P.B., Camacho, R., Gama, J. (eds.) PKDD 2005. LNCS (LNAI), vol. 3721, pp. 675–683. Springer, Heidelberg (2005)
17. Freund, Y., Schapire, R.E.: Experiments with a new boosting algorithm. In: Thirteenth International Conference on Machine Learning, San Francisco, pp. 148–156 (1996)
18. Witten, I.H., Frank, E.: Practical Machine Learning Tools, 2nd edn. Morgan Kaufmann Series in Data Management. Morgan Kaufmann Publishers Inc., USA (2005)
19. Breiman, L.: Random forests. Machine Learning 45(1), 5–32 (2001)

Early Visual Processing for Pattern Recognition in Natural Environments

Rosana Matuk Herrera

Department of Computer Science, Facultad de Ciencias Exactas y Naturales,
Universidad de Buenos Aires, Argentina
rmatuk@dc.uba.ar

Abstract. In this article, the performance of hierarchical architectures for computer vision of biological inspiration is analyzed. In particular, the role of the lateral geniculate nucleus (LGN) for the robustness in the recognition of ring shaped patterns under gradual changes in illumination was analyzed. Changes in illumination are common in everyday environments and thus, it is a crucial factor to be considered for the recognition of objects in everyday environments.

1 Introduction

In this article, we analyze a computational model of the visual cortex, and in particular the role of the early visual processing system, for the recognition of patterns under different levels of illumination. This is also a fundamental problem for robotics in uncontrolled environments, because illumination strongly affects the visual perception of the environment by the robots.

2 Biological Background

During visual perception, light entering the eye is detected by the retina, an array of photoreceptors and related cells on the inside of the rear surface of the eye. The cells in the retina encode the light levels at a given location as patterns of electrical activity in neurons called ganglion cells. Output from the ganglion cells travels through neural connections to the lateral geniculate nucleus of the thalamus, or LGN, at the base of each side of the brain. From the LGN, the signals continue to the primary visual cortex, or V1 at the rear of the brain (Fig. 1). The output from V1 goes on to many different higher cortical areas, including areas that underlie object and face processing.

Retinal ganglion cells perform a type of edge detection on the input, responding most strongly to borders between bright and dark areas. The two main types of such neurons are the ON-center and OFF-center. An ON center retinal ganglion cell responds most strongly to a spot of light surrounded by dark, located in a region of the retina called its receptive field, or RF. An OFF-center ganglion cell instead prefers a dark area surrounded by light. The size of the preferred

L. Alvarez et al. (Eds.): CIARP 2012, LNCS 7441, pp. 543–550, 2012.

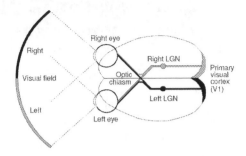

Fig. 1. Human visual pathway (extracted from [1])

spot determines the spatial frequency preference of the neuron; neurons prefer-
ring large spots have a low preferred spatial frequency, and vice versa.

Neurons in the LGN have properties similar to retinal ganglion cells, and
are also arranged retinotopically, so that nearby LGN cells respond to nearby
portions of the retina. The ON-center cells in the retina connect to the ON cells
in the LGN, and the OFF cells in the retina connect to the OFF cells in the
LGN. Because of this independence, the ON and OFF cells are often described
as separate processing channels: the ON channel and the OFF channel.

Like LGN neurons, nearby neurons in V1 also respond to nearby portions
of the retina and are selective for spatial frequency. Unlike LGN neurons, most
V1 neurons are binocular, responding to some degree to stimuli from either eye,
although they usually prefer one eye or the other. They are also selective for
the orientation of the stimulus and its direction of movement. In addition, some
V1 cells prefer particular color combinations (such as red/green or blue/yellow
borders), and disparity (relative positions on the two retinas). V1 neurons respond most strongly to stimuli that match their feature preferences, although
they respond to approximate matches as well (see [2] for a review).

3   Computational Maps of the Visual Cortex

The LISSOM model (laterally interconnected synergetically self organizing map;
[3] [4] [5] [1]) was designed as a computational map model of V1.

The V1 network in LISSOM is a sheet of $N \times N$ interconnected computational units, or neurons (Fig. 2). Because the focus is on the two-dimensional
organization of the cortex, each neuron in V1 corresponds to a vertical column of
cells through the six layers of the biological cortex. This columnar organization
helps make the problem of simulating such a large number of neurons tractable,
and is viable because the cells in a column generally fire in response to the same
inputs.

Each cortical neuron receives external input from two types of neurons in
the LGN: ON-center and OFF-center. The LGN neurons in turn receive input
from a small area of the retina, represented as an $R \times R$ array of photoreceptor
cells. The afferent input connections from the retina to LGN and LGN to V1

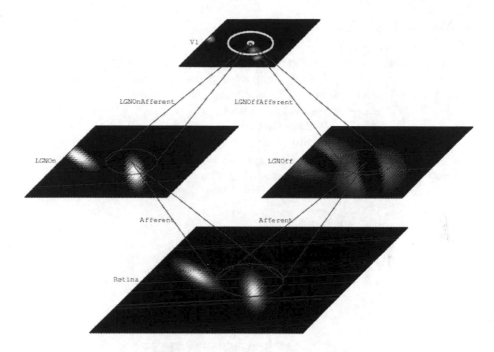

Fig. 2. Architecture of the LISSOM model. The large circle in V1 corresponds to the range of lateral inhibitory connections, and the small circle to the range of lateral excitatory connections, regarding to the neuron situated at the center of the V1 sheet.

are all excitatory. In addition to the afferent connections, each cortical neuron has reciprocal excitatory and inhibitory lateral connections with other neurons. Lateral excitatory connections have a short range, connecting only close neighbors in the map. Lateral inhibitory connections run for long distances, but may be patchy, connecting only selected neurons.

The ON and OFF neurons in the LGN represent the entire pathway from photoreceptor output to the V1 input, including the ON/OFF processing in the retinal ganglion cells and the LGN. Although the ON and OFF neurons are not always physically separated in the biological pathways, for conceptual clarity they are divided into separate channels in LISSOM. Each of these channels is further organized into an $L \times L$ array corresponding to the retinotopic organization of the LGN.

Each neuron develops an initial response as a weighted sum (scalar product) of the activation in its afferent input connections. The lateral interactions between cortical neurons then focus the initial activation pattern into a localized response on the map. After the pattern has stabilized, the connection weights of cortical neurons are modified. As the self-organization progresses, these neurons grow more nonlinear and weak connections die off. The result is a self-organized structure in a dynamic equilibrium with the input.

4 Method

For the experiments, we use Topographica [6] which is a software package for computational modeling of neural maps based on LISSOM, developed by the Institute for Adaptive and Neural Computation at the University of Edinburgh and the Neural Networks Research Group at the University of Texas at Austin.

In order to analyze the role of the ON/OFF channels, two different architectures were tested. The first architecture is the basic LISSOM model (Fig. 2), which has a retina network at its bottom level, ON and OFF networks at its middle level, and a V1 network at its top level. The second architecture, is similar to the the first architecture, but without the ON and OFF networks (Fig. 3).

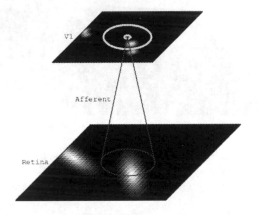

Fig. 3. Architecture without the ON/OFF channels

The following dimensions were used: a 54x54 retina, a 36x36 LGN (composed of one 36x36 OFF channel sheet, and one 36x36 ON channel sheet), and a 48x48 V1. Both architectures were trained presenting 10000 pairs of oriented Gaussian patterns at random angles and positions.

5 Results

The training of the networks lasted around 5 minutes on a computer with an Intel Core i5 processor. The response of the network after the training, when a test pattern was presented, was very fast (less than 1 second).

The orientation Preference/Selectivity maps and Fourier spectrums obtained are shown in Fig. 4. Figure 5 shows the responses of the V1 activity under testing. The test patterns consisted of a ring shaped pattern, increasing its level of smoothing.

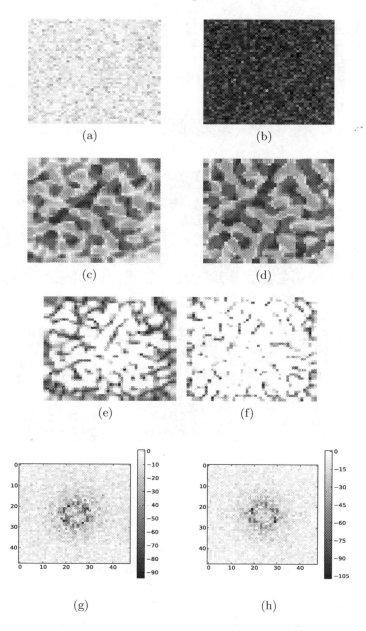

Fig. 4. Orientation Preference/Selectivity maps and Fourier spectrums. (a) initial orientation preference/selectivity map before the training; (b) initial selectivity map; orientation preference/selectivity maps after the training of the architecture without the LGN level (c) and with the LGN level (d); selectivity maps after the training of the architectures without the LGN level and(e) with the LGN level (f); Fourier spectrums of the orientation preference/selectivity maps for the architecture without the LGN level (g) and with the LGN level (h). The selectivity maps show that before training (b) the neurons are unselective (i.e. dark), and after training (e) and (f) nearly all of the neurons are highly selective (light)

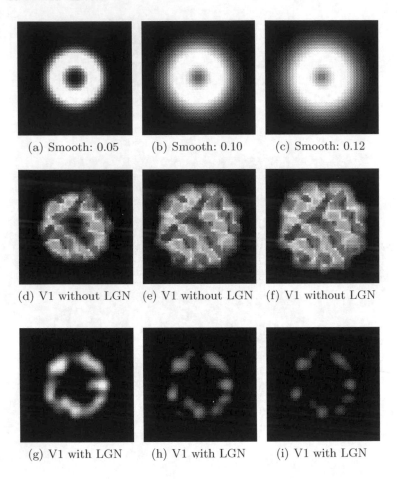

Fig. 5. V1 activity testing with the same ring shaped pattern, increasing its level of smoothing. Ring test patterns corresponding to (a) smoothing of 0.05, (b) smoothing of 0.10, (c) smoothing of 0.12. The middle row of the figure show the V1 activity responses corresponding to the architecture without the LGN level. The last row of the figure show the V1 activity responses corresponding to the architecture with the LGN level. The V1 answer is patchy due to the orientation preference and selectivity of the V1 neurons.

6   Discussion

The orientation preference/selectivity maps of Fig. 4 show that the training was successful in obtaining smoothly varying orientation and selectivity maps. An interesting property of orientation maps measured in animals is that their Fourier spectrums usually show a ring shape, because the orientations repeat at a constant spatial frequency in all directions. The subfigures 4(g) and 4(h) show ring shaped Fourier spectrums for both architectures, which thus indicates that the orientation preference/selectivity maps are similar to biological maps. The selectivity map for the neurons in the architecture with the LGN level (Fig. 4(f)), is lighter that the selectivity map for the architecture without the LGN level (Fig. 4(e)). This result indicates higher selectivity for the neurons in the architecture with the LGN level, which coincides with previous results in [1].

The V1 activities of Fig. 5, show that when the level of smoothing is increased, the recognition of the ring shaped pattern is more difficult for both architectures. The architecture without the LGN level get the worst performance, because when the level of smoothing is increased, the answer of the V1 seems a disk instead of a ring. Thus, the architecture with the LGN level seems more robust to gradual changes in illumination in a ring shaped pattern. This result gives more strength to the result in [1] regarding the robustness of an architecture with LGN in natural environments, because smoothing is an important visual characteristic in natural images.

7   Conclusions and Future Work

In this article, the performance of hierarchical architectures for computer vision based on LISSOM was analyzed. In particular, the importance of the LGN level for the robustness under gradual changes in illumination was analyzed. Changes in illumination are common in everyday environments and are therefore a crucial factor that affects the recognition of objects in everyday environments. The LISSOM architecture with the LGN level showed a good level of robustness for ring shaped pattern recognition under changes of illumination.

Only single ON and OFF channels are used in LISSOM simulations in this article. Multiple channels representing different spatial frequencies are currently being analyzed to be included in the models, in order to improve the computational early visual processing.

Regarding the velocity of the answer of V1, it was very fast, after the training, which could be suitable for real time applications. However, the dimension of the networks was small, and the dimension of the network affects the capacity of the model to recognize patterns. Thus, parallel implementation of the model are currently being analyzed to increase its velocity and use larger networks in realistic environments.

Processing in the brain in general and visual processing in particular is organized in a hierarchical fashion, from simple localized features to complex, large scale features. The visual system consists of a hierarchy, in which neurons in early visual areas extract simple image features (e.g., orientation) over a small local region of visual space, which are then transmitted to neurons in higher visual areas responding to more complex features (e.g. shape) over a larger region of visual space. Hierarchical representations can derive and organize features at multiple levels. However, although all neurophysiologic evidence suggests that in the human visual system quite a number of levels are realized, it has turned out that the design and/or learning of such deep hierarchical systems is a very difficult task. Most existing computer vision systems are 'flat' (e.g., having rather simple features as input) and hence cannot make use of the advantages connected to deep hierarchies. Here in particular the generalization capabilities are crucial for any form of cognitive intelligence. As a consequence, the issue of establishing deep hierarchies is considered as one major challenge for the establishment of truly cognitive systems. This paper deals with the computational modeling at the level of the early visual processing, and is at the base of a hierarchical cognitive system. Thus, the study, design and optimization of early visual processing levels is also relevant to achieve truly cognitive systems.

References

1. Miikkulainen, R., Bednar, J., Choe, Y., Sirosh, J.: Computational Maps in the Visual Cortex. Springer (2005)
2. Ringach, D.: Mapping receptive fields in primary visual cortex. The Journal of Physiology (558), 717–728 (2004)
3. Miikkulainen, R.: Self-organizing process based on lateral inhibition and synaptic resource redistribution. In: Kohonen, T., Makisara, K., Simula, O., Kangas, J. (eds.) Proceedings of the 1991 International Conference on Artificial Neural Networks (1991)
4. Miikkulainen, R., Bednar, J., Choe, Y., Sirosh, J.: Self-organization, plasticity, and low-level visual phenomena in a laterally connected map model of the primary visual cortex. Psychology of Learning and Motivation 36, 257–308 (1997)
5. Sirosh, J.: A self-organizing neural network model of the primary visual cortex. PhD thesis, Department of Computer Sciences, The University of Texas at Austin, Austin, TX (1995)
6. http://www.topographica.org

Motor Intention Recognition in EEG: In Pursuit of a Relevant Feature Set

Pablo A. Iturralde[1], Martín Patrone[1], Federico Lecumberry[2],
and Alicia Fernández[2]

[1] Department of Physics, School of Engineering, UdelaR, Montevideo, Uruguay
[2] Department of Electrical Engineering, School of Engineering, UdelaR,
Montevideo, Uruguay
{iturral,mpatrone,fefo,aliciaf}@fing.edu.uy

Abstract. Brain-computer interfaces (BCIs) based on electroencephalograms (EEG) are a noninvasive and cheap alternative to get a communication channel between brain and computers. Some of the main issues with EEG signals are its high dimensionality, high inter-user variance, and non-stationarity. In this work we present different approaches to deal with the high dimensionality of the data, finding relevant descriptors in EEG signals for motor intention recognition: first, a classical dimensionality reduction method using Diffusion Distance, second a technique based on spectral analysis of EEG channels associated with the frontal and prefrontal cortex, and third a projection over average signals. Performance analysis for different sets of features is done, showing that some of them are more robust to user variability.

1 Introduction

In recent years, Brain-Computer Interfaces (BCIs) have become an active topic of research. Such interfaces could provide an alternative communication channel between humans and computers, replacing the normal output channel of nerves and muscles. As its main application, BCIs could be used by paralyzed patients or others suffering some type of motor impairment but who are cognitively intact as a means to interact with the environment.

BCIs register brain states (relating to thoughts and intentions) as signals that are interpreted and translated into actions. The signal acquisition process is critical to the performance of the whole system, and several technologies have been proposed to carry out such a task. Signal registering through electroencephalograms (EEG) are one of the most promising systems because of its noninvasive nature that allows for simpler and cheaper devices with almost no associated risks, as opposed to invasive technologies such as electrocorticographic (ECoG) signals which require medical procedures for its implantation. However, EEG signals provide only a diffuse access to brain signals, since currents in the brain cortex are volume conducted through the skull before being sensed at the scalp. This means that more sophisticated processing and recognition systems are needed in order to obtain information about brain states from such signals [12,10].

L. Alvarez et al. (Eds.): CIARP 2012, LNCS 7441, pp. 551–558, 2012.

One of the main issues with EEG signals is its high dimensionality. Usually, signals from over ten and up to hundreds of channels are acquired at sampling rates of at least 100 Hz to ensure that no aliasing occurs. This implies that even for short trials that last for about a second, the raw feature space has a dimension between 1000 and 60000, making it very difficult to work with. One of the most used [3,2] is to perform component analysis (PCA, ICA or equivalent) in order to reduce redundancy in both time (over-sampled signals) and space (EEG electrodes that are nearby have similar EEG signals). This type of analysis (particularly ICA) has also been used to deduce the actual location of brain activity from EEG signals, see [3].

Another common approach [13] after the component analysis is to divide the remaining signals in several frequency bands along different time windows for the duration of the trial (time-frequency analysis [11]), using these spectral components to perform the classification. While the amplitude of the spectral components is widely used particularly in the mu and beta bands [2], the phase of the components has received special attention because of its relation to Event Related (De)Synchronization (ERS/ERD) [8,11].

Dimensionality reduction is a major topic of research, and several algorithms have been proposed to perform such task. Data laying in high dimensional spaces generally presents complex geometries, and probably not enough samples for accurate statistics. This kind of problem requires new strategies to deal with it instead of the classical PCA or Multi-Dimensional Scaling (MDS). One reason is the non linearity of the manifold where the original high dimensional data points lies. Another is the computational cost of traditional methods applied to data of high dimension, as it grows exponentially with dimension. Additionally, the sparse sampling leads to poor convergence of the algorithms, a phenomenon referred to as "the curse of dimensionality". Although input data may present a high dimensionality, it is common that the "real" or intrinsic dimensionality of the source that generates this data is much lower due to significant correlations between many of the coordinates. Finding meaningful structures in the data and obtaining those "principal coordinates" is one of the goals of the machine learning algorithms. In past years kernel based methods have concentrated the attention with good results and a solid background theory; a brief list of these methods include Locally Linear Embedding [9], Laplacian Eigenmaps [1], Hessian Eigenmaps [4] and Diffusion Maps [5].

In this paper we deal with a motor imagery task, consisting of several trials in where a user decided to release, and actually released, a button or not. The situation has the same high dimensionality problem that was described before, consisting of instances containing 31 EEG signals originally sampled at 1kHz for a time frame of one second. To reduce the amount of data preserving the spectral components of interest, downsampling to 100Hz was performed. Data also presents high inter-user variance, and non-stationarity.

We present different approaches to deal with the high dimensionality of the data, finding relevant descriptors in EEG signals for motor intention recognition: first, a classical dimensionality reduction method using Diffusion Distance, second a technique based on spectral analysis of EEG channels associated with the frontal and prefrontal cortex [11], and third a projection over average signals as proposed in [3].

This paper is structured as follows. On section Methods we describe the dataset that was used, and we detail the three different approaches used. On section Results we present the performance analysis in all three cases for all the users in the dataset, as well as some other results obtained from different variants of these strategies. Discussion regarding the results and future lines of work are mentioned on the last section.

2 Methods

2.1 Data Description

The EEG data files of the experiment were made available by A. Delorme in (http://sccn.ucsd.edu/~arno/fam2data/data/). Fourteen subjects of several ages and both sexes were tested in two recording phases on different days. Each day consisted of at least 10 series with 100 images per series. The subjects were asked to identify target images and non-target images, equally likely presented. In each instance, the image was shown for 20 msec. in a computer (avoiding the use of exploratory eye movement), and the subject had to gave their response following a go/nogo paradigm. For each target they had to lift their finger from a button as quickly as possible, and for each distractor had to keep pressing the button during at least 1 sec (nogo response).

Scalp EEGs were recorded from 31 channels (placed according to the international 10/20 system [6], see figure 1) with a 1 kHz sampling rate during 1s for each instance. Every instance consists of a single image experiment; it starts with the image being displayed for 20 msec., and lasts for a second, which was the maximum time the users had to respond. The database includes at least 1000 images per subject and fourteen different subjects, which results in 14000 instances with a feature set of 31000 dimensions. However, since EEGs depends on personal physiological factors [6], there is an important variability in the characteristics of the signals between subjects (signal mean and energy). This is the reason to use the data as fourteen independent sets, one for each subject.

Pre-processing of the data was performed to correct for a DC drift between instances. Therefore, signals from every channel in each instance were forced to start at zero by substracting a DC level. Signals were also downsampled to 100 Hz, since spectral analysis showed that no energy was present over 50 Hz, making the elevated original sampling rate unnecesary.

2.2 High-Dimensionality Analysis Tools

A first step for dimension reduction is to estimate the intrinsic dimension of the problem.

We found the best results (regarding consistency in the estimation) using the Maximum Likelihood Estimator for dimensionality, which gave values ranging

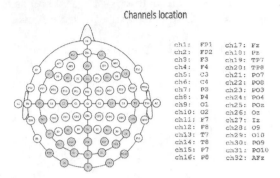

Fig. 1. Channel locations used in the EEG recordings, according to the 10/20 system. Image adapted from `http://www.mariusthart.net/`

from 29 to 35 for the different users. Independently from the estimator used, a mapping tool was selected in order to reduce the feature space. Locally Linear Embedding, Laplacian Eigenmaps, Hessian Eigenmaps and Diffusion Maps (DM) were considered. In this case the best results were obtained with the use of Diffusion Maps. DM is a general framework for data analysis based on a diffusion process over an undirected weighted graph, defining a new metric on the data called Diffusion Distance [7]. This distance is equivalent to the Euclidean distance in the space with coordinates given by the mapping function. In order to compute the weights on the graph we used a Gaussian kernel with an adequate (manually) selected variance, fixed for all subjects.

Once the reduced feature space was obtained, a classifier was trained with these new features.

2.3   Channel and Time Window Selection from Active Zones

Plotting the data corresponding to the EEG signals over a single trial, different zones of activity (both in the spatial and temporal senses) become visible. Approximately 100msec after the image is shown, the occipital region becomes active. Since the occipital lobe is where visual information is processed, this seems to indicate that an analysis of the image is being performed. After about 550msec pre-frontal cortex becomes active, which is consistent with the expected motor control actions that need to be carried out. While it could be expected that the activity be more noticeable when a motor action is indeed executed (target class), both classes seem to present some of this activity (see figure 2, which show average signals for target and non-target instances). Furthermore, it is in these channels and time-window that the greatest differential activity is observed.

From both the functional analysis of the cerebral lobes and the activity zones shown in the signals, follows that considering a feature space consisting only of the signals corresponding to frontal and pre-frontal channels (F-channels, see figure 1) might allow to reduce dimensionality while still allowing to differentiate

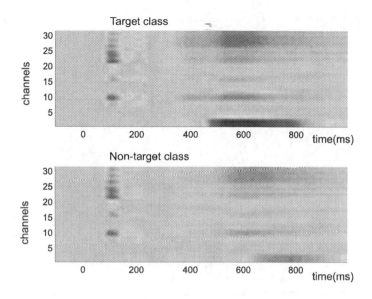

Fig. 2. Average signals for target and non-target classes

between the two types of instances. Spectral analysis was then performed over these channels. Frequencies finally considered for the training of classifiers where in the 0-10Hz band, resulting in a feature vector of dimension 275.

2.4   Projection over Average Signals

An average signal –over instances– was extracted for each of the 31 available channels, for each class. Thus, 62 reference signals were obtained, 31 corresponding to the average in all the EEG channels in the target class (T) and 31 for the channels in the non-target class (NT). Let us call s_i^j the time signal corresponding to the i-th channel for the j-th instance, s_i^T the time signal corresponding to the i-th channel in the average over the target class in the training set, and s_i^{NT} the time signal corresponding to the i-th channel in the average over the non-target class in the training set (see Equations 1, 2). For each instance, a projection over the reference signals was performed (channel by channel, by means of a scalar product over time), resulting in a feature vector $c = (c_i^T, c_i^{NT})$ of 62 scalar features for each instance (see Equations 4, 3). The first 31 of these features (c_i^T) refer to the projection of the instance's signals into the averaged signals for the target class, and the last 31 (c_i^{NT}) for the non-target class. From this new feature space different classifiers were trained. Results were validated over the test set.

$$s_i^{NT} = \frac{1}{N} \sum_{j \in NT} s_i^j, \ i \in [1, 31] \tag{1}$$

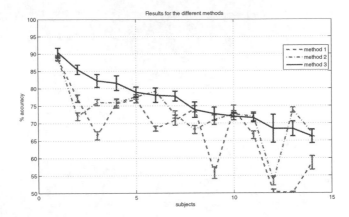

Fig. 3. Results obtained for the different users. Method 1: Diffusion Maps. Method 2: Channel and time window selection from active zones. Method 3: Projection over average signals. The classification was made with a two-layer feedforward perceptron, with 3 neurons in each layer, a learning rate of 0.3 and backpropagation as the training algorithm.

$$s_i^T = \frac{1}{N} \sum_{j \in T} s_i^j,\; i \in [1, 31] \tag{2}$$

$$c_i^{NT} = < s_i^j, s_i^{NT} >,\; i \in [1, 31] \tag{3}$$

$$c_i^T = < s_i^j, s_i^T >,\; i \in [1, 31] \tag{4}$$

Experiments were also conducted considering only F-channels, as is suggested by the analysis of the previous section. However results were worse in that case than when considering all channels.

3   Results

The results obtained with the methods described in the previous section are shown in figure 3. For all cases different classifiers were trained and tested (multilayer perceptrons, C4.5 trees) but since results did not differ significantly among them, only best results concerning multilayer perceptrons are presented.

There are two major observations that arise from figure 3. First of all, for most subject the best results are obtained by making the projection over average signals (Method 3), even over Method 2 (spectral analysis in frontal and prefrontal channels) which is the most common approach found in literature. This indicates that there is useful information in the shape of the signals (in time) that could complement the frequency analysis.

Second, the inter-user variance is significantly lower for Method 3 which indicates that this method is more consistent among the different subjects. On

Table 1. Average results and variance for the tested methods over all users

	Method 1	Method 2	Method 3
mean	68.1%	72.9%	76.3%
variance	11.0%	7.7%	7.0%

the other hand, DM (Method 1) presents an extreme inter-user variance (with accuracy going over 85% for some users and as low as 50% for others).

Method 3 presents the best results regarding both classifier performance and inter-user variance (see Table 1). Although this method uses a feature set dependent on information extracted from the actual signals (averages over instances) it can be generalized, which allows an automatic process of feature extraction and classification for new users.

It is worth noting that results drop notoriously if instances are not randomly mixed before the train and test groups are separated. This seems to be due to the temporal non-stationarity that exists between signal from the same subject, where significant differences can be found between signals from different experiments. Even more, these differences seem to increase with time.

The results are consistent with the foreseen need to include expert knowledge in the feature extraction. The dimension of the original feature space has proved to be too big for most automatic algorithms of dimensionality reduction.

4   Conclusion

We proposed and tested three different approaches to perform feature selection/extraction in EEG signals. All the methods make a classifier independent selection. Performance evaluation of motor intention recognition, using the selected features with a two layer perceptron show that the results are user dependent for all the methods, but projection over average signals (Method 3) shows the least variability between users. The classifier based on DM has the same high performance for the best users but a very low one for others; further analysis in the parameter selection process is needed in order to generalize this method to new users. As an advantage, DM shows lower dependability with the training/test data set split.

Discarding channels that are not related with the frontal cortex works well for reducing dimensionality, and thus helps to increase classifier performance, as was shown with results for Method 2. However for Method 3 discarding channels seemed to show a decrease in performance, suggesting that there is indeed relevant information associated with these channels. It is worth noticing that in the latter case dimensionality is no longer an issue, since the projection over average signals yields a feature space of dimension 62, as opposed to the thousands originally present.

In the future we will try to obtain results while making embedded feature selection with different classifiers (SVM, C4.5, etc.) and try combining the three tested methods in order to improve the performance for each user. Some promising early results along this line show that an improvement of 4% over the best single classifier is possible at least for some users.

References

1. Belkin, M., Niyogi, P.: Laplacian eigenmaps and spectral techniques for embedding and clustering (2002)
2. Bigdely-Shamlo, N., Vankov, A., Ramirez, R.R., Makeig, S.: Brain activity-based image classification from rapid serial visual presentation. IEEE Transactions on Neural Systems and Rehabilitation Engineering 16(5), 432–441 (2008)
3. Delorme, A., Makeig, S., Fabre-Thorpe, M., Sejnowski, T.: From single-trial eeg to brain area dynamics. Neurocomputing 44-46, 1057–1064 (2002); Computational Neuroscience Trends in Research 2002
4. Donoho, D.L., Grimes, C.: Hessian eigenmaps: Locally linear embedding techniques for high-dimensional data. Proceedings of the National Academy of Sciences 100(10), 5591–5596 (2003)
5. Lafon, S., Keller, Y., Coifman, R.R.: Data fusion and multicue data matching by diffusion maps. IEEE Transactions on Pattern Analysis and Machine Intelligence 28(11), 1784–1797 (2006)
6. Malmivuo, J., Plonsey, R.: Bioelectromagnetism: principles and applications of bioelectric and biomagnetic fields. Oxford University Press (1995)
7. Nadler, B., Lafon, S., Coifman, R.R., Kevrekidis, I.G.: Diffusion maps, spectral clustering and reaction coordinates of dynamical systems. Applied and Computational Harmonic Analysis 21(1), 113–127 (2006); Special Issue: Diffusion Maps and Wavelets.
8. Pfurtscheller, G., Lopes da Silva, F.H.: Event-related eeg/meg synchronization and desynchronization: basic principles. Clinical Neurophysiology 110(11), 1842–1857 (1999)
9. Roweis, S.T., Saul, L.K.: Nonlinear dimensionality reduction by locally linear embedding. Science 290(5500), 2323–2326 (2000)
10. Vaughan, T.M.: Guest editorial brain-computer interface technology: a review of the second international meeting. IEEE Transactions on Neural Systems and Rehabilitation Engineering 11(2), 94–109 (2003)
11. Wang, T., Deng, J., He, B.: Classifying eeg-based motor imagery tasks by means of time–frequency synthesized spatial patterns. Clinical Neurophysiology 115(12), 2744–2753 (2004)
12. Wolpaw, J.R., Birbaumer, N., McFarland, D.J., Pfurtscheller, G., Vaughan, T.M.: Brain–computer interfaces for communication and control. Clinical Neurophysiology 113(6), 767–791 (2002)
13. Wolpaw, J.R., Birbaumer, N., Heetderks, W.J., McFarland, D.J., Peckham, P.H., Schalk, G., Donchin, E., Quatrano, L.A., Robinson, C.J., Vaughan, T.M.: Brain-computer interface technology: a review of the first international meeting. IEEE Transactions on Rehabilitation Engineering 8(2), 164–173 (2000)

Bag of Features for Automatic Classification of Alzheimer's Disease in Magnetic Resonance Images

Andrea Rueda, John Arevalo, Angel Cruz, Eduardo Romero, and Fabio A. González

BioIngenium Research Group, Universidad Nacional de Colombia, Bogotá, Colombia
{adruedao,jearevaloo,aacruzr,edromero,fagonzalezo}@unal.edu.co

Abstract. The goal of this paper is to evaluate the suitability of a bag-of-feature representation for automatic classification of Alzheimer's disease brain magnetic resonance (MR) images. The evaluated method uses a bag-of-features (BOF) to represent the MR images, which are then fed to a support vector machine, which has been trained to distinguish between normal control and Alzheimer's disease. The method was applied to a set of images from the OASIS data set. An exhaustive exploration of different BOF parameters was performed, i.e. feature extraction, dictionary construction and classification model. The experimental results show that the evaluated method reaches competitive performance in terms of accuracy, sensibility and specificity. In particular, the method based on a BOF representation outperforms the best published result in this data set improving the equal error classification rate in about 10% (0.80 to 0.95 for Group 1 and 0.71 to 0.81 for Group 2).

1 Introduction

Alzheimer's disease (AD) is a slow, progressive and incurable brain disease, characterized by a progressive memory impairment together with reasoning, planning, language, and perception disturbances. The clinical onset is still poorly understood and the diagnosis is mainly accomplished using psychological tests that become positive when the disease is practically irreversible. Yet MR (Magnetic resonance) images are a useful information source to study the neurodegenerative process in specific regions [13], their role is quite blurry in the early disease stages. Lately, several researchers have focused on automatic detection of the Alzheimer's disease in MR, aiming to identify the early stages by investigating certain subtle anatomical changes of the primary cortex, looking for morphological biomarkers.

The main problem regarding a proper AD characterization is the large brain anatomical variability. This noise is increased with some physiological processes, for instance the aging itself leads to a natural neurodegenerative process. An opportune diagnosis is crucial towards delaying the neurodegenerative process and depends upon the possibility of establishing objective differences among brains, a very up-to-date research problem known as morphometry. This brain comparison has been previously approached by characterizing spatial regions with different estimations of the differences between a particular brain and a statistical brain template: voxel-based morphometry [1,18], tensor-based morphometry [2,16,6,15,10] and object-based morphometry [11,14]. Recently, it has been proposed to compare relevant brain features rather than anatomical

L. Alvarez et al. (Eds.): CIARP 2012, LNCS 7441, pp. 559–566, 2012.

structures, a technique known as Feature-Based Morphometry (FBM) [17]. This method combines local, spatial and scale invariant features and a probabilistic model to characterize the relative differences between groups, reporting an Equal Error Classification Rate (EER) of about 0.80. The objective of these methods is to diminish the amount of recorded noise by determining a set of zones that may be invariant under different noise conditions.

This article establishes brain similarities by calculating the differences of a part-based brain representation, the Bag Of Features (BOF). The basic idea behind this method is to represent the image visual content as a probability distribution (histogram) of local features (visual words) and collect a knowledge base from a set of images, previously labeled. In fact, this approach has been successfully used in medical image analysis. [9] used a BOF approach in classification of histopathology images using local features (SIFT, raw-patches) and a new strategy that separated semantically the basic stain components. Cruz-Roa et al. in [7] proposed a strategy for automatic visual mining of histopathology images using a BOF representation. The results showed that BOF is a good alternative for representing histology images. It allows to extract implicit patterns and use them to perform automatic annotation, reaching a F-score of 90%. This method was extended using a non-negative matrix factorization from a BOF image representation [8].

This paper evaluates the BOF approach to represent 3D MRI images for automatic Alzheimer's disease classification. For doing so, an exhaustive exploration of different variations from classical BOF approaches was performed and compared with our proposed method. Main contributions of this paper are: an adapted BOF method, an exhaustive evaluation of each BOF stage (feature detection and description, dictionary construction, classification method) from different BOF approaches for 2D and 3D images, and a new strategy from automatic classification of Alzheimer's disease.

The rest of paper is organized as follows: Section 2 presents the proposed method, Section 3 presents the MRI Alzheimer data set and the experimental setup used to evaluate the classification performance of our method. Section 4 shows the experimental results and discussion. Finally Section 5 presents the conclusions and future work.

2   Automatic BOF Classification of Alzheimer's Disease

The proposed method, illustrated in Figure 1, is composed of two main phases: first, a BOF image representation of MRI images, and, second, an AD automatic classifier, i.e. a Support Vector Machine (SVM) with a RBF (Radial Basis Function) Kernel trained to distinguish between normal controls or subjects diagnosed with Alzheimer's disease.

2.1   BOF Image Representation

A BOF represents an image as a frequency histogram of an unordered collection of individual regions (patches or blocks). This collection is constructed by selecting the most common regions in a whole image collection. Extracted regions correspond to squared image pieces, known as image patches or local image features, which are vectorized (linearized) by concatenating each patch row one after the other. With these patches,

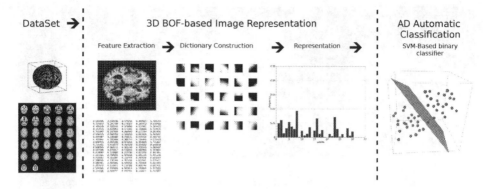

Fig. 1. The proposed method with BOF MRI scans and a Binary SVM Classifier

a visual dictionary is built by applying a clustering algorithm, and each cluster centroid will represent the set of patches as a visual word. The complete representation procedure is described as follows:

1. *Local feature detection and description:* In the first step, the main goal is to detect visual patterns and to describe each image in terms of their visual appearance. In our particular case, the whole 3D MRI volume is processed in a slice-by-slice basis, following the volume acquisition direction. The detection method starts by defining a regular 2D grid on the whole slice, and extracting every patch, which is then linearized as a vector with the gray pixel intensities. Patch description is enriched with spatial information, by also concatenating each vector 3D coordinates (x, y, z). As the original BoF representation does not take into account the spatial location of each patch, including this information into the descriptor could be useful in posterior stages. Patches belonging to the background (black homogeneous patches) are discarded, i.e., patches with null mean and variance. In addition, following the proposed scheme in [3], a normalization process is performed on each patch, in order to deal with luminance variations of MRI volumes, through a transformation for each point x_i in a patch X with null mean μ and unitary standard deviation σ as follows:

$$x_i' = \frac{(x_i - \mu)}{\sigma}$$

2. *Dictionary construction:* The second step comprises a clustering k-means algorithm on the extracted patches, allowing to construct a visual dictionary by finding the most representative patches in the image collection. Each cluster centroid is then considered as a visual word of the dictionary.

3. *Histogram image representation:* As mentioned before, the idea behind the BOF model is to represent an image using the most common regions in the whole image collection. For a given dictionary, it is possible to describe an image as the frequency of visual words. Then, the final image representation will be a histogram with as many elements as dictionary visual words. The complete 3D representation of a MR volume is obtained by merging each 2D slice histograms as a single 3D histogram.

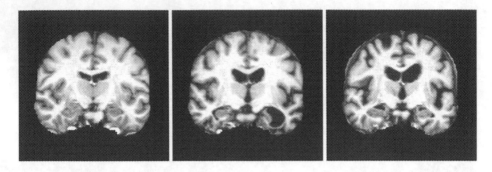

Fig. 2. Coronal example slices of brain MR volumes from OASIS data set. Left: normal control subject, Middle: patient diagnosed with very mild AD, Right: patient diagnosed with mild AD.

2.2 SVM-Based Binary Classifier

A first approximation to the problem of classifying Alzheimer's cases is binary since the clinical meaningful task consists in detecting the early stages, i.e., when no clinical sign is present at all and the disease is still hidden. At this point, anatomical information may be valuable to determine any abnormality. From a machine learning perspective, for the binary classification problem, patients classified with Alzheimer's disease are modeled as the positive class, while the normal controls corresponds to the negative class. Every histogram bin is considered as a model feature, trained by an RBF Kernel, already used in some biomedical problems [5].

3 Experimental Setup

A set of brain MR images from healthy and pathological subjects were extracted from the OASIS (Open Access Series of Imaging Studies) database [12]. Each subject has been previously analyzed with a Mini-Mental State Examination (MMSE) and a Clinical Dementia Rating (CDR), and diagnosed as normal controls (NC) or with probable Alzheimer's disease (AD) using the scores obtained in the MMSE and CDR tests. The OASIS database provides a number of images per subject, from which we have selected the skull-stripped gain-field corrected atlas-registered image to the 1988 atlas space of Talairach and Tournoux [4]. To evaluate the performance of the proposed approach, results are reported on a subset of the available images composed by two different divisions:

1. *Group 1*: 86 subjects aged 60-80 years, mild AD ($CDR = 1$): 20 AD, 66 NC
2. *Group 2*: 136 subjects aged 60-80 years, mild and very mild AD ($CDR = \{1, 0.5\}$): 70 AD, 66 NC

Figure 2 shows coronal example slices of MR volumes from a normal subject, a patient clinically diagnosed with very mild AD and a patient clinically diagnosed with mild AD.

The local feature detection was performed on a regular grid (without patch overlapping) with patch sizes of 8×8 and 16×16 pixels. The used descriptor consists of a linearized patch, known as *raw patch*, in four different configurations according to the inclusion of spatial information and the patch normalization: Raw Patch (RP), Normalized Raw Patch (NRP), Spatial Raw Patch (SRP) and Spatial Normalized Raw Patch (SNRP). Dictionary construction was carried out with a k-means algorithm for different dictionary sizes, $k = 100, 200, 400, 800, 1600$ and 3200 visual words. For the classification phase, each group was divided into two sets: training (70%) and test (30%), maintaining the class proportions within each set. With the training set, SVM parameters (C and γ in RBF) were adjusted using a 10-fold cross-validation, and the best parameter combination was used to train the SVM model. Finally, images in the test set were classified using the trained model. Classification performance evaluation was calculated using standard classification measures, such as sensibility (SEN), specificity (SPC), balanced accuracy (BAC) and equal error classification rate (EER). Following [17], the EER is defined as the value of the true positive rate corresponding to the point of the ROC curve where the false positive rate is equal to the false negative rate.

4   Results and Discussion

Figures 3 and 4 presents the obtained performance in terms of BAC measure for each configuration in Group 1 and Group 2, respectively. These results suggest that normalization process of patches worsens the discrimination capability of BOF representation. This could be explained because the visual variability of local patches is reduced whereas without normalization the visual appearance of patches is wider.

Other interesting results are that spatial information does not seem to contribute significantly to distinguish between normal control and Alzheimer in this image representation approach. A probable explanation is that BOF is a histogram of local patterns occurrences, given by the set of visual words of the dictionary, which captures the representative visual variations to represent the MRI volume. However the fact of including spatial patch description information increases the number of possible spatially located

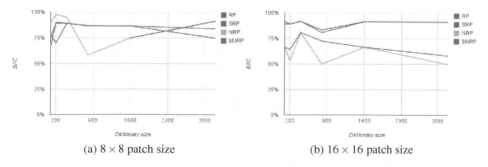

(a) 8×8 patch size   (b) 16×16 patch size

Fig. 3. Performance comparison, in terms of BAC, in Group 1 for each feature descriptor: Raw Patch (RP), Normalized Raw Patch (NRP), Spatial Raw Patch (SRP) and Spatial Normalized Raw Patch (SNRP), varying the dictionary size for patch sizes of 8×8 (left) and 16×16 (right)

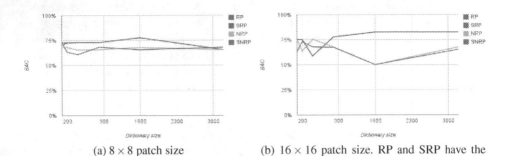

(a) 8 × 8 patch size

(b) 16 × 16 patch size. RP and SRP have the same values.

Fig. 4. Performance comparison, in terms of BAC, in Group 2 for each feature descriptor: Raw Patch (RP), Normalized Raw Patch (NRP), Spatial Raw Patch (SRP) and Spatial Normalized Raw Patch (SNRP), varying the dictionary size for patch sizes of 8 × 8 (left) and 16 × 16 (right)

Table 1. Summary of best results in terms of EER for the two evaluated groups. Value within parenthesis refers to the best dictionary size for the corresponding configuration. The baseline is reported at top, Feature Based Morphometry (FBM), and the different feature descriptors combined with patch size are reported in the following rows: Raw Patch (RP), Normalized Raw Patch (NRP), Spatial Raw Patch (SRP) and Spatial Normalized Raw Patch (SNRP).

		Group 1	Group 2
Baseline (FBM)		0.80	0.71
8 × 8	RP	0.90 (1600)	**0.81 (400)**
	NRP	**0.95 (200)**	0.71 (400)
	SRP	0.90 (200)	**0.81(400)**
	SNRP	**0.95 (100)**	0.71 (400)
16 × 16	RP	**0.95 (1600)**	**0.81 (100)**
	NRP	0.90 (1600)	0.76 (400)
	SRP	**0.95 (1600)**	**0.81 (400)**
	SNRP	0.80 (400)	0.76 (400)

visual patterns. Then the dictionary size required when spatial information is added must be larger.

Under these results results, it is clear that the improvement obtained when the dictionary size increases (two times) is mild, whereas patch sizes of 16 × 16 provide a better performance than 8 × 8 patch size. These results suggest that a moderate wider local region is better to detect the local visual changes that characterize the Alzheimer of the normal controls.

Table 1 reports the EER for different configurations using the best dictionary size. At the top, the first classification results on the OASIS dataset, reported by Toews et al. with the FBM approach are included as a baseline [17]. It is important to notice that Toews' result were produced using a leave-one-out evaluation setup, different to the setup used in this work, which has a test data set with a stratified sample of the 30% of the data. The leave-one-out strategy generally overestimates the performance of the evaluated model, in fact some of the configurations got 98% EER when evaluated using leave-one-out cross validation, however we chose to report the results with our setup since it generates a better estimation of the classifier performance. In both groups, the proposed strategy outperforms the baseline.

In general, the results suggest that the best classification results can be obtained by using a patch size of 16×16 and a dictionary size between 100 and 400. The inclusion of spatial information into the descriptor vector did not show a clear advantage, but normalization seems to degrade the results.

5   Conclusion and Future Work

This paper presents a BOF image representation scheme for brain MR images, which, combined with a SVM, allows classification of normal controls and patients clinically diagnosed with Alzheimer's disease. The experimental results shows that the proposed method has a competitive performance that improves results reported by state-of-art methods. The results are encouraging and suggest that the BOF representation has the ability to capture visual patterns useful for discriminating healthy MR brain volumes from those exhibiting the Alzheimer's disease. Our future work includes a thorough evaluation including additional data sets, an exploration of feature descriptors such as SIFT, HOG and feature combinations, among others, the analysis of the visual dictionary to find the most discriminating visual words that characterize the Alzheimer's disease, and improvements to the method to enhance its interpretability paving the way to automatic methods that could effectively support clinical diagnosis.

Acknowledgements. This work was partially funded by the project "Anotación Automática y Recuperación por Contenido de Imágenes Radiológicas usando Semántica Latente" number 110152128803 and project "Sistema para la Recuperación de Imágenes Médicas utilizando Indexación Multimodal" number 110152128767 by Convocatoria Colciencias 521 de 2010.

References

1. Ashburner, J., Friston, K.J.: Voxel-based morphometry–the methods. Neuroimage 11(6), 805–821 (2000)
2. Ashburner, J., Hutton, C., Frackowiak, R., Johnsrude, I., Price, C., Friston, K.: et al. Identifying global anatomical differences: deformation-based morphometry. Human Brain Mapping 6(5-6), 348–357 (1998)
3. Avni, U., Greenspan, H., Sharon, M., Konen, E., Goldberger, J.: X-ray image categorization and retrieval using patch-based visualwords representation. In: IEEE International Symposium on Biomedical Imaging, ISBI 2009, pp. 350–353. IEEE (2009)
4. Buckner, R.L., Head, D., Parker, J., Fotenos, A.F., Marcus, D., Morris, J.C., Snyder, A.Z.: A unified approach for morphometric and functional data analysis in young, old, and demented adults using automated atlas-based head size normalization: reliability and validation against manual measurement of total intracranial volume. Neuroimage 23(2), 724–738 (2004)

5. Caicedo, J.C., Cruz, A., Gonzalez, F.A.: Histopathology Image Classification Using Bag of Features and Kernel Functions. In: Combi, C., Shahar, Y., Abu-Hanna, A. (eds.) AIME 2009. LNCS, vol. 5651, pp. 126–135. Springer, Heidelberg (2009)

6. Chung, M.K., Worsley, K.J., Paus, T., Cherif, C., Collins, D.L., Giedd, J.N., Rapoport, J.L., Evans, A.C.: A unified statistical approach to deformation-based morphometry. NeuroImage 14(3), 595–606 (2001)

7. Cruz-Roa, A., Caicedo, J.C., González, F.A.: Visual pattern mining in histology image collections using bag of features. In: Artificial Intelligence in Medicine (2011)

8. Cruz-Roa, A., Díaz, G., Romero, E., González, F.A.: Automatic Annotation of Histopathological Images Using a Latent Topic Model Based On Non-negative Matrix Factorization. J. Path Inform. 2(1), 4 (2011)

9. Diaz, G., Romero, E.: Micro-structural tissue analysis for automatic histopathological image annotation. Microscopy Research and Technique, pp. 343–358 (2011)

10. Lao, Z., Shen, D., Xue, Z., Karacali, B., Resnick, S.M., Davatzikos, C.: Morphological classification of brains via high-dimensional shape transformations and machine learning methods. NeuroImage 21(1), 46–57 (2004)

11. Mangin, J.F., Riviere, D., Cachia, A., Duchesnay, E., Cointepas, Y., Papadopoulos-Orfanos, D., Collins, D.L., Evans, A.C., Régis, J.: Object-based morphometry of the cerebral cortex. IEEE Transactions on Medical Imaging 23(8), 968–982 (2004)

12. Marcus, D.S., Wang, T.H., Parker, J., Csernansky, J.G., Morris, J.C., Buckner, R.L.: Open access series of imaging studies (oasis): cross-sectional mri data in young, middle aged, nondemented, and demented older adults. Journal of Cognitive Neuroscience 19(9), 1498–1507 (2007)

13. Nestor, P.J., Scheltens, P., Hodges, J.R.: Advances in the early detection of alzheimer's disease. Nature Reviews Neuroscience (2004)

14. Pohl, K.M., Sabuncu, M.R.: A Unified Framework for MR Based Disease Classification. In: Prince, J.L., Pham, D.L., Myers, K.J. (eds.) IPMI 2009. LNCS, vol. 5636, pp. 300–313. Springer, Heidelberg (2009)

15. Studholme, C., Drapaca, C., Iordanova, B., Cardenas, V.: Deformation-based mapping of volume change from serial brain mri in the presence of local tissue contrast change. IEEE Transactions on Medical Imaging 25(5), 626–639 (2006)

16. Thompson, P.M., Giedd, J.N., Woods, R.P., MacDonald, D., Evans, A.C., Toga, A.W., et al.: Growth patterns in the developing brain detected by using continuum mechanical tensor maps. Nature 404(6774), 190–192 (2000)

17. Toews, M., Wells III, W., Collins, D.L., Arbel, T.: Feature-based morphometry: Discovering group-related anatomical patterns. NeuroImage 49(3), 2318–2327 (2010)

18. Toga, A.W., Thompson, P.M., Mega, M.S., Narr, K.L., Blanton, R.E.: Probabilistic approaches for atlasing normal and disease-specific brain variability. Anatomy and Embryology 204(4), 267–282 (2001)

An Automatic Segmentation Approach
of Epithelial Cells Nuclei

Claudia Mazo[1], Maria Trujillo[1], and Liliana Salazar[2]

[1] Escuela de Ingeniería de Sistemas y Computación
[2] Departamento de Morfología
[3] Universidad del Valle,
Ciudadela Universitaria Melendez, Cali, Colombia
{claudia.mazo,maria.trujillo,liliana.salazar}@correounivalle.edu.co

Abstract. Histology images are used to identify biological structures present in living organisms — cells, tissues, organs, and parts of organs. E-Learning systems can use images to aid teaching how morphological features relate to function and understanding which features are most diagnostic of organs. The structure of cells varies according to the type and function of the cell. Automatic cell segmentation is one of the challenging tasks in histology image processing. This problem has been addressed using morphological gradient, region-based methods and shape-based method approaches, among others. In this paper, automatic segmentation of nuclei of epithelial cells is addressed by including morphological information. Image segmentation is commonly evaluated in isolation. This is either done by observing results, via manual segmentation or via some other goodness measure that does not rely on ground truth images. Expert criteria along with images manually segmented are used to validate automatic segmentation results. Experimental results show that the proposed approach segments epithelial cells in a close way to expert manual segmentations. An average sensitivity of 76% and an average specificity of 77% were obtained on a selected set of images.

1 Introduction

Tissue samples are used to study biological structures present in living organisms. The samples contain information about cells and their distribution. Tissue samples allow identifying large amount of pathologies by analysing cells normality or abnormality, besides supporting diagnosis in daily medical practice of histologists, biologists, pathologists and related disciplines. Cells are the basic element in histology. The structure of cells varies according to the type and function of the cell. Pathologies are detected by analysing cells, in the daily practice of physicians [16]. Epithelia is one of the four basic body tissues. The lining epithelia have two locations: the lumen — the inner region — of hollow internal organs and external body surfaces coated, epidermis. These locations are always close to areas of light. A cell nucleus is a key part in identifying biological structures. A light region is labeled in Fig. 1 (a). Cell nuclei is enlarged and shown in Fig. 1 (b).

L. Alvarez et al. (Eds.): CIARP 2012, LNCS 7441, pp. 567–574, 2012.

(a)   (b)

Fig. 1. Illustration of Cell Nuclei in Epithelial Tissue. (a) Epithelia Tissue. (b) Cell Nuclei.

On the other hand, digital technologies development has made available, to physicians and biologists, microscopes connected to digital cameras for capturing images in order to preserve information. Different components of a tissue under a microscope are visualised and large repositories of images are gathered to preserve information. The cell image analysis process has two steps: segmenting cell nuclei and measuring morphological descriptions. The segmentation of cell nuclei has been addressed using morphological gradient [8], region-based methods [4], shape-based methods [12], minimax algorithm and thresholding [1], geometric active contours [17] and binary graph cuts [19]. However, these techniques require manual parameters setting. Moreover, histology images contain cell variations, due to photoelectronic and thermal noise, that make the segmentation of cell nuclei an open problem. Automatic segmentation of a cell nuclei involves several problems: the presence of similar cell nuclei that do not belong to the epithelial tissue, image noise acquired by capture devices, cell nuclei size to recognise, and low definition in image areas such as: borders, among others.

In this paper, an automatic segmentation of nuclei of epithelial cells is addressed by including morphological information. As original contribution, segmentation is performed using information in a manner similar to histologists, biologists and pathologists do. The segmentation is addressed in two parts: on the one hand, initially performs the segmentation of cell nuclei and on the other hand, light regions are identified. The distance between those cells and light regions is used to identify epithelia. Experimental results show that the proposed approach correctly segmented epithelial cell nuclei in histological images.

2   A Segmentation Approach of Epithelial Cell Nuclei

An automatic segmentation approach of epithelial cell nuclei is build using tissue morphological information. The samples were prepared with hematoxylin-eosin staining and by this technique nuclei are distinguished by an intense violet hue, which allows the differentiation of morphological characteristics of this cell structure: the shape, thickness, separation between a cell and other. The segmentation of cell nuclei is addressed in two parts: on the one hand, obtained segmentation with the largest eigenvalue of structure tensor algorithm along with the red and the green color channels are used as input into the K-means algorithm in order to obtain cell nuclei. On the other hand, the green color channel is segmented

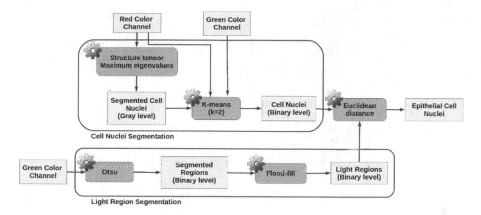

Fig. 2. Diagram of the automatic segmentation Process

using the Otsu algorithm follows by the Flood-fill algorithm in order to identified light regions — regions represented by large intensity values in an image. Finally, distances between cell nuclei and light regions are calculated to identify epithelial cell nuclei. The complete process is illustrated in Fig. 2.

2.1 Cell Nuclei Segmentation

Initially, different segmentation algorithms were evaluated in order to obtain cell nuclei of epithelial tissue; obtained results are: Fig. 3 (a) using the edge segmentation by computing the gradient-magnitude [2], [7]; Fig. 3 (b) using the gradient-magnitude combining with non-maximum gradient suppress [2], [7]; Fig. 3 (c) using the Hessian tensor maximum eigenvalues [5], [6], [9]; Fig. 3 (d) using the Hessian tensor minimum eigenvalues [5], [6], [9]; Fig. 3 (e) using the Structure tensor maximum eigenvalues [3], [10]; Fig. 3 (f) using the Structure tensor minimum eigenvalues [3], [10]; Fig. 3 (g) using the Normalised cut edge detection simple [18]; Fig. 3 (h) using the normalised cut edge detection with T=3000 [18].

The largest eigenvalue of structure tensor was chosen according to the best segmentation results in terms of cell nuclei segmentation, as it can be observed in Fig. 3 (e). The proposed cell nuclei segmentation combines results of the largest eigenvalue of structure tensor with the red and the green color channels into the K-means algorithm.

Largest Eigenvalue of Structure Tensor. The largest eigenvalue of structure tensor [15] is described as follows. Given the red channel of an image the structure tensor J_0 is defined as the outer product of the gradient vector $\bigtriangledown I$:

$$J_0 = \bigtriangledown I \left(\bigtriangledown I\right)^T = \begin{pmatrix} I_x^2 & I_x I_y \\ I_x I_y & I_y^2 \end{pmatrix}, \tag{1}$$

where $\left(\bigtriangledown I\right)^T$ symbolised the transpose of $\bigtriangledown I$. J_0 is extended to the linear structure tensor by a convolution of the components of J_0 with a Gaussian kernel K_p (Gaussian smoothing)in order to consider neighbouring information:

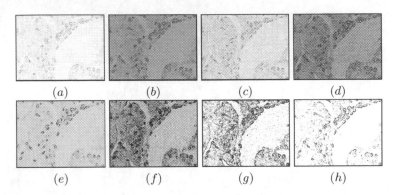

Fig. 3. Segmentation results obtained using Fig. 1 by (a) Using the Gradient-magnitude. (b) Using the gradient-magnitude combining with non-maximum gradient suppress. (c) Using the Hessian tensor maximum eigenvalues. d) Using the Hessian tensor minimum eigenvalues. (e) Using the Structure tensor maximum eigenvalues. (f) Using the Structure tensor minimum eigenvalues. (g) Using the Normalized cut edge detection simple. (h) Using the normalised cut edge detection with T=3000.

$$J_\rho = J_0 * K_\rho = \begin{pmatrix} j_{11} & j_{12} \\ j_{12} & j_{22} \end{pmatrix}. \tag{2}$$

The matrix J_p has orthonormal eigenvectors v_1 and v_2 with v_1 parallel to

$$\left(\frac{2j_{11}}{j_{11} + j_{22} - \sqrt{j_{11} - j_{22}^2 + 4j_{12}^2}} \right). \tag{3}$$

The eigenvalues are given by

$$\mu_1 = \frac{1}{2}\left[j_{11} + j_{22} + \sqrt{j_{11} - j_{22}^2 + 4j_{12}^2} \right], \tag{4}$$

and

$$\mu_2 = \frac{1}{2}\left[j_{11} + j_{22} - \sqrt{j_{11} - j_{22}^2 + 4j_{12}^2} \right]. \tag{5}$$

The eigenvalues describe the average contrast in the eigen-directions within a neighbourhood of size (ρ). The vector v_1 indicates the orientation with the highest red value fluctuations, while v_2 gives the preferred local orientation, the coherence direction. Furthermore, μ_1 and μ_2 serve as descriptors of local structure. Isotropic areas are characterised by $\mu_1 \cong \mu_2$, straight edges gives $\mu_1 \gg \mu_2 = 0$ and corner by $\mu_1 \geq \mu_2 \gg 0$ [15]. Fig. 4 (b) shows obtained results using the larger eigenvalues on the red channel.

The K-means Algorithm. It can be observed in Fig. 4 (b) small regions like cells contours. However, the obtained results are in gray level. The K-means algorithm, with k=2, is used to refine this segmentation. The segmentation of cell nuclei is conducted using the red and the green color channels along with the tensor values — obtained in the previous step — by the K-means algorithm [11].

However, obtained K-means segmentation contains cell nuclei which do not belong to epithelial tissue, it can be observed in Fig. 4 (c). The light regions are commonly used by histologists, biologists and pathologists as information, since epithelial cells are always found close to the light regions. Thus, light regions will be identified in the next section, in order to refine the obtained K-means segmentation.

2.2 Light Regions Segmentation

Light regions are observed in white color in an image. Initially, the Otsu algorithm [14] is used to segment light regions on the green color channel. However, there exit small and large regions identified as light. Thus, segmented regions, using the Otsu algorithm, are not useful. It can be observed in Fig. 4 (d), Otsu segmented many small regions, which are not of interest. The Flood-fill algorithm [13] is used to filter and select larger regions identified as light. Larger regions are identifed using a threshold. Larger regions are shown in Fig. 4 (e) as white areas.

2.3 Combining Segmentation Results

Once light regions are identified and cell nuclei are segmented, distances between cell nuclei and light regions are calculated using the Euclidean measure [20]. A threshold is used to determine if a segmented cell nucleus belongs or not to epithelial tissue. In this way, we keep only segmented cells that are close to light regions. Fig. 4 shows results step by step of the proposed approach.

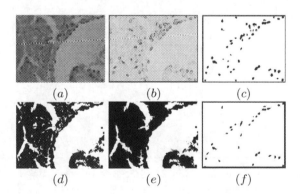

Fig. 4. Illustration of the proposed approach. (a) Original image, (b) Segmented cell nuclei using the largest eigenvalue, (c) Refined segmented cell nuclei by the K-means algorithm, (d) Obtained lighter regions using Otsu's algorithm, (e) Refined lighted regions by the Flood-fill algorithm, (f) Final segmentation of the cell nuclei of epithelial tissue.

3   Experimental Validation

In order to assess the proposed approach, epithelial tissue samples were processed with hematoxylin-eosin staining to highlight the cell nuclei. A set of 30 images were obtained and used to validate the proposed approach. Automatic segmentation results are evaluated by experts in a qualitative way. Also, expert manual segmentations are used as ground-truth to calculate the sensitivity and specificity measures. Sensitivity relates to the ability to segment epithelial cell nuclei and specificity relates to the ability not to segment non-epithelial cell nuclei.

Automatic segmentation and manual segmentation results of selected images are in Fig. 5. It can be observed that the proposed approach segmented all epithelial cell nuclei. However, non-epithelial cell nuclei are segmented as well, when they are close to light regions. Those cells have additional features that we are not taken into account, yet. A quantitative evaluation of the obtained results is in Table 1. The automatic segmentation results are compared with the manual segmentation – as ground truth.

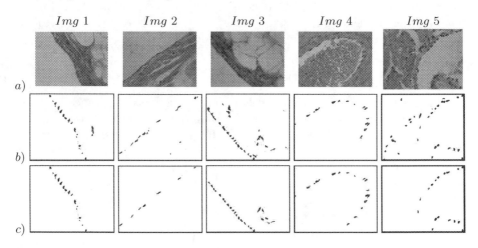

Fig. 5. Results obtained using automatic and manual segmentation of the epithelial cell nuclei. (a) Original images. (b) Automatic segmentation results. (c)Expert manual segmentation results.

Table 1. Performance evaluation of selected images

Confusion Matrix	Img 1	Img 2	Img 3	Img 4	Img 5	Avg 30 Imgs
True Positive	18	6	22	17	17	19
False Negative	6	6	9	0	15	6
False Positive	3	7	7	0	13	7
True Negative	25	18	23	54	30	24
Sensitivity	0.75	0.50	0.71	1	0.53	0.76
Specificity	0.89	0.72	0.77	1	0.30	0.77

Expert criteria are used to validate the automatic segmentation results. Table 2 contains the expert judgements using poor, average, good, very good and excellent in the evaluation of the automatic segmentation results of the images in Fig. 5. The evaluation of the expert 1 was based on observing nuclei, not morphology. The evaluation of the expert 2 took into account morphology, shape of nuclei and location these aspects are not taked into account in the proposed approach. According to the experts, the proposed approach is a promising tool since there is a discrimination of nuclei by their location to recognise epithelial tissue.

Table 2. Performance evaluation of selected images by expert

Expert	Img 1	Img 2	Img 3	Img 4	Img 5
Expert 1	Very good	Excelent	Good	Excelent	Good
Expert 2	Good	Good	Good	Very good	Good

Summarising, the segmentation results are guided by light regions as histologists, biologists and pathologists do. Images 1, 2, 3 and 5 contain non-epithelial cells close to light regions which mislead the segmentation. Those cells and enclosing areas contain additional information that histologists, biologists and pathologists use during the analysis. This information will be included as a constraint.

4   Conclusions

Cells are the foundation for recognising tissues present in an organ. Once cells are segmented, it is possible to identify a tissue or tissues. Segmentation is an initial step in a cell analysis process. In this paper, an automatic segmentation of epithelial cell nuclei was presented. The cell nuclei segmentation combines different source of information as input to the K-means algorithm. The proposed epithelial cell nuclei segmentation is based on combining segmented cell nuclei and identified light regions. Obtained results provided a closer segmentation to the expert-eye segmentation, according to the expert opinions.

As original contribution, the segmentation is performed using information in a manner similar to histologists, biologists and pathologists do. That is, perform the segmentation of cell nuclei, identify light regions, and calculate the distance between those cells and light regions to identify epithelia.

References

1. Swank, P., Greenberg, S., Winkler, D., Hunter, N., Spjut, H., Estrada, R., Taylor, G.: Nuclear Segmentation of Bronchial Epithelial Cells by Minimax and Thresholding Techniques. A Comparison. Analytical and Quantitative Cytology 5(3), 153–158 (1983)
2. Canny, J.: A Computational Approach to Edge Detection. IEEE Computer Society 8, 679–698 (1986)

3. Rao, A., Schunck, B.: Computing Oriented Texture Fields. In: Proceedings of IEEE Computer Society Conference on Computer Vision and Pattern Recognition, CVPR 1989, pp. 61–68 (1989)
4. Pham, D.L., Xu, C., Prince, J.L.: A Survey of Current Methods in Medical Image Segmentation. Annual Review of Biomedical Engineering, 315–338 (1998)
5. Sato, Y., Nakajima, S., Shiraga, N., Atsumi, H., Yoshida, S., Koller, T., Gerig, G., Kikinis, R.: Three-dimensional Multi-scale Line Filter for Segmentation and Visualization of Curvilinear Structures in Medical Images. Med. Image Anal. 2, 143–168 (1998)
6. Frangi, A., Niessen, W., Hoogeveen, R., van Walsum, T., Viergever, M.: Model-based Quantitation of 3-D Magnetic Resonance Angiographic Images. IEEE Transactions on Medical Imaging 18(10), 946–956 (1999)
7. Sonka, M., Hlavac, V., Boyle, R.: Image Processing, Analysis and Machine Vision. Chapman. Signal Processing 35, 102–104 (1999)
8. Nedzved, A., Ablameyko, S., Pitas, I.: Morphological Segmentation of Histology Cell Images. In: Pattern Recognition International Conference, vol. 1 (2000)
9. Rohr, K.: Landmark-based Image Analysis: Using Geometric and Intensity Models. In: Computational Imaging and Vision (2001)
10. Weickert, J.: A Scheme for Coherence-Enhancing Diffusion Filtering with Optimized Rotation Invariance. Journal of Visual Communication and Image Representation 13(1-2), 103–118 (2002)
11. Tapas, K., David, M., Mount, N.S., Netanyahu, C.D., Piatko, R.S., Angela, Y.: An Efficient K-means Clustering Algorithm: Analysis and Implementation. IEEE Transactions on Pattern Analysis and Machine Intelligence 24(7), 881–892 (2002)
12. Tsai, A., Yezzi Jr., A., Wells, W., Tempany, C., Tucker, D., Fan, A., Grimson, W., Willsky, A.: A Shape-based Approach to the Segmentation of Medical Imagery Using Level Sets. IEEE Transactions on Medical Imaging 22(2), 137–154 (2003)
13. Nosal, E.: Flood-fill Algorithms Used for Passive Acoustic Detection and Tracking. In: New Trends for Environmental Monitoring Using Passive Systems, pp. 1–5 (2008)
14. Dongju, L., Jian, Y.: Otsu Method and K-means. In: Ninth International Conference on Hybrid Intelligent Systems, HIS 2009, vol. 1, pp. 344–349 (2009)
15. Bibo, L., Chunli, M., Hui, W.: Pixel Level Image Fusion Based on Linear Structure Tensor. In: 2010 IEEE Youth Conference on Information Computing and Telecommunications (YC-ICT), pp. 303–306 (2010)
16. Gartner, L., Hiatt, J., Strum, J.: Cell Biology and Histology, 6th edn. Lippincott Williams & Wilkins (2010)
17. Harandi, N., Sadri, S., Moghaddam, N., Amirfattahi, R.: An Automated Method for Segmentation of Epithelial Cervical Cells in Images of ThinPrep. Journal of Medical Systems 34(6), 1043–1058 (2010)
18. Barrientos, M., Madrid, H.: Normalized Cut Based Edge Detection. In: Proceedings of the Third Mexican Conference on Pattern Recognition, pp. 211–219 (2011)
19. Eramian, M., Daley, M., Neilson, D., Daley, T.: Segmentation of Epithelium in H&E Stained Odontogenic Cysts. Journal of Microscopy 244(3), 273–292 (2011)
20. Deza, M.M., Elena, D.: Encyclopedia of Distances, pp. 94–95. Springer (2009)

Evaluation and Selection of Morphological Procedures for Automatic Detection of Micro-calcifications in Mammography Images

Claudia C. Diaz-Huerta[1], Edgardo M. Felipe-Riverón[2,*], Luis M. Montaño-Zetina[1]

[1] Research and Higher Studies Center, National Polytechnic Institute A.P. 14-740,
07000 Mexico City, Mexico
{celia,lmontano}@fis.cinvestav.mx
[2] Center for Computing Research, National Polytechnic Institute,
Av. Juan de Dios Batiz w/n and Miguel Othon de Mendizabal, P.O. 07738,
Mexico City, Mexico
edgardo@cic.ipn.mx

Abstract. In this paper, we present an evaluation of four different algorithms, based on Mathematical Morphology, to detect the occurrence of micro-calcifications in digital mammogram images from the mini-MIAS database. Results provided by TMVA produced the ranking of features that allowed discrimination between real micro-calcifications and normal tissue. ROC area measures the performance of automatic classification, which produced its highest value 0.976 for Gaussian kernel, followed by polynomial kernel, which produced 0.972. An additional parameter, called Signal Efficiency*Purity (SE*P), is proposed as a measure of the number of micro-calcifications with the lowest quantity of noise.

Keywords: Mammography image, mage reconstruction, digital mammography, micro-calcification detection, Mathematical Morphology.

1   Introduction

Breast cancer is the most common malignant neoplasm in western women, being the main cause of death in some countries around the world. Clinical studies revealed that 30% to 50% of breast cancer cases showed micro-calcifications in mammography images and between 60% and 80% were confirmed by histological examination.

Different methods for automatic detection of micro-calcification clusters in digital mammograms have been developed in the past [1, 2]. Recently, research has been focused on simulation 3D of micro-calcification obtained from a micro-CT [3]. However, mammography (which provides information of breast in 2D) is still considered as the most suitable method for detection of micro-calcifications.

The purpose of this work is to analyze the performance of four processing algorithms based on morphological operators reported in the literature for detection of micro-calcifications, and choose the one with the highest sensitivity in order to make an

---

* Corresponding author.

L. Alvarez et al. (Eds.): CIARP 2012, LNCS 7441, pp. 575–582, 2012.

automatic classification. Morphological operators were used because the characteristics analyzed by the specialists are based on their morphology, as described in [4,5].

2   Materials and Methods

Data were obtained from the mini-MIAS database [6]. It consisted of mammograms of pixel size 200 microns, dimensions 1024×1024 pixels with 8 bits per pixel (0-black, 255-white). The four algorithms were implemented in MATLAB. First, we remove labels and artifacts on mammograms using reconstruction by dilation [7,8]. The four image processing algorithms evaluated in this work were applied on each entire image. After thresholding, we evaluated the sensitivity and selected the algorithm that retrieved most of micro-calcification. The number of false positives was reduced using a set of features that were inputs of a support vector machine (SVM).

3   Background

Mathematical Morphology was developed by Serra [9]. It is a broad set of operations that process images based on shapes, extracting the relevant information using a structuring element. Two basic operations are erosion and dilation. They produce other operators, known as opening and closing, whose combination give rise to White Top Hat (WTH) and Black Top Hat (BTH) and contrast enhancement κ_{TH} operators [7].

4   Algorithms Analysis

In what follows, four processing algorithms are listed.

4.1   Algorithm 1: Morphological Reconstruction and Extended Maxima Segmentation

This classical algorithm was originally proposed by Soille [7]. The steps were:

1. To apply erosion $\varepsilon_B^{(1)}(f)$ to the entire original image f.

2. To apply Opening by Reconstruction: $\gamma_R^{(1)}(f) = R_f^\delta \left[\varepsilon^{(1)}(f) \right]$, where R_f^δ is the reconstruction by dilation of f, from the eroded image of step 1.

3. To apply White Top-Hat by Reconstruction: $RWTH(f) = f - \gamma_R^{(n)}(f)$.

4. To apply the extended maxima thresholding, for different values of h.

4.2   Algorithm 2: Contrast Operator and Extended Maxima Segmentation

This algorithm was also proposed by Soille [7]. The steps were the following:

1. To apply the Contrast Enhancement Operator κ_{TH} [7] to the original image f.
2. To apply the maxima extended thresholding for different thresholding values of h.
3. To remove objects whose area was greater than 55 pixels. A specialist analyzed the size of micro-calcifications; most of them have less than 50 pixels.

4.3   Algorithm 3: Bicubic Interpolation and Segmentation by Histogram

Part of this algorithm was proposed by Papadopoulos et al. [1]. The steps were:

1. Each entire image f was split in 32 sub-regions.
2. To calculate the mean gray level in the lower 70% region for each sub-region.
3. To apply bicubic interpolation. It produced the image f_{bkg}.
4. To subtract f_{bkg} from the original f. That is $f_{micro} = f - f_{bkg}$.
5. To threshold in two parallel steps:

   5.1. Local thresholding: (a) to split f_{micro} in 32×32 sub-regions. (b) To select a percentage of pixels with the highest gray level, producing f_1. (c) To test different percentage values.

   5.2. Global thresholding: (a) To apply the operator White Top-Hat (WTH) to f. (b) To select pixels with the highest gray level values, producing the image f_2. (c) To test different percentage values for the thresholding.

6. To apply the intersection f_1 AND f_2.

4.4   Algorithm 4: Bicubic Interpolation and Extended Maxima Segmentation

The procedure started with the image f_{micro}, obtained in Section 4.3.

1. To threshold f_{micro} in two parallel processes:

   1.1. Local thresholding: (a) to split f_{micro} in 32×32 sub regions. (b) To threshold each with the maxima extended transformation, producing a binary image f_1. (c) To test different values for maxima extended parameter.

   1.2. Global thresholding: (a) to apply maxima extended transformation, after applying the White Top-Hat Operator (WTH) to the original image f, producing a binary image f_2. (b) To test different values for maxima extended parameter.

2. To apply intersection of both images: f_1 AND f_2.
3. To eliminate objects whose area is greater than 55 pixels.

Results of the four algorithms were evaluated using the ground truth information,. The algorithm with the highest sensitivity was selected as the most suitable.

5   Feature Extraction

After enhancement and segmentation for the most suitable processing algorithm, we extracted a set of 65 features in the spatial domain, texture and spectral domains.

6   Spatial Domain Features

They are shown in Table 1 for each object in the binary image. Features f1 and f17 are the same (the area in pixels) so intentionally established for the purpose of proving the effectiveness of ordering in importance, as will be seen in Section 6. Another group of spatial features was computed in blocks of size 17 x 17 pixels, corresponding to the size of micro-calcifications and normal tissue, as explained in Section 5.3.

Table 1. Spatial features

Feature No.	Name	Feature No.	Name	Feature No.	Name
1	Area	5	Orientation	15	Compactness
2	Eccentricity	6	Solidity	16	Elongation
3	Major axis length	7	Perimeter	17	Area
4	Minor axis length	8-14	Seven Invariant moments of Hu		

For each block centered on the centroid of the object, two new features were obtained: pixel intensity variance $i\,var$ (f62) and energy variance $e\,var$ (f63), defined in [2] as:

$$i\,var = \sum_{m=1}^{M}\sum_{n=1}^{N}[f(m,n) - avg]^2$$

$$e\,var = \sum_{m=1}^{M}\sum_{n=1}^{N}[f(m,n) - eavg]^2 .$$

The quantity avg is the average of image block and *eavg* is the energy average [2].

7   Texture Features

Textural properties are based on the Gray Level Co-occurrence matrices [10]. They are built from information of a small block of size 17 x 17 pixels centered on the centroid of each potential micro-calcification. For each angle between adjacent pixels 0°, 45°, 90° and 135° and a distance d = 1, a set of 11 features is obtained, as shown in Tables 2 and 3. The total number of textural features is 44.

8   Spectral Domain Features

Spectral domain features involve the block activity A (feature f64) and the spectral entropy E (feature f65), defined in [14] as:

$$A = \sum_{j=1}^{N}\sum_{i=1}^{M}|c(i,j)|$$

$$E = -\sum_{i=1}^{M}\sum_{j=1}^{N}a(i,j)\ln(a(i,j))$$

where $a(i,j)$ is related with the coefficients of the discrete cosines transform (DCT) as:

$$a(i,j) = \frac{|c(i,j)|}{A}.$$

Table 2. Texture features for $\theta = 0°$ between adjacent pixels

Feat No.	Name	Feat No.	Name	Feat No.	Name
f18	Contrast	f22	Variance	f26	Difference of variances
f19	Correlation	f23	Sum average	f27	Difference of entropies
f20	Energy	f24	Sum variance	f28	Inverse difference of normalized moments
f21	Entropy	f25	Sum entropy		

Table 3. Remainder of features considered

Feat No.	Name	Feat No.	Name	Feat No.	Name
f29-f39	Idem for $\theta = 45°$	f62	Intensity variance	f65	Spectral entropy
f40-f50	Idem for $\theta = 90°$	f63	Energy variance		
f51-f61	Idem for $\theta = 135°$	f64	Block activity		

9   Results and Discussion

A specialist found 354 micro-calcifications in the mini-MIAS database [6]. Table 4 included parameters of thresholding, sensitivity and the number of false positives for each algorithm. Maxima extended transformation produced higher sensitivity.

Algorithms 1 and 2 used only one control parameter, which resulted in higher sensitivity than 3 and 4. Algorithm 2 retrieved most of the micro-calcifications keeping their morphology. We selected it as the most suitable. Figure 2 shows the results.

Our study quantitatively justified the use of a specific processing algorithm, taking into account the number of true-positives (TP), parameters of each algorithm, the type of breast and the morphology of micro-calcifications.

Table 4. Sensitivity and false positives per algorithm for different parameter values

Algorithm	Parameter type	Parameter value	True Positives	Sensitivity (TP/P)	False positives	Observations
1	extended maxima h	2.5	344	0.9718	1811	(a)
		3	337	0.9520	985	
		4	324	0.9153	578	
2	extended maxima h	6	346	0.9774	2144	(b)
		8	342	0.9661	1218	
		10	335	0.9463	663	
		13	318	0.8993	275	
		15	295	0.8333	151	
3	(c)	5%; 5%	257	0.7260	1041	(d)
		5%; 10%	257	0.7260	1387	
		10%; 5%	272	0.7684	1394	
		10%; 10%	268	0.7571	1909	
4	(e)	2.5; 2.5	335	0.9463	1870	(f)
		2.5; 5	314	0.8870	673	
		5; 5	296	0.8362	325	

(a)   Segmentation did not produce the size neither the shape of the original.
(b)   Distinguish between two closely micro-calcifications.
(c)   Percentage of pixels for Local threshold $pctg_{loc}$; Global threshold $pctg_{glob}$
(d)   Not appropriate for detection in dense-glandular breast.
(e)   Global extended maxima h_{glob}; Local extended maxima h_{loc}.
(f)   More parameters in segmentation process than in algorithms 1 and 2.

Articles [1, 2] reported in the literature used a specific processing algorithm, but did not mention the number of true-positives retrieved after application.

The stage of automatic classification was done with the Toolkit for Multivariate Analysis (TMVA), which is a software for multivariate classification [11, 12]. Signal and background corresponded to true micro-calcifications and normal tissue.

First, TMVA ranked features that discriminate signal from background. The most significant feature corresponded to the largest separation between signal and background histograms. Table 5 shows the ranking of 65 features. As mentioned in Section 5.1, area was labeled two times (f1 and f17) and TMVA ranked in the first two positions. It means that TMVA effectively ranked features.

For automatic classification data were subdivided into 70% for training and 30% for test. SVM output goes from 0 to 1 as shown in Figure 2(a). Each value corresponded to a specific value of the following quantities [11]: signal efficiency ratio (SE) is the sensitivity; background efficiency ratio (BE) is the specificity; signal purity (SP) is the ratio of objects well detected as signal and the total of objects classified as signal and background; the product of signal efficiency and signal purity (SE*P) is a measure of the highest quantity of signal with the lowest quantity of noise; significance (Sig) is the ratio of the number of instances well detected as signal and the Poisson error associated to detection. TMVA also provided results for the area under ROC curve, as shown in figure 2(b). It plots sensitivity versus specificity.

The statistical significance of a signal in High Energy Physics (HEP) is used as a measure of how good a signal measurement is. A way of maximizing it is to maximize the product Signal Efficiency*Purity. We propose this parameter as another measure of how good the detection system is. Maximizing this value is equivalent to maximize performance.

Fig. 1. (Left) Region diagnosed with micro-calcifications on image mdb253; (center) Image after contrast enhancement operator; (right) Binary image after maxima extended thresholding

Table 5. Ranking of 65 features in spatial domain, texture and spectral domain

Rank	Feat	Rank	Feat	Rank	Feat	Rank	Feat	Rank	Feat	Rank	Feat
1	1	12	23	23	39	34	53	45	49	56	24
2	17	13	56	24	43	35	32	46	35	57	52
3	64	14	63	25	42	36	6	47	57	58	60
4	7	15	45	26	21	37	16	48	59	59	19
5	3	16	34	27	31	38	62	49	30	60	27
6	15	17	55	28	61	39	65	50	38	61	18
7	4	18	33	29	54	40	9	51	51	62	48
8	25	19	44	30	28	41	10	52	26	63	13
9	47	20	22	31	2	42	46	53	11	64	14
10	58	21	8	32	5	43	40	54	29	65	12
11	36	22	50	33	20	44	41	55	37		

It weights the number of micro-calcifications detected with the diagnosis made by the specialist and the detection of all objects made by the classifier. Typical values of SE*P reported in literature of HEP are higher than 0.50 [13]. In the next step, we found the suitable values of kernel parameters in order to obtain the highest value of ROC area, SE and SE*P. They are shown in Table 6.

In Table 6, notice that for linear SVM, the lower the number of features (15 for the linear kernel), the lower both SE*P and the ROC area. Meanwhile, SE is random. However the same number of features for different SVM kernels produced similar results (Gauss $\sigma = 10$ and polynomial). The highest ROC area in this study was 0.976, which corresponded to Gaussian kernel, followed by polynomial kernel, with 0.972. In terms of the parameter SE*P, Gaussian kernel had the highest value (50.07%), as shown in Table 6, which is an acceptable result from the point of view of HEP [13].

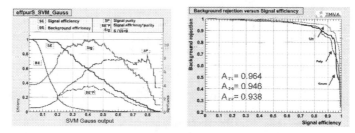

Fig. 2. TMVA results for Gaussian kernel with $\sigma = 10$, 50 features and $C = 10$ (left). Areas under ROC curves for lineal, Gaussian and polynomial kernels (right)

Table 6. Results from the automatic classification carried out with SVM

Kernel	Number of features	C	ROC Area	SE (%)	SE*Purity (%)
Gauss $\sigma = 10$	50	10	0.971	82.81	50.07
Gauss $\sigma = 100$	60	100	0.976	81.25	49.33
Linear	15	0.5	0.949	82.81	40.88
Linear	45	0.5	0.959	87.50	41.65
Polynomial $p = 2, \theta = 1$	50	0.1	0.972	82.81	48.23

10   Conclusions

We have presented a quantitative evaluation of four algorithms of processing images based on Mathematical Morphology. The algorithm based on contrast enhancement and thresholding with extended maxima had the highest sensitivity. We proposed the parameter Signal Efficiency*Purity (SE*P) in detection. It provided the higher quantity of micro-calcifications with the lower quantity of background.

Finally, we evaluated performance of SVM for linear, Gaussian and polynomial kernels, testing variations of cost parameter C, kernel parameters and number of features. Gaussian kernel gave the best result for both ROC area and SE*P parameter.

Acknowledgements. The authors would like to thank Secretaría de Investigación y Posgrado, Centro de Investigación en Computación (CIC) of the Instituto Politécnico Nacional (IPN), Instituto de Ciencia y Tecnología del Distrito Federal (ICyT-DF) and also Consejo Nacional de Ciencia y Tecnología (CONACyT) and Sistema Nacional de Investigadores (SNI), Mexico, for their economic support to this research.

References

1. Papadopoulos, A., Fotiadis, D.I., Costaridou, L.: Computers in Biology and Medicine 38, 1045–1055 (2008)
2. Zheng, B., Qian, W., Clarke, L.: Digital mammography: mixed feature neural network with spectral entropy decision for detection of microcalcifications. IEEE Trans. Med. Imaging. 15(5), 589–597 (1996)
3. Shaheen, E., Van Ongeval, C., Zanca, F., Cockmarin, L., Marshall, N., Jacobs, J.: The simulation of 3D Microcalcification clusters in D digital mammography and breast tomosynthesis. Medical Physics 38(12), 6659–6670 (2011)
4. Sickles, E.: American Journal of Roentgenology 143, 461–464 (1984)
5. Hong, W.K., Bast, R.C., Hait, W.N., Kufe, E.W., Pollock, R., Weischelbaum, R.R., Holland, J.F., Frei, E.: Holland-Frei Cancer Medicine. People's Medical Publishing House, USA (2010)
6. http://peipa.essex.ac.uk/info/mias.html
7. Soille, P.: Morphological Image Analysis. Principles and ApplicationsGermany. Springer, Germany (2003)
8. Gonzalez, R.C., Woods, R.E.: Digital Image Processing. Pearson Prentice Hall, New Jersey (2008)
9. Serra, J.: Mathematical Morphology, vol. 1. Academic Press, London (1982)
10. Haralick, R.M., Shanmugam, K., Distein, I.: Textural Features for Image Classification. IEEE Transactions on Systems, Man and Cybernetics SMC-3(6), 610–621 (1973)
11. Hoecker, A., Speckmayer, P., Stelzer, J., Therhaag, J., Von Toerne, E.: Voss H. TMVA-Toolkit for Multivariate Data Analysis. PoS ACAT 040 (2007)
12. http://tmva.sourceforge.net/
13. http://www.docstoc.com/docs/105178797/Machine-Learning-with-T-MVA

Detection of Chickenpox Vesicles in Digital Images of Skin Lesions

Julián Oyola, Virginia Arroyo, Ana Ruedin, and Daniel Acevedo

Departamento de Computación, Facultad de Ciencias Exactas y Naturales,
Universidad de Buenos Aires
Ciudad Universitaria, Pab. I. (C1428EGA), Ciudad de Buenos Aires
{joyola,ana.ruedin,dacevedo}@dc.uba.ar, virginia.arroyo@gmail.com

Abstract. Chickenpox is a viral disease characterized by itchy skin vesicles that can have severe complications in adults. A tool for automatic detection of these lesions in patients' photographs is highly desirable to help the physician in the diagnosis. In this work we design a method for detection of chickenpox skin lesions in images. It is a combination of image processing techniques - color transform, equalization, edge detection, circular Hough transform- and statistical tests. We obtain highly satisfactory results in the detection of chickenpox vesicles, the elimination of false detections using the Kullback Leibler divergence, and in preliminary tests for discrimination between chickenpox and herpes zoster.

Keywords: skin lesions, chickenpox, detection, image processing.

1 Introduction

Chickenpox or varicella, caused by the varicella-zoster virus of the herpes group, is a very contagious infection that causes itchy outbreaks of skin vesicles. The disease is spread by droplet or direct contact. The incubation period for chickenpox ranges from 11 to 21 days. Early symptoms consist of low-grade fever, headache, unrest and anorexia. On the following day, the characteristic rash begins to appear. The lesions evolve to form small papules, and then vesicles. Over the next several days, the vesicles rupture and then crust. The rash begins on the chest and back and spreads to involve the face, scalp, and the extremities. New lesions of chickenpox arise in crops over a period of several days.

This viral infection is most common amongst children, for whom it evolves as a mild disease: children recover uneventfully or with a few minor scars. However, teenagers and adults can also get chickenpox in which case it can be extremely severe. Complications from chickenpox include pneumonia, encephalitis, and skin infection; some of the mentioned complications can end in the patient's death. Chickenpox can also lead to severe problems in pregnant women, causing birth defects of the newborn. Persons with weakened immune systems are also at risk for complications resulting from chickenpox. It is highly desirable to have a tool for early detection of chickenpox vesicles, specially in the case of adults.

L. Alvarez et al. (Eds.): CIARP 2012, LNCS 7441, pp. 583–590, 2012.

After a chickenpox infection, varicella-zoster virus can become latent in the nerve cell bodies, without causing any symptoms. Years or decades later, the virus can become active again, break out of nerve cell bodies and travel down nerve axons to cause viral infection of the skin in the region of the nerve, accompanied by headaches and sensitivity to light. This disease is herpes zoster, also known as shingles or zona. Although the rash usually heals within two to four weeks, some patients experience residual nerve pain for months or years. It is also desirable to have a tool to distinguish chickenpox from herpes zoster.

The object of this paper is to develop a method capable of detecting chickenpox vesicles, and analyze and extract their characteristics in order to discriminate them from other diseases, such as herpes-zoster. In the long run it is intended to become a part of a general tool designed to assist physicians in the task of diagnosing skin diseases. To do this we apply a combination of image processing and pattern recognition techniques. These aim at increasing global contrast, detecting edges, detecting circles, and extracting color information. Global contrast is increased by histogram equalization, edges are detected with a Canny edge detector, circles are detected by means of the circular Hough transform, and color information is used twice: with the Kullback Leibler divergence to eliminate false positives, and with statistical tests to discriminate chickenpox from herpes zoster.

Databases with images of skin lesions -varicella vesicles, and other diseases- are difficult to find, and generally lacking. As a consequence, there is little or no research on such images. But many of the tools that we have integrated into our algorithm have been applied in the past. Histogram equalization has been used to improve contrast [1]. A Canny edge detector was applied on facial recognition to detect facial expressions [2]. The circular Hough transform has been used to detect circular shapes in images, namely to find coconuts [3]. Color information was used to detect other skin lesions, such as malignant melanoma [4].

This paper is organized as follows. In Sec. 2 we give some considerations on available images of skin lesions. Sec. 3 addresses the detection of chickenpox vesicles: edge detection, circular shape detection, elimination of duplicate detections, and elimination of false detections. In Sec. 4 we give concluding remarks.

2   Some Considerations on Images of Skin Lesions

The images we worked with for detection of varicella vesicles were downloaded from the University of Iowa website[1]. Great differences in the resolution, the scale and the lighting conditions were observed – see Fig. 1. Moreover, there were variations in the colors of the patients' skin, as well as differences in the stages of the illness- skin rash in the early days, then vesicles, and finally crusts. All these differences contribute to the difficulty of detecting varicella from photographic images. Another added difficulty are hairs, moles and inscriptions present in the image. In order to work with a more homogeneous set of images, we have discarded those having very small skin lesions, such as Fig. 1(a).

---

[1] http://www.lib.uiowa.edu/hardin/md/dermpictures.html

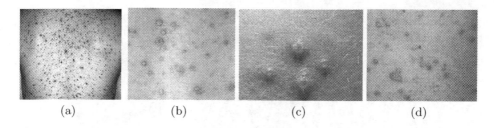

(a)   (b)   (c)   (d)

Fig. 1. Varicella skin lesions of differently coloured skins, at different scales and different illumination conditions

3 Detection of Varicella Vesicles

3.1 Luminance Information for Edge Detection

To increase global contrast in each image, histogram equalization was performed as a first step in the detection of skin vesicles. Next the luminance component was extracted by converting the images to YCbCr and L*a*b* color spaces- both color representations separate luminance from chrominance.

To find the edges of an image we used a Canny edge detector [5] on the luminance component. This detector is robust, and provides localized edges as well as connectivity of contours. It consists of 4 steps: Gaussian smoothing, gradient filtering, non-maximum suppression to obtain thin borders, and hysteresis thresholding. Since chickenpox vesicles are generally circular, extracted edges having circular shape are listed as candidates for vesicles.

3.2 Detection of Circles

The Circular Hough Transform was used to determine circular shapes in the image of extracted edges. The classical version of this transform was first introduced by Paul Hough in [6] to detect lines in a binary image and later it was popularized by Ballard [7] for gray-scale images and arbitrary shapes. The rough idea behind the Hough transform is that every circle can be represented by a center point and a radius (this is the parameter space in the Hough transform). Then, for each point on an edge in the image plane (and for a specific radius), circles are drawn and accumulated on a mask image. The following geometric property is used: *given a circle with center c and radius r, if along each point of the circumference we draw a circle –of radius r– centered upon that point, then all these circles will intersect at c.*

The circles drawn -centered on the edge of the image - accumulate votes for the centre of a possible circle, if the shape of the edge is circular. We may detect circle-centers by searching for the most voted points in the accumulator mask [8]. This is done by trying with different circle radii (one accumulator mask for each radius). Given a circle with a determined radius, the number of points or pixels that lie on its border is known. Accordingly, the ideal number of votes

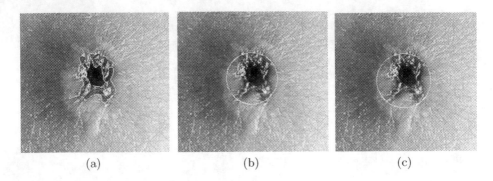

(a)   (b)   (c)

Fig. 2. In white: (a) edges of vesicle and circle detection with radii (b) $r = 40$ and (c) $r = 43$

that the center should have is also known. A circular shape is detected, when in the accumulator mask a point has enough votes to exceed a given threshold– a percentage (70 % – 90 %) of the ideal score. In Fig. 2 we observe the edges of a vesicle, and detected circles with different radii. In Fig. 3 we observe the edges of the image, where some edges are circular and some (marked in red) are only approximately circular. Circles detected with thresholds 70% and 90% are also shown. Notice that with a threshold of 70%, some spurious circles - false positives- are detected, as well as the approximately circular vesicles; these disappear with the 90% threshold.

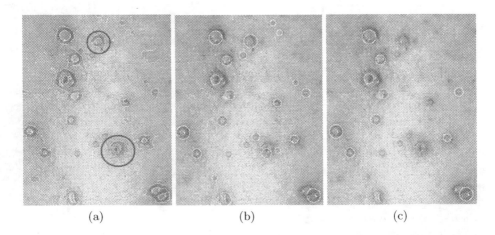

(a)   (b)   (c)

Fig. 3. (a) Vesicles and detected edges in white. Some edges having a very approximate circular shape are marked in red. (b) Circles detected with a threshold of 70%, in white. (c) Circles detected with a threshold of 90%, in white.

3.3 Dealing with Duplicate Detected Circles

When detecting circles it may happen that duplicate detections occur, or that the algorithm finds a profusion of circles near the same spot. We have chosen 2 different criterions to decide that 2 circles are in this situation:

i) We consider a case of duplicate detections when circle $C(c^{(a)}, r_a)$ (having center $c^{(a)}$ and radius r_a) and circle $C(c^{(b)}, r_b)$, satisfy $\|c^{(a)} - c^{(b)}\| < \max\{r_a, r_b\}$, in which case the center of the smaller circle is inside the larger one.

ii) We consider a case of duplicate detections when circles $C(c^{(a)}, r_a), C(c^{(b)}, r_b)$, satisfy $\|c^{(a)} - c^{(b)}\| < r_a + r_b$, in which case both circles intersect.

In the presence of duplicate detections we eliminate the circle having less votes in the acumulator mask. In Fig. 4 we show the result of eliminating duplicate circles with each criterion, the second criterion being the one giving better results.

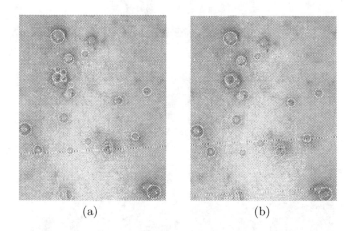

(a)   (b)

Fig. 4. (a) Result of eliminating duplicate circles with criterion i). (b) Result of eliminating duplicate circles with criterion ii) –see text.

3.4 Chrominance Information to Eliminate False Positives

As mentioned earlier, the original RGB images were transformed to L*a*b* color space. The CIE L*a*b* was specified by the "Commission internationale de l'éclairage", its aim was that uniform changes of components in the L*a*b* color space would correspond to uniform changes in perceived color. To eliminate false vesicle detections, we worked on component a* of this color representation. The pixels inside each detected vesicle were extracted, and their a* chromatic component was analyzed. First we calculated the empirical histogram of all the pixels in the true varicella vesicles. The Kullback Leibler distance between this all-varicella-histogram and the empirical histograms of each detected circle, whether it were a false positive(skin) or true positive (varicella). In Table 1 we list the KLD between histograms of 10 false detection -and 10 true detections - versus the histogram of all varicella pixels. Notice that false detections all have much higher KLD values, which helps to get rid of these false positives.

Table 1. Row 1: KLD between empirical histogram of pixels (component a*) inside 10 spurious detected circles versus the histogram of all varicella pixels (component a*). Row 2: KLD between empirical histogram of pixels (component a*) inside 10 truly detected varicella vesicles versus the histogram of all varicella pixels (component a*).

Skin	24.26	25.30	23.94	23.63	27.54	28.98	38.66	25.71	18.89	22.52
Varicella	0.334	0.515	1.131	0.679	2.771	2.005	2.168	0.684	1.486	1.833

4 Discriminating between Chickenpox and Herpes Zoster Vesicles

We have made preliminary tests in order to discriminate chickenpox vesicles from herpes zoster vesicles. These we carried out on 4 images - see Fig. 5[2].

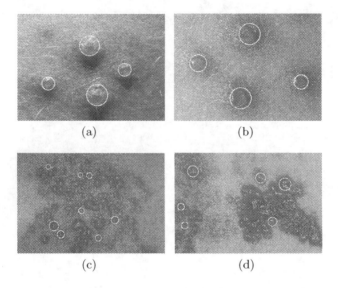

(a)   (b)

(c)   (d)

Fig. 5. Skin lesions and detected vesicles. (a) - (b) Examples of chickenpox lesions. (c) - (d) Examples of herpes zoster lesions.

Different tests were performed on the 3 components of L*a*b* color system, assuming normal distributed values and equal variances in the data. We found statistical evidence of differences between the means of the 2 classes (chickenpox and herpes zoster) on component a*. This component indicates the position of the pixel's color between green and red/magenta (a* negative values indicate green, while positive values indicate magenta). In Fig. 6 are given the histograms of component a* in the vesicles of each image of Fig. 5. Notice that the sample means are much smaller for herpes zoster lesions than for chickenpox lesions.

---

[2] The original images (chickenpox_primary_lesions_03, varicella_34, herpes_zoster_114, herpes_zoster_8) are larger. A detail containing all detected vesicles is shown.

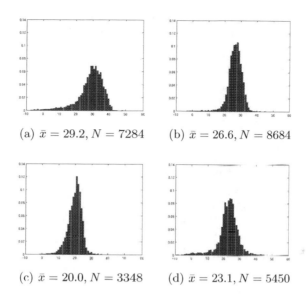

(a) $\bar{x} = 29.2, N = 7284$ (b) $\bar{x} = 26.6, N = 8684$

(c) $\bar{x} = 20.0, N = 3348$ (d) $\bar{x} = 23.1, N = 5450$

Fig. 6. Histograms of component a* of pixels inside vesicles, $\bar{x}$ is the sample mean, N is the number of samples; (a) - (b): chickenpox lesions; (c) - (d): herpes zoster lesions

An ANOVA (Analysis of variance) test was carried out to compare the mean values of pixels (component a*) belonging to the 2 classes. There were $N = 15968$ samples in the chickenpox class, and $N = 8798$ samples in the herpes zoster class. With probability 1 ($p = 0$) the null hypothesis –that the means of the 2 classes are equal– was rejected. The estimated value for the difference between the means was $\mu_{(chickenpox)} - \mu_{(herpeszoster)} = 5.8608$, with a 100% confidence interval of $[5.7044, 6.0171]$. The test indicates that the error between classes was much greater than the intraclass error.

Next four vectors were built gathering information from inside the vesicles of each mentioned image (component a*). An ANOVA was performed on these four vectors, and multiple comparisons were done between the vectors. We list the estimated value for the difference between the means, and give the 100% confidence intervals. Recall that (a) and (b) belong to chickenpox class, (c) and (d) to herpes zoster class.

Interclass comparisons:

$\mu_{(a)} - \mu_{(c)} = 9.1967 \in [8.8831, 9.5104]$; $\mu_{(a)} - \mu_{(d)} = 6.1135 \in [5.8445, 6.3826]$.
$\mu_{(b)} - \mu_{(c)} = 6.5746 \in [6.2689, 6.8802]$; $\mu_{(b)} - \mu_{(d)} = 3.4913 \in [3.2317, 3.7509]$.

Intraclass comparisons:

$\mu_{(a)} - \mu_{(b)} = 2.6222 \in [2.3835, 2.8609]$; $\mu_{(c)} - \mu_{(d)} = -3.0832 \in [-3.4131, -2.7533]$.

From these results we conclude that there is sufficient statistical evidence to reject the (null) hypothesis that the difference between the means of 2 images belonging to different classes is 0 (i.e., the means of images belonging to different classes are significantly different). However, although the difference of means was smaller for intraclass comparisons than for interclass comparisons, there is too much variability in the data to be able to accept the other (null) hypothesis that images belonging to the same class have equal means. The last 2 confidence intervals should have contained 0 to be able to accept this hypothesis.

5   Conclusions

A tool for detection of chickenpox vesicles was designed, giving satisfactory results when applied over a group of pictures belonging to patients that suffer from this illness. Most vesicles were successfully detected by applying different image processing and pattern recognition techniques, and the method has proven to be robust under different illumination scenarios. Both lumninance and chrominance information were used to obtain result. Once vesicles were detected, preliminary statistical tests for discrimination between herpez zoster and chickenpox classes achieved promising results, although intraclass variance was high.

References

[1] Yeganeh, H., Ziaei, A., Rezaie, A.: A novel approach for contrast enhancement based on Histogram Equalization. In: IEEE Int. Conf. Computer and Communication Eng., pp. 256–260 (2008)
[2] Peng, Z.-Y., Zhu, Y.-H., Zhou, Y.: Real-time Facial Expression Recognition Based on Adaptive Canny Operator Edge Detection. In: IEEE Int. Conf. Multimedia and Information Technology, pp. 154–157 (2010)
[3] Rizon, M., Yazid, H., Saad, P., Md Shakaff, A., Saad, A., Sugisaka, M., Yaacob, S., Mamat, M., Karthigayan, M.: Object Detection using Circular Hough Transform. American Journal of Applied Sciences 2(12), 1606–1609 (2005)
[4] Coll, L., Chinchilla, D., Coll, C., Stengel, F., Cabo, H.: Análisis digital de imágenes en lesiones pigmentadas de la piel. Diagnóstico precoz del melanoma. Dermatología Argentina 14(3) (2008)
[5] Canny, J.F.: A Computational Approach to Edge Detection. IEEE PAMI 8(6), 679–698 (1986)
[6] Hough, P.V.: Machine analysis of bubble chamber pictures. In: Kowarski, L. (ed.) Int. Conf. on High Energy Accelerators and Instrumentation, pp. 554–556 (1959)
[7] Ballard, D.H.: Generalizing the Hough Transform to Detect Arbitrary Shapes. Pattern Recognition 13(2), 111–122 (1981)
[8] Pedersen, S.: Circular Hough Transform. Aalborg University, Vision, Graphics, and Interactive Systems (November 2007)

Real-Time On-Board Image Processing Using an Embedded GPU for Monocular Vision-Based Navigation

Matías Alejandro Nitsche and Pablo De Cristóforis

Buenos Aires University, Faculty of Exact and Natural Sciences,
Computer Science Department
{mnitsche,pdecris}@dc.uba.ar

Abstract. In this work we present a new image-based navigation method for guiding a mobile robot equipped only with a monocular camera through a naturally delimited path. The method is based on segmenting the image and classifying each super-pixel to infer a contour of navigable space. While image segmentation is a costly computation, in this case we use a low-power embedded GPU to obtain the necessary framerate in order to achieve a reactive control for the robot. Starting from an existing GPU implementation of the quick-shift segmentation algorithm, we introduce some simple optimizations which result in a speedup which makes real-time processing on board a mobile robot possible. Performed experiments using both a dataset of images and an online on-board execution of the system in an outdoor environment demonstrate the validity of this approach.

Keywords: monocular vision-based navigation, image segmentation, GPU.

1 Introduction

Vision-based robot navigation has long been a fundamental goal in both robotics and computer vision research in last years. Most vision-based navigation techniques assume that a sequence of images is acquired during a human-guided training step that allows the robot to build a map of the environment. However, this is a tedious process as it involves human intervention every time a robot moves to a new workspace. Therefore, to achieve a completely autonomous navigation system it is necessary to remove human intervention [1] [2].

The final aim of this work is to facilitate a mobile robot equipped only with a monocular camera to autonomously drive through a naturally delimited path. This robot should perform all processing on-board, given real-time constraints imposed by the robot motion.

While in previous works classification in navigable or non-navigable ground is done at the pixel level [3], in this work we follow more recent proposals that segment images into regions to perform a better classification [4] [5]. The advantage of the segmentation is that the pixels belonging to a certain region have

L. Alvarez et al. (Eds.): CIARP 2012, LNCS 7441, pp. 591–598, 2012.
© Springer-Verlag Berlin Heidelberg 2012

low internal contrast. This facilitates the search of the navigable terrain, since it is fair to assume that this area is more or less uniformly colored or textured and the edges will most likely be of high-contrast. On the other side, the disadvantage is usually the associated high computational cost. For this reason, real-time image segmentation is difficult to achieve using low-power embedded processors on autonomous robots, which is the current target of this work.

In this work we present a new image-based navigation method for guiding a mobile robot equipped only with a monocular camera through a naturally delimited path. The method is based on segmenting the image and classifying each super-pixel to infer a contour of navigable space. We use a low-power embedded GPU to obtain an acceptable framerate in order to achieve a reactive control for the robot. Starting from an existing GPU implementation of the quick-shift segmentation algorithm [6], we introduce some optimizations which result in a speedup of approximately five times. This increased speed makes real-time processing on board a mobile robot possible.

2   Related Work

There are previous works that perform visual navigation using only monocular system and pixel classification. If we can assume that the robot is operating on a flat surface and all objects have their bases on the ground, the problem is reduced to classifying pixels into two classes: obstacle or traversable floor. This approach, that is suitable for robots that operate on benign flat terrains, has been used in in a variety of works. In [3] classification is done at the pixel level. First the image is filtered with a Gaussian filter. Second the RGB values are transformed into the HSV (hue, saturation, and value) color space. In the third step, an area in front of the mobile robot is used for reference and valid hue and intensity values inside this area are histogrammed. In the fourth step, all pixels of the input image are compared to the hue and intensity histograms. A pixel is classified as an obstacle if its hue or intensity histogram bin value is below some threshold. Otherwise the pixel is classified as belonging to the ground. This method is fast, as no complex computation is involved. The main drawback of this method is it is very unstable at the robot's movements and sensitive to noise.

Thus, the idea of segmenting the image into a number of super-pixels (i.e., contiguous regions with fairly uniform color and texture) arises. In [4] a graph-based image segmentation algorithm [7] is used. Once the image is over-segmented in super-pixels, each one is labeled as belonging to the ground or non-ground region using the HSV histogram approach as in [3]. While this method is more stable and robust, it is quite computational expensive, so the exploration algorithm that uses this method has to stop the robot periodically to capture and process images of the workspace. Using the same image segmentation algorithm, in [5] super-pixels that are likely be classified equal are grouped into constellations. Constellations can be the labeled as floor or non-floor with an estimator of confidence depending on whether all super-pixels in the constellation have the same label. This is a more robust method, but computationally expensive. In contrast to these methods, this work proposes a real-time segmentation algorithm that allows a reactive control for guiding the robot.

3   Proposed Method

The global idea of the proposed method can be summarized as follows. First, the image obtained from the camera is smoothed using a median blur filter[1]. Then, the image is segmented into a number of super-pixels, allowing the discrimination of individual chunks of pixels with low internal contrast. Given an example of what the navigable space looks like (by using a sub-region of the image corresponding to the area directly in front of the robot), each segment is classified as being similar to it or not. After individual classification, the resulting positively classified group of super-pixels nearest to the example area are assumed to correspond to the most likely navigable path. Finally, by computing the contour of this area, a motion line can be extracted and used for reactive control. A control law is defined that restricts the robot to remain inside this detected navigable area. From these steps, the most computationally demanding corresponds to the image segmentation. Therefore, we focus on optimizing this portion of the method to allow real-time execution.

3.1   Image Segmentation

The quick-shift segmentation algorithm is a simpler and faster alternative to other segmentation algorithm. In listing 1.1 a pseudo-code implementation is shown. The algorithm first computes the density ρ of each pixel, which is a measure of local contrast in the vicinity of size 3σ. Next, each pixel is linked to the nearest neighbor in a vicinity of τ which has a higher density than the current one. In this fashion, trees are formed where each root is a pixel with the highest local contrast in the vicinity. Each tree then represents a segment or super-pixel.

Since with this algorithm the computation can be performed in parallel for each pixel in the image, it is a good candidate for a GPU implementation. In fact, such an implementation already exists and reports considerable advantage when compared to the CPU-based version[8]. The code used in this work by Fulkerson and Soatto is available on line. Moreover, this code actually includes a further speedup proposed by James Fung where authors report a $2x$ relation to the original. This code was used in the present work, but introducing a series of simple optimizations, obtaining a speedup of up to four times when performing all experiments on a low-power embedded GPU (which is used in the experiments with the robot).

---

[1] In contrast to the commonly used Gaussian blur, the median blur preserves high contrast edges, which is important for road-detection.

```
function density
 for i in all pixels
    ρi = 0
    for j in neighborhood of size 3σ
```
$$\rho_i \mathrel{+}= exp(\frac{-||RGB[i]-RGB[j]||^2}{2*\sigma^2})$$

```
function neighbors
 for i in all pixels
    for j in neighborhood of size τ
       if ρi > ρj and distance(i,j) is smallest among all neighbors
          di = distance(i,j)
          parent[i] = j
```

Listing 1.1. Quickshift algorithm pseudocode

The first optimizations that were introduced consist of careful tuning of the number of concurrent threads executed, the registers required for code compilation (which affects the efficiency of the thread scheduling and thus the paralellization level), taking into account the capabilities of the specific card to be used. The second main optimization that was introduced involves a simpler handling of out-of-bound accesses which arise when searching the neighborhood of pixels near the edges of the image. In the original implementation these were avoided explicitly, where in our case, the *clamping mode* of the texture memory is used. Here, these accesses simply return the nearest valid pixel in the image (effectively repeating pixels in the image outwards). By introducing this change, the code can be simpler and more efficient. Finally, memory accesses in general were reduced by delaying them up to the point where they were for certain to be required.

3.2   Super-Pixel Classification

Once a list of super-pixels has been obtained, the following task is to classify each as belonging to free or non-free space. For this classification, a positive example of the floor appearance is provided. As in [3], a sub-region of the image corresponding to the ground immediately ahead of the robot was chosen for this example. In this work a rectangular region is used, instead of a trapezoid, to simplify the computations.

In order to classify each super-pixel according to this example region, a measure is taken from each and compared. By establishing a certain threshold, the classification is performed. In this work the measure consists of a simple average of pixel values belonging to the segment and to the rectangular region. This measure is not as computationally demanding as other histogram-based methods generally used, and also produces satisfying results.

While pixel values are generally processed in RGB, alternative color spaces exist. In particular, the HSV color space is particularly useful since it separates the tonal and illumination aspects of the image. Even further, in most cases, the hue channel provides enough information to discern a path (for example, a gray pavement road delimited by green vegetation). Since the RGB to HSV conversion can be computationally demanding if performed on all the pixels of each frame, in this work we reduce this cost by first computing the average in the RGB space and then converting the final results to HSV. Besides the computational aspect, this solves the problem of taking the average HSV value of a group of pixels, since the hue channel is actually a continuous measure that wraps around.

3.3   Control Law

After the super-pixels are classified, several contiguous unconnected regions may appear as possible ground. Among these, the candidate region which includes the center point of the rectangular example area is chosen.

In order to achieve a reactive control to guide the robot so that it maintains its position inside the chosen region, its contour in the image is obtained and processed in several steps. First, by going through every point of this contour from bottom to top (up to a predefined row, related to the horizon position), the horizontal middle position is computed using the left-most and right-most contour pixels. The resulting middle points are then fitted using a linear regression, which approximates the middle of the visible free space with a straight line called motion line. From this line, both its angle and its horizontal deviation with respect to the image's middle vertical are computed. These deviations are scaled in the range $[-1, 1]$ and are identified as ω and d, respectively.

Since these two values indicate the direction and position of the road with respect to the robot, a simple control law is used to compute turning (v_a) and forward (v_x) speeds which allow the robot to remain in the road:

$$v_a = \alpha \cdot \omega + \beta \cdot d$$
$$v_x = 1 - |v_a|$$

where α and β are constants between $[0, 1]$. In the tests performed, these constants were set to 0.5, giving equal impact by both values to the angular speed. In other words, when either the fitted road line deviates or turns, the robot will turn in the same direction. Regarding the forward speed, the control law generates a constant forward motion whenever the robot is not turning. Otherwise, the robot reduces (in an inverse proportion) its speed while turning.

4   Results

The system was tested using a previously recorded dataset and also on-line in an outdoor scenario. In the former case the road-detection capability of the system was evaluated. In the latter, the complete system was tested including the control-law that drives the robot, in order to ensure the capability of remaining inside the road limits.

The robot used in the experiments, the ExaBot[9], consists of a differential-drive base with an embedded Mini-ITX board (AT5ION-T Deluxe) and a firewire camera (model 21F04, from *Imaging Source*) with a $3.5 - 8mm$ zoom lens. The embedded computer features a GPU capable of general purpose computing, using the CUDA technology from NVIDIA. This graphic card features 16 cores running at 1.1Ghz and with 256MB of memory.

While the camera is capable of capturing images at 640×480 px images at 15 fps, a smaller resolution of 320×240 px (at 30 fps) was chosen since it was enough for proper road detection. This smaller resolution also decreases computation times. The zoom lens was set-up at 3.5mm, providing a fairly wide-angle of view.

Additionally, an analysis of the computational times obtained by using the optimized segmentation step is included.

4.1   Performance Improvement

In this section we measure the execution speed of the segmentation algorithm, compared to the original GPU-targeted unmodified version. The segmentation algorithm depends on two parameters (σ and τ) which ultimately control segment size and affects computational speed. Through several tests with real-world images, it was experimentally found that the acceptable results were obtained with values $\sigma = 4$ and $\tau = 10$. Therefore, performance results are here presented with these fixed values.

The speedup obtained when compared to the original implementation running on the same low-power GPU is around 4.8 times. This relation does not change with different image resolutions since only an improved implementation of the same algorithm is used. For a 320×240 resolution (which was used in the on-line tests) the execution time of the segmentation step is around 145 milliseconds. This accounts for 60% of the total time required for one processing step, which is about 240 milliseconds. In the following experiments it can be seen that this it is enough for on-line processing on the robot.

4.2   Offline Tests

The dataset used for this test was produced by a *Pioneer* robot, on a several hundred meter long trajectory, on an outdoor park in Prague, Czech Republic[2]. This dataset was processed and the road contour along the middle line used for control was drawn. In figures 1(a) to 1(e) some example frames are presented[3]. While in some frames the system classified some distant parts as road (near the horizon), what is used for controlling the robot motion is the line fitted from the yellow middle points which are below of the last row configured by the user. This way, the road following is reduced to detecting the nearby edges and attempting to remain away from them.

---

[2] Dataset: `http://robotica.exp.dc.uba.ar/trac/exabot/export/85/trunk/` `src/gpu/floordetection/dataset/dataset.avi`

[3] Full video: `http://robotica.exp.dc.uba.ar/trac/exabot/export/85/trunk/` `src/gpu/floordetection/dataset/frontier.avi`

4.3   Online Tests

The system performance running on a robot was evaluated on an outdoor scenario, where the control-law and system reactiveness was put to test. The trials consisted of several initial positions were the robot was in the middle of the road and near the sides, both looking straight forward and also deviated towards a side. This allowed testing not only of the stability of a good initial configuration but also of extreme cases (which did not normally occur since the robot always remained on track) where the robot quickly returned to the middle of the road. Example frames from the complete video [4] are presented in figures 1(f) to 1(i).

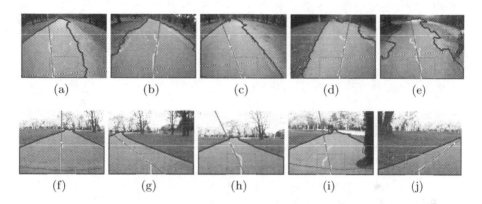

Fig. 1. Example frames from the processed images obtained during off-line (1(a)-1(e)) and on-line (1(f)-1(i)) testing. The green square represents the area defined as ground, the blue contour corresponds to the detected road, the red line is obtained by fitting the middle yellow points (which is then used for motion commands) and the horizontal yellow line is the last row that is processed for adding middle points.

5   Conclusions and Future Work

In this work we present a real-time implementation of a navigable floor detection algorithm for a mobile robot equipped only with a monocular camera.

The main computational requirement of this method is the image-segmentation step. By using an on-board low-power graphics card which is capable of general purpose computation, we achieve a reactive control for the robot. Based on an existing GPU implementation of the quick-shift segmentation algorithm, we introduce some simple optimizations which result in a speedup of approximately five times. This reduces computational times to a level that allows real-time execution on the robot.

The capability of the method to detect a road in an outdoor natural scenario was tested using a pre-recorded dataset. Also, several tests were performed on a

---

[4] http://robotica.exp.dc.uba.ar/trac/exabot/export/85/trunk/
    src/gpu/floordetection/results-bien/frontier.avi

mobile robot featuring the specified hardware. Besides starting the robot in the middle of the road and verifying its stability, several extreme initial positions and orientations were tested. In these conditions the robot quickly returned to the center line demonstrating the general stability of the road-detection.

After obtaining satisfying results, there are several aspects that can be improved. First, the classification of each segments as road or non-road (based on a single average measure in HSV color-space) could rely on the fact that a contiguous (i.e.: without holes) region is expected to be detected as road. Therefore, it could be better if the classification of a single segment could depend on the classification of nearby segments. Second, while framerate is already sufficient, the algorithm could possibly be sped up by attempting to utilize the GPU for other steps than image segmentation alone. Furthermore, robustness of this method in the long-term (and also to varying illumination) would have to be addressed by including some form of learning of positive (and possibly negative) examples of the area considered as free-space. Finally, the classification itself could be improved by considering not only pixel values (color) but also texture.

References

1. DeSouza, G., Kak, A.: Vision for mobile robot navigation: A survey. IEEE Transactions on Pattern Analysis and Machine Intelligence 24(2), 237–267 (2002)
2. Bonin-Font, F., Ortiz, A., Oliver, G.: Visual navigation for mobile robots: a survey. Journal of Intelligent & Robotic Systems 53(3), 263–296 (2008)
3. Ulrich, I., Nourbakhsh, I.: Appearance-based obstacle detection with monocular color vision. In: Proceedings of the National Conference on Artificial Intelligence, pp. 866–871. AAAI Press, MIT Press, Menlo Park, Cambridge (2000)
4. Santosh, D., Achar, S., Jawahar, C.: Autonomous image-based exploration for mobile robot navigation. In: IEEE International Conference on Robotics and Automation, ICRA 2008, pp. 2717–2722. IEEE (2008)
5. Wang, Y., Fang, S., Cao, Y., Sun, H.: Image-based exploration obstacle avoidance for mobile robot. In: Control and Decision Conference, CCDC 2009, pp. 3019–3023. IEEE, Chinese (2009)
6. Vedaldi, A., Soatto, S.: Quick Shift and Kernel Methods for Mode Seeking. In: Forsyth, D., Torr, P., Zisserman, A. (eds.) ECCV 2008, Part IV. LNCS, vol. 5305, pp. 705–718. Springer, Heidelberg (2008)
7. Felzenszwalb, P., Huttenlocher, D.: Efficient graph-based image segmentation. International Journal of Computer Vision 59(2), 167–181 (2004)
8. Fulkerson, B., Soatto, S.: Really quick shift: Image segmentation on a gpu. In: ECCV 2010 Workshop on Computer Vision on GPUs, CVGPU 2010 (2010)
9. Pedre, S., De Cristóforis, P., Caccavelli, J.: A mobile mini-robot architecture for research, education and popularization of science. Journal of Applied Computer Science Methods 2(1) (2010)

Hardware/Software Co-design for Real Time Embedded Image Processing: A Case Study

Sol Pedre[1], Tomáš Krajník[2], Elías Todorovich[3], and Patricia Borensztejn[1]

[1] Departamento de Computación, FCEN-UBA, Argentina
{spedre,patricia}@dc.uba.ar
[2] Czech Technical University in Prague, Czech Republic
tkrajnik@labe.felk.cvut.cz
[3] Departamento de Computación y Sistemas, FCE-UNICEN, Argentina
etodorov@exa.unicen.edu.ar

Abstract. Many image processing applications need real time performance, while having restrictions of size, weight and power consumption. These include a wide range of embedded systems from remote sensing applications to mobile phones. FPGA-based solutions are common for these applications, their main drawback being long development time. In this work a co-design methodology for processor-centric embedded systems with hardware acceleration using FPGAs is applied to an image processing method for localization of multiple robots. The goal of the methodology is to achieve a real-time embedded solution using hardware acceleration, but with development time similar to software projects. The final embedded co-designed solution processes 1600×1200 pixel images at a rate of 25 fps, achieving a $12.6\times$ acceleration from the original software solution. This solution runs with a comparable speed as up-to-date PC-based systems, and it is smaller, cheaper and demands less power.

Keywords: real time image processing, hardware/software co-design methodology, FPGA, robotics.

1 Introduction

Many image processing applications require solutions that achieve real time performance. A usual approach for accelerating is to exploit their inherent parallel sections, building implementations on parallel architectures such as GPUs or FPGAs. The appearance of the CUDA [1] framework allowed to implement image processing methods on GPUs (graphical hardware of common PCs) with relative small coding effort resulting in their significant speedup [2, 3]. Although these implementations are based on affordable computational hardware, they are unsuitable for applications that also require small and low power consuming solutions. These cover a wide range of embedded systems from remote sensing applications and robotics to mobile phones and consumer electronics.

An alternative solution is to use Field Programmable Gate Arrays. FPGAs are devices made up of thousands of logic cells and memory. Both the logic cells

L. Alvarez et al. (Eds.): CIARP 2012, LNCS 7441, pp. 599–606, 2012.
© Springer-Verlag Berlin Heidelberg 2012

and their interconnections are programmable using a standard computer. Their highly parallel architecture with low power consumption, small size and weight provide an excellent platform for achieving real time performance on embedded applications. The inclusion of processor cores embedded in programmable logic has also made FPGAs an excellent platform for hardware/software co-designed solutions. These solutions try to combine the best of both software and hardware worlds, making use of the ease of programming a processor while designing tailored hardware modules for the most time consuming sections of the application. Several authors [4–6] reported successful implementation of image processing algorithms on FPGA-based hardware, including co-designed solutions [7, 8].

The main drawback of FPGA-based methods is time consuming development, that raise exponentially as the complexity of the application increases. This led to the proposal of new methodologies, tools and language aimed at reducing design time by raising the abstraction level of design and implementation. These approaches are commonly known as Electronic System Level (ESL) [9], although they differ in language, abstraction level and tool support.

In this work an image processing case study of a co-design methodology for processor-centric embedded systems with hardware acceleration using FPGAs is presented. The case study is an image processing algorithm for real-time localization and identification of multiple robots, integrated in a remote access robotic laboratory. Results indicate that the proposed methodology is suitable to achieve real-time performance in embedded image processing applications, while reducing the design and coding effort usually needed for this type of tailored co-designed solutions.

2   Methodology Overview

The proposed co-design methodology, described in detail in [10], is aimed at reducing design and coding effort. It has four broad stages: A) Design, B) Implementation and Testing in a general purpose processor, C) Hardware/Software partition and D) Implementation, testing and integration of each hardware module in the final embedded platform.

Taking advantage of the processor centric approach, the whole system is designed using well established high level modeling techniques, languages and tools from the software domain. That is, an Object Oriented Programming (OOP) design approach expressed in Unified Modeling Language (UML) and implemented in C++. This helps to reduce design effort by raising abstraction level while not imposing the need to learn new languages and tools. There are several related works that use domain-specific specializations of UML profiles for hardware or co-design specifications [11] [12] [13]. However, different degrees of hardware details still need to be specified in these approaches. In our approach, the UML design is done prior to hardware/software partition, abstracting away the implementation details related to both hardware and software.

The C++ implementation is then tested in a general purpose processor using debugging resources available in these processors. This implementation not only provides a golden reference model, but may also be used as part of the final embedded software. In this manner, software coding effort is reduced.

To perform hardware/software partition, the complete software solution must be migrated to the final embedded processor. The required hardware resources to make the embedded processor run are characterized and the hardware platform is generated. The software platform for the embedded processor is generated and the software solution is migrated. Using profiling tools in the embedded processor, the methods that need to be accelerated by hardware are identified completing the hardware/software partition phase. The modular OOP design facilitates to find the exact methods that need to be accelerated, preventing useless translations to hardware and hence reducing hardware coding effort.

Finally, each hardware module is implemented, tested and integrated in the complete system. Related work in the area of High-Level synthesis include semi-automatic tools to translate code in C to Hardware Description Language (HDL) code for FPGAs [14] [15] [16]. All these require rewriting effort on the original code to particular C language subset, and hardware knowledge in order to generate correct HDL. Our approach is to use the two-process structured VHDL design method [17] for hardware implementation by translating the C++ object methods by hand in a guided way. This method has proven to reduce man-years, code lines and bugs in many major projects [18].

3 Multiple Robot Localization

The System for Robotic Teleeducation (SyRoTek)[19] is a system developed by the Intelligent and Mobile Robotics Group at the Czech Technical University in Prague. This virtual lab provides remote access from anywhere around the world to real mobile robots located in an arena.

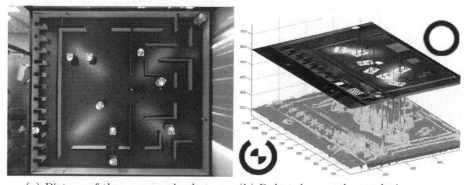

(a) Picture of the arena and robots   (b) Robot dress and convolution response

Fig. 1. Localization system in SyroTek

In order to perform localization, each robot carries a unique ring-like pattern that allows to calculate its position and orientation in a 1600×1200 gray scale image taken by an overhead camera (see Fig. 1). The image is processed in several steps. First, the radial distortion caused by camera lens imprecision is removed. Then, the image is transformed to make the arena appear as a rectangle aligned with the image edges. Using the intrinsic and extrinsic parameters of the camera, a look-up table mapping pixel coordinates of the rectified image to pixel coordinates of the captured image is computed. Using this look-up table, both transformations are performed in a single step, achieving a faster undistortion. For more accurate results, bilinear interpolation with four surrounding pixels is used to calculate the gray level of the destination pixel.

The rectified image is then convolved with a 40×40 annulus pattern. The maximal values of the convolution filter indicate robot positions on the arena, see Fig.1. Knowing robot positions allows to find the endpoints of the robot dress arc and to determine the robot heading. When orientations are found, each robot is identified by a binary code in the dress center.

The convolution of the entire image is slower than the camera frame rate and therefore it is performed only at system start. After that, the convolution is computed in a neighborhood of each robot's position in the previous frame. Therefore, the correction for image distortion is only performed in those neighborhoods, greatly diminishing the amount of memory accesses needed.

4   Hardware/Software Co-designed Solution

4.1   UML Structural and Behavioral Design

The overall structural design of the solution is shown in the Fig. 2.

The `Robot` class contains the information of each robot, i.e position, heading and id. The class `PositionCalculator` calculates the new position of a robot implementing the image convolution in the `exec` method. The class `Angle-Calculator` calculates the new heading of a robot.

A `Matrix` class was created to encapsulate matrix operations. Since most matrices are sub-matrices of bigger ones (e.g. an image section is a sub-matrix of image), memory is only dealt with in very specific moments. The `LoadableMatrix` class inherits from `Matrix` and encapsulates actual memory movements. Finally, the `Image` class is a particular `LoadableMatrix` that knows about image undistortion operation. This class implements both bilinear and nearest neighbor interpolation for comparison purposes.

4.2   Hardware-Software Partition

An Avnet development kit including a Virtex4-FX12 FPGA with a PowerPC405 embedded processor was used. The development tools used are Xilinx's Design Suite 11.2 for hardware and embedded software development and GNU valgrind and gprof for preliminary resource characterization.

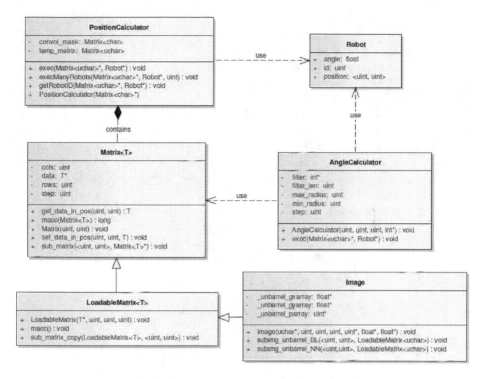

Fig. 2. Structural Design

First, the resources needed to run the software solution in the embedded processor were characterized. Profiling results in a Core i5 M480 (2 cores@2.67GHz) show that the `Matrix::macc` method uses 87% of the time, and is a clear candidate for hardware implementation. This method is called 100 times in `PositionCalculator::exec` that searches for the new position of a robot. The modularity of the OOP design and the encapsulation of the matrix operations in a separate class allows the profiling to accurately point where the most time consuming operation is, preventing useless translations to hardware.

Next, the needed hardware platform to run the software solution in the embedded processor is generated. From the previous analysis, the memories included are Flash, SDRAM and Block RAMs (memory embedded in the FPGA), connected through an IBM PLB bus to the processor. Internal caches were configured. The PowerPC405 is set at its maximum frequency (300 MHz). A standalone (no operating system) software platform was generated for the processor.

The migration of the complete software solution to the embedded processor required only two minor changes. In the embedded solution, images that were opened with OpenCV are loaded from the Flash memory, and dynamic memory for image sections is replaced by BlockRAMs. These interface changes were encapsulated in a single configuration file, so the rest of the code is unchanged.

Finally, the complete software solution is profiled in the embedded processor. Since the PowerPC405 has no FPU, all floating point operations are emulated by Xilinx's compiler. Hence, software optimizations were developed for the PowerPC's particular architecture. Profiling results for each code version are shown in Table 1. The first column corresponds to the original code. The second column uses pre-calculated cosine and sine masks for angle estimation. The third column corresponds to changing all floating point operations to fixed point arithmetics. The fourth column keeps previous changes but performs image undistortion without bilinear interpolation. The fifth column simplifies angle calculation, removing bilinear interpolation for pixel brightness calculation. The last two changes add a 1.6% error in worst case for angle estimation.

All these changes were first implemented and tested in the Corei5, using its debugging and testing resources, and keeping the golden reference model up to date. Migration to the PowerPC did not require code changes. The test suite were images with 14 robots in the arena loaded in the Flash memory. Results for profiling in the Corei5 processor are also shown in this table. The fastest code was used for this test (including all optimizations and floating point arithmetics).

Table 1. Profiling results. All times in miliseconds.

	PPC405@300 MHz					i5@2.67GHz
	orig. code	cos_mask	fixed pt.	unbarrel_NI	angle_NI	all opt.
Matrix::macc	117.7	117.7	117.7	117.7	117.7	28.69
angleCalc::exec	246.9	48.3	17.7	17.7	7.3	0.84
Image::unbarrel	120.0	120.0	120.0	4.5	4.5	0.72
complete solution	*489.5*	*295.6*	*264.0*	*141.7*	*130.2*	*30.74*

An output of this stage is the complete, correct and optimized software version running in the embedded PowerPC405 processor. Also, the definite hardware-software partition is to translate the `Matrix::macc` method to hardware.

4.3 Hardware Implementation, Testing and Integration

Next, the hardware module for the `Matrix::macc` is implemented, including its interface with the memory and embedded processor. Hardware and software changes are introduced to integrate this hardware module in the solution.

The `macc` does the convolution of two matrices. To access data, it is connected to two Block RAMs, one per matrix. The PowerPC is connected to the other port of each Block RAM so it can load data (i.e, the image section and the convolution mask). The `macc` module is also connected by a Device-Control Register(DCR) bus to the PowerPC. This is a simple bus that can connect many slave modules in a daisy chain manner. Through this bus, the PowerPC tells the `macc` module in which address of each Block RAM the matrix to be multiplied starts. When the multiplication is over, the `macc` returns the accumulated value through this DCR bus to the PPC. The six modules and seven interface packages needed for the solution were implemented following the two-process VHDL design method.

In Table 2 a comparison between the complete software solution and the solution with hardware acceleration and software optimizations can be found.

Table 2. Solution comparison in the Virtex4 FPGA

		all software	hard accelerated
	Slices	3,575	3,718
Area	BRAM	13	15
	DSP48	0	1
	Matrix::macc	117.7	22.4
Time (ms)	angleCalc::exec	246.9	7.3
	Image::unbarrel	120.0	4.5
	complete solution	*489.5*	*38.7*

The best possible complete-system performance is achieved since each part (hardware and software) runs at its maximum frequency. For this, a Digital Clock Manager (DCM) is included and the connection between the embedded processor and hardware is done in an asynchronous way (i.e, using memories and the DCR bus).

The final hardware accelerated solution processes 25 fps of 1600×1200 pixel images, achieving a real-time embedded solution for the problem. The acceleration from the original solution to the final software optimized and hardware accelerated solution is $12.6\times$. The extra FPGA area required is one DSP48 (i.e, a hardware multiplier), 2 Block RAMs and 143 slices, only 4% area penalty. The hardware accelerated solution takes 38.7 ms to process an image while the most optimized software solution in a Corei5 (2 cores@2.67GHz) takes 30.4 ms.

5   Conclusions

The stages of a co-design methodology for processor-centric embedded systems with hardware acceleration using FPGAs were applied to an image processing case study for localization of multiple robots. The aim of the methodology is to achieve a real-time embedded solution using hardware acceleration, but with development times similar to software projects. Results indicate that the proposed methodology is suitable to achieve real-time performance in embedded image processing applications, while reducing design time and coding effort usually needed for this type of tailored co-designed solutions. The achieved embedded solution successfully processes 1600×1200 pixel images at a rate of 25 fps. It runs with a comparable speed as the method implementation on an up-to-date general purpose processor, but is smaller, cheaper and demands less power.

Acknowledgments. Xilinx Design Suite was donated by Xilinx University Program. This work has been partially supported by Czech project No. 7AMB12AR022, and Argentinien projects MINCyT RC/11/20, UBACyT 200158 and PICT-2009-0041.

References

1. NVIDIA: CUDA: Parallel Programming (January 2012), http://www.nvidia.com
2. Jošth, R., et al.: Real-time PCA calculation for spectral imaging (using SIMD and GP-GPU). Journal of Real-Time Image Processing, 1–9 (2012)
3. Cornelis, N., van Gool, L.: Fast scale invariant feature detection and matching on programmable graphics hardware. In: IEEE International Conference on Computer Vision and Pattern Recognition, CVPR, Anchorage Alaska (June 2008)
4. Diaz, J., et al.: FPGA-based real-time optical-flow system. IEEE Transactions on Circuits and Systems for Video Technology 16(2), 274–279 (2006)
5. Pedre, S., Stoliar, A., Borensztejn, P.: Real Time Hot Spot Detection using FPGA. In: 14th Iberoamerican Congress on Pattern Recognition, pp. 595–602. Springer (2009)
6. Bonato, V., Marques, E., Constantinides, G.A.: A Parallel Hardware Architecture for Scale and Rotation Invariant Feature Detection. Transactions on Circuits and Systems for Video Technology 18(12), 1703–1712 (2008)
7. Jordan, H., Dyck, W., Smodic, R.: A co-processed contour tracing algorithm for a smart camera. Journal of RealTime Image Processing 6(1), 23–31 (2010)
8. Castillo, A., Shkvarko, Y., Torres Roman, D., Perez Meana, H.: Convex regularization based hardware/software co-design for real-time enhancement of remote sensing imagery. Journal of Real-Time Image Processing 4, 261–272 (2009)
9. Bailey, B., Martin, G., Piziali, A.: ESL Design and Verification: A prescription for Electronic System-Level Methodology. Morgan Kaufmann (2007)
10. Pedre, S., Krajník, T., Todorovich, E., Borensztejn, P.: A co-design methodology for processor-centric embedded systems with hardware acceleration using FPGA. In: IEEE 8th Southern Programmable Logic Conference, pp. 7–14. IEEE, Brazil (2012)
11. Mallet, F., André, C., DeAntoni, J.: Executing AADL Models with UML/MARTE. In: International Conference of Engineering of Complex Computer Systems, pp. 371–376. IEEE, Germany (2009)
12. Mueller, W., Rosti, A., Bocchio, S., Riccobene, E., Scandurra, P., Dehaene, W., Vanderperren, Y., Ku, L.: UML for ESL Design - Basic Principles, Tools, and Applications. In: IEEE/ACM Int. Conf. on Computer Aided Design, pp. 73–80 (November 2006)
13. Silva-Filho, A.G., et al.: An ESL Approach for Energy Consumption Analysis of Cache Memories in SoC Platforms. International Journal of Reconfigurable Computing, 1–12 (2011)
14. Jacquard: ROCCC 2.0 (October 2011), http://www.jacquardcomputing.com/roccc/
15. Mentor-Graphics: CatapultC (October 2011), http://www.mentor.com/esl/catapult
16. Nallatech: DIME-C (October 2011), www.nallatech.com/Development-Tools/dime-c.html
17. Gaisler, J.: A structured VHDL design method. In: Fault-tolerant Microprocessors for Space Applications. Gaisler Research, pp. 41–50 (2004)
18. ESA: European Space Agency VHDL (October 2011), http://www.esa.int
19. Kulich, M., et al.: SyRoTek - On an e-Learning System for Mobile Robotics and Artificial Intelligence. In: ICAART 2009, pp. 275–280. INSTICC Press, Setúbal (2009)

Dynamic Textures Segmentation with GPU

Juan Manuel Rodríguez, Francisco Gómez Fernández,
María Elena Buemi, and Julio Jacobo-Berlles

Departamento de Computación, Facultad de Ciencias Exactas y Naturales,
Universidad de Buenos Aires, Buenos Aires, Argentina

Abstract. This work addresses the problem of motion segmentation in video sequences using dynamic textures. Motion can be globally modeled as a statistical visual process know as dynamic texture. Specifically, we use the mixtures of dynamic textures model which can simultaneously handle different visual processes. Nowadays, GPU are becoming increasingly popular in computer vision applications because of their cost-benefit ratio. However, GPU programming is not a trivial task and not all algorithms can be easily switched to GPU. In this paper, we made two implementations of a known motion segmentation algorithm based on mixtures of dynamic textures. One using CPU and the other ported to GPU. The performance analyses show the scenarios for which it is worthwhile to do the full GPU implementation of the motion segmentation process.

1 Introduction

Motion and texture are key characteristics for video interpretation. The recognition of textures in motion allows video analysis in the presence of water, fire, smoke, crowds, among others. Understanding these visual processes has been very challenging in computer vision. Some motion segmentation methods are based on optical flow [1,2]. This approach presents difficulties like aperture and noise problems. The classical solution is to regularize the optical flow field, however, this produces unwanted effects in motion, smoothing edges or regions where the movement is smooth (for example, vegetation in outdoor scenes).

To analyze the dynamical visual processes we need a model that can describe them. To fully understand the properties of dynamical visual processing, learning a model, given our measurements (a finite sequence of images), it is necessary to recover the scene that was generated. The recognition of textures in movement based on observed video sequences sampled from stochastic processes taking into account the variations in time and space is called dynamic textures (DT) [3].

Dynamic textures have been used for segmentation of visual processes in video. However, when multiple dynamic textures (possibly superimposed) occur in a same scene, this model is not capable of discriminating them well. To face this problem, a Mixture of Dynamic Textures (MDT) [4] model has been proposed, to handle this issue as a constituent part of the model. The MDT algorithm can classify a set of input video sequences into different categories, given the number

L. Alvarez et al. (Eds.): CIARP 2012, LNCS 7441, pp. 607–614, 2012.

of different visual processes to model. Thus, to segment a single video, we can easily partition it into a group of sub-videos (spatio-temporal patches that fulfill the entire video) and then classify them using MDT. The main drawback using this video segmentation procedure is that the visual process is reduced as a result of the patch-based partition, similar to the aperture problem in optical flow. To address this problem, a global generative model called Layered Dynamic Texture (LDT) [5] has been introduced, which has co-occurring dynamic textures as part of the model. Even considering the new approaches to LDT [5], using them for motion segmentation is slow and will not be part of our study. Implementing these statistical models is computationally demanding. Thus, taking advantage of cutting-edge technology is a necessity. Nowadays, the use of Graphics Processing Units (GPU) in computer vision applications are becoming increasingly popular because of their cost-benefit ratio and their suitability to general purpose computing. In this work, we implement two versions of a motion segmentation algorithm based on the MDT model [5]: one using a traditional CPU processor and other using a GPU-translated optimized implementation with library modules. Computing time tests are carried out to evaluate the benefits of porting to this technology. No quality tests were performed; those were already exposed in previous publications, and the results we obtained are the same here. The structure of this paper is as follows: section 2 describes the dynamic textures and the mixture dynamic models, section 3 shows the implementation developed in this paper, in section 4 we discuss the testing results for dynamic texture segmentation in videos with mixtures of dynamic textures in CPU and GPU. Finally, in section 5 we present the conclusions and future work.

2   Dynamic Texture Model

A dynamic texture [3] is a generative model for both the appearance and the dynamics of video sequences. It consists of a random process containing an observed variable y_t, which encodes the appearance component (video frame y at time t), and a hidden state variable x_t, which encodes the dynamics (evolution of the video over time). The state and observed variables are related through the LDS (Linear Dynamical System) defined by:

$$\begin{cases} x_{t+1} = Ax_t + v_t \\ y_t = Cx_t + w_t \end{cases} \tag{1}$$

where $x_t \in \mathbb{R}^n$ and $y_t \in \mathbb{R}^m$ (typically $n \leq m$). The parameter $A \in \mathbb{R}^{n \times n}$ is a state-transition matrix, and $C \in \mathbb{R}^{m \times n}$ is an observation matrix. The driving noise processes v_t and w_t are normally distributed with zero mean and covariances Q and R respectively, that is, $v_t \sim \mathcal{N}(0, Q)$ and $w_t \sim \mathcal{N}(0, R)$. This model is extended to an initial state x_1 of arbitrary mean μ and arbitrary covariance S, that is, $x_1 \sim \mathcal{N}(\mu, S)$. This extension produces a richer video model that can capture variability in the initial frame and is necessary for learning a dynamic texture from multiple video samples with different initial frames (as is the case in clustering and segmentation problems). The dynamic texture is specified by the parameters $\Theta = \{A, Q, C, R, \mu, S\}$. It can be shown [6] from this definition that the distributions of the initial state, the conditional state, and the conditional observation are:

$$p(x_1) = G(x_1, \mu, S), \quad p(x_t|x_{t-1}) = G(x_t, Ax_{t-1}, Q), \quad p(y_t|x_t) = G(y_t, Cx_t, R)$$

where $G(x, \mu, \Sigma) = (2\pi)^{-n/2}|\Sigma|^{-1/2}e^{-\frac{1}{2}\|x-\mu\|_\Sigma^2}$ is the n-dimensional multivariate Gaussian distribution, and $\|x\|_\Sigma^2 = x^T\Sigma^{-1}x$ is the Mahalanobis distance with respect to the covariance matrix Σ. Let $x_1^\tau = (x_1, \cdots, x_\tau)$ and $y_1^\tau = (y_1, \cdots, y_\tau)$ be the sequence of states and the sequence of observations, respectively. Then, their joint distribution is $p(x_1^\tau, y_1^\tau) = p(x_1) \prod_{t=2}^\tau p(x_t|x_{t-1}) \prod_{t=1}^\tau p(y_t|x_t)$.

2.1 Mixtures of Dynamic Textures

Under the mixtures of dynamic textures model, an observed video sequence y_1^τ is sampled from one of K dynamic textures, each having some nonzero probability of occurrence. This is a useful extension for two classes of applications. The first class involves a video that is homogeneous and the second class involves an inhomogeneous video, that is, a video composed of multiple processes that can be individually modelled as a dynamic texture with different parameters. In this model, the random variable $z \sim multinomial(\alpha_1, ..., \alpha_K)$ with $\sum_{j=1}^K \alpha_j - 1$ indicates which of the K dynamic textures, each with probability α_j of occurrence, is used to represent the observed sequence. The model parameters are given by $\{\Theta_1, \ldots, \Theta_K\}$, where $\Theta_i = \{A_i, Q_i, C_i, R_i, \mu_i, S_i\}$ as described before. The probability of y_1^τ is given by:

$$p(y_1^\tau) = \sum_{j=1}^K \alpha_j p(y_1^\tau|z = j),$$

where $p(y_1^\tau|z = j)$ is the class conditional probability of the j-th dynamic texture, i.e., the texture component parametrized by $\Theta_i = \{A_i, Q_i, C_i, R_i, \mu_i, S_i\}$. Fig. 1 shows the MDT as a graphical model.

2.2 Parameter Estimation

The parameters of K dynamic textures to fit a set $\{y^{(i)}\}_{i=1}^N$ of N video sequences, are estimated using the Expectation-Maximization (EM) algorithm [7], that is, an iterative procedure for estimating the parameters of a probability distribution, given that the distribution depends on hidden variables. For the mixtures of dynamic textures model, the observed data is a set of video sequences $\{y^{(i)}\}_{i=1}^N$, and the missing information consists of: 1) the assignments $z^{(i)}$ of each sequence to a mixture component, 2) the hidden state sequence $x^{(i)}$ that produces $y^{(i)}$, and 3) the parameter vector $\Theta = \{\Theta_j\}_{j=1}^K$. Each iteration of the EM algorithm consists of two steps:

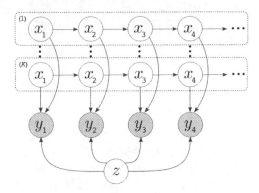

Fig. 1. Graphical model for mixtures of dynamic textures

- **E-step**: $\mathcal{Q}(\Theta; \hat{\Theta}) = \mathbb{E}_{X,Z|Y;\hat{\Theta}}(\log p(X, Y, Z; \Theta))$
- **M-step**: $\hat{\Theta}^* = \arg\max_{\Theta} \mathcal{Q}(\Theta; \hat{\Theta})$

Step E estimates hidden states, and hidden assignment variables with the current parameters, and step M computes new parameters given the previous estimates. Function $p(X, Y, Z; \Theta)$ is the complete-data likelihood of the observations, hidden states, and hidden assignment variables, parametrized by Θ. In mixtures of dynamic textures, the training data are considered to be a set of independent video sequences. In [4] the authors present EM for the mixtures of dynamic textures algorithm. In this method, the E-step relies on the Kalman smoothing filter to compute: 1) the expectations of the hidden state variables x_t, given the observed sequence $y^{(i)}$ and the component assignment $z^{(i)}$, and 2) the likelihood of observation $y^{(i)}$ given the assignment $z^{(i)}$. Then, the M-step computes the maximum-likelihood parameter values for each dynamic texture component j by averaging over all sequences $\{y^{(i)}\}_{i=1}^{N}$, weighted by the posterior probability of assigning $z^{(i)} = j$. The initialization of the EM algorithm is done setting each Θ_j using the method in [3] on a random video sequence from the training set.

3   Video Classification and Motion Segmentation

Mixtures of dynamic textures (MDT) are well suited to motion segmentation, where a moving object or a group of them can be characterized by a dynamic texture. If the model of a dynamic texture is known, then one can estimate the probability of an observed sequence y is generated by the model. In the context of MDT, given a set of video sequences $\{y_i\}$, once the MDT model is learned for $\{y_i\}$ (i.e. all parameters Θ of K dynamic dextures are estimated), each sequence y_i can be classified as the j-th mixture component with the largest posterior probability of being generated by j.

$$\ell_i = \arg\max_{j} \left(\log p(y^{(i)}; \Theta_j) + \log \alpha_j \right) \tag{2}$$

This procedure automatically performs a classification of a video dataset into K categories, useful for video retrieval or video semantics. The aim of motion segmentation is to create a static image describing the regions from a video with homogeneous appearance and motion, i.e. annotate each video location with the number of component to which it belongs, such as fire, water, crowd, traffic jam, etc. This can be achieved generating a set of spatio-temporal patches from a single video, then classifying them using MDT as mentioned before, and finally extracting a new patch at each pixel location and assigning it to a mixture component, according to Equation (2). Algorithm 1 summarizes the motion segmentation process.

Algorithm 1. Motion segmentation with MDT

Input: video y, number of components K
Output: segmentation image M

  1. Extract N non-overlapping spatio-temporal patches $\{y^{(i)}\}_{i=1}^{N}$ from input video y
  2. Call EM algorithm with $\{y^{(i)}\}_{i=1}^{N}$ and K
  3. For each p pixel location in y
    3.1. Let $y^{(i)}$ a spatio-temporal patch centered at p
    3.2. Let ℓ_i given by Equation (2), Set $M_p \leftarrow \ell_i$
  4. Return matrix M segmented into K components

---

4   Results

This section presents computer time performance results of the MDT algorithm presented in the previous section. Both CPU and GPU implementations were developed in order to compare each other. Most important parameters and video frame size were tried to test their impact in the execution time.

To carry out time performance tests, the Synthetic Dynamic Texture Segmentation Database (SynthDB) [8] was used. This database is composed of 299 synthetic videos especially generated to assess video segmentation of visual processes. Each video is composed of K components ($K = \{2, 3, 4\}$), of different temporal textures like water, fire, moving plants, etc. Also, they contain ground-truth template and an initial segmentation contour. Video dimensions are 160×110 with 60 frames at 30 fps.

Algorithm implementations were tested on a CPU computer with an AMD Phenom processor and an NVIDIA Tesla C2070 1.15 GHz GPU. The NVIDIA Tesla C2070 has 448 streaming processor cores and a total amount of global memory of 5376 MBytes. The CPU implementation was developed using Matlab and translated into GPU using functions built in the Parallel Computing Toolbox.

To perform the tests, 3 runs of the entire segmentation process were done over 3 different videos (and the one with minimum time was selected), for 3 different components $K = \{2, 3, 4\}$ and 4 different resized videos (when memory limitations were satisfied). Resized videos were generated scaling the original

Fig. 2. Video frame examples from SynthDB with $K = \{2, 3, 4, 4\}$, respectively (first row). Their segmentation (best viewed in color) and Rand index r is shown below.

image sequence ($160 \times 110 \times 60$) by a scaling factor of $SF = \{0.5, 1, 1.5, 2\}$, obtaining in this way, for each K, 3 more videos of 80×55, 240×165, and 320×220 all with 60 frames.

Fig. 2 shows segmentation examples over SynthDB. The segmentation quality is computed with the Rand index metric [9]. Following [10], in order to avoid the bottleneck of computing the inverse of a covariance matrix in the Kalman Filter at the expectation step, a C++ implementation [11] of the Cholesky factorization using GPU [12] and CUBLAS [13] was used. This implementation is based on the fact that, as covariance matrices are positive-definite, it is possible to perform the Cholesky factorization and then solve the (upper and lower) triangular systems using TRSM (Triangle Solve Multiple) function of CUBLAS.

Fig. 3 shows computing times with and without the GPU's inverse implementation described below. Darker bars show GPU times. We ran the tests using videos scaled using $SF = \{0.5, 1, 1.5, 2\}$ and $K = \{2, 3, 4\}$. It can be observed a reduction in computing times for large videos. This is due to the fact that the ratio of data transfer time (to and from GPU) with respect to GPU processing time is lower for larger videos. For smaller videos, computing times are better for CPU processing than for GPU processing.

Fig. 4 shows the GPU performance against CPU for all the segmentation process with $K = \{2, 3, 4\}$ and scaling factor $SF = \{0.5, 1, 1.5\}$, and $SF = 2$ only for $K = 2$ due to GPU memory limitations.

Using the same argument as before, the overhead in time of switching data back and forth to GPU has to be lower than the processing time. Therefore, as expected, the GPU implementation outperforms the CPU implementation only when the video is bigger than the original size (1.5 and 2 times bigger).

Finally, most important parameters and video frame size were tried to assess their impact in the execution time. As expected, frame size, sub-video size m and number of components to find K affect directly the computer execution time. However, varying the size n of the hidden state x and fixing the remaining parameters, computer times keep on approximately constant. Also, it was found that the best parameters are $m = 100$, $n = 10$ with respect to Rand index and execution time.

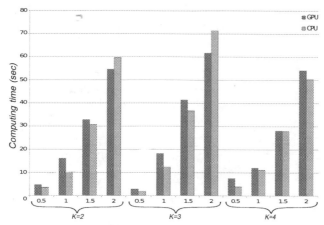

Fig. 3. Time comparisons of two implementations of the inverse using CPU and GPU. Horizontal axis show different scaling factor grouped by segmentation component K.

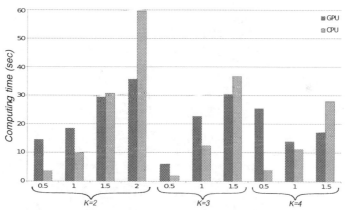

Fig. 4. Computing time performances of the segmentation process on GPU and CPU. Horizontal axis show different scaling factors grouped by segmentation components K.

5   Conclusions and Future Work

In this work we presented CPU and GPU implementations of the motion segmentation algorithm described in [4]. Our GPU implementation is an adaptation from the CPU implementation using library modules that run directly over a GPU card. The importance of this work resides in the analysis of the cases where making a full GPU implementation is a worthwhile work. Performance tests were carried out in order to evaluate benefits and drawbacks of porting algorithms to GPU. Our performance evaluation showed that computing time is reduced significantly with the use of GPU when video size equals or exceeds 320×240, which is the case for video applications of most practical interest.

When analyzing the bottleneck of the MDT algorithm, matrix operations and specially computing the inverse, are the most time-consuming tasks. Our results showed that a meaningful acceleration can be achieved with the use of a specialized GPU function to compute the inverse.

As future work, we are interested in implementing the segmentation algorithm based on layered dynamic textures [14]. This showed better quality results but has a more complex model. Another line of work is to split the learning part of the algorithm from the segmentation part, in order to achieve real time motion segmentation. In this approach, the effort would be put on making the segmentation part online, leaving the learning part as an offline process.

References

1. Horn, B.K.P., Schunck, B.G.: Determining optical flow. Artificial Intelligence 17(1-3), 185–203 (1981)
2. Lucas, B.D., Kanade, T.: An iterative image registration technique with an application to stereo vision. In: IJCAI 1981, pp. 674–679 (1981)
3. Doretto, G.: Dynamic textures: Modeling, learning, synthesis, animation, segmentation, and recognition, Thesis (Ph.D.)–University of California, Los Angeles
4. Chan, A.B., Vasconcelos, N.: Modeling, clustering, and segmenting video with mixtures of dynamic textures. PAMI 30 (May 2008)
5. Chan, A.B., Vasconcelos, N.: Variational layered dynamic textures. In: CVPR, pp. 1062–1069 (June 2009)
6. Roweis, S., Ghahramani, Z.: A unifying review of linear Gaussian models. Neural Comput. 11(2), 305–345 (1999)
7. Dempster, A.P., Laird, N.M., Rubin, D.B.: Maximum Likelihood from Incomplete Data via the EM Algorithm. J. Roy. Statist. Soc. Ser. B, Meth. 39(1), 1–38 (1977)
8. Chan, A.: Synthetic Dynamic Texture Segmentation Database (July 2009), http://www.svcl.ucsd.edu/projects/motiondytex/db/dytex_synthdb.zip
9. Hubert, L., Arabie, P.: Comparing partitions (1985)
10. Huang, M.-Y., Wei, S.-C., Huang, B., Chang, Y.-L.: Accelerating the Kalman Filter on a GPU. In: ICPADS (2011)
11. Bouckaert, R.: Matrix inverse with Cuda and CUBLAS, http://www.cs.waikato.ac.nz/~remco/
12. Ltaief, H., Tomov, S., Nath, R., Du, P., Dongarra, J.: A Scalable High Performant Cholesky Factorization for Multicore with GPU Accelerators. In: Palma, J.M.L.M., Daydé, M., Marques, O., Lopes, J.C. (eds.) VECPAR 2010. LNCS, vol. 6449, pp. 93–101. Springer, Heidelberg (2011)
13. NVIDIA, Cuda cublas library, Version 4.1 (January 2012)
14. Chan, A.B., Vasconcelos, N.: Layered Dynamic Textures. IEEE Transactions on Pattern Analysis and Machine Intelligence 31, 1862–1879 (2009)

Fast Tracking Algorithm
with Borders 1-D Histogram Correlation

María Curetti, *Member, IEEE*, Santiago Garcia Bravo, *Member, IEEE*,
Gabriela Soledad Arri, and Ladislao Mathé, *Member, IEEE*

Abstract. This paper presents a fast algorithm for object tracking in an image sequence. It is a method that models the borders of the image as one-dimensional histograms which are then used instead of templates in the matching procedure. The algorithm models the item being tracked as well as the background in the vicinity so as to then suppress it. It uses cross correlation to find the best match and weighted average to renew the model.

Keywords: Image matching, Image sequence analysis, Video signal processing.

1 Introduction

Object tracking through image sequences is one of the problems of image processing most often studied. Besides its inherent worth, tracking is the previous step for any navigation system based on images. To this end, a wide variety of algorithms that model the object of interest and then look for it in the image are used. One of the first methods to be applied in object tracking is template matching. This algorithm takes a known intensity mask of the item being tracked and compares it with the image until it finds the place where their correlation takes its maximum value. [1], [2], [3], [5].

This method presents a series of problems, among them, the changes that the object appearance suffers with time is one of the most significant ones. Variations in the light and in the shape of the image must be taken into account among other case scenarios. To overcome this, a variety of approaches with different amount of computational load have been employed. [4], [7].

Updating the template after a certain amount of frames is a basic method often applied to outline a valid solution for some of those problems. The main failure of this algorithm is that the object may drift from the mask. To keep the element centered in the template, in [6] the approach proposed is to preserve the first mask and use it in the new template to prevent the drift. Transitory occlusion may occur deteriorating the mask in algorithms that lack robustness. In [8], Kalman filters are used to estimate the intensity of the new template to improve robustness against occlusions. In newer approaches, in [10] for example, the step of matching based on local brightness was replaced with a search for a model. The main reason that leads to this new tactic is the limitation in the brightness mask's constancy originated by light appearance changes.

The objective of this work is to model the object through a set of one-dimensional histograms that describe the borders of the tracked object; then these profiles are used to find the same border distribution in the next frame. Here "border" is defined as the

L. Alvarez et al. (Eds.): CIARP 2012, LNCS 7441, pp. 615–623, 2012.

dividing line or frontier between regions with different intensity on the image. This one-dimensional model is not fixed and allows amendments to take into account the changes in the appearance and size of the object. To avoid the disturbance caused by the background borders, their profiles in the vicinity of the target are modeled and suppressed. These models are not only continuously updated but they also drift from the target position; therefore, they must be correlated before suppression. With heterogeneous backgrounds, this last step is not only essential but also enables the algorithm to estimate the relative movements of the object, taking the background as reference. The main advantage of this algorithm is that, as it models the mask (section of the picture that contains the target) through 1-D signals, the computational load grows proportionally to the object's size to the first power instead of the square power, as it usually happens. Furthermore, the background suppression avoids erroneous changes of the mask's size that can arise when borders are the basis of this choice.

In [9], the tracked object pixel's color distribution is also modeled by a histogram. Then the central computational module, based on mean shift iterations, finds the most probable target position in the current frame. The histograms employed in that work, unlike the ones used in this paper, had bins with no relation to the position of the pixel classified, thus making the description of the target appearance generic. With a 240x360 image and a variable mask from 25x39 to 9x9 following the changes of the object, a processing speed of more than 660 fps is achieved in an Intel(R) Core(TM) i7-2600 CPU 3.4 GHz.

2   System Outline

The tracking system proposed has an initialization stage and five sequential stages that iterate for every frame. Before the sequence of images is processed, the first location and the target size must be input, and the models of the background and target are initialized. The first step in each iteration is to model the region near the location expected for the object in the new frame. Then, the drift of the background is estimated correlating its model with the borders extracted from the frame. Next, the background model is subtracted from the total image model calculated in the new sample. After that, the location that maximizes the correlation with the model of the target is found. Finally, both, the background and target models are updated with a weighted average, and everything is ready for the next iteration.

At the end of each iteration, the algorithm determines whether the mask needs to grow or shrink, and if the target is centered. The algorithm calculates a set of coefficients that reflect the presence of borders near the boundaries of the mask. Then, it compares them to the threshold values that change depending on the target size. Thus, the object will not drift from the mask and the whole target will be contained within.

Prior to explaining each stage of the system, it is necessary to define the model proposed to describe the borders in the image.

3   Model

This model's main objective is to locate the borders of the image through a set of one-dimensional histograms that accumulate the number of pixels corresponding to the target border in each column and row. The system selects four kinds of borders, namely vertical and horizontal borders, which may be positive or negative. This leaves us with eight histograms, four that integrate all the data in a column in one value and four that summarize the rows information.

The first step to calculate this model is to locate the borders in the image. To confirm whether a pixel belongs to any of the target borders proposed, the difference between its intensity and its neighbor's intensity is calculated. Then, the absolute value is compared to a threshold. If the value is greater than this threshold, the pixel will be classified depending on the sign of the difference and the location of the neighbor. This method is applied to the pixels located to the right and below the evaluated pixel Consequently, a pixel will be classified as a positive border if its intensity is higher than the intensity of the one in the row or column immediately next to it, as shown in this expressions:

$$I_{r,c} - I_{r+1,c} > \alpha \Rightarrow hor.\,border\,(+)\,;\; I_{r,c} - I_{r+1,c} < \alpha \Rightarrow hor.\,border\,(-)$$
$$I_{r,c} - I_{r,c+1} > \alpha \Rightarrow vert.\,border\,(+)\,;\; I_{r,c} - I_{r,c+1} < \alpha \Rightarrow vert.\,border\,(-)$$

Fig. 1. Sample image

With this classification method, four matrices will be obtained with unitary value in the border locations. In Fig. 2 a representation of them can be observed.

Fig. 2. Four classification matrices: the vertical borders on the first and third image, and a negative value on the first two images may be observed

From these matrices the computation of the histograms (Fig. 3) is simple.

If the matrices are called M_i, with $i \in \{1,2,3,4\}$, then the calculation needed to complete the model would be:

$$H_{ci} = \sum_c M_i \;;\; H_{ri} = \sum_r M_i$$

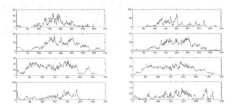

Fig. 3. Eight histograms obtained

4   Initialization

In this stage, it is important to define the target location and size in the first frame. Once these data are input, the system will estimate the target model (tgt) and the background model (bkg). It is convenient not to start with a mask larger than the target since it may incorporate more background borders than necessary. Then, the system will suppress the background borders from the object model, assuming that the target only covers a small section of the background and that the borders will continue inside with some homogeneity. A more detailed explanation of this stage procedure is included below.

First, the system will extract the section of the image centered on the target location. This section has to be twice as large as the mask. Next, all the pixels in this section are classified. Then, the model for the central region is calculated. This will be the first estimate of the target model. All the pixels in this central region are set to zero and then the remaining section is modeled as an approximation of "bkg".

To estimate the central values that belonged to the background and that have been erased, the horizontal borders interrupted by the target will be completed horizontally. The same approximation is applied to the vertical borders to finish "bkg".

Once the background model is estimated, the target model is modified, subtracting the pixels that were decided to belong to borders of the background from the histograms.

5   Stages 1 to 3

The first three stages are similar to the initialization. The main difference is that then the position was known.

The double sized section will be extracted from the vicinity of the estimated position, calculated from the previous positions. All the pixels from this extracted section are classified and modeled (tot). This model (b&t) will include both background and target.

To subtract the modeled background (bkg) from this model (b&t), first the background drift must be determined. Instead of working with the total model the central region in the matrices is turned to zero, and the same estimations made in the initialization are applied to estimate an approximate model of the background alone (bap) in the new frame. The region that must be turned to zero is bigger than the target mask size because the current location is just an estimation that has uncertainty.

To establish the relative position of the two signals that makes the match maximum, the cross correlation method is adopted. This technique calculates for each relative position the scalar product of the displaced signals.

$$C_u = \sum_x f_x t_{x-u}$$

Before the cross correlation is applied, the mean of each vector should be subtracted. Otherwise, the relative position that maximizes C_u, may not be the best match. For instance, if a histogram, with peaks and valleys, is correlated with a signal composed of this same histogram next to other vector of the same size, but with all its elements equal to the maximum of the histogram; the relative position that will maximize the result will be the one that aligns the first signal to the second part of this assembled signal. This can be avoided with the mean subtraction.

$$t'_x = t_x - \bar{t}$$
$$f'_x = f_x - \bar{f}$$
$$\gamma'_u = \sum_x f'_x t'_{x-u}$$

Once the background drift that maximizes the summed cross correlations of each of the eight signals of the models (bkg and bap) is determined, it is used to subtract the background model (bkg) from the total model calculated at the beginning (b&t). As a result, an estimated model (tonly), where only the target borders are modeled, is obtained for the current sample.

6   Stage 4 and 5

In the fourth stage, the correlations of the eight signals of the models "tgt" and "tap" are calculated and added. The resulting value is used to determine a more accurate position of the target in the current frame.

The last stage, where the models (bkg and tgt) are updated, is a very important one. To perform the update, weighted averages are used, and the drift is taken into account. To update "tgt" the model used is "tap", because it's the estimated model of the target alone. A new model (bkn) will be calculated to renew "bkg", this can be obtained from the difference between the overall model (b&t) and the target (tgt), in the position estimated during the last stage. The coefficients that establish the update rate are to be picked carefully. The weight given to the refreshing models should be low enough so as not to add erroneous information, but the renewal must be quick enough so as to follow the changes in the object and improve the model.

$$fond_m = fond'_{m-1} \times (1 - \beta) + totr'_m \times \beta \text{ with } \beta < 1$$
$$yyu_m = yyu'_{m-1} \times (1 - \varepsilon) + totp'_m \times \varepsilon \text{ with } \varepsilon < 1$$

Before the weighted average is calculated, the models must be centered and sectioned considering the misalignment and changes in size. In the background model (bkg), new values that were not modeled in the previous step may be modeled; these are taken from the refreshing model directly (without the previous weighting).

7   Resizing and Centering

This stage allows the model to follow the changes in the size of the object, and it keeps the object centered. Keeping the model as small as possible is useful to avoid entering erroneous information and to decrease the computational load. But, if the model does not include the whole object, some information will not be taken into account and the chances of finding the target are lower.

To decide if the model must grow, every histogram will have its extreme values close to zero (there are no borders in the limit of the mask). If the sum of these extreme values exceeds a certain threshold the model will grow, adding two zeros to the extremes of the four histograms that follow the expanded dimension. It is worth mentioning that the change in size of each dimension is independent.

To resolve shrinking procedure, once we verified that the model will not grow, the values to be checked are those that are next to the extreme ones. If the sum of all these values does not exceed another threshold, that must be lower than the last one, the model will shrink. The extreme values of each of the four histogram of the dimension that is decreasing will be removed. If the threshold is not smaller than the one to which the extreme values were compared, then in the next frame this model will probably grow and this oscillation may continue for a while.

To ensure that the model will follow the size of the object; there is one more situation that must be considered. If the profiles are not centered, the target may shrink and the condition verified to diminish the model can be false. To prevent that from happening, the first three and the last three values of the model are added separately. If one of these trios is below the threshold picked in the last case, the model will shrink by removing the two values in that extreme.

Lastly, it should be pointed out that the threshold should depend on the dimensions of the mask. In this system, a percentage of the size of the dimension that is not being evaluated is used as threshold. It is logical to pick this value because it is also a percentage of the maximum value the histogram can have for this dimension.

8   Experimental Results

This tracking system was designed to find the position of a flying plane; it works as a module of a camera control project. The position of the tracked object in the image is the input of a control system in charge of centering the aircraft in the frame. Thus, the camera will be able to use the optic zoom to its full extent, preventing the target from escaping from the frame. It can only work correctly when applied in objects that fill a small region of the image (60x60 pixels top) that move relative to the background.

To test this algorithm effectiveness, its behavior was studied in two sequences of images: one of a UAV (Unmanned Air Vehicle) taking off and one of a flying plane. These sequences were taken from videos captured previously during another stage of this project's development. To evaluate the obtained results, they were contrasted with the ones attained by using two template matching algorithms: one that simply uses a fixed template and the other with adapting template. During the experience, the threshold values where adjusted so as to not lead to unstable behavior (such as size oscillation, continuous growth or shrinking).

The first sequence taken from the video contains 1500 frames, during the sequence, the UAV shape and its size change drastically. The adapting template technique and the proposed algorithm, both succeed in finding the UAV during the whole succession (Fig.4). The one with the fixed template fails due to the object sudden changes (Fig. 5 (a)). The rate of the adapting template method was of 256 fps, while the profile based algorithm processed 660 images per second. During the second sequence the results where similar, except for the algorithm with the fixed template that this time could follow the target.

Besides the position of the plane for each frame, the system described in this paper has other results that are worth mentioning. In Fig. 5 (b), the horizontal background's accumulated drift is plotted. The plane acceleration is perceptible to the eye. In Fig. 6, the evolution of one of the horizontal signal of background model is shown; here the relative movement is also clear. Finally, the evolution of one of the target model histogram is presented in Fig. 7. Here the model's shrinking accompanying the target changes in size is visible. As the model's histogram always starts in the first line, when the number of bins diminishes, small stepped lines appear in the otherwise gradual changes of the model.

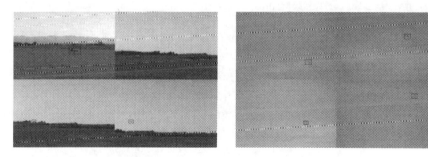

Fig. 4. Samples trough the sequence first and second sequence

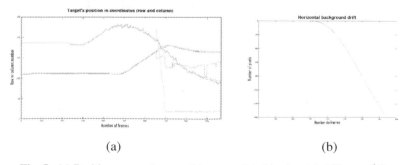

(a)   (b)

Fig. 5. (a) Position versus frames, (b) accumulated horizontal drift versus frames

Fig. 6. Background model evolution

Fig. 7. Target's model evolution

9   Conclusions

The method proposed in this paper to track an object through a sequence of images, uses one-dimensional signals to model the borders in the image and improve the processing speed. It applies procedures of gradual renewal for the models, size adjustment and centering of the object. It also models the background, to suppress it in the new frame, and it makes trajectory predictions. It can run in real-time with images of 360x240 pixels of resolution and at frequencies of up to 660 fps (2.5 times faster than the results obtained with the adaptive mask method). It is robust to changes of the target's appearance, and partial occlusions.

In the future, the performance of this algorithm will be evaluated in sequences where the background is not static. For example, a scenery with trees being moved by the wind.

Acknowledgment. This work was supported by the Ministry of Defense of the Nation, within the framework of the project PIDDEF 019/2010, in charge of Ing. L. Mathé.

It was developed in the facilities of the "Centro de Investigaciones Aplicadas" dependent on the "Instituto Universitario Aeronáutico", Córdoba, Argentina.

References

1. Black, M., Jepson, A.: Eigen-Tracking: Robust Matching and tracking of Articulated Objects Using a View-Based Representation. Int'l. J. Computer Vision 36(2), 63–84 (1998)
2. Hager, G., Belhumeur, P.: Efficient Region Tracking with Parametric Models of Geometry and Illumination. IEEE Trans. Pattern Analysis and Machine Intelligence 20(10), 1025–1039 (1998)
3. Cootes, T., Edwards, G., Taylor, C.: Active Appearance Models. IEEE Trans. Pattern Analysis and Machine Intelligence 23(6), 681–685 (2001)

4. Xiao, J., Kanade, T., Cohn, J.: Robust Full-Motion Recovery of Head by Dynamic Templates and Re-Registration Techniques. In: Proc. IEEE Int'l Conf. Automatic Face and Gesture Recognition, pp. 163–169 (2002)
5. Baker, S., Matthews, I.: Lucas-Kanade 20 Years on: A Unifying Framework. Int'l. J. Computer Vision 53(3), 221–255 (2004)
6. Matthews, I., Ishikawa, T., Baker, S.: The Template Update Problem. IEEE Trans. on Pattern Analysis and Machine Intelligence 26(6) (2004)
7. Zhong, Y., Jain, A.K., Dubuisson-Jolly, M.-P.: Object Tracking Using Deformable Templates. IEEE Trans. on Pattern Analysis and Machine Intelligence 22(5) (May 2000)
8. Nguyen, H.T., Worring, M., van den Boomgaard, R.: Occlusion robust adaptive template tracking. In: Eighth IEEE International Conference on Computer Vision (2001)
9. Comaniciu, D., Ramesh, V., Meer, P.: Real-Time Tracking of Non-Rigid Objects using Mean Shift. IEEE (2000)
10. Wu, Y., Fan, J.: Contextual Flow. In: IEEE Conference on Computer Vision and Pattern Recognition (2009)

Disparity Confidence Measures on Engineered and Outdoor Data

Ralf Haeusler and Reinhard Klette

Department of Computer Science, The University of Auckland
Auckland, New Zealand
rhae001@aucklanduni.ac.nz

Abstract. Confidence measures for stereo analysis are not yet a subject of detailed comparative evaluations. There have been some studies, but still insufficient for estimating the performance of these measures. We comparatively discuss confidence measures whose performance appeared to be 'promising' to us, by evaluating their performance on commonly used stereo test data. Those data are either engineered and come with accurate ground truth (for disparities), or they are recorded outdoors and come with approximate ground truth. The performance of confidence measures varies widely between these two types of data. We propose modifications of confidence measures which can improve their performance on outdoor data.

1 Errors or Confidence Values in Stereo Analysis

With the current application of stereo vision to a variety of imaging tasks, the *reliability* of stereo vision became also a research topic in itself. On rendered or engineered data (e.g., data discussed in [14], or Sets 2 and 7 on [2]), state-of-the-art stereo analysis algorithms are capable of computing depth maps of satisfying quality. However, this differs on image data taken under adverse lighting conditions as they are common for outdoor scenes (e.g., real-world stereo video data on [2]). Outdoor scenes are classified in *situations* in [8], defined by *events* such as lighting artefacts, traffic scenes in the night and sun strikes. Stereo reconstruction appears to be impossible with current methods for such situations. In an abstract sense, critical situations are, for example, if both camera recordings do not satisfy the brightness constancy assumption, or if (e.g. around a recorded light such as in the "Night" sequence in Set 5 on [2]) intensities are nearly constant in some image regions.

The quality of disparity maps is usually rated globally (i.e. summarizing for one disparity map of a given stereo frame). If disparity ground truth is available, common *error measures* are the *root-mean squared error* (RMS) or the *normalized cross-correlation* (NCC) between given and calculated disparities. [14] initiated a ranking of a large number of stereo matchers but only on a small number of stereo frames. Current results on those stereo frames show that they do not represent a true challenge anymore for state-of-the-art stereo algorithms. Prediction error analysis in [16] for the case of optical flow analysis has been adapted

L. Alvarez et al. (Eds.): CIARP 2012, LNCS 7441, pp. 624–631, 2012.

to disparity error analysis in [10] for stereo frames where disparity ground truth is not available. The used error measures provide again only one summarizing value for each stereo frame of a stereo video sequence. Such values are likely to be meaningless in critical situations as specified above.

Confidence measures are designed to provide local (i.e. *pixelwise*) evaluations for identifying regions of failure. Such pixelwise measures are defined based on values of the data cost function (used in the stereo matcher) at a pixel; the global minimum of those values defines usually the selected disparity (ignoring for simplicity the influence of a smoothness term in the stereo matcher). See Fig. 1 for an example; in our experiments we use semi-global matching [5] with the census cost function and 8-path optimization (SGM). An example is shown in Fig. 2.

Confidence measures may be defined on data derived from the cost function (e.g. "around" the global minimum) of the used stereo matcher. The *left-right consistency check* is a common way in stereo matching to accept only results where left-to-right and right-to-left matching defines (about) the same disparity. For a compilation of a number of confidence measures, see [1,7]. Both papers do not provide a comprehensive evaluation of the performance of confidence measures, in particular for stereo data recorded outdoors.

Sophisticated, but computationally more expensive disparity confidence measures have been proposed by [13] (used here directly for the stereo matching process), or in [9] (a perturbation measure) when aiming at improved 3D reconstructions of outdoor scenes. For these two measures, every single cost value contributes, and this makes these measures computationally expensive.

A popular confidence measure is the *opening of the parabola* fitted to the global minimum (and its immediate neighbours) of the cost function. This opening is equivalent to the curvature at the vertex of the parabola. It is assumed that a "wide valley" around the minimum indicates a mismatch, whereas a "narrow valley" is likely to indicate a correct match. [17] used this confidence measure for improving scene flow by enhancing the used stereo-analysis module.

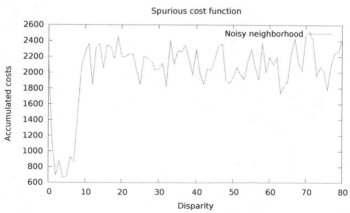

Fig. 1. Values of the census cost function at one pixel (of a recorded stereo video)

Fig. 2. Top row: Outdoor stereo pair (from Set 1 on [2]) and depth map (SGM as specified in the text without any post-processing). Bottom row: Labels from the left-right consistency check (green for occluded, red for other mismatches), manually assigned labels of bad matches (green), and of areas excluded from evaluation (blue); depth map after interpolating manually labelled areas.

The *peak ratio* (basic idea as known from feature matching) is a confidence measure based on comparing two values of a cost function. The second-smallest cost value is usually a neighbour of the global minimum; the peak ratio uses that local minimum of the cost function having the second smallest cost value (considered to be a competing matching candidate). Figure 1 illustrates a pixel where the peak ratio would not be a 'reasonable' confidence value.

There is still a lack of comparative evaluations of such *disparity confidence measures*, and also of a more systematic approach towards the possible design of new measures. Due to the general lack of disparity ground truth for outdoor scenes, evaluations are typically restricted to rendered or engineered indoor stereo data, and only in a few rare cases to outdoor stereo data with approximated disparity ground truth. This paper contributes to such comparative evaluations, suggests new ways for designing confidence measures, and also shows ways how to use recorded outdoor stereo data more widely in these studies.

The paper is structured as follows: Section 2 provides formal definitions of confidence measures with our proposed modifications. Section 3 explains the evaluation method for confidence measures. Section 4 contains results and discussion. Section 5 concludes.

2   Disparity Confidence Measures

A confidence measure C is defined pixelwise for the selected disparity values. These disparities are usually defined by the global minimum of a cost function c. In our case, c is resulting from enforcing smoothness constraints to the disparity values by aggregating according to the semi global matching heuristic. For a pixel in the left image, c is defined for disparities in an interval $[d_{min}, d_{max}]$; $c(d)$ is the cost for disparity d.

We identify two special disparities: d_0, where $c(d_0)$ is the global minimum, and d_1, where $c(d_1)$ also defines a local minimum but which is only the second smallest globally.

Curvature. Local curvature of c at the cost minimum d_0 is a widely used confidence measure. We use the inverse of the opening of a fitted parabola:

$$C_0 = \frac{1}{-2c(d_0) + c(d_0 - 1) + c(d_0 + 1)} \tag{1}$$

Perturbation. The perturbation measure, proposed in [9], computes the deviation from an ideal cost function that has a single minimum at location d_0 and is 'very large' everywhere else. Nonlinear scaling is applied:

$$C_1 = \sum_{d \neq d_0} e^{-\frac{(c(d_0) - c(d))^2}{\sigma^2}} \tag{2}$$

Parameter σ is chosen to obtain a valid range of confidence values regarding numerical precision limits.

Peak ratio. The peak ratio indicates low confidence if there are two candidates with similar matching costs. It is defined as

$$C_2 = \frac{c(d_0)}{c(d_1)} \tag{3}$$

Right-left consistency check. Right-left consistency compares the selected disparities of left-to-right and right-to-left matching. Let d_0^R be the global minimum of the cost function for right-to-left. Then,

$$C_4 = |d_0 - d_0^R| \tag{4}$$

Large disparity differences between both views show an incorrect match, at least for one of both. In practice, a difference of more than one pixel is considered to be an indication of a mismatch. Defining values smaller than 1 is of questionable value for a confidence measure.

Proposed Modifications. Inspired by the observation that the neighbourhood of the global cost function minimum on recorded stereo frames contains little information about the correctness of the match (see the plot of the curvature measure in Fig. 4), we exclude a neighbourhood of size n from the confidence computation, where n equals (about) half of the matching window size. The perturbation measure is then defined as follows:

$$C_1(x, y) = \sum_{d \in [d_{min}, d_0 - n] \cup [d_0 + n, d_{max}]} e^{-\frac{(c(d_0) - c(d))^2}{\sigma^2}} \tag{5}$$

For the peak ratio, in addition to being a local minimum of c, the following constraint is applied for the selection of d_1: $d_1 < d_0 - n$ and $d_1 > d_0 + n$.

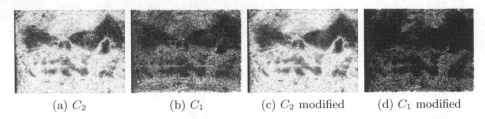

(a) C_2 (b) C_1 (c) C_2 modified   (d) C_1 modified

Fig. 3. Visualisation of peak ratio (a) and perturbation measure (b) and their modified counterparts (c),(d) for the stereo frame displayed in Fig. 2. Lighter grey values indicate locations with lower confidence into the calculated disparity.

3   Synthetic, Engineered and Recorded Data

We tested confidence measures defined on accumulated cost of SGM (defined above) using a census [3] cost function instead of the originally used mutual information [5]. This choice is justified by good overall performance of census costs, as, for example, reported in [6].

We use a *sparsification strategy* for comparing the performance of measures: initially, the number of bad pixels is counted on the disparity map with full density; successively, pixels with lowest confidence (or highest score assigned, respectively) are removed, resulting in semi-dense disparity maps; for each disparity density, the number of bad pixels is counted, until the set of points in the disparity map is empty.

This evaluation requires disparity ground truth. For synthetic scenes, ground truth is available with very high accuracy, without any mismatches; see Set 2 on [2]. Accurate ground truth for indoor scenes can be obtained using the structured lighting technique [15]. Subpixel accuracy is available on downsampled images. Several data sets with ground truth, generated using structured lighting, have been published in conjunction with [14,12].

For outdoor scenes, one of the few methods to generate depth measurements is using a laser range-finder [4,11]. Drawbacks of this technique include: misregistration of camera and range-finder sensors, non-overlapping occluded areas, low density of laser measurements, and numerous measurement artefacts on specular surfaces.

For the evaluation of disparity confidence measures we count the number of bad pixels (according to some criterion), not the total deviation from ground truth (e.g., as done with RMS). Therefore it is more important to have accurate maps of gross mismatches than very accurate disparity measurements itself. For the evaluation of recorded data, we choose to manually enhance a disparity map by labelling bad pixels; see Fig. 2. To compensate for unavoidable inaccuracies on real-world data, we identify as bad matches only disparities that differ from the ground truth value by eight units or more. On synthetic and engineered data, a difference of more than 1 defines a bad match.

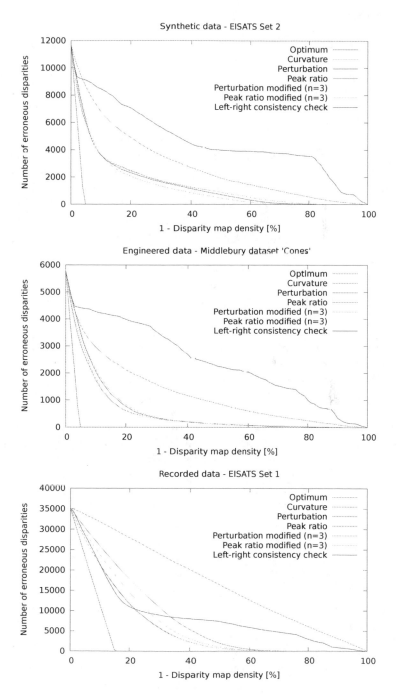

Fig. 4. Sparsification plots of confidence measures. Top to bottom: synthetic, engineered, and outdoor-recorded stereo input data.

4 Results

Results from sparsification are plotted in Fig. 4. The curvature measure is generally the worst performing one, despite its popularity. On the recorded data set it even provides no information about confidence at all. The proposed modifications of perturbation and peak ratio measure are not advantageous on synthetic and engineered data. The modified peak ratio significantly outperforms the original peak ratio measure on the recorded dataset. Improvements in sparsification (see Fig. 4)for the modified perturbation measure are minor for the used dataset, in contrast to what the visualization in Figure 3 suggests. With the modification of the peak ratio feature, an effective noise reduction in feature space can be achieved: See, e.g., in Fig. 3 that areas depicting trees in the recorded images (see Fig. 2) are well estimated by the used stereo matcher, and the modified peak ratio measure better reflects this than the original one. The main advantage of the proposed feature modification is avoiding false positives in detecting stereo errors.

In the following, we discuss reasons for deviations in confidence measure accuracies. For the curvature measure, it is important to note that due to limited sharpness in recorded data, the global minimum of the accumulated cost function is never a sharp peak. Therefore, parabola fits at the cost minimum (and immediate neighbours) never yield large values for curvature, except at noisy patches. However, such patches may not generate a correct match. Extending the parabola fit to, for example, a least-squares fit of a wider neighbourhood might help. In the perturbation measure, for the same reason as explained above, excluding a neighbourhood of the global cost minimum gives more weight to other minima, and can enhance the distinctiveness of this feature. The largest potential for confidence measure accuracy improvements seems to be in peak ratio modifications: In recorded data, due to inherent noise, there is often another local minimum only a few (e.g. two) disparities away from the global minimum (see, e.g., Fig. 1). This local minimum usually has an associated cost very close to that of the global minimum, hence produces a very high peak ratio, or a low confidence, respectively. However, such matches are often correct or have a minor disparity inaccuracy. So, it is not desirable to exclude them from subsequent computations using these disparities. It may be of interest to scale n, the exclusion window size, depending on disparity d, as matching errors in more distant objects produce larger absolute errors in object space. Note, however, that this does not influence evaluations based on metrics using the number of bad pixels.

5 Conclusion

We have shown that popular confidence features behave significantly different on synthetic or engineered data on the one hand, compared to outdoor data on the other hand. We conclude that conclusions from evaluations of such measures on synthetic or engineered data are of no value for outdoor data.

However, characterizing different confidence measures on outdoor data in terms of their properties (e.g. performance in dependence of given situations, as discussed in [8]) requires more extensive experiments than reported in this paper. This will also help to identify particular signal or geometry cases where stereo matchers may fail and need to be improved.

References

1. Banks, J., Corke, P.I.: Quantitative evaluation of matching methods and validity measures for stereo vision. Int. J. Robotic Research 20, 512–532 (2001)
2. EISATS (.enpeda.. image sequence analysis test site): The University of Auckland, www.mi.auckland.ac.nz/EISATS (last visit: February 13, 2012)
3. Egnal, G.: Mutual information as a stereo correspondence measure. Computer and Information Science, University of Pennsylvania, Philadelphia, Tech. Rep. MS-CIS-00-20 (2000)
4. Haeusler, R., Klette, R.: Evaluation of Stereo Confidence Measures on Synthetic and Recorded Image Data. In: Proc. IEEE ICIEV (to appear, 2012)
5. Hirschmüller, H.: Stereo processing by semiglobal matching and mutual information. IEEE Trans. Pattern Analysis Machine Intelligence 30, 328–341 (2008)
6. Hirschmüller, H., Scharstein, D.: Evaluation of cost functions for stereo matching. In: Proc. CVPR, pp. 1–8 (2007)
7. Hu, X., Mordohai, P.: A quantitative evaluation of confidence measures for stereo vision. In: IEEE Trans. Pattern Analysis Machine Intelligence (2012), doi:10.1109/TPAMI.2012.46
8. Klette, R., Krüger, N., Vaudrey, T., Pauwels, K., van Hulle, M., Morales, S., Kandil, F., Haeusler, R., Pugeault, N., Rabe, C., Lappe, M.: Performance of correspondence algorithms in vision-based driver assistance using an online image sequence database. IEEE Trans. Vehicular Technology 60, 2012–2026 (2011)
9. Merrell, P., Akbarzadeh, A., Wang, L., Mordohai, P., Frahm, J.-M., Yang, R., Nister, D., Pollefeys, M.: Real-time visibility-based fusion of depth maps. In: Proc. ICCV, pp. 1–8 (2007)
10. Morales, S., Klette, R.: A Third Eye for Performance Evaluation in Stereo Sequence Analysis. In: Jiang, X., Petkov, N. (eds.) CAIP 2009. LNCS, vol. 5702, pp. 1078–1086. Springer, Heidelberg (2009)
11. Morales, S., Klette, R.: Ground Truth Evaluation of Stereo Algorithms for Real World Applications. In: Koch, R., Huang, F. (eds.) ACCV Workshops 2010, Part II. LNCS, vol. 6469, pp. 152–162. Springer, Heidelberg (2011)
12. Scharstein, D., Pal, C.: Learning conditional random fields for stereo. In: Proc. CVPR, pp. 1–8 (2007)
13. Scharstein, D., Szeliski, R.: Stereo matching with nonlinear diffusion. Int. J. Computer Vision 28, 155–174 (1998)
14. Scharstein, D., Szeliski, R.: A taxonomy and evaluation of dense two-frame stereo correspondence algorithms. Int. J. Computer Vision 47, 7–42 (2002)
15. Scharstein, D., Szeliski, R.: High-accuracy stereo depth maps using structured light. In: Proc. CVPR, pp. 195–202 (2003)
16. Szeliski, R.: Prediction error as a quality metric for motion and stereo. In: Proc. ICCV, pp. 781–788 (1999)
17. Wedel, A., Brox, T., Vaudrey, T., Rabe, C., Franke, U., Cremers, D.: Stereoscopic scene flow computation for 3D motion understanding. Int. J. Computer Vision 95, 29–51 (2011)

Speckle Reduction Using Stochastic Distances

Leonardo Torres, Tamer Cavalcante, and Alejandro C. Frery*

Universidade Federal de Alagoas – UFAL
Laboratório de Computação Científica e Análise Numérca – LaCCAN
57072-970, Maceió, AL – Brazil

Abstract. This paper presents a new approach for filter design based on stochastic distances and tests between distributions. A window is defined around each pixel, samples are compared and only those which pass a goodness-of-fit test are used to compute the filtered value. The technique is applied to intensity Synthetic Aperture Radar (SAR) data, using the Gamma model with varying number of looks allowing, thus, changes in heterogeneity. Modified Nagao-Matsuyama windows are used to define the samples. The proposal is compared with the Lee's filter which is considered a standard, using a protocol based on simulation. Among the criteria used to quantify the quality of filters, we employ the equivalent number of looks (related to the signal-to-noise ratio), line contrast, and edge preservation. Moreover, we also assessed the filters by the Universal Image Quality Index and the Pearson's correlation between edges.

Keywords: information theory, SAR, speckle reduction.

1   Introduction

SAR plays an important role in Remote Sensing since they provide complementary information to that provided by optical sensors. SAR data are subjected to speckle noise, which is also present in laser, ultrasound-B, and sonar imagery [4]. This noise degrades the SAR information content and makes image interpretation classification difficult [5].

Statistical analysis is essential for dealing with speckle. In addition, statistical modeling provides support for the development of algorithms for interpreting the data efficiently, and for the simulation of plausible images. Different statistical distributions are proposed in the literature to describe speckled data. We used the multiplicative model in intensity format for homogeneous areas, ergo the Gamma distribution was employed to describe the data [3].

This work presents new filters based on stochastic distances and tests between distributions, as presented in Nascimento et al. [8]. The filters are compared to Lee's filter using a protocol proposed by Moschetti et al. [6] using Monte Carlo simulation. The criteria used to evaluate this filters are the equivalent number of looks, line contrast, edge preserving, the Q index [10] and Pearson's correlation between edges.

* The authors are grateful to CNPq and Fapeal for supporting this research.

L. Alvarez et al. (Eds.): CIARP 2012, LNCS 7441, pp. 632–639, 2012.

The paper is organized as follows: In Section 2 we summarise the model for speckle data. Section 3 describe the new filters. Section 4 presents the measures for assessing the quality of filtered images, with conclusions drawn in Section 5.

2   The Multiplicative Model

According to Goodman [4], the multiplicative model can be used to describe SAR data. This model asserts that the intensity observed in each pixel is the outcome of the random variable $Z\colon \Omega \to \mathbb{R}_+$ which is the product of two independent random variables: $X\colon \Omega \to \mathbb{R}_+$, that characterizes the backscatter; and $Y\colon \Omega \to \mathbb{R}_+$, which models the speckle noise. The distribution of the observed intensity $Z = XY$ is completely specified by the distributions of X and Y.

This proposal deals with homogeneous regions in intensity images, so a constant $X \sim \lambda > 0$ defines the backscatter, and the speckle noise is described by a Gamma distribution $Y \sim \Gamma(L, L)$ with unitary mean $\mathbb{E}(Y) = 1$, where $L \geq 1$ is number of looks. Thus, it follows that $Z \sim \Gamma(L, L/\lambda)$ with density

$$f_Z(z; L, \lambda) = \frac{L^L}{\lambda^L \Gamma(L)} z^{L-1} \exp\left\{\frac{-Lz}{\lambda}\right\}, \tag{1}$$

where Γ is the gamma function, $z, \lambda > 0$ and $L \geq 1$.

3   Stochastic Distances Filter

The proposed filter is based on stochastic distances and tests between distributions [8], obtained from the class of (h, ϕ)-divergences. It employs neighborhoods as defined by Nagao and Matsuyama [7], presented in Figure 1(a), and extended versions as shown in Figure 1(b).

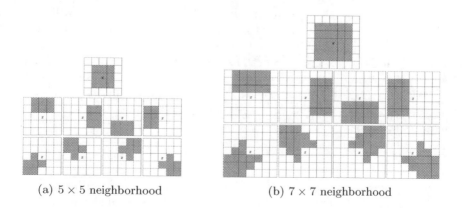

(a) 5×5 neighborhood   (b) 7×7 neighborhood

Fig. 1. Nagao-Matsuyama neighbourhoods

Each filtered pixel has a 5×5 neighborhood (see Figure 1(a)) or a 7×7 neighborhood (see Figure 1(b)), within which nine disjoint areas are defined. Denote $\widehat{\boldsymbol{\theta}}_1$ the estimated parameter in the central 3×3 or 5×5 neighborhood, respectively, and $(\widehat{\boldsymbol{\theta}}_2, \ldots, \widehat{\boldsymbol{\theta}}_9)$ the estimated parameters in the eight remaining areas. To account for possible departures from the homogeneous model, we estimate $\widehat{\boldsymbol{\theta}}_i = (L_i, \lambda_i)$ by maximum likelihood; reduced equivalent number of looks are related to heterogeneous areas [1].

Based on a random sample of size n, $\boldsymbol{z} = (z_1, z_2, \ldots, z_n)$, the likelihood function related to the $\Gamma(L, L/\lambda)$ distribution is given by

$$\mathcal{L}(L, \lambda; \boldsymbol{z}) = \left(\frac{L^L}{\lambda^L \Gamma(L)} \right)^n \prod_{j=1}^{n} z_j^{L-1} \exp\left\{ \frac{-Lz_j}{\lambda} \right\}. \tag{2}$$

Thus, maximum likelihood estimators for (L, λ), namely, $(\widehat{L}, \widehat{\lambda})$, are the solution of the following system of non-linear equations:

$$\begin{cases} \ln \widehat{L} - \psi^0(\widehat{L}) - \ln\left(\frac{1}{n} \sum_{j=1}^{n} z_j \right) + \frac{1}{n} \sum_{j=1}^{n} \ln z_j = 0, \\ \qquad\qquad -\frac{n\widehat{L}}{\widehat{\lambda}} + \frac{\widehat{L}}{\widehat{\lambda}^2} \sum_{j=1}^{n} z_j = 0, \end{cases}$$

where ψ^0 is the digamma function.

The proposal is based on the use of stochastic distances on small areas within the filtering window. Consider Z_1 and Z_i random variables defined on the same probability space, whose distributions are characterized by the densities $f_{Z_1}(z_1; \boldsymbol{\theta}_1)$ and $f_{Z_i}(z_i; \boldsymbol{\theta}_i)$, respectively, where $\boldsymbol{\theta}_1$ and $\boldsymbol{\theta}_i$ are parameters. Assuming that the densities have the same support $I \subset \mathbb{R}$, the h-ϕ divergence between f_{Z_1} and f_{Z_i} is given by

$$D_\phi^h(Z_1, Z_i) = h\left(\int_{x \in I} \phi\left(\frac{f_{Z_1}(x; \boldsymbol{\theta}_1)}{f_{Z_i}(x; \boldsymbol{\theta}_i)} \right) f_{Z_i}(x; \boldsymbol{\theta}_i) \, \mathrm{d}x \right), \tag{3}$$

where $h: (0, \infty) \to [0, \infty)$ is a strictly increasing function with $h(0) = 0$ and $h'(x) > 0$ for every $x \in \mathbb{R}$, and $\phi: (0, \infty) \to [0, \infty)$ is a convex function [9]. Choices of functions h and ϕ result in several divergences.

Divergences sometimes are not distances because they are not symmetric. A simple solution, described in [8], is to define a new measure d_ϕ^h given by $d_\phi^h(Z_1, Z_i) = \left(D_\phi^h(Z_1, Z_i) + D_\phi^h(Z_i, Z_1) \right)/2$. Distances, in turn, can be conveniently scaled to present good statistical properties that make them statistical hypothesis tests [8]:

$$S_\phi^h(\widehat{\boldsymbol{\theta}}_1, \widehat{\boldsymbol{\theta}}_i) = \frac{2mnk}{m+n} \, d_\phi^h(\widehat{\boldsymbol{\theta}}_1, \widehat{\boldsymbol{\theta}}_i), \tag{4}$$

where $\widehat{\boldsymbol{\theta}}_1$ and $\widehat{\boldsymbol{\theta}}_i$ are maximum likelihood estimators based on samples size m and n, respectively, and $k = (h'(0)\phi'')^{-1}$. When $\boldsymbol{\theta}_1 = \boldsymbol{\theta}_i$, under mild conditions $S_\phi^h(\widehat{\boldsymbol{\theta}}_1, \widehat{\boldsymbol{\theta}}_i)$ is asymptotically χ_M^2 distributed, being M the dimension of $\boldsymbol{\theta}_1$. Observing $S_\phi^h(\widehat{\boldsymbol{\theta}}_1, \widehat{\boldsymbol{\theta}}_i) = s$, the null hypothesis $\boldsymbol{\theta}_1 = \boldsymbol{\theta}_i$ can be rejected at level η if $\Pr(\chi_M^2 > s) \le \eta$. Details can be seen in the work by Salicrú et al. [9].

Since we are using the same sample for eight tests, we modified the value of η by a Bonferroni-like correction, namely, Šidák correction, that is given by $\eta = 1 - (1 - \alpha)^{1/t}$, where t is the number of tests and, α the level of significance for the whole series of tests.

Nascimento et al. [8] derived several distances for the $\mathcal{G}^0$ model, which includes the one presented in Equation (1). We opted for the latter, due to the numerical complexity of the former; the lack of flexibility is alleviated by allowing the number of looks to vary locally. The statistical tests used in this paper are then:

Hellinger test: $S_H = \frac{8mn}{m+n} \left(1 - \frac{2^{\widehat{L}} (\widehat{\lambda}_1 \widehat{\lambda}_i)^{\widehat{L}/2}}{(\widehat{\lambda}_1 + \widehat{\lambda}_i)^{\widehat{L}}} \right)$.

Kulback-Leibler test: $S_{KL} = \frac{2mn}{m+n} \widehat{L} \left(\frac{\widehat{\lambda}_1^2 + \widehat{\lambda}_i^2}{2\widehat{\lambda}_1 \widehat{\lambda}_i} - 1 \right)$.

Rényi test of order β: $S_R^\beta = \frac{2mn}{m+n} \frac{\widehat{L}}{2\beta(\beta-1)} \log \frac{\widehat{\lambda}_1 \widehat{\lambda}_i}{\left(\beta\widehat{\lambda}_i + (1-\beta)\widehat{\lambda}_1 \right) \left(\beta\widehat{\lambda}_1 + (1-\beta)\widehat{\lambda}_i \right)}$, in which $0 < \beta < 1$.

Although these are all different tests, in practice they led to exactly the same decisions in all situations here considered. We, therefore, chose to work only with the test based on the Hellinger distance since it has the smallest computational cost in terms of number of operations.

The filtering procedure consists in checking which regions can be considered as coming from the same distribution that produced the data in the central block. The sets which are not rejected are used to compute a local mean. If all the sets are rejected, the filtered value is updated with the average on the central neighborhood around the filtered pixel.

4   Results

Image quality assessment in general, and filter performance evaluation in particular, are hard tasks [6]. A "good" technique must combat noise and, at the same time, preserve details as well as relevant information. In the following we assess the filters by two approaches. Firstly, we use simulated data; with this, we are able to compare the true image (phantom) with the result of applying filters to corrupted version of the phantom. Secondly, we apply measures of quality to a real image and its filtered version.

4.1   Simulated Data

The Monte Carlo experiment discussed in Moschetti et al. [6] consists of simulating corrupted images with different parameters. Each simulated image is subjected to filters, and quality measures are computed from each result. The quality of the filter with respect to each measure can then be assessed analyzing the data, not just a single image. We use a phantom image (see Figure 2(a)) which consists of light strips and points on a dark background, and we corrupt it with speckle noise (see Figure 2(b)). The following measures of quality on the filtered versions as, for instance, Figures 2(c) and 2(d), are then computed:

Equivalent Number of Looks: In intensity imagery and homogeneous areas, it can be estimated by $\mathsf{NEL} = (\bar{z}/\hat{\sigma}_Z)^2$, i.e., the square of the reciprocal of the coefficient of variation. In this case, the bigger the better.

Line Contrast: The preservation of the line of one pixel width will be assessed by computing three means: in the coordinates of the original line (x_ℓ) and in two lines around it $(x_{\ell_1}$ and $x_{\ell_2})$. The contrast is then defined as $2x_\ell - (x_{\ell_1} + x_{\ell_2})$, and compared with the contrast in the phantom. The best values are the smallest.

Edge Preserving: It is measured by means of the edge gradient (the absolute difference of the means of strip around edges) and variance (same as the former but using variances instead of means). The best values are the smallest.

The Q Index: $Q = \frac{s_{xy}}{s_x s_y} \frac{2\bar{x}\bar{y}}{\bar{x}^2 + \bar{y}^2} \frac{2s_x s_y}{s_x^2 + s_y^2}$, where $s_\bullet^2$ and $\bar{\bullet}$ denote the sample variance and mean, respectively. The range of Q is $[-1, 1]$, being 1 the best value.

The β_ρ index: $\beta_\rho = \frac{\sum_{j=1}^{n}(x_j - \bar{x})(y_j - \bar{y})}{\sqrt{\sum_{j=1}^{n}(x_j - \bar{x})^2 \sum_{j=1}^{n}(y_j - \bar{y})^2}}$, it is a correlation measure is between the Laplacians of images X and Y, where $\bullet_j$ and $\bar{\bullet}$ denote the gradient values of the jth pixel and mean of the images $\nabla^2 X$ and $\nabla^2 Y$, respectively. The range of β_ρ is $[-1, 1]$, being 1 the perfect correlation.

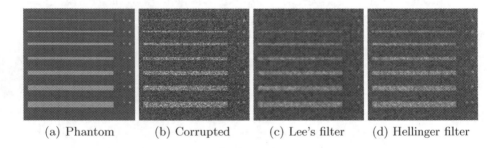

(a) Phantom   (b) Corrupted   (c) Lee's filter   (d) Hellinger filter

Fig. 2. Lee's Protocol, speckled data and filtered images

The proposed filter was compared with Lee's filter [5] which is considered a standard. All filters were applied only once for the whole series of tests. The results obtained are summarized by means of boxplots. Each boxplot describes the results of one filter applied to 100 images formed by independent samples of the $\Gamma(L, L/\lambda)$ distribution with the parameters shown in Table 1. These parameters describes situations usually found when analyzing SAR imagery in homogeneous regions. The tests were performed at the 80%, 90% and 99% level of significance.

Figure 3 shows the boxplot of six measures corresponding to four filters. Vertical axes are coded by the filter ('L' for Lee and 'H' for Hellinger), the situation ID (from 1 to 4, see Table 1), the filter size (5×5 and 7×7). Only results at the 99% level of significance are shown; the rest is consistent with this discussion.

Lee's filter presents better results than our proposal with respect to Edge Variance and the β_ρ index in most of the considered situations, c.f. figures 3(d)

Table 1. Simulated situations with the $\Gamma(L, L/\lambda)$ distribution

Situation ID	L	λ	Background mean
#1	1	200	70
#2	3	195	55
#3	5	150	30
#4	7	170	35

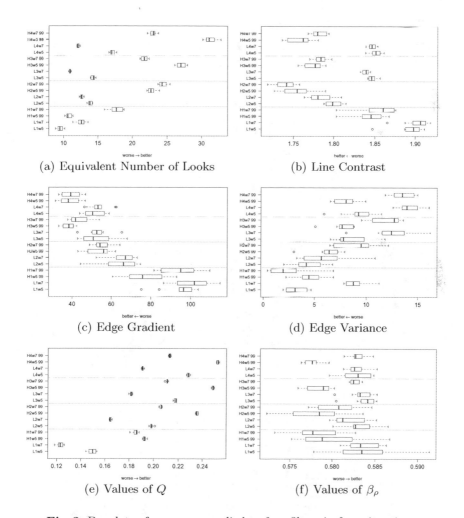

(a) Equivalent Number of Looks (b) Line Contrast

(c) Edge Gradient (d) Edge Variance

(e) Values of Q (f) Values of β_ρ

Fig. 3. Boxplots of measures applied to four filters in four situations

and 3(f). The filters based on stochastic distances consistently outperform Lee's filter with respect to all the other criteria, namely Number of Looks (figure 3(a)), Line Contrast (figure 3(b)), Edge Gradient (figure 3(c)), and the Universal Index Quality measure (figure 3(e)).

4.2 Real Data

Not all the quality measures presented in Section 4.1 can be applied to real data, unless the ground truth is known. For this reason, the following metrics will be used in this case [2], where the smaller is the better (they are all error measures):

Mean Absolute Error: $\mathsf{MAE} = n^{-1} \sum_{j=1}^{n} |x_j - y_j|$.

Mean Square Error: $\mathsf{MSE} = n^{-1} \sum_{j=1}^{n} (x_j - y_j)^2$.

Normalized Mean Square Error: $\mathsf{NMSE} = \frac{\sum_{j=1}^{n} (x_j - y_j)^2}{\sum_{j=1}^{n} x_j^2}$.

Distortion Contrast: $\mathsf{DCON} = n^{-1} \sum_{j=1}^{n} \frac{|x_j - y_j|}{\alpha + x_i + y_j}$, where α depends on the relationship between luminance and gray level of the display; we used $\alpha = 23/255$.

Figure 4 presents the real image, its filtered versions and analysis 1-D of the $row = 50$. The original data were produced by the E-SAR sensor in the L band (HH polarization) with $2.2 \times 3.0\,\mathrm{m}$ of ground resolution and four nominal looks. Nascimento et al. [8] analyzed this image, and the equivalent number of looks in homogeneous areas is always below three.

The Lee filtered image is smoother that the ones obtained with stochastic distances, but comparing figures 4(b) and 4(c) one notices that our proposal

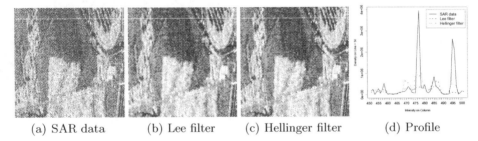

(a) SAR data   (b) Lee filter   (c) Hellinger filter   (d) Profile

Fig. 4. SAR data, filtered images and 1D analysis

Table 2. Image quality indexes in the real SAR image

α	Speckle Filter	Measures of Quality				Q index	
		MAE	MSE	NMSE	DCON	$\bar{Q}$	s_Q
	Lee_w5	0.145	0.037	0.110	0.184	0.142	0.138
	Lee_w7	0.156	0.042	0.126	0.195	0.082	0.127
80%	H_w5	**0.117**	**0.025**	**0.076**	**0.155**	**0.486**	0.170
	H_w7	0.141	0.035	0.104	0.180	0.265	0.187
90%	H_w5	0.120	0.026	0.080	0.159	0.453	0.176
	H_w7	0.142	0.035	0.106	0.182	0.250	0.189
99%	H_w5	0.127	0.029	0.085	0.166	0.397	0.180
	H_w7	0.145	0.036	0.109	0.185	0.222	0.189

retains much more detail than the classical technique. Figure 4(d) presents the profile of the images in the highlighted line. While combating speckle with almost the same success: the bright spots in the upper right corner, which are seldom visible after applying the Lee filter, stand out in the image filtered with the Hellinger distance and windows of side 5 at a level $\alpha = 80\%$.

Table 2 presents the assessment of the filters, and we note that the Hellinger filter of order 5 with $\alpha = 80\%$ achieved the best results.

5   Conclusions

We presented new filters based on stochastic distances for speckle noise reduction. The proposal was compared with the classical Lee filter, using a protocol based on Monte Carlo experiences, showing that it is competitive. An applications to real SAR data was presented and, numerical methods were used to assert the proposal. The proposed filters behave nearly alike, and they outperform the Lee filter in almost all quality measures. However, other significance levels will be tested, along with different points of parameter space to have a yet more complete assessment of proposal. The proposal can be extended to any problem, requiring only the computation of stochastic distances.

References

1. Anfinsen, S.N., Doulgeris, A.P., Eltoft, T.: Estimation of the equivalent number of looks in polarimetric synthetic aperture radar imagery. IEEE Transactions on Geoscience and Remote Sensing 47(11), 3795–3809 (2009)
2. Baxter, R., Seibert, M.: Synthetic aperture radar image coding. MIT Lincoln Laboratory Journal 11(2), 121–158 (1998)
3. Gao, G.: Statistical modeling of SAR images: A Survey. Sensors 10, 775–795 (2010)
4. Goodman, J.W.: Some fundamental properties of speckle. Journal of the Optical Society of America 66(11), 1145–1150 (1976)
5. Lee, J.-S.: Speckle suppression and analysis for synthetic aperture radar images. Optical Engineering 25(5), 636–645 (1986) ISSN 0091-3286
6. Moschetti, E., Palacio, M.G., Picco, M., Bustos, O.H., Frery, A.C.: On the use of Lee's protocol for speckle-reducing techniques. Latin American Applied Research 36(2), 115–121 (2006)
7. Nagao, M., Matsuyama, T.: Edge preserving smoothing. Computer Graphics and Image Processing 9(4), 394–407 (1979)
8. Nascimento, A.D.C., Cintra, R.J., Frery, A.C.: Hypothesis testing in speckled data with stochastic distances. IEEE Transactions on Geoscience and Remote Sensing 48(1), 373–385 (2010)
9. Salicrú, M., Morales, D., Menéndez, M.L., Pardo, L.: On the applications of divergence type measures in testing statistical hypotheses. Journal of Multivariate Analysis 21(2), 372–391 (1994)
10. Wang, Z., Bovik, A.C.: A universal image quality index. IEEE Signal Process. Letters 9(3), 81–84 (2002)

Automatic Classification of Volcanic Earthquakes in HMM-Induced Vector Spaces

Riccardo Avesani[1], Alessio Azzoni[1],
Manuele Bicego[1], and Mauricio Orozco-Alzate[2]

[1] Dipartimento di Informatica, Università degli Studi di Verona, Ca' Vignal 2, Strada
Le Grazie 15, 37134, Verona, Italy
[2] Departamento de Informática y Computación, Universidad Nacional de Colombia -
Sede Manizales, Kilómetro 7 Vía al Aeropuerto, Manizales (Caldas), Colombia

Abstract. Even though hidden Markov models (HMMs) have been used
for the automatic classification of volcanic earthquakes, their usage has
been so far limited to the Bayesian scheme. Recently proposed alternatives, proven in other application scenarios, consist in building HMM-
induced vector spaces where discriminative classification techniques can
be applied. In this paper, a simple vector space is induced by considering log-likelihoods of the HMMs (per-class) as dimensions. Experimental
results show that the discriminative classification in such an induced
space leads to better performances than those obtained with the standard Bayesian scheme.

Keywords: Automatic classification, generative embedding, hidden
Markov models, model-induced feature space, seismic-volcanic signals.

1 Introduction

South America is geologically very active, having a relatively young and seis-
mically restless mountain range —the Andes— which runs parallel to the west
coast of the continent. Volcanism in the Andes results from subduction of the
Nazca and Antarctic oceanic plates below South America and occurs in four
separate regions named the Northern, Central, Southern and Austral volcanic
zones [1]. The fist zone includes 19 volcanoes in Colombia and 55 in Ecuador,
where among the largest and more hazardous ones is Nevado del Ruiz volcano
(NRV), whose eruption in 1985 triggered deadly lahars that killed more than
23000 people. Since 1985 and in order to avoid further tragedies, NRV is permanently monitored by the Volcanological and Seismological Observatory at
Manizales, Colombia (OVSM by its acronym in Spanish). Monitoring activities
include the measurement and analysis of tilt, gas emissions, physicochemical
properties of hot springs and seismic events. The latter are registered by several
seismic stations that the OVSM has deployed in strategic places at NRV.

In spite of the availability of several studies on the application of pattern
recognition techniques to the automated identification of seismic-volcanic events

L. Alvarez et al. (Eds.): CIARP 2012, LNCS 7441, pp. 640–647, 2012.

(see [2] for a comprehensive inventory), the OVSM staff members still visually analyze and manually label every incoming seismic signal registered by the monitoring network. Class labels assigned at OVSM to the registered signals encompass volcano tectonic events, long period events, tremors, hybrid events, teleseismic events, regional and local earthquakes, rock falls, explosions, landslides, avalanches, icequakes and lightnings. The manual assignment of these labels is time and labor consuming as well as prone to human error. Such a tedious task can be significantly simplified by the design and deployment of an automatic classification system.

Several feature extraction[1] and classification approaches have been tested in previous studies [2]. Among the classification approaches, hidden Markov models (HMMs) have proved to be convenient classification tools for the sequential and unequal-length nature of the seismic signals [3–5] (conference papers and other older publications are not cited here due to space constraints, refer again to [2] for additional references). Even though these studies show the usefulness of such approaches, the full potentialities of HMM-based classification systems have not been completely exploited.

In this paper we propose an alternative approach, which explores the possibility of employing recent advancements in the HMM theory to the seismic classification problem. In particular, we use a generative embedding scheme, where the basic idea is to exploit the HMM to map the objects to be classified into a feature space (also called HMM-induced Vector Space), where discriminative techniques (e.g., kernel-based support vector machines) can be used. Actually, it has been shown in many different applications and scenarios [6–10] that the typical HMM classification scheme can be largely improved when enriched with such a discriminative step. We also compare the classical Bayes rule (representing the typical approach in the HMM-based seismic classification systems) with a simple generative embedding scheme [9], showing on a set of signals coming from the NRV the superiority of the latter approach.

The remaining part of the paper is organized as follows. The proposed seismic signals classification system, including the data preprocessing step and the HMM-based classification scheme, is presented in Sec. 2. A brief description of the classes in the data set and all the details about the algorithms application and their parameters are provided in Sec. 3. Experimental results are presented in Sec. 4. Finally, observations and concluding remarks are given in Sec. 5.

2 Methods

2.1 Data Preprocessing

Seismic signals recorded by OVSM instruments are acquired by using a 12-bit analog-to-digital converter that provides unsigned integers. As a result, an offset is introduced, which must be removed by subtracting the mean value before the feature extraction stage.

---

[1] More generally: representation approaches.

Second, seismic waveforms are transformed into the frequency domain. In particular we employed spectrograms for representation, mainly because spectral analysis, either in the frequency or the time-frequency domain, is widely used for both visual and computer-based [11] inspection of seismic phenomena. In particular, spectrograms are computed by using a fast Fourier transform (FFT) and a Hann (Hanning) window with a given overlap. Length of the FFT and the percentage of overlap where varied as indicated in Sec. 3.2. The magnitude in decibels is computed as $20 \log_{10} |X|$, where X is a matrix containing the short-time Fourier transform of a signal x. In this way we have an observation sequence, able to be modelled with a HMM, in which every symbol is the FFT of the given window. In order to reduce the dimensionality of every symbol, we finally applied a Discrete Cosine Transform (DCT), retaining only the first four values.

2.2   Classification

Hidden Markov Models (HMMs). A discrete-time HMM λ is defined by the following entities [12]:

- a set $S = \{S_1, S_2, \cdots, S_N\}$ of (hidden) states;
- a transition matrix $\mathbf{A} = \{a_{ij}\}$, where $a_{ij} \geq 0$ represents the probability of going from state S_i to state S_j;
- an emission matrix $\mathbf{B} = \{b(o|S_j)\}$, indicating the probability of emission of symbol o from state S_j;
- an initial state probability distribution $\boldsymbol{\pi} = \{\pi_i\}$, representing the probability of the first state $\pi_i = P[Q_1 = S_i]$.

For a sequence $\mathbf{O}$ and a HMM λ, there is a standard recursive procedure, called the *forward-backward* procedure [12], able to compute the probability $P(\mathbf{O}|\lambda)$. Given a set of observed sequences $\{\mathbf{O}_i\}$, the learning of the HMM parameters is usually performed using the well-known Baum-Welch algorithm [12], which is able to determine the parameters maximizing the log-likelihood: $\log P(\{\mathbf{O}_i\}|\lambda)$.

Classification with the Bayes Rule. The Bayes Decision Rule starts from the idea of determining a probability density function for each class, which can be used to find the probability that a given x element belongs to that class. The Bayes decision rule then dictates to assign that given element to the class with the higher probability (also called a posteriori probability). Now, to find those probabilities we chose a HMM approach, i.e. we represent each function with a HMM. In particular, in the training phase, a HMM λ_c is trained for every class c, using only the training sequences belonging to such class. At the end of the training process, we have a set of HMMs $\lambda_1, ..., \lambda_C$. In the testing phase, then, an unknown sequence $\boldsymbol{o} = (o_1, ..., o_T)$ is assigned to the class whose model shows the highest likelihood (assigning to each class the same prior probability), namely the label $\ell(\boldsymbol{o})$ is determined as: $\ell(\boldsymbol{o}) = \arg\max_c \log P(\boldsymbol{o}|\lambda_c)$.

Classifying Using the Generative Embedding Theory. The Generative Embedding Theory is based on the idea that both performance and interpretability of conventional approaches could be improved by taking into account available prior knowledge about the process generating the observed data. The term generative embedding is sometimes used to denote a particular model-induced feature space, or so-called generative score space, in which case the associated line of research is said to be concerned with generative embeddings. Here, we will use the term in singular form to denote the process of using a generative model to project the data into a generative score space, rather than using the term to denote the space itself. Generative embedding rests on two components: a generative model for the feature selection and a discriminative method for classification.

In particular, we employed the set of trained HMMs to project every sequence o (both training and testing sequences) into a feature space, using the following mapping, firstly introduced in [9]:

$$\phi(o, \lambda_1, \lambda_2, \cdots, \lambda_C) = [\log P(o|\lambda_1) \log P(o|\lambda_2) \cdots \log P(o|\lambda_C)] \in \mathbb{R}^C$$

Here the idea is to project a sequence in a feature space where every direction represents the log-likelihood of the model. Even if very simple, such generative embedding has been shown to be very effective in different applications. In such HMM-induced vector space, then, every standard classifier can be used. In our experiments we tried many different techniques (see Sec. 3.2), showing promising results.

3 Experimental Setup

3.1 Data Set

The data set we have been provided is composed by a total of 1359 signals, distributed per classes as follows[2]: *volcano tectonic* events (VT, 276), *long period* events (LP, 212), *regional tectonic* events (RE, 601) and *local tectonic* events: (TL, 270). VT and LP classes are related to volcanic phenomena: fracture of solid rock in the volcano and transport of fluid, e.g. gases or magma, within it; respectively. The other two classes correspond to seismic events of tectonic origin, which are localized either far (RE) or near (TL) the volcano. Even though RE and TL events are of less interest to monitor the volcanic activity, they anyway have to be distinguished and labeled.

3.2 Experimental Details

The proposed approach has been compared with the standard Bayes rule in the above described data set. HMMs have been trained using the standard

---

[2] Class names are indicated together with a pair (Abbreviation, Number of signals).

Baum-Welch procedure[3], stopping after likelihood convergence (or after 500 iterations). Choosing a higher number of iterations will probably lead to a massive waste of time and computational resources, because experiments show that the convergence threshold is achieved with less than 500 iterations. For a higher number of states, however, when the training becomes difficult, slightly increasing the number of iterations may actually be useful, even if still time consuming. Initialization has been carried out, as in many applications, with a clustering based on Gaussian mixture models. The Gaussians in the emission probabilities were assumed to have diagonal covariance matrix (due to the high dimensionality of the signal, full covariance matrices would have been poorly estimated). The number of states used is a parameter of interest, which we have diversified during the various experiments.

For the generative embedding approach, in the resulting vector space, different classifiers have been tested[4], namely the linear bayesian classifier (ldc), the quadratic bayesian classifier (qdc), the Parzen classifier (parzenc), the linear perceptron classifier (perlc), the fisher classifier (fisherc), the logistic classifier (logc), the quadratic discriminant classifier (quadr) and the k-nearest neighbor classifier (knnc).

The parameters of the preprocessing approach —the window length and the overlap— as well as the number of HMM states have been largely varied, in order to understand the impact of such parameters in the final classification. In particular, states were varied from 2 to 8, the window length was analyzed in the range [64, 128, 256, 512, 1024] and the window overlap in the range [0, 0.25, 0.5, 0.75].

Classification accuracies have been computed using cross-validation: for ten times the data set has been split in 75% for training and 25% for testing, using every split only once for training, to ensure more variability between elements of the original data set composing the training and test set. However, when conducting the experiments for the Embedding Classification System, we used the same splits and the same trained HMM used with the Bayes Classifier: this is meant to reduce the effect of the random chance as an explanation to the outcomes of the experiments and thus enhance the quality of the comparisons.

4   Results

For the sake of simplicity, we tried to analyze them from different points of view. In particular we kept a parameter fixed, averaging (or maximizing) the results over the remaining two. In this way we can inspect the impact of every parameter on the results, as well as the robustness of the two classification approaches with respect to such parameters. Results are reported in Fig. 1, for the window length, the window overlap and the number of states, respectively. In particular, for the generative embedding case, the best classifier result has been shown.

---

[3] As implemented in the Bayes Net Toolbox for Matlab by Kevin Murphy. See http://code.google.com/p/bnt/

[4] Implementation given in PRTools. See http://www.prtools.org

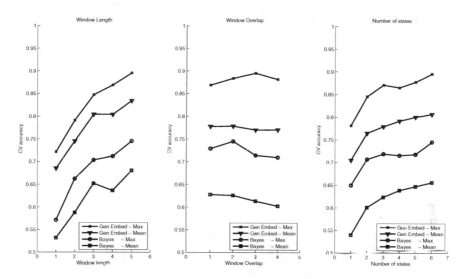

Fig. 1. Accuracy varying the different parameters. Values in horizontal axes correspond to indexes of the explored ranges as described in Sec. 3.2.

4.1   Window Length

We can see a clear trend for this parameter. From a length of 64 through a length of 1024 the efficacy of the classification keeps rising. We would also want to point out that preliminary experiments on 2048 long frames do not permit a so impressive increasing. Actually, it has been impossible to train the HMM in all cases, because the training with such higher lengths becomes impracticable: this happens because the longer the frames, the shorter the sequence. Looking both at average and maximum values of the two algorithms, it is evident that the Embedded Classification System seems to work better.

4.2   Window Overlap

Regarding this parameter we can easily notice that there is no significant trend as the experimental results are very similar. Just like with the previous parameter the average values as well as the maximum value indicate the superiority of the generative embedding approach. Eventually, we can conclude that this parameter does not seem to be that important since all the tested values delivered the same results.

4.3   Number of States

Observing this parameter, it seems clear that Embedded Classifier Systems results achieve a better efficacy when compared with the ones from the Bayes classifier; this happens not only with the maximum values, but also with the average ones.

Classifiers in the Original Space. A final experiment has been done in order to understand if the HMM-based embedding is actually useful for the classification of seismic signals if compared with standard approaches. In particular, we built a vector space by averaging the frames of every sequence, applying the same classifiers used in the HMM-induced vector spaces. Results are presented in Fig. 2, for different classifiers. It is evident the improvement obtained with the generative embedding approach.

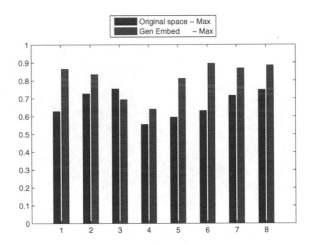

Fig. 2. Comparison with baseline classification approach. Indexes in the horizontal axis correspond to classifiers: ldc, qdc, parzenc, perlc, fisherc, logc, quadr and knnc; respectively.

5   Observations and Conclusions

As can be seen from the charts in Fig. 1, we can state that the Generative Embedding Classification System actually surpasses the Bayes Classification System (and thus the Bayes Theory) in its maximum values. However, in two over three cases it also shows a higher standard deviation so it is quite safe to say that the results may be better but they also suffer a little more from shifting chances and luck. The window length and the number of states really showed themselves as important parameters, whose values can abruptly change the eventual efficacy of the algorithm. The window overlap, however, does not really shine as vital. Its variation looks quite flat and while the average efficacy seems to slightly drop when the overlap is rising, the maximum efficacy actually slightly ascends. This is probably due to the fact that with longer frames its harder to train a decent HMM, but when successful the result is actually improved. As Fig. 2 shows, the Generative Embedded Classification System obtains better results than the simple application of classifiers in a standard vector space.

References

1. Stern, C.R.: Active Andean volcanism: its geologic and tectonic setting. Andean Geology 31(2), 161–206 (2004)
2. Orozco-Alzate, M., Acosta-Muñoz, C., Londoño-Bonilla, J.M.: The Automated Identification of Volcanic Earthquakes: Concepts, Applications and Challenges. In: D'Amico, S. (ed.) Earthquake Research and Analysis - Seismology, Seismotectonic and Earthquake Geology, pp. 345–370. InTech, Rijeka (2012)
3. Benítez, M.C., Ramírez, J., Segura, J.C., Ibáñez, J.M., Almendros, J., García-Yeguas, A., Cortés, G.: Continuous HMM-based seismic event classification at Deception Island, Antarctica. IEEE Transactions on Geoscience and Remote Sensing 45(1), 138 146 (2007)
4. Beyreuther, M., Wassermann, J.: Continuous earthquake detection and classification using discrete hidden Markov models. Geophysical Journal International 175(3), 1055–1066 (2008)
5. Ibáñez, J.M., Benítez, C., Gutiérrez, L.A., Cortés, G., García-Yeguas, A., Alguacil, G.: The classification of seismo-volcanic signals using Hidden Markov Models as applied to the Stromboli and Etna volcanoes. Journal of Volcanology and Geothermal Research 187(3-4), 218–226 (2009)
6. Tsuda, K., Kawanabe, M., Rätsch, G., Sonnenburg, S., Müller, K.R.: A new discriminative kernel from probabilistic models. Neural Computation 14(10), 2397–2414 (2002)
7. Bosch, A., Zisserman, A., Muñoz, X.: Scene Classification Via pLSA. In: Leonardis, A., Bischof, H., Pinz, A. (eds.) ECCV 2006, Part IV. LNCS, vol. 3954, pp. 517–530. Springer, Heidelberg (2006)
8. Perina, A., Cristani, M., Castellani, U., Murino, V., Jojic, N.: A hybrid generative/discriminative classification framework based on free-energy terms. In: 2009 IEEE 12th International Conference on Computer Vision, pp. 2058–2065. IEEE (2009)
9. Bicego, M., Murino, V., Figueiredo, M.A.T.: Similarity-based classification of sequences using hidden Markov models. Pattern Recognition 37(12), 2281–2291 (2004)
10. Bicego, M., Pekalska, E., Tax, D.M.J., Duin, R.P.W.: Component-based discriminative classification for hidden Markov models. Pattern Recognition 42(11), 2637–2648 (2009)
11. Lesage, P.: Interactive Matlab software for the analysis of seismic volcanic signals. Computers & Geosciences 35(10), 2137–2144 (2009)
12. Rabiner, L.R.: A tutorial on hidden Markov models and selected applications in speech recognition. Proceedings of the IEEE 77(2), 257–286 (1989)

Building Change Detection from Uniform Regions

Charles Beumier and Mahamadou Idrissa

Signal & Image Centre, Royal Military Academy, 1000 Brussels, Belgium
{charles.beumier,idrissa}@elec.rma.ac.be

Abstract. This paper deals with building change detection by supervised classification of image regions into 'built' and 'non-built' areas. Regions are the connected components of low gradient values in a multi-spectral aerial image. Classes are learnt from spectral (colour, vegetation index) and elevation cues relatively to building polygons and non building areas as defined in the existing database. Possible candidate building regions are then filtered by geometrical features. Inconsistencies in the database with the recent image are automatically detected. Tests in cooperation with the Belgian National Geographical Institute on an area with sufficient buildings and landscape variety have shown that the system allows for the effective verification of unchanged buildings, and detection of destructions and new candidate buildings.

Keywords. Building verification, building detection, spectral cues, geometrical cues, Digital Surface Model.

1   Introduction

The production of cartographic or digital geographic information is currently living an important change. The ever increasing demand for up-to-date data requires the development of procedures keeping the human intervention to an acceptable level.

One traditional approach for geographical data update requires the analyst to observe aerial images and update the digital data accordingly. Recent projects (e.g. project WIPKA, Germany [1]; project MAJEC, France [2]; project ATOMI, Switzerland [3]; DB TOP10DK, Denmark [4]) try to help the analyst in localising semi-automatically plausible changes from recent aerial imagery.

Our research department has been active in change detection in remote sensing for nearly 10 years, in cooperation with the Belgian Geographical National Institute. After considering the detection of change from satellite images at the level of building blocks, the team has concentrated its effort on DSM (Digital Surface Model) extraction from stereoscopic pairs and change detection from aerial images at 0.3 m resolution. In this respect, the previous publication [10] described the detection of building changes from spectral cues (colour, NDVI) and local elevation.

In this paper, we present building change detection thanks to the inclusion of geometrical clues as a way to reduce false alarms and improve the detection of candidate new buildings.

L. Alvarez et al. (Eds.): CIARP 2012, LNCS 7441, pp. 648–655, 2012.

2   Change Detection

Conventional solutions for topographic database production generally rely on stereo-scopic aerial colour images with resolution better than 50cm. To reduce the amount of work to keep the database up to date, only changes are looked for as the majority of data remains valid.

As confirmed by the activities about change detection organised by EuroSDR [5], National Mapping Agencies and other map suppliers are looking for (semi-) auto-matic solutions in order to lighten the needed human resources and shorten the update latency. Considering the bibliography about change detection for topo-geographic database update in the case of aerial images [1-8], most approaches rely on the same extracted information: colour, vegetation index and elevation (DSM and DTM, Digi-tal Terrain Model). For instance the works of N. Champion [2] and M. Niederöst [3] both exploited a vegetation mask obtained from the multispectral data and a normal-ised Digital Surface Model derived from the DSM. In [2] candidate buildings are looked for thanks to DSM contours and 3D line segments, while in [3] blob detection or rectangle fitting are used to try to reconstruct a 3D building shape.

We believe that 3D lines are indeed a fundamental clue as a way to confirm or highlight man made structures. However we preferred first to segment the image and look for regions consistent with being a building roof. For this, colour, vegetation and elevation features are measured and averaged over the regions and compared to val-ues encountered in building regions of the database. In comparison with our previous work [10], the pixel analysis is replaced by a region analysis, normally more robust, fast and enabling geometrical constraints to be applied. A prospective goal, not yet implemented, is the possible integration of topological clues (presence of shadow neighbouring regions, alignment of buildings and proximity of road parts).

3   Spectral Cues

The most direct information extracted from the multispectral image concerns the red (R), green (G), blue (B) and near Infrared (nIR) pixel values.

3.1   Exploiting R, G, B, nIR

R, G and B values are highly correlated by intensity so that derived values like HSI or Lab are preferable to better discriminate objects based on colour hue and intensity. The uniformity of spectral features is a good criterion to find objects or part of them.

If buildings are quite easily delineated thanks to elevation (DSM), one common difficulty is to eliminate false targets due to vegetation (trees). The near infra-red channel allows for the computation of an index highlighting vegetated areas.

3.2   Shadow

Shadow areas do not receive much of the sun illumination and are henceforth imaged with little intensity and contrast. They typically suffer from a decrease in spectral specificity, bad vegetation discrimination and errors in a DSM obtained from stereo image matching. Identifying shadow regions is appealing either to reject doubtful conclusions related to such areas or to use them as evidence for the presence of elevated object in the sun direction.

4   Geometrical Cues

Stereoscopic pairs of images enable ortho-rectification so that produced maps are geometrically correct. They also allow for the capture of a digital surface model (DSM) which can provide for elevation values in the vector databases.

For change detection, the DSM usually helps localising potential building candidates using the local elevation relatively to a DTM, digital model of the terrain.

Other potential geometric features concern the planar extent of elevated objects. The objective is to detect image objects having some characteristics related to size and shape. As such, a building is rather blob shaped while road segments are elongated. The difficulty is to find the real building extent because roofs are rarely uniform, possibly containing different faces with different intensities.

We propose to segment the image into regions of uniform spectral values, representing parts or whole of landscape objects like roofs, roads, water areas or fields. We prefer to design a many-to-one approach (many regions, one building object) since an object usually consists of parts with different spectral properties.

4.1   Region Segmentation

We handle image segmentation with the most forward, simple and fast approach that we know: connected component labelling. Typically designed for binary images, this procedure consists in assigning a unique label to all connected pixels. The algorithm first scans the image to assign a label to each pixel, propagating labels already assigned in case of connectivity. Some regions appear to be connected quite late, so their labels have to be merged in a second image scan.

The key point of this approach is to get an adequate binary image. Since we are looking for spectrally uniform areas, we propose to threshold the image based on the gradient defined by the Euclidian distance of RGB values (and not only luminance). Low threshold values are chosen since we prefer over-segmentation with regions that will be later grouped into possible objects. The threshold value is therefore not very critical and we used the percentile 80 of the histogram of gradient values. We had to include the elevation in the process since regions in shadow sometimes contain roof and ground pixels due to the lack of gradient in dark areas. We added to the gradient image the edge pixels of the normalised DSM thresholded at 2.5m.

Fig. 1. Segmentation results with regions represented with random colours

For the kind of images we are working with, there are about 4000 regions (of at least 44 pixel = 4m2) per km^2.

4.2   Digital Surface Model

A Digital Surface Model is a collection of elevation values over a geographical area. In our department, DSMs are produced by stereo matching of image pairs with proprietary software using multiple size windows and a regularization procedure [9]. For change detection, DSMs are very powerful at highlighting potential buildings, if vegetation is filtered out (trees, woods). Since the terrain is rarely a flat surface, it has to be subtracted to the DSM to form the normalised DSM (nDSM = DSM − DTM). The nDSM is thresholded to find candidate buildings. DTMs can be derived from the DSM [2] or are available from national mapping agencies or from the SRTM campaign.

4.3   Feature Extraction

Each region, made of pixels with similar spectral values, is attributed average values for the luminance L ((R+G+B)/3), the colour factors a' (R-G) and b' (G-B) and the vegetation index NDVI. (Mention that a' and b' are not the components of the famous L*a*b* colour space.)

The first geometrical feature is the area of the region which allows for the filtering of tiny objects ($< 4m^2$) and huge areas ($> 2000m^2$).

The second geometrical clue is the average elevation nZ (from the normalised DSM). A 2m threshold is used as garden huts possibly populate the database.

The next two geometrical values are derived from the 2D pixel distribution of the region: the extreme moments Mmin and Mmax. Their ratio Mmax/Mmin gives an idea of the elongation of the region. This ratio has been limited to 10 to reject elongated shapes like road or railway segments.

Finally, for large regions, the external outline was analysed to look for linear parts of at least 5m. This helps distinguishing natural objects from man-made structures.

4.4   Discussion

Segmentation into regions of uniform spectral values brings many advantages. First, it groups similar pixels into entities closer to the searched objects and allows for a compact representation (mean feature values). Secondly, it simplifies the computation of geometric parameters (area, elevation, elongation and outline). Finally it allows for the elimination of shadow regions which usually disturb approaches due to their poor colour content, weak NDVI estimation and erroneous DSM values.

Moreover regions will be particularly well suited in future developments to check contextual rules like the building alignment or distance and road proximity.

5   Classification

We handle building change detection by supervised classification of image regions into 'built' and 'non-built' classes. Since the database (to be updated) generally contains a small percentage of changes, it may be used to learn the two classes. Regions of the built class which do not satisfy geometrical constraints are then discarded.

5.1   Learning

Learning building likelihood from features consists in filling a 5-dimensional histogram containing the 'in' (built, according to the database) and 'out' (non-built) region counts for feature values (L, a', b', NDVI, nZ). Each feature range is divided into a few intervals based on the value distribution (regular spacing). The nZ and NDVI have only 2 bins as they can be handled by a threshold. L has 7 bins since its dynamic range is large while a' and b' have both 5 bins. Each histogram cell receives a feature vector likelihood based on the proportion of in and out counts of region, normalised by the global proportion for the entire set of regions. Empty cells are attributed a likelihood of -1 to label the corresponding feature vector as 'Class unknown'.

Mention that if the number of regions is small, the histogram approach is preferably replaced by nearest neighbour counting, comparing the proportion of in and out count of regions with similar feature vector.

5.2   Change Detection

Each region receives a 'built up' likelihood corresponding to the 5D feature vector thanks to the histogram. For building verification (modification/destruction or 'No Change'), each DB building polygon is assigned the maximum likelihood of all the regions mainly (at least 50% of the area) contained in the polygon. For new building detection, any region with high likelihood is proposed for confirmation. The threshold on likelihood is adapted by the operator who solves the trade-off between low false alarms and low miss rate. For Fig. 2, the threshold on the likelihood was set to 0.6.

In order to reduce the number of false alarms for new candidate buildings, geometrical constraints were applied. The tiny and huge regions were discarded. The moment ratio helped removing elongated regions corresponding to road or railway segments or long shadow areas. The difficult shadow regions, having poor spectral specificity and possibly elevated, were rejected based on an intensity threshold obtained from the known building side opposite to the sun [11]. Finally, large regions whose external outline does not contain linear parts (> 5m) were also discarded.

According to the database (old) and image (new) classes, four cases arise: a) the building still exists (green); b) the building is destroyed/modified (blue); c) a new building appeared (red); there was never a building (transparent). We take for granted that a polygon is verified as soon as one region has sufficient likelihood. As visible on Fig. 2, many regions of gable roofs are in shadow and receive little support from spectral or geometrical clues. This explains why there are many blue areas in the results.

Fig. 2. Classified regions. Green for built regions mainly in building database polygon, Blue for polygon part not verified, Red for built regions not in the database.

5.3   Building Completion

A last step is welcome to obtain an accurate change detection map. We noticed in Fig. 2 that many buildings are only partially covered by supporting regions. In order to detect object boundaries as close as possible to reality, the seed regions (green and red) have to be enlarged. We propose to use the normalized DSM and NDVI and create a building mask which is converted into regions by a connected component labeling. Each region is a candidate building if it contains at least a red or green classified region.

6   Results

A first zone representative for tests has been proposed by our client. The data set, covering 4 km^2 around Leuven, consists of the database vectors as well as the RGB and Near Infrared images (stereo pairs at 0.3 m resolution). We produced a DSM at 0.3m and extracted the regions from the RGB ortho-rectified images. We derived the spectral and geometrical features for each region.

The classification results produced by the histogram approach and geometrical constraints were displayed for quality analysis by inspection (Fig. 2 is a small part). Results displayed with 3 colours facilitate the counting of the different cases. For a region of 4 km^2 containing about 1200 polygons, we observed:

Table 1. Change detection results in number of cases (database polygons or regions)

Cases	All polygons (1164)	Polygons > 30m2 (974)
Unchanged buildings (at least partly green)	1012	927
Not verified (totally blue)	141	47
New buildings (red)	117	59
Bad New	66	28

Although the numbers of detected changes appear too high to relieve the operator of much image interaction, most errors are due to helpless situations or unimportant cases. We noticed several houses hidden in the woods. Many undetected buildings concern the small and low annexes or garden huts. This is secondary change information for the database provider which can hardly be dealt with the current image resolution. For that reason, we derived the statistics for building larger than 30 m2 as well.

In the reasonable situation focusing on large polygons (> 30m2), we obtained about 4% of bad verification, some cases of which are helpless (hidden by trees). 59 regions were detected as potential building parts, half of which were not real buildings although some of them could be considered as such (e.g. containers).

7   Conclusions

This paper has presented building change detection between a digital vector database and stereo aerial imagery. The colour image is segmented into regions of uniform colours and elevation. These regions receive attribute values for L, a', b', NDVI, local elevation (nDSM) and other geometrical features. These attributes help classifying regions with a histogram approach after a learning procedure using the a priori classes building / non-building as stated in the database to update. Many regions are discarded thanks to geometrical features. Compared to previous results, the region approach has similar verification performance for known database building polygons but reduces the number of false alarms when looking for new candidate buildings.

We intend to use the region approach to add contextual constraints like the relation between dark areas (shadow) and elevated regions, and the link between the road network and the presence of buildings.

References

1. Busch, A., Gerke, M., Grünreich, D., Heipke, C., Liedtke, C.-E., Müller, S.: Automated Verification of a Topographic Reference Dataset: System Design and Practical Results. In: Int. Archives of Photogrammetry and Remote Sensing IAPRS, Istanbul, Turkey, vol. XXXV, B2, pp. 735–740 (2004)
2. Champion, N., Stamon, G., Pierrot-Deseilligny, M.: Automatic Revision of 2D Building Databases from High Resolution Satellite Imagery: A 3D Photogrammetric Approach. In: AGILE, Hannover Germany (2009)
3. Niederöst, M.: Detection and Reconstruction of Buildings for Automated Map updating, These Institut für Geodäsie und Photogrammetrie, ETH Zürich (2003)
4. Olsen, B.: Automatic Change Detection for Validation of Digital Map Databases. In: ISPRS XX, Commission II, Istambul, vol. XXXV, pp. 569–574 (2004)
5. Heipke, C., Mooney, K.: EuroSDR – A research organisation serving Europe's geospatial information needs. In: Fritsch, D. (hrsg.) Photogrammetric Week 2009, pp. 321–330. Wichmann, Heidelberg (2009)
6. Baltsavias, E.: Object Extraction and Revision by Image Analysis using Existing Geodata and Knowledge: Current Status and Steps towards Operational Systems. ISPRS Journal of Photogrammetry and Remote Sensing 58, 129–151 (2004)
7. Matikainen, I., Hyyppä, J., Ahokas, E., Markelin, L., Kartinen, H.: Automatic Detection of Buildings and Changes in Buildings for Updating of Maps. Remote Sensing 2, 1217–1248 (2010)
8. Rottensteiner, F.: Building Change Detection from Digital Surface Models and Multispectral Images. In: Photogrammetric Image Analysis, Munich, Germany, pp. 145–150 (2007)
9. Idrissa, M., Lacroix, V.: A Multiresolution-MRF Approach for Stereo Dense Disparity Estimation. In: IEEE-GRSS/ISPRS Joint Urban Remote Sensing Event, Shanghai, China (2009)
10. Beumier, C., Idrissa, M.: Building Change Detection by Histogram Classification. In: Int. Conf. on Signal-Image Technology and Internet-Based Systems, Dijon, France (2011)
11. Beumier, C.: Building verification from geometrical and photometric cues. In: Applic. of Digital Image Processing XXX, San Diego, California. Proc. of SPIE, vol. 6696 (2007)

Generalized Statistical Complexity
of SAR Imagery

Eliana S. de Almeida[1], Antonio Carlos de Medeiros[1],
Osvaldo A. Rosso[1,2], and Alejandro C. Frery[1,*]

[1] Universidade Federal de Alagoas – UFAL
Laboratório de Computação Científica e Análise Numérca – LaCCAN
57072-970, Maceió, AL – Brazil
[2] Laboratorio de Sistemas Complejos
Facultad de Ingeniería
Universidad de Buenos Aires
Av. Paseo Colón 840, Ciudad Autónoma de Buenos Aires, 1063 Argentina

Abstract. A new generalized Statistical Complexity Measure (SCM) was proposed by Rosso et al in 2010. It is a functional that captures the notions of order/disorder and of distance to an equilibrium distribution. The former is computed by a measure of entropy, while the latter depends on the definition of a stochastic divergence. When the scene is illuminated by coherent radiation, image data is corrupted by speckle noise, as is the case of ultrasound-B, sonar, laser and Synthetic Aperture Radar (SAR) sensors. In the amplitude and intensity formats, this noise is multiplicative and non-Gaussian requiring, thus, specialized techniques for image processing and understanding. One of the most successful family of models for describing these images is the Multiplicative Model which leads, among other probability distributions, to the $\mathcal{G}^0$ law. This distribution has been validated in the literature as an expressive and tractable model, deserving the "universal" denomination for its ability to describe most types of targets. In order to compute the statistical complexity of a site in an image corrupted by speckle noise, we assume that the equilibrium distribution is that of fully developed speckle, namely the Gamma law in intensity format, which appears in areas with little or no texture. We use the Shannon entropy along with the Hellinger distance to measure the statistical complexity of intensity SAR images, and we show that it is an expressive feature capable of identifying many types of targets.

Keywords: information theory, speckle, feature extraction.

1 Introduction

Synthetic Aperture Radar (SAR) is a prominent source of information for many Remote Sensing applications. The data these devices provides carries information which is mostly absent in conventional sensors which operate in the optical

* The authors are grateful to CNPq and Fapeal for supporting this research.

L. Alvarez et al. (Eds.): CIARP 2012, LNCS 7441, pp. 656–663, 2012.
© Springer-Verlag Berlin Heidelberg 2012

spectrum or in its vicinity. SAR sensors are active, in the sense that they carry their own illumination source and, therefore, are able to operate any time. Since they operate in the microwaves region of the spectrum, they are mostly sensitive to the roughness and to the dielectric properties of the target. The price to pay for these advantages is that these images are corrupted by a signal-dependent noise, called *speckle*, which in the mostly used formats of SAR imagery is non-Gaussian and enters the signal in a non-additive manner. This noise makes both automatic and visual analysis a hard task, and defies the use of classical features.

This paper presents a new feature for SAR image analysis called Generalized Statistical Complexity. It was originally proposed and assessed for one-dimensional signals, for which it was shown to be able to detect transition points between different regimes [18]. This feature is the product of an entropy and a stochastic distance between the model which best describes the data and an equilibrium distribution [12,13].

The statistical nature of speckled data allows to propose a Gamma law as the equilibrium distribution, while the $\mathcal{G}^0$ model describes the observed data with accuracy. Both the entropy and the stochastic distance are derived within the framework of the so-called (h, ϕ) entropies and divergences, respectively, which stem from studies in Information Theory.

We show that the Statistical Complexity of SAR data, using the Shannon entropy and the Hellinger distance, stems as a powerful new feature for the analysis of this kind of data.

2   The Multiplicative Model

The multiplicative model is one of the most successful frameworks for describing data corrupted by speckle noise. It can be traced back to the work by Goodman [9], where stems from the image formation being, therefore, phenomenological. The multiplicative model for the intensity format states that the observation in every pixel is the outcome of a random variable $Z \colon \Omega \to \mathbb{R}_+$ which is the product of two independent random variables: $X \colon \Omega \to \mathbb{R}_+$, the ground truth or backscatter, related to the intrinsic dielectric properties of the target, and $Y \colon \Omega \to \mathbb{R}_+$, the speckle noise, obeying a unitary mean Gamma law. The distribution of the return, $Z = XY$, is completely specified by the distributions X and Y obey.

The univariate multiplicative model began as a single distribution for the amplitude format, namely the Rayleigh law [10], was extended by Yueh et al. [23] to accommodate the K law and later improved further by Frery et al. [7] to the G distribution, that generalizes all the previous probability distributions. Gao [8] provides a complete and updated account of the distributions employed in the description of SAR data.

For the intensity format which we deal with in this article, the multiplicative model reduces to, essentially, two important distributions, namely the Gamma and the $\mathcal{G}^0$ laws. The Gamma distribution is characterized by the density function

$$f(z) = \frac{(L/c)^L}{\Gamma(L)} z^{L-1} \exp\{-Lz/c\}, \qquad (1)$$

being $c > 0$ the mean, $z > 0$ and $L \geq 1$, denoted $\Gamma(L, L/c)$. This is an adequate model for homogeneous regions as, for instance, pastures over flat relief. The $\mathcal{G}^0$ law has density function

$$f(z) = \frac{L^L \Gamma(L - \alpha)}{\gamma^\alpha \Gamma(L) \Gamma(-\alpha)} \frac{z^{L-1}}{(\gamma + Lz)^{L-\alpha}}, \qquad (2)$$

where $-\alpha, \gamma, z > 0$, $L \geq 1$, denoted $\mathcal{G}^0(\alpha, \gamma, L)$. This distribution was proposed as a model for extremely heterogeneous areas [7], and Mejail et al. [15,16] demonstrated it can be considered a universal model for speckled data.

Data obeying the Γ law are referred to as "fully developed speckle", meaning that there is no texture in the wavelength of the illumination (which is in the order of centimeters). The absolute value of the parameter α in Equation (1) is, on the contrary, a measure of the number of distinct objects of size of the order of the wavelength with which the scene is illuminated. As $\alpha \to -\infty$, the $\mathcal{G}^0$ distribution becomes the Γ law.

3   Generalized Measure of Statistical Complexity

The information content of a system is typically evaluated via a probability distribution function (PDF) describing the apportionment of some measurable or observable quantity (i.e. a time series $\mathcal{S}(t)$). An information measure can primarily be viewed as a quantity that characterizes this given probability distribution P. The Shannon entropy is often used as a the "natural" one [21]. Given a discrete probability distribution $P = \{p_i : i = 1, \cdots, M\}$, with M the degrees of freedom, Shannon's logarithmic information measure reads $\mathrm{S}[P] = -\sum_{i=1}^{M} p_i \ln(p_i)$. It can be regarded as a measure of the uncertainty associated to the physical process described by P. From now on we assume that the only restriction on the PDF representing the state of our system is $\sum_{j=1}^{N} p_j = 1$ (micro-canonical representation). If $\mathrm{S}[P] = \mathrm{S}_{min} = 0$ we are in position to predict with complete certainty which of the possible outcomes i, whose probabilities are given by p_i, will actually take place. Our knowledge of the underlying process described by the probability distribution is then maximal. In contrast, our knowledge is minimal for a uniform distribution and the uncertainty is maximal, $\mathrm{S}[P_e] = \mathrm{S}_{max}$.

It is known that an entropic measure does not quantify the degree of structure or patterns present in a process [4]. Moreover, it was recently shown that measures of statistical or structural complexity are necessary for a better understanding of chaotic time series because they are able to capture their organizational properties [5]. This kind of information is not revealed by measures of randomness. The extremes perfect order (like a periodic sequence) and maximal randomness (fair coin toss) possess no complex structure and exhibit zero statistical complexity. There is a wide range of possible degrees of physical structure these extremes that should be quantified by *statistical complexity measures*. Rosso and coworkers introduced an effective statistical complexity measure (SCM) that is able to detect essential details of the dynamics and differentiate different degrees of periodicity and chaos [12]. This specific SCM, abbreviated as MPR, provides important additional information regarding the peculiarities of the underlying probability distribution, not already detected by the entropy.

The statistical complexity measure is defined, following the seminal, intuitive notion advanced by López-Ruiz et al. [13], via the product

$$C[P] = H[P] \cdot D[P, P_{ref}].$$ (3)

The idea behind the Statistical Complexity is measuring at the same time the order/disorder of the system (H) and how far the system is from its equilibrium state (the so-called disequilibrium D) [14,17]. The first component can be obtained by means of an entropy, while the second requires computing a stochastic distance between the actual (observed) model and a reference one. Salicrú et al. [19,20] provide a very convenient conceptual framework for both of these measures.

Let $f_Z(Z'; \theta)$ be a probability density function with parameter vector θ which characterizes the distribution of the (possibly multivariate) random variable Z. The (h, ϕ)-entropy relative to Z is defined by

$$H_\phi^h(\theta) = h\left(\int_{\mathcal{A}} \phi(f_Z(Z'; \theta)) \mathrm{d}Z' \right),$$

where either $\phi : [0, \infty) \to \mathbb{R}$ is concave and $h : \mathbb{R} \to \mathbb{R}$ is increasing, or ϕ is convex and h is decreasing. The differential element $\mathrm{d}Z'$ sweeps the whole support $\mathcal{A}$. In this work we only employ the Shannon entropy, for which $h(y) = y$ and $\phi(x) = -x \ln x$.

Consider now the (possibly multivariate) random variables X and Y with densities $f_X(Z; \theta_1)$ and $f_Y(Z; \theta_2)$, respectively, where θ_1 and θ_2 are parameter vectors. The densities are assumed to have the same support $\mathcal{A}$. The (h, ϕ)-divergence between f_X and f_Y is defined by

$$D_\phi^h(X, Y) = h\left(\int_{\mathcal{A}} \phi\left(\frac{f_X(Z; \theta_1)}{f_Y(Z; \theta_2)} \right) f_Y(Z; \theta_2) \mathrm{d}Z \right),$$ (4)

where $h: (0, \infty) \to [0, \infty)$ is a strictly increasing function with $h(0) = 0$ and $\phi: (0, \infty) \to [0, \infty)$ is a convex function such that $0 \phi(0/0) = 0$ and $0 \phi(x/0) = \lim_{x \to \infty} \phi(x)/x$. The differential element $\mathrm{d}Z$ sweeps the support. In the following we will only employ the Hellinger divergence which is also a distance, for which $h(y) = y/2$, $0 \le y < 2$ and $\phi(x) = (\sqrt{x} - 1)^2$.

The influence of the choice of a distance when computing statistical complexities is studied in Reference [11]. Following Rosso et al. [17], we work with the Hellinger distance and we define the Statistical Complexity of coordinate (i, j) in an intensity SAR image as the product

$$C(i, j) = H(i, j) \cdot D(i, j),$$ (5)

where $H(i,j)$ is the Shannon entropy observed in (i,j) under the $\mathcal{G}^0$ model, and $D(i,j)$ is the observed Hellinger distance between the universal model (the $\mathcal{G}^0$ distribution) and the reference model of fully developed speckle (the Γ law).

As previously noted, if an homogeneous area is being analyzed, the $\mathcal{G}^0$ and Γ model can be arbitrarily close, and the distance between them tends to zero. The entropy of the $\mathcal{G}^0$ model is closely related to the roughness of the target, as will be seen later, that is measured by α.

Computing these observed quantities requires the estimation of the parameters which characterize the Γ distribution (c, the sample mean) and the $\mathcal{G}^0$ law (α and γ), provided the number of looks L is known. The former is immediate, while estimating the later by maximum likelihood requires solving a nonlinear optimization problem. The estimation is done using data in a vicinity of (i,j). Once obtained $\widehat{c}$ and $(\widehat{\alpha}, \widehat{\gamma})$, the terms in Equation (5) are computed by numerical integration. References [1,6] discuss venues for estimating the parameters of the $\mathcal{G}^0$ law safely.

4   Results

Figure 1 presents the main results obtained with the proposed measures. Figure 1(a) shows the original image which was obtained by the E-SAR sensor, an airborne experimental polarimetric SAR, over Munich, Germany. Only the intensity HH channel is employed in this study. The image was acquired with three nominal looks. The scene consists mostly of different types of crops (the dark areas), forest and urban areas (the bright targets). 2 Figure 1(b) shows the Shannon entropy as shades of gray whose brightness is proportional to the observed value. It is remarkable that this measure is closely related to the roughness of the target, i.e., the brighter the pixel the more heterogeneous the area. The entropy is also able to discriminate between different types of homogeneous targets, as shown in the various types of dark shades.

Figure 1(c) shows the Hellinger distance between the universal model and the model for fully developed speckle. As expected, the darkest values are related to areas of low level of roughness, while the brightest spots are the linear strips in the uppermost right corner, since they are man-made structures.

The Statistical Complexity is shown in Figure 1(d). It summarizes the evidence provided by the entropy (Figure 1(b)) and by the stochastic distance between models (Figure 1(c)). As it can be seen in the image, the values exhibit more variation than their constituents, allowing a fine discrimination of targets. As such, it stems as a new and relevant feature for SAR image analysis.

The data were read, processed, analyzed and visualized using R v. 2.14.0 [22] on a MacBook Pro running Mac OS X v. 10.7.3. This platform is freely available at http://www.r-project.org for a diversity of computational platforms, and its excellent numerical properties have been attested in [2,3].

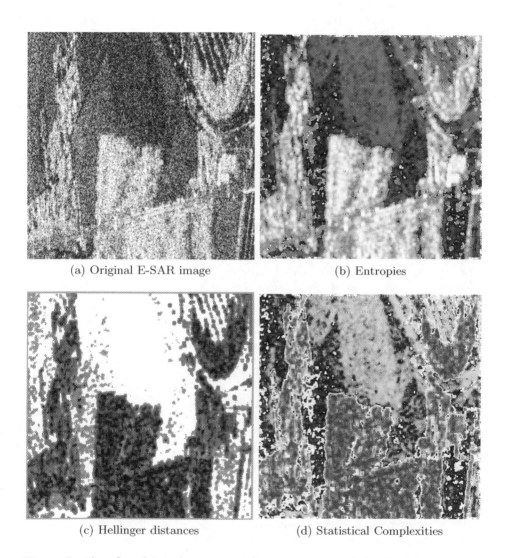

(a) Original E-SAR image   (b) Entropies

(c) Hellinger distances   (d) Statistical Complexities

Fig. 1. Results of applying the proposed feature extraction to an E-SAR image over Munich, Germany

5 Conclusions

The Statistical Complexity of SAR images reveals information which is not available either through the mean (which is the parameter of the model for homogeneous areas) or by the parameters of the model for extremely heterogeneous areas. As such, it appears as a promising feature for SAR image analysis.

Ongoing studies include the derivation of analytical expressions for the entropy and the Hellinger distance, other stochastic distances, the sample properties of the Statistical Complexity and its generalization for other models including Polarimetric SAR.

References

1. Allende, H., Frery, A.C., Galbiati, J., Pizarro, L.: M-estimators with asymmetric influence functions: the GA0 distribution case. Journal of Statistical Computation and Simulation 76(11), 941–956 (2006)
2. Almeida, E.S., Medeiros, A.C., Frery, A.C.: Are Octave, Scilab and Matlab reliable? Computational and Applied Mathematics (in press)
3. Almiron, M., Almeida, E.S., Miranda, M.: The reliability of statistical functions in four software packages freely used in numerical computation. Brazilian Journal of Probability and Statistics Special Issue on Statistical Image and Signal Processing, 107–119 (2009), http://www.imstat.org/bjps/
4. Feldman, D.P., Crutchfield, J.P.: Measures of statistical complexity: Why? Physics Letters A 238(4-5), 244–252 (1998), http://www.sciencedirect.com/science/article/pii/S0375960197008554
5. Feldman, D.P., McTague, C.S., Crutchfield, J.P.: The organization of intrinsic computation: Complexity-entropy diagrams and the diversity of natural information processing. Chaos 18, 043106 (2008), http://dx.doi.org.ez9.periodicos.capes.gov.br/10.1063/1.2991106
6. Frery, A.C., Cribari-Neto, F., Souza, M.O.: Analysis of minute features in speckled imagery with maximum likelihood estimation. EURASIP Journal on Applied Signal Processing (16), 2476–2491 (2004)
7. Frery, A.C., Müller, H.J., Yanasse, C.C.F., Sant'Anna, S.J.S.: A model for extremely heterogeneous clutter. IEEE Transactions on Geoscience and Remote Sensing 35(3), 648–659 (1997)
8. Gao, G.: Statistical modeling of SAR images: A survey. Sensors 10, 775–795 (2010)
9. Goodman, J.W.: Some fundamental properties of speckle. Journal of the Optical Society of America 66, 1145–1150 (1976)
10. Jakeman, E., Pusey, P.N.: A model for non-Rayleigh sea echo. IEEE Transactions on Antennas and Propagation 24(6), 806–814 (1976)
11. Kowalski, A.M., Martín, M.T., Plastino, A., Rosso, O.A., Casas, M.: Distances in probability space and the statistical complexity setup. Entropy 13(6), 1055–1075 (2011), http://www.mdpi.com/1099-4300/13/6/1055/
12. Lamberti, P.W., Martín, M.T., Plastino, A., Rosso, O.A.: Intensive entropic non-triviality measure. Physica A: Statistical Mechanics and its Applications 334(1-2), 119–131 (2004), http://www.sciencedirect.com/science/article/pii/S0378437103010963

13. López-Ruiz, R., Mancini, H., Calbet, X.: A statistical measure of complexity. Physics Letters A 209(5-6), 321–326 (1995), http://www.sciencedirect.com/science/article/pii/0375960195008675
14. Martin, M.T., Plastino, A., Rosso, O.A.: Generalized statistical complexity measures: Geometrical and analytical properties. Physica A 369, 439–462 (2006)
15. Mejail, M.E., Frery, A.C., Jacobo-Berlles, J., Bustos, O.H.: Approximation of distributions for SAR images: proposal, evaluation and practical consequences. Latin American Applied Research 31, 83–92 (2001)
16. Mejail, M.E., Jacobo-Berlles, J., Frery, A.C., Bustos, O.H.: Classification of SAR images using a general and tractable multiplicative model. International Journal of Remote Sensing 24(18), 3565–3582 (2003)
17. Rosso, O.A., De Micco, L., Larrondo, H.A., Martín, M.T., Plastino, A.: Generalized statistical complexity measure. International Journal of Bifurcation and Chaos 20(3), 775–785 (2010)
18. Rosso, O.A., Larrondo, H.A., Martín, M.T., Plastino, A., Fuentes, M.A.: Distinguishing noise from chaos. Physical Review Letters 99, 154102 (2007), http://link.aps.org/doi/10.1103/PhysRevLett.99.154102
19. Salicrú, M., Mendéndez, M.L., Pardo, L.: Asymptotic distribution of (h, ϕ)-entropy. Communications in Statistics - Theory Methods 22(7), 2015–2031 (1993)
20. Salicrú, M., Morales, D., Menéndez, M.L.: On the application of divergence type measures in testing statistical hypothesis. Journal of Multivariate Analysis 51, 372–391 (1994)
21. Shannon, C., Weaver, W.: The Mathematical Theory of Communication. University of Illinois Press (1949)
22. Team, R.D.C.: R: A Language and Environment for Statistical Computing. R Foundation for Statistical Computing, Vienna, Austria (2011) ISBN 3-900051-07-0, http://www.R-project.org/
23. Yueh, S.H., Kong, J.A., Jao, J.K., Shin, R.T., Novak, L.M.: K-distribution and polarimetric terrain radar clutter. Journal of Electromagnetic Waves and Applications 3(8), 747–768 (1989)

New Metrics to Evaluate Pattern Recognition in Remote Sensing Images

Manel Kallel, Mohamed Naouai, and Yosr Slama

Faculty of Science of Tunis, University Tunis el Manar DSI 2092 Tunis Belvidaire-Tunisia,
manel.kallel@yahoo.fr, naouai@polytech.unice.fr,
yosr.slama@fst.rnu.tn

Abstract. The continuous development of pattern recognition approaches increases the need for evaluation tools to quantify algorithms performance and establish precise inter-algorithm comparison. So far, few performance evaluating metrics in pattern recognition algorithms are known in the literature, especially in remote sensing images. In this paper, four metrics are proposed for this purpose. The advantages and drawbacks of these metrics are first described, then some experimentation results are the presented in order to validate our contribution.

Keywords: Evaluating metrics, pattern recognition, performance evaluation, remote sensing.

1 Introduction

Pattern recognition (PR) covers a wide range of problems, and it is hard to find a unified view or approach. PR is used particularly in Engineering problems, such as character readers and waveform analysis, as well as to brain modeling in biology and psychology (brain modeling) [1].

The goal of a PR algorithm is to determine boundaries that separate forms of different classes and provide the best possible performance. PR consists of one of the following two tasks [2]: supervised classification (e.g. discriminant analysis) in which the input pattern is identified as a member of a predefined class, or unsupervised classification (e.g. clustering) where the pattern is assigned to a hitherto unknown class.

Performance evaluation of PR algorithms is more than an objective ; it is a necessity. In fact, there are two standard metrics, namely recall and precision, which are not reliable in some specific fields. We believe that these metrics do not accurately measure the different aspects of performance of PR algorithms especially in remote sensing images.

In this paper, we propose several metrics which can be used to determine how much the result of PR algorithms matches the ground truth. We attempted to propose these metrics as a result of a need for performance evaluation of PR algorithms in remote sensing images.

The remainder of the paper is organized as follows. In section 2, we detail our motivation. Section 3 is devoted to a brief state-of-the-art. In section 4, four proposed performance metrics are described. Section 5 first describes the experimental setup used to perform the evaluation and comparison of the metrics. Our experimental results and comments are then detailed. Finally, Section 6 provides a conclusion to this paper.

L. Alvarez et al. (Eds.): CIARP 2012, LNCS 7441, pp. 664–673, 2012.

2 Motivation (Remote Sensing Specificity)

Remote sensing images involve very specific forms and structures. Recognizing these objects and their spatial positions and evaluating the relationships between them is considered as a PR problem. However, their extraction is difficult and many works have been devoted to studying this topic.

Extracting objects from a satellite image is proved to be a hard problem because of its large variability. But, the difficulty degree depends on the types of existing scenes in images. In fact, there are two types of scenes i.e. city and rural ones.

A rural scene is different from a city scene. In the former, most of the area is farmland and most folk houses have similar appearance [3]. So rural visualization has a small amount of data, this makes recognition of objects easy. But the complexity of the urban landscape makes it difficult to produce efficient and reliable algorithms.

Several algorithms have been developed to extract the objects of these images for both types of scenes. The complexity of recognition and extraction vary, so we need reliable means to evaluate the performance of these algorithms and compare them.

So far, most of PR algorithms are evaluated through two metrics: precision and recall. Precision is the fraction of retrieved instances that are relevant, while recall is the ratio of relevant instances that are retrieved. However, counting the number of objects correctly recognized compared to those relevant or compared to those returned is not sufficient. We must also consider the exact location of these objects and their areas i.e. the number of pixels spanning these objects.

In fact, we consider five types of object recognition: correct recognition, over-recognition, under recognition, misses, and noise. Over-recognition or multiple detections of a single object, results is not a correct recognition. Under-recognition, results is a subset of the correct recognition. A missed recognition is used when an algorithm fails to find an object which appears in the image (false negative). A noise is used when the algorithm assumes the existence of an object which is not in the image (false positive). Obviously, these measures may have various importance in different applications.

For these reasons, we propose metrics that will be most useful for evaluating performance for PR algorithms especially for remote sensing images.

3 Related Work

Performance evaluation is necessary for researchers to compare a new algorithm to those already existing and for users to choose an algorithm and adjust its settings depending on the problem to suit.

Several metrics have been proposed for evaluating PR algorithms. In object detection, Yi et al. [4] proposed a set of seven metrics for quantifying different aspects of a detection algorithm performance. As their names indicate, two of the metrics, i.e. Area-Based Recall for frame and Area-Based Precision for frame, are two variants of recall and precision, taking into account area of objects instead of their numbers. They are based on pixel count and they treat each pixel in the ground-truth as object/non-object and the output pixels as detected/non-detected.

Regarding evaluation of image segmentation with reference (ground-truth), Zhao and al. [5] suggested two precision measures to quantitatively evaluate the result segments of different algorithms. The region precision measures how many pixels are correctly classified and the boundary precision measures how close is the segment boundary to the real one. Yasnoff et al. [6] presented a new generalized quantitative error measure, based on comparison of both pixel class proportions and spatial distributions of ground truth and test segmentations.

Philipp-Foliguet and Guigues [7] proposed new criteria for evaluation image segmentation when no ground-truth is available. These criteria, based on an energy formalism, take into account both the complexity of the segmented image and the goodness-of-fit of an underlying model with the initial data. These evaluation criteria are thus multi-scale criteria. Various forms of energy formulation are experimentally compared.

4 Proposed Metrics

Our proposed metrics are described in the following subsections with their advantages and drawbacks. All the metrics values range from zero to one where one means every object is correctly recognized (perfect).

The first metric is general. It can be used to evaluate PR algorithms for any type of images including remote sensing images. It is inspired by the two metrics recall and precision. The second one is based on the area covered by the objects. The third one measures how well the ground truth is close to recognition result. The fourth has the same principle as the previous, except that the superposition is done object by object.

4.1 Object Correspondence (OC)

This metric is an object-count-based metric. It is inspired from both recall and precision metrics and merges them. It can be used for any type of image, not only remote sensing ones.

Let O_G be the set of relevant objects i.e. those of the ground-truth and O_R be the set of retrieved objects i.e. those of the result.

Therefore, recall and precision can be written in these forms:

$$recall = \frac{\mathrm{Card}(O_G \cap O_R)}{\mathrm{Card}(O_G)}$$

$$precision = \frac{\mathrm{Card}(O_G \cap O_R)}{\mathrm{Card}(O_R)}$$

We define the Correspondence Object metric CO as the ratio of relevant objects retrieved with the total of retrieved objects and relevant ones:

$$CO = \frac{\mathrm{Card}(O_G \cap O_R)}{\mathrm{Card}(O_G \cup O_R)}$$

This metric provides a single significant measure to compare different algorithms using the objects number criteria. In fact, if we want to compare the performance of two PR algorithms, the two metrics recall and precision by returning two distinct values may not be enough significant, especially if the first one gives the best recall whereas the second gives the best precision as shown in Fig. 1. Therefore, it seems more interesting to combine the two metrics into a single one.

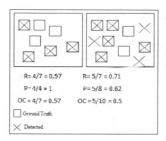

Fig. 1. Example illustrating Correspondence Object Metric

Despite its usefulness, the drawback of this metric as well as of both recall and precision is that they do not take into account the accuracy of the recognized object location or area relatively to the ground truth.

An object is deemed relevant or not using a visual assessment i.e. the user compares the retrieved objects to those of the ground truth and evaluates the relevance with the human eye. An over or under-recognized object can be declared as a relevant object.

In remote sensing images, another drawback is clear for the counting of objects because they can be infinitely small and the number is obvious.

4.2   Global Area (GA)

This metric is a pixel-count-based metric that measures how much the result of the algorithm approaches the ground-truth in terms of global area covered by the objects recognized in the same class. Among these classes, we find building, road, vacant land, vegetation and water.

We thought of offering this metric in order to solve the problem of counting objects that seem difficult. Instead of counting the number of objects and comparing the result with the ground-truth, we thought to proceed by their surface i.e. the number of pixels covered by these objects.

Hence, the metric consists of comparing the pixel number of the ground-truth objects of the same class with the pixel number of recognized objects. The number of pixels presents area or spatial union of objects of the same class.

Let U_G and U_R be the spatial union of all objects of the same class in ground-truth and result respectively. We have:

$$GA = 1 - \frac{|\text{Card}(U_G) - \text{Card}(U_R)|}{U_G}$$

To compute this metric for many classes, we can simply sum the values of this metric for all the classes and divide the sum by the class number.

Despite the ability of computing this metric, it presents a major drawback. In fact, the area of ground-truth objects may be close to the result objects, when recognition is not really well done (see Fig. 2).

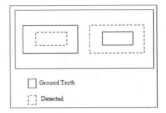

Fig. 2. Example illustrating GA metric limit

4.3   Superposed Area (SA)

This metric is a pixel-count-based metric that measures how much the result of the algorithm approaches the ground-truth.

The contribution of this metric compared to the previous is that it takes into account the detection error and not only the part well detected and this is defined by the union of the ground truth with the result of algorithm.

The objective of this metric is to determine the recognition rate for one class by taking into account the locations of objects. We have :

$$SA = \frac{\mathrm{Card}(U_G \cap U_R)}{\mathrm{Card}(U_G \cup U_R)}$$

The disadvantage of this metric is that the recognition of very close objects in one may produce a good result for the surface existing between these objects is very negligible see(Fig. 3).

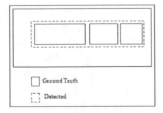

Fig. 3. Example illustrating SA metric limit

4.4   Superposed Per Object Area (SOA)

This metric is a pixel-count-based metric that measures how well the result of the algorithm approaches the ground-truth and assesses the spatial positions of the objects.

This metric considers first the number of pixels for each object and secondly its exact location. In this metric, the ground-truth and the algorithm output must be superposed to derive the recognized objects. A ground truth object is considered detected if a minimum proportion of its area is covered by the output object. A matching algorithm is used here to make correspondence between real and detected objects. It is based on maximizing the common area between correspondent objects. It should be noted that roads are treated as one object because they constitute a connected circuit. Thus, the matching algorithm principle is different from objects of other classes. In this case, many detected objects can be matched to the same ground truth object (road).

Let n be the total number of all the types of objects: correct recognition, over recognition, under-recognition, missed, and noise, $U_{OG}(i)$ the spatial union of the object i in ground-truth and $U_{OR}(i)$ the spatial union of result object corresponding to i. We get :

$$SOA = \frac{\sum_{i=1}^{n} \mathrm{Card}(U_{OG}(i) \cap U_{OR}(i))}{\sum_{i=1}^{n} \mathrm{Card}(U_{OG}(i) \cup U_{OR}(i))}$$

5 Experimental Study

In order to provide a set of baseline results allowing a first evaluation of these metrics, we have considered the same experiments site on which we have applied three representative PR algorithms. The proposed metrics as well as recall and precision are then computed for each recognition result and each algorithm.

5.1 Experiment Site

For our experiment site, we consider a remote sensing image of the city of Strasbourg, France. Fig. 4 shows this image as well as the ground truth of the three classes it includes i.e. buildings, roads and vegetation. We have prepared these three images representing ground truth, especially for this work, as a first step in constructing a remote sensing image benchmark.

5.2 Experiment Algorithms

Three chosen PR algorithms to be evaluated in our experimental study are K-means [8], Particle swarm optimization [9] and Hierarchical Classification-based Region Growing [10]. These algorithms are able to detect buildings, roads and vegetations. We present in the following the description of each algorithm as well as the results we obtained.

K-Means. Algorithm K-means is the best known and most widely clustering algorithm due to the easiness of its implementation. It has been applied to our experiment image and has given the results shown in Fig. 5.

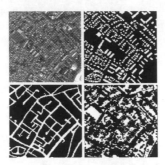

Fig. 4. Experiment site with buildings, roads and vegetation ground-truth

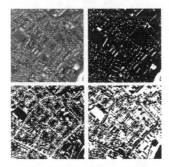

Fig. 5. K-means algorithm results

Particle Swam Optimization (PSO). The Particle Swarm Optimization algorithm belongs to the broad class of stochastic optimization algorithms that may be used to find optimal (or near optimal) solutions of numerical and qualitative problems. The recognition results of this algorithm is shown in Fig. 6.

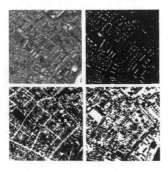

Fig. 6. PSO algorithm results

Hierarchical Classification-Based Region Growing (HCBRG). The algorithm is a hierarchical classification based on a region growing approach driven by expert knowledge represented in a hierarchical concept. A first classification will associate a

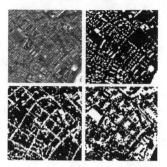

Fig. 7. HCBRG algorithm results

confidence score to each region in the image. This score will be used through an iterative step which allows interaction between segmentation and classification at each iteration. The region with the highest score will be taken as seeds in the growing step in each iteration and the approach allows the semantic growing based on the class of the seeds. This algorithm has given the results shown in Fig. 7.

5.3 Results

The performance evaluation of buildings, roads and vegetation recognition by the three chosen algorithms applied to the experiment image are depicted in Table 1.

We can notice from the above results that the values of each metric differ depending on both the PR algorithm used and the detected class. In fact, each algorithm has its own

Table 1. Proposed metrics values for three algorithms and three detection classes

Algorithms	Detected Classes		
	Buildings	Roads	Vegetation
K-means	GA = 0.38 SA = 0.19 SOA = 0.16 P = 0.41 R = 0.9	GA = 0.41 SA = 0.3 SOA = 0.3 P = 0.39 R = 0.93	GA = 0.36 SA = 0.55 SOA = 0.21 P = 0.14 R = 0.19
PSO	GA = 0.21 SA = 0.16 SOA = 0.14 P = 0.39 R = 0.85	GA = 0.65 SA = 0.33 SOA = 0.34 P = 0.41 R = 0.93	GA = 0.6 SA = 0.59 SOA = 0.28 P = 0.17 R = 0.35
HCBRG	GA = 0.8 SA = 0.41 SOA = 0.35 P = 0.7 R = 0.84	GA = 0.79 SA = 0.49 SOA = 0.49 P = 0.65 R = 0.92	GA = 0.89 SA = 0.9 SOA = 0.67 P = 0.71 R = 0.8

recognition ability and it depends on the nature of the objects to recognize. One can easily see that for the processed images, the first metric is sufficient to note that the last algorithm (HCBRG) is significantly better than the others for the three detected classes. This result was confirmed by the two other metrics giving more accurate comparisons. In addition, for the three metrics, K-means gives better (resp. worse) performances than PSO for buildings (resp. roads) recognition. However, we can, for example, remark that GA metric is not sufficient to accurately compare vegetation recognition by K-means and PSO algorithms. In fact, this metric leads us to think that PSO is much better than K-means (compare 0.6 to 0.36), whereas for SA and SOA metrics the two algorithms performance are quite close.

On the other hand, it is also noteworthy that the metrics values are in most cases decreasing in the order they are presented (i.e. GA then SA then SOA). This order is inversely proportional to the metrics accuracy as explained in their theoretical study. Therefore, these three metrics may be used according to the cascading priority criterion in our evaluation. Indeed, if the overall area of detected objects is the most important criterion, GA is the best to provide this information. However, if objects localization is also important, then SA can add more accuracy. SOA is the one that finally gives the most accurate information because it takes into account, in the same time, both the object sizes and their localization, and it also degrades for each missed or over detected object.

We finally note that only in the case of detecting roads, the last metric gives results very similar to the previous one. This is due to the different way of implementing connections between real objects and detected ones as explained in section 4.4.

6   Conclusion

Performance evaluation of image processing algorithms especially those of pattern recognition (PR), presents a major difficulty for researchers, because of the lack of performance evaluating metrics, particularly in the field of remote sensing. In this paper we proposed a set of metrics in order to provide specific and personalized performance evaluation of PR algorithms. The first metric, called Object Correspondence (OC), is based on object numbers and is proposed to combine the two metrics commonly used in pattern recognition i.e. Recall and Precision, in order to have only one value taking into account missed as well as over detected objects. The other three proposed metrics are rather specific to remote sensing images and principally based on the objects area. They have been introduced in an order proportional to their accuracy and inversely proportional to their respective complexities. The Global Area metric (GA) is based on a comparison of the global areas of ground truth objects and result ones. This metric is simply computed and is useful when one has a large number of small objects. However, it does not allow the evaluation of the good localization of detected objects. The Superposed Area metric (SA) measures how well the ground truth is close to recognition result by superposing their areas, This metric is usually most accurate than the previous one, but it does not take in account the corresponding objects. The last metric, called Superposition per Object Area (SOA) is finally proposed to allow the most accuracy level of performance evaluation. It takes into account localization and sizes of detected objects as well as missed or over detected ones. We implemented the last three metrics on three significant algorithms: K-means, Particle Swarm Optimization and Hierarchical Classification-based Region Growing using as experiments site an RS image of the city of Strasbourg. The results obtained with these algorithms in buildings, roads and vegetation recognition were discussed in order to analyze the usefulness of each metric in performance evaluation. Thus, Our theoretical study of metrics has been validated. In addition, we deduced that the different metrics may be used in cascade according to chosen priorities of evaluation criterion. As a future work, it will be useful to extend our experimental study to other PR algorithms and other experiments sites. Besides, we intend to focus on another aspect in performance evaluation which is a standard benchmark construction for PR methods in remote sensing field. The experimental images of the benchmark must cover major challenges for PR such as light and shadow effects.

References

1. Fukunaga, K.: Introduction to statistical Pattern Recognition. Academic Press (1990)
2. Watanabe, S.: Pattern Recognition: Human and Mechanical. Wiley, New York (1985)
3. Li, D., Liu, Y., Chen, Y.: Computer and Computing Technologies in Agriculture IV. In: 4th IFIPTC 12 Conference, CCTA, China (2010)
4. Mariano, V.Y., et al.: Performance evaluation of object Detection Algorithms. Pattern Recognition 3, 965–969 (2002)
5. Zhao, Y., et al.: A benchmark for interactive image segmentation algorithms. In: Person-Oriented Vision (POV), pp. 33–38 (2011)
6. Yasnoff, W.A., Galbraith, W., Bacus, J.W.: Errormeasures for objective assessment of scene segmentation algorithms. AQC 1, 107–121 (1979)
7. Philipp-Foliguet, S., Guigues, L.: Evaluation de la segmentation d'images: état de l'art, nouveaux indices et comparaison. TS. Traitement du Signal 23(2), 109–124 (2006) ISSN 0765-0019
8. McQueen, J.: Some Methods for Classification and Analysis of Multivariate Observations. In: Proc. Fifth Berkeley Symp. Math. Statistics and Probability, pp. 281–297 (1967)
9. Kennedy, J., Eberhart, R.C.: Particle swarm optimization. In: Proceedings of the IEEE International Conference on Neural Networks IV, pp. 1942–1948. IEEE, Piscataway (1995)
10. Sellaouti, A., Hamouda, A., Deruyver, A., Wemmert, C.: Hierarchical Classification-Based Region Growing (HCBRG): A Collaborative Approach for Object Segmentation and Classification. In: Campilho, A., Kamel, M. (eds.) ICIAR 2012, Part I. LNCS, vol. 7324, pp. 51–60. Springer, Heidelberg (2012)

Polarimetric SAR Image Smoothing
with Stochastic Distances

Leonardo Torres, Antonio C. Medeiros, and Alejandro C. Frery*

Universidade Federal de Alagoas – UFAL
Laboratório de Computação Científica e Análise Numérca – LaCCAN
57072-970, Maceió, AL – Brazil

Abstract. Polarimetric Synthetic Aperture Radar (PolSAR) images are establishing as an important source of information in remote sensing applications. The most complete format this type of imaging produces consists of complex-valued Hermitian matrices in every image coordinate and, as such, their visualization is challenging. They also suffer from speckle noise which reduces the signal-to-noise ratio. Smoothing techniques have been proposed in the literature aiming at preserving different features and, analogously, projections from the cone of Hermitian positive matrices to different color representation spaces are used for enhancing certain characteristics. In this work we propose the use of stochastic distances between models that describe this type of data in a Nagao-Matsuyama-type of smoothing technique. The resulting images are shown to present good visualization properties (noise reduction with preservation of fine details) in all the considered visualization spaces.

Keywords: information theory, polarimetric SAR, speckle.

1 Introduction

Among the remote sensing technologies, PolSAR has achieved a prominent position. PolSAR imaging is a well-developed coherent and microwave remote sensing technique for providing large-scaled two-dimensional (2-D) high spatial resolution images of the Earths surface reflectivity; see Lee and Pottier [4].

The phenomenon speckle in SAR data hinders the interpretation these data and reduces the accuracy of segmentation, classification and analyses of objects contained within the image. Therefore, reducing the noise effect is an important task, and multilook processing is often used for this purpose in single-channel data.

According to Lee and Pottier [4], the principle to preserve the polarimetric signature and Polarimetric SAR image smoothing requires: (i) for each element of the image should be filtered in a way similar to multilook processing by averaging the covariance matrix of neighboring pixels; (ii) the filtering should be executed independently for each element of the covariance matrix; and (iii) homogeneous

* The authors are grateful to CNPq and Fapeal for supporting this research.

L. Alvarez et al. (Eds.): CIARP 2012, LNCS 7441, pp. 674–681, 2012.

regions in the neighborhood should be adaptively selected to preserve resolution, edges and the image quality.

The statistical modeling provides a good support for the development of algorithms for interpreting PolSAR data efficiently, and for the simulation of plausible images. Frery et al. [2,3] introduce statistical tests for analyzing contrast in PolSAR images under the scaled multilook complex Wishart distribution, which has been successfully employed as a statistical model in such images for homogeneous regions. Frery et al. [3] derive several distances and tests for the complex Wishart model.

This work presents a new smoothing process for PolSAR imagery based on stochastic distances and tests between distributions. This process, beyond reducing the noise effect, maintains geometric features of the PolSAR data. Vasile et al. [10] use a similar adaptive technique, but the decisions are based on the intensity information while we use the complete complex covariance matrix.

The paper is organized as follows: In Section 2 we summarise the model for polarimetric data. Section 3 we describe the smoothing process for PolSAR images using stochastic distances between complex Wishart distributions, and the visualization of this kind of data. Results are presented in Section 4, while Section 5 concludes the paper.

2   The Complex Wishart Distribution

PolSAR imaging results in a complex scattering matrix, which includes intensity and relative phase data [3]. Such matrices have possibly four distinct complex elements, namely S_{VV}, S_{VH}, S_{HV}, and S_{HH}, where H and V refer to the horizontal and vertical wave polarization states, respectively. The complex signal backscattered from each resolution cell is characterized by the p-tuple scattering matrix vector $\boldsymbol{y}$, where $p = 3$ for a reciprocal medium ($S_{VH} = S_{HV}$); see Ulaby and Elachi [9].

Thus, we have a scattering complex random vector $\boldsymbol{y} = [S_{VV}, S_{VH}, S_{HH}]^t$, where $[\cdot]^t$ indicates vector transposition. In PolSAR data, the speckle might be modeled as a multiplicative independent zero-mean complex circular Gaussian process that modules the scene reflectivity [9,8], whose probability density function is

$$f(y; \boldsymbol{\Sigma}) = \frac{1}{\pi^3 |\boldsymbol{\Sigma}|} \exp\{-y^* \boldsymbol{\Sigma}^{-1} y\},$$

where $|\cdot|$ is the determinant, the superscript '$*$' denotes the complex conjugate transpose of a vector, $\boldsymbol{\Sigma}$ is the covariance matrix of $\boldsymbol{y}$. The covariance matrix $\boldsymbol{\Sigma}$, besides being Hermitian and positive definite, has all the information which characterizes the backscattering under analysis.

Multilook processing is intended to enhance the signal-to-noise ratio, thus, is calculated the averaged over L ideally independent looks of the same scene. This results in the sample covariance matrix $\boldsymbol{Z}$ given by $\boldsymbol{Z} = L^{-1} \sum_{\ell=1}^{L} \boldsymbol{y}_\ell \boldsymbol{y}_\ell^*$, where L is the number of looks $\boldsymbol{y}_\ell$, for $\ell = \{1, 2, \ldots, L\}$, and the superscript '$*$' denotes the complex conjugate transposition.

According to Anfinsen et al. [1], $\boldsymbol{Z}$ follows a multilook scaled complex Wishart distribution, denoted by $\boldsymbol{Z} \sim \mathcal{W}(\boldsymbol{\Sigma}, L)$. Having $\boldsymbol{\Sigma}$ and L as parameters, it is characterized by the following probability density function:

$$f_{\boldsymbol{Z}}(\boldsymbol{Z}'; \boldsymbol{\Sigma}, L) = \frac{L^{3L}|\boldsymbol{Z}'|^{L-3}}{|\boldsymbol{\Sigma}|^{L}\Gamma_3(L)} \exp\{-L \operatorname{tr}(\boldsymbol{\Sigma}^{-1}\boldsymbol{Z}')\}, \tag{1}$$

where $\Gamma_3(L) = \pi^3 \prod_{i=0}^{2} \Gamma(L - i)$, $\Gamma(\cdot)$ is the gamma function, $\operatorname{tr}(\cdot)$ is the trace operator, and the covariance matrix of $\boldsymbol{Z}$ is given by

$$\boldsymbol{\Sigma} = E\{\boldsymbol{yy}^*\} = \begin{bmatrix} E\{S_1 S_1^*\} & E\{S_1 S_2^*\} & E\{S_1 S_3^*\} \\ E\{S_2 S_1^*\} & E\{S_2 S_2^*\} & E\{S_2 S_3^*\} \\ E\{S_3 S_1^*\} & E\{S_3 S_2^*\} & E\{S_3 S_3^*\} \end{bmatrix},$$

where $E\{\cdot\}$ and the superscript '$*$' denote expectation and complex conjugation, respectively.

3   Stochastic Distances Filter

The proposed filter is based on stochastic distances and tests between distributions [3] obtained from the class of (h, ϕ)-divergences. It employs in a modified Nagao-Matsuyama set of neighbors [5], presented in Figure 1.

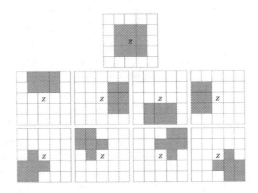

Fig. 1. Nagao-Matsuyama neighbourhoods

The filtering procedure consists in checking which regions can be considered as coming from the same distribution that produced the data in the central block. The sets which are not rejected are used to compute a local mean of covariance matrices. If all the sets are rejected, the filtered value is updated with the average on the central neighborhood around the filtered pixel.

Each filtered pixel has a 5×5 neighborhood, within which nine overlapping areas are defined. Denote $\widehat{\boldsymbol{\theta}}_1$ the estimated parameter in the central 3×3 neighborhood, and $(\widehat{\boldsymbol{\theta}}_2, \ldots, \widehat{\boldsymbol{\theta}}_9)$ the estimated parameters in the eight remaining areas.

We estimate $\widehat{\boldsymbol{\theta}}_i = (\widehat{\boldsymbol{\Sigma}}_i)$ by maximum likelihood, assuming that the number looks L is known; details can be seen in Anfinsen et al. [1]. Based on a random sample of size n, let $\{\boldsymbol{Z}_1, \boldsymbol{Z}_2, \ldots, \boldsymbol{Z}_n\}$, the likelihood function related to the $\mathcal{W}(\boldsymbol{\Sigma}, L)$ distribution is given by

$$\mathcal{L}(\boldsymbol{\Sigma}; \boldsymbol{Z}') = \left(\frac{L^{3L}}{|\boldsymbol{\Sigma}|^L \Gamma_3(L)}\right)^n \prod_{j=1}^n |\boldsymbol{Z}'|^{L-3} \exp\{-L \operatorname{tr}(\boldsymbol{\Sigma}^{-1} \boldsymbol{Z}')\}. \qquad (2)$$

Thus, the maximum likelihood estimator for $\boldsymbol{\Sigma}$ is $\widehat{\boldsymbol{\Sigma}} = n^{-1} \sum_{j=1}^n \boldsymbol{Z}_j$.

The proposal is based on the use of stochastic distances on small areas within the filtering window. Consider that $\boldsymbol{Z}_1$ and $\boldsymbol{Z}_i$ are random matrices defined on the same probability space, whose distributions are characterized by the densities $f_{\boldsymbol{Z}_1}(\boldsymbol{Z}'; \boldsymbol{\theta}_1)$ and $f_{\boldsymbol{Z}_i}(\boldsymbol{Z}'; \boldsymbol{\theta}_i)$, respectively, where $\boldsymbol{\theta}_1$ and $\boldsymbol{\theta}_i$ are parameters. Assuming that the densities have the same support given by the cone of Hermitian positive definite matrices $\boldsymbol{\mathcal{A}}$, the h-ϕ divergence between $f_{\boldsymbol{Z}_1}$ and $f_{\boldsymbol{Z}_i}$ is given by

$$D_\phi^h(\boldsymbol{Z}_1, \boldsymbol{Z}_i) = h\left(\int_{\boldsymbol{\mathcal{A}}} \phi\left(\frac{f_{\boldsymbol{Z}_1}(\boldsymbol{Z}'; \boldsymbol{\theta}_1)}{f_{\boldsymbol{Z}_i}(\boldsymbol{Z}'; \boldsymbol{\theta}_i)}\right) f_{\boldsymbol{Z}_i}(\boldsymbol{Z}'; \boldsymbol{\theta}_i) \, \mathrm{d}\boldsymbol{Z}'\right), \qquad (3)$$

where $h \colon (0, \infty) \to [0, \infty)$ is a strictly increasing function with $h(0) = 0$ and $h'(x) > 0$ for every $x \in \mathbb{R}$, and $\phi \colon (0, \infty) \to [0, \infty)$ is a convex function [7]. Choices of functions h and ϕ result in several divergences.

Divergences sometimes are not distances because they are not symmetric. A simple solution, described in [2,3,6], is to define a new measure d_ϕ^h given by

$$d_\phi^h(\boldsymbol{Z}_1, \boldsymbol{Z}_i) = \frac{D_\phi^h(\boldsymbol{Z}_1, \boldsymbol{Z}_i) + D_\phi^h(\boldsymbol{Z}_i, \boldsymbol{Z}_1)}{2}. \qquad (4)$$

Distances, in turn, can be conveniently scaled to present good statistical properties that make them suitable as test statistics [3,6]:

$$S_\phi^h(\widehat{\boldsymbol{\theta}}_1, \widehat{\boldsymbol{\theta}}_i) = \frac{2mnk}{m+n} d_\phi^h(\widehat{\boldsymbol{\theta}}_1, \widehat{\boldsymbol{\theta}}_i), \qquad (5)$$

where $\widehat{\boldsymbol{\theta}}_1$ and $\widehat{\boldsymbol{\theta}}_i$ are maximum likelihood estimators based on samples size m and n, respectively, and $k = (h'(0)\phi'')^{-1}$. When $\boldsymbol{\theta}_1 = \boldsymbol{\theta}_i$, under mild conditions $S_\phi^h(\widehat{\boldsymbol{\theta}}_1, \widehat{\boldsymbol{\theta}}_i)$ is asymptotically χ_M^2 distributed, being M the dimension of $\boldsymbol{\theta}_1$. Observing $S_\phi^h(\widehat{\boldsymbol{\theta}}_1, \widehat{\boldsymbol{\theta}}_i) = s$, the null hypothesis $\boldsymbol{\theta}_1 = \boldsymbol{\theta}_i$ can be rejected at level η if $\Pr(\chi_M^2 > s) \le \eta$. Details can be seen in the work by Salicrú et al. [7].

Since we are using the same sample for eight tests, we modified the value of η by a Bonferroni-like correction, namely, the Šidák correction, that is given by $\eta = 1 - (1 - \alpha)^{1/t}$, where t is the number of tests and, α the level of significance for the whole series of tests.

678   L. Torres, A.C. Medeiros, and A.C. Frery

Frery et al. [3] derived several distances for the $\mathcal{W}(\boldsymbol{\Sigma}, L)$ model, the one presented in Equation (1) among them. The statistical test used in this paper was derived from the Hellinger distance, yielding:

$$
\mathcal{S}_H = \frac{8mn}{m+n}\left[1 - \left(\frac{\left|\left(\frac{\boldsymbol{\Sigma}_1^{-1}+\boldsymbol{\Sigma}_i^{-1}}{2}\right)^{-1}\right|}{\sqrt{|\boldsymbol{\Sigma}_1|\,|\boldsymbol{\Sigma}_i|}}\right)^L\right].
\tag{6}
$$

PolSAR is used to measure the target's reflectivity with four polarization channel combinations (HH, HV, VH and VV), which can be expressed as a complex scattering matrix [4,9]. Transformations on these channels polarization makes it possible to visualize the PolSAR data as a color image.

Two ways of visualizing the covariance matrix in false color are the Pauli (in the horizontal basis) and Sinclair decompositions. They assign $|S_{HH} - S_{VV}|^2$, $|2S_{HV}|^2$ and $|S_{HH} + S_{VV}|^2$, and $|S_{VV}|$, $|2S_{HV}|$ and $|S_{HH}|$ to the red, green and blue channels, respectively.

4   Results

The NASA/Jet Propulsion Laboratory Airborne SAR (AIRSAR) of the San Francisco Bay was used for evaluating the quality of the procedure. The original polarimetric SAR data was generated with 4-looks and 900×1024 pixels. Figure 2 presents results in the Pauli decomposition, while Figure 3 shows their counterparts using the Sinclair decomposition. Figures 2(a) and 2(b) (Figures 3(a) and 3(b), respectively) show the original data set and a zoom.

Figures 2(c) and 2(d) (Figures 3(c) and 3(d), resp.) show the effect of the mean computed on windows of size 5×5 over the whole image. Albeit the noise reduction is evident, it is also clear that the blurring introduced eliminates useful information as, for instance, curvilinear details in the forested area.

Figures 2(e) and 2(f) (Figures 3(e) and 3(f), resp.) present the result of smoothing the original data set computing means which pass the Hellinger test at the level significance $\alpha = 80\%$. The noise effect is alleviated, c.f. the reduced graininess specially in the forest and over the urban areas, but fine details are more preserved than when the mean is employed. The directional selectiveness of the proposed filter retains linear structures as, for instance, the streets and the docks. Bright structures within the forest are enhanced, and their linear appearance is maintained.

5   Conclusions

The proposed technique combats the effect of speckle noise in all the areas of the test image. The filter is selective, producing stronger noise reduction in untextured areas, while it preserves fine details as linear structures and the forest texture. The proposal was compared with the simple mean filter using the decomposition process for PolSAR images.

(a) PolSAR data

(b) Zoom PolSAR data

(c) Mean filter

(d) Zoom Mean filter

(e) Stochastic Distances filter

(f) Zoom Stochastic Distances filter

Fig. 2. PolSAR data on Pauli Decomposition

(a) PolSAR data

(b) Zoom PolSAR data

(c) Mean filter

(d) Zoom Mean filter

(e) Stochastic Distances filter

(f) Zoom Stochastic Distances filter

Fig. 3. PolSAR data on Sinclair Decomposition

Next steps will be assessing quantitatively the proposal, using iterated filters (since the complex Wishart distribution is closed under convolutions), and estimating the equivalent number of looks in order to consider possible departures from the homogeneous model.

References

1. Anfinsen, S.N., Doulgeris, A.P., Eltoft, T.: Estimation of the equivalent number of looks in polarimetric synthetic aperture radar imagery. IEEE Transactions on Geoscience and Remote Sensing 47(11), 3795–3809 (2009)
2. Frery, A.C., Cintra, R.J., Nascimento, A.D.C.: Hypothesis test in complex Wishart distributions. In: Proceedings of the 5th International Workshop on Science and Applications of SAR Polarimetry and Polarimetric Interferometry, Frascati, Italy (January 2011)
3. Frery, A.C., Nascimento, A.D.C., Cintra, R.J.: Information theory and image understanding: An application to polarimetric SAR imagery. Chilean Journal of Statistics 2(2), 81–100 (2011)
4. Lee, J.S., Pottier, E.: Polarimetric Radar Imaging: From Basics to Applications. CRC Pres, Boca Raton (2009)
5. Nagao, M., Matsuyama, T.: Edge preserving smoothing. Computer Graphics and Image Processing 9(4), 394–407 (1979)
6. Nascimento, A.D.C., Cintra, R.J., Frery, A.C.: Hypothesis testing in speckled data with stochastic distances. IEEE Transactions on Geoscience and Remote Sensing 48(1), 373–385 (2010)
7. Salicrú, M., Morales, D., Menéndez, M.L., Pardo, L.: On the applications of divergence type measures in testing statistical hypotheses. Journal of Multivariate Analysis 21(2), 372–391 (1994)
8. Touzi, R., Boerner, W.M., Lee, J.S., Lueneburg, E.: A review of polarimetry in the context of synthetic aperture radar: concepts and information extraction. Canadian Journal of Remote Sensing 30(3), 380–407 (2004)
9. Ulaby, F.T., Elachi, C.: Radar Polarimetriy for Geoscience Applications. Artech House, Norwood (1990)
10. Vasile, G., Trouve, E., Lee, J.S., Buzuloiu, V.: Intensity-driven adaptive-neighborhood technique for polarimetric and interferometric SAR parameters estimation. IEEE Transactions on Geoscience and Remote Sensing 44(6), 1609–1621 (2006)

Recognition and Real-Time Detection of Blinking Eyes on Electroencephalographic Signals Using Wavelet Transform

Renato Salinas[1], Enzo Schachter[1], and Michael Miranda[2]

[1] Departamento de Ingeniería Mecánica
[2] Programa de Doctorado en Automatización
Facultad de Ingeniería, Universidad de Santiago de Chile, Santiago, Chile
{renato.salinas,enzo.schachter,michael.mirandas}@usach.cl

Abstract. In this paper we study the detection of a specific pattern associated with the blinking of an eye in real time using electroencephalogram (EEG) signals of a single channel. This paper takes into account the theoretical and practical principles enabling the design and implementation of a system for real-time detection of time location, regardless of scale and multiple incidences. By using wavelet transform it permits us the fulfillment of our objective. The multiple detection and real-time operation is achieved by working with a pop-up window giving the projection of an ongoing analysis of the signal sampled by the EEG.

Keywords: biological signals, electroencephalogram EEG, brain computer interface BCI, eye blink detection, pattern recognition, wavelet transform.

1   Introduction

The electroencephalogram or EEG was first used in humans by Hans Berger in 1924 [1], with the purpose of recording electric potentials of the brain. These signals are acquired from sensors called electrodes attached to the scalp of the subject. The function of an electrode is to passively collect electrical potentials from neuron banks that are located mainly in the cerebral cortex. The level of these signals is typically within the range of 40 to 100 microvolts [2]. Given their low electrical levels, EEG signals can be easily contaminated by other sources. An EEG signal that does not originate in the brain is called an artifact. The artifacts fall into two categories: physiological and non-physiological. Any source in the body that has an electric dipole generates an electric field capable of producing physiological artifacts. The non-physiological artifacts are produced by electrical and mechanical devices [3]. The human eye, similar to an electrical system, acts as a dipole with a positive charge in front and a negative charge in the back; the exercise of closing and opening the eyes produces artifacts of EEG signals [4]. Given that the artifacts are usually considered an unwanted signal or signal interference, this work is focused on real-time detection of a specific pattern generated by the blink of an eye so that they can be removed. The artifact generated by the blink of an eye is not necessarily a problem, but an opportunity, because its

L. Alvarez et al. (Eds.): CIARP 2012, LNCS 7441, pp. 682–690, 2012.

one-dimensional representation on a graph of microvolts vs. time is specific and independent of the individual from which the EEG signals are obtained [4]. Therefore, the artifact represents a clear identifiable pattern that can be used in brain computer interfaces -BCI-, if the artifacts are generated voluntarily by the user it can translate simple commands to help people with disabilities. Currently, there are numerous researches aimed at finding processing algorithms and classification of EEG patterns that will produce better results in the BCI [5] [6] [7]. At first glance, you may assume that having a specific pattern makes it easier to detect the presence of artifacts produced by the blinking of the eyes, but in practice it is not, because the pattern is presented at different scales and in multiple instances. In order for the detection algorithm to be robust it is necessary to consider an invariant model both in scale, translation and instances in which the pattern appears in the window of study, all in real time. This study takes advantage of the non-stationary signal analysis capabilities of the wavelet transform that, unlike the Fourier transform, it is a simultaneous representation of the time and the frequency domains [8].

2   Acquisition and Processing of the EEG Signal

2.1   Signal Acquisition and Signal Transmission

Human electroencephalography signals are typically below 256Hz [9] (fmax), by the foregoing and in consideration of the Nyquist-Shannon sampling theorem, it is necessary to use a sampling frequency equal to or greater than twice the maximum frequency, i.e., at least 512Hz. For a practical reason we preferred to use dry contact sensors or active electrodes, which have an electrical microcircuit in the electrode to improve the quality of the acquired signal.

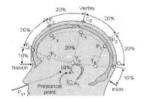 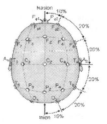

Fig. 1. The international 10-20 system. A = Ear lobe, C = central, Pg = nasopharyngeal, P = parietal, F = frontal, Fp = frontal polar, O = occipital. [9].

In the study of EEG signals, the cerebral cortex is divided into different zones; of which the nomenclature used depends on the system [10] [11]; in the case of the international system our goal of study focuses on the polar frontal areas FP1 and FP2 (Fig. 1). For the development of this work we used the Mindset of Neurosky Inc. This unit has only one dry contact EEG electrode that is located in the FP1, its frequency is 512Hz, and it includes a rechargeable battery, as well as a blue-tooth transmitter that sends the signal to the computer wirelessly.

2.2   EEG Signal Processing

Upon receiving the signal on the computer, we construct a continuous recording of EEG data at 512 samples per second. The samples are extracted, one at a time from this record to build the analysis segment in the form of a moving window of 500[ms], i.e. a vector of 256 samples or components that are being renewed by entering a new sample. A sample data flow is shown in Fig 2.

$$\cdots \rightarrow s^{n+1} \rightarrow [s_{256}^n \rightarrow s_{255}^{n-1} \rightarrow \cdots \rightarrow s_2^{n-2} \rightarrow s_1^{n-255}] \rightarrow s^{n-256} \rightarrow \cdots$$

Fig. 2. A schematic example of the data flow within the analysis window of 256 components. The subscript represents the component in the analysis window; the superscript represents the number of signal sample under study.

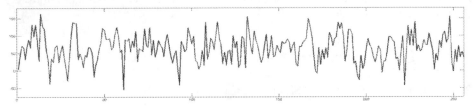

Fig. 3. Typical EEG signal without the presence of artifacts, captured by the processing system in an analysis window of 256 components, equal to 500ms

The number of components of the window was selected given the duration of a blink of an eye [12]. An example of EEG signal without artifacts is shown in Fig. 3. The moving window is processed with the low pass filter.

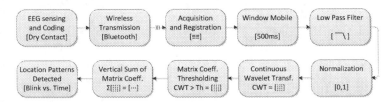

Fig. 4. Overall scheme of the recognition system and real-time detection of eye blinking in electroencephalographic EEG signals using wavelet transform

The step of acquiring and processing data in a global context is presented in the first row of the scheme depicted in Fig. 4. Once processed the analysis of the signal segment, the algorithm proceeds to the next step of detecting the eye-blinking pattern shown in the second row of the scheme of Fig. 4, the detection block yields the temporal location of each artifact caused by the blinking of the eyes.

3   Characteristics and Effects of Eye Blinking in EEG Signals

The artifact in the EEG signal produced by the blinking of an eye has a positive maxi-mum and a negative minimum, associated with eye opening and eye closing, respectively. In this paper we use a feature associated with shape that has low symmetry and a variable amplitude, duration and frequency, as shown in Fig. 5.

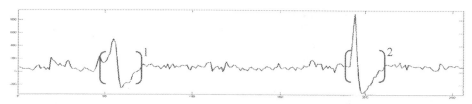

Fig. 5. EEG signal with two artifacts produced by blinking eyes. The artifacts are shown enclosed in square brackets.

Determining a unique shape pattern for the recursive detection of eye blinking present in a stochastic signal is useless, since it would only apply to a group of shapes that present some similarity to the chosen pattern. To improve the condition one may increase the number of different patterns in amplitude and duration, and then perform a recursive search, but it would consume enough time for each process cycle to damage the final condition of real-time analysis. Requiring a group of interrelated patterns is not entirely negative, as one might think of a family of patterns derived from a "mother" pattern that passes down the characteristics to the children patterns, to perform multi-resolution analysis. In our case, this paper deals with the analysis using wavelet transform.

4   Wavelet Transform

The analysis of signals with stationary components highlights the Fourier Transform FT, thanks to the ability to deliver a representation of frequency content present in the signal. However, it is not very useful for analyzing signals that do not possess stationary behavior, or those which have abrupt changes in very small intervals.

$$\text{Short Time FT (STFT)} \qquad STFT(f) = \int_{-\infty}^{\infty} x(t)g^*(t-b)e^{-i2\pi ft}\,dt \qquad (1)$$

To counteract the disadvantages there is an adapted version of the Fourier Transform called Short Time Fourier Transform STFT (Eq. 3), also known as Gabor Transform. In the equation 1 is given a function $g(t)$ used for analysis window moving over the data to determine the spectrum locally, variable b indicates the position in which the analysis is made and * denotes the complex conjugate. The disadvantage of this transform is that the analysis window is of a fixed size and therefore cannot adapt to the characteristics of the signal at certain points of interest to analyze.

Analysis by Wavelet Transform is a logical step following the STFT, using windows regions of variable sizes. Wavelet analysis allows the use of large time intervals in those segments where greater accuracy is required at low frequencies and smaller regions where information is required at high frequency. A wavelet is a waveform of limited duration that has average value zero. Wavelet analysis decomposes the signal into shifted and scaled versions of another signal called mother wavelet [13]. The

Wavelet has a limited duration, it also tends to be irregular and asymmetric, allowing for greater adaptability and better convergence; for this reason, it is important to properly select the mother wavelet depending on the signal analyzed. There are two classes of wavelets with applications in different domains. The continuous wavelet transform and the discrete wavelet; these classes determine their particular properties. The discrete wavelet transform or DWT arises from a discretization in time and scale, unlike the continuous wavelet transform or CWT, which is used in this work.

4.1 Continuous Wavelet Transform

The continuous wavelet transform can be defined as the integral in the entire interval of time t of the signal $x(t)$ multiplied by the scale of a shifted version of the mother function $\Psi(t)$ (equation 2).

$$\text{Mother Wavelet} \qquad \Psi_{a,b}(t) = \frac{1}{\sqrt{a}} \Psi \left(\frac{t-b}{a} \right) \qquad (a,b) \in R, a \neq 0. \qquad (2)$$

$$\begin{array}{c} \text{Continuous Wavelet} \\ \text{Transform (CWT)} \end{array} \qquad CWT(a,b) = \frac{1}{\sqrt{a}} \int_{-\infty}^{\infty} x(t) \Psi \left(\frac{t-b}{a} \right) dt \qquad (3)$$

The CWT (equation 3) delivers as a result coefficients depending on the scale a and position b of the mother wavelet generating a family of wavelets from the original, which is scaled and translated in each of these two subscripts, respectively. The application of these operations on this function generates the different areas of detail.

The main families of wavelets are Haar, Daubechies, Biorthogonal (bior), Coiflet, Morlet, Mexican Hut, Meyer and Symlet [14]. All have a specific equation that shows their differences in shape, as shown in Fig 6.

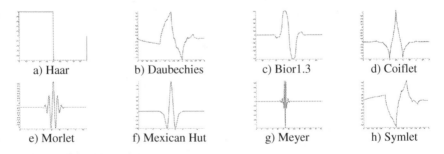

Fig. 6. Typical shapes of the main wavelet families. (Source: Wavelet Toolbox Matlab®).

5 Characteristic Pattern Detection

Given the waveform pattern associated with eye blinking shown in Fig. 5, it is simple to find similarities with the Biorthogonal wavelet family, specifically bior1.3 (see Fig. 6c and Fig. 7); the condition of similarity is sufficient to use this wavelet in the analysis because it is a variant pattern which has different versions of scale and translation, which is a problem to be solved using the wavelet transform analysis. As seen in

Fig. 4 the algorithm comprises a detection step which starts with the normalization of the analyzed signal, then bior1.3 continuous wavelet transform is applied to obtain the coefficients which will be subsequently processed to obtain the location of each artifact. Using the signal shown in Fig. 5 and applying the continuous wavelets transform, we obtain a coefficient matrix, equation 4. The dimensions of the matrix depend on the number of components or samples of the analyzed signal and the level or number of scales in the decomposition by the wavelet transform.

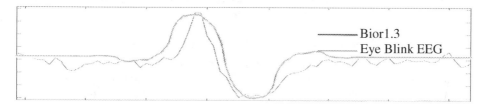

Fig. 7. Overlay of the artifact produced by eye blinking and the wavelet bior1.3

$$C(a,b) = CWT(\text{'input signal'}, \text{'bior1.3'})$$

where $C(a,b)$ is the coefficients matrix and CWT is the continuous wavelet transform, applied to input signal. (4)

This matrix can be plotted as if it were a gray scale image, with this you get the graph scale vs. time, i.e. coefficients a vs. b respectively obtained from equation 4, see Fig. 8, in which white vertical lines indicate the level of agreement of the wavelet used for signal analysis and study, like the images in grayscale, the higher-value components tend to be represented with a color ever closer to white [15]. In Fig. 8(a) there is a dark horizontal band corresponding to the first wavelet decomposition level, i.e., the high frequency; therefore, we can deduce that the searched pattern has no presence in a high frequency band. As you would in a grayscale image analysis [15], it is possible to apply thresholding to the matrix of wavelet coefficients, as defined in equation 5.

$$T(a,b) = \begin{cases} 0 & if \quad C(a,b) < Threshold_{fixed} \\ C(a,b) & , \qquad otherwise \end{cases}$$ (5)

Fig. 8(b) shows the presence of two white vertical lines that represent the detection of the searched pattern and its location in time. The aim of this work is to automate the detection and do it in real time, so that speed of each process is very important.

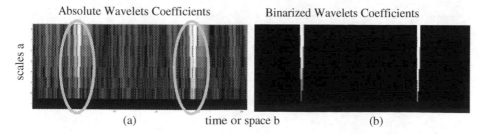

Absolute Wavelets Coefficients   Binarized Wavelets Coefficients

scales a

(a)   time or space b   (b)

Fig. 8. (a) Applications of the continuous wavelet transform bior 1.3 to the signal shown in Fig. 5. (b) Binarization of the wavelet coefficient matrix using thresholding.

In the case under study for this work the number of components or the analysis window size is of 256 samples and 8 levels of decomposition, which involves obtaining a coefficient matrix [C] of 8x256 elements. Any way you can use parameters other than those indicated for detection, which do not have a strong impact on the algorithm for the next step, reduces the number of rows in the matrix to just one row. To perform the dimensional reduction, the columns of the coefficient matrix $T(a, b)$ are added as shown in equation 6. The vector V obtained in equation 6 gives us the actual location in time of the artifact produced by the eye blinking. Since the analysis is in real time, the data was smoothed with a 10ms. moving average.

$$V(1,2,\dots, n) = \sum_a T(a,b), \quad b = 1,2,\dots,n \tag{6}$$

Applying the identification process to the signal shown in Fig. 5 results in the signal shown in Fig. 9, which overlap the input signal or analysis signal with the filtered output signal along with the location of artifacts detected produced by the blinking of an eye.

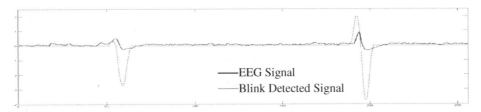

Fig. 9. Overlay of original EEG signal with the filtered EEG signal, highlighting the detected artifacts produced by eye blinking

6   Results and Discussion

Results from this work have been tested with real-time EEG introducing eye blinking artifacts alternately with different frequencies and amplitudes, proving to be a robust algorithm to filter artifacts produced by other sources that do not share similarity in shape, as well as detecting a target pattern in its many versions independent of the number of occurrences, the extent and the level of symmetry in the study window.

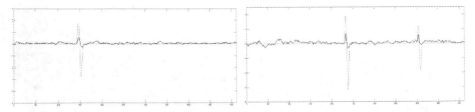

Fig. 10. Examples of real-time detection of a few eye blinks with an analysis window of 1000ms

As seen in Fig. 10 the pattern is always well-detected independent of the size of the analysis window.

7   Conclusions

The use of wavelet transform in analyzing non-stationary signals, such as electroen-cephalograms, shows comparative advantages with respect to the Fourier transform. Among these advantages is the multi-resolution analysis which involves looking at the same time multiple versions of the same signal, the versions are band-pass filtered which are determined by the scale. Incorporating features of shape, amplitude, and phase shift for detecting patterns using one-dimensional wavelet transform ensures a robust recognition system prior to detection. This work contributes to the science related to bioengineering dedicated to brain computer interfaces or BCI, allowing real-time detection of artifacts or Eye Blinking; which generated voluntarily by the user can translate into simple commands for helping people with disabilities, for example, commanding the motor forward or reverse of a wheelchair. From the results of our work we conclude that filtering the artifact due to eye blinking in electroencepha-logram EEG signals will be straightforward, now that the timing information of occurrence is well defined. It should be noted that although there are alternative ana-lyses for eye blinking detection from EEG data, those approaches operate off-line, and our method operates in real time.

Acknowledgement. The authors gratefully acknowledge the support of DIMEC-USACH and the support of VRID-USACH.

References

1. Gloor, P.: Hans Berger on the Electroencephalogram of Man. Elsevier Publishing Compa-ny, Amsterdam (1969)
2. Fisch, B.: EEG PRIMER Basic principles of digital and analog EEG, 3rd edn. Elsevier Academic Press (1999) ISBN: 0-444-82147-3
3. Binnie, C., Cooper, R., Mauguire, F., Osselton, J., Prior, P., Tedman, B.: Clinical Neuro-physiology. Elsevier Academic Press (2003) ISBN: 0-444-51257-8
4. Polkko, J.: A Method for Detecting Eye Blinks from Single-Channel Biopotential Signal in the Intensive Care Unit. Master's Thesis (2007)
5. Slep, M.: Single Trial Analysis of EEG Signals, COS 497/498 (2003)
6. Bayliss, J.: A Flexible Brain-Computer Interface. Ph.D. Thesis, Computer Science Dept., U. Rochester (August 2001)
7. Chambayil, B., Singla, R., Jha, R.: EEG Eye Blink Classification Using Neural Network. In: Proceedings of the World Congress on Engineering, WCE 2010, London, U.K., vol. I (June 2010)
8. Walker, J.S.: Fourier Analysis and Wavelet Analysis. University of Wiconsin-Eau Claire. Notices of the Ams. 44(6) (1997)
9. Aeschbach, D., Borb'ely, A.A.: All-night dynamics of the human sleep EEG. J. Sleep Res. 2(2), 70–81 (1993)
10. Gilmore, R.L.: American Electroencephalographic Society guidelines in electroencephalo-graphy, evoked potentials, and polysomnography. J. Clin. Neurophysiol. 11, 147 (1994)
11. Sharbrough, F., Chatrian, G.-E., Lesser, R.P., Lüders, H., Nuwer, M., Picton, T.W.: Amer-ican Electroencephalographic Society Guidelines for Standard Electrode Position Nomen-clature. J. Clin. Neurophysiol. 8, 200–202 (1991)

12. Divjak, M., Bischof, H.: Eye blink based fatigue detection for prevention of Computer Vi-sion Syndrome. In: IAPR Conference on Machine Vision Applications (MVA 2009), Tokyo, Japan, May 20-22, pp. 350–353 (2009)
13. Mallat, S.: A theory for multiresolution signal decomposition: the wavelet repre-sentation. IEEE Pattern Anal. and Machine Intell. 11(7), 674–693 (1989)
14. Misiti, M., Misiti, Y., Oppenheim, G., Poggi, J.M.: Wavelet Toolbox for use with Matlab. The MathWorks Inc. EEUU (2004)
15. González, R., Woods, R.: Digital Image Processing, 3rd edn. Prentice-Hall (2008)

Finite Rank Series Modeling for Discrimination of Non-stationary Signals

Lina Maria Sepulveda-Cano, Carlos Daniel Acosta-Medina,
and Germán Castellanos-Dominguez

Signal Processing and Recognition Group, Universidad Nacional de Colombia,
Km. 9, Vía al aeropuerto, Campus la Nubia, Manizales, Colombia
lmsepulvedac@bt.unal.edu.co

Abstract. The analysis of time-variant biosignals for classification tasks, usually requires a modeling that may handel their different dynamics and non–stationary components. Although determination of proper stationary data length and the model parameters remains as an open issue. In this work, time–variant signal decomposition through Finite Rank Series Modeling is carried out, aiming to find the model parameters. Three schemes are tested for OSA detection based on HRV recordings: SSA and DLM as linear decompositions and EDS as non–linear decomposition. Results show that EDS decomposition presents the best performance, followed by SSA. As a conclusion, it can be inferred that adding complexity at the linear model the trend is approximate to a simple non–linear model.

1 Introduction

As regards the analysis and processing of biosignals, stochastic modeling has been under continuous formulation for extracting valuable information due to the high non–stationarity inherent of this kind of time series. Mostly, a methodology for analysis of non–stationary time series is based on the assumption that there is a processing time window of such a length that the piecewise stationary–based approach of analysis holds. Although determination of proper stationary data length and the model parameters remains as an open issue [1]. Grounded on piecewise stationary approach, several time-variant linear decomposition techniques had been proposed for non–stationarity characterization: time-frequency representation, smoothing techniques based on ortogonal polynomials, linear splines, wavelets, empirical mode decomposition, and regressive modeling, among others.

Based on generalized spectral representation, a more elaborated approximation, termed *Finite-rank Series Modeling*, can be carried out by decomposing the underlying biosignal into a linear combination of products of harmonics, exponential, or even polynomial series [2], that is, the problem is addressed as modeling multiple time-evolving data streams governed by some linear recurrent formula, and inferring similarities and relationships between these data over prescribed time window lags. Although, a single input signal can be decomposed by

L. Alvarez et al. (Eds.): CIARP 2012, LNCS 7441, pp. 691–698, 2012.

an unknown number of recurrent sequences, which may vary from observation to observation, a strong constrain on this decomposition approach is related with modeling time series holding itself different stochastic structures [3].

This paper considers the extension of Finite Order Series Modeling behind baseline Singular Spectrum Analysis (SSA), explained in [2]. Namely, Dynamic Linear Modeling (DLM) as linear scheme [4], and Exponentially Damped Sinusoids (EDS) as non–linear scheme [5] are also considered. As a demonstrative example, we analyze discrimination of hear rate variability recordings, which are a multi-process exhibiting high non-stationary behavior, for detection of Obstructive Sleep Apnoea [3]. The remainder of the paper is organized as follows: In Section 2.1, the fundamentals of finite rank modeling is briefly introduced. In Section 3 the methodology for parameters estimation is explained. Lastly, in Sections 4 and 5, the effectiveness of each decomposition is illustrated for the considered task detection through cross–validation using a k-nearest neighbors (k-nn) classifier, followed by a discussion of the obtained results.

2   Background

2.1   Basic Finite Rank Series Modeling

Assume a real-valued time series $x = \{x_n : i, \ldots, N\}$, with $x \in \mathbb{R}^N$, which is mapped into the multidimensional time series set $\tilde{X} = \{\tilde{x}_k : k, \ldots, K\}$, $\tilde{X} \in \mathbb{R}^{K \times L}$, termed *Hankel Matrix*, comprising L-lagged vectors $\tilde{x}_k = [x_{i-1}, \ldots, x_{i+L-2}]^\top$; $\tilde{x}_k \in \mathbb{R}^L$, where $K = N - L$, being $3 \leq L \leq N$ [6]. Furthermore, if the dimension $\dim \mathfrak{L}^{(L)}\{x\} = \text{span}\{\tilde{x}_k : \forall k\} = d$, for $0 \leq d \leq L$, then, the series is regarded as L-rank d, noted as $\text{rank}_L\{x\}$. In turn, when the equality $\text{rank}_L\{x = d\}$ holds for all suitable L, the series x has rank d, that is, $\text{rank}\{x\} = d$. If such d exists, the time series is called a *finite rank series* [2].

Generally, a nonzero series x is governed by the following linear sequence of dimension not exceeding $d \geq 1$ if

$$x_{i+d} = \sum_{k=1}^{d} w_k x_{i+d-k}, \tag{1}$$

for a certain set $\{w_i \in \mathbb{R} : i = 1, \ldots, d\}$ with $w_d \neq 0$, and $0 \leq i \leq N - d$.

Since $\text{rank}_L\{x\} = \text{rank}_L\{\tilde{X}\} = \text{rank}_L\{\tilde{X}\tilde{X}^\top\}$, the orthonormal system of eigenvectors $\{u_l : l = 1, \ldots, d\}$ (corresponding to d positive eigenvalues of the matrix $\text{rank}_L\{\tilde{X}\tilde{X}^\top\}$) constitutes the left singular vectors of the singular value decomposition of the matrix $\tilde{X}$. This concrete model of Finite Rank Series is known as *Singular Spectral Analysis* (SSA) [7].

Suppose a sufficiently large N of the series x, under assumption that $d < \min(L, K)$, so, taking into account Eq. (2), the L-lagged vectors $\{\tilde{x}_k\}$ satisfy the following vector recurrent equation:

$$\tilde{x}_{i+d} = \sum_{k=1}^{d} w_k \tilde{x}_{i+d-k}, \tag{2}$$

The coefficient set in Eq. (2) can be found as follows:

$$w = \frac{1}{1-\mu^2} \sum_{i=1}^{d} u_{di} u_d^{\nabla},$$ (3)

where ∇ is the truncation operator, $w = [w_d, \ldots, w_1]^\top$ is the coefficient vector, $u_d^{\nabla} = [u_{1i}, \ldots, u_{di}]$ is the i–th eigenvector, and $\mu^2 = \sum_{i=1}^{d} u_{di}^2$ is the *verticality coefficient*.

2.2   Extended Finite Rank Series Modeling

For sake of generalization, model (2) can be rewritten in terms of an *autoregressive model*, as follows:

$$x_{i+d} = w x_{i-k-1},$$ (4)

where $x_{i-k-1} = [x_{i-k-1} \ldots x_{i+d-k}]^\top$ is the *autoregressive vector* and $w \in \mathbb{R}^{d\times 1}$ is the corresponding *parameter vector*, given by: $w = [w_1, \ldots, w_d]$; that is assumed to be constant in time. However, model (2) can be also extended for representing time–varying autoregressive model of order d, termed TVAR(d), if

$$x_i = \sum_{k=1}^{d} w_{k,i} x_{i-k},$$ (5)

where w_i is the autoregressive parameter at i–th time sample.

An alternative structure of (5) is the Dynamic Linear Model (DLM). Thus, it is important to be able to embed an TVAR model in the DLM form in order to distinguish, and ultimately infer, the process structure from contaminating noise [8]. Particularly, a DLM describing an TVAR process, at moment time i, has the form of Eq. (4) and is given by [4]:

$$x_i = \mathbf{1}^\top H_i W_i x_{i-1} + \delta_i,$$ (6)

where $\mathbf{1} = [1, \ldots, 1] \in \mathbb{R}^{d\times 1}$, $H_i = \mathrm{diag}\{U_i^\top f\} U_i^{-1}$, with $H_i \in \mathbb{R}^{d\times d}$, $f = [1, 0 \ldots 0]^\top \in \mathbb{R}^{d\times 1}$ is the *vector of regressors*, δ a zero–mean normal innovation vector, and $W_i \in \mathbb{R}^{d\times d}$ is the parameter matrix expressed as:

$$W_i = U_i A_i U_i^{-1} = \begin{bmatrix} w_{1,i} & w_{2,i} & \cdots & w_{d-1,i} & w_{d,i} \\ 1 & 0 & \cdots & 0 & 0 \\ \vdots & \vdots & \vdots & \vdots & 0 \\ 0 & 0 & \cdots & 1 & 0 \end{bmatrix}, \quad i = 1+d, \ldots, N-d$$ (7)

being $U_i \in \mathbb{R}^{d\times d}$ the eigenvector matrix and $A_i \in \mathbb{R}^{d\times d}$ the eigenvalues of W_i, respectively, at moment time i.

So, a TVAR model in Eq. (5) can be rewritten by means of vector recurrent expression (2), namely:

$$x_i = \sum_{k=1}^{d} h_{k,i} a_{k,i} \boldsymbol{u}_{k,i} x_{i-k} + \delta_i, \tag{8}$$

where $\boldsymbol{h}_i \in \mathbb{R}^d$ is the principal diagonal of $\text{diag}\{\boldsymbol{U}_i^\top \boldsymbol{f}\}$ and $\boldsymbol{a}_i \in \mathbb{R}^d$ is the eigenvalue vector of $\boldsymbol{W}_i$.

Lastly, the model (2) can be represented as a linear combination of *Exponentially Damped Sinusoidals* (EDS), when the signal is modeled as a finite sum of discrete-time exponentially damped complex sinusoids, as follows [5]:

$$x_i = \sum_{k=1}^{d} a_k \exp(j\phi_k) \exp((-h_k + j2\pi f_k) i \Delta n) \tag{9}$$

The amplitudes a_k, damping factors h_k, phases ϕ_k, frequencies f_k, and the model order d are free parameters of the non–linear model. Through Prony analysis exposed in [9], the non–linear problem stated in Eq. (9) can be decoupled by solving two introduced sets of linear equations, given in least square sense. Thus, model (9) is rewritten by using Eq. (2), as follows:

$$x_{i+d} = - \sum_{k=1}^{d} w_k x_{i+d-k}, \tag{10}$$

where the the parameter vector $\boldsymbol{w}$ is given as [10]:

$$\boldsymbol{w} = \sum_{k=1}^{d} \sigma_k \boldsymbol{u}_k \boldsymbol{v_k}^\top, \tag{11}$$

being $\boldsymbol{\sigma}$ the principle singular vector of $\tilde{\boldsymbol{X}}$. $\{\boldsymbol{v}_k : k = 1, \dots, d\}$ constitutes the right singular vectors of the singular value decomposition of the matrix $\tilde{\boldsymbol{X}}$. At the end, the EDS model can be expressed as:

$$x_{i+d-k} = \boldsymbol{w} \boldsymbol{x}_{i+d-1}, \tag{12}$$

3   Experimental Set–Up

The methodology is divided into five steps: *i*) Preprocessing *ii*) Signal Decomposition and *iii*) Classification, where a simple k-nearest neighbors (k–NN) classifier is used.

3.1   Database and Preprocessing

This collection holds $M = 70$ electrocardiographic recordings (modified lead V2) from PhysioNet [11], each one including a set of reference annotations added every minute of the recording indicating either the presence or absence of apnoea during each segment of time. The recordings were subdivided in three groups: apneic patients, with more than 100 minutes in apnea, borderline patients, with total apnea duration more than 5 and less than 99 minutes and control or normal patients, with less than 5 minutes in apnea. These recordings were obtained from men and women between the ages 27 through 63 years old, with weights ranging from 53 to 135 kg. From the database, 25 recordings were used as a training set for the classification algorithms. A second group with 25 recordings was used as a test set to measure the performance of the algorithms. It mus be quoted that OSA diagnosis requires the extraction of HRV time series from each ECG recording, which can be estimated of the QRS complex. In this work, complex detection is carried out including linear filtering, followed by a non linear transformation, and adaptive decision rules, as well. Then, the HRV time serie is normalized, termed x', as recommended in [3]:

$$x' = \frac{2(x - \mathcal{E}\{x\})}{\max_{\forall n}\{x\} - \min_{\forall n}\{x\}}, \ n \in N$$

3.2   Training Based on Signal Time Decomposition

The HRV signal is highly non–stationary, due to this, is necessary a better representation of the signal. In this work, for signal decomposition, three approaches are considered: the signal is decomposed directly through SSA, EDS and DLM. Tuning of the different schemes of considered signal decomposition throughout this training procedure is carried out by using the average classification accuracy for the automatic OSA detection, which is estimated using a k-nn classifier, followed by the well–known cross–validation methodology.

Singular Spectrum Analysis : for SSA tuning, the model order is chosen according to the classification accuracy, as shown in Figure 1(a). Since the lowest order presents a better result, then, order 1 is selected for considered model.

Dynamic Linear Model: the Bayesian information criterion (BIC) is used as order estimator, with the aim to find the recurrent coefficient of the embedded TVAR model, in terms of DLM form. The estimated mean of the order, given by BIC, is 10. Nevertheless, higher and lower orders are tested. The best classification accuracy is presented by the higher order, as seen in Figure 1(b).

Exponentially Damped Sinusoidal: Likewise, the model order is chosen according to the classification accuracy, as shown in Figure 1(c). Since the lowest order presents a better result, then, order 1 is chosen for this model.

4   Results and Discussion

Due to a huge dimension, which is inherent to the signal decomposition training space, the k-nn classifier requires a high computational cost with large memory

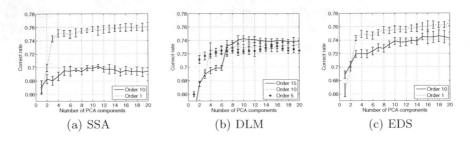

Fig. 1. Tuning of the different schemes of considered signal decomposition

amount. So, strong dimension reduction of such large training feature set should be carried out. Since there is a need for finding groups that are highly correlated (as it is the case with time series decomposition data), the principal component analysis is used throughout this study as unsupervised method to perform dimensionality reduction over the input training set in hand as recommended in [1].

Figure 2 illustrates how the estimated performance changes when ranging from 1 to 20 the number of considered principal components, which are a mutually linear independent combination of original variables. As seen, for the compared cases of signal decomposition, the proposed methodology is able to find differences between control and apneic events.

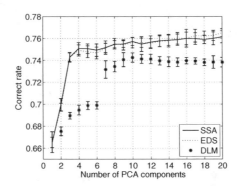

Fig. 2. Accuracy performance depending upon the signal decomposition when varying the number of used principal components

Table 1 summarizes the best performance obtained after the parameter tuning for each approach tested and the comparison between another outcomes related to OSA diagnosis. In the case of the results presented by [12], several approaches for the spectral splitting upon time–frequency planes in the concrete case of OSA detection are studied.

The model based on EDS presents the best performance, with $76.50 \pm 0.37\%$, followed by SSA with $76.13 \pm 0.55\%$. The linear model SSA and the non–linear

Table 1. Performance outcomes for time series analysis using a single tuned k-nn classifier

Approach	Ac	$Number of Features$
SSA	$76.13 \pm 0.55\%$	20
DLM	$74.25 \pm 0.42\%$	10
EDS	$76.50 \pm 0.37\%$	20
[12] Heuristic Approach	$75.42 \pm 0.88\%$	6
[12] Relevance Maximum variance	$75.22 \pm 0.58\%$	7

model EDS are very similar. That similar behavior can be explained. So, if adding complexity at the linear model SSA, the trend becomes more approximate to a simple non–linear model, as in case of EDS. Both models represent the signal with a lower order, i.e. the decomposition converges to the original signal through the highest principal eigenvalue, associated to the Hankel matrix in the projections (12) and (3). Besides, the order increases, on the opposite, the accuracy decreases; this can be explained because the other eigenvalues are informativeness for the process, adding just noise.

In the case of DLM, despite being a TVAR model, the accuracy is the lowest of the tested decompositions. The criterion for order selection is not coherent with the results of Figure 1(b), i.e. the order mean is not an adequate estimator due to the difference between orders in the training group are over five points. Additionally, the dynamic imposed by the model requires a higher order, near to the signal length, aiming to follow the signal trend as the other models. However, even with the above problem, the decomposition is able to find differences between control and apneic events with an acceptable precision.

5 Conclusions

A methodology for non–stationary signal discrimination is explored that imposes a finite rank modeling for a considered time series signal. The training procedure appraises the time-variant signal decomposition, aiming to find the model parameters. In this work, three approaches are tested: Singular Spectrum Analysis and Dynamic Linear Model as linear schemes, and Exponentially Damped Sinusoids as non–linear scheme. The methodology is proved particularity on biosignal data, namely, for Obstructive Sleep Apnoea syndrome detection. This data collection is chosen due to the fact that the interaction between the sympathetic and parasympathetic systems on the HRV recordings, gives rise to several non-stationary components added to the signal [3].

According to the performance of each time-variant signal decomposition, it can be concluded that the linear model SSA and the non–linear model EDS are very similar. It is possible because adding complexity at the linear model SSA, the trend is more approximate to a simple non–linear model as EDS. Regarding to DLM, the dynamic imposed by the model requires a higher order, near to the signal length, aiming to follow the signal trend as the other models. Therefore, for OSA detection, it would be of benefit to explore needed enhancement by using more elaborated non–linear models.

Acknowledgments. This research is supported by *"Becas para estudiantes sobresalientes de Posgrado - Universidad Nacional de Colombia"*

References

1. Sepulveda-Cano, L., Gil, E., Laguna, P., Castellanos-Dominguez, G.: Selection of Nonstationary Dynamic Features for Obstructive Sleep Apnoea Detection in Children. EURASIP Journal on Advances in Signal Processing 2011, 10 (2011)
2. Golyandina, N., Osipov, E.: The "caterpillar"-ssa method for analysis of time series with missing values. Journal of Statistical Planning and Inference 137(8), 2642–2653 (2007)
3. Martínez-Vargas, J., Sepulveda-Cano, L., Travieso-Gonzalez, C., Castellanos-Dominguez, G.: Detection of obstructive sleep apnoea using dynamic filter-banked features. Expert Systems with Applications 39, 9118–9128 (2012)
4. West, M., Prado, R., Krystal, A.D.: Evaluation and comparison of eeg traces: Latent structure in nonstationary time series. Journal of the American Statistical Association 94, 1083–1095 (1999)
5. De Clercq, W., Vanrumste, B., Papy, J.M., Van Paesschen, W., Van Huffel, S.: Modeling common dynamics in multichannel signals with applications to artifact and background removal in eeg recordings. IEEE Transactions on Biomedical Engineering 52, 2006–2015 (2005)
6. Mahmoudvand, R., Zokaeo, M.: On the singular values of the hankel matrix with application in singular spectrum analysis. Chilean Journal of Statistics 3, 43–56 (2012)
7. Thomakos, D.: Optimal linear filtering, smoothing and trend extraction for m-period differences of processes with a unit root. Technical report (2008)
8. West, M., Harrison, J.: Bayesian forecasting and dynamic models, 2nd edn. Springer-Verlag New York, Inc., New York (1997)
9. Allu, G.K.: Estimating the parameters of exponentially damped sinusoids in noise. Technical report, Electrical Engineering Department, University of Rhode Island, Kingston, Rhode Island (2003)
10. Li, S., Lv, X., Sun, H., Hu, W.: Multiple scattering centers measurements using the kumaresan-tufts method. In: 2006 IET International Conference on Wireless, Mobile and Multimedia Networks, pp. 1–4 (2006)
11. Mendez, M., Corthout, J., Huffel, S., Matteucci, M., Penzel, T., Cerutti, S., Bianchi, A.: Automatic screening of obstructive sleep apnea from the ecg based on empirical mode decomposition and wavelet analysis. Physiol. Meas. 31, 273–289 (2010)
12. Martínez-Vargas, J., Sepúlveda-Cano, L., Castellanos-Domínguez, G.: On determining available stochastic features by spectral splitting in obstructive sleep apnea detection. In: 33rd Annual International Conference of the IEEE EMBS, Boston, Massachusetts USA, August 30-September 3, pp. 6079–6082. IEEE (2011)

Quaternionic Analytic Signal Using Atomic Functions

E. Ulises Moya-Sánchez and Eduardo Bayro-Corrochano

CINVESTAV, Unidad Guadalajara
Electrical and Computer Sciences Department
{emoya,edb}@gdl.cinvestav.mx

Abstract. Atomic Functions are widely used in different applications in image processing, pattern recognition, computational physics and also in the digital interpretation of signal measurements. In 1D signals, is usual to compute the phase and the magnitude of a signal using the analytic signal (the signal and its Hilbert transform using complex numbers). However, for high dimensional signals the monogenic signal (the signal and its Riesz transform) has been used to obtain the local phase and orientation with good results. The main aim of this work is to present a new way to make the computation of the Hilbert transform using the atomic function. The computation of the Hilbert transform take relevance when the phase computation is required.

Keywords: Quaternion Algebra, Atomic functions, Image Processing, 2D Phase Information.

1 Introduction

The visual system is the most advanced of our senses. Therefore, it is easy to understand that the processing of the images plays an important role in human perception and computer vision implementation [8,9]. For 1D signals is usual to compute the phase and the magnitude using the signal and its Hilbert transform with a complex number [9]. Additionally, the phase information can be used to detect low-level geometric characteristics such as lines or edges [9,5,17]. Moreover, the phase can also be used to measure the local decomposition of the image according to its symmetries [9,8,10]. As will be shown in this work, the atomic function $up(x)$ in addition to hypercomplex numbers can be used as a building block to get multiple operations commonly used in image processing and analysis, such as low/high-pass filter, n-order derivatives, local phase, local amplitude, local orientation etc.

2 Atomic Functions

The Atomic Functions AF are compactly supported infinitely differentiable solutions of differential equations with a shifted argument [1] i.e.

$$Lf(x) = \lambda \sum_{k=1}^{M} c(k)f(ax - b(k)), |a| > 1, \tag{1}$$

L. Alvarez et al. (Eds.): CIARP 2012, LNCS 7441, pp. 699–706, 2012.

where $L = \frac{d^n}{dx^n} + a_1 \frac{d^{n-1}}{dx^{n-1}} + ... + a_n$ is a linear differential operator with constant coefficients. In the AF class, the function $up(x)$ is the simplest and at the same time, the most useful primitive function to generate other kinds of atomic functions [1]. It satisfies the equation 1 as

$$f(x)' = 2\left(f(2x+1) - f(2x-1)\right), \tag{2}$$
$$dup(x) = 2\left(up(2x+1) - up(2x-1)\right) \tag{3}$$

Function $up(x)$ is infinitely differentiable but non-analytical; $up(0) = 1$, $up(-x) = up(x)$. In general the Atomic Function $up(x)$ is generated by infinite convolutions of rectangular impulses. The function $up(x)$ has the following representation in terms of the Fourier transform:

$$up(x) = \frac{1}{2\pi} \int_{-\infty}^{\infty} e^{iux} \prod_{k=1}^{\infty} \frac{\sin(u2^{-k})}{u2^{-k}} du. \tag{4}$$

Figure 1 shows the $up(x)$ and the Fourier Transform of $F(up)$. Atomic windows were compared with classic ones [1] by means of the system of parameters such as: the equivalent noise bandwidth, the 50% overlapping region correlation, the parasitic modulation amplitude, the maximum conversion losses (in decibels), the maximum side lobe level (in decibels), the asymptotic decay rate of the side lobes (in decibels per octave), the window width at the six-decibel level, the coherent gain. All atomic windows exceed classic ones in terms of the asymptotic decay rate [1].

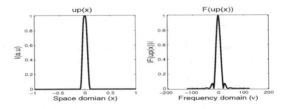

Fig. 1. Atomic function $up(x)$ and the Fourier Transform of $up(x)$

3   Quaternion Algebra

The even subalgebra $\mathcal{G}_{3,0,0}^{+}$ (bivector basis) is isomorphic to $\mathcal{H}$, which is an associative, noncommutative, four-dimensional algebra that consists of one real element and three imaginary elements.

$$q = a + bi + cj + dk \ \ a, b, c, d \ \epsilon \ \Re \tag{5}$$

The units i, j obey the relations $i^2 = j^2 = -1, ij = k$. $\mathcal{H}$ is geometrically inspired, and the imaginary components can be described in terms of the basis of $\mathcal{R}^3$ space, $i \to e_{23}, j \to e_{12}, k \to e_{31}$. Another important property of $\mathcal{H}$ is the phase concept. A polar representation of q is

$$q = |q|e^{i\phi}e^{k\psi}e^{j\theta}, \qquad (6)$$

where $|q| = \sqrt{q\bar{q}}$ where $\bar{q}$ is a conjugate of $q = a - bi - cj - dk$ and the angles (ϕ, θ, ψ) represent the three quaternionic phases[3].

3.1 Quaternionic Atomic Function $Qup(x, y)$

Since any 2D function $f(x, y)$ can be split into even (e) and odd (o) parts [3],

$$f(x, y) = f_{ee}(x, y) + f_{oe}(x, y) + f_{eo}(x, y) + f_{oo}(x, y), \qquad (7)$$

we can separate the four components of $up(x, y)$ function and represent it as a quaternion as follows [17,10]:

$$\begin{aligned} Qup(x, y) &= up(x, y)[\cos(w_x)\cos(w_y) + i(\sin(w_x)\cos(w_y)) + \\ &+ j(\cos(w_x)\sin(w_y)) + k(\sin(w_x)\sin(w_y))] \\ &= Qup_{ee} + iQup_{oe} + jQup_{eo} + kQup_{oo}. \end{aligned} \qquad (8)$$

Figure 2 shows a $Qup(x, y)$ in a space domain with its four components: the real part Qup_{ee} and the imaginary parts $Qup_{eo}, Qup_{oe}, andQup_{oo}$. We can see even and odd symmetries in the horizontal, vertical, and diagonal axes.

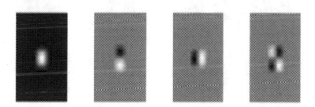

Fig. 2. From left to right. Qup_{ee}, Qup_{oe}, Qup_{eo}, and Qup_{oo}.

4 Quaternionic Local Phase Information

In this paper, we refer to the phase information as the local phase in order to separate the structure or geometric information and the amplitude in a certain part of the signal. Moreover, the phase information permits us to obtain invariant or equivariant[1] response. For instance, it has been shown that the phase has an invariant response to changes in image brightness and the phase can be used to measure the symmetry or asymmetry of objects [5,9,8]. These invariant and

---

[1] Equivariance: monotonic dependency of value or parameter under some transformation.

equivariant responses are the key part to link the low-level processing with the image analysis and the upper layers in computer vision applications.

The local phase means the computation of the phase at a certain position in a real signal. In 1D signals, the analytic signal based on the Hilbert transform $(f_\mathbf{H}(x))$ [3] is given by

$$f_A(f(x)) = f(x) + if_\mathbf{H}(x), \tag{9}$$
$$f_A(f(x)) = |A|e^{i\theta}, \tag{10}$$

where $|A| = \sqrt{f(x)^2 + f_\mathbf{H}(x)^2}$ and $\theta = arctan(\frac{f(x)}{f_\mathbf{H}(x)})$ permits us to extract the magnitude and phase independently. In 2D signals, the Hilbert transform is not enough to compute the magnitude and phase independently in any direction [18]. Then, in order to solve this, the quaternionic analytic (see Eq. 11) signal and the monogenic signal have been proposed by Bülow [3] and Felsberg [18], respectively. Until now, we have used an approximation of the quaternionic analytic signal based on the basis of QFT to extract some oriented axis symmetries.

Figure (3)contains, at the top, an image with lines and edges, at the center an image profile, and at the bottom the profiles of the three quaternionic phases. In phase profiles, we can distinguish between a line (even) and an edge (odd) using the phase (θ). These results are similar to the results reported by Granlund [9] using only a complex phase, because they used an image that changes in one direction.

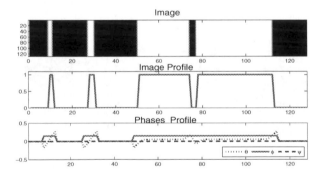

Fig. 3. From top to bottom: image, image profile, and three quaternionic phases: profile, line, and edge

4.1 Quaternionic Analytic Signal

The quaternionic analytic signal in the space domain is defined as [3]

$$f_A^q(x, y) = f(x, y) + if_{\mathbf{H}i}(x, y) + jf_{\mathbf{H}j}(x, y) + kf_{\mathbf{H}k}(x, y), \tag{11}$$

where $f_{\mathbf{H}i}(x, y) = f(x, y) * \frac{1}{\pi x}$ and $f_{\mathbf{H}j}(x, y) = f(x, y) * \frac{1}{\pi y}$ are the partial Hilbert transforms and $f_{\mathbf{H}k}(x, y) = f(x, y) * \frac{1}{\pi^2 xy}$ is the total Hilbert transform. Bülow has shown that the QFT kernel is expressed in terms of the Hilbert transforms. The phases can be computed easily using a 3D rotation matrix $\mathcal{M}$, which can be factored into three rotations, $R = R_x(2\phi), R_z(2\psi), R_y(2\theta)$, in the coordinate axes [3], i.e.,

$$\mathcal{M}(q) = \mathcal{M}(q_1)\mathcal{M}(q_2)\mathcal{M}(q_3) \tag{12}$$
$$q_1 = e^{i\phi}, q_2 = e^{j\theta}, q_3 = e^{k\psi}, \tag{13}$$

$$\mathcal{M}(q) = \begin{pmatrix} a^2 + b^2 - c^2 - d^2 & 2(bc - ad) & 2(bd + ac) \\ 2(bc + ad) & a^2 - b^2 + c^2 - d^2 & 2(cd - ab) \\ 2(bd - ac) & 2(cd + ab) & a^2 - b^2 - c^2 + d^2, \end{pmatrix} \tag{14}$$

where a, b, c and d are defined in the Eq 5. Then, the phases are expressed by the following rules:

$$\psi = -\frac{\arcsin\left(2(bc - ad)\right)}{2} \tag{15}$$

- If $\psi \in]-\frac{\pi}{4}, \frac{\pi}{4}[$, then $\phi = \frac{arg_i(\boldsymbol{q}\mathcal{T}_j(\bar{\boldsymbol{q}}))}{2}$ and $\theta = \frac{arg_j(\mathcal{T}_i(\bar{\boldsymbol{q}})\boldsymbol{q})}{2}$.
- If $\psi = \pm\frac{\pi}{4}$, then select either $\phi=0$ and $\theta = \frac{arg_j(\mathcal{T}_k(\bar{\boldsymbol{q}})\boldsymbol{q})}{2}$ or $\theta=0$ and $\phi = \frac{arg_i(\boldsymbol{q}\mathcal{T}_k(\bar{\boldsymbol{q}}))}{2}$.
- If $e^{i\phi}e^{k\psi}e^{j\theta} = -\boldsymbol{q}$ and $\phi \geq 0$, then $\phi \rightarrow \phi - \pi$.
- If $e^{i\phi}e^{k\psi}e^{j\theta} = -\boldsymbol{q}$ and $\phi < 0$, then $\phi \rightarrow \phi + \pi$.

The phase ranges are $(\phi, \theta, \psi) \in [-\pi, \pi[\times [-\frac{\pi}{2}, \frac{\pi}{2}[\times, \pi[- \times [-\frac{\pi}{4}, \frac{\pi}{4}]$.

4.2   Hilbert Transform Using AF

The main aim of this section is to present a new way to make the computation of the Hilbert transform using the atomic function. The Hilbert transform and the derivative are closely related, and the Hilbert transform can actually be done using a derivative and some convolution $(\star)$ properties[14]:

$$f \star (g \star h) = (f \star g) \star h \tag{16}$$
$$\nabla(f \star g) = \nabla f \star g = f \star \nabla g, \tag{17}$$

where $f(x,y), g(x,y)h(x,y) \in \mathcal{R}^2$, $\nabla = e_1\frac{\partial}{\partial x} + e_2\frac{\partial}{\partial y}$. If $g(x,y) = -\frac{1}{\pi}\log(|x|)$ $\log(|y|)$ where $\log(|x|)$ is the fundamental solution of Laplace equation. Moreover if we use the convolution distribution properties, we can express the Hilbert transform and the partial Hilbert transform (see Eq. 11) as

$$f_{\mathbf{H_i}}(x,y) = \frac{\partial f(x,y)}{\partial x} \star -\frac{1}{\pi}\log(|x|) \tag{18}$$

$$f_{\mathbf{H_j}}(x,y) = \frac{\partial f(x,y)}{\partial y} \star -\frac{1}{\pi}\log(|y|) \tag{19}$$

$$f_{\mathbf{H_k}}(x,y) = \frac{\partial^2 f(x,y)}{\partial x \partial y} \star -\frac{1}{\pi^2}\log(|x|)\log(|y|) \tag{20}$$

and we can use the convolution association property to get the equation of a certain part of the signal in terms of $dup(x)$ (see Eq 3):

$$f_{\mathbf{H_i}}(x,y) = f(x,y) \star \left(dup(x,y)_x \star -\frac{1}{\pi}\log(|x|) \right) \tag{21}$$

$$f_{\mathbf{H_j}}(x,y) = f(x,y) \star \left(dup(x,y)_y \star -\frac{1}{\pi}\log(|y|) \right) \tag{22}$$

$$f_{\mathbf{H_k}}(x,y) = f(x,y) \star \left(dup(x,y)_{xy} \star -\frac{1}{\pi^2}\log(|x|)\log(|y|). \right) \tag{23}$$

The figure 4 shows the $up(x)$ and its Hilbert transform.

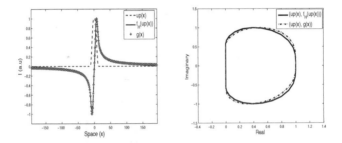

Fig. 4. $up(x)$, its Hilbert transform and Eq 21. Rigth Dot-line $up(x)$(real part) and the Hilbert transform (imaginary).

5   Results

Figure 5 illustrates the convolution of the first derivative, $dup(x,y)$, and a shadow chessboard. The convolution with dup can be used as an oriented change detector with a simple rotation, the convoluted images has a low response in the shadow part.

Figure (6) illustrates an image with lines and geometric objects. In this case, we can use the quaternionic phases to extract different oriented edges of geometric objects or different oriented line textures. The θ and ϕ phases detect lines or edges in some vertical and horizontal directions, while the ψ phase detects the diagonal response and the corners in squares or geometric figures. Even if the geometric objects have lines inside, different illuminations or positions, the edges of each square can be detected in ϕ and θ images. Moreover, in the ϕ phase, the horizontal lines are highlighted, whereas the vertical lines dont appear. The θ phases show a similar result, but in this case the vertical edges and lines are highlighted. In the ψ phase, the vertical lines or edges are highlighted.

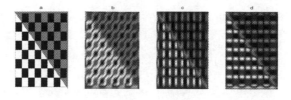

Fig. 5. Convolution of $dup(x, y)$ with the test image. (a) Test image; (b)result of the convolution of the image with $dup(x, y, 0°)$; (c) $dup(x, y, 45°)$; (d) $dup(x, y, 135°)$.

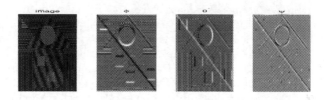

Fig. 6. Image and 2D quaternionic phases. A texture based on lines can be detected or discriminated, and at the same time, the phase information can highlight the edges.

6   Conclusion

We have shown that the $Qup(x, y)$ is useful to detect lines or edges in a specific orientation using the quaternionic phase concept. Additionally, an oriented texture can be chosen using the quaternionic phases. As an initial step, we have shown how to do the image analysis of geometric objects in $\Re^2$ using the symmetry. As in other applications in geometric algebra GA, we can take advantage of the constraints. Since the information from the three phases is independent of illumination changes, algorithms using the quaternionic atomic function can be less sensitive than other methods based on the illumination changes. These results motivated us to find other invariants such as rotation invariants using the Riesz transform. In a future work, we can develop a complete computer vision approach based on GA.

References

1. Kravchenko, V.F., Perez-Meana, H.M., Ponomaryov, V.I.: Adaptive digital processing of multidimensional signals with applications. In: MOSCOW FIZMATLIT (2009)
2. Bayro-Corrochano: Geometric Computing for Wavelet Transforms, Robot Vision, Learning, Control and Action. Springer, London (2010)
3. Bülow, T.: Hypercomplex Spectral Signal Representations for the Processing and Analysis of Images. Christian- Albert, Kiel University. Ph.D Thesis (1999)
4. Jähne, B.: Digital Image Processing. Springer, Germany (2002)
5. Kovesi, P.: Invariant measures of images features from phase information. University of Western Australia. PhD Thesis (1996)

6. Bayro, E.: Geometric Computing for Wavelet Transforms, Robot Vision, Learning, Control and Action. Springer, London (2010)
7. Hestenes, D.: New Foundations for Classical Mechanics, 2nd edn. Kluwer Academic Publishers, Arizona (2002)
8. Josef Bigun.: Vision with Direction. Springer (2006)
9. Granlund, G., Kutsson, H.: Signal Processing for Computer Vision. Lippincott Williams and Wilkins, Philaphia (2002)
10. Moya-Sánchez, E.U., Vázquez-Santacruz, E.: A Geometric Bio-inspired Model for Recognition of Low-Level Structures. In: Honkela, T. (ed.) ICANN 2011, Part II. LNCS, vol. 6792, pp. 429–436. Springer, Heidelberg (2011)
11. Dorts, L., Mann, S.: Geometric algebra: A computational framework for geometrical applications. In: IEEE Computer Graphics ans Applications, pp. 25–31 (2002)
12. Kovesi, P.: Invariant measures of images features from phase information. PhD thesis, University of Western Australia, Autralia (1996)
13. Lennart, W.: Local feature detection by higher order riesz transforms on images. Master thesis, Christian- Albert, Kiel University, Kiel Germany (2008)
14. Svensson, B.: A Multidimensional Filtering Framework with Applications to Local Structure Analysis and Image Enhancement. PhD thesis, Linkoping University, Linkoping, Sweden (2008)
15. Kolodyazhnya, V.M., Rvachev, V.A.: Cybernetics and Systems Analysis, vol. 43 (2007)
16. Treil, S., Petermichl, S., Volberg, A.: Why the riesz transforms are averages of the dyadic shifts? Publ. Mat. 46(6) (2002)
17. Moya-Sánchez, E.U., Bayro-Corrochano, E.: Quaternion Atomic Function Wavelet for Applications in Image Processing. In: Bloch, I., Cesar Jr., R.M. (eds.) CIARP 2010. LNCS, vol. 6419, pp. 346–353. Springer, Heidelberg (2010)
18. Felsberg, M.: Low-level image processing with the structure multivector. PhD thesis, Christian- Albert, Kiel University, Kiel, Germany (2002)

Separation and Classification of Harmonic Sounds for Singing Voice Detection

Martín Rocamora[1] and Alvaro Pardo[2]

[1] Institute of Electrical Engineering - School of Engineering
Universidad de la República, Uruguay
[2] Department of Electrical Engineering - School of Engineering and Technologies
Universidad Católica del Uruguay, Uruguay

Abstract. This paper presents a novel method for the automatic detection of singing voice in polyphonic music recordings, that involves the extraction of harmonic sounds from the audio mixture and their classification. After being separated, sounds can be better characterized by computing features that are otherwise obscured in the mixture. A set of descriptors of typical pitch fluctuations of the singing voice is proposed, that is combined with classical spectral timbre features. The evaluation conducted shows the usefulness of the proposed pitch features and indicates that the approach is a promising alternative for tackling the problem, in particular for not much dense polyphonies where singing voice can be correctly tracked. As an outcome of this work an automatic singing voice separation system is obtained with encouraging results.

1 Introduction

Much research in audio signal processing over the last years has been devoted to music information retrieval, i.e. the extraction of musically meaningful content information from the automatic analysis of an audio recording. This involves diverse music related problems and applications, from computer aided musicology to automatic music transcription and recommendation. Not surprisingly, several research works deal with the singing voice, such as singing voice separation and melody transcription. This kind of research would benefit from a reliable segmentation of a song into singing voice fragments. Furthermore, singing voice segments of a piece are valuable information for music structure analysis.

The goal of this work is to build a computer system for the automatic detection of singing voice in polyphonic music recordings; i.e. classifying each time interval into vocal or non-vocal. The most common approach found in the literature is to extract features from audio signal frames, and then classify them using a statistical classifier. For instance, Mel Frequency Cepstral Coefficientes (MFCC)[1] and Gaussian Mixture Models are applied in [1], which can be considered an example of the standard solution. Several other classifiers have been explored, such as Hidden Markov Models, Artificial Neural Networks and Support Vector Machines. With regards to descriptors, most common features used in previous

---

[1] Section 3.2 describes these classical audio features traditionally used in speech.

L. Alvarez et al. (Eds.): CIARP 2012, LNCS 7441, pp. 707–714, 2012.

work are different ways of characterizing spectral energy distribution. In [2] a study is conducted which concludes that MFCC are the most appropriate among the features reported to be used for the task. Most recent work began to explore other types of information, such as frequency and amplitude modulation features of the sining voice [3], with a limited success.

In our research on the problem a significant effort has been put into the improvement of the standard solution by considering different acoustic features and machine learning techniques. Results indicate that it seems rather difficult to surpass certain performance bound by variations on this approach. For this reason, in this work we propose a different strategy which involves the extraction of harmonic sound sources from the mixture and their individual classification. This pursues a better characterization of the different musical instruments present in the piece, in a way which is not feasible when dealing with the audio mixture.

2   Harmonic Sounds Separation

An existing harmonic sound sources extraction front-end is applied, which is very briefly summarized in what follows. It involves a time-frequency analysis, followed by polyphonic pitch tracking and sound sources separation.

The time-frequency analysis is based on [4], in which the application of the Fan Chirp Transform (FChT) to polyphonic music is introduced. The FChT offers optimal resolution for the components of an harmonic linear chirp, i.e. harmonically related sinusoids with linear frequency modulation. This is well suited for music analysis since many sounds have an harmonic structure and their frequency modulation can be approximated as linear within short time intervals. The FChT can be formulated as [4],

$$X(f, \alpha) = \int_{-\infty}^{\infty} x(t) \, \phi_\alpha'(t) \, e^{-j2\pi f \phi_\alpha(t)} dt, \tag{1}$$

where $\phi_\alpha(t) = (1 + \frac{1}{2}\alpha t) t$, is a time warping function. The parameter α is the variation rate of the instantaneous frequency of the analysis chirp.

In addition, based on the FChT analysis, a pitch salience representation called F0gram is proposed in [4], which reveals the evolution of pitch contours in the signal, as depicted in Figures 1 and 3. Given the FChT of a frame $X(f, \alpha)$, salience (or prominence) of fundamental frequency f_0 is obtained by summing the log-spectrum at the positions of the corresponding harmonics,

$$\rho(f_0, \alpha) = \frac{1}{n_H} \sum_{i=1}^{n_H} \log |X(if_0, \alpha)|, \tag{2}$$

where n_H is the number of harmonics considered. Polyphonic pitch tracking is carried out by means of the technique described in [5], which is based on unsupervised clustering of F0gram peaks. Finally, each of the identified pitch contours are separated from the sound mixture. To do this, the FChT spectrum is band-pass filtered at the location of the harmonics of the f_0 value, and the inverse FChT is performed to obtain the waveform of the separated sound.

3 Audio Features

3.1 Pitch Related Features

In a musical piece, pitch variations are used by a singer to convey different expressive intentions and to stand out from the accompaniment. Most typical expressive features are *vibrato*, a periodic pitch modulation, and *glissando*, a slide between two pitches [6]. Although this is by no means an exclusive feature of the singing voice, in a music performance where singing voice takes part as a leading instrument, continuous modulations of its fundamental frequency are of common use. In addition, the accompaniment frequently comprises fixed-pitch musical instruments, such as piano or fretted strings. Thus, low frequency modulations of a pitch contour are considered as an indication of singing voice. Nevertheless, since other musical instruments can produce such modulations, this feature shall be combined with other sources of information.

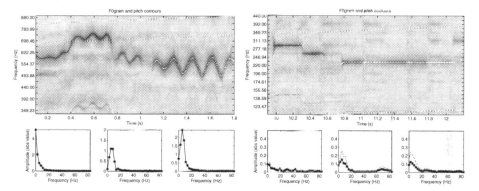

Fig. 1. Vocal notes with vibrato and low frequency modulation (*left*) and saxophone notes without pitch fluctuations (*right*) for two audio files from the MIREX melody extraction test set. Summary spectrum $c[k]$ is depicted at the bottom for each contour.

In order to describe the pitch variations, the contour is regarded as a time dependent signal and the following procedure is applied. The pitch values $f_0[n]$ are represented in a logarithmic scale using a 16th semitone grid. After removing the mean value, the contour is processed by a sliding window and a spectral analysis is applied to each signal frame i using the Discrete Cosine Transform,[2]

$$c[k]^i = \sum_{n=1}^{N} f_0[n]^i \cos \frac{\pi(2n-1)(k-1)}{2N}, \quad k = 1 \dots N.$$

Frame length is set to ~ 180 ms, to have two frequency components in the range of a typical vibrato. Frames are highly overlapped, using a hop size of ~ 20 ms.

---

[2] Normalized by $1/\sqrt{N}$ for $k = 1$ and by $\sqrt{2/N}$ for $k = 2, \dots, N$.

After analysing all the frames, the $c[k]^i$ coefficients are summed up in a single spectrum $\tilde{c}[k]$ as follows. Since we are interested in high values in low frequency, the maximum absolute value for each frequency bin is taken, namely $\hat{c}[k]$. However, it was observed that this over estimates frames with high low energy values that occasionally arise in noisy contours due to tracking errors. Thus, the median of the absolute value of each frequency bin $\bar{c}[k]$ is also considered and both spectrums are combined as,

$$\tilde{c}[k] = \frac{\hat{c}[k] + \bar{c}[k]}{2}, \quad \text{where} \begin{cases} \hat{c}[k] = \max_i\{|c[k]^i|\} \\ \bar{c}[k] = \text{median}_i\{|c[k]^i|\}. \end{cases}$$

Examples of the behaviour of $\tilde{c}[k]$ are given in Figure 1. Then, two features are derived from this spectrum. The low frequency power (LFP) is computed as the sum of absolute values up to 20 Hz ($k = k_L$). Since well-behaved pitch contours do not exhibit prominent components in the high frequency range, a low to high frequency power ratio is considered (PR), which tries to exploit this property,

$$\text{LFP} = \sum_{k=1}^{k_L} \tilde{c}[k], \quad \text{PR} = \frac{\text{LFP}}{\sum_{k_L+1}^{N} \tilde{c}[k]}. \tag{3}$$

Besides, two additional pitch related features are computed. One of them is simply the extent of pitch variation,

$$\Delta f_0 = \max_n\{f_0[n]\} - \min_n\{f_0[n]\}. \tag{4}$$

The other is the mean value of pitch salience in the contour,

$$\Gamma_{f_0} = \text{mean}_n\{\rho(f_0[n])\}. \tag{5}$$

This gives an indication of the prominence of the sound source, but it also includes some additional information. As noted in [4], pitch salience computation favours harmonic sounds with high number of harmonics, such as the singing voice. Besides, as done in [4], a *pitch preference* weighting function is introduced that highlights most probable values for a singing voice in the f_0 selected range.

3.2   Mel-Frequency Cepstral Coefficients

Mel-frequency Cepstral Coefficients (MFCC) are one of the most common features used in speech and music modeling for describing the spectral timbre of audio signals. The implementation of MFCC is based on [7]. Frame length is set to 25 ms, using a Hamming window and a hop size of 10 ms. The signal frame is processed by a filter bank of 40 bands, whose center frequencies are equally-spaced according to the mel scale (approximately linear in log frequency). An FFT is applied and log-power on each band is computed. The elements of these vectors are highly correlated so a DCT is applied and only the 13 lowest order coefficients are retained. Temporal integration is done by computing median and standard deviation of the frame-based coefficients within the whole pitch contour. In order to capture temporal information first order derivatives of the coefficients are also included, for a total of 50 audio features.

4   Classification Methods

4.1   Training Database

An advantage of the proposed method over the classical polyphonic audio approach is that monophonic audio clips can be used for training, that is music in which only a single musical instrument takes part. There is a lot of monophonic music available and collecting such a database requires much less effort than manually labeling songs. A training database was built based on more than 2000 audio files, comprising singing voice on one hand and typical musical instruments found in popular music on the other.

The procedure for building the database involves the FChT analysis followed by pitch tracking and sound source extraction. Finally the audio features are computed for each extracted sound. In this way, a database of 13598 audio sounds was obtained, where vocal/non-vocal classes are exactly balanced.

4.2   Classifiers and Training

First of all, to assess the discrimination ability of the proposed pitch related features, histograms and box-plots are presented in Figure 2 for the training patterns. Although these features should be combined with other sources of information, it seems they are informative about the class of the sound. In addition, using only the proposed pitch related features, a Polynomial Kernel SVM operating as a linear discriminant reaches 93.7% of correctly classified instances when trained and tested by 10-fold cross validation (CV) on the training data.[3]

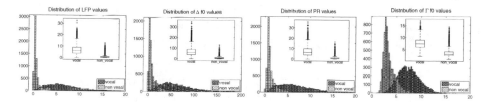

Fig. 2. Analysis of the pitch related features on the training database

A feature selection experiment on the pitch related features using the Correlation Based selection method and the Best First searching algorithm [8] indicates all features provide some relevant information. An SVM classifier with a Gaussian RBF Kernel was selected for further classification experiments. Optimal values for the γ kernel parameter and the penalty factor C were selected by grid-search. Performance estimated by 10-fold CV on the training set is presented in Table 1 for the MFCC set and by adding the pitch features. Some remarks can be made on these results. Firstly, the performance is encouraging, though it is based on training data. Then, pitch related features seem to contribute to the discrimination between classes (considering that an increase of 1%

---

[3] All classification and selection experiments are performed using Weka software [8].

Table 1. Percentage of correctly classified instances and confusion matrix for each set of features, obtained by 10-fold CV on the training dataset using an SVM classifier

class	MFCC classified as vocal	MFCC classified as non-vocal	MFCC + Pitch classified as vocal	MFCC + Pitch classified as non-vocal
vocal	6671	128	6740	59
non-vocal	123	6676	38	6761
performance	98.2%		99.3%	

is more relevant in a high performance level). Finally, the confusion matrix is well balanced, so there seems not to be a significant classification bias.

4.3 Automatic Labeling of Polyphonic Music

In order to deal with polyphonic music the following procedure is applied. The audio is processed with the sound source extraction front-end. Each extracted sound is classified based on MFCC and pitch features. A time interval of the polyphonic audio file is labeled as vocal if any of the identified pitch contours it contains is classified as vocal. This is shown in the examples of Figure 3.

When manual labeling a musical piece, very short pure instrumental regions are usually ignored. For this reason, the automatic labels are further processed and two vocal regions are merged if they are separated by less than 500 ms. It is important to notice that manually generated labels include unvoiced sounds (such as fricative consonants). Although this type of sounds are shrunk when singing, this constitute a systematic source of errors of the proposed approach.

The analysis of pitch fluctuations described in section 3.1 imposes a certain minimum contour length, so a threshold of approximately 200 ms is applied and pitch fluctuations analysis is avoided for shorter segments.

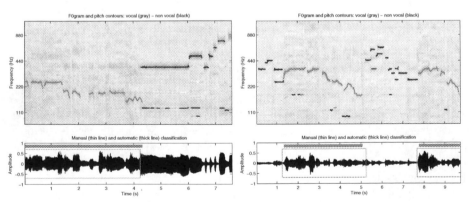

Fig. 3. Examples of automatic vocal labeling. *Left:* Fragment of the song *For no one* by The Beatles. A singing voice in the beginning is followed by a French horn solo. There is a soft accompaniment of bass and tambourine. *Right:* Blues song excerpt from the testing dataset. It comprises singing voice, piano, bass and drums. Singing voice notes are correctly distinguished from piano and bass notes that are also detected.

5   Evaluation and Results

An evaluation was conducted to estimate the performance of the singing voice detection approach applied on polyphonic music audio files, and to assess the usefulness of the proposed pitch related features. For this purpose a testing database of 30 manually labeled audio fragments of 10 seconds length was utilized. Music was extracted from Magnatune[4] recordings labeled as: blues, country, funk, pop, rock and soul. A few musical genres were avoided, such as heavy-metal or electronica, because of the high density of sources and the ubiquity of prominent noise-like sounds, what makes the pitch tracking rather troublesome. Classification results are presented in Figure 4. Performance is measured as the percentage of time in which the manual and automatic labeling match. The addition of pitch information produces a noticeable performance increase in the overall results, as well as for almost every file of the database. The performance of the standard approach, MFCC of the audio mixture and an SVM classifier [2], is also reported.

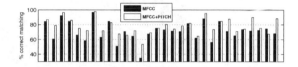

	matching
MFCC	71.3%
MFCC + Pitch	78.0%
MFCC [2]	73.7%

Fig. 4. Classification performance as percentage of time in which the manual and automatic vocal labels match, for both set of features and for the standard approach

6   Discussion and Future Work

A novel approach for singing voice detection in polyphonic music was introduced that makes use of an harmonic sound sources extraction front-end [4,5]. The extracted sounds are then classified based on the classical MFCC coefficients and on some new features devised to capture characteristic of typical singing voice pitch contours. Results obtained indicate that the proposed features provide additional information for singing voice discrimination. Besides, an advantage of the sound source separation approach is that it enables the application of other acoustic features for describing isolated sounds that are otherwise obscured in the polyphonic sound mixture (e.g. the estimation of formants will be tackled in future work). Although the sound sources extraction introduces new challenges, the proposed approach seems a feasible alternative to the standard solution.

As an interesting outcome of this research an automatic singing voice separation system is obtained which yields very promising results, mainly for not much dense polyphonies where singing voice can be correctly tracked. Examples of the automatic singing voice separation are provided in Figure 5, for the audio excerpts previously introduced.[5] The improvement of this tool and its application to different music scenarios are the most appealing ideas for future research.

---

[4] http://magnatune.com/

[5] Audio and more examples at http://iie.fing.edu.uy/~rocamora/mscthesis/

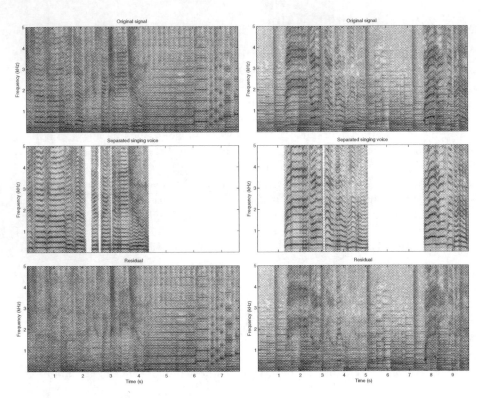

Fig. 5. Automatic singing voice separation for the audio introduced in Figure 3

References

1. Tsai, W.H., Wang, H.M.: Automatic singer recognition of popular music recordings via estimation and modeling of solo vocal signal. IEEE Transactions on Speech and Audio Processing 14(1) (2006)
2. Rocamora, M., Herrera, P.: Comparing audio descriptors for singing voice detection in music audio files. In: 11th Brazilian Symposium on Computer Music, São Paulo, Brazil (2007)
3. Regnier, L., Peeters, G.: Singing voice detection in music tracks using direct voice vibrato detection. In: ICASSP IEEE Int. Conf., pp. 1685–1688 (2009)
4. Cancela, P., López, E., Rocamora, M.: Fan chirp transform for music representation. In: 13th DAFx-10 Int. Conf. on Digital Audio Effects, Graz, Austria (2010)
5. Rocamora, M., Cancela, P.: Pitch tracking in polyphonic audio by clustering local fundamental frequency estimates. In: 9th Brazilian AES Audio Engineering Congress, São Paulo, Brazil (2011)
6. Sundberg, J.: The science of the singing voice. De Kalb, Il. Northern Illinois University Press (1987)
7. Ellis, D.P.W.: PLP and RASTA (and MFCC, and inversion) in Matlab (2005)
8. Witten, I.H., Frank, E.: Data Mining: Practical machine learning tools and techniques, 2nd edn. Morgan Kaufmann, San Francisco (2005)

Online Signature Verification Based on Legendre Series Representation. Consistency Analysis of Different Feature Combinations

Marianela Parodi and Juan Carlos Gómez

Laboratory for System Dynamics and Signal Processing,
FCEIA, Universidad Nacional de Rosario, CIFASIS, CONICET
{parodi,gomez}@cifasis-conicet.gov.ar

Abstract. In this paper, orthogonal polynomial series are used to approximate the time functions associated to the signatures and the coefficients in these series are used as features to model them. A novel consistency factor is proposed to quantify the discriminative power of different combinations of time functions related to the signing process. Pen coordinates, incremental variation of pen coordinates and pen pressure are analyzed for two different signature styles, namely, Western signatures and Chinese signatures from a publicly available Signature Database. Two state-of-the-art classifiers, namely, Support Vector Machines and Random Forests are used in the verification experiments. The obtained error rates are comparable to results reported over the same signature datasets in a recent signature verification competition.

Keywords: Online Signature Verification, Legendre Polynomials, Consistency Factor.

1 Introduction

Signature verification is the most popular method for identity verification. It is a non-invasive biometric technique, and people are familiar with the use of signatures for identity verification in their everyday life.

Electronic pen-input devices, such as digitizer tablets and PDAs, are gaining popularity for signature acquisition in several daily applications, increasing the interest in online signature verification. In online systems, the signature is parameterized by different discrete time functions, *e.g.*, pen coordinates, pressure and inclination angles. Researchers have long argued about the effectiveness of these different time functions for verification purposes. During the First International Signature Verification Competition (SVC2004), the results using only pen coordinates outperformed those adding pen pressure and inclination angles [1]. Since then, several works have been presented concerning the best set of features to model the signatures. A desirable property for any feature is that it must have high consistency. The feature values of the genuine signatures should be close to each other while the ones of genuine and forged signatures should be not. A consistency model is introduced in [2], where several features are compared. Pen coordinates and some derived features proved to be the most reliable

L. Alvarez et al. (Eds.): CIARP 2012, LNCS 7441, pp. 715–723, 2012.

ones. In [3], the authors assert that using pen coordinates leads to better results than adding pen pressure. On the other hand, some works showed improvements when combining pen coordinates with pen pressure and inclination angles [4]. The conflicting results observed in the literature and the lack of a widely used consistency model, make the discussion still open. Moreover, most of the works do not consider the cultural origin of the signatures.

The main contributions of this paper are the following:
- A new feature extraction approach based on Legendre series representation of the time functions associated to the signatures is proposed. To the best of the authors' knowledge this is the first time that this approach is used in the context of signature verification.
- A novel consistency factor is proposed to quantify the discriminative power of different combinations of the time functions associated to the signing process. The pros and cons of these different combinations are analyzed.
- The experiments are performed on the most recent signature datasets, containing Western and Chinese signatures, which have been used in the latest signature verification competition. Two state-of-the-art classifiers, namely, Support Vector Machines (SVMs) and Random Forests (RFs), are used to perform the verification experiments. For the results, the EER (Equal Error Rate) and the cost of the log-likelihood ratios $\hat{C}_{llr}$ are reported.

2   Feature Extraction

Several features have been proposed for online signature verification. In this paper, features composed by the orthogonal polynomial approximation coefficients of the different time functions associated to the signatures are proposed.

Under certain conditions, a function f in an inner product space $H([a, b])$ can be uniquely represented by $f = \sum_{i=0}^{\infty} \alpha_i L_i$, where $\{L_i\}_{i=0}^{\infty}$ are orthonormal basis and $\alpha_i = \langle f, L_i \rangle$, where $\langle \cdot, \cdot \rangle$ stands for the inner product.

It is not difficult to prove that the best (in the sense of the metric induced by the inner product) approximation of $f \in H([a, b])$ in an N-dimensional subspace is given by

$$f \approx \sum_{i=0}^{N} \alpha_i L_i \ . \tag{1}$$

The idea here is to approximate the time functions measured during the acquisition of the signature by a finite series expansion in orthonormal polynomials in the interval $[0, 1]$, and to use their coefficients as features. Particularly, orthonormal Legendre polynomials are considered as the basis functions L_i in this paper.

Since the time functions $f(t)$ are unknown, the coefficients in (1) cannot be computed as $\alpha_i = \langle f, L_i \rangle$, but rather they have to be estimated from a set of M (usually larger than $N + 1$) samples of the function at the time instants $\{t_1, t_2, \cdots, t_M\}$, resorting to least squares estimation techniques.

A similar approach to represent handwritten symbols but using function moments instead of the corresponding series expansions was presented in [5].

3   Consistency Measure

A desirable property for a feature is its consistency. Features associated to genuine signatures should be close to each other while distances between features associated to genuine and forged signatures should be relatively large. A measure of consistency based on the features would be difficult to compute since they may have different lengths. It is then more reasonable to define a consistency measure based on the distances among features and not on the features themselves. In this paper, the consistency of a given feature will be computed based on the statistics of the intraclass (for the genuine signature class) and interclass (between the genuine and forged signature classes) distances. A consistency factor d, for each writer, could then be defined as follows:

$$ d = \frac{\mu_D(C_g, C_f) - \mu_D(C_g, C_g)}{\sqrt{\sigma_D^2(C_g, C_g)} + \sqrt{\sigma_D^2(C_g, C_f)}}, \tag{2} $$

where C_g and C_f stand for the genuine and the forged classes, respectively, and where $\mu_D(C_g, C_g)$ and $\sigma_D^2(C_g, C_g)$, and $\mu_D(C_g, C_f)$ and $\sigma_D^2(C_g, C_f)$ are the sample means and sample variances of the genuine intraclass distances and the genuine-forged interclass distances, respectively.

The consistency factor in (2) is normalized in such a way that, under the assumption of Gaussian distributions for the involved distances, it equals 1 when $\mu_D(C_g, C_f)$ and $\mu_D(C_g, C_g)$ are separated by the sum of the respective standard deviations. This is illustrated in Fig. 1. The larger the consistency factor, the more consistent the features are. A slightly different definition for the consistency measure is presented in [2].

4   Evaluation Protocol

The publicly available SigComp2011 Dataset [6] is used. It has two separate datasets, one containing genuine and forged Western signatures (Dutch ones) and the other one containing genuine and forged Chinese signatures. The available forgeries are skilled forgeries, which are simulated signatures in which forgers (different writers than the reference one) are allowed to practice the reference signature for as long as they deem it necessary. The data was collected from

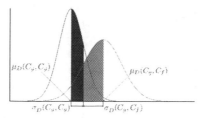

Fig. 1. Genuine intraclass distance distribution (blue) and genuine-forged interclass distance distribution (grey)

realistic and forensically relevant scenarios. The signatures were acquired using a ballpoint pen on paper (WACOM Intuos3 A3 Wide USB Pen Tablet), which is the natural writing process.

The measured data consists of three discrete time functions: pen coordinates x and y, and pen pressure p. In addition to the raw data, the incremental variation of the x and y pen coordinates (Δx and Δy, respectively) are computed. In [2] and [3] the authors list x,y, Δx and Δy among the most reliable features.

In [2], the most common time functions were individually compared based on a consistency model. In this paper, a novel consistency factor is proposed and several combinations of time functions (modeled by the Legendre series coefficients) are tested. In particular, the following combinations will be considered to compute their consistency factors and to assess the verification performance: *i.* pen coordinates: x, y; *ii.* pen coordinates and pen pressure: x, y, p; *iii.* incremental variation of pen coordinates: $\Delta x, \Delta y$; *iv.* incremental variation of pen coordinates and pen pressure: $\Delta x, \Delta y, p$; *v.* pen coordinates and incremental variation of pen coordinates: $x, y, \Delta x, \Delta y$; *vi.* pen coordinates, incremental variation of pen coordinates and pen pressure: $x, y, \Delta x, \Delta y, p$.

4.1   Consistency Computation

The consistency factor quantifies the discriminative power of a particular combination of time functions. Based on this value, it is possible to select the most suitable combination of time functions to be used in a verification system. This selection has to be done in the training stage. The consistency factor should then be computed with the signatures available during this stage. It is the common case that, when training a verification system, skilled forgeries are not available. For this reason, the consistency factor for a particular writer will be computed using the genuine signatures corresponding to all the remaining writers as forgeries (usually called random forgeries). This will result in larger consistency factors compared with the ones that would be obtained using skilled forgeries for each writer. In any case, since the used database does contain skilled forgeries, the consistency factor will also be computed using them, for comparison purposes.

4.2   Verification Performance Evaluation

Two well known state-of-the-art classifiers, SVMs [7] and RFs [8], are used to assess the verification performance of the different time function combinations.

The datasets in the SigComp2011 database are divided into two sets, namely, the Training Set and the Testing Set (see [6] for a detailed description). For each of the datasets, namely, Dutch and Chinese, the optimization of the meta-parameters of the system is performed over the corresponding Training Set while the corresponding Testing Set is used for independent testing purposes.

The tuning parameters to adjust are the order of the Legendre polynomials[1] and the internal parameters of the classifiers. For SVMs, the parameters[2] are

---

[1] To select the optimal order, this parameter was varied from 1 to 25.
[2] Optimized, within the range 10^{-10} to 10^{10}, using tune.svm of the e1071 Package [9].

the scale σ^2 in the Radial Basis Functions (RBF) kernel[3], and the regularization parameter C. For RFs, the parameters are the number of trees to grow and the number of randomly selected splitting variables to be considered at each node.[4]

To obtain statistically significant results, a 5-fold cross-validation (5-fold CV) is performed over the Testing Set to estimate the testing errors. For each instance of the 5-fold CV, a signature model is trained for each writer, using only genuine signatures. To train the signature model for a particular writer, the genuine class was formed with the genuine signatures of the writer in the corresponding training set of the 5-fold CV, while the forged class was formed with the genuine signatures of all the remaining writers in the dataset available in the same training set. The genuine and forged signatures of the writer under consideration in the corresponding testing set of the 5-fold CV are used for testing. Only skilled forgeries are considered to calculate the testing errors. Random forgeries are not considered for testing since they seldom appear in real situations.

To evaluate the performance, the EER is calculated, using the Bosaris toolkit [10], from the Detection Error TradeOff (DET) Curve as the point in the curve where the FRR (False Rejection Rate) equals the FAR (False Acceptance Rate). The cost of the log-likelihood ratios $\hat{C}_{llr}$ and its minimal possible value $\hat{C}_{llr}^{min}$ [10] are computed using the toolkit as well. A smaller value of $\hat{C}_{llr}^{min}$ indicates a better performance of the system. Using these measurements to evaluate the performance of a signature verification system is proposed in [6], where the importance of computing the likelihood ratios was highlighted since they make Forensic Handwriting Experts (FHEs) able to combine the results obtained from an automatic verification system with other evidence presented in a court of law.

5   Results and Discussion

Figure 2 shows the boxplots associated to the consistency factors for each feature combination over the 54 writers for the Dutch dataset (first row) and over the 10 writers for the Chinese dataset (second row).

The consistency factors computed resorting to random and skilled forgeries lead to the same conclusion that the most consistent (largest value of the consistency factor) time function combination is $\Delta x, \Delta y, p$, for both datasets. This agreement is important since, in real situations, the verification system can be subjected to skilled forgeries but the decisions about which combination is to be used must be necessarily made based on consistency factors computed with random forgeries, since skilled forgeries are usually not available for training.

The pen pressure, when combined with the other considered time functions, improves the consistency factor of the combinations, for both datasets. In addition, the pen coordinates x and y are not included in the most consistent combination ($\Delta x, \Delta y, p$). This suggests that, based on the consistency factor, using the pen coordinates x and y is not a good choice for any of the datasets.

---

[3] The RBF kernel is defined as $K(\mathbf{x}(n), \mathbf{x}(k)) = e^{\|\mathbf{x}(n) - \mathbf{x}(k)\|^2 / \sigma^2}$.

[4] In general, the default values are a good choice for these parameters.

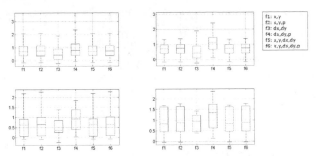

Fig. 2. Boxplots for the consistency factor: over the 54 Dutch authors, computed with skilled (top left) and random (top right) forgeries; over the 10 Chinese authors, computed with skilled (bottom left) and random (bottom right) forgeries

Table 1 presents the verification results for the Dutch and Chinese datasets.[5] In addition to making the combination more consistent, incorporating the pen pressure improves the performance in most of the cases for Dutch and Chinese data, independently of the classifier being used. This is in agreement with the ideas presented in [4], where the authors stated that adding pen pressure could improved the results depending on the classification algorithm. In addition, in almost all the cases, using the computed sequences Δx and Δy leads to a better performance than using directly the measured sequences x and y, which are also less consistent. These experimental results agree with the ones in [2], where the pen coordinates and the speed are listed among the most reliable features.

The results obtained with RF are better than those obtained with SVM. In addition, for some time functions, the results depend on the classifier being used. For Dutch data, whenever using pen coordinates together with SVMs, the performance is strongly degraded, then they are not robust against the different classifiers. For Chinese data, x and y coordinates appear to be more robust than Δx and Δy, nevertheless, whenever using the pen pressure, the results improve, then pen pressure is robust against the different classifiers. The consistency factor, on the other hand, does not depend on the classifier being used. Then, it can be used to indicate the potential of a particular combination for being effective in the verification stage, independently of the classification method.

The position information is likely to be better suited, in the sense of the verification errors, for the Chinese data than for the Dutch data. Chinese signature style is, in most of the cases, close to the Chinese handwriting style, consisting of one or more multi-trace ideograms, while Western signatures can adopt several different styles. Since Chinese characters usually convey their meaning through pictorial resemblance to a physical object, it is likely that the position information has more discriminative power than in the case of Dutch data.

---

[5] The following tuning parameters were used: SVM: $\sigma^2 = 10^7$ and $C = 1$ (Dutch dataset), and $\sigma^2 = 10^7$ and $C = 10$ (Chinese dataset); RF: number of trees = 500, number of randomly selected splitting variables = $\sqrt{P}$, where P is the dimension of the feature vector, and Legendre polynomials: $N = 21$ (both datasets).

Table 1. Verification results for the Dutch (left) and Chinese (right) Datasets

Features	Class.	Dutch Dataset			Chinese Dataset		
		EER	$\hat{C}_{llr}$	$\hat{C}_{llr}^{min}$	EER	$\hat{C}_{llr}$	$\hat{C}_{llr}^{min}$
x,y	SVM	12.32	0.461	0.3832	12.67	0.5222	0.4419
	RF	8.94	0.3265	0.288	12.18	0.4587	0.3808
x,y,p	SVM	12.39	0.4322	0.373	11.03	0.4164	0.3435
	RF	7.39	0.2751	0.2396	10.32	0.3849	0.3159
$\Delta x,\Delta y$	SVM	8.55	0.3482	0.3032	14.42	0.5467	0.4458
	RF	5.92	0.2648	0.2035	10.8	0.4	0.3266
$\Delta x,\Delta y,p$	SVM	7.63	0.3501	0.2657	12.74	0.5086	0.4187
	RF	**5.91**	**0.237**	**0.195**	11.09	0.3938	0.2994
$x,y,\Delta x,\Delta y$	SVM	12.35	0.461	0.3833	13.44	0.5084	0.4418
	RF	6.46	0.2497	0.2122	11.83	0.4293	0.354
$x,y,\Delta x,\Delta y,p$	SVM	12.54	0.4478	0.3744	10.8	0.4393	0.3696
	RF	7.24	0.2676	0.251	**10.03**	**0.36**	**0.2969**

System	Acc.	$\hat{C}_{llr}$	$\hat{C}_{llr}^{min}$	Acc.	$\hat{C}_{llr}$	$\hat{C}_{llr}^{min}$
commercial	96.27	0.2589	0.1226	93.17	0.4134	0.2179
1st. non-commercial	93.49	0.4928	0.2375	84.81	0.5651	0.3511

The best result for the Dutch data is obtained using the $\Delta x,\Delta y,p$ combination. This makes sense since pen coordinates are not reliable for this data, and adding the pen pressure improves the results. This also confirms what the consistency factor is indicating, being $\Delta x,\Delta y,p$ the most consistent combination. The best result for the Chinese data is obtained combining all the time functions available, viz, $x,y,\Delta x,\Delta y,p$. Despite the fact that the most consistent combination is the one containing only $\Delta x,\Delta y$ and p, Chinese signatures appear to be more complex than Dutch ones, then it is not surprising that more features are needed to model the signature, in order to reach better verification results.

A straightforward relationship between the consistency of the features and the corresponding verification performance can be observed. For instance, adding the pen pressure results in a larger consistency factor and in a better verification performance. It was also argued that x and y coordinates are not consistent and results using the incremental coordinates Δx and Δy outperform them. This close relationship is also observed in the case of the most consistent combination for the Dutch data $(\Delta x,\Delta y,p)$ which is the best one in the sense of the verification results as well. On the other hand, the combination achieving the best verification results for the Chinese data $(x,y,\Delta x,\Delta y,p)$ is not the most consistent one. This is probably due to the complexity of this data as mentioned above.

For the purposes of comparison, the results for the best commercial and non-commercial systems in the SigComp2011 competition are included in the last two rows of Table 1. Even tough the results are not as good as the corresponding to the best commercial system ($xyzmo$, see [6]), they would have ranked first among the non-commercial systems and second among all the participants. Finally, the results for the Dutch signatures are better than those for the Chinese ones, confirming the observations in [6] and indicating that Chinese data is more challenging and that a lot of research has to be done on this type of data.

6   Conclusions

A novel consistency factor was proposed to quantify the discriminative power of different combinations of time functions related to the signing process. Several combinations were studied for two different signature styles, namely, Western and Chinese, of the most recent publicly available Signature Database. The proposed consistency factor proved to be well suited since it is robust against skilled forgeries and a close relationship between its value and the verification performance associated to a time function combination can be found.

The experiments showed that combining the pen pressure with the other time functions makes the combination more consistent and leads to a better verification performance for both datasets, independently of the classifier being used. In addition, in most of the cases, using Δx and Δy leads to a better performance than using directly x and y, which are also less consistent.

The $\Delta x, \Delta y, p$ combination achieved the best verification performance for the Dutch data, and resulted to be the most consistent combination as well. For the Chinese data, the $x, y, \Delta x, \Delta y, p$ combination achieved the best verification results. Although this is not the most consistent combination, it is not surprising that more features are needed to model Chinese signatures since they appear to be more complex than Dutch ones.

The results obtained with RF are better than the ones obtained with SVM, for both signature styles. Nevertheless, since the consistency factor does not depend on the classifier being used, it indicates the potential of a particular combination for the verification, independently of the classification method.

The use of Legendre polynomials to model the signatures proved to be a good choice, resulting in verification performances comparable to those of other state-of-the-art verification systems, tested on the same datasets. In addition, the proposed signature model would allow for a dimensionality reduction with respect to the case of using all the points in the time functions.

References

1. Yeung, D.-Y., Chang, H., Xiong, Y., George, S.E., Kashi, R.S., Matsumoto, T., Rigoll, G.: SVC2004: First International Signature Verification Competition. In: Zhang, D., Jain, A.K. (eds.) ICBA 2004. LNCS, vol. 3072, pp. 16–22. Springer, Heidelberg (2004)
2. Lei, H., Govindaraju, V.: A Comparative Study on the Consistency of Features in On-line Signature Verification. Pattern Recogn. Lett. 147, 2483–2489 (2005)
3. Kholmatov, A., Yanikoglu, B.: Identity Authentication Using Improved Online Signature Verification Method. Pattern Recogn. Lett. 26, 2400–2408 (2005)
4. Muramatsu, D., Matsumoto, T.: Effectiveness of Pen Pressure, Azimuth, and Altitude Features for Online Signature Verification. In: Lee, S.-W., Li, S.Z. (eds.) ICB 2007. LNCS, vol. 4642, pp. 503–512. Springer, Heidelberg (2007)

5. Golubitsky, O., Watt, S.M.: Distance-Based Classification of Handwritten Symbols. Int. Journal of Doc. Anal. and Recogn. 13, 133–146 (2010)
6. Liwicki, M., Malik, M.I., den Heuvel, C.E., Chen, X., Berger, C., Stoel, R., Blumenstein, M., Found, B.: Signature Verification Competition for Online and Offline Skilled Forgeries (SigComp 2011). In: Int. Conf. on Doc. Anal. and Recogn. (2011)
7. Vapnik, V.: The Nature of Statistical Learning Theory. Springer, NY (1995)
8. Breiman, L.: Random Forests. Technical Report, Statistics Department, University of California, Berkeley (2001)
9. Dimitriadou, E., Hornik, K., Leisch, F., Meyer, D., Weingessel, A.: Misc. Functions of the Department of Statistics (e1071). TU Wien (2010)
10. Brümmer, N., du Preez, J.: Application-Independent Evaluation of Speaker Detection. Comput. Speech and Lang. 20, 230–275 (2006)

Gaussian Selection for Speaker Recognition Using Cumulative Vectors

Flavio J. Reyes Díaz, José Ramón Calvo de Lara, and Gabriel Hernández-Sierra

Advanced Technologies Application Center
{freyes,jcalvo,gsierra}@cenatav.co.cu
http://www.cenatav.co.cu

Abstract. Speaker recognition systems frequently use GMM - MAP method for modeling speakers. This method represents a speaker using a Gaussian mixture. However in this mixture not all the Gaussian components are truly representative of the speaker. In order to remove the model redundancy, this work proposes a Gaussian selection method to achieve a new GMM model only with the more representative Gaussian components. Speaker verification experiments applying the proposal show a similar performance to baseline; however the speaker models have a reduction of 80 % regarding the speaker model used for baseline. The application of this Gaussian selection method in real or embedded speaker verification systems could be very useful for reducing computational and memory cost.

Keywords: speaker verification, gaussian components selection, cumulative vector.

1 Introduction

Speaker recognition state of the art approaches are mainly based on statistical modeling of the acoustical space. Speaker utterances information has been modeled using the Gaussian Mixture Model-Universal Background model (GMM-UBM) Reynolds's paradigm [1]. The usual approach is to train an UBM model, through the estimation of a large number of "Gaussian components", using as much data as possible from many different speakers of impostor's population. Then, each GMM speaker model can be adapted from the UBM using much less data through Maximum a Posteriori (MAP) adaptation of the UBM means [2], while variance and weight are unchanged.

GMM-UBM method includes a natural hierarchy between the UBM and each speaker model; for each UBM Gaussian component, there is a corresponding adapted component in the GMM-UBM speaker model. In real or embedded applications these method is not efficient enough because there are some aspects that increase the computational and memory cost:

(1) The GMM-UBM speaker model has a high number of Gaussian components, commonly M= 1024 or 2048, because the MAP adaptation from UBM to speaker data uses all the UBM Gaussian components.

L. Alvarez et al. (Eds.): CIARP 2012, LNCS 7441, pp. 724–731, 2012.

(2) The GMM-UBM speaker model has only some Gaussian components that represent better the acoustic space of each speaker utterance and the rest are redundant, in other words:

    a) A sub-set of Gaussian components represents better the speaker utterance (best discriminative for the target)

    b) Another subset of components represents better the utterances of many speakers (non discriminative between targets)

    c) The rest of the components represents better utterances of other speakers (discriminative for impostors)

So, it is convenient to apply some Gaussian components selection method, in order to reduce this redundancy and to bring more effective classification methods, mainly in front of real and embedded applications, and to reduce the storage size of the models, too.

Well known and more extended criterion is proposed by Reynolds et al. in [1] which performs at the verification stage, a selection of Gaussian components from the GMM-UBM target model, using the top-C "better classified gaussian components" of the UBM for each feature vector of test signal, creating a sub-model with R components for each feature vector, obtaining as many sub-models as feature vectors contain a test utterance. In this variant it is possible to perform a reuse of Gaussian components in different sub-models causing an increase of the computational load and runtime of the verification stage; this method is used in our work as a baseline for comparison.

A recent article of Saeidi et al. [3] refers a good overview of previous works that deal with another Gaussian selection in GMM models for speaker recognition systems:

    - Auckenthaler and Mason [4] applied UBM-like hash model; for each speaker Gaussian component, there is a shortlist of indices of the expected best scoring components of UBM model.

    - Xiang and Berger [5] construct a tree structure for the UBM and multilevel MAP adaptation is used for generating the speaker model with a tree structure. In the verification phase, target speaker scores and UBM scores are combined using an MLP neural network.

    - Kinnunen, T. et al. [6] pre-quantize the test sequence prior to matching, reducing the number of test vectors and prune out unlikely speakers during the identification process, generalizing best variants to $GMM-UBM$ based modeling.

Previous methods degrade the system performance in exchange for gaining speed-up. Saeidi et al in [3] proposed an optimization of the sorted function exposed by Mohammadi et al. in [7], obtaining better results than GMM-UBM baseline. They use the Particle Swarm Optimization (PSO) method, evaluating the search width in power of 2. Results obtained with search width of 512 are better than those obtained with the sorted function in [7].

More recently, another extension of the method explained in [3] is proposed by Saeidi et al. in [8], using a two-dimensional indexation, allowing simultaneous selection of Gaussian and frames. The evaluation was developed using several values of a control parameter to specify the neighborhood of the optimization (2%, 3%, 5%, 10%, 15% and 20%) obtaining speed-up ratios of 157:1, 85:1, 37:1, 11:1, 5:1 and 3:1, respectively.

Lately, Liu et al. in [9] proposed a Gaussians selection method using only the components selected by cluster UBM (CUBM) as input for calculating a EM statistic with the objective to improve the speed of estimating the factor analysis model (FA) obtaining a good balance between the efficiency and performance. The efficiency of CUBM-FA is much better than baseline factor analysis (the cost time has been reduced from 9.53 sec to 1.24 sec) while having similar performance (both around 3.8% in EER and 0.02 in minDCF).

These recent methods obtain similar performance than baseline reducing the processing time.

Our work focuses the attention in the redundant information present in speaker models and proposes a method to reduce this, performing a simple selection of Gaussian components of the GMM-UBM and the UBM models, based on cumulative vectors of number of activations of better classified components for each feature vector of the acoustic utterances. As our intention is to evaluate the reduction of redundant information in speaker models only, we will use GMM-UBM speaker verification experimental framework under Reynolds's paradigm [1].

2 Proposed Methods

2.1 The Cumulative Vector

This algorithm is similar to the recently proposed by Anguera in [10], but using a universal background model (UBM) instead of anchor models. The process consists in obtaining the most likely component of the UBM regarding each frame of speech utterance, and storing in a vector the sum of reached activations in all frames of the utterance. See figure 1.

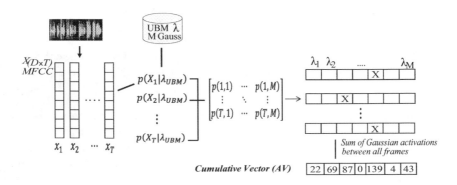

Fig. 1. Cumulative vectors method

The likelihood is calculated for each speech utterance frame, regarding all Gaussian components of the UBM, obtaining a likelihood matrix $LLH(X|\lambda_{UBM})_{(T,M)}$, where T is the number of frames and M is the number of Gaussian components of UBM.

From the LLH matrix, a row (frame) search of the most likely component is done and it is identified as activated, then a sum by columns of activated components is performed (over all frames of utterance), and the result is stored in the cumulative vector (CV). The cumulative vector contains M accumulative values, reflecting the number of activations of each Gaussian component, for the utterance.

2.2   Gaussian Component Selection through Cumulative Vectors

As described above, there are several Gaussian component selection methods based on the feature vector likelihood given the Gaussian component $p(x|\lambda)$; hence the goal of our proposal is to select a set of Gaussian components that better characterize the acoustic classes of a speaker utterance, based on the k greatest accumulative values of cumulative vector. Using the cumulative vector obtained from UBM in 2.1, the Gaussian components with the k greatest accumulative values are selected. See figure 2.

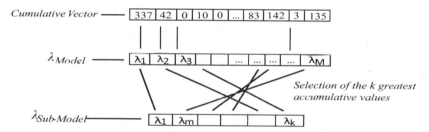

Fig. 2. Gaussian component selection criteria using cumulative vector (GCS-CV)

This method brings an important reduction of model from M to only k components. These k components are the most likely components in all utterances, so the new model would be more discriminative.

2.3   Two New Classification Methods for Speaker Recognition

Two methods of classification using the GMM-UBM framework [2] will be proposed; both methods use the UBM Gaussian component selection based on cumulative vector (GCS-CV) explained above to select the Gaussian components and obtain a reduced model which better represents the speaker utterance. The methods were applied using training and test utterances.

Classification Method Using the Training Utterance. Using the feature vectors of the training utterance and the UBM, a speaker model is obtained with MAP adaptation; simultaneously CV is obtained as explained in section 2.1, using the same input data. With GMM-UBM model and CV, GCS-CV method is applied as explained in 2.2, obtaining a new k-components model of the training utterance. Lastly, test utterance is classified in GMM-UBM framework, but using the new model of the training utterance. See figure 3A.

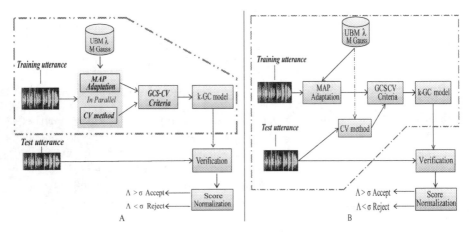

Fig. 3. Both classification method

Classification Method Using the Test Utterance. This method makes the selection of the Gaussian components using the feature vectors of the test utterance, based on the method proposed by Reynolds in [1].

Hence, we propose the use of GCS-CV method on the test utterance together with the target model to obtain a new model of the target and make the classification. In contrast to the one proposed by Reynolds, here we obtain only one model for test utterance.

Using the feature vectors of the training utterance and the UBM, a speaker model is obtained with MAP adaptation; in the test session, using the feature vectors of the test utterance and the UBM, CV is obtained as explained in 2.1. With GMM-UBM model and CV, GCS-CV method is applied as explained in 2.2, obtaining a new k-components model of the training utterance. Finally, the test utterance is classified in GMM-UBM framework, but using the new model of the training utterance. See figure 3B.

3 Experimental Results

Databases, front-end and score normalization used for all experiments are explained in this section.

The UBM model is obtained from "SALA: SpeechDat across Latin America" telephone speech database (Venezuelan version). It contains 1000 speakers uttering in each telephone call a total of 45 read and spontaneous items. For training and test utterances, NIST2001 Ahumada database was used. Ahumada is a speech database of 104 male Spanish speakers. Each speaker utters a spontaneous expression of about 60 sec. in each telephone session; eliminating the pauses, speech is about 48 sec. as average, in each utterance.

Well known MFCC features have been used to represent the short time speech spectra. All telephone speech signals are quantized at 16 *bits* at 8000 Hz sample rate, pre-emphasized with a factor of 0.97, and an energy based silence removal scheme is used. At last, the Δ cepstral features from MFCC normalized cepstral feature are obtained and appended to MFCC features conforming a 24-dimensional $MFCC + \Delta$ feature vector.

Score normalization method for small evaluation databases is proposed. For each score L between a target X_A and a test X_B, the normalized score is

$$Lnorm(X_A, X_B) = L(X_A, X_B) - mean(L(X_A, I_s)) \tag{1}$$

Where I_s is a subset of impostors. As the evaluation database is small, we divided the experiment into two subsets, a and b, each of them composed of half of the speakers. When the subset a is used to perform the speaker recognition test, the speakers from the subset b are used as impostors for the normalization and viceversa. The test from the two subset is polled together in order to obtain the global performance of a given system.

4   Speaker Verification Experiments

4.1   GMM-UBM Speaker Verification Baseline

First, a GMM-UBM speaker verification baseline using the data and methods explained in Section 3 was established. A UBM model with $M = 2048$ Gaussian components was trained with 1989 speech utterances from SALA database. GMM-UBM models of 100 speakers were MAP adapted [2] using as training utterances their spontaneous utterances of session T1 of Ahumada database. For verification, testing spontaneous utterances was obtained from the same speakers but in session $T2$ of Ahumada database, and the comparison was based on the criteria to reduce the verification load, proposed in [1] and explained in section 2.3, using R=10 components. Score normalization is applied as described in section 3. Results were evaluated on DET curve, obtaining and EER = 4%; the NIST evaluation criteria, minimal of "detection cost function" was evaluated too, minDCF= 2.29%.

4.2   Speaker Verification Experiments Using Training and Test Data to Select Gaussian Components from de UBM Model

Two experiments were performed with both classification methods explained in section 2.3, selecting k= 250, 300, 350, 400 and 500 Gaussian components. Table 1 reflects the results of both experiments for different k.

Table 1. EER and minDCF results of experiments

k	Selection with Method 1		Selection with Method 2	
	% EER	% minDCF	% EER	% minDCF
250	5.00	2.47	4.00	2.28
300	4.52	2.39	4.36	2.41
350	4.00	2.22	4.05	2.28
400	5.00	2.29	4.20	2.22
500	5.00	2.23	4.18	2.21

Experimental results of the proposed methods show:

a. Redundancy reduction in the selected Gaussian components:
   As shown, experiment using method 1 with $k = 350$ Gaussian component and experiment using method 2 with $k = 250$ Gaussian components, get the same % EER and less % minDCF related to the GMM-UBM baseline, with a respective reduction of 82.9% and 87.7% of the Gaussian components of the original GMM-UBM speaker model (2048). The non-selected Gaussian components are less discriminative of the speaker or not discriminative at all. This reduction of information lowers verification phase computational burden, due to the use of fewer number of Gaussian components.
b. Classification method using the test utterance is better:
   Method 2 obtains similar results as method 1 with less Gaussian components (250 vs. 350); this method is more adjusted to the test speaker because it selects the components of the GMM-UBM model from the test utterance, very similar to Reynolds method [1] but less expensive.

5   Conclusion and Future Work

In the presence of real or embedded applications of speaker verification, classical GMM-UBM [1] method is not sufficient enough because of the high dimensionality of the GMM-UBM model and the existence of non-discriminative and redundant information in them.

Experimental results show that GMM-MAP adaptation of UBM model represent speech utterances not efficiently , containing many non-discrimative and useless Gaussian components. So we can argue that only about 20% of the Gaussian components of the speaker model is as effective as all the model. In conclusion, this results using GSC-CV criteria show that an important reduction of the models, more than 80%, is reached, with similar performance in speaker verification experiments. Of course, the volume reduction will depend on the databases used, but it is present. The use of the GSC-CV method of Gaussian components selection would reduce the computational and memory cost of classifying stage in real applications of speaker verification.

As future work, we propose to obtain another method to select the Gaussian components of the model, using an Adaboosting classifier, considering the

Gaussian component as weak classifiers and utterances of target and impostors speakers as positive and negative samples. The proposal would be to obtain an optimal value of k Gaussian components as a strong classifier of each target speaker, to be used as speaker model for speaker verification experiments.

References

1. Reynolds, D.A.: Speaker identification and verification using Gaussian mixture speaker models. Speech Communication 17(1), 91–108 (1995)
2. Reynolds, D.A., Quatieri, T., Dunn, R.: Speaker verification using adapted gaussian mixture models. Digital Signal Processing 10(1), 19–41 (2000)
3. Saeidi, R., Sadegh Mohammadi, H.R., Ganchev, T., Rodman, R.D.: Particle Swarm Optimization for Sorted Adapted Gaussian Mixture Models. IEEE Trans. on Audio, Speech, and Language Processing 17(2), 344–353 (2009)
4. Auckenthaler, R., Mason, J.: Gaussian selection applied to text independent speaker verification. In: Proceedings of Speaker Odyssey: the Speaker Recognition Workshop, Crete, Greece, pp. 83–88 (2001)
5. Xiang, B., Berger, T.: Efficient text-independent speaker verification with structural Gaussian mixture models and neural network. IEEE Transactions on Speech and Audio Processing, 447–456 (2003)
6. Kinnunen, T., Karpov, E., Franti, P.: Real-time speaker identification and verification. IEEE Transaction on Audio, Speech and Language Processing 14(1), 277–288 (2006)
7. Mohammadi, H.R.S., Saeidi, R.: Efficient implementation of GMM based speaker verification using sorted Gaussian mixture model. In: Proc. EUSIPCO 2006, Florence, Italy (2006)
8. Saeidi, R., Kinnunen, T., Mohammadi, H.R.S., Rodman, R., Fränti, P.: Joint frame and gaussian selection for text independent speaker verification. In: IEEE Trans. ICASSP 2010, pp. 4530–4533 (2010)
9. Liu, Q., Huang, W., Xu, D., Cai, H., Dai, B.: A fast implementation of factor analysis for speaker verification In: Interspeech 2010, pp. 1077–1080 (2010)
10. Anguera, X., Bonastre, J.F.: A Novel Speaker Binary Key Derived from Anchor Models. In: Proceedings of Interspeech (2010)

Speaker Recognition Using a Binary Representation and Specificities Models

Gabriel Hernández-Sierra[1,2], Jean-François Bonastre[2],
and José Ramón Calvo de Lara[1]

[1] Advanced Technologies Application Center, Havana, Cuba
{gsierra,jcalvo}@cenatav.co.cu
[2] University of Avignon, LIA, France
jean-francois.bonastre@univ-avignon.fr

Abstract. State of the Art speaker recognition methods are mainly based on GMM/UBM based supervector paradigm. Recently, a simple representation of speech based on local binary decision taken on each acoustic frame have been proposed, allowing to represent a speech excerpt as a binary matrix. This article is based on a similar approach. A new temporal block representation of the binary transformed data as well as three simple algorithms to obtain an efficient similarity measure are proposed. The experimental results show a better robustness of the proposed approach and a similar or better overall performance over classical approaches.

Keywords: speaker recognition, binary values, accumulative vector.

1   Introduction

During last years information of identity of speakers has been modeled using Gaussian Mixture Models/Universal Background Model (GMM/UBM) paradigm, a weighted sum of Gaussian density functions models the space of acoustic classes. Each GMM model of speaker target is adapted from the UBM using Maximum a Posteriori (MAP) adaptation [1] of the UBM.

The efficiency of GMM-MAP (with or without supervector) based approaches in speaker recognition is well known. But is associated with two main drawbacks. Firstly, these approaches show large and complex models and high computational cost which constitute a limiting factor for some real life applications where small memory resources, fast response and high accuracy are needed. Secondly, it is not easy to work with segmental/temporal information as the approaches usually work at the file level.

This work presents a new approach to reduce these limitations thanks to a novel binary representation of the speech proposed in [2]. But in this work, a dynamic Generator Model is used to generate the binary vectors. Our approach uses a variable number of specificities for each feature vector to perform the test, ensuring that only the amount of necessary specificities to characterize the acoustic vector will be selected. This approach is used to explore temporal/segmental speaker specific information also.

L. Alvarez et al. (Eds.): CIARP 2012, LNCS 7441, pp. 732–739, 2012.

In this article new similarity measures driven by the binary information are proposed. The measures work over the intersection and symmetric difference between two discrete vectors, obtained from the binary representation.

This paper is organized as follows. Section 2 explains the process to obtain the binary representation of speech. Section 3 and 4 present the models used at the utterance level and for the temporal/segmental information. Section 5 describes the new similarity measure. Section 6 describes the different adaptation of the main principle for speaker recognition. Experimental protocols and the results are shown in section 7. Finally, section 8 presents some conclusions.

2   Algorithm to Obtain a Binary Representation

This method to obtain the specificities of the model is similar to the one presented in [2], [6], [7], but different compared to amount and type of specificities for each Gaussian component. The logic behind the model is based on increasing the discriminative power of a UBM; new model is composed of components which are selected from a classical UBM and specificities living within each acoustic class are represented by these selected components.

The selection consists in choosing those components of UBM that achieve the highest likelihood at least once from the same features used to train the UBM, this new set is named by us as Activated Gaussian Component Model (AGCM). Each component in the AGCM is adapted as often as feature files were used to train the UBM, obtaining a set of components adapted for each component in the AGCM. Finally, the specificities living within each component of the AGCM are obtained by a selection (similarly to the selection of the components for the AGCM) of the components in the corresponding set.

As GMM is a clustering algorithm with overlapping between classes, each acoustic feature will be assigned with most likely acoustic class, obtaining a distribution of the acoustic features for each class. In our approach each component in the AGCM has a different amount of specificities (Gaussian components), if we normalize the weights and equalize the variances they can be seen as a GMM embedded in each component. Each embedded model has a variable number of components defined by the nature of each acoustic class of the original UBM. We will call the new whole AGCM and its specificities as Generator Model.

The aim of this new Generator Model consists in obtaining a binary matrix for each speech utterance that represents the best relationships between each acoustic vector and its groups of specificities.

To obtain the binary matrix, for each frame the "3" top AGCM components with highest likelihood scores are extracted. Within each of these components the specificities with greater likelihood superior to a given threshold are obtained. So, for each component, different numbers of specificities are selected. With this process it is possible to obtain a spatial information about the acoustic features that is not possible in classical GMM algorithms.

Each utterance is represented by a KxN-dimensional binary matrix called Bk, where K is the number of specificities and N is the number of acoustic vectors of

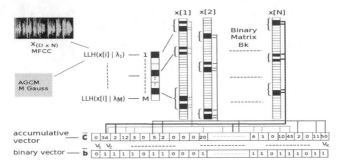

Fig. 1. Steps to obtain the binary matrix, accumulative vector and binary vector

the signal. Each column of Bk corresponds to an acoustic vector and reflects the labeled probabilities of each vector with respect to each specificities, where the top percent of highest likelihood scores are labeled as "*1*" (activated component) and the rest labeled as "*0*" (not activated) [2], [6]. The size of the accumulative vector and the resulting binary vector is the amount of specificities (K) of the entire Generator Model.

3 GA, a General Model for a Speech Utterance

The process to obtain a general model from a binary matrix Bk is very simple. It only involves a sum of "*1*" in each matrix row, resulting in the number of activations of each specificities. We define a speech utterance General model (GA) as an M-dimensional accumulative vector, $\bar{c} = \{v_1, \ldots, v_M\}$, $\bar{c} \in \mathbb{N}$. Each vector position j in $\bar{c}$, $j = 1, \ldots, M$, represents a specificity that is clustered by a Gaussian component of AGCM, and each value v_j of the vector $\bar{c}$ is the number of activations ("*1*") of each specificity. The General Model defined here is the same as defined in [2] as "accumulative vector (vc)".

Like in [2], a global binary vector is extracted from the matrix, by setting to "*1*" the coefficients corresponding to n-best highest accumulative values of vc. In contrast to [2] we will now use jointly the binary vector and the accumulative vector. Because the binary vector reflects the specificities that best represent the expression while the accumulative vector weights the influence of each specificity (the level of activation), this model may present a higher discriminative power.

A speech excerpt is therefore represented by two simple and sparse vectors which compose a new speaker model, causing a drastic reduction of the necessary information for speaker recognition compared to classical GMM models. It is also important to notice that all the needed information is present in the (sparse) accumulative vector, allowing efficient implementations.

4 TA, Trajectory Model for a Speech Utterance

Not only the General Model of the utterance but also information about different temporal segments in the utterance can be extracted from the binary matrix.

To obtain the Trajectory Model, we apply a windowing procedure to select over-lapped blocks of the binary matrix. Each block has a size k and, between two consecutive blocks, there is z frames displacement.

Then, given a binary matrix Bk and parameters k -size of the blocks- and z -displacement between them-, we obtain T blocks, $T = (N - k)/z$, where N is the number of acoustic vectors in the utterance.

We define the Trajectory Model of a speech utterance, as a set of accumulative vectors, $TA = \{\bar{c}_1, \bar{c}_2, \ldots, \bar{c}_T\}$, where T is the number of blocks obtained from the binary matrix, and each $\bar{c}_t$ is a accumulative vector obtained in the same way as the General Model but on the corresponding temporal segment. It is important to observe that T depends on the utterance duration. Fig 2 reflects the process to obtain the trajectory model. Similarly with the GA model, we extract also the binary vector for each temporal block.

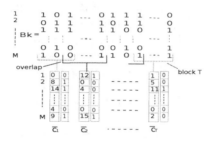

Fig. 2. Process for obtaining the trajectory model

The trajectory model of one utterance should be able to extract complementary information v.s. the general model. Accumulative vectors in a segment of the utterance reflect a distribution of specificities related to the phonetic and prosodic contents of the segment, different to others segments and to the whole utterance. Adequate overlapping of segments ensures a soft transition between values of the accumulative vectors. A speech segment contaminated by noise should be considered as a weak feature set for speaker discrimination, but an adequate segmentation and overlapping of speech could reduce the effect of noise and increase the robustness of the whole model.

5   New Similarity Measures

These new representations of speech characteristics involve finding new and simple ways to measure the similarity between two models. We define two set-based operations to evaluate the elements involved in the comparison of two models, A and B. These operations are the intersection and the symmetric difference. These operations are explained in Fig 3 where:

Although the pairs of (0,0) elements at the intersection are interesting (they identify the common not activated components), they were not analyzed in this work. Therefore the analyzed elements in the intersection are only the (1,1) pairs.

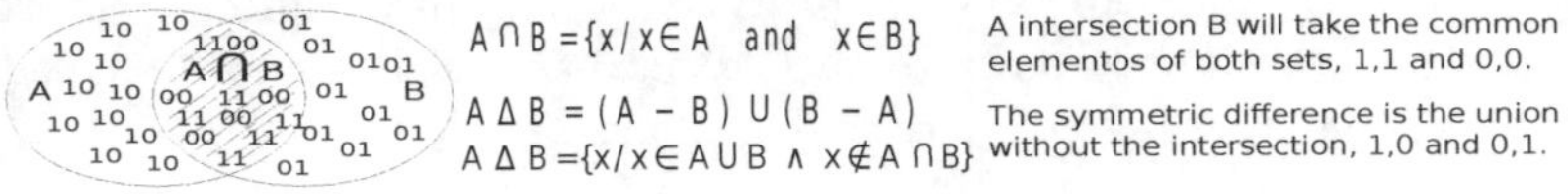

$A \cap B = \{x / x \in A \text{ and } x \in B\}$ A intersection B will take the common elementos of both sets, 1,1 and 0,0.

$A \triangle B = (A - B) \cup (B - A)$ The symmetric difference is the union

$A \triangle B = \{x / x \in A \cup B \wedge x \notin A \cap B\}$ without the intersection, 1,0 and 0,1.

Fig. 3. Binary set operations within two utterances

5.1 Using the Intersection as a Similarity Measure

In [2] the authors propose a measure that reflects the size of the intersection, defined by the pairs (1,1).

$$IS(A, B) = \frac{|A \cap B|}{|A|}, \qquad |A| = |B| \qquad (1)$$

This measure works on the binary vectors only and corresponds to the number of common active components in both models. We call it "intersection similarity (IS)". IS measure has advantages with respect to the classical Maximum Likelihood Estimation measure such that it is easy to program, the computational cost is very small and it allows to characterize each speaker utterance with a simple binary vector, reducing dramatically the memory size.

But it also has disadvantages: to use only the binary vector as a simplification of general model may cause it to lose information of the speaker utterance, that has to do with the level of activation of the specificities in each utterance.

5.2 New Similarity Measure Using the Intersection and Symmetric Difference (ISDS)

In this section we define a new measure driven by the binary vector of A and B but applied on the corresponding accumulative vectors. The use of accumulative vectors instead of binary vectors to obtain a similarity between speech utterances brings us a new dimension in the comparison, because accumulative vectors not only contain the selection of the top best specificities (which models mainly the utterance) but also contain the information of the strength of these selected specificities. This is the main difference of our proposal with respect to [2], [6].

This new similarity measure is based on two independent terms, which work on the intersection and symmetric difference between the two sets. These terms can be viewed as similarity measures separately; the first new similarity measure reflects the difference that exists in the intersection (ID) of two sets, regarding the cumulative values of each, and is defined as follows.

Let two General models A and B of two utterances, represented by their respective accumulative vectors. Let the binary operation be driven by the binary vectors corresponding to A and B like in the previous section.

$$ID(A, B) = \frac{1}{\sum_{i=1}^{|A \cap B|} |a_i - b_i|} \qquad \{\forall a \in A, \forall b \in B \mid \exists(a, b) \in A \cap B \text{ and } a \neq b\} \qquad (2)$$

The cumulative values in each model are the number of activations of the specificities in the complete utterance, they have a close relationship with the duration of the utterance, then it is necessary to normalize the accumulative vector in each set with respect to the sum of the cumulative values in it respectively.

The second proposed measure consists in the sum of the cumulative values of the elements in the intersection divided by the sum of the cumulative values found in the symmetric difference ISD of sets A and B.

$$ISD(A,B) = \frac{\sum_{i=1}^{|A \cap B|} a_i + b_i}{\sum_{j=1}^{A-B} a_j + \sum_{j=1}^{B-A} b_j} \qquad \{\forall a \in A, \forall b \in B \mid A - B \neq \emptyset\}^1 \qquad (3)$$

This term determines the similarity between the intersection and symmetric difference for two accumulative vectors. The more the activations of the specificities in the intersection the greater the similarity between two utterances.

Finally the union of the two previous measures makes up our new similarity measure ("Interception and Symmetric Difference Similarity" ISDS).

$$ISDS(A,B) = \frac{\sum_{i=1}^{|A \cap B|} a_i + b_i}{(\sum_{j=1}^{A-B} a_j + \sum_{j=1}^{B-A} b_j) * \sum_{i=1}^{|A \cap B|} |a_i - b_i|} \qquad (4)$$

$$\{\forall a \in A, \forall b \in B \mid A - B \neq \emptyset \text{ and } \exists a \neq b \mid (a,b) \in A \cap B\}$$

6   Using the ISDS Measure

Below we describe the use of the General Model (GA) and Trajectory Model (TA) of an utterance in the framework of speaker recognition applications. First we focus on the use of the general model.

The first step for all algorithms is the normalization of accumulative vector, eliminating its dependence on the duration of the speech utterance, then vector $\bar{x}$ will be the normalized accumulative vector.

Let one accumulative vector $\bar{c}$.

$$\bar{x} = \frac{\bar{c}(i)}{\sum_{j=1}^{M} \bar{c}(j)} \qquad (5)$$

where $i = 1, 2, \ldots, M$, $\sum_{i=1}^{M} \bar{x}(i) = 1$.

Let A, a target speaker and B, an unknown test speaker.
Algorithm 1: Apply ISDS measure for general model of speech

1. Obtain the binary matrix for both speaker, $\{Bk^A, Bk^B\}$.
2. Obtain the general model, $\{Bk^A, Bk^B\} \Rightarrow \{GA^A, GA^B\}$.
3. The similarity measure for test speaker by comparing it to the target speaker:

$$S(GA^B, GA^A) = ISDS(GA^B, GA^A) \qquad (6)$$

Next, we describe the use of both models, the GA and the TA of a utterance. It is important to note that each TA could have a different number of vectors, which are related to the duration of the corresponding utterance.

This algorithm performs a comparison between the general model of A with the trajectory model of B and vice versa. We call GT, the coupling of GA and TA in the same context, $GT = (GA, TA)$.

---

[1] Note: Given the nature of our sets that ensures that all sets have the same number of elements, the cases $A \supset B$ or $B \supset A$ do not exist, therefore $A - B \neq \emptyset \Leftrightarrow B - A \neq \emptyset$.

Algorithm 2: Cross-comparison with GA and TA

1. Obtain the binary matrix for both speaker, $\{Bk^A, Bk^B\}$.
2. Obtain the GA and TA for each binary matrix, $\{Bk^A, Bk^B\} \Rightarrow \{GT^A, GT^B\}$
3. The similarity measure for test speaker by comparing it to the target speaker:

$$S(GT^A, GT^B) = \frac{1}{2}(\frac{1}{T^B}\sum_{t=1}^{T^B} ISDS(TA^B[t], GA^A) + \frac{1}{T^A}\sum_{t=1}^{T^A} ISDS(TA^A[t], GA^B)) \quad (7)$$

Finally, the following algorithm combines the information in the general model and the trajectory model.

Algorithm 3: Combination of the algorithms 1 and 2

Steps 1 and 2 are the same as in Algorithm 2.

1. Combination of the algorithms:

$$S(GT^A, GT^B) = \frac{1}{3}(\frac{1}{T^B}\sum_{t=1}^{T^B} ISDS(TA^B[t], GA^A) + \qquad (8)$$

$$\frac{1}{T^A}\sum_{t=1}^{T^A} ISDS(TA^A[t], GA^B) + ISDS(GA^B, GA^A))$$

7   Speaker Recognition Experiments

In order to test the feasibility of the proposed measures and the Trajectory Model for the speaker verification task, we have performed several tests using the SALA [3] and AHUMADA [4] databases. The SALA database was used to create a 512 mixtures UBM, using 1990 sequences of digits from 500 speakers, about 2.5 hours of telephone speech; 459 components were selected with 22000 specificities components. The front end of experiments was 12 MFCC + 12 deltas with cepstral normalization.

7.1   Text Independent Speaker Recognition Experiment

Text independent speaker verification experiment are performed using telephone sessions of Ahumada called T1 and T2. Each session has 100 speakers uttering about 1.5 minutes of spontaneous speech; utterances of session T1 are used as train set and utterances session T2 as test set. It gives a total of 100 target tests and 9900 impostor tests. The experiment focuses on the comparison of the four measures -IS and the three proposed ISDS algorithms- using as baseline a GMM-MAP approach [1] based on ALIZE toolkit [5].

For general models, GA, the binary vectors are extracted from the corresponding accumulative vectors using the 1000 best values. For the trajectory models TA, we use blocks of size k=300 vectors, displacement between blocks z=150 vectors and top 250 values for the binary vector extraction.

Table 1 presents the results of this experiment in terms of EER and DCF. It shows the advantages of using accumulative vectors and new similarity measures compared to IS measure and binary information only. Taken alone, the performance of the general models and trajectory models TA using the accumulative vectors (algorithm 1 y 2) remains modest results regarding the GMM baseline. Nevertheless, when combining the complementary information between them, as shown by algorithm 3 results, the performance is little better than the GMM-MAP baseline results.

Table 1. Results in text-independent speaker recognition

system	DCF(*100)	EER %
IS	3.9	6
Algorithm 1	2.97	5.48
Algorithm 2	4.33	6.8
Algorithm 3	**2.19**	**5**
GMM-Map	2.51	5.42

8 Conclusions and Future Work

This paper presents preliminary results of a new approach based on speech binary representation. Both, a new trajectory model (able to take into account successive temporal block information) and new similarities which measures associate binary representation and accumulative vectors were proposed.

Compared to state-of-the-art approaches, these new representation and similarity measures require less memory/computational resources and are able to take into account segmental information when the proposed approach shows a level of performance comparable to GMM/MAP approach. Besides these advantages, this approach opens a large avenue for further investigations. First, new techniques in order to deal with channel and session mismatch problems could be proposed, taking advantage of the binary/discrete (and sparse) speech representation. Second, the proposed approach allows to work on temporal/trajectory speaker specific information as it is based on a segmental block speech representation (until a frame-based representation). Moreover, the latter will directly benefit GMM-based knowledge as well as session mismatch progress, allowing to associate newest variability modeling techniques and trajectory models.

References

1. Reynolds, D.A., Quatieri, T.F., Dunn, R.B.: Speaker Verification Using Adapted Gaussian Mixture Models. In: Digital Signal Processing, pp. 19–41 (2000)
2. Anguera, X., Bonastre, J.: A novel speaker binary key derived from anchor models. In: Proc. Interspeech, pp. 2118–2121 (2010)
3. Moreno, A.-H., Koler, H., et al.: SpeechDat Across Latin America. Project SALA. In: Proc. of the First International Conference on Language Resources and Evaluation, Granada, Spain, vol. I, pp. 367–370 (1998)
4. Ortega, J., et al.: AHUMADA: A large speech corpus in Spanish for speaker characterization and identification. Speech Communication, 255–264 (2000)
5. Bonastre, J.-F., Wils, F., Meignier, S.: ALIZE, a free toolkit for speaker recognition. In: Proc. ICASSP, pp. 737–740 (2005)
6. Bonastre, J.-F., Anguera, X.: H. Sierra, G., et al.: Speaker modeling using local binary decisions. In: Proc. Interspeech, pp. 13–16 (2011)
7. Bonastre, J.-F., Bousquet, P.M., Matrouf, D., et al.: Discriminant binary data representation for speaker recognition. In: Proc. ICASSP, pp. 5284–5287 (2011)

Analysis of the Multifractal Nature of Speech Signals

Diana Cristina González, Lee Luan Ling, and Fábio Violaro

DECOM – FEEC, Universidade Estadual de Campinas (UNICAMP)
{dianigon,lee,fabio}@decom.fee.unicamp.br

Abstract. Frame duration is an essential parameter to ensure correct application of multifractal signal processing. This paper aims to identify the multifractal nature of speech signals through theoretical study and experimental verification. One important part of this pursuit is to select adequate ranges of frame duration that effectively display evidence of multifractal nature. An overview of multifractal theory is given, including definitions and methods for analyzing and estimating multifractal characteristics and behavior. Based on these methods, we evaluate the utterances from two different Portuguese speech databases by studying their singularity curves $(\tau(q)$ and $f(\alpha))$.We conclude that the frame duration between 50 and 100 ms is more suitable and useful for multifractal speech signal processing in terms of speaker recognition performance [11].

Keywords: Multifractal Spectrum, Hölder Exponent, Speech Signals, Scaling Analysis, Multifractal Characteristics.

1   Introduction

In recent years, the use of the multifractal theory as an alternative method for non-stationary signal modeling has considerably increased. Most traditional approaches for signal modeling and analysis are based on the use of short-time spectral approach performed by the DFT [1], [2], mainly focusing on the signal's stationary properties [3]. Those traditional methods fail largely to characterize non-stationary behavior in signals and therefore are unable to explore the information contained in most of their transient and non-stationary parts. In fact, most real world signals and processes, such as speech and video, can be better characterized by their non-stationary behavior [4]. In literature, there are some works reporting the use of multifractal techniques in speech processing. In [3] a multifractal-based approach was employed for characterization of speech consonants. In [5], [6], fractal parameters were extracted and used as new nonlinear feature of speech signals. In terms of analysis of the multifractal nature of speech signals, in [7] the geometry of speech turbulence was fractally modeled. In [8] [9], the authors concluded that multifractal methods of can be used for signal processing such as decomposition, representation and spectrum characterization. In [10] the multifractal nature of unvoiced speech signals was studied and demonstrated.

The current work arises from the necessity of determining the appropriate frame duration to perform the multifractal analysis of speech signals. The results of this study have provided a solid basis for the design and implementation of the speaker

L. Alvarez et al. (Eds.): CIARP 2012, LNCS 7441, pp. 740–748, 2012.

recognition system in [11]. More specifically, multifractal characteristics presented in speech signals are studied using multifractal curves including the multifractal spectrum $f(\alpha)$ and the scaling functions $\tau(q)$. These curves (also called singularity curves) are capable of providing some essential information for speech signal processing, such as signal decomposition, representation and characterization, similar to that performed by traditional Fourier approaches [8]. Two databases with different sampling rates were tested in order to observe and determine the multifractal nature of speech signals under different time scaling conditions.

2   Multifractal Processes

Multifractal signals, as well as multifractal processes, are usually characterized by their highly irregular behavior. In other words, time functions exhibit abrupt and varying levels of instantaneous transitions in time, also known as singular points, at which the time function is non-differentiable. This singularity level measure can be obtained through estimation of the Lipschitz exponent, which provides the so-called uniform measures of regularity, either evaluating it on small time intervals (neighborhood) or at isolated points (pointwise) [12]. In multifractal processes, the Lipschitz exponent, also known as the Hölder exponent α_t, is a series of time dependent values. In literature, there are two widely adopted definitions for "multifractals" in terms of their nonlinear characteristics of statistical moments, observed under different time scales, measured locally or pointwisely:

Definition 1.
The first definition of multifractals can be viewed as a generalization of monofractals [13]. Thus, it is said that a process $X(t)$ is multifractal when it obeys the following scale relationship $X(ct) \overset{d}{=} c^{H(c)}X(t)$, where $c^{H(c)}$ represents the scaling factor with $0 < H(c) < 1$ and $c>0$. The equality operator "$\overset{d}{=}$" indicates equality in statistical distribution. For monofractal processes, $H(c) = H$ is a constant which can be characterized by a single scale factor, known as the Hurst parameter. For multifractal processes, the generalized Hurst parameter becomes a Hölder exponent.

Definition 2.
The second definition of multifractal processes is based on the analysis of local scaling properties of the random paths of the process $X(t)$, by way of its local Hölder exponent, which is roughly defined as follows:

$$|X(t) - P_n(t)| \leq C|t - t_0|^{h(t_0)} \tag{1}$$

where $P_n(t)$ is a Taylor polynomial of X in t of degree n, for t sufficiently close to t_0, The degree n of the polynomial indicates the number of times that the tion $X(t)$ is differentiable at t_0. Therefore, $h(t_0)$ provides a measure of the singularity (or regularity) level at t_0. A complete and more rigorous version of this definition can be found in [13].

3   Estimation of Multifractal Characteristics

This section presents two practical approaches to study the multifractal behavior of a time series. The first approach is based on the estimation of the partition function of the process using the method of moments, while the second relies on the analysis of regularity of the process through its "multifractal spectrum".

3.1   The Method of Moments

The method of moments assumes that the signal holds major characteristics of a multiplicative cascade process [14]. The basic idea of this approach consists in acquire knowledge of the Hölder exponent distribution, by analyzing singularity property of the cascade. A procedure widely used for this analysis is the partition function. Let $\{X_i\}_{i=1}^{2^N}$ be the time series that represents a level of the cascade with a measure on the interval [0, 1] on the scale $1/2^N$. The partition function for the moment of order q is defined as [14]:

$$\mathcal{X}_m^X(q) := \sum_{k=1}^{N/m} \left(\overline{X_k^{(m)}}\right)^q \tag{2}$$

where,

$$\overline{X_k^{(m)}} := \sum_{i=1}^{m} X_{(k-1)m+i}^m \tag{3}$$

where m define the aggregation number for the construction of the cascade processes, for instance, process with dyadic partition $m = 2, 4, 8 \ldots 2^N$. the time series elements $X_{(k-1)m+i}^m$ represent the aggregate data, generating the new interval of next cascade stage for a fixed value of m. The scaling nature of the partition function can be evaluated by using the scaling function $\tau(q)$ as follows,

$$log\, X_m^X(q) = \tau(q)\, log\, m + C \tag{4}$$

where C is constant. For the special case of multifractal processes, $log\, X_m^X(q)$ exhibits linearity with $log\, m$ and $\tau(q)$ is not linear in terms of q.

3.2   Multifractal Spectrum

The multifractal spectrum $f(\alpha)$ is a representation of the distribution of its Hölder exponents. The spectral function can be determined using some techniques such as coarse graining spectrum, Hausdorff spectrum, and Legendre spectrum. Due to its simplicity of the technique, this study focuses on the Legendre spectrum [12] which can be obtained by means of the Legendre transform of $\tau(q)$ (scaling function) [14], as $f(\alpha) = \min_q\{q\alpha - \tau(q)\}$. Typically the spectrum of a multifractal process has negative concave shape, where the horizontal axis indicates the Hölder exponent values and the vertical axis the total amount of points with the same exponent value. In particular, when a signal process is monofractal, the scaling function becomes as $\tau(q) = \beta q - 1$, which is linear in q with a constant angular coefficient β. As a result, the Hölder exponent holds a unique value graphically represented by a single non-zero point or a straight line.

4   Tests, Results and Discussion

In this section, we use the theory and procedures described in the previous section to study and determine possible multifractal nature and behavior of speech signals. The main purpose is to verify the conditions under which a speech signal reliably reveals its multifractal behavior.

4.1   Description of Speech Signals

Two speech signal databases were used for this experimental investigation [15]. The speech signals of these two databases were collected via a high-quality microphone and recorded under a low noise, controlled environment. The speech signals of the first database are collected from 30 speakers under the 11.025 kHz sample rate. The utterances have an average duration of 2.5 s. The second database, contributed by 71 speakers, has their speech signal sampled at rate of 22.05 kHz. The average duration of each speech utterance is approximately 3 s. Before the speech signals were submitted to multifractal analysis, they underwent a pre-processing procedure which consisted of three operations in sequel: pre-emphasis [16], normalization and elimination of silence intervals.

4.2   Experimental Investigation

In this subsection, we graphically evaluate the multifractal behavior of the speech signals. First, applying the moment method we obtain the partition function and the scaling function $\tau(q)$. Then, via the Legendre spectrum, we observe the scaling behavior and any particular event appearing on each speech segment, namely consonants, vowel transitions, vowel-consonant pairs.

*Experimental Test 1:*The moment method determines graphically the behavior of the partition functions in terms of moment order q. In this experiment test we randomly selected 30 speech phrases recorded from different speakers (with varying genders and ages) of each database. For illustration purpose, Figs. 1.a and 1.c show the curves of the partition functions ($\log X_m^X$ versus $\log m$) of two phrases arbitrarily selected from the two different databases. In fact, similar graphic behaviors are observed for most of the evaluated utterances. Notice that the partition functions exhibit linearity in relation to $\log m$, despite some soft inflection points, regardless of the sampling frequency and utterance duration. This suggests that speech signals may hold fractal behavior or characteristics, presenting different scaling properties that are monofractal or multifractal behaviors at different scales. In contrast, the curves of the scaling function $\tau(q)$, as illustrated by Figs. 1.b and 1.d, show some nonlinearity, what suggests the existence of a multifractal spectrum. The vertical bars represent 95% confidence intervals of the estimated values of the scaling function $\tau(q)$ for each moment der q, all estimated confidence intervals are small and present similar dynamic shapes in q. This visual inspection alone, although suggesting the presence of different properties of scaling, may not be definitive or conclusive. Therefore, a complementary analysis approach was adopted, using a multifractal spectrum (spectrum of Legendre). This approach is usually more reliable and informative [14].

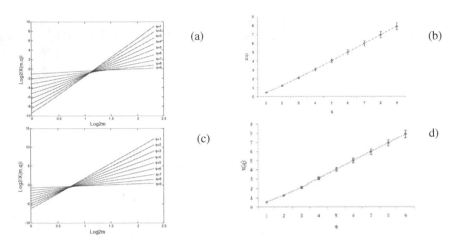

Fig. 1. Partition functions: (a) Database Ynoguti 1 (c) Database Ynoguti 2; scaling function $\tau(q)$ vs q; (b) Database Ynoguti 1, (d) Database Ynoguti 2

Experimental Test 2: In this experimental test, the speech signals are analyzed in terms of phonemes (the smallest sound units that conforms a word) as well as the relationship to their neighbor phonemes. As explained in Section 3-B, the multifractal spectrum provides information regarding the singularity degree of a time signal and, therefore, about the variation of its Hölder exponent function. Through this variation in time, the multifractal behavior of speech signals is determined. Here, the multifractal spectrum is obtained by applying Legendre Transform [1] (implemented in MATLAB) using the FRACLAB Tool [17].

Table 1. Phonetic classes

Classes	Phonemes	Classes	Phonemes
Silences (s)	#	Fricatives (f)	f, s, ʃ, v, z, ʒ
Vowels (v)	a, e, ɛ, i, j, o, ɔ, u	Lateral (l)	l, ʎ
Nasal vowels (ns)	ã, ẽ, ĩ, õ, ũ	Nasals (n)	n, m, ɲ
Plosives (p)	p, t, tʃ, k, b, d, ʤ, g	Tap	r, r̄, R

---

[1] More information on the Legendre Transform can be found in Appendix B from [14].

Since there are phoneme variations according to languages, this work focuses on 36 phones of the Brazilian Portuguese language. Table 1 shows to which class each phone belongs. After segmentation of speech, we analyzed the behavior of those segments. These segments were analyzed in different time scales (20-, 50-, 100- and 500-ms) in order to observe the dynamics of the speech in different scales and its singularities distribution. For smaller scales, the analysis focused on sub-segments of phonemes, implying practically the behavior analysis of isolated phonemes. For large time scales, the studied speech segments consist of a phoneme and its neighbor phonemes. The first phonetic class analyzed was "vowels". Vowels were chosen in different conditions, including start, end and middle of a word. For example, Fig. 2 illustrates the distribution of the Hölder exponents for the first vowel "a" in word "Para". Due to space limitation, only predominating and informative results are presented.

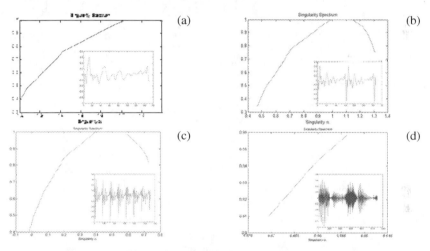

Fig. 2. Legendre spectrum of the phoneme "a". (a) One pitch period of the phoneme *"a"*, (b) Two pitch period of the phoneme *"a"*,   (c)100 ms, (d) 500 ms.

The second studied phonetic class was "plosive consonants". Traditionally consonants can be characterized by their very short duration and are usually followed by vowels, and cause almost non-significant changes on the vowel sound. Therefore, in the vicinity of the plosive phoneme, the multifractal behavior is maintained in a similar manner to that given by the vowel phonemes. Fig. 3 shows two examples of such a phenomenon through the spectra of singularities of consonants *"t"* and *"b"*.

Fig. 3. Legendre spectrum around of the plosive, with 20 ms of duration. (a). *"t"*. (b). *"b"*.

The third phonetic class analyzed was "fricative consonants". Fricative sounds are consequences of the turbulence produced by lungs when the air is forced to pass through a constricted vocal tract [7]. During the analysis of fricatives, we observed two different behaviors which are exemplified by the "f" and "x" phonemes as shown in Fig. 4 and Fig. 5. Accordingly, the phoneme "f" of the word "foi", shown by Fig. 4, has random behavior similar to that of a random signal, which is usually characterized by monofractal processes. According to [7], the sound produced by one phone can be represented by one fractal dimension, and therefore can be better modeled by a mono-fractal process.

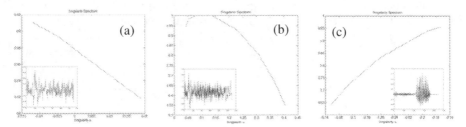

Fig. 4. Legendre spectrum of the phoneme "*f*". (a) 50 ms, (b) 100 ms, (c) 500 ms.

For spontaneous speech, fricative is usually accompanied by audible sounds in order to present multifractal characteristics at scales close to 100 ms. An example of this kind is illustrated by Fig. 4.b. We also observed that most of the fricative phones have similar behavior above mentioned. Another interesting phenomenon of fricatives is exemplified by the phoneme "s" in the word "próxima ['prɔsimɐ]". The length of this fricative sound is very short; as a consequence, it rapidly connects to the followed vowel sound, as shown in Figs. 5.a and 5.b. As a result, the fricative component presents a multifractal behavior similar to that of vowel sounds, especially at low time scales (20- and100-ms).

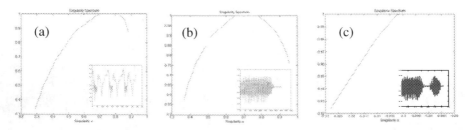

Fig. 5. Legendre spectrum of the phoneme "*x*". (a) 20 ms, (b) 100 ms, (c) 500 ms .

Generally speaking, every studied speech segment has demonstrated monofractal behavior on large time scales and multifractal behavior on small time scales. However, the range of small time scales on which the multifractal characteristics are observed varies. For instance, the phoneme "b" (Fig. 3) and the phoneme "f"

(Fig. 4.a show multifractal behavior on time scales shorter than 20 ms and greater than 50 ms, respectively. After detailed analysis and comparison, we found that spontaneous speech signals reliably present multifractal behavior on the range between 50m and 100ms time scales.

5   Conclusions

After extensive tests and evaluations performed on speech signals selected from two different speech databases, we summarize our conclusions as the following:

- Speech signals may present either monofractal or multifractal behavior depending on the time scales under which observation and analysis are performed. Experimental results show that speech signals composed of some phonetics classes (fricatives or taps) present monofractal behavior under short time interval analysis. This same behavior was found for long speech segment for all studied signals. However, definitely there is no rigid boundary for fractal behavior classification, due to fact that speech signal dynamics varies and is highly affected by both the speaker's speech rate and the signal's structure.
- It was found that, in general, all speech signals reveal multifractal behavior under a time frame analysis ranging from 50ms to 100ms. As this time interval includes a phone or a phone transition, we believe that this result is independent of the language.
- A new speaker recognition system in [11] that incorporates some multifractal features has reported a 3% increase in recognition rate with respect to one using only classical Mel-Cepstral features. This implies that multifractal features have increased and provided additional pattern discriminating capabilities.

References

1. Campell, J.: Speaker Recognition: A Tutorial. Proceeding of the IEEE 85(9) (1998)
2. Reynolds, D.A., Rose, R.C.: Robust Text-Independent Speaker Identification Using Mixture Speaker Model. IEEE Trans. Speech Audio Processing 3(1), 72–82 (1995)
3. Langi, A., Kinsner, W.: Consonant Characterization Using Correlation Fractal Dimension for Speech Recognition. In: Proc. on IEEE Western Canada Conference on Communications, Computer, and Power in the Modem Environment, Winnipeg, Canada, vol. 1, pp. 208–213 (1995)
4. Jayant, N., Noll, P.: Digital Coding of Waveforms: Principles and Applications to Speech and Video, 688 p. Prentice-Hall, Englewood Cliffs (1984)
5. Sant'Ana, R., Coelho, R., Alcaim, A.: Text-Independent Speaker Recognition Based on the Hurst Parameter and the Multidimensional Fractional Brownian Motion Model. IEEE Trans. on Audio, Speech, and Language Processing 14(3), 931–940 (2006)
6. Zhou, Y., Wang, J., Zhang, X.: Research on Speaker Recognition Based on Multifractal Spectrum Feature. In: Second International Conference on Computer Modeling and Simulation, pp. 463–466 (2010)

7. Maragos, P.: Fractal Aspects of Speech Signals: Dimension and Interpolation. In: Proc. IEEE ICASSP, vol. 1, pp. 417–420 (1991)
8. Langitt, A., Soemintapurat, K., Kinsners, W.: Multifractal Processing of Speech Signals Information, Communications and Signal Processing. In: Han, Y., Quing, S. (eds.) ICICS 1997. LNCS, vol. 1334, pp. 527–531. Springer, Heidelberg (1997)
9. Kinsner, W., Grieder, W.: Speech Segmentation Using Multifractal Measures and Amplification of Signal Features. In: Proc. 7th IEEE Int. Conf. on Cognitive Informatics (ICCI 2008), pp. 351–357 (2008)
10. Adeyemi, O.A.: Multifractal Analysis of Unvoiced Speech Signals. ETD Collection for University of Rhode Island. Paper AAI9805227 (1997)
11. González, D.C., Lee, L.L., Violaro, F.: Use of Multifractal Parameters for Speaker Recognition. M. Eng. thesis, FEEC/UNCAMP, Campinas, Brazil (2011)
12. Sténico, J.W., Lee, L.L.: Estimation of Loss Probability and an Admission Control Scheme for Multifractal Network Traffic. M. Eng. thesis, FEEC/UNCAMP, Campinas, Brazil (2009)
13. Riedi, R.H., Crouse, M.S., Ribeiro, V.J., Baraniuk, R.G.: A Multifractal Wavelet Model with Application to Network Traffic. IEEE Trans. on Information Theory 45(3), 992–1018 (1999)
14. Krishna, M.P., Gadre, V.M., Dessay, U.B.: Multifractal Based Network Traffic Modeling. Kluwer Academic Publishers., Ed. Bombay (2003)
15. Ynoguti, C., Violaro, F.: Continuous Speech Recognition Using Hidden Markov Models. D. Eng. thesis, FEEC/UNCAMP, Campinas, Brazil (1999)
16. Holmes, J., Holmes, W.: Speech Synthesis and Recognition, 2nd edn. Tayor & Francis, London (2001)
17. Research Center INRIA Saclay, http://fraclab.saclay.inria.fr/

Beam-Search Formant Tracking Algorithm Based on Trajectory Functions for Continuous Speech

José Enrique García Laínez[1], Dayana Ribas González[2],
Antonio Miguel Artiaga[1], Eduardo Lleida Solano[1],
and José Ramón Calvo de Lara[2]

[1] Communications Technology Group (GTC),
Aragon Institute for Engineering Research (I3A), University of Zaragoza, Spain
{jegarlai,amiguel,lleida}@unizar.es
[2] Advanced Technologies Application Center (CENATAV), 7a # 21812 e/ 218 y 222,
Rpto. Siboney, Playa, C.P. 12200, La Habana, Cuba
{dribas,jcalvo}@cenatav.co.cu

Abstract. This paper presents a formant frequency tracking algorithm
for continuous speech processing. First, it uses spectral information for
generating frequency candidates. For this purpose, the roots of the polynomial of a Linear Predictive Coding (LPC) and peak picking of Chirp
Group Delay Function (CGD) were tested. The second stage is a beam-
search algorithm that tries to find the best sequence of formants given the
frequency candidates, applying a cost function based on local and global
evidences. The main advantage of this beam-search algorithm compared
with previous dynamic programming approaches lies in that a trajectory
function that takes into account several frames can be optimally incorporated to the cost function. The performance was evaluated using a
labeled formant database and the Wavesurfer formant tracker, achieving
promising results.

Keywords: formant tracking, chirp group delay, beam-search algorithm,
speech processing.

1 Introduction

The resonance frequencies of the vocal tract, known as formants, carry useful information to identify the phonetic content and articulatory information of speech
as well as speaker discriminative information and emotion. That is why formant
tracking methods are widely used in automatic speech processing applications
like speech synthesis, speaker identification, speech and emotions recognition.
Those methods have to deal with the problem of the variability of the amount of
formants depending on phoneme and the merging and demerging of neighboring
formants over time, very common with F2 and F3. This is why, formant tracking
is a hard task to face [1].

For decades, a number of works have been dedicated to designing formant
tracking methods. Formant trackers usually consists of two stages: firstly the

L. Alvarez et al. (Eds.): CIARP 2012, LNCS 7441, pp. 749–756, 2012.

speech is represented and analyzed for obtaining some formant frequency candidates and secondly the selection of those candidates is done, taking into account some constraints. Those constraints are related with the acoustical features of the formant frequencies, the continuity of formant trajectory, etc. Traditionally LPC has been used for extracting the formant candidates, by means of solving the roots of the filter coefficients. Several types of those models have been designed for this task [2].On the other hand, previous works [3] have demonstrated that spectral representation based on phase (Group Delay Function (GDF)) shows better spectral resolution than LPC spectra. After that, some works have been focused on develop spectral representations based on GDF that are robust to additive noise, as in the case of Chirp Group Delay Zero Phase (CGDZP) representation [4]. In this work we obtained formant frequencies candidates by using both spectral representation: LPC and CGD.

The stage of formant selection has been in the focus of the scientific community in the last years. Probabilistic methods for estimating formant trajectories have been used successfully in recent years. Within this group are methods based on the Bayesian filtering like Kalman Filters [5] and particle filters [6] or Hidden Markov Models (HMM) [7]. Previous algorithms based on continuity constraints made use of dynamic programming and the Viterbi algorithm [8][9][10]. However, it has the limitation that the cost function of a hypothesis only depends on the current observation, and the last state. In this paper we propose a beam-search algorithm that is able to incorporate trajectory information to the cost function, overcoming the limitation of the Viterbi search. This algorithm consists of propagating the M-best hypotheses in each frame, that are evaluated by means of a cost function that makes use of local observations and the trajectory function of neighbor frames. It's main advantage is to make no Markovian assumptions about the problem, i.e the evaluation of hypothesis in a frame takes into account the hypothesis defined in all previous frames unlike the Viterbi search which only use previous state (frame in this case). This feature allows to incorporate the algorithm within an online system due to its incremental processing mechanism.

2   The Proposed Method

The proposed formant detector can be decomposed in two main stages: The first state is the formant frequency candidate extractor, where a set of frequencies and their bandwidths are chosen as possible formants. For this stage, two different spectral analyzers were tested: the first one is based on LPC, as proposed by [8][10]. In this extractor, a set of frequencies and bandwidths are extracted from the roots of the polynomial of the linear predictor. The second frequency candidate extractor is a peak picking technique computed over a phase spectrum, CGD, that has been demonstrated to enhance spectral peaks in formant regions [4].

The second stage is a beam-search algorithm for finding the best sequence of formants, given the frequency candidates. A mapping as proposed in [8][10] of frequency candidates to all possible combinations of formants is chosen. The algorithm tries to find the best sequence of mappings, by applying a cost function that makes use of both local and global information.

2.1   CGDZP Feature Extractor

For computing CGDZP, first the zero-phase version of the signal is obtained, which for a short-term speech segment is computed by taking the inverse Fourier transform of its magnitude spectrum. The conversion to zero-phase guarantees that all of the zeros occur very close to the unit circle, therefore the resulting CGD representation (Fig. 1 b) will be very smooth, with higher resolution than the magnitude spectrum (Fig. 1 a). After that the chirp group delay (CGD) is computed, defined as the negative derivative of the phase spectrum computed from z-transform [11] on a circle other than the unit circle. Given a short-term discrete-time signal $x(n), n = \{0, 1, ..., N-1\}$, a zero z-transform (ZZT) representation for a signal and provided that $x(0)$ is non-zero, it can compute its chirp Fourier Transform by the following equation:

$$X(w) = x(0)(\rho e^{jw})^{(-N+1)} \prod_{n=1}^{N-1} (\rho e^{jw} - Z_m) \tag{1}$$

where ρ is the radius of the analysis circle and Z_m is a zero of the signal.

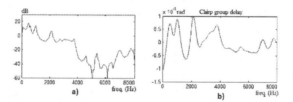

Fig. 1. a) Magnitude spectrum, b) CGDZP spectrum

A simple peak picking procedure is implemented for selecting the maximums of the CGDZP. The corresponding bandwidth of each maximum is extracted using the CGDZP spectrum. These extracted frequencies and their associated bandwidths will serve as formant candidates to the search stage.

2.2   Formant Selection

The main objective of the formant selection block in a formant tracking system is to choose the best formant candidates, taking a global decision by means of exploiting temporal information between contiguous sounds.

Let $X = \{x_1, ..., x_t, ..., x_T\}$ be the sequence of candidates in T frames, where $x_t = \{f_1, b_1, .., f_k, b_k, ...f_N, b_N\}$ is a set of N candidate frequencies and bandwidths in frame t, $h_t = \{F_1, B_1, F_2, B_2, F_3, B_3, F_4, B_4\}$ is a possible formant tuple at frame t, obtained by means of a mapping from frequency candidates.

The algorithm tries to find the best sequence of formants $H = \{h_1, ..., h_t, ..., h_T\}$, that minimizes a cost function f.

$$H = \underset{H}{argmin} \, f(X, H) \tag{2}$$

Computing all possible sequences of mappings in T frames is computationally intractable, even for small values of T and N, and this is why an approximated search algorithm must be used. Previous approaches of formant selection made use of dynamic programming and the Viterbi algorithm [8][10]. However, the states defined in the search only were able to manage cost functions that depend on the current observation and the last frame. This structural assumption is a limitation if a cost function that makes use of several frames wants to be incorporated.

In this paper we propose a tree beam-search algorithm for finding the best sequence of formants, that tries to solve the search problem using information of both local and neighbor frames. In each frame, the current hypotheses are sorted, and only the M best hypotheses are propagated. As defined in [8], [9], [10], our selection algorithm considers joint formant hypotheses h_t. With this search procedure, transition costs that make use of several frames can be applied in an optimal way. Such beam-search algorithm has been applied successfully in speech coding problems [12][13].

The method consists of a synchronous evaluation algorithm, where in a frame by frame basis the M-best hypotheses (with minimum accumulated cost) are maintained. Before frame t is evaluated, a hypothesis x is composed of an accumulated cost $a_{x,t-1}$ and a formant history $z_{t-1} = \{h_1, ..., h_{t-1}\}$.

Each one of the M active hypotheses at frame t are propagated through all possible combinations of formant candidates $o_t = \{h_{t1}, ..., h_{tw}, ..., h_{tU}\}$. Where U is the number of possible frequency mappings at frame t. The resultant number of hypotheses at frame t is $N = M * U$. These hypotheses are evaluated by means of the cost function:

$$c_{x,t} = cfrequency + cbandwidth + ctrajectory + cmapping \qquad (3)$$

that takes into account the frequency values of the formants, the bandwidth and the trajectory of such formants and a cost of the chosen frequency mapping. Then, the accumulated cost of the hypothesis is the previous accumulated cost summed with the current cost.

$$acc_{x,t} = acc_{x,t-1} + c_{x,t} \qquad (4)$$

Just after the hypotheses of the current frame have been computed, the hypotheses list is sorted, and only the M-best are conserved for propagating in the next frame. The M value represents a compromise between accuracy and execution speed. The trajectory term that makes use of several past frames justifies the use of the tree beam-search algorithm in place of the Viterbi decoding algorithm. One of the main benefits of this trajectory model is that it allows to recover observation errors in frames between obstruent and vowel, thanks to contiguous frame evidences.

2.3   Cost Function

The defined cost function uses both local and global observations for choosing the best sequence of formants. The part of the cost function that makes use of local information (it is, the current frame) contains the terms cfrequency, cbandwidth (defined as in [8]) and cmapping:

$$cfrequency = \alpha \sum_i |(F_i - norm_i)/norm_i|$$ (5)

$$cbandwidth = \beta \sum_i (B_i)$$ (6)

where $norm_i = 500, 1500, 2500, 3500$ and $i = \{1, ..., 4\}$ is the formant number.

$$cmapping_i = \begin{cases} 0 & if\ BWmin_i > THR \\ \frac{THR - BWmin_i}{\gamma_i} & if\ BWmin_i < THR \end{cases}$$ (7)

$$cmapping = \sum_i cmapping_i$$ (8)

where $BWmin_i$ is the minimum bandwidth of the frequency candidates that are discarded and that would be valid for the formant i in this mapping; γ_i and THR are constants. The part of the cost function that employs global information assumes that the frequency of each formant follows a smooth trajectory. This term is intended to take into account when a mapping is discarding some frequency peak with a low bandwidth.

$$ctrajectory = \theta \sqrt{\sum_{i,w} \frac{F_{i,w} - F_{i,\widehat{w}}}{B_i}}$$ (9)

Where $w = \{0, ..., W - 1\}$ and W is the order of the trajectory function and $\widehat{F}_{i,t-w}$ is the estimated value of formant i, at frame $t - w$, assuming that $F_{i,t}, ..., F_{i,t-(W-1)}$ is approximated by a known function; $1/B_i$ is the weighted term of the trajectory, in order to give more importance to frames that have lower bandwidth; α, β and θ are constant for representing the weight of the terms. In the experiments, linear and quadratic functions were used, approximated with the least squares method. However, we assume that there is room for improvement in the modeling of such trajectory.

An advantage of this continuity constraint compared with previous works is that this function does not increment costs when a change in the value of two consecutive frequencies occurs, as considered in [8][10]. In addition, this global function will help the algorithm to correct errors in difficult frames where the frequency candidates do not give clear evidences. Within this group are frames between obstruent and vowel and frames corrupted by noise.

3   Experiments and Results

The performance of the proposed formant tracking method was measured carrying a quantitative evaluation using the VTR-Formant database [14]. This database contains the formant labels of a representative subset of the TIMIT corpus with respect to speaker, gender, dialect and phonetic context. In these experiments, 420 signals from VTR database were processed and the mean absolute error (MAE) between formants estimated for our proposal and VTR database were computed. For comparative purposes, we also computed the MAE for the formants estimated by Wavesurfer's methods from Snack toolkit [15]. The pitch ESPS algorithm from Snack toolkit was used, for obtaining the MAE only taking into account voiced frames.

When LPC is considered the speech signal is sampled at 10KHz. After that, a first order preemphasis filter of the form $1 - 0.7z^{-1}$ is applied. Autocorrelation LPC analysis is performed each 10 ms, using a 49ms duration hamming window. The poles of the estimated model are obtained by solving for the zeros of a 12th order linear predictor polynomial. Real poles, which merely contribute to overall spectral slope, are eliminated. The remaining complex poles are then expressed as frequency-bandwidth pairs. In order to make a clear comparison of the tracking algorithm in Snack the same frequency candidates generator was used. With this frequency candidate generator, two families of trajectory functions were tested: quadratic and linear. The second was made using CGDZP as spectral representation for obtaining formant candidates and beam-search algorithm for formant selection. The order of trajectory function was $W = 10$ and the number of hypothesis propagated were $M = 20$. The constants of the cost function where optimized manually with a small subset of 8 signals of the database.

Table 1. MAE (Hz) for formant estimations obtained with Wavesurfer and proposed method. All experiments use LPC representation, except for the last one (CGD-Quad). Unless stated explicitly, the weights of the trajectory function were set to 1 and the term cmapping were set to 0. Lin indicates an order 10 linear trajectory; Quad indicates an order 10 quadratic trajectory; Mp indicates that the term cmapping is included in the cost function. Weight indicates that the trajectory function consider weights defined in (9).

Fmt	Wavesurfer	Lin	Quad	Lin+Mp	Quad+Mp	Quad+Mp+Weight	CGD-Quad
F1	18.46	18.33	18.35	18.37	18.39	18.38	24.07
F2	30.84	28.77	28.55	29.27	27.96	27.82	66.50
F3	46.33	48.41	42.81	36.66	35.26	36.66	84.42
F4	70.78	63.87	63.42	68.13	69.01	68.71	117.17

It can be observed in table 1 how the proposed tracking algorithm outperforms consistently Snack formant extractor in most cases. Notice that F1 achieved a lesser improvement than the other formants, because of its stable behavior. From that, Wavesurfer is pretty accurate with F1. However for F2 the relative improvement of our method is near 10 percent and for F3 we obtained a significative improvement of 20 percent, taking into account that these are the harder resonances to follow. For F4 the improvement is slight, but this formant have less importance because in VTRdatabase F4 it is not manually labeled. It is important to note that the performance of the quadratic trajectory is slightly better than linear's, also weighted quadratic has a similar performance than quadratic. As the table 1

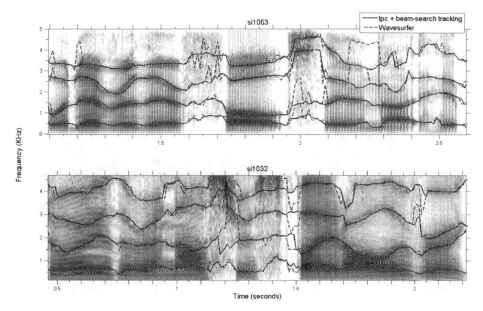

Fig. 2. Example results of two signals of TIMIT database with the proposed formant tracker with LPC and Wavesurfer

shows, the cmapping term (named Mp) is very important in order to detect correctly F3. A wrong detection of F3 can occurs in sounds that have more than 4 formants. The penalty associated to a mapping that discards some intermediate frequency peaks allows to choose the first 4 frequency candidates as formants.

On the other hand, the last column shows CGD results, which were not capable of outperforming Wavesurfer estimation. During the experiments we observed that spectral representation obtained from CGD could isolate very well formant areas, however, it is not very accurate in locating the exact frequency.

Figure 2 shows the formant estimation achieved with the proposal of two selected speech signals of TIMIT database, that enhances the benefits of our tracking algorithm. The signal in the bottom shows how the proposed formant tracker is able to produce more accurate formant frequencies than Wavesurfer, in a region located in the middle of two voiced sounds. On the top, it is shown how the proposal is able to track F3 correctly unlike Wavesurfer.

4   Conclusions

A method of formant tracking has been proposed and tested in the TIMIT database, showing significative improvement compared with the Wavesurfer tracking algorithm and achieving smoother trajectories. The proposal has demonstrated benefits in two key aspects: 1)- In the transition between voiced segments, the algorithm is able to follow the correct trajectory of the formants where the local evidence is not clear; 2)- In regions of ascendent / descendent formants, the algorithm is able to track the formant correctly and better than previous dynamic programming approaches, based on the Viterbi algorithm. The spectral representation CGD has been able to isolate well the formant areas, however it did not locate with enough accuracy the exact frequency of the formant. We plan in future works to improve this method by using a combination between phase spectrum for locate formant regions, and magnitude spectrum for obtain the exact value; in order to evaluated the hypothesis and for replacement of the cost functions use statistical models; to evaluate the robustness of the proposal using noisy signals.

Acknowledgements. This work has been partially funded by Spanish national program INNPACTO IPT-2011-1696-390000.

References

1. Rose, P.: Forensic Speaker Identification. In: Robertson, J. (ed.) Taylor and Francis Forensic Science Series. Taylor and Francis, London (2002)
2. McCandless, S.: An algorithm for automatic formant extraction using linear prediction spectra. IEEE TASSP ASSP-22, 135–141 (1974)
3. Yegnanarayana: Formant extraction from linear prediction phase spectrum. Journal of Acoustic Society of America 63, 1638–1640 (1978)
4. Bozkurt, B., Couvreur, L., Dutoit, T.: Chirp group delay analysis of speech signals. Speech Communications (2007)
5. Mehta, D.D., Rudoy, D., Wolfe, P.J.: KARMA: Kalman-based autoregressive moving average modeling and inference for formant and antiformant tracking. stat. AP (2011)
6. Gläser, C., Heckmann, M., Joublin, F., Goerick, C.: Combining auditory preprocessing and Bayesian Estimation for Robust Formant Tracking. IEEE Trans. Audio Speech Lang. Process. (2010)
7. Messaoud, Z.B., Gargouri, D., Zribi, S., Hamida, A.B.: Formant Tracking Linear Prediction Model using HMMs for Noisy Speech Processing. Int. Journal of Inf. and Comm. Eng. 5(4) (2009)
8. Talkin, D.: Speech formant trajectory estimation using dynamic programming with modulated transition costs. JASA 82(S1), 55 (1987)
9. Deng, L., Bazzi, I., Acero, A.: Tracking Vocal Tract Resonances Using an Analytical Nonlinear Predictor and a Target-Guided Temporal Constraint (2003)
10. Xia, K., Espy-Wilson, C.: A new strategy of formant tracking based on dynamic programming. In: Proc. ICSLP (2000)
11. Rabiner, L.R., Shafer, R.W.: The Chirp z-Transform Algorithm. IEEE Transactions on Audio and Electroacoustics au-17(2) (1969)
12. Garcia, J.E., Ortega, A., Miguel, A., Lleida, E.: Predictive vector quantization using the M-algorithm for distributed speech recognition. In: FALA (2010)
13. Jelinek, F., Anderson, J.B.: Instrumentable Tree Encoding of Information Sources. IEEE Trans. on Information Theory, 118–119 (1971)
14. Deng, L., Cui, X., Pruvenok, R., Huang, J., Momen, S., Chen, Y., Alwan, A.: A Database of Vocal Tract Resonance Trajectories for Research in Speech Processing. In: ICASSP (2006)
15. Snack toolkit: http://www.speech.kth.se/wavesurfer

Multi-level Modeling of Manuscripts for Authorship Identification with Collective Decision Systems

Salvador Godoy-Calderón, Edgardo M. Felipe-Riverón[*], and Edith C. Herrera-Luna

Center for Computing Research, National Polytechnic Institute,
Juan de Dios Bátiz and Miguel Othón de Mendizábal, P.O. 07738, Gustavo A Madero, México
{sgodoyc,edgardo}@cic.ipn.mx, edith.hluna@gmail.com

Abstract. In the context of forensic and criminalistics studies the problem of identifying the author of a manuscript is generally expressed as a supervised-classification problem. In this paper a new approach for modeling a manuscript at the word and text line levels is presented. This new approach introduces an eclectic paradigm between texture-related and structure-related modeling approaches. Compared to previously published works, the proposed method significantly reduces the number and complexity of the text-features to be extracted from the text. Extensive experimentation with the proposed model shows it to be faster and easier to implement than other models, making it ideal for extensive use in forensic and criminalistics studies.

Keywords: Collective decision, Author identification, Manuscript text, Supervised pattern recognition.

1 Introduction

The analysis of handwritten text, for the purpose of authentication and author identification, is a tool that allows researchers to study text from many different points of view according to the number of authors, the type and quantity of characteristics extracted from the text, the classification algorithms used for its recognition, and so on. The analysis of manuscripts is at the core of graphoscopic analysis techniques and plays an important role in a number of practical problems, included, but not limited to, forensic and criminalist processing of evidence, validation of legal documents, historiography, psychological profiling, etc.

Since the 1950's several manuscript author identification and verification methods have been developed for forensic document analysis. Before the era of digital communication, the wide range of implements and supports for writing motivated several approaches to characterize handwriting. Those approaches differ among themselves by their way of capturing data and by their dependence on the semantics of the written text.

Computer aided manuscript analysis is a broad field of study that encompasses two main areas: Optical Character Recognition (OCR) and Writing Identification and

---

[*] Corresponding author.

L. Alvarez et al. (Eds.): CIARP 2012, LNCS 7441, pp. 757–764, 2012.

Verification (WIV). OCR has been widely studied and consists of recognizing characters from a digital image of a manuscript in such a way that the text may be interpreted word by word or even symbol by symbol [19].

The WIV area deals with the recognition of a manuscript's author, the relationship of several authors to different documents, the identification of document alterations, etc. In some WIV approaches it is necessary to know the semantic contents of the words that make-up the text (text-dependent methods) [20], and in others, the method does not depend on semantic contents (text-independent methods) [2].

Computer-related characteristics extracted from the text may be texture-related or structure-related [3]. When extracting texture characteristics, the document is seen and processed as an image (not as a text), but when structural characteristics are extracted, a description similar to that given by a graphoscopic expert is sought in order to characterize the properties of the author's writing style.

This paper introduces a new approach to modeling handwritten text by extracting off-line static features from the manuscript at the line and word levels. This method allows the use of collective decision algorithms for author recognition tasks. The proposed approach is independent of the semantics and represents a hybrid or eclectic approach between texture and structural characteristics.

2   Related Works

Recently, amongst already published papers are [1] and [4], where the identification efficiency is considerably reduced due to the high number of authors in the supervision sample. The paper [5] propose a manuscript's texture analysis technique using Gabor's filters and grey-scale co-occurrence matrices (GSCM) using the weighted Euclidean distance and a K-NN classifier [6] to identify 40 different authors. Authors in [7] propose the use of horizontal projections and morphological operators together with the texture characteristics of English and Greek words, using a multilayer perceptron and a Bayesian classifier.

The method proposed in [3] splits words into graphemes and at the same time combine the local characteristics extracted from regions of text. Finally they employ a commonly used model for information retrieval, known as vector space model, for the task of identifying the author of a manuscript. The research outlined in [8] presents an algorithm that extracts structural features from characters and graphemes, by means of a genetic algorithm, to look for optimal characteristics after extracting 31 characteristics from each selected word and using a neural network classifier. In their doctoral dissertation [2] extract textural features from manuscripts and then use probability functions and an Euclidean and Hamming distance-based K-NN classifier to identify and verify the author. In [9] is extracted a set of structural features from text lines, as well as a set of fractal-based features, resulting in a 90% plus efficiency of author recognition.

In [10] a study can be found about handwritten text recognition, taking into account methodologies for working in-line and off-line. In [11] the IAM database is described in a general way and an analysis is made about the way in which images included were segmented. The last two papers include references that detail recent research work on manuscript analysis.

More recently, in [17] a segmentation methodology, in text lines and words, of handwritten documents is presented. Text line segmentation is achieved by applying Hough transform on a subset of the document image connected components. With careful post-processing steps authors claim to achieve an efficient separation of vertically connected characters using a novel method based on skeletonization. They use several performance measures to compare the text line segmentation and word segmentation results against the available supervision sample. Paper [19] shows a methodology for off-line handwritten character recognition. The proposed methodology relies on a new feature extraction technique based on recursive subdivisions of the character image so that the resulting sub-images have an approximately equal number of foreground pixels. Feature extraction is followed by a two-stage classification scheme based on the level of granularity of the feature extraction method.

Until today the most reliable results achieved in authorship recognition over manuscripts can be found in [3], [4], [5], [8], [12] and [17].

3   Proposed Model

The basic idea behind the proposed model is to extract from the manuscript a different set of features at the line and word levels. The final model uses patterns that describe the manuscript at the paragraph level by selecting and averaging all features extracted from lines that comprise each paragraph. Extracted features are then processed at different stages by an algorithm that assigns a potential author to each paragraph and then decides the authorship of the whole manuscript by collecting all the evidence learned from each paragraph in the text.

Manuscript images are first pre-processed in order to sharpen the digital image and remove noise. A binary image of the manuscript is obtained by thresholding over the green plane of the original color image with Otsu [13] and Khashman - Sekeroglu [14] methods. Finally, a geodesic reconstruction of each manuscript is obtained by erosion using the Otsu-processed image as a marker (see Figure 1). All features are extracted from the binary image of each manuscript.

At the line level the space percentage occupied by the left margin, the right margin, the separation between subsequent lines, the general direction of the writing and the inter-word space are considered. Features extracted at the word level include the proportions of the middle zone of the writing compared to that of the upper and lower zones, word inclination and the presence of a crest and an axis in all words. Figure 2 shows the semantics of all features extracted at the line and word levels.

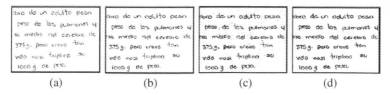

(a)   (b)   (c)   (d)

Fig. 1. (a) Sample manuscript color image, (b) Otsu-thresholding over the green plane, (c) Khashman – Sekeroglu thresholding, (d) final noise-free binary image

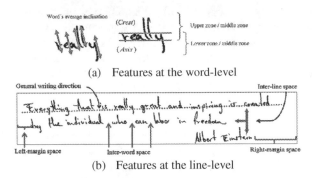

(a)   Features at the word-level

(b)   Features at the line-level

Fig. 2. Features extracted at different levels

Each manuscript's text line is represented by a 22-tuple with word-level and line-level features. Word-level features are extracted from words with and without upper-zone, as well as from words with and without lower-zone. All features are positive real or integer numbers, except for the Average inclination of words, which takes values in the interval [-1, 1] of real numbers. Nevertheless a good recognition method must be independent of the representation space for the objects. Table 1 sums up the features extracted at the word and line levels.

Table 1. Features representing a line of text

Word-level features	Line-level features
Average upper/middle zone ratio	Left and right margins space percentage
Average lower/middle zone ratio	Current/previous line ratio
Average inclination of words	Current/next line ratio
Number of words in the line	Average inter-word space
	General direction of writing.

4   Recognition Process

The manuscript whose author is to be recognized is pre-processed and the aforementioned features are extracted to form several line and paragraph patterns and a weighted syntactic-distance function is used for comparison between patterns. The particular differentiated-weighting scheme used assigns a different feature weight value depending on the class being tested. This mechanism provides enough flexibility to accurately discriminate patterns belonging to classes where the same sub-set of features is relevant but with a different proportion in each case. Details about such a scheme and its use for author recognition can be found on [15].

Each text-line pattern is independently classified and then a collective decision rule is applied, issuing a final decision regarding the authorship of the text. This final decision may be one of the authors included in the supervision sample or an unknown author not included in the sample, if certain similarity thresholds previously established are not met. Pseudo code of the specific procedure looks as follows:

1. For each pattern in the supervision sample, determine its class representativeness.
2. Select only the most representative patterns to form a Reduced Supervision Sample.
3. Compare each control pattern with the reduced supervision sample formed in step 2.
4. Calculate the average similarities of control patterns vs representative patterns.
5. Use the highest average similarity as the final decision rule.
6. If considered convenient, add the recently identified patterns to the supervision sample and recalculate the set of objects that are representative of each class.

The classification of the manuscript is a collective decision based on the lines contained in a given text. The procedure for its classification looks as follows:

1. Create a pattern for each text-line in the manuscript and classify it.
2. The whole manuscript is labeled as the class which contains the majority of its line-patterns, allowing a maximum of classes.

This multiple-pattern representation of each manuscript, along with the collective decision criteria used by the solution rule, establishes a new and not previously explored approach for this kind of problems. The resulting impact over the precision and general efficiency of the identification process can be seen on the next section.

5 Experimental Results

An *ad hoc* database was created with manuscripts written by 50 test subjects. Each subjected wrote three handwritten texts, always using print-type letters. Each manuscript contains from 5 to 9 text lines, giving closely a total of 600 lines. Text contents were selected arbitrarily from non-technical books with no restrictions on the logic or semantics. Images of those manuscripts were digitally scanned at 300dpi with a conventional scanner and all manuscripts were written with the same black ink pen and white paper.

Three supervision and control samples were built for the experiments to take place. For experiment type #1, the supervision sample contains the most representative patterns in each class. In experiment type #2 the total number of manuscripts is randomly divided between the supervision sample and the control sample. Finally, for experiment type #3 only the least representative patterns from each class was selected for the supervision sample. In each experiment type the objects from the control sample are classified taking the supervision sample objects as a reference. Three class-representative patterns were selected from each class within the supervision sample, according to the previously described procedure.

The following rule was used for assessing the efficiency of the manuscript classification: identification is considered correct if and only if the manuscript is classified in less than q classes and one of them is the correct one. Table 2 shows some experimental results obtained, for all three experiments types, when using a differentiated feature-weighting scheme.

Table 1. Results from the first experiment set

Experiment type	% of text-lines recognition	% of manuscript recognition
1	60.16	72.22
1	61.79	72.22
2	67.72	88.89
2	64.57	94.44
3	65.35	88.89
3	62.99	83.33

Although the percentage of correct text-line recognition seems unacceptably low, results only got better for the manuscript level, reaching levels higher than 80% in several cases. Although the classification at the line level was substantially altered, the impact of the differentiated feature-weighting scheme becomes evident in the results at a text level.

A second set of experiments was carried out, considering the centroid of each class as the only representative pattern for that same class. This raised the effectiveness of the recognition for the line level and to a lesser degree for the classification of the whole manuscript (See Table 3).

Table 4 shows this research's results compared with those by other authors (taken from Bensefia et al. 2005). The comparison is summarized and some details are added on the type of methodology applied.

Table 2. Results from the second experiment set

Experiment type	% of text-lines recognition	% of manuscript recognition
1	73.17	94.44
2	70.08	88.89
3	72.44	94.44

Table 3. Comparison of manuscript's author identification

Publication	Number of writers	Supervision Sample	Lexicon dependency	Reported Performance (%)
Said et al. (2000) [5]	40	Few lines handwritten text	No	95.0
Zois and Anastassopoulos (2000) [7]	50	45 examples, the same word	Yes	92.48
Marti et al. (2001) [16]	20	5 examples of the same text	Yes	90.00
Bensefia et al. (2005)[3]	88	Paragraphs / 3-4 words	No	93.0 / 90.0
This paper	**30**	**3 examples of the same text**	**No**	**94.44**

6   Conclusions

A collective decision algorithm with a differentiated feature-weighting scheme is used to identify the author of a manuscript by means of the individual classification of the text lines that comprise the manuscript. The descriptive features used to make up the patterns representing such lines include features extracted at the word-level as well as at the line-level. When all the text lines have been classified, a final collective decision regarding the author of such text is applied. The highest efficiency percentages on identification are achieved in those experiments in which centroids are used as class representative patterns.

A comparison with previously published works shows that the modeling approach herein proposed yields better results than previous related works, with the added advantage that the recognition process needs not to be dependent on the semantic contents of the text. The implementation of these improvements may be extremely useful for the identification of authors of handwritten texts, mainly in forensic control situations as well as in authentication and security institutions.

Acknowledgements. The authors would like to thank the Academic Secretary, COFAA, Postgraduate and Research Secretary, and Centre for Computing Research of the National Polytechnic Institute (IPN), CONACyT and SNI, for their economic support to carry out this work.

References

1. Srihari, S.N., Cha, S.-H., Arora, H., Lee, S.: Individuality of Handwriting. Journal of Forensic Sciences 47(4), Paper ID JFS2001227-474 (2001)
2. Pecharromán-Balbás, S.: Reconocimiento de escritor independiente de texto basado en características de textura. Tesis doctoral. Escuela Politécnica Superior, Universidad Autónoma de Madrid (2007)
3. Bensefia, A., Paquet, T., Heutte, L.: A writer identification and verification system. Pattern Recognition Letters 26, 2080–2092 (2005)
4. Srihari, S.N.: Recognition of handwritten and machine-printed text for postal address interpretation. Pattern Recognition Letters 14(4), 291–302 (1993)
5. Said, H., Tan, T., Baker, K.: Personal Identification Based on Handwriting. Pattern Recognition 33(1), 149–160 (2000)
6. Cover, T.M., Hart, P.E.: Nearest neighbour pattern classification. IEEE Trans. Inform. Theory, IT-13(1), 21–27 (1967)
7. Zois, E., Anastassopoulos, V.: Morphological waveform coding for writer identification. Pattern Recognition 33(3), 385–398 (2000)
8. Pervouchine, V., Leedham, G.: Extraction and analysis of forensic document examiner features used for writer identification. Pattern Recognition 40, 1004–1013 (2007)
9. Hertel, C., Bunke, H.: A Set of Novel Features for Writer Identification. In: Proc. Fourth Int'l Conf. Audio and Video-Based Biometric Person Authentication, pp. 679–687 (2003)
10. Plamondon, R., Srihari, S.N.: On-line and off-line handwriting recognition: A comprehensive survey. IEEE Transactions on Pattern Analysis and Machine Intelligence 22, 63–84 (2000)
11. Zimmermann, M., Bunke, H.: Automatic segmentation of the IAM off-line handwritten {English} text database. In: 16th International Conf. on Pattern Recognition, Canada, vol. 4, pp. 35–39 (2002)

12. Srihari, S.N.: Handwriting identification: research to study validity of individuality of handwriting and develop computer-assisted procedures for comparing handwriting. University of Buffalo, U.S.A. Center of Excellence for Document Analysis and Recognition. Tech. Rep. CEDAR-TR-01-1 (2001)

13. Otsu, N.: A threshold selection method from gray-level histograms. IEEE Trans. Sys., Man., Cyber. 9, 62–66 (1979)

14. Khashman, A., Sekeroglu, B.: A Novel Thresholding Method for Text Separation and Document Enhancement. In: Proceedings of the 11th Pan-Hellenic Conference in Informatics, Greece, pp. 324–330 (2007)

15. Herrera-Luna, E., Felipe-Riverón, E., Godoy-Calderón, S.: A supervised algorithm with a new differentiated-weighting scheme for identifying the author of a handwritten text. Pattern Recognition Letters 32(2), 1139–1144 (2011)

16. Marti, U.V., Messerli, R., Bunke, H.: Writer identification using text line based features. In: Proc. ICDAR 2001, pp. 101–105 (2001)

17. Louloudis, G., Gatos, B., Pratikakis, I., Halatsis, C.: Text line and word segmentation of handwritten documents. Pattern Recognition 42, 3169–3183 (2009)

18. Bertolami, R., Bunke, H.: Hidden Markov model-based ensemble methods for offline handwritten text line recognition. Pattern Recognition 41, 3452–3460 (2008)

19. Vamvakas, G., Gatos, B., Perantonis, S.J.: Handwritten character recognition through two-stage foreground sub-sampling. Pattern Recognition 43, 2807–2816 (2010)

20. Jou, C., Lee, H.C.: Handwritten numeral recognition based on simplified structural classification and fuzzy memberships. Expert Systems with Applications 36, 11858–11863 (2009)

Extraction of Stationary Spectral Components Using Stochastic Variability

David Cárdenas-Peña,
Juan David Martínez-Vargas, and Germán Castellanos-Dominguez

Signal Processing and Recognition Group, Universidad Nacional de Colombia,
Km. 9, Vía al aeropuerto, Campus la Nubia, Caldas, Manizales, Colombia
{dcardenasp,jmartinezv,cgcastellanosd}@unal.edu.co

Abstract. Biosignal recordings are widely used in the medical environment to support the evaluation and the diagnosis of pathologies. Nevertheless, the main difficulty lies in the non-stationary behavior of the biosignals, making difficult the obtention of patterns characterizing the changes in physiological or pathological states. Thus, the obtention of the stationary and non-stationary components of a biosignal poses still an open issue. This work proposes a methodology to detect time-homogeneities based on time-frequency analysis aiming to extract the non-stationary behavior of the biosignal. Two homogeneity constraints are introduced as the measure of stochastic variability of the considered dataset. The first one is the relevance value, which gives information about the contribution of the spectral component to the process. The second one is based on the first and second moments of stochastic variability map, being related to the uniformity along the time of each spectral component. Results show an increase in the stationarity of the reconstructions from the enhanced time-frequency representations. Moreover, the inter class distance for the reconstructed time-series show more discrimination on the stationary component than on the non-stationary one. Those extracted components tend to meet the requirement of most algorithms proposed for other tasks, such as biosignal classification problems, leading to a performance increase of the methodologies.

Keywords: Time-evolving Latent Variable Decomposition, Multivariate Locally Stationary Time Series, Stationarity Enhancement.

1 Introduction

In biosignal applications, it is often of interest to be able to separate an observed time series into two or more groups with different stochastic behavior [4]. In particular, there is a need for distinguishing stationary from non-stationary components, either because its assumption is a pre-requisite for applying most of standard algorithms devoted to steady-state regimes, or because its breakdown conveys specific information in evolutive contexts, as remarked in [8,1]. In the analysis of biomedical data, corresponding recordings usually appear non-stationary (temporal and spectral characteristics of the signal vary over time),

L. Alvarez et al. (Eds.): CIARP 2012, LNCS 7441, pp. 765–772, 2012.

although there exist stationary sources, these are not discernible, since superpositions of stationary and non-stationary components can be measured.

Commonly, the time domain non-stationariness can be quantitative measured by the variation of either first two statistical moments over time (second order process). Instead, the non-stationary upon the spectrum domain of biological signals has been emphasized more recently, because of the corresponding physiological meanings of some spectral components [3], for instance, for Heat Rate Variability (HRV) recordings, the spectral components can provide information about the relative inputs of the two autonomic nervous system mutually antagonistic components the sympathetic one, which acts to increase heart rate, and the parasympathetic component acting to slow the heart and to dilate blood vessels [4]. Nevertheless, even the traditional time-averaged spectrum of non-stationary signals, being widely used, is not appropriate for quantifying the temporal variability in the spectrum. Therefore, techniques devoted to provide clear images of the energy distribution on the time-frequency (t–f) plane, directly demonstrating the non-stationarity of the signal, have been proposed for decomposition into stationary and non-stationary components, namely, t–f localized linear splines, t–f representations, wavelets, empirical mode decomposition, and stationary subspace analysis [7]. Generally, extraction of stationary components from real-valued biosignal can be provided by using the following two subsequent stages: i) decomposition of underlying time series, by properly handling the signal model within a stochastic subspace framework, and ii) searching of the needed number of components to match *a priori* given stationary homogeneity constrains.

This work is based on evolutionary time-frequency (t-f) analysis, for which testing of the time-homogeneity constraints of the evolutionary spectra is evaluated at different instants of time by using multivariate time series subspace representation. In this sense, a new methodology for stationarity enhancement on biosignals is introduced. The paper is organized as follows: The Section 2 is dedicated to the description of the methods required to perform the stationarity enhancement; in Section 3, the experimental setup is described and obtained results are presented. Finally, the results are properly discussed in Section 4.

2   Background

2.1   Enhanced t-f Representation

Decomposition into stationary and non-stationary components is carried out upon enhanced t-f representation of the input data. In particular, the short time Fourier transform is employed introducing a time localization concept by means of a tapering window function of short duration, ϕ, that is going along the underlying biosignal, $y(t)$, as follows:

$$\boldsymbol{S}_y(t, f) = \left| \int_T y(\tau)\phi(\tau - t)e^{-j2\pi f\tau} d\tau \right|^2, \; \boldsymbol{S}_y(t, f) \in \mathbb{R}^+ \tag{1}$$

with $t, \tau \in T, f \in F$. Based on introduced *spectrogram* of Eq. (1), the corresponding t–f representation matrix, $\boldsymbol{S}_y \in \mathbb{R}^{T \times F}$, can be described by the row vector set, $\boldsymbol{S}_y = [\boldsymbol{s}_1 \ldots \boldsymbol{s}_f \ldots \boldsymbol{s}_F]^\top$, with $\boldsymbol{s}_f \in \mathbb{R}^{1 \times T}$, where the vector $\boldsymbol{s}_f = [s(f,1) \ldots s(f,t) \ldots (f,T)]$, with $s(f,t) \in \mathbb{R}$, is each one of the time–variant spectral decomposition components at frequency f, and equally sampled through the time axis.

2.2 Measure of Stochastic Variability

Several variability analysis techniques suitable for clinical applications had been proposed, including statistical, geometric, energetic, informational, and invariant measures [2]. In this research, the amount of stochastic variability of the spectral component set is computed following the approach given in [4], that is based on time-variant decomposition estimated by adapting in time any of commonly used latent variable techniques, upon which a piecewise stationary restriction is imposed [6]. So, under the locally stationary assumption, consistent estimates of the time-varying spectral density matrix are obtained and consequently consistent estimates of the time-varying eigenvalues and eigenvectors may be accomplished [5]. Namely, the time–evolving principal component analysis is extended to the dynamic feature modeling by stacking the input observation matrix in the following manner:

$$\boldsymbol{\Xi}_y = \begin{bmatrix} s_1^1 & s_2^1 & \cdots & s_F^1 \\ s_1^2 & s_2^2 & \cdots & s_F^2 \\ \vdots & \vdots & \vdots & \vdots \\ s_1^M & s_2^M & \cdots & s_F^M \end{bmatrix}, \ \boldsymbol{\Xi}_y \subset \mathbb{R}^{M \times FT} \tag{2}$$

where vector $\boldsymbol{s}_f^i$ corresponds to f-th short–term spectral component estimated from the i-th spectrogram matrix, $\boldsymbol{S}_y^i$, which is related to the i-th object, with $i \in M$. Accordingly, the amount of stochastic variability of the spectral component set is computed by the singular value decomposition calculation over observation matrix in Eq. (2). So, the following time–variant relevance measure is carried out [6]:

$$\boldsymbol{g}(\boldsymbol{\Xi}_y; \tau) = [\chi(1) \ \cdots \ \chi(\tau) \ \cdots \ \chi(FT)]^\top, \in \mathbb{R}^{FT \times 1} \tag{3}$$

being $\chi(\tau) = \boldsymbol{E}\{|\lambda_f^2 v_f(\tau)| : \forall f \in F\}$, where $\{\lambda_f\}$ is the relevance eigenvalue set of matrix $\boldsymbol{\Xi}_y$, and scalar–valued $v_f(\tau)$ is the respective element at τ moment, with $\tau = 1, \ldots, FT$ that indexes every one of the relevance values computed for the whole time–variant data set (notation $\boldsymbol{E}\{\cdot\}$ stands for the expectation operator). At the end of the multivariate procedure, a relevance map $\boldsymbol{\Gamma}(t,f) = [g(\boldsymbol{s}_1) \ldots g(\boldsymbol{s}_f) \ldots g(\boldsymbol{s}_F)], \in \mathbb{R}^{T \times F}$ is achieved that contains stochastic variability measured for the whole spectral component set, $\{\boldsymbol{s}_f\}$.

Matching stochastic homogeneity constrains: From the relevance map $\boldsymbol{\Gamma}(t,f)$, the amount of information given for each spectral component, $\boldsymbol{s}_f$, can be derived by averaging the relevance matrix over the frequency axis, yielding the relevance marginal $\gamma(f)$. Thus, the higher the value of $\gamma(f)$, the more relevant the spectral component s_f. With this constrains in mind, a weighting t–f function can be built with those frequency components exceeding a relevance threshold η, as follows:

$$\omega_f(\eta) = \begin{cases} 1, & \text{if } \gamma(f) > \eta \\ 0, & \text{otherwise} \end{cases}, \quad \forall f \in F. \tag{4}$$

Additionally, taking each relevant spectral component as a time-series s_f, regarded as stochastic process, any randomness structure estimator must remain constant in time, by instance, the mean value. This work proposes to take the following assumption:

$$\|\boldsymbol{E}\{g(\boldsymbol{s}_f); t\} - \boldsymbol{E}\{g(\boldsymbol{s}_f); t - \tau\}\| \leq \varepsilon, \quad \forall t, \tau \in T \tag{5}$$

with $\varepsilon \to 0$. Thus, the weighting t–f function can be redefined with those relevant frequency bands satisfying the previous conditions, becoming in a η, ε dependant function, $\boldsymbol{\omega}_f(\eta, \varepsilon)$.

In practice, the extraction of non–stationary components from a random signal formally can be related as filtration task, carried out under the following assumptions [7]:

- the observed signals are linear superpositions of stationary and non-stationary sources, so, an observable given time series vector, $\boldsymbol{y}$, is separated into two unobservable components, i.e., a stationary and non–stationary, respectively;

$$\boldsymbol{y} = \boldsymbol{y}^* + \varsigma,$$

- the non-stationarity component, ς, is a second order measurable stochastic process.

Hence, the main assumption in this research is that by selecting the relevant and stationary frequency bands of the t–f maps, according with the level of stochastic homogeneity of the random variable s_f, a given time series $\boldsymbol{y}$ can be split into the stationary $\boldsymbol{y}^*$ and non–stationary ς parts.

Measuring the stationarity degree of the time series: As proposed in [1], firstly, a set of J stationary surrogate signals $\{s_j : j = 1, \ldots, J\}$ is computed from a given signal. Then, a contrast measure, for a given time series y, is defined as:

$$c_n(y) := d(\boldsymbol{S}_y(t, f), \boldsymbol{E}\{\boldsymbol{S}_y(t, f) : \forall t \in T\}) \tag{6}$$

where $d \in \mathbb{R}^+$ is some suitable spectral distance, in this case the Kullback-Leibler distance was used. Finally, the index of non-stationarity is determined as:

$$\kappa = \sqrt{\frac{\text{var}(c_n(y) : \forall t \in T)}{\boldsymbol{E}\{\text{var}(c_n(s_j) : \forall t \in T) : \forall j\}}} \tag{7}$$

3   Experimental Set-up

3.1   Database Description

The database holds a available collection of 1-*min* HRV segments selected from **Physionet**, which holds 70 electrocardiographic recordings, each one including a set of reference annotations added every minute of the recording indicating either the presence of absence of apnoea during each segment. Finally, 600 HRV segments of 1-minute length (300 apneic and 300 normal labeled) were selected from 25 training recordings to build the dataset [4].

3.2   Splitting into Stationary and Non-stationary Subspaces

Time-Frequency Representations Enhancement of Estimated Time Series: In this work, according to the spectral HRV signal properties, the STFT based quadratic spectrogram is computed by sliding windows for the following set of estimation parameters: a 32.5 *ms* hamming window, 50% of overlapping, and 512 frequency bins within a range of 0 to 1 *Hz*. For the sake of medical interpretation, the whole frequency rank is splitted into sub–frequency bands, termed Low Frequency (LF) spectral band ($f \in [0.04 - 0.15]Hz$) and High Frequency (HF) spectral band ($f \in [0.15 - 0.5]Hz$).

Weighting Function Selection: The main core of this approach is to find the stationary and non-stationary components of a given time series. For this aim, the weighting t–f function derived from the relevance map, must be tuned to optimize the level of stationarity of the time-series, by assuming: (i) the higher the relevance threshold η, the more relevant the selected spectral components s_f^*; and (ii) the larger value of ε, the more presence of non-stationary components to the signal. Thus, once the thresholds η and ε are selected, the stationary y^* and non–stationary ς parts of the time series can be derived by the inverse STFT.

To test the performance of the proposed methodology, two measures are established. Firstly, the κ index assessing the degree of signal non-stationarity is used. So, the κ values are computed for each recording on the dataset (κ_y) and its stationary (κ_{y^*}) and non-stationary (κ_ς) reconstructions, obtained with the proposed approach. Consequently, the lower the κ index, the more stationary the time-series.

Secondly, intra and inter class distance functions are employed to measure quantitatively the influence of the stationarity and non-stationarity on the grouping of the signals. A Hausdorff distance scheme was employed as the distance between two sets (classes). Since such scheme requires the comparison of all possible pairs of time-variant subjects, the correlation distance was choosen as the pairwise subject comparison.

Since the relevance map is computed for both spectral bands, η and ε have to be estimated for each of them. The marginals $\gamma_{LF}(f)$ and $\gamma_{HF}(f)$ are estimated for their respective bands as follows:

$$\gamma_{LF}(f) = \boldsymbol{E}\{g(\boldsymbol{s}_f); t\}; \forall f \in [0.04 - 0.15]Hz$$
$$\gamma_{HF}(f) = \boldsymbol{E}\{g(\boldsymbol{s}_f); t\}; \forall f \in [0.15 - 0.5]Hz,$$

while the ratios $\varepsilon_{LF}(f)$ and $\varepsilon_{HF}(f)$ are defined as, $\varepsilon(f) = \boldsymbol{\sigma}(f)/\boldsymbol{\gamma}(f)$, being $\boldsymbol{\sigma}(f)$ the standard deviation of $g(\boldsymbol{s}_f)$. Finally, the marginals $\boldsymbol{\gamma}(f)$ and ratios $\varepsilon(f)$ are normalized in the interval $[0, 1]$.

4   Results and Discussion

Figure 1(a) shows the results of k for the iterative procedure, while varying the relevance threshold η between $[0.1, 0.8]$ with steps of 0.1, and the stationarity threshold ε between $[0.1, 0.7]$ with steps of 0.1. As expected, the higher values of $k(\kappa_\varsigma > \kappa_{y^*})$, are presented for lower values of ε. In that case, the variability of the spectral components is highly restricted, therefore the presence of non-stationary components is low.

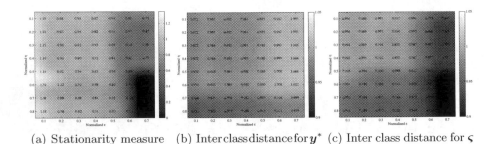

(a) Stationarity measure   (b) Inter class distance for y^* (c) Inter class distance for ς

Fig. 1. Experimental results for tested configurations of ε and η

Figures 1(b) and 1(c) depict the distance measure between apneic and normal classes for both reconstructions, stationary and non-stationary, respectively. Two facts have to be highlighted in those results. Firstly, the larger the ε threshold, the larger the inter-class distance for the stationary reconstruction (y^*) and the shorter the inter-class distance for the non-stationary reconstruction (ς). Which means that the stationary components of such biosignals contain the inner class dynamics. Secondly, it is expected to obtain higher distances on lower values of the η threshold. Such behavior is related to the number of relevant components used on the reconstructions. Since higher thresholds turn off more components on each class, all subjects are equally represented on such frequencies, reducing the pairwise correlation distance of the subjects.

Figure 2 shows an example of the estimated t-f representation (left), along to the obtained relevance map for both spectral bands (center) and the relevance marginal $\gamma(f)$, as well as its standard deviation $\sigma(f)$ (right). Moreover, as an example, the frequency weighting function for $\eta = \varepsilon = 0.6$ is plotted as a blue line over the marginal. It can be seen that the proposed measure attempts to select not only the more relevant but also the more steady components of the map. Frequencies with higher relevance are allowed to have higher variance and the less relevant frequencies require a more steady behavior to be taken into account.

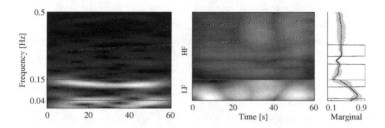

Fig. 2. Relevance map and relevance marginal estimation for each spectral band of the HRV database. Frequency weighting function in blue.

An example of the reconstruction procedure is shown in Figure 3. In the left side, a common pathological signal is depicted along with its t-f representation; the relevant stationary and relevant non stationary component of the t-f enhanced by the weighting function are presented in the middle top and middle bottom, respectively; in the right side are shown the reconstructions of each part of the signal. It must be highlighted that the stationary reconstruction is smoother than the non-stationary side. This kind of signals tends to meet the requirements of most of the standard algorithms devoted to steady-state regimes.

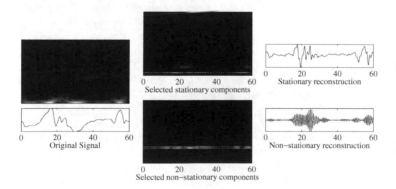

Fig. 3. Reconstruction procedure for both stationary and non-stationary components of the signal

5   Conclusions

A new methodology for stationarity enhancement on biosignals is presented. The performance is tested on a well known database, which comprise non-stationary behaviors, namely, heart rate variability recordings. The methodology estimates a spectral weighting function from a stochastic variability map. Such function is applied as a filter enhancing the stationary components of the signal. As measure of the non-stationarity the κ, proposed by [1] is used. Results show an increase in the stationarity of the reconstructions from the enhanced t-f representations as well as an improvement on the representation of each class As future work, the use of several non-stationarity measures is proposed, as well as the use of the methodology for solving non-stationary signal discrimination issues.

Acknowledgments. This work is supported by *"Centro de Investigación e Innovaciónn de Excelencia - ARTICA*, and *Programa Nacional de Formación de Investigadores "Generación del Bicentenario", 2011*, financed by COLCIENCIAS".

References

1. Borgnat, P., Flandrin, P., Honeine, P., Richard, C., Xiao, J.: Testing stationarity with surrogates: A time-frequency approach. Submitted to IEEE Trans. Signal Processing 58(7), 3459–3470 (2009)
2. Bravi, A., Longtin, A., Seely, A.: Review and classification of variability analysis techniques with clinical applications. BioMedical Engineering OnLine 10(1), 90 (2011)
3. Cao, C., Slobounov, S.: Application of a novel measure of eeg non-stationarity as shannon- entropy of the peak frequency shifting for detecting residual abnormalities in concussed individuals. Clinical Neurophysiology 122(7), 1314–1321 (2011)
4. Martinez-Vargas, J.D., Sepulveda-Cano, L.M., Travieso-Gonzalez, C., Castellanos-Dominguez, G.: Detection of obstructive sleep apnoea using dynamic filter-banked features. Expert Systems with Applications 39(10), 9118–9128 (2012)
5. Ombao, H., Ringo Ho, M.: Time-dependent frequency domain principal components analysis of multichannel non-stationary signals. Comput. Stat. Data Anal. 50(9), 2339–2360 (2006)
6. Sepulveda-Cano, L., Acosta-Medina, C.: Castellanos-Dominguez G. Relevance Analysis of Stochastic Biosignals for Identification of Pathologies. EURASIP Journal on Advances in Signal Processing 2011, 10 (2011)
7. Von Buenau, P., Meinecke, F., Kiraly, F., Mueller, K.: Finding stationary subspaces in multivariate time series. Physical Review Letters 103(21), 214101-1–214101-4 (2009)
8. Weng, X., Shen, J.: Finding discordant subsequence in multivariate time series. In: 2007 IEEE International Conference on Automation and Logistics, pp. 1731–1735 (August 2007)

Finding Edges by a Contrario Detection of Periodic Subsequences

Mariano Tepper[1,*], Pablo Musé[2], Andrés Almansa[3], and Marta Mejail[1]

[1] Departamento de Computación, Facultad de Ciencias Exactas y Naturales,
Universidad de Buenos Aires, Argentina
{mtepper,marta}@dc.uba.ar
[2] Instituto de Ingeniería Eléctrica, Facultad de Ingeniería,
Universidad de la República, Uruguay
pmuse@fing.edu.uy
[3] CNRS - LTCI UMR5141, Telecom ParisTech, France
andres.almansa@telecom-paristech.fr

Abstract. A new method to detect salient pieces of boundaries in an image is presented. After detecting perceptually meaningful level lines, periodic binary sequences are built by labeling each point in close curves as salient or non-salient. We propose a general and automatic method to detect meaningful subsequences within these binary sequences. Experimental results show its good performance.

Keywords: topographic maps, level lines, periodic binary sequences, edge detection, Helmholtz principle.

1   Introduction

Shape plays a key role in our cognitive system: in the perception of shape lies the beginning of concept formation. Formally, shapes in an image can be defined by extracting contours from solid objects. Shapes can be represented and analyzed as the locus of an infinite number of points, which leads to level-sets methods [7].

We define an image as a function $u : \mathbb{R}^2 \to \mathbb{R}$ with continuous first derivatives. Level sets [7], or level lines, provide a complete and contrast-invariant image description. We define the boundaries of the connected components of a level set as a level line. These level lines have the following properties: (1) level lines are closed Jordan curves; (2) level lines at different levels are disjoint; (3) by topological inclusion, level lines form a partially ordered set.

We call the collection of level lines (along with their level) a topographic map. The inclusion relation allows to embed the topographic map in a tree-like representation. For extracting the level lines of a digital image we use the Fast Level Set Transform (FLST) [6] which computes level lines by bilinear interpolation. In general, the topographic map is an infinite set and so only quantized grey levels are considered, ensuring that the set is finite.

---

* Present address: Department of Electrical and Computer Engineering, University of Minnesota.

L. Alvarez et al. (Eds.): CIARP 2012, LNCS 7441, pp. 773–780, 2012.
© Springer-Verlag Berlin Heidelberg 2012

Edge detectors, from which the most renowned is Canny's [1], rely on the fact that information is concentrated along contours (regions where contrast changes abruptly). From one side, only a subset of the topographic map is necessary to obtain a *perceptually* complete description. Going to a deeper level, perceptually important level lines, in general, are so because they contain contrasted *pieces*. In summary, we have to prune the topographic map and then prune inside the level lines themselves.

The search for perceptually important contours will focus on unexpected configurations, rising from the perceptual laws of Gestalt Theory [5]. From an algorithmic point of view, the main problem with the Gestalt rules is their qualitative nature. Desolneux et al. [3] developed the Computational Gestalt detection theory which seeks to provide a quantitative assessment of gestalts. It is primarily based on the Helmholtz principle which states that conspicuous structures may be viewed as exceptions to randomness. In this approach, there is no need to characterize the elements one wishes to detect but contrarily, the elements one wishes to avoid detecting, i.e., the background model. When an element sufficiently deviates from the background model, it is considered meaningful and thus, detected.

Within this framework, Desolneux et al. [3] proposed an algorithm to detect contrasted level lines in grey level images, called meaningful boundaries. Further improvements to this algorithm were proposed by Cao et al. [2] and by Tepper et al. [8,9]. In this work we address the dissection of meaningful boundaries, developing an algorithm to select salient pieces contained in them. Each level line is considered as a periodic binary sequence where, following a partial saliency model, each point is labeled as salient or non-salient. Then, the goal is to extract meaningful subsequences of salient points. In order to do so, we extend to the periodic case an algorithm for binary subsequence detection proposed by Grompone et al [4].

The remainder of this paper is organized as follows. In Section 2 we recall the definition by Tepper of meaningful boundaries[8]. In Section 3 we describe the proposed algorithm. In Section 4 we show examples that prove the pertinence of the approach and provide some final remarks.

2   Meaningful Contrasted Boundaries

We begin by formally explaining the meaningful boundaries algorithm, as defined by Tepper et al. [8,9].

Let C be a level line of the image u and let us denote by $\{x_i\}_{i=0...n-1}$ the n regularly sampled points of C, with arc-length two pixels, which in the a contrario noise model are assumed to be independent. In particular the gradients at these points are independent random variables (the image gradient norm $|Du|$ can be computed by standard finite differences on a 2×2 neighborhood). We note by μ_k $(0 \leq k < n)$ the k-th value of the values $|Du|(x_i)$ sorted in ascending order.

The detection algorithm consists in rejecting the null hypothesis $\mathcal{H}_0$: *the line C with contrasts $\{\mu_k\}_{k=0...n-1}$ is observed only by chance.* For this we assume that the values of $|Du|$ are i.i.d., extracted from a noise image with the same gradient histogram as the image u itself.

Desolneux et al. [3] present a thorough study of the binomial tail $\mathcal{B}(n, k; p)$ and its use in the detection of geometric structures. The regularized incomplete beta function, defined by $I(x; a, b)$ is an interpolation $\widetilde{\mathcal{B}}$ of the binomial tail to the continuous domain $\widetilde{\mathcal{B}}(n, k; p) = I(p; k, n - k + 1)$ where $n, k \in \mathbb{R}$ [3]. Additionally the regularized incomplete beta function can be computed very efficiently.

Let $H_c(\mu) = \mathrm{P}(|Du| > \mu)$. For a given line of length l, the probability under $\mathcal{H}_0$ that, some parts with total length greater or equal than $l_{(s,n)}(n - k)$ have a contrast greater than μ can be modeled by $\widetilde{\mathcal{B}}(n \cdot l_{(s,n)}, k \cdot l_{(s,n)}; H_c(\mu))$, where $l_{(s,n)} = \frac{l}{s \cdot n}$ acts as a normalization factor [8,9].

Definition 1. *Let $\mathcal{C}$ be a finite set of N_{ll} level lines of u. A level line $C \in \mathcal{C}$ is a ε-meaningful boundary if $N_{ll} \cdot K \cdot \min\limits_{k < K} \widetilde{\mathcal{B}}(n \cdot l_{(2,n)}, k \cdot l_{(2,n)}; H_c(\mu_k)) < \varepsilon$ where K is a parameter of the algorithm. We also note*

$$k_{\min} = \arg\min_{k < K} \widetilde{\mathcal{B}}(n \cdot l_{(2,n)}, k \cdot l_{(2,n)}; H_c(\mu_k)) \tag{1}$$

The parameter K controls the number of points that we allow to be likely generated by noise, that is a line must have no more than K points with a "high" probability of belonging to the background model. It is simply chosen as a percentile of the total number of points in the line.

Def. 1 is motivated by the following proposition (we refer to the work by Tepper [8] for a complete proof).

Proposition 1. *The expected number of ε-meaningful boundaries, in a finite set of random level lines is smaller than ε.*

3   Boundary Clean-up by Detecting Meaningful Periodic Subsequences

Prop. 1 asserts that if a level line is a meaningful boundary, then it cannot be entirely generated in white noise (up to ε false detections on the average) but it can have parts that are likely to be contained in noise.

Cao et al. [2] propose to give an upper bound to the size of those parts. Assume that C is a piece of level line with L independent points, contained in a non-edge part, described by the noise model. The probability that L is larger than $l > 0$ needs to be estimated, knowing that $|Du| \geq \mu$. This is exactly the a posteriori length distribution $p(\mu; l) \overset{\text{def}}{=} P(L \geq l \mid |Du| \geq \mu)$. The estimation of this distribution was studied by Cao et al. [2].

Let us now consider an image u with N_{ll} (quantized) level lines. Let us also denote by N_l the number of all possible sampled subcurves of these level lines. ($N_l = \sum_{i=1}^{N_{ll}} n_i(n_i - 1)/2$, where n_i is the number of independent points in line i). As in Prop. 1, it can be proved that $N_l \cdot p(\mu; l)$ is an upper bound of the expected number of pieces of lines of length larger than l with gradient larger than μ. For a fixed μ, let be l such that $N_l \cdot p(\mu; l) < \varepsilon$. Then, we know that on a white noise image, on the average, we cannot observe more than ε pieces of level line with a length larger than l and a gradient everywhere larger than μ. Then one can define $\mathcal{L}(\mu) = \inf\{l, N_l \cdot p(\mu; l) < \varepsilon\}$ and keep every subcurve of any meaningful boundary with length equal or greater than $\mathcal{L}(\mu)$, where $|Du| \geq \mu$.

The value of μ can be seen as a new parameter of the method. Its value can be fixed arbitrarily using a conservative approach [2]: letting $|Du|$ be less than 1, means that edges with an accuracy less than one pixel may be detected. Thus, taking $\mu = 1$ is the least restrictive choice. For μ about 1, values of $\mathcal{L}(\mu)$ less than a few hundreds are obtained.

Since $\mathcal{L}(\mu)$ is a decreasing function of μ, fixing it at a small value produces large lengths. We are imposing that the contrasted pieces have to be very large and this is not always the case, as argued before. Furthermore the probability distribution $p(\mu; l)$ has to be estimated. We propose to take a different path to remove non-contrasted boundary parts.

In Def. 1, pieces of a meaningful boundary are explicitly allowed to be generated in white noise. We are certainly not interested in these pieces and this relaxation responds to the fact that we want to retrieve the remaining pieces of that boundary (i.e. edge region). The desired detection of contrasted parts in a boundary is very close in spirit to periodic subsequence detection.

3.1 Detecting Periodic Subsequences

Grompone et al. [4] proposed a method for accurately detecting straight line segments in a digital image. It is based on the Helmholtz principle and hence parameterless. In the authors' words, "at the core of the work lies a new way to interpret binary sequences in terms of unions of segments".

A sequence $S = (s_i)_{1 \leq i \leq L}$ of length L is binary if $\forall i, s_i \in \{0, 1\}$. A subsequence $a \subseteq S$ is defined by a pair of indices $(a^{(1)}, a^{(2)})$ with $1 \leq a^{(1)} < a^{(2)} \leq L$, such that $(\forall s_i, a^{(1)} \leq i \leq a^{(2)})\ s_i \in a$. Given a binary sequence S of length L, an n-subsequence is an n-tuple $(a_1, \ldots, a_n)$ of n disjoints subsequences $a_i \subseteq S$. The set of all n-subsequences in S will be denoted by $\mathcal{M}(n, S)$. We define $k(a) = \#\{s_i \mid i \in [a^{(1)}, a^{(2)}] \wedge s_i = 1\}$ and $l(a) = a^{(2)} - a^{(1)} + 1$ (i.e. the length of a). Notice that $\#\mathcal{M}(n, S) = \binom{L}{2n}$ [4].

Definition 2. (Grompone et al. [4]) *Given a binary sequence S of length L, an n-subsequence $(a_1, \ldots, a_n)$ in $\mathcal{M}(n, S)$ is said ε-meaningful if*

$$\text{NFA}(a_1, \ldots, a_n) \stackrel{\text{def}}{=} \binom{L}{2n} \prod_{i=1}^{n} (l(a_i) + 1)\mathcal{B}(l(a_i), k(a_i), p) < \varepsilon \tag{2}$$

where $p = \Pr(s_i = 1), 1 \leq i \leq L$. This number is called number of false alarms (NFA) of $(a_1, \ldots, a_n)$.

Proposition 2. *The expected number of ε-meaningful n-subsequences in a random binary sequence is smaller than ε.*

We refer to the work by Grompone et al. [4] for a complete proof.

Fig. 1. A periodic sequence where runs are represented in green. If treated as a non-periodic sequence, any subsequence detector would detect four subsequences at best, when in fact the desired result is to detect three subsequences.

A run in S is a maximal subsequence only containing ones, i.e.

$$\left(\forall i \in [a^{(1)}, a^{(2)}],\ s_i = 1\right) \wedge \left(a^{(1)} = 1 \vee s_{a^{(1)}-1} = 0\right) \wedge \left(a^{(2)} = L \vee s_{a^{(2)}+1} = 0\right).$$

One can restrict the search for n-subsequences to the ones where each of the n subsequences starts at a run start and ends at a run end [4]. We denote by R the number of runs in S.

Definition 3. *Given a binary sequence S, its maximal ε-meaningful subsequence $(a_1, \ldots, a_n)^*$ is defined as*

$$(a_1, \ldots, a_n)^* \overset{\text{def}}{=} \underset{\substack{1 \leq n \leq R \\ (a_1, \ldots, a_n) \in \mathcal{M}(n,S)}}{\arg\min}\ \mathrm{NFA}(a_1, \ldots, a_n).$$

We propose now to extend the above definitions to support periodic binary sequences. A binary sequence $S = (s_i)_{1 \leq i \leq L}$ is made periodic by considering L its period. Periodic sequences are different in nature from their non-periodic counterparts, see Fig. 1. A definition suitable for the periodic case is needed.

In the periodic case, a subsequence must be defined more carefully. Now a subsequence $a \subseteq S$, defined by a pair of indices $\left(a^{(1)}, a^{(2)}\right)$, can belong to one of two different types:

Intra-subsequences: if $a^{(1)} < a^{(2)}$ then the non-periodic definition holds, i.e.,
 $1 \leq a^{(1)} < a^{(2)} \leq L$, and $\left(\forall s_i,\ a^{(1)} \leq s_i \leq a^{(2)}\right)\ s_i \in a$.
Inter-subsequences: if $a^{(1)} > a^{(2)}\ \left(\forall s_i,\ 1 \leq s_i \leq a^{(2)} \vee a^{(1)} \leq s_i \leq L\right)\ s_i \in a$.

Runs are modified accordingly to also cover inter-subsequences. Given a periodic binary sequence S of period L, a periodic n-subsequence is an n-tuple $(a_1, \ldots, a_n)$ of n disjoints subsequences $a_i \subseteq S$. The set of all n-subsequences in S will be denoted by $\mathcal{M}(n, S)$.

We define $k(a) = \#\{s_i \mid i \in [a^{(1)}, a^{(2)}] \wedge s_i = 1\}$ and the length of a as

$$l(a) = \begin{cases} a^{(2)} - a^{(1)} + 1, & \text{if } a \text{ is an intra-subsequence;} \\ a^{(2)} + L - a^{(1)} + 1, & \text{if } a \text{ is an inter-subsequence.} \end{cases}$$

Notice that $\#\mathcal{M}(n, S) = 2\binom{L}{2n}$ since from each pair of points in S two subsequences can be constructed.

Definition 4. *Given a periodic binary sequence S of period L, an n-subsequence $(a_1, \ldots, a_n)$ in $\mathcal{M}(n, S)$ is said ε-meaningful if*

$$\mathrm{NFA}(a_1, \ldots, a_n) \overset{\text{def}}{=} 2 \binom{L}{2n} \prod_{i=1}^{n} (l(a_i) + 1) \, \mathcal{B}(l(a_i), k(a_i), p) < \varepsilon$$

where $p = \Pr(s_i = 1), 1 \le i \le L$. This number is called number of false alarms (NFA) of $(a_1, \ldots, a_n)$.

Proposition 3. *The expected number of ε-meaningful n-subsequences in a random periodic binary sequence is smaller than ε.*

Proof. This proof follows closely the one by Grompone et al. [4] but adapted to periodic sequences. The expected number of ε-meaningful n-subsequences is given by

$$\mathbb{E}\left(\sum_{(a_1, \ldots, a_n) \in \mathcal{M}(n, S)} \mathbf{1}_{\mathrm{NFA}(a_1, \ldots, a_n) < \varepsilon} \right) = \sum_{(a_1, \ldots, a_n) \in \mathcal{M}(n, S)} \mathrm{P}\left(\mathrm{NFA}(a_1, \ldots, a_n) < \varepsilon \right).$$

$\mathrm{NFA}(a_1, \ldots, a_n) < \varepsilon$ implies that $\prod_{i=1}^{n} \mathcal{B}(l(a_i), k(a_i), p) < \frac{\varepsilon}{2 \binom{L}{2n} \prod_{i=1}^{n} (l(a_i) + 1)}$.

Let $U_i = \mathcal{B}(l(a_i), k(a_i), p)$ be a random variable, let $\alpha \in \mathbb{R}^+$, and let $\mathrm{P}_U^\alpha = \mathrm{P}\left(\prod_{i=1}^{n} U_i < \alpha \right)$. Then,

$$\mathrm{P}_U^\alpha = \sum_{u_2, \ldots, u_n} \mathrm{P}\left(\prod_{i=1}^{n} U_i < \alpha \,\middle|\, U_2 = u_2, \ldots, U_n = u_n \right) \mathrm{P}\left(U_2 = u_2, \ldots, U_n = u_n \right).$$

Since the a_i are disjoint, the U_i are independent. Then

$$\mathrm{P}_U^\alpha = \sum_{u_2, \ldots, u_n} \mathrm{P}\left(\prod_{i=1}^{n} U_i < \frac{\alpha}{u_2 \ldots u_n} \right) \cdot \mathrm{P}\left(U_2 = u_2, \ldots, U_n = u_n \right).$$

Using the classical lemma $\mathrm{P}(U_i < \alpha) < \alpha$, that $\mathrm{P}\left(U_2 = u_2, \ldots, U_n = u_n \right) \le \mathrm{P}\left(U_2 \le u_2, \ldots, U_n \le u_n \right)$, and that there are $l(a_i) + 1$ possible values for U_i,

$$\mathrm{P}\left(\prod_{i=1}^{n} U_i < \alpha \right) < \prod_{i=2}^{n} (l(a_i) + 1) \, \alpha < \prod_{i=1}^{n} (l(a_i) + 1) \, \alpha.$$

Let us recall that $\#\mathcal{M}(n, S) = 2 \binom{L}{2n}$, then setting $\alpha = \frac{\varepsilon}{2 \binom{L}{2n} \prod_{i=1}^{n} (l(a_i) + 1)}$ gives the wanted result. $\qquad \square$

The maximality rule from Def. 3 holds unchanged in the periodic case.

On the implementation side, Grompone et al. [4] describe a dynamic programming scheme for the non-periodic case that eases the heavy computational burden. We show now that implementing the algorithm for detecting periodic subsequences is indeed straightforward.

IMAGE   MB   MB+CU   MB+MPS

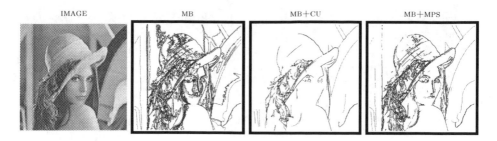

Fig. 2. Comparison of the results obtained with both clean-up algorithms. The one by Cao et al. (CU) [2] produces underdetection; this is corrected by using MPS.

IMAGE   MB   MB+MPS

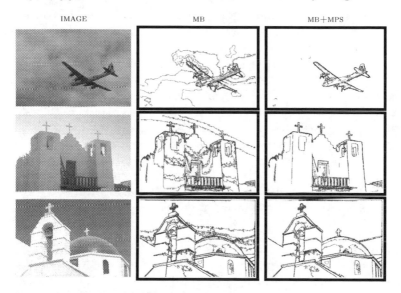

Fig. 3. Results of the presented clean-up algorithm. MPS eliminates the vast majority of the unwanted pieces of level line.

We begin by shifting the periodic sequence S (with R runs), to transform inter-subsequences into intra-subsequences. A circular shift to the left is used. We then form a non-periodic sequence $S^{(2)}$ of length $2L$ from two periods of the periodic sequence S of period L. Let $R^{(2)}$ be the number of runs in $S^{(2)}$. Two key tricks allow us to solve the problem: (1) restrict the number of tested subsequences. In the non-periodic case, we test for n-subsequences for $S^{(2)}$ where $1 \leq n \leq R^{(2)}$. In the periodic case, we only test for n-subsequences where $1 \leq n \leq R$; (2) subsequences longer than L are not tested. With these two restrictions, one can simply detect non-periodic subsequences in non-periodic sequence $S^{(2)}$ and the result will be optimal.

4   Results and Final Remarks

Before applying the detector of meaningful periodic subsequences (MPS) to any boundary, we need to binarize it since its contrast (or its regularity) takes on real values. This former problem is solved by thresholding on the contrast (or on the regularity). In this direction, we claim that a natural choice is $\mu_{k_{\min}}$ (see Def. 1, p. 775). A maximal ε-meaningful boundary is thus converted into a periodic binary sequence. We want to apply the periodic subsequence detection algorithm from Def. 4 and 3 to that sequence. The only parameter left is $p = \Pr(s_i = 1), 1 \le i \le L$ and it is straightforward defined as $p \overset{\text{def}}{=} H_c(\mu_{k_{\min}})$.

We finally define the following clean-up rule: *For any meaningful boundary, keep every subcurve belonging to its maximal 1-meaningful subsequence.*

This clean-up mechanism does not impose a minimal length to contrasted parts. The length is adjusted automatically, by choosing the most meaningful subsequence in the level line. As an additional advantage, there is no need to estimate any probability distribution. Fig. 2 shows an example of the benefits of the proposed clean-up method over the one by Cao et al. [2]. Their version clearly produces underdetection: visually important structures are missed (notice the face in the third image). The proposed algorithm produces a very mild overdetection: some small noisy parts are not eliminated but no important structure is lost. Fig. 3 shows two more examples on images from the BSD database. Notice that, on the last row, MPS does not remove a few pieces of lines that should be removed (e.g., the lower wall and the roof). This does not occur because of a failure in MPS, but because of a faulty binarization, that is, the $\mu_{k_{\min}}$ was not optimal in those cases.

In summary, we presented a general and fully automatic algorithm to detect meaningful subsequences within periodic binary sequences. We apply it to select salient pieces of level lines in an image, showing good results on natural images.

References

1. Canny, J.: A Computational Approach to Edge Detection. IEEE Transactions on Pattern Analysis and Machine Intelligence 8(6), 679–698 (1986)
2. Cao, F., Lisani, J.L., Morel, J.M., Musé, P., Sur, F.: A Theory of Shape Identification. Lecture Notes in Mathematics, vol. 1948. Springer (2008)
3. Desolneux, A., Moisan, L., Morel, J.M.: From Gestalt Theory to Image Analysis, vol. 34. Springer (2008)
4. Grompone, R., Jakubowicz, J., Morel, J.M., Randall, G.: On Straight Line Segment Detection. Journal of Mathematical Imaging and Vision 32(3), 313–347 (2008)
5. Kanizsa, G.: Organization in Vision: Essays on Gestalt Perception. Praeger (1979)
6. Monasse, P., Guichard, F.: Fast Computation of a Contrast Invariant Image Representation. IEEE Transactions on Image Processing 9(5), 860–872 (2000)
7. Serra, J.: Image Analysis and Mathematical Morphology. Academic Press (1983)
8. Tepper, M.: Detecting clusters and boundaries: a twofold study on shape representation. Ph.D. thesis, Universidad de Buenos Aires (March 2011)
9. Tepper, M., Gómez, F., Musé, P., Almansa, A., Mejail, M.: Morphological Shape Context: Semi-locality and Robust Matching in Shape Recognition. In: Bayro-Corrochano, E., Eklundh, J.-O. (eds.) CIARP 2009. LNCS, vol. 5856, pp. 129–136. Springer, Heidelberg (2009)

A Non Bayesian Predictive Approach for Functional Calibration

Noslen Hernández[1], Rolando J. Biscay[2], and Isneri Talavera[1]

[1] Advanced Technologies Application Center, CENATAV, Cuba
[2] Universidad de Valparaíso, Chile
{nhernandez,italavera}@cenatav.co.cu, rolando.biscay@uv.cl

Abstract. A non Bayesian predictive approach for statistical calibration with functional data is introduced. This is based on extending to the functional calibration setting the definition of non Bayesian predictive probability density proposed by Harris (1989). The new method is elaborated in detail in case of Gaussian functional linear models. It is shown through numerical simulations that the introduced non Bayesian predictive estimator of the unknown parameter of interest in calibration (commonly, a substance concentration) has negligible bias and compares favorably with the classical estimator, particularly in extrapolation problems. A further advantage of the new approach, which is also briefly illustrated, is that it provides not only point estimates but also a predictive likelihood function that allows the researcher to explore the plausibility of any possible parameter value.

Keywords: statistical calibration, functional data analysis, regression.

1 Introduction

Statistical calibration plays a crucial role in many areas of technology such as pharmacology and chemometrics ([1–6]). In general, the calibration problem can be described as follows. A training sample $(z_i, x_i)_{1 \leq i \leq n}$ of n independent observations in some space $\mathcal{Z} \times \mathcal{X}$ is available, which are generated according to conditional probability distributions $F(X/z_i)$ that belong to some specified statistical model $\{F_\theta(X/Z) : \theta \in \Theta\}$. The observations z_i may be non random (case of fixed design) or random (case of random design). Given a new observation X generated according to the distribution $F(X/z)$ with an unknown value z, it is desired to obtain an estimate or prediction $\hat{z}$ of z.

There are several works that deal with this problem in the setting in which $z_1, ..., z_n, z$ are observations of a real random variable and X is a random function. All of them are based on different approximations $\hat{z}$ to the conditional mean $\tilde{z} = E(Z/X)$ [7, 8]. This estimator $\tilde{z}$ is optimal in the sense of minimizing the quadratic Bayesian risk $E(\tilde{z} - Z)^2$. However, these approaches have two fundamental shortcomings: a) they focus on the case of random design; b) the estimator $\tilde{z}$ has poor performance for extrapolation, i.e., when the unknown quantity Z is not generated by the same probabilistic mechanism as the previous data $z_1, ..., z_n$ and lies far away from this cluster of points.

L. Alvarez et al. (Eds.): CIARP 2012, LNCS 7441, pp. 781–788, 2012.

The calibration problem has also been studied in [9] for the setting in which Z and X are functions, the mean $\mu(z)$ of the statistical model $F_\theta(X/Z)$ is linear with respect to z, and the design is fixed. For this problem, a non Bayesian estimate estimator $\widehat{z}$ is introduced on the basis of a regularized inversion of the linear operator defined by the mean function μ. This generalizes to a functional framework the regularization of the so-called classical estimator for calibration proposed in [10] for the scalar linear model.

In the present work we are interested in the specific functional setting, common in chemometrics, in which the variable X is a function (e.g., a spectral curve), the variable $\mathbf{z}$ is a finite-dimensional vector (e.g., concentrations of some substances), and the statistical model is linear and Gaussian with respect to $\mathbf{z}$. In contrast to previous methods, we introduce an approach for statistical calibration based on a non Bayesian predictive framework. This extends to such functional setting the non Bayesian predictive approach for statistical calibration proposed in [11] for the scalar linear model.

More specifically, the non Bayesian predictive density introduced by Harris [12] is extended to the calibration setting just described, so providing, on the basis of the training sample, a non Bayesian *predictive density* $f_P(x; \mathbf{z})$, for a new observation x corresponding to the unknown $\mathbf{z}$. This allows one to define the non Bayesian *predictive likelihood* by

$$L(\mathbf{z}) = f_P(x; \mathbf{z}),$$

and the non Bayesian *predictive estimator* $\widehat{\mathbf{z}} = \arg\max_{\mathbf{z}} L(\mathbf{z})$.

It is shown that this new approach has a number of potential advantages: *i*) good performance for extrapolation; *ii*) negligible bias; *iii*) it can be applied to both random and fixed designs, *iv*) it offers not only a point estimate $\widehat{\mathbf{z}}$ but also a predictive likelihood function $l_P(z)$ that allows one to explore the likelihoods of all the possible values of the unknown $\mathbf{z}$; it permits to incorporate the information that some components of the vector $\mathbf{z}$ are known, when such information is available.

The rest of the paper is organized as follows. Section 2 presents the functional Non Bayesian Predictive estimator. Sections 3 illustrates its performance in a simulation study. Finally, some concluding remarks are given in Section 4.

2   Functional Non Bayesian Predictive Estimator

Let be given a sample of previous (training) data $(\mathbf{z}_i, x_i) = (z_{i1}, ..., z_{iq}, x_i)$ $(i = 1, ..., n)$ that follow the model:

$$x_i(t) = \beta_1(t) z_{i1} + ... + \beta_q(t) z_{iq} + e_i(t).$$

Here, $x_i \in \mathcal{X} = L_2(t, \mathbb{R})$ is a functional responses ($t \in [0, 1]$); $\mathbf{z}_i \in \mathbb{R}^q$ is vector of covariates; $\boldsymbol{\beta}(t) = (\beta_1(t), ..., \beta_q(t))^\mathsf{T}$ is a vector of non random functions (coefficients); and $e_1, e_2, ...$ are independent zero-mean Gaussian functions in L_2

with covariance function σ_e. We will denote by $N_{L_2}(\mu, \sigma)$ the Gaussian distribution of a random function with mean μ and covariance function σ. Thus, the distribution of e_i is $P_e = N_{L_2}(0, \sigma_e)$.

This model can be written

$$\mathbf{x}(t) = \mathbf{Z}\boldsymbol{\beta}(t) + \mathbf{e}(t), \tag{1}$$

where $\mathbf{Z} = (Z_{ij})$ is the $n \times q$ design matrix, $\mathbf{x}(t) = (x_1(t), ..., x_n(t))^\mathsf{T}$, and $\mathbf{e}(t) = (e_1(t), ..., e_n(t))^\mathsf{T}$.

It is assumed that a new data x is available which follows model (1), that is

$$x(t) = \beta_1(t)z_1 + ... + \beta_q(t)z_q + e(t) = \boldsymbol{\beta}^\mathsf{T}(t)\mathbf{z} + e(t). \tag{2}$$

The problem of interest is to estimate the vector of variables $\mathbf{z}$ on the basis of the current observation x and the training data $(\mathbf{z}_i, x_i), i = 1, ..., n$.

Let $\widehat{\boldsymbol{\beta}}$ be the least squares estimate of $\boldsymbol{\beta}$:

$$\widehat{\boldsymbol{\beta}}(t) = (\mathbf{Z}^\mathsf{T}\mathbf{Z})^{-1}\mathbf{Z}^\mathsf{T}\mathbf{x}(t),$$

and $\widehat{\sigma}_e$ be the usual estimator of σ_e based on the residuals:

$$\widehat{\sigma}_e = \frac{1}{n}\sum_{i=1}^{n}(x_i - \widehat{x}_i) \otimes (x_i - \widehat{x}_i),$$

where $\widehat{x}_i = \mathbf{z}_i^\mathsf{T}\widehat{\boldsymbol{\beta}}$. Since the training vector of observations $\mathbf{x}$ is a Gaussian process with distribution $N_{L_2^n}(\mathbf{Z}\boldsymbol{\beta}, \mathbf{I}\sigma_e)$, where $\mathbf{I}$ is the $n \times n$ identity matrix, $\widehat{\boldsymbol{\beta}}$ is a Gaussian process with distribution $P_{\widehat{\boldsymbol{\beta}}}(\cdot; \boldsymbol{\beta}, \sigma_e) = N_{L_2^q}(\boldsymbol{\beta}, (\mathbf{Z}^\mathsf{T}\mathbf{Z})^{-1}\sigma_e)$. Define the probability distribution

$$\mu_P(\cdot; \mathbf{z}, \boldsymbol{\beta}, \sigma_e) = \int P_X(\cdot; \mathbf{z}, \boldsymbol{\gamma}, \sigma_e) P_{\widehat{\boldsymbol{\beta}}}(d\boldsymbol{\gamma}; \boldsymbol{\beta}, \sigma_e),$$

where $P_X(\cdot; \mathbf{z}, \boldsymbol{\beta}, \sigma_e) = N_{L_2}(\mathbf{z}^\mathsf{T}\boldsymbol{\beta}, \sigma_e)$ is the distribution of the observation X according to the model. Thus, $\mu_P(\cdot; \mathbf{z}, \boldsymbol{\beta}, \sigma_e) = N_{L_2}\left(\mathbf{z}^\mathsf{T}\boldsymbol{\beta}, \left(1 + \mathbf{z}^\mathsf{T}(\mathbf{Z}^\mathsf{T}\mathbf{Z})^{-1}\mathbf{z}\right)\sigma_e\right)$. Under mild conditions, this measure has a density $g(\cdot; \mathbf{z}, \boldsymbol{\beta}, \sigma_e)$ with respect to the measure P_e, which is given by

$$g(\cdot; \mathbf{z}, \boldsymbol{\beta}, \sigma_e) = \int f_X(\cdot; \mathbf{z}, \boldsymbol{\gamma}, \sigma_e) P_{\widehat{\boldsymbol{\beta}}}(d\boldsymbol{\gamma}; \boldsymbol{\beta}, \sigma_e),$$

where $f_X(\cdot; \mathbf{z}, \boldsymbol{\gamma}, \sigma_e) = dP_X(\cdot; \mathbf{z}, \boldsymbol{\gamma}, \sigma_e)/P_e$ is the density of $P_X(\cdot; \mathbf{z}, \boldsymbol{\gamma}, \sigma_e)$ with respect to P_e.

Let φ_l, λ_l be, respectively, the eigenfunctions and eigenvalues of the covariance function σ_e. From known results on equivalence of Gaussian measures [13] it follows that

$$g(\cdot; \mathbf{z}, \boldsymbol{\beta}, \sigma_e) = \frac{1}{\sqrt{1 + \mathbf{z}^\mathsf{T}(\mathbf{Z}^\mathsf{T}\mathbf{Z})^{-1}\mathbf{z}}}\exp\left\{\frac{1}{1 + \mathbf{z}^\mathsf{T}(\mathbf{Z}^\mathsf{T}\mathbf{Z})^{-1}\mathbf{z}}\sum_{l=1}^{\infty}\frac{\mathbf{z}^\mathsf{T}\boldsymbol{\beta}^l}{\lambda_l}\left(x^l - \frac{\mathbf{z}^\mathsf{T}\boldsymbol{\beta}^l}{2}\right)\right\},$$

where

$$\beta^l = \left(\langle \beta_j, \varphi_l \rangle\right)_{1 \le j \le q},$$
$$x^l = \langle x, \varphi_l \rangle.$$

Here, $\langle \cdot, \cdot \rangle$ denotes the inner product in $L_2\left([0, T]\right)$.

Note that $g\left(\cdot; \mathbf{z}, \boldsymbol{\beta}, \sigma_e\right)$ takes into consideration the uncertainty about $\boldsymbol{\beta}$ in determining the true density $f_X\left(\cdot; \mathbf{z}, \boldsymbol{\beta}, \sigma_e\right)$ through the estimate $\widehat{\boldsymbol{\beta}}$. On this basis it is possible, by extending to the functional setting the approach initiated in [12], to define a non Bayesian *predictive density* for the new observation x corresponding to $\mathbf{z}$ as the following empirical version of $g\left(\cdot; \mathbf{z}, \boldsymbol{\beta}, \sigma_e\right)$:

$$f_P\left(x; \mathbf{z}\right) = \frac{1}{\sqrt{1 + \mathbf{z}^\mathsf{T}\left(\mathbf{Z}^\mathsf{T}\mathbf{Z}\right)^{-1}\mathbf{z}}} \exp\left\{\frac{1}{1 + \mathbf{z}^\mathsf{T}\left(\mathbf{Z}^\mathsf{T}\mathbf{Z}\right)^{-1}\mathbf{z}} \sum_{l=1}^{m} \frac{\mathbf{z}^\mathsf{T}\widehat{\boldsymbol{\beta}}^l}{\widehat{\lambda}_l}\left(x^l - \frac{\mathbf{z}^\mathsf{T}\widehat{\boldsymbol{\beta}}^l}{2}\right)\right\},$$

where $m = m\left(n\right)$ is a specified integer such that $m \to \infty$ as $n \to \infty$; $\widehat{\varphi}_k, \widehat{\lambda}_k$ are, respectively, the eigenfunctions and eigenvalues of the covariance function $\widehat{\sigma}_e$; and

$$\widehat{\boldsymbol{\beta}}^l = \left(\left\langle \widehat{\boldsymbol{\beta}}_j, \widehat{\varphi}_l \right\rangle\right)_{1 \le j \le q},$$
$$x^l = \langle x, \widehat{\varphi}_l \rangle.$$

We also define the non Bayesian *predictive likelihood* function by

$$L\left(\mathbf{z}\right) = f_P\left(x; \mathbf{z}\right),$$

and the non Bayesian *predictive estimator* $\widehat{\mathbf{z}}$ of $\mathbf{z}$ by

$$\widehat{\mathbf{z}}_P = \arg\max_{\mathbf{z}} L\left(\mathbf{z}\right).$$

In cases in which some components of the vector $\mathbf{z}$ are known, they are not considered in this maximization.

3   A Simulation Study

The feasibility and the performance of the introduced functional calibration method are here explored through a simulation study. For simplicity, we consider models with only one covariate z (i.e., $q = 1$), so they have the specific form:

$$x(t) = \beta(t)z + e(t).$$

The covariate values in the training data were generated following a normal distribution $z_i \sim N(15, 1.5)$, $i = 1, ..., n$. The size of the training sample was set to $n = 300$.

The Gaussian error process $e(t)$ was simulated with the covariance function

$$\sigma_e(s,t) = \sum_{i=1}^{200} \lambda_i \phi_i(s) \phi_i(t),$$

where $(\phi_i(t))_i$ is the trigonometric basis on $L_2([0,1])$ (i.e., $\phi_{2k-1} = \sqrt{2}\cos(2\pi kt)$, $\phi_{2k} = \sqrt{2}\sin(2\pi kt)$), and the eigenvalues were set to $\lambda_i = 0.06/(i^{1.01})$.

The coefficient functions were specified to be of the form $\beta(t) = Cg(t)\sin(2\pi t)$, where $g(t)$ is the density function $N(0.5, 0.05)$ (i.e., a peak) and C is a constant.

Different simulation settings were considered according to the signal (β) to noise (σ_e) ratio by varying the constant C in the mean function: "good", "moderate" and "bad" scenarios correspond to $C = 2.5$, $C = 1$ and $C = 0.2$, respectively. The means functions for different scenarios are shown in Figure 1.

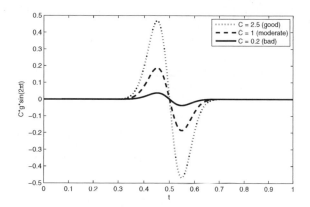

Fig. 1. Mean curves for the good, moderate and bad scenarios

Our interest is in methods with good performance for extrapolation, thus we focus comparisons with the classical estimator

$$\hat{z}_C = \frac{\left\langle x, \widehat{\beta} \right\rangle}{\left\| \widehat{\beta} \right\|^2}.$$

The Mean Square Error (MSE) $E(z - \hat{z})^2$ is used as comparison criteria, which is computed on the basis of $B = 3000$ sample repetitions.

Figure 2 shows the MSE curves for both estimators and all the settings. It can be observed that, in all simulation settings, both estimators perform worse as the covariate value z goes away from the center of the calibration range. In the good setting the difference between the estimators is not so noticeable. As the setting becomes worse, differences between the estimators become remarkable. Inside the calibration range, the performance of both estimators is quite similar, but

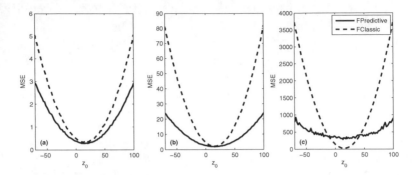

Fig. 2. Curves of RMSE as function of z for the estimators $\hat{z}_C$ and $\hat{z}_P$ in scenarios good(a), moderate (b) and bad (c)

outside such range (i.e., for extrapolation) the non Bayesian predictive estimator shows much less MSE than the classical estimator.

Figure 3 shows plots of mean values of the estimates (predictions) versus true values of the covariate in the bad scenarios for both estimators. It can be appreciated that the classical estimator is highly biased while the introduced estimator has negligible bias.

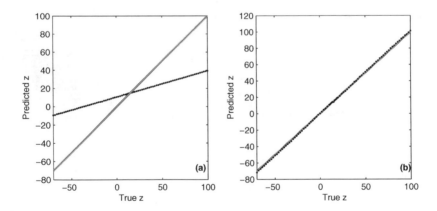

Fig. 3. Points represent predicted z values versus true z values in the bad setting for the (a) Classic estimator and the (b) Non Bayesian Predictive estimator. The diagonal line is also shown, for reference.

An attractive feature of the non Bayesian predictive approach for functional calibration is that it provides not only point estimates of the covariate z but also predictive likelihoods of all possible values of this parameter. This allows one to complement the point estimate $\hat{z}_P$ with a likelihood-based appreciation of the location of z by plotting the relative predictive likelihood curve. As an illustration, Figure 4 shows the relative predictive likelihood curves for two samples generated from the good and the bad setting. It can be observed that predictive

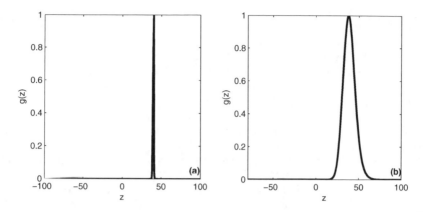

Fig. 4. Relative predictive likelihood functions for samples from the a) good and b) bad scenarios corresponding to the true value $z = 40$ of the covariate

likelihood curves show more precision in the assessment of z (i.e., they are more spiky) for good settings than for bad settings.

4 Conclusions

This papers introduces a non Bayesian predictive calibration approach for functional data. Its rationality comes from taking into consideration model uncertainty by averaging with respect to the distribution of the parameter estimator, a device that shows to have a regularizing effect in the resulting solution to the calibration (inverse) problem. By construction, the introduced method can be applied to both random and fixed designs. It shows negligible bias, and much better performance for extrapolation than the classical estimator. It also has the following advantageous feature that is lacking in previous Bayesian and non Bayesian approaches to calibration: it provides not only a point estimate but also a non Bayesian predictive likelihood function that can be used to assess the plausibility of any possible value of the covariate to be predicted. Finally, it is worth of note that the introduced approach can be extended to a wide variety of statistical models. In case of very complex models it might be implemented by means of a bootstrap approximation to the predictive density.

References

1. Osborne, C.: Statistical calibration: A review. Int. Stat. Rev. 59, 309–336 (1991)
2. Martens, H., Naes, T.: Multivariate calibration. Wiley, Chichester (1989)
3. Brown, P.J.: Measurement, Regression, and Calibration. Clarendon Press, Oxford (1993)
4. Massart, D.L., Vandeginste, B.G.M., Buydens, L., Jong, S.D., Lewi, P.J., Smeyers-Verbeke, J.: Handbook of Chemometrics and Qualimetrics: Part B. Elsevier Science B. V., The Netherlands (1997)

5. Lavine, B.K., Workman, J.: Fundamental reviews: Chemometrics. Anal. Chem. 74, 2763–2770 (2002)
6. Walters, F.H., Rizzuto, G.T.: The calibration problem in statistics and its application to chemistry. Anal. Lett. 21, 2069–2076 (1988)
7. Ferraty, F., Vieu, P.: Nonparametric Functional Data Analysis: Theory and Practice (Springer Series in Statistics). Springer, New York (2006)
8. Ramsay, J., Silverman, B.: Functional Data Analysis. Springer, Berlin (1997)
9. Cuevas, A., Febrero, M., Fraiman, R.: Linear functional regression: the case of fixed design and functional response. The Canadian Journal of Statistics 30, 285–300 (2002)
10. Hagwood, C.: The calibration problem as an ill-posed inverse problem. J. Stat. Plan. Infer. 31, 179–185 (1992)
11. Hernández, N., Biscay, R.J., Talavera, I.: A non-bayesian predictive approach for statistical calibration. Journal of Statistical Computation and Simulation 82, 529–545 (2012)
12. Harris, I.R.: Predictive fit for natural exponential families. Biometrika 76, 675–684 (1989)
13. Grenander, U.: Abstract Inference. Wiley, New York (1981)

Classifier Combination Using Random Walks on the Space of Concepts

Jorge Sánchez[1,2] and Javier Redolfi[2]

[1] CIEM-CONICET, Universidad Nacional de Córdoba
[2] CIII, Universidad Tecnológica Nacional, Fac. Reg. Córdoba
jsanchez@scdt.frc.utn.edu.ar

Abstract. We propose a novel approach for the combination of classifiers based on two commonly adopted strategies in multiclass classification: one-vs-all and one-vs-one. The method relies on establishing the relevance of nodes in a graph defined in the space of concepts. Following a similar approach as in the ranking of websites, the relative strength of the nodes is given by the stationary distribution of a Markov chain defined on that graph. The proposed approach do not requires the base classifiers to provide calibrated probabilities. Experiments on the challenging problem of multiclass image classification show the potentiality of our approach.

Keywords: multiclass, classification, random walks, image classification, Fisher vectors.

1 Introduction

Multiclass classification is a fundamental problem in pattern recognition. Here, the task is to assign a given sample to one or more instances from a predefined set of concepts or classes. According to whether a sample can belong either to just one or to several of such concepts, the classification problem can be further characterized as a multiclass single-label (MCSL) or a multiclass multi-label (MCML) task. In what follows, we assume the availability of a training set consisting of a fair amount of manually annotated samples of each class.

Although a large number of methods exists aiming to solve the multiclass problem as a whole, the most common approach is to decompose the classification task into a set of binary subproblems and to solve them independently. This class of methods have been shown to perform on par with more elaborated techniques when used properly [15,4]. Let $\mathcal{C} = \{1, \ldots, C\}$ denote the set of classes. A common binarization strategy, known as *one-vs-all* (OVA) or *one-vs-the-rest*, is to generate a set of C binary classifiers trained by using as positives the samples form each class and as negatives those from the others, i.e. each model is trained to separate one class from the rest. Given a new sample, each classifier provides a score s_i, $1 \leq i \leq C$, reflecting its confidence in assigning the input sample to the class $i \in \mathcal{C}$. The final decision regarding class membership is generally made using the "argmax" rule (MCSL), i.e. $\hat{i} = \arg\max_i s_i$, or via

L. Alvarez et al. (Eds.): CIARP 2012, LNCS 7441, pp. 789–796, 2012.

a simple threshold (MCML), i.e. the input sample belongs to class $\hat{i} \subset \mathcal{C} \iff s_i > threshold$.

Another strategy, known as *one-vs-one* classification (OVO), consists in training a set of $\binom{C}{2}$ binary classifiers to discriminate between every pairs of classes. Let r_{ij} be the output of the classifier trained with samples of the ith and $j$the classes as positives and negatives respectively. In order to decide which class the input sample belongs, a common approach is to compute a weighted vote, e.g. $\sum_j r_{ij}$, followed by the application of one of the above assignment strategies.

As the OVA and OVO schemes use different subsets of data for learning the classifiers, they are likely to provide complementary information about the structure of the feature space they act on. Based on this hypothesis, we propose a novel approach for combining the scores of OVA and OVO classifiers based on the stationary distribution of a Markov chain defined in the space of concepts. The approach does not requires the base classifiers to provide calibrated probabilities, nevertheless the combined scores do. We demonstrate the effectiveness and potentiality of the approach on the challenging problem of multiclass image classification, for both the single- and multi-label settings.

Related Work. Next, we provide a summary of the methods most closely related to our work in the context of multiclass classification.

Garcia-Pedrajas and Ortiz-Boyer [5] proposed a method for the combination of OVO and OVA classifiers. The method is a two-stage approach in which the best two scoring classes of an OVA scheme are used as hypothesis for OVO classification. The method relies on the following observations: *i)* in many cases, when an OVA scheme using the "argmax" rule fails, the correct class is given by the second best performing classifier; and *ii)* most of the errors in OVO classification are due to *incompetent classifiers*, i.e. those classifiers that have not been trained using the correct class of the query sample. Our method differs from [5] in that we take into account not only the second but all the scores provided by the pool of OVA classifiers in a principled way, avoiding early decisions that may affect the final classification. Reid [14] proposed to weight each pairwise (OVO) prediction by an estimate of the probability that the sample belongs to that pair. The method is very computationally demanding as it involves the training and evaluation of $C(C - 1)$ classifiers, half of which must be learned using all available sample instances. Moreover, an additional calibration step must be performed in order to use state-of-the-art classifiers, e.g. Support Vector Machines (SVM). Also close to our work is the first of the methods proposed by Wu *et al.* [16]. The authors formulate an optimization problem involving all pairwise (OVO) estimates and the unknown class-probabilities. The solution to this problem is shown to be the stationary distribution of an irreductible Markov chain (cf. Sec. 2) whose transition matrix involves the set of (calibrated) pairwise predictions. Our method differs from [16] in the following: *a)* we go beyond simple OVO classification, *b)* we do not require the base classifiers to provide calibrated probabilities and *c)* we do not assume the training data to be balanced.

This paper is organized as follows: we first give a brief introduction to the theory of random walks on graphs and its application to the node ranking problem (Sec. 2). In Sec. 3 we formalize our approach for classifier combination. In Sec. 4 we give a detailed explanation of the experimental setup. Results of our experiments are shown in Sec. 5. Finally, we draw some conclusions in Sec. 6.

2   Preliminaries

Let $G = (\mathcal{V}, \mathcal{E}, A)$ be a weighted directed graph with nodes $\mathcal{V} = \{1, \ldots, n\}$ and edges $\mathcal{E} = \{(i, j) | i \in \mathcal{V}, j \in \mathcal{V}\}$. The $n \times n$ adjacency matrix $A = [a_{ij}]$ is defined such that $a_{ij} > 0 \iff (i, j) \in \mathcal{E}$ and 0 otherwise. Let us now consider the following random walk on G: starting from an arbitrary node, if at time t the walker is at node i, it makes a jumps to node j with probability $p_{ij} := \hat{a}_{ij} = a_{ij} / \sum_{j=1}^{n} a_{ij}$ (independent of t). Each "step" of the process can be associated with a random variable X_t taking values on $\mathcal{V}$. The sequence $X_1, X_2, \ldots, X_t, \ldots$ corresponds to a Markov chain defined on the space of nodes and $P(X_{t+1} = j | X_t = i) = p_{ij}$. Thus, a random walk on G is a Markov chain with states in $\mathcal{V}$ and transition matrix $P = [\hat{a}_{ij}]$. The distribution $\mathbf{\Pi}$ is said to be stationary if

$$\mathbf{\Pi}^T = \mathbf{\Pi}^T P \ . \tag{1}$$

It can be shown that such a distribution exists if the Markov chain encoded by P is *irreducible* (any state must be reachable from any other state in a finite number of steps) and *aperiodic* (returning to state i can occur at irregular number of steps). Given P, the stationary distribution $\mathbf{\Pi}$ can be found by solving the eigenvalue problem (1) with the constraint $\mathbf{\Pi}^T \mathbf{e} - 1$. Here, $\mathbf{e}$ denotes the n-dimensional vector whose elements are all equal to 1. The solution to this problem can be found numerically, e.g. by the power-method.

PageRank and the Relevance of Nodes in a Graph. PageRank [10] was proposed as a model to determine the relevance of web-pages. The model considers the hyperlink structure of the web as a directed graph, on which a random walker located at node i can jump to any of the nodes linked by i with equal probability, i.e. $p_{ij} = 1 / \sum_k a_{ik}$. Here, $a_{ij} = 1$ if $(i, j) \in \mathcal{E}$ and 0 otherwise. A particularity of this structure is the presence of nodes with no out-going links ("dangling" links). For these nodes, the corresponding row of the transition matrix contains only zeros. Beeing non-stochastic, the resulting P do not corresponds to a valid transition matrix. Page *et al.* proposed the following definition for P:

$$\tilde{P} = \alpha P + (1 - \alpha) \frac{\mathbf{e}\mathbf{e}^T}{n} \tag{2}$$

where $0 \leq \alpha \leq 1$. Here, the convex combination of P with the perturbation matrix $E = \frac{\mathbf{e}\mathbf{e}^T}{n}$ ensures $\tilde{P}$ to be irreducible by definition[1] [7]. The intuition behind this approach is to model the behaviour of a "random surfer" that with

---

[1] Note that by adding E we are effectively creating an arc between every pair of nodes.

probability $(1-\alpha)$ gets bored and makes a jump to an arbitrary site. An extension to this model –known as *personalization*– consists on replacing $\mathbf{e}^T/n$ by $\mathbf{v}^T$: a distribution over states reflecting the preferences of each particular user [6].

3   Random Walks for Classifier Combination

Let G^C be a graph with nodes $\mathcal{V} = \mathcal{C}$, i.e. a graph defined on the space of concepts. Let us consider a random walk on G^C with a transition matrix defined as the convex combination of two terms, as follows:

$$\tilde{P} = \alpha P_O + (1 - \alpha)P_A \; , \tag{3}$$

where $0 \le \alpha \le 1$. Let us also define the matrix $A = [a_{ij}]$, with elements:

$$a_{ij} = \begin{cases} \sigma(\beta r_{ij}), & \text{if } i \ne j \\ 0, & \text{otherwise} \end{cases} \; , \tag{4}$$

where $\beta > 0$ corresponds to a tuning parameter and $\sigma(x) = (1 + \exp{(-x)})^{-1}$ is the logistic function. The matrix A can be seen as the adjacency matrix of the graph corresponding to the first term in (3). The $C \times C$ matrix P_O is defined as the the row-normalized version of the adjacency matrix (4). The matrix P_A is defined as $P_A = \mathbf{e}\mathbf{q}^T$, where the "personalization" vector $\mathbf{q} = (q_1, \dots, q_C)^T$ takes the form:

$$q_i = \frac{\sigma(\beta s_i)}{\sum_{k=1}^{C} \sigma(\beta s_k)} \; . \tag{5}$$

Using (4) and (5) in the definition of $\tilde{P}$ makes it a valid transition matrix[2]. It comprises two terms: the first, reflecting all pairwise relations between nodes; the second, modelling the behaviour of a "random surfer" which prefers those nodes with a high one-vs-all classification score. The trade-off between these terms is controlled by the parameter α.

Given a new sample $\mathbf{x}$ and a set of trained OVO and OVA classifiers, we define the *classification score w.r.t. the ith class as the corresponding element of the stationary distribution vector of the Markov chain having $\tilde{P}$ as transition matrix*.

The computation of $\tilde{P}$ involves the evaluation of $C(C + 1)/2$ classifiers. It is interesting to see that in the case of $\alpha = 0$, i.e. when considering only the OVA-terms, the stationary distribution is $\mathbf{\Pi} = \mathbf{q}$. From the definition of q_i in eq. (5), it follows that the "argmax" rule will make the same prediction as with a traditional OVA scheme.

4   Experimental Setup

We evaluate our approach in the context of multiclass image classification. The evaluation was performed using two challenging image datasets: PASCAL

---

[2] It corresponds to a fully connected graph, as $q_i > 0$, $\forall i$.

VOC2007 [3] and MIT Indoor Scenes [13]. The image representation we used was the improved Fisher Vector (FV) but without spatial pyramids (cf. [12]). Before going into details regarding the experimental procedure, we give a brief overview of this state-of-the-art image signature. Details can be found in [11,12].

4.1 Image Signature

Let $X = \{x_t, t = 1 \ldots T\}$ be the set of D-dimensional local descriptors extracted from a given image. Let $u_\lambda : \mathbb{R}^D \to \mathbb{R}_+$ be a pdf with parameters λ modelling the generation process of low-level descriptors in *any* image. Here, u_λ is defined to be a mixture of N Gaussians with diagonal covariances: $u_\lambda(x) = \sum_{i=1}^{N} w_i u_i(x)$, $\lambda = \{w_i, \mu_i, \sigma_i, i = 1 \ldots N\}$. w_i, μ_i and σ_i^2 denote, respectively, the mixing weight, mean and variance vectors corresponding to the ith component of the mixture. The FV is defined as $\mathcal{G}_\lambda^X = L_\lambda G_\lambda^X$, where G_λ^X corresponds to the gradient of the (average) log-likelihood of X, i.e. $\frac{1}{T} \sum_{t=1}^{T} \nabla_\lambda \log u_\lambda(x_t)$ and L_λ a diagonal normalizer. The image signature is the concatenation of normalized partial derivatives, resulting in a vector of dimensionality $2ND$. Following [12], we apply the transformation $f(z) = sign(z)\sqrt{|z|}$ on each dimension and L_2-normalize the resulting vector as it was shown to improve classification accuracy.

Low-Level Features. We used 128-dimensional SIFT descriptors [9] extracted from image patches of 32×32 pixels uniformly distributed on the image (from the nodes of a regular grid with a step size of 8 pixels). We did not perform any normalization on the image patches before computations. The dimensionality of the resulting descriptors were further reduced to 80 by Principal Components Analysis (PCA). To account for variations in scale, we extracted patches at 5 different resolutions using a scale factor of 0.707 between levels.

Generative Model. We trained a GMM under a Maximum Likelihood (ML) criterion using the Expectation-Maximization (EM) algorithm. We used $1M$ random samples from the training set of PASCAL VOC2007. We initialized the EM iterations by running k-means and using the statistics of cluster assignments (relative count, mean and variance vectors) as initial estimates.

4.2 Base Classifiers

As base classifiers we used linear SVMs trained on the primal using Stochastic Gradient Descent (SGD) [1], i.e. minimizing the L_2 regularized hinge-loss in a sample-by-sample basis. The regularization parameter λ was chosen by cross-validation on the training set.

4.3 Datasets

PASCAL VOC2007. This dataset contain images of 20 object categories. The set of images for each class exhibits a large degree of intra-class variation, including changes in viewpoint, illumination, scale, partial occlusions, etc.. Images from this dataset are split into three groups: *train*, *val* and *test*. We followed the recommended procedure of tuning parameters on the *train* set while using the *val* set for testing. Once the best choice for the parameters have been selected, the system was re-trained using the *train+val* sets. Classification performance is measured using the mean Average Precision (mAP) computed on the *test* set.

MIT Indoor Scenes. This dataset consists on more than $15K$ images depicting 67 different indoor environments. We created 10 different train/test splits by randomly selecting 50% of the images for training and 50% for testing. In order to adjust model parameters, we ran a 5-fold cross validation on the training set of the first of such splits. The best configuration was used in all runs. Classification performance was measured using the *multiclass prediction accuracy* (MPA), i.e. the mean over the diagonal elements of the confusion matrix [13]. We report the mean as well as standard deviation over runs.

5   Results

We observed that finely tuning the parameter β has little effect on performance. For the hyperparameter α, we found that a value of 0.6 was the optimal choice in most situations. We set $\alpha = 0.6$ and $\beta = 2$ in all our experiments.

Table 1 show classification performances obtained on PASCAL VOC 2007 as a function of the model complexity (the number of Gaussian components, N) for two classification schemes: one-vs-all (OVA) and our RW based approach (RWC). We compare only against OVA because it is the best performing method on this dataset[3]. It can be observed that the gain brought by our method decreases as the model complexity increases. For instance, our approach achieves a better score on 16, 15, 14, 13, 10 and 7 classes out of 20 for model complexities of $N = 8, 16, 32, 64, 128$ and 256 respectively. This seems to indicate that the proposed approach helps to ameliorate –in the final stage of the classification pipeline– the use of representations with less expressive power. For this dataset, the feature space induced by models with more than 64 Gaussians makes OVA classification a good multiclass scheme, provided this particular representation. From this point, a better performance can be expected due to a more descriptive (complex) model and not to the capabilities of the system on solving possible ambiguities between concepts.

Table 2 show the performance obtained by the OVA and RWC systems on a problem involving a larger number of classes (MIT Indoor Scenes). As before, it can be seen that the gain in performance is greater for systems based on less complex representations. In this particular case, the RWC approach allows a model with a small number of Gaussians to achieve a performance comparable to that achieved by a model using twice as many components.

---

[3] In preliminary experiments we also considered the use of OVO classification with voting, but its performance was consistently lower compared to the simpler and more usual OVA strategy.

Table 1. PASCAL VOC2007. Classification performance for one-vs-all (OVA) and the proposed approach (RWC), for increasing model complexity (number of Gaussians, N).

Class	N=8 OVA	RWC	N=16 OVA	RWC	N=32 OVA	RWC	N=64 OVA	RWC	N=128 OVA	RWC	N=256 OVA	RWC
aeroplane	69.3	**72.4**	71.0	**72.1**	72.6	**73.9**	**75.8**	75.3	**78.2**	77.5	**78.4**	77.2
bicycle	50.8	**53.7**	53.0	**54.9**	59.0	**60.4**	61.2	**62.2**	**64.7**	64.5	**65.9**	65.8
bird	31.8	**35.6**	39.2	**39.5**	43.9	**46.5**	46.0	**47.3**	45.4	**46.7**	**48.3**	47.8
boat	62.0	**63.9**	64.6	**66.1**	65.1	**66.4**	68.2	**69.0**	**68.7**	68.4	69.6	**69.7**
bottle	24.2	**24.9**	28.3	**29.0**	**32.3**	31.3	**31.1**	30.9	**31.9**	**31.9**	**33.6**	32.2
bus	54.9	**55.3**	56.5	**59.1**	59.2	**61.0**	63.7	**65.0**	64.0	**64.8**	**64.7**	**64.7**
car	70.5	**73.4**	73.2	**76.1**	75.9	**77.6**	76.7	**78.9**	78.1	**79.2**	79.9	**80.5**
cat	46.5	**46.2**	**51.0**	49.5	**54.0**	53.9	55.8	**56.8**	**56.8**	55.4	**58.6**	57.2
chair	45.3	**46.6**	43.2	**46.4**	46.6	**48.6**	48.5	**50.1**	48.4	**49.0**	49.8	**51.1**
cow	**30.0**	26.8	**35.2**	32.5	35.3	**36.6**	**41.4**	41.1	**42.5**	39.8	**45.2**	42.5
diningtable	41.0	**41.6**	42.8	**43.0**	48.0	**48.2**	50.7	**51.4**	53.7	**54.8**	**55.3**	54.7
dog	31.0	**41.9**	36.3	**44.8**	40.4	**45.1**	40.2	**46.6**	41.5	**46.1**	45.5	**48.3**
horse	**68.9**	67.9	72.8	**73.6**	**74.5**	74.3	**75.1**	74.7	**76.4**	75.6	**77.6**	76.8
motorbike	**51.3**	50.4	**57.5**	56.7	**62.3**	60.9	**64.0**	63.6	**66.5**	65.2	**65.7**	65.4
person	**76.6**	74.7	**79.2**	78.1	**81.1**	80.8	**81.5**	80.9	**82.2**	81.5	**82.6**	82.3
pottedplant	14.1	**15.7**	21.9	**25.3**	24.2	**26.5**	27.5	**28.9**	30.9	**32.0**	30.1	**31.2**
sheep	30.6	**34.4**	**38.4**	36.8	**40.6**	39.8	**40.2**	38.5	**38.9**	38.0	**43.3**	40.2
sofa	43.7	**45.1**	43.5	**45.5**	45.8	**47.4**	49.9	**51.1**	49.2	**49.8**	**51.9**	51.7
train	68.2	**70.2**	72.0	**73.6**	74.2	**76.1**	75.1	**76.2**	77.6	**77.8**	**79.2**	79.1
tvmonitor	44.6	**46.8**	46.0	**48.9**	47.6	**50.1**	49.8	**51.9**	50.8	**54.4**	51.8	**54.1**
average	47.8	**49.4**	51.3	**52.6**	54.1	**55.3**	56.1	**57.0**	57.3	**57.6**	58.8	58.6
gain		+1.6		+1.3		+1.2		+0.9		+0.3		-0.2

Table 2. MIT Indoor Scenes. Multiclass prediction accuracy (in %). OVA vs. RWC (*left*). Comparison with the state-of-the-art (*right*).

	N=16 OVA	RWC	N=32 OVA	RWC	N=64 OVA	RWC	N=128 OVA	RWC	N=256 OVA	RWC
avg.	46.3	**48.7**	48.9	**50.8**	51.2	**52.6**	52.9	**53.9**	53.6	**54.4**
s.d.	0.6	0.7	0.6	0.6	0.5	0.5	0.6	0.6	0.6	0.6
gain		+2.4		+1.9		+1.4		+1.0		+0.8

Method	MPA
OB [8]	37.6
NNbMF [2]	47.0
OVA	50.7
RWC	52.3

As a final comparison, we ran experiments using the same train/test as in [13]. We compare the OVA and RWC schemes based on Fisher vectors ($N = 128$) and simple linear classifiers against the *Object Bank* (OB) approach of Li *et al.* [8] and the *Nearest-Neighbor based Metric Functions* (NNbMF) of Çakir *et al.* [2]. Results are shown in Table 2 (right). It can be observed that the system based on FVs and linear OVA classification outperforms the state-of-the-art on this dataset and that even such a powerful representation can benefit from the proposed classifier combination scheme.

6   Conclusions and Future Work

We proposed a method to combine the scores of two common multiclass classification schemes: one-vs-all and one-vs-one. The approach is based on the stationary distribution of a Markov chain defined in the space of concepts. Results on the challenging problem of image classification showed the potentiality of our approach. In a future work we will investigate other types of graph connectivity structures, specially those leading to sparse transition matrices.

References

1. Bottou, L.: SGD, http://leon.bottou.org/projects/sgd
2. Çakir, F., Güdükbay, U., Ulusoy, Ö.: Nearest-neighbor based metric functions for indoor scene recognition. Computer Vision and Image Understanding 115(11), 1483–1492 (2011)
3. Everingham, M., Van Gool, L., Williams, C.K.I., Winn, J., Zisserman, A.: The PASCAL Visual Object Classes Challenge 2007 (VOC 2007) Results, http://www.pascal-network.org/challenges/VOC/voc2007/workshop/index.html
4. Galar, M., Fernández, A., Tartas, E.B., Sola, H.B., Herrera, F.: An overview of ensemble methods for binary classifiers in multi-class problems: Experimental study on one-vs-one and one-vs-all schemes. Pattern Recognition 44(8), 1761–1776 (2011)
5. García-Pedrajas, N., Ortiz-Boyer, D.: Improving multiclass pattern recognition by the combination of two strategies. IEEE Tr. on Pattern Analysis and Machine Intelligence 28(6), 1001–1006 (2006)
6. Haveliwala, T.H.: Topic-sensitive pagerank: A context-sensitive ranking algorithm for web search. IEEE Tr. on Knowledge and Data Eng. 15(4), 784–796 (2003)
7. Langville, A.N., Meyer, C.D.: Deeper inside PageRank. Internet Mathematics 1(3), 335–400 (2004)
8. Li, L.-J., Su, H., Xing, E.P., Li, F.-F.: Object bank: A high-level image representation for scene classification & semantic feature sparsification. In: Proc. NIPS (2010)
9. Lowe, D.G.: Distinctive image features from scale-invariant keypoints. Intl. Jrnl. on Computer Vision 60(2) (2004)
10. Page, L., Brin, S., Motwani, R., Winograd, T.: The pagerank citation ranking: Bringing order to the web. Technical report, Stanford InfoLab (1999)
11. Perronnin, F., Dance, C.: Fisher kernels on visual vocabularies for image categorization. In: Proc. CVPR (2007)
12. Perronnin, F., Sánchez, J., Mensink, T.: Improving the Fisher Kernel for Large-Scale Image Classification. In: Daniilidis, K., Maragos, P., Paragios, N. (eds.) ECCV 2010, Part IV. LNCS, vol. 6314, pp. 143–156. Springer, Heidelberg (2010)
13. Quattoni, A., Torralba, A.: Recognizing indoor scenes. In: Proc. CVPR (2009)
14. Reid, S.R.: Model Combination in Multiclass Classification. Ph.D. thesis, Univ. of Colorado (2010)
15. Rifkin, R.M., Klautau, A.: In: defense of one-vs-all classification. Jrnl. of Machine Learning Research 5, 101–141 (2004)
16. Wu, T.F., Lin, C.J., Weng, R.C.: Probability estimates for multi-class classification by pairwise coupling. Jrnl. of Machine Learning Research 5, 975–1005 (2004)

Stochastic Approaches of Minimum Distance Method for Region Based Classification

Rogério G. Negri, Luciano V. Dutra, and Sidnei J.S. Sant'Anna

Instituto Nacional de Pesquisas Espaciais – INPE, São José dos Campos - SP, Brasil
Divisão de Processamento de Imagens – DPI
{rogerio,dutra,sidnei}@dpi.inpe.br

Abstract. Normally remote sensing image classification is performed pixelwise which produces a noisy classification. One way of improving such results is dividing the classification process in two steps. First, uniform regions by some criterion are detected and afterwards each unlabeled region is assigned to class of the "nearest" class using a so-called stochastic distance. The statistics are estimated by taking in account all the reference pixels. Three variations are investigated. The first variation is to assign to the unlabeled region a class that has the minimum average distance between this region and each one of reference samples of that class. The second is to assign the class of the closest reference sample. The third is to assign the most frequent class of the k closest reference regions. A simulation study is done to assess the performances. The simulations suggested that the most robust and simple approach is the second variation.

Keywords: region based classification, stochastic distances, image simulation, remote sensing.

1 Introduction

Traditionally land cover classification, using remote sensing data, is performed pixelwise, also known as pixel based classification. The main drawback of this approach is producing a noisy classification map.

One way of improving such results is using what is called a *contextual classifier*, where the pixel classification depends somehow on the state of its neighbours [1]. Another traditional approach is dividing the image classification process in two steps. First, uniform regions by some criterion are detected in the imagery and afterwards each region is assigned to just one class. This unknown region is assigned to the class closest to it, in terms of a so-called stochastic distance [2].

Stochastic distance is a generic name to a class of distances that measures the *difference* between two distributions, it is zero when two distributions are equal. The reference statistics is calculated using all data of the several training samples of a particular class.

In this paper we will investigate three variations of the aforementioned approach. A Monte Carlo study is done to assess the performance of the proposed modifications.

L. Alvarez et al. (Eds.): CIARP 2012, LNCS 7441, pp. 797–804, 2012.

2   Stochastic Distances

The Jeffries-Matusita (JM), a well known stochastic distance between two distributions is defined as [3]:

$$JM(\mathbf{U}, \mathbf{V}) = \int_{\mathbf{x} \in \mathcal{X}} \left[\sqrt{f_\mathbf{U}(\mathbf{x}; \Theta_U)} - \sqrt{f_\mathbf{V}(\mathbf{x}; \Theta_V)} \right]^2 d\mathbf{x} \tag{1}$$

where $f_\mathbf{U}$ and $f_\mathbf{V}$ are probability density functions with parameters $\Theta_\mathbf{U}$ and $\Theta_\mathbf{V}$, respectively, related to the random variables $\mathbf{U}$ and $\mathbf{V}$, defined on the same probability space $\mathcal{X}$.

From the equation (1) one can observe that if $f_\mathbf{U}$ and $f_\mathbf{V}$ are equal this distance is zero, and if these distributions are totally different this distance comes to two. For classes normally distribuited the JM distance is written as [3]:

$$JM(\mathbf{U}, \mathbf{V}) = 2 \left(1 - e^{-B(\mathbf{U}, \mathbf{V})} \right) \tag{2}$$

where $B(\cdot, \cdot)$ is the Bhattacharyya distance, which for normal distributions is written as:

$$B(\mathbf{U}, \mathbf{V}) = \frac{1}{8} (\mu_\mathbf{U} - \mu_\mathbf{V})^T \left(\frac{\Sigma_\mathbf{U} + \Sigma_\mathbf{V}}{2} \right)^{-1} (\mu_\mathbf{U} - \mu_\mathbf{V}) + \frac{1}{2} \ln \left(\frac{0.5 |\Sigma_\mathbf{U} + \Sigma_\mathbf{V}|}{|\Sigma_\mathbf{U}| + |\Sigma_\mathbf{V}|} \right) \tag{3}$$

where $\mu_\mathbf{Z}$ and $\Sigma_\mathbf{Z}$ are the average vector and covariance matrix estimated for the random variable $\mathbf{Z}$, with $(\cdot)^T$, $|\cdot|$ and $(\cdot)^{-1}$ denoting respectively the transpose, determinant and inverse operations.

3   Region Based Classification Using Stochastic Distances

Formally, the pixel based classification process consists in associating the classes $\omega_j \in \Omega$, $j = 1, 2, \ldots, c$; for each pattern (pixel) $\mathbf{x}_i \in \mathcal{I} \subset \mathcal{X}$, $i = 1, 2, \ldots, n$, from a function $g : \mathcal{X} \to \Omega$, called classifier. In this context, $\mathcal{I}$ represents an image composed by patterns $\mathbf{x}$ defined on the *atribute space* $\mathcal{X}$. The different image classification methods can be understood as different ways of modeling the function g and applying on $\mathcal{I}$.

For region based classification the images are initially organized into different regions using *image segmentation* techniques. More details about these techniques can be found in [4].

In the region based approach the object is no longer pixels but regions. A region $\mathbf{R}_l$, $l = 1, \ldots, L$ is a set of spatially connected pixels that attends a particular uniformity criterion defined by the segmentor, $\bigcup_{l=1}^{L} \mathbf{R}_l = \mathcal{I}$. In region based classification the whole region is assigned at once, to a particular class. All pixels in the $\mathbf{R}_l$ region has the same class.

To train a supervised region based methodology it is required a set of labelled regions $\mathcal{D} = \{(\mathbf{R}_l, \omega_j) \in \mathcal{X} \times \Omega, l = 1, \ldots, N; j = 1, \ldots, c\}$, where N is the total number of training regions. The standard *Minimum Stochastic Distance Classifier* uses the information of pixels distribution inside the unlabelled region to associate it to the class which has the closest distribution. The classes distributions are modeled using the information of $\mathcal{D}$. Being $\mathbf{R}_l$ an unlabelled region, i.e. $l \notin \mathcal{D}$, $M(f_{\mathbf{R}_l}, f_{\omega_j})$ a stochastic distance between $f_{\mathbf{R}_l}$, the distribution of $\mathbf{R}_l$ and f_{ω_j}, the distribution of the class ω_j, an assignment of ω_j to $\mathbf{R}_l$, denoted by $(\mathbf{R}_l, \omega_j)$, is made if the following rule is satisfied:

$$(\mathbf{R}_l, \omega_j) \Leftrightarrow j = \underset{j=1,\ldots,c}{\arg\min}\ M(f_{\mathbf{R}_l}, f_{\omega_j}) \tag{4}$$

The class distribution are estimated taking into account all the pixels that are present inside the many labelled regions taken as reference to a particular class. In this work we investigate other alternatives for the standard classification rule defined in (4).

The *Minimum Mean Stochastic Distance* rule (M_{mean}) is obtained by the arithmetic mean of the stochastic distances between a given unlabelled region and each one of training regions of the same class. This distance can be defined as:

$$M_{mean}(f_{\mathbf{R}_l}, f_{\omega_j}) = \frac{1}{t_j} \sum_{k=1}^{t_j} M(f_{\mathbf{R}_l}, f_{\omega_{j\mathbf{R}_k}}) \tag{5}$$

where $f_{\omega_{j\mathbf{R}_k}}$ is a probability density function that models the k-th training region of ω_j, which has t_j training regions in $\mathcal{D}$.

Other option is the M_{min} distance, which is the minimum distance between an unlabelled region $\mathbf{R}_l$ and each one of the training regions of ω_j. This rule is written as:

$$M_{min}(f_{\mathbf{R}_l}, f_{\omega_j}) = \min\left\{ M(f_{\mathbf{R}_l}, f_{\omega_{j\mathbf{R}_k}}) : k = 1, \ldots, t_j \right\} \tag{6}$$

Another option is suggested by (6). It would be the stochastic distance form of the k-Nearest-Neighbors classifier (M_{knn}), which is defined by associating a class to an unabelled region as the most frequent class of the k-nearest training regions.

4   Experiments and Results

To evaluate the classification results a Monte Carlo study was performed. The study was based on simulated images having optical characteristics. The simulation process is divided into three main steps: creating phantom image, computing statistical parameters and simulating image patches. The phantom image is an idealized cartoon model, which contains the image regions. Mean vector and covariance matrix are statistics extracted from different targets (classes) in real image. The adopted image model is introduced in the image patch simulation step (image synthesis).

For this study its was created a phantom image that is formed by concatenating six identical blocks of 512×512 pixels, partitioned in 44 segments having different forms and sizes. Each block will represent a distinct class. For classification purposes the upper quarter of each block was selected as training samples. Figure 1(a) illustrates the phantom image and the respective training regions.

A four band (visible and near infrared) LANDSAT5/TM image was used to estimate statistical parameters (mean vector and covariance matrix) of six distinct classes. The TM image was acquired on September 26th 2010 and covers an area located along BR-163 highway, next to the Tapajós National Forest in Pará State, Brazil. The land cover classes used on the statistical estimation procedure were *primary forest, old regeneration* (secondary forest older than 20 years old), *new regeneration* (secondary forest newer than eight years old), *clean pasture, dirty pasture* and *agriculture fields*.

As mentioned, the optical characteristics are required for the simulated images, therefore a Multivariate Gaussian distribution is assumed for the data distribution. The image synthesis step consists of a joint Gaussian distribution and the expression (7) which defines the covariance structure of the simulated image patches. The expression for a single pixel $\widetilde{\mathbf{p}}_{ab}$ of the segment b of block a is given by:

$$\widetilde{\mathbf{p}}_{ab} = [(E_a \times L_a \times \nu) \times \zeta_b] + (\mu_a \times \psi_b) \tag{7}$$

where μ_a represents a q-dimensional mean vector of the class a, E_a is the eigenvectors matrix derived from the covariance matrix of class a (Σ_a), L_a is the diagonal matrix defined by the square root of the eigenvalues of Σ_a and ν is a q-dimensional random vector generated by a standard Multivariate Gaussian distribution. The parameters ζ_b and ψ_b are random scalars uniformly distributed, with $b \in \{1, 2, \ldots, 44\}$ indexing each segment. They were adopted to model the mean and variance intraclass fluctuations. Note that the index a, in this simulation case, ranges from 1 to 6, since it is used to distinguish each image block.

The columns of E_a are organized according to the descending order of their respective eigenvalues, as well as the diagonal elements of L_a. The variance information of each band is determined by L_a. It is important to notice that for this simulation experiment the values of ζ_b and ψ_b ranged from 0.55 to 1.45 and from 0.90 to 1.10, respectively, as they are commonly found in real case. The classification results were analyzed based on 100 simulated images having four spectral bands and six classes. In Figure 1(b) is illustrated one spectral band of a simulated image, where the fluctuations can be clearly observed.

The simulated images have been classified by the *Minimum Distance Classifier* defined in (4) and by its derivatives M_{mean}, M_{min} and M_{knn}, described, respectively by (5), (6), and the last phrase of section 3. To conduct the Monte Carlo study three different scenarios were employed for the classification analysis. The scenarios were characterized by the number of classes (six, four or two) present on the images. The images having four classes were designed by grouping the image blocks 1, 4 and 5 (*primary forest, clean pasture* and *new regeneration* classes) as a single class. On the other hand, grouping the image blocks 1, 5 and 6 (*primary forest, new regeneration* and *dirty pasture* classes) as a single class and the image blocks 2, 3 and 4 (*agriculture, old regeneration* and *clean pasture*

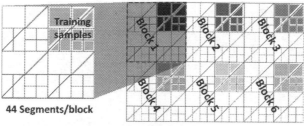

(a) Phantom image and location of the training regions

(b) A band of the simulated image, in gray scale

Fig. 1. The *primary forest*, *agriculture*, *old regeneration*, *clean pasture*, *new regeneration* and *dirty pasture* classes are represented by blocks 1 to 6, respectively

classes) in another single class generate the two classes images. These grouping process aims to verify the classifier capability of dealing with heterogeneous classes.

Classification is performed for all set of classes using the JM distance as M in the (2) and its derivatives. It was adopted $k = 3$ for M_{knn}. Overall accuracy is computed for each classification case considering the 33 segments not used as training regions.

Figures 2, 3 and 4 present the simulation results for images containing 6, 4 and 2 classes respectively. Table 1 brings the mean overall accuracy (OA) and its standard deviation for the simulated results. It is possible to observe that M_{min} and M_{knn} produce the highest OA values for all studied cases, indicating that they are quite robust to multi-modality, which is also reflected in Table 1. The average overall accuracy of M_{min} and M_{knn} have been found statiscally indifferent at 95% of confidence level. Figure 5(a) is the reference map, Figures 5(b), (c) and (d) are typical examples of M_{knn}, M_{mean} and M classifications for two classes.

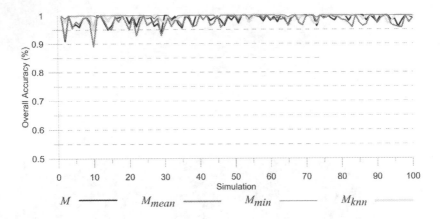

Fig. 2. Overall accuracy results for six classes image

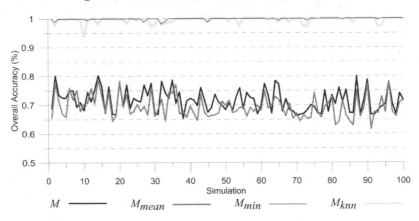

Fig. 3. Overall accuracy results for four classes image

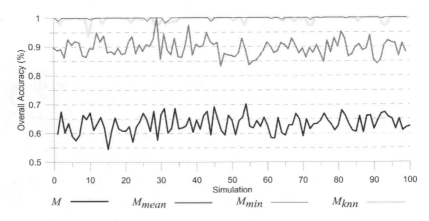

Fig. 4. Overall accuracy results for two classes image

Table 1. Overall accuracy results

# Classes		M	M_{mean}	M_{min}	M_{knn}
6	Average	0.987	0.981	0.999	0.996
	Std. Deviation	0.016	0.020	0.003	0.009
4	Average	0.716	0.694	0.999	0.995
	Std. Deviation	0.039	0.039	0.003	0.010
2	Average	0.632	0.896	0.999	0.995
	Std. Deviation	0.030	0.029	0.003	0.010

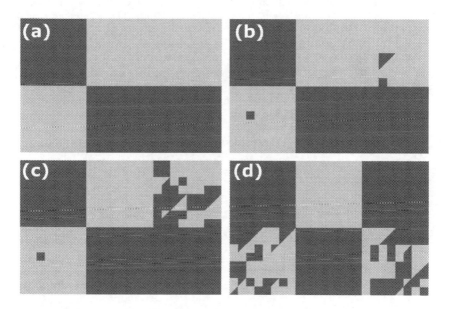

Fig. 5. Typical examples of classification results for two classes: (a) reference map, (b) M_{min} classification, (c) M_{mean} classification, (d) M classification

5   Conclusions

Unlike what is commonly used for region based classification which is the M function based on JM distance, the M_{min} or M_{knn} rule would be prefered because its robustness. Also as the M_{min} rule is not statistically different from the M_{knn} rule then M_{min} is preferred because it is simpler and quicker.

The conclusion implies that the user have to be careful to collect training samples, at least one representative for each aspect of the class to be mapped. One example is the use of region based classification for classifying roofs tops in high resolution imagery, which is a problem intrinsically multi-modal. Instead of training each type of roof tops separately, it is possible to add samples of each type of roof in a general roof top category, and then the classification is expected to work properly using the M_{min} version.

Acknowledgments. This work was supported by CAPES, CNPq (Grant # 307666/2011-5) and FAPESP (Grant # 08/58112-0 and 08/57719-9).

References

1. Kartikeyan, B., Gopalakrishna, B., Kalubarme, M.H., Majumder, K.L.: Contextual techniques for classification of high and low resolution remote sensing data. International Journal of Remote Sensing 15(5), 1037–1051 (1994)
2. Silva, W.B., Pereira, L.O., Sant'Anna, S.J.S., Freitas, C.C., Guimarães, R.J.P.S., Frery, A.C.: Land cover discrimination at brazilian Amazon using region based classifier and stochastic distance. In: 2011 IEEE International Geoscience and Remote Sensing Symposium, pp. 2900–2903 (2011)
3. Richards, J.A., Jia, X.: Remote Sensing Digital Image Analysis: An Introduction. Springer (2005)
4. Gonzalez, R.C., Woods, R.E.: Digital Image Processing, 3rd edn. Prentice-Hall, Inc., Upper Saddle River (2006)

Skills Assessment of Users in Medical Training Based on Virtual Reality Using Bayesian Networks

Ronei M. Moraes[1], Liliane S. Machado[1], and Leandro C. Souza[2]

[1] Federal University of Paraíba, João Pessoa/PB, Brazil
ronei@de.ufpb.br
[2] Federal University of Pernambuco, Recife/PE, Brazil
liliane@di.ufpb.br

Abstract. Virtual reality allows the development of digital environments that can explore users' senses to provide realistic and immersive experiences. When used for training purposes, interaction data can be used to verify users skills. In order to do that, intelligent methodologies must be coupled to the simulations to classify users´ skills into N a priori defined classes of expertise. To reach that, models based on intelligent methodologies are composed from data provided by experts. However, online Single User's Assessment System (SUAS) for training must have low complexity algorithms to do not compromise the performance of the simulator. Several approaches to perform it have been proposed. In this paper, it is made an analysis of performance of SUAS based on a Bayesian Network and also a comparison between that SUAS and another methodology based on Classical Bayes Rule.

Keywords: Medical Training, User's Assessment, Bayesian Networks, Virtual Reality.

1   Introduction

Virtual Reality (VR) environments can provide realistic systems for several areas and have been used since a long time [1]. In such immersive and interactive environments, users perform tasks that simulate real situations. Interaction data feed the system and are processed in real time to generate feedback for users, as new points of view, force feedback and sound effects. This data can also be collected to monitor users´ actions in order to analyze how tasks are accomplished and classify users performance. This is particularly interesting when the virtual environments are used for training purposes.

Researches on training assessment for simulators based on VR has less than 20 years old and the methodologies for assessment make possible to know users' performance during the training to analyze if they are prepared to perform the procedure in real situations. Probably the pioneer works for Single User's Assessment System (SUAS) were proposed by Dinsmore et al. [3] using a quiz to assess users in the identification of subcutaneous tumors in a training system based on VR. The quiz was composed by questions related to the diagnosis and hardness of tumor. Other research group [16] created a minimally invasive system in which each task could be programmed for different difficulty levels. Performance data of each user could be saved to post analysis (offline) by an expert or using statistical methods [15].

L. Alvarez et al. (Eds.): CIARP 2012, LNCS 7441, pp. 805–812, 2012.

Since 90's, several assessment methods were proposed [8,13], mainly for medical training. With continuous advances on computers performance, SUAS evolved too. Nowadays, a SUAS must continuously monitor all users interactions on VR environment and compare their performance with pre-defined expert's classes of performance to recognize users level of training. Basically, there are two types of SUAS: off-line and on-line.

Off-line SUAS can be defined as methods which can be or not coupled to VR systems, whose assessment results are provided some time (which can be minutes, hours or days) after the end of the VR-based training [15]. On the other hand, on-line SUAS must coupled to the training system based on VR [10] and should be able to collect interaction data to provide a result of performance in lower than one second after the end of the simulation [12]. It occurs by comparing a model composed by users' interaction data with classes of performance previously defined from experts knowledge. A SUAS must be able to monitor user's interactions with the VR simulator by variables such as spatial position (of user and of interaction tools used in the VR simulation), touch force and resistance, user's angle of visualization, sound, smell, sense of temperature, velocity and acceleration of interactions and felt shapes. All the information are sent to the SUAS which analyzes the data and emits, at the end of the training, an assessment report about user's performance according pre-defined classes of performance (Figure 1). An on-line SUAS must have low complexity to does not compromise VR simulations performance, but it must have high accuracy to does not compromise the assessment and they are normally based on pattern recognition techniques. Then, several methodologies developed for SUAS can be potentially applied to other research areas.

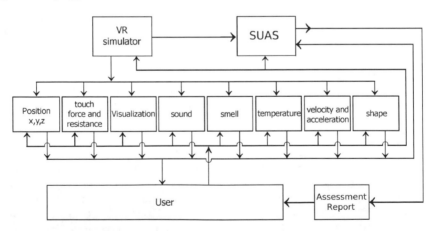

Fig. 1. Diagram of a training system based on VR with a SUAS coupled on it [9]

An approach based on a Bayesian Network for an online SUAS was proposed by [11]. In the present paper we provide an analysis of performance of that approach and also a comparison between that approach and another one based on Classical Bayes Rule [9,12].

In medical training assessment, is necessary to find the better SUAS to assess users with high accuracy. Since patients' life or their health conditions can depend on physicians skills, a good assessment method is important to provide feedback about training status. However, the choice of a methodology will depend on the features of the training simulator that can provide qualitative and/or quantitative data as input for the assessment. Since the kind of input data is known, models can be composed and integrated into a SUAS. For performance reasons, supervised methods are the most used in SUAS, but an exhaustive comparison them was not found in the literature. Then, the main contribution of this paper is the presentation of a methodology for SUAS bases on Bayesian Networks and its comparison with another methodology based on Classical Bayes Rule. A simulator for training of a medical procedure is presented as an example of application of the SUAS.

2   Theoretical Aspects

This section presents theoretical aspects of the SUAS based on Bayesian Network. For reader's better understanding, it is presented a short review about the Classical Bayes Rule and in the following, is presented the Bayesian Network.

2.1   Classical Bayes Rule

Formally, let be the classes of performance in space of decision $\Omega = \{1,....,M\}$ where M is the total number of classes of performance. Let be w_i, $i \in \Omega$ the class of performance for an user. The Classical Bayes Rule (CBR) [9,12] computes conditional class probabilities and then predict the most probable class of a vector of training data X, according to sample data D, where X is a vector with n features obtained when a training is performed, i.e. $X = \{X_1, X_2, ..., X_n\}$. Using the Bayes Theorem:

$$P(w_i \mid X) = [P(X \mid w_i) \, P(w_i)] / P(X) \Leftrightarrow P(w_i \mid X_1, X_2, ..., X_n) = \qquad (1)$$
$$= [P(X_1, X_2, ..., X_n \setminus w_i) \, P(w_i)] / P(X)$$

However, as $P(X)$ is the same for all classes w_i, then it is not relevant for data classification. Then, the equation (1) can be expressed by:

$$P(w_i \mid X_1, X_2, ..., X_n) = P(w_i) \, P(X_1, X_2, ..., X_n \mid w_i) \qquad (2)$$

Then, the assessment rule for CBR is done by:

$$X \in w_i \ \ if \ \ P(w_i \mid X_1, X_2, ..., X_n) > P(w_j \mid X_1, X_2, ..., X_n)$$
$$for \ all \ i \neq j \ and \ i, j \in \Omega \qquad (3)$$

2.2   Bayesian Network

Formally, a Bayesian network is defined as directed acyclic graphs, denoted by G and a probabilistic distribution denoted by P. The graph G is a set of nodes and oriented arcs, where nodes represent variables in process and oriented arcs encode conditional dependencies between that variables [14]. The dependencies are modeled by specific conditional probabilistic distributions [6].

Several kinds of Bayesian networks can be found in literature [2]. They can differ on their graph structure and types of dependencies relationship which they can model. According to statistical relationship between variables which describe that process a specific Bayesian network should be chosen. This is critical, because it changes the final results. The General Bayesian Network (GBN) is a generalized form of Bayesian networks, which allows nodes to form an arbitrary graph [2]. Another important characteristic is that each child node cannot be connected to the final classes of assessment and the dependencies between nodes can adjust itself to real dependencies. Thus, it is possible to verify dependencies between variables during network modeling and put them in structure nodes of GBN, which did not occur in other structures [5].

Formally, let be the same M classes of performance, w_j, $i \in \Omega$ the class of performance for a user and X_k, $1 \leq k \leq n$, represents a node in GBN with n as the number of nodes in a graph. The joint probability distribution in GBN for an event is done by:

$$P(X_1, X_2, ..., X_n) = \prod^n_{k=1} P(X_n \mid X_{n-1}, X_{n-2}, ..., X_1) \qquad (4)$$

where $P(X_1, X_2, ..., X_n)$ is the joint probability distribution and $P(X_n \mid X_{n-1}, X_{n-2}, ..., X_1)$ is the conditional probability of X_n conditioned by its predecessor nodes $X_{n-1}, X_{n-2}, ..., X_1$.

The probability nodes are associated to probability distribution, which can be different for each node. For example, a node A can have a Gaussian distribution and a node B, which depends on A, can have a bivariate Gaussian distribution. The structure of GBN is learned from data, finding dependencies among nodes, as well as the parameters of conditional probabilities. Scores are used to help estimate the final structure of GBN for each class of assessment. In a first moment a network is created with all independent nodes and an initial score is calculated. Next, all combinations are searched and an arc is designed between two nodes for which an increment of initial score is obtained. Then, the parameters for that nodes set are re-estimated using linear regression. This cycle is repeated until total network score is less than a predetermined value or a fixed number of cycles [11].

3   The Bone Marrow Harvest Simulator

A bone marrow harvest simulator was developed to allow training of the bone marrow harvest for transplant [7]. The procedure is composed by three steps which were considered in the development of the simulator. The first step is related to the observation of the anatomy, the second to the palpation of the patient pelvic region, and the third to the puncture process to harvest bone marrow. Since the main activity of the procedure is related to the third step, the simulator was designed in details to represent this step. Also, a haptic device was used to provide realism and co-relation between real and virtual environments.

Since this simulator included a rigorous process of design, a framework called CyberMed [8] was used to decrease the development effort and speed up this process. The framework is expansible and several methodologies for a SUAS can be included in its functions. This makes possible to observe the performance and the efficiency of the assessment methodologies in a simulated training. In this case, the haptic interaction data of the puncture step is acquired and used to assess the user in order to indicate their dexterity a ability to perform the procedure.

In a usual situation, a physician should calibrate the SUAS previously, according M classes of performance defined, where M may be any integer number greater than one. The calibration process consists on execute several times the procedure in the simulator and to label each execution according to classes of performance. This calibration occurs in a simulation previously designed to capture physician interactions. This simulation is similar to the final simulator but the physician interaction data is collected and labeled for each execution of the procedure. The number of classes of performance is defined by the physician, e.g. as $M=3$: 1) correct procedures, 2) acceptable procedures, 3) badly executed procedures. So, the classes of performance for a trainee could mean: "you are well qualified", "you need some training yet", "you need more training".

A SUAS based on GBN was implemented in Cybermed, expanding the framework capabilities. This implementation added a new class in the CybAssess class. In this implementation, the default value for network score is 10^{-4} and the fixed number of cycles is 100.

4   Results

To test the GBN method, four classes of performance were simulated from seven different Gaussian distributions, which were mixture. From that procedure, several kinds of statistical distributions could be generated. Only one restriction was used: at least 30% of data generated by a statistical distribution should be intersection with another one. This makes a more realistic simulation, when compared with real data provide from physicians. For each of four classes were generated 30 thousand vectors, from which 10 thousand were used to calibrate the system and the other 20 thousand were used to check the assessment method based on GBN. Each vector contained 10000 positions, which is equivalent to 10 seconds simulation and the calibration time to build the General Bayesian Network was 19 minutes and 6 seconds.

A comparison of the classification agreement between SUAS based on GBN and the generated data was performed using the Cohen's Kappa Coefficient, according to recommended by literature [4] because it is known to be over conservative. The classification matrix obtained is presented in the Table 1. Each line of that matrix represents the real class of performance which data belongs and the column represents class assign by the SUAS. The Kappa coefficient was $K=99.9767\%$ with variance 3.8882×10^{-9}. In 14 cases, the SUAS based on GBN made mistakes and all of them were made in classes of performance C1 and C2. That performance is good and shows that General Bayesian Network is a competitive approach in the solution of assessment problems.

Table 1. Assessment results using a SUAS based on General Bayesian Network

	C_1	C_2	C_3	C_4
C_1	19994	6	0	0
C_2	8	19992	0	0
C_3	0	0	20000	0
C_4	0	0	0	20000

Those tests were performed in a commodity computer (Dual Core computer with 256Mb graphic card and 2 Gb of RAM). That computer run Linux operational system and CyberMed version 1.2. The average of CPU time consumed for assessment of a sample vector contained 10000 elements was 0.5 ms, i.e. that system is able to assess an user in lower than one second and characterizes an online assessment.

5   Comparison with SUAS Based on CBR

Some comparison tests were made to check performance of SUAS based on GBN in relation to the SUAS based on CBR [9], which was implemented in the CyberMed. Tests were performed with respect to time of execution, time of parameters learning and accuracy of that assessment for each SUAS.

All comparative tests were made in the same commodity computer using the same methodology (10 thousand vectors were used to calibrate the system and the other 20 thousand vectors were used to check the performance of the SUAS based on CBR), where each vector contained 10000 elements. The calibration time to build the Classical Bayes Rule was 7 minutes and 50 seconds.

The classification matrix obtained for the CBR is presented in the Table 2. The Kappa coefficient was K=92.7267% with variance 1.1403×10^{-6}. Besides the SUAS based on CBR made correct all assessments for classes of performance C3 and C4, it made several mistakes for C1 and C2 class. The reason for that bad performance can be credited to the restriction made in simulation, which at least 30% of data generated by a statistical distribution should be intersection with another one. That number of assessment errors can be considered high in a condition of medical training assessment, where the patient's life may depend on the physician skills.

Performance tests were conducted for both SUAS, by varying the number of elements in vector, between 1000 and 20000 elements, adding 1000 elements in vector to each test. The Figure 2 presents a comparative graph of performance for two SUAS, in which is possible to note the superior computational performance of SUAS based on CBR over SUAS based on GBN for all number of elements in vector, which were analyzed.

From the Figure 2, it is possible to infer when the performance of the SUAS based on GBN will not be sufficient to be characterized as online: around 40000 elements in the vector for that commodity computer used. However, for those same situations, the SUAS based on CBR probably reach that limit in around 100000 elements in vector.

Table 2. Assessment results using a SUAS based on Classical Bayes Rule

	C_1	C_2	C_3	C_4
C_1	16208	3792	0	0
C_2	0	19428	572	0
C_3	0	0	20000	0
C_4	0	0	0	20000

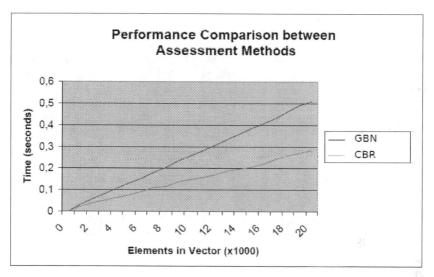

Fig. 2. Performance comparison between SUAS based on GBN and based on CBR according to number of elements in vector

6   Conclusions

In this paper, it was proposed a SUAS based on GBN, which was implemented in CyberMed and is available in the last version of that framework. Tests were performed using statistical simulation and results showed that assessment methodology as an appropriate approach in the solution of assessment problems, with high accuracy and low computational complexity. A comparison of this approach with another SUAS based on CBR was performed.

Quantitative data was generated according to the medical procedure chosen as case for the SUAS. This data generated by Gaussian distribution guarantee that both SUAS used the same data in its calibration and in the comparison of its performance. Both SUAS are able to perform online assessments and could be applied in other kind of training. However, the SUAS based on CBR is faster and can support around 100000 elements in vector, while the SUAS based on GBN can lead with 40000 elements approximately. It is important to note that in all those tests a commodity computer was used. The SUAS based on GBN achieve better results according to Cohen's Kappa Coefficient and for any number of elements in vector its accuracy is always higher from the same input vectors.

A performance statistical comparison with others SUAS, as well as with other kind of computer configurations, are planning as future works to achieve application limits for SUAS based on GBN.

Acknowledgments. This work is partially supported by Brazilian Council for Scientific and Technological Development, CNPq (Processes 310339/2009-0, 312375/2009-3 and 573710/2008-2).

References

1. Burdea, G., Coiffet, P.: Virtual Reality Technology, 2nd ed. Wiley Interscience (2003)
2. Cheng, J., Greiner, R.: Learning Bayesian Belief Network Classifiers: Algorithms and System. In: Proc. of the Fourteenth Canadian Conference on Artificial Intelligence (2001)
3. Dinsmore, M.: VR simulation: training for palpation of subsurface tumors. Master's Thesis, Dep. Mechanical and Aerospace Eng., Rutgers University (October 1996)
4. Duda, R., Hart, P., Stork, D.: Pattern Classification, 2nd edn. Wiley-Interscience (2000)
5. Gaba, D.M., et al.: Assessment of clinical performance during simulated crises using both technical and behavioral ratings. Anesthesiology 89, 8–18 (1998)
6. Krause, P.J.: Learning Probabilistic Networks. Knowledge Engineering Review 13, 321–351 (1998)
7. Machado, L.S., et al.: A Virtual Reality Simulator for Bone Marrow Harvest for Pediatric Transplant. Studies in Health Technology and Informatics 81, 293–297 (2001)
8. Machado, L.S., et al.: A Framework for Development of Virtual Reality-Based Training Simulators. Studies in Health Technology and Informatics 142, 174–176 (2009)
9. Machado, L.S., Moraes, R.M.: Intelligent Decision Making in Training Based on VR. In: Ruan, D. (org.) Computational Intelligence in Complex Decision Systems, ch. 4, pp. 85–123. Atlantis Press (2010)
10. Moraes, R.M., Machado, L.S.: Fuzzy Gaussian Mixture Models for On-line Training Evaluation in Virtual Reality Simulators. In: Int. Conference on Fuzzy Information Processing, China, pp. 733–740 (2003)
11. Moraes, R.M., Machado, L.S., Souza, L.C.: Online Assessment of Training in Virtual Reality Simulators Based on General Bayesian Networks. In: VI International Conference on Engineering and Computer Education (CDROM) (2009)
12. Moraes, R., Machado, L.: Development of a Medical Training System with Integration of Users' Assessment. In: Kim, J.-J. (ed.) Virtual Reality, pp. 325–348. Intech, Vienna (2011)
13. Moraes, R.M., Rocha, A.V., Machado, L.S.: Intelligent Assessment Based on Beta Regression for Realistic Training in Medical Simulators. Knowledge-Based Systems (in press, 2012)
14. Neapolitan, R.E.: Learning Bayesian Networks. Prentice Hall Series in Artificial Intelligence (2003)
15. Scott, et al.: Measuring Operative Performance after Laparoscopic Skills Training: Edited Videotape versus Direct Observation. Journal of Laparoendoscopic & Advanced Surgical Techniques 10(4), 183–190 (2000)
16. Wilson, M.S., et al.: MIST VR: a virtual reality trainer for surgery assesses performance. Annals of the Royal College of Surgeons of England 79, 4034 (1997)

New Strategies for Evaluating the Performance of Typical Testor Algorithms

Eduardo Alba, Diego Guilcapi, and Julio Ibarra

Universidad San Francisco de Quito, Colegio de Ciencias e Ingeniería,
Diego de Robles y Vía Interoceánica, Quito, Ecuador
{ealba,jibarra}@usfq.edu.ec, diego.guilcapi@estud.usfq.edu.ec
http://www.usfq.edu.ec

Abstract. Typical testors have been used in feature selection and supervised classification problems in the logical combinatorial pattern recognition. Several algorithms have been used to find the set of all typical testors of a basic matrix. This algorithms are based on different heuristics. There is no doubt these algorithms find the set of all typical testors. However, the time spent on this search strategies, differs between them. Due to size of this set, the search time is a critical factor. There is not a standard procedure to evaluate the time performance of typical testors algorithms. In this paper we introduce a strategy to solve this problem through a new set of test matrices. These test matrices have the property that the set's cardinality of all typical testors is known in advance.

Keywords: Logical combinatorial PR, feature selection, testor theory, typical testors algorithms, test matrices.

1 Introduction

When is used the logical combinatorial approach in the solution of supervised pattern recognition problems, typical testors play a very important role [1],[2]. In a basic approximation, a testor is a collection of features that discriminates all descriptions of objects belonging to different classes, and is minimal in the partial order determined by set inclusion. Through the stages of the problem solution, typical testors can be applied to satisfy different goals. For example, to construct a hierarchical order of features according to their relevance [3],[4],[5],[6] and/or to determine the support sets in the partial precedence algorithms [2]. In recent works, typical testors have been used in text mining [7], [8],[9].

In the logical combinatorial approach, the data of a supervised pattern recognition problem can be reduced to a matrix [2]. The typical testors are searched among all possible subsets of column labels of this matrix. The computation of the set of all typical testors may take a lot of time. Several deterministic heuristics have been used to find this set [10], [16]. Also evolutionary algorithms have been introduced to deal with matrices of high dimension [12], [13].

It is necessary to have a set of instances for testing the performances of the different proposed algorithms to calculate the typical testors. On the other hand,

L. Alvarez et al. (Eds.): CIARP 2012, LNCS 7441, pp. 813–820, 2012.

having these test matrices the typical testor problem becomes an useful bench-mark problem to evaluate stochastic optimization algorithms. In [15] were given the first steps for solving this topic. Test matrices should be built so that the set of all typical testors can be determined a priori. Moreover, these matrices should allow controlling aspects such as: dimension, cardinality of each typical testor and the number of typical testors.

The paper is organized as follows: first, we formally introduce the concept of typical testor for boolean matrices. Then, we present theoretical results for the construction of test matrices. Finally, we illustrate how to generate some classes of test matrices.

2   The Concept of Testor and Typical Testor

Let U be a collection of objects. These objects are described by a set of n features and are grouped into l classes. By comparing feature to feature, each pair of objects belonging to different classes, we obtain a matrix $M = [m_{ij}]_{l \times n}$ where $m_{ij} \in \{0, 1\}$ and l is the number of pairs. $m_{ij} = 1\,(0)$ means that the objects of pair denoted by i are different (similar) in the feature j. Let $I = \{i_1, \ldots, i_j\}$ be the set of the rows of M and $J = \{j_1, \ldots, j_n\}$ the set of labels of its columns (features). Let $T \subseteq J$, $M_{/T}$ is the matrix obtained from M eliminating all columns not belonging to the set T.

Definition 1. *A set $T = \{j_{k_1}, \ldots, j_{k_l}\} \subseteq J$ is a testor of M if there is not any zero row in $M_{/T}$.*

Definition 2. *The feature $j_{k_r} \in T$ is typical with respect to (wrt) T and M if $\exists q,\ q \in \{1, \ldots, l\}$ such that $a_{i_q j_{k_r}} = 1$ and for $s > 1$ $a_{i_q j_{k_p}} = 0$, $\forall p, p \in \{1, \ldots, s\}\, p \neq r$.*

Definition 3. *A set T has the property of typicality wrt a matrix M if all fea-tures in T are typical wrt T and M.*

Proposition 1. *A set $T = \{j_{k_1}, \ldots, j_{k_l}\} \subseteq J$ has the property of typicality wrt matrix M if and only if identity matrix can be obtained in $M_{/T}$, by eliminating some rows.*

Definition 4. *A set $T = \{j_{k_1}, \ldots, j_{k_s}\} \subseteq J$ is denominated typical testor of M, if T is a testor and it has the property of typicality wrt M .*

Let $\mathbf{a}$ and $\mathbf{b}$ be two rows from M.

Definition 5. *We say that $\mathbf{a}$ is less than $\mathbf{b}$ ($\mathbf{a} < \mathbf{b}$) if $\forall i\, a_i \leq b_i$ and $\exists j$ such that $a_j \neq b_j$.*

Definition 6. *$\mathbf{a}$ is a basic row from M if there is not any row less than $\mathbf{a}$ in M.*

Definition 7. *The basic matrix of M is the matrix M' that only containing all different basic rows of M.*

The following proposition [10] is a characterization of the basic matrix:

Proposition 2. *M′ is a basic matrix if and only for any two rows* $\mathbf{a}$, $\mathbf{b} \in M'$, *there exist two columns i and j that $a_i = b_j = 1$ and $a_j = b_i = 0$.*

Given a matrix A, let $\Psi^*(A)$ be the set of all typical testors of matrix A.

Proposition 3. $\Psi^*(M) = \Psi^*(M')$.

According with the proposition 3, to obtain the set $\Psi^*(M)$, it is very convenient to find the matrix M', and then, to calculate the set $\Psi^*(M')$. Taking into account that M' has equal or less number of rows than M, the efficiency of the algorithms should be better for M'. In fact, all generated test matrices described in this paper are basic.

3 Matrix Operators and It's Properties

We will define the operator *concatenation* denoted by φ :

$$\varphi : \mathcal{M}_{p \times q} \times \mathcal{M}_{p \times q'} \to \mathcal{M}_{p \times (q+q')}, \; q > 0, \, p > 0 \tag{1}$$

Given two matrices $A \in \mathcal{M}_{p \times q}$ and $B \in \mathcal{M}_{p \times q'}$, $\varphi(A, B) = [A\,B]$ i.e. the matrix $C = \varphi(A, B)$ is the matrix formed by two blocks: A and B.
   Properties of operator φ:

1. $\varphi(\varphi(A, B), C) = \varphi(A, \varphi(B, C)) = \varphi(A, B, C)$.
2. Let A and B be boolean matrices. If A or B are basic matrices then $\varphi(A, B)$ is a basic matrix.

The first property is trivial starting from the characteristics of the *concatenation* operator. The second property can be demonstrated starting from the characteristics of this operator and the proposition 2.
   We will define the operator *combinatory merge* denoted by θ:

$$\theta : \mathcal{M}_{p \times q} \times \mathcal{M}_{p' \times q'} \to \mathcal{M}_{pp' \times (q+q')} \tag{2}$$

Given two matrices $A = [a_{ij}]_{p \times q}$ and $B = [b_{ij}]_{p' \times q'}$ the operation θ is defined as follows:

$$\theta(A, B) = \begin{bmatrix} A(1,:) \; B(1,:) \\ \cdots \quad \cdots \\ A(1,:) \; B(p',:) \\ \cdots \quad \cdots \\ A(p,:) \; B(1,:) \\ \cdots \quad \cdots \\ A(p,:) \; B(p',:) \end{bmatrix} \tag{3}$$

Properties of operator θ

1. $\theta\left(\theta\left(A,B\right),C\right) = \theta\left(A,\theta\left(B,C\right)\right) = \theta\left(A,B,C\right)$.
2. Let A and B be boolean matrices. If A and B are basic matrices, then $\theta\left(A,B\right)$ is a basic matrix.

Note that for this operation both matrices should be basic.

Let I_n be an $n \times n$ identity matrix.

Properties of matrix I_n:

1. I_n is a basic matrix.
2. The number of all typical testors of matrix I_n is equal to 1, i.e. $|\Psi^*\left(I_n\right)| = 1$
3. $\Psi^*\left(I_n\right) = \{J_{I_n}\}$ where J_{I_n} is the set of all column labels of matrix I_n.

Once defined these operators we will present the theoretical framework that we use to develop the strategies to construct test matrices.

4   Theoretical Results on the Determination of Ψ^*

Let Q denote the concatenation of N $(N > 1)$ matrices $B \in \mathcal{M}_{p \times q}$. Let $\Psi^*\left(B\right) = \{T_1, \ldots, T_\nu\}$.

Theorem 1. $|\Psi^*\left(Q\right)| = N^{|T_1|} + \ldots + N^{|T_\nu|}$

Let $A_1, \ldots, A_m$ be m matrices such as $A_i = I_{n_i} \forall i \in \{1, \ldots, m\}$. Let $J_{A_1}, \ldots, J_{A_m}$ denote the sets of all column labels of these matrices and $\{J_{A_i} \cap J_{A_j}\} = \emptyset \forall i, j \in \{1, \ldots, m\}$, $i \neq j$. Let A be a matrix, which is obtained applying the combinatory merge operator to matrices A_i, i. e. $A = \theta\left(A_1, \ldots, A_m\right)$.

Theorem 2. $\Psi^*(A) = \{\Psi^*(A_1), \ldots, \Psi^*(A_m)\} = \{J_{A_1}, \ldots, J_{A_m}\}$

Corollary 1. $|\Psi^*(A)| = m$

Let P denote the concatenation of N $(N > 1)$ matrices A.

Corollary 2. $|\Psi^*\left(P\right)| = N^{n_1} + \ldots + N^{n_m}$

The proof of these results are provided in [15].

5   Strategies to Generate Test Matrices

In this section, we describe new ways to generate the following test matrices: Matrices of equal size and different number of Typical Testors (TT) and Matrices with different dimensions and the same number of TT, based on the operators φ and θ introduced before.

5.1 Matrices with Equal Size and Different Number of Typical Testors (TT)

Two matrices Q_1 and Q_2, with equal size and different number of T, satisfy two conditions: $dim(Q_1) = dim(Q_2)$ and $|\Psi^*(Q_1)| \neq |\Psi^*(Q_2)|$.

And these matrices are generated as follows:

Suppose $B_1 = I_4$ and $B_2 = \theta(I_2, I_2)$. So $Q_1 = \varphi(\underbrace{B_1, ..., B_1}_{N\ times}), Q_2 = \varphi(\underbrace{B_2, ..., B_2}_{N\ times})$

By Theorem 1: $|\Psi^*(Q_1)| = N^4$, $|\Psi^*(Q_2)| = 2 \times N^2$ and $dim(Q_i) = 4 \times 4N$ for $i = 1, 2$.

Note that, because the structure of Q_2, the difference between the number of TT of these matrices increases in a quadratic form. We know $Q_2 = \varphi(\underbrace{B_2, ..., B_2}_{N\ times}) = \varphi(\underbrace{\theta(I_2, I_2), ..., \theta(I_2, I_2)}_{N\ times})$. So, the operator θ used to build B_2, helps increase the size of the matrix, but does not change the cardinality of its TT. That means, when we apply the operator φ to B_1 and B_2 respectively $(Q_1 = \varphi(\underbrace{B_1, ..., B_1}_{N\ times}); Q_2 = \varphi(\underbrace{B_2, ..., B_2}_{N\ times}))$, the number of TT of these matrices will be influenced by the cardinality of the TT of the involved matrices Q_1 and Q_2. Thus, $|\Psi^*(Q_1)| > |\Psi^*(Q_2)|$ for $N > 1$.

We have generated two types of matrices with equal size and different number of TT; however, we can generate 46 additional matrices with this features. Twenty-three $(4! - 1)$ matrices from $B_1 = I_4$ through transpositions and permutations of the columns of this matrix, and then applying the concatenation operator (φ). Similarly, 23 matrices from $B_2 = \theta(I_2, I_2)$ and then applying the concatenation operator. These kind of matrices have the same number of TT and the same size of Q_1 and Q_2 respectively, but they look different.

Moreover, we can appreciate that the number of rows of Q_1 and Q_2 is 4. But, there exist some results that can help us to generate matrices with more rows:

Let n an even number $(n = 2, 4, 6, ...)$,

Proposition 4. $dim(I_{n^2}) = dim(\varphi(\underbrace{\theta(I_n, I_n), ..., \theta(I_n, I_n)}_{n/2\ times})) = n^2 \times n^2$

Proof. $dim(I_{n^2}) = n^2 \times n^2$, $dim(\theta(I_n, I_n)) = n^2 \times 2n$

$dim(\varphi(\underbrace{\theta(I_n, I_n), ..., \theta(I_n, I_n)}_{n/2\ times})) = n^2 \times \underbrace{2n + 2n + ... + 2n}_{n/2\ times}$

$= n^2 \times 2n\,[n/2] = n^2 \times n^2$

Proposition 5. $|\Psi^*(I_{n^2})| \neq \left| \Psi^*(\varphi(\underbrace{\theta(I_n, I_n), ..., \theta(I_n, I_n)}_{n/2\ times})) \right|$

Proof. $|\Psi^*(I_{n^2})| = 1$

$$\left| \Psi^*(\varphi(\underbrace{\theta(I_n, I_n), ..., \theta(I_n, I_n)}_{n/2 \; times})) \right| = \frac{n^n}{2^{n-1}} \; since \; \theta(I_n, I_n) \; has \; two \; TT, \; each \; one$$

with cardinality n. Thus, when we concatenate $\frac{n}{2}$ times , we get $\left[\frac{n}{2}\right]^n + \left[\frac{n}{2}\right]^n = 2\left[\frac{n}{2}\right]^n = \frac{n^n}{2^{n-1}}$.

Anyway, we can generate matrices with the same size and different number of TT, but with more than 4 rows.

Considering the above results we can generalize the construction of new matrices of this type using φ operator. Let $Q_3 = \varphi(I_{n^2}, ..., I_{n^2})$ and

$$Q_4 = \varphi \left[\underbrace{\varphi(\underbrace{\theta(I_n, I_n), ..., \theta(I_n, I_n)}_{n/2 \; times}), ..., \varphi(\underbrace{\theta(I_n, I_n), ..., \theta(I_n, I_n)}_{n/2 \; times})}_{N \; times} \right]$$

where:
$dim(Q_3) = dim(Q_4) = n^2 \times n^2 * N$, $|\Psi^*(Q_3)| = N^{n^2}$
$|\Psi^*(Q_4)| = 2N^n$, $|\Psi^*(Q_3)| \neq |\Psi^*(Q_4)|$

The next table shows the number of TT when we modify the number of concatenated matrices

Table 1. Number of typical testors when we modify the number of concatenated matrices

Concatenated Matrices (N)	Dimension : $n^2 \times n^2 * N$	$|\Psi^*(Q_3)| = N^{n^2}$	$|\Psi^*(Q_4)| = 2N^n$
1	$n^2 \times n^2$	1	2
2	$n^2 \times 2n^2$	2^{n^2}	$2 * 2^n$
$\vdots$	$\vdots$	$\vdots$	$\vdots$

5.2 Matrices with Different Dimensions and the Same Number of Typical Testors (TT)

Two matrices Q_1 and Q_2 with different dimensions and the same number of typical testors, satisfy two conditions: $dim(Q_1) \neq dim(Q_2)$, $|\Psi^*(Q_1)| = |\Psi^*(Q_2)|$

These matrices are $Q_1 = \varphi \left[\underbrace{I_{n_1}, ..., I_{n_1}}_{N_1 \; times} \right]$ and $Q_2 = \varphi \left[\underbrace{I_{n_2}, ..., I_{n_2}}_{N_2 \; times} \right]$

where $n_1 \neq n_2$, $N_1^{n_1} = N_2^{n_2}$
However, note if $n_1, n_2 \geq 2$ and
$n_2 = 2n_1$
$N_1 = N_2^2$
we get $n_1 \neq n_2$ and $N_1^{n_1} = \left[N_2^2\right]^{n_1} = N_2^{n_2}$

Thus, we can generate several matrices that satisfy this features. The next table illustrate some examples

Table 2. Test Matrices with the same number of TT and different size, for different values of n_1, n_2, N_1 y N_2

n_1	n_2	N_1	N_2	$dim(Q_1) =$ $n_1 \times n_1 * N_1$	$dim(Q_2) =$ $n_2 \times n_2 * N_2$	$\|\Psi^*(Q_1)\|$ $= N_1^{n_1}$	$\|\Psi^*(Q_2)\|$ $= N_2^{n_2}$
2	4	4	2	2×8	4×8	4^2	2^4
2	4	9	3	2×18	4×12	9^2	3^4
2	4	16	4	2×32	4×16	16^2	4^4
2	4	25	5	2×50	4×20	25^2	5^4
2	4	36	6	2×72	4×24	36^2	6^4

On the other hand, there exist other way to generate matrices of this category. We observe that identity matrices of order $2, 3, 4, ...$ have different size, but the same number of TT. So, when we apply θ operator n times we get matrices with different number of TT ($from\ 1\ to\ n$) and different dimension.

Other way to generate matrices of this category, is applying θ operator to n identity matrices of different order. The general form of this kind of matrix is $\theta(I_{s_1}, I_{s_2}, ..., I_{s_n})$ where s_i ,with $i=1, 2, 3, ...$, can take the next values: $2, 3, 4, ...$ Its number of TT is n and its dimension is $\prod_{i-1}^{n} s_i \times \sum_{i-1}^{n} s_i$.

For example, when $n = 3$, $s_1 - 5$, $s_2 = 7$, $s_3 = 12$; the resulting matrix is $\theta(I_5, I_7, I_{12})$ whose dimension is $(5 * 7 * 12) \times (5 + 7 + 12)$, and it has 3 TT.

Note when $s_i = s_j (i \neq j)$ we get matrices with high dimensions and few typical testors.

6   Conclusions

The objective of this work is applying a general method to create test matrices for evaluating the performance of strategies to search typical testors. The method proposed is based on theoretical results that are simple in their formulation. However, these results are a solid support to obtain different instances that allow to test several edges of the typical testor search problems.

In this paper, we have described new ways to generate the following test matrices: Matrices of equal size and different number of TT and Matrices with different dimensions and the same number of TT. We found that θ operator helps increase the size of the matrix, but does not change the cardinality of its TT. Moreover, when we combine this operator with operator φ, we have showed that we can generate several kinds of test matrices.

We have presented some examples that illustrate how to generate the instance needed to test the influence of a particular feature on the typical testor search algorithms. Taking into account that we have introduced a flexible and general tool for the construction of test matrices, we expect that this work will allow standarize the procedures to evaluate the performance of Typical Testor algorithms.

References

1. Dmitriev, A.N., Zhuravlev, Y.I., Krendeleiev, F.: On the mathematical principles of patterns and phenomena classification. Diskretnyi Analiz. 7, 3–15 (1966); Smith, T.F., Waterman, M.S.: Identification of Common Molecular Subsequences. J. Mol. Biol. 147, 195–197 (1981)
2. Ruiz, J., Lazo, M., Alba, E.: An overview of the concept of testor. Pattern Recognition 34, 13–21 (2001)
3. Lazo, M., Ruiz, J.: Determining the feature relevance for non classically described objects and a new algorithm to compute typical fuzzy testors. Pattern Recognition Letters 16, 1259–1265 (1995)
4. Carrasco-Ochoa, J.A., Martínez-Trinidad, J.F.: Feature Selection for Natural Disaster Texts Classification Using Testors. In: Yang, Z.R., Yin, H., Everson, R.M. (eds.) IDEAL 2004. LNCS, vol. 3177, pp. 424–429. Springer, Heidelberg (2004)
5. Vázquez, R., Godoy, S.: Using testor theory to reduce the dimension of neural network models. Special Issue in Neural Networks and Associative Memories 28, 93–103 (2007)
6. Santos, J., Carrasco, A., Martínez, J.: Feature selection using typical testors applied to estimation of stellar parameters. Computación y Sistemas 8, 15–23 (2004)
7. Pons-Porrata, A., Gil-García, R.J., Berlanga-Llavori, R.: Using Typical Testors for Feature Selection in Text Categorization. In: Rueda, L., Mery, D., Kittler, J. (eds.) CIARP 2007. LNCS, vol. 4756, pp. 643–652. Springer, Heidelberg (2007)
8. Pons-Porrata, A., Ruiz-Shulcloper, J., Berlanga-Llavori, R.: A Method for the Automatic Summarization of Topic-Based Clusters of Documents. In: Sanfeliu, A., Ruiz-Shulcloper, J. (eds.) CIARP 2003. LNCS, vol. 2905, pp. 596–603. Springer, Heidelberg (2003)
9. Li, F., Zhu, Q., Lin, X.: Topic discovery in research literature based on non-negative matrix factorization and testor theory. In: Asia-Pacific Conference on Information Processing, vol. 2, pp. 266–269 (2009)
10. Sánchez, G.: Efficient algorithms to calculate typical testors from a basic matrix. In: Design and Program. Master Thesis, BUAP, México (1997)
11. Morales-Manilla, L.R., Sanchez-Diaz, G.: FS-EX Plus: A New Algorithm for the Calculation of Typical FS-Testor Set. In: Rueda, L., Mery, D., Kittler, J. (eds.) CIARP 2007. LNCS, vol. 4756, pp. 380–386. Springer, Heidelberg (2007)
12. Sánchez, G., Lazo, M., Fuentes, O.: Genetic algorithm to calculate minimal typical testors. In: Proceedings of the IV Iberoamerican Symposium on Pattern Recognition, pp. 207–214 (1999)
13. Alba, E., Santana, R., Ochoa, A., Lazo, M.: Finding typical testors by using an evolutionary strategy. In: Proceedings of the V Ibero American Symposium on Pattern Recognition, pp. 267–278 (2000)
14. Garey, M., Johnson, D.: Computers and intractability: A guide to the theory of NP-completeness. W. H. Freeman and Company, New York (1979)
15. Alba, E., Santana, R.: Generación de matrices para evaluar el desempeño de estrategias de búsqueda de testores típicos. Avances en Ciencias e Ingenierías, 30–35 (2010)
16. Sanchez-Diaz, G., Piza-Davila, I., Lazo-Cortes, M., Mora-Gonzalez, M., Salinas-Luna, J.: A Fast Implementation of the CT_EXT Algorithm for the Testor Property Identification. In: Sidorov, G., Hernández Aguirre, A., Reyes García, C.A. (eds.) MICAI 2010, Part II. LNCS, vol. 6438, pp. 92–103. Springer, Heidelberg (2010)

Hierarchies and Climbing Energies

Jean Serra, Bangalore Ravi Kiran, and Jean Cousty

Université Paris-Est, Laboratoire d'Informatique Gaspard-Monge, A3SI, ESIEE
{j.serra,kiranr,j.cousty}@esiee.fr

Abstract. A new approach is proposed for finding the "best cut" in
a hierarchy of partitions by energy minimization. Said energy must
be "climbing" i.e. it must be hierarchically and scale increasing. It
encompasses separable energies [5], [9] and those which composed under
supremum [14], [12]. It opens the door to multivariate data processing
by providing laws of combination by extrema and by products of
composition.

1 Introduction

A hierarchy of image transforms, or of image operators, intuitively is a series of
progressive simplified versions of the said image. This hierarchical sequence is
also called a pyramid. In the particular case that we take up here, the image
transforms will always consist in segmentations, and lead to increasing *partitions*
of the space. Now, a multi-scale image description can rarely be considered as an
end in itself. It often requires to be completed by some operation that summarizes
the hierarchy into the "best cut" in a given sense. Two questions arise then,
namely:

1. Given a hierarchy H of partitions and an energy ω on its partial partitions,
   how to combine classes of this hierarchy for obtaining a new partition that
   minimizes ω?
2. When ω depends on integer j, i.e. $\omega = \omega^j$, how to generate a sequence
   of minimum partitions that increase with j, which therefore should form a
   minimum hierarchy?

These questions have been taken up by several authors. The present work
pursues, indeed, the method initiated by Ph. Salembier and L. Garrido for
generating thumbnails [9], well formalized for additive energies by L.Guigues
et al [5], [5] and extended by J. Serra in [10]. In [9], the superlative "best", in
"best cut", is interpreted as the most accurate image simplification for a given
compression rate. We take up this Lagrangian approach again in the example of
section below. In [5], the "best" cut requires linearity and affinity assumptions.
However, one can wonder whether these two hypotheses are the very cause
of the properties found by the authors. Indeed, for solving problem 1 above,
the alternative and simpler condition of hierarchical increasingness is proposed
in [10], and is shown to encompass optimizations which are neither linear nor

L. Alvarez et al. (Eds.): CIARP 2012, LNCS 7441, pp. 821–828, 2012.
© Springer-Verlag Berlin Heidelberg 2012

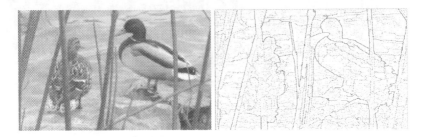

Fig. 1. Left: Initial image, Right: Saliency map of the hierarchy H obtained from image

affine, such as P. Soille's constraint connectivity [12], or Zanoguerra's lasso based segmentations [14].

Our study is related to the ideas developed by P. Arbelaez et al [1] in learning strategies for segmentation. It is also related to the approach of J. Cardelino et al [3] where Mumford and Shah functional is modified by the introduction of shape descriptors. Similarly C. Ballester et al. [2] use shape descriptors to yield compact representations.

The present paper aims to solve the above questions, 1 and 2. The former was partly treated in [10], where the concept of h-increasingness was introduced as a sufficient condition. More deeply, it is proved in [10] that an energy satisfies the two minimizations of questions 1 and 2 if and only if it is climbing. The present paper summarizes without proofs the major results of the technical report [10], yet unpublished. The results of [10] are briefly reminded in section 2; the next section introduces the climbing energies (definition 3) and states the main result of the text (theorem 2); the last section, number 4, develops an example.

2   Hierarchical Increasingness (Reminder)

The space under study (Euclidean, digital, or else) is denoted by E and the set of subsets of E by $P(E)$. A partition $\pi(S)$ associated with a set $S \in P(E)$ is called *partial partition* of E of support S [8]. The family of all partial partitions of set E is denoted by $\mathcal{D}(E)$, or simply by $\mathcal{D}$. A hierarchy H is a finite chain of partitions π_i, i.e.

$$H = \{\pi_i, 0 \leq i \leq n \mid i \leq k \leq n \Rightarrow \pi_i \leq \pi_k\}, \tag{1}$$

where π_n is the partition $\{E\}$ of E in a single class.

The partitions of a hierarchy may be represented by their classes, or by the saliency map of the edges[6],[4], as depicted in Figure 1, or again by a family tree where each node of bifurcation is a class S, as depicted in Figure 2. The classes of π_{i-1} at level $i-1$ which are included in class S_i are said to be *the sons* of S_i.

Denote by $\mathcal{S}(H)$ the set of all classes S of all partitions involved in H. Clearly, the descendants of each S form in turn a hierarchy $H(S)$ of summit S, which is included in the complete hierarchy $H = H(E)$.

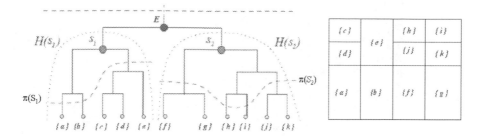

Fig. 2. Left, hierarchical tree; right, the corresponding space structure. S_1 and S_2 are the nodes sons of E, and $H(S_1)$ and $H(S_1)$ are the associated sub-hierarchies. π_1 and π_2 are cuts of $H(S_1)$ and $H(S_1)$ respectively, and $\pi_1 \sqcup \pi_2$ is a cut of E.

2.1 Cuts in a Hierarchy

Any partition π of E whose classes are taken in S defines a *cut* in hierarchy H. The set of all cuts of E is denoted by $\Pi(E) = \Pi$. Every "horizontal" section $\pi_i(H)$ at level i is obviously a cut, but several levels can cooperate in a same cut, such as $\pi(S_1)$ and $\pi(S_2)$, drawn with thick dotted lines in Figure 2. Similarly, the partition $\pi(S_1) \sqcup \pi(S_2)$ generates a cut of $H(E)$. The symbol $\sqcup$ is used here for expressing that groups of classes are concatenated. Each class S may be in turn the root of sub-hierarchy $H(S)$ where S is the summit, and in which (partial) cuts may be defined. whose it is the summit. Let $\Pi(S)$ be the family of all cuts of $H(S)$. The union of all these cuts, when node S spans hierarchy H is denoted by

$$\widetilde{\Pi}(H) = \cup\{\Pi(S), S \in \mathcal{S}(H)\}. \tag{2}$$

2.2 Cuts of Minimum Energy and h-Increasingness

Definition 1. *An energy $\omega : \mathcal{D}(E) \to \mathbb{R}^+$ is a non negative numerical function over the family $\mathcal{D}(E)$ of all partial partitions of set E. An optimum cut $\pi^* \in \Pi(E)$ of E, is one that minimizes ω, i.e. $\omega(\pi^*) = \inf\{\omega(\pi) \mid \pi \in \Pi(E)\}$.*

The problem of unicity of optimum cut is not treated here (refer [11]).

Definition 2. *[10] Let π_1 and π_2 be two partial partitions of same support, and π_0 be a partial partition disjoint from π_1 and π_2. An energy ω on $\mathcal{D}(E)$ is said to be* hierarchically increasing, *or h-increasing, in $\mathcal{D}(E)$ when, $\pi_0, \pi_1, \pi_2 \in \mathcal{D}(E)$, π_0 disjoint of π_1 and π_2, we have*

$$\omega(\pi_1) \le \omega(\pi_2) \quad \Rightarrow \quad \omega(\pi_1 \sqcup \pi_0) \le \omega(\pi_2 \sqcup \pi_0). \tag{3}$$

Implication (3) is illustrated in Figure 3. When the partial partitions are embedded in a hierarchy H, then Rel.(3) allows us an easy characterization of the cuts of minimum energy of H, according to the following property, valid for the class $\mathcal{H}$ of all finite hierarchies on E.

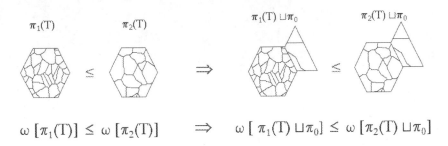

$$\omega \left[\pi_1(T)\right] \leq \omega \left[\pi_2(T)\right] \quad \Longrightarrow \quad \omega \left[\pi_1(T) \sqcup \pi_0\right] \leq \omega \left[\pi_2(T) \sqcup \pi_0\right]$$

Fig. 3. Hierachical increasingness

Theorem 1. *Let $H \in \mathcal{H}$ be a finite hierarchy, and ω be an energy on $\mathcal{D}(E)$. Consider a node S of H with p sons $T_1..T_p$ of optimum cuts $\pi_1^*, ..\pi_p^*$. The cut of optimum energy of summit S is, in a non exclusive manner, either the cut*

$$\pi_1^* \sqcup \pi_2^*.. \sqcup \pi_p^*, \tag{4}$$

or the partition of S into a unique class, if and only if S is h-increasing (proof given in [11])

The condition of h-increasingness (3) opens into a broad range of energies, and is easy to check. It encompasses that of Mumford and Shah, the separable energies of Guigues [5] [9], as well as energies composed by suprema [12] [14], and many other ones [11]. Moreover, any weighted sum $\Sigma \lambda_j \omega^j$ of h-*increasing* energies with positive λ_j is still h-*increasing* energies, as well as, under some conditions, any supremum and infimum of h-*increasing* energies [11]. The condition (3) yields a dynamic algorithm, due to Guigues, for finding the optimum cut $\pi^*(H)$ in one pass [5].

2.3   Generation of h-Increasing Energies

The energy $\omega : \mathcal{D}(E) \to \mathbb{R}^+$ has to be defined on the family $\mathcal{D}(E)$ of all partial partitions of E. An easy way to obtain a h-increasing energy consists in taking, firstly, an arbitrary energy ω on all sets $S \in \mathcal{P}(E)$, considered as one class partial partitions $\{S\}$, and then in extending ω to all partial partitions by some law of composition. The h-increasingness is introduced here by the law of composition, and not by $\omega[\mathcal{P}(E)]$. The first laws which come to mind are, of course, addition, supremum, and infimum, and indeed we can state:

Proposition 1. *Let E be a set and $\omega : \mathcal{P}(E) \to \mathbb{R}^+$ an arbitrary energy defined on $\mathcal{P}(E)$, and let $\pi \in \mathcal{D}(E)$ be a partial partition of classes $\{S_i, 1 \leq i \leq n\}$. Then the three extensions of ω to the partial partitions $\mathcal{D}(E)$*

$$\omega(\pi) = \bigvee_i \omega(S_i), \quad \omega(\pi) = \bigwedge_i \omega(S_i), \quad and \;\; \omega(\pi) = \textstyle\sum_i \omega(S_i), \tag{5}$$

are h-increasing energies.

A number of other laws are compatible with h-increasingness. One could use the product of energies, the difference sup-inf, the quadratic sum, and their combinations. Moreover, one can make depend ω on more than one class, on the proximity of the edges, on another hierarchy, etc..

3   Climbing Energies

The usual energies are often given by finite sequences $\{\omega^j, 1 \leq j \leq p\}$ that depend on a positive index, or parameter, j. Therefore, the processing of hierarchy H results in a sequence of p optimum cuts π^{j*}, of labels $1 \leq j \leq p$. A priori, the π^{j*} are not ordered, but if they were, i.e. if

$$j \leq k \quad \Rightarrow \quad \pi^{j*} \leq \pi^{k*}, \qquad j, k \in J, \tag{6}$$

then we should obtain a nice progressive simplification of the optimum cuts. For getting it, we need to combine h-increasingness with the supplementary axiom (7) of scale increasingness, which results in the following climbing energies.

Definition 3. We call climbing energy any family $\{\omega^j, 1 \leq j \leq p\}$ of energies over $\widetilde{\Pi}$ which satisfies the three following axioms, valid for $\omega^j, 1 \leq j \leq p$ and for all $\pi \in \Pi(S), S \in \mathcal{S}$

- i) each ω^j is h-increasing,
- ii) each ω^j admits a single optimum cutting,
- iii) the $\{\omega^j\}$ are scale increasingness, i.e. for $j \leq k$, each support $S \in \mathcal{S}$ and each partition $\pi \in \Pi(S)$, we have that

$$j \leq k \ \text{ and } \omega^j(S) \leq \omega^j(\pi) \Rightarrow \omega^k(S) \leq \omega^k(\pi), \qquad \pi \in \Pi(S), \ \ S \in \mathcal{S}. \tag{7}$$

Axiom i) and ii) allow us to compare the same energy at two different levels, whereas iii) compares two different energies at the same level. The relation (7) means that, as j increases, the ω^j's preserve the sense of energetic differences between the nodes of hierarchy H and their partial partitions. In particular, all energies of the type $\omega^j = j\omega$ are scale increasing.

The climbing energies satisfy the very nice property to order the optimum cuts with respect to the parameter j:

Theorem 2. Let $\{\omega^j, 1 \leq j \leq p\}$ be a family of energies, and let π^{j*} (resp. π^{k*}) be the optimum cut of hierarchy H according to the energy ω^j (resp. ω^k). The family $\{\pi^{j*}, 1 \leq j \leq p\}$ of the optimum cuts generates a unique hierarchy H^* of partitions, i.e.

$$j \leq k \quad \Rightarrow \quad \pi^{j*} \leq \pi^{k*}, \qquad 1 \leq j \leq k \leq p \tag{8}$$

if and only if the family $\{\omega^j\}$ is a climbing energy (proof given in [11]).

Such a family is climbing in two senses: for each j the energy climbs pyramid H up to its best cut (h-increasingness), and as j varies, it generates a new pyramid to be climbed (scale-increasingness). Relation (8) has been established by L. Guigues in his Phd thesis [5] for affine and separable energies, called by him multiscale energies. However, the core of the assumption (7) concerns the propagation of energy through the scales $(1...p)$, rather than affinity or linearity, and allows non additive laws. In addition, the set of axioms of the climbing energies 3 leads to an implementation simpler than that of [5].

4   Examples

We now present two examples of energies composed by rule of supremum and another by addition. In all cases, the energies depend on a scalar parameter k such that the three families $\{\omega^k\}$ are climbing. The reader may find several particular climbing energies in the examples treated in [5],[14],[13],and [9].

4.1   Increasing Binary Energies

The simplest energies are the binary ones, which take values 1 and 0 only. We firstly observe that the relation $\pi \sqsubseteq \pi_1$, where $\pi_1 = \pi \sqcup \pi'$ is made of the classes of π plus other ones, is an ordering. A binary energy ω such that for all $\pi, \pi_0, \pi_1, \pi_2 \in \mathcal{D}(E)$

$$\omega \text{ is } \sqsubseteq\text{-increasing, i.e. } \omega(\pi) = 1 \quad \Rightarrow \quad \omega(\pi \sqcup \pi_0) = 1$$

$$\omega(\pi_1) = \omega(\pi_2) = 0 \quad \Rightarrow \quad \omega(\pi_1 \sqcup \pi_0) = \omega(\pi_2 \sqcup \pi_0),$$

is obviously h-increasing, and conversely. Here are two examples of this type.

Large classes removal. One wants to suppress the very small classes, considered as noise, and also the largest ones, considered as not significant. Associate with each $S \in \mathcal{P}(E)$ the energy $\omega^k(\langle S \rangle) = 0$ when $area(S) \leq k$, and $\omega^k(\langle S \rangle) = 1$ when not, and compose them by sum, $\pi = \sqcup \langle S_i \rangle \Rightarrow \omega^k(\pi) = \sum_i \omega^k(\langle S_i \rangle)$. Therefore the energy of a partition equals the number of its classes whose areas are larger than k. Then the class of the optimum cut at point $x \in E$ is the larger class of the hierarchy that contains x and has an area not greater than k.

Soille-Grazzini minimization [13],[12]. A numerical function f is now associated with hierarchy H. Consider the range of variation $\delta(S) = \max\{f(x), x \in S\} - \min\{f(x), x \in S\}$ of f inside set S, and the h-increasing binary energy $\omega^k(\langle S \rangle) = 0$ when $\delta(S) \leq k$, and $\omega^k(\langle S \rangle) = 1$ when not. Compose ω according the law of the supremum, i.e. $\pi = \sqcup \langle S_i \rangle \Rightarrow \omega^k(\pi) = \bigvee_i \omega^k(\langle S_i \rangle)$. Then the class of the optimum cut at point $x \in E$ is the larger class of H whose range of variation is $\leq j$. When the energy ω^k of a father equals that of its sons, one keeps the father when $\omega^k = 0$, and the sons when not.

4.2   Additive Energies under Constraint

The example of additive energy that we now develop is a variant of the creation of thumbnails by Ph. Salembier and L. Garrido [9]. We aim to generate "the best" simplified version of a colour image f, of components (r, g, b), when the compression rate is imposed equal to 20. The bit depth of f is 24 and the size of f is $= 600x480$ pixels. A hierarchy H has been obtained by previous segmentations of the luminance $l = (r+g+b)/3$ based on [4]. In each class S of H, the reduction consists in replacing the function f by its colour mean $m(S)$. The quality of this approximation is estimated by the L_2 norm, i.e.

$$\omega_\mu(S) = \sum_{x \in S} \| l(x) - m(S) \|^2 . \qquad (9)$$

The coding cost for a frontier element is $\simeq 2$, which gives, for the whole S

$$\omega_\partial(S) = 24+ \mid \partial S \mid \qquad (10)$$

with 24 bits for $m(S)$. We want to minimize $\omega_\mu(S)$, while preserving the cost. According to Lagrange formalism, the total energy of class S is thus written $\omega(S) = \omega_\mu(S) + \lambda^j \omega_\partial(S)$. Classically one reaches the minimum under constraint $\omega(S)$ by means of a system of partial derivatives. Now remarkably our approach replaces the of computation of derivatives by a climbing. Indeed we can access the energy a cut π by summing up that of its classes, which leads to $\omega(\pi) = \lambda^j \omega_\mu(\pi) + \omega_\partial(\pi)$. The cost $\omega_\partial(\pi)$ decreases as λ^j increases, therefore we can climb the pyramid of the best cuts and stop when $\omega_\partial(\pi) \simeq n/20$. It results in Figure 4 (left), where we see the female duck is not nicely simplified.

However, there is no particular reason to choose the same luminance l for generating the pyramid, and later as the quantity to involve in the quality estimate (9). In the RGB space, a colour vector $\overrightarrow{x}$ (r, g, b) can be decomposed in its two orthogonal projections on the grey axis, namely $\overrightarrow{l}$ of components $(l/3, l/3, l/3)$, and on the chromatic plane orthogonal to the grey axis at the origin, namely $\overrightarrow{c}$ of components $(3/\sqrt{2})(2r - g - b, 2g - b - r, 2b - r - g)$. We

Fig. 4. Left: Best cut of Duck image by optimizing by Luminance, Right: and by Chrominance

have $\vec{x} = \vec{l} + \vec{c}$. Let us repeat the optimization by replacing the luminance $l(x)$ in (9) by the module $|\vec{c}(x)|$ of the chrominance in x. We now find for best cut the segmentation depicted in Figure 4, where, for the same compression rate, the animals are correctly rendered, but the river background is more simplified than previously.

5   Conclusion

This paper has introduced the new concept of increasing energies. It allows to find best cuts in hierarchies of partitions, encompasses the known optimizations of such hierarchies and opens the way to combinations of energies by supremum, by infimum, and by scalar product of Lagrangian constraints. This work was funded by Agence Nationale de la Recherche through contract ANR-2010-BLAN-0205-03 KIDIKO.

References

1. Arbelaez, P., Maire, M., Fowlkes, C., Malik, J.: Contour Detection and Hierarchical Image Segmentation. IEEE PAMI 33 (2011)
2. Ballester, C., Caselles, V., Igual, L., Garrido, L.: Level lines selection with variational models for segmentation and encoding. JMIV 27, 5–27 (2007)
3. Cardelino, J., Caselles, V., Bertalmío, M., Randall, G.: A contrario hierarchical image segmentation. In: IEEE ICIP 2009, Cairo, Egypt (2009)
4. Cousty, J., Najman, L.: Incremental Algorithm for Hierarchical Minimum Spanning Forests and Saliency of Watershed Cuts. In: Soille, P., Pesaresi, M., Ouzounis, G.K. (eds.) ISMM 2011. LNCS, vol. 6671, pp. 272–283. Springer, Heidelberg (2011)
5. Guigues, L.: Modèles multi-échelles pour la segmentation d'images.Thèse doctorale Université de Cergy-Pontoise (Décembre 2003)
6. Najman, L., Schmitt, M.: Geodesic Saliency of Watershed Contours and Hierarchical Segmentation. IEEE Trans. PAMI (1996)
7. Najman, L.: On the Equivalence Between Hierarchical Segmentations and Ultrametric Watersheds. JMIV 40(3), 231–247 (2011)
8. Ronse, C.: Partial partitions, partial connections and connective segmentation. JMIV 32, 97–125 (2008)
9. Salembier, Ph., Garrido, L.: Binary Partition Tree as an Efficient Representation for Image Processing, Segmentation, and Information Retrieval. IEEE TIP 9(4), 561–576 (2000)
10. Serra, J.: Hierarchies and optima. In: Domenjoud, E. (ed.) DGCI 2011. LNCS, vol. 6607, pp. 35–46. Springer, Heidelberg (2011)
11. Serra, J., Kiran, B.R.: Climbing the pyramids. Techn. report ESIEE (March 2012)
12. Soille, P.: Constrained connectivity for hierarchical image partitioning and simplification. IEEE PAMI 30, 1132–1145 (2008)
13. Soille, P., Grazzini, J.: Constrained Connectivity and Transition Regions. In: Wilkinson, M.H.F., Roerdink, J.B.T.M. (eds.) ISMM 2009. LNCS, vol. 5720, pp. 59–69. Springer, Heidelberg (2009)
14. Zanoguera, F., Marcotegui, B., Meyer, F.: A toolbox for interactive segmentation based on nested partitions. In: Proc. of ICIP 1999, Kobe, Japan (1999)

A Method for Reducing the Cardinality
of the Pareto Front

Ivan Cabezas and Maria Trujillo

Laboratorio de Investigación en Multimedia y Visión,
Escuela de Ingeniería de Sistemas y Computación,
Ciudad Universitaria Meléndez, Cali, Colombia
{ivan.cabezas,maria.trujillo}@correounivalle.edu.co

Abstract. Multi-objective problems are characterised by the presence of a set of optimal trade-off solutions –a Pareto front–, from which a solution has to be selected by a decision maker. However, selecting a solution from a Pareto front depends on large quantities of solutions to select from and dimensional complexity due to many involved objectives, among others. Commonly, the selection of a solution is based on preferences specified by a decision maker. Nevertheless a decision maker may have not preferences at all. Thus, an informed decision making process has to be done, which is difficult to achieve. In this paper, selecting a solution from a Pareto front is addressed as a multi-objective problem using two utility functions and operating in the objective space. A quantitative comparison of stereo correspondence algorithms performance is used as an application domain.

Keywords: Multi-objective problems, Pareto front, decision making, computer vision, stereo correspondence, quantitative evaluation.

1   Introduction

A Multi-objective Optimisation Problem (MOP) involves several conflicting and incommensurable objectives [1]. A MOP can be addressed using a Multi-objective Evolutionary Algorithm (MOEA), such as the non-dominated sorting genetic algorithm [2], the strength Pareto approach [3], and the Pareto archived evolutionary strategy [4], among others. In a MOP, a single solution simultaneously optimising all objectives may not exist [5]. Thus, a MOEA solves a MOP by computing an approximation to the Pareto front, which is a set of mathematically equally good compromise solutions. As part of a decision making process, a solution from the Pareto front has to be selected in order to solve the problem being optimised. This selection is a responsibility of a decision maker (DM). However, in most of cases, a Pareto front may overload the judging capabilities of a DM, due to factors such as its large cardinality [1], the multidimensional complexity of the problem being solved [6], plus inherent limitations of a DM for effectively handling large amounts of data and more than several factors at once [7], among others. Although a visualisation of the Pareto front may assist a DM, a visualisation becomes complex with several solutions and

L. Alvarez et al. (Eds.): CIARP 2012, LNCS 7441, pp. 829–836, 2012.

three objectives or more, as well as visualised information for making a decision may become difficult to use [8]. Difficulties in a decision making process may be alleviated by introducing preferences [9]. Preferences can be seen as knowledge and/or expectations about a problem solution. They can be used as a mechanism to decide if a specific solution is preferable than other solutions [10]. Nevertheless, in some cases a DM may lack of information for selecting a solution and/or has not preferences among all objectives. In the absence of preferences, it is generally assumed that the most preferable solution correspond to a region in the maximum convex bulge of a Pareto curve/surface, termed as the *knee* region [8]. However, identifying the *knee* region of a Pareto front requires solving a non-linear optimisation problem, as well as some a priori knowledge on a Pareto front. In addition, determining the *knee* region(s) may become prohibitively complex as the dimensionality of a problem increases [11].

In this paper, without loss of generalisation, a quantitative comparison of stereo correspondence algorithms (SCAs) performance [12, 13] is used as an application domain. An SCA takes as input a stereo image pair, estimates projections from points in 3D space into image plains, and produces as output a disparity map. A quantitative comparison of SCAs should be conducted following an evaluation methodology, which is composed by a set of evaluation elements and methods interacting in an ordered sequence of steps, in order to produce evaluation results. A comparison of SCAs is addressed as a MOP in the **A*** Groups evaluation methodology presented in [13]. This methodology computes a Pareto front using vectors of error measure scores, from which a solution, or solutions, should be selected as part of evaluation results interpretation. In this case a methodology user is acting in the role of decision maker. Thus, if preferences are introduced at this stage of an evaluation process, it may bias results interpretation.

In this context, a decision making scenario is addressed with the following characteristics:

— The decision making process is posterior to the search process.
— The DM lacks of preferences about the problem for selecting a solution.
— It is not possible to assign an importance to involved objective functions.
— Although at least one *knee* region should exist, the selection of a solution is not based on the proximity to that region.
— The problem on which a solution should be selected involves many objectives.

The selection of a solution from the Pareto front is seen as a MOP, based on two utility functions computed over the objective space. The paper is structured as follows. Related works are presented in Section 2. The proposed method is introduced in Section 3. Experimental validation is included and discussed in Section 4. Final remarks are stated in Section 5.

2   Related Works

Preferences can be specified by a DM in three ways: *a priori*, *interactive* and *a posteriori*. In the *a priori* way, preferences are specified before the beginning of search process by the aggregation of objective function into lexicographic order or into a linear/nonlinear combination, among others [9]. A deep knowledge of the problem and a clear understanding of the search space are required. In the *interactive* way, preferences are specified during the search, based on a progressively and interactively acquired knowledge of the problem [1]. An intensive effort of a DM is required, since, he/she is asked to give preference information at each algorithm's iteration, commonly consisting in specifying aspiration levels for each objective function, classifying objective functions according to their relevance, or introducing references points, among others. However, a DM may have large optimistic or pessimistic aspiration levels. In addition, when there are two or more DMs may arise disagrees about preferences. Preferences specified in *a priori* or *interactive* way have an impact on search results. In the *a posteriori* way, the search is executed first, and after that, a decision method is applied into the Pareto front [14]. In this case, a DM has too many choices to select from, and a fair comparison among them is not an easy task to achieve due to the inherent dimensional complexity. There are two main approaches, to perform *a posteriori* multi-criteria decision making: utility functions and outranking methods [5]. Utility functions assign a numerical value to each solution. Outranking methods are based on pairwise comparisons of all solutions, in order to establish if there exists preference, indifference or incomparability. However, commonly used methods under these two approaches rely on weights that should be specified by a DM [14]. Consequently, these methods cannot be used in the problem context specified in this paper. Methods such as the average rank, the maximum rank, and the favour rank do not require weights [10]. The average and the maximum rank can be seen as utility functions. The average rank uses multiple ranks considering each objective independently and a final rank is calculated as the average of previously assigned ranks, whilst the maximum rank takes the best rank as the global rank for each solution. In the favour rank, a solution x is preferred over a solution y, only if x outperforms y on more objectives than those on which y outperforms x. However, the maximum rank method tends to favour solutions with high performance in some of the objectives, but with a poor overall performance. In addition, the average rank and the favour rank may produce even ranks, or indifferences, respectively, very often. Moreover, none of them considers the magnitude on which a solution outperforms another according to the involved objective functions.

3   A Method for Reducing the Cardinality of the Pareto Front

Without loss of generalisation, a MOP consists in finding the vector of decision variables $x = (x_1, x_2, \dots, x_n)^T$ that optimises the following equation.

$$Min_x f(x) = \left(f_1(x), f_2(x), \dots, f_K(x) \right)^T, \tag{1}$$

subject to:

$$g_i(x) \leq 0 \quad i = 1, \dots, P, \tag{2}$$

$$h_j(x) = 0 \quad j = 1, \dots, Q, \tag{3}$$

where $f_k: \mathbb{R}^n \to \mathbb{R}$ $(k = 1, \dots, K)$ are the objective functions, and g_i and $h_j: \mathbb{R}^n \to \mathbb{R}$ $(i = 1, \dots, P; \ j = 1, \dots, Q)$ are the constraints of the problem.

In addition, some key definitions are presented for the sake of completeness.

Definition 1 *(Pareto dominance relation).* Given two solutions $x, y \in \mathbb{R}^n$, x is said to dominate y, denoted as $x \prec y$, if and only if: $f_a(x) \leq f_a(y) \, \forall \, a \in \{1,..,K\}$ and $\exists \, b \in \{1,..,K\}$ where $f_b(x) < f_b(y)$.

Definition 2 *(Non-dominated solution).* A solution $x \in \mathbb{R}^n$ is said to be non-dominated if and only if there does not exist another solution $y \in \mathbb{R}^n$, such that $y \prec x$.

Definition 3 *(Pareto optimal solution).* A solution $x \in F \subseteq \mathbb{R}^n$, where F is the decision space, is said to be Pareto optimal if it is non-dominated with respect to F.

Definition 4 *(Pareto optimal set).* Let P^* be the Pareto optimal set defined as $P^* = \{x \in F, \ x \text{ is Pareto optimal}\}$.

Definition 5 *(Pareto front).* Let PF^* be the Pareto front, defined as $PF^* = \{f(x) \in \mathbb{R}^K, \ x \in P^*\}$.

In the proposed method, the selection of a solution from the Pareto front is addressed as a MOP, based on two utility functions and the Pareto dominance relation. The utility functions are adapted from [15] in order to avoid the use of weights. They are computed over the vectors composing the Pareto front from which a solution should be selected. Thus, the proposed method consists in finding the vector $s = (f_1(x), f_2(x), ..., f_K(x))^T$ that optimises the following equation:

$$Min_s \, u(s) = \big(u_1(s), u_2(s)\big)^T, \tag{4}$$

subject to:

$$s \in PF^* , \tag{5}$$

where $u_l: \mathbb{R}^K \to \mathbb{R} \ (l = 1, 2)$ are the objective functions.

Let u_1 be the sum of ranks assigned to $f_k: \mathbb{R}^n \to \mathbb{R} \ (k = 1, ..., K)$ in the Pareto front:

$$u_1 (s) = \sum_{k=1}^{K} Rank(f_k(x)). \tag{6}$$

Let u_2 be the sum of ratios of $f_k: \mathbb{R}^n \to \mathbb{R} \ (k = 1, ..., K)$ in the Pareto front:

$$u_2 (s) = \sum_{k=1}^{K} \frac{(f_k(x) - Min(f_k(x)))}{(Max(f_k(x) - Min(f_k(x))))}, \tag{7}$$

where $Min(f_k(x))$ and $Max(f_k(x))$, are the minimum and the maximum score of the kth objective, respectively. The lowest sum of ranks is associated with the solution that, comparatively with other solutions in the Pareto front, minimises most of involved objectives, whilst the lowest sum of ratios is associated with the solution with the best objective function values. The selection of a final solution may be based on the above criteria, which are problem context independent. Thus, the set of possible solutions to select from is turned into a set of a small cardinality, or even into a single solution, depending on data, by the proposed method. The set that corresponds to a reduction of the original PF^* set is denoted as RPF^*. In addition, the reduction of cardinality allows the use of a parallel coordinates plotting diagram [6] as a visualisation tool for assisting a solution selection. Moreover, the values computed by the u_2 function can be used for plotting the diagram.

4   Experimental Validation

In the application domain context, the **A*** Groups evaluation methodology [13] conceives the comparison of SCAs as a MOP. In the evaluation model of the **A*** Groups methodology, the decision space is a discrete and finite set composed by the SCAs under comparison, whilst the objective space is a set composed by a set of vectors of error scores, calculated according to selected evaluation elements and methods. In this problem, a user of the methodology requires, not only the set of SCAs composing the Pareto front –denoted in the methodology as the A_1^* set–, but also an impartial interpretation of results and assistance for selecting a single solution (i.e. in an intra-technique comparison), or solutions (i.e. in an inter-technique comparison). Thus, the discussed evaluation scenario is mathematically equivalent to the scenario which arises using an *a posteriori* MOEA, for addressing a MOP. Three evaluation scenarios are considered for validating the proposed method. All of them use a test-bed of four images (the Tsukuba, the Venus, the Teddy and the Cones stereo image pairs) [12] and the SCAs repository available in [16], as well as a combination of different evaluation criteria and evaluation measures. In regard to evaluation criteria, the depth discontinuity areas –*disc*–, the non-occluded areas –*nonocc*–, and the entire image –*all*– are used as evaluation criteria. Three error measures are used as evaluation measures. The percentage of Bad Matched Pixels (BMP) measures the quantity of disparity estimation errors exceeding a threshold δ (equals to 1 pixel) [12]. The Sigma-Z-Error (SZE) measures the impact of estimation errors on a 3D reconstruction based on the distance between the real depth and the estimated depth, based on ground-truth disparity and estimated disparity, respectively [17]. The Mean Relative Error (MRE) is based on the ratio between the absolute difference of estimated disparity against ground-truth disparity, and ground-truth disparity [18].

4.1   Evaluation Scenario Suited for Semi-dense Disparity Maps

The first evaluation scenario is devised for selecting the best performance algorithm from the SCAs repository using the *disc* and the *nonocc* criteria. In addition, the BMP and the SZE, which are conceptually different measures, are used, for a total of 16 objectives. The cardinality of the Pareto front (A_1^*) and the reduced Pareto front (RPF^*) sets, for the first evaluation scenario, are shown in the first column of Table 1. It can be observed that the proposed method reduces in 96.0% the cardinality of the Pareto front. This reduction considerably alleviates the judging overload of a DM. The SCAs composing the RPF^* set and the utility function values are also shown in Table 1. It can be observed that, in this case, a decision should be taken between the *SubPixelDoubleBP* and the *GC+SegmBorder* algorithms [16]. However, the two solutions show similar sum of ratios values. This similarity may influence a DM in order to make a decision based on the sum of ranks. The parallel coordinates plotting diagram associated to the obtained RPF^* set is shown in Fig 1. It allows to a DM an analysis of the achieved trade-off in objective functions by solutions to finally select from.

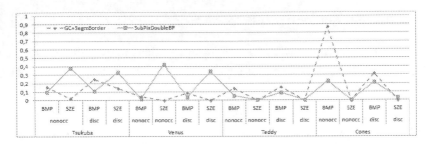

Fig. 1. Parallel coordinates plot of elements composing the *RPF** set in the first evaluation scenario

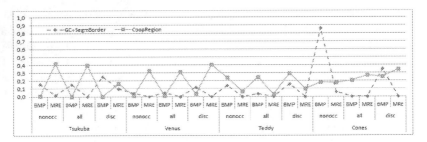

Fig. 2. Parallel coordinates plot of elements composing the *RPF** set in the second evaluation scenario

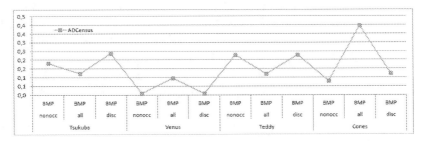

Fig. 3. Parallel coordinates plot of elements composing the *RPF** set in the third evaluation scenario

Table 1. Experimental validation data according to used evaluation scenarios

Evaluation Criteria	*disc & nonocc*		*all & disc & nonocc*		*all & disc & nonocc*	
Error Measures	BMP & SZE		BMP & MRE		BMP	
$|A_1^*|$	51		46		20	
$|RPF^*|$	2		2		1	
Reduction %	96.0		95.6		95.0	
Utility Functions SCAs	u_1	u_2	u_1	u_2	u_1	u_2
SubPixDoubleBP	**184.0**	2.363				
GC+SegmBorder	214.5	**2.170**	251.0	**2.487**		
CoopRegion			**239.5**	4.494		
ADCensus					59.0	1.826

4.2   Evaluation Scenario Suited for Dense Disparity Maps

The second evaluation scenario is based on the *all*, the *disc*, and the *nonocc* evaluation criteria. The BMP and the MRE measures are used, for a total of 24 objectives. These measures may be conflicting since the MRE considers the inverse relation between depth and disparity. The cardinality of the A_1^* and the RPF^* sets, as well as the SCAs composing the RPF^* set and utility function values are shown in Table 1. It can be observed that the proposed method reduces in 95.6% the cardinality of the Pareto front. In this case, a decision should be taken between the *CoopRegion* and the *GC+SegmBorder* algorithms [16]. The parallel coordinates plotting diagram associated to the obtained RPF^* set is shown in Fig 2.

4.3   Evaluation Scenario of the Middlebury's Evaluation Methodology

The third evaluation scenario is devised in the same way that the one used in [16]. It considers the *all*, the *disc* and the *nonocc* evaluation criteria, and the BMP measure, for a total of 12 objectives. The cardinality of the A_1^*, and the RPF^* sets, as well as the single element composing the RPF^* set and utility function values are shown in the third column of Table 1. It can be observed that the proposed method reduces in a 95.0% the cardinality of the Pareto front. In this case, the proposed method reports a single solution, the *ADCensus* algorithm [16]. The parallel coordinates plotting diagram associated to the obtained RPF^* set is shown in Fig 3.

5   Final Remarks

In this paper, a challenging decision making scenario is addressed, in which decisions are taken *a posteriori*, and the DM lacks of preferences and information about the importance of many involved objectives. As innovative aspect, it addresses the selection of a solution from a Pareto front as a MOP, based on two utility functions and the Pareto dominance. The considered utility functions do not require weight specifications by a DM. A quantitative comparison of SCAs, using an evaluation model which produces as output a Pareto front, was used as an application domain. The experimental validation shows that the proposed method significantly reduces the cardinality of the Pareto front, even to a single solution, depending on data. Moreover, this cardinality reduction makes possible the use of conventional aids for making decision such as visualisation tools. The proposed method may alleviate the judging overload of a DM.

References

1. Ben Said, L., Bechikn, S., Ghédira, K.: The r-Dominance: A New Dominance Relation for Interactive Evolution Multi-criteria Decision Making. IEEE Trans. on Evolutionary Computation 14(5), 801–818 (2010)
2. Deb, K., Pratap, P., Agarwal, S., Meyarivan, T.: A Fast and Elitist Multiobjective Genetic Algorithm: NSGA-II. IEEE Trans. Evolutionary Computation 6(2), 182–197 (2002)

3. Zitzler, E., Laumanns, L., Thiele, L.: SPEA 2: Improving the Strength Pareto Evolutionary Algorithm for Multiobjective Optimisation. In: Giannakoglou, K.C. (ed.) Evolutionary Methods for Design, Optimisation and Control with Application to Industrial Problems, pp. 95–100 (2002)

4. Knowles, J., Corne, D.: Approximating the Nondominated FrontUsing the Pareto Archived Evolutionary Strategy. In: Proc. IEEE Congress on Evolutionary Computation, vol. 8(2), pp. 173–195 (2000)

5. Cvetkovic, D., Coello, C.: Human Preferences and their Applications in Evolutionary Multi-objective Optimisation. In: Yaochun, J. (ed.) Knowledge Incorporation in Evolutionary Computation, pp. 479–502. Springer, Heidelberg (2005)

6. Brockhoff, D., Zitzler, E.: Are All Objectives Necessary? On Dimensionality Reduction in Evolutionary Multiobjective Optimization. In: Runarsson, T.P., Beyer, H.-G., Burke, E.K., Merelo-Guervós, J.J., Whitley, L.D., Yao, X. (eds.) PPSN 2006. LNCS, vol. 4193, pp. 533–542. Springer, Heidelberg (2006)

7. Cvetkovic, D., Parmee, I.: Preferences and their Application in Evolutionary Multiobjective Optimisation. IEEE Trans. Evolutionary Computation 6(1), 42–57 (2002)

8. Das, I.: On Characterizing the "knee" of the Pareto Curve Based on Normal-Boundary Intersection. Structural and Multidisciplinary Optimization 18(2), 107–115 (1999)

9. Rachmawati, L., Srinivasan, D.: Preference Incorporation in Multi-objective Evolutionary Algorithms: A Survey. In: Proc. IEEE Congress on Evolutionary Computation, pp. 962–968 (2006)

10. López, A., Coello, C.: Study of preference relations in many-objective optimization. In: Proc. Genetic and Evolutionary Computation Conference, pp. 611–618 (2009)

11. Rachmawati, L., Srinivasan, D.: Multiobjective Evolutionary Algorithm withControllable Focus on the Knees of the Pareto Front. IEEE Trans. Evolutionary Computation 13(4), 810–824 (2009)

12. Scharstein, D., Szeliski, R.: A Taxonomy and Evaluation of Dense Two-Frame Stereo Correspondence Algorithms. International Journal of Computer Vision 47, 7–42 (2002)

13. Cabezas, I., Trujillo, M., Florian, M.: An Evaluation Methodology for Stereo Correspondence Algorithms. In: Proc. Intl. Joint Conference on Computer Vision and Computer Graphics Theory and Applications, pp. 154–163 (2012)

14. Parreiras, R., Maciel, J., Vasconcelos, J.: The a posteriori decision in multiobjective optimization problems with smarts, promethee II, and a fuzzy algorithm. IEEE Trans. Magnetics 42(4), 1139–1142 (2006)

15. Bentley, P., Wakefield, J.: Finding Acceptable solutions in the Pareto-Optimal Range using Multiobjective Genetic Algorithms. In: Chawdhry, P., et al. (eds.) Soft Computing in Engineering Design and Manufacturing, pp. 231–240 (1997)

16. Scharstein, D., Szeliski, R.: Middlebury Stereo Evaluation - Version 2, http://vision.middlebury.edu/stereo/eval/

17. Cabezas, I., Padilla, V., Trujillo, M.: A Measure for Accuracy Disparity Maps Evaluation. In: San Martin, C., Kim, S.-W. (eds.) CIARP 2011. LNCS, vol. 7042, pp. 223–231. Springer, Heidelberg (2011)

18. Van der Mark, W., Gavrila, D.: Real Time Dense Stereo for Intelligent Vehicles. IEEE Trans. Intelligent Transportation Systems 7(1), 38–50 (2006)

Feature Selection by Relevance Analysis for Abandoned Object Classification

Johanna Carvajal-González,
Andrés M. Álvarez-Meza, and German Castellanos-Domínguez

Signal Processing and Recognition Group, Universidad Nacional de Colombia,
Manizales, Colombia
{jpcarvajalg,amalvarezme,cgcastellanosd}@unal.edu.co

Abstract. A methodology to classify abandoned objects in video surveillance environments is proposed. Our aim is to determine a set of relevant features that properly describes the main patterns of the objects. Assuming that the abandoned object was previously detected by a visual surveillance framework, a preprocessing stage to segment the region of interest from a given detected object is also presented. Then, some geometric and Hu's moments features are estimated. Moreover, a relevance analysis is employed to identify which features reveal the major variability of the input space to discriminate among different objects. Attained results over a real-world video surveillance dataset show how our approach is able to select a subset of features for achieving stable classification performance. Our approach seems to be a good alternative to support the development of automated video surveillance systems.

Keywords: Video surveillance, abandoned object classification, feature relevance analysis.

1 Introduction

Video surveillance has always been a vital component of security systems. High-level video interpretation tasks related to surveillance are usually completely performed by human operators, who have to process large amounts of visual information presented to them through one or more monitor [1]. Recent years have seen a growing demand of automated video surveillance systems for public safety and security enhancement [2]. Unattended objects in public premises such as airports, terminal bus and train stations include mainly bags and trolleys. Bags are a threat for these places because they can be used as a means of terrorist attack, especially for bombs [3]. Trolleys are left abandoned, and they are not a threat for the secured areas, causing nuisance alarms. In [4] address the problem of determining which feature estimation technique proves more useful for accurate object classification in a video surveillance context (scale invariant image transformed key points vs. geometric primitive features), concluding that the classifier based on the set of statistics of geometric primitive features achieved the highest recognition accuracy, and the lowest false alarm rate. However, they need a high dimensional feature set to represent the objects, and no model for reducing dimensionality is

L. Alvarez et al. (Eds.): CIARP 2012, LNCS 7441, pp. 837–844, 2012.

used. Another work attempts in the classification of different types of bags [5], selecting the optimal feature subset by iterative training a Support Vector Machines classifier with all the possible combinations of the input feature space. Nonetheless, it leads in an exhaustive and complex procedure. On the other hand, besides the geometric and shape features, both based on edge detection or contours, Hu's invariant moments have been extensively applied to image pattern recognition, image registration, and image reconstruction [6]. In this sense, it is necessary to identify a set of features that suitable highlights discriminating patterns to classify abandoned objects, achieving a stable performance with low complexity in automated video surveillance systems.

In this work, a methodology to classify abandoned objects in video surveillance environments is proposed. We aim to identify a set of relevant features that properly highlights discriminating patterns to classify abandoned objects, in order to support the development of automated video surveillance systems. It is important to note that our approach assumes that the abandoned object was previously detected by a visual surveillance framework. Besides, a preprocessing stage to segment the region of interest from a given detected object is also described. Then, some geometric and Hu's moments features are estimated. Moreover, a relevance analysis is employed to select which features reveal the major variability of the input space to discriminate among different objects. Some previous works [7,8] have shown how analyzing the amount of variability that each feature provides to the studied process, allows to identify discriminative subsets of features for enhancing the classification performance while diminishing the computational complexity. The methodology is experimentally verified on a real-world video surveillance data set, which aim to differentiate among bags, trolleys, and humans in public buildings under potential terrorism attacks.

The remainder of this work is organized as follows. In section 2, the proposed methodology is described. In section 3, the experimental conditions and results are presented. Finally, in sections 4 and 5 we discuss and conclude about the attained results.

2   Abandoned Object Classification

The main structure of a video surveillance system involves detection, tracking, and recognition of objects. Considering the objects involved in a video surveillance environment can be either moving (e.g., people, groups of people etc.), or abandoned (e.g., bags, trolleys, etc.) [9], our aim is to develop a methodology that automatically classifies abandoned objects, finding a set of relevant features that highlight appropriate patterns. For such purpose, we assume that the abandoned object was detected by a visual surveillance framework, using for example, a background subtraction method [10]. Following, the main sketch of our approach is described.

2.1   Image Preprocessing

Given an image I_{in} of a bounding box that includes an abandoned object, which is left unattended for a specific period of time, it is necessary to develop some previous preprocessing steps that allow to properly segment and characterize the object. Regarding, I_{in} is transformed to gray-scale color space (I_{gray}). After that, the image is smoothed using a filter to reduce possible image noise components. Then, an adaptive thresholding operation is performed, obtaining a binary image I_b, which encoded the region of interest of the bounding box. This image is taken as the input to the contour detection method, needed to segment the object of interest, removing the presented background. It is important to note that the segmentation is based on the assumption that the bigger contour corresponds to the object of interest, which is drawn as I_{mask}. Finally, the object is cropped using this mask and the segmented unknown object of interest is obtained.

2.2 Feature Estimation

Let I_{mask} be a binary image containing the region of interest, in order to describe properly the shape of an abandoned object, some geometric features are estimated to infer the shape properties of the studied objects. These geometric features can contain corners, circles, lines, fitting ellipses, bounding box properties, among others [5,4,11]. Moreover, the moment invariants (Hu's Moments) are also considered, which have been proven to be the adequate measures for tracing patterns regarding the images' translation, scaling and rotation, under the assumption of images with continuous functions and noise-free [6]. A full list of the considered features is illustrated in Table 1.

Table 1. Considered features for abandoned object classification

Lines	Corners	Ellipses	Other Features
- Percentage of lines: diagonal, horizontal and vertical.	- Total of corners.	- Fitting ellipse aspect ratio.	- Bounding box ratio.
- Vertical lines: percentage of lines placed at the left, right and in the center.	- Percentage of corners: left, right, top and bottom.	- Fitting ellipse area ratio.	- Hu's moments.
- Horizontal lines: percentage of lines placed at the top, bottom and in the middle.	- Horizontal and vertical standard deviation.		

2.3 Feature Selection Based on Relevance Analysis

Principal Component Analysis (PCA) is a statistical technique applied to find out a low-dimensional representation of the original feature space, searching for directions with greater variance to project the data. Although PCA is commonly used as a feature extraction method, it can be useful to select a relevant subset of the original features that better represent the studied process [7,8]. Given a set of features ($\xi_k : k = 1, \ldots, p$) corresponding to each column of the input data matrix $\mathbf{X} \in \Re^{n \times p}$ (e.g., a set of p features describing n abandoned objects), the relevance of ξ_k can be identified looking at the values of the relevance vector $\rho \in \Re^{p \times 1}$. Based on a variability analysis as in traditional PCA, ρ is computed as $\rho = \sum_{j=1}^{m} |\lambda_j \mathbf{v}_j|$, where λ_j and $\mathbf{v}_j$ are the eigenvalues and eigenvectors of the covariance matrix $\mathbf{S} \in \Re^{p \times p}$ computed as $\mathbf{S} = \mathbf{X}^\top \mathbf{X}$.

Therefore, the main assumption is that the largest values of ρ_k point out to the best input attributes, since they exhibit higher overall correlations with principal components. Traditionally, the m value is fixed as the number of dimensions needed to conserve a percentage of the input data variability. Regarding, the eigenvalues λ_j can be analyzed to infer m [7]. Hence, it is expected that a subset containing the most relevant input features according to ρ are enough to achieve a reliable classification performance. The proposed methodology for abandoned object classification can be summarized as in Fig. 1.

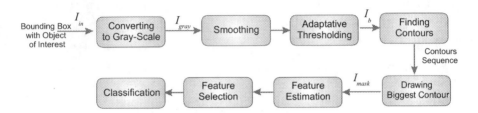

Fig. 1. Abandoned object classification: General Scheme

3   Experiments and Results

We aim to test the capability of our approach to identify a relevant set of features for abandoned object classification in video surveillance environments. In this sense, a set of footages from a real-world video surveillance data set provided by the partner company is considered. The footages were recorded in airports, train stations and other public buildings under potential terrorism attacks. The objects of interest were manually cropped, choosing bags, trolleys and people. Furthermore, the studied dataset is completed with some web images to achieve a representative sample. The images were taken under different conditions, varying the lighting, the pose, and the resolution. Therefore, 82 images of bags, 96 images of trolleys, and 70 images of people (one person per image) are considered. All images are stored as 24-bit JPEG images using the RGB color space (8 bits per color channel). Fig. 2 shows some images of the tested data set.

Then, a preprocessing stage is performed over the samples in order to detect the region of interest from each image, as mentioned in section 2.1. Particularly, a gaussian filter is used to remove noise from the original bounding box, using a 3×3 window, and a kernel-width of 0.95. The adaptive threshold is calculated in a pixel by pixel basis, by computing a weighted average (according to a Gaussian Function of their distance from that center point) of a 151×151 region around each pixel location minus 10. The above mentioned free parameters were empirically fixed. Moreover, the geometric features and the Hu's moments described in section 2.2 are computed over each detected object. Thus, an input space with 248 samples, 27 features, and 3 classes is obtained ($\mathbf{X} \in \Re^{248 \times 27}$). The Open Computer Vision library (OpenCV) was used to calculate the feature set. Besides, to identify the discriminant feature capability, a feature selection stage based on relevance analysis is performed according to section 2.3. Here, a 10-fold cross validation scheme is made to generate a mean weighted vector $\bar{\rho}$, with $\bar{\rho_k} = 1/10 \sum_{i=1}^{10} \rho_{ki}$, being ρ_{ki} the weight of relevance of the k-th feature in the i-th fold. The number of considered eigenvectors and eigenvalues m to computed ρ_{ki} is estimated looking for a 95% of retained input data variability.

A soft-margin Support Vector Machines (SVM) classifier and a k-nearest neighbors classifier (KNN) are trained. We generate a curve of performance adding one by one the features, which are sorted according to $\bar{\rho}$. For a given subset, the optimum working point is fixed using a 10-fold cross validation to fix the tradeoff parameter $C \in \Re^+$ between the solution size and training errors, and the gaussian kernel band-width σ value in SVM, and to choose the number of neighbors in KNN. Fig. 3 shows some image preprocessing results. Finally, Fig. 4 presents the classification performances.

Fig. 2. Database image examples

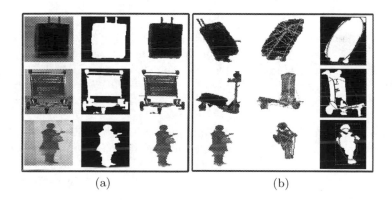

(a)   (b)

Fig. 3. Image preprocessing examples results. (a) Segmentation: I_{gray} at the left side, I_{mask} in the center and I_{segm} at the right side. (b) Geometric features: Corners at the left side, lines in the center and fitting shapes at the right side.

4 Discussion

From Fig. 3(a) it can be seen how the proposed preprocessing scheme (section 2.1) is able to segment the object of interest, given the bounding box by a video surveillance framework for abandoned object detection. Hence, the attained segmented images are useful to characterize the shape properties of the object. Now, Fig. 3(b) exhibits how some of the proposed geometric features seem to be suitable to find discriminant patterns among objects.

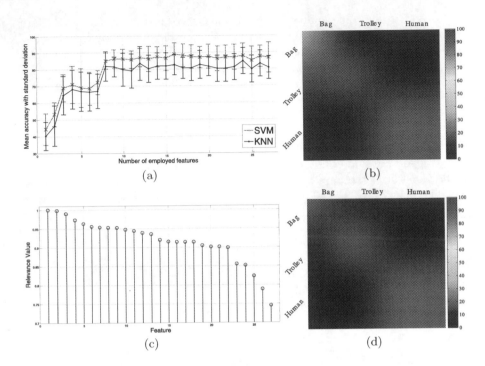

Fig. 4. Classification Results. (a): Feature selection training curve using relevance analysis. (b): KNN confusion matrix using the 16 most relevant features - testing set accuracy: 82.73 ± 06.17. (c): Normalized relevance values of the input feature. (d): SVM confusion matrix using the 16 most relevant features - testing set accuracy: 89.07 ± 06.69.

On the other hand, regarding to the attained relevance feature analysis, Fig. 4(c) shows how the described feature selection methodology based on relevance analysis (section 2.3), identifies a decreasing behavior. The relevance curve has a significant fall before the tenth most relevant feature. The above statement can be verified by the obtained classification performance shown in Fig. 4(a), where it is possible to notice how the system performance is reliable before employing the first eight most relevant features. Note that the classification accuracy, and the standard deviation of the system is stable for both classifiers (SVM and KNN), before employing those eight most relevant features. Therefore, the classifiers can achieve success rates with a small subset of features, diminishing the complexity of the problem.

The eight first most relevant features correspond to (1) the percentage of vertical lines, (2) the percentage of diagonal lines, (3) the horizontal standard deviation of the corners, (4) the percentage of vertical lines in the center, (5) the fifth, (6) the sixth, and (7) the third Hu's moments and (8) the bounding box ratio. Lines are the features that best discriminate the objects, with three of them on the top 4. From Fig. 3(b) is evident that the distribution of the lines are well defined in the three objects analyzed, bag and humans have more vertical lines in the center than trolleys (blue lines), and trolleys have more diagonal lines (green lines). The Hu's moments also provide a high discriminant power, which proofs the hypothesis that Hu's moments can also describe successfully shapes or contours. Finally, the bounding box ratio depicts the proportion of actual pixels in the object and the total pixels in the region, with humans and bags showing a bigger proportion (see left column in Fig. 3(b)).

The five less relevant features are: the percentage of horizontal lines in the center of the object (being the worst), followed by the fitting ellipse aspect ratio, percentage of horizontal lines in the top, the second Hu's moment and the percentage of vertical lines at the right side. Bags, trolleys and humans have horizontal lines in the center and in the top, which explains why these features are part of the less relevant ones. Fitting ellipse aspect ratio is not a good attribute for this classification task, it can be explained because the ellipse fitting can have a similar ratio in the three objects of interest, it would have been better to have included the orientation of the ellipse. The percentage of vertical lines at the right side (weighted at the position 23 in the relevance analysis process) and also at the left side (weighted at the position 19) are not discriminant for humans and bags, as both are mainly placed in the middle of the bounding box, however, trolley can have more lines in one side depending of their orientation, but in this work this orientation is not considered.

Overall, SVM obtains a better performance than KNN, which can be explained by its generalization capability controlled by the regularization term and the kernel band-width. The presented confusion matrixes in Figs. 4(b) and 4(d) corroborate the latter statement, where is evident how KNN shows higher overlaps among different classes, especially for bags and trolleys.

5   Conclusions

In this work, an abandoned object classification methodology to support video surveillance systems was presented, which identifies a set of relevant features to find discriminant patterns. We assumed that the abandoned object was previously detected by a visual surveillance framework, and a preprocessing stage to segment the region of interest from a given object is also presented. Then, some geometric and Hu's moments features are estimated. Given the input feature set, a relevance analysis is employed to identify which features reveal the major variability of the input space to discriminate among different objects samples. Besides, a set of footages from a real-world video surveillance data set was tested. Attained results show how our approach is able to select a subset of relevant features for achieving stable classification performances. Thus, we can conclude that lines are the features that best discriminate our objects of interest. Moreover, the Hu's moments also provided a high discriminant power, successfully describing the object shapes. Therefore, presented approach is able to support the classification stage in automated video surveillance systems, diminishing its complexity while ensuring a stable performance. As future work, we are interested in test our methodology using other kinds of abandoned objects, and we also pretend to couple some nonlinear feature extraction methods based on similarity/dissimilarity measures, in order to enhance the classification accuracy. Moreover, it would be interesting to couple the proposed approach with a robust preprocessing stage, in order to provide stable results against noisy scene conditions, such as, light variations, scale changes, occlusions, among others.

Acknowledgments. Research carried out under grants provided by a PhD. scholarship and the project 20201006570 funded by Universidad Nacional de Colombia, and project 20201006594 funded by Universidad Nacional de Colombia and Universidad de Caldas.

References

1. Silvia, F., Gianluca, G., Carlo, R.: Classification of unattended and stolen objects in video-surveillance system. In: Proceedings of the IEEE International Conference on Video and Signal Based Surveillance, AVSS 2006 (2006)
2. Fan, Q., Pankanti, S.: Modeling of temporarily static objects for robust abandoned object detection in urban surveillance. In: 8th IEEE International Conference on Advanced Video and Signal-Based Surveillance, pp. 36–41 (2011)
3. Kwak, S., Bae, G., Byun, H.: Abandoned luggage detection using a finite state automaton in surveillance video. Opt. Eng. 49 (2010)
4. Otoom, A.F., Gunes, H., Piccardi, M.: Feature extraction techniques for abandoned object classification in video surveillance. In: ICIP, pp. 1368–1371 (2008)
5. Kartoun, U., Stern, H., Edan, Y.: Bag classification using support vector machines. In: Applied Soft Computing Technologies: The Challenge of Complexity Series: Advances in Soft Computing (2006)
6. Huang, Z., Leng, J.: Analysis of hu's moment invariants on image scaling and rotation. In: Computer Engineering and Technology, ICCET 2010 (2010)
7. Daza, G., Arias, J.D., Godino, J.I., Sáenz, N., Osma, V., Castellanos, G.: Dynamic feature extraction: An application to voice pathology detection. Intelligent Automation and Soft Computing (2009)
8. Orozco, J.R., Murillo, S., Álvarez, A.M., Arias, J.D., Delgado, E., Vargas, J.F., Castellanos, G.: Automatic selection of acoustic and non-linear dynamic features in voice. In: INTERSPEECH 2011 (2011)
9. Otoom, A.F., Hatice Gunes, M.P.: Automatic classification of abandoned objects for surveillance of public premises. In: Congress on Image and Signal Processing (2008)
10. Hu, W., Tan, T., Wang, L., Maybank, S.: A survey on visual surveillance of object motion and behaviors. IEEE Transactions on Systems, Man and Cybernetics-Part C, 334–352 (2004)
11. Shotton, J., Blake, A., Cipolla, R.: Contour-based learning for object detection. In: Tenth IEEE International Conference on Computer Vision, ICCV 2005 (2005)

Fusion of Local and Global Descriptors for Content-Based Image and Video Retrieval

Felipe S.P. Andrade, Jurandy Almeida,
Hélio Pedrini, and Ricardo da S. Torres*

Institute of Computing, University of Campinas – UNICAMP
13083-852, Campinas, SP – Brazil
felipe.andrade@students.ic.unicamp.br,
{jurandy.almeida,helio,rtorres}@ic.unicamp.br

Abstract. Recently, fusion of descriptors has become a trend for improving the performance in image and video retrieval tasks. Descriptors can be global or local, depending on how they analyze visual content. Most of existing works have focused on the fusion of a single type of descriptor. Different from all of them, this paper aims to analyze the impact of combining global and local descriptors. Here, we perform a comparative study of different types of descriptors and all of their possible combinations. Extensive experiments of a rigorous experimental design show that global and local descriptors complement each other, such that, when combined, they outperform other combinations or single descriptors.

Keywords: visual information retrieval, image and video descriptor, information fusion, genetic programming, performance evaluation.

1 Introduction

Recent advances in technology have increased the availability of image and video data, creating a strong requirement for efficient systems to manage those materials. Making efficient use of visual information requires the development of powerful tools to quickly find similar contents. For this, it is necessary (1) to design a feature extractor for encoding visual properties into feature vectors and (2) to define a similarity measure for comparing image and video data from their vectors, a pair known as descriptor [10].

In the literature, two main strategies have been considered for extracting visual features [7]: global descriptors, which are computed using the whole data and have the ability of generalizing the visual content with a single feature vector; or local descriptors, which are computed on boundaries between regions or points of interest.

To improve the performance of image and video retrieval systems, a new trend is the fusion of visual features. A common approach is the use of learning methods for combining different descriptors, such as Genetic Programming (GP) [6]. Most of existing works have focused on the fusion of a single type of descriptor (i.e., global or local) [5,9,12]. In spite of all the advances, it is still unclear how the

---

* Thanks to Brazilian agencies FAPESP, CNPq, and CAPES for funding.

L. Alvarez et al. (Eds.): CIARP 2012, LNCS 7441, pp. 845–853, 2012.
© Springer-Verlag Berlin Heidelberg 2012

fusion of different types of descriptors affects the performance of those systems. A major difficulty of dealing with different types of descriptors is the different nature of data [6].

This paper aims to fill such a gap. Here, we perform a comparative study of different types of descriptors, including all of their possible combinations. Moreover, we carry out those analysis on the GP framework [11], which provides an effective way for combining descriptors. To the best of our knowledge, although this approach has been used for combining descriptors of the same type, it has never been employed in the fusion of different types of descriptors.

Extensive experiments were conducted on three large collections, comprising of both image and video data. Results from a rigorous experimental comparison of twelve descriptors, covering a variety of visual features, show that different types of descriptors act in a complementary manner, improving the performance in retrieval tasks.

The remainder of this paper is organized as follows. Section 2 briefly reviews the definition and the taxonomy of descriptors. Section 3 presents the GP framework and shows how to apply it for combining descriptors. Section 4 reports the results of our experiments and compares different combinations of descriptors. Finally, we offer our conclusions and directions for future work in Section 5.

2 Image and Video Descriptors

Both the effectiveness and the efficiency of image and video retrieval systems are very dependent on *descriptors*. A descriptor is responsible for characterizing visual properties and for computing their similarities, making it possible the ranking of images and videos based on their visual content.

Formally, a descriptor D can be defined as a pair (ϵ_D, δ_D) [10], where ϵ_D is a *feature-extraction algorithm* for encoding visual properties (e.g., color, shape, and texture) into feature vectors; and δ_D is a *similarity function* for comparing visual data from their corresponding feature vectors.

Figure 1(a) illustrates the use of a simple descriptor D to compute the similarity between two images (or videos) $\hat{I}_A$ and $\hat{I}_B$. First, the feature-extraction algorithm ϵ_D is used to compute the feature vectors $\vec{v}_{\hat{I}_A}$ and $\vec{v}_{\hat{I}_B}$ associated with $\hat{I}_A$ and $\hat{I}_B$, respectively. Next, the similarity function δ_D is used to determine the similarity value s between $\hat{I}_A$ and $\hat{I}_B$.

The feature-extraction algorithm ϵ_D can produce either a single feature vector or a set of feature vectors. In the former case, when a single feature vector must capture the entire information of the visual content, we say it is a *global descriptor*. In the latter case, a set of feature vectors is associated with different features of the visual content (regions, edges, or small patches around points of interest) and it is called *local descriptor*.

The similarity function δ_D can also be calculated as the inverse of a *distance function*. The most simple and widely used distance functions are the Manhattan distance (L_1) and the Euclidean distance (L_2). There are also more complex functions, such as the Earth Mover's Distance (EMD).

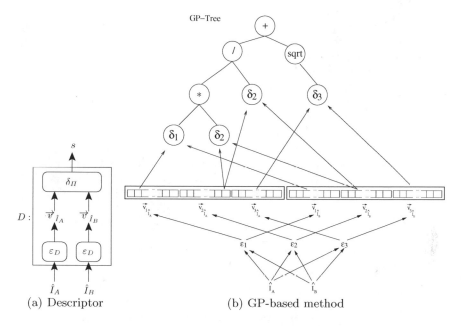

Fig. 1. Comparison between a simple descriptor and a GP-based similarity function

3   The GP Framework

Genetic programming (GP) [6] is a set of artificial intelligence search algorithms designed following the principles of biological inheritance and evolution. The solution to a problem is represented as an individual in a population pool. The population of individuals evolves generation by generation through genetic transformation operations - such as reproduction, crossover, and mutation - with the aim at creating more diverse and better performing individuals with better fitness values in subsequent generations. A fitness function is available to assign the fitness value for each individual.

The entire discovery framework can be seen as an iterative process. Starting with a set of training data with known relevance judgements, GP first operates on a large population of random combination functions. These combination functions are then evaluated based on the relevance information from training data. If the stopping criteria is not met, it will go through the genetic transformation steps to create and evaluate the next generation population iteratively.

In this paper, we adopted the GP framework proposed by Torres et al. [11] for combining image and video descriptors to support queries based on visual content. In this context, such a framework can be used for building the so-called *Content-Based Image and Video Retrieval systems*. These systems can be characterized as follows: assume that we have a image (or video) database containing a large number of images (or videos). Given a user-defined query pattern (i.e., image or video), retrieve a list of the images (or videos) from the database which are most "similar" to the query pattern according to the visual content (i.e., the objects represented therein and their properties, such as shape, color, and texture, encoded through image and video descriptors).

Figure 1(b) illustrates the whole process to generate a GP-based similarity function. Let $\mathcal{D} = \{D_1 = (\epsilon_1, \delta_1), D_2 = (\epsilon_2, \delta_2), D_3 = (\epsilon_3, \delta_3)\}$ be a set composed by 3 pre-defined descriptors. First, their extraction algorithms ϵ_i are executed for each image (or video), and the resulting feature vectors are concatenated. In the following, a new similarity function is obtained by combining the similarity functions δ_i, through the GP framework. This new function can now be used to compute the similarity between images (or videos) $\hat{I}_A$ and $\hat{I}_B$, by using their feature vector representations. Usually, the computation of the GP-base similarity function is performed completely offline and, hence, does not impact on the search time. The overall framework is presented in Algorithm 1.

Algorithm 1. GP Framework

1: Generate an initial population of random "similarity trees"
2: **while** number of generations $\leq N_{gen}$ **do**
3:     Calculate the fitness of each similarity tree
4:     Record the top N_{top} similarity trees
5:     **for all** the N_{top} individuals **do**
6:         Create a new population by reproduction, crossover, and mutation operations.
7:     **end for**
8: **end while**
9: Apply the "best similarity tree" (i.e., the first tree of the last generation) on a set of testing (query) data

---

The GP framework for the image and video retrieval problem is considered "global", in the sense it tries to find the best descriptor combination (represented as just one tree), which optimizes the number of the relevant results returned.

4   Experiments and Results

Experiments were conducted on three large collections: FreeFoto Nature, Caltech25, and Youtube10. FreeFoto Nature is a subset of the FreeFoto dataset[1] containing 3,461 natural images divided into 9 classes. Caltech25 contains 4,991 images from 25 classes of the Caltech101 dataset[2]. The number of images per class varies from 80 to 800. YouTube10 is a ten-class collection with 696 videos (245,402 frames) downloaded from YouTube[3] that we have created based on well-defined semantic categories. To reduce the amount of redundant information, a sampling method was used to extract one frame at each 2 seconds of video, totaling 115,082 frames. It is important to highlight that a better compression can be obtained by employing more elaborate techniques, such as summarization methods [2,3]. Examples of categories are Apple, Soccer, and World Trade Center. The average number of videos per class is 70.

---

[1] http://www.freefoto.com/browse/205-00-0/Nature As of April 2012.
[2] http://www.vision.caltech.edu/Image_Datasets/Caltech101/ As of April 2012.
[3] http://www.youtube.com As of April 2012.

For describing those visual data, we used six global descriptors: ACC, BIC, GCH, and JAC, for encoding the color information; LAS and QCCH, for analyzing the texture property. For more details regarding those global descriptors, refer to [8]. In addition, we also extracted SIFT and SURF features, from which six local descriptors were generated. Two of them employ the EMD for comparing local features [4] and are referred to as SIFT and SURF, respectively. The others consist of a Bag-of-Words (BoW) representation defined by a 500-word vocabulary. When L_1 is used as distance function, they are named as SIFTBOF and SURFBOF; and for L_2, we call them L2SIFTBOF and L2SURFBOF. It is important to realize that any descriptor could be used for feature extraction.

To combine those descriptors, we evolved a population of 30 individuals along 10 generations using the GP framework (Section 3). For applying genetic operators, we used the tournament selection technique for selecting individuals. The reproduction, mutation, and crossover rates employed were 0.05, 0.2, and 0.8, respectively. A 5-fold cross validation was performed for each dataset in order to ensure statistically sound results. The reported results refer to the average scores obtained for the effectiveness measures.

We assess the effectiveness of each approach using Precision×Recall curves. Precision is the ratio of the number of relevant images/videos retrieved to the total number of irrelevant and relevant images/videos retrieved. Recall is the ratio of the number of relevant images/videos retrieved to the total number of relevant images/videos in the database. Some unique-value measurements are also used in the validation: Mean Average Precision (MAP), which is the area below Precision×Recall curves; and Precision at 5 (P@5), which is the average precision after 5 images/videos are returned.

Figure 2 presents the Precision×Recall curves observed for the different approaches. Those graphs compare the effectiveness of the global descriptors (first column) and the local descriptors (second column) for the FreeFoto (first row), Caltech (second row), and YouTube (third row) datasets. Our GP-based methods (third column) are also included: *GP-Global*, which combines the global descriptors; *GP-Local*, which combines the local descriptors; and *GP-GlobalLocal*, which combines both the global and local descriptors.

As we can observe, the GP based similarity functions perform better than all the descriptors. Observe that *GP-Global* performs slightly better than the global descriptors. However, the same does not happen for the *GP-Local*, which did not significantly improve the effectiveness of the local descriptors. On the other hand, the combination of both the global and local descriptors is promising, yielding the best results. Note the superiority of *GP-GlobalLocal* when compared with the use of the best global and local descriptors in isolation.

Table 1 presents the comparison of descriptors and GP-based methods with respect to the MAP and P@5 measures. MAP is a good indication of the effectiveness considering all positions of obtained ranked lists. P@5, in turn, focuses on the effectiveness of the methods considering only the first positions of the ranked lists. For each dataset, we highlight the best result of each approach (i.e., global descriptors, local descriptors, and GP-based methods). Again, similar results to those observed for the Precision×Recall curves were obtained.

Paired t-tests were performed to verify the statistical significance of those results. For that, the confidence intervals for the differences between paired means of each class from the database were computed to compare every pair of approaches. If the confidence interval includes zero, the difference is not significant at that confidence level. If the confidence interval does not include zero, then the sign of the difference indicates which alternative is better.

Tables 2 and 3 present the confidence intervals (with a confidence of 95%) of the differences between the GP-based methods and the best global and local descriptors for the MAP and P@5 measures, respectively. In addition, we also include a comparison of *GP-GlobalLocal* with *GP-Global* and *GP-Local*.

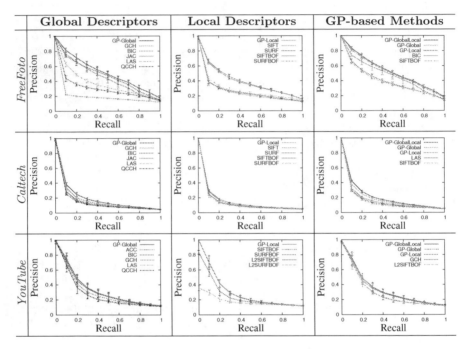

Fig. 2. Precision×Recall curves obtained by the global descriptors (first column), local descriptors (second column), and GP-based methods (third column) for the FreeFoto (first row), Caltech (second row), and YouTube (third row) datasets

The results show that *GP-Global* exhibits a similar performance to the best global descriptor, but is always better than the best local descriptor. As we also can see, the effectiveness of *GP-Local* is bounded by the poor performance of some local descriptors, reason for what the combination of them offers no performance gain. Despite the low effectiveness observed for the local descriptors, their combination with the global ones outperforms all the other approaches.

Figure 3 shows three query patterns and their top-5 results retrieved using the different approaches. The first position in each list of results is the query itself and the remaining ones are ranked in decreasing order of similarity regarding the query. The relevant results of each query are marked with a rectangular box.

Note that the global descriptors perform better than the local ones for the query *Starfish*, whereas the opposite behavior is performed for the query *Moun-*

Table 1. MAP and P@5 scores obtained by the global descriptors, local descriptors, and GP-based methods for the FreeFoto, Caltech, and Youtube datasets

Approach		MAP			P@5		
		FreeFoto	*Caltech*	*YouTube*	*FreeFoto*	*Caltech*	*Youtube*
Global Descriptors	GCH	0.1596	0.1526	**0.3147**	0.1682	0.3249	**0.3934**
	BIC	**0.4648**	0.1681	0.3092	0.7668	**0.3599**	0.3902
	JAC	0.4453	0.1455	–	**0.7767**	0.3082	–
	ACC	–	–	0.2894	–	–	0.3575
	LAS	0.3575	**0.1703**	0.2635	0.6196	0.3500	0.3180
	QCCH	0.2914	0.1469	0.2673	0.4608	0.3076	0.3224
Local Descriptors	SIFT	0.2396	0.1350	–	0.4269	0.2920	–
	SURF	0.2477	0.1361	–	0.4247	0.2870	–
	SIFTBOF	**0.3802**	**0.1435**	0.2852	**0.6506**	**0.2950**	0.3534
	SURFBOF	0.2635	0.1253	0.2358	0.4760	0.2553	0.2965
	L2SIFTBOF	–	–	**0.2866**	–	–	**0.3544**
	L2SURFBOF	–	–	0.1547	–	–	0.1262
GP-based Methods	GP-Global	0.5063	0.1916	0.3215	0.8191	0.3838	0.4023
	GP-Local	0.3906	0.1582	0.2854	0.6656	0.3324	0.3523
	GP-GlobalLocal	**0.5211**	**0.2086**	**0.3280**	**0.8321**	**0.4051**	**0.4143**

Table 2. Differences between MAP of the different approaches at a confidence of 95%

Approach	*FreeFoto*		*Caltech*		*Youtube*	
	min.	max.	min.	max.	min.	max.
GP-Global – Best Global	-0.0201	0.1031	0.0091	0.0333	-0.0031	0.0168
GP-Global – Best Local	0.0617	0.1904	0.0049	0.0911	0.0067	0.0630
GP-Local – Best Global	-0.0503	0.0238	-0.0345	0.0103	-0.0603	0.0018
GP-Local – Best Local	0.0377	0.0273	-0.0102	0.0396	-0.0043	0.0019
GP-GlobalLocal – Best Global	-0.0229	0.1355	0.0131	0.0633	0.0052	0.0213
GP-GLobalLocal – Best Local	0.0887	0.1929	0.0139	0.1161	0.0148	0.0678
GP-GlobalLocal – GP-Global	-0.0078	0.0375	0.0024	0.0315	0.0001	0.0128
GP-GlobalLocal – GP-Local	0.0728	0.1881	0.0184	0.0822	0.0151	0.0699

Table 3. Differences between P@5 of the different approaches at a confidence of 95%

Approach	*FreeFoto*		*Caltech*		*Youtube*	
	min.	max.	min.	max.	min.	max.
GP-Global – Best Global	0.0139	0.0709	-0.0050	0.0529	-0.0040	0.0218
GP-Global – Best Local	0.0967	0.2402	0.0126	0.1650	0.0183	0.0777
GP-Local – Best Global	-0.1868	-0.0352	-0.0651	0.0100	-0.0721	-0.0101
GP-Local – Best Local	-0.0047	0.0348	-0.0214	0.0961	-0.0060	0.0060
GP-GlobalLocal – Best Global	0.0197	0.0910	0.0197	0.0707	0.0055	0.0362
GP-GLobalLocal – Best Local	0.1214	0.2415	0.0301	0.1900	0.0344	0.0855
GP-GlobalLocal – GP-Global	-0.0054	0.0313	0.0044	0.0380	-0.0002	0.0241
GP-GlobalLocal – GP-Local	0.1121	0.2207	0.0347	0.1107	0.0374	0.0865

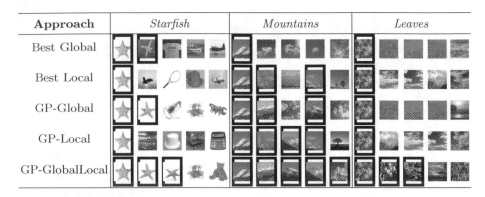

Approach	*Starfish*	*Mountains*	*Leaves*
Best Global			
Best Local			
GP-Global			
GP-Local			
GP-GlobalLocal			

Fig. 3. Top-5 results retrieved by the different approaches in three queries: *Starfish* from Caltech, *Mountains* and *Leaves* from FreeFoto

tains. The results of both types of descriptors in isolation are improved by their combination, as shown by *GP-Global* and *GP-Local*. However, the same does not happen for the query *Leaves*, in which those approaches exhibit a poor performance. In spite of that, the fusion of the global and local descriptors takes the advantages of each type of descriptor, yielding significantly improved performance. Clearly, *GP-GlobalLocal* outperforms all the other approaches.

5   Conclusions

This paper has discussed the impact of combining different types of descriptors in the content-based image and video retrieval. Here, we have used a genetic-programming framework in the fusion of global and local descriptors.

We have conducted an extensive performance evaluation of twelve descriptors and all of their possible combinations, covering a variety of visual features. Results from a rigorous experimental comparison on three large datasets show that global and local features offer different and complementary information that can be exploited in order to improve the performance in retrieval tasks.

Future work includes the evaluation of other visual features for image and video retrieval (e.g., motion patterns [1]). We also plan to consider other learning-to-rank methods for combining global and local descriptors. Finally, we want to investigate the effects of their use in other applications.

References

1. Almeida, J., Leite, N.J., Torres, R.S.: Comparison of video sequences with histograms of motion patterns. In: Int. Conf. Image Proc. (ICIP), pp. 3673–3676 (2011)
2. Almeida, J., Leite, N.J., Torres, R.S.: VISON: VIdeo Summarization for ONline applications. Pattern Recognition Letters 33(4), 397–409 (2012)
3. Almeida, J., Torres, R.S., Leite, N.J.: Rapid video summarization on compressed video. In: Int. Symp. Multimedia (ISM), pp. 113–120 (2010)
4. Almeida, J., Rocha, A., Torres, R.S., Goldenstein, S.: Making colors worth more than a thousand words. In: Int. Symp. Appl. Comput. (SAC), pp. 1180–1186 (2008)

5. Ferreira, C.D., Santos, J.A., Torres, R.S., Gonçalves, M.A., Rezende, R.C., Fan, W.: Relevance feedback based on genetic programming for image retrieval. Pattern Recognition Letters 32(1), 27–37 (2011)
6. Koza, J.R.: Genetic Programming: On the Programming of Computers by Means of Natural Selection. MIT Press (1992)
7. Liu, Y., Zhang, D., Lu, G., Ma, W.Y.: A survey of content-based image retrieval with high-level semantics. Pattern Recognition 40(1), 262–282 (2007)
8. Penatti, O.A.B., Valle, E., Torres, R.S.: Comparative study of global color and texture descriptors for web image retrieval. J. Visual Commun. Image Representation 23(2), 359–380 (2012)
9. Salgian, A.: Combining local descriptors for 3D object recognition and categorization. In: Int. Conf. Pattern Recognition (ICPR), pp. 1–4 (2008)
10. Torres, R.S., Falcão, A.X.: Content-Based Image Retrieval: Theory and Applications. J. Theoretical and Applied Informatics 13(2), 161–185 (2006)
11. Torres, R.S., Falcão, A.X., Gonçalves, M.A., Papa, J.P., Zhang, B., Fan, W., Fox, E.A.: A genetic programming framework for content-based image retrieval. Pattern Recognition 42(2), 283–292 (2009)
12. Wu, Y.: Shape-based image retrieval using combining global and local shape features. In: Int. Congress Image and Signal Processing (CISP), pp. 1–5 (2009)

Speed Estimation Thanks to Two Images from One Stationary Camera

Charles Beumier

Signal & Image Centre, Royal Military Academy, 1000 Brussels, Belgium
Charles.beumier@elec.rma.ac.be

Abstract. This paper presents speed estimation of a moving object thanks to two images captured within a known time interval from one stationary un-calibrated camera. The development is currently applicable to rigid objects animated by a pure translation and requires the localization of corresponding points in both images and the specification of one real dimension. An interesting solution based on an equivalent stereo problem is suggested. It considers the object stationary and searches for the virtual camera motion which would produce the same images. The mathematical formulation is simple using 3D vectors and the camera parameters: focal length, CCD size and pixel size. The developed software package was tested for vehicle speed second assessment of the velocity captured by the LIDAR system LMS-06 distributed by secuRoad SA.

Keywords: Speed estimation, 3D translation, vehicle speed, LIDAR.

1   Introduction

More and more control systems are based on cameras. These generally offer flexibility, limited costs, easier installation and maintenance compared to alternative solutions. Images possibly contain additional information directly interpretable by any analyst. The use of camera for control has also been observed in traffic surveillance [1], application domain of the present work.

In the literature about vehicle speed estimation with one camera, most techniques track individual objects over a sequence of video images and derive a displacement in pixel. This displacement is converted into speed thanks to the known time interval and a conversion pixel to meter taking into account the homography which maps 3D world to image coordinates [2, 3, 4]. Refer to [2] for a precise explanation of the homography and its automatic estimation. In [3], the camera is automatically calibrated from image lane markings to get the world to image projection. In those references, real distances about lane marking are used. Strictly speaking, as mentioned in [2], features should be tracked at the road level since the homography, derived from lane markings, is only valid at that level.

In the present work, we propose to estimate the speed of any rigid object animated by a translation from two images with timestamps captured with a stationary un-calibrated camera. Compared to studies concerned with traffic surveillance for which the camera tilt is important, our camera is pointed to capture the frontal or rear licence

L. Alvarez et al. (Eds.): CIARP 2012, LNCS 7441, pp. 854–861, 2012.

plate for vehicle identification and speed estimation. The high camera resolution allows for a precise estimation of the 3D object motion thanks to triangulation and licence plate dimensions. The program developed has been applied to images captured by the cameras of a LIDAR system for vehicle speed second assessment.

In what follows, section 2 states the problem of speed estimation with camera and gives associated hypotheses. Section 3 details the mathematical background used for motion estimation. Section 4 describes the application for vehicle speed estimation and section 5 presents motion and speed estimation. Section 6 concludes the paper.

2   Problem Statement

The presented approach has been originally developed for vehicle speed estimation as second assessment for the LIDAR speed system LMS-06 used for law enforcement. For certification in Belgium, the deviation between speeds measured by each method must not exceed 10 %.

The LIDAR system LMS-06 consists of a sweeping laser which extracts horizontal profiles of range distances. Speed is estimated from profile range values over time. Compared to Doppler radar, the LIDAR is much more precise in speed and localisation. Several road lanes may be supervised simultaneously with their own speed limit. A LMS-06 system can control traffic in both driving directions and is equipped with two cameras pointing in opposite directions (Fig. 1.). A typical functional setup is to measure LIDAR speed when the vehicle is approaching and if this speed exceeds the limit, a set of images are captured. Up to two images can be taken by each camera, the first camera capturing the vehicle front and the second one its rear.

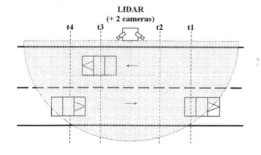

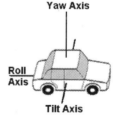

Fig. 1. LIDAR system with two cameras   **Fig. 2.** Vehicle angles

The speed measured by camera is estimated from the distance travelled in a time interval. The time interval, of about 250 ms in our application (due to camera latency time between shots), is known with a precision of +/- 1 ms. Motion estimation is derived from points localised in two images. In our application, 3 hypotheses simplify the approach and its implementation.

First, the camera is expected to be stationary, as claimed by the LIDAR system operator. This simplifies the approach which can focus on object displacement, without estimating the camera motion. The stationary condition is easily confirmed. Secondly, motion can be approximated by a translation. This is certainly true for vehicles on a straight lane. Vehicle flows are generally approximated by lines as mentioned in the introduction. Considering the three possible angles of a vehicle (Fig. 2.), tilt mainly corresponds to braking or acceleration, yaw to lane changes and roll intervenes when in a curve. These rotations are likely to be negligible in our application. We finally suppose that rigid object points are visible in both images and that at least one real dimension is available. In the vehicle application, the license plate corners are valid candidate points since the plate is used for vehicle identification and is normally of known size.

3   3D Motion Estimation

We propose 3D motion estimation thanks to object points whose projections are specified in both images. The simple pinhole model (3.1) is used to derive 3D lines from both images that should intersect (3.3) at best if the proper motion is found (3.4).

3.1   Camera Model

The camera model used here to solve 3D motion estimation is the classical pinhole model. The perspective projection depends on the focal length and the CCD pixel size (derived from the CCD size and image resolution).

Due to the quality of the image sensors (CCD of Nikon D70S and D90) and the relatively large focal length values (initially 35 or 50mm), distortion parameters could be neglected. In such a situation, a simple relation links the 3D coordinates of a point (X,Y,Z) and its projection in the images (x,y), especially if the optical centre of the camera is used as object coordinate centre Oc $(0,0,0)$.

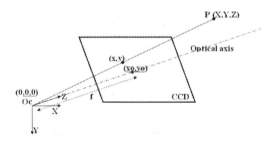

Fig. 3. Axis system and pinhole model

Instead of the analytical formulation linking x,y and X,Y,Z, we preferred a geometrical view which simply need vectors. The 3D line through a scene point P(X, Y, Z) and Oc will intersect the image plane at coordinates (Kx*(x-xo), Ky*(y-yo), f), all expressed in mm in our real world coordinate system. Kx and Ky are the pixel size in mm and (xo, yo) are the image coordinates of the optical centre (supposed to be at the image centre). Conversely, an image point (x, y) directly defines the 3D line specified by point Oc = (0,0,0) and the 3D vector (Kx*(x-xo), Ky*(y-yo), f).

3.2   Triangulation

Triangulation refers to the localization of a 3D point thanks to two projections of known point of view.

We adopted a reverse approach to object motion. We tried to identify the virtual camera motion which would compensate for object motion, allowing for a static description of object 3D points. The problem is then equivalent to stereo computing, where a moving camera captures two images of a stationary object (Fig. 4.).

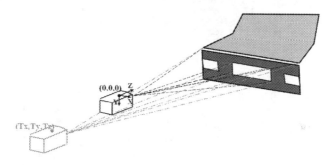

Fig. 4. Triangulation for a virtual camera motion and stationary object

Using triangulation enables to enforce that image points from both images are consistent projections of the 3D object. The problem defined as such is ill-posed, as similar objects of different scales at different distances can produce the same projections. To solve this scale indeterminate, one distance on object has to be specified.

Triangulation simply consists of 3D line intersection. More specifically, for each pair of corresponding points in images, a 3D line is constructed with optical centre 0c (0,0,0) for image1 and optical centre (Tx,Ty,Tz) for image2. The virtual motion of the camera is formalized by the translation of the optical centre of image 2.

The (stationary) coordinates of 3D object points are found at the intersection of two 3D lines. To follow with our geometrical formalism based on vector processing, we designed an elegant and fast algorithm detailed in the next section.

3.3   3D Line Intersection

3D line intersection is not as simple as for planar line intersection since two 3D lines are more likely to have no intersection (even if not parallel). The geometrical algorithm presented here first computes the intersection error which is the minimal distance between the two lines. Then it returns the intersection position which is the midpoint of the shortest segment separating the two 3D lines.

Consider the two 3D lines of Fig. 5, each specified by a point and a vector (p1, **v1** and p2, **v2**). **v1** and **v2** define a normal vector **pln**, perpendicular to **v1** and **v2** and simply obtained by vector product **v1*v2** and normalisation to have a unit vector.

From the family of parallel planes with perpendicular direction **pln**, the distance between planes is in the difference of the scalar product **p.pln**, where p has the coordinates of a point belonging to a plane. The distance between the two 3D lines is the distance between the planes containing p1 and p2 respectively, hence $dist$ = (**p1-p2).pln**. Mention that the distance 'dist' is signed.

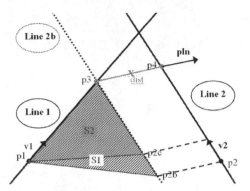

Fig. 5. 3D line intersection

The coordinates of the intersection needs a definition because two 3D lines only intersect if 'dist' is 0. We decided to look for the mid point where the distance between the two lines is minimal. Consider the dashed line 2b in Fig. 5., parallel to line2 and translated by the signed distance 'dist' obtained previously. Line 2b, in the plane (p1, **v1**), intersects line 1 at point p3. Surface S1 of triangle (p2b p1 p3) is given by half of $((\mathbf{p1-p2b})*k\mathbf{v1}).\mathbf{pln}$ (k, unknown, will disappear). For point p2c, which is p2b shifted by **v2**, we have surface $S2 = ((\mathbf{p1-p2c})*k\mathbf{v1}).\mathbf{pln}$. The ratio of S2 and S1 allows in one operation to get where point p3 is located: from p2b, along **v2** and at a distance of S1/(S1-S2) (independent of k).

Similarly point p4 could be estimated, but the desired midpoint, halfway between p3 and p4 is directly obtained from p3, at a distance dist/2 in the **pln** direction. Special conditions, like parallel or coinciding lines, are easily detected in our algorithm.

3.4   Translation Estimation

To sum up, object speed estimation requires in our approach the virtual camera translation which makes both images the valid projections of the 3D object. The object is materialized by a set of 3D points localized by the user in both images. Each pair of corresponding image points defines two 3D lines whose intersection is computed to derive an intersection position and error.

The virtual camera translation (Tx,Ty,Tz) associated to image 2 is obtained from the minimization of the error E consisting of two terms:

$$E = w1*RMS (\ dist(\ pt\ )\ ) + w2*RMS\_plate\_size$$

The first term concerns the reconstruction error of all 3D points *pt* and is computed as the root mean square (RMS) value of the intersection errors (*dist* in Fig. 5). The second term, associated with scaling, is the RMS value of the differences between known distances (at least one is required) and reconstructed distances (distance between intersection positions). Both terms can be weighed according to their relative importance (we used a balanced weight: w1 = w2 = 0.5).

The minimization procedure to find the smallest error E follows a coarse-to-fine approach. The Tx, Ty and Tz values span their range with some increment at a level and their best estimates (minimum of E) are used as central values for the next level which will be evaluated in a smaller extent and with finer increments. In order to limit computation time, it is advised to restrict the ranges of each parameter, as explained below for our application.

After optimization, the algorithm returns the residual error E and the individual deviations for all points and given distances.

4   Vehicle Speed Estimation

4.1   Graphical Interface

The developed system has a graphical user interface displaying two images and superimposed points which can be manipulated (added, moved or deleted).

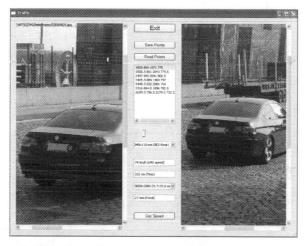

Fig. 6. Graphical interface: 2 images with points and camera parameters

The four licence plate corners must be first localised manually and the plate dimensions have to be specified (country, front/rear, or values typed in). A few additional points, preferably at another range (car bonnet, window corners) make speed estimation more robust. Manual point localisation represents a small time overhead which satisfies the client compared to the risk of failure of a fully automatic solution. Finally, camera details have to be specified (focal length, CCD size in pixel and mm).

Once all the information has been entered, the system can search the optimal translation and derive the vehicle speed and its deviation with the measured LIDAR speed. The residual error E is displayed for all the coarse-to-fine levels to highlight possible convergence problems. For the best solution, the residual error for each point and for the four plate sides is listed. This enables the detection of bad point localisation.

4.2   Uncontrolled Deviation

Our camera based speed estimation has been compared with LIDAR measurements considered as ground truth. Some uncontrolled influences explain their difference.

First, the LMS-06 LIDAR system gets its velocity estimation from the average of measures taken frontally before any image is acquired. The instants of LIDAR speed measurement and camera capture may differ from a few tenths of second to more than one second.

Secondly, the focal length is returned by the camera as an integer value in mm. For 25 mm, this may represent +/-2 % error on speed estimation.

Thirdly, point localization is crucial to the optimization. Although the operator is warned by the reported point residuals, the precision is limited by the object size in pixel. This is particularly true for small focal values.

Fourthly, licence plate dimensions may differ from the official size.

5   Results

Two types of tests were conducted with a vehicle plate as object of interest.

The first test considered a stationary vehicle placed at known relative distances on a line. In the following table, the measured and estimated distance between successive positions are given. The first position P0 is about 10m from the camera and P6 at about 36m. After 36m, the plate has only 80x15 pixel and the lack in resolution leads to imprecise estimation notified by a very large residue. This test made us confident to perform speed measurements in real traffic situations.

Table 1. Estimated distance in the case of a stationary vehicle moved along a line

Distance	P0-P1	P1-P2	P2-P3	P3-P4	P4-P5	P5-P6	P6-P7
Measured	3.00	3.00	5.00	5.00	5.00	5.00	5.00
Estimated	3.17	3.02	5.01	5.03	4.79	4.74	3.10
Residue	3.68	5.63	6.51	6.37	3.91	4.96	31.84

The second test concerned vehicle speed estimation in real circumstances. Analysing the convergence data, we could check that the estimated translation vectors have a similar direction, arguing for a rectilinear movement. The global residue ranged roughly from 3 to 10 mm after point refinement. Individual intersection error maxima amounted to 5 mm for worse points after refinement although the majority of point errors lied below 2 mm.

The image based speeds were compared to the LIDAR measurements. Although influences mentioned in 4.2 were expected, the large majority of the tests revealed a speed deviation inferior to 10%, as required by the client. Worst deviations were observed when the driver braked, what can be checked in rear pictures thanks to the brake lights. There was no large positive speed deviation (like a strong acceleration). The speed deviation average of more than 100 tests in different conditions (different cameras, focal length, speed and plate type) for acceptable situations (no brake) is about -3%.

More difficult cases concern vehicle slow down due to road or traffic conditions (hill climbing, road crossing). There is little evidence of such conditions if the driver simply releases gas without braking.

6   Conclusions

This paper has presented an algorithm for speed estimation based on two images with known timestamps captured by a stationary camera.

The solution has been developed so far for pure translation movements. It is based on the 3D reconstruction of points manually localised in the images with at least one known distance. It has been applied to vehicle speed estimation on straight lanes. Many tests confirmed the translational motion hypothesis and showed that the estimated velocity lies within 10% of a LIDAR measurement in normal conditions.

We hope to get test data with better speed stability or with a closer ground truth in order to get better statistical results about speed deviation.

References

1. Kastrinaki, V., Zervakis, M., Kalaitzakis, K.: A survey of video processing techniques for traffic applications. In: Image and Vision Computing, vol. 21, pp. 359–381. Elsevier, Amsterdam (2003)
2. Grammatikopoulos, L., Karras, G., Petsa, E.: Automatic estimation of vehicle speed from uncalibrated video sequences. In: Proc. of Int. Symposium on Modern Technologies, Education and Professional Practice in Geodesy and Related Fields, Sofia, pp. 332–338 (2005)
3. Tocino Diaz, J.C., Houben, Q., Czyz, J., Debeir, O., Warzée, N.: A Camera Auto-Calibration Algorithm for Real-Time Road Traffic Analysis. In: Proc. of VISAPP 2009 Int. Conf. on Computer Vision Theory and Applications, Lisboa, Portugal, pp. 625–631 (2009)
4. Beymer, D., McLauchlan, P., Coifman, B., Malik, J.: A Real-Time Computer Vision System for measuring Traffic Parameters. In: Proceedings of Computer Vision and Pattern Recognition, pp. 495–501. IEEE (1997)
5. Beumier, C.: Vehicle Speed Estimation from Two Images for LIDAR Second Assessment. In: Proc. of VISAPP 2012 Int. Conf. on Computer Vision Theory and Applications, Roma, Italy (2012)

An Algorithm for Highlights Identification
and Summarization of Broadcast Soccer Videos

Waldez Azevedo Gomes Junior and Díbio Leandro Borges

Department of Computer Science, University of Brasilia,
70910-900 Brasília, DF, Brazil
waldezjr14@gmail.com, dibio@unb.br

Abstract. This paper presents an algorithm that aims to perform automatic summarization in broadcast soccer videos. The summarization considers identifying and keeping only the highlights of the match. A situation that could be considered a highlight is defined as one with high convergence of players to a spot. Our approach considers velocities and positions of the players, and an inferred movement of the TV camera as basic features to be extracted. The movement of the TV cameras are approximated using the movement of all the players in the image. A motion field is computed over the image in order to analyze aspects of the match. The algorithm was tested with real data of a soccer match and results are promising considering the approach uses as input broadcast videos only, and it has no a priori knowledge of cameras positions or other fixed parameters.

Keywords: Motion field analysis, soccer video analysis, video summarization.

1 Introduction

Broadcast soccer matches are probably the sport TV shows mostly viewed on the planet nowadays. Automatic analysis of soccer video sequences and complete matches has captured the interest of the Computer Vision research community since there are challenges in object, scene recognition and classification to be dealt with, and also a handful of needed applications to be developed and deployed. Automatic identification of highlights (e.g. situations leading to a goal or closer) and further summarization of the match based on those highlights are examples these challenges.

There has been a great deal of recent works in the literature considering automatic analysis of soccer videos. In [5] and [3] the authors consider tracking the players and the ball in order to study the detection of a highlight in the match. However, those works are based in a manual (i.e. prefixed) initialization of the position of the ball. The work done in [8] also approached the problem by tracking the players and it showed good results, but it assumes a fixed and controlled camera view .

The work reported in [6] has taken a different approach to this problem of highlights identification and summarization. It considers the relative position of the soccer field and the surrounding stadium in the video as main objects to be identified in the initial

L. Alvarez et al. (Eds.): CIARP 2012, LNCS 7441, pp. 862–869, 2012.

steps. Sequences to be considered as highlights are classified based on a relative classification of those regions in a frame. Results achieved there are interesting since different matches in complete different stadiums and transmission are tested. [4] an analysis of motion fields resulted from the movement of the players throughout a match is realized. The authors suggest that the movement of all the players may be a good indication of the position of the ball. Their work however aimed to have a dynamic scene analysis methodology to be used in situations where they would have complete knowledge and control of camera setups and positions. Contextual flow [9], a motion analysis methodology based on contextual matching is also a promising technique for target tracking that can be used for video summaries based on motion.

Our approach here considers a global analysis of the movement of the players. We consider that the players on the field have the best view of the game, therefore, analyzing their movement should provide a good indication of what is happening during the match. we make the hypothesis that when the movement of the players highly converges to one place on the field and the cameraman moves the camera with a higher speed than usual there is a relevant event of the match going on, and possibly a highlight. For summarizing a highlight we associate these detected frames as more likely sequences to be extracted. The algorithm starts with the identification of the players on the field, then tracking of the players, the construction of a dense velocity field based on the velocities of the players, the identification of the highlights, and the sorting of the highlight flags. In the next sections the details of those steps are presented followed by the results and evaluation of the algorithm.

2   Identification of the Players

In long shots of a soccer broadcast the prevailing color is the green color of the grass. In order to identify such prevailing color the image was divided in three channels and for each channel the histogram is calculated. With the histograms we obtain the most frequent color for each channel $R_{peak}, G_{peak}, B_{peak}$. Before obtaining such values the image is normalized to decrease the effect of light on the processing.

Fig. 1. The input image at left and segmented image at right. The segmented image is white where there is no grass in the pitch, including players and advertisement boards.

To segment the grass regions on the image, a binary image is computed using peak values of the channels and thresholding the grass similar values out. To improve the identification of the players and reduce the noise in I_{NG} some erosions and dilations are applied to it (Fig.1). This step of the algorithm is similar to the work in [5]. At this point, after the normalization and segmentation of the image the algorithm is already able to classify the image as a long/medium distance shot, or a short distance shot.

A shot is classified as long, medium, or short distance according to the following [6]: If it is possible to segment more than 65% of the image as grass for more than 100 frames it is a long distance shot; if it happens for less than 100 frames the shot is classified as of medium distance; and finally, if less than 65% of the image is segmented as grass the shot is classified as of short distance.

Fig. 2. The input image at left, and a modification of I_{PLACTR} at right. The image at right also shows the velocities outputted by the optical flow.

The next step is to apply morphological filters to the binary image and then to identify the contours in I_{NG} comparing the area in each contour to two threshold values that are the maximum and minimum values of area for a region of players in the field. Those threshold values already take into account that a contour in I_{NG} possibly covers more than one player. This is done to differentiate the players from any other contour found in I_{NG} such as the audience or advertisement signs. Then, for each contour that is between the thresholds the minimum rectangle possible to contour it is chosen and then filled with white and put into another image I_{PLA} which will act as a mask for the tracking of the players. To increase the rate of success finding the players the box is enlarged a few pixels before being put in I_{PLA} . The tracking of the players is done in a new image, I_{PLACTR} (Fig. 2), that contains circles centered in the centroids of the boxes at I_{PLA}. To track the players a similar algorithm by Shi and Tomasi [7] is applied, followed by computing the optical flow.

3　Construction of a Dense Velocity Field

To construct the dense velocity field we have to interpolate the velocities of each player, in this case we are interpolating the features extracted and tracked in the previous step. This velocity field should also be smooth so that any inference done by checking it should not be biased by points where the interpolation does not work well.

This is a surface interpolation problem, and it can be solved [4]   using a radial basis function. The interpolation function used in this work is:

$$f(x) = c(x) + \sum_{i=0}^{n-1} \lambda_i \cdot \varphi(\|x - x_i\|) \tag{1}$$

Where n is the number of points being interpolated, x is the position (x,y) of a pixel in an image, λ_i are coefficients, $c(x)$ is a polynomial function, here:

$$c(x,y) = c_0 + c_1 x + c_2 y \tag{2}$$

The function $\varphi(\|x - x_i\|)$ is a radial basis function, as mentioned in [1], some popular choices of φ are: $\varphi = r$ (linear); $\varphi = r^2 \log r$ (thin-plate spline); $\varphi = e^{-ar}$ (Gaussian); $\varphi = \sqrt{r^2 + c^2}$ (Multi-quadratic); with

$$r = \|x - x_i\| \tag{3}$$

As in [4] and [1] we also chose the thin-plate spline. The thin-plate, or 2-D biharmonic spline, models the deflection of an infinite thin plate. While the linear radial basis function will interpolate the data, the thin-plate spline is more attractive since it also provides C^1 continuity and minimizes the energy function:

$$\int \left(\frac{\partial^2 \phi}{\partial x^2}\right)^2 + 2\left(\frac{\partial^2 \phi}{\partial y \partial x}\right)^2 + \left(\frac{\partial^2 \phi}{\partial y^2}\right)^2 dxdy \tag{4}$$

In this sense the thin-plate spline is the smoothest interpolating of $\varphi(x, y)$ [1].

In our implementation it was used a slight modification of the thin plate spline:

$$\varphi = r^2 \log(r + 1) \tag{5}$$

Solving the interpolation means to find the values of the coefficients λ_i, c_0, c_1, c_2. Since there are two components of the velocity of each point there must be done two interpolations in order to have the complete field. It ends to solving the following linear system for each component of the velocities [1]:

$$\begin{bmatrix} A & Q \\ Q^T & 0 \end{bmatrix} + \begin{bmatrix} \lambda \\ c \end{bmatrix} = \begin{bmatrix} U \\ 0 \end{bmatrix} \tag{6}$$

$$A = (a_{ij}) = \varphi(\|x_i - x_j\|) \tag{7}$$

$$c = \begin{bmatrix} c_0, c_1, c_2 \end{bmatrix}^T \tag{8}$$

$$\lambda = (\lambda_0, \dots, \lambda_{n-1}) \tag{9}$$

$$Q=\begin{pmatrix} 1 & x_0 & y_0 \\ .. & .. & .. \\ 1 & x_{n-1} & y_{n-1} \end{pmatrix} \tag{10}$$

Where **U** is just a matrix with the velocities from each point being interpolated. After interpolating for both components of velocity we have:

$$\phi(x,y)=f(x,y)i+g(x,y)j \tag{11}$$

Where, $\phi(x,y)$ is the dense velocity field, and $f(x,y), g(x,y)$ are its x and y components. Finally, to create smoother transitions between frames we apply a half-gaussian filter with $\sigma=1$ to the last four values of ϕ calculated in the last four frames. The results of the interpolation can be seen in Fig. 3.

4   Identification of the Highlights

In order to identify a frame as a highlight we propose to quantify the convergence of the movements of the players, and the velocity of the camera. If the camera was hold still, the only movement seen would be of the players and the ball, therefore, the motion flow could be represented as $\phi_1(x,y)$. Since the camera moves while the action is happening inside the pitch, the flow that is seen on the video is:

$$\phi(x,y)=\phi_1(x,y)+V_{CAM}(x,y) \tag{12}$$

The divergence of this dense velocity field is able to quantify the convergence of the movements of the players. Furthermore, $V_{CAM}(x,y)$ does not depend on the variation of x, or the variation of y, so:

$$\nabla.\phi(x,y)=\nabla.\phi_1(x,y)+\nabla.V_{CAM} \tag{13}$$

$$\nabla.\phi(x,y)=\nabla.\phi_1+\frac{\partial V_{CAMX}}{\partial x}+\frac{\partial V_{CAMY}}{\partial y} \tag{14}$$

$$\nabla.\phi(x,y)=\frac{\partial u}{\partial x}+\frac{\partial v}{\partial y} \tag{15}$$

Where, u, v are the components x and y of the dense velocity field. This shows that the divergence of ϕ not only quantifies the convergence of the movement of the players but it is also robust to the motion of the camera. The numeric computation was done in Matlab® , where the equations resulted in:

$$r=\sqrt{\left(x-x_i\right)^2+\left(y-y_i\right)^2} \tag{16}$$

$$\frac{\partial u}{\partial x} = c_1 + \sum_{i=0}^{n-1} \lambda_i \cdot \left(-\log(r+1) - \frac{r}{2(r+1)} \right) \cdot (2x_i - 2x) \tag{17}$$

$$\frac{\partial v}{\partial y} = c_2 + \sum_{i=0}^{n-1} \lambda_i \cdot \left(-\log(r+1) - \frac{r}{2(r+1)} \right) \cdot (2y_i - 2y) \tag{18}$$

The divergence is computed all over the image and then sampled at a grid. The negative values are threshold and then summed so that quantifying the convergence of the movement of the players could be easily done. In Fig.4 the threshold divergent is represented as a circle, the lower the value of the divergent, the redder the circle will appear in that image. The velocity seen in the video is the velocity of the camera plus the velocity of the players. And assuming that the velocities of the players are insignificant when the camera moves very fast, in a highlight for example, the velocity of the camera is approximated as:

$$V_{CAM} \simeq \frac{\sum_{i=0}^{n-1} u_i i + \sum_{i=0}^{n-1} v_i j}{n} \tag{19}$$

In the highlight frame of Fig.4 the blue arrow is V_{CAM}. A frame is defined as a highlight when these two conditions are satisfied:

- $\|V_{CAM}\|$ is large enough;
- The sum of threshold negative values of $\nabla . \varphi$ is low enough.

Each time a frame is identified as a highlight a flag is turned on, and the algorithm assumes that a region of 120 frames before and after that frame should be considered for further analysis.

5 Results and Evaluation

The evaluation of the algorithm was realized with the input of a full broadcast video of the match "Flamengo x Fluminense" played at Maracana Stadium, Brazil (2010). In Fig. 4 it can be observed that the convergence of the movement of the players works properly indicating where the play tends to continue. There were 322 frames considered as highlight frames, of those, 48 were false positives due to wrong classification of the scene, a total of 17.90% of false positive frames only.

One of the huge concerns in the development of the algorithm was to decrease the false positives due to camera movements that were fast but did not indicate any relevant event on the match, such as the movement of the camera after a goal kick for example. In this case the algorithm identified false positives just in 15 frames, a rate of 4.65% of false positives due to movement of the camera that was mainly caused by mistakes

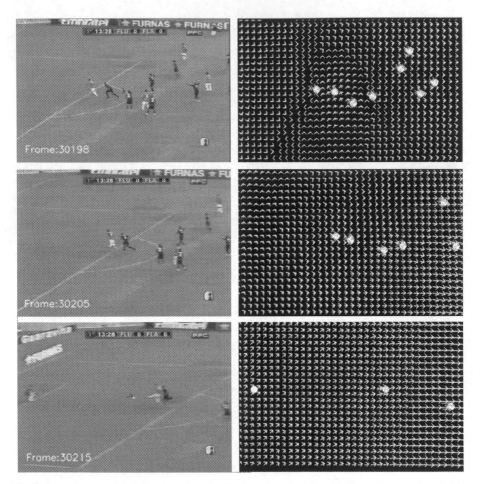

Fig. 3. Input image with the camera's velocity (as a blue arrow) at left, and the motion field at right represented with white arrows

Fig. 4. Frame identified as a highlight. The higher the value of the convergence, the redder is the circle. This image also contains the players boxes and the blue arrow at the center representing the camera velocity. This frame is within the sequence shown in Fig.3.

in the identification of the players. The full video of 109 minutes was summarized into a video of 18 minutes and 30 seconds, therefore a compression rate of 83.02%. The approach of analyzing global movements of the players and the movement of the camera showed good results, even with some amount of false positives. A significant amount of relevant plays on the match were successfully identified.

6   Conclusion and Future Work

In this work we proposed an algorithm for highlights identification and summarization of broadcast soccer videos. Results have shown that the movement of the players and the movement of the camera may indicate successfully relevant events in a soccer match. Most part of the false positives was due to flaws in the processing of the images. It was possible to obtain a compression rate of 83.02% which is a significant compression, which would help most of the public that would benefit from this summarization. A natural next step to the work in here would be to improve the study on the classification of the scenes and identification of the players in order to increase the compression rate of the algorithm.

Acknowledgments. This work was partially supported by FAPDF, DPP-UnB, and CIC-UnB.

References

1. Carr, J.C., et al.: Surface Interpolation with Radial Basis Functions for Medical Imaging. IEEE Transactions on Medical Imaging 16(1), 96–107 (1997)
2. Choi, K., Seo, Y.: Tracking Soccer Ball in TV Broadcast Video. In: Roli, F., Vitulano, S. (eds.) ICIAP 2005. LNCS, vol. 3617, pp. 661–668. Springer, Heidelberg (2005)
3. Choi, K., Seo, Y.: Probabilistic Tracking of the Soccer Ball. In: Comaniciu, D., Mester, R., Kanatani, K., Suter, D. (eds.) SMVP 2004. LNCS, vol. 3247, pp. 50–60. Springer, Heidelberg (2004)
4. Kim, K., et al.: Motion Fields to Predict Play Evolution in Dynamic Sport Scenes. In: Proceedings of CVPR 2010, pp. 840–847 (2010)
5. Seo, Y., et al.: Where are the Ball and the Players? Soccer Game Analysis with Color-based Tracking and Image Mosaick. In: Del Bimbo, A. (ed.) ICIAP 1997. LNCS, vol. 1311, pp. 196–203. Springer, Heidelberg (1997)
6. Sgarbi, E., Borges, D.L.: Structure in Soccer Videos: Detecting and Classifying Highlights for Automatic Summarization. In: Sanfeliu, A., Cortés, M.L. (eds.) CIARP 2005. LNCS, vol. 3773, pp. 691–700. Springer, Heidelberg (2005)
7. Shi, J., Tomasi, C.: Good Features to Track. In: Proceedings of CVPR, pp. 593–600 (1994)
8. Mountney, P.: Tracking Football Players using Conditional Density Propagation. Master Thesis, University of Bristol UK (2003)
9. Wu, Y., Fan, J.: Contextual flow. In: Proceedings of CVPR, pp. 33–40 (2009)

Bubble Identification Based on High Speed Videometry Data: Algorithm and Validation

Carlos E.F. do Amaral, Rafael F. Alves, Marco J. da Silva, Lúcia V.R. Arruda, Leyza B. Dorini, and Rigoberto E.M. Morales

Federal University of Technology - Paraná. 3165 Sete de Setembro Av., CEP: 80230-901 Curitiba-Paraná, Brazil

Abstract. The simultaneous flow of gas and liquid in a pipe is commonly found in several industrial activities, such as crude oil extraction and processing. In order to analyze this (two-phase) flow, many measurement techniques have been proposed, including X-ray, ultrasound, impedance and optical measurement. In this context, although the high speed videometry use is limited in practical cases, it is an important tool to validate other methods in experimental essays. Approaches based on image segmentation have already been considered to analyze gas-liquid flows along vertical pipes, but just a few have focused horizontal experiments, which are also widely found in many applications. This article describes a new technique developed to automatically measure the bubble volume through video analysis. The tests carried out considering horizontal air-water flow images yielded results with good correlation with known volume data, thus showing that the measurements are accurate enough to be considered for the validation of other technologies.

Keywords: Two-phase flow, watershed segmentation, bubble identification.

1 Introduction

Gas-liquid two-phase flows are present in a wide range of industrial cases, including food, nuclear, aerospace, geothermal and petroleum industry. In these cases, such flows are typically constrained to pipes or vessels and may have an important role in determining the safety and efficiency of the plant processes [1]. Thus, detailed information about flow behavior under controlled conditions with accurate non- or minimal intrusive measurement techniques is essential for flow modeling and prediction.

The measurement and imaging of two-phase flows have received much attention recently. Several techniques have already been used and developed to analyze the phenomena in two-phase flow, including high-speed videometry [2], capacitive probes [3] and ultrasound [4], X-ray tomographic imaging [5] and impedanciometry [6]. High-speed videometry offers many interesting characteristics for laboratories essays, such as non-invasiveness, advances in instrumentation technology and signal processing algorithms [7]. Image processing techniques also constitute a powerful tool to study the two-phase flow phenomena, being typically non-intrusive and relatively simple to design and implement. To separate the different substances (phases) flowing inside the pipe, filtering [2] and wavelets [8] have been applied. Although

L. Alvarez et al. (Eds.): CIARP 2012, LNCS 7441, pp. 870–876, 2012.

many works have addressed vertical applications, just a few studies have been done in horizontal cases [9].

In this paper, we propose an algorithm to automatically extract quantitative information of air bubble volumes from high-speed camera acquisitions in horizontal two-phase flows. The obtained images are processed using mathematical morphology operations and the watershed transform. The obtained results have shown to be accurate when compared to known volume data and, thus, can be considered for the validation of other technologies.

2   Experimental Setup

The experimental loop (Fig. 1), located in the Thermal Sciences Laboratory (LACIT) at the Federal University of Technology - Paraná (UTFPR), is able to produce different flow patterns of air and tap water mixtures. In this paper, we consider only the slug pattern, which has as main characteristic the alternation between bubbles and a liquid region between them. This intermittent regime has large bubbles, called Taylor bubbles [7].

The horizontal acrylic pipe has an internal diameter of 26 millimeters and is 9 meters long. The water flow rate is independently measured through a Coriolis flow meter for water. The air is provided by a system that controls the exactly gas volume before the mixing entrance. In the tube exit, a separator/reservatory expels the air to the atmosphere and store the water.

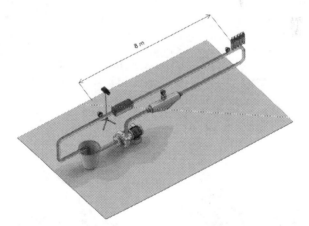

Fig. 1. Schematic representation from the experimental plant

The control of the temperature of the phase, as well as of the pressure of the two-phase mixture at the entrance and in the measurement point is made by a host computer connected to sensors via Foundation Field Bus. In such a way, it is possible to measure the total air volume at the video images based on the difference between the pressures measured at the pipe entrance and at the measurement position, as defined by Eq. (1):

$$P_1 V_1 = P_2 V_2 \tag{1}$$

where P_1 and P_2 denote the pressure in the entrance and in the measurement position and V_1 and V_2 represent, respectively, the volume (in m³) of the gas-system input (which may vary for each measurement) and of the position where the sensors are placed.

The two-phase flow images were acquired using a high speed camera (NanoSense MKIII, Dantec Dynamics A/S) at a resolution of 320x500 pixels and with a frame rate of 60 Hz. A 140 μs exposure time was chosen to avoid blurry images. A rectangular transparent acrylic box (200 mm x 100 mm x 100 mm) filled with water was used to better match the refraction indices of the water and the acrylic pipe, thus reducing light refraction in the pipe borders. A strong and pulsed illumination source was placed 100 mm behind this acrylic box. The light source contains 19 high light bright leds (MotionLEDs – IDT). To ensure an uniform illumination all over the test section, a diffuser was placed between the light source and the acrylic box.

A total of 10 injection volumes, repeated 10 times, have been measured by the high-speed camera. For each experimental condition, an air volume were injected in the pipe at a constant liquid flow rate set up to 1911.34 l/h. The measurements were stored over 10 seconds, time enough to acquire the gas passing the test section. The proposed methodology was implemented using the MatLab plataform, due the great number of functions already available for statistics and image treatment. The running time to process all data ($9,6x10^9$ pixels) was 2 hours and 42 minutes on an Intel Quad Core 2 i7 (@ 2.66 GHz) with 6 Gb of RAM memory and running Windows 7 64 bits.

3   Image Segmentation and Bubble Detection

In a morphological framework, considered in the approach proposed in this paper, gray-scale image segmentation is typically implemented by first extracting markers of the significant structures, and then using the watershed transform to extract the contours of these structures as accurately as possible.

Intuitively, the watershed transform can be defined as a flood simulation, where an image is seen as a topographical surface whose pixel values correspond to the elevation at that point, as illustrated in Fig. 2(a). The flooding process starts with the water filling markers such as the image minima (or "valleys"). When the flooding of two minima met, a dam is built to identify this boundary, allowing segmentation of objects in different regions [11]. Fig. 2 (b) shows the top view of the image after watershed treatment.

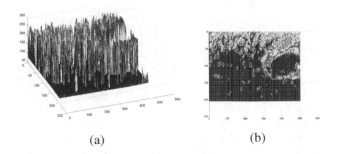

(a)   (b)

Fig. 2. (a) 3D view of the watershed performance after the H-minima transform (b) Top view of the same landscape after flooding process

However, image extrema (frequently used as markers in the watershed transform) can correspond to insignificant structures or noise, conducing to the over-segmentation problem. To prevent it, image extrema are usually selected according to some criteria, such as contrast, area and so forth. A typical approach consists on considering the h-maxima (h-minima) transform to suppress all image maxima (minima), whose contrast is lower than a specified value h, and use the extended extrema as markers [10].

Fig. 3 depicts an example. The watershed transform is applied to the original high speed camera image (Fig 3(a)) considering a set of extended extrema as markers, yielding the segmentation shown in Fig. 3(b). Since the test images correspond to the slug flow pattern, we can assume that the main air volume is found in the Taylor bubble body. Thus, we mark as interest regions only that with a segmented area larger than 4 % of the total frame surface, as illustrated in Fig. 3 (c).

Observe that the algorithm may also mark regions that correspond to the gap between dispersed bubbles, which does not contribute significantly to the total air volume. To avoid this problem, we discard all regions that are not in contact with the right or left boards of the image. Also note that small parts of the main bubble may be segmented separately. In order to still consider these areas, the software assigns the regions connected to the main bubble as part of the resulting segmentation, as presented in Fig. 3 (d).

(a)

(b)

(c)

(d)

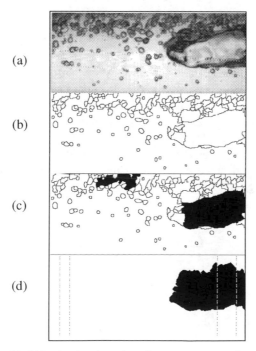

Fig. 3. Detection of bubbles borders based on the watershed transform segmentation results

Based on this procedure, it is possible to determine the bubble edges and, further, the bubble nose coordinates, thus allowing the volume computation, as described in the following.

4   Bubble Volume Calculation

To approximate the bubble volume, it is necessary to build a panoramic image. One example is illustrated in Fig. 4.

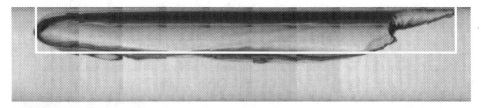

Fig. 4. Gas bubble reconstructed from 8 frames acquisition and marked with bubble nose, tail and mean high coordinates

   To perform this task, the images used in the test section are subjected to a reconstruction process, which takes into account the velocity of the bubble to join the frames and produce the panoramic image. The velocity of image data can be computed based on the difference between the nose frames cordinates, as defined   in Eq. (2).

$$U_B = \frac{\Delta K_P}{\Delta_P}.(P_S).(F_R) \tag{2}$$

where U_B is the bubble nose velocity (meters per second), ΔK_P is the difference in pixels between the K position on the considered frames (pixels), Δ_P is the number of frames showing the bubble nose (frames), P_S is the pixel size (meters per pixel) calculated by dividing the field of view length by the number of horizontal pixels in the frame and F_R is the frame rate (frames/second).

   Using the image segmentation approach detailed in Section 3, it is possible to estimate the bubble height, denoted here by h. This parameter is illustrated as the highlighted segment in Fig. 5.

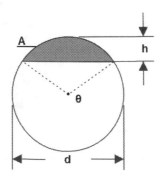

Fig. 5. Determination of bubble frame area where d is the pipe diameter, h is the air bubble high

The angle θ (rad) from the arc can be found using the Eq. (3):

$$\theta = 2\arcsin\left(1 - \frac{2h}{d}\right) \qquad (3)$$

where d (meters) is the diameter from the pipe and h (meters) the height of gas column.

After computing the circular segment shape, it is assumed that the bubble has the same format from the beginning to the end. Then, the approximate bubble volume is calculated as shown in Eq. (4).

$$V = \left(\left(1 - \frac{\left(\theta - \sin\left(\theta\right)\right)}{2\pi}\right)\cdot\frac{\pi d^2}{4}\right)\cdot n \qquad (4)$$

where d (meters) is the diameter from the pipe, n is the number of the pixels in the k axis that compose the bubble and V (m³) the bubble volume.

We emphasize that this method is an approximation for the regular shape of bubbles and only works for horizontal flows, where the gravity forces the gas bubble at the top of pipe.

5   Results and Discussion

Fig. 6 shows the bubble volume results obtained using the proposed approach compared with the correct reference volume from gas injection system considering a ±10% error boundaries. One can notice a video treatment tendency to decrease the real bubble volume in around 10 %. This can be explained due the fact that small dispersed bubbles may be not detected by the computer algorithm.

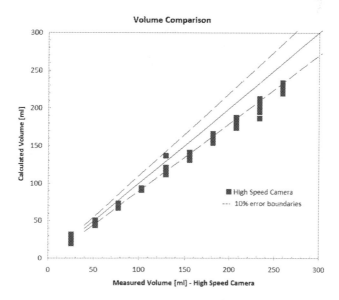

Fig. 6. Bubbles volume comparison between High Speed Camera and know amount of air mixed to the water

6   Conclusion

The operation principle of image treatment was reviewed, as well as the steps for extraction of air flow volume based in the high speed videometry data. We have developed and tested an algorithm for bubble segmentation in gas-liquid flows based in the watershed transform and on mathematical morphology operations. Subsequently, derived parameters such as bubble size and velocity distributions can be obtained. The develop technique obtained satisfactory results for bubbles volume measurements when compared with the real values, validating the proposed algorithm.

References

1. Shoham, O.: Mechanistic Modeling of Gas-Liquid Two-phase Flow in Pipes. Society of Petroleum (2006)
2. Mayor, T., Pinto, a., Campos, J.: Vertical slug flow in laminar regime in the liquid and turbulent regime in the bubble wake—Comparison with fully turbulent and fully laminar regimes. Chemical Engineering Science 63, 3614–3631 (2008)
3. Ahmed, W., Ismail, B.: Innovative Techniques For Two-Phase Flow Measurements. Recent Patents on Electrical Engineering 1, 1–13 (2008)
4. Skwarek, V., Windorfer, H., Hans, V.: Measuring pulsating flow with ultrasound. Measurement 29, 225–236 (2001)
5. Hervieu, E., Jouet, E., Desbat, L.: Development and validation of an X-ray tomograph for two-phase flow. Annals of the New York Academy of Sciences 972, 87–94 (2002)
6. Wang, M.: Impedance mapping of particulate multiphase flows. Flow Measurement and Instrumentation 16, 183–189
7. Falcone, G., Hewitt, G.F., Alimonti, C.: Multiphase Flow Metering: Principles and Applications. Elsevier Science & Technology (2009)
8. Guo, F., Yang, Y., Chen, B., Guo, L.: A novel multi-scale edge detection technique based on wavelet analysis with application in multiphase flows. Powder Technology 202, 171–177 (2010)
9. Hout, R.V., Barnea, D., Shemer, L.: Translational velocities of elongated bubbles in continuous slug flow 28, 1333-1350 (2002)
10. Soille, P.: Morphological Image Analysis: Principles and Applications. Springer (2003)
11. Pratikakis, I.: Low level image partitioning guided by the gradient watershed hierarchy. Signal Processing 75, 173–195 (1999)

Object and Gesture Recognition to Assist Children with Autism during the Discrimination Training

Eduardo Quintana[1], Catalina Ibarra[2], Lizbeth Escobedo[2],
Monica Tentori[1], and Jesus Favela[1]

[1] Department of Computer Science, CICESE, México
{equintan,mtentori,favela}@cicese.mx
[2] School of Computer Science, UABC, México
{cibarra,lescobedo}@uabc.edu.mx

Abstract. Teachers prompt children with autism to redirect their attention to the object discrimination training and reduce the time they spend "off task". In this paper, we describe MOBIS, a mobile augmented reality application enabling multi-modal interaction to provide guidance to students with autism during the object discrimination training. The system uses a vision-based object recognition algorithm to associate visual and verbal prompts to the object being discriminated (i.e., "object of interest"). The results of a performance evaluation of the system show that the object recognition component achieves an accuracy of 90%, processing an image every 0.5 seconds. Accelerometers placed on objects of interest are used to detect interaction gestures with an accuracy of 87%. The performance of both algorithms is sufficient to support the object discrimination training in real-time.

Keywords: Augmented reality, object recognition, multimodal interaction.

1   Introduction

Teachers of children with autism[1] use real objects and paper-based visual supports during the object discrimination training (Fig 1 right). These supports, along with prompts from the teacher help students match a real object to its corresponding visual support. Paper-based visual supports, however, are not interactive and appealing to students that spend considerable time "off task". Technological interventions that provide interactive visual supports (*e.g.*, vSked [6]) help teachers to keep students "on task" [6]. However, these tools still lack some realism to help students generalize from the classroom to other environments. Thus, a new type of interactive visual supports capable of augmenting the physical form of a traditional object with digital information is needed.

---

[1] For simplicity of reading we will refer as students to the children with autism attending to the object discrimination training at Pasitos - a specialized clinic attending to close to 60 low-functioning students http://www.pasitos.org

L. Alvarez et al. (Eds.): CIARP 2012, LNCS 7441, pp. 877–884, 2012.

One possible solution to this problem is the use of Augmented Reality (AR) due its capability to seamlessly superimpose digital information on real objects. Previous work has demonstrated that AR technology [3, 10] is suitable for children with autism. Additionally, AR enables the automated record-keeping, relieving teachers of this onerous burden. In this paper, we present the design and implementation of MOBIS, a mobile augmented reality system that combines the benefits of digital and physical supports, and helps teachers to keep students "on task". MOBIS relies on a vision-based object recognition component using the Speeded-Up Robust Features (SURF) algorithm [1], and uses an algorithm for recognizing interactions gestures to facilitate the record-keeping. Teachers can upload new images to the system at any time and use them to annotate new objects of interest. In the reminder of the paper we motivate the problem, describe the system and present the results of its evaluation.

2   Related Work: Ubicomp in Support of Autism

The Ubicomp community has proposed several applications to support the training of students with autism. Over the last decade, ubiquitous technologies that use visual supports have mainly supported children with autism to manage their visual schedules [5] or remediate their speech and language disabilities [2], serving most of the time as an augmentative communication tool [2]. For example, the GreceApp or DynaVox [2] uses a speech-generating system running in tablets, that enables children with autism to communicate effectively by building semantic sequences from relevant images to form sentences based on the Picture Exchange Communication System (PECS). Other ubiquitous solutions use virtual characters as communication intermediaries between children with autism and their peers [9].

Several projects have researched the use of interactive displays to support the use of visual schedules inside the classroom (*e.g.*, vSked [6]), and mobile technology for the generalization of skills (*e.g.*, MOSOCO [3, 10]). The deployment studies of these applications have proven that ubiquitous solutions in support of students with autism reduces the quantity of educator-initiated prompts [3] and enables skills generalization in real life situations [3]. This work shows that there is great potential in the use of ubiquitous tools in support of the training of students with autism. However, leaves open questions as to how the benefits students gained using digital visual supports could be obtained when using real objects –often used during the discrimination training.

3   Discrimination Training for Autism

To supplement our understanding from our literature review we conducted a qualitative study at Pasitos. For a period of 3 months we conducted 13 semi-structured interviews with 11 teachers working at this clinic and we complemented our interviews with 75 hours of passive observation.

The results of our study uncover current practices around the object discrimination training. Teachers at Pasitos use the *combined blocking procedure* [11] to teach a student how to discriminate objects. This method demands from the student to conduct repetitions about a particular task, called trials. The task for each trial involves the discrimination of one object or one color. Most of the observed teachers conduct a total of 10 trials per object per student, and after 10 completed trials the teacher will change the object or color used to discriminate. A trial is considered complete if the student successfully chooses the object being discriminated without the need of teacher-initiated prompts. Teacher-initiated prompts include:

- verbal, a spoken instruction or follow-up to a request,
- physical or model, hand-over-hand physical interaction or demonstrate the behavior being requested, and/or
- visual, sometimes called positional, placement of objects in such a way that the correct choice is closer to the student or pointing to the correct choice.

Each trial is reinforced with a reward (*e.g.*, tickles, spoken congratulations). To exemplify how teachers conduct an object discrimination lesson at Pasitos here we present a scenario.

Alexa, a low-functioning child with autism, is learning how to discriminate the orange fruit. The teacher Adie starts the trial placing in the table four paper-based laminated cards each one with different fruits (Fig 1). Then, Adie starts the first trial of 10 and asks Alexa to grab the card that contains an orange. Alexa grabs the chips card instead and starts playing with it. So Adie prompts her saying, "Alexa! Grab the orange!", and points towards the orange card. Alexa loses concentration and starts looking around. Adie grabs Alexa's hand to help her grab the orange card saying: "Alexa! Grab the orange card!" Alexa grabs the orange card and gives it to Adie. Adie rewards her by saying: "Good job!" while marking the trial.

Fig. 1. A student with autism attending to an object discrimination lesson (left) Paper-based visual supports used during the object discrimination training (right)

This scenario shows the workload teachers have during the training, and how much effort they invest in keeping the student "on task" constantly giving prompts while maintaining a detailed record of students' interactions with objects.

4   The Mobile OBject Identification System (MOBIS)

We used the results of the study to iteratively design and implement our system MOBIS, a mobile augmented reality application that combines the benefits of visual and physical supports to help teachers cope with the challenges faced during the object discrimination training. MOBIS consists of three interfaces: (1) one running in a tablet teachers use to set up the therapy and monitor each trial, (2) a second one running in a smartphone a student uses as a "visor"[4] to uncover visual and verbal prompts added on top of physical objects (Fig 2 right), and (3) the third one is a Tangible User Interface (TUI) housing accelerometers that could be attached to the objects being discriminated to detect students' interaction gestures to facilitate the record-keeping for the teacher. MOBIS architecture includes 4 main subsystems: the **Tag Manager**, the **coordinationNotepad,** an extended version of the **Ambient Notification System (ANS)** [8], and **Augmented Objects** using accelerometers to detect students' interaction gestures [7]. The Tag Manager and the ANS rely on an object recognition module that uses SURF algorithm [1], robust against variations in illumination, viewpoint, rotation and scale.

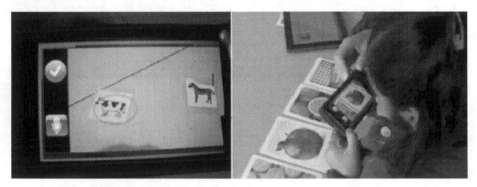

Fig. 2. MOBIS giving visual prompts to a student with autism

4.1   The Tag Manager

Teachers use the **Tag Manager** to upload captured photographs of relevant objects, and associate tags to photos and tagged photos to therapies. To create a new tag, teachers select the object and associate a visual support (*e.g.*, a circle) to an audio or a text message. This message will be displayed to the student with autism as a prompt superimposed over the detected object (Fig 2 left). This subsystem is deployed on a server and is also responsible for feature extraction and object recognition.

The Tag Manager displays all the photographs associated to that therapy from which the teacher can select one that shows the object to which s/he wants to associate the tag. The system automatically displays other photographs where the same object is recognized, allowing the teacher to select the object and increase the number of features that will be used to compare with the query image. To retrieve these images, first, the SURF algorithm selects the interest points (IPs) of the "object of interest" (*i.e.,* the object being discriminated) at distinctive locations in the image (*e.g.*, corners, blobs). The most valuable property of an IP detector is its repeatability, i.e. whether it reliably finds the same IPs under different viewing conditions. Then, the IP-neighborhood is represented with a 64-feature vector distinctive and robust to noise, detection errors, and geometric and photometric deformations. Finally, the Euclidean distance is used to match feature vectors from all images.

4.2   coordinationNotepad

Teachers use the **coordinationNotepad** on a tablet, to select the object the student will need to discriminate, the number of trials, and the amount of prompts and rewards available per trial. Teachers first select the number of students that will participate in a trial, as the system supports multiple users. Then the teacher selects the object the student will learn to discriminate. The ANS Tag Search Engine (see 4.3.2), to improve performance, only considers the tagged objects that match the object selected by the teacher. Next, the teacher selects the number of prompts, including visual and audio prompts, vibration, and a combination of the three, to be provided to students. The level of prompting will depend on the functioning level of the student and should be faded out as the student executes the skill being taught without needing object-initiated prompts. Having these different forms of visualization support multiple modes of interaction. Then, the teacher selects the rewards associated to each trial and to the complete activity. Finally, the teacher selects the number of trials per activity, and initiates the activity. This will activate the ANS Client running in the student's smartphone. The coordinationNotepad is paired up with the objects augmented with accelerometers to enable the assisted-automatic capture of students' interactions with the "objects of interest".

4.3   The Ambient Notification System

The Ambient Notification System (ANS) runs on the smartphone used by the students. It continuously captures images using the camera in the mobile device and sends them to the server. When the server notifies the mobile application that a tag has been found, the ANS alerts the student with an audio notification and/or vibrating. Then the ANS superimposes the tag on the image of the detected physical object. Students uncover the tag using the camera of the smartphone as a visor to physical objects (Fig 2 right). This application mimics educator-initiated prompts supporting multiple modes of interaction based on teachers' configuration and available tagged images. First, the system shows the student his/her photograph on the screen's top left and a traffic light on its right indicating they have to wait for a teacher's request (Fig 2 left). When the teacher activates the trial, the system exchanges the traffic light with the image of the object the teacher is asking the student to discriminate. To achieve this functionality ANS executes two main processes:

- Request tags: This process runs continuously in the background and it is only suspended to allow the server to process the client's request. The client application sends the captured photograph to the server, which performs a matching process against the associated tagged object the teacher is using to discriminate. The client has a simplified copy of the tag repository (keeping only audio and text files, and leaving out IPs files), which is used to prompt the students according to pre-configured modes of interaction (audio, visual prompt, vibration, etc.).

- Update tag repository: This process is executed every minute. The client sends an "update request" message to the server, which checks a changelog file to monitor changes in the Tag Manager.

When a new photograph is received from the smartphone, the server extracts the interest points and matches them to the IPs of the "object of interest" selected by the teacher for each therapy.

4.4   Augmented Objects

Objects augmented with accelerometers [7] attached to the "objects of interest" assist teachers with the capture of students' interactions with objects detecting when the student grabs, releases and shakes an object. If the teacher does not receive a correct response from the object, the system will start prompting the student based on the pre-configured modes of interaction. When the teacher receives the correct student's response the system displays the reward to the student. Augmented objects work in pair with the coordinationNotePad, assisting the teacher to monitor the therapy and allowing her to manually correct the detected interaction gesture if needed.

The approach for gesture recognition uses windows of 0.5sec containing 25 accelerometer readings. The algorithm uses the mean, variance and RMS of these readings as features and a linear classifier, to detect three interaction gestures: grabbing, shaking and releasing. To evaluate the performance of this approach we conducted an experiment with 8 participants using the augmented objects imitating the interaction gestures used during a therapy for a period of 3 minutes. Each interaction gesture was continuously performed for at least 30 sec. The results of this evaluation shows our approach is able to detect the grabbing gesture with 82.5% accuracy, releasing with 85.70% and shaking with 92.95%, for an average of 87.08%.

5   Evaluation

In this section we present the main results from the performance evaluation of the object recognition component of MOBIS used to define appropriate operation parameters for the system and to evaluate the system under realistic conditions of use.

We used a digital camera to collect a dataset of 197 800x600 images portraying the use of different objects. Photographs were taken from different angles in the classroom. From this set, 39 images were used as queries and 158 were used to create 32 tags associated to objects considered relevant to one particular training activity. Additional 800x480 images were captured by the children using a smartphone when conducting a training session and are used to evaluate the performance under real operating conditions.

We used the 39 query images in the first dataset to assess the accuracy of the system. In 35 of the 39 queries the system retrieved the correct tag, resulting in an accuracy of 89.7%. In this test the search is performed in all 32 tags. However, during the therapy the student is asked to discriminate only one object at a time and the search can be performed only with this tag.

We compared the system performance when searching for only one to five tags (formed by all IPs obtained from all the objects selected from those images where the object appears), with all the tags created for a given therapy (32), and with all 159 images available in the dataset. On average, with 1 to 5 tags with 39 queries, the server takes 1.7 seconds to process each query, 5.4 seconds with 32 tags and 11 seconds searching in all images. Clearly, adapting the search in real-time to look only for the tag of interest for the task at hand considerably improves performance.

We conducted additional tests with 6 sequences of images gathered in real-time when students used MOBIS during an object discrimination lesson (Figure 4). As it can be seen, several images are blurry or partially covered. This happens because students continuously move the smartphone and often block the camera with a finger while holding the smartphone. In the sequence shown in Figure 4 the student was asked to grab the card with the red train, which was accurately recognized in the first two images. We estimated the accuracy of the system with 6 different sequences with a total of 205 images, in which the student was asked to grab 6 different objects. In contrast with the evaluation described above, in this case the comparison was made only between the photographs used as query and a single tag associated to the object of interest. The average accuracy obtained was 71.6%. The ground truth was defined as any image recognized by a person as the target object. For instance, of the 6 images in Figure 4, a human can recognize the object in 4 of them. False negatives however, were often followed by true positives in the next or subsequent query where the object might be more visible. Of the 205 images processed, only once was an object not recognized by the system while being somewhat visible in 5 consecutive images, and 3 times it was not detected in 3 consecutive images. The queries were performed on average every 0.7 seconds. Thus, the object was correctly recognized within 2 seconds, except in one case, which required 3.5s. The performance of the system improved with respect to the previous test (0.7s vs. 1.7s) since the images obtained from the smartphone have a lower resolution, the query is compared with only 1 tag (instead of 1 to 5), and also because less IPs are detected when images are blurry. Using the 205 images as queries the system produced 7 false positives, but none of them were consecutive. Thus, restricting the notification of a new object found to two consecutive true positives would eliminate false notifications. This makes sense during the actual therapy, since a new image is processed in less than one second and we don't want the system to notify the student of the presence of an object when the camera is moved randomly from one place to another, but rather when it is pointed to an object decisively.

Fig. 3. Sequence of images obtained from the ANS Client during a discrimination therapy

6   Conclusion

We presented MOBIS, a multimodal system assisting students during the object discrimination training. MOBIS combines the benefits of digital and visual supports using augmented reality technology relying on a vision-based object recognition algorithm and augmented objects for gesture recognition. Several experiments were conducted to establish the appropriate parameters of MOBIS by adequately balancing performance and accuracy. We used contextual information (*i.e.*, the activity and location) to reduce the search space. Our results show that MOBIS achieves an adequate performance to efficiently support the object discrimination training using a smartphone.

We are currently running a deployment study of MOBIS in three classrooms at Pasitos to measure the efficacy of the system and its impact in current practices.

References

1. Bay, H., Ess, A., Tuytelaars, T., Van-Gool, L.: Speeded-up robust features. Computer Vision and Image Understanding 110(3), 346–359 (2008)
2. Binger, C.: Classroom-Based Language Goals and Intervention for Children Who Use AAC: Back to Basics. Perspective on Augmentative and Alternative Communication 17, 20–26 (2008)
3. Escobedo, L., Nguyen, D., Hayes, G., Boyd, L., Rangel, A., García, D., Hirano, S., Tentori, M.: MOSOCO: A Mobile Assistive Tool to Support Children with Autism Practicing Social Skills in Real-Life Situations. In: CHI 2012. ACM, Austin (2012)
4. García-Macías, J.A., Alvarez-Lozano, J., Estrada, P.E., Aviles-Lopez, E.: Browsing the Internet of Things with Sentient Visors. IEEE Computer 44(5), 46–52 (2011)
5. Hayes, G.R., Hirano, S., Marcu, G., Monibi, M., Nguyen, D.H., Yeganyan, M.: Interactive Visual Supports for Children with Autism. Personal and Ubiquitous Computing 14(7) (2010)
6. Hirano, S.H., Yeganyan, M.T., Marcu, G., Nguyen, D.H., Boyd, L., Hayes, G.R.: vSked: evaluation of a system to support classroom activities for children with autism. In: 28th CHI 2010. ACM Press, Atlanta (2010)
7. Ibarra, C., Escobedo, L., Tentori, M.: Smart objects to support the discrimination training of children with autism. In: UBICOMP 2012 (submitted, 2012)
8. Quintana, E., Favela, J.: Ambient Notifications as Memory Aids for People Suffering from Dementia. In: 5th Intl. Conf. on Ubiquitous Computing and Ambient Intelligence (UCAMI 2011), Riviera Maya, Mexico (2011)
9. Tartaro, A., Cassell, J.: Playing with virtual peers: bootstrapping contingent discourse in children with autism. In: International Conference of the Learning Sciences (2008)
10. Tentori, M., Hayes, G.R.: Designing for interaction immediacy to Enhance Social Skills of Children with Autism. In: UBICOMP 2010, Denmark, Copehaguen, pp. 51–60 (2010)
11. Williams, G., Pérez-González, L.A., Muller, A.: Using a combined blocking procedure to teach color discrimination to a child with autism. Journal of Applied Behavior Analysis 38(4), 555–558 (2005)

Pedestrian Detection Using a Feature Space Based on Colored Level Lines

Pablo Negri[1,2] and Pablo Lotito[1,3]

[1] CONICET, Av. Rivadavia 1917, Capital Federal, Argentina
[2] Instituto de Tecnologia, UADE, Lima 717, Capital Federal, Argentina
[3] PLADEMA-UNCPBA, Campus Universitario, Tandil, Argentina

Abstract. This work gives the guidelines to develop a pedestrian detection system using a feature space based on colored level lines, called Movement Feature Space (MFS). Besides detecting the movement in the scene, this feature space defines the descriptors used by the classifiers to identify pedestrians. The multi-channel level lines approach has been tested on the HSV color space, which improves the one-channel (gray scale) level lines calculation. Locations hypotheses of pedestrian are performed by a cascade of boosted classifiers. The validation of these regions of interest is carry out by a Support Vector Machine classifier. Results give more than 78.5 % of good detections on urban video sequences.

1 Introduction

This work aims to detect pedestrians in street video sequences using a pattern recognition system. Our main contribution is the development of the Movement Feature Space (MFS) based on level lines [6,2]. Using an adaptive background model, the MFS identify moving level lines of objects, preserving their gradient orientation and a factor similar to the gradient modulus. This MFS has two objectives in this system. First, it generates a descriptor of the moving objects in the scene and then, it becomes the input of the detector to classify between pedestrian and non-pedestrian classes.

Working with the MFS has interesting advantages. For instance, it adapts well to slow changes in the scene while it is robust to rapid variations (i.e. illumination changes or weather conditions). In these situations, the people appearance on the MFS does not change significantly compared to normal conditions and thus, they are easily detected by the classifiers. On a transformed HSV color space, called Texton Color Space (TCS) [1], we compute the level lines of each channel. The performance of this color approach has been contrasted with that from the B&W monochromatic MFS (hereafter called MFS-TCS for the former and MFS-gray for the latter).

The pedestrian detection algorithm has three steps. The first one consists in identify the movement on the scene with our MFS. Then, a cascade of boosted classifiers generates several hypotheses. Finally and using a Support Vector Machine (SVM) classifier, these hypotheses are thus confirmed.

L. Alvarez et al. (Eds.): CIARP 2012, LNCS 7441, pp. 885–892, 2012.

The paper is structured as follows. Section 2 gives the guidelines to obtain the MFS in the video sequences. In section 3, we introduce changes to extend the MFS to color images. Section 4.1 describe the input descriptors and the classifiers used in the pedestrian detection. Experimental results over a dataset built for this particular purpose are given in section 5. Finally, we give our final remarks and future extensions in section 6.

2   Movement Feature Space Based on Level Lines

2.1   Definition of Level Lines

Let I be a monochromatic image with $h \times w$ pixels, where $I(p)$ is the intensity value at pixel p whose coordinates are (x, y). The (upper) level set X_λ of I for the level λ is the set of pixels $\mathbf{p} \in I$, so that their intensity is greater than or equal to λ, $X_\lambda = \{\mathbf{p}/I(\mathbf{p}) \geq \lambda\}$.

For each λ, the associated level line is the boundary of the corresponding level set X_λ, see [6]. Finally, we consider a family of N level lines $\mathcal{C}$ of the image I obtained from a given set of N thresholds $\Lambda = \{\lambda_1, ..., \lambda_N\}$. From these level lines we compute two arrays S and O of order $h \times w$ defined as follows:

- $S(p)$ is the number of level lines C_λ superimposed at p. When considering all the gray levels, this quantity is highly correlated with the gradient module.
- $O(p)$ is the gradient orientation at p. In this paper, it is computed in the level set X_λ using a Sobel filter of 3×3 pixels, then, orientations are quantized in η values. Here, we do not make difference between a dark-bright transition and a bright-dark one in order to be robust to the high variability in human appearance. For each pixel p, we have a set of $S(p)$ orientation values, one for each level line passing over p. The value assigned to $O(p)$ is the most repeated orientation in the set.

Generally, in the practical implementation, only those pixels for which $S(\mathbf{p})$ is greater than a fixed threshold δ are considered, simplifying the analysis and preserving meaningful contours. In our system, best results where obtained with $N = 48$ and $\delta = 2$.

2.2   Movement Detection

As described in [4], level lines have many properties, being invariant to contrast changes. It means that a regular contrast change (monotonic and upper semi-continuous) can either create or remove level lines from a pixel, changing the $S(p)$ quantity, but it could never create a new level line intersecting the original ones [2]. This is crucial because we will use level line intersections to detect movements. The last assertion means that our method will be robust to regular contrast variations.

Now, let two consecutive images I_{t-1} and I_t obtained at times $t - 1$ and t. When looking for scene changes at pixel p, the variation of $S(p)$ could correspond

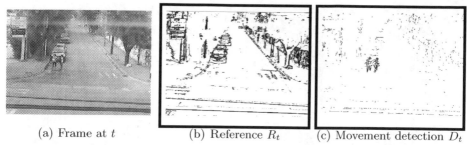

(a) Frame at t (b) Reference R_t (c) Movement detection D_t

Fig. 1. Movement detection of the same sequence, showing the background model reference and the movement detection

to a movement but also to a change in contrast. A more reliable indicator is a variation on $O(p)$, i.e., $O_{t-1}(p) \neq O_t(p)$. However, the number of points verifying that condition between two consecutive images could be very few. Bouchafa and Aubert [3,2] showed that it is better to work with background reference. They defined an adaptive background reference model, composed of the set of pixel p which are stable over an horizon of time, together with the corresponding values S^R and O^R. More precisely, given a horizon of time T we define R_t as the set

$$R_t = \{p \in I_t : O_{t-1}(p) = O_{t-2}(p) = \cdots = O_{t-T}(p)\},$$

together with O_t^R whose value at p is the preserved orientation, i.e., $O_t^R(p) = O_{t-1}(p)$ for any $p \in R_t$. In practice, the equality constraints in the definition of the reference space R_t can be mollified to allow for small variations of orientation due to noise or other perturbations.

Thus, at time t, the set of pixels p that are not in the reference or have an orientation other than the reference: $O_t(p) \neq O_t^R(p)$, are more likely to correspond to moving objects. These pixels will make up the detected set D_t. Figure 1 shows an example of the reference model of the video sequence at time t. Detected set D_t is presented in fig. 1(c). Note that for this frame, parked cars belong to the reference model and do not appear in D_t.

Below, we will focus the analysis only on pixels in the detected set D_t, and their values of S_t and O_t. This set can be considered as a virtual image with two associated scalar fields, or a kind of feature space referred to as *Movement Feature Space*, or MFS.

3 Colored Level Lines

Gray Scale Limitation

The color of an object in the scene is the result of the body reflection. It depends on two characteristics related to the physical properties of the material: the penetration of the light and the scattering of the body's pigments [11]. Clothes are opaque bodies and reflect light in a way that difficult the detection of color transitions between the person and the background. This difficulty becomes harder

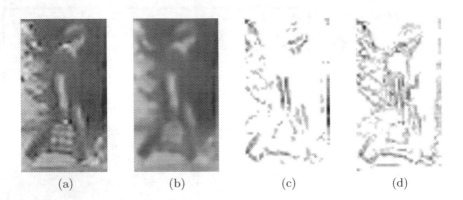

(a)   (b)   (c)   (d)

Fig. 2. RGB and Graylevel color spaces. Level line comparison.

for detecting small-sized objects and when the capture is converted into a gray scale.

Fig. 2(a) shows a person wearing a red t-shirt walking in front of a green hedge. If we transform the color image in its gray-scale representation (see fig. 2(b)), the RGB average approaches both color and it is impossible to find a transition between them without generating any level line (see fig. 2(c)).

HSV Transformed Space

We thus propose to work with a transformed HSV color space, where it is possible to recover the transition between the body (clothes) and the background finding the level lines showed in fig. 2(d). In this space, Hue (H) is the color feature, Saturation (S) measures the degree of purity of the Hue, and Intensity (V) is the average gray level. Carron [5] proposes this transformation scheme because color features are less sensitive to non-linear effects, being less correlated than the RGB color space.

If Saturation has high values, the Hue is very pertinent. In contrast, when Saturation has small values, Hue is noisy or unstable, and thus it may be irrelevant [5]. The last means that Hue is ill-defined in the unsaturated cases, and this channel can generate irrelevant level lines [11].

To overcome this, Alvarez et al. [1] introduce a simplification of the Carron's method called Color Texton Space (CTS). In this space, two new channels are generated: $S \cdot cos(H)$, and $S \cdot sin(H)$. The intensity V remains unchanged. In this way, in a pixel where H is not relevant because of the low value of S, those channels have not an important value.

First, we calculate for each channel of the Texton Space, $S_t^x(p)$ and $O_t^x(p)$, where $x = \{SsinH, ScosH, V\}$. Then, in order to obtain $S_t^{CTS}(p)$ and $O_t^{CTS}(p)$, it is choose, for each pixel p, the orientation and the modulus of the greatest $S_t^x(p)$. Finally, we obtain D_t, as was explained early, from $S_t^{CTS}(p)$ and $O_t^{CTS}(p)$.

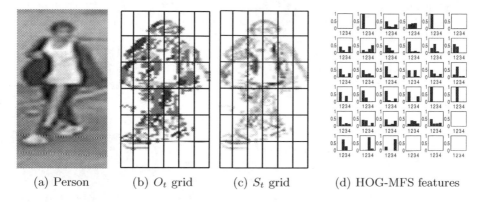

(a) Person   (b) O_t grid   (c) S_t grid   (d) HOG-MFS features

Fig. 3. HOG-MFS calculation on defined grids. In (b), each color correspond to a one of the four directions of the gradient. In (c), darker pixels have highest S_t values.

4 Pedestrian Detector System

Features and descriptors extract information from the image. The choice of a good representation space (feature space), helps the classifier to discriminate whether a person is present inside a region of interest (RoI) or a pattern. Using a learning dataset, positive samples (patterns with a person inside) and negative samples (patterns without persons) are grouped into two classes by the classifier by a decision boundary.

4.1 Feature Space

The chosen pattern is a rectangle of 12x36 pixels size. The information inside the pattern generates a set of descriptors called feature space.

Two types of feature spaces are used by the classifiers. First ones are calculated from the MFS and the second ones are the Haar-like features [13], which are computed from the gray scale representation of the image.

Feature Space from the MFS. First set is a HOG-like features, called HOG-MFS, calculated on rectangular patches inside the RoI using S_t and O_t information of the D_t pixels (the MFS space).

HOG-MFS results in a concatenated set of Histograms of Oriented Gradients (HOG) [9]. A RoI is subdivided into a grid of rectangular patches. Within each patch, we compute HOG descriptors as follow:

- a histogram has $\eta = 8$ bins (one for each direction),
- the value for a bin is the sum of the $S(p)$ for the p with this orientation,
- the histogram values are normalized.

Figure 3 shows the 6x6 grid and the HOG-MFS calculated in each grid on figure 3(d). For the sake of simplicity, we consider four gradient directions, where the histogram bin 1 corresponds to the vertical direction, bin 3 corresponds to horizontal direction, and the other two are the diagonals directions.

The second set of features, called MAG-MFS computes the sum of the S_t values inside each patch. This feature helps with the fact that HOG descriptors can make difference between a strong edge in the patch, generating a one in the corresponding bin, and only one pixel of noise, which generates the same histogram after the normalization.

Haar-Like Filters. Rectangular filters or Haar-like features provide information about the gray-level distribution of two adjacent regions in an image. These filters consist of two, three or four rectangles, as proposed by Viola [13]. To compute the output of a filter on a certain region of image, the sum of all pixels values in the gray region is subtracted from the sum of all pixels values in the white one (and normalized by a coefficient in case of a filter with three rectangles). The total number of Haar-like features calculated on the person pattern is 4893.

4.2   Pedestrian Classification

Datasets. The dataset is composed of seven video sequences. Five of them are employed to train the classifiers, having 3793 labeled pedestrian in more than 5000 frames. Negative samples are obtained from captures without pedestrians. Test sequence have 1324 labeled pedestrians in 4200 frames.

Hypothesis Generation. In the hypothesis generation, the whole image is analyzed using a sliding window approach [9] to identify pedestrians in these regions.

The detector is an Adaboost Cascade of 20 boosted classifiers [13] discriminating pedestrian and non-pedestrian hypothesis. The implemented methodology is analogous to the one presented in [12][1]. This classifier has a good performance, it evaluates about 25.000 RoIs in some milliseconds and deliver to the next detection step only most probable hypothesis.

The input descriptors of the cascade will be: MAG-MFS, HOG-MFS as a generative function (calculated using a pedestrian model, see [12]), HOG-MFS as a discriminant function, and Haar-like features. At each iteration of the learning process of a strong classifier, the learner chooses between one of those sets of features and their weak classification function associated. The HOG-MFS and the MAG-MFS descriptors are computed on a dense grid of 3707 overlapped square and rectangular patches with different sizes on the pattern.

It is important to note that in the learning process, initially the boosted classifiers of the cascade are chosen among HOG-MFS and MAG-MFS descriptors, which discriminate the movement in the scene. Then, at later steps, classifiers choose Haar-like features, they are highly discriminant and help to identify pedestrians from others moving objects, as circulating vehicles.

---

[1] http://pablonegri.free.fr/Downloads/RealAdaboost_PANKit.htm

(a) Hypothesis generation   (b) Hypothesis validated   (c) Final RoIs

Fig. 4. The three steps of the detection algorithm

Hypothesis Validation. The hypothesis validation is carried out by a SVM classifier. Once the Adaboost classifiers have finished their work, only remains hypothesis which can be considered as harder samples.

The SVM classifier has better discriminant properties than the Adaboost cascade, but it is very time consuming. To speed it up, we use a limited set of HOG-MFS. The RoI is divided in a set of 2x2, 4x4 and 6x6 non-overlapped patches (as show fig. 3(b)). In addition, we have calculated three more grids overlapping the others of 1 patch size (overlapping the grid of 2x2), 3x3 patches, and 5x5 patches. This set of 91 HOG-MFS features is the input of the SVM classifier. Positive samples are the labeled pedestrians of the training datasets, and negative samples are those RoIs validated by the Adaboost cascade. To train the classifier we use the LIBSVM [7] and their default parameters.

Hypothesis Filtering. Validated RoIs, as shown in fig. 4(b), are then grouped using a Mean Shift Clustering method [8,10]. This is an iterative algorithm that chooses a mean position from the position of neighbouring RoIs. Returned clusters (RoI positions) are considered the system response (see figure 4(c)). Finally, the system output, i.e., the estimated pedestrian positions, is given by the position of those resulting RoIs.

5   Experimental Results

Video sequences were recorded by a Vivotek SD7151 camera, filming a street in the city of Tandil (Argentina). The recording format is MJPEG of 640x480 pixels size. We have chosen the minimum JPEG compression to reduce blocking artifacts in captures, moreover a bilinear interpolation is applied to input frames: on each HSV channel and on the gray scale image. With this JPEG resolution, the limited network bandwidth reduces the recording process to one capture every three seconds on average.

Two approaches are compared: a MFS-gray system calculated on monochromatic images, and a MFS-TCS system using the Texton Color Space. Detection results, in percentage, are 76.9 % for the MFS-Gray system, and **78.6 %** for the MFS-TCS system. The former made 833 false alarms on the test dataset (4200 frames), and the later 899 false alarms. System performance is given by the mean values of individual systems obtained by a 3-fold training. As we see, MFS-TCS outperforms the system using monochromatic images in detection, having few more false alarms at the same time.

6   Conclusions and Future Work

This article presented a pedestrian detector system, which obtains promising results on urban video sequences. It proposed a Movement Feature Space that help to detect movements and to generate descriptors to identify pedestrians in the scene. The MFS calculated on color images, using a Texton Color Space, improves a system which employs the MFS calculated on monochromatic images.

These are preliminary results and there is a work in progress to improve the detection. This detection system will be employed later to analyze the behavior of pedestrians crossing the street in an intersection and their interaction with moving vehicles.

Acknowledgments. This work was supported by the PICT-2283 of ANPCyT, the ACyT R11020 of UADE and CONICET (Argentina).

References

1. Alvarez, S., Salvatella, A., Vanrell, M., Otazu, X.: 3d texton spaces for color-texture retrieval. In: Image Analysis and Recognition, pp. 354–363 (2010)
2. Aubert, D., Guichard, F., Bouchafa, S.: Time-scale change detection applied to real-time abnormal stationarity monitoring. Real-Time Imaging 10, 9–22 (2004)
3. Bouchafa, S.: Motion detection invariant to contrast changes. Application to detection abnormal motion in subway corridors. Ph.D. thesis, UPMC Paris VI (1998)
4. Cao, F., Musse, P., Sur, F.: Extracting meaningful curves from images. Journal of Mathematical Imaging and Vision 22, 1519–1581 (2005)
5. Carron, T., Lambert, P.: Color edge detector using jointly hue, saturation, and intensity. In: ICIP, pp. 977–981 (1994)
6. Caselles, V., Col, I.B., Morel, J.: Topographic maps and local contrast changes in natural images. International Journal on Computer Vision 33, 5–27 (1999)
7. Chang, C.C., Lin, C.J.: Libsvm: a library for support vector machines, http://www.csie.ntu.edu.tw/~cjlin/libsvm (accessed November 2011)
8. Comaniciu, D.: Mean shift: A robust approach toward feature space analysis. IEEE Transactions on Pattern Analysis and Machine Intelligence 24(5), 603–619 (2002)
9. Dalal, N., Triggs, B.: Histograms of oriented gradients for human detection. In: Computer Vision and Pattern Recognition, pp. 886–893 (2005)
10. Finkston, B.: http://www.mathworks.com/matlabcentral/fileexchange/10161-mean-shift-clustering (accessed on March 2012)
11. Gouiffes, M., Zavidovique, B.: A color topographic map based on the dichromatic reflectance model. EURASIP JIVP, 1–14 (2008)
12. Negri, P., Clady, X., Hanif, S., Prevost, L.: A cascade of boosted generative and discriminative classifiers for vehicle detection. EURASIP JASP, 1–12 (2008)
13. Viola, P., Jones, M.: Rapid object detection using a boosted cascade of simple features. In: CVPR, vol. 1, pp. 511–518 (December 2001)

Author Index